Constitutional Law for a Changing America

In honor of our parents
Ann and Kenneth Spole
Josephine and George Walker

EIGHTH EDITION

CONSTITUTIONAL LAW FOR A CHANGING AMERICA

Rights, Liberties, and Justice

LEE EPSTEIN
GOULD SCHOOL OF LAW,
UNIVERSITY OF SOUTHERN CALIFORNIA

THOMAS G. WALKER
EMORY UNIVERSITY

Los Angeles | London | New Delhi
Singapore | Washington DC

Los Angeles | London | New Delhi
Singapore | Washington DC

FOR INFORMATION:

CQ Press

An Imprint of SAGE Publications, Inc.

2455 Teller Road

Thousand Oaks, California 91320

E-mail: order@sagepub.com

SAGE Publications Ltd.

1 Oliver's Yard

55 City Road

London EC1Y 1SP

United Kingdom

SAGE Publications India Pvt. Ltd.

B 1/I 1 Mohan Cooperative Industrial Area

Mathura Road, New Delhi 110 044

India

SAGE Publications Asia-Pacific Pte. Ltd.

3 Church Street

#10-04 Samsung Hub

Singapore 049483

Acquisitions Editor: Charisse Kiino

Editorial Assistant: Marcelle Maginnis

Production Editor: Astrid Virding

Copy Editor: Judy Selhorst

Typesetter: C&M Digitals (P) Ltd.

Proofreader: Dennis Webb

Indexer: Gloria Tierney

Cover Designer: Michael Dubowe

Marketing Manager: Jonathan Mason

Permissions Editor: Adele Hutchinson

Printed in the United States of America

Library of Congress Cataloging-in-Publication Data

Epstein, Lee, 1958-

Constitutional law for a changing America: rights, liberties, and justice / Lee Epstein, Thomas G. Walker.—8th ed.

p. cm.
Includes bibliographical references and index.

ISBN 978-1-4522-2674-3 (pbk. : alk. paper)

1. Civil rights—United States. 2. Constitutional law—United States. I. Walker, Thomas G. II. Title. III. Title: Rights, liberties, and justice.

KF4748.E67 2013
342.73—dc23   2012027064

This book is printed on acid-free paper.

12 13 14 15 16 10 9 8 7 6 5 4 3 2 1

CONTENTS

CHRONOLOGICAL TABLE OF CASES

TABLES, FIGURES, AND BOXES

PREFACE

Twenty-one years have passed since *Constitutional Law for a Changing America: Rights, Liberties, and Justice* made its debut in a discipline already supplied with many fine casebooks by law professors, historians, and social scientists. We believed then, as we do now, that a fresh approach was needed because, as professors who regularly teach courses on public law, and as scholars concerned with judicial processes, we saw a growing disparity between what we taught and what our research taught us.

We had adopted books for our classes that focused primarily on Supreme Court decisions and how the Court applied the resulting legal precedents to subsequent disputes, but as scholars we understood that to know the law is to know only part of the story. A host of political factors—internal and external—influence the Court's decisions and shape the development of constitutional law. These include the ways lawyers and interest groups frame legal disputes, the ideological and behavioral propensities of the justices, the politics of judicial selection, public opinion, and the positions elected officials take, to name just a few.

Because we thought no existing book adequately combined legal factors with the influences of the political process, we wrote one. In most respects, our book follows tradition: readers will find that we include excerpts from the classic cases that best illustrate the development of constitutional law. But our focus is different, as is the appearance of this volume. We emphasize the arguments raised by lawyers and interest groups and the politics surrounding litigation. We include tables and figures on Court trends and other materials that bring out the rich legal, social, historical, economic, and political contexts in which the Court reaches its decisions. As a result, students and instructors will find this work both similar to and different from casebooks they may have read before.

Integrating traditional teaching and research concerns was only one of our goals. Another was to animate the subject of constitutional law. As instructors, we find our subject inherently interesting—to us con law is exciting stuff. Many of the books available, however, could not be less inviting in design, presentation, or prose. That kind of book seems to dampen enthusiasm. We have written a book that we hope mirrors the excitement we feel for our subject. We describe the events that led to the suits and include photographs of litigants and relevant exhibits from the cases. Moreover, because students often ask us about the fates of particular litigants—for example, what happened to the "Scottsboro boys"?—and hearing that colleagues elsewhere are asked similar questions, we decided to attach "Aftermath" boxes to a select set of cases. In addition to providing final chapters to these stories, the focus on the human element leads to interesting discussions about the decisions' impacts on the lives of ordinary Americans. We hope these materials demonstrate to students that Supreme Court cases are more than just legal names and citations, that they involve real people engaged in real disputes.

Finally, to broaden students' perspectives on the U.S. legal system, we have added boxes on the laws and legal practices of other countries. Students and instructors can use these to compare and contrast U.S. Supreme Court decisions over a wide range of issues, such as the death penalty, prayer in schools, and libel, with policies developed in other countries. The use of foreign law sources in their opinions has sparked some dissension among the justices, and we have found that the material we include here inspires lively debates in our classes. We hope it will do so in yours as well.

Important Revisions

In preparing this eighth edition, we have strengthened the distinctive features of the earlier versions by making changes at all three levels of the book—organization, chapters, and cases. Material on the boundaries of free expression has been reorganized so that we focus not only on the traditional topics of libel and obscenity but also on emerging areas of government concern—for example, cruelty and violence. To date, the government's efforts at regulating expression have not been especially successful. But whether the Court will stick to its position of defining only a limited number of categories of expression—notably, obscenity and libel—as beyond the reach of the First Amendment is anyone's guess.

The most significant changes are in the individual chapters. All have been thoroughly updated to include important opinions handed down through the 2011 term. Since Chief Justice Roberts took office in 2005, the Court has taken up many pressing issues of the day, including gun control (*District of Columbia v. Heller*), the use of the death penalty for child rapists (*Kennedy v. Louisiana*), the extent to which defendants have the right to confront witnesses against them (including *Davis v. Washington* and *Harmon v. Indiana*), and, as we just mentioned, cruelty and violence (*United States v. Stevens*; *Brown v. Entertainment Merchants Association*).

The chapters that follow contain discussions of these cases, along with many others from the Roberts Court. For example, Chapter 4 houses new material on government involvement in the internal affairs of religious organizations, with an excerpt from *Hosanna-Tabor Evangelical Lutheran Church and School v. Equal Employment Opportunity Commission* (2012). Chapter 5 provides expanded coverage of hateful and offensive speech and now includes an excerpt from *Snyder v. Phelps* (2011)—an attempt by Westboro Baptist Church to win First Amendment protection for its anti-gay, anti-Catholic demonstrations at military funerals. We have updated Chapter 11 to include a discussion of the Court's reintroduction of the importance of physical intrusions in determining Fourth Amendment search and seizure violations, highlighted by an excerpt from the GPS tracking case of *United States v. Jones* (2012). And last but certainly not least, to Chapter 14's coverage of campaign finance issues we have added an excerpt from the Court's controversial decision in *Citizens United v. Federal Election Commission* (2010).

For the seventh edition, we made a change in our presentation of the case material: for each excerpted case, we noted key arguments made by the attorneys on both sides. Our goal was to highlight the array of important claims before the Court, and not simply those the justices chose to highlight. This addition proved popular with students and instructors alike, and so we have retained it in this new edition.

We have also retained and enhanced other features pertaining to case presentation that have proved to be useful. The Aftermath boxes not only remain but have increased in number—a testament to the positive feedback we have received. We continue to excerpt concurring and dissenting opinions; in fact, virtually all cases analyzed in the text now include one or the other or both. Although these opinions lack the force of precedent, they are useful in helping students to see alternative points of view.

We also continue to provide universal resource locators (URLs) to the full texts of the opinions and, where available, to a Web site containing audio recordings of oral arguments in many landmark cases. We have taken this step for much the same reason that we now highlight attorneys' arguments: reading decisions in their entirety and listening to oral arguments can help students to develop the important skill of differentiating between compelling and less compelling arguments. Finally, we continue to retain the historical flavor of the decisions, reprinting verbatim the original language used in *U.S. Reports* to introduce the justices' writings. Students will see that during most of its history the Court used the courtesy title "Mr." to refer to justices, as in "Mr. Justice Holmes delivered the opinion of the Court" or "Mr. Justice Harlan, dissenting." In 1980 the Court dropped the "Mr." This point may seem minor, but we think it is evidence that the justices, like other Americans, updated their usage to reflect fundamental changes in American society—in this case, the emergence of women as a force in the legal profession and shortly thereafter on the Court itself.

We have made some cuts along the way as well. Most notably, adopters of previous editions will see that we've trimmed the number of appendixes in the "Reference Material" section. Because so much of the material they contained is now readily available from reliable sources on the Internet, we made the decision to delete them to make room for more case material and narrative.

Student and Instructor Resources

We continue to update and improve our Online Con Law Resource Center located at http://clca.cqpress.com and hope instructors find this a valuable resource for assigning supplemental cases and useful study aids, as well as for accessing helpful instructor resources. Through the supplemental case archive professors and students can access excerpts of important decisions that we mention in the text but that space limitations and other considerations counsel against excerpting. Cases included in the online archive are indicated by boldface italic type in the text, and a complete list appears in Appendix 4; in the archive these cases are introduced and excerpted in the same fashion as they are in the book. The archive now houses more than two hundred cases; we will continue to keep it current, adding important decisions as the Court hands them down.

The Online Resource Center also features some very handy study tools for students: a set of interactive flash cards for each chapter that will help students review key terms and concepts, and links to a wealth of data and background material from CQ Press's reference sources, such as *Guide to the U.S. Supreme Court, The Supreme Court A to Z,* and our *Supreme Court Compendium* (which we coauthored with the Harold J. Spaeth and Jeffrey A. Segal). Students can click to a bio of any justice, read a background piece on the origins of the Court, and view selected data tables on ideological means or on voting interagreements among justices by issue area. Also available are new hypothetical cases—sixteen for this volume—written by Stephen Daniels of the American Bar Foundation and Northwestern University and James Bowers of St. John Fisher College. These rich, detailed hypotheticals, tied

to specific chapters, are accompanied by both discussion and writing questions that will help spark conversation and serve as the basis for writing assignments.

We are grateful to Tim Johnson of the University of Minnesota for producing a great set of instructor's resources. In addition to a test bank that includes multiple-choice, short-answer, and hypothetical questions, he has created a set of discussion questions for each chapter. There are also case briefs for every case excerpted in the book and a full set of PowerPoint lecture slides. We'd also like to thank Rorie Spill Solberg of Oregon State University and Liane Kosaki of the University of Wisconsin–Madison for their Moot Court Simulation in the Resource Center. Instructors can choose hypothetical cases and utilize their guidelines so students can play the roles of counsel or chief or associate justice. Rorie and Liane also blog for the Resource Center, tying current news events and developments to content in *Constitutional Law for a Changing America.* We encourage all of our readers to check out "Without Prejudice" on the home page of the Resource Center.

Instructors can also download all the tables, figures, and charts from our book (in PowerPoint or JPG formats) for use during lecture. To access all of these resources, be sure to click on "instructor resources" once at clca.cqpress.com so you can register and start downloading.

Acknowledgments

Although the first edition of this volume was published twenty-one years ago, it had been in the works for many more. During those developmental years, numerous people provided guidance, but none as much as Joanne Daniels, a former editor at CQ Press. It was Joanne who conceived of a constitutional law book that would be accessible, sophisticated, and contemporary. And it was Joanne who brought that concept to our attention and helped us develop it into a book. We are forever in her debt.

Because this new edition charts the same course as the first seven, we remain grateful to all of those who had a hand in the previous editions. They include David Tarr and Jeanne Ferris at CQ Press, Jack Knight at Duke University, Joseph A. Kobylka of Southern Methodist University, Jeffrey A. Segal of the State University of New York at Stony Brook, and our many colleagues who reviewed and commented on our work: Judith A. Baer, Ralph Baker, Lawrence Baum, John Brigham, Gregory A. Caldeira, Bradley C. Canon, Robert A. Carp, James Cauthen, Phillip J. Cooper, Sue Davis, John Fliter, John B. Gates, Edward V. Heck, David Korman, John A. Maltese, Wendy Martinek, Kevin McGuire, Wayne McIntosh, Susan Mezey, Richard J. Pacelle Jr., C. K. Rowland, Donald R. Songer, Harry P. Stumpf, and Artemus Ward. We are also indebted to the many scholars who took the time to send us suggestions, including (again) Greg Caldeira, as well as Akiba J. Covitz, Jolly Emrey, Alec C. Ewald, Leslie Goldstein, and Neil Snortland. Many thanks also go to Jeff Segal for his frank appraisal of the earlier volumes; to Segal (again), Rebecca Brown, David Cruz, Micheal Giles, Linda Greenhouse, and Adam Liptak for their willingness to share their expertise in all matters of constitutional law; to Judith Baer and Leslie Goldstein for their help with the revision of the discrimination chapter in previous editions and their answers to innumerable e-mail messages; to Jack Knight for his comments on the drafts of several chapters; and to Harold J. Spaeth for his wonderful data set. We also thank the following reviewers for their help on this edition: John Forren (Miami University), Joshua Kaplan (University of Notre Dame), Peter Kierst (University of New Mexico), David Korman (University of Pittsburgh), Cynthia Lebow (University of California, Los Angeles), Wendy Martinek (University of Binghamton, SUNY), Richard J. Pacelle Jr. (Georgia Southern University), Chris Shortell (Portland State University), and Joseph Smith (University of Alabama).

Most of all, we acknowledge the contributions of our editors at CQ Press, Brenda Carter and Charisse Kiino. Brenda saw *Constitutional Law for a Changing America* through the first five editions; Charisse came on board on the fifth and worked with us throughout the eighth. Both are just terrific, somehow knowing exactly when to steer us and when to steer clear. We are equally indebted to Carolyn Goldinger, our copy editor on the first four editions and on the sixth edition. Her imprint, without exaggeration, remains everywhere. Over the years, she made our prose more accessible, questioned our interpretation of certain events and opinions—and was all too often right—and made our tables and figures understandable. There is not a better copy editor in this business. Period.

For this edition, we express our sincere thanks to our new copy editor, Judy Selhorst. Judy continued the tradition of strong CQ Press editors. Her expertise and attention to detail not only enhanced our prose but worked to improve the accuracy and relevance of what we wrote. We also express many thanks to Nancy Loh for help with photo research and to Astrid Virding for her fine work as production editor.

Finally, we acknowledge the support of our home institutions and of our colleagues and friends. We are forever grateful to our former professors for instilling in us their genuine interest in and curiosity about things judicial and legal, and to our parents for their unequivocal support.

Shortly before the fifth edition went to press, we learned that the *Constitutional Law for a Changing America* volumes had won the award for teaching and mentoring presented by the Law and Courts section of the American Political Science Association. Each and every one of the editors and scholars we thank above deserves credit for whatever success our books have enjoyed. Any errors of omission or commission, however, remain our sole responsibility. We encourage students and instructors alike to comment on the book and to inform us of any errors. Contact us at lepstein@ law.usc.edu or polstw@emory.edu.

L.E., *Los Angeles*
T.G.W., *Atlanta*

The Supreme Court and the Constitution

PART I

The Living Constitution

The Living Constitution

TWO BUILDING BLOCKS undergird virtually every book on rights, liberties, and justice in the United States: the U.S. Supreme Court and the amendments to the U.S. Constitution. No matter which approach these volumes take, their purpose is to help you understand how the Court has interpreted the Bill of Rights and other amendments to the Constitution.

Constitutional Law for a Changing America is no different. Although we also develop some unique themes, including the legal, economic, and political factors that explain why the Court reaches the decisions it does, our primary goal is to provide the narrative and opinion excerpts necessary for you to develop a clear understanding of the Supreme Court's approach to the Constitution's provisions concerning rights, liberties, and justice.

We devote the first part of the book to the two building blocks: the Court and the amendments to the Constitution. In what follows, we consider the events leading up to the drafting of the Bill of Rights and some of the debates over its adoption. Chapter 1 looks at the Court, examining the procedures it uses to decide cases and its approaches to decision making. In the next two chapters, we begin to put the two building blocks together by considering how the Court has interpreted its own power (Chapter 2) and how it has analyzed the general nature and applicability of the Bill of Rights (Chapter 3).

THE ROAD TO THE BILL OF RIGHTS

Before the adoption of the Declaration of Independence, the Continental Congress selected a group of delegates to make recommendations for the formation of a national government. Composed of representatives of each of the thirteen colonies, this committee proposed a national charter, the Articles of Confederation, which Congress approved and submitted to the states for ratification in November 1777. Ratification was achieved in March 1781.

The Articles of Confederation was the nation's first written charter, but it changed the way the government operated very little; instead, it merely formalized practices that had developed prior to 1774. For example, rather than provide for a compact between the people and the government, the charter institutionalized "a league of friendship" among the states, and its guiding principle was state sovereignty. This is not to suggest that the charter failed to provide for a central government; it created a national governing apparatus with a one-house legislature but no formal federal executive or judiciary. The legislature had some power, most notably in the area of foreign affairs, but it derived its authority from the states that had created it, not from the people.

The weaknesses in the system soon became apparent, and the Congress issued a call for a convention to meet in May 1787 in Philadelphia "for the sole and express purpose of revising the Articles of Confederation."

Within a month, however, the fifty-five delegates had dramatically altered their mission. Viewing the articles as unworkable, they decided to start afresh. What emerged just four months later, on September 17, was an entirely new government scheme embodied in the U.S. Constitution.

Pleased with their handiwork, the framers "adjourned to City Tavern, dined together and took cordial leave of each other."[1] Most of the delegates were more than ready to go home after the long, hot summer in Philadelphia, and they departed with confidence that the new document would receive speedy approval by the states. At first, their optimism appeared justified. As Table I-1 depicts, between December 7, 1787, and January 8, 1788, five states ratified the Constitution—three by unanimous votes. But after that auspicious beginning, the drive lost momentum. An opposition movement was marshaling arguments to persuade state convention delegates to vote against ratification. What these opponents, the Anti-Federalists, feared most of all was the Constitution's new balance of power. They believed that strong state governments provided the best defense against the concentration of too much power in the national government and that the proposed Constitution tipped the scales the other way. These fears were countered by the Federalists, who favored ratification. The Federalists' arguments and writings took many forms, but among the most important was a series of eighty-five articles published in New York newspapers under the pen name "Publius." Written by John Jay, James Madison, and Alexander Hamilton, *The Federalist Papers* continue to provide insight into the objectives and intent of the founders.[2]

Debates between the Federalists and their opponents were often highly philosophical, with emphasis on the appropriate roles and powers of national institutions. In the states, however, ratification drives were marked by the stuff of ordinary politics—deal making. Massachusetts provides a case in point. After three weeks of debate among delegates, Federalist leaders realized that they would never achieve victory without the support of Governor John Hancock. They went to his house and proposed that he endorse ratification on condition that a series of amendments be tacked on for consideration by Congress. The governor agreed, but

in return he wanted to become president of the United States if Virginia failed to ratify or George Washington refused to serve. Or he would accept the vice presidency. With the deal cut, Hancock went to the state convention to propose a compromise—the ratification of the Constitution with amendments. The delegates agreed, and Massachusetts became the sixth state to ratify.

This compromise—the call for a bill of rights—caught on, and Madison began to advocate it whenever close votes were likely. As it turned out, he and other Federalists needed to mention it quite often: as Table I-1 indicates, of the eight states ratifying after January 1788, seven recommended that the new Congress consider amendments. New York and Virginia probably would not have agreed to the Constitution without such additions, and Virginia even called for a second constitutional convention for that purpose. Other states began devising their own wish lists—enumerations of specific rights they wanted put into the document.

Why were states so reluctant to ratify the Constitution without a bill of rights? Some viewed the new government scheme with downright suspicion because of the extensive powers granted to the proposed national government. But more tended to agree with Thomas Jefferson, who, in a letter to Madison, argued that "a bill of rights is what the people are entitled to against every government on earth, general and particular, and what no just government should refuse, or rest on inference."

What Jefferson's remark suggests is that although many people thought well of the new system of government, they were troubled by the lack of a declaration of rights. At the time, Americans clearly understood concepts of *fundamental* and *inalienable* rights, those that inherently belonged to them and that no government could deny. Even England, the country they fought to gain their freedom, had such guarantees. The Magna Carta of 1215 and the Bill of Rights of 1689 gave Britons the right to a jury trial, to protection against cruel and unusual punishments, and so forth. Moreover, after the American Revolution, almost every state constitution included a philosophical statement about the relationship between citizens and their government and/or a list of fifteen to twenty inalienable rights, such as religious freedom and electoral independence. Small wonder that the call for such a statement or enumeration of rights became a battle cry. If it was so widespread, why did the framers fail to include a bill of rights in the original document? Did they not anticipate the reaction?

---

1. *1787,* compiled by historians of the Independence National Historical Park (New York: Exeter Books, 1987), 191.

2. *The Federalist Papers* are available at http://thomas.loc.gov/home/histdox/fedpapers.html.

TABLE I-1   The Ratification of the Constitution

STATE	DATE OF ACTION	DECISION	VOTE
Delaware	December 7, 1787	Ratified	30–0
Pennsylvania	December 12, 1787	Ratified	46–23
New Jersey	December 18, 1787	Ratified	38–0
Georgia	January 2, 1788	Ratified	26–0
Connecticut	January 8, 1788	Ratified	128–40
Massachusetts	February 6, 1788	Ratified with amendments	187–168
Maryland	April 28, 1788	Ratified	63–11
South Carolina	May 23, 1788	Ratified with amendments	149–73
New Hampshire	June 21, 1788	Ratified with amendments	57–46
Virginia	June 26, 1788	Ratified with amendments	89–79
New York	July 26, 1788	Ratified with amendments	30–27
North Carolina	August 4, 1788	Rejected	75–193
	November 21, 1789	Ratified with amendments	194–77
Rhode Island	May 29, 1790	Ratified with amendments	34–32

SOURCES: Ratifying documents in the Avalon Project at Yale Law School (http://avalon.law.yale.edu/subject_menus/constpap.asp); Ralph Mitchell, *CQ's Guide to the U.S. Constitution,* 2nd ed. (Washington, DC: Congressional Quarterly, 1994), 28–30.

Records of the 1787 constitutional debates indicate that, in fact, the delegates considered specific individual guarantees on at least four separate occasions.[3] On August 20, Charles Pinckney submitted a proposal that included several guarantees, such as freedom of the press and the eradication of religious tests, but the various committees never considered his plan. On September 12, 14, and 16, just before the close of the convention, some delegates tried, again without success, to persuade the convention to enumerate specific guarantees. At one point, George Mason said that a bill of rights "would give great quiet to the people; and with the aid of the state delegations, a bill might be prepared in a few hours." This motion was unanimously defeated by those remaining in attendance. On the convention's last day, Edmund Randolph made a desperate plea that the delegates allow the states to submit amendments and then convene a second convention. Although he favored a bill of rights, Pinckney responded, "Conventions are serious things, and ought not to be repeated."

Why the majority of delegates showed little enthusiasm for these suggestions is a matter of scholarly debate. Some say the pleas came too late, that the framers wanted to complete their mission by September 15 and were simply unwilling to stay in Philadelphia even one day longer. Others disagree, arguing that the framers of the Constitution were more concerned with the structure of government than with individual rights and that the plan they devised—one based on enumerated, not unlimited, powers—would foreclose the need for a bill of rights. Hamilton wrote, "The Constitution is itself . . . a BILL OF RIGHTS."[4] Under it the government could exercise only those functions specifically bestowed upon it; all remaining rights belonged to the people. He also asserted that "independent of those which relate to the structure of government," the Constitution did, in fact, contain some of the more necessary specific guarantees.[5] For example, Article I, Section 9, prohibits bills of attainder, ex post facto laws, and the suspension of writs of habeas corpus. Hamilton and others further argued that the specification of rights was not only unnecessary but also could even be dangerous because no list could be complete.

Despite these misgivings, the reality of the political environment caused many Federalists to change their views on including a bill of rights. They realized

3. The following discussion comes from Daniel A. Farber and Suzanna Sherry, *A History of the American Constitution,* 2nd ed. (St. Paul, MN: Thomson/West, 2005), 316–317. This book reprints verbatim debates over the Constitution and the Bill of Rights.

4. *The Federalist Papers,* No. 84.

5. Ibid.

that if they did not accede to state demands, either the Constitution would not be ratified or a new convention would be necessary. As neither alternative was particularly attractive, they agreed to amend the Constitution as soon as the new government came into power.

In May 1789, one month after the start of the First Congress, Madison announced to the House of Representatives that he would draft a bill of rights and submit it within the coming month. As it turned out, the task proved more difficult than Madison had anticipated; the state conventions had suggested to Congress more than two hundred amendments, some of which would have significantly decreased the power of the national government. After sifting through these lists, Madison at first thought it might be best to incorporate the amendments into the Constitution's text, but he soon changed his mind. Instead, he presented the House with the following statement, echoing the views expressed in the Declaration of Independence:

That there be prefixed to the Constitution a declaration—That all power is originally vested in, and consequently derived from, the people.[6]

The legislators rejected this proposal, preferring a catalog of rights rather than a philosophical statement. Madison returned to his task, eventually fashioning a list of seventeen amendments. When he took it back to the House, however, the list was greeted with suspicion and opposition. Some members of Congress, even those who had argued for a bill of rights, now did not want to be bothered with the proposals, insisting that they had more important business to settle. One suggested that other nations would not see the United States "as a serious trading partner as it was still tinkering with its constitution instead of organizing its government."[7]

Finally, in July, after Madison had prodded and even begged, the House considered his proposals. A special committee scrutinized them and reported a few days later, and the House adopted, with some modification, Madison's seventeen amendments. The Senate approved some and rejected others so that by the time the Bill of Rights was submitted to the states on October 2, only twelve remained.[8]

The states ended up ratifying ten of the twelve. The amendments that did not receive approval were the original Articles I and II. Article I dealt with the number of representatives:

After the first enumeration required by the first article of the Constitution, there shall be one Representative for every thirty thousand, until the number shall amount to one hundred, after which the proportion shall be so regulated by Congress, that there shall be not less than one hundred Representatives, nor less than one Representative for every forty thousand persons, until the number of Representatives shall amount to two hundred; after which the proportion shall be so regulated by Congress, that there shall not be less than two hundred Representatives, nor more than one Representative for every fifty thousand persons.

Article II contained the following provision:

No law varying the compensation for the services of the Senators and Representatives shall take effect, until an election of Representatives shall have intervened.

This article also failed to garner sufficient support from the states in the 1790s and did not become a part of the Bill of Rights. Unlike the original Article I, however, this provision eventually took its place in the Constitution. In 1992, more than two hundred years after it was proposed, the states ratified it as the Twenty-seventh Amendment to the U.S. Constitution.

Why the states originally refused to pass this amendment, along with the original Article I, is a mystery, for few records of state ratification proceedings exist. What we do know is that on December 15, 1791, when Virginia ratified, the Bill of Rights became part of the U.S. Constitution.

THE AMENDMENT PROCESS

It is truly remarkable that Congress proposed and the states ratified ten amendments to the Constitution in three years: since then, only seventeen others have been

6. The full text of Madison's statement is available in *Contexts of the Constitution: A Documentary Collection on Principles of American Constitutional Law* by Neil H. Cogan (New York: Foundation Press, 1999), 813–815.

7. Quoted in Farber and Sherry, *American Constitution,* 330.

8. Among those rejected was the one Madison "prized above all others": that the states would have to abide by many of the enumerated guarantees. See Chapter 3 on incorporation of the Bill of Rights.

TABLE I-2   Methods of Amending the Constitution

PROPOSED BY	RATIFIED BY	USED FOR
Two-thirds vote in both houses of Congress	State legislatures in three-fourths of the states	Twenty-six amendments
Two-thirds vote in both houses of Congress	Ratifying conventions in three-fourths of the states	Twenty-first Amendment
Constitutional convention (called at the request of two-thirds of the states)	State legislatures in three-fourths of the states	Never used
Constitutional convention (called at the request of two-thirds of the states)	Ratifying conventions in three-fourths of the states	Never used

added! Such reticence would have pleased the writers of the Constitution. They wanted to create a government that would have permanence, even though they also recognized the need for flexibility. One of the major flaws in the Articles of Confederation, some thought, was the amending process: changing that document required the approval of all thirteen states. The framers imagined an amending procedure that would be "bendable but not trendable, tough but not insurmountable, responsive to genuine waves of popular desire, yet impervious to self-serving campaigns of factional groups."[9]

In Article V, the framers established a two-step procedure for altering the Constitution *(see Table I-2)*. Proposing a constitutional amendment is the first step. This may be done either by a two-thirds vote of both houses of Congress or by two-thirds of the states petitioning for a constitutional convention. To date, all proposed constitutional amendments have been the product of congressional action. A second constitutional convention has never been called.[10] This method has been avoided because it raises serious questions. Would the delegates to such a convention deliberate only the amendments under consideration, or would they be able to take up any or all parts of the Constitution?

The second step is ratification. Here, too, the framers allowed two options. Proposed amendments may be ratified by three-fourths of the state legislatures or by three-fourths of special state ratifying conventions.

Historically, only the Twenty-first Amendment, which repealed Prohibition, was ratified by state conventions. The others were all ratified by the required number of state legislatures.

Through the 2000s Congress has considered more than ten thousand amendments and sent thirty-three of them to the states. Among those thirty-three were the child labor amendment (proposed in 1924), prohibiting the "labor of persons under eighteen years of age," and the equal rights amendment (ERA; proposed in 1972), stating that "equality of rights under law shall not be denied or abridged by the United States or any State on account of sex." In both instances, an insufficient number of states agreed to their ratification. Suggestions for new constitutional amendments continue to be advanced. In 2006, for example, the House of Representatives voted on the Federal Marriage Amendment, which defines marriage as "the union of a man and a woman." The Amendment failed to obtain the necessary two-thirds vote. Today, efforts remain to persuade Congress to propose an amendment limiting the number of terms that U.S. representatives and senators may serve. Along similar lines, some law scholars (and, more recently, politicians) have proposed limiting the tenure of U.S. Supreme Court justices to one nonrenewable eighteen-year term.[11]

THE SUPREME COURT AND THE AMENDMENT PROCESS

So far, our discussion of the amendment process has not mentioned the president or the Supreme Court. The reason is that neither has any formal constitutional role in it. We do not mean to suggest, however,

9. J. T. Keenan, *The Constitution of the United States: An Unfolding Story*, 2nd ed. (Chicago: Dorsey Press, 1988), 41.

10. This is not to say that attempts to call a constitutional convention have never been made. Perhaps the most widely reported was the effort by Everett Dirksen, R-Ill. (Senate, 1951–1969), to convince the states to request a national convention with the purpose of overturning *Reynolds v. Sims,* the Supreme Court's 1964 reapportionment decision. He failed, by one state, to do so. A later attempt by the states to initiate constitutional change was a proposed amendment to require a balanced federal budget. This effort stalled with just two additional states required to call a convention.

11. See, for example, Roger C. Cramton and Paul D. Carrington, eds., *Reforming the Court: Term Limits for Supreme Court Justices* (Durham, NC: Carolina Academic Press, 2006).

TABLE I-3	Five Amendments that Overturned Supreme Court Decisions	
AMENDMENT	DATE RATIFIED	SUPREME COURT DECISION OVERTURNED
Eleventh	February 7, 1795	*Chisholm v. Georgia* (1793) In its first major decision, the Court authorized citizens of one state to sue another state in the Supreme Court. The decision angered advocates of states' rights.
Thirteenth	December 6, 1865	*Scott v. Sandford* (1857) The Court ruled slaves are property with which Congress may not interfere, and that neither slaves nor their descendants are citizens under the Constitution. Ratified in the wake of the Civil War, the Thirteenth and Fourteenth Amendments rectified the Court's decision.
Fourteenth	July 9, 1868	*Scott v. Sandford* (1857)
Sixteenth	February 3, 1913	*Pollock v. Farmers' Loan and Trust Co.* (1895) The Court declared the federal income tax unconstitutional, occasioning the adoption of the Sixteenth Amendment eighteen years later.
Twenty-sixth	July 1, 1971	*Oregon v. Mitchell* (1970) The Court ruled that Congress has the power to lower the voting age to eighteen only for federal, not state and local, elections. At a period when eighteen-year-olds were drafted to serve in the Vietnam War, Congress quickly responded to *Mitchell*, proposing the Twenty-sixth Amendment in March 1971.

SOURCE: Lee Epstein, Jeffrey A. Segal, Harold J. Spaeth, and Thomas G. Walker, *The Supreme Court Compendium: Data, Decisions, and Developments*, 5th ed. (Washington, DC: CQ Press, 2012), Tables 1-1 and 7-1.

that these institutions have nothing to do with the process: both have significant, albeit informal, functions. Presidents often instigate and support proposals for constitutional amendments. Indeed, virtually every chief executive has wanted some alteration to the Constitution. In his first inaugural address, George Washington urged the adoption of a bill of rights; more than two hundred years later, presidents continue to call for the ratification of amendments. During his presidency, George W. Bush, in response to state court rulings allowing same-sex marriages, endorsed the Federal Marriage Amendment; his successor, Barack Obama, has stated his opposition to any proposal to ban gays and lesbians from marrying. The Court also has played three important roles in the process.

First, the Court has served as a nationalizer of the Bill of Rights. Though many of the guarantees in the Bill of Rights seemed aimed at safeguarding personal freedoms against tyranny by the *federal* government—the First Amendment, for example, states that "Congress shall make no law . . . abridging the freedom of speech"—the Court has applied most of the guarantees to the states as well. We take a close look at how the Court has done this in Chapter 3.

Second, the Court has played the role of "instigator" of constitutional amendments. Of the seventeen additions to the Constitution after the Bill of Rights, Congress proposed five to overturn Supreme Court decisions *(see Table I-3).* Many consider one of these—the Fourteenth—the single most important amendment since 1791.

A healthy portion of the ten thousand or so proposals Congress has considered were aimed at similar objectives, among them the failed child labor and equal rights amendments, both of which emanated, at least in part, from Supreme Court rulings rejecting their premises.[12] Others Congress has considered to overturn Court decisions include a human life amendment that would make abortions illegal (in response to *Roe v. Wade,* 1973); a school prayer amendment that would allow public school children to engage in prayer (in response to *Engel v. Vitale,* 1962, and *School District of Abington Township v. Schempp,* 1963); a flag desecration amendment that would prohibit mutilation of the American flag (in response to *Texas v. Johnson,* 1989); and a congressional term limits amendment (to overturn the Supreme Court's ruling in *U.S. Term Limits v. Thornton,* 1995).

Finally, the Court has been asked to interpret Article V, which deals with the amendment process, but

---

12. In 1916 Congress passed a child labor law that prohibited the shipment in interstate commerce of anything made by children under age fourteen. When the Court struck down this act (and another like it) as an unconstitutional use of congressional power (*Hammer v. Dagenhart,* 1918), Congress proposed a child labor amendment.

it has been hesitant to do so. One example is ***Coleman v. Miller*** (1939), which involved the actions of the Kansas legislature over the child labor amendment.[13] Proposed by Congress in 1924, the amendment stated: "The Congress shall have power to limit, regulate, and prohibit the labor of persons under eighteen years of age." In January 1925, Kansas legislators rejected the amendment. The issue arose again, however, when the state senate reconsidered it in January 1937. At that time, the legislative body split 20–20, with the lieutenant governor casting the decisive vote to approve it. Members of the Kansas legislature (mostly those who had opposed the proposal) challenged the 1937 vote on two grounds: they questioned the ability of the lieutenant governor to break the tie and, more generally, they questioned the reconsideration of an amendment that previously had been rejected. Writing for the Court, Chief Justice Charles Evans Hughes refused to address these points. Rather, he asserted that the suit raised questions, particularly those pertaining to rescission, that were political and, therefore, nonjusticiable, meaning that a court was not an appropriate place to settle them. In his words, the "ultimate authority" over the amendment process was Congress, not the Court.

Over the years, the Court has followed the *Coleman* approach, leaving questions regarding the interpretation of Article V to Congress. Consider how it treated its most recent Article V case, ***NOW v. Idaho*** (1982). At issue was a 1978 act of Congress that extended the original deadline for state ratification of the equal rights amendment from 1979 to 1982; the act also rejected a clause that would have permitted state legislatures to rescind their prior approval. In the wake of a strong anti-ERA movement, Idaho, which had passed the amendment in the early 1970s, decided to ignore

federal law and retract its original vote.[14] The National Organization for Women challenged the state's action, and in 1982 the Court docketed the case for argument. But, upon the request of the United States, it dismissed the suit as moot: the congressionally extended time period for ratification had run out, and the controversy was no longer viable.

The Court could be confronted with even more difficult questions. For example, if the drive for a balanced budget amendment succeeded in attaining the support of two-thirds of the states, the Court might have to consider issues relating to a second constitutional convention. Would that mean only the amendments under consideration could be debated, or would the entire Constitution be subject to revision? Addressing this question might be one of the most significant tasks the Supreme Court has ever faced. Remember that the 1787 delegates met to amend the Articles of Confederation but instead reframed the entire system of government. Perhaps that is why those same men were so vehemently opposed to the notion of holding another convention to propose a bill of rights. Jefferson, for one, believed that a second convention could significantly weaken the government.

In any event, it may be a while before the Court must address this delicate issue. Since 1983 no state has passed the balanced budget amendment, a situation some analysts have credited to the budget surpluses of the 1990s and, more recently, to arguments that it may not be effective at solving economic problems. Others point to the formation of an anticonvention movement that strongly opposes any tinkering with the original document. To appreciate the seriousness of such an enterprise, we need only remind ourselves that the U.S. Constitution is the world's oldest surviving ruling charter and that the Bill of Rights is its heart.

---

13. Boldface type indicates that the opinions in the case can be found in the online archive at http://clca.cqpress.com.

14. Three other states, Kentucky, Nebraska, and Tennessee, also rescinded.

1 Understanding the U.S. Supreme Court

THIS BOOK IS DEVOTED to narrative and opinion excerpts showing how the U.S. Supreme Court has interpreted many of the amendments to the Constitution. As a student approaching civil rights, civil liberties, and justice, perhaps for the first time, you may think it is odd that the subject requires more than 770 pages of text. After all, in length, the U.S. Constitution and the amendments to it could fit easily into many Court decisions. Moreover, the document itself—its language—seems so clear.

First impressions, however, can be deceiving. Even apparently clear constitutional scriptures do not necessarily lend themselves to clear constitutional interpretation. For example, according to the First Amendment, "Congress shall make no law . . . prohibiting the free exercise" of religion. Sounds simple enough, but could you, based on those words, answer the following questions, all of which have been posed to the Court?

- May a state refuse to give unemployment benefits to an individual who quits her job because her employer wants her to work on Saturday, the day of rest in her religion?
- May the military retain a policy that forbids Jews in service from wearing yarmulkes?
- May a city prohibit the sacrificing of animals for religious purposes?

What these and other questions arising from the different guarantees contained in the Constitution illustrate is that a gap sometimes exists between the document's words and reality. Although the language seems explicit, its meaning can be elusive and difficult to interpret. Accordingly, justices have developed various approaches to resolving disputes.

But, as Figure 1-1 shows, a great deal happens before the justices actually decide cases. We begin our discussion with a brief overview of the steps depicted in the figure. Next, we consider explanations for the choices justices make at the final and most important stage, the resolution of disputes.

PROCESSING SUPREME COURT CASES

During the 2009–2010 term nearly 8,200 cases arrived at the Supreme Court's doorstep, but the justices decided only 73 with written opinions.[1] The disparity between the number of parties that want the Court to resolve their disputes and the number the Court agrees to resolve raises some important questions: How do the justices decide which cases to hear? What happens to the cases they reject? Those the Court agrees to resolve? We address these and other questions by describing how the Court processes its cases.

---

1. Data from the Chief Justice's 2010 Year-End Report on the Federal Judiciary.

FIGURE 1-1   The Processing of Cases

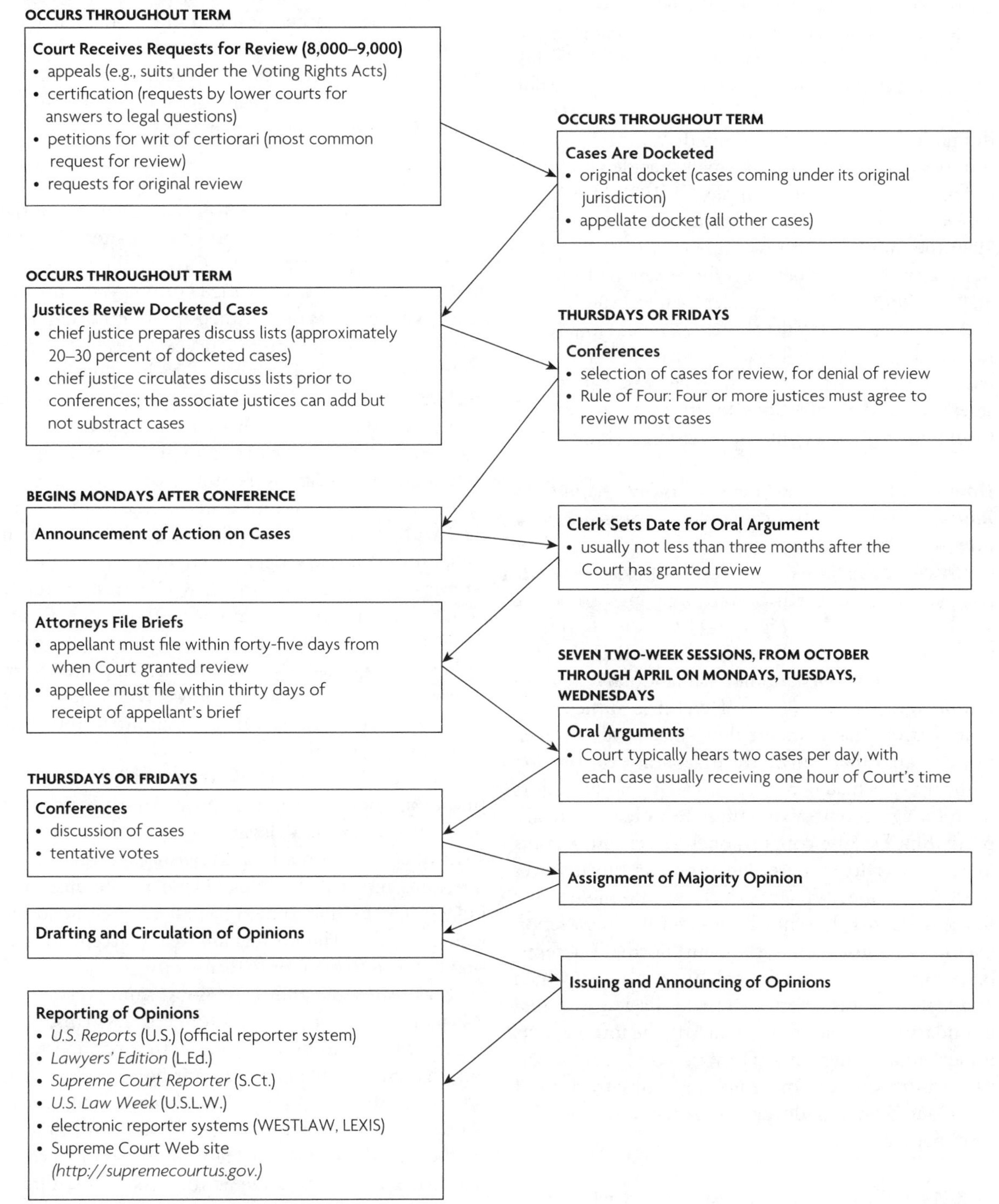

OCCURS THROUGHOUT TERM

Court Receives Requests for Review (8,000–9,000)
- appeals (e.g., suits under the Voting Rights Acts)
- certification (requests by lower courts for answers to legal questions)
- petitions for writ of certiorari (most common request for review)
- requests for original review

OCCURS THROUGHOUT TERM

Cases Are Docketed
- original docket (cases coming under its original jurisdiction)
- appellate docket (all other cases)

OCCURS THROUGHOUT TERM

Justices Review Docketed Cases
- chief justice prepares discuss lists (approximately 20–30 percent of docketed cases)
- chief justice circulates discuss lists prior to conferences; the associate justices can add but not substract cases

THURSDAYS OR FRIDAYS

Conferences
- selection of cases for review, for denial of review
- Rule of Four: Four or more justices must agree to review most cases

BEGINS MONDAYS AFTER CONFERENCE

Announcement of Action on Cases

Clerk Sets Date for Oral Argument
- usually not less than three months after the Court has granted review

Attorneys File Briefs
- appellant must file within forty-five days from when Court granted review
- appellee must file within thirty days of receipt of appellant's brief

SEVEN TWO-WEEK SESSIONS, FROM OCTOBER THROUGH APRIL ON MONDAYS, TUESDAYS, WEDNESDAYS

Oral Arguments
- Court typically hears two cases per day, with each case usually receiving one hour of Court's time

THURSDAYS OR FRIDAYS

Conferences
- discussion of cases
- tentative votes

Assignment of Majority Opinion

Drafting and Circulation of Opinions

Issuing and Announcing of Opinions

Reporting of Opinions
- *U.S. Reports* (U.S.) (official reporter system)
- *Lawyers' Edition* (L.Ed.)
- *Supreme Court Reporter* (S.Ct.)
- *U.S. Law Week* (U.S.L.W.)
- electronic reporter systems (WESTLAW, LEXIS)
- Supreme Court Web site (*http://supremecourtus.gov.*)

SOURCE: Compiled by authors.

Deciding to Decide: The Supreme Court's Caseload

As the figures for the 2009–2010 term indicate, the Court heard and decided less than 1 percent of the cases it received. This percentage is quite low, but it follows the general trend in Supreme Court decision making: the number of requests for review increased dramatically during the twentieth century, but the number of cases the Court formally decided each year did not increase. For example, in 1930 the Court agreed to decide 159 of the 726 disputes sent to it. In 1990 the number of cases granted review fell to 141, but the sum total of petitions for review had risen to 6,302—nearly nine times greater than in 1930.[2]

How do cases get to the Supreme Court? How do the justices decide which will get a formal review and which will be rejected? What affects their choices? Let us consider each of these questions, for they are fundamental to an understanding of judicial decision making.

How Cases Get to the Court: Jurisdiction and the Routes of Appeal. Cases come to the Court in one of four ways: either by a request for review under the Court's original jurisdiction or by three appellate routes—appeals, certification, and petitions for writs of certiorari *(see Figure 1-1).* Chapter 2 explains more about the Court's original jurisdiction, as it is central to understanding the landmark case of *Marbury v. Madison* (1803). Here, it is sufficient to note that original cases are those that have not been heard by any other court. Article III of the Constitution authorizes such suits in cases involving ambassadors from foreign countries and those to which a state is a party. But, because congressional legislation permits lower courts to exercise concurrent authority over most cases meeting Article III requirements, the Supreme Court does not have exclusive jurisdiction over them. Consequently, the Court normally accepts, on its original jurisdiction, only those cases in which one state is suing another (usually over a disputed boundary) and sends the rest back to the lower courts for an initial ruling. That is why, in recent years, original jurisdiction cases make up only a tiny fraction of the Court's overall docket—between one and five cases per term.

Most cases reach the Court under its appellate jurisdiction, meaning that a lower federal or state court has already rendered a decision and one of the parties is asking the Supreme Court to review that decision. As Figure 1-2 shows, such cases typically come from one of the U.S. courts of appeals or state supreme courts. The U.S. Supreme Court, the nation's highest tribunal, is the court of last resort.

To invoke the Court's appellate jurisdiction, litigants can take one of three routes, depending on the nature of their dispute: appeal as a matter of right, certification, and certiorari. Cases falling into the first category (normally called "on appeal") involve issues Congress has determined are so important that a ruling by the Supreme Court is necessary. Before 1988 these included cases in which a lower court declared a state or federal law unconstitutional or in which a state court upheld a state law challenged on the ground that it violated the U.S. Constitution. Although the justices were supposed to decide such appeals, they often found a more expedient way to deal with them—by either failing to consider them or issuing summary decisions (shorthand rulings). At the Court's urging, in 1988 Congress virtually eliminated "mandatory" appeals. Today, the Court is legally obliged to hear only those few cases (typically involving the Voting Rights Act) appealed from special three-judge district courts. When the Court agrees to hear such cases, it issues an order noting its "probable jurisdiction."

A second, but rarely used, route to the Court is certification. Under the Court's appellate jurisdiction and by an act of Congress, lower appellate courts can file writs of certification asking the justices to respond to questions aimed at clarifying federal law. Because only judges may use this route, very few cases come to the Court this way. The justices are free to accept a question certified to them or to dismiss it.

That leaves the third and most common appellate path, a request for a writ of certiorari (from the Latin meaning "to be informed"). In a petition for a writ of certiorari, the litigants desiring Supreme Court review ask the Court, literally, to become "informed" about their cases by requesting the lower court to send up the record. Most of the eight thousand or so cases that arrive each year come as requests for certiorari. The Court, exercising its ability to choose the cases to review, grants "cert" to less than 1 percent of the petitions. A grant of cert means that the justices have

---

2. Data are from Lee Epstein, Jeffrey A. Segal, Harold J. Spaeth, and Thomas G. Walker, *The Supreme Court Compendium: Data, Decisions, and Developments,* 5th ed. (Washington, DC: CQ Press, 2011), Tables 2-5 and 2-6.

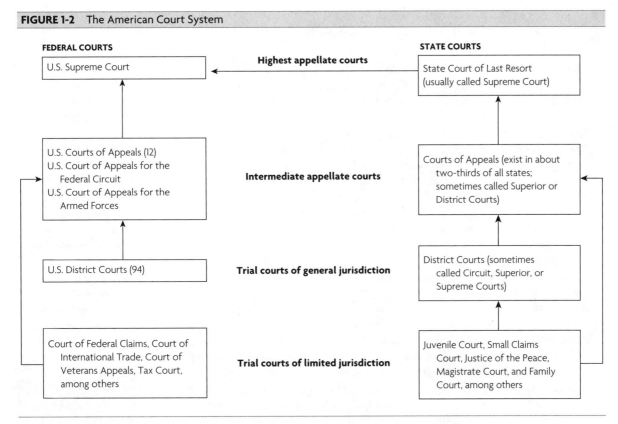

FIGURE 1-2   The American Court System

SOURCE: Compiled by authors.

decided to give the case full review; a denial means that the decision of the lower court remains in force.

In sum, Article III of the U.S. Constitution enables the Supreme Court to decide cases that have not been heard by any other court, but the vast majority of disputes that reach the justices have already been resolved by another judicial body. The United States' approach is not the only way to design a legal system. For example, in a society that has created a single constitutional court, that tribunal may have a judicial monopoly on interpreting matters of constitutional law; it may be the only forum in which citizens can bring constitutional claims *(see Box 1-1)*.

How the Court Decides: The Case Selection Process.
Regardless of the specific design of a legal system, in many countries jurists must confront the task of "deciding to decide"—that is, choosing which cases among many hundreds or even thousands they will actually resolve. The U.S. Supreme Court is no exception; it too has the job of deciding to decide, or identifying

those cases to which it will grant cert. This task presents something of a mixed blessing to the justices. Selecting the approximately ninety cases to review from the large number of requests is an arduous undertaking that requires the justices or their law clerks to look over hundreds of thousands of pages of briefs and other memoranda. The ability to exercise discretion, however, frees the Court from one of the major constraints on judicial bodies: the lack of agenda control. The justices may not be able to reach out and propose cases for review the way members of Congress can propose legislation, but the enormous number of petitions ensures that they can resolve at least some issues important to them.

Many scholars and lawyers have tried to determine what makes a case "certworthy," that is, worthy of review by the Supreme Court. Before we look at some of their findings, let us consider the case selection process itself. The original pool of about eight thousand petitions faces several checkpoints along the way *(see Figure 1-1)*, which significantly reduce the amount of

BOX 1-1   THE AMERICAN LEGAL SYSTEM IN GLOBAL PERSPECTIVE

The American legal system can be described as *dual, parallel,* and (for the most part) *three tiered.* It is dual because one federal system and fifty state systems coexist, each ruling on disputes falling under its particular purview. This duality does not mean, however, that state courts never hear cases involving claims made under the U.S. Constitution or that federal courts necessarily shun cases arising out of state law. In fact, the U.S. Supreme Court can review cases involving federal questions on which state supreme courts have ruled and can strike down state laws if they are incompatible with the U.S. Constitution. Similarly, many cases arising from state law and heard in state courts also contain federal issues that must be resolved.

Differences exist among the states' court systems, but most today roughly parallel the federal system. Trial courts—the lowest rungs on the ladder—are the entry points into the system. In the middle of the ladder are appellate courts, those that upon request review the records of trial court proceedings. Finally, both systems have supreme courts, bodies that provide final answers to legal questions in their own domains.

Although a supreme court sits atop each ladder, the U.S. Supreme Court plays a unique role—it is the apex of both state and federal court systems. Because it can hear cases and ultimately overturn the rulings of federal and state court judges, it is presumably *the* authoritative legal body in the United States.

Many nations have created legal systems that, to greater or lesser extents, resemble the American system. For example, Japan, whose constitutional document was largely drafted by Americans, also has a three-tiered structure. Cases begin at the district (trial) court level, move to high courts (Japan's version of midlevel appellate courts) and, finally, to the Supreme Court.[1] But other nations—first Germany and Italy, and later Belgium, Portugal, South Africa, Spain, and most of the countries of Eastern Europe—took a much different approach. In these countries, the highest court is not a supreme court but a single constitutional court, which has a judicial monopoly on interpreting matters of constitutional law. These constitutional courts are not part of the "ordinary" court system; litigants do not typically petition the justices to review decisions of lower courts. Rather, when judges confront a law whose constitutionality they doubt, they are obliged to send the case directly to the constitutional court. This tribunal receives evidence on the constitutional issue, sometimes gathers evidence on its own, hears arguments, perhaps consults sources that counsel overlooked, and hands down a decision. But, unlike in the United States, the constitutional court does not decide the case because it has not heard a case; it has only addressed a question of constitutional interpretation. Although the court publishes an opinion justifying its ruling and explaining the controlling principles, the case still must be decided by regular tribunals. In some countries—for example, Germany, Italy, and Russia—public officials also may bring suits in their constitutional courts challenging the legitimacy of legislative, executive, or judicial acts, and, under some circumstances, private citizens may initiate similar litigation. Where judicial action is challenged, the constitutional court in effect reviews a decision of another court, but the form of the action is very different from an appeal in the United States.

This type of court system is often called "centralized" because the power of judicial review—that is, the power to review government acts for their compatibility with the nation's constitution and strike down those acts that are not compatible—rests in one constitutional court; other courts are typically barred from exercising judicial review, although they may refer constitutional questions to the constitutional tribunal. In contrast, the U.S. system is deemed "decentralized" because ordinary courts—not just supreme courts—can engage in judicial review. We shall return to this distinction in Chapter 2 (*see Box 2-1*).

---

[1] Japan has summary courts with jurisdiction over minor civil and criminal cases. District courts (trial courts of general jurisdiction) can hear civil appeals from summary courts. For more details, see Herbert Jacob, ed., *Courts, Law, and Politics* (New Haven, CT: Yale University Press, 1996), chap. 6.

time the Court, acting as a collegial body, spends deciding what to decide. The staff members in the office of the Supreme Court clerk act as the first gatekeepers. When a petition for certiorari arrives, the clerk's office examines it to make sure it is in proper form, that it conforms to the Court's precise rules. Briefs must be "prepared in a 6 1/8- by 9 1/4-inch booklet, . . . typeset in a Century family 12-point type with 2-point or more leading between lines." Exceptions are made for litigants who cannot afford to pay the Court's fees.

FIGURE 1-3   A Page from Justice Blackmun's Docket Books

	HOLD FOR	DEFER		CERT.			JURISDICTIONAL STATEMENT				MERITS		MOTION		
		RELIST	CVSG	G	D	G & R	N	POST	DIS	AFF	REV	AFF	G	D	
Rehnquist, Ch. J............					✓							✓			
White, J............				3								✓			
Blackmun, J............				✓							✓				
Stevens, J............				✓							✓				
O'Connor, J............				3								✓			
Scalia, J............					✓							✓			
Kennedy, J............				✓							✓				
Souter, J............				✓								✓			
Thomas, J............					✓							✓			

SOURCE: Dockets of Harry A. Blackmun, Manuscript Division, Library of Congress, Washington, D.C.

NOTE: As the docket sheet shows, the justices have a number of options when they meet to vote on cert. They can grant (G) the petition or deny (D) it. They also can cast a "Join 3" (3) vote. Justices may have different interpretations of a Join 3 but, at the very least, it tells the others that the justice agrees to supply a vote in favor of cert if three other justices support granting review. In the MERITS column, REV = reverse the decision of the court below; AFF = affirm the decision of the court below.

The rules governing these petitions, known as *in forma pauperis* briefs, are somewhat looser, allowing indigents to submit briefs on 8½-by-11-inch paper. The Court's major concern, or so it seems, is that the document "be legible."[3]

The clerk's office gives all acceptable petitions an identification number, called a "docket number," and forwards copies to the chambers of the individual justices. On the current (2012) Court, all of the justices but Samuel Alito use the "certiorari pool system" in which clerks from the different chambers collaborate in reading and then writing memos on the petitions.[4] Upon receiving the preliminary or pool memos, the individual justices may ask their own clerks for their thoughts about the petitions. The justices then use the pool memos, along with their clerks' reports, as a basis for making their own independent determinations about which cases they believe are worthy of a full hearing.

During this process, the chief justice plays a special role, serving as yet another checkpoint on petitions.

Before the justices meet to make case selection decisions, the chief circulates a "discuss list" containing those cases he feels the Court should consider; any justice (in order of seniority) may add cases to this list but may not remove any. About 20 percent to 30 percent of the cases that come to the Court make it to the list and are actually discussed by the justices in conference. The rest are automatically denied review, leaving the lower court decision intact.[5]

This much we know. Because only the justices attend the Court's conferences, we cannot say precisely what transpires. We can offer only a rough picture based on scholarly writings, the comments of justices, and our examination of the private papers of a few retired justices. These sources tell us that the discussion of each petition begins with the chief justice presenting a short summary of the facts and, typically, stating his vote. The associate justices, who sit at a rectangular table in order of seniority, then comment on each petition, with the most senior justice speaking first and the newest member last. The associate justices usually provide some indication of how they will vote on the merits of the case if it is accepted. Indeed, as Figure 1-3 shows, the justices record certiorari and merits votes in their

---

3. Rules 33 and 39 of the Rules of the Supreme Court of the United States. All Supreme Court rules are available at http://www.supremecourt.gov/ctrules/ctrules.aspx

4. Supreme Court justices are authorized to hire four law clerks each. Typically, these clerks are outstanding recent graduates of the nation's top law schools. Pool (or preliminary) memos, as well as other documents pertaining to the Court's case selection process, are available at http://epstein.usc.edu/blackmun.php.

5. For information on the discuss list, see Gregory A. Caldeira and John R. Wright, "The Discuss List: Agenda Building in the Supreme Court," *Law and Society Review* 24 (1990): 807–836.

docket books. But, given the large number of petitions, the justices apparently discuss few cases in detail.

By tradition, the Court adheres to the so-called Rule of Four: it grants certiorari to those cases receiving the affirmative vote of at least four justices. The Court identifies the cases accepted and rejected on a "certified orders list," which is released to the public. For cases granted certiorari or in which probable jurisdiction is noted, the clerk informs participating attorneys, who then have specified time limits in which to turn in their written legal arguments (briefs), and the case is scheduled for oral argument.

Considerations Affecting Case Selection Decisions. This is how the Court considers petitions, but why do the justices make the decisions that they do? Scholars have developed several answers to this question. Two sets are worthy of our attention: legal considerations and political considerations.[6]

Legal considerations are listed in Rule 10, which the Court has established to govern the certiorari decision-making process:

Review on a writ of certiorari is not a matter of right, but of judicial discretion. A petition for a writ of certiorari will be granted only for compelling reasons. The following, although neither controlling nor fully measuring the Court's discretion, indicate the character of the reasons the Court considers:

(a)   a United States court of appeals has entered a decision in conflict with the decision of another United States court of appeals on the same important matter; has decided an important federal question in a way that conflicts with a decision by a state court of last resort; or has so far departed from the accepted and usual course of judicial proceedings, or sanctioned such a departure by a lower court, as to call for an exercise of this Court's supervisory power;

(b)   a state court of last resort has decided an important federal question in a way that conflicts with the decision of another state court of last resort or of a United States court of appeals;

(c)   a state court or a United States court of appeals has decided an important question of federal law that has not been, but should be, settled by this Court, or has decided an important federal question in a way that conflicts with relevant decisions of this Court.

A petition for a writ of certiorari is rarely granted when the asserted error consists of erroneous factual findings or the misapplication of a properly stated rule of law.

To what extent do the considerations outlined in Rule 10 affect the Court? The answer is mixed. On one hand, the Court seems to follow its dictates. The presence of actual conflict between or among federal courts, a major concern of Rule 10, substantially increases the likelihood of review; if actual conflict is present in a case, it has a 33 percent chance of gaining Court review—as compared with the usual 1 percent certiorari rate.[7] On the other hand, as political scientists Gregory A. Caldeira and John R. Wright explain, Rule 10 is not all that helpful in understanding "how the Court makes gatekeeping decisions."[8] The Court may use the existence of actual conflict as a threshold (cases that do not present conflict *may* be rejected); it does not accept all cases with conflict because there are too many.[9]

The legal considerations listed in Rule 10 may act as constraints on the justices' behavior, but they do not necessarily further our understanding of what occurs in cases meeting the criteria. That is why scholars have looked to *political* factors that may influence the Court's case selection process. Three are particularly important. The first is the U.S. solicitor general (SG), the attorney who represents the U.S. government before the Supreme Court. Simply stated, when the SG files a petition, the Court is very likely to grant certiorari. In fact, the Court accepts about 70 percent to 80 percent of the cases in which the federal government is the petitioning party.

Scholars have posited a number of reasons for the solicitor general's success as a petitioner. One is that the Court is cognizant of the SG's special role. A presidential appointee whose decisions often reflect the

---

6. Some scholars have noted a third set: procedural considerations. These emanate from Article III, which—under the Court's interpretation—places constraints on the ability of federal tribunals to hear and decide cases. These constraints are reviewed in Chapter 2. Here we note the two that are particularly important for the review decision: the case must be appropriate for judicial resolution in that it presents a real "case" and "controversy" (justiciability) and the appropriate person must bring the case (standing). Unless these procedural criteria are met, the Court—at least theoretically—will deny review.

7. See Gregory A. Caldeira and John R. Wright, "Organized Interests and Agenda Setting in the U.S. Supreme Court," *American Political Science Review* 82 (1988): 1109–1127.

8. Ibid., 1115.

9. In fact, during any given term, the Court rejects hundreds of cases in which real conflicts exist. See Lawrence Baum, *The Supreme Court*, 10th ed. (Washington, DC: CQ Press, 2009), 92–93.

administration's philosophy, the SG also represents the interests of the United States. As the nation's highest court, the Supreme Court cannot ignore these interests. In addition, the justices rely on the solicitor general to act as a filter; that is, they expect the SG to examine carefully the cases to which the government is a party and bring only the most important to their attention. Finally, because solicitors general are involved in so much Supreme Court litigation, they acquire a great deal of knowledge about the Court that other litigants do not. They are "repeat players" who know the "rules of the game" and can use them to their advantage. For example, they know how to structure their petitions to attract the attention and interest of the justices.

The second political factor is the amicus curiae (friend of the court) brief. These briefs are usually filed by interest groups and other third parties after the Court makes its decision to hear a case, but they can also be filed at the certiorari stage *(see Box 1-2)*. Research by political scientists shows that amicus briefs significantly enhance a case's chances of being heard, and multiple briefs have a greater effect.[10] Another interesting finding of these studies is that even when groups file *in opposition* to granting certiorari, they increase—rather than decrease—the probability that the Court will hear the case.

What can we make of these findings? Most important is this: the justices may not be strongly influenced by the arguments contained in these briefs (if they were, why would briefs in opposition to certiorari have the opposite effect?), but they seem to use them as cues. In other words, because amicus curiae briefs filed at the certiorari stage are somewhat uncommon—less than 10 percent of all petitions are accompanied by amicus briefs—they do draw the justices' attention. If major organizations are sufficiently interested in an appeal to pay the cost of filing briefs in support of (or against) Court review, then the petition for certiorari is probably worth the justices' serious consideration.

In addition, we have strong reasons to suspect that a third political factor—the ideology of the justices—affects actions on certiorari petitions. Researchers tell us that the justices during the liberal period under Chief Justice Earl Warren (1953–1969) were more

likely to grant review to cases in which the lower court reached a conservative decision so that they could reverse, while those of the moderately conservative Court during the years of Chief Justice Warren Burger (1969–1986) took liberal results to reverse. It would be difficult to believe that the current justices would be any less likely than their predecessors to vote on the basis of their ideologies. Scholarly studies also suggest that justices engage in strategic voting behavior at the cert stage. In other words, justices are forward thinking; they consider the implications of their cert vote for the later merits stage, asking themselves: If I vote to grant a particular petition, what are the odds of my position winning down the road? As one justice explained his calculations, "I might think the Nebraska Supreme Court made a horrible decision, but I wouldn't want to take the case, for if we take the case and affirm it, then it would become precedent."[11]

The Role of Attorneys

Once the Supreme Court agrees to decide a case, the clerk of the Court informs the parties. The parties present their side of the dispute to the justices in written and oral arguments.

Written Arguments. Written arguments, called briefs, are the major vehicles for parties to Supreme Court cases to document their positions. Under the Court's rules, the appealing party (known as the appellant or petitioner) must submit its brief within forty-five days of the time the Court grants certiorari; the opposing party (known as the appellee or respondent) has thirty days after receipt of the appellant's brief to respond with arguments urging affirmance of the lower court ruling.

As is the case for cert petitions, the Court maintains specific rules covering the presentation and format of merits briefs. For example, the briefs of both parties must be submitted in forty copies and may not exceed 15,000 words. Rule 24 outlines the material that briefs must contain, such as a description of the questions presented for review, a list of the parties, and a statement describing the Court's authority to hear the case.

The clerk sends the briefs to the justices, who normally study them before oral argument. Written briefs

10. Caldeira and Wright, "Organized Interests and Agenda Setting"; Ryan C. Black and Ryan J. Owens, "Agenda Setting in the Supreme Court: The Collision of Policy and Jurisprudence," *Journal of Politics* 71 (2009): 1062–1075.

11. Quoted in H. W. Perry Jr., *Deciding to Decide: Agenda Setting in the United States Supreme Court* (Cambridge, MA: Harvard University Press, 1991), 200.

BOX 1-2   THE AMICUS CURIAE BRIEF

The amicus curiae practice probably originates in Roman law. A judge would often appoint a *consilium* (officer of the court) to advise him on points where the judge was in doubt. That may be why the term *amicus curiae* translates from the Latin as "friend of the court." But today it is the rare amicus who is a friend of the court. Instead, contemporary briefs almost always are a friend of a party, supporting one side over the other at the certiorari and merits stages. Consider the brief filed in *United States v. Virginia* (1996), the cover of which is reprinted here. In that case, the National Women's Law Center and other organizations supported the federal government's request to have the Court hear the case. They, along with the United States, believed that the court below erred when it allowed the state of Virginia to maintain a single-sex admissions policy at Virginia Military Institute. These groups were anything but neutral participants.

How does an organization become an amicus curiae participant in the Supreme Court of the United States? Under the Court's rules, groups wishing to file an amicus brief at the certiorari or merits stage must obtain the written consent of the parties to the litigation (the federal and state governments are exempt from this requirement). If the parties refuse to give their consent, the group can file a motion with the Court asking for its permission. The Court today almost always grants these motions.

IN THE
Supreme Court of the United States
OCTOBER TERM, 1994
JUNE 26, 1995
NO. 94-1941

------------●------------

UNITED STATES OF AMERICA, *Petitioner*

—V.—

COMMONWEALTH OF VIRGINIA, et al., *Respondents*.

ON PETITION FOR A WRIT OF CERTIORARI TO THE UNITED STATES COURT OF APPEALS FOR THE FOURTH CIRCUIT BRIEF OF AMICI CURIAE NATIONAL WOMEN'S LAW CENTER, AMERICAN CIVIL LIBERTIES UNION, THE AMERICAN ASSOCIATION OF UNIVERSITY WOMEN, B'NAI B'RITH WOMEN, CENTER FOR ADVANCEMENT OF PUBLIC POLICY, CENTER FOR WOMEN POLICY STUDIES, COALITION OF LABOR UNION WOMEN,

CONNECTICUT WOMEN'S EDUCATION AND LEGAL FUND, EQUAL RIGHTS ADVOCATES, FEDERALLY EMPLOYED WOMEN, INC., NATIONAL COUNCIL OF JEWISH WOMEN, INC., NATIONAL COUNCIL OF NEGRO WOMEN, NATIONAL EDUCATION ASSOCIATION, THE NATIONAL GAY AND LESBIAN TASK FORCE, NATIONAL ORGANIZATION FOR WOMEN, THE NATIONAL WOMAN'S PARTY, NATIONAL WOMEN'S CONFERENCE COMMITTEE, NATIONAL WOMEN'S POLITICAL CAUCUS, NOW LEGAL DEFENSE AND EDUCATION FUND, TRIAL LAWYERS FOR PUBLIC JUSTICE, WOMEN EMPLOYED, WOMEN'S LAW PROJECT, AND THE WOMEN'S LEGAL DEFENSE FUND IN SUPPORT OF THE PETITION

MARCIA D. GREENBERGER, DEBORAH L. BRAKE
National Women's Law Center, 11 Dupont Circle, Suite 800,
Washington, D.C. 20036
SARA L. MANDELBAUM, STEVEN R. SHAPIRO, JANET GALLAGHER
American Civil Liberties Union, 132 W. 43rd Street, New York, NY 10036

ROBERT N. WEINER, Counsel for Record, WALTER J. ROCKLER,
PETER G. NEIMAN, MARK ECKENWILER, ARNOLD & PORTER
555 12th Street, N.W., Washington, D.C. 20004
(202) 942-5000
Counsel for Amici Curiae

are important because the justices may use them to formulate the questions they ask the lawyers representing the parties. The briefs also serve as a permanent record of the positions of the parties, available to the justices for consultation after oral argument when they decide the case outcome. A well-crafted brief can place into the hands of the justices arguments, legal references, and suggested remedies that later may be incorporated into the opinion.

In addition to the briefs submitted by the parties to the suit, Court rules allow interested persons, organizations, and government units to participate as amici curiae on the merits—just as they are permitted to file such briefs at the review stage. Those wishing to submit friend of the court briefs must obtain the written permission of the parties or the Court. Only the federal government and state governments are exempt from this requirement *(see Box 1-2)*.

Oral Arguments. Attorneys also have the opportunity to present their cases orally before the justices. Each side has thirty minutes to convince the Court of the merits of its position and to field questions from the justices, though sometimes the Court makes small exceptions to this rule. In the 2011 term, it made a particularly big one, hearing six hours of oral argument, over three days, on the Patient Protection and Affordable Care Act, the health care law passed in 2010. This was unprecedented in the modern era, but not in the Court's early years. In the past, because attorneys did not always prepare written briefs, the justices relied on oral arguments to learn about the cases and to help them marshal their arguments for the next stage. Orals were considered important public events, opportunities to see the most prominent attorneys of the day at work. Arguments often went on for days: *Gibbons v. Ogden* (1824), the landmark commerce clause case, was argued for five days, and *McCulloch v. Maryland* (1819), the litigation challenging the constitutionality of the national bank, took nine days to argue.

The justices are allowed to interrupt the attorneys at any time with comments and questions, as the following exchange between Justice Byron White and Sarah Weddington, the attorney representing Jane Roe in *Roe v. Wade* (1973), illustrates. White got the ball rolling when he asked Weddington to respond to an issue her brief had not addressed: whether abortions should be performed during all stages of pregnancy or should somehow be limited. The following discussion ensued:

WHITE: And the statute doesn't make any distinction based upon at what period of pregnancy the abortion is performed?

WEDDINGTON: No, Your Honor. There is no time limit or indication of time, whatsoever. So I think—

WHITE: What is your constitutional position there?

WEDDINGTON: As to a time limit—

WHITE: What about whatever clause of the Constitution you rest on—Ninth Amendment, due process . . .— that takes you right up to the time of birth?

WEDDINGTON: It is our position that the freedom involved is that of a woman to determine whether or not to continue a pregnancy. Obviously, I have a much more difficult time saying that the State has no interest in late pregnancy.

WHITE: Why? Why is that?

WEDDINGTON: I think that's more the emotional response to a late pregnancy, rather than it is any constitutional—

WHITE: Emotional response by whom?

WEDDINGTON: I guess by persons considering the issue outside the legal context, I think, as far as the State—

WHITE: Well, do you or don't you say that the constitutional—

WEDDINGTON: I would say constitutional—

WHITE: —right you insist on reaches up to the time of birth, or—

WEDDINGTON: The Constitution, as I read it . . . attaches protection to the person at the time of birth.

In the Court's early years, there was little doubt about the importance of such exchanges, and of oral arguments in general, because, as noted above, the justices did not always have the benefit of written briefs. Today, however, some have questioned the effectiveness of oral arguments and their role in decision making. Chief Justice Earl Warren maintained that they made little difference to the outcome. Once the justices have read the briefs and studied related cases, most have relatively firm views on how the case should be decided, and orals change few minds. Justice William J. Brennan Jr., however, maintained that they are extremely important because they help justices to clarify core arguments. Recent scholarly work seems to come down on Brennan's side. According to a study by Timothy Johnson and his colleagues, the justices are more likely to vote for the side with the better showing at orals. Along somewhat different lines, a study by Epstein, Landes, and Posner shows that orals may be a good predictor of the Court's final votes: the side that receives more questions tends to lose.[12] One possible explanation is that the justices use oral argument as a way to express their opinions and attempt to influence their colleagues, because formal deliberation (described below) is often limited and highly structured.

The debate will likely continue. Even if oral arguments turn out to have little effect on the justices' decisions, we should not forget their symbolic importance: they are the only part of the Court's decision-making process that occurs in public and that you now have the opportunity to hear. Political scientist Jerry Goldman has made the oral arguments of many cases available online at http://www.oyez.org. Throughout this book you will find references to this Web site, indicating that you can listen to the arguments in the case you are reading.

The Supreme Court Decides: Some Preliminaries

After the Court hears oral arguments, it meets in a private conference to discuss the case and to take a preliminary vote. Below, we describe the Court's conference procedures and the two stages that follow the conference: the assignment of the opinion of the Court and the opinion circulation period.

The Conference. Despite popular support for "government in the sunshine," the Supreme Court insists that its decisions take place in a private conference, with no one in attendance except the justices. Congress has agreed to this demand, exempting the federal courts from open government and freedom of information legislation. There are two basic reasons for the Court's insistence on the private conference. First, the Court—which, unlike Congress, lacks an electoral

connection—is supposed to base its decisions on factors other than public opinion. Opening up deliberations to press scrutiny, for example, might encourage the justices to take notice of popular sentiment, which is not supposed to influence them. Or so the argument goes. Second, although in conference the Court reaches tentative decisions on cases, the opinions explaining the decisions remain to be written. This process can take many weeks or even months, and a decision is not final until the opinions have been written, circulated, and approved. Because the Court's decisions can have major impacts on politics and the economy, any party having advance knowledge of case outcomes could use that information for unfair business and political advantage.

The system works so well that with only a few exceptions, the justices have not experienced information leaks. It is therefore impossible to know precisely what occurs in the deliberation of any particular case. We can, however, piece together the procedures and the general nature of the Court's discussions from the papers of retired justices and the comments of others. We have learned the following. First, we know that the chief justice presides over the deliberations. He calls up the case for discussion and then presents his views about the issues and how the case should be decided. The remaining justices state their views and vote in order of seniority.

The level and intensity of discussion, as the justices' notes from conference deliberations reveal, differ from case to case. In some, it appears that the justices had very little to say. The chief presented his views, and the rest noted their agreement. In others, every Court member had something to add. Whether the discussion is subdued or lively, it is unclear to what extent conferences affect the final decisions. It would be unusual for a justice to enter the conference room without having reached a tentative position on the cases to be discussed; after all, he or she has read the briefs and listened to oral arguments. But the conference, in addition to oral arguments, provides an opportunity for the justices to size up the positions of their colleagues. This sort of information, as we shall see, may be important as the justices begin the process of crafting and circulating opinions.

Opinion Assignment. The conference typically leads to a tentative outcome and vote. What happens at this point is critical because it determines who assigns the opinion of the Court—the Court's only authoritative

12. Timothy R. Johnson, Paul J. Wahlbeck, and James F. Spriggs, II, "The Influence of Oral Arguments on the U.S. Supreme Court," *American Political Science Review* 100 (2006): 99–113; Lee Epstein, William Landes, and Richard A. Posner, "Inferring the Winning Party in the Supreme Court from the Pattern of Questioning at Oral Argument," *Journal of Legal Studies* 39 (2010): 433–467.

policy statement, the only one that establishes precedent. Under Court norms, when the chief justice votes with the majority, he assigns the writing of the opinion. The chief may decide to write the opinion or assign it to one of the other justices who voted with the majority. When the chief justice votes with the minority, the assignment task falls to the most senior member of the Court who voted with the majority.

In making the assignment, the chief justice (or the senior associate in the majority) takes many factors into account. Legal scholars Forrest Maltzman and Paul J. Wahlbeck examined the opinion assignments of Chief Justice William Rehnquist and found that the chief tried to equalize the distribution of the Court's workload. [13] Rehnquist's management made sense: the Court will not run efficiently, given the burdensome nature of opinion writing, if some justices are given many more assignments than others. The research also suggests that Rehnquist took into account the justices' particular areas of expertise. He recognized that some of his colleagues had more knowledge of particular areas of the law than others, and he tended to assign accordingly. By encouraging specialization, Rehnquist may have been trying to increase the quality of opinions and reduce the time required to write them. Maltzman and Wahlbeck also noted that when a case was decided by a one-vote margin, Rehnquist assigned the opinion to a moderate member of the majority rather than to an extreme member. His reasoning seemed clear: if the writer in a close case drafts an opinion with which other members of the majority are uncomfortable, the opinion may drive justices to the other side, causing the majority to become a minority. Rehnquist tried to minimize this risk by asking justices squarely in the middle of the majority coalition to write the opinion. Whether Chief Justice Roberts has followed suit, we will know only when a justice who served under Roberts opens his or her papers to the public.

Opinion Circulation. Regardless of the factors the chief considers in making assignments, one thing is clear: the opinion writer is a critical player in the opinion circulation phase, which eventually leads to the final decision of the Court. The writer begins the process by circulating an opinion draft to the others.

Once the justices receive the first draft of the opinion, they have many options. First, they can join the opinion, meaning that they agree with it and want no changes. Second, they can ask the opinion writer to make changes, that is, *bargain* with the writer over the content of and even the disposition—to reverse or affirm the lower court ruling—offered in the draft. The following memo sent from Brennan to White is exemplary: "I've mentioned to you that I favor your approach to this case and want if possible to join your opinion. If you find the following suggestions . . . acceptable, I can join you."[14]

Third, they can tell the opinion writer that they plan to circulate a dissenting or concurring opinion. A concurring opinion generally agrees with the disposition but not with the rationale; a dissenting opinion means that the writer disagrees with the disposition the majority opinion reaches and with the rationale it invokes. Finally, justices can tell the opinion writer that they await further writings, meaning that they want to study various dissents or concurrences before they decide what to do.

As justices circulate their opinions and revise them—the average majority opinion undergoes three to four revisions in response to colleagues' comments—many different opinions on the same case, at various stages of development, will be floating around the Court over the course of several months. Because this process is replicated for each case the Court decides with a formal written opinion, it is possible that scores of different opinions may be working their way from office to office at any point in time.

Eventually, the final version of the opinion is reached, and each justice expresses a position in writing or by signing an opinion of another justice. This is how the final vote is taken. When all of the justices have declared themselves, the only remaining step is for the Court to announce its decision and the vote to the public.

SUPREME COURT DECISION MAKING: THE ROLE OF LAW AND LEGAL METHODS

So far, we have examined the processes the justices follow to reach decisions on the disputes brought before them. We have answered basic questions about the institutional procedures the Court uses to carry out its

13. Forrest Maltzman and Paul J. Wahlbeck, "May It Please the Chief? Opinion Assignments in the Rehnquist Court," *American Journal of Political Science* 40 (1996): 421–443.

14. Memorandum from Justice Brennan to Justice White, 12/9/76, re: 75-104, *United Jewish Organizations v. Carey.*

responsibilities. The questions we have not addressed concern why the justices reach particular decisions and what forces play a role in determining their choices.

As you might imagine, the responses to these questions are many, but they can be categorized into two groups. One focuses on the role of law, broadly defined, and legal methods in determining how justices interpret the Constitution, emphasizing, among other things, the importance of its words, American history and tradition, and precedent (previously decided constitutional rulings). Judge Richard Posner and his coauthors have referred to this as a legalistic theory of judicial decision making.[15] The other—what Posner et al. call a realistic theory of judging—emphasizes nonlegalistic factors, including the role of politics. "Politics" can take many forms, such as the particular ideological views of the justices, the mood of the public, and the political preferences of the executive and legislative branches.

Often commentators define these two sides as "should" versus "do." That is, they say the justices *should* interpret the Constitution in line with, say, the language of the text of the document or in accord with precedent. They reason that justices are supposed to shed all of their personal biases, preferences, and partisan attachments when they take their seats on the bench. But, it is argued, justices *do not* shed these biases, preferences, and attachments; rather, their decisions often reflect the justices' own politics or the political views of those around them.

To the extent that approaches grounded in law originated to answer the question of how justices *should* decide pending disputes, we understand why the difference between the two groups is often cast in terms of "should" versus "do." But, for several reasons, we ask you to think about whether, in fact, the justices actually do use these "should" approaches to reach decisions, and not merely to camouflage their politics. One reason is that the justices themselves often say they look to the founding period, the words of the Constitution, previously decided cases, and other "law" approaches to resolve disputes because they consider them appropriate criteria for reaching decisions. Another is that some scholars express agreement with the justices, arguing that Court members cannot follow their own personal preferences, the whims of the public, or other

non–legally relevant factors "if they are to have the continued respect of their colleagues, the wider legal community, citizens, and leaders." Rather, they "must be principled in their decision-making process."[16]

Whether they are principled in their decision making is for you to determine as you read the cases to come. First, however, it is necessary to have some sense of the various analytical approaches—or what some call methods of constitutional interpretation—that the justices frequently say they employ. We consider some of the most important approaches and describe the philosophies that support their use: original intent, textualism, original meaning, polling other jurisdictions, stare decisis analysis, appeals to tradition, and pragmatism.[17] Table 1-1 provides a brief summary of each, using the Second Amendment as an example; in what follows, we supply more details, including the philosophies that support their use.

The Second Amendment of the U.S. Constitution reads as follows: "A well regulated Militia, being necessary to the security of a free State, the right of the people to keep and bear Arms, shall not be infringed." In *District of Columbia v. Heller (excerpted on pages 390-395),* the U.S. Supreme Court ruled that the amendment protects the right of individuals who are not affiliated with any state-regulated militia to keep handguns and other firearms in their homes for their own private use.

Legal briefs filed with the Court, as well as media and academic commentary on the case, employed diverse methods of constitutional interpretation. Notice that no method seems to dictate a particular outcome; rather, lawyers for either side of the lawsuit could plausibly employ a variety of approaches to support their side.

Original Intent

The Supreme Court first invoked the term *the intention of the framers* in 1796. In *Hylton v. United States* the Court said, "It was . . . obviously the intention of

---

15. Lee Epstein, William M. Landes, and Richard A. Posner, *The Behavior of Federal Judges: A Theoretical and Empirical Study of Rational Choice* (Cambridge, MA: Harvard University Press, 2012).

16. Ronald Kahn, "Institutional Norms and Supreme Court Decision Making: The Rehnquist Court on Privacy and Religion," in *Supreme Court Decision-Making,* ed. Cornell W. Clayton and Howard Gillman (Chicago: University of Chicago Press, 1999), 176.

17. For overviews (and critiques) of these and other approaches, see Eugene Volokh, "Using the Second Amendment as a Teaching Tool—Modalities of Constitutional Argument" (available at http://www.law.ucla.edu/volokh/2amteach/interp.htm); Philip Bobbitt, *Constitutional Fate: Theory of the Constitution* (New York: Oxford University Press, 1982).

TABLE 1-1   Methods of Constitutional Interpretation

METHOD	EXAMPLE
Original Intent. Asks what the framers wanted to do.	"The Framers would have been shocked by the notion of the government taking away our handguns."
	OR
	"The Framers would have been shocked by the notion of people being entitled to own guns in a society where guns cause so much death and violence."
Textualism. Places emphasis on what the Constitution says.	"The Second Amendment says 'right of the people to keep and bear arms,' so the people have a right to keep and bear arms."
	OR
	"The Second Amendment says 'A well regulated militia . . . ,' so the right is limited only to the militia."
Original Meaning. Considers what a clause meant (or how it was understood) to those who enacted it.	"'Militia' meant 'armed adult male citizenry' when the Amendment was enacted, so that's how we should interpret it today."
	OR
	"'Arms' meant flintlocks and the like when the Amendment was enacted, so that's how we should interpret it today."
Stare Decisis. Looks to what courts have written about the clause.	"Courts have held that the Second Amendment protects weapons that are part of ordinary military equipment, and handguns certainly qualify."
	OR
	"Courts have held that the Second Amendment was meant to keep the Militia as an effective force, and they can be nicely effective just with rifles."
Polling Jurisdictions. Examines practices in the United States and even abroad.	"The Legislatures of all fifty States are united in their rejection of bans on private handgun ownership. Every State in the Union permits private citizens to own handguns. Practices in other countries are immaterial to the task of interpreting the U.S. Constitution."
	OR
	"The largest cities in the United States have local laws banning handguns or tightly regulating their possession and use; and many industrialized countries also ban handguns or grant permits in only exceptional cases.
Pragmatism. Considers the effect of various interpretations, suggesting that courts should adopt the one that avoids bad consequences.	"The Second Amendment should be interpreted as protecting the right to own handguns for self-defense, because otherwise only criminals will have guns and crime will skyrocket."
	OR
	"The Second Amendment should be interpreted as not protecting the right to own handguns for self-defense, because otherwise we'll never solve our crime problems."

SOURCE: We adopt much of the material in this table from Eugene Volokh, "Using the Second Amendment as a Teaching Tool—Modalities of Constitutional Argument," at http://www.law.ucla.edu/volokh/2amteach/interp.htm. Other material comes from the briefs filed in *District of Columbia v. Heller.*

the framers of the Constitution, that Congress should possess full power over every species of taxable property, except exports. The term taxes, is generical, and was made use of to vest in Congress plenary authority in all cases of taxation."[18] In *Hustler Magazine v. Falwell* (1988), the Court used the same grounds to find that cartoon parodies,

however obnoxious, constitute expression protected by the First Amendment.

Undoubtedly, justices over the years have frequently looked to the intent of the framers to reach conclusions about the disputes before them.[19] But why? What possible relevance could the framers' intentions have

18. Example cited by Boris I. Bittker in "The Bicentennial of the Jurisprudence of Original Intent: The Recent Past," *California Law Review* 77 (1989): 235.

19. Given the subject of this volume, we deal here exclusively with the intent of the framers of the U.S. Constitution and its amendments, but one also could apply this approach to statutory construction by considering the intent of those who drafted and enacted the laws in question.

for today's controversies? Advocates of this approach offer several answers. First, they assert that the framers acted in a calculated manner; that is, they knew what they were doing, so why should we disregard their precepts? One adherent said: "Those who framed the Constitution chose their words carefully; they debated at great length the most minute points. The language they chose meant something. It is incumbent upon the Court to determine what that meaning was."[20]

Second, it is argued that, if they scrutinize the intent of the framers, justices can deduce "constitutional truths," which they can apply to cases. Doing so, proponents say, produces neutral principles of law and eliminates value-laden decisions.[21] Consider, for example, speech advocating the violent overthrow of the government. Suppose the government enacted a law prohibiting such expression and arrested members of a radical political party for violating it. Justices could scrutinize this law in several ways. A liberal might conclude, solely because of his or her liberal values, that the First Amendment prohibits a ban on such expression. Conservative jurists might reach the opposite conclusion. Neither would be proper jurisprudence in the opinion of those who advocate an original intent approach, because both are value laden, and ideological preferences should not creep into the law. Rather, justices should examine the framers' intent as a way to keep the law value-free. Applying this approach to free speech, one adherent argues, leads to a clear, unbiased result:

Speech advocating violent overthrow is . . . not [protected] "political speech" . . . as that term must be defined by a Madisonian system of government. It is not political speech because it violates constitutional truths about processes and because it is not aimed at a new definition of political truth by a legislative majority.[22]

Finally, supporters of this mode of analysis argue that it fosters stability in law. They maintain that the law today is far too labile, that it changes with the ideological whims of the justices, creating havoc for those who must interpret and implement Court decisions. Lower court judges, lawyers, and even ordinary citizens

do not know if today's rights will still exist tomorrow. Following a jurisprudence of original intent would eliminate such confusion because it provides a principle that justices would consistently follow.

Many Supreme Court opinions contemplate the original intent of the framers (or its variants, which we describe below), and at least one justice on the current Court—Clarence Thomas—regularly invokes forms of originalism to answer a wide range of questions, from limits on campaign spending to the appropriate balance of power between the states and the federal government.[23] Such a jurisprudential course would have angered Thomas's predecessor, Thurgood Marshall, who did not believe that the Constitution was "forever 'fixed' at the Philadelphia Convention." Nor did Marshall find "the wisdom, foresight, and sense of justice exhibited by the framers," in light of the 1787 Constitution's treatment of women and blacks, "particularly profound."[24]

Marshall was not the only critic of an originalist approach to the Constitution; it has generated many others over the years. One reason for the controversy is that the doctrine became highly politicized in the 1980s. Those who advocated it, particularly Edwin Meese, an attorney general in President Ronald Reagan's administration, and defeated Supreme Court nominee Robert Bork, were widely viewed as conservatives who were using the doctrine to promote their own ideological ends.

Others joined Marshall, however, in raising several more concrete objections to this jurisprudence. Justice Brennan in 1985 argued that if the justices employed only this approach, the Constitution would lose its applicability and be rendered useless:

We current Justices read the Constitution in the only way that we can: as Twentieth Century Americans. We look to the history of the time of the framing and to the intervening history of interpretation. But the ultimate question must be, what do the words of the text mean in our time? For the

---

20. Edwin Meese III, address before the American Bar Association, July 9, 1983, Washington, D.C.

21. See, for example, Robert Bork, "Neutral Principles and Some First Amendment Problems," *Indiana Law Journal* 47 (1971): 1–35.

22. Ibid., 31.

23. Many scholars also advocate originalism. For a particularly intelligent defense, see Keith E. Whittington, *Constitutional Interpretation: Textual Meaning, Original Intent, and Judicial Review* (Lawrence: University Press of Kansas, 1999). We should note that contemporary justices are more likely to look at the original meaning of the words—that is, what the words would have ordinarily meant to the people at the time of the framing—rather than the intent of the framers. We discuss this form of originalism below.

24. Thurgood Marshall, "Reflections on the Bicentennial of the United States Constitution," *Harvard Law Review* 101 (1987): 1.

genius of the Constitution rests not in any static meaning it might have had in a world that is dead and gone, but in the adaptability of its great principles to cope with current problems and current needs.[25]

Another criticism is that the Constitution embodies not one intent, but many. Political scientists Jeffrey A. Segal and Harold J. Spaeth pose some interesting questions: "Who were the Framers? All fifty-five of the delegates who showed up at one time or another in Philadelphia during the summer of 1787? Some came and went. . . . Some probably had not read [the Constitution]. Assuredly, they were not all of a single mind."[26]

Finally, from which sources should justices divine the original intentions of the framers? They could look at the records of the constitutional debates and at the founders' journals and papers, but some of what passes for "records" of the Philadelphia convention is jumbled, even forged. During the debates, the secretary became confused and thoroughly botched the minutes. James Madison, who took the most complete and probably the most reliable notes on what was said, edited them after the convention adjourned. Perhaps this is why Justice Robert H. Jackson once wrote:

Just what our forefathers did envision, or would have envisioned had they foreseen modern conditions, must be divined from materials almost as enigmatic as the dreams Joseph was called upon to interpret for Pharaoh. A century and a half of partisan debate and scholarly specification yields no net result but only supplies more or less apt quotations from respected sources on each side of any question. They largely cancel each other.[27]

Textualism

On the surface, textualism resembles the doctrine of original intent: it values the Constitution itself as a guide above all else. But this is where the similarity ends. In an effort to prevent the infusion of new meanings from sources outside the text of the Constitution, adherents of original intent seek to deduce constitutional truths by examining the *intended* meanings behind the words. Textualists look no further than the words of the Constitution to reach decisions. Justice Antonin Scalia explained the differences between the approaches:

I belong to a school, a small but hardy school, called "textualists" or "originalists." That used to be "constitutional orthodoxy" in the United States. The theory of originalism treats a constitution like a statute, and gives it the meaning that its words were understood to bear at the time they were promulgated. You will sometimes hear it described as the theory of original intent. You will never hear me refer to original intent, because as I say I am first of all a textualist, and secondly an originalist. If you are a textualist, you don't care about the intent, and I don't care if the framers of the Constitution had some secret meaning in mind when they adopted its words. I take the words as they were promulgated to the people of the United States, and what is the fairly understood meaning of those words.[28]

Under Scalia's brand of textualism, it is fair game for justices to go beyond the literal meaning of the words and consider what they would have ordinarily meant to the people of that time—a type of textual analysis to which we return presently. To other textualists, those we might call pure textualists or *literalists,* it is only the words in the constitutional text, and the words alone, that justices ought to consider.

This apparently subtle distinction between original intent and literalism can lead to radically different results. To use the example of speech aimed at overthrowing the U.S. government, original intent advocates would hold that the meaning behind the First Amendment prohibits such expression. Those who consider themselves *pure* literalists, on the other hand, might scrutinize the words of the First Amendment—"Congress shall make no law . . . abridging the freedom of speech"—and construe them literally: *no law* means *no law.* Therefore, any statute infringing on speech, even a law that prohibits expression advocating the overthrow of the government, would violate the First Amendment.

25. William J. Brennan Jr., address to the Text and Teaching Symposium, Georgetown University, October 12, 1985, Washington, D.C.

26. Jeffrey A. Segal and Harold J. Spaeth, *The Supreme Court and the Attitudinal Model Revisited* (New York: Cambridge University Press, 2002), 68. See also William Anderson, "The Intention of the Framers: A Note on Constitutional Interpretation," *American Political Science Review* 49 (1955): 340.

27. *Youngstown Sheet & Tube Co. v. Sawyer* (1952).

28. Antonin Scalia, "A Theory of Constitutional Interpretation," remarks at the Catholic University of America, Washington, D.C., October 18, 1996.

Original intent and literalism sometimes overlap. When it comes to the right to privacy, particularly where it is leveraged to create other rights, such as legalized abortion, *some* original intent adherents and literalists would reach the same conclusion: it does not exist. The former would argue that it was not the intent of the framers to confer privacy; the latter, that because the Constitution does not expressly mention this right, it does not exist.

Textual analysis is quite common in Supreme Court opinions: many, if not most, opinions look to the Constitution and ask what it says about the matter at hand. Hugo Black is most closely associated with this view—at least in its pure form. During his thirty-four-year tenure on the Court, Justice Black continually emphasized his literalist philosophy. His own words best describe his position:

My view is, without deviation, without exception, without any ifs, buts, or whereases, that freedom of speech means that government shall not do anything to people . . . either for the views they have or the views they express or the words they speak or write. Some people would have you believe that this is a very radical position, and maybe it is. But all I am doing is following what to me is the clear wording of the First Amendment. . . . As I have said innumerable times before I simply believe that "Congress shall make no law" means Congress shall make no law. . . . Thus we have the absolute command of the First Amendment that no law shall be passed by Congress abridging freedom of speech or the press.[29]

Why did Black advocate literalism? Like original intent adherents, he viewed it as a value-free form of jurisprudence. If justices looked only at the words of the Constitution, their decisions would not reflect ideological or political values, but rather those of the document. Black's opinions provide good illustrations. Although he almost always supported claims of free *speech* against government challenges, he refused to extend constitutional protection to *expression* that was not strictly speech. He believed that activities such as flag burning and the wearing of armbands, even if calculated to express political views, fell outside the protections of the First Amendment.

Moreover, literalists maintain that their approach is superior to the doctrine of original intent. They say that some provisions of the Constitution are so transparent that were the government to violate them, justices could "almost instantaneously and without analysis identify the violation"; they would not need to undertake an extensive search to uncover the framers' understanding.[30] Often-cited examples include the "mathematical" provisions of the Constitution, such as the command that the president's term be four years and that the president be at least thirty-five years old.

Despite the seeming logic of these justifications and the high regard scholars have for Black, many have actively attacked his brand of jurisprudence. Some assert that it led him to take some rather odd positions, particularly in cases involving the First Amendment. Most analysts and justices—even those considered liberal—agree that obscene materials fall outside of First Amendment protection and that states can prohibit their dissemination. But in opinion after opinion, Black clung to the view that no publication could be banned on the grounds that it was obscene.

A second objection is that literalism can result in inconsistent outcomes. For example, is it really sensible for Black to hold that obscenity is constitutionally protected while other types of expression, such as desecration of the flag, are not?

Segal and Spaeth raise yet a third problem with literalism: it presupposes a precision in the English language that does not exist. Not only may words, including those used by the framers, have multiple meanings, but the meanings themselves may be contrary. For example, the common legal word *sanction*, as Segal and Spaeth note, means to punish *and* to approve.[31] How, then, would a literalist construe it?

Finally, even when the words are crystal clear, literalism may not be on firm ground. Despite the precision of the mathematical provisions, law professor Frank Easterbrook has suggested that they, like all the others, are loaded with "reasons, goals, values, and the like."[32] The framers might have imposed the presidential age limit "as a percentage of average life expectancy"—to ensure that presidents have a good

---

29. Hugo L. Black, *A Constitutional Faith* (New York: Knopf, 1969), 45–46.

30. We draw this material and the related discussion to follow from Mark V. Tushnet, "A Note on the Revival of Textualism," *Southern California Law Review* 58 (1985): 683.

31. Segal and Spaeth, *The Supreme Court and the Attitudinal Model Revisited*, 54.

32. Frank Easterbrook, "Statutes' Domains," *University of Chicago Law Review* 50 (1983): 536.

deal of practical political experience before ascending to the presidency and little opportunity to engage in politicking after they leave—or "as a minimum number of years after puberty"—to guarantee that they are sufficiently mature while avoiding unduly limiting the pool of eligible candidates. Seen in this way, the words "thirty-five Years" in the Constitution may not have much value: they may be "simply the framers' shorthand for their more complex policies, and we could replace them by 'fifty years' or 'thirty years' without impairing the integrity of the constitutional structure."[33] More generally, as Justice Oliver Wendell Holmes Jr. once put it, "A word is not a crystal, transparent and unchanged, it is the skin of a living thought and may vary greatly in color and content according to the circumstances and the time in which it is used."[34]

Original Meaning or Understanding

As we noted above, advocates of textual approaches suggest that justices need look no further than the words of the Constitution to reach decisions. But as we also suggested, adherents do not necessarily approach the task of interpreting the "words" in the same way. Black claimed to be loath to go beyond the literal meaning of the words, but Scalia is not so reticent. Indeed, under his "meaning of the words" brand of textualism—what some call original meaning understanding—it is appropriate for justices to ask what the words would have ordinarily meant to the people of that time.[35]

Seen in this way, the meaning of the words approach to constitutional interpretation has its roots in both literalism and originalism: it emphasizes the words of the Constitution at the time the framers wrote them. But there are differences. While literalists stress the words themselves, this mode highlights their meaning; and while originalism focuses on the intent behind phrases, at least some variants of the meaning of the words approach emphasize "lexicographic skill"—asking justices to interpret the words of the Constitution according to their meaning at the time they were written.[36]

The merits of this approach are similar to those of literalism and originalism. By focusing on how the framers defined their own words and then applying their definitions to disputes over those constitutional provisions containing them, this approach seeks to generate value-free and ideology-free jurisprudence. Indeed, one of the most important developers of this approach, historian William W. Crosskey, specifically embraced it to counter "sophistries" of the "living-document" view of the Constitution.[37]

Chief Justice Rehnquist's opinion in *Nixon v. United States* (1993) provides a particularly good illustration of the value of this approach. Here, the Court considered a challenge to the procedures the Senate used to impeach a federal judge, Walter L. Nixon Jr. The entire Senate did not try the case; instead, a special twelve-member committee heard it and reported to the full body. Nixon argued that this procedure violated Article I of the Constitution, which states, "The Senate shall have the sole power to try all Impeachments." But before addressing Nixon's claim, Rehnquist sought to determine whether courts had any business resolving such disputes. He used a meaning of the words approach to consider the word *try* in Article I:

Petitioner argues that the word "try" in the first sentence imposes by implication an additional requirement on the Senate in that the proceedings must be in the nature of a judicial trial. . . . There are several difficulties with this position which lead us ultimately to reject it. The word "try," both in 1787 and later, has considerably broader meanings than those to which petitioner would limit it. Older dictionaries define try as "[t]o examine" or "[t]o examine as a judge." See 2 S. Johnson, A Dictionary of the English Language (1785). In more modern usage the term has various meanings. For example, try can mean "to examine or investigate judicially," "to conduct the trial of," or "to put to the test by experiment, investigation. . . ." Webster's Third New International Dictionary (1971).

Like the other modes we have examined, the meaning of the words approach is not without its critics. One objection is similar to that leveled at originalism: it is too static. Political scientist C. Herman Pritchett noted that like originalism, it can "make a nation the

---

33. Tushnet, "A Note on the Revival of Textualism," 686.

34. *Towne v. Eisner* (1918).

35. See Scalia's "Originalism: The Lesser Evil," *University of Cincinnati Law Review* 849 (1989).

36. David W. Rohde and Harold J. Spaeth, *Supreme Court Decision Making* (San Francisco: W. H. Freeman, 1976), 41.

37. W. W. Crosskey, *Politics and the Constitution in the History of the United States* (Chicago: University of Chicago Press, 1953), 1172–1173.

prisoner of its past, and reject any constitutional development save constitutional amendment."[38]

Another criticism is that it may be just as difficult for justices to establish the original meaning of the words as it is to establish the original intent behind them. Attempting to understand what the framers meant by each word can be a far more daunting task in the run-of-the-mill case than it was for Rehnquist in *Nixon*. It might even require the development of a specialized dictionary, which could take years of research to compile and still not have any value—determinate or otherwise. Besides, scholars argue, even if we could create a dictionary that would help shed light on the meaning of particular words, it would tell us little about the significance of such constitutional phrases as "due process of law" or "cruel and unusual punishment."[39] Some say the same of other sources to which the justices could turn—such as the profusion of pamphlets (heavily outnumbering the entire population) that argued for and against ratification of the new Constitution. But this mass of literature demonstrates not one but maybe dozens of understandings of what it all meant. In other words, the documents often fail to provide a single clear message.

Polls of Other Jurisdictions

Aside from turning to originalism, textualism, or other historical approaches, a justice might probe English traditions or early colonial or state practices to determine how public officials of the times—or of contemporary times—interpreted similar words or phrases.[40]

The Supreme Court has frequently used such evidence. For instance, when *Wolf v. Colorado* (1949) presented the Court with the question whether the Fourth Amendment barred use in state courts of evidence obtained through an unconstitutional search, Justice Felix Frankfurter surveyed the law in all the states and in ten jurisdictions within the British Commonwealth. He used the information to bolster a conclusion that although the Constitution forbade unreasonable searches and seizures, it did not prohibit state officials from using such questionably obtained evidence against a defendant.

In 1952, however, when ***Rochin v. California*** asked the justices whether a state could use evidence it had obtained from a defendant by pumping his stomach—evidence admissible in the overwhelming majority of states at that time—Frankfurter declined to call the roll. Instead, he declared that gathering evidence by a stomach pump was "conduct that shocks the conscience" whose fruits could not be used in either state or federal courts. When in 1961 *Mapp v. Ohio* overruled *Wolf* and held that state courts must *exclude* all unconstitutionally obtained evidence, the justices again surveyed the field. For the Court, Justice Tom C. Clark said, "While in 1949 almost two-thirds of the States were opposed to the exclusionary rule, now, despite the *Wolf* case, more than half of those since passing upon it, by their own legislative or judicial decision, have wholly or partly adopted or adhered to the [rule]."

The point of this set of examples is not that Frankfurter or the Court was inconsistent but that the method itself—although it offers insights—is, according to some commentators, far from foolproof. First of all, the Constitution of 1787 as it initially stood and has since been amended rejects many English and some colonial and state practices. Second, even a steady stream of precedents from the states may signify nothing more than the fact that judges, too busy to give the issue much thought, imitated each other under the rubric of stare decisis. Third, if justices are searching for original intent or understanding, it is difficult to imagine the relevance of what was in the minds of people in the eighteenth century to state practices in the twentieth and twenty-first centuries. Polls are useful if we want to know what other judges, now and in the recent past, have thought about the Constitution, writ large or small. Nevertheless, they say nothing about the correctness of those thoughts—and the correctness

38. C. Herman Pritchett, *Constitutional Law of the Federal System* (Englewood Cliffs, NJ: Prentice Hall, 1984), 37.

39. Crosskey did, in fact, develop "a specialized dictionary of the eighteenth-century word-usages, and political and legal ideas." He believed that such a work was "needed for a true understanding of the Constitution." But some scholars have been skeptical of the understandings to which it led him, as many were highly "unorthodox." Bittker, "The Bicentennial of the Jurisprudence of Original Intent," 237–238. Some applauded Crosskey's conclusions. Charles E. Clark, for example, in "Professor Crosskey and the Brooding Omnipresence of Erie-Tompkins," *University of Chicago Law Review* 21 (1953): 24, called it "a major scholastic effort of our times." Others were appalled. See Julius Goebel Jr., "Ex Parte Clio," *Columbia Law Review* 54 (1954): 450. Goebel wrote, "[M]easured by even the least exacting of scholarly standards, [the work] is in the reviewer's opinion without merit."

40. We adopt the material in this section from Walter F. Murphy, C. Herman Pritchett, Lee Epstein, and Jack Knight, *Courts, Judges, and Politics*, 6th ed. (New York: McGraw-Hill, 2006).

of a lower court's interpretation may be precisely the issue before the Supreme Court.

Despite these criticisms, the Supreme Court continues to take into account the practices of other U.S. jurisdictions, just as courts in other societies occasionally look to their counterparts elsewhere—including the U.S. Supreme Court—for guidance. The South African ruling in *The State v. Makwanyane* (1995) provides a vivid example. To determine whether the death penalty violated its nation's constitution, South Africa's Constitutional Court surveyed practices elsewhere, including those in the United States. At the end of the day, the justices decided not to follow the path taken by the U.S. Supreme Court, ruling instead that their constitution prohibited the state from imposing capital punishment. Rejection of U.S. practice was made all the more interesting in light of a speech delivered by Justice Harry Blackmun only a year before *Makwanyane*.[41] In that address, Blackmun chastised his colleagues for failing to take into account a decision of South Africa's court to dismiss a prosecution against a person kidnapped from a neighboring country. This ruling, Blackmun argued, was far more faithful to international conventions than the one his court had reached in *United States v. Alvarez-Machain* (1992), which permitted U.S. agents to abduct a Mexican national.

Alvarez-Machain aside, the tendency seems to be growing for American justices to consider the rulings of courts abroad and practices elsewhere as they interpret the U.S. Constitution. This trend is particularly evident in opinions regarding capital punishment; justices opposed to this form of retribution often point to the nearly one hundred countries that have abolished the death penalty.

Whether this practice will become more widespread or filter into other legal areas is an intriguing question, and one likely to cause debate among the justices. Although some support efforts to expand their horizons beyond U.S. borders, others apparently agree with Justice Scalia, who has argued that "the views of other nations, however enlightened the Justices of this court may think them to be, cannot be imposed upon Americans through the Constitution."[42]

Stare Decisis

Translated from Latin, the term *stare decisis* means "let the decision stand." What this concept suggests is that, as a general rule, jurists should decide cases on the basis of previously established rulings, or precedent. In shorthand terms, judicial tribunals should honor prior rulings.

The benefits of this approach are fairly evident. If justices rely on past cases to resolve current cases, some scholars argue, the law they generate becomes predictable and stable. Justice Harlan F. Stone acknowledged the value of precedent in a somewhat more ironic way: "The rule of stare decisis embodies a wise policy because it is often more important that a rule of law be settled than that it be settled right."[43] The message, however, is the same: if the Court adheres to past decisions, it provides some direction to all who labor in the legal enterprise. Lower court judges know how they should and should not decide cases; lawyers can frame their arguments in accordance with the lessons of past cases; legislators understand what they can and cannot enact or regulate, and so forth.

Precedent, then, can be an important and useful factor in Supreme Court decision making. Along these lines, it is interesting to note that the Court rarely reverses itself—it has done so less than three hundred times over its entire history. Even modern-day Courts, as Table 1-2 shows, have been loath to overrule precedents. In the fifty-eight terms covered in the table, the Court has overturned only 143 precedents, or, on average, about 2.5 per term. What is more, the justices almost always cite previous rulings in their decisions; indeed, it is the rare Court opinion that does not mention other cases.[44] Finally, several scholars have verified that precedent helps to explain Court decisions in some areas of the law. In one study, analysts found that the Court reacted quite consistently to legal doctrine presented in more than fifteen years of death penalty litigation. Put differently, using precedent from past cases, the researchers could correctly categorize the outcomes (for or against the death penalty) in 75 percent of sixty-four cases decided since 1972.[45] Scholarly

---

41. "Justice Blackmun Addresses the ASIL Annual Dinner," *American Society of International Law Newsletter,* March 1994.

42. *Thompson v. Oklahoma* (1987); see also his dissent in *Atkins v. Virginia* (2002).

43. *United States v. Underwriters Association* (1944).

44. See Jack Knight and Lee Epstein, "The Norm of Stare Decisis," *American Journal of Political Science* 40 (1996): 1018–1035.

45. Tracey E. George and Lee Epstein, "On the Nature of Supreme Court Decision Making," *American Political Science Review* 86 (1992): 323–337.

TABLE 1-2 Precedents Overruled, 1953–2010 Terms

COURT ERA (TERMS)	NUMBER OF TERMS	NUMBER OF OVERRULED PRECEDENTS	AVERAGE NUMBER OF OVERRULINGS PER TERM
Warren Court (1953–1968)	16	43	2.7
Burger Court (1969–1985)	17	47	2.8
Rehnquist Court (1986–2004)	16	45	2.8
Roberts Court (2005–2010)	6	8	1.3

SOURCE: Calculated by the authors from data available on the U.S. Supreme Court Judicial Database (http://supremecourtdatabase.org).

work considering precedent in search and seizure litigation had similar success.[46]

Despite these data, we should not conclude that the justices necessarily follow this approach. Many allege that judicial appeal to precedent often is mere window dressing, used to hide ideologies and values, rather than a substantive form of analysis. There are several reasons for this allegation.

First, the Supreme Court has generated so much precedent that it is usually possible to find support for any conclusion. By way of proof, turn to any page of any opinion in this book and you probably will find the writers—both for the majority and the dissenters—citing precedent.

Second, it may be difficult to locate the rule of law emerging in a majority opinion. To decide whether a previous decision qualifies as a precedent, judges and commentators often say, one must strip away the non-essentials of a case and expose the basic reasons for the Supreme Court's decision. This process is generally referred to as "establishing the principle of the case," or the ratio decidendi. Other points made in a given opinion—obiter dicta (any expression in an opinion that is unnecessary to the decision reached in the case or that relates to a factual situation other than the one actually before the court)—have no legal weight, and judges are not bound by them. It is up to courts to separate the ratio decidendi from dicta. This task can be difficult, but it provides a way for justices to skirt precedent with which they do not agree. All they need to do is declare parts of it to be dicta. Or justices

can brush aside even the ratio decidendi when it suits their interests. Because the Supreme Court, at least today, is so selective about the cases it decides, it probably would not take a case for which clear precedent existed. Even in the past, two cases that were precisely identical probably would not be accepted. What this means is that justices can always deal with "problematic" ratio decidendi by distinguishing the case at hand from those that have already been decided.

A scholarly study of the role of precedent in Supreme Court decision making offers a third reason. Two political scientists hypothesized that if precedent matters, it ought to affect the subsequent decisions of members of the Court. If a justice dissented from a decision establishing a particular precedent, the same justice would not dissent from a subsequent application of the precedent. But that was not the case. Of the eighteen justices included in the study, only two occasionally subjugated their preferences to precedent.[47]

Finally, and most interesting, many justices recognize the limits of stare decisis in cases involving constitutional interpretation. Indeed, the justices often say that when constitutional issues are involved, stare decisis is a less rigid rule than it might normally be. This view strikes some as prudent, for the Constitution is difficult to amend and judges make mistakes or come to see problems quite differently as their perspectives change. As Justice Black once said:

Ordinarily it is sound policy to adhere to prior decisions but this practice has quite properly never been a blind, inflexible rule. Courts are not omniscient. Like every other human agency, they too can profit from trial and error, from experience and reflection. As others have demonstrated, the principle commonly referred to as stare decisis has never been thought to extend so far as to prevent the courts from correcting their own errors. . . . Indeed, the Court has a special responsibility where questions of constitutional law are involved to review its decisions from time to time and where compelling reasons present themselves to refuse to follow erroneous precedents; otherwise mistakes in interpreting the Constitution are extremely difficult to alleviate and needlessly so.[48]

---

46. Jeffrey A. Segal, "Predicting Supreme Court Cases Probabilistically: The Search and Seizure Cases, 1962–1984," *American Political Science Review* 78 (1984): 891–900.

---

47. Jeffrey A. Segal and Harold J. Spaeth, "The Influence of Stare Decisis on the Votes of U.S. Supreme Court Justices," *American Journal of Political Science* 40 (1996): 971–1003.

48. *Green v. United States* (1958).

In fact, of the 143 precedents overruled between the 1953 and 2010 terms *(see Table 1-2)*, nearly two-thirds involved constitutional issues.[49]

Pragmatism

What these data suggest is that the Court does not always feel bound to follow its own precedent. Perhaps the rule was in error. Or perhaps circumstances have changed and the justices wish to announce a rule consistent with the new circumstances, even if it is inconsistent with the old rule. The justices might even consider the consequences of overturning a precedent or more generally of interpreting a precedent in a particular way. This is known as pragmatic analysis, and it entails appraising alternative rulings by forecasting their consequences. Presumably, justices who engage in this form of analysis will select among plausible constitutional interpretations the one that has the best consequences and reject the ones that have the worst.

Pragmatism makes an appearance in many Supreme Court opinions, occasionally in the form of an explicit cost-benefit analysis in which the justices attempt to create rules, or analyze existing ones, so that they maximize benefits and minimize costs. Consider the exclusionary rule, which forbids use in criminal proceedings of evidence obtained in violation of the Fourth Amendment. Claims that the rule hampers the conviction of criminals have affected judicial attitudes, as Justice White frankly admitted in *United States v. Leon* (1984): "The substantial social costs exacted by the exclusionary rule for the vindication of Fourth Amendment rights have long been a source of concern." In *Leon* a majority of the justices applied a "cost-benefit" calculus to justify a "good faith" seizure by police on an invalid search warrant.

When you encounter cases that engage in this sort of analysis, you might ask questions raised by some critics of the approach: By what account of values should judges weigh costs and benefits? How do they take into account the different people whom a decision may simultaneously punish and reward?

---

49. We computed this figure from the U.S. Supreme Court Judicial Database.

SUPREME COURT DECISION MAKING: THE ROLE OF POLITICS

So far in our discussion we have not mentioned the justices' ideologies, their political party affiliations, or their personal views on various public policy issues. The reason is that legal approaches to Supreme Court decision making do not admit that these factors figure into the way the Court arrives at its decisions. Instead, they suggest that justices divorce themselves from their personal and political biases and settle disputes based upon the law. The approaches we consider below posit a quite different vision of Supreme Court decision making. They argue that the forces that drive the justices are anything but legal in composition and that it is unrealistic to expect justices to shed all their preferences and values or to ignore public opinion when they put on their black robes. Indeed, the justices are people like all of us whose political biases and partisan attachments are strong and pervasive.

Because justices usually do not admit that they are swayed by the public or that they vote according to their ideologies, our discussion of the role politics plays in Supreme Court decision making is distinct from that of the role of law. Here you will find little in the way of supporting statements from Court members, for it is an unusual justice indeed who admits to following anything but precedent, history, the text of the Constitution, and the like in deciding cases. Instead, we offer the results of decades of research by scholars who think that political and other extralegal forces shape judicial decisions. We organize these approaches into three categories: preference-based, strategic, and external forces. See if you think these scholarly accounts are persuasive.

Preference-Based Approaches

Preference-based approaches see the justices as rational decision makers who hold certain values they would like to see reflected in the outcomes of Court cases. Two prevalent preference-based approaches stress the importance of judicial attitudes and the judicial role.

Judicial Attitudes. Attitudinal approaches emphasize the importance of the justices' political ideologies. Typically, scholars examining the ideologies of the

FIGURE 1-4　Liberal Voting of the Chief Justices, 1953–2010 Terms

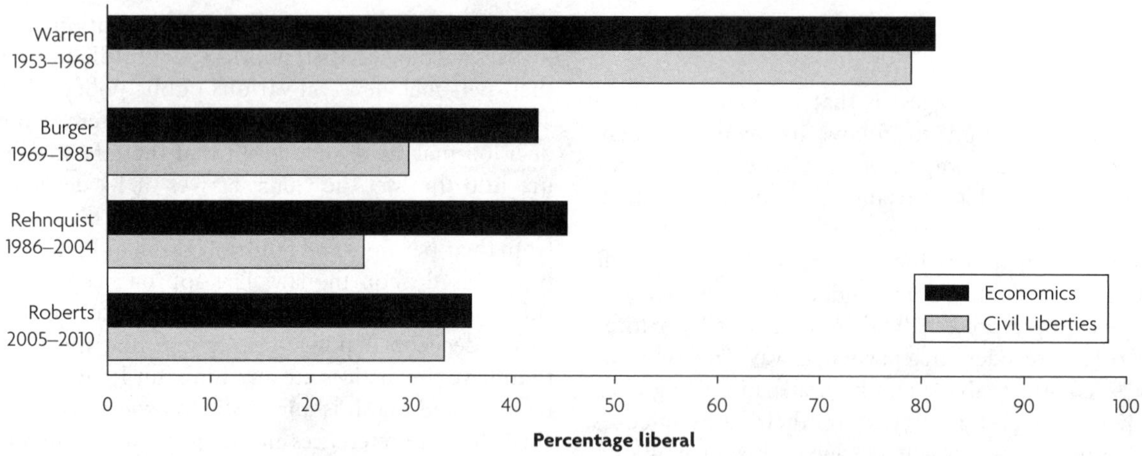

SOURCE: Calculated by the authors from data available on the U.S. Supreme Court Judicial Database (http://supremecourtdatabase.org).

justices discuss the degree to which a justice is conservative or liberal—as in "Justice X holds conservative views on issues of criminal law" or "Justice Y holds liberal views on free speech." This school of thought maintains that when a case comes before the Court each justice evaluates the facts of the dispute and arrives at a decision consistent with his or her personal ideology.

One of the first scholars to study systematically the importance of the justices' personal attitudes was C. Herman Pritchett.[50] Examining the Court during the 1930s and '40s, Pritchett observed that dissent had become an institutionalized feature of judicial decisions. During the early 1900s, in no more than 20 percent of the cases did one or more justices file a dissenting opinion; by the 1940s, that figure was more than 60 percent. If precedent and other legal factors drove Court rulings, why did various justices interpreting the same legal provisions frequently reach different results? Pritchett concluded that the justices were not following precedent but were "motivated by their own preferences."[51]

Pritchett's findings touched off an explosion of research on the influence of attitudes on Supreme Court decision making.[52] Much of this scholarship describes how liberal or conservative the various justices were and attempts to predict their voting behavior based on their attitudinal preferences. To understand some of these differences, consider Figure 1-4, which presents the voting records of the present Chief Justice, John Roberts, and his three immediate predecessors: Earl Warren, Warren Burger, and William Rehnquist. The data report the percentage of times each voted in the liberal direction in two different issue areas: civil liberties and economic liberties.

The data show dramatic differences among these four important jurists, especially in civil liberties. Cases in this category include disputes over issues such as the First Amendment freedoms of religion, speech, and press; the right to privacy; the rights of the criminally accused; and illegal discrimination. The liberal position is a vote in favor of the individual who is claiming a denial of these basic

---

50. C. Herman Pritchett, *The Roosevelt Court* (New York: Macmillan, 1948); and Pritchett, "Divisions of Opinion among Justices of the U.S. Supreme Court, 1939–1941," *American Political Science Review* 35 (1941): 890–898.

51. Pritchett, *The Roosevelt Court*, xiii.

52. The classic works in this area are Glendon Schubert, *The Judicial Mind* (Evanston, IL: Northwestern University Press, 1965); and Rohde and Spaeth, *Supreme Court Decision Making*. For a lucid modern-day treatment, see Segal and Spaeth, *The Supreme Court and the Attitudinal Model Revisited*, chaps. 3 and 8.

rights. Warren supported the liberal side almost 80 percent of the time, but Burger, Rehnquist, and now Roberts did so in no more than about one-third of such cases.

Economics cases involve challenges to the government's authority to regulate the economy. The liberal position supports an active role by the government in controlling business and economic activity. Here, too, the four justices show different ideological positions. Warren is the most liberal of the four, ruling in favor of government regulatory activity in better than 80 percent of the cases, while Burger, Rehnquist, and Roberts support such government activity in less than half. The data depicted in Figure 1-4 are typical of the findings of most attitudinal studies: within given issue areas, individual justices tend to show consistent ideological predispositions.

Moreover, we often hear that a particular Court is ideologically predisposed toward one side or the other. For example, on May 29, 2002, the *New York Times* ran a story claiming that "Chief Justice William Rehnquist and his fellow conservatives have made no secret of their desire to alter the balance of federalism, shifting power from Washington to the states." Three years later, in September 2005, it titled the chief justice's obituary "William H. Rehnquist, Architect of Conservative Court, Dies

at 80." After President George W. Bush appointed Rehnquist's replacement, John Roberts, and a new associate justice, Samuel Alito, the press was quick to label both "reliable members of the conservative bloc." And now Sonia Sotomayor and Elena Kagan, President Obama's appointees, are often deemed "liberal." Sometimes an entire Court era is described in terms of its political preferences, such as the "liberal" Warren Court or the "conservative" Rehnquist Court. The data in Figure 1-5 confirm that these labels have some basis in fact. Looking at the two lines from left to right, from the 1950s through the early 2000s, note the mostly downward trend, indicating the increased conservatism of the Court in economics and civil liberties cases.

How valuable are the ideological terms used to describe particular justices or Courts in helping us understand judicial decision making? On one hand, knowledge of justices' ideologies can lead to fairly accurate predictions about their voting behavior. Suppose that the Roberts Court handed down a decision dealing with the death penalty and that the vote was 5–4 in favor of the criminal defendant. The most conservative members of that Court on death penalty cases are Chief Justice Roberts and Justices Antonin Scalia, Clarence Thomas, and Samuel Alito—they almost always vote against the defendant. If we predicted that

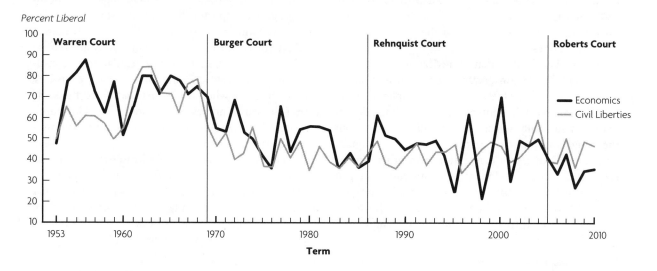

FIGURE 1-5   Court Decisions on Economics and Civil Liberties, 1953–2010 Terms

SOURCE: Calculated by the authors from data available on the U.S. Supreme Court Judicial Database (http://supremecourtdatabase.org).

Roberts, Scalia, Thomas, and Alito cast the dissenting votes in our hypothetical death penalty case, we would almost certainly be right.[53]

On the other hand, preference-based approaches are not foolproof. First, how do we know if a particular justice is liberal or conservative? The answer typically is that we know a justice is liberal or conservative because he or she casts liberal or conservative votes. Scalia favors conservative positions on the Court because he is a conservative, and we know he is a conservative because he favors conservative positions in the cases he decides. This is circular reasoning indeed. Second, knowing that a justice is liberal or conservative or that the Court decided a case in a liberal or conservative way does not tell us much about the Court's (or the country's) policy positions. To say that *Roe v. Wade* is a liberal decision is to say little about the policies governing abortion in the United States. If it did, this book would be nothing more than a list of cases labeled liberal or conservative. But such labels would give us no sense of more than two hundred years of constitutional interpretation.

Finally, we must understand that ideological labels are occasionally time dependent, that they are bound to particular historical eras. In *Muller v. Oregon* (1908) the Supreme Court upheld a state law that set a maximum number on the hours women (but not men) could work. How would you, as a student in the twenty-first century, view such an opinion? You probably would classify it as conservative because it seems to patronize and protect women. But when it was decided most considered *Muller* a liberal ruling because it allowed the government to regulate business.

A related problem is that some decisions do not fall neatly on a single conservative-liberal dimension. In *Wisconsin v. Mitchell* (1993), the Court upheld a state law that increased the sentence for crimes if the defendant "intentionally selects the person against whom the crime is committed" on the basis of race, religion, national origin, sexual orientation, and other similar criteria. Is this ruling liberal or conservative? If you view the law as penalizing racial or ethnic hatred, you would likely see it as a liberal decision. If, however, you see the law as treating criminal defendants more

harshly and penalizing a person because of what he or she believes or says, the ruling is conservative.

Judicial Role. Another concept within the preference-based category is the judicial role, which scholars have defined as norms that constrain the behavior of jurists.[54] Some students of the Court argue that each justice has a view of his or her role, a view that is based far less on political ideology and far more on fundamental beliefs of what a good judge should do or what the proper role of the Court should be. Some scholars claim that jurists vote in accordance with these role conceptions.

Analysts typically discuss judicial roles in terms of activism and restraint. An activist justice believes that the proper role of the Court is to assert independent positions in deciding cases, to review the actions of the other branches vigorously, to be willing to strike down acts the justice believes are unconstitutional, and to impose far-reaching remedies for legal wrongs whenever necessary. Restraint-oriented justices take the opposite position. Courts should not become involved in the operations of the other branches unless absolutely necessary. The benefit of the doubt should be given to actions taken by elected officials. Courts should impose remedies that are narrowly tailored to correct a specific legal wrong.

Based on these definitions, we might expect to find activist justices more willing than their opposites to strike down legislation. Therefore, a natural question to ask is this: To what extent have specific jurists practiced judicial activism or restraint? The data in Table 1-3 address this question by reporting the votes of justices serving on the Court sometime between the 1994 and 2010 terms (and are still on the Court) in cases in which the majority declared federal, state, or local legislation unconstitutional. Note the wide variation among the justices, even for the five who sat together and heard the same cases (Kennedy, Thomas, Scalia, Breyer, and Ginsburg). Of particular interest is that some of the Court's conservative members—Kennedy, Scalia, and Thomas—were more likely to vote with the majority to strike down federal laws than those on the left (Breyer and Ginsburg).

These patterns are suggestive: judicial activism and restraint do not necessarily equal judicial liberalism and conservatism. An activist judge need not be liberal, and a judge who practices restraint need not be conservative.

---

53. We adopt this example from Jeffrey A. Segal and Harold J. Spaeth, *The Supreme Court and the Attitudinal Model* (New York: Cambridge University Press, 1993), 223.

54. See James L. Gibson, "Judges' Role Orientations, Attitudes, and Decisions," *American Political Science Review* 72 (1978): 917.

TABLE 1-3   Percentage of Votes to Declare Legislation Unconstitutional, 1994–2010 Terms

JUSTICE	FEDERAL LAWS	STATE AND LOCAL LAWS
Kennedy	94.44%	88.64%
Roberts	85.71	83.33
Thomas	80.56	56.82
Scalia	72.22	59.09
Alito	57.14	66.67
Breyer	50.00	75.00
Ginsburg	50.00	70.45

SOURCE: Calculated by the authors from data available on the U.S. Supreme Court Judicial Database (http://supremecourtdatabase.org).

NOTE: Percentages indicate the percentage of cases in which the justice voted with the majority to declare legislation unconstitutional. The number of cases is 36 for federal laws and 44 for state and local laws, although some justices may not have participated in all cases. We do not show Sonia Sotomayor or Elena Kagan because the numbers are too small to compute meaningful percentages.

It is also true that so-called liberal Courts are no more likely to strike down legislation than are conservative Courts. Figure 1-6 shows the number of federal, state, and local laws struck down since 1789. Note the relatively high numbers of statutes declared unconstitutional during the 1920s, 1970s, and 1980s, all periods of relative conservatism on the Court. Such activism calls into question a strong relationship between ideology and judicial role.

Although scholars have used measures, such as the number of laws struck down, to assess the extent to which justices practice judicial activism or restraint, the question arises: To what extent does this information help us understand Supreme Court decision making? This question is difficult to answer because few scholars have studied the relationship between roles and voting in a systematic way.

The paucity of scholarly work on judicial roles leads to a criticism of the approach, namely, that it is virtually impossible to separate roles from attitudes. When Scalia votes to uphold a law restricting access to abortions, can we conclude that he was practicing restraint? The answer, quite clearly, is no. It may be his attitude toward abortion—not restraint—that guides him. Another criticism of role approaches is similar to that leveled at attitudinal factors—they tell us very little about the resulting policy in a case. Again, to say that *Roe v. Wade* was an activist decision because it struck down abortion laws nationwide is to say nothing about the policy content of the opinion.

FIGURE 1-6   Provisions of Federal, State, and Local Laws and Ordinances Held Unconstitutional by the Supreme Court, 1789–2010

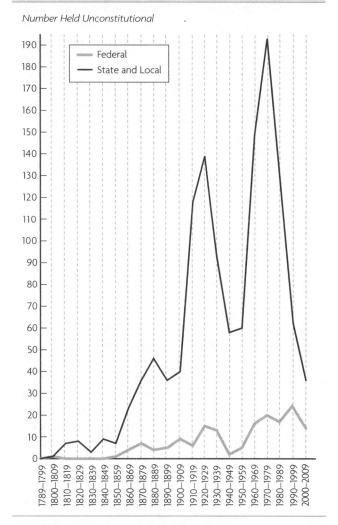

Number Held Unconstitutional

SOURCES: Harold W. Stanley and Richard G. Niemi, *Vital Statistics on American Politics*, 5th ed. (Washington, DC: CQ Press, 1995), 286; and data updated by Stanley and Niemi: Table 7-12, "Federal, State, and Local Laws Declared Unconstitutional by U.S. Supreme Court, by Decade, 1789–2010," in *Vital Statistics on American Politics, 2011-2012*, edited by Harold W. Stanley and Richard G. Niemi (Washington, DC: CQ Press, 2011), 285. Available at http://library.cqpress.com/vsap/vsap11_tab7-12.

Strategic Approaches

Strategic accounts of judicial decisions rest on a few simple propositions: justices may be primarily seekers of legal policy (as the attitudinal adherents claim) or they may be motivated by jurisprudential principles (as approaches grounded in law suggest), but they are not unconstrained actors who make decisions based solely on their own ideological attitudes or jurisprudential desires. Rather, justices are strategic actors who realize that their ability to achieve their goals—whatever those goals might be—depends on a consideration of the preferences of other relevant actors (such as their colleagues and members of other political institutions), the choices they expect others to make, and the institutional context in which they act. Scholars term this approach "strategic" because the ideas it contains are derived from the rational choice paradigm, on which strategic analysis is based and as it has been advanced by economists and political scientists working in other fields. Accordingly, we can restate the strategic argument in this way: we can best explain the choices of justices as strategic behavior and not merely as responses to ideological or jurisprudential values.[55]

Such arguments about Supreme Court decision making seem to be sensible: a justice can do very little alone. It takes a majority vote to decide a case and a majority agreeing on a single opinion to set precedent. Under such conditions, human interaction is important, and case outcomes—not to mention the rationale of decisions—can be influenced by the nature of relations among the members of the group.

Although scholars have not considered strategic approaches to the same degree that they have studied judicial attitudes, a number of influential works point to their importance. Research started in the 1960s and continuing today into the private papers of former justices consistently has shown that through intellectual persuasion, effective bargaining over opinion writing, informal lobbying, and so forth, justices have influenced the actions of their colleagues.[56]

How does strategic behavior manifest itself? One way is in the frequency of vote changes. During the deliberations that take place after oral arguments, the justices discuss the case and vote on it. These votes do not become final until the opinions are completed and the decision is made public *(see Figure 1-1)*. Research has shown that between the initial vote on the merits of cases and the official announcement of the decision, at least one vote switch occurs more than 50 percent of the time.[57] This figure indicates that justices change their minds—perhaps reevaluating their initial positions or succumbing to the persuasion of their colleagues—which seems inexplicable if we believe that justices are simply liberals or conservatives and always vote in accord with their preferences.

Vote shifts are just one manifestation of the interdependence of the Court's decision-making process. Another is the revision of opinions that occurs in almost every Court case.[58] As opinion writers try to accommodate their colleagues' wishes, their drafts may undergo five, ten, even fifteen revisions. Bargaining over the content of an opinion is important because it can significantly alter the policy ultimately expressed. A clear example is *Griswold v. Connecticut* (1965), in which the Court considered the constitutionality of a state law that prohibited the dissemination of birth control information and devices, even to married couples. In his initial draft of the majority opinion, Justice William O. Douglas struck down the law on the ground that it interfered with the First Amendment's right of association. A memorandum from Brennan convinced Douglas to alter his rationale and to establish the foundation for a right to privacy. "Had the Douglas draft been issued as the *Griswold* opinion of the Court, the case would stand as a precedent on the freedom of association," rather than serve as the landmark ruling it became.[59]

External Factors

In addition to internal bargaining, strategic approaches (as well as others) also take account of political pressures that come from outside the Court. We consider three sources of such influence: public opinion, partisan politics, and interest groups. While reading about

55. For more details on this approach, see Lee Epstein and Jack Knight, *The Choices Justices Make* (Washington, DC: CQ Press, 1998).

56. Walter F. Murphy, *Elements of Judicial Strategy* (Chicago: University of Chicago Press, 1964); David J. Danelski, "The Influence of the Chief Justice in the Decisional Process of the Supreme Court," in *The Federal Judicial System,* ed. Thomas P. Jahnige and Sheldon Goldman (New York: Holt, Rinehart & Winston, 1968); J. Woodford Howard, "On the Fluidity of Judicial Choice," *American Political Science Review* 62 (1968): 43–56; Epstein and Knight, *The Choices Justices Make*; Forrest Maltzman, Paul J. Wahlbeck, and James Spriggs, *Crafting Law on the Supreme Court: The Collegial Game* (New York: Cambridge University Press, 2000).

57. Saul Brenner, "Fluidity on the Supreme Court, 1956–1967," *American Journal of Political Science* 26 (1982): 388–390; Brenner, "Fluidity on the United States Supreme Court: A Re-examination," *American Journal of Political Science* 24 (1980): 526–535; Forrest Maltzman and Paul J. Wahlbeck, "Strategic Considerations and Vote Fluidity on the Burger Court," *American Political Science Review* 90 (1996): 581–592.

58. Epstein and Knight, *The Choices Justices Make,* chap. 3.

59. See Bernard Schwartz, *The Unpublished Opinions of the Warren Court* (New York: Oxford University Press, 1985), chap. 7.

these sources of influence, keep in mind that one of the fundamental differences between the Supreme Court and the political branches is the lack of a direct electoral connection between the justices and the public. Once appointed, justices may serve for life. They are not accountable to the public and are not required to undergo any periodic reevaluation of their decisions. So why would they let the stuff of ordinary partisan politics, such as public opinion and interest groups, influence their opinions?

Public Opinion. To address this question, let us first look at public opinion as a source of influence on the Court. We know that the president and members of Congress are always trying to find out what the people are thinking. Conducting and analyzing public opinion polls is a never-ending task, and those who commission the polls have a good reason for this activity. The political branches are supposed to represent the people, and incumbents can jeopardize their reelection prospects by straying too far from what the public wants. But federal judges—including Supreme Court justices—are not dependent upon pleasing the public to stay in office, and they do not serve in the same kind of representative capacity that legislators do.

Does that mean that the justices are not affected by public opinion? Some scholars say they are, and offer three reasons for this claim.[60] First, because justices are political appointees, nominated and approved by popularly elected officials, it is logical that they should reflect, however subtly, the views of the majority. It is probably true that an individual radically out of step with either the president or the Senate would not be nominated, much less confirmed. Second, the Court, at least occasionally, views public opinion as a legitimate guide for decisions. It has even gone so far as to incorporate that consideration into some of its jurisprudential standards. For example, in evaluating whether certain kinds of punishments violate the Eighth Amendment's prohibition against cruel and unusual punishment, the Court proclaimed that it would look toward "evolving standards of decency,"

as defined by public sentiment.[61] The third reason relates to the Court as an institution. Put simply, the justices have no mechanism for enforcing their decisions. Instead, they depend on other political officials to support their positions and on general public compliance, especially when controversial Court opinions have ramifications beyond the particular concerns of the parties to the suit.

Certainly, we can think of cases that lend support to these claims—cases in which the Court seems to have embraced public opinion, especially under conditions of extreme national stress. One example occurred during World War II. In *Korematsu v. United States* (1944) the justices endorsed the government's program to remove all Japanese Americans from the Pacific Coast states and relocate them to inland detention centers. It seems clear that the justices were swept up in the same wartime apprehensions as the rest of the nation. But it is equally easy to summon examples of the Court handing down rulings that fly in the face of what the public wants. The most obvious example occurred after Franklin D. Roosevelt's 1932 election to the presidency. By choosing Roosevelt and electing many Democrats to Congress, the voters sent a clear signal that they wanted the government to take vigorous action to end the Great Depression. The president and Congress responded with many laws—the so-called New Deal legislation—but the Court remained unmoved by the public's endorsement of Roosevelt and his legislation. In case after case, at least until 1937, the justices struck down many of the laws and administrative programs designed to get the nation's economy moving again.

And, in fact, some scholars remain unconvinced of the role of public opinion in Court decision making. After systematically analyzing the data, Helmut Norpoth and Jeffrey A. Segal conclude: "Does public opinion influence Supreme Court decisions? If the model of influence is of the sort where the justices set aside their own (ideological) preferences and abide by what they divine as the vox populi, our answer is a resounding no."[62] What Norpoth and Segal find instead is that Court appointments made by Richard Nixon in the early 1970s caused a "sizable ideological shift" in the direction of Court decisions *(see Figure 1-5).*

---

60. See, for example, Barry Friedman, *The Will of the People* (New York: Farrar, Straus & Giroux, 2009); William Mishler and Reginald S. Sheehan, "The Supreme Court as a Counter-majoritarian Institution? The Impact of Public Opinion on Supreme Court Decisions," *American Political Science Review* 87 (1993): 89.

---

61. *Trop v. Dulles* (1958).

62. Helmut Norpoth and Jeffrey A. Segal, "Popular Influence in Supreme Court Decisions," *American Political Science Review* 88 (1994): 711–716.

The entry of conservative justices created the illusion that the Court was echoing public opinion; it was not that sitting justices modified their voting patterns to conform to the changing views of the public.

This finding reinforces yet another criticism of this approach: that public opinion affects the Court only indirectly through presidential appointments, not through the justices' reading of public opinion polls. This distinction is important, for if justices were truly influenced by the public, their decisions would change with the ebb and flow of opinion. But if they merely share their appointing president's ideology, which must mirror the majority of the citizens *at the time of the president's election,* their decisions would remain constant over time. They would not fluctuate, as public opinion often does.

The question of whether public opinion affects Supreme Court decision making is still open for discussion, as illustrated by a more recent article, "Does Public Opinion Influence the Supreme Court? Possibly Yes (But We're Not Sure Why)."[63] The authors find that when the "mood" is liberal (conservative), the Court is significantly more likely to issue liberal (conservative) decisions. But why, as the article's title suggests, is anyone's guess. It could be that the justices bend to the will of the people because the Court requires public support to remain an efficacious branch of government. Or it could be that "the people" include the justices. The justices do not respond to public opinion directly but rather respond to the same events or forces that affect the opinions of other members of the public. As Justice Benjamin Cardozo once put it, "The great tides and currents which engulf the rest of men do not turn aside in their course and pass the judge by."[64]

Partisan Politics. Public opinion is not the only political factor that allegedly influences the justices. As political scientist Jonathan Casper wrote, we cannot overestimate "the importance of the political context in which the Court does its work." In his view, the statement that the Court follows the election returns "recognizes that the choices the Court makes are related to developments in the broader political system."[65] In other words, the political environment has an effect on Court behavior. In fact, many assert that the Court is responsive to the influence of partisan politics, both internally and externally.

On the inner workings of the Court, social scientists long have argued that political creatures inhabit the Court, that justices are not simply neutral arbiters of the law. Since 1789, the beginning of constitutional government in the United States, those who have ascended to the bench have come from the political institutions of government or, at the very least, have affiliated with particular political parties. Judicial scholars recognize that justices bring with them the philosophies of those partisan attachments. Just as the members of the present Court tend to reflect the views of the Republican Party or Democratic Party, so too did the justices who came from the ranks of the Federalists and Jeffersonians. As one might expect, justices who affiliate with the Democratic Party tend to be more liberal in their decision making than those who are Republicans. Some commentators say that *Bush v. Gore* (2000), in which the Supreme Court issued a ruling that virtually ensured that George W. Bush would become president, provides an example *(see Chapter 14).* In that case, five of the Court's seven Republicans "voted" for Bush, and its two Democrats "voted" for Gore.

Political pressures from the outside also can affect the Court. Although the justices have no electoral connection or mandate of responsiveness, the other institutions of government have some influence on judicial behavior, and, naturally, the direction of that influence reflects the partisan composition of those branches. The Court has always had a complex relationship with the president, a relationship that provides the president with several possible ways to influence judicial decisions. The president has some direct links with the Court, including (1) the power to nominate justices and shape the Court; (2) personal relationships with sitting justices, such as Franklin Roosevelt's with James Byrnes, Lyndon Johnson's with Abe Fortas, and Richard Nixon's with Warren Burger; and (3) the notion that the president, having been elected within the previous four years, may carry a popular mandate, reflecting the preferences of the people, which would affect the environment within which the Court operates.

---

63. Lee Epstein and Andrew D. Martin, "Does Public Opinion Influence the Supreme Court? Possibly Yes (But We're Not Sure Why)," *University of Pennsylvania Journal of Constitutional Law* 13 (2010): 263–281.

64. Benjamin Cardozo, *The Nature of the Judicial Process* (New Haven, CT: Yale University Press, 1921), 168.

65. Jonathan Casper, *The Politics of Civil Liberties* (New York: Harper & Row, 1972), 293.

A less direct source of influence is the executive branch, which operates under the president's command. The bureaucracy can assist the Court in implementing its policies, or it can hinder the Court by refusing to do so, a fact of which the justices are well aware. As a judicial body, the Supreme Court cannot implement or execute its own decisions. It often must depend on the executive branch to give its decisions legitimacy through action. The Court, therefore, may act strategically, anticipate the wishes of the executive branch, and respond accordingly to avoid a confrontation that could threaten its legitimacy. *Marbury v. Madison,* in which the Court enunciated the doctrine of judicial review, is the classic example *(see Chapter 2 for an excerpt).* Some scholars suggest that the justices knew if they ruled a certain way, the Jefferson administration would not carry out their orders. Because the Court felt that such a failure would threaten the legitimacy of judicial institutions, it crafted its opinion in a way that would not force the administration to take any action but would send a message about its displeasure with the administration's politics.

Another indirect source of presidential influence is the U.S. solicitor general. In addition to the SG's success as a petitioning party, the office can have an equally pronounced effect at the merits stage. In fact, data indicate that whether acting as an amicus curiae or as a party to a suit, the SG's office is generally able to convince the justices to adopt the position advocated by the SG.[66]

Presidential influence is also demonstrated in the kinds of arguments a solicitor general brings into the Court. That is, SGs representing Democratic administrations tend to present more liberal arguments; those from the ranks of the Republican Party, more conservative arguments. The transition from George H. W. Bush's administration to Bill Clinton's administration provides an interesting illustration. Bush's SG had filed amicus curiae briefs—many of which took a conservative position—in a number of cases heard by the Court during the 1993–1994 term. Drew S. Days III, Clinton's first solicitor general, rewrote at least four of those briefs to reflect the new administration's more liberal posture. For example, Days argued that the Civil Rights Act of 1991 should be applied retroactively, whereas

the Bush administration had suggested that it should not be. In another case, Days claimed trial attorneys could not systematically challenge prospective jurors on the basis of sex; his predecessor had argued that such dismissals were constitutional.

Congress, too—or so some argue—can influence Supreme Court decision making. Like the president, the legislature has many powers over the Court the justices cannot ignore.[67] Some of these resemble presidential powers—the Senate's role in confirmation proceedings, the implementation of judicial decisions—but there are others. Congress can restrict the Court's jurisdiction to hear cases, enact legislation or propose constitutional amendments to recast Court decisions, and hold judicial salaries constant. To forestall a congressional attack, the Court might accede to legislative wishes. Often-cited examples include the Court's willingness to defer to the Radical Republican Congress after the Civil War and to approve New Deal legislation after Roosevelt proposed his Court-packing plan in 1937. Some argue that these examples represent anomalies, not the rule. The Court, they say, has no reason to respond strategically to Congress because it is so rare that the legislature threatens, much less takes action against, the judiciary. Only infrequently has Congress taken away the jurisdiction of the Supreme Court to hear particular kinds of cases, most prominently just after the Civil War and far more recently in response to the war on terrorism *(see Chapter 2 for more details).* You should keep this argument in mind as you read the cases that pit the Court against Congress and the president.

Interest Groups. In *Federalist* No. 78, Alexander Hamilton wrote that the U.S. Supreme Court was "to declare the sense of the law" through "inflexible and uniform adherence to the rights of the constitution and individuals." Despite this expectation, Supreme Court litigation has become political over time. We see manifestations of politics in virtually every aspect of the Court's work, from the nomination and confirmation of justices to the factors that influence their decisions, but perhaps the most striking example of this politicization is the incursion of organized interest groups into the judicial process.

---

66. See Epstein et al., *Supreme Court Compendium,* Tables 7-15 and 7-16.

67. See Gerald N. Rosenberg, "Judicial Independence and the Reality of Political Power," *Review of Politics* 54 (1992): 369–398.

Naturally, interest groups may not attempt to persuade the Supreme Court the same way lobbyists deal with Congress. It would be grossly improper for the representatives of an interest group to approach a Supreme Court justice directly. Instead, interest groups try to influence Court decisions by submitting amicus curiae briefs *(see Box 1-2)*. Presenting a written legal argument to the Court allows interest groups to make their views known to the justices, even when the group is not a direct party to the litigation.

These days, it is a rare case before the U.S. Supreme Court that does not attract such submissions. On average, organized interests in recent years filed at least one amicus brief in nearly 90 percent of all cases decided by full opinion between 1986 and 2007.[68] Some cases, particularly those involving controversial issues such as abortion and affirmative action, are especially attractive to interest groups. In *Regents of the University of California v. Bakke* (1978), involving admission of minority students to medical school, more than one hundred organizations filed fifty-eight amici briefs: forty-two backed the university's admissions policy, and sixteen supported Bakke. A more recent affirmative action case, *Grutter v. Bollinger* (2003), drew eighty-four briefs, and from a wide range of interests: colleges and universities, *Fortune* 500 companies, and retired military officers, to name just a few.[69] In addition to participating as amici, groups are sponsoring cases—that is, providing litigants with attorneys and the money necessary to pursue their cases—in record numbers.

The explosion of interest group participation in Supreme Court litigation raises two questions. First, why do groups go to the Court? One answer is obvious: they want to influence the Court's decisions. But groups also go to the Supreme Court to achieve other, subtler, ends. One is the setting of institutional agendas: by filing amicus curiae briefs at the case selection stage or by bringing cases to the Court's attention, organizations seek to influence the justices' decisions on which disputes to hear. Group participation also may serve as a counterbalance to other interests that have competing goals. So if Planned Parenthood, a pro-choice group, knows that Life Legal Defense

Foundation, a pro-life group, is filing an amicus curiae brief in an abortion case (or vice versa), it too may enter the dispute to ensure that its side is represented in the proceedings. Finally, groups go to the Court to publicize their causes and their organizations. The NAACP (National Association for the Advancement of Colored People) Legal Defense Fund's legendary litigation campaign to end school segregation provides an excellent example. It not only resulted in a favorable policy decision in *Brown v. Board of Education* (1954) but also established the Legal Defense Fund as the foremost organizational litigant of this issue *(for an excerpt of the decision, see pages 620-624)*.

The second question is this: Can groups influence the outcomes of Supreme Court decisions?[70] This question has no simple answer. When interest groups participate on both sides, it is reasonable to speculate that one or more exerted some intellectual influence or at least that intervention of groups on the winning side neutralized the arguments of those who lost. To determine how much influence any group or private party exerted, a researcher would have to interview all the justices who participated in the decision (and they do not grant such interviews), since even a direct citation to an argument advanced in one of the parties' or amici's briefs may indicate merely that a justice is seeking support for a conclusion he or she had already reached.

We can be more certain that many cases would not get into any court, much less the U.S. Supreme Court, without the help of an interest group. Therefore, we can say that because judges have to wait for cases to come before them, groups help set the judicial agenda. It may be that many judges, especially judges on appellate courts, look on interest groups as sources of important information that otherwise would not come to their attention. Caldeira and Wright's research on amici participation at the agenda-setting stage supports this contention.[71] The growing percentage of U.S. Supreme Court opinions that cite amici's arguments reinforces the point. During the Warren Court, the justices cited amicus curiae briefs in about 40 percent of their opinions;

68. See Ryan J. Owens and Lee Epstein, "Amici Curiae during the Rehnquist Years," *Judicature* 89 (2005): 127–133.

69. We adopt some of this material from Pritchett et al., *Courts, Judges, and Politics*, chap. 6.

70. See Linda Greenhouse, "What Got into the Court? What Happens Next?," *Maine Law Review* 57 (2005): 6. Greenhouse wrote that "more than 100 briefs, a record number, were filed" in the 2003 affirmative action cases. Our figure (eighty-four) for *Grutter* excludes briefs filed by individuals.

71. Caldeira and Wright, "Organized Interests and Agenda Setting."

that figure rose to 66 percent for Burger Court justices and to 68 percent for the Rehnquist Court.[72] It seems clear that the justices—now more than ever—are at least learning enough from amici briefs to cite them in their opinions.

Having once gained the attention of a Court, attorneys for some groups, such as the Women's Rights Project of the American Civil Liberties Union and the NAACP, are often more experienced and their staffs more adept at research than counsel for what law professor Marc Galanter called "one-shotters."[73] When he was chief counsel for the NAACP, Thurgood Marshall would solicit help from allied groups and orchestrate their cooperation on a case, dividing the labor among them by assigning specific arguments to each while enlisting sympathetic social scientists to muster supporting data. Before going to the Supreme Court for oral argument, he would sometimes have a practice session with friendly law professors, each one playing the role of a particular justice and trying to pose the sorts of questions that justice would be likely to ask. Such preparation can pay off, but it need not be decisive. In oral argument, Allan Bakke's attorney displayed a surprising ignorance of constitutional law and curtly told one justice who tried to help him that he would like to argue the case his own way. Despite this poor performance, Bakke won.

Some evidence, however, suggests that attorneys working for interest groups are no more successful than private counsel. One study paired similar cases decided by the same district court judge, the same year, with the only major difference being that one case was sponsored by a group and the other was brought by attorneys unaffiliated with an organized interest. Despite Galanter's contentions about the obstacles confronting one-shotters, the study found no major differences between the two.[74]

In short, the debate over the influence of interest groups continues, and it is a debate that you will have ample opportunity to consider. With the case excerpts in this volume, we often provide information on the arguments of amici and attorneys so that you can compare these points with the justices' opinions.

CONDUCTING RESEARCH ON THE SUPREME COURT

As you can see, considerable disagreement exists in the scholarly and legal communities about how justices should interpret the Constitution, and even why they decide cases the way they do. These approaches show up in many of the Court's opinions in this book. Keep in mind, however, that the opinions are not presented here in full; the excerpts included here are intended to highlight the most important points of the various majority, dissenting, and concurring opinions. Occasionally, you may want to read the decisions in their entirety. Following is an explanation of how to find opinions and other kinds of information on the Court and its members.

Locating Supreme Court Decisions

U.S. Supreme Court decisions are published by various reporters. The four major reporters are *U.S. Reports, Lawyers' Edition, Supreme Court Reporter,* and *U.S. Law Week.* All contain the opinions of the Court, but they vary in the kinds of ancillary material they provide. For example, as Table 1-4 shows, the *Lawyers' Edition* contains excerpts of the briefs of attorneys submitted in orally argued cases, *U.S. Law Week* provides a topical index of cases on the Court's docket, and so forth.

Locating cases within these reporters is easy if you know the case *citation.* Case citations, as the table shows, take different forms, but they all work in roughly the same way. To see how, turn to pages 234–238 to find an excerpt of *Texas v. Johnson* (1989). Directly under the case name is a citation: 491 U.S. 397, which means that *Texas v. Johnson* appears in volume 491, page 397, of *U.S. Reports.*[75] The first set of numbers is the volume number; the U.S. is the form of citation

---

72. See Epstein et al., *Supreme Court Compendium,* Table 7-25.

73. Marc Galanter, "Why the 'Haves' Come Out Ahead: Speculations on the Limits of Legal Change," *Law and Society Review* 9 (1974): 95–160.

74. Lee Epstein and C. K. Rowland, "Debunking the Myth of Interest Group Invincibility in the Court," *American Political Science Review* 85 (1991): 205–217.

---

75. In this book, we list only the *U.S. Reports* cite for each case because *U.S. Reports* is the official record of Supreme Court decisions. It is the only reporter published by the federal government; the three others are privately printed. Almost every law library has *U.S. Reports.* If your college or university does not have a law school, check with your librarians. If they have any Court reporter, it is probably *U.S. Reports.*

TABLE 1-4 Reporting Systems

REPORTER/PUBLISHER	FORM OF CITATION (TERMS)	DESCRIPTION
United States Reports Government Printing Office	Dall. 1–4 (1790–1800) Cr. 1–15 (1801–1815) Wheat. 1–12 (1816–1827) Pet. 1–16 (1828–1843) How. 1–24 (1843–1861) Bl. 1–2 (1861–1862) Wall. 1–23 (1863–1875) U.S. 91– (1875–)	Contains official text of opinions of the Court. Includes tables of cases reported, cases and statutes cited, miscellaneous materials, and subject index. Includes most of the Court's decisions. Court opinions prior to 1875 are cited by the name of the reporter of the Court. For example, Dall. stands for Alexander J. Dallas, the first reporter.
United States Supreme Court Reports, Lawyers' Edition Lawyers' Cooperative Publishing Company	L. Ed. L. Ed. 2d	Contains official reports of opinions of the Court. Additionally, provides per curiam and other decisions not found elsewhere. Summarizes individual majority and dissenting opinions and counsel briefs.
Supreme Court Reporter West Publishing Company	S. Ct.	Contains official reports of opinions of the Court. Contains annotated reports and indexes of case names. Includes opinions of justices in chambers. Appears semimonthly.
United States Law Week Bureau of National Affairs	U.S.L.W.	Weekly periodical service containing full text of Court decisions. Includes four indexes: topical, table of cases, docket number table, and proceedings section. Contains summary of cases filed recently, journal of proceedings, summary of orders, arguments before the Court, argued cases awaiting decisions, review of Court's work, and review of Court's docket.

SOURCES: Lee Epstein, Jeffrey A. Segal, Harold J. Spaeth, and Thomas G. Walker, *The Supreme Court Compendium: Data, Decisions, and Developments,* 5th ed. (Washington, DC: CQ Press, 2012), Table 2-9. Dates of reporters are from David Savage, *Guide to the U.S. Supreme Court,* 5th ed. (Washington, DC: CQ Press, 2010).

for *U.S. Reports*; and the second set of numbers is the starting page of the case.

Texas v. Johnson also can be located in the three other reporters. The citations are as follows:

Lawyers' Edition: 105 L. Ed. 2d 342 (1989)

Supreme Court Reporter: 109 S. Ct. 2533 (1989)

U.S. Law Week: 57 U.S.L.W. 4770 (1989)

Note that the abbreviations vary by reporter, but in form the citations parallel *U.S. Reports* in that the first set of numbers is the volume number and the second set is the starting page number.

These days, however, many students turn to electronic sources to locate Supreme Court decisions. Several companies maintain databases of the decisions of federal and state courts, along with a wealth of other information. In some institutions these services—LEXIS-NEXIS and Westlaw—are available only to law school students. Check with your librarians to see if your school provides access to other students, perhaps through Academic Universe (a subset of the LEXIS-NEXIS service). Also, the Legal Information Institute (LII) at Cornell Law School (http://www .law.cornell.edu/supct), FindLaw (http://www.findlaw .com/casecode/supreme.html), and now the Supreme Court itself (http://www.supremecourtus.gov)—to name just three—house Supreme Court opinions and offer an array of search capabilities. You can read the opinions online, have them e-mailed to you, or download them immediately. If a case we excerpt here is located in these archives, we note the Web address after the case citation.

Locating Other Information on the Supreme Court and Its Members

As you might imagine, there is no shortage of reference material on the Court. Three (print) starting points are the following:

1. *The Supreme Court Compendium: Data, Decisions, and Developments,* 5th edition, contains information on the following dimensions of Court activity: the Court's development, review process, opinions and decisions, judicial background, voting patterns, and impact.[76] You will find data as varied as the number of cases the Court decided during a particular

---

76. Epstein et al., *Supreme Court Compendium.*

term, the votes in the Senate on Supreme Court nominees, and the law schools the justices attended.

2. *Guide to the U.S. Supreme Court,* 5th edition, provides a fairly detailed history of the Court. It also summarizes the holdings in landmark cases and provides brief biographies of the justices.[77]

3. *The Oxford Companion to the Supreme Court of the United States,* 2nd edition, is an encyclopedia containing entries on the justices, important Court cases, the amendments to the Constitution, and so forth.[78]

The U.S. Supreme Court also gets a great deal of attention on the Internet. The Legal Information Institute (http://www.law.cornell.edu) is particularly useful. In addition to Supreme Court decisions, the LII contains links to various documents (such as the U.S. Code and state statutes) and to a vast array of legal indexes and libraries. If you are unable to find the material you are looking for on the LII site, you may locate it by clicking on one of the links.

Another worthwhile site is SCOTUSblog, a project of a law firm (http://www.scotusblog.com). This site provides extensive summaries of pending Court cases, as well as links to briefs filed by the parties and amici.

As already mentioned, you can listen to selected oral arguments of the Court at the Oyez Project site (http://www.oyez.org/oyez/frontpage). Oyez contains audio files of Supreme Court oral arguments for selected constitutional cases decided since the 1950s.

These are just a few of the many sites—perhaps hundreds—that contain information on the federal courts. But there is at least one other important electronic source of information on the Court worthy of mention—Harold J. Spaeth's computer-dependent U.S. Supreme Court Judicial Databases. These databases provide a wealth of data beginning with the Vinson Court (1946 term) to the present. Among the many attributes of Court decisions coded by Spaeth are the names of the courts making the original decisions, the identities of the parties to the cases, the policy context of the cases, and the votes of each justice. Indeed, we deployed one of Spaeth's databases to create many of the charts and

tables presented in this chapter. You can obtain all the databases and accompanying documentation free of charge at http://supremecourtdatabase.org.

In this chapter, we have examined Supreme Court procedures and attempted to shed some light on how and why justices make the choices they do. Our consideration of preference-based factors, for example, highlighted the role ideology plays in Court decision making, and our discussion of political explanations emphasized public opinion and interest groups. After reading this chapter, you may have concluded that the justices are relatively free to go about their business as they please. But, as you shall see in the next chapter, that is not necessarily so. Although Court members have a good deal of power and the freedom to exercise it, they also face considerable institutional obstacles. It is to the subjects of judicial power and constraints that we now turn.

ANNOTATED READINGS

In the text and footnotes, we mention many interesting studies on the Supreme Court. Our goal in each chapter's "Annotated Readings" section is to highlight a few books for the interested reader.

Lawrence Baum's *The Supreme Court,* 10th ed. (Washington, DC: CQ Press, 2011), provides a modern-day introduction to the Court and its work. For insightful historical-political analyses, see Robert G. McCloskey's *The American Supreme Court* (Chicago: University of Chicago Press, 2004) and Barry Friedman's *The Will of the People* (New York: Farrar, Straus & Giroux, 2009). Several of the current justices have written books outlining their approaches to interpreting the Constitution. See Stephen Breyer's *Active Liberty: Interpreting Our Democratic Constitution* (New York: Knopf, 2005) and Antonin Scalia's *A Matter of Interpretation: Federal Courts and the Law* (Princeton, NJ: Princeton University Press, 1997), which includes responses from prominent legal scholars. For other studies of approaches to constitutional interpretation, see Philip Bobbit, *Constitutional Fate: Theory of the Constitution* (New York: Oxford University Press, 1982); Leslie Friedman Goldstein, *In Defense of the Text* (Savage, MD: Rowman & Littlefield, 1991); Ronald Kahn, *The Supreme Court and Constitutional Theory* (Lawrence: University Press of Kansas, 1994); Jack N. Rakove, *Original Meanings: Politics and Ideas in the Making of the Constitution* (New York: Vintage

---

77. David Savage, *Guide to the U.S. Supreme Court,* 5th ed. (Washington, DC: CQ Press, 2010).

78. Kermit Hall, ed., *The Oxford Companion to the Supreme Court of the United States,* 2nd ed. (New York: Oxford University Press, 2005).

Books, 1996); Keith E. Whittington, *Constitutional Interpretation: Textual Meaning, Original Intent, and Judicial Review* (Lawrence: University Press of Kansas, 1999); Richard H. Fallon Jr., *Implementing the Constitution* (Cambridge, MA: Harvard University Press, 2001); Michael J. Gerhardt, *The Power of Precedent* (New York: Oxford University Press, 2008); Gary L. McDowell, *The Language of Law and the Foundations of American Constitutionalism* (New York: Cambridge University Press, 2010).

Leading political science studies of judicial decision making (including case selection) are C. Herman Pritchett, *The Roosevelt Court* (New York: Macmillan, 1948); Glendon Schubert, *The Judicial Mind* (Evanston, IL: Northwestern University Press, 1965); Walter J. Murphy, *Elements of Judicial Strategy* (Chicago: University of Chicago Press, 1964); H. W. Perry Jr., *Deciding to Decide: Agenda Setting in the United States Supreme Court* (Cambridge, MA: Harvard University Press, 1991); Lee Epstein and Jack Knight, *The Choices Justices Make* (Washington, DC: CQ Press, 1998); Forrest Maltzman, Paul J. Wahlbeck, and James Spriggs, *Crafting Law on the Supreme Court: The Collegial Game* (New York: Cambridge University Press, 2000); Jeffrey A. Segal and Harold J. Spaeth, *The Supreme Court and the Attitudinal Model Revisited* (New York: Cambridge University Press, 2002); Stefanie A. Lindquist and Frank B. Cross, *Measuring Judicial Activism* (New York: Oxford University Press, 2009).

On the work of interest groups and attorneys, see Kevin T. McGuire, *The Supreme Court Bar: Legal Elites in the Washington Community* (Charlottesville: University Press of Virginia, 1993); Timothy R. Johnson, *Oral Arguments and the United States Supreme Court* (Albany: State University of New York Press, 2004); Paul M. Collins Jr., *Friends of the Supreme Court: Interest Groups and Judicial Decision Making* (New York: Oxford University Press, 2008).

2 The Judiciary: Institutional Powers and Constraints

ONCERNED ABOUT THE proliferation of child pornography, especially on the Internet, Congress passed the Child Pornography Prevention Act of 1996. The law forbade "any visual depiction . . . [that] is, or appears to be, of a minor engaging in sexually explicit conduct." The prohibition covered a wide range of depictions, including "virtual child pornography," computer-generated images that do not show actual children but that Congress reasoned could threaten children in other, less direct, ways. For example, pedophiles could use virtual child pornography to encourage children to participate in sexual activity. Six years after the legislation was passed, in *Ashcroft v. Free Speech Coalition* (2002), the U.S. Supreme Court struck down the law as a violation of the First Amendment.

What the Court did was an uncommon, but not unexpected, act. For more than two centuries federal courts have exerted the power of judicial review, the power to review acts of government to determine their compatibility with the U.S. Constitution. Even though the Constitution does not explicitly give them such power, the courts' authority to do so has rarely been challenged. Today, we take for granted the notion that federal courts may review government actions and strike them down if they violate constitutional mandates.

Nevertheless, when courts exert this power, as the U.S. Supreme Court did in *Ashcroft*, they provoke controversy. Look at it from this perspective: Congress,

composed of officials we *elect*, passed the Child Pornography Prevention Act, which was then rendered invalid by a Supreme Court of *unelected* judges. Such an occurrence strikes some people as odd, perhaps even antidemocratic. Why should we Americans allow a branch of government, over which we have no electoral control, to review and nullify the actions of the government officials we elect to represent us?

As we shall see throughout this book, the alleged antidemocratic nature of judicial review is just one of many controversies surrounding the practice. To appreciate them fully, it is important to have a firm grasp of the development of judicial review in the United States. Many of the early justifications for its practice are still fueling disputes.

Judicial review is the primary weapon that federal courts have to keep the other branches of government in check. Because the power could be awesome in scope, many critics tend to emphasize it to the neglect of factors that constrain its use. In the second part of this chapter, we explore the limits on judicial power. An appreciation of both aspects of judicial power is necessary to understand the cases in this chapter and those to come.

JUDICIAL REVIEW

Even though judicial review is an extremely powerful tool and there is evidence that the framers intended for federal courts to have it, it is not mentioned in the Constitution. Early in U.S. history, federal courts claimed it for themselves. In *Hylton v. United States* (1796), Daniel Hylton challenged the constitutionality of a 1793 federal tax on carriages. According to Hylton, the act violated the constitutional mandate that direct taxes must be apportioned on the basis of population. With only three justices participating, the Court upheld the act. But, by even considering it, the Court in effect used its authority to review acts of Congress.

Not until 1803, however, did the Court invoke judicial review to strike down legislation deemed incompatible with the U.S. Constitution. That decision came in the landmark case *Marbury v. Madison*. How does Chief Justice John Marshall justify the Court's power to strike down legislation when the newly framed Constitution failed to confer judicial review on the Court?

William Marbury

Marbury v. Madison

5 U.S. (1 CR.) 137 (1803)
http://laws.findlaw.com/US/5/137.html
Vote: 4 (Chase, Marshall, Paterson, Washington)
    0

OPINION OF THE COURT: *Marshall*

NOT PARTICIPATING: *Cushing, Moore*

FACTS:

When voting in the presidential election of 1800 was over, it was apparent that President John Adams, the Federalist candidate, had lost after a long and bitter campaign, but it was not clear who the winner was. In those days voters did not elect a single ticket consisting of a candidate for president and a candidate for vice president; rather, the person with the most votes became president, and the second-place person became vice president. In 1800 the voting resulted in a tie between Republican candidate Thomas Jefferson and his running mate, Aaron Burr, and the election had to be settled in the House of Representatives, which in February 1801 elected Jefferson. Because the Federalists had lost both the presidential election and their majority in Congress, they took steps to maintain control of the third branch of government, the judiciary.

The lame-duck Congress enacted the Circuit Court Act of 1801, which created six new circuit courts and several district courts to accommodate the new states

John Marshall

of Kentucky, Tennessee, and Vermont. These new courts needed judges and support staff such as attorneys, marshals, and clerks. As a result, during his last six months in office, Adams made more than two hundred nominations, with sixteen judgeships (the "midnight appointments") approved by the Senate during his final two weeks as president.

An even more important opportunity arose in December 1800, when the third chief justice of the United States, Federalist Oliver Ellsworth, resigned so that Adams—not Jefferson—could name his replacement. Adams offered the post to John Jay, who had served as the first chief justice before leaving to take what was in those days a more prestigious job—the governorship of New York. When Jay refused, Adams turned to his secretary of state, John Marshall, an ardent Federalist. The Senate confirmed Marshall in January 1801, but he also continued as secretary of state.

In addition, the Federalist Congress passed the Organic Act, authorizing Adams to appoint forty-two justices of the peace for the District of Columbia. It was this seemingly innocuous law that set the stage for the drama of *Marbury v. Madison.* In the confusion of the Adams administration's last days in office, Marshall, the outgoing secretary of state, failed to deliver some of these commissions. When the new administration came into office, James Madison, the new secretary of state, acting under orders from Jefferson, refused to deliver at least five commissions.[1] Some years later, Jefferson explained the situation this way: "I found the commissions on the table of the Department of State, on my entrance into office, and I forbade their delivery. Whatever is in the Executive offices is certainly deemed to be in the hands of the President, and in this case, was actually in my hands, because when I countermanded them, there was as yet no Secretary of State."[2]

As a result, in 1801 William Marbury and three others who were denied their commissions went *directly* to the Supreme Court (that is, they invoked the Court's original jurisdiction rather than beginning the case in

---

1. Historical accounts differ, but it seems that Jefferson decreased the number of Adams's appointments to justice of the peace positions to thirty from forty-two. Twenty-five of the thirty appointees received their commissions, but five—including William Marbury—did not. See Francis N. Stites, *John Marshall* (Boston: Little, Brown, 1981), 84.

2. Quoted in Charles Warren, *The Supreme Court in United States History,* vol. 1 (Boston: Little, Brown, 1922), 244.

James Madison

Thomas Jefferson

a lower court) and asked it to issue a writ of mandamus ordering Madison to deliver the commissions. Marbury believed he could take his case directly to the Court because Section 13 of the 1789 Judiciary Act gave the Court the power to issue writs of mandamus to anyone holding federal office:

The Supreme Court . . . shall have power to issue . . . writs of mandamus, in cases warranted by the principles and usages of law, to any courts appointed, or persons holding office, under the authority of the United States.

In this volatile political climate, Marshall, now serving as chief justice, was perhaps in the most tenuous position of all. He had been a supporter of the Federalist Party, which now looked to him to "scold" the Jefferson administration. Marshall, however, wanted to avoid a confrontation between the Jefferson administration and the Supreme Court, which not only seemed imminent but also could end in disaster for the struggling nation. Note the year in which the Court handed down the decision in *Marbury.* The case was not decided until two years after Marbury filed suit because Congress and the Jefferson administration had abolished the 1802 term of the Court.

ARGUMENTS:

For the applicant, William Marbury:

- After the president has signed a commission for an office, and it comes to the secretary to be sealed, the president has done with it, and nothing remains, but that the secretary perform those ministerial acts which the law imposes upon him. It immediately becomes his duty to seal, record, and deliver it on demand. In such a case the appointment becomes complete by the signing and sealing; and the secretary does wrong if he withholds the commission.
- Congress has expressly given the Supreme Court the power of issuing writs of mandamus.
- Congress can confer original jurisdiction in cases other than those mentioned in the Constitution. The Supreme Court has entertained jurisdiction on mandamus in several cases. See, e.g., *United States v. Lawrence,* 3 U.S. 42 (1795). In this case and in others, the power of the Court to issue writs of mandamus was taken for granted in the arguments of counsel on both sides. Hence it appears there has been a legislative construction of the Constitution upon this point, and a judicial practice under it, since the formation of that government.

For Secretary of State James Madison:
(Madison and Jefferson intentionally did not show up in order to emphasize their position that the proceedings had no legitimacy. So it seems that Madison was unrepresented and no argument was made on his behalf.)

 MR. CHIEF JUSTICE MARSHALL DELIVERED THE OPINION OF THE COURT.

The peculiar delicacy of this case, the novelty of some of its circumstances, and the real difficulty attending the points which occur in it, require a complete exposition of the principles, on which the opinion to be given by the court, is founded. . . .

In the order in which the court has viewed this subject, the following questions have been considered and decided.

1st. Has the applicant a right to the commission he demands?

2dly. If he has a right, and that right has been violated, do the laws of his country afford him a remedy?

3dly. If they do afford him a remedy, is it a *mandamus* issuing from this court?

The first object of enquiry is,

1st. Has the applicant a right to the commission he demands? . . .

It is . . . decidedly the opinion of the court, that when a commission has been signed by the President, the appointment is made; and that the commission is complete, when the seal of the United States has been affixed to it by the secretary of state. . . .

Mr. Marbury, then, since his commission was signed by the President, and sealed by the secretary of state, was appointed; and as the law creating the office, gave the officer a right to hold for five years, independent of the executive, the appointment was not revocable; but vested in the officer legal rights, which are protected by the laws of his country.

To withhold his commission, therefore, is an act deemed by the court not warranted by law, but violative of a vested legal right.

This brings us to the second enquiry; which is,

2dly. If he has a right, and that right has been violated, do the laws of his country afford him a remedy?

The very essence of civil liberty certainly consists in the right of every individual to claim the protection of the laws, whenever he receives an injury. One of the first duties of government is to afford that protection. . . .

The government of the United States has been emphatically termed a government of laws, and not of men. It will certainly cease to deserve this high appellation, if the laws furnish no remedy for the violation of a vested legal right. . . .

If this obloquy is to be cast on the jurisprudence of our country, it must arise from the peculiar character of the case. . . .

The conclusion . . . is, that where the heads of departments are the political or confidential agents of the Executive, merely to execute the will of the President, or rather to act in cases in which the Executive possesses a constitutional or legal discretion, nothing can be more perfectly clear than that their acts are only politically examinable. But where a specific duty is assigned by law, and individual rights depend upon the performance of that duty, it seems equally clear that the individual who considers himself injured, has a right to resort to the laws of his country for a remedy.

If this be the rule, let us enquire how it applies to the case under the consideration of the court.

The power of nominating to the senate, and the power of appointing the person nominated, are political powers, to be exercised by the President according to his own discretion. When he has made an appointment, he has exercised his whole power, and his discretion has been completely applied to the case. If, by law, the officer be removable at the will of the President, then a new appointment may be immediately made, and the rights of the officer are terminated. But as a fact which has existed cannot be made never to have existed, the appointment cannot be annihilated; and consequently if the officer is by law not removable at the will of the President; the rights he has acquired are protected by the law, and are not resumable by the President. They cannot be extinguished by executive authority, and he has the privilege of asserting them in like manner as if they had been derived from any other source.

The question whether a right has vested or not, is, in its nature, judicial, and must be tried by the judicial authority. If, for example, Mr. Marbury had taken the oaths of a magistrate, and proceeded to act as one; in consequence of which a suit had been instituted against him, in which his defence had depended on his being a magistrate; the validity of his appointment must have been determined by judicial authority.

So, if he conceives that, by virtue of his appointment, he has a legal right, either to the commission which has been made out for him, or to a copy of that commission, it is equally a question examinable in a court, and the decision of the court upon it must depend on the opinion entertained of his appointment.

That question has been discussed, and the opinion is, that the latest point of time which can be taken as that at which the appointment was complete, and evidenced, was when, after the signature of the president, the seal of the United States was affixed to the commission.

It is then the opinion of the court,

1st. That by signing the commission of Mr. Marbury, the president of the United States appointed him a justice of peace, for the county of Washington in the district of Columbia; and that the seal of the United States, affixed thereto by the secretary of state, is conclusive testimony of the verity of the signature, and of the completion of the appointment; and that the appointment conferred on him a legal right to the office for the space of five years.

2dly. That, having this legal title to the office, he has a consequent right to the commission; a refusal to deliver which, is a plain violation of that right, for which the laws of his country afford him a remedy.

It remains to be enquired whether,

3dly. He is entitled to the remedy for which he applies. This depends on,

1st. The nature of the writ applied for; and,

2dly. The power of this court. . . .

The act to establish the judicial courts of the United States authorizes the Supreme Court "to issue writs of mandamus, in cases warranted by the principles and usages of law, to any courts appointed, or persons holding office, under the authority of the United States."

The secretary of state, being a person holding an office under the authority of the United States, is precisely within the letter of the description; and if this court is not authorized to issue a writ of mandamus to such an officer, it must be because the law is unconstitutional, and therefore absolutely incapable of conferring the authority, and assigning the duties which its words purport to confer and assign.

The constitution vests the whole judicial power of the United States in one Supreme Court, and such inferior courts as congress shall, from time to time, ordain and establish. This power is expressly extended to all cases arising under the laws of the United States; and consequently, in some form, may be exercised over the present case; because the right claimed is given by a law of the United States.

In the distribution of this power it is declared that "the supreme court shall have original jurisdiction in all cases affecting ambassadors, other public ministers and consuls, and those in which a state shall be a party. In all other cases, the supreme court shall have appellate jurisdiction."

It has been insisted, at the bar, that as the original grant of jurisdiction, to the supreme and inferior courts, is general, and the clause, assigning original jurisdiction to the Supreme Court, contains no negative or restrictive words; the power remains to the legislature, to assign original jurisdiction to that court in other cases than those specified in the article which has been recited; provided those cases belong to the judicial power of the United States.

If it had been intended to leave it in the discretion of the legislature to apportion the judicial power between the supreme and inferior courts according to the will of that body, it would certainly have been useless to have proceeded further than to have defined the judicial power, and the tribunals in which it should be vested. The subsequent part of the section is mere surplussage, is entirely without meaning, if such is to be the construction. If congress remains at liberty to give this court appellate jurisdiction, where the constitution has declared their jurisdiction shall be original; and original jurisdiction where the constitution has declared it shall be appellate; the distribution of jurisdiction, made in the constitution, is form without substance.

Affirmative words are often, in their operation, negative of other objects than those affirmed; and in this case, a negative or exclusive sense must be given to them or they have no operation at all.

It cannot be presumed that any clause in the constitution is intended to be without effect; and therefore such a construction is inadmissible, unless the words require it. . . .

To enable this court then to issue a mandamus, it must be shown to be an exercise of appellate jurisdiction, or to be necessary to enable them to exercise appellate jurisdiction.

It has been stated at the bar that the appellate jurisdiction may be exercised in a variety of forms, and that if it be the will of the legislature that a mandamus should be used for that purpose, that will must be obeyed. This is true, yet the jurisdiction must be appellate, not original.

It is the essential criterion of appellate jurisdiction, that it revises and corrects the proceedings in a cause already instituted, and does not create that cause. Although, therefore, a mandamus may be directed to courts, yet to issue such a writ to an officer for the delivery of a paper, is in effect the same as to sustain an original action for that paper, and therefore seems not to belong to appellate, but to original jurisdiction. Neither is it necessary in such a case as this, to enable the court to exercise its appellate jurisdiction.

The authority, therefore, given to the Supreme Court, by the act establishing the judicial courts of the United States, to issue writs of mandamus to public officers, appears not to be warranted by the constitution; and it becomes necessary to enquire whether a jurisdiction, so conferred, can be exercised.

The question, whether an act, repugnant to the constitution, can become the law of the land, is a question deeply interesting to the United States; but, happily, not of an intricacy proportioned to its interest. It seems only necessary to recognise certain principles, supposed to have been long and well established, to decide it.

That the people have an original right to establish, for their future government, such principles as, in their opinion, shall most conduce to their own happiness, is the basis, on which the whole American fabric has been erected. The exercise of this original right is a very great exertion; nor can it, nor ought it to be frequently repeated. The principles, therefore, so established, are deemed fundamental. And as the authority, from which they proceed, is supreme, and can seldom act, they are designed to be permanent.

This original and supreme will organizes the government, and assigns, to different departments, their respective powers. It may either stop here; or establish certain limits not to be transcended by those departments.

The government of the United States is of the latter description. The powers of the legislature are defined, and limited; and that those limits may not be mistaken, or forgotten, the constitution is written. To what purpose are powers limited, and to what purpose is that limitation committed to writing, if these limits may, at any time, be passed by those intended to be restrained? The distinction, between a government with limited and unlimited powers, is abolished, if those limits do not confine the persons on whom they are imposed, and if acts prohibited and acts allowed, are of equal obligation. It is a proposition too plain to be contested, that the constitution controls any legislative act repugnant to it; or, that the legislature may alter the constitution by an ordinary act.

Between these alternatives there is no middle ground. The constitution is either a superior, paramount law, unchangeable by ordinary means, or it is on a level with ordinary legislative acts, and like other acts, is alterable when the legislature shall please to alter it.

If the former part of the alternative be true, then a legislative act contrary to the constitution is not law: if the latter part be true, then written constitutions are absurd attempts, on the part of the people, to limit a power, in its own nature illimitable.

Certainly all those who have framed written constitutions contemplate them as forming the fundamental and paramount law of the nation, and consequently the theory of every such government must be, that an act of the legislature, repugnant to the constitution, is void.

This theory is essentially attached to a written constitution, and is consequently to be considered, by this court, as one of the fundamental principles of our society. It is not therefore to be lost sight of in the further consideration of this subject.

If an act of the legislature, repugnant to the constitution, is void, does it, notwithstanding its invalidity, bind the courts, and oblige them to give it effect? Or, in other words, though it be not law, does it constitute a rule as operative as if it was a law? This would be to overthrow in fact what was established in theory; and would seem, at first view, an absurdity too gross to be insisted on. It shall, however, receive a more attentive consideration.

It is emphatically the province and duty of the judicial department to say what the law is. Those who apply the rule to particular cases, must of necessity expound and interpret that rule. If two laws conflict with each other, the courts must decide on the operation of each.

So if a law be in opposition to the constitution; if both the law and the constitution apply to a particular case, so that the court must either decide that case conformably to the law, disregarding the constitution; or conformably to the constitution, disregarding the law; the court must determine which of these conflicting rules governs the case. This is of the very essence of judicial duty.

If then the courts are to regard the constitution; and the constitution is superior to any ordinary act of the legislature; the constitution, and not such ordinary act, must govern the case to which they both apply.

Those then who controvert the principle that the constitution is to be considered, in court, as a paramount law, are reduced to the necessity of maintaining that courts must close their eyes on the constitution, and see only the law.

This doctrine would subvert the very foundation of all written constitutions. It would declare that an act, which, according to the principles and theory of our government, is entirely void; is yet, in practice, completely obligatory. It would declare, that if the legislature shall do what is expressly forbidden, such act, notwithstanding the express prohibition, is in reality effectual. It would be giving to the legislature a practical and real omnipotence, with the same breath which professes to restrict their powers within narrow limits. It is prescribing limits, and declaring that those limits may be passed at pleasure.

That it thus reduces to nothing what we have deemed the greatest improvement on political institutions—a written constitution—would of itself be sufficient, in America, where written constitutions have been viewed with so much reverence, for rejecting the construction. But the peculiar expressions of the constitution of the United States furnish additional arguments in favour of its rejection.

The judicial power of the United States is extended to all cases arising under the constitution.

Could it be the intention of those who gave this power, to say that, in using it, the constitution should not be looked into? That a case arising under the constitution should be decided without examining the instrument under which it arises?

This is too extravagant to be maintained.

In some cases then, the constitution must be looked into by the judges. And if they can open it at all, what part of it are they forbidden to read, or to obey?

There are many other parts of the constitution which serve to illustrate this subject.

It is declared that "no tax or duty shall be laid on articles exported from any state." Suppose a duty on the export of cotton, of tobacco, or of flour; and a suit instituted to recover it. Ought judgment to be rendered in such a case? ought the judges to close their eyes on the constitution, and only see the law.

The constitution declares that "no bill of attainder or *ex post facto* law shall be passed."

If, however, such a bill should be passed and a person should be prosecuted under it; must the court condemn to death those victims whom the constitution endeavours to preserve?

"No person," says the constitution, "shall be convicted of treason unless on the testimony of two witnesses to the same overt act, or on confession in open court."

Here the language of the constitution is addressed especially to the courts. It prescribes, directly for them, a rule of evidence not to be departed from. If the legislature should change that rule, and declare *one* witness, or a confession *out* of court, sufficient for conviction, must the constitutional principle yield to the legislative act?

From these, and many other selections which might be made, it is apparent, that the Framers of the constitution contemplated that instrument, as a rule for the government of *courts*, as well as of the legislature.

Why otherwise does it direct the judges to take an oath to support it? This oath certainly applies, in an especial manner, to their conduct in their official character.

How immoral to impose it on them, if they were to be used as the instruments, and the knowing instruments, for violating what they swear to support!

The oath of office, too, imposed by the legislature, is completely demonstrative of the legislative opinion on this subject. It is in these words, "I do solemnly swear that I will administer justice without respect to persons, and do equal right to the poor and to the rich; and that I will faithfully and impartially discharge all the duties incumbent on me as according to the best of my abilities and understanding, agreeably to *the constitution*, and laws of the United States."

Why does a judge swear to discharge his duties agreeably to the constitution of the United States, if that *constitution* forms no rule for his government? if it is closed upon him, and cannot be inspected by him?

If such be the real state of things, this is worse than solemn mockery. To prescribe, or to take this oath, becomes equally a crime.

It is also not entirely unworthy of observation, that in declaring what shall be the *supreme law* of the land, the *constitution* itself is first mentioned; and not the laws of the United States generally, but those only which shall be made in *pursuance* of the constitution, have that rank.

Thus, the particular phraseology of the constitution of the United States confirms and strengthens the principle, supposed to be essential to all written constitutions, that a law repugnant to the constitution is void; and that *courts*, as well as other departments, are bound by that instrument.

The rule must be discharged.

Scholars differ about Marshall's opinion in *Marbury*, but even his critics acknowledge Marshall's shrewdness. Think about the way the chief justice dealt with a most delicate political situation. By ruling against Marbury, who never did receive his commission *(see Box 2-1)*, Marshall avoided a potentially devastating clash with the new president; but, by exerting the power of judicial review, he sent a clear signal to Jefferson that the Court was going to be an important part of the American government.

The decision helped to fix Marshall's reputation as perhaps the greatest justice in Supreme Court history. More relevant to our concerns, *Marbury* asserted the Court's authority to review and strike down government actions that were incompatible with the Constitution.[3] In Marshall's view, such authority, while not explicit in the Constitution, was clearly intended by the framers. Was he correct? His opinion makes a plausible argument, and current justices more than occasionally invoke the logic of *Marbury*, even though universal acceptance of judicial review built only gradually during the nineteenth century.[4] Consider the Court's decision in *City of Boerne v. Flores* (1997). At issue was the Religious Freedom Restoration Act of 1993 (RFRA), which Congress passed in response to *Employment Division v. Smith* (1990) *(pages 114–120)*. RFRA directed the Court to adopt a particular standard of law in constitutional cases involving the free exercise clause of the First Amendment—a standard the Court had rejected in *Smith*.

In striking down Congress's effort at constitutional interpretation, the Court did not hesitate to cite *Marbury*:

Our national experience teaches that the Constitution is preserved best when each part of the government respects both the Constitution and the proper actions and determinations of the other branches. When the Court has interpreted the Constitution, it has acted within the province of the Judicial Branch, which embraces the duty to say what the law is. *Marbury v. Madison.* When the political branches of the Government act against the background of a judicial interpretation of the Constitution already issued, it must be understood that in later cases and controversies the Court will treat its precedents with the respect due them under settled principles, including *stare decisis*, and contrary expectations must be disappointed. RFRA was designed to control cases and controversies, such as the one before us; but as the provisions of the federal statute here invoked are beyond congressional authority, it is this Court's precedent, not RFRA, which must control.

---

3. In *Marbury* the Court addressed only the power to review acts of the federal government. Could the Court exert judicial review over the states? According to Section 25 of the 1789 Judiciary Act, it could. Congress gave the Court appellate jurisdiction to cover appeals from a state's highest court if that court upheld a state law against challenges of unconstitutionality or denied some claim based on the U.S. Constitution, federal laws, or treaties. In *Martin v. Hunter's Lessee* (1816) and *Cohens v. Virginia* (1821), the justices upheld Section 25 of the Judiciary Act.

4. Mark A. Graber, "Establishing Judicial Review? *Schooner Peggy* and the Early Marshall Court," *Political Research Quarterly* 51 (1998): 221–239.

BOX 2-1   AFTERMATH . . . *MARBURY V. MADISON*

From meager beginnings, William Marbury gained political and economic influence in his home state of Maryland and became a strong supporter of John Adams and the Federalist Party. Unlike others of his day who rose in wealth through agriculture or trade, Marbury made his way to prominence through banking and finance. At age thirty-eight, he saw his appointment to be a justice of the peace as a public validation of his rising economic status and social prestige. Marbury never received his judicial position; instead, he returned to his financial activities, ultimately becoming the president of a bank in George-town. He died in 1835, the same year as Chief Justice John Marshall.

Other participants in the famous decision played major roles in the early history of our nation. Thomas Jefferson, who refused to honor Marbury's appointment, served two terms as chief executive, leaving office in 1809 as one of the nation's most revered presidents. James Madison, the secretary of state who carried out Jefferson's order depriving Marbury of his judgeship,

became the nation's fourth president, serving from 1809 to 1817. Following the *Marbury* decision, Chief Justice Marshall led the Court for an additional thirty-two years. His tenure was marked with fundamental rulings expanding the power of the judiciary and enhancing the position of the federal government relative to the states. He is rightfully regarded as history's most influential chief justice.

Although the *Marbury* decision established the power of judicial review, it is ironic that the Marshall Court never again used its authority to strike down a piece of congressional legislation. In fact, it was not until *Scott v. Sandford* (1857), more than two decades after Marshall's death, that the Court once again invalidated a congressional statute.

SOURCES: John A. Garraty, "The Case of the Missing Commissions," in John A. Garraty, *Quarrels That Have Shaped the Constitution* (New York: Harper and Row, 1962); David F. Forte, "Marbury's Travail: Federalist Politics and William Marbury's Appointment as Justice of the Peace," *Catholic University Law Review* 45 (1996): 349–402.

It is not only justices serving in the contemporary era who continue to cite *Marbury* with approval. Many countries have written judicial review into their constitutions, refusing to leave its establishment to chance (*see Box 2-2*).

Even so, some judges and scholars have pointed out problems with *Marbury*. Table 2-1 summarizes the arguments over judicial review, many of which will resurface in the pages to come.[5] These controversies are important because they place judicial review into a theoretical context for debate. But the questions may

never be resolved: as one side finds support for its position, the other side always does too.

Let us consider instead several issues arising from the way the Court actually has exercised the power of judicial review: the number of times it has invoked the power to strike laws and the significance of those decisions. As Lawrence Baum suggests, investigation of these issues can help us achieve a better understanding of judicial review and place it in a realistic context.[6] First, how often has the Court overturned a federal, state, or local law or ordinance? Figure 1-6 *(page 35)* depicts those numbers over time. The data seem to indicate that the Court has made frequent use of the power, striking down close to fifteen hundred government acts since 1790. Baum notes, however, that those acts are but a "minute fraction" of the laws enacted at various levels of government. Since 1790, for example, Congress has passed more than sixty thousand laws, and the Court has struck down far less than 1 percent of them.

---

5. Some critics attack specific aspects of the ruling. Jefferson argued that once Marshall ruled that the Court did not have jurisdiction, he should have dismissed it. Another criticism is that Section 13 of the 1789 Judiciary Act—which *Marbury* held unconstitutional—did not "even remotely suggest an expansion of the Supreme Court's original jurisdiction"; Jeffrey Segal and Harold Spaeth, *The Supreme Court and the Attitudinal Model Revisited* (New York: Cambridge University Press, 2002), 23. If this is so, then Marshall "had nothing to declare unconstitutional!" A counterargument is that Section 13 was seen as expanding the Court's original jurisdiction, or else why did Marbury bring his suit directly to the Court? And why did his attorney specifically note that the act was constitutional?

6. Lawrence Baum, *The Supreme Court*, 9th ed. (Washington, DC: CQ Press, 2007), 164–170.

BOX 2-2   JUDICIAL REVIEW IN GLOBAL PERSPECTIVE

Judicial authority to invalidate acts of coordinate branches is not unique to the United States, although it is fair to say that the prestige of the U.S. Supreme Court has provided a model and incentive for other countries. By the middle of the nineteenth century, the Judicial Committee of the British Privy Council was functioning as a kind of constitutional arbiter for colonial governments within the British Empire—but not for the United Kingdom itself. Then in the late nineteenth century Canada and in the first years of the twentieth Australia created their own systems of constitutional review.

In the nineteenth century Argentina also modeled its Corte Suprema on that of the United States and even instructed its judges to pay special attention to precedents of the American tribunal. In the twentieth century Austria, Ireland, India, and the Philippines adopted judicial review, and variations of this power can be found in Norway, Switzerland, much of Latin America, and some countries in Africa.

After World War II the three defeated Axis powers—Italy, Japan, and (West) Germany—all institutionalized judicial review in their new constitutions. This development was due in part to a revulsion against their recent experiences with unchecked political power and in part to the influence of American occupying authorities. Japan, where the constitutional document was largely drafted by Americans, follows the decentralized model of the United States: the power of constitutional review is diffused throughout the entire judicial system.[1] Any court of general jurisdiction can declare a legislative or executive act invalid.

Germany and Italy, and later Belgium, Portugal, and Spain, followed a centralized model first adopted in the Austrian constitution of 1920. Each country has a single constitutional court (although some sit in divisions or senates) that has a judicial monopoly on reviewing acts of government for their compatibility with their constitutions. The most a lower court judge can do when a constitutional issue is raised is to refer the problem to the specialized constitutional court. *(See Box 1-1, page 14.)*

After the Berlin Wall collapsed in 1989, and the Soviet Union disintegrated soon after, many East European republics looked to protect their new-found liberties through judges' interpreting a constitutional text with a bill of rights. Most opted for centralized systems of constitutional review, establishing ordinary tribunals and a separate constitutional court. They made this choice despite familiarity with Chief Justice John Marshall's argument for a decentralized court system in *Marbury*; namely, all judges may face the problem of a conflict between a statute or executive order and the terms of a constitutional document. If judges cannot give preference to the constitutional provision over ordinary legislation or an executive act, they violate their oath to support the constitution.

The experience of these tribunals has been quite varied. The German Constitutional Court, for example, is largely regarded as a success story. In its first thirty-eight years, that tribunal invalidated 292 Bund (national) and 130 Land (state) laws, provoking frequent complaints that it "judicializes" politics.[2] The Court, however, has survived these attacks and has gone on to create a new and politically significant jurisprudence in the fields of federalism and civil liberties. The Russian Constitutional Court stands (or teeters) in stark contrast. It too began to make extensive use of judicial review to strike down government acts but quickly paid a steep price: In 1993 President Boris Yeltsin suspended the court's operations; it did not resume its activities until nearly two years later.

SOURCE: Adapted from C. Herman Pritchett, Walter F. Murphy, Lee Epstein, and Jack Knight, *Courts, Judges and Politics*, 6th ed. (New York: McGraw-Hill, 2005), chap. 6.

[1] Walter F. Murphy and Joseph Tanenhaus, eds., *Comparative Constitutional Law* (New York: St. Martin's Press, 1977), chaps. 1–6; C. Neal Tate and Torbjörn Vallinder, eds., *The Global Expansion of Judicial Power: The Judicialization of Politics* (New York: New York University Press, 1995).

[2] Donald P. Kommers, *The Constitutional Jurisprudence of the Federal Republic of Germany*, 2nd ed. (Durham, NC: Duke University Press, 1997), 52.

TABLE 2-1   Major Controversies over Judicial Review

CONTROVERSY	SUPPORTING JUDICIAL REVIEW	OPPOSING JUDICIAL REVIEW
Framers' Intent: Did the framers intend the federal courts to exercise judicial review?	The framers knew about judicial review. Evidence shows that the concept was adopted in England in the 1600s. Moreover, between 1776 and 1787, eight of the thirteen colonies incorporated judicial review into their constitutions, and by 1789 various state courts had struck down as unconstitutional eight acts passed by their legislatures.	Even though some states adopted judicial review, their courts rarely exercised the power. When they did, the public outrage that followed provides some indication that the practice was not widely accepted.
	The framers left judicial review out of the Constitution because they did not want to heighten controversy over Article III review, not because they opposed the practice.	The participants at the Constitutional Convention rejected the proposed Council of Revision, which would have enabled Supreme Court justices and the president to veto legislative acts.
	The framers implicitly accepted judicial review. Historians have established that more than half of the delegates to the Constitutional Convention approved of it. In *The Federalist*, Hamilton argued that one branch of government must safeguard the Constitution and that the courts were best suited for that task.	
Judicial Restraint: Should unelected courts defer to the elected institutions of government?	The government needs an umpire who will act neutrally and fairly in interpreting the constitutional strictures.	Unelected judges should defer to the wishes of elected officials, who represent the best interests of the people and who can be removed from office when they do not.
Democratic Checks: Are there sufficient checks on courts to prevent them from using judicial review in a way repugnant to the best interests of the people?	Acting in different combinations, Congress, the president, and the states can, for example, ratify a constitutional amendment to overturn a decision, change the size of the Court, or remove the Court's appellate jurisdiction.	The problem with these checks, some analysts say, is that they are rarely invoked: only five amendments have overturned Court decisions; the Court's size has not been changed since 1869; and only rarely has Congress removed the Court's appellate jurisdiction.
	Although Congress rarely takes direct action against the Court, the fact that the legislature has weapons to use against the judiciary may influence the justices, who might try to accommodate the wishes of Congress rather than risk the reversal of a ruling. It is the existence of congressional threat—not its actual use—that may affect how the Court rules in a given case, which may explain why the justices rarely strike down congressional acts.	
Role of Courts in a Democratic Society: Do courts need the power of judicial review to protect minority interests?	The Court must have the power of judicial review if it is to fulfill its most important constitutional assignment: protection of minority rights. Because legislatures and executives are popularly elected, they reflect the interests of the majority. So that the majority cannot tyrannize a minority, it is necessary for the one branch of government that lacks any electoral connection to have the power of judicial review.	This position conflicts with the idea of the Court as a body that defers to the elected branches.
		Courts have not always used judicial review to protect minorities: some of the acts they strike down are those that harmed a "privileged class." For example, in *City of Richmond v. J. A. Croson Co.* (1989) and *Adarand Constructors v. Pena* (1995), the justices struck down programs designed to help minority interests.

SOURCE: We adopt this framework from David Adamany, "The Supreme Court," in *The American Courts: A Critical Assessment*, ed. John B. Gates and Charles A. Johnson (Washington, DC: CQ Press, 1991).

Second, how significant are the laws the Court strikes down? Using **Scott v. Sandford** (1857) as an illustration, some argue that the Court often strikes down significant legislation. Undoubtedly, that opinion had major consequences: by ruling that Congress could not prohibit slavery in the territories and by striking down the Missouri Compromise, even though the law had already been repealed, the Court fueled the growing divisions between the North and South, providing a major impetus for the Civil War. The decision also tarnished the prestige of the Court and the reputation of Chief Justice Roger B. Taney.

Some other Court opinions striking down government acts have been almost as important as *Scott*—for example, those nullifying state abortion and segregation laws, the federal child labor acts, and many pieces of New Deal legislation. But many others were minor. Consider *Monongahela Navigation Co. v. United States* (1893), in which the Court struck down, on Fifth Amendment grounds, a law concerning the amount of money to be paid by the United States to companies for the "purchase or condemnation of a certain lock and dam in the Monongahela River."

Despite the ambiguous record, we can reach two conclusions about the Court's use of judicial review. One is that "important as judicial review has been, it has not given the Court anything like a dominant position in the national government."[7] The other is that the Court's *use* of judicial review may not be what is significant. Rather, like the president's ability to veto congressional legislation, its power may lie in the threat of its invocation. In either case, it has provided federal courts with their most significant political weapon.

CONSTRAINTS ON JUDICIAL POWER

Given all the attention paid to judicial review, it is easy to forget that the power of courts to exercise it and courts' judicial authority, more generally, has substantial limits. Article III—or the Court's interpretation of it—places three major constraints on the ability of federal tribunals to hear and decide cases: the court must have authority to hear a case (jurisdiction); the case must be appropriate for judicial resolution (justiciability); and the appropriate party must bring the case (standing). Following is a brief review of the doctrine

surrounding these constraints. As you read, consider not only the Court's interpretation of its own limits but also the justifications it offers. Note in particular how fluid these can be: some Courts tend toward loose constructions of the rules, while others are anxious to enforce them. What factors might explain these different tendencies? Or, to put it another way, to what extent do these constraints limit the Court's authority?

Jurisdiction

According to Chief Justice Salmon P. Chase, "Without jurisdiction the court cannot proceed at all in any cause. Jurisdiction is power to declare the law, and when it ceases to exist, the only function remaining to the court is that of announcing the fact and dismissing the cause."[8] In other words, a court cannot hear a case unless it has the authority—the jurisdiction—to do so.

Article III, Section 2, defines the jurisdiction of U.S. federal courts. Lower courts have the authority to hear disputes involving particular parties and subject matter. The U.S. Supreme Court's jurisdiction is divided into original and appellate: the former are classes of cases that originate in the Court; the latter are those it hears after a lower court.

To what extent does jurisdiction constrain the federal courts? *Marbury v. Madison* provides some answers, although contradictory, to this question. Chief Justice Marshall informed Congress that it could not alter the original jurisdiction of the Court. Having reached this conclusion, perhaps Marshall should have dismissed the case on the grounds that the Court lacked authority to hear it, but that is not what he did.

The issue of appellate jurisdiction is a bit more complex. Article III explicitly states that for those cases over which the Court does not have original jurisdiction, it "shall have appellate Jurisdiction . . . with such Exceptions, and under such Regulations as the Congress shall make." The exceptions clause seems to give Congress authority to alter the Court's appellate jurisdiction.

Has the Supreme Court allowed Congress to do so? In **Martin v. Hunter's Lessee** (1816) the Supreme Court allowed Congress to authorize it to hear appeals from the highest state courts, if those tribunals upheld a state law against challenges of unconstitutionality or denied some claim based on the U.S. Constitution, federal laws, or treaties (*see footnote 3*). The question the Court addressed in *Ex parte McCardle* was a bit different. Here

---

7. Ibid., 170.

8. *Ex parte McCardle* (1869).

the justices determined whether Congress could use its power under the exceptions clause to *remove* the Court's appellate jurisdiction over a particular category of cases.

Ex parte McCardle

74 U.S. (7 WALL.) 506 (1869)
http://laws.findlaw.com/US/74/506.html
Vote: 8 (Chase, Clifford, Davis, Field, Grier, Miller, Nelson, Swayne)
    0

OPINION OF THE COURT: *Chase*

FACTS:

After the Civil War, the Radical Republican Congress imposed a series of restrictions on the South.[9] Known as the Reconstruction laws, they in effect placed the region under military rule. Journalist William McCardle opposed these measures and wrote editorials urging resistance to them. He was arrested for publishing allegedly "incendiary and libelous articles" and held for a trial before a military tribunal, established under Reconstruction.

Because he was a civilian, not a member of any militia, McCardle claimed that he was being illegally held. He petitioned the U.S. circuit court in Mississippi for a writ of habeas corpus (an order issued to determine whether a person held in custody is lawfully detained or imprisoned) under an 1867 act, which enabled federal judges "to grant habeas corpus to persons detained in violation" of the U.S. Constitution. When this effort failed, McCardle appealed to the U.S. Supreme Court, which had gained appellate jurisdiction in such cases with passage of the 1867 law.

In early March 1868, *McCardle* "was very thoroughly and ably [presented] upon the merits" to the U.S. Supreme Court. It was clear to most observers that "no Justice was still making up his mind": the Court's sympathies, as was widely known, lay with McCardle.[10] But before the justices issued their decision, Congress, on March 27, 1868, repealed the 1867 Habeas Corpus Act and removed the Supreme Court's authority to hear appeals emanating from it. This action was meant to punish the Court or, at the very least, to send it a strong message. In 1866, two years before *McCardle,* the Court had invalidated President Abraham Lincoln's use of military tribunals in certain areas.[11] Congress did not want to see the Court take similar action in this dispute. Congress was so adamant on this issue that after President Andrew Johnson vetoed the 1868 repealer act, the legislature overrode the veto.

The Court responded by redocketing the case for oral arguments in March 1869. During the arguments and in its briefs, the government contended that the Court no longer had authority to hear the case and should dismiss it.

ARGUMENTS:

For the appellant, William McCardle:

- According to the Constitution, the judicial power extends to "the laws of the United States." The Constitution also vests that judicial power in one Supreme Court. The jurisdiction of this Court, then, comes directly from the Constitution, not from Congress.

- Suppose that Congress never made any exceptions or any regulations regarding the Court's appellate jurisdiction. Under the argument that Congress must define when, and where, and how the Supreme Court shall exercise its jurisdiction, what becomes of the "judicial power of the United States," given to this Court? It would cease to exist. But the Court is coexistent and coordinate with Congress, and must be able to exercise judicial power even if Congress passed no act on the subject.

- This case had been argued in this Court. Congress has interfered with a case on which this Court has passed, or is passing, judgment. This amounts to an exercise by the Congress of judicial power.

For the appellee, U.S. Government:

- The Constitution gives Congress the power to "except" any or all of the cases mentioned in the jurisdiction clause of Article III from the appellate jurisdiction of the Supreme Court. It was clearly Congress's intention, in the repealer act, to exercise its power to "except."

- The Court has no authority to pronounce any opinion or render any judgment in this cause because the act conferring the jurisdiction has been repealed and so jurisdiction ceases.

---

9. For more information on *McCardle,* see Thomas G. Walker and Lee Epstein, "The Role of the Supreme Court in American Society: Playing the Reconstruction Game," in *Contemplating Courts,* ed. Lee Epstein (Washington, DC: CQ Press, 1995), 315–346.

10. Charles Fairman, *Reconstruction and Reunion,* vol. 7 of *History of the Supreme Court of the United States* (New York: Macmillan, 1971), 456.

11. That action came in *Ex parte Milligan* (1866).

- No court can act in any case without jurisdiction, and it does not matter at what period in the progress of the case the jurisdiction ceases. After it has ceased no judicial act can be performed.

THE CHIEF JUSTICE DELIVERED THE OPINION OF THE COURT.

It is unnecessary to consider whether, if Congress had made no exceptions and no regulations, this court might not have exercised general appellate jurisdiction under rules prescribed by itself. From among the earliest Acts of the first Congress, at its first session, was the Act of September 24th, 1789, to establish the judicial courts of the United States. That Act provided for the organization of this court, and prescribed regulations for the exercise of its jurisdiction. . . .

The exception to appellate jurisdiction in the case before us . . . is not an inference from the affirmation of other appellate jurisdiction. It is made in terms. The provision of the Act of 1867, affirming the appellate jurisdiction of this court in cases of habeas corpus, is expressly repealed. It is hardly possible to imagine a plainer instance of positive exception.

We are not at liberty to inquire into the motives of the Legislature. We can only examine into its power under the Constitution; and the power to make exceptions to the appellate jurisdiction of this court is given by express words.

What, then, is the effect of the repealing Act upon the case before us? We cannot doubt as to this. Without jurisdiction the court cannot proceed at all in any cause. Jurisdiction is power to declare the law, and when it ceases to exist, the only function remaining to the court is that of announcing the fact and dismissing the cause. And this is not less clear upon authority than upon principle. . . .

It is quite clear, therefore, that this court cannot proceed to pronounce judgment in this case, for it has no longer jurisdiction of the appeal; and judicial duty is not less fitly performed by declining ungranted jurisdiction than in exercising firmly that which the Constitution and the laws confer. . . .

The appeal of the petitioner in this case must be dismissed for want of jurisdiction.

As we can see, the Court acceded and declined to hear the case. *McCardle* suggests that Congress has the authority to remove the Court's appellate jurisdiction

as it deems necessary. As Justice Felix Frankfurter put it in 1949, "Congress need not give this Court any appellate power; it may withdraw appellate jurisdiction once conferred and it may do so even while a case is *sub judice* [before a judge]."[12] On the other hand, thirteen years later, Justice William O. Douglas remarked, "There is a serious question whether the *McCardle* case could command a majority view today."[13] And even Chief Justice Chase himself suggested limits on congressional power in this area. After *McCardle* had been decided, he noted that use of the exceptions clause was "unusual and hardly to be justified except upon some imperious public exigency."[14]

To this day, then, *McCardle's* status remains an open question. To Frankfurter and others in his camp, the *McCardle* precedent, not to mention the text of the exceptions clause, makes it quite clear that Congress can remove the Court's appellate jurisdiction. To Douglas and other commentators, *McCardle* was something of an oddity that does not square with American traditions: before *McCardle*, Congress had never stripped the Court's jurisdiction, and since *McCardle*, Congress has only rarely taken this step, and did not take it in the wake of some of the Court's most controversial decisions, such as *Roe v. Wade* and *Brown v. Board of Education*. Then there is the related argument that, taken to its extreme, jurisdiction stripping could render the Court virtually powerless. Would the framers have created an institution only to allow Congress to destroy it? Many scholars say no.

Justiciability

According to Article III, the judicial power of the federal courts is restricted to "cases" and "controversies." Taken together, these words mean that a litigation must be justiciable—appropriate or suitable for a federal tribunal to hear or to solve. As Chief Justice Earl Warren asserted, cases and controversies

are two complementary but somewhat different limitations. In part those words limit the business of federal courts to questions presented in an adversary context and in a form historically viewed as capable of resolution through the judicial process. And in part those words define the role assigned to the judiciary in a tripartite allocation of power

---

12. *National Mutual Insurance Co. v. Tidewater Transfer Co.* (1949).

13. *Glidden Co. v. Zdanok* (1962).

14. *Ex parte Yerger* (1869).

to assure that the federal courts will not intrude into areas committed to the other branches of government. Justiciability is the term of art employed to give expression to this dual limitation placed upon federal courts by the case-and-controversy doctrine.[15]

Although Warren also suggested that "justiciability is itself a concept of uncertain meaning and scope," he elucidated several types of cases or characteristics of litigation that would render it nonjusticiable. In this section, we treat five: advisory opinions, collusion, mootness, ripeness, and political questions. In the following section, we deal with another concept related to justiciability—standing to sue.

Advisory Opinions. A few states and some foreign countries require judges of the highest court to advise the executive or legislature, when requested to do so, as to their views on the constitutionality of a proposed policy. Since the time of Chief Justice Jay, however, federal judges in the United States have refused to issue advisory opinions. They do not render advice in hypothetical suits, because if litigation is abstract, it possesses no real controversy. The language of the Constitution does not prohibit advisory opinions as opinions, but the framers rejected a proposal that would have permitted the other branches of government to request judicial rulings "upon important questions of law, and upon solemn occasions." Madison was critical of the proposal on the grounds that the judiciary should have jurisdiction only over "cases of a Judiciary Nature."

The Supreme Court agreed with Madison. In July 1793, Secretary of State Thomas Jefferson asked the justices if they would be willing to address questions concerning the appropriate role America should play in the ongoing British-French war. Jefferson wrote that President George Washington "would be much relieved if he found himself free to refer questions [involving the war] to the opinions of the judges of the Supreme Court in the United States, whose knowledge . . . would secure us against errors dangerous to the peace of the United States."[16] Less than a

month later, in a written response sent directly to the president, the justices denied Jefferson's request:

We have considered [the] letter written by your direction to us by the Secretary of State [regarding] the lines of separation drawn by the Constitution between the three departments of government. These being in certain respects checks upon each other, and our being judges of a court in the last resort, are considerations which afford strong arguments against the propriety of our extra-judicially deciding the questions alluded to, especially as the power given by the Constitution to the President, of calling on the heads of departments for opinions, seems to have been *purposely* as well as expressly united to the *executive* departments.

With these words, the justices sounded the death knell for advisory opinions: they would violate the separation of powers principle embedded in the Constitution. The subject has resurfaced only a few times in U.S. history; in the 1930s, for example, President Franklin Roosevelt considered a proposal that would require the Court to issue advisory opinions on the constitutionality of federal laws. But Roosevelt quickly gave up on the idea at least in part because of its dubious constitutionality.

Nevertheless, scholars still debate the Court's 1793 letter to Washington. Some agree with the justices' logic, but others assert that more institutional concerns were at work; perhaps the Court was concerned about being thrust into disputes prematurely. Whatever the reason, all subsequent Courts have followed that 1793 precedent: requests for advisory opinions to the U.S. Supreme Court present nonjusticiable disputes.

But justices have found other ways of offering advice.[17] For example, they have sometimes offered political leaders informal suggestions in private conversations or correspondence.[18] Furthermore, justices of the Supreme Court have often given advice in an institutional but indirect manner. Justice Willis Van Devanter had a hand in drafting the Judiciary Act of 1925, which granted the Court wide discretion in controlling its docket, and Chief Justice

---

15. *Flast v. Cohen* (1968).

16. For the full text of Jefferson's request and the justices' response, see Henry M. Hart Jr. and Albert M. Sacks, *The Legal Process: Basic Problems in the Making and Application of Law*, prepared for publication from the 1958 tentative edition by and containing an introductory essay by William N. Eskridge Jr. and Philip P. Frickey (Westbury, NY: Foundation Press, 1994), 630.

17. We adopt some of the material to follow from Walter F. Murphy, C. Herman Pritchett, Lee Epstein, and Jack Knight, *Courts, Judges, and Politics* (New York: McGraw-Hill, 2006), chap. 6.

18. See, for example, Stewart Jay, *Most Humble Servants: The Advisory Role of Early Judges* (New Haven, CT: Yale University Press, 1997).

William Howard Taft and several associate justices openly lobbied for its passage, "patrolling the halls of Congress," as Taft put it. In 1937, when the Senate was considering President Roosevelt's Court-packing plan, opponents arranged for Chief Justice Charles Evans Hughes to send a letter to Senator Burton K. Wheeler, D-Mont., advising him that raising the number of justices would impede rather than facilitate the Court's work and that the justices' sitting in separate panels to hear cases—a procedure that increasing the number of justices was supposed to allow—would probably violate the constitutional command that there be "one supreme Court." More recent chief justices have sent annual reports on the state of the judiciary to Congress explaining not only what kinds of legislation they deemed good for the courts but also the likely impact of proposed legislation on the federal judicial system.

Finally, judges have occasionally used their opinions to provide advice to decision makers. In *Regents of the University of California v. Bakke* (1978) *(excerpted on pages 691–698),* for example, the Court held that a state medical school's version of affirmative action had deprived a white applicant of equal protection of the laws by rejecting him in favor of minority applicants whom the school ranked lower on all the relevant academic criteria. But, in his opinion, Justice Lewis F. Powell Jr. proffered the advice that the kind of affirmative action program operated by Harvard University would be constitutionally acceptable.

Collusive Suits. A second corollary of justiciability is collusion. The Court will not decide cases in which the litigants (1) want the same outcome, (2) evince no real adversity between them, or (3) are merely testing the law. Why the Court deems collusive suits nonjusticiable is well illustrated in **Muskrat v. United States** (1911). At issue here were several federal laws involving land distribution and appropriations to Native Americans. To determine whether these laws were constitutional, Congress enacted a statute authorizing David Muskrat and other Native Americans to challenge the land distribution law in court. This legislation also ordered the courts to give priority to Muskrat's suit and allowed the attorney general to defend his claim. Furthermore, Congress agreed to pay Muskrat's legal fees if his suit was successful. When the dispute

reached the U.S. Supreme Court, it was dismissed. Justice William Day wrote:

This attempt to obtain a judicial declaration of the validity of the act of Congress is not presented in a "case" or "controversy," to which, under the Constitution of the United States, the judicial power alone extends. It is true the United States is made a defendant to this action, but it has no interest adverse to the claimants. The object is not to assert a property right as against the Government, or to demand compensation for alleged wrongs because of action upon its part. The whole purpose of the law is to determine the constitutional validity of this class of legislation, in a suit not arising between parties concerning a property right necessarily involved in the decision in question, but in a proceeding against the Government in its sovereign capacity, and concerning which the only judgment required is to settle the doubtful character of the legislation in question.

The Court has not always followed the *Muskrat* precedent, however. Several landmark decisions were the result of collusive suits, including *Pollock v. Farmers' Loan and Trust Co.* (1895), in which the Court declared the federal income tax unconstitutional. The litigants in this dispute, a bank and a stockholder in the bank, both wanted the same outcome—the demise of the tax. And in *Carter v. Carter Coal Co.* (1936) the Court agreed to resolve a dispute over a major piece of New Deal legislation despite the fact that the litigants, a company president and the company, which included the president's father, both wanted the same outcome—the eradication of the legislation.

Why did the justices resolve these disputes? "The Court's decision to hear or dismiss such a test case," David Savage claims, "usually turns on whether it presents an actual conflict of legal rights susceptible to judicial resolution."[19] So the Court might overlook some element of collusion if the suit presents a real controversy or the potential for one. Other scholars are more skeptical. The temptation to set "good" public policy (or strike down "bad" public policy) is sometimes too strong for the justices to follow their own rules.

Mootness. In general, the Court will not decide cases in which the controversy is no longer live by the time it

---

19. David Savage, *Guide to the U.S. Supreme Court,* 4th ed. (Washington, DC: CQ Press, 2004), 316.

reaches the Court's doorstep. *DeFunis v. Odegaard* (1974) provides an example. Rejected for admission to the University of Washington Law School, Marco DeFunis Jr. brought suit against the school, alleging that it had engaged in reverse discrimination because it had denied him a place but accepted statistically less qualified minority students. In 1971 a trial court found merit in his claim and ordered that the university admit him. While DeFunis was in his second year of law school, the state supreme court reversed the trial judge's ruling. He then appealed to the U.S. Supreme Court. By that time, DeFunis had registered for his final quarter in school. In a per curiam opinion, the Court refused to rule on the merits of DeFunis's claim, asserting that it was moot.

Because [DeFunis] will complete his law school studies at the end of the term for which he has now registered regardless of any decision this Court might reach on the merits of this litigation, we conclude that the Court cannot, consistently with the limitations of Art. III of the Constitution, consider the substantive constitutional issues tendered by the parties.

In his dissent, Justice Brennan noted that DeFunis could conceivably not complete his studies that quarter, and so the issue was not necessarily moot. This suggests that the rules governing mootness are a bit fuzzier than the *DeFunis* majority opinion characterized them. In another example, in the well-known case of *Roe v. Wade* (1973) *(see pages 409-416),* in which the Court legalized abortions performed during the first two trimesters of pregnancy, Norma McCorvey, also known as Jane Roe, was pregnant when she filed suit in 1970. When the Court handed down the decision in 1973, she had long since given birth and put her baby up for adoption. But the justices did not declare this case moot. Why not? What made *Roe* different from *DeFunis*?

The justices provided two legal justifications. First, DeFunis brought the litigation in his own behalf, while *Roe* was a class action—a lawsuit brought by one or more persons who represent themselves and all others similarly situated. Second, DeFunis had been admitted to law school, and he would "never again be required to run the gauntlet." Roe could become pregnant again; that is, pregnancy is a situation capable of repetition or recurrence. Are these reasonable points? Or is it possible, as some suspect, that the

Court developed them to avoid particular legal issues? In either case, it is clear that mootness may be a rather slippery concept, open to interpretation by different justices and Courts.

Ripeness. Related to the concepts of advisory opinions and mootness is that of ripeness. Under existing Court interpretation, a case is nonjusticiable if the controversy is premature—has insufficiently gelled—for review. *International Longshoremen's Union v. Boyd* (1954) illustrates this concept. In 1952 Congress passed a law mandating that all aliens seeking admission into the United States from Alaska be "examined" as if they were entering from a foreign country. Believing that the law might affect seasonal American laborers working in Alaska temporarily, a union challenged the law. Writing for the Court, Justice Frankfurter dismissed the suit. In his view,

Appellants in effect asked [the Court] to rule that a statute the sanctions of which had not been set in motion against individuals on whose behalf relief was sought, because an occasion for doing so had not arisen, would not be applied to them if in the future such a contingency should arise. That is not a lawsuit to enforce a right; it is an endeavor to obtain a court's assurance that a statute does not govern hypothetical situations that may or may not make the challenged statute applicable. Determination of the . . . constitutionality of the legislation in advance of its immediate adverse effect in the context of a concrete case involves too remote and abstract an inquiry for the proper exercise of the judicial function.

Political Questions. Another type of nonjusticiable suit involves what is deemed a political question. Chief Justice Marshall stated in *Marbury v. Madison*:

The province of the court is, solely, to decide on the rights of individuals, not to inquire how the executive, or executive officers, perform duties in which they have a discretion. Questions in their nature political, or which are, by the constitution and laws, submitted to the executive, can never be made in this court.

In other words, the Court recognizes that there is a class of questions that may be constitutional in nature, but the Court will not address them because they are better solved by other branches of government

But what exactly constitutes a political question? In the case of **Baker v. Carr** (1962), Justice William J. Brennan Jr. set out the following definition:

Prominent on the surface of any case held to involve a political question is found a textually demonstrable constitutional commitment of the issue to a coordinate political department; or a lack of judicially discoverable and manageable standards for resolving it; or the impossibility of deciding without an initial policy determination of a kind clearly for nonjudicial discretion; or the impossibility of a court's undertaking independent resolution without expressing lack of the respect due coordinate branches of government; or an unusual need for unquestioning adherence to a political decision already made; or the potentiality of embarrassment from multifarious pronouncements by various departments on one question.

Note that this definition contains two major prongs. First, the Court will look to the Constitution to see if there is a "textually demonstrable commitment" to another branch of government. The justices also consider whether particular questions should be left to another branch of government as a matter of prudence. This is where factors such as the lack of judicially discoverable standards, embarrassment, and so forth come into play.

Nixon v. United States (1993) provides an example of both. There the Court held that impeachment procedures are not subject to judicial review because, first, Article I of the Constitution assigns the task of impeachment to Congress, and second, judicial intrusion into impeachment proceedings could create confusion. Imagine the kinds of problems that would emerge if a U.S. president could challenge his impeachment in the federal courts. Would he still be president as his case made its way through the courts or would his successor be the president? This is not a scenario for which the Court wanted to take responsibility.

While *Baker* established a relatively clear doctrinal base for determining political questions, the doctrine itself remains controversial. Some commentators say that the Court has a responsibility to address constitutional questions; that failure to do so is anathemic to *Marbury v. Madison*–type review. Others, however, agree with the justices and suggest that the federal courts continue to avoid cases raising political questions, with *Nixon* a good example.

Standing to Sue

Another constraint on federal judicial power is the requirement that the party bringing a lawsuit have "standing to sue." Not everyone is entitled to the use of the federal courts to challenge the constitutionality of a law or government action. A party must have standing to qualify as an appropriate litigant. According to the Court's interpretation of Article III, standing requires that (1) the party must have suffered a concrete injury or be in imminent danger of suffering such a loss; (2) the injury must be "fairly traceable" to the challenged action of the defendant (usually the government in constitutional cases); and (3) the party must show that a favorable court decision is likely to provide redress.[20] In general, the requirement of these three elements is designed, as Justice Brennan noted in *Baker,* "to assure . . . concrete adverseness which sharpens the presentation of issues upon which the Court so largely depends for illumination of difficult constitutional questions."

In many disputes, the litigants have little difficulty meeting the standing requirements mandated by Article III. A citizen who has been denied the right to vote on the basis of race, a criminal defendant sentenced to death, and a church member jailed for religious proselytizing would have sufficient standing to challenge the federal or state laws that may have deprived them of their rights. But what about parties who wish to challenge some government action on the ground that they are taxpayers? Such claims raise an important question: Does the mere fact that one pays taxes provide a sufficient basis for standing?

In general, the answer is no. In addition to the three constitutionally derived requirements, the Court has articulated several prudential considerations to govern standing. Among the most prominent are those that limit generalized grievance suits—mostly those brought by parties whose only injury is as taxpayers who want to prevent the government from spending money.[21]

---

20. See, for example, *Lujan v. Defenders of Wildlife* (1992), which lays out these three elements. See also **Raines v. Byrd** (1997), which defines an injury relevant for redress from the Court as personal rather than institutional.

21. The exception, based on the establishment clause, is quite narrow. See *Flast v. Cohen* (1968) and **Hein v. Freedom from Religion Foundation** (2007).

Separation of Powers/Checks and Balances

The jurisdiction, justiciability, and standing requirements place considerable constraints on the exercise of judicial power. Yet it is important to note that these doctrines largely come from the Court's own interpretation of Article III and its view of the proper role of the judiciary—the constraints are largely self-imposed.

It would be a mistake, however, to conclude that the use of judicial power is limited only by self-imposed constraints. Indeed, scholars have argued that when it comes to making decisions, the justices are restrained in another way: if they want to generate enduring policy, the justices must be attentive to the preferences of the elected institutions and the actions they expect those institutions to take.

This claim flows from the concept underlying the U.S. Constitution—the separation of powers/checks and balances—and the system of government it created. That system, along with informal rules that have evolved over time—such as the power of judicial review—endows each branch of government with significant power and authority over its own sphere. At the same time, it provides explicit checks on the exercise of those powers, with each branch exercising some control over the others. So, for example, the judiciary may interpret the law and even strike down laws as being in violation of the Constitution, but Congress can pass new legislation, which the president may sign or veto.

Seen in this way, the rule of checks and balances inherent in the system of separation of powers provides justices (and all other government actors) with important information: *policy in the United States emanates not from separate actions of the branches of government but from interaction among them.* For any set of actors to make authoritative policy—be they justices, legislators, or executives—they may have to take this institutional constraint into account by formulating expectations about the preferences of the other relevant actors and what they expect them to do when making their own choices.[22]

This general claim requires some clarification. Although it may be true that the separation of powers system operates across a range of substantive issues, many scholars argue that it imposes a more significant constraint on powers of the statutory variety than on those of the constitutional variety. It is easy to understand why this might be the case when the Court construes a federal law, for Congress can, by a simple majority vote, overturn or modify the justices' interpretation. For example, in *Grove City College v. Bell* (1984), the Court held that Title IX of the 1972 Education Amendments, which prohibits sex discrimination in any "program or activity" receiving federal aid, applies only to the particular program receiving the aid, not to every program at an institution. Congress believed that the Court had misconstrued its intent that Title IX should have an institutionwide scope, and in 1988 simply enacted new legislation—essentially overruling *Grove City*—that made this assumption clear to the Court.[23]

Cases involving constitutional interpretation present a different situation. Although the separation of powers system endows Congress and the president with weapons that they can deploy against the Court, which we will describe, they do not use them very often. This point is important because the infrequency of congressional responses to constitutional decisions (coupled with the difficulty in overturning them) may encourage justices to pay less attention to the preferences and likely actions of other government actors in constitutional disputes than in statutory cases. Yet, for three reasons, we would not expect the Court to ignore completely

---

22. Some argue that the constraint imposed by the separation of powers system subsumes Article III constraints. In *Constitutional Law* (St. Paul, MN: West, 1993), 1028, Daniel A. Farber, William N. Eskridge Jr., and Philip P. Frickey note that the political questions doctrine centers on the notion that the branches have distinct responsibilities. Others suggest—as we have above—that it comes directly from the words of Article III.

23. See William N. Eskridge Jr., "Reneging on History?," *California Law Review* 79 (1991): 613–684. Congress's action in *Grove City* was not all that unusual; indeed, between 1967 and 1990, it disturbed some 120 Court decisions. The sheer number of overrides raises an interesting question: If the Court takes into account government preferences and likely actions when it reaches decisions, why does it occasionally produce inefficacious policy, which Congress or the president later overturns? One explanation is that the Court fails to take account of the external constraint imposed by the separation of powers system. Another is that the Court believes its decisions can provide information to the legislature that may lead members of Congress to reevaluate their positions. Or the justices do not know with certainty what other government actors will do. In these situations, the justices can only make estimates, which may be wrong.

the external constraint imposed by the separation of powers system in constitutional cases.[24]

First, the other branches of government possess the power to alter constitutional policy established by the Court. Congress has attempted to enact legislation to override constitutional decisions, with RFRA providing a case in point (see page 52). It can also propose constitutional amendments to overturn Court decisions. This constraint on the Court is especially effective because once an amendment is part of the Constitution it is "constitutional," meaning that the justices are bound by it. In addition, once the amendment process is set in motion, the Court usually is reluctant to interfere.[25]

It is worth reiterating that Congress does not often propose legislation or constitutional amendments to override the Court. In fact, it has succeeded only five times in overriding the Court with constitutional amendments, and overrulings by legislation may be equally rare. And when the legislature attempts to direct the justices on how to adjudicate constitutional cases, the justices may decline to take such direction— as the majority's reaction to RFRA in *City of Boerne* indicates. Yet the battle over RFRA continued. In 2000, Congress enacted another, albeit watered-down, version of RFRA, called the Religious Land Use and Institutionalized Persons Act, thereby generating the possibility that the Court might eventually buckle. The more general point, however, is this: because

Congress has overridden the Court in the past, the justices must assume it will do so in the future. And this threat may be sufficient to constrain the justices, even in constitutional disputes.

A second reason stems from the U.S. Constitution itself. That document provides the elected institutions with general weapons they can use to "punish" justices for their (constitutional) policy decisions. Congress, for example, can hold judicial salaries constant, impeach justices, change the size of the Court, and make "exceptions" to the Court's appellate jurisdiction. These weapons can have an effect on the doctrine the Court produces, as evident in *Ex parte McCardle.* Perhaps to protect the Court's institutional legitimacy, the justices chose not to rule the way they really wanted—in favor of McCardle. Instead, they dismissed the suit, thereby lending credence to the notion that Congress can remove the Court's appellate jurisdiction as it deems necessary.

McCardle is unusual in constitutional history because the political branches rarely deploy these weapons, but their mere existence may serve to constrain policy-oriented justices from acting on their preferences, which may explain *Marbury.* Certainly, Chief Justice Marshall—himself an Adams appointee— wanted to give Marbury his commission. At the same time, however, Marshall was well aware of the serious repercussions of ordering the administration to do so: President Jefferson made no secret of his disdain for Marshall, and impeachment of the chief justice was a distinct possibility in his (and Marshall's) mind. Therefore, the chief justice was confronted with a dilemma: he could vote his sincere political preferences and risk the institutional integrity of the Court and his own job, or he could act in a sophisticated fashion with regard to his political preferences by refusing to give Marbury his commission and elevate judicial supremacy (establish judicial review) in a way that Jefferson could accept. Not surprisingly, Marshall chose the latter course of action.

Finally, government actors can refuse, implicitly or explicitly, to implement particular constitutional decisions, thereby decreasing the Court's ability to create efficacious policy. *Immigration and Naturalization Services v. Chadha* (1983) provides a case in point. Theoretically speaking, *Chadha* nullified on constitutional grounds the practice of legislative vetoes, by which the vote by one house of Congress can overturn an executive agency policy or decision. In practice, however, Congress continues to pass new laws containing legislative vetoes since *Chadha,* and agencies continue

---

24. For studies suggesting that the constraint may be equally (if not more) operative in constitutional cases, see Lee Epstein, Jack Knight, and Andrew D. Martin, "The Supreme Court as a *Strategic* National Policy Maker," *Emory Law Journal* 50 (2001): 583–611; James Meernik and Joseph Ignagni, "Judicial Review and Coordinate Construction of the Constitution," *American Journal of Political Science* 41 (1997): 447–467; Jeffrey A. Segal, Chad Westerland, and Stefanie A. Lindquist, "Congress, the Supreme Court, and Judicial Review: Testing a Constitutional Separation of Powers Model," *American Journal of Political Science* 55 (2011): 89–104.

25. *Coleman v. Miller* (1939) concerned the actions of the Kansas legislature on the child labor amendment. Proposed by Congress in 1924, the amendment stated: "The Congress shall have power to limit, regulate, and prohibit the labor of persons under eighteen years of age." Kansas legislators rejected the amendment in January 1925. The state senate reconsidered it in January 1937, when the legislative body split 20–20, with the lieutenant governor casting the decisive vote in its favor. Some Kansas legislators (mostly those who opposed the proposal) challenged the 1937 vote on two grounds: the ability of the lieutenant governor to break the tie and the reconsideration of an already rejected amendment. Writing for the Court, Chief Justice Hughes refused to address these points. Rather, he asserted that the suit raised a political question. In his words, "the ultimate authority" over the amendment process was Congress, not the Court.

to pay heed to congressional rejections of their policies. The problem, so it seems, was that the Court fashioned a rule that was "unacceptable" to the other branches of government and that had, as a result, been "eroded by open defiance and subtle evasion."[26] Why the Court would establish such an inefficacious rule is open to speculation, but the relevant point is simple enough: once the Court reached its decision, it had to depend on Congress to implement it. Because Congress failed to do so, the Court was unable to set long-term policy.

In sum, Article III is not the only source of constraint on the Court's power. Although those constraints that emanate from the separation of powers system may play greater roles in cases involving statutory, rather than constitutional, interpretation, they seem to have had some effect in constitutional disputes—as *McCardle* illustrates. What *McCardle* and many other cases you will read in this book demonstrate is that justices, in their quest to create sound policy, occasionally consider how other government actors will respond. If they are not attentive in this fashion, then a *Chadha*-like situation may result, in which the other branches either fail to comply with Court policy or seek to overturn it.

ANNOTATED READINGS

For studies of judicial power, consult the citations in the footnotes in this chapter. Here we only wish to

highlight several interesting books that explore how the Court interprets (or should interpret) its powers in Article III, along with the role the Court plays (or should play) in American society. These books include Alexander M. Bickel, *The Least Dangerous Branch* (New York: Bobbs-Merrill, 1962); Jesse H. Choper, *Judicial Review and the National Political Process* (Chicago: University of Chicago Press, 1980); John Hart Ely, *Democracy and Distrust* (Cambridge, MA: Harvard University Press, 1980); Thomas M. Franck, *Political Questions/Judicial Answers: Does the Rule of Law Apply in Foreign Affairs?* (Princeton, NJ: Princeton University Press, 2009); Larry D. Kramer, *The People Themselves: Popular Constitutionalism and Judicial Review* (New York: Oxford University Press, 2004); William Lasser, *The Limits of Judicial Power* (Chapel Hill: University of North Carolina Press, 1988); Philippa Strum, *The Supreme Court and Political Questions* (Tuscaloosa: University of Alabama Press, 1974); Cass R. Sunstein, *One Case at a Time: Judicial Minimalism on the Supreme Court* (Cambridge, MA: Harvard University Press, 1999).

To greater and lesser extents, these works cover *Marbury v. Madison*. Books more explicitly about the case include Robert Lowry Clinton, Marbury v. Madison *and Judicial Review* (Lawrence: University Press of Kansas, 1989); William E. Nelson, Marbury v. Madison: *The Origins and Legacy of Judicial Review* (Lawrence: University Press of Kansas, 2000); Cliff Sloan and David McKean, *The Great Decision: Jefferson, Adams, Marshall, and the Battle for the Supreme Court* (New York: PublicAffairs, 2009).

---

26. Louis Fisher, "The Legislative Veto: Invalidated, It Survives," *Law & Contemporary Problems* 56 (1993): 273–288.

3

Incorporation of the Bill of Rights

THE FIRST AMENDMENT to the U.S. Constitution contains a clear prohibition: "Congress shall make no law . . . abridging the freedom of speech." The wording specifically and exclusively limits the powers of Congress, reflecting the fact that the Bill of Rights was added to the Constitution because of fear that the *federal* government might become too powerful and encroach upon individual rights. Does the language of the First Amendment mean that state legislatures *may* enact laws curtailing their citizens' free speech? For more than a hundred years it did. The U.S. Supreme Court, following historical interpretations and emphasizing the intention of the framers of the Constitution, refused to nationalize the Bill of Rights by making its protections binding on the state governments. The states were free to recognize those freedoms they deemed important and to develop their own guarantees against state violations of those rights.

Because of a process known as selective incorporation, however, this interpretation is no longer valid. As the nation entered the twentieth century, the Supreme Court slowly began to inform state governments that they too must abide by most guarantees contained in the first eight amendments of the federal Constitution. Today, we take for granted that the states in which we live may not infringe on our right to exercise our religion freely, that no officer of the state may enter our homes without a warrant, and so forth. But the process by which we obtained these rights was long, and the supporters of incorporation lost many disputes

along the way. The process caused acrimonious debates among Supreme Court justices. In fact, the question of whether states must honor the guarantees contained in the Bill of Rights is almost as old as the nation and has been debated by modern Courts as well.

MUST STATES ABIDE BY THE BILL OF RIGHTS? INITIAL RESPONSES

In drafting the original version of the Constitution of 1787, as we noted in the Part I opening essay, the delegates to the convention did not include a bill of rights, believing that such a list was unnecessary.[1] Much of the nation thought otherwise, however, and in order to achieve ratification, supporters of the new government found it necessary to promise that a bill of rights promptly would be added to the new Constitution. Subsequently, James Madison submitted to the First Congress a list of seventeen articles (amendments), mostly aimed at safeguarding personal freedoms against tyranny by the federal government. In a speech to the House, he suggested that "in revising the Constitution, we may throw into that section, which interdicts the abuse of certain powers of the State legislatures, some other provisions of equal, if not greater

---

1. Before the framers adjourned, "It was moved and seconded to appoint a Committee to prepare a Bill of Rights." The motion, however, was defeated.

importance than those already made." To that end, Madison's proposed fourteenth amendment said, "[N]o State shall violate the equal right of conscience, freedom of the press, or trial by jury in criminal cases."[2] This article failed to garner congressional approval, so the states never considered it.

Although scholars now agree that Madison viewed this amendment as the most significant among the seventeen he proposed, Congress's refusal to adopt it may have meant that the founders never intended for the Bill of Rights to be applied to the states or local governments. Chief Justice John Marshall's opinion in *Barron v. Baltimore* (1833), the first case in which the U.S. Supreme Court considered nationalizing the Bill of Rights, supports this conclusion. While reading *Barron,* note the relative ease with which Marshall reached the conclusion that historical circumstances could not possibly have implied that states were bound by the federal Bill of Rights.

Barron v. Baltimore

32 U.S. (7 PET.) 243 (1833)
http://laws.findlaw.com/US/32/243.html
Vote: 6 (Duvall, Johnson, Marshall, McLean, Story, Thompson)
0

OPINION OF THE COURT: *Marshall*

NOT PARTICIPATING: *Baldwin*

FACTS:

The story of this case begins in Baltimore, a city undergoing major economic changes in the early 1800s.[3] Because of its busy harbor, Baltimore was becoming a major hub of economic activity in the United States. Such growth necessitated constant construction and excavation. While entrepreneurs erected new buildings, the city began to repair its badly worn streets.

Most of Baltimore's residents welcomed the activity, but a group of wharf owners saw problems. They noticed that the city's street construction altered the flow of streams coming into Baltimore Harbor. This redirection of water, the owners argued in a letter to the city, led to the accumulation of sand and earth near their wharves, causing the surrounding water to

2. James Madison, speech before the House of Representatives, June 7, 1789.

3. For an interesting account of this case, see Fred Friendly and Martha J. H. Elliot, *The Constitution: That Delicate Balance* (New York: Random House, 1984).

become too shallow for large ships. Because their livelihood depended on accommodating these ships, which unloaded goods on the wharves for storage in nearby warehouses, the owners wanted the city to dredge the harbor at its expense. But the city paid no heed to their request.

John Barron and John Craig owned a particularly profitable wharf in the eastern section of the city. When they acquired the wharf it enjoyed the deepest water in the harbor and was therefore capable of servicing the largest ships. As a consequence of the city's construction program, however, sand and silt deposits had rendered the water in front of their wharf so shallow that their business had lost nearly all its value. In 1822 they brought city representatives to county court in Maryland, asking for $20,000 in damages. The court ordered the city to pay them $4,500. When a state appellate court reversed the county court's decision, a determined Barron appealed to the U.S. Supreme Court.

Although Barron's lawyer wanted to discuss the specific facts surrounding the wharf's lost value, the justices were more concerned with a constitutional question. Specifically, under what authority did the United States Supreme Court have jurisdiction to review this local matter that had already been decided by the state courts?

ARGUMENTS:

For the plaintiff-in-error, John Barron:

- The Fifth Amendment to the United States Constitution, which holds that "private property cannot be taken for public use, without just compensation," gives the Court authority over this dispute.
- The Constitution was intended to secure rights against state abuse as well as federal.
- The City of Baltimore, through its public works project, has taken the value of the wharf without providing the owners just compensation.

For the defendants-in-error, the Mayor and the City Council of Baltimore:

- Although the city opposed Barron's position, attorney Roger Brook Taney, a future Supreme Court chief justice, was not allowed to present an argument. As soon as Taney rose to address the Court, the justices cut him off, apparently having already made up their minds.

MR. CHIEF JUSTICE MARSHALL DELIVERED THE OPINION OF THE COURT.

The constitution was ordained and established by the people of the United States for themselves, for their own government, and not for the government of the individual states. Each state established a constitution for itself, and, in that constitution, provided such limitations and restrictions on the powers of its particular government as its judgment dictated. The people of the United States framed such a government for the United States as they supposed best adapted to their situation, and best calculated to promote their interests. The powers they conferred on this government were to be exercised by itself; and the limitations on power, if expressed in general terms, are naturally, and, we think, necessarily applicable to the government created by the instrument. They are limitations of power granted in the instrument itself; not of distinct governments, framed by different persons and for different purposes.

If these propositions be correct, the fifth amendment must be understood as restraining the power of the general government, not as applicable to the states. In their several constitutions they have imposed such restrictions on their respective governments as their own wisdom suggested; such as they deemed most proper for themselves. It is a subject on which they judge exclusively, and with which others interfere no farther than they are supposed to have a common interest.

The counsel for the plaintiff-in-error insists, that the constitution was intended to secure the people of the several states against the undue exercise of power by their respective state governments; as well as against that which might be attempted by their general government. In support of this argument he relies on the inhibitions contained in the tenth section of the first article. We think, that section affords a strong, if not a conclusive, argument in support of the opinion already indicated by the court. The [ninth section] contains restrictions which are obviously intended for the exclusive purpose of restraining the exercise of power by the departments of the general government. Some of them use language applicable only to congress; others are expressed in general terms. The third clause, for example, declares, that 'no bill of attainder or ex post facto law shall be passed.' No language can be more general; yet the demonstration is complete, that it applies solely to the government of the United States. [The tenth section] . . . , the avowed purpose of which is to restrain state legislation, contains in terms the very prohibition.

It declares, that 'no state shall pass any bill of attainder or ex post facto law.' This provision, then, of the ninth section, however comprehensive its language, contains no restriction on state legislation.

. . . Perceiving, that in a constitution framed by the people of the United States, for the government of all, no limitation of the action of government on the people would apply to the state government, unless expressed in terms, the restrictions contained in the tenth section are in direct words so applied to the states. . . .

If the original constitution, in the ninth and tenth sections of the first article, draws this plain and marked line of discrimination between the limitations it imposes on the powers of the general government, and on those of the state; if, in every inhibition intended to act on state power, words are employed, which directly express that intent; some strong reason must be assigned for departing from this safe and judicious course, in framing the amendments, before that departure can be assumed. We search in vain for that reason.

Had the people of the several states, or any of them, required changes in their constitutions; had they required additional safeguards to liberty from the apprehended encroachments of their particular governments, the remedy was in their own hands, and would have been applied by themselves. A convention would have been assembled by the discontented state, and the required improvements would have been made by itself. The unwieldy and cumbrous machinery of procuring a recommendation from two-thirds of congress, and the assent of three-fourths of their sister states, could never have occurred to any human being as a mode of doing that which might be effected by the state itself. Had the framers of these amendments intended them to be limitations on the powers of the state governments, they would have imitated the framers of the original constitution, and have expressed that intention. Had congress engaged in the extraordinary occupation of improving the constitutions of the several states by affording the people additional protection from the exercise of power by their own governments in matters which concerned themselves alone, they would have declared this purpose in plain and intelligible language.

But it is universally understood, it is a part of the history of the day, that the great revolution which established the constitution of the United States, was not effected without immense opposition. Serious fears were extensively entertained that those powers which the patriot statesmen, who then watched over the interests of our country, deemed essential to union, and to the attainment of those invaluable objects for which union was sought, might be exercised in a manner dangerous to liberty. In almost every convention by which the constitution was adopted, amendments to guard against the abuse of power were recommended. These amendments demanded security against the apprehended encroachments of the general government—not against those of the local governments. In compliance with a sentiment thus generally expressed, to quiet fears thus extensively entertained, amendments were proposed by the required majority in congress, and adopted by the states. These amendments contain no expression indicating an intention to apply them to the state governments. This court cannot so apply them.

We are of opinion that the provision in the fifth amendment to the constitution, declaring that private property shall not be taken for public use without just compensation, is intended solely as a limitation on the exercise of power by the government of the United States, and is not applicable to the legislation of the states. We are therefore of opinion that there is no repugnancy between the several acts of the general assembly of Maryland, given in evidence by the defendants at the trial of this cause, in the court of that state, and the constitution of the United States. This court, therefore, has no jurisdiction of the cause; and it is dismissed.

Writing for a unanimous Court, in one of his last major opinions, Chief Justice John Marshall, who previously had shown a propensity to enlarge the powers of national government, sent a clear message to the states on the question of nationalizing the Bill of Rights. The Bill of Rights was intended only to protect the people against abusive actions of the federal government, not the states. Instead, guarantees against state violations of individual liberties would have to be found in the laws and constitutions of the respective individual states.

INCORPORATION THROUGH THE FOURTEENTH AMENDMENT: EARLY INTERPRETATIONS

Marshall quipped that the Court did not have "much difficulty" in addressing the question at issue in *Barron*, but the question of the applicability of the Bill of Rights to state and local governments would not disappear with similar ease. Although Marshall's opinion settled the issue for the time being, members of the legal community continued to search for opportunities to reverse the Court's decision. A chance to do so emerged in 1868 when the nation ratified the Fourteen Amendment. The intended purpose of this post–Civil War amendment was to secure the Union and to ensure equality for African Americans, but two of its provisions—the privileges or immunities clause and the due process clause—were viewed by some as possible vehicles for nationalizing the Bill of Rights.

The privileges or immunities clause declares, "No State shall make or enforce any law which shall abridge the privileges or immunities of citizens of the United States." Supporters of applying the Bill of Rights to the states argued that the "privileges or immunities" of U.S. citizenship were nothing more or less than those rights guaranteed by the first eight amendments to the Constitution. If accepted, this interpretation would mean that no state could violate the liberties protected by the Bill of Rights. In other words, the proponents argued, the privileges or immunities clause "incorporated" or "absorbed" the Bill of Rights guarantees and obliged the states to honor them. Achieving this result, however, would require the Supreme Court to be quite expansive in its interpretation of the amendment.

The Supreme Court had its first opportunity to scrutinize this claim in the *Slaughterhouse Cases* (1873). This litigation grew out of the Industrial Revolution—an economic diversification that touched the whole country. Although industrialization changed the United States for the better in many ways, it also had negative effects. In Louisiana, for example, the state legislature claimed that the Mississippi River had become polluted because New Orleans butchers dumped garbage into it. To remedy this problem (or, as some have suggested, to use it as an excuse to form a monopolistic enterprise), the legislature created the Crescent City Live Stock Landing & Slaughter House Company to receive and slaughter all city livestock for twenty-five years.

Because they were forced to use its facilities, and to pay top dollar for the privilege, the butchers despised the new corporation. They formed their own organization, the Butchers' Benevolent Association, and hired John A. Campbell, a former U.S. Supreme Court justice, to sue the corporation for depriving them of their right to pursue their business—a basic guarantee, they argued, granted by the Fourteenth Amendment's privileges or immunities clause. After a state district court and the Louisiana Supreme Court ruled in favor of the corporation, the butchers' association appealed to the U.S. Supreme Court.

Writing for a five-person majority, Justice Samuel F. Miller affirmed the judgment of the Louisiana court. As he put it:

Was it the purpose of the fourteenth amendment, by the simple declaration that no State should make or enforce any law which shall abridge the privileges and immunities of *citizens of the United States,* to transfer the security and protection of all the civil rights which we have mentioned, from the States to the Federal government? And where it is declared that Congress shall have the power to enforce that article, was it intended to bring within the power of Congress the entire domain of civil rights heretofore belonging exclusively to the States?

All this and more must follow, if the proposition of the plaintiffs . . . be sound. For not only are these rights subject to the control of Congress whenever in its discretion any of them are supposed to be abridged by State legislation, but that body may also pass laws in advance, limiting and restricting the exercise of legislative power by the States, in their most ordinary and usual functions, as in its judgment it may think proper on all such subjects. And still further, such a construction followed by the reversal of the judgments of the Supreme Court of Louisiana in these cases, would constitute this court a perpetual censor upon all legislation of the States, on the civil rights of their own citizens, with authority to nullify such as it did not approve as consistent with those rights, as they existed at the time of the adoption of this amendment. The argument we admit is not always the most conclusive which is drawn from the consequences urged against the adoption of a particular construction of an instrument. But when, as in the case before us, these consequences are so serious, so far-reaching and pervading, so great a departure from the structure and spirit of our institutions; when the effect is to fetter and degrade the State governments by subjecting them to the control of Congress, in the exercise of powers heretofore universally conceded to them of the most ordinary and fundamental character; when in fact it radically changes the whole theory of the relations of the State and Federal governments to each other and of both these governments to the people; the argument has a force that is irresistible, in the absence of language which expresses such a purpose too clearly to admit of doubt.

We are convinced that no such results were intended by the Congress which proposed these amendments, nor by the legislatures of the States which ratified them.

Justice Miller's majority opinion had at least two major effects on the development of the law. First, its severely limited interpretation rendered the privileges or immunities clause of the Fourteenth Amendment almost useless, a condition that has changed little since then.[4] Second, and more relevant to our understanding of incorporation, the Court made clear that it would not use this clause as a vehicle by which to nationalize the Bill of Rights.

With the *Slaughterhouse Cases* sounding the death knell for incorporation via the privileges or immunities clause, attorneys turned to yet another section of the Fourteenth Amendment, the due process clause, which says, "Nor shall any State deprive any person of life, liberty, or property, without due process of law." The advocates of nationalizing the Bill of Rights hoped to convince the Court that the words *due process of law* subsumed those rights protected by the first eight amendments. If this argument proved successful, the due process clause would prohibit the states from violating any of the liberties protected under the federal Bill of Rights. But would the justices be willing to use this section as a mechanism for incorporation?

In its first opportunity to evaluate this claim, *Hurtado v. California* (1884), the Court rejected that interpretation of the due process clause. While reading the opinions in *Hurtado,* consider two questions. First, did the Court completely shut the door on the use of the clause to incorporate the Bill of Rights? Second, how did Justice John Marshall Harlan's lone dissent differ from the views of the Court's majority?

Hurtado v. California

110 U.S. 516 (1884)
http://laws.findlaw.com/US/110/516.html
Vote: 7 (Blatchford, Bradley, Gray, Matthews, Miller, Waite, Woods)
  1 (Harlan)

OPINION OF THE COURT: *Matthews*
DISSENTING OPINION: *Harlan*
NOT PARTICIPATING: *Field*

FACTS:

Joseph Hurtado and his wife, Susie, lived in Sacramento, California, where they met and became friends with Jose Antonio Estuardo, an immigrant from Chile. Their relationship disintegrated, however, when Hurtado learned of Estuardo's affair with Susie. Hurtado asked

---

4. But see the Court's 1999 opinion in ***Saenz v. Roe*** in which the majority relies on the "previously dormant" privileges or immunities clause to address the question of whether states can deny welfare assistance to residents who had lived in their jurisdictions for less than one year.

his former friend to leave the city, but Estuardo continued to court Susie until Hurtado sent her to live with her parents. This arrangement proved only temporary; when Susie returned to Sacramento, Estuardo again pursued her. Faced with this continuing threat, Hurtado confronted Estuardo in a bar, and the police arrested him on battery charges. While his trial on the battery charge was pending, Hurtado shot and killed Estuardo.[5] The state charged him with murder, an offense punishable by death.

At the time, many states provided for grand jury hearings before a defendant went to trial. Typically, a grand jury comprising some two dozen people listens to the prosecutor's side of a case and decides whether enough evidence exists to bring a defendant to trial. The California Constitution of 1879, however, specified that prosecutors could initiate a trial from an *information,* a document filed by the prosecutor charging a person with a crime after evidence is presented to a judge, rather than a grand jury. Using such a document, the state brought Hurtado to trial for murder. He was found guilty and sentenced to death. The California Supreme Court affirmed the sentence, and a date was set for his execution. Hurtado asked the U.S. Supreme Court to reverse the conviction on the grounds that the state had denied him his right to a grand jury hearing.

ARGUMENTS:

For the plaintiff-in-error, Joseph Hurtado:

- The due process of law provision of the Fourteenth Amendment is broad enough to include the right to a grand jury hearing as guaranteed by the Fifth Amendment.
- By convicting and sentencing him to death without benefit of a grand jury hearing, the state denied Hurtado due process of law in violation of the Fourteenth Amendment.

For the defendant-in-error, People of the State of Utah:

- It has been settled law since *Barron v. Baltimore* that the protections of the Bill of Rights apply only to the federal government and not to the states.

---

5. For more details on this case, see Richard C. Cortner, *The Supreme Court and the Second Bill of Rights* (Madison: University of Wisconsin Press, 1981).

 MR. JUSTICE MATTHEWS DELIVERED THE OPINION OF THE COURT.

It is claimed on behalf of the prisoner that the conviction and sentence are void, on the ground that they are repugnant to that clause of the Fourteenth Article of Amendment of the Constitution of the United States which is in these words:

"Nor shall any State deprive any person of life, liberty, or property without due process of law."

The proposition of law we are asked to affirm is that an indictment or presentment by a grand jury, as known to the common law of England, is essential to that "due process of law," when applied to prosecutions for felonies, which is secured and guaranteed by this provision of the Constitution of the United States, and which accordingly it is forbidden to the States respectively to dispense with in the administration of criminal law.

The question is one of grave and serious import, affecting both private and public rights and interests of great magnitude, and involves a consideration of what additional restrictions upon the legislative policy of the States has been imposed by the Fourteenth Amendment to the Constitution of the United States. . . .

We are to construe this phrase in the Fourteenth Amendment by the *usus loquendi* [common usage of ordinary speech] of the Constitution itself. The same words are contained in the Fifth Amendment. That article makes specific and express provision for perpetuating the institution of the grand jury, so far as relates to prosecution for the more aggravated crimes under the laws of the United States. . . .

According to a recognized canon of interpretation, especially applicable to formal and solemn instruments of constitutional law, we are forbidden to assume, without clear reason to the contrary, that any part of this most important amendment is superfluous. The natural and obvious inference is, that in the sense of the Constitution, "due process of law" was not meant or intended to include, *en vi termini* [by the force of the term], the institution and procedure of a grand jury in any case. The conclusion is equally irresistible, that when the same phrase was employed in the Fourteenth Amendment to restrain the action of the States, it was used in the same sense and with no greater extent; and that if in the adoption of that amendment it had been part of its purpose to perpetuate the institution of the grand jury in all the States, it would have embodied, as did the Fifth Amendment, express declarations to that effect. Due process of law in the latter refers to that law of the land which derives its authority from the legislative powers conferred upon Congress by the Constitution of the United States, exercised within the limits therein prescribed, and interpreted according to the principles of the common law. In the Fourteenth Amendment, by parity of reason, it refers to that law of the land in each State, which derives its authority from the inherent and reserved powers of the State, exerted within the limits of those fundamental principles of liberty and justice which lie at the base of all our civil and political institutions, and the greatest security for which resides in the right of the people to make their own laws, and alter them at their pleasure. . . .

But it is not to be supposed that these legislative powers are absolute and despotic, and that the amendment prescribing due process of law is too vague and indefinite to operate as a practical restraint. It is not every act, legislative in form, that is law. Law is something more than mere will exerted as an act of power. It must be not a special rule for a particular person or a particular case, but . . . "the general law, a law which hears before it condemns, which proceeds upon inquiry, and renders judgment only after trial," so "that every citizen shall hold his life, liberty, property and immunities under the protection of the general rules which govern society," and thus excluding, as not due process of law, acts of attainder, bills of pains and penalties, acts of confiscation, acts reversing judgments, and acts directly transferring one man's estate to another, legislative judgments and decrees, and other similar special, partial and arbitrary exertions of power under the forms of legislation. Arbitrary power, enforcing its edicts to the injury of the persons and property of its subjects, is not law, whether manifested as the decree of a personal monarch or of an impersonal multitude. And the limitations imposed by our constitutional law upon the action of the governments, both State and national, are essential to the preservation of public and private rights, notwithstanding the representative character of our political institutions. The enforcement of these limitations by judicial process is the device of self-governing communities to protect the rights of individuals and minorities, as well against the power of numbers, as against the violence of public agents transcending the limits of lawful authority, even when acting in the name and wielding the force of the government. . . .

It follows that any legal proceeding enforced by public authority, whether sanctioned by age and custom, or newly devised in the discretion of the legislative power, in furtherance of the general public good, which regards and preserves these principles of liberty and justice, must be held to be due process of law. . . .

Tried by these principles, we are unable to say that the substitution for a presentment or indictment by a grand jury of the proceeding by information, after examination and commitment by a magistrate, certifying to the probable guilt of the defendant, with the right on his part to the aid of counsel, and to the cross-examination of the witnesses produced for the prosecution, is not due process of law. It is . . . an ancient proceeding at common law, which might include every case of an offence of less grade than a felony, except misprision of treason; and in every circumstance of its administration, as authorized by the statute of California, it carefully considers and guards the substantial interest of the prisoner. It is merely a preliminary proceeding, and can result in no final judgment, except as the consequence of a regular judicial trial, conducted precisely as in cases of indictments. . . .

For these reasons, finding no error therein, the judgment of the Supreme Court of California is

Affirmed.

MR. JUSTICE HARLAN, *dissenting.*

My brethren concede that there are principles of liberty and justice lying at the foundation of our civil and political institutions which no State can violate consistently with that due process of law required by the Fourteenth Amendment in proceedings involving life, liberty, or property. Some of these principles are enumerated in the opinion of the court. But, for reasons which do not impress my mind as satisfactory, they exclude from that enumeration the exemption from prosecution, by information, for a public offence involving life. By what authority is that exclusion made? . . .

. . . [I]t is said that the framers of the Constitution did not suppose that due process of law necessarily required for a capital offence the institution and procedure of a grand jury, else they would not in the same amendment prohibiting the deprivation of life, liberty, or property, without due process of law, have made specific and express provision for a grand jury where the crime is capital or otherwise infamous; therefore, it is argued, the requirement by the Fourteenth Amendment of due process of law in all proceedings involving life, liberty, and property, without specific reference to grand juries in any case whatever, was not intended as a restriction upon the power which it is claimed the States previously had, so far as the express restrictions of the national Constitution are concerned, to dispense altogether with grand juries. . . .

It seems to me that too much stress is put upon the fact that the framers of the Constitution made express provision for the security of those rights which at common law were protected by the requirement of due process of law, and, in addition, declared, generally, that no person shall "be deprived of life, liberty or property without due process of law." The rights, for the security of which these express provisions were made, were of a character so essential to the safety of the people that it was deemed wise to avoid the possibility that Congress, in regulating the processes of law, would impair or destroy them. Hence, their specific enumeration in the earlier amendments of the Constitution, in connection with the general requirement of due process of law, the latter itself being broad enough to cover every right of life, liberty or property secured by the settled usages and modes of proceeding existing under the common and statute law of England at the time our government was founded. . . .

. . . [T]he court, in this case, while conceding that the requirement of due process of law protects the fundamental principles of liberty and justice, adjudges, in effect, that an immunity or right, recognized at the common law to be essential to personal security, jealously guarded by our national Constitution against violation by any tribunal or body exercising authority under the general government, and expressly or impliedly recognized, when the Fourteenth Amendment was adopted in the Bill of Rights or Constitution of every State in the Union, is, yet, not a fundamental principle in governments established, as those of the States of the Union are, to secure to the citizen liberty and justice, and, therefore, is not involved in that due process of law required in proceedings conducted under the sanction of a State. My sense of duty constrains me to dissent from this interpretation of the supreme law of the land.

Although it failed to adopt Hurtado's claims, the Court did not completely preclude the possibility of incorporation. The majority reasoned that because due process is but one part of the Fifth Amendment, it could not at the same time be the equivalent of the entire Bill of Rights. Thus, the Court concluded that the due process clause could not be used to apply the entire Bill of Rights to the states. But, as Richard C. Cortner points out, the Court ruled that the due process clause "did protect against state encroachment

those 'fundamental principles of liberty and justice which lie at the base of all our civil and political institutions.'"[6] For the legal community and citizens of the United States, however, the Court left a critical question unresolved: Did the "fundamental principles of liberty" include any of the guarantees contained in the Bill of Rights?

Chicago, Burlington & Quincy Railroad v. Chicago (1897), one of the most important cases to come to the Court after *Hurtado*, involved an economic issue rather than criminal procedure. This case, like *Barron* and the *Slaughterhouse Cases*, grew out of a controversy caused by industrialization. As Chicago began to expand, it acquired, under the principle of eminent domain, large pieces of property belonging to railroad companies and private citizens. The city needed the property as part of a street improvement project. Based on local ordinances, the city offered property owners what it considered just compensation for the land. If the owners considered the offers unacceptable, they could challenge the city in county court, and many did so. In one county court, an interesting pattern emerged: individual property owners received almost $13,000 for their lands, and the railroad companies were given $1.

Viewing this apparent inequity as a violation of the Fifth Amendment's guarantee that private property shall not "be taken for public use, without just compensation," an aggrieved railroad company took its case to the Illinois Supreme Court. When the judges affirmed the county court's decision, the company appealed to the U.S. Supreme Court, asking the justices to interpret the Fifth Amendment the same way John Barron had demanded sixty-four years before: that the just compensation (or takings) clause should apply to states. The railroads, however, had a weapon that did not exist in Barron's day—the Fourteenth Amendment's due process clause. And this Court did what the justices under John Marshall had refused to do: it ruled that the states must abide by the Fifth Amendment's commands regarding government seizure of private property for a public purpose. Writing for the majority, Justice Harlan had an opportunity to see the logic of his dissent in *Hurtado* become the basis for the opinion of the Court:

In determining what is due process of law regard must be had to substance, not to form. . . . If compensation for private property taken for public use is an essential element of due

6. Ibid., 21.

process of law as ordained by the Fourteenth Amendment, then the final judgment of a state court . . . is to be decreed the act of the State within the meaning of that amendment.

Harlan added that just compensation indeed constituted "a vital principle of republican institutions" without which "almost all other rights would become worthless." As a consequence, a state violated the due process clause of the Fourteenth Amendment when it did not provide just payment for seized private property.

The Court finally had incorporated, via the Fourteenth Amendment, a clause contained in the Bill of Rights. But it failed to bridge the apparent contradictions between *Hurtado* and *Chicago Railroad,* leaving open the question of which would provide controlling precedent in this area. In other words, why was the Court willing to incorporate the Fifth Amendment's guarantee of just compensation, but not the grand jury provision?

The next incorporation case, *Maxwell v. Dow* (1900), did little to shed light on this puzzling question. At issue were the antics of Charles L. "Gunplay" Maxwell, who robbed a Utah bank in 1898. Under the state's newly adopted constitution, an individual charged with a non-capital offense, such as armed robbery, could be tried by a jury of eight persons instead of the traditional twelve, and no provision was made for a defendant's right to a grand jury hearing. After an eight-person jury found him guilty and he was sentenced to eighteen years in prison, Maxwell hired an experienced criminal lawyer, J. W. N. Whitecotton, to represent him in the state supreme court. Whitecotton argued that the state's denial of grand jury proceedings and its jury trial system deprived Maxwell of his federal Fifth and Sixth Amendment rights, which should be incorporated under the Fourteenth Amendment's due process and privileges or immunities clauses. Utah's highest court rejected this claim, and Maxwell filed for a writ of error with the U.S. Supreme Court, asking the justices specifically to rectify contradictions of interpretation between *Hurtado* and *Chicago Railroad.* The Court, 8–1, refused to do so and, in fact, virtually ignored the entire incorporation argument. Writing for the majority, Justice Rufus W. Peckham noted, "Trial by jury has never been affirmed to be a necessary requisite of due process of law."

The three major cases following the *Slaughterhouse* decision—*Hurtado, Chicago Railroad,* and *Maxwell*—provided no clear answers to a legal community seeking direction on incorporation. If anything, more questions than answers remained because of the apparent contradictions among these decisions.

A STANDARD EMERGES

As legal scholars debated incorporation, the Court took a case that allowed the justices to impose some order on what had become a very confusing area of constitutional interpretation. In *Twining v. New Jersey* (1908) the Court moved one cautious step closer to enunciating the doctrine of selective incorporation.

The case involved state fraud charges against Albert Twining and other officers of a bank trust. At his trial in state court, Twining refused to take the stand, invoking his guarantee against self-incrimination. The judge allowed him to do this, but in his charge to the jury he made reference to Twining's refusal to testify, insinuating that it implied guilt. If the federal Fifth Amendment provision against self-incrimination were applicable to the states, such comments clearly would be impermissible. Twining's attorney appealed to the state's supreme court, alleging that the judge's words denied Twining due process of law. But the New Jersey court upheld the judge's right to highlight in his instructions to the jury a defendant's refusal to testify. Twining appealed to the U.S. Supreme Court, asking it to incorporate the Fifth Amendment protection against self-incrimination.

With only Harlan dissenting, the Court, 8–1, rejected Twining's claim that the Fourteenth Amendment's due process clause prohibited a state from denying a criminal defendant the right against compulsory self-incrimination. In Justice William H. Moody's words, "We think that the exemption from self-incrimination in the courts of the States is not secured by any part of the Federal Constitution." By so concluding, the Court affirmed New Jersey's ruling against Twining.

The importance of this case, however, is not that the justices ruled against Twining, but that the Court for the first time articulated a position that opened the door for the future application of some Bill of Rights provisions to the states. In his majority opinion, Moody declared:

It is possible that some of the personal rights safeguarded by the first eight Amendments against National action may also be safeguarded against state action, because a denial of them would be a denial of due process of law. If this is so, it is not because those rights are enumerated in the first eight Amendments, but because they are of such a nature that they are included in the conception of due process of law. Few phrases of the law are so elusive of exact apprehension as this. Doubtless the difficulties of ascertaining its connotation have been increased in American jurisprudence, where it has been embodied in constitutions and put to new uses as a limit on legislative power. This court has always declined to give a comprehensive definition of it, and has preferred that its full meaning should be gradually ascertained by the process of inclusion and exclusion in the course of the decisions of cases as they arise. There are certain general principles well settled, however, which narrow the field of discussion and may serve as helps to correct conclusions. . . .

But . . . we prefer to rest our decision on broader grounds, and inquire whether the exemption from self-incrimination is of such a nature that it must be included in the conception of due process. Is it a fundamental principle of liberty and justice which inheres in the very idea of free government and is the inalienable right of a citizen of such a government? If it is, and if it is of a nature that pertains to process of law, this court has declared it to be essential to due process of law.

The Court's words in *Twining* established three important principles. First, some provisions of the Bill of Rights might be protected against state abridgment through the due process clause of the Fourteenth Amendment. Second, the liberties included in due process of law attain such status not because they are enumerated in the first eight amendments, but because they are "fundamental and inalienable" rights. Third, the Court will not incorporate the entire Bill of Rights but will consider rights individually when necessary as cases come before it. In this way, the Court moved cautiously toward an endorsement of selective incorporation. The justices would consider making the provisions of the Bill of Rights binding on the states on a case-by-case, right-by-right basis.

In the final analysis, the opinion in *Twining* is narrow in its approach to incorporation. The Court refused to make the entire Bill of Rights applicable to the states and denied that the specific right at issue—the exemption from compulsory self-incrimination—should be protected against state action. Still, *Twining* is important because it created the *possibility* of incorporation by future Courts, if they could identify rights deemed fundamental and inalienable.

In *Twining* Justice Moody provided several examples of fundamental and inalienable rights: a court must have jurisdiction to hear a case, it must provide adequate notice of trial dates and charges, and it must grant a trial for those accused of committing a crime. Beyond these, Moody did not specify what other guarantees might fall under this rubric; nor did he provide an adequate definition of what the Court meant by "fundamental and inalienable."

This gap put the burden on lawyers litigating claims of civil rights, civil liberties, and criminal justice to bring cases testing the boundaries of *Twining*. These lawyers had a vested interest in securing federal guarantees for their clients for whom such rights remained inapplicable in state courts. They recognized that cases involving free speech, religion, and search and seizure, which they were losing in state trial courts, could be won if the Supreme Court agreed that these and other rights were fundamental. It is not surprising, therefore, that one of the cases assessing the boundaries of *Twining* involved a free speech claim brought to the Court's attention by the American Civil Liberties Union.

The issues in *Gitlow v. New York* (1925) *(excerpted on pages 205–209)* arose during the early 1900s when the United States was gripped by a fear of Communist subversion. To combat the "red menace," several states, including New York, created commissions to investigate subversive organizations. The New York commission in 1919 raided one such group, arrested several Socialist Party leaders, and seized their materials. Among those arrested was Benjamin Gitlow, a leader in the Left Wing Section of the party, who had produced a pamphlet titled *Left Wing Manifesto* that called for mass action to overthrow the capitalist system in the United States.

Gitlow was prosecuted in a New York trial court for violating the state's criminal anarchy law. Under the leadership of Clarence Darrow, Gitlow's defense attorneys alleged that the statute violated the First Amendment's guarantee of free speech, a fundamental right deserving incorporation under the due process clause.

In a 7–2 decision, the Supreme Court affirmed Gitlow's conviction, but it also adopted Darrow's argument and incorporated the free speech and press clauses. As Justice Edward T. Sanford wrote for the majority:

For present purposes we may and do assume that freedom of speech and of the press . . . are among the fundamental personal rights and "liberties" protected by the due process clause of the Fourteenth Amendment from impairment by the states. . . . Reasonably limited . . . this freedom is an inestimable privilege in a free government.

The Court went no further; once again it refused to provide a more general principle by which to identify fundamental rights.

Gitlow is important because it represents the Court's first meaningful steps toward the selective incorporation doctrine. In *Twining* the Court had declared that incorporation of some rights was possible; in *Gitlow* the justices made particular provisions of the Bill of Rights binding on the states. *Gitlow* was a portent of decisions to come, but it took the Court another twelve years to provide the next indication of what it meant by "fundamental rights." *Palko v. Connecticut* (1937), a case involving the Fifth Amendment's prohibition against double jeopardy, was the vehicle. While reading *Palko,* consider the signals it sent to lawyers across the nation. How did it help them to determine which rights were fundamental?

Palko v. Connecticut

302 U.S. 319 (1937)
http://laws.findlaw.com/US/302/319.html
Vote: 8 (Black, Brandeis, Cardozo, Hughes, McReynolds,
     Roberts, Stone, Sutherland)
    1 (Butler)
OPINION OF THE COURT: *Cardozo*

FACTS:

The story of Frank Palka (whose name was misspelled as *Palko* in Court documents) begins in Connecticut, where he robbed a store and shot and killed two police officers. Arrested in Buffalo, New York, Palka confessed to the killings. At his trial for first-degree murder, the Connecticut judge refused to admit the confession, and, in the absence of such evidence, the jury found him guilty only of second-degree murder, for which Palka received a mandatory life sentence. State prosecutors appealed to the Connecticut Supreme Court of Errors, which reversed the trial judge's exclusion of Palka's confession and ordered a new trial. Palka's attorney objected, claiming that a new trial violated the Fifth Amendment's prohibition of double jeopardy. Nevertheless, Palka was tried and convicted again, but this time of first-degree murder, and he was sentenced to death. When his appeal to the Connecticut high court failed, Palka turned to the U.S. Supreme Court.

ARGUMENTS:

For the appellant, Frank Palko:
- The right against double jeopardy is a fundamental and immutable principle of law not to be abridged by the state.
- The right against double jeopardy is protected and made applicable to the states through the due process clause of the Fourteenth Amendment.

For the appellee, State of Connecticut:
- Double jeopardy is not a fundamental principle of law.

- The prohibition against double jeopardy is not implied by the due process clause of the Fourteenth Amendment.
- The laws of Connecticut rightfully do not allow Palko to benefit from the trial court's erroneous decision to deny the jury access to his confession.

 MR. JUSTICE CARDOZO DELIVERED THE OPINION OF THE COURT.

The argument for appellant is that whatever is forbidden by the Fifth Amendment is forbidden by the Fourteenth also. The Fifth Amendment, which is not directed to the states, but solely to the federal government, creates immunity from double jeopardy. No person shall be "subject for the same offense to be twice put in jeopardy of life or limb." The Fourteenth Amendment ordains, "nor shall any State deprive any person of life, liberty, or property, without due process of law." To retry a defendant, though under one indictment and only one, subjects him, it is said, to double jeopardy in violation of the Fifth Amendment, if the prosecution is one on behalf of the United States. From this the consequence is said to follow that there is a denial of life or liberty without due process of law, if the prosecution is one on behalf of the People of a State. . . .

We have said that in appellant's view the Fourteenth Amendment is to be taken as embodying the prohibitions of the Fifth. His thesis is even broader. Whatever would be a violation of the original bill of rights (Amendments I to VIII) if done by the federal government is now equally unlawful by force of the Fourteenth Amendment if done by a state. There is no such general rule.

The Fifth Amendment provides, among other things, that no person shall be held to answer for a capital or otherwise infamous crime unless on presentment or indictment of a grand jury. This court has held that, in prosecutions by a state, presentment or indictment by a grand jury may give way to information at the instance of a public officer. The Fifth Amendment provides also that no person shall be compelled in any criminal case to be a witness against himself. This court has said that, in prosecutions by a state, the exemption will fail if the state elects to end it. The Sixth Amendment calls for a jury trial in criminal cases and the Seventh for a jury trial in civil cases at common law where the value in controversy shall exceed twenty dollars. This court has ruled that consistently with those amendments trial by jury may be modified by a state or abolished altogether. . . .

On the other hand, the due process clause of the Fourteenth Amendment may make it unlawful for a state to abridge by its statutes the freedom of speech which the First Amendment safeguards against encroachment by the Congress, or the like freedom of the press, or the free exercise of religion, or the right of peaceable assembly, without which speech would be unduly trammeled, or the right of one accused of crime to the benefit of counsel. In these and other situations immunities that are valid as against the federal government by force of the specific pledges of particular amendments have been found to be implicit in the concept of ordered liberty, and thus, through the Fourteenth Amendment, become valid as against the states.

The line of division may seem to be wavering and broken if there is a hasty catalogue of the cases on the one side and the other. Reflection and analysis will induce a different view. There emerges the perception of a rationalizing principle which gives to discrete instances a proper order and coherence. The right to trial by jury and the immunity from prosecution except as the result of an indictment may have value and importance. Even so, they are not of the very essence of a scheme of ordered liberty. To abolish them is not to violate a "principle of justice so rooted in the traditions and conscience of our people as to be ranked as fundamental." Few would be so narrow or provincial as to maintain that a fair and enlightened system of justice would be impossible without them. What is true of jury trials and indictments is true also, as the cases show, of the immunity from compulsory self-incrimination. This too might be lost, and justice still be done. Indeed, today as in the past there are students of our penal system who look upon the immunity as a mischief rather than a benefit, and who would limit its scope, or destroy it altogether. No doubt there would remain the need to give protection against torture, physical or mental. Justice, however, would not perish if the accused were subject to a duty to respond to orderly inquiry. The exclusion of these immunities and privileges from the privileges and immunities protected against the action of the states has not been arbitrary or casual. It has been dictated by a study and appreciation of the meaning, the essential implications, of liberty itself.

We reach a different plane of social and moral values when we pass to the privileges and immunities that have been taken over from the earlier articles of the federal bill of rights and brought within the Fourteenth Amendment by a process of absorption. These in their origin were effective against the federal government alone. If the Fourteenth Amendment has absorbed them, the process of absorption has had its source in the belief that neither liberty nor justice would exist if they were sacrificed. This is true, for illustration, of freedom of thought, and speech. Of that freedom one may say that it is the matrix, the indispensable condition, of nearly every other form of freedom. With rare aberrations a pervasive recognition of that truth can be traced in our history, political and legal. So it has come about that the domain of liberty, withdrawn by the Fourteenth Amendment from encroachment by the states, has been enlarged by latter-day judgments to include liberty of the mind as well as liberty of action. The extension became, indeed, a logical imperative when once it was recognized, as long ago it was, that liberty is something more than exemption from physical restraint, and that even in the field of substantive rights and duties the legislative judgment, if oppressive and arbitrary, may be overridden by the courts. Fundamental too in the concept of due process, and so in that of liberty, is the thought that condemnation shall be rendered only after trial. The hearing, moreover, must be a real one, not a sham or a pretense. . . .

Our survey of the cases serves, we think, to justify the statement that the dividing line between them, if not unfaltering throughout its course, has been true for the most part to a unifying principle. On which side of the line the case made out by the appellant has appropriate location must be the next inquiry and the final one. Is that kind of double jeopardy to which the statute has subjected him a hardship so acute and shocking that our polity will not endure it? Does it violate those "fundamental principles of liberty and justice which lie at the base of all our civil and political institutions"? The answer surely must be "no." What the answer would have to be if the state were permitted after a trial free from error to try the accused over again or to bring another case against him, we have no occasion to consider. We deal with the statute before us and no other. The state is not attempting to wear the accused out by a multitude of cases with accumulated trials. It asks no more than this, that the case against him shall go on until there shall be a trial free from the corrosion of substantial legal error. This is not cruelty at all, nor even vexation in any immoderate degree. If the trial had been infected with error adverse to the accused, there might have been review at his instance, and as often as necessary to purge the vicious taint. A reciprocal privilege, subject at all times to the discretion of the presiding judge, has now been granted to the state. There is here no seismic innovation. The edifice of justice stands, its symmetry, to many, greater than before. . . .

The judgment is

Affirmed.

BOX 3-1 AFTERMATH . . . FRANK PALKA

On the evening of September 30, 1935, Frank Palka allegedly shot and killed two police officers in Bridgeport, Connecticut, after he had smashed a window of a music store and stolen a radio. Palka, a twenty-three-year-old aircraft riveter, had previously been in legal trouble for juvenile delinquency and statutory rape. He was found guilty of first-degree murder after an earlier trial had found him guilty of murder in the second degree. Palka's attorneys appealed to the U.S. Supreme Court, claiming that the second trial violated Palka's Fifth Amendment right against double jeopardy.

The Court in 1937 ruled against Palka, holding that the double jeopardy clause was not binding on the states, but only on the federal government. However, in his opinion for the Court, Justice Benjamin Cardozo modified the standards of the selective incorporation doctrine, making it easier for specific provisions of the Bill of Rights to be made applicable to the states. This doctrinal shift was a significant one for the expansion of civil liberties, but it did not help Frank Palka. On April 12, 1938, he was put to death in the Connecticut electric chair. Thirty-one years later, in *Benton v. Maryland* (1969), the Supreme Court

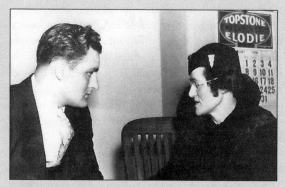

Frank Palka as photographed with his mother in 1935. Palka was convicted of shooting to death two police officers, Sergeant Thomas Kearney and patrolman Wilfred Walker, who confronted him during a burglary.

reversed its position and made the double jeopardy clause binding on the states through the due process clause of the Fourteenth Amendment.

SOURCE: Richard Polenberg, "Cardozo and the Criminal Law: *Palko v. Connecticut* Reconsidered," *Journal of Supreme Court History* 21, no. 2 (1996): 92–105.

In 1937 the Court did not consider the protection against double jeopardy a fundamental right, and this ruling set the groundwork for Palka's execution *(see Box 3-1)*. But did the Court provide attorneys with any further guidance as to what this elusive term included? To some extent it did. It defined fundamental rights as those without which liberty and justice could not exist, rights implicit in the concept of ordered liberty. But the process by which the Court planned to make known exactly which rights fall into that category remained unchanged from *Twining* and *Gitlow*. The majority of justices adopted the doctrine of selective incorporation, from which they would determine fundamental rights on a case-by-case basis.

INCORPORATION IN THE AFTERMATH OF *PALKO*

What happened after *Palko*? As Table 3-1 shows, the Court continued to incorporate the various guarantees contained in the Bill of Rights. At first, the Court limited itself to those rights contained in the First Amendment,

but in the 1960s it began to incorporate guarantees the Constitution affords to people accused of crimes.

Selective incorporation of these guarantees came about through the Warren Court's revolutionary decisions regarding the rights of criminal defendants. For example, under the Warren Court, indigents were guaranteed the right to counsel in certain kinds of cases, and police were required to read suspected offenders a set of statements known as Miranda warnings. In the coming chapters we shall have more to say about the Warren Court and its liberalizing decisions in this area and others involving rights and liberties. Here, we point out that the Warren Court revolution would have had far less impact had it not incorporated these guarantees and made them applicable to actions by the states. Without incorporation, only indigents accused of federal—not state—crimes would be given attorneys; only federal agents—not state or local police officers—would be forced to read Miranda warnings; and so on. Because the majority of criminal prosecutions are filed in state courts, and federal prosecutions are a small percentage of the total nationwide, very few defendants would have benefited from the Warren Court's decisions. Instead,

TABLE 3-1   Cases Incorporating Provisions of the Bill of Rights into the Due Process Clause of the Fourteenth Amendment

CONSTITUTIONAL PROVISION	CASE	YEAR
First Amendment		
Freedom of speech and press	*Gitlow v. New York*	1925
Freedom of assembly	*DeJonge v. Oregon*	1937
Freedom of petition	*Hague v. CIO*	1939
Free exercise of religion	*Cantwell v. Connecticut*	1940
Establishment of religion	*Everson v. Board of Education*	1947
Second Amendment		
Right to keep and bear arms	*McDonald v. Chicago*	2010
Fourth Amendment		
Unreasonable search and seizure	*Wolf v. Colorado*	1949
Exclusionary rule	*Mapp v. Ohio*	1961
Fifth Amendment		
Payment of compensation for the taking of private property	*Chicago, Burlington and Quincy R. Co. v. Chicago*	1897
Self-incrimination	*Malloy v. Hogan*	1964
Double jeopardy	*Benton v. Maryland*	1969
When jeopardy attaches	*Crist v. Bretz*	1978
Sixth Amendment		
Public trial	*In re Oliver*	1948
Due notice	*Cole v. Arkansas*	1948
Right to counsel (felonies)	*Gideon v. Wainwright*	1963
Confrontation and cross-examination of adverse witnesses	*Pointer v. Texas*	1965
Speedy trial	*Klopfer v. North Carolina*	1967
Compulsory process to obtain witnesses	*Washington v. Texas*	1967
Jury trial	*Duncan v. Louisiana*	1968
Right to counsel (misdemeanor when jail is possible)	Argersinger v. Hamlin	1972
Eighth Amendment		
Cruel and unusual punishment	*Louisiana ex rel. Francis v. Resweber*	1947
Ninth Amendment		
Privacy[a]	*Griswold v. Connecticut*	1965

NOTE: Provisions the Court has not incorporated: Third Amendment right against quartering soldiers; Fifth Amendment right to a grand jury hearing; Seventh Amendment right to a jury trial in civil cases; and Eighth Amendment right against excessive bail and fines.

a. The word *privacy* does not appear in the Ninth Amendment (nor anywhere in the text of the Constitution). In *Griswold* several members of the Court viewed the Ninth Amendment as guaranteeing (and incorporating) that right.

with incorporation, all levels of government must abide by the selected constitutional guarantees.

A second development after *Palko* is that justices continued to advocate different solutions to this long-standing problem. Most remained loyal to the selective incorporation doctrine. For example, in **Adamson v. California** (1947), an appeal that asked the Court to apply the Fifth Amendment self-incrimination clause to the states, Justice Stanley F. Reed spoke for the majority: "*Palko* held that such provisions of the Bill of Rights as were 'implicit in the concept of ordered liberty' became secure from state interference by the [due process] clause. But it held nothing more."

In applying *Palko,* the Court declined to incorporate self-incrimination.

Other justices expressed different views. Some offered a more cramped version of incorporation, and others a more expansive perspective. Justices John Marshall Harlan (II)[7] and Potter Stewart represent the

---

7. Two justices had the name John Marshall Harlan. To distinguish them, scholars and other writers call the elder one John Marshall Harlan (I). He served on the Court from 1877 to 1911. His grandson, identified as John Marshall Harlan (II), served from 1955 to 1971. Harlan (I) took quite liberal positions on issues such as incorporation and civil rights, often in dissent. Harlan (II) was conservative, frequently dissenting from liberal Warren Court rulings.

more restricted position. Their approach, according to observers, is close to *Twining*. They viewed the term *due process of law* as requiring only that criminal trials "be fundamentally fair." Their solution, as Harlan writes, involves

a much more discriminating process of adjudication than does "incorporation." . . . It entails a "gradual process of judicial inclusion and exclusion," seeking, with due recognition of constitutional tolerance for state experimentation and disparity, to ascertain those immutable principles of justice which inhere in the very idea . . . of free government which no member of the Union may disregard.[8]

The expansive approach was argued by justices such as Frank Murphy, Hugo Black, and William Douglas. They supported, as did John Marshall Harlan (I), complete incorporation of the Bill of Rights. Black's dissent in *Adamson*, joined by Douglas, states their view:

If the choice must be between the selective process of the *Palko* decision, applying some of the Bill of Rights to the States, or the *Twining* rule, applying none of them, I would choose the *Palko* selective process. But, rather than accept either of these choices, I would follow what I believe was the original purpose of the Fourteenth Amendment—to extend to all the people of the nation the complete protection of the Bill of Rights.

These two developments after *Palko*—the Warren Court's use of selective incorporation and the support for distinct approaches to incorporation—are well illustrated in *Duncan v. Louisiana* (1968). As you read the various opinions in the case, consider how they encapsulate a historical range of perspectives on the incorporation of the Bill of Rights.

Duncan v. Louisiana

391 U.S. 145 (1968)
http://laws.findlaw.com/US/391/145.html
Oral arguments are available at http://www.oyez.org.
Vote: 7 (Black, Brennan, Douglas, Fortas, Marshall, Warren, White)
    2 (Harlan, Stewart)

OPINION OF THE COURT: *White*
CONCURRING OPINIONS: *Black, Fortas*
DISSENTING OPINION: *Harlan*

---

8. Harlan (II), dissenting in *Duncan v. Louisiana* (1968).

FACTS:

In October 1966, Gary Duncan, a nineteen-year-old black man, was driving down a highway when he spotted two of his younger cousins on the side of the road with four white youths. Duncan apparently became alarmed because his cousins had recently transferred to a formerly all-white school where "racial incidents" had occurred. He pulled over and asked his cousins to get into his car. What happened next is in dispute. The white youths asserted that Duncan slapped one of them, Herman M. Landry Jr., before getting back into his car; Duncan and his cousins maintained that he "touched" Landry rather than slapped him.

Just after Duncan pulled away, P. E. Lathum, the principal of a private school formed in response to the desegregation of the area's public schools, called the police. He had observed the encounter and alleged that Duncan hit Landry. The police questioned Duncan and let him go in the belief that he had not committed an offense. But, just a few days later, they arrested Duncan on the charge of cruelty to juveniles.[9]

Believing that their son's arrest was racially motivated, Duncan's parents contacted Richard Sobol, an attorney for the Lawyers Constitutional Defense Committee, a civil rights organization with offices in New Orleans. Sobol agreed to represent Duncan after he became convinced that "Duncan's case was part of a pattern of anti–civil rights intimidation and harassment" in the area.

Sobol filed a motion with a state trial court judge to dismiss the charge against Duncan. He asserted that Louisiana law permitted a cruelty to juveniles conviction only against an individual having supervision over the juveniles, which did not apply to Duncan. The prosecuting attorney reported to Landry's family that they would not be able to win the case.

Rather than see Duncan set free, Landry's mother asked the police to rearrest him on charges of simple battery, a misdemeanor punishable in Louisiana by a maximum of two years in jail and a $300 fine. Sobol went back to court, this time to request that Duncan be tried by a jury. The judge refused, citing the Louisiana Constitution, which grants jury trials only in cases involving punishments of hard labor or death.

Duncan was tried without a jury, found guilty by the judge, and sentenced to sixty days in a local jail and a $150

---

9. We adopt this paragraph and those that follow from Cortner, *The Supreme Court,* 248–251.

fine. His appeal to the state supreme court was unsuccessful, and he appealed to the U.S. Supreme Court.

ARGUMENTS:

For the appellant, Gary Duncan:

- The Supreme Court's earlier position refusing to incorporate the right to a jury trial has long since been abandoned.
- The right to a jury trial in criminal cases is a fundamental right as evidenced by the importance the framers and the Supreme Court have placed on this right and the fact that thirty-eight states recognize the right to a jury trial for offenses carrying potential sentences of six months incarceration or more.
- The Court should make the Sixth Amendment jury trial provision binding on the states through the Fourteenth Amendment due process clause.

For the appellee, State of Louisiana:

- The Court has long held that the right to a jury trial is not a fundamental right.
- Offenses punished by sentences of six months incarceration or less are considered petty offenses not subject to jury trial rights.

 MR. JUSTICE WHITE DELIVERED THE OPINION OF THE COURT.

The test for determining whether a right extended by the Fifth and Sixth Amendments with respect to federal criminal proceedings is also protected against state action by the Fourteenth Amendment has been phrased in a variety of ways in the opinions of this Court. The question has been asked whether a right is among those "'fundamental principles of liberty and justice which lie at the base of all our civil and political institutions,'" . . . whether it is "basic in our system of jurisprudence," . . . and whether it is "a fundamental right, essential to a fair trial." . . . The claim before us is that the right to trial by jury guaranteed by the Sixth Amendment meets these tests. The position of Louisiana, on the other hand, is that the Constitution imposes upon the States no duty to give a jury trial in any criminal case, regardless of the seriousness of the crime or the size of the punishment which may be imposed. Because we believe that trial by jury in criminal cases is fundamental to the American scheme of justice, we hold that the Fourteenth Amendment guarantees a right of jury trial in all criminal cases which—were they to be tried in a

federal court—would come within the Sixth Amendment's guarantee. Since we consider the appeal before us to be such a case, we hold that the Constitution was violated when appellant's demand for jury trial was refused.

The history of trial by jury in criminal cases has been frequently told. It is sufficient for present purposes to say that by the time our Constitution was written, jury trial in criminal cases had been in existence in England for several centuries and carried impressive credentials traced by many to Magna Carta. Its preservation and proper operation as a protection against arbitrary rule were among the major objectives of the revolutionary settlement which was expressed in the Declaration and Bill of Rights of 1689. . . .

Jury trial came to America with English colonists, and received strong support from them. Royal interference with the jury trial was deeply resented. . . .

The Declaration of Independence stated solemn objections to the King's making "Judges dependent on his Will alone, for the tenure of their offices, and the amount and payment of their salaries," to his "depriving us in many cases, of the benefits of Trial by Jury," and to his "transporting us beyond Seas to be tried for pretended offenses." The Constitution itself, in Art. III, §2, commanded:

The Trial of all Crimes, except in Cases of Impeachment, shall be by Jury; and such Trial shall be held in the State where the said Crimes shall have been committed.

Objections to the Constitution because of the absence of a bill of rights were met by the immediate submission and adoption of the Bill of Rights. Included was the Sixth Amendment which, among other things, provided:

In all criminal prosecutions, the accused shall enjoy the right to a speedy and public trial, by an impartial jury of the State and district wherein the crime shall have been committed.

The constitutions adopted by the original States guaranteed jury trial. Also, the constitution of every State entering the Union thereafter in one form or another protected the right to jury trial in criminal cases.

Even such skeletal history is impressive support for considering the right to jury trial in criminal cases to be fundamental to our system of justice. . . .

Jury trial continues to receive strong support. The laws of every State guarantee a right to jury trial in serious criminal cases; no State has dispensed with it; nor are there significant movements underway to do so. . . .

We are aware of prior cases in this Court in which the prevailing opinion contains statements contrary to our holding today that the right to jury trial in serious criminal cases is a fundamental right and hence must be recognized by the States as part of their obligation to extend due process of law to all persons within their jurisdiction. Louisiana relies especially on *Maxwell v. Dow* (1900); *Palko v. Connecticut* (1937); and *Snyder v. Massachusetts* (1934). None of these cases, however, dealt with a State which had purported to dispense entirely with a jury trial in serious criminal cases. *Maxwell* held that no provision of the Bill of Rights applied to the States—a position long since repudiated—and that the Due Process Clause of the Fourteenth Amendment did not prevent a State from trying a defendant for a noncapital offense with fewer than 12 men on the jury. It did not deal with a case in which no jury at all had been provided. In neither *Palko* nor *Snyder* was jury trial actually at issue, although both cases contain important dicta asserting that the right to jury trial is not essential to ordered liberty and may be dispensed with by the States regardless of the Sixth and Fourteenth Amendments. These observations, though weighty and respectable, are nevertheless dicta, unsupported by holdings in this Court that a State may refuse a defendant's demand for a jury trial when he is charged with a serious crime. . . . Respectfully, we reject the prior dicta regarding jury trial in criminal cases.

The guarantees of jury trial in the Federal and State Constitutions reflect a profound judgment about the way in which law should be enforced and justice administered. A right to jury trial is granted to criminal defendants in order to prevent oppression by the Government. Those who wrote our constitutions knew from history and experience that it was necessary to protect against unfounded criminal charges brought to eliminate enemies and against judges too responsive to the voice of higher authority. The framers of the constitutions strove to create an independent judiciary but insisted upon further protection against arbitrary action. Providing an accused with the right to be tried by a jury of his peers gave him an inestimable safeguard against the corrupt or overzealous prosecutor and against the compliant, biased, or eccentric judge. If the defendant preferred the common-sense judgment of a jury to the more tutored but perhaps less sympathetic reaction of the single judge, he was to have it. Beyond this, the jury trial provisions in the Federal and State Constitutions reflect a fundamental decision about the exercise of official power—a reluctance to entrust plenary powers over the life and liberty of the citizen to one judge or to a group of judges. Fear of unchecked power, so typical of our State and Federal Governments in other respects, found expression in the criminal law in this insistence upon community participation in the determination of guilt or innocence. The deep commitment of the Nation to the right of jury trial in serious criminal cases as a defense against arbitrary law enforcement qualifies for protection under the Due Process Clause of the Fourteenth Amendment, and must therefore be respected by the States. . . .

The State of Louisiana urges that holding that the Fourteenth Amendment assures a right to jury trial will cast doubt on the integrity of every trial conducted without a jury. Plainly, this is not the import of our holding. Our conclusion is that in the American States, as in the federal judicial system, a general grant of jury trial for serious offenses is a fundamental right, essential for preventing miscarriages of justice and for assuring that fair trials are provided for all defendants. We would not assert, however, that every criminal trial—or any particular trial—held before a judge alone is unfair or that a defendant may never be as fairly treated by a judge as he would be by a jury. Thus we hold no constitutional doubts about the practices, common in both federal and state courts, of accepting waivers of jury trial and prosecuting petty crimes without extending a right to jury trial. However, the fact is that in most places more trials for serious crimes are to juries than to a court alone; a great many defendants prefer the judgment of a jury to that of a court. Even where defendants are satisfied with bench trials, the right to a jury trial very likely serves its intended purpose of making judicial or prosecutorial unfairness less likely.

Louisiana's final contention is that even if it must grant jury trials in serious criminal cases, the conviction before us is valid and constitutional because here the petitioner was tried for simple battery and was sentenced to only 60 days in the parish prison. We are not persuaded. It is doubtless true that there is a category of petty crimes or offenses which is not subject to the Sixth Amendment jury trial provision and should not be subject to the Fourteenth Amendment jury trial requirement here applied to the States. Crimes carrying possible penalties up to six months do not require a jury trial if they otherwise qualify as petty offenses. . . . But the penalty authorized for a particular crime is of major relevance in determining whether it is serious or not and may in itself, if severe enough, subject the trial to the mandates of the Sixth Amendment. The penalty authorized by the law of the locality may be taken 'as a gauge of its social and ethical judgments' of the crime in question. . . . In the case before us the Legislature of Louisiana has made simple battery a criminal offense punishable by imprisonment for up to two years and a fine. The question, then, is whether a crime carrying such a penalty is an offense which Louisiana may insist on trying without a jury.

We think not. So-called petty offenses were tried without juries both in England and in the Colonies and have always been held to be exempt from the otherwise comprehensive language of the Sixth Amendment's jury trial provisions. There is no substantial evidence that the Framers intended to depart from this established common-law practice, and the possible consequences to defendants from convictions for petty offenses have been thought insufficient to outweigh the benefits to efficient law enforcement and simplified judicial administration resulting from the availability of speedy and inexpensive nonjury adjudications. These same considerations compel the same result under the Fourteenth Amendment. . . .

We need not . . . settle in this case the exact location of the line between petty offenses and serious crimes. It is sufficient for our purposes to hold that a crime punishable by two years in prison is, based on past and contemporary standards in this country, a serious crime and not a petty offense. Consequently, appellant was entitled to a jury trial and it was error to deny it.

The judgment below is reversed and the case is remanded for proceedings not inconsistent with this opinion.

Reversed and remanded.

MR. JUSTICE BLACK with whom MR. JUSTICE DOUGLAS joins, concurring.

The Court today holds that the right to trial by jury guaranteed defendants in criminal cases in federal courts by Art. III of the United States Constitution and by the Sixth Amendment is also guaranteed by the Fourteenth Amendment to defendants tried in state courts. With this holding I agree for reasons given by the Court. I also agree because of reasons given in my dissent in *Adamson v. California.* In that dissent, I took the position, contrary to the holding in *Twining v. New Jersey,* that the Fourteenth Amendment made all of the provisions of the Bill of Rights applicable to the States. This Court in *Palko v. Connecticut,* decided in 1937, . . . explain[ed] that certain Bill of Rights' provisions were made applicable to the States by bringing them "within the Fourteenth Amendment by a process of absorption." Thus

Twining v. New Jersey refused to hold that any one of the Bill of Rights' provisions was made applicable to the States by the Fourteenth Amendment, but *Palko,* which must be read as overruling *Twining* on this point, concluded that the Bill of Rights Amendments that are "implicit in the concept of ordered liberty" are "absorbed" by the Fourteenth as protections against state invasion. In this situation I said in *Adamson v. California* that, while "I would . . . extend to all the people of the nation the complete protection of the Bill of Rights," that "if the choice must be between the selective process of the *Palko* decision applying some of the Bill of Rights to the States, or the *Twining* rule applying none of them, I would choose the *Palko* selective process." . . . And I am very happy to support this selective process through which our Court has since the *Adamson* case held most of the specific Bill of Rights' protections applicable to the States to the same extent they are applicable to the Federal Government. . . .

While I do not wish at this time to discuss at length my disagreement with Brother Harlan's forthright and frank restatement of the now discredited *Twining* doctrine, I do want to point out what appears to me to be the basic difference between us. . . . [D]ue process, according to my Brother Harlan, is to be a phrase with no permanent meaning, but one which is found to shift from time to time in accordance with judges' predilections and understandings of what is best for the country. If due process means this, the Fourteenth Amendment, in my opinion, might as well have been written that "no person shall be deprived of life, liberty or property except by laws that the judges of the United States Supreme Court shall find to be consistent with the immutable principles of free government." It is impossible for me to believe that such unconfined power is given to judges in our Constitution that is a written one in order to limit governmental power. . . .

In closing I want to emphasize that I believe as strongly as ever that the Fourteenth Amendment was intended to make the Bill of Rights applicable to the States. I have been willing to support the selective incorporation doctrine, however, as an alternative, although perhaps less historically supportable than complete incorporation. The selective incorporation process, if used properly, does limit the Supreme Court in the Fourteenth Amendment field to specific Bill of Rights' protections only and keeps judges from roaming at will in their own notions of what policies outside the Bill of Rights are desirable and what are not. And, most importantly for me, the selective incorporation process has the virtue of having already worked to make most of the Bill of Rights' protections applicable to the States.

MR. JUSTICE FORTAS, concurring.

[A]lthough I agree with the decision of the Court, I cannot agree with the implication that the tail must go with the hide: that when we hold, influenced by the Sixth Amendment, that "due process" requires that the States accord the right of jury trial for all but petty offenses, we automatically import all of the ancillary rules which have been or may hereafter be developed incidental to the right to jury trial in the federal courts. I see no reason whatever, for example, to assume that our decision today should require us to impose federal requirements such as unanimous verdicts or a jury of 12 upon the States. We may well conclude that these and other features of federal jury practice are by no means fundamental—that they are not essential to due process of law—and that they are not obligatory on the States.

I would make these points clear today. Neither logic nor history nor the intent of the draftsmen of the Fourteenth Amendment can possibly be said to require that the Sixth Amendment or its jury trial provision be applied to the States together with the total gloss that this Court's decisions have supplied. The draftsmen of the Fourteenth Amendment intended what they said, not more or less: that no State shall deprive any person of life, liberty, or property without due process of law. It is ultimately the duty of this Court to interpret, to ascribe specific meaning to this phrase. There is no reason whatever for us to conclude that, in so doing, we are bound slavishly to follow not only the Sixth Amendment but all of its bag and baggage, however securely or insecurely affixed they may be by law and precedent to federal proceedings. To take this course, in my judgment, would be not only unnecessary but mischievous because it would inflict a serious blow upon the principle of federalism. The Due Process Clause commands us to apply its great standard to state court proceedings to assure basic fairness. It does not command us rigidly and arbitrarily to impose the exact pattern of federal proceedings upon the 50 States. On the contrary, the Constitution's command, in my view, is that in our insistence upon state observance of due process, we should, so far as possible, allow the greatest latitude for state differences. It requires, within the limits of the lofty basic standards that it prescribes for the States as well as the Federal Government, maximum opportunity for diversity and minimal imposition of uniformity of method and detail upon the States. Our Constitution sets up a federal union, not a monolith.

MR. JUSTICE HARLAN, whom MR. JUSTICE STEWART joins, dissenting.

The States have always borne primary responsibility for operating the machinery of criminal justice within their borders, and adapting it to their particular circumstances. In exercising this responsibility, each State is compelled to conform its procedures to the requirements of the Federal Constitution. The Due Process Clause of the Fourteenth Amendment requires that those procedures be fundamentally fair in all respects. It does not, in my view, impose or encourage nationwide uniformity for its own sake; it does not command adherence to forms that happen to be old; and it does not impose on the States the rules that may be in force in the federal courts except where such rules are also found to be essential to basic fairness.

The Court's approach to this case is an uneasy and illogical compromise among the views of various Justices on how the Due Process Clause should be interpreted. The Court does not say that those who framed the Fourteenth Amendment intended to make the Sixth Amendment applicable to the States. And the Court concedes that it finds nothing unfair about the procedure by which the present appellant was tried. Nevertheless, the Court reverses his conviction: it holds, for some reason not apparent to me, that the Due Process Clause incorporates the particular clause of the Sixth Amendment that requires trial by jury in federal criminal cases—including, as I read its opinion, the sometimes trivial accompanying baggage of judicial interpretation in federal contexts. I have raised my voice many times before against the Court's continuing undiscriminating insistence upon fastening on the States federal notions of criminal justice, and I must do so again in this instance. With all respect, the Court's approach and its reading of history are altogether topsy-turvy. . . .

. . . In my view, often expressed elsewhere, the first section of the Fourteenth Amendment was meant neither to incorporate, nor to be limited to, the specific guarantees of the first eight Amendments. The overwhelming historical evidence . . . demonstrates, to me conclusively, that the Congressmen and state legislators who wrote, debated, and ratified the Fourteenth Amendment did not think they were "incorporating" the Bill of Rights and the very breadth and generality of the Amendment's provisions suggest that its authors did not suppose that the Nation would always be limited to mid-19th century conceptions of "liberty" and "due process of law" but that the increasing experience and evolving conscience of the American people would add new "intermediate premises." In short, neither history, nor sense, supports using the Fourteenth Amendment to put the States in a constitutional straitjacket with respect to their own development in the administration of criminal or civil law.

Although I therefore fundamentally disagree with the total incorporation view of the Fourteenth Amendment, it seems to me that such a position does at least have the virtue, lacking in the Court's selective incorporation approach, of internal consistency: we look to the Bill of Rights, word for word, clause for clause, precedent for precedent because, it is said, the men who wrote the Amendment wanted it that way. For those who do not accept this "history," a different source of "intermediate premises" must be found. The Bill of Rights is not necessarily irrelevant to the search for guidance in interpreting the Fourteenth Amendment, but the reason for and the nature of its relevance must be articulated.

Apart from the approach taken by the absolute incorporationists, I can see only one method of analysis that has any internal logic. That is to start with the words "liberty" and "due process of law" and attempt to define them in a way that accords with American traditions and our system of government. This approach, involving a much more discriminating process of adjudication than does "incorporation," is, albeit difficult, the one that was followed throughout the 19th and most of the present century. It entails a "gradual process of judicial inclusion and exclusion," seeking, with due recognition of constitutional tolerance for state experimentation and disparity, to ascertain those "immutable principles . . . of free government which no member of the Union may disregard." . . .

Through this gradual process, this Court sought to define "liberty" by isolating freedoms that Americans of the past and of the present considered more important than any suggested countervailing public objective. The Court also, by interpretation of the phrase "due process of law," enforced the Constitution's guarantee that no State may imprison an individual except by fair and impartial procedures.

The relationship of the Bill of Rights to this "gradual process" seems to me to be twofold. In the first place it has long been clear that the Due Process Clause imposes some restrictions on state action that parallel Bill of Rights restrictions on federal action. Second, and more important than this accidental overlap, is the fact that the Bill of Rights is evidence, at various points, of the content Americans find in the term "liberty" and of American standards of fundamental fairness. . . .

The Court has justified neither its starting place nor its conclusion. If the problem is to discover and articulate the rules of fundamental fairness in criminal proceedings, there is no reason to assume that the whole body of rules developed in this Court constituting Sixth Amendment jury trial must be regarded as a unit. The requirement of trial by jury in federal criminal cases has given rise to numerous subsidiary questions respecting the exact scope and content of the right. It surely cannot be that every answer the Court has given, or will give, to such a question is attributable to the Founders; or even that every rule announced carries equal conviction of this Court; still less can it be that every such subprinciple is equally fundamental to ordered liberty. . . .

Even if I could agree that the question before us is whether Sixth Amendment jury trial is totally "in" or totally "out," I can find in the Court's opinion no real reasons for concluding that it should be "in." The basis for differentiating among clauses in the Bill of Rights cannot be that only some clauses are in the Bill of Rights, or that only some are old and much praised, or that only some have played an important role in the development of federal law. These things are true of all. The Court says that some clauses are more "fundamental" than others, but it turns out to be using this word in a sense that would have astonished Mr. Justice Cardozo and which, in addition, is of no help. The word does not mean "analytically critical to procedural fairness" for no real analysis of the role of the jury in making procedures fair is even attempted. Instead, the word turns out to mean "old," "much praised," and "found in the Bill of Rights." The definition of "fundamental" thus turns out to be circular. . . .

The argument that jury trial is not a requisite of due process is quite simple. The central proposition of *Palko,* a proposition to which I would adhere, is that "due process of law" requires only that criminal trials be fundamentally fair. As stated above, apart from the theory that it was historically intended as a mere shorthand for the Bill of Rights, I do not see what else "due process of law" can intelligibly be thought to mean. If due process of law requires only fundamental fairness, then the inquiry in each case must be whether a state trial process was a fair one. The Court has held, properly I think, that in an adversary process it is a requisite of fairness, for which there is no adequate substitute, that a criminal defendant be afforded a right to counsel and to cross-examine opposing witnesses. But it simply has not been demonstrated, nor, I think, can it be demonstrated, that trial by jury is the only fair means of resolving issues of fact. . . .

This Court, other courts, and the political process are available to correct any experiments in criminal procedure that prove fundamentally unfair to defendants. That is not what is being done today: instead, and quite without reason, the Court has chosen to impose upon every State one means of trying criminal cases; it is a good means, but it is not the only fair means, and it is not demonstrably better than the alternatives States might devise.

I would affirm the judgment of the Supreme Court of Louisiana.

As *Duncan* illustrates, the Court continued to abide by the compromise position of selective incorporation, applying only those rights about which the justices believed "that neither liberty nor justice would exist if they were sacrificed." But, *in practice,* the total incorporation approach favored by the first John Marshall Harlan and Hugo Black has predominated. As depicted in Table 3-1, over the years the Court has incorporated and made applicable to the states almost every guarantee contained in the Bill of Rights, and in several cases reversed earlier decisions that declined to incorporate specific provisions.

The most recent addition was the Second Amendment's right to keep and bear arms. As we shall see in Chapter 9, in *District of Columbia v. Heller* (2008) *(excerpted on pages 390-395)* the Supreme Court expanded the rights of gun owners against federal gun control regulations. Two years later, in **McDonald v. Chicago** (2010), it incorporated the guarantee, making it applicable to states and localities. Writing for a 5–4 Court, Justice Samuel Alito held that the use of handguns for self-defense is "fundamental to the Nation's scheme of ordered liberty" and "deeply rooted in this Nation's history and tradition." Interestingly, Justice Clarence Thomas, in a concurring opinion, tried to revive the privileges or immunities clause as a vehicle for incorporating the Second Amendment. But the other four justices in the majority rejected this position, holding instead that incorporation should be done through the due process clause. As Justice Alito wrote, "For many decades, the question of the rights protected by the Fourteenth Amendment against state infringement has been analyzed under the Due Process Clause of that Amendment and not under the Privileges or Immunities Clause. We therefore decline to disturb the *Slaughter-House* holding."

Justice Stephen Breyer, writing in dissent for Justices Ruth Bader Ginsburg and Sonia Sotomayor, could "find nothing in the Second Amendment's text, history, or underlying rationale that could warrant characterizing it as 'fundamental' insofar as it seeks to protect the keeping and bearing of arms for private self-defense purposes." Justice John Paul Stevens, reiterating parts of his dissent in *Heller,* wrote, "By its terms, the Second Amendment does not apply to the States; read properly, it does not even apply to individuals outside of the militia context." He also noted that "the Fourteenth Amendment has never been understood by the Court to have 'incorporated' the entire Bill of Rights. There was nothing foreordained about today's outcome."

Even so, as Table 3-1 shows, the Court has read the Constitution to ensure that almost all civil liberties are protected uniformly against infringement by any government entity—federal, state, or local. This is the legacy of the doctrine of selective incorporation.

ANNOTATED READINGS

Some interesting articles on the incorporation debate are available, including Charles Fairman, "Does the Fourteenth Amendment Incorporate the Bill of Rights?," *Stanford Law Review* 2 (1949): 5–173; Felix Frankfurter, "Memorandum on 'Incorporation' of the Bill of Rights into the Due Process Clause of the Fourteenth Amendment," *Harvard Law Review* 78 (1965): 746–783; Louis Henkin, "Selective Incorporation in the Fourteenth Amendment," *Yale Law Journal* 73 (1963): 74–88; Frank H. Walker, "Constitutional Law—Was It Intended That the Fourteenth Amendment Incorporate the Bill of Rights?," *North Carolina Law Review* 42 (1964): 925–936.

Books on the incorporation debate are not many in number. We recommend Richard C. Cortner, *The Supreme Court and the Second Bill of Rights* (Madison: University of Wisconsin Press, 1981); and Leonard Levy, *Introduction to the Fourteenth Amendment and the Bill of Rights: The Incorporation Theory* (New York: Da Capo, 1970).

PART II Civil Liberties

Approaching Civil Liberties

Approaching Civil Liberties

THE NEXT SEVEN chapters explore Supreme Court interpretation of guarantees contained in the First and Second Amendments and those that have been seen as relating to the right of privacy. These constitutional provisions allow Americans to live their lives as they please; to worship in whatever manner they wish; to hold and express political and social views of their own conviction; to place demands upon the government; to print, post, and read whatever satisfies them; and to keep government out of those areas of human life that are considered private and personal. In contemporary society, however, few freedoms are absolute. To maintain order, the government must regulate in ways that may restrict some of these liberties. The history of the Supreme Court is a chronicle of how it has played its role as an interpreter of these fundamental rights and as an umpire between the often contradictory values of freedom and order.

As a student approaching the subject of civil liberties, perhaps for the first time, you might be wondering why we devote so much space in Chapter 4 (on religion) and Chapters 5 through 8 (on expression) to the following few phrases:

Congress shall make no law respecting an establishment of religion, or prohibiting the free exercise thereof; or abridging the freedom of speech, or of the press; or the right of the people peaceably to assemble, and to petition the Government for a redress of grievances.

After all, the guarantees contained in the First Amendment seem specific enough. Or do they? Suppose we read about a religion that required its members to smoke marijuana before religious services, or about students who were so fed up with university policies they burned down the administration building in protest, or about a radio station that regularly allowed its announcers to use profanity. Taking the opening words of the First Amendment, "Congress shall make no law," to heart, we might conclude that the amendment's language—the guarantees of freedom of religion, speech, and press—protects these activities. Is that conclusion correct? Is society obliged to condone such practices and forms of expression? What our examples and the subsequent cases illustrate is that a gap sometimes exists between the words of the First Amendment and reality. Although the language of the amendment may seem explicit, its meaning can be elusive and therefore difficult to apply to actual circumstances.

In contrast, the constitutional problems presented by the Second Amendment center on what exactly the amendment covers. Some argue that it creates only a narrow right—that of the states to maintain "a well regulated militia"; others suggest that it creates a broader right that enables citizens to "keep and bear" guns. In Chapter 9, we sort through these competing approaches, as well as the Court's statements on the subject.

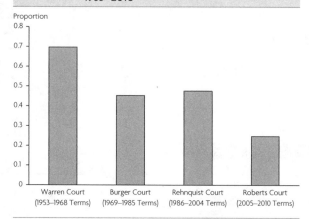

FIGURE II-1 Proportion of First Amendment and Privacy Cases Decided in Favor of the Claimant, 1953–2010

SOURCE: Calculated by the authors from data available on the U.S. Supreme Court Judicial Database (http://supremecourtdatabase.org).

NOTE: The numbers of cases for the Court eras are as follows: Warren Court, N = 158; Burger Court, N = 250; Rehnquist Court, N = 173; and Roberts Court, N = 36.

Supreme Court formulation and interpretation of a right to privacy, as we discuss in Chapter 10, present even more difficulties, primarily because the Constitution contains no explicit mention of such a guarantee. Even though most justices agree that it exists, they have disagreed over various questions, including from what provision of the Constitution the right to privacy arises and how far it extends.

It is the gap between what the Constitution says (or does not say) and the kinds of questions litigants ask the Court to address that explains why we devote so much space to civil liberties. Because the meaning of those rights is less than crystal clear, the institution charged with interpreting and applying them—the Supreme Court of the United States—has approached its task in a somewhat erratic way. Throughout the Court's history, justices have brought different modes of interpretation to the guarantees of religion, expression, and the press, and to the right to privacy, which in turn have significantly affected the ways citizens enjoy those rights.

Figure II-1 provides one way of looking at how differently the Court has treated First Amendment and privacy claims over five decades. The Court led by Earl Warren was generally supportive of such claims, ruling in favor of the party alleging some abridgment of his or her rights in more than two-thirds of the cases. The Court under Chief Justice Warren Burger and Chief Justices William Rehnquist, and now John Roberts, moved in the opposite direction, with its support of the individual rights position well below that of the Warren Court.

Figure II-1 helps to reinforce the point that the amendments are open to interpretation, that the words of the Constitution alone do not necessarily provide a sufficient guidepost for the justices as they resolve cases. Even so, the data raise many questions: Why did the Burger and Rehnquist Courts, and now the Roberts Court, evince patterns of decision making distinctly different from that of the Warren Court? Is it merely because recent Courts have had more conservative members? Or have the cases and the precedents governing their resolution changed? Perhaps the more recent justices have invoked different modes of analysis to resolve these disputes. Might it also be that the Court has responded to the public or to the other institutions of government? Another possibility is that the Warren Court was far more supportive of First Amendment and privacy claims than its predecessors, and the Burger, Rehnquist, and Roberts Courts, in turn, rebalanced the scales. Finally, we must consider the possibility that traditional definitions of "liberal" and "conservative" may not be particularly useful today. If the Court upholds a law that punishes "hate speech," has it ruled in a liberal or conservative direction? If the Court strikes down regulations placed on individuals who use First Amendment protections to harass abortion seekers, has it rendered a conservative or liberal decision? Last but not least, if the Court invalidates restrictions on campaign financing, as the Roberts Court has done in several cases,[1] is that a liberal First Amendment decision or a conservative ruling because it may limit government's ability to regulate corruption in elections? More generally, does support for First Amendment values continue to provide a—if not the—defining characteristic of liberalism, as so many analysts once assumed? Answering these questions will require careful study of the cases to come.

---

1. Of these decisions, *Citizens United v. Federal Elections Commission,* 130 S.CT. 876 (2010), garnered a great deal of attention. In this case, the Court ruled that limits on corporate and union funding of political broadcasts violate the First Amendment.

Another interesting feature of these personal rights cases is how they have generally increased in terms of the proportion of the docket the Court devotes to them. In the six years immediately prior to Warren's appointment as chief justice, slightly more than 6 percent of the Court's rulings dealt with religion, expression, and privacy issues. Since then, that figure has increased to nearly 10 percent, and in some terms it was far higher. In 1970, for example, 23 of the Court's 124 cases (18.6 percent) touched on these issues.

Why the proportion of the Court's docket devoted to these cases has generally grown with time is an interesting question. One answer is that the justices themselves contributed to the growth with two decisions in the late 1930s, *Palko v. Connecticut* (1937) and **United States v. Carolene Products** (1938).[2] In *Palko,* as we saw in Chapter 3, a majority of the justices adopted the doctrine of selective incorporation, which would eventually lead the Court to apply most of the Bill of Rights to the states. This step, in turn, provided the Court with jurisdiction over a range of personal liberty disputes that it had previously denied itself.

Carolene Products, on its face, seems a less dramatic step than *Palko.* In fact, at issue in this dispute was an economic, not civil liberties, regulation—a 1923 law that prohibited the interstate shipment of milk blended with oil or fat. Justice Harlan Fiske Stone wrote for the Court in the case, asserting that the justices would generally uphold such laws. He also said, in what would become widely known as Footnote Four:

There may be narrower scope for operation of the presumption of constitutionality when legislation appears on its face to be within a specific prohibition of the Constitution, such as those of the first ten amendments, which are deemed equally specific when held to be embraced within the Fourteenth.

It is unnecessary to consider now whether legislation which restricts those political processes which can ordinarily be expected to bring about repeal of undesirable legislation, is to be subjected to more exacting judicial scrutiny under the general prohibitions of the Fourteenth Amendment than are most other types of legislation.

Nor need we enquire whether similar considerations enter into the review of statutes directed at particular religious, or national, or racial minorities; whether prejudice against discrete and insular minorities may be a special condition, which tends seriously to curtail the operation of those political processes ordinarily to be relied upon to protect minorities, and which may call for a correspondingly more searching judicial inquiry.[3]

With these words, Justice Stone advanced a doctrine that has become known as "preferred freedoms."[4] Under it, the Court presumes that *most* laws are constitutional; it is up to the challenger, not the government, to undermine that presumption. The presumption, however, shifts if the law in question abridges individual rights or liberties. In such cases, it is the government's responsibility to show that the law in question is narrowly tailored to achieve a compelling governmental interest. By articulating the preferred freedoms doctrine, which first appeared in a majority opinion in *Murdock v. Pennsylvania* (1943), the Court signaled its willingness to give closer scrutiny to civil liberties (and rights) disputes and to remove itself from those involving economic issues.[5]

Another explanation for the increasing number of cases is that actors outside the Court—most notably, lawyers and organized interests such as the American Civil Liberties Union and the NAACP—who had adequate, if not substantial, sources of financial support, generated something of a "rights revolution."[6]

Whatever the cause of the growth, it is true that civil liberties cases represent some of the most

2. See Richard L. Pacelle, *The Transformation of the Supreme Court's Agenda* (Boulder, CO: Westview Press, 1991); Jeffrey A. Segal and Harold J. Spaeth, *The Supreme Court and the Attitudinal Model Revisited* (New York: Cambridge University Press, 2002).

3. We have omitted the cases Stone cited in the footnote. For the full version, see FindLaw at http://laws.findlaw.com/US/304/144.html.

4. See Chapter 5 for more details.

5. *Erie Railroad v. Tompkins* (1938), decided the same day as *Carolene Products,* reinforced the message that the Court was interested in closing the door on ordinary economic disputes, which had long been "staples" of its agenda. In this case, the Court held that the federal courts were not free to make their own common law to resolve diversity cases—those between citizens of different states. As the Court put it, "There is no general federal common law." See Pacelle, *Transformation of the Supreme Court's Agenda.*

6. Charles R. Epp, *The Rights Revolution* (Chicago: University of Chicago Press, 1998), 69.

interesting—and difficult—issues in American constitutional law. Disputes involving aid to religious institutions, prayer in schools, the rights of protesters, censorship of the press, libel, obscenity, and reproductive rights all fall into this category. The Court's responses to these issues determine the extent to which the government can constitutionally impose regulations that impinge on personal freedom.

Each decade brings to the Court new questions regarding these fundamental freedoms, as well as novel approaches to more traditional issues. In the coming pages, we examine the major controversies the justices have been asked to settle. In some areas they have been successful in developing coherent and settled doctrine. In others they have repeatedly returned to the same conflicts between personal freedoms and government authority without reaching conclusions that stand the test of time. This is not surprising. As you read the next chapters you will discover that these issues often present conflicts among values that go to the very core of what it means to be an American citizen.

4 Religion: Exercise and Establishment

"O N MY ARRIVAL in the United States," wrote Alexis de Tocqueville in the 1830s, "the religious aspect of the country was the first thing that struck my attention; and the longer I stayed there, the more I perceived the great political consequences resulting from this new state of things. In France I had almost always seen the spirit of religion and the spirit of freedom marching in opposite directions. But in America I found they were intimately united and that they reigned in common over the same country."[1] Tocqueville's astute observations remain valid today. The United States is one of the world's more religious nations. More than 80 percent of Americans report an affiliation with a particular faith tradition. Some 40 percent attend a place of worship one or more times a week, and almost 60 percent say that they engage in prayer daily. By contrast, only 5 percent of American reject the existence of a God.[2] Consequently, it should not be surprising that religion plays an important role in the lives of most Americans and that religious values significantly influence our culture and our politics.

Indeed, as Tocqueville observed, Americans have always been a religious people. All of us learned in

elementary school that the first settlers came to America to escape religious persecution in Europe and to practice their religion freely in a new land. What we often forget, however, is that as the colonies developed during the seventeenth century, they too became intolerant toward "minority" religions: many passed anti-Catholic laws or imposed ecclesiastical views on their citizens. Prior to the adoption of the Constitution, only two states (Maryland and Rhode Island) provided full religious freedoms—the remaining eleven had some restrictive laws. Six states had established state religions. Puritanism was the official faith of the Massachusetts Bay Colony, and Virginia established itself under the Church of England.

More tolerant attitudes toward religious liberty developed with time. After independence was declared, some states adopted constitutions that contained guarantees of religious freedom. For example, North Carolina's 1776 constitution proclaimed, "All men have a natural and unalienable right to worship Almighty God according to the dictates of their own consciences." But other constitutions continued to favor some religions over others. Delaware's said, "There shall be no establishment of any religious sect in this State in preference to another," but it required all state officers to "profess faith in God the Father, and in Jesus Christ His Only Son."

It would be fair to say that when the framers gathered in Philadelphia, they—like modern-day

---

1. Alexis de Tocqueville, *Democracy in America,* vol. 1 (New York: Vintage Books, 1954), 319.

2. Data on religious practices from Pew Forum on Religion and Public Life (http://pewforum.org).

Americans—held divergent views about the relationship between religion and the state. Even so, the subject of religion arose only occasionally during the course of the debates. After one particularly difficult session, Benjamin Franklin moved that the delegates pray "for the assistance of Heaven, and its blessings on our deliberations." With virtual unanimity, the delegates attacked Franklin, arguing that a prayer session might offend some members and that the public would perceive it as an act of desperation.[3] In the end, the founders mentioned religion only once in the Constitution. Article VI provides that all government officials must take an oath to "support this Constitution; but no religious Test shall ever be required as a Qualification to any Office or public Trust under the United States."

Opponents of the new Constitution objected to its lack of any guarantees of religious liberty. New York Anti-Federalists, for example, condemned the document for "not securing the rights of conscience in matters of religion, of granting the liberty of worshipping God agreeable to the mode thereby dictated."[4] Many states proposed amendments that centered on religious liberty. When James Madison drew up what would become the Bill of Rights, he included the following: "The Civil Rights of none shall be abridged on account of religious belief or worship, nor shall any national religion be established, nor shall the full and equal rights of conscience be in any manner, or on any pretext, infringed." After several rounds of changes, the framers adopted two provisions to protect religious liberty: the establishment clause and the free exercise clause. Together they became the first two guarantees contained in the First Amendment of the Constitution: "Congress shall make no law respecting an establishment of religion, or prohibiting the free exercise thereof."

How has the Court interpreted these two clauses? Are their meanings the same today as when the framers wrote them? In this chapter, we examine these and other questions. We begin with a basic question that has implications for both clauses: What is religion?

---

3. Daniel A. Farber and Suzanna Sherry, *A History of the American Constitution,* 2nd ed. (St. Paul, MN: Thomson/West, 2005), 172–173.

4. Address of the Albany Antifederal Committee, April 26, 1788, excerpted in ibid., 256.

DEFINING RELIGION

Suppose some prisoners form a religion holding that God requires them to eat filet mignon and drink Cabernet Sauvignon every day. Members of this new religion ask prison officials to serve them these things, but the officials, believing that the religion is nothing more than a ploy to get expensive meat and wine, refuse the request. The prisoners file a lawsuit to force the prison to comply. They claim that the government is depriving them of their right to exercise their religion freely.

This dispute may strike you as easy to resolve; after all, it seems clear that the prisoners formed this religion only to obtain steak and wine. But how would you distinguish their "religion" from others that also seek to obtain benefits for their members at society's expense? For example, if an Orthodox Jew is fired from her job because she refuses to work on Saturdays, may the state deny her unemployment benefits? Is she using her religion to take money from the state? You would probably answer no to both questions because you perceive a difference between the religion of the prisoners and the religion of the unemployed worker. But what is that difference? How do we distinguish a genuine religion from a sham?

These questions are critical to our discussion, because if a religion is not genuine or bona fide, it is not entitled to protection under the religion clauses of the First Amendment. But the cases that come before the Supreme Court are rarely simple to resolve. In fact, the Court has had a good deal of difficulty in defining religion in terms of the First Amendment. Its first attempt came in 1879 in **Reynolds v. United States.** In the next section, which deals with the free exercise of religion, we discuss this case in some detail. Here, it is enough to say that it involved the Mormon Church, whose adherents at the time of this dispute lived mostly in the Utah Territory. Apparently, because the church was relatively new (it had formed in 1830) and its practices, particularly polygamy, were unfamiliar, if not distasteful, to the Court, the justices felt the need to consider whether it was a religion at all. Writing for the Court, Chief Justice Morrison R. Waite suggested:

The word "religion" is not defined in the Constitution. We must go elsewhere, therefore, to ascertain its meaning, and nowhere more appropriately, we think, than to the history of the times in the midst of which the provision was adopted.

Using this approach, Waite did not declare that Mormonism was not a religion, but he did say that the government could outlaw one of its teachings—the practice of polygamy—because there was no support for it at the time of the founding of the nation.

In fact, at the time the Mormon religion was founded, its adherents were persecuted and even attacked by hostile mobs. Many Mormons moved to the West because other states would not tolerate their presence. For example, in 1838 Missouri called out the militia because, as the state governor wrote, "The Mormons must be treated as enemies, and must be exterminated."[5] As *Reynolds* indicates, government efforts to undermine the religion did not stop after the Mormons settled in Utah. In addition to the antipolygamy law, Congress in 1887 passed an act that allowed the government to "disenfranchise Mormon voters, remove corporate status from the Mormon church, and confiscate all church property."[6] About thirteen hundred Mormons were arrested.

A decade or so after the decision in *Reynolds,* the Court had an opportunity to reconsider it when a Mormon challenged a law that disqualified individuals from voting if they refused to take an oath "abjuring bigamy or polygamy." But in *Davis v. Beason* (1890), the Court only reinforced *Reynolds,* this time with a statement about beliefs in God and "morals":

The term "religion" has reference to one's views of his relations to his Creator, and to the obligations they impose of reverence for his being and character, and of obedience to his will. . . . With man's relations to his Maker and the obligations he may think they impose, and the manner in which an expression shall be made by him of his belief on those subjects, no interference can be permitted, provided always the laws of society, designed to secure its peace and prosperity, and the morals of its people, are not interfered with.

These are narrow approaches to religion; *Reynolds* suggests that government may regulate religious practices that are new or were unknown to the framers. When we consider that during the eighteenth century there were only a few dozen major religions or sects, compared with more than 250 today—to say nothing of the hundreds of small "fringe" groups—we can see

why this ruling was so underinclusive.[7] *Davis v. Beason* binds religion to a belief in God, a belief that some religions do not hold or about which some "religious" individuals are skeptical. It also permits regulation of religious practices if those practices interfere with the "morals" of the people. In short, through the nineteenth century, courts defined religion, as legal scholar Laurence Tribe has written, in terms of "theistic notions respecting divinity, morality, and worship. In order to be considered legitimate, religions had to be viewed as 'civilized' by Western standards."[8] Fortunately for adherents of nonmainstream religions, *Reynolds* and *Davis* were not the Court's last words on the subject. Since the 1940s two types of cases have provided the Court with opportunities to reconsider Chief Justice Waite's approach. The first centers on religions that appear to be shams and is well exemplified by **United States v. Ballard** (1944).

The *Ballard* case concerned the "I Am" movement, which was founded in California by Guy Ballard, who had a long-standing interest in the occult. He claimed that while hiking on Mount Shasta in 1930 he encountered a young man who identified himself as Comte de Saint Germain. Saint Germain supposedly asserted that he was several centuries old and was, along with Jesus, one of the Ascended Masters. According to Ballard's account, Saint Germain explained that the Ascended Masters had chosen Ballard and his wife, Edna, and their son, Donald, to be their divine messengers on earth. In response the Ballards started the I Am movement, a variation of which remains active today. As the spiritual leader of I Am, Ballard claimed supernatural healing powers and told his followers that he needed money to continue his work. In return he promised health, wealth, and happiness. Ballard used the U.S. Postal Service to collect these funds, making a good deal of money along the way.

Asserting that the I Am sect was not a religion, the federal government accused Ballard of using the mail to defraud people. When the case reached the Supreme Court, it addressed the question of what a jury could consider in determining whether to convict Ballard. The trial court judge had told the jury that it could not take into account the truth of Ballard's views (for example, whether Saint Germain had chosen Ballard as a messenger); rather, it could consider only the sincerity

---

5. Quoted in Laurence Tribe, *American Constitutional Law* (Mineola, NY: Foundation Press, 1988), 1271.

6. Ibid.

7. These figures are quoted in ibid., 1179.

8. Ibid.

with which Ballard held his views. The Supreme Court agreed with this approach. Writing for the majority, Justice William O. Douglas asserted:

Men may believe what they cannot prove. They may not be put to the proof of their religious doctrines or beliefs. Religious experiences which are as real as life to some may be incomprehensible to others. Yet the fact that they may be beyond the ken of mortals does not mean that they can be made suspect before the law. Many take their gospel from the New Testament. But it would hardly be supposed that they could be tried before a jury charged with the duty of determining whether those teachings contained false representations. The miracles of the New Testament, the Divinity of Christ, life after death, the power of prayer are deep in the religious convictions of many. If one could be sent to jail because a jury in a hostile environment found those teachings false, little indeed would be left of religious freedom.

As for the Ballards, Douglas had this to say:

The religious views espoused by [Ballard] might seem incredible, if not preposterous, to most people. But if those doctrines are subject to trial before a jury charged with finding their truth or falsity, then the same can be done with the religious beliefs of any sect. When the triers of fact undertake that task, they enter a forbidden domain.

Under the *Ballard* approach, the proper test of a constitutionally protected religious belief is not the truth of its doctrine but the sincerity with which it is held. For our would-be gourmet prisoners, then, we would ask if they sincerely held their religious views, rather than if those views were factually accurate.

The second category of cases in which the Court has considered what religion is involves conscientious objector exemptions from the military. In the Universal Military Training and Service Act of 1940, Congress provided exemptions from military combat to individuals "who, by reason of religious training and belief, [are] conscientiously opposed to participation in war in any form." The law defined religious training and belief as "an individual's belief in a relation to a Supreme Being involving duties superior to those arising by any human relation but [not including] essentially political, sociological, or philosophical views or a merely personal moral code."

Using Congress's definition, members of some organized religions, such as the Quakers, would qualify for exemptions. But what about those who are not members of a traditional, organized religion or those who do not necessarily frame their religious views with reference to a supreme being? Could they obtain religious exemptions from military service?

As the Vietnam War raged on in the 1960s, several cases presented the Court with opportunities to answer these questions. In *United States v. Seeger* (1965) the justices considered whether an individual who was not a member of an organized religion could obtain a military exemption on religious grounds. Daniel Seeger asserted that, although he opposed participation in the war on the basis of his religious belief, "he preferred to leave the question as to his belief in a Supreme Being open 'rather than answer yes or no.'" Did his declared "skepticism or disbelief in the existence of God" disqualify him from a religious exemption? Writing for the Court, Justice Tom C. Clark said it did not, for

Congress, in using the expression "Supreme Being" rather than the designation "God," was merely clarifying the meaning of religious training and belief so as to embrace all religions and to exclude essentially political, sociological, or philosophical views.

Clark then provided a standard to govern future litigation, one that again stressed the sincerity of the beliefs held:

[T]he test of belief "in relation to a Supreme Being" is whether a given belief that is sincere and meaningful occupies a place in the life of its possessor parallel to . . . the orthodox belief in God.

In response to the Court's ruling in *Seeger*, Congress removed from the 1940 law the words "in relation to a Supreme Being." But more litigation ensued. In *Welsh v. United States* (1970) the Court considered another section of the law, which excluded from exemption coverage individuals whose views were "essentially political, sociological, or philosophical." In a judgment for the Court,[9] Justice Hugo L. Black explained that even if a draftee's objection to the war was not based strictly on traditional religious grounds, he could obtain a religious exemption if his moral and ethical beliefs were sincerely held—as sincerely held as traditionally defined religious beliefs. For if those views are that

---

9. A judgment represents the view of a plurality, not a majority, of the Court's members. Unlike a majority opinion (or "opinion of the Court"), a judgment lacks precedential value.

strong, they take on a religious character falling within the protection of the law.

In the conscientious objector cases, the Court moved away from the strictly theistic view of religion it had expressed in *Reynolds*. To be considered "religious"—that is, to come under the protection of the free exercise clause—one need not profess a religion based in a belief in God. Rather, since *Welsh* the Court's inquiries have focused on the sincerity (but not the truth) with which someone (or one's religion) holds a particular view.

The cases and narrative to come provide many opportunities for you to think about what elements define religion. As you read them, ask yourself: Does the Court still evince a bias toward established, major religions, or has it significantly changed its approach in response to the expanding diversity of religions in contemporary America? You may also want to consider the competing charge that the Court has gone too far, that it extends First Amendment coverage to religions that are undeserving.

FREE EXERCISE OF RELIGION

Imagine a religious sect whose members handle poisonous snakes in the belief that such activity demonstrates their faith in God. Should government prohibit such activity because it is dangerous? Or would a law banning this behavior violate the First Amendment's free exercise clause, which proclaims that there can be "no law . . . prohibiting the free exercise" of religion?

A literal approach to the free exercise clause would suggest that religious denominations can pursue any exercise of their religion they desire. Yet it seems clear that the majority of Americans did not think the free exercise of religion meant any such thing at the time the clause was framed. Although we do not know specifically what the framers intended by the words "free exercise" (congressional debates over religious guarantees tended to focus on the establishment clause rather than the free exercise clause), writings and documents of the day point to a universally accepted limit.[10] As Thomas Jefferson set it out in an 1802 letter to the Danbury Baptist Association: "[I believe] that religion is a matter

which lies solely between man and his God; that he owes account to none other for his faith or his worship; that the legislative powers of the Government reach actions only, and not opinion."[11] In other words, the free exercise of religion is not limitless, as a literal reading of the amendment would suggest. Rather, at least under Jefferson's interpretation, governments can regulate "actions."

Belief-Action Distinction and Valid Secular Policy Test

Like Jefferson, the Court has never taken a literal approach to the free exercise clause. Rather, in its first major decision in this area, it seized on his words to proclaim that some religious activities lie beyond First Amendment protections. As we mentioned, that case was **Reynolds v. United States**, which involved the Mormon practice of polygamy. Mormons believed that males "had the duty . . . to practice polygamy" and that failure to do so would result in "damnation in the life to come." Word of this practice found its way to the U.S. Congress, which was charged with governing the Utah Territory, where many Mormons lived. In 1874 Congress outlawed polygamy. After Mormon follower George Reynolds married his second wife, he was charged with violating the law. In his defense, Reynolds argued that he was following the dictates of his faith, a right reserved to him under the free exercise clause.

The U.S. Supreme Court disagreed. In a unanimous opinion, the justices rejected an absolutist interpretation of the clause and instead sought to draw a distinction between the behaviors it did and did not protect. Chief Justice Waite's opinion for the Court asserted, "Congress was deprived of all legislative power over mere opinion, but was left free to reach actions which were in violation of social duties or subversive of the good order." This distinction between opinions (or beliefs) and actions (or practices) became, as we shall see, the centerpiece for several future religion cases.

Some have argued that the belief-action distinction was simply a way for the Court to uphold a government prohibition of an almost universally condemned practice advocated by a particularly unpopular church.[12] This view receives support from the Court's failure to use the distinction in its next major free exercise clause

---

10. For an interesting view, see Michael W. McConnell, "Free Exercise as the Framers Understood It," in *The Bill of Rights*, ed. Eugene W. Hickok Jr. (Charlottesville: University of Virginia Press, 1991).

11. Letter to the Danbury Baptist Association, 1802, quoted in *Reynolds v. United States* (1879).

12. John Brigham, *Civil Liberties and American Democracy* (Washington, DC: CQ Press, 1984), 77.

BOX 4-1   THE JEHOVAH'S WITNESSES AND THE COURT

The Jehovah's Witnesses began in the 1870s in Pittsburgh, Pennsylvania. Starting as a Bible study class directed by eighteen-year-old Charles Taze Russell, the sect became a powerful grassroots movement. By the late 1930s, under the leadership of Joseph Franklin Rutherford, the Witnesses were preaching all over the United States and in several foreign countries. The Witnesses claim more than 6 million active members worldwide today.

Members see themselves as evangelical ministers with the mission to preach about Jehovah's struggle with Satan. They denounce organized religion, particularly Catholicism, and reject the notion of the trinity and the deity of Christ. The Witnesses interpret the Bible as prohibiting them from honoring secular symbols, such as national flags, and from receiving blood transfusions and other medical treatments. They preach and distribute literature door-to-door and on street corners. Because of their active proselytizing and unpopular views, members of the church have been prosecuted for violating local ordinances. The Witnesses have a long history of turning to the courts for relief when their constitutional rights were threatened.

The Jehovah's Witnesses have secured many legal victories at the Supreme Court level, including the following:

Murdock v. Pennsylvania (1943). A local government may not impose a tax on the privilege of religious solicitation.

West Virginia State Board of Education v. Barnette (1943). A state may not require students to recite the Pledge of Allegiance.

Martin v. Struthers (1943). A city may not forbid knocking on doors without the resident's permission.

Niemotko v. Maryland (1951). A city may not deny a permit for a public meeting because it finds a group's beliefs objectionable.

Wooley v. Maynard (1977). A state may not require automobile owners to display license plates that include state mottos that the person finds offensive to his or her religious creed.

Thomas v. Review Board (1981). A state may not deny unemployment compensation to an otherwise eligible individual who for religious reasons refuses to work in a weapons plant.

Watchtower Bible and Tract Society v. Stratton (2002). A city may not require a permit as a condition for engaging in door-to-door religious solicitation.

---

case, ***Pierce v. Society of Sisters*** (1925). In 1922, Oregon had passed a compulsory public school education act, requiring children between the ages of eight and sixteen to attend public school. A diverse body of interests supported this measure for equally diverse reasons: progressives hailed it as a necessary step for the assimilation of immigrants, and the Ku Klux Klan backed it because it was viewed as anti-Catholic. Indeed, the ultimate effect of the Oregon law was to force closure of the state's privately run schools, many of which were Roman Catholic. The Society of Sisters, organized in 1880 to provide secular and religious instruction to children, faced dissolution because it derived more than $30,000 of its annual income from its school.

Rather than shut its doors, the society chose to sue the state. Because the free exercise clause had not yet been incorporated, the society relied on a direct application of the Fourteenth Amendment, arguing that the law deprived parents of their fundamental liberty to determine how their children would be educated without due process of law. The sisters received support from organizations representing the spectrum of religions in the United States. Jews, Lutherans, Episcopalians, and Seventh-Day Adventists had a vested interest in the case's outcome because they also ran private schools. In addition, they wanted to show their unity of distaste for the Klan-backed law, believing it repressed "pluralism in education."[13]

In a unanimous opinion, the Court held for the Society of Sisters but virtually ignored the *Reynolds* belief-action distinction. Instead, the Court rested its ruling on the view that the sisters (as opposed to the Mormons) engaged in a "useful and meritorious" undertaking. Justice James McReynolds wrote:

The inevitable practical result of enforcing the act . . . would be the destruction of appellees' primary schools. . . . Appellees are engaged in a kind of undertaking not inherently harmful but long regarded as useful and meritorious. Certainly, there is nothing in the present record to indicate that they have failed to discharge their obligations to patrons, students, or the state.

---

13. For more details on this case, see Clement E. Vose, *Constitutional Change* (Lexington, MA: Lexington Books, 1972).

The Court did not return to the belief-action dichotomy until 1940, when, for the first time, the justices specifically applied the free exercise clause to state action, this time taken against the Jehovah's Witnesses *(see Box 4-1)*. The Jehovah's Witnesses denomination actively promotes its religion and vigorously proselytizes to gain converts to the faith. Church members regularly distribute religious pamphlets and solicit money, activities regulated by laws in many states. In *Cantwell v. Connecticut*, among other cases, the Witnesses asked the Court to strike down such regulation as infringements on their right to practice their religion freely.

Cantwell v. Connecticut

310 U.S. 296 (1940)
http://laws.findlaw.com/US/310/296.html
Vote: 9 (Black, Douglas, Frankfurter, Hughes,
      McReynolds, Murphy, Reed, Roberts, Stone)
      0

OPINION OF THE COURT: *Roberts*

FACTS:

Newton Cantwell and his sons, Jesse, age sixteen, and Russell, eighteen, members of the Jehovah's Witnesses sect, were playing records, soliciting contributions, and distributing pamphlets to citizens house-to-house in New Haven, Connecticut, in an area that was predominantly Catholic. Two passersby took offense at the anti-Catholic messages in the material and complained. The next day, police arrested the Cantwells for violating a state law prohibiting individuals "from soliciting money for any cause" without a license. The law required those who wanted to solicit to obtain a "certificate of approval" from the state's secretary of the Public Welfare Council. The state charged this official with determining whether "the cause is a religious one" or one of a "bona fide object of charity." If the official found neither, he was authorized to withhold the necessary certificate.

After unsuccessfully fighting these charges in the lower courts, the Cantwells appealed to the U.S. Supreme Court. Two important issues were at stake. First, the justices had to confront the question of whether the First Amendment's free exercise clause should be incorporated and made applicable to the states through the Fourteenth Amendment. If the answer to that question was yes, then the Court would have to determine if the Connecticut solicitation license policy violated the Cantwells' rights.

ARGUMENTS:

***For the appellants, Jesse, Newton,
and Russell Cantwell:***

- The Connecticut statute deprives the appellants of their freedom of worship, as well as their freedoms of speech and press, and is therefore invalid under the due process clause of the Fourteenth Amendment.
- The "imprescriptible right" to worship Almighty God is clearly one of the "liberties" that the Fourteenth Amendment protects against state invasion.
- The right to worship Almighty God by going door-to-door as Jesus and his apostles did is an essential privilege granted to every person who resides in the United States.

For the appellee, State of Connecticut:

- The sole purpose of the statute is to protect citizens from fraudulent solicitation. The state police powers give Connecticut ample authority to do so.
- The statute does not censor or discriminate against any ideas or teachings, nor does it prohibit the appellants from worshipping in any way they see fit. It applies only to those who solicit funds.
- It is reasonable for the state to delegate to the secretary of the Public Welfare Council the authority to certify solicitors as representing legitimate religious, charitable, or philanthropic causes.

MR. JUSTICE ROBERTS DELIVERED THE OPINION OF THE COURT.

We hold that the statute, as construed and applied to the appellants, deprives them of their liberty without due process of law in contravention of the Fourteenth Amendment. The fundamental concept of liberty embodied in that Amendment embraces the liberties guaranteed by the First Amendment. The First Amendment declares that Congress shall make no law respecting an establishment of religion or prohibiting the free exercise thereof. The Fourteenth Amendment has rendered the legislatures of the states as incompetent as Congress to enact such laws. The constitutional inhibition of legislation on the subject of religion has a double aspect. On the one hand, it forestalls compulsion by law of the acceptance of any creed or the practice of any form of worship. Freedom of conscience and freedom to adhere to such religious organization or form of worship as the individual may choose cannot be restricted by law. On the other hand, it safeguards the free exercise of the chosen form of religion. Thus the Amendment embraces two concepts—freedom to believe and freedom to act. The first is absolute but, in the nature of things, the second cannot be. Conduct remains subject to regulation for the protection of society. The freedom to act must have appropriate definition to preserve the enforcement of that protection. In every case the power to regulate must be so exercised as not, in attaining a permissible end, unduly to infringe the protected freedom. No one would contest the proposition that a state may not, by statute, wholly deny the right to preach or to disseminate religious views. Plainly such a previous and absolute restraint would violate the terms of the guarantee. It is equally clear that a state may by general and nondiscriminatory legislation regulate the times, the places, and the manner of soliciting upon its streets, and of holding meetings thereon; and may in other respects safeguard the peace, good order and comfort of the community, without unconstitutionally invading the liberties protected by the Fourteenth Amendment. The appellants are right in their insistence that the Act in question is not such a regulation. If a certificate is procured, solicitation is permitted without restraint but, in the absence of a certificate, solicitation is altogether prohibited.

The appellants urge that to require them to obtain a certificate as a condition of soliciting support for their views amounts to a prior restraint on the exercise of their religion within the meaning of the Constitution. The State insists that the Act, as construed by the Supreme Court of Connecticut, imposes no previous restraint upon the dissemination of religious views or teaching but merely safeguards against the perpetration of frauds under the cloak of religion. Conceding that this is so, the question remains whether the method adopted by Connecticut to that end transgresses the liberty safeguarded by the Constitution.

The general regulation, in the public interest, of solicitation, which does not involve any religious test and does not unreasonably obstruct or delay the collection of funds, is not open to any constitutional objection, even though the collection be for a religious purpose. Such regulation would not constitute a prohibited previous restraint on the free exercise of religion or interpose an inadmissible obstacle to its exercise.

It will be noted, however, that the Act requires an application to the secretary of the public welfare council of the State; that he is empowered to determine whether the cause is a religious one, and that the issue of a certificate depends upon his affirmative action. If he finds that the cause is not that of religion, to solicit for it

becomes a crime. He is not to issue a certificate as a matter of course. His decision to issue or refuse it involves appraisal of facts, the exercise of judgment, and the formation of an opinion. He is authorized to withhold his approval if he determines that the cause is not a religious one. Such a censorship of religion as the means of determining its right to survive is a denial of liberty protected by the First Amendment and included in the liberty which is within the protection of the Fourteenth. . . .

Nothing we have said is intended even remotely to imply that, under the cloak of religion, persons may, with impunity, commit frauds upon the public. Certainly penal laws are available to punish such conduct. Even the exercise of religion may be at some slight inconvenience in order that the state may protect its citizens from injury. Without doubt a state may protect its citizens from fraudulent solicitation by requiring a stranger in the community, before permitting him publicly to solicit funds for any purpose, to establish his identity and his authority to act for the cause which he purports to represent. The state is likewise free to regulate the time and manner of solicitation generally, in the interest of public safety, peace, comfort, or convenience. But to condition the solicitation of aid for the perpetuation of religious views or systems upon a license, the grant of which rests in the exercise of a determination by state authority as to what is a religious cause, is to lay a forbidden burden upon the exercise of liberty protected by the Constitution. . . .

The judgment affirming the convictions . . . is reversed and the cause is remanded for further proceedings not inconsistent with this opinion. So ordered.

Reversed and remanded.

As to the first major question posed in this case, the justices unequivocally ruled that the free exercise clause is applicable to state and local governments through the due process clause of the Fourteenth Amendment. Having held that the states must comply with free exercise guarantees, the Court focused its attention on the question of whether the Connecticut statute violated the Cantwells' religious rights. To resolve this issue, Justice Owen Roberts, speaking for the unanimous Court, returned to the belief-action dichotomy, but he treated it in a slightly different manner. He claimed that although the free exercise clause covered belief and action, "The first is absolute but, in the nature of things, the second cannot be." How then would the Court distinguish protected action from illegal action? Under the principles articulated in *Cantwell,* which some analysts refer to as the "valid secular policy" test, the Court looks at the particular legislation or policy adopted by the government. If the policy serves a legitimate nonreligious government goal, not directed at any particular religion, the Court will uphold it, even if the legislation has the effect of conflicting with religious practices. In *Cantwell* the Court said that the state could regulate the collection of funds, even if those funds were for a religious purpose, because it has a valid interest in protecting its citizens from fraudulent solicitation. If Connecticut's law had not empowered government officials to use their own discretion in determining whether a cause is religious or not, the Court probably would have upheld it as a legitimate secular policy.[14]

Had the Court upheld the law, the Jehovah's Witnesses would have found it more difficult to carry out the dictates of their religion. By the same token, all other would-be solicitors—charitable organizations and the like—would be similarly affected. In other words, the religious and the nonreligious alike would be subject to the regulations. Looking at *Cantwell* this way reveals an important underpinning of the logic of the valid secular policy test: neutrality. If the government has a valid secular reason for its policy, then, in the eyes of the justices, religions should not be exempt from its coverage simply because they are religions. Exempting them would give religions an elevated position in society. By adopting the valid secular policy test, the Court suggested that the effect on the Jehovah's Witnesses amounts to only an incidental intrusion on religion that comes about as the government pursues a legitimate interest.

Application of the Valid Secular Policy Test

How has this test worked? In particular, what constitutes a valid secular policy, a legitimate state interest? In *Cantwell,* Justice Roberts provided some clues as to what these concepts might encompass: the prevention of fraud, the reasonable regulation of the time and manner of solicitation, and the preservation of "public safety, peace, comfort or convenience." Shortly after *Cantwell,* the Court added to Roberts's list when it reviewed cases involving mandatory flag salutes and child labor laws.

At issue in the first flag salute case, ***Minersville School District v. Gobitis*** (1940), were the recitation of the Pledge of Allegiance and the hand gesture or salute that accompanied it. For most individuals, particularly schoolchildren, the pledge and salute are noncontroversial routines that illustrate their loyalty to the basic tenets of American society. Such is not the case for the Jehovah's Witnesses, who exalt religious laws over all others. They claim that the salute and the pledge violate a teaching from Exodus:

Thou shalt not make unto thee any graven image, or any likeness of anything that is in heaven above, or that is in earth beneath, or that is in the water under the earth; thou shalt not bow down thyself to them, nor serve them.

Accordingly, Jehovah's Witnesses do not want their children to recite the pledge or salute the flag. The problem, at the time of this case, was that public schools made the pledge and salute to the flag mandatory for all children attending the schools. Flag salute laws became particularly pervasive after World War I as a show of patriotism. Before the war only five states required flag salutes; by 1935 that figure had risen to eighteen, with many local school boards compelling the salute in the absence of state legislation.[15]

Beginning in the mid-1930s, the Witnesses actively campaigned to do away with the salutes. The effort began in Nazi Germany, where Jehovah's Witnesses who refused to salute Hitler with raised arms were sent to concentration camps. Joseph Rutherford, the Witnesses' leader in the United States, spoke out against the American flag salute, which, at that time, was regularly done with a straight, extended arm, resembling the Nazi-Fascist salute. He asserted that Witnesses "do not 'Heil Hitler' nor any other creature."

After Rutherford's speech, some members of the Jehovah's Witnesses asked their children not to salute the flag. Among these was Walter Gobitas, whose two children—twelve-year-old Lillian and her younger brother, William—attended a Pennsylvania public school with a mandatory flag salute policy.[16] When the children refused to salute the flag, they were expelled. Represented by attorneys from the Witnesses, Gobitas

14. See, however, a more recent case, *Watchtower Bible and Tract Society v. Stratton* (2002), in which the Court, in response to another legal action by the Jehovah's Witnesses, struck down a city's permit requirement for door-to-door solicitation even when local officials were not given such discretion. The challenged ordinance applied to solicitation for any cause, not just for religious purposes. The Court said the ordinance violated First Amendment freedom of speech protections.

15. See Peter Irons, *The Courage of Their Convictions* (New York: Free Press, 1988), 16–24.

16. The family name, Gobitas, was misspelled as Gobitis in the Court records.

Walter Gobitas sued the Minersville, Pennsylvania, school district after his children, William and Lillian, were expelled for refusing to salute the flag because of their Jehovah's Witnesses faith.

brought suit against the school board, arguing that the expulsion violated his children's free exercise of religion rights. Writing for an eight-justice majority, Felix Frankfurter used the valid secular policy rationale to uphold the flag salute requirement. Frankfurter claimed that the state had a legitimate secular reason for requiring flag salutes: to foster patriotism. That the law affected the religious practice of the Jehovah's Witnesses did not, in Frankfurter's view, detract from its constitutionality. Besides, Frankfurter believed that the Court should not interfere with local policies because that "would in effect make [the Court] the school board for the country."

The repercussions from the Court's decision in *Gobitis* were extraordinary. After the ruling, many states either retained or passed laws that required flag salutes and pledges for all public school children and threatened to expel anyone who did not comply. What was startling was the violence against Jehovah's Witnesses. "Within two weeks of the Court's decision," two federal officials later wrote, "hundreds of attacks upon the Witnesses were reported to the Department of Justice."[17] Viewing their refusal to salute the flag as unpatriotic—especially

as the country fought in World War II—mobs throughout the United States stoned, kidnapped, beat, and even castrated Jehovah's Witnesses.[18]

The justices' response to the issues raised in ***Prince v. Massachusetts*** (1944) provides a second example of the valid secular policy test, this time applied in the area of child welfare. *Prince* involved a Massachusetts statute declaring it unlawful for minors (girls under eighteen and boys under twelve) "to sell, expose, or offer for sale any newspapers, magazines, periodicals or any other articles of merchandise of any description . . . in any street or public place." It further specified that any parent or guardian allowing minors to perform such activity would be engaging in criminal behavior. Sarah Prince, a Jehovah's Witness, allowed her nine-year-old niece, Betty Simmons, for whom Prince was the legal guardian, to help her distribute religious pamphlets. Prince knew she was violating the law—she had been warned by school authorities—but she continued and was arrested.

---

17. Irons, *Courage of Their Convictions*, 22–23.

18. As we will see in Chapter 5, three years after *Gobitis* the Court in *West Virginia Board of Education v. Barnette* (1943) struck down compulsory flag salute laws. That decision, however, was based primarily on freedom of speech grounds.

At the trial court level some doubt arose whether the child actually had sold materials, but when the case reached the Supreme Court, it dealt exclusively with this question: Did the state law violate First Amendment principles? The Court divided 5 to 4 to hold that it did not. Writing for the majority, Justice Wiley Rutledge asserted:

The State's authority over children's activities is broader than over like actions of adults. This is peculiarly true of public activities and in matters of employment. A democratic society rests . . . upon the healthy, well-rounded growth of young people into full maturity as citizens. . . . It may secure this against impeding restraints and dangers, within a broad range of selection. Among evils most appropriate for such action are the crippling effects of child employment . . . and the possible harms arising from other activities subject to all the diverse influences of the street. It is too late now to doubt that legislation appropriately designed to reach such evils is within the state's police power, whether against the parent's claim to control of the child or one that religious scruples dictate contrary action.

Clearly, state legislatures can regulate religious practices that could harm children as well as those of questionable morality and safety. Such laws, in the eyes of the justices, present a reasonable use of state police power, which is the ability of states to regulate in the best interests of their citizens. In other words, child labor laws represent a valid secular policy that will prevail over claims that some forms of child labor constitute the free exercise of one's religion.

The *Sherbert-Yoder* Compelling Interest Test

Cantwell, Gobitis, and *Prince* have several traits in common: they were lawsuits filed by a minority religion; they were decided during the 1940s, a period when the Court was neither particularly conservative nor liberal in ideological outlook; and they often involved free exercise arguments combined with other constitutional claims, such as freedom of expression. In addition, the Court's approach to the cases was relatively consistent. Religious beliefs were not questioned, but when a person's religious actions were at issue, the Court invoked the valid secular policy test to resolve the disputes. This approach occasionally led the justices to strike down state policies (*Cantwell*), as well as to uphold them (*Gobitis* and *Prince*).

In the 1960s, however, major changes began to occur in the Court's free exercise jurisprudence. The first signs came in **Braunfeld v. Brown**, which was one of several cases the Court heard in 1961 involving "blue laws." These ordinances required businesses offering nonessential goods and services to close on Sundays. Abraham Braunfeld, an Orthodox Jew, owned a retail clothing and home furnishing store in Philadelphia. Because under state law such stores were not among those permitted to remain open on Sunday, Braunfeld wanted the Court to issue a permanent injunction against the law. His religious principles dictated that he could not work on Saturday, the Jewish Sabbath, but he needed to be open six days a week for economic reasons. He challenged the law as a violation of, among other things, his right to exercise his religion.

Writing for a plurality, Chief Justice Earl Warren upheld the constitutionality of blue laws and restated the belief-action dichotomy:

Certain aspects of religious exercise cannot, in any way, be restricted or burdened by either federal or state legislation. Compulsion by law of the acceptance of any creed or the practice of any form of worship is strictly forbidden. The freedom to hold religious beliefs and opinions is absolute. . . .

However, the freedom to act, even where the action is in accord with one's religious convictions, is not totally free from legislative restrictions. . . . [L]egislative power over mere opinion is forbidden but it may reach people's action when they are found to be in violation of important social duties or subversive of good order, even when the actions are demanded by one's religion.

But, according to many observers, Warren's opinion veered significantly from established precedent. Consider the following passage:

If the purpose or effect of a law is to impede the observance of one or all religions or is to discriminate invidiously between religions, that law is constitutionally invalid even though the burden may be characterized as being only indirect. But if the State regulates conduct by enacting a general law within its power, the purpose and effect of which is to advance the State's secular goals, the statute is valid despite its indirect burden on religious observance *unless the State may accomplish its purpose by means which do not impose such a burden.* [emphasis added].

In some ways, this merely restates the logic of *Cantwell* and the valid secular policy test. But note the italicized phrase. It suggests that the state must show that its legislation achieves an important secular end that it cannot achieve with legislation that places less of a burden on religious freedom.

Sunday closing laws, Warren reasoned, met both of these standards. According to the chief justice, in passing blue laws, the state intended to set up a day of "rest, repose, recreation and tranquillity—a day which all members of the family and community have the opportunity to spend and enjoy together." In other words, the Sunday closing laws reflect a valid secular purpose. They also are the least restrictive way of accomplishing that purpose. Even though the laws indirectly burden members of some religions (for example, Orthodox Jews), Warren reasoned that the states had adopted a relatively unburdensome way of accomplishing their goal of creating a uniform "weekly respite from all labor."

Other members of the Court took issue with Warren's analysis, which represented the views of only a plurality of the justices. Especially memorable were dissents by William Brennan and Potter Stewart. Brennan thought the Court had taken a misguided approach to the issue: "I would approach this case differently, from the point of view of the individuals whose liberty is—concededly—curtailed by these enactments. For the values of the First Amendment . . . look primarily towards the preservation of personal liberty, rather than towards the fulfillment of collective goals." In a one-paragraph dissent, Stewart put the issue even more starkly:

Pennsylvania has passed a law which compels an Orthodox Jew to choose between his religious faith and his economic survival. That is a cruel choice. It is a choice which I think no State can constitutionally demand. For me this is not something that can be swept under the rug and forgotten in the interest of enforced Sunday togetherness. I think the impact of this law upon the appellants grossly violates their constitutional right to free exercise of their religion.

The divided opinion in *Braunfeld* created something of a quandary for legal scholars: Was the plurality—through its articulation of a least restrictive means approach—signaling a change in the way the Court would resolve free exercise disputes? Or was *Braunfeld* an aberration? Consider these questions as you read *Sherbert v. Verner*, decided just two years later.

Sherbert v. Verner

374 U.S. 398 (1963)
http://laws.findlaw.com/US/374/398.html
Oral arguments are available at http://www.oyez.org.
Vote: 7 (Black, Brennan, Clark, Douglas, Goldberg, Stewart, Warren)
    2 (Harlan, White)

OPINION OF THE COURT: *Brennan*
CONCURRING OPINIONS: *Douglas, Stewart*
DISSENTING OPINION: *Harlan*

FACTS:

Adell Sherbert was a spool tender in a Spartanburg, South Carolina, textile mill, a job she had held for thirty-five years. Sherbert worked Monday through Friday from 7:00 A.M. to 3:00 P.M. She had the option of working Saturdays but chose not to. Sherbert was a member of the Seventh-Day Adventist Church, which held that no work could be performed between sundown on Friday and sundown on Saturday. In other words, Saturday was her church's Sabbath.

On June 5, 1959, Sherbert's employer informed her that starting the next day work on Saturdays would no longer be voluntary: to retain her job she would need to report to the mill every Saturday. Sherbert continued to work Monday through Friday but, in observance of her religious beliefs, did not work on six successive Saturdays. Her employer fired her on July 27.

Between June 5 and July 27, Sherbert had tried to find a job at three other textile mills, but they too operated on Saturdays. Sherbert filed for state unemployment benefits. Under South Carolina law, a claimant who is eligible for benefits must be "able to work . . . and available for work"; a claimant is ineligible for benefits if he or she has "failed, without good cause . . . to accept available suitable work when offered . . . by the employment office or the employer." The benefits examiner in charge of Sherbert's claim turned her down on the ground that she failed, without good cause, to accept "suitable work when offered" by her employer. In other words, her religious preference was insufficient justification for refusing to accept a job.

Sherbert and her lawyers filed suit in a South Carolina state court, which ruled in favor of the employment office. After the state supreme court affirmed that decision, Sherbert's attorneys asked the U.S. Supreme Court to review the case.

ARGUMENTS:

For the appellant, Adell Sherbert:

- Conditioning state unemployment benefits on a person's willingness to work on her Sabbath requires Sherbert to repudiate her religious belief by doing something that directly conflicts with the tenets of her church. Denying her unemployment benefits constitutes economic coercion to give up a religious belief.

- The Saturday work requirement is not essential to accomplish the state's policy objectives.
- Requiring work on Saturday but not Sunday is discriminatory and arbitrary in violation of the First and Fourteenth Amendments.

***For the appellee, Charlie Verner and the
other members of the South Carolina
Employment Security Commission:***
- Denying Sherbert her unemployment benefits does not constitute coercion to work on the Sabbath in violation of the free exercise clause.
- The benefits policy is a valid and necessary regulation to advance the state's secular interest in achieving stable employment by awarding benefits to those who have tried and failed to find work, while denying benefits to those who have turned down a job.
- The law does not prohibit any form of religious belief or practice and was not designed to discriminate against those who observe the Sabbath on Saturday. The economic burden on Sherbert is no greater than the Court previously permitted in *Braunfeld v. Brown*.

MR. JUSTICE BRENNAN DELIVERED THE OPINION OF THE COURT.

The door of the Free Exercise Clause stands tightly closed against any governmental regulation of religious beliefs as such, *Cantwell v. Connecticut.* . . . On the other hand, the Court has rejected challenges under the Free Exercise Clause to governmental regulation of certain overt acts prompted by religious beliefs or principles, for "even when the action is in accord with one's religious convictions, [it] is not totally free from legislative restrictions." *Braunfeld v. Brown.* The conduct or actions so regulated have invariably posed some substantial threat to public safety, peace or order. See, e.g., *Reynolds v. United States; Prince v. Massachusetts.* . . .

Plainly enough, appellant's conscientious objection to Saturday work constitutes no conduct prompted by religious principles of a kind within the reach of state legislation. If, therefore, the decision of the South Carolina Supreme Court is to withstand appellant's constitutional challenge, it must be either because her disqualification as a beneficiary represents no infringement by the State of her constitutional rights of free exercise, or because any incidental burden on the free exercise of appellant's religion may be justified by a "compelling

state interest in the regulation of a subject within the State's constitutional power to regulate. . . ."

We turn first to the question whether the disqualification for benefits imposes any burden on the free exercise of appellant's religion. We think it is clear that it does. In a sense the consequences of such a disqualification to religious principles and practices may be only an indirect result of welfare legislation within the State's general competence to enact; it is true that no criminal sanctions directly compel appellant to work a six-day week. But this is only the beginning, not the end, of our inquiry. For "if the purpose or effect of a law is to impede the observance of one or all religions or is to discriminate invidiously between religions, that law is constitutionally invalid even though the burden may be characterized as being only indirect." *Braunfeld v. Brown.* Here not only is it apparent that appellant's declared ineligibility for benefits derives solely from the practice of her religion, but the pressure upon her to forego that practice is unmistakable. The ruling forces her to choose between following the precepts of her religion and forfeiting benefits, on the one hand, and abandoning one of the precepts of her religion in order to accept work, on the other hand. Governmental imposition of such a choice puts the same kind of burden upon the free exercise of religion as would a fine imposed against appellant for her Saturday worship.

Nor may the South Carolina court's construction of the statute be saved from constitutional infirmity on the ground that unemployment compensation benefits are not appellant's "right" but merely a "privilege." It is too late in the day to doubt that the liberties of religion and expression may be infringed by the denial of or placing of conditions upon a benefit or privilege. . . .

We must next consider whether some compelling state interest enforced in the eligibility provisions of the South Carolina statute justifies the substantial infringement of appellant's First Amendment right. It is basic that no showing merely of a rational relationship to some colorable state interest would suffice; in this highly sensitive constitutional area, "[o]nly the gravest abuses, endangering paramount interests, give occasion for permissible limitation." . . . No such abuse or danger has been advanced in the present case. The appellees suggest no more than a possibility that the filing of fraudulent claims by unscrupulous claimants feigning religious objections to Saturday work might not only dilute the unemployment compensation fund but also hinder the scheduling by employers of necessary Saturday work. But that possibility is not apposite here because no such objection appears to have been made before the South Carolina Supreme Court, and we are unwilling to assess the importance of an asserted state interest without the views of the state court. Nor, if the contention had been made below, would the record appear to sustain it; there is no proof whatever to warrant such fears of malingering or deceit as those which the respondents now advance. Even if consideration of such evidence is not foreclosed by the prohibition against judicial inquiry into the truth or falsity of religious beliefs, *United States v. Ballard*, . . . it is highly doubtful whether such evidence would be sufficient to warrant a substantial infringement of religious liberties. For even if the possibility of spurious claims did threaten to dilute the fund and disrupt the scheduling of work, it would plainly be incumbent upon the appellees to demonstrate that no alternative forms of regulation would combat such abuses without infringing First Amendment rights. . . .

In these respects, then, the state interest asserted in the present case is wholly dissimilar to the interests which were found to justify the less direct burden upon religious practices in *Braunfeld v. Brown*. The Court recognized that the Sunday closing law which that decision sustained undoubtedly served "to make the practice of [the Orthodox Jewish merchants'] . . . religious beliefs more expensive." But the statute was nevertheless saved by a countervailing factor which finds no equivalent in the instant case—a strong state interest in providing one uniform day of rest for all workers. That secular objective could be achieved, the Court found, only by declaring Sunday to be that day of rest. Requiring exemptions for Sabbatarians, while theoretically possible, appeared to present an administrative problem of such magnitude, or to afford the exempted class so great a competitive advantage, that such a requirement would have rendered the entire statutory scheme unworkable. In the present case no such justifications underlie the determination of the state court that appellant's religion makes her ineligible to receive benefits. . . .

The judgment of the South Carolina Supreme Court is reversed and the case is remanded for further proceedings not inconsistent with this opinion.

It is so ordered.

MR. JUSTICE DOUGLAS, concurring.

The case we have for decision seems to me to be of small dimensions, though profoundly important. The question is whether the South Carolina law which denies unemployment compensation to a Seventh-day Adventist who, because of her religion, has declined to work on her Sabbath, is a law "prohibiting the free exercise" of religion as those words are used in the First Amendment. It seems obvious to me that this law does run afoul of that clause. . . .

Some have thought that a majority of a community can, through state action, compel a minority to observe their particular religious scruples so long as the majority's rule can be said to perform some valid secular function. That was the essence of the Court's decision in the Sunday Blue Law Cases . . . a ruling from which I then dissented and still dissent.

That ruling of the Court travels part of the distance that South Carolina asks us to go now. She asks us to hold that when it comes to a day of rest a Sabbatarian must conform with the scruples of the majority in order to obtain unemployment benefits.

The result turns not on the degree of injury, which may indeed be nonexistent by ordinary standards. The harm is the interference with the individual's scruples or conscience—an important area of privacy which the First Amendment fences off from government. The interference here is as plain as it is in Soviet Russia, where a churchgoer is given a second-class citizenship, resulting in harm though perhaps not in measurable damages. . . .

MR. JUSTICE STEWART, concurring in the result.

My . . . difference with the Court's opinion is that I cannot agree that today's decision can stand consistently with *Braunfeld v. Brown*. The Court says that there was a "less direct burden upon religious practices" in that case than in this. With all respect, I think the Court is mistaken, simply as a matter of fact. The *Braunfeld* case involved a state criminal statute. The undisputed effect of that statute, as pointed out by MR. JUSTICE BRENNAN in his dissenting opinion in that case, was that

"'Plaintiff, Abraham Braunfeld, will be unable to continue in his business if he may not stay open on Sunday and he will thereby lose his capital investment.' In other words, the issue in this case—and we do not understand either appellees or the Court to contend otherwise—is whether a State may put an individual to a choice between his business and his religion."

The impact upon the appellant's religious freedom in the present case is considerably less onerous. We deal here not with a criminal statute, but with the particularized administration of South Carolina's Unemployment

Compensation Act. Even upon the unlikely assumption that the appellant could not find suitable non-Saturday employment, the appellant at the worst would be denied a maximum of 22 weeks of compensation payments. I agree with the Court that the possibility of that denial is enough to infringe upon the appellant's constitutional right to the free exercise of her religion. But it is clear to me that in order to reach this conclusion the Court must explicitly reject the reasoning of *Braunfeld v. Brown.* I think the *Braunfeld* case was wrongly decided and should be overruled, and accordingly I concur in the result reached by the Court in the case before us.

MR. JUSTICE HARLAN, whom MR. JUSTICE WHITE joins, dissenting.

Today's decision is disturbing both in its rejection of existing precedent and in its implications for the future. . . .

. . . What the Court is holding is that if the State chooses to condition unemployment compensation on the applicant's availability for work, it is constitutionally compelled to *carve out an exception*—and to provide benefits—for those whose unavailability is due to their religious convictions. Such a holding has particular significance in two respects.

First, despite the Court's protestations to the contrary, the decision necessarily overrules *Braunfeld v. Brown,* which held that it did not offend the "Free Exercise" Clause of the Constitution for a State to forbid a Sabbatarian to do business on Sunday. The secular purpose of the statute before us today is even clearer than that involved in *Braunfeld.* And . . . the indirect financial burden of the present law is far less than that involved in *Braunfeld.* Forcing a store owner to close his business on Sunday may well have the effect of depriving him of a satisfactory livelihood if his religious convictions require him to close on Saturday as well. Here we are dealing only with temporary benefits, amounting to a fraction of regular weekly wages and running for not more than 22 weeks. Clearly, any differences between this case and *Braunfeld* cut against the present appellant.

Second, the implications of the present decision are far more troublesome than its apparently narrow dimensions would indicate at first glance. The meaning of today's holding, as already noted, is that the State must furnish unemployment benefits to one who is unavailable for work if the unavailability stems from the exercise of religious convictions. The State, in other words, must *single out* for financial assistance those whose behavior is religiously motivated, even though it denies such assistance to others whose identical behavior (in this case, inability to work on Saturdays) is not religiously motivated. . . .

. . . I cannot subscribe to the conclusion that the State is constitutionally compelled to carve out an exception to its general rule of eligibility in the present case. Those situations in which the Constitution may require special treatment on account of religion are, in my view, few and far between, and this view is amply supported by the course of constitutional litigation in this area. . . . Such compulsion in the present case is particularly inappropriate in light of the indirect, remote, and insubstantial effect of the decision below on the exercise of appellant's religion and in light of the direct financial assistance to religion that today's decision requires.

For these reasons I respectfully dissent from the opinion and judgment of the Court.

Brennan's majority opinion represents a significant break from past free exercise claims. No longer would a secular legislative purpose suffice; rather, under *Sherbert,* when the government enacts a law that burdens the free exercise of religion, it must show that it is protecting a compelling government interest and doing it in the least restrictive manner possible. How would the Court use this new standard? Many analysts believed that the compelling interest/least restrictive means approach would almost always result in a victory for the free exercise claimant. Governments would have to demonstrate that policies burdening religion are of sufficient magnitude to override the free exercise interest and that the policy is cast in the least restrictive manner possible. As indicated by *Sherbert,* this is a very difficult task.

Although the Warren Court ushered in a change in free exercise standards with its decisions in *Braunfeld* and *Sherbert,* it was left to the justices on the Court led by Warren's successor as chief justice, Warren Burger, to apply those standards, because under Earl Warren the Court heard very few free exercise cases after *Sherbert.*

The opportunity for the Burger Court to put its stamp on this area of the law arose early in the new chief justice's tenure. The case was *Wisconsin v. Yoder* (1972). As you read the excerpt from *Yoder,* consider how the Burger Court dealt with the standard it inherited from its predecessor. Do you detect any differences in approach? Or does Burger's opinion parallel Warren's in *Braunfeld* and Brennan's in *Sherbert?*

Wisconsin v. Yoder

406 U.S. 205 (1972)
http://laws.findlaw.com/US/406/205.html
Oral arguments are available at http://www.oyez.org.
Vote: 6 (Blackmun, Brennan, Burger, Marshall, Stewart, White)
  1 (Douglas)

OPINION OF THE COURT: *Burger*
CONCURRING OPINIONS: *Stewart, White*
DISSENTING IN PART: *Douglas*
NOT PARTICIPATING: *Powell, Rehnquist*

FACTS:

Like many states, Wisconsin had a compulsory education law, mandating that children attend public or private schools until the age of sixteen. This law violated the norms of the Old Order Amish, who were among the first religious groups to arrive in the United States. The Amish eschew technology, including automobiles and electricity, and they do not permit their children to attend public school after the eighth grade, believing that they will be adversely exposed "to worldly influences in terms of attitudes, goals, and values contrary to their beliefs." Instead, they prefer to educate their older children at home.

For several decades prior to the 1970s, the Amish had many skirmishes with education officials over this issue. In response to this history of hostility, a group of professors, lawyers, and clergy formed the National Committee for Amish Religious Freedom (NCARF) in 1967 to provide legal defense services for the Amish. NCARF's leaders included the general counsel of the American Jewish Committee, the dean of Boston University Law School, and the executive director of the Commission on Religious Liberty of the National Council of Churches.

Among the suits for which NCARF provided legal assistance was one concerning a controversy that emanated from New Glarus, Wisconsin, where the school district administrator brought criminal complaints against Jonas Yoder, Wallace Miller, and Adin Yutzy for removing their children (Frieda Yoder, Barbara Miller, and Vernon Yutzy) from school after they had completed the eighth grade. The Yoder and Miller families were part of the Old Order Amish community and Yutzy a member of the Conservative Amish Mennonite Church. The parents claimed that the compulsory attendance law violated their First and Fourteenth Amendment rights, but they were found guilty and each fined $5 by the county court. After being convicted in the lower courts, the Amish parents won their appeal at the Wisconsin Supreme Court. The state, however, requested that the decision be reviewed by the U.S. Supreme Court.

ARGUMENTS:

For the petitioner, State of Wisconsin:

- Compulsory education laws have existed in the United States since colonial times, and the courts have consistently upheld their validity.
- Under *Prince v. Massachusetts* (1943) the state has a compelling interest in protecting a child from the disease of ignorance. Additionally, the child has a right to an education.
- Without a formal education, those Amish who choose to leave their community later in life will enter the secular world without the intellectual tools to survive.

For the respondents, Jonas Yoder and the other Amish parents:

- Applying the compulsory education law to the Amish and their children interferes with their right to free exercise of religion.
- This dispute should be controlled by *Sherbert v. Verner* (1963), not *Prince v. Massachusetts* (1943).
- The Amish support education. The training their children receive at home is rigorous and appropriate for their agrarian lives. Exempting the Amish from the compulsory education law would not significantly interfere with the state's realizing its educational policy goals.

MR. CHIEF JUSTICE BURGER DELIVERED THE OPINION OF THE COURT.

On petition of the State of Wisconsin, we granted the writ of certiorari in this case to review a decision of the Wisconsin Supreme Court holding that respondents' convictions for violating the State's compulsory school-attendance law were invalid under the Free Exercise Clause of the First Amendment to the United States Constitution made applicable to the States by the Fourteenth Amendment. For the reasons hereafter stated we affirm the judgment of the Supreme Court of Wisconsin. . . .

Amish objection to formal education beyond the eighth grade is firmly grounded in . . . central religious concepts. They object to the high school, and higher education generally, because the values they teach are in marked variance with Amish values and the Amish way of life; they view secondary school education as an impermissible exposure of their children to a "worldly" influence in conflict with their beliefs. The high school tends to emphasize intellectual and scientific accomplishments, self-distinction, competitiveness, worldly success, and social life with other students. Amish society emphasizes informal learning-through-doing; a life of "goodness," rather than a life of intellect; wisdom, rather than technical knowledge; community welfare, rather than competition; and separation from, rather than integration with, contemporary worldly society.

Formal high school education beyond the eighth grade is contrary to Amish beliefs, not only because it places Amish children in an environment hostile to Amish beliefs with increasing emphasis on competition in class work and sports and with pressure to conform to the styles, manners, and ways of the peer group, but also because it takes them away from their community, physically and emotionally, during the crucial and formative adolescent period of life. During this period, the children must acquire Amish attitudes favoring manual work and self-reliance and the specific skills needed to perform the adult role of an Amish farmer or housewife. . . .

The Amish do not object to elementary education through the first eight grades as a general proposition because they agree that their children must have basic skills in the "three R's" in order to read the Bible, to be good farmers and citizens, and to be able to deal with non-Amish people when necessary in the course of daily affairs. They view such a basic education as acceptable because it does not significantly expose their children to worldly values or interfere with their development in the Amish community during the crucial adolescent period. While Amish accept compulsory elementary education generally, wherever possible they have established their own elementary schools in many respects like the small local schools of the past. In the Amish belief higher learning tends to develop values they reject as influences that alienate man from God. . . .

There is no doubt as to the power of a State, having a high responsibility for education of its citizens, to impose reasonable regulations for the control and duration of basic education. . . . [But] a State's interest in universal education, however highly we rank it, is not totally free from a balancing process when it impinges on fundamental rights and interests, such as those specifically protected by the Free Exercise Clause of the First Amendment, and the traditional interest of parents with respect to the religious upbringing of their children so long as they . . . "prepare them for additional obligations."

It follows that in order for Wisconsin to compel school attendance beyond the eighth grade against a claim that such attendance interferes with the practice of a legitimate religious belief, it must appear either that the State does not deny the free exercise of religious belief by its requirement, or that there is a state interest of sufficient magnitude to override the interest claiming protection under the Free Exercise Clause. . . .

The essence of all that has been said and written on the subject is that only those interests of the highest order and those not otherwise served can overbalance legitimate claims of free exercise of religion. We can accept it as settled, therefore, that, however strong the State's interest in universal compulsory education, it is by no means absolute to the exclusion or subordination of all other interests. *E.g., Sherbert v. Verner* (1963). . . .

We come then to the quality of the claims of the respondents concerning the alleged encroachment of Wisconsin's compulsory school-attendance statute on their rights and the rights of their children to the free exercise of the religious beliefs they and their forebears have adhered to for almost three centuries. In evaluating those claims we must be careful to determine whether the Amish religion and their mode of life are, as they claim, inseparable and interdependent. A way of life, however virtuous and admirable, may not be interposed as a barrier to reasonable state regulation of education if it is based on purely secular considerations: to have the protection of the Religion Clauses, the claims must be rooted in religious belief. . . .

Giving no weight to . . . secular considerations . . . we see that the record in this case abundantly supports the claim that the traditional way of life of the Amish is not merely a matter of personal preference, but one of deep religious conviction, shared by an organized group, and intimately related to daily living. . . .

. . . The conclusion is inescapable that secondary schooling, by exposing Amish children to worldly influences in terms of attitudes, goals, and values contrary to beliefs, and by substantially interfering with the religious development of the Amish child and his integration into the way of life of the Amish faith community at the crucial adolescent stage of development, contravenes the basic religious tenets and practice of the Amish faith, both as to the parent and the child. . . .

In sum . . . the State's requirement of compulsory formal education after the eighth grade would gravely endanger if not destroy the free exercise of respondents' religious beliefs.

Neither the findings of the trial court nor the Amish claims as to the nature of their faith are challenged in this Court by the State of Wisconsin. Its position is that the State's interest in universal compulsory formal secondary education to age 16 is so great that it is paramount to the undisputed claims of respondents that their mode of preparing their youth for Amish life, after the traditional elementary education, is an essential part of their religious belief and practice. Nor does the State undertake to meet the claim that the Amish mode of life and education is inseparable from and a part of the basic tenets of their religion—indeed, as much a part of their religious belief and practices as baptism, the confessional, or a sabbath may be for others.

Wisconsin concedes that under the Religion Clauses religious beliefs are absolutely free from the State's control, but it argues that "actions," even though religiously grounded, are outside the protection of the First Amendment. But our decisions have rejected the idea that religiously grounded conduct is always outside the protection of the Free Exercise Clause. . . . This case, therefore, does not become easier because respondents were convicted for their "actions" in refusing to send their children to the public high school; in this context belief and action cannot be neatly confined in logic-tight compartments. . . .

Nor can this case be disposed of on the grounds that Wisconsin's requirement for school attendance to age 16 applies uniformly to all citizens of the State and does not, on its face, discriminate against religions or a particular religion, or that it is motivated by legitimate secular concerns. A regulation neutral on its face may, in its application, nonetheless offend the constitutional requirement for governmental neutrality if it unduly burdens free exercise of religion. *Sherbert v. Verner*. . . .

We turn, then, to the State's broader contention that its interest in its system of compulsory education is so compelling that even the established religious practices of the Amish must give way. Where fundamental claims of religious freedom are at stake, however, we cannot accept such a sweeping claim; despite its admitted validity in the generality of cases, we must searchingly examine the interests that the State seeks to promote by its requirement for compulsory education to age 16, and the impediment to those objectives that would flow from recognizing the claimed Amish exemption. . . .

The State advances two primary arguments in support of its system of compulsory education. It notes . . . that some degree of education is necessary to prepare citizens to participate effectively and intelligently in our open political system if we are to preserve freedom and independence. Further, education prepares individuals to be self-reliant and self-sufficient. We accept these propositions.

However, the evidence adduced by the Amish in this case is persuasively to the effect that an additional one or two years of formal high school for Amish children in place of their long-established program of informal vocational education would do little to serve those interests. . . . It is one thing to say that compulsory education for a year or two beyond the eighth grade may be necessary when its goal is the preparation of the child for life in modern society as the majority live, but it is quite another if the goal of education be viewed as the preparation of the child for life in the separated agrarian community that is the keystone of the Amish faith. . . .

The State attacks respondents' position as one fostering "ignorance" from which the child must be protected by the State. No one can question the State's duty to protect children from ignorance but this argument does not square with the facts disclosed in the record. Whatever their idiosyncrasies as seen by the majority, this record strongly shows that the Amish community has been a highly successful social unit within our society, even if apart from the conventional "mainstream." Its members are productive and very law- abiding members of society. . . .

Insofar as the State's claim rests on the view that a brief additional period of formal education is imperative to enable the Amish to participate effectively and intelligently in our democratic process, it must fall. The Amish alternative to formal secondary school education has enabled them to function effectively in their day-to-day life under self-imposed limitations on relations with the world, and to survive and prosper in contemporary society as a separate, sharply identifiable and highly self-sufficient community for more than 200 years in this country. In itself this is strong evidence that they are capable of fulfilling the social and political responsibilities of citizenship without compelled attendance beyond the eighth grade at the price of jeopardizing their free exercise of religious belief. When Thomas Jefferson emphasized the need for education as a bulwark of a free people against tyranny, there is nothing to indicate he had in mind compulsory education through any fixed age beyond a basic education. Indeed, the Amish communities singularly parallel and reflect many of the virtues of Jefferson's ideal of the "sturdy yeoman" who would form the basis of what he considered as the ideal of a democratic society. Even their idiosyncratic separateness exemplifies the diversity we profess to admire and encourage. . . .

Finally, the State, on authority of *Prince v. Massachusetts*, argues that a decision exempting Amish children from the State's requirement fails to recognize the substantive right of the Amish child to a secondary education, and fails to give due regard to the power of the State as *parens patriae* to extend the benefit of secondary education to children regardless of the wishes of their parents. Taken at its broadest sweep, the Court's language in *Prince* might be read to give support to the State's position. However, the Court was not confronted in *Prince* with a situation comparable to that of the Amish as revealed in this record; this is shown by the Court's severe characterization of the evils that it thought the legislature could legitimately associate with child labor, even when performed in the company of an adult. . . .

This case, of course, is not one in which any harm to the physical or mental health of the child or to the public safety, peace, order, or welfare has been demonstrated or may be properly inferred. The record is to the contrary, and any reliance on that theory would find no support in the evidence. . . .

For the reasons stated we hold, with the Supreme Court of Wisconsin, that the First and Fourteenth Amendments prevent the State from compelling respondents to cause their children to attend formal high school to age 16. Our disposition of this case, however, in no way alters our recognition of the obvious fact that courts are not school boards or legislatures, and are ill-equipped to determine the "necessity" of discrete aspects of a State's program of compulsory education. This should suggest that courts must move with great circumspection in performing the sensitive and delicate task of weighing a State's legitimate social concern when faced with religious claims for exemption from generally applicable educational requirements. . . .

Affirmed.

MR. JUSTICE WHITE with whom MR. JUSTICE BRENNAN and MR. JUSTICE STEWART join, concurring.
Cases such as this one inevitably call for a delicate balancing of important but conflicting interests. I join the opinion and judgment of the Court because I cannot say that the State's interest in requiring two more years of compulsory education in the ninth and tenth grades outweighs the importance of the concededly sincere Amish religious practice to the survival of that sect.

This would be a very different case for me if respondents' claim were that their religion forbade their children from attending any school at any time and from complying in any way with the educational standards set by the State. Since the Amish children are permitted to acquire the basic tools of literacy to survive in modern society by attending grades one through eight, and since the deviation from the State's compulsory education law is relatively slight, I conclude that respondents' claim must prevail. . . .

. . . *Pierce v. Society of Sisters* (1925) lends no support to the contention that parents may replace state educational requirements with their own idiosyncratic views of what knowledge a child needs to be a productive and happy member of society. . . . A State has a legitimate interest not only in seeking to develop the latent talents of its children, but also in seeking to prepare them for the lifestyle that they may later choose, or at least to provide them with an option other than the life they have led in the past. In the circumstances of this case, although the question is close, I am unable to say that the State has demonstrated that Amish children who leave school in the eighth grade will be intellectually stultified or unable to acquire new academic skills later. The statutory minimum school attendance age set by the State is, after all, only 16.

. . . I join the Court because the sincerity of the Amish religious policy here is uncontested, because the potentially adverse impact of the state requirement is great, and because the State's valid interest in education has already been largely satisfied by the eight years the children have already spent in school.

MR. JUSTICE DOUGLAS, dissenting in part.
I agree with the Court that the religious scruples of the Amish are opposed to the education of their children beyond the grade schools, yet I disagree with the Court's conclusion that the matter is within the dispensation of parents alone. The Court's analysis assumes that the only interests at stake in the case are those of the Amish parents on the one hand, and those of the State on the other. The difficulty with this approach is that, despite the Court's claim, the parents are seeking to vindicate not only their own free exercise claims, but also those of their high-school-age children. . . .

. . . [N]o analysis of religious-liberty claims can take place in a vacuum. If the parents in this case are allowed religious exemption, the inevitable effect is to impose the parents' notions of religious duty upon their children. Where the child is mature enough to express potential conflicting desires, it would be an invasion of the child's rights to permit such an imposition without canvassing his views. . . . As the child has no other effective forum, it is in this litigation that his rights should be considered. And, if an Amish child desires to attend high school, and is mature enough to have that desire respected, the State may well be able to override the parents' religiously motivated objections.

What are we to make of Chief Justice Burger's first major statement on the free exercise of religion? He cited *Sherbert* with approval and invoked its approach to find that the state's interest was not sufficiently compelling to outweigh the free exercise claim. That Burger found for the religious claimants lends support to those analysts who argue that the *Sherbert* standard would almost always lead to such a conclusion. But some scholars maintain that Burger grounded his opinion on respect for the history and the practices of the Amish rather than the logic of *Sherbert.* If Burger had followed such a course, he would not be the first nor probably the last to do so. Remember Chief Justice Waite's opinion in *Reynolds*? Did it not rest as much on the Court's perception of the Mormons as a strange and bizarre sect as it did on legal factors?

Whatever Burger's motivation, it looked as if the Court would continue to apply the compelling interest standard to free exercise claims. Less than a decade after *Yoder,* the justices decided **Thomas v. Review Board of Indiana Employment Security Division** (1981), the facts of which bore a marked resemblance to *Sherbert.* Eddie Thomas was a Jehovah's Witness who worked in a steel mill. When the owners closed the mill down, they transferred Thomas to another plant. Because his new job required him to make tanks for use by the military, Thomas quit on religious grounds and filed for unemployment benefits, which the state denied. Writing for the Court, Burger acknowledged the parallels between *Sherbert* and this dispute: "Here, as in *Sherbert,* the employee was put to a choice between fidelity to his religious beliefs or cessation of work; the coercive impact on Thomas is indistinguishable from *Sherbert.*" Accordingly, he said, "Unless we are prepared to overrule *Sherbert,* Thomas can not be denied the benefits due him."

Two years after *Thomas,* in **Bob Jones University v. United States** (1983), the Supreme Court examined yet another free exercise question: May the government punish a sectarian institution for its religiously divined racist policy? Bob Jones University was not affiliated with any religious denomination but described itself as "dedicated to the teaching and propagation of . . . fundamentalist Christian beliefs." These beliefs included, among others, a strong prohibition

against interracial dating and marriage. To enforce this particular tenet, the school excluded African Americans until 1971, when it began to accept applications from married blacks only. Litigation forced the school to begin admitting unmarried blacks in 1976, but only if they adhered to a strict set of rules; for example, interracial dating or marriage would lead to expulsion. The school continued to deny admission to individuals in interracial marriages. The Internal Revenue Service (IRS) revoked Bob Jones's tax-exempt status on the ground that the school's policies were racist. The university challenged the decision, saying that the IRS action punished the practice of religious beliefs. When the case reached the Court, one of the issues for the justices to decide was whether the government's interest in prohibiting race discrimination was sufficiently compelling to abridge free exercise guarantees.

Writing for the Court, Burger applied the compelling interest/least restrictive means standard of *Sherbert* to rule against Bob Jones:

The governmental interest at stake here is compelling. . . . [T]he government has a fundamental, overriding interest in eradicating racial discrimination in education—discrimination that prevailed . . . for the first 165 years of this Nation's constitutional history. That governmental interest substantially outweighs whatever burden denial of tax benefits places on petitioners' exercise of their religious beliefs. The interests asserted by petitioners cannot be accommodated with that compelling governmental interest, and no "less restrictive means" are available to achieve the governmental interest.

Burger also noted that this policy—unlike the one at issue in *Yoder*—would not prevent Bob Jones from practicing its religion. Seen in this way, the IRS policy was more akin to Sunday closing laws. In *Braunfeld,* Warren acknowledged that blue laws would place an economic burden on some Orthodox Jews but would not stop them from practicing their religion. In this case Burger wrote: "Denial of tax benefits will inevitably have a substantial impact on the operation of private religious schools, but will not prevent these schools from observing their religious tenets."

Bob Jones is also interesting because it demonstrates the Court's use of the compelling interest/least restrictive means standard to uphold a government policy that allegedly infringes on the free exercise of religion. The eradication of racism, in the eyes of the justices, is a compelling government objective.

Demise of *Sherbert-Yoder* and Adoption of the Smith Test

Despite the Burger Court's application of the compelling interest standard in *Bob Jones,* signs began to appear in the early to mid-1980s that some of the justices wanted to rethink that standard or at least make it easier for the state to respond to free exercise challenges. ***United States v. Lee***—decided in 1982, a year before *Bob Jones*—was the first of these signs.

Edwin Lee, a member of the Amish faith, owned a farm and a carpentry shop. In violation of federal law, he refused to withhold Social Security taxes or pay the employer's share of those taxes, arguing that the payment of taxes and the receipt of Social Security benefits violated his religious beliefs. To support his argument, Lee's attorneys pointed out that Congress had provided a Social Security tax exemption to self-employed Amish. Although Lee did not fall under that specific exemption—he employed others—the very existence of the exemption demonstrated Congress's sensitivity toward the Amish.

In a short opinion for the Court, Burger disagreed. To be sure, he conceded, "compulsory participation" in the Social Security system interferes with the free exercise rights of the Amish. But the government was able to justify that burden on religion by showing that compulsory participation is "essential to accomplish an overriding governmental interest" in the maintenance of the Social Security system. As Burger put it: "To maintain an organized society that guarantees religious freedom to a great variety of faiths requires that some religious practices yield to the common good."

Some critics cite *Lee* as the first sign that the Court was about to back away from the *Sherbert-Yoder* standard. These observers were unconvinced that Burger had adequately justified how it was consistent under *Sherbert-Yoder* to exempt the Amish from compulsory education laws but compel them to comply with the requirements of the Social Security system.

Goldman v. Weinberger (1986), one of the last major free exercise cases of the Burger Court era, did little to dispel these and other suspicions about the direction the Court was taking. S. Simcha Goldman, an Orthodox Jew, was an ordained rabbi and a captain in the U.S. Air Force. He was stationed at March Air Force Base in Riverside, California, as a clinical psychologist in the base hospital. From the time Goldman began his service at the base, he wore a yarmulke (skull cap) while in and out of uniform. Goldman did so because his religion requires its male adherents to keep their heads covered at all times.

After a superior told him that the yarmulke violated Air Force Dress Code Regulation (AFR) 35-10, a 190-page regulation that describes in minute detail all of the various items of apparel that constitute the Air Force uniform, Goldman brought suit against the U.S. secretary of defense, arguing that the regulation violated his First Amendment free exercise rights. A U.S. district court judge agreed, but a panel of judges on the U.S. Court of Appeals for the District of Columbia circuit reversed.

Following the rejection by the court of appeals, Goldman brought the case to the Supreme Court. There, his attorneys argued that Goldman's conduct was of a nonintrusive nature that "interferes with no one else, does not harm the public health, and imposes no burden on accommodation." They were attempting to show that Goldman's behavior was markedly different from religious activities the Court had allowed the government to regulate in *Reynolds* and *Prince.* They also maintained that the Air Force lacked any overriding government interest that would justify this intrusion into Goldman's religious practice.

The government's response was that "there can be no serious doubt that uniform dress and appearance standards serve the military interest in maintaining discipline, morale, and esprit de corps" and that enforcement of the dress code "is a necessary means to the undeniably critical ends of molding soldiers into an effective fighting force." The government also urged the justices to consider what might happen if the Air Force allowed Goldman to wear his yarmulke: followers of other religions could request exemptions to wear turbans, dreadlocks, saffron robes, and so forth.

Writing for the majority, Justice William Rehnquist agreed with the government and ruled against Goldman. His opinion emphasized that the military is a specialized society separate from civilian society. To be successful the military requires a subordination of individual desires to the needs of the service. Further, he noted that the courts have traditionally and wisely given wide deference to the military to set standards of conduct necessary to achieve the military's goals.

The Court's decision in *Goldman* fueled debate in political and academic circles. Taking up an invitation issued by Justice Brennan in a dissenting opinion— "The Court and the military have refused these servicemen their constitutional rights; we must hope that

Congress will correct this wrong"—Congress passed legislation in 1987 allowing members of the armed forces "to wear an item of religious apparel while in uniform" so long as the item is "neat and conservative" and does not "interfere with the performance" of military duties.

Academic and legal debate centered on the rationale the Court invoked to resolve *Goldman.* Was *Goldman* a substantial break from the *Sherbert-Yoder* standard? Clearly, the four dissenters saw it that way. Justice Sandra Day O'Connor's opinion is particularly interesting. After noting that Court cases in this area adopted slightly different versions of a similar standard, she set out the "two consistent themes" running through precedent from *Sherbert* to *Lee.* First, the government "must show that an unusually important interest is at stake, whether or not that interest is denominated 'compelling.'" Second, "the government must show that granting the requested exemption will do substantial harm to that interest, whether by showing that the means adopted is the 'least restrictive' or 'essential.'" O'Connor saw no reason to jettison this two-pronged standard—as she thought the majority had done in *Goldman*—simply because the military was involved.

In contrast, some scholars (along with a few members of the Court) did not think *Goldman* represented a significant shift in the Court's jurisprudence. They argued that *Goldman* was an exceptional case: it involved the interests of the armed forces, interests to which the justices traditionally defer. Accordingly, they asserted that the Court would return to the compelling interest/least restrictive means standard in future cases.

Predictions about a return to the *Sherbert-Yoder* standard proved to be inaccurate. In 1986 William Rehnquist, the author of the majority opinion in *Goldman,* became chief justice. Rehnquist's promotion was quickly followed by the appointments of conservative justices Antonin Scalia and Anthony Kennedy. This shift in the ideological balance of the Court set the stage for a serious rethinking of the Court's free exercise jurisprudence.

In 1990 the justices not only reconsidered their previous free exercise rulings but also completely rejected the *Sherbert-Yoder* standard. In *Employment Division, Department of Human Resources of Oregon v. Smith* (1990) the Court seemed to turn its back on nearly three decades of free exercise cases and adopt a new standard. How did the majority justify its position? Do you find its logic compelling? Keep these questions in mind as you read about this highly controversial case.

Employment Division, Department of Human Resources of Oregon v. Smith

494 U.S. 872 (1990)
http://laws.findlaw.com/US/494/872.html
Oral arguments are available at http://www.oyez.org.
Vote: 6 (Kennedy, O'Connor, Rehnquist, Scalia, Stevens, White)
3 (Blackmun, Brennan, Marshall)

OPINION OF THE COURT: *Scalia*
CONCURRING OPINION: *O'Connor*
DISSENTING OPINION: *Blackmun*

FACTS:

This case centers on the use of peyote, which is illegal to possess in Oregon unless it is prescribed by a doctor. Peyote is a hallucinogen produced by certain cactus plants found in the southwestern United States and northern Mexico. Unlike other hallucinogenic drugs, such as LSD, peyote has never been widely used or deemed especially problematic. One reason is that peyote users ingest the drug by eating the buds of the cactus, which have an unpleasant taste and also frequently cause nausea and vomiting. The members of one group, however, use peyote on a regular basis as part of the practice of their bona fide religion—the Native American Church. To members of this church, peyote is a sacramental substance, necessary for religious rituals. Twenty-three states (all with large Native American populations), as well as the federal government, allow religious use of peyote even though the substance is criminalized for nonreligious uses. The federal government even provides licenses to grow peyote for sacramental purposes.

The dispute at issue in *Smith* arose when two members of the Native American Church, Alfred Smith and Galen Black, were fired from their jobs as counselors at a private drug and alcohol abuse clinic after they used peyote at a religious ceremony. The men applied for unemployment benefits, but the state turned them down because they had been fired for "misconduct," which made them ineligible for benefits under state law.

Smith and Black brought suit in state court, citing the Court's holdings in *Sherbert* and *Thomas.* The issue, they argued, was not that the state had criminalized peyote (they were not charged with any crime) but that the state had denied them unemployment benefits for refusing to give up a religious practice. Oregon argued that it could deny the benefits, regardless of Smith and Black's free exercise claim, because the use of peyote was prohibited by a general criminal statute that did not target any religion. The state also pointed out that it had a compelling interest in regulating drug use and that the state's law represented the least intrusive means of doing that.

The Oregon Supreme Court thought otherwise, relying on *Sherbert* and *Thomas* to find in favor of the fired employees. The state appealed to the U.S. Supreme Court, which heard arguments in the case in 1987. After the Court remanded the case to Oregon to decide a preliminary issue, the case came back to the Court in 1990, where both sides assumed that the Court would use the *Sherbert* standard to resolve the dispute.

ARGUMENTS:

For the petitioner, the Employment Division of the Department of Human Resources of the state of Oregon:

- The state has a compelling interest in controlling the use and availability of dangerous drugs.
- Peyote is a dangerous drug.
- The state cannot accommodate religiously motivated drug use without seriously compromising its drug control policies.

For the respondents, Alfred Smith and Galen Black:

- The petitioners are entitled to unemployment compensation under such precedents as *Sherbert v. Verner* (1963) and *Thomas v. Review Board* (1981).
- The experience of other states that have exempted religious use of peyote has not shown any adverse impact on drug enforcement policies.
- The free exercise clause requires that the religious practices of the respondents be accommodated.

JUSTICE SCALIA DELIVERED THE OPINION OF THE COURT.

The free exercise of religion means, first and foremost, the right to believe and profess whatever religious doctrine one desires. Thus, the First Amendment obviously excludes all "governmental regulation of religious *beliefs* as such." . . .

But the "exercise of religion" often involves not only belief and profession but the performance of (or abstention from) physical acts: assembling with others for a worship service, participating in sacramental use of bread and wine, proselytizing, abstaining from certain foods or certain modes of transportation. It would be true, we think (though no case of ours has involved the point), that a state would be "prohibiting the free exercise [of religion]" if it sought to ban such acts or abstentions

only when they are engaged in for religious reasons, or only because of the religious belief that they display. It would doubtless be unconstitutional, for example, to ban the casting of "statues that are to be used for worship purposes," or to prohibit bowing down before a golden calf.

Respondents in the present case, however, seek to carry the meaning of "prohibiting the free exercise [of religion]" one large step further. They contend that their religious motivation for using peyote places them beyond the reach of a criminal law that is not specifically directed at their religious practice, and that is concededly constitutional as applied to those who use the drug for other reasons. . . .

. . . We have never held that an individual's religious beliefs excuse him from compliance with an otherwise valid law prohibiting conduct that the State is free to regulate. On the contrary, the record of more than a century of our free exercise jurisprudence contradicts that proposition. . . . We first had occasion to assert that principle in *Reynolds v. United States* (1879), where we rejected the claim that criminal laws against polygamy could not be constitutionally applied to those whose religion commanded the practice. . . .

Subsequent decisions have consistently held that the right of free exercise does not relieve an individual of the obligation to comply with a "valid and neutral law of general applicability on the ground that the law proscribes (or prescribes) conduct that his religion prescribes (or proscribes)." *United States v. Lee* (1982). . . . In *Prince v. Massachusetts* (1944) we held that a mother could be prosecuted under the child labor laws for using her children to dispense literature in the streets, her religious motivation notwithstanding. We found no constitutional infirmity in "excluding [these children] from doing there what no other children may do." In *Braunfeld v. Brown* (1961) (plurality opinion) we upheld Sunday-closing laws against the claim that they burdened the religious practices of persons whose religions compelled them to refrain from work on other days. . . .

The only decisions in which we have held that the First Amendment bars application of a neutral, generally applicable law to religiously motivated action have involved not the Free Exercise Clause alone, but the Free Exercise Clause in conjunction with other constitutional protections, such as freedom of speech and of the press, see *Cantwell v. Connecticut,* . . . *Pierce v. Society of Sisters,* . . . *Wisconsin v. Yoder.* . . .

The present case does not present such a hybrid situation, but a free exercise claim unconnected with any communicative activity or parental right. Respondents urge us to hold, quite simply, that when otherwise prohibitable conduct is accompanied by religious convictions, not only the convictions but the conduct itself must be free from governmental regulation. We have never held that, and decline to do so now. There being no contention that Oregon's drug law represents an attempt to regulate religious beliefs, the communication of religious beliefs, or the raising of one's children in those beliefs, the rule to which we have adhered ever since *Reynolds* plainly controls. "Our cases do not at their farthest reach support the proposition that a stance of conscientious opposition relieves an objector from any colliding duty fixed by a democratic government." . . .

Respondents argue that even though exemption from generally applicable criminal laws need not automatically be extended to religiously motivated actors, at least the claim for a religious exemption must be evaluated under the balancing test set forth in *Sherbert v. Verner* (1963). Under the *Sherbert* test, governmental actions that substantially burden a religious practice must be justified by a compelling governmental interest. . . . Applying that test we have, on three occasions, invalidated state unemployment compensation rules that conditioned the availability of benefits upon an applicant's willingness to work under conditions forbidden by his religion. See *Sherbert v. Verner; Thomas v. Review Bd. of Indiana Employment Security Div.* (1981); *Hobbie v. Unemployment Appeals Comm'n of Florida* (1987). We have never invalidated any governmental action on the basis of the *Sherbert* test except the denial of unemployment compensation. Although we have sometimes purported to apply the *Sherbert* test in contexts other than that, we have always found the test satisfied. . . . In recent years we have abstained from applying the *Sherbert* test (outside the unemployment compensation field) at all. . . . In *Goldman v. Weinberger* (1986) we rejected application of the *Sherbert* test to military dress regulations that forbade the wearing of yarmulkes. . . .

Even if we were inclined to breathe into *Sherbert* some life beyond the unemployment compensation field, we would not apply it to require exemptions from a generally applicable criminal law. The *Sherbert* test, it must be recalled, was developed in a context that lent itself to individualized governmental assessment of the reasons for the relevant conduct. . . .

Whether or not the decisions are that limited, they at least have nothing to do with an across-the-board

criminal prohibition on a particular form of conduct. Although, as noted earlier, we have sometimes used the *Sherbert* test to analyze free exercise challenges to such laws . . . we have never applied the test to invalidate one. We conclude today that the sounder approach, and the approach in accord with the vast majority of our precedents, is to hold the test inapplicable to such challenges. The government's ability to enforce generally applicable prohibitions of socially harmful conduct, like its ability to carry out other aspects of public policy, "cannot depend on measuring the effects of a governmental action on a religious objector's spiritual development." . . . To make an individual's obligation to obey such a law contingent upon the law's coincidence with his religious beliefs, except where the State's interest is "compelling"—permitting him, by virtue of his beliefs, "to become a law unto himself," *Reynolds v. United States*—contradicts both constitutional tradition and common sense.

The "compelling government interest" requirement seems benign, because it is familiar from other fields. But using it as the standard that must be met before the government may accord different treatment on the basis of race . . . or before the government may regulate the content of speech . . . is not remotely comparable to using it for the purpose asserted here. What it produces in those other fields—equality of treatment and an unrestricted flow of contending speech—are constitutional norms; what it would produce here—a private right to ignore generally applicable laws—is a constitutional anomaly.

Nor is it possible to limit the impact of respondents' proposal by requiring a "compelling state interest" only when the conduct prohibited is "central" to the individual's religion. . . . It is no more appropriate for judges to determine the "centrality" of religious beliefs before applying a "compelling interest" test in the free exercise field, than it would be for them to determine the "importance" of ideas before applying the "compelling interest" test in the free speech field. What principle of law or logic can be brought to bear to contradict a believer's assertion that a particular act is "central" to his personal faith? Judging the centrality of different religious practices is akin to the unacceptable "business of evaluating the relative merits of differing religious claims." . . . Repeatedly and in many different contexts, we have warned that courts must not presume to determine the place of a particular belief in a religion or the plausibility of a religious claim. . . .

If the "compelling interest" test is to be applied at all, then, it must be applied across the board, to all actions thought to be religiously commanded. Moreover, if "compelling interest" really means what it says (and watering it down here would subvert its rigor in the other fields where it is applied), many laws will not meet the test. Any society adopting such a system would be courting anarchy, but that danger increases in direct proportion to the society's diversity of religious beliefs, and its determination to coerce or suppress none of them. Precisely because "we are a cosmopolitan nation made up of people of almost every conceivable religious preference," *Braunfeld v. Brown,* and precisely because we value and protect that religious divergence, we cannot afford the luxury of deeming presumptively invalid, as applied to the religious objector, every regulation of conduct that does not protect an interest of the highest order. The rule respondents favor would open the prospect of constitutionally required religious exemptions from civic obligations of almost every conceivable kind—ranging from compulsory military service . . . to the payment of taxes . . . to health and safety regulation such as manslaughter and child neglect laws . . . compulsory vaccination laws . . . drug laws . . . and traffic laws . . . to social welfare legislation such as minimum wage laws . . . child labor laws . . . animal cruelty laws . . . environmental protection laws . . . and laws providing for equality of opportunity for the races. . . . The First Amendment's protection of religious liberty does not require this.

Values that are protected against government interference through enshrinement in the Bill of Rights are not thereby banished from the political process. Just as a society that believes in the negative protection accorded to the press by the First Amendment is likely to enact laws that affirmatively foster the dissemination of the printed word, so also a society that believes in the negative protection accorded to religious belief can be expected to be solicitous of that value in its legislation as well. It is therefore not surprising that a number of States have made an exception to their drug laws for sacramental peyote use. . . . But to say that a nondiscriminatory religious-practice exemption is permitted, or even that it is desirable, is not to say that it is constitutionally required, and that the appropriate occasions for its creation can be discerned by the courts. It may fairly be said that leaving accommodation to the political process will place at a relative disadvantage those religious practices that are not widely engaged in; but

that unavoidable consequence of democratic government must be preferred to a system in which each conscience is a law unto itself or in which judges weigh the social importance of all laws against the centrality of all religious beliefs.

Because respondents' ingestion of peyote was prohibited under Oregon law, and because that prohibition is constitutional, Oregon may, consistent with the Free Exercise Clause, deny respondents unemployment compensation when their dismissal results from use of the drug. The decision of the Oregon Supreme Court is accordingly reversed.

It is so ordered.

JUSTICE O'CONNOR, with whom JUSTICE BRENNAN, JUSTICE MARSHALL, and JUSTICE BLACKMUN join as to Parts I and II, concurring in the judgment. [JUSTICE BRENNAN, JUSTICE MARSHALL, and JUSTICE BLACKMUN join as to Parts I and II of this opinion, but they do not concur in the judgment.]

Although I agree with the result the Court reaches in this case, I cannot join its opinion. In my view, today's holding dramatically departs from well-settled First Amendment jurisprudence, appears unnecessary to resolve the question presented, and is incompatible with our Nation's fundamental commitment to individual religious liberty.

[Part I, a short clarification of the issue before the Court, is omitted.]

II

The Court today extracts from our long history of free exercise precedents the single categorical rule that "if prohibiting the exercise of religion . . . is . . . merely the incidental effect of a generally applicable and otherwise valid provision, the First Amendment has not been offended." Indeed, the Court holds that where the law is a generally applicable criminal prohibition, our usual free exercise jurisprudence does not even apply. To reach this sweeping result, however, the Court must not only give a strained reading of the First Amendment but must also disregard our consistent application of free exercise doctrine to cases involving generally applicable regulations that burden religious conduct.

The Free Exercise Clause of the First Amendment commands that "Congress shall make no law . . . prohibiting the free exercise [of religion]." In *Cantwell v.*

Connecticut (1940) we held that this prohibition applies to the States by incorporation into the Fourteenth Amendment and that it categorically forbids government regulation of religious beliefs. As the Court recognizes, however, the "free exercise" of religion often, if not invariably, requires the performance of (or abstention from) certain acts. . . . Because the First Amendment does not distinguish between religious belief and religious conduct, conduct motivated by sincere religious belief, like the belief itself, must be at least presumptively protected by the Free Exercise Clause.

The Court today, however, interprets the Clause to permit the government to prohibit, without justification, conduct mandated by an individual's religious beliefs, so long as that prohibition is generally applicable. But a law that prohibits certain conduct—conduct that happens to be an act of worship for someone—manifestly does prohibit that person's free exercise of his religion. A person who is barred from engaging in religiously motivated conduct is barred from freely exercising his religion. Moreover, that person is barred from freely exercising his religion regardless of whether the law prohibits the conduct only when engaged in for religious reasons, only by members of that religion, or by all persons. It is difficult to deny that a law that prohibits religiously motivated conduct, even if the law is generally applicable, does not at least implicate First Amendment concerns.

The Court responds that generally applicable laws are "one large step" removed from laws aimed at specific religious practices. The First Amendment, however, does not distinguish between laws that are generally applicable and laws that target particular religious practices. Indeed, few States would be so naive as to enact a law directly prohibiting or burdening a religious practice as such. Our free exercise cases have all concerned generally applicable laws that had the effect of significantly burdening a religious practice. If the First Amendment is to have any vitality, it ought not be construed to cover only the extreme and hypothetical situation in which a State directly targets a religious practice. . . .

To say that a person's right to free exercise has been burdened, of course, does not mean that he has an absolute right to engage in the conduct. Under our established First Amendment jurisprudence, we have recognized that the freedom to act, unlike the freedom to believe, cannot be absolute. See, e.g., *Cantwell; Reynolds v. United States* (1879). Instead, we have respected both the First Amendment's express textual mandate and the governmental interest in regulation of conduct by requiring the government to justify any substantial burden on religiously motivated conduct by a compelling state interest and by means narrowly tailored to achieve that interest. . . .

The Court attempts to support its narrow reading of the Clause by claiming that "[w]e have never held that an individual's religious beliefs excuse him from compliance with an otherwise valid law prohibiting conduct that the State is free to regulate." But as the Court later notes, as it must, in cases such as *Cantwell* and *Yoder* we have in fact interpreted the Free Exercise Clause to forbid application of a generally applicable prohibition to religiously motivated conduct. . . . Indeed, in *Yoder* we expressly rejected the interpretation the Court now adopts. . . .

The Court endeavors to escape from our decisions in *Cantwell* and *Yoder* by labeling them "hybrid" decisions, but there is no denying that both cases expressly relied on the Free Exercise Clause . . . and that we have consistently regarded those cases as part of the mainstream of our free exercise jurisprudence. Moreover, in each of the other cases cited by the Court to support its categorical rule, we rejected the particular constitutional claims before us only after carefully weighing the competing interests. See *Prince v. Massachusetts* . . . *Braunfeld v. Brown.* . . . That we rejected the free exercise claims in those cases hardly calls into question the applicability of First Amendment doctrine in the first place. Indeed, it is surely unusual to judge the vitality of a constitutional doctrine by looking to the win-loss record of the plaintiffs who happen to come before us.

Respondents, of course, do not contend that their conduct is automatically immune from all governmental regulation simply because it is motivated by their sincere religious beliefs. The Court's rejection of that argument might therefore be regarded as merely harmless dictum. Rather, respondents invoke our traditional compelling interest test to argue that the Free Exercise Clause requires the State to grant them a limited exemption from its general criminal prohibition against the possession of peyote. The Court today, however, denies them even the opportunity to make that argument, concluding that "the sounder approach, and the approach in accord with the vast majority of our precedents, is to hold the [compelling interest] test inapplicable to" challenges to general criminal prohibitions.

In my view, however, the essence of a free exercise claim is relief from a burden imposed by government on religious practices or beliefs, whether the burden is imposed directly through laws that prohibit or compel specific religious practices, or indirectly through laws that, in effect, make abandonment of one's own religion or conformity to the religious beliefs of others the price of an equal place in the civil community. . . . A State that makes criminal an individual's religiously motivated conduct burdens that individual's free exercise of religion in the severest manner possible, for it "results in the choice to the individual of either abandoning his religious principle or facing criminal prosecution." . . . I would have thought it beyond argument that such laws implicate free exercise concerns.

Indeed, we have never distinguished between cases in which a State conditions receipt of a benefit on conduct prohibited by religious beliefs and cases in which a State affirmatively prohibits such conduct. The *Sherbert* compelling interest test applies in both kinds of cases. . . . I would reaffirm that principle today: a neutral criminal law prohibiting conduct that a State may legitimately regulate is, if anything, more burdensome than a neutral civil statute placing legitimate conditions on the award of a state benefit.

Legislatures, of course, have always been "left free to reach actions which were in violation of social duties or subversive of good order." . . . Yet because of the close relationship between conduct and religious belief, "[i]n every case the power to regulate must be so exercised as not, in attaining a permissible end, unduly to infringe the protected freedom." . . . Once it has been shown that a government regulation or criminal prohibition burdens the free exercise of religion, we have consistently asked the Government to demonstrate that unbending application of its regulation to the religious objector "is essential to accomplish an overriding governmental interest," or represents "the least restrictive means of achieving some compelling state interest." . . . To me, the sounder approach—the approach more consistent with our role as judges to decide each case on its individual merits—is to apply this test in each case to determine whether the burden on the specific plaintiffs before us is constitutionally significant and whether the particular criminal interest asserted by the State before us is compelling. Even if, as an empirical matter, a government's criminal laws might usually serve a compelling interest in health, safety, or public order, the First Amendment at least requires a case-by-case determination of the question, sensitive to the facts of each particular claim. . . . Given the range of conduct that a State

might legitimately make criminal, we cannot assume, merely because a law carries criminal sanctions and is generally applicable, that the First Amendment never requires the State to grant a limited exemption for religiously motivated conduct. . . .

The Court today gives no convincing reason to depart from settled First Amendment jurisprudence. There is nothing talismanic about neutral laws of general applicability or general criminal prohibitions, for laws neutral toward religion can coerce a person to violate his religious conscience or intrude upon his religious duties just as effectively as laws aimed at religion. Although the Court suggests that the compelling interest test, as applied to generally applicable laws, would result in a "constitutional anomaly," the First Amendment unequivocally makes freedom of religion, like freedom from race discrimination and freedom of speech, a "constitutional nor[m]," not an "anomaly." . . . The Court's parade of horribles not only fails as a reason for discarding the compelling interest test, it instead demonstrates just the opposite: that courts have been quite capable of applying our free exercise jurisprudence to strike sensible balances between religious liberty and competing state interests.

Finally, the Court today suggests that the disfavoring of minority religions is an "unavoidable consequence" under our system of government and that accommodation of such religions must be left to the political process. In my view, however, the First Amendment was enacted precisely to protect the rights of those whose religious practices are not shared by the majority and may be viewed with hostility. The history of our free exercise doctrine amply demonstrates the harsh impact majoritarian rule has had on unpopular or emerging religious groups such as the Jehovah's Witnesses and the Amish. . . .

III

The Court's holding today not only misreads settled First Amendment precedent; it appears to be unnecessary to this case. I would reach the same result applying our established free exercise jurisprudence.

There is no dispute that Oregon's criminal prohibition of peyote places a severe burden on the ability of respondents to freely exercise their religion. Peyote is a sacrament of the Native American Church and is regarded as vital to respondents' ability to practice their religion. . . .

There is also no dispute that Oregon has a significant interest in enforcing laws that control the possession and use of controlled substances by its citizens. . . .

Thus, the critical question in this case is whether exempting respondents from the State's general criminal prohibition "will unduly interfere with fulfillment of the governmental interest." . . . Although the question is close, I would conclude that uniform application of Oregon's criminal prohibition is "essential to accomplish" . . . its overriding interest in preventing the physical harm caused by the use of a . . . controlled substance. Oregon's criminal prohibition represents that State's judgment that the possession and use of controlled substances, even by only one person, is inherently harmful and dangerous. Because the health effects caused by the use of controlled substances exist regardless of the motivation of the user, the use of such substances, even for religious purposes, violates the very purpose of the laws that prohibit them. . . . Moreover, in view of the societal interest in preventing trafficking in controlled substances, uniform application of the criminal prohibition at issue is essential to the effectiveness of Oregon's stated interest in preventing any possession of peyote. . . .

I would therefore adhere to our established free exercise jurisprudence and hold that the State in this case has a compelling interest in regulating peyote use by its citizens and that accommodating respondents' religiously motivated conduct "will unduly interfere with fulfillment of the governmental interest." . . .

Accordingly, I concur in the judgment of the Court.

JUSTICE BLACKMUN, with whom JUSTICE BRENNAN and JUSTICE MARSHALL join, dissenting.

[The majority's] . . . distorted view of our precedents leads [it] . . . to conclude that strict scrutiny of a state law burdening the free exercise of religion is a "luxury" that a well-ordered society cannot afford, and that the repression of minority religions is an "unavoidable consequence of democratic government." I do not believe the Founders thought their dearly bought freedom from religious persecution a "luxury," but an essential element of liberty—and they could not have thought religious intolerance "unavoidable," for they drafted the Religion Clauses precisely in order to avoid that intolerance. . . .

In weighing the clear interest of respondents Smith and Black (hereinafter respondents) in the free exercise of their religion against Oregon's asserted interest in enforcing its drug laws, it is important to articulate in precise terms the state interest involved. It is not the State's broad interest in fighting the critical "war on drugs" that must be weighed against respondents' claim, but the State's narrow interest in refusing to make an exception for the religious, ceremonial use of peyote. . . .

The State's interest in enforcing its prohibition, in order to be sufficiently compelling to outweigh a free exercise claim, cannot be merely abstract or symbolic. The State cannot plausibly assert that unbending application of a criminal prohibition is essential to fulfill any compelling interest, if it does not, in fact, attempt to enforce that prohibition. In this case, the State actually has not evinced any concrete interest in enforcing its drug laws against religious users of peyote. Oregon has never sought to prosecute respondents, and does not claim that it has made significant enforcement efforts against other religious users of peyote. The State's asserted interest thus amounts only to the symbolic preservation of an unenforced prohibition. But a government interest in "symbolism, even symbolism for so worthy a cause as the abolition of unlawful drugs," cannot suffice to abrogate the constitutional rights of individuals.

Similarly, this Court's prior decisions have not allowed a government to rely on mere speculation about potential harms, but have demanded evidentiary support for a refusal to allow a religious exception. . . . In this case, the State's justification for refusing to recognize an exception to its criminal laws for religious peyote use is entirely speculative. . . .

I dissent.

Smith represents a change in the standards governing free exercise disputes. For the first time since it was articulated, the Court explicitly rejected the *Sherbert* test. To be sure, the justices had failed to apply it in cases such as *Goldman,* but here the Court was eradicating the *Sherbert-Yoder* line of cases and returning to the kind of analysis it used in *Reynolds v. United States.* As Scalia wrote:

To make an individual's obligation to obey . . . a law contingent upon the law's coincidence with his religious beliefs, except where the State's interest is "compelling"—permitting him, by virtue of his beliefs, "to become a law unto himself," *Reynolds v. United States*—contradicts both constitutional tradition and common sense.

In place of the *Sherbert* test, the Court now held that the free exercise clause does not relieve an individual from the obligation to comply with a valid and neutral law of general applicability on the ground that the law commands behavior inconsistent with a person's religious teachings. The articulation of this new standard meant, as one scholar put it, that the Court had "brought free exercise jurisprudence full circle by reaffirming the . . . doctrine of *Reynolds*" and rejecting the compelling interest approach of *Sherbert*.[19]

As you might expect, *Smith* generated enormous controversy. O'Connor's and Blackmun's opinions made clear their displeasure with the majority's break from precedent, asserting that the Court should stick with the compelling interest/least restrictive means approach of *Sherbert* and *Yoder*. Members of Congress also voiced their disapproval. Soon after the justices handed down *Smith*, interest groups began to lobby Congress to overturn the decision. As Senator Edward M. Kennedy, D-Mass., put it, these interests feared that, under the new standard, "dry communities could ban the use of wine in communion services, government meat inspectors could require changes in the preparation of kosher food and school boards could force children to attend sex education classes [contrary to their religious beliefs]."[20] Led by politicians as varied in ideological approach as Kennedy and Senator Orrin Hatch, R-Utah, Congress began debating legislative options to counteract the Supreme Court's newly articulated position on religious liberty.

Before Congress could arrive at a legislative response to *Smith*, the Supreme Court heard another free exercise case. In ***Church of the Lukumi Babalu Aye v. City of Hialeah*** (1993) the justices considered whether ordinances prohibiting animal slaughter for religious purposes violate the free exercise clause. The particular targets of this law were adherents of the Santeria religion, a faith that has a mixture of African, Caribbean, and Roman Catholic roots. Central to this religion is animal sacrifice. Practitioners sacrifice chickens, pigeons, doves, ducks, guinea pigs, goats, sheep, and turtles at various events, including the initiations of new priests, weddings, births, and deaths, and as cures for the sick. The animals, which are killed by cutting the carotid arteries in the neck, are cooked and eaten after some of the rituals. Santerians may sacrifice as many as thirty animals during a single ritual.

Members of the Hialeah, Florida, community— who apparently were less than enthusiastic about the practice—enacted six ordinances limiting animal sacrifice, which was defined as "to unnecessarily kill, torment, or mutilate an animal in a public or private ritual or ceremony not for the primary purpose of food consumption."

The Supreme Court struck down the Hialeah ordinances, 9–0. Although the justices were no more in agreement over the appropriate standard to use than they were in *Smith*, they unanimously concluded that the city had violated the free exercise clause. Even though the ordinances were generally worded, no one doubted that the laws were passed to prohibit the practices of a particular religious group, the Santerians. As such, the statutes would fall under either the *Sherbert-Yoder* or the *Smith* test. As Justice Blackmun put it in a concurring opinion, "Because the respondent [Hialeah] here does single out religion in this way, the present case is an easy one to decide."

That the Court unanimously had supported a religious practice over state regulation did not stop Congress from continuing to find ways to blunt the impact of the *Smith* decision. In ruling for the Santerians, the majority opinion liberally cited *Smith* as the governing standard in religious liberty cases. Almost no one viewed *Lukumi Babalu* as a retreat from the *Smith* test.

The *Smith* decision gave governments more latitude to restrict religious exercise than they had under the *Sherbert-Yoder* approach to the First Amendment, but governments may use their discretion in exercising that power. Congress and the state legislatures can always give greater protection to rights than the Constitution requires. Even Justice Scalia, who wrote the majority opinion in *Smith*, acknowledged that Oregon was free to accommodate the religious use of peyote if it wanted to do so.

Pursuing just such a course, Congress passed the Religious Freedom Restoration Act (RFRA) in November 1993. RFRA received the support of a coalition of more than sixty religious and civil liberties groups. Congressional approval for the proposed law was overwhelming. The Senate, for example, passed the statute on a vote of 97 to 0.

RFRA expanded protection of religious exercise by restricting the use of government authority to regulate it. The law's most important provision, which applied to both state and federal governments, reads as follows:

Government shall not substantially burden a person's exercise of religion even if the burden results from a rule of general applicability [unless the government can show that the

---

19. Frederick Mark Gedicks, "Religion," in *The Oxford Companion to the Supreme Court,* ed. Kermit L. Hall (New York: Oxford University Press, 1992), 725.

20. Quoted in Adam Clymer, "Congress Moves to Ease Curb on Religious Acts," *New York Times,* May 10, 1993, A9.

burden] (1) is in furtherance of a compelling governmental interest; and (2) is the least restrictive means of furthering that compelling governmental interest.

The language should sound familiar: the statute codified the compelling interest/least restrictive means test used in *Sherbert* and *Yoder*. It explicitly rejected the general applicability approach ushered in by *Smith*. Congress was extending more protection to religious exercise rights than the Court was offering through its interpretation of the First Amendment.

RFRA applied to all federal departments, agencies, and officials and to all state and local governments. This included federal and state judges. The applicability of the statute raised two significant constitutional questions. First, could Congress require judges to employ a particular constitutional test of the First Amendment? And second, did the federal government have the power to impose its view of liberty on state officials?

Although most religious groups praised RFRA, state and local officials were troubled by it. Did the act mean that a city would violate federal civil rights laws if it enforced an anti-noise ordinance against a religious group that used sound trucks to spread its message, or arrested for disorderly conduct a group of religious zealots who paraded down streets blocking traffic, or failed to make religious accommodations for jail inmates? What did the statute mean when it prohibited a government from imposing a substantial burden on a person's religious exercise? What standards would be used to determine a compelling government interest and the least restrictive means?

It did not take long for the statute to be challenged. The case arose from a dispute between a local Catholic church and the city of Boerne, Texas. The city had denied the church permission to tear down its existing building, which had historic landmark status, and erect a new structure. The Catholic archdiocese claimed that under RFRA the city was without power to block construction.

City of Boerne v. Flores

521 U.S. 507 (1997)
http://laws.findlaw.com/US/521/507.html
Oral arguments are available at http://www.oyez.org.
Vote: 6 (Ginsburg, Kennedy, Rehnquist, Scalia, Stevens, Thomas)
    3 (Breyer, O'Connor, Souter)
OPINION OF THE COURT: Kennedy
CONCURRING OPINIONS: Scalia, Stevens
DISSENTING OPINIONS: Breyer, O'Connor, Souter

FACTS:

In 1991 the Catholic parish of St. Peter the Apostle in Boerne, Texas, determined that it could no longer function effectively because its church was too small to accommodate its rapidly growing membership. Pastor Tony Cummins received permission from Patrick Flores, the archbishop of San Antonio, to demolish the current structure and to build a new church with more than three times the capacity of the old building. When the parish applied for the necessary building permits, however, city officials rejected the project on the ground that the existing church, built in 1923, was covered by the city's historic preservation program. Archbishop Flores, on behalf of the church, sued in federal court, claiming that constructing a new church was a form of religious exercise that was protected against government interference by the Religious Freedom Restoration Act. The city countered by arguing that the statute was unconstitutional, that Congress lacked the authority to restrict the power of the states to regulate religious exercise. The district court agreed with the city, striking down the law. But the court of appeals reversed, concluding that the law was a proper exercise of federal legislative power. The city

Father Tony Cummins in front of St. Peter the Apostle Catholic Church in Boerne, Texas. In 1997 the church lost its battle to replace the structure, which the city had declared a historic landmark.

appealed to the U.S. Supreme Court, setting up a test of RFRA's constitutionality.

For the petitioner, City of Boerne, Texas:

- The Religious Freedom Restoration Act violates the separation of powers doctrine. It is the role of the judiciary, not the legislature, to interpret the Constitution.
- *Employment Division v. Smith* (1990) is the appropriate standard for determining the state's regulatory power over religious exercise.
- The Religious Freedom Restoration Act is not a valid exercise of the power given to Congress to enforce the Fourteenth Amendment.

For the respondent, Patrick Flores, Archbishop of San Antonio:

- The Fourteenth Amendment authorizes Congress to pass laws that prohibit states from infringing on various constitutionally guaranteed liberties, including freedom of religious exercise.
- The Religious Freedom Restoration Act permissibly provides additional protections for religious liberty beyond what the Constitution guarantees.
- The law does not infringe on the judiciary's authority to interpret the Constitution.

JUSTICE KENNEDY DELIVERED THE OPINION OF THE COURT.

A decision by local zoning authorities to deny a church a building permit was challenged under the Religious Freedom Restoration Act of 1993 (RFRA). The case calls into question the authority of Congress to enact RFRA. We conclude the statute exceeds Congress' power. . . .

Congress enacted RFRA in direct response to the Court's decision in *Employment Div., Dept. of Human Resources of Ore. v. Smith* (1990). . . . In evaluating the claim, we declined to apply the balancing test set forth in *Sherbert v. Verner* (1963), under which we would have asked whether Oregon's prohibition substantially burdened a religious practice and, if it did, whether the burden was justified by a compelling government interest. . . .

The application of the *Sherbert* test, the *Smith* decision explained, would have produced an anomaly in the law, a constitutional right to ignore neutral laws of general applicability. The anomaly would have been accentuated, the Court reasoned, by the difficulty of determining whether a particular practice was central to

an individual's religion. We explained, moreover, that it "is not within the judicial ken to question the centrality of particular beliefs or practices to a faith, or the validity of particular litigants' interpretations of those creeds." . . .

Four Members of the Court disagreed. They argued the law placed a substantial burden on the Native American Church members so that it could be upheld only if the law served a compelling state interest and was narrowly tailored to achieve that end. Justice O'Connor concluded Oregon had satisfied the test, while Justice Blackmun, joined by Justice Brennan and Justice Marshall, could see no compelling interest justifying the law's application to the members.

These points of constitutional interpretation were debated by Members of Congress in hearings and floor debates. Many criticized the Court's reasoning, and this disagreement resulted in the passage of RFRA. Congress announced.

"(1) [T]he framers of the Constitution, recognizing free exercise of religion as an unalienable right, secured its protection in the First Amendment to the Constitution;

"(2) laws 'neutral' toward religion may burden religious exercise as surely as laws intended to interfere with religious exercise;

"(3) governments should not substantially burden religious exercise without compelling justification;

"(4) in *Employment Division v. Smith* (1990), the Supreme Court virtually eliminated the requirement that the government justify burdens on religious exercise imposed by laws neutral toward religion; and

"(5) the compelling interest test as set forth in prior Federal court rulings is a workable test for striking sensible balances between religious liberty and competing prior governmental interests."

The Act's stated purposes are:

"(1) to restore the compelling interest test as set forth in *Sherbert v. Verner* (1963) and *Wisconsin v. Yoder* (1972) and to guarantee its application in all cases where free exercise of religion is substantially burdened; and

"(2) to provide a claim or defense to persons whose religious exercise is substantially burdened by government."

RFRA prohibits "[g]overnment" from "substantially burden[ing]" a person's exercise of religion even if the burden results from a rule of general applicability unless the government can demonstrate the burden "(1) is in furtherance of a compelling governmental interest; and (2) is the least restrictive means of furthering that compelling governmental interest." The Act's mandate applies to any "branch, department, agency, instrumentality, and official (or other person acting under color of law) of the United States," as well as to any "State, or . . . subdivision of a State." . . .

Under our Constitution, the Federal Government is one of enumerated powers. *McCulloch v. Maryland* (1819). The judicial authority to determine the constitutionality of laws, in cases and controversies, is based on the premise that the "powers of the legislature are defined and limited; and that those limits may not be mistaken, or forgotten, the constitution is written." *Marbury v. Madison* (1803). . . .

Congress relied on its Fourteenth Amendment enforcement power in enacting the most far reaching and substantial of RFRA's provisions, those which impose its requirements on the States. The Fourteenth Amendment provides, in relevant part:

"Section 1. . . . No State shall make or enforce any law which shall abridge the privileges or immunities of citizens of the United States; nor shall any State deprive any person of life, liberty, or property, without due process of law; nor deny to any person within its jurisdiction the equal protection of the laws.

"Section 5. The Congress shall have power to enforce, by appropriate legislation, the provisions of this article."

The parties disagree over whether RFRA is a proper exercise of Congress' §5 power "to enforce" by "appropriate legislation" the constitutional guarantee that no State shall deprive any person of "life, liberty, or property, without due process of law" nor deny any person "equal protection of the laws." . . .

Legislation which deters or remedies constitutional violations can fall within the sweep of Congress' enforcement power even if in the process it prohibits conduct which is not itself unconstitutional and intrudes into "legislative spheres of autonomy previously reserved to the States." *Fitzpatrick v. Bitzer* (1976). . . .

It is also true, however, that "[a]s broad as the congressional enforcement power is, it is not unlimited." *Oregon v. Mitchell* [1970]. . . .

Congress' power under §5 . . . extends only to "enforc[ing]" the provisions of the Fourteenth Amendment. The Court has described this power as "remedial," *South Carolina v. Katzenbach* [1966]. The design of the Amendment and the text of §5 are inconsistent with the suggestion that Congress has the power to decree the substance of the Fourteenth Amendment's restrictions on the States. Legislation which alters the meaning of the Free Exercise Clause cannot be said to be enforcing

the Clause. Congress does not enforce a constitutional right by changing what the right is. It has been given the power "to enforce," not the power to determine what constitutes a constitutional violation. Were it not so, what Congress would be enforcing would no longer be, in any meaningful sense, the "provisions of [the Fourteenth Amendment]." . . .

While the line between measures that remedy or prevent unconstitutional actions and measures that make a substantive change in the governing law is not easy to discern, and Congress must have wide latitude in determining where it lies, the distinction exists and must be observed. There must be a congruence and proportionality between the injury to be prevented or remedied and the means adopted to that end. Lacking such a connection, legislation may become substantive in operation and effect. . . .

The design of the Fourteenth Amendment has proved significant also in maintaining the traditional separation of powers between Congress and the Judiciary. The first eight Amendments to the Constitution set forth self-executing prohibitions on governmental action, and this Court has had primary authority to interpret those prohibitions. . . . As enacted, the Fourteenth Amendment confers substantive rights against the States which, like the provisions of the Bill of Rights, are self-executing. The power to interpret the Constitution in a case or controversy remains in the Judiciary.

The remedial and preventive nature of Congress' enforcement power, and the limitation inherent in the power, were confirmed in our earliest cases on the Fourteenth Amendment. In the *Civil Rights* Cases (1883), the Court invalidated sections of the Civil Rights Act of 1875 which prescribed criminal penalties for denying to any person "the full enjoyment of" public accommodations and conveyances, on the grounds that it exceeded Congress' power by seeking to regulate private conduct. The Enforcement Clause, the Court said, did not authorize Congress to pass "general legislation upon the rights of the citizen, but corrective legislation; that is, such as may be necessary and proper for counteracting such laws as the States may adopt or enforce, and which, by the amendment, they are prohibited from making or enforcing. . . ."

Any suggestion that Congress has a substantive, nonremedial power under the Fourteenth Amendment is not supported by our case law. . . .

If Congress could define its own powers by altering the Fourteenth Amendment's meaning, no longer would the Constitution be "superior paramount law, unchangeable by ordinary means." It would be "on a level with ordinary legislative acts, and, like other acts, . . . alterable when the legislature shall please to alter it." *Marbury v. Madison*. Under this approach, it is difficult to conceive of a principle that would limit congressional power. Shifting legislative majorities could change the Constitution and effectively circumvent the difficult and detailed amendment process contained in Article V.

We now turn to consider whether RFRA can be considered enforcement legislation under §5 of the Fourteenth Amendment.

Respondent contends that RFRA is a proper exercise of Congress' remedial or preventive power. The Act, it is said, is a reasonable means of protecting the free exercise of religion as defined by *Smith*. . . . If Congress can prohibit laws with discriminatory effects in order to prevent racial discrimination in violation of the Equal Protection Clause, then it can do the same, respondent argues, to promote religious liberty.

While preventive rules are sometimes appropriate remedial measures, there must be a congruence between the means used and the ends to be achieved. The appropriateness of remedial measures must be considered in light of the evil presented. Strong measures appropriate to address one harm may be an unwarranted response to another, lesser one.

A comparison between RFRA and the Voting Rights Act is instructive. In contrast to the record which confronted Congress and the judiciary in the voting rights cases, RFRA's legislative record lacks examples of modern instances of generally applicable laws passed because of religious bigotry. The history of persecution in this country detailed in the hearings mentions no episodes occurring in the past 40 years. . . .

Regardless of the state of the legislative record, RFRA cannot be considered remedial, preventive legislation, if those terms are to have any meaning. RFRA is so out of proportion to a supposed remedial or preventive object that it cannot be understood as responsive to, or designed to prevent, unconstitutional behavior. It appears, instead, to attempt a substantive change in constitutional protections. Preventive measures prohibiting certain types of laws may be appropriate when there is reason to believe that many of the laws affected by the congressional enactment have a significant likelihood of being unconstitutional. Remedial legislation under §5 "should be adapted to the mischief and wrong which the [Fourteenth] [A]mendment was intended to provide against." *Civil Rights Cases.*

RFRA is not so confined. Sweeping coverage ensures its intrusion at every level of government, displacing laws and prohibiting official actions of almost every description and regardless of subject matter. RFRA's restrictions apply to every agency and official of the Federal, State, and local Governments. RFRA applies to all federal and state law, statutory or otherwise, whether adopted before or after its enactment. RFRA has no termination date or termination mechanism. Any law is subject to challenge at any time by any individual who alleges a substantial burden on his or her free exercise of religion. . . .

The stringent test RFRA demands of state laws reflects a lack of proportionality or congruence between the means adopted and the legitimate end to be achieved. If an objector can show a substantial burden on his free exercise, the State must demonstrate a compelling governmental interest and show that the law is the least restrictive means of furthering its interest. Claims that a law substantially burdens someone's exercise of religion will often be difficult to contest. Requiring a State to demonstrate a compelling interest and show that it has adopted the least restrictive means of achieving that interest is the most demanding test known to constitutional law. . . . This is a considerable congressional intrusion into the States' traditional prerogatives and general authority to regulate for the health and welfare of their citizens.

. . . It is a reality of the modern regulatory state that numerous state laws, such as the zoning regulations at issue here, impose a substantial burden on a large class of individuals. When the exercise of religion has been burdened in an incidental way by a law of general application, it does not follow that the persons affected have been burdened any more than other citizens, let alone burdened because of their religious beliefs. . . .

Our national experience teaches that the Constitution is preserved best when each part of the government respects both the Constitution and the proper actions and determinations of the other branches. When the Court has interpreted the Constitution, it has acted within the province of the Judicial Branch, which embraces the duty to say what the law is. *Marbury v. Madison*. When the political branches of the Government act against the background of a judicial interpretation of the Constitution already issued, it must be understood that in later cases and controversies the Court will treat its precedents with the respect due them under settled principles, including *stare decisis,* and contrary expectations must be disappointed. RFRA was designed to control cases and controversies, such as the one before us; but as the provisions of the federal statute here invoked are beyond congressional authority, it is this Court's precedent, not RFRA, which must control.

It is for Congress in the first instance to "determin[e] whether and what legislation is needed to secure the guarantees of the Fourteenth Amendment," and its conclusions are entitled to much deference. Congress' discretion is not unlimited, however, and the courts retain the power, as they have since *Marbury v. Madison,* to determine if Congress has exceeded its authority under the Constitution. Broad as the power of Congress is under the Enforcement Clause of the Fourteenth Amendment, RFRA contradicts vital principles necessary to maintain separation of powers and the federal balance. The judgment of the Court of Appeals sustaining the Act's constitutionality is reversed.

It is so ordered.

JUSTICE STEVENS, concurring.

In my opinion, the Religious Freedom Restoration Act of 1993 (RFRA) is a "law respecting an establishment of religion" that violates the First Amendment to the Constitution.

If the historic landmark on the hill in Boerne happened to be a museum or an art gallery owned by an atheist, it would not be eligible for an exemption from the city ordinances that forbid an enlargement of the structure. Because the landmark is owned by the Catholic Church, it is claimed that RFRA gives its owner a federal statutory entitlement to an exemption from a generally applicable, neutral civil law. Whether the Church would actually prevail under the statute or not, the statute has provided the Church with a legal weapon that no atheist or agnostic can obtain. This governmental preference for religion, as opposed to irreligion, is forbidden by the First Amendment. *Wallace v. Jaffree* (1985).

JUSTICE SCALIA, with whom JUSTICE STEVENS joins, concurring in part.

Who can possibly be against the abstract proposition that government should not, even in its general, nondiscriminatory laws, place unreasonable burdens upon religious practice? Unfortunately, however, that abstract proposition must ultimately be reduced to concrete cases. The issue presented by *Smith* is, quite simply, whether the people, through their elected representatives, or rather this Court, shall control the outcome of those concrete cases. For example, shall it be the determination of this Court, or rather of the people, whether (as the dissent apparently believes) church construction will be exempt from zoning laws? The historical evidence put forward by the dissent does nothing to

undermine the conclusion we reached in *Smith:* It shall be the people.

JUSTICE O'CONNOR, with whom JUSTICE BREYER joins . . . dissenting.

I dissent from the Court's disposition of this case. I agree with the Court that the issue before us is whether the Religious Freedom Restoration Act (RFRA) is a proper exercise of Congress' power to enforce §5 of the Fourteenth Amendment. But as a yardstick for measuring the constitutionality of RFRA, the Court uses its holding in *Employment Div., Dept. of Human Resources of Ore. v. Smith* (1990), the decision that prompted Congress to enact RFRA as a means of more rigorously enforcing the Free Exercise Clause. I remain of the view that *Smith* was wrongly decided, and I would use this case to reexamine the Court's holding there. Therefore, I would direct the parties to brief the question whether *Smith* represents the correct understanding of the Free Exercise Clause and set the case for reargument. If the Court were to correct the misinterpretation of the Free Exercise Clause set forth in *Smith*, it would simultaneously put our First Amendment jurisprudence back on course and allay the legitimate concerns of a majority in Congress who believed that *Smith* improperly restricted religious liberty. We would then be in a position to review RFRA in light of a proper interpretation of the Free Exercise Clause. . . .

Accordingly, I believe that we should reexamine our holding in *Smith*, and do so in this very case. In its place, I would return to a rule that requires government to justify any substantial burden on religiously motivated conduct by a compelling state interest and to impose that burden only by means narrowly tailored to achieve that interest. . . .

JUSTICE SOUTER, dissenting.

To decide whether the Fourteenth Amendment gives Congress sufficient power to enact the Religious Freedom Restoration Act, the Court measures the legislation against the free exercise standard of *Employment Div., Dept. of Human Resources of Ore. v. Smith* (1990). For the reasons stated in my opinion in *Church of Lukumi Babalu Aye, Inc. v. Hialeah* (1993) (opinion concurring in part and concurring in judgment), I have serious doubts about the precedential value of the *Smith* rule and its entitlement to adherence. . . . But without briefing and argument on the merits of that rule (which this Court has never had in any case, including *Smith* itself), I am not now prepared to join Justice O'Connor in rejecting it or the majority in assuming it to be correct.

The decision was a victory for the city in its fight to preserve the historically important church building, but in the end the two parties to this litigation reached a compromise that satisfied the interests of both *(see Box 4-2)*. But the ruling had significance well beyond the dispute over the construction of a new church. The Court's majority remained loyal to the *Smith* interpretation of the scope of the government's power to regulate religious exercise and steadfastly maintained that the judiciary, and not the legislature, had the ultimate authority to determine the meaning of the Constitution. Yet the decision

---

BOX 4-2   AFTERMATH . . . *CITY OF BOERNE V. FLORES*

Although the Supreme Court stuck down the provisions of the Religious Freedom Restoration Act that would have protected the Catholic Church from city efforts to stop the expansion of St. Peter the Apostle Church, the two sides continued to negotiate. Two months after the Supreme Court's 1997 ruling, they reached a compromise. The city approved a new renovation plan for the church that preserved 80 percent of the original 1923 structure but added seven hundred seats. The compromise allowed the parish to serve its growing congregation and the city to preserve a building of historical importance. The remodeled church won a national award for its architecture.

Archbishop Patrick Flores, who invoked the Religious Freedom Restoration Act as a legal defense against the city's attempt to stop the church expansion, led the Catholic Archdiocese of San Antonio for a quarter century. He was appointed to the position in 1978, becoming the first Mexican American bishop of the Roman Catholic Church. Flores was extremely popular with the people of his San Antonio diocese. Considered a man of the people, he maintained an open-door policy, meeting with any individuals who might come to him for help.

The archbishop's policy of openness led to an unfortunate incident in 2000 when Nelson Antonio Escolero paid a visit to Flores at the diocese offices. The forty-year-old, unemployed Escolero, a legal resident of the United States for twenty-five years, feared that his recent arrest for driving with a suspended license would result in his deportation to his native El Salvador. He initially came to ask the archbishop for assistance with this problem, but the visit quickly turned into a crisis when Escolero produced a grenade, pushed the archbishop to the floor, and took Flores and his seventy-three-year-old secretary, Myrtle Sanchez, hostage. Another office worker escaped and notified police. More than fifty law enforcement officers evacuated other church employees and surrounded the building. After holding his captives for more than two hours, Escolero allowed the secretary to leave unharmed.

Archbishop Patrick Flores

The standoff continued for seven more hours but ended peacefully when Escolero was persuaded to give himself up to police. Escolero and Flores walked out of the building with no one hurt. The grenade turned out to be fake.

Prosecutors charged Escolero with two counts of aggravated kidnapping. In April of 2002, he was found guilty and sentenced to sixty-five years in prison for the kidnapping of Archbishop Flores and twenty-five years for the kidnapping of Myrtle Sanchez.

Flores stepped down as archbishop of San Antonio in 2004 when he reached the church's mandatory retirement age of seventy-five.

Father Tony Cummins, who headed the church renovation effort, remains pastor of St. Peter the Apostle Church today, having served in that position for more than twenty years.

SOURCES: *Amarillo Globe-News*, April 5, May 28, June 30, June 29, and August 9, 2000; Colin L. Black, "The Free Exercise Clause and Historic Preservation Law: Suggestions for a More Coherent Free Exercise Analysis," *Tulane Law Review* 72 (1997–1998): 1767–1807; CNN, June 28, 2000; *Dallas Morning News*, June 30, 2000; John Thomas Noonan, *Narrowing the Nation's Power: The Supreme Court Sides with the States* (Berkeley: University of California Press, 2003).

was relatively narrow, holding only that Congress could not use the Fourteenth Amendment to impose its interpretation of the free exercise clause on the states. The decision left open the possibility that Congress might use another constitutional provision to accomplish its goals.

It did not take Congress long to do so. Three years after the Court issued its decision in *City of Boerne*, President Bill Clinton signed into law the Religious Land Use and Institutionalized Persons Act (RLUIPA), a scaled-back version of RFRA applying primarily to zoning issues and the religious rights of prisoners. Congress based this law on the power of the federal government to regulate interstate commerce and to spend for the general welfare. Specifically, the provisions of the law affected any zoning activity or prison facility that received federal financial assistance or affected interstate or foreign commerce. Under the law, religious exercise rights could not be restricted without a compelling reason to do so using the least restrictive means possible.

Shortly after RLUIPA was enacted, a group of inmates sued the Ohio Department of Rehabilitation and Correction for violating their rights under the statute. The prisoners, members of the Satanist, Wicca, and Asatru sects along with adherents of the Church of Jesus Christ Christian, claimed that Ohio authorities discriminated against them. They were not allowed access to religious literature, opportunities for group worship, freedom to engage in religious dress, or the use of ceremonial items that were available to members of mainstream religions. In *Cutter v. Wilkinson* (2005) the Court unanimously upheld the law. The justices ruled that Congress was within its authority to require accommodation of the religious liberty of persons institutionalized in prison systems receiving federal assistance.

The decision in *City of Boerne* struck down RFRA only as it applied to Congress placing demands on the states. The decision did not speak to the constitutionality of RFRA's applicability to the federal government, an issue raised in *Gonzales v. O Centro Espirita Beneficente Uniao Do Vegetal* (2006). The case involved a Christian Spiritist sect based in Brazil. Only about 130 of its members reside in the United States. Central to the group's practices is the use of hoasca, a sacramental tea made from two plants unique to the Amazon region. The tea's ingredients contain hallucinogens that are outlawed under the federal Controlled Substances Act. When a shipment of the tea was intercepted by U.S. customs agents, the group filed suit claiming that the confiscation of the sect's sacramental substance violated the group members' rights under RFRA.

The Court unanimously upheld RFRA and its applicability in this case. The federal government has the power to restrict the degree to which its own officials and agencies can limit religious exercise. Under RFRA, the Controlled Substances Act could not be enforced against drugs used for sacramental purposes without a compelling reason to do so.

In spite of the Court's willingness to allow government to provide additional protections for religious liberty, the justices have not changed their view of the free exercise clause. The *Smith* test prevails. Under this approach, the government, if it wishes to do so, is free to make and enforce valid and neutral laws of general applicability even if they restrict religious exercise.

RELIGIOUS ESTABLISHMENT

In an 1802 letter to the Danbury Baptist Association, Thomas Jefferson proclaimed that the First Amendment built "a wall of separation between Church and State." But what sort of wall did Jefferson conceive? Was it to be porous, allowing some commingling between church and state so long as government does not establish a national religion? Or did he envision a solid barrier preventing all cooperative interactions between church and state? Or something in between?

Underlying the cases involving the religious establishment clause is that persistent question: What is the nature of the wall that separates church from state? To answer it, many Court opinions look to the intent of the framers, a highly elusive concept, particularly in this area of the law. As the nation's founders were of many minds, it is possible to find evidence supporting three major interpretations of the establishment clause:

1. The religious establishment clause erects a solid wall of separation between church and state, prohibiting most, if not all, forms of public aid for or support of religion.

2. The religious establishment clause may erect a wall of separation between church and state, but that wall of separation only bars the state from favoring one religion over another. Nondiscriminatory support or aid for all religions is constitutionally permissible.

3. The religious establishment clause simply prohibits the establishment of an official national religion.

In a detailed analysis of the framers' intent, Michael J. Malbin found that the *majority* of the framers subscribed to views 2 or 3 (accommodationist positions), but not to view 1 (a separationist position), which erects the most impermeable wall.[21] But the founders did not speak with one voice on the constitutional relationship between church and state, leaving a difficult task for those who use an "intent of the framers" approach to constitutional interpretation. Consider the following, often contradictory, actions taken by influential figures of the time:[22]

- James Madison and Thomas Jefferson, considered the most influential of the framers on establishment clause matters, publicly advocated a clear separation of church and state both in their home state of Virginia and at the national level. Their most important statements on the issue are Jefferson's "Letter to the Danbury Baptist Association" and Madison's "Memorial and Remonstrance against Religious Assessments."
- Patrick Henry introduced a bill in the Virginia legislature to use tax dollars to support the Christian religion, inspiring Jefferson's comment on the need to pray devoutly for Henry's death.
- Madison's original draft of the establishment clause stated only that Congress shall not establish a "national religion."
- In 1789, the same year Congress passed the establishment clause, the legislature passed a law making land grants to sectarian schools. Later, Congress granted land to the Society of the United Brethren for "propagating the Gospel among the Heathen."
- In the early 1800s Congress approved treaties requiring financial support of the religious education of the Native American tribes.

21. Michael J. Malbin, *Religion and Politics: The Intentions of the Authors of the First Amendment* (Washington, DC: American Enterprise Institute, 1978).

22. For interpretations of the founders' positions on religious establishment, see Robert S. Alley, *The Supreme Court on Church and State* (New York: Oxford University Press, 1988); Leonard W. Levy, *Constitutional Opinions* (New York: Oxford University Press, 1986); Levy, *The Establishment Clause* (New York: Macmillan, 1986); William H. Rehnquist, dissenting opinion in *Wallace v. Jaffree*, 472 U.S. 38 (1985); Joseph Story, *Commentaries on the Constitution of the United States*, vol. 2, 5th ed. (1891; repr., Buffalo, NY: William S. Hein, 1994); and Garry Wills, *Under God* (New York: Simon & Schuster, 1990).

- Presidents George Washington and John Adams issued Thanksgiving Day proclamations, but President Jefferson refused to do so on religious establishment grounds.

Due in part to these inconsistencies, the Supreme Court has fluctuated between some version of views 1 and 2. But its treatment of the conflicts between church and state have been neither clear nor consistent.

In the remainder of this chapter, we review the Court's attempts to develop a workable understanding of the meaning of the establishment clause and then turn our attention to some of the major controversies surrounding the elusive wall of separation.

The Search for a Standard: Controversies over Government Aid to Religious Institutions

The Supreme Court began its search for the meaning of the establishment clause in 1899, and more than a century later the justices are still having difficulty developing a coherent and consistent approach. At the center of this process are legal battles over the use of public funds to support religious institutions. These controversies most commonly focus on challenges to government programs aiding parochial schools, with less than satisfying legal results. As one scholar explained, "From a lawyer's point of view, the Establishment Clause is the most frustrating part of First Amendment law. The cases are an impossible tangle of divergent doctrines and seemingly conflicting results."[23]

Initial Attempts. Bradfield v. Roberts (1899) was the Court's first establishment clause dispute. It involved a $30,000 congressional appropriation to a hospital in Washington, D.C., for the construction of facilities to be used to treat indigent patients. The appropriation was challenged because the hospital was operated by Roman Catholic nuns. The justices, however, unanimously rejected the challenge, finding little relevance in the fact that Catholic nuns administered the hospital. It was the purpose of the facility that mattered to the Court, and in this case the justices found the hospital to have a secular, not religious, purpose.

Bradfield was important because it demonstrated from the start the Court's willingness to allow some

23. Daniel A. Farber, *The First Amendment* (New York: Foundation Press, 1998), 263.

public money to go to religious institutions, if the aid was intended to advance a clear secular purpose. Although the Court did not offer a comprehensive legal standard by which to adjudicate future claims, the secular purpose requirement first articulated in *Bradfield* remained a core principle in establishment clause jurisprudence.

Almost fifty years elapsed between *Bradfield* and the next important religious establishment case, *Everson v. Board of Education* (1947). While reading the Court's decision in *Everson,* consider these questions: Did the Court establish any legal standards by which to determine whether state practices violate the establishment clause? What view of the establishment clause did it adopt?

Everson v. Board of Education

330 U.S. 1 (1947)
http://laws.findlaw.com/US/330/1.html
Vote: 5 (Black, Douglas, Murphy, Reed, Vinson)
    4 (Burton, Frankfurter, Jackson, Rutledge)

OPINION OF THE COURT: Black
DISSENTING OPINIONS: Jackson, Rutledge

FACTS:

In 1941 New Jersey passed a law authorizing local school boards that provided "any transportation for public school children to and from school" also to supply transportation to children living in the district who attended nonprofit private schools. At the time New Jersey enacted this legislation, at least fifteen other states had similar laws.

Ewing Township decided to use tax dollars to reimburse parents for transportation costs incurred in sending their children to school. Because the township had no public high schools of its own, the reimbursement policy covered transportation expenses to parents sending their children to three neighboring public high schools. It also covered four private schools, all of which were affiliated with the Roman Catholic Church and provided regular religious instruction along with normal secular subjects. The average payment to parents sending their children to public or Catholic schools was $40 per student.

Arch Everson, a taxpayer living in the district, challenged the reimbursements to parents sending their children to religious schools. He claimed that this money supported religion in violation of the establishment clause of the First Amendment.

ARGUMENTS:

For the appellant, Arch R. Everson:

- The concept of liberty embodied in the due process clause of the Fourteenth Amendment embraces the fundamental freedoms protected by the First Amendment.

- This transportation program allows public money to be used in support of a religious purpose contrary to the First and Fourteenth Amendments.

For the appellee, Board of Education of the Township of Ewing:

- In *Cochran v. Board of Education* (1930) the Court upheld making textbooks available to schoolchildren regardless of what schools they attended. Transportation should be similarly treated.

- The transportation program is a valid use of the state's police powers. It facilitates the state's compulsory education requirements and promotes the health, safety, and welfare of schoolchildren.

- The state law authorizes local districts to fund transportation for all students attending nonprofit schools, public or private. There is no establishment of religion. Aid does not go to any religious institution.

 MR. JUSTICE BLACK DELIVERED THE OPINION OF THE COURT.

The New Jersey statute is challenged as a "law respecting an establishment of religion." The First Amendment . . . commands that a state "shall make no law respecting an establishment of religion, or prohibiting the free exercise thereof." These words of the First Amendment reflected in the minds of early Americans a vivid mental picture of conditions and practices which they fervently wished to stamp out in order to preserve liberty for themselves and for their posterity. Doubtless their goal has not been entirely reached; but so far has the Nation moved toward it that the expression "law respecting an establishment of religion," probably does not so vividly remind present-day Americans of the evils, fears, and political problems that caused that expression to be written into our Bill of Rights. Whether this New Jersey law is one respecting the "establishment of religion" requires an understanding of the meaning of that language, particularly with respect to the imposition of taxes. Once again, therefore, it is not inappropriate briefly to review the background and environment of the period in which that constitutional language was fashioned and adopted.

A large proportion of the early settlers of this country came here from Europe to escape the bondage of laws which compelled them to support and attend government favored churches. The centuries immediately before and contemporaneous with the colonization of America had been filled with turmoil, civil strife, and persecutions, generated in large part by established sects determined to maintain their absolute political and religious supremacy. With the power of government supporting them, at various times and places, Catholics had persecuted Protestants, Protestants had persecuted Catholics, Protestant sects had persecuted other Protestant sects, Catholics of one shade of belief had persecuted Catholics of another shade of belief, and all of these had from time to time persecuted Jews. In efforts to force loyalty to whatever religious group happened to be on top and in league with the government of a particular time and place, men and women had been fined, cast in jail, cruelly tortured, and killed. . . .

These practices of the old world were transplanted to and began to thrive in the soil of the new America. The very charters granted by the English Crown to the individuals and companies designated to make the laws which would control the destinies of the colonials authorized these individuals and companies to erect religious establishments which all, whether believers or non-believers, would be required to support and attend. An exercise of this authority was accompanied by a repetition of many of the old world practices and persecutions. Catholics found themselves hounded and proscribed because of their faith; Quakers who followed their conscience went to jail; Baptists were peculiarly obnoxious to certain dominant Protestant sects; men and women of varied faiths who happened to be in a minority in a particular locality were persecuted because they steadfastly persisted in worshipping God only as their own consciences dictated. And all of these dissenters were compelled to pay tithes and taxes to support government-sponsored churches whose ministers preached inflammatory sermons designed to strengthen and consolidate the established faith by generating a burning hatred against dissenters.

These practices became so commonplace as to shock the freedom-loving colonials into a feeling of abhorrence. The imposition of taxes to pay ministers' salaries and to build and maintain churches and church property aroused their indignation. It was these feelings which found expression in the First Amendment. No one locality and no one group throughout the Colonies can rightly be given entire credit for having aroused the sentiment that culminated in an adoption of the Bill of Rights' provisions embracing religious liberty. But Virginia, where the established church had achieved a dominant influence in political affairs and where many excesses attracted wide public attention, provided a great stimulus and able leadership for the movement. The people there, as elsewhere, reached the conviction that individual religious liberty could be achieved best under a government which was stripped of all power to tax, to support, or otherwise to assist any or all religions, or to interfere with the beliefs of any religious individual or group.

The movement toward this end reached its dramatic climax in Virginia in 1785–86 when the Virginia legislative body was about to renew Virginia's tax levy for the support of the established church. Thomas Jefferson and James Madison led the fight against this tax. Madison wrote his great Memorial and Remonstrance against the law. In it, he eloquently argued that a true religion did not need the support of law; that no person, either believer or non-believer, should be taxed to support a religious institution of any kind; that the best interest of a society required that the minds of men always be wholly free; and that cruel persecutions were the inevitable result of government-established religions. . . .

The meaning and scope of the First Amendment, preventing establishment of religion or prohibiting the free exercise thereof, in the light of its history and the evils it was designed forever to suppress, have been several times elaborated by the decisions of this Court prior to the application of the First Amendment to the states by the Fourteenth. The broad meaning given the Amendment by these earlier cases has been accepted by this Court in its decisions concerning an individual's religious freedom rendered since the Fourteenth Amendment was interpreted to make the prohibitions of the First applicable to state action abridging religious freedom. There is every reason to give the same application and broad interpretation to the "establishment of religion" clause. . . .

The "establishment of religion" clause of the First Amendment means at least this: Neither a state nor the Federal Government can set up a church. Neither can pass laws which aid one religion, aid all religions, or prefer one religion over another. Neither can force nor influence a person to go to or to remain away from church against his will or force him to profess a belief or disbelief in any religion. No person can be punished for entertaining or professing religious beliefs or disbeliefs, for church attendance or nonattendance. No tax in any amount, large or small, can be levied to support any religious activities or institutions, whatever they may be called, or whatever form they may adopt to teach or practice religion. Neither a state nor the Federal Government can, openly or secretly, participate in the affairs of any religious organizations or groups and vice versa. In the words of Jefferson, the clause against establishment of religion by law was intended to erect "a wall of separation between Church and State."

We must consider the New Jersey statute in accordance with the foregoing limitations imposed by the First Amendment. But we must not strike that state statute down if it is within the state's constitutional power even though it approaches the verge of that power. New Jersey cannot consistently with the "establishment of religion" clause of the First Amendment contribute tax-raised funds to the support of an institution which teaches the tenets and faith of any church. On the other hand, other language of the amendment commands that New Jersey cannot hamper its citizens in the free exercise of their own religion. Consequently, it cannot exclude individual Catholics, Lutherans, Mohammedans, Baptists, Jews, Methodists, Nonbelievers, Presbyterians, or the members of any other faith, *because of their faith, or lack of it,* from receiving the benefits of public welfare legislation. While we do not mean to intimate that a state could not provide transportation only to children attending public schools, we must be careful, in protecting the citizens of New Jersey against state-established churches, to be sure that we do not inadvertently prohibit New Jersey from extending its general State law benefits to all its citizens without regard to their religious belief.

Measured by these standards, we cannot say that the First Amendment prohibits New Jersey from spending tax-raised funds to pay the bus fares of parochial school pupils as a part of a general program under which it pays the fares of pupils attending public and other schools. It is undoubtedly true that children are helped to get to church schools. There is even a possibility that some of the children might not be sent to the church schools if the parents were compelled to pay their children's bus fares out of their own pockets when transportation to a public school would have been paid for by the State. The same possibility exists where the state requires a local transit company to provide reduced fares to school children including those attending parochial schools, or where a municipally owned transportation system undertakes to carry all school children free of charge. Moreover, state-paid policemen, detailed to protect children going to and from church schools from the very real hazards of traffic, would serve much the same purpose and accomplish much the same result as state provisions intended to guarantee free transportation of a kind which the state deems to be best for the school children's welfare. And parents might refuse to risk their children to the serious danger of traffic accidents going to and from parochial schools, the approaches to which were not protected by policemen. Similarly, parents might be reluctant to permit their children to attend schools which the state had cut off from such general government services as ordinary police and fire protection, connections for sewage disposal, public highways and sidewalks. Of course, cutting off church schools from these services, so separate and so indisputably marked off from the religious function, would make it far more difficult for the schools to operate. But such is obviously not the purpose of the First Amendment. That Amendment requires the state to be a neutral in its relations with groups of religious believers and non-believers; it does not require the state to be their adversary. State power is no more to be used so as to handicap religions, than it is to favor them.

This Court has said that parents may, in the discharge of their duty under state compulsory education laws, send their children to a religious rather than a public school if the school meets the secular educational requirements which the state has power to impose. It appears that these parochial schools meet New Jersey's requirements. The State contributes no money to the schools. It does not support them. Its legislation, as applied, does no more than provide a general program to help parents get their children, regardless of their religion, safely and expeditiously to and from accredited schools.

The First Amendment has erected a wall between church and state. That wall must be kept high and impregnable. We could not approve the slightest breach. New Jersey has not breached it here.

Affirmed.

MR. JUSTICE JACKSON, dissenting.

I find myself, contrary to first impressions, unable to join in this decision. I have a sympathy, though it is not ideological, with Catholic citizens who are compelled by law to pay taxes for public schools, and also feel constrained by conscience and discipline to support other schools for their own children. Such relief to them as this case involves is not in itself a serious burden to taxpayers and I had assumed it to be as little serious in principle. Study of this case convinces me otherwise. . . .

If we are to decide this case on the facts before us, our question is simply this: Is it constitutional to tax this complainant to pay the cost of carrying pupils to Church schools of one specified denomination? . . .

. . . Of course, the state may pay out tax-raised funds to relieve pauperism, but it may not under our Constitution do so to induce or reward piety. It may spend funds to secure old age against want, but it may not spend funds to secure religion against skepticism. It may compensate individuals for loss of employment, but it cannot compensate them for adherence to a creed.

It seems to me that the basic fallacy in the Court's reasoning, which accounts for its failure to apply the principles it avows, is in ignoring the essentially religious test by which beneficiaries of this expenditure are selected. A policeman protects a Catholic, of course— but not because he is a Catholic; it is because he is a man and a member of our society. The fireman protects the Church school—but not because it is a Church school; it is because it is property, part of the assets of our society. Neither the fireman nor the policeman has to ask before he renders aid "Is this man or building identified with the Catholic Church?" But before these school authorities draw a check to reimburse for a student's fare they must ask just that question, and if the school is a Catholic one they may render aid because it is such, while if it is of any other faith or is run for profit, the help must be withheld. To consider the converse of the Court's reasoning will best disclose its fallacy. That there is no parallel between police and fire protection and this plan of reimbursement is apparent from the incongruity of the limitation of this Act if applied to police and fire service. Could we sustain an Act that said the police shall protect pupils on the way to or from public schools and Catholic schools but not while going to and coming from other schools, and firemen shall extinguish a blaze in public or Catholic school buildings but shall not put out a blaze in Protestant Church schools or private schools operated for profit? That is the true analogy to the case we have before us and I should think it pretty plain that such a scheme would not be valid.

The Court's holding is that this taxpayer has no grievance because the state has decided to make the reimbursement a public purpose and therefore we are bound to regard it as such. I agree that this Court has left, and always should leave to each state, great latitude in deciding for itself, in the light of its own conditions, what shall be public purposes in its scheme of things. It may socialize utilities and economic enterprises and make taxpayers' business out of what conventionally had been private business. It may make public business of individual welfare, health, education, entertainment or security. But it cannot make public business of religious worship or instruction, or of attendance at religious institutions of any character. . . .

MR. JUSTICE FRANKFURTER joins in this opinion.

MR. JUSTICE RUTLEDGE, with whom MR. JUSTICE FRANKFURTER, MR. JUSTICE JACKSON, and MR. JUSTICE BURTON agree, dissenting.

"Congress shall make no law respecting an establishment of religion, or prohibiting the free exercise thereof. . . ." U.S. Const., Amend. . . .

"We, the General Assembly, do enact, That no man shall be compelled to frequent or support any religious worship, place, or ministry whatsoever, nor shall be enforced, restrained, molested, or burthened in his body or goods, nor shall otherwise suffer, on account of his religious opinions or belief. . . ."*

I cannot believe that the great author of those words, or the men who made them law, could have joined in this decision. Neither so high nor so impregnable today as yesterday is the wall raised between church and state by Virginia's great statute of religious freedom and the First Amendment, now made applicable to all the states by the Fourteenth. . . .

The Amendment's purpose was not to strike merely at the official establishment of a single sect, creed or religion, outlawing only a formal relation such as had prevailed in England and some of the colonies. Necessarily it was to uproot all such relationships. But the object was broader than separating church and state in this narrow sense. It was to create a complete and permanent separation of the spheres of religious activity and civil authority by comprehensively forbidding every form of public aid or support for religion. In proof the Amendment's wording and history unite with this Court's consistent utterances whenever attention has been fixed directly upon the question. . . .

As the Remonstrance discloses throughout, Madison opposed every form and degree of official relation between religion and civil authority. For him religion was a wholly private matter beyond the scope of civil power either to restrain or to support. Denial or abridgment of religious freedom was a violation of rights both of conscience and of natural equality. State aid was no less obnoxious or destructive to freedom and to religion

---

*"A Bill for Establishing Religious Freedom," enacted by the General Assembly of Virginia, January 19, 1786.

itself than other forms of state interference. "Establishment" and "free exercise" were correlative and coextensive ideas, representing only different facets of the single great and fundamental freedom. The Remonstrance, following the Virginia statute's example, referred to the history of religious conflicts and the effects of all sorts of establishments, current and historical, to suppress religion's free exercise. With Jefferson, Madison believed that to tolerate any fragment of establishment would be by so much to perpetuate restraint upon that freedom. Hence he sought to tear out the institution not partially but root and branch, and to bar its return forever. . . .

Does New Jersey's action furnish support for religion by use of the taxing power? Certainly it does, if the test remains undiluted as Jefferson and Madison made it, that money taken by taxation from one is not to be used or given to support another's religious training or belief, or indeed one's own. Today as then the furnishing of "contributions of money for the propagation of opinions which he disbelieves" is the forbidden exaction; and the prohibition is absolute for whatever measure brings that consequence and whatever amount may be sought or given to that end. . . .

Two great drives are constantly in motion to abridge, in the name of education, the complete division of religion and civil authority which our forefathers made. One is to introduce religious education and observances into the public schools. The other, to obtain public funds for the aid and support of various private religious schools. In my opinion both avenues were closed by the Constitution. Neither should be opened by this Court. The matter is not one of quantity, to be measured by the amount of money expended. Now as in Madison's day it is one of principle, to keep separate the separate spheres as the First Amendment drew them; to prevent the first experiment upon our liberties; and to keep the question from becoming entangled in corrosive precedents. We should not be less strict to keep strong and untarnished the one side of the shield of religious freedom than we have been of the other.

The judgment should be reversed.

The Court's decision in *Everson* is notable for a number of reasons. First, it applied the establishment clause to the states, an important step because the Court had not received many cases in this area. With incorporation, the Court now opened its doors to challenges to state and local practices on establishment grounds.

After nearly 150 years of dormancy, the establishment clause would become, on average, an annual issue for the justices.

Second, even though Black's opinion for the majority ruled in favor of the state's funding program, it etched into law an interpretation of Madison's and Jefferson's philosophies that supports a clear division between government and religion. Black even quoted Jefferson's comment that the clause was intended to build "a wall of separation between Church and State," thereby "constitutionalizing" the phrase. Although Black's opinion does not lay down a concrete legal standard, it stresses several fundamental ideas, most notably that the aid was secular in purpose (to provide safe transportation to students); that the aid was indirect (it was not paid directly to the religious institution); and that the beneficiaries of the aid were children (not churches). As we shall see, these themes recur in later Court opinions and foreshadow aspects of a legal standard the Court eventually formulates.

Third, *Everson* provides the first indication of the sensitive and salient nature of religious establishment questions. After the Court issued its ruling, Roman Catholic bishops in the United States mounted a public attack on it. Even though the decision supported reimbursements for costs incurred in sending children to Catholic schools, the bishops lambasted the justices for fundamentally misconstruing Jefferson's position on church and state. They argued that the founders supported the view that "the First Amendment means only that the Federal government may not prefer one religion over another."[24]

Finally, and perhaps most important, *Everson* indicates the divisive and complex nature of religious establishment questions. On one hand, all the justices—the majority and dissenters alike—agreed with Black's portrayal of the intent of the framers. In other words, the entire Court believed that Jefferson and Madison preferred strict separation of church and state. On the other hand—and this is the crux of the matter—the justices applied that historical framework to reach wholly disparate conclusions about the reimbursement plan. The majority, as Frank Sorauf put it, "succeeded . . . in combining the strictest separationist rhetoric with an accommodationist outcome."[25] Black's opinion, while

---

24. Quoted in Milton R. Konvitz, *Bill of Rights Reader* (Ithaca, NY: Cornell University Press, 1973), 31.

25. Frank Sorauf, *The Wall of Separation* (Princeton, NJ: Princeton University Press, 1976), 20.

TABLE 4-1 Major Religious Establishment Cases from Everson (1947) to Epperson (1968)

CASE	ISSUE	VOTE (OUTCOME)	RATIONALE
Everson v. Board of Education (1947)	Reimbursement for transportation costs incurred by parents sending their children to private schools	5–4 (accommodationist)	Secular purpose; child benefits; neutral
Illinois ex rel. McCollum v. Board of Education (1948)	Time-release program in which religious instructors come to public school weekly and provide religious training for students whose parents so desire	8–1 (separationist)	State provides "invaluable aid" to religious education efforts of local churches.
Zorach v. Clauson (1952)	Time-release program in which students are released an hour or so early one day each week to obtain religious instruction off school premises	6–3 (accommodationist)	State and religion need not be "hostile, suspicious, and even unfriendly"
Engel v. Vitale (1962)	Prayer, recited by public school children each morning, written by state's board of regents	8–1 (separationist)	Government cannot be in the business of prayer writing
School District of Abington Township v. Schempp (1963)	Reading of the Lord's Prayer and verses from the Bible in public schools	8–1 (separationist)	Public school prayer does not have (1) a secular legislative purpose or (2) a primary purpose that neither advances nor inhibits religion
Board of Education v. Allen (1968)	Public school loans of secular textbooks to students attending private schools	6–3 (accommodationist)	Primary purpose of the law furthers education, not religion
Epperson v. Arkansas (1968)	Barring the teaching of evolutionary theory in public schools	9–0 (separationist)	Not neutral; nonsecular purpose

adopting Jefferson's metaphor, at the same time found in favor of the township. The dissenters also advocated the same general approach but thought it led to a disposition against the township. Indeed, they took Black to task for heading in one direction and landing in another.

That the adoption of a similar historical vision of religious establishment could lead to such disparate outcomes was a problem that continued to confound this area of the law, at least through the Warren Court (and, as we shall see, still crops up today). As Table 4-1 illustrates, between the Court's decision in *Everson* in 1947 and the end of the Warren era in 1968 the justices decided seven major cases involving the establishment clause. Three led to an accommodationist outcome (upholding a government policy challenged as a violation of the establishment clause), and four to a separationist outcome (striking down a government policy as a violation of the establishment clause). Many of these cases will be discussed in detail later, but here we simply underscore several points.

First, although the Court continued to adhere to Black's (and Rutledge's) historical account of the separation between church and state, it was willing to uphold some kinds of support for religion, as it had in *Everson,* while ruling others unconstitutional. But,

as Table 4-1 shows, a pattern began to emerge from the Court's rulings. The justices seemed more willing to tolerate some public support of private education, such as transporting children to school (*Everson*) and loaning secular subject textbooks (***Board of Education v. Allen***, 1968) than it was to permit the entry of religion into public education, such as prayer in school (*Abington School District v. Schempp,* 1963) and the teaching of creationism (*Epperson v. Arkansas,* 1968).

A second point highlighted in Table 4-1 is this: after *Everson,* the Court began to formulate a test, flowing from Jefferson's metaphor and Black's *Everson* opinion, to determine whether government actions violated the establishment clause. During the Warren Court era, that test received its fullest articulation in *Abington Township* (excerpted on pages 170–175). Writing for the majority, Justice Clark explained that standard:

The test may be stated as follows: What are the purpose and primary effect of the enactment? If either is the advancement or inhibition of religion then the enactment exceeds the scope of legislative power as circumscribed by the Constitution. That is to say that to withstand the strictures of the Establishment Clause there must be a secular legislative purpose and a primary effect that neither advances nor inhibits religion.

With these words, Clark accomplished what Black had failed to do in *Everson*: provide attorneys and lower court judges with a benchmark for future litigation and decisions.

Early on, some analysts argued that this standard would always lead to separationist outcomes. These scholars thought it would be difficult for government attorneys to show that their policies met the two-pronged standard reached in *Abington*: that the policy has a secular legislative purpose and that its primary effect neither advances nor inhibits religion. But, as Table 4-1 shows, those commentators were wrong. In *Allen*, for example, the Court considered a New York State requirement that public schools lend, upon request, secular books to private school students in the seventh to twelfth grades. Attorneys for the American Civil Liberties Union (ACLU) argued that the requirement violated the establishment clause, but the Court disagreed. Writing for a six-person majority, Justice Byron White asserted:

The express purpose [of the law] was stated by the New York legislature to be furtherance of the educational opportunities available to the young. Appellants have shown us nothing about the necessary effects of the statute that is contrary to this stated purpose. The law merely makes available to all children the benefits of a general program to lend school books free of charge. Perhaps free books make it more likely that some children choose to attend a sectarian school, but that was true of the state-paid bus fare in *Everson* and does not alone demonstrate an unconstitutional degree of support for a religious institution.

In other words, White used the *Abington* "purpose" prong to reach an accommodationist outcome. Three justices—Abe Fortas, Douglas, and Black, the author of *Everson*—dissented. Both Black and Douglas differentiated between the kind of aid at issue in *Everson* (reimbursement for transportation costs) and in *Allen* (book loans). As Douglas put it:

Whatever may be said of *Everson*, there is nothing ideological about a bus. . . . [But] the textbook goes to the very heart of education in a parochial school. It is the chief, although not solitary, instrumentality for propagating a particular religious creed or faith. How can we possibly approve such state aid to a religion?

The third point about the Warren Court's handling of religious establishment cases is that although the justices generally adopted Jefferson's wall of separation

metaphor and agreed on the test for adjudicating establishment clause cases, they continued to split on case outcomes. Note the votes depicted in Table 4-1: with the exception of the evolution issues raised in *Epperson v. Arkansas,* the justices were divided over the resolution of cases.

Lemon Test. By the time Warren Burger became chief justice in 1969, observers were predicting that the Court would change its approach to adjudicating establishment clause cases. Even though the justices generally coalesced around the *Everson* historical understanding and the *Abington* standard, they were divided over how to apply those approaches to particular disputes. What is more, organized interest groups reacted to perceived inconsistencies in the Court's handling of these cases and were pressing the justices to formulate more coherent standards. Separationist groups such as the ACLU and Americans United for Separation of Church and State wanted the Court to reach outcomes in line with a strict separation of church and state, while accommodationist interests were asking the Court to move in precisely the opposite direction *(see Box 4-3)*. These competing groups were unrelenting in sponsoring and supporting cases brought to the Supreme Court.

In addition, observers expected that Burger would be more inclined than Warren to rule with the government in many areas of the law. Indeed, analysts predicted that Burger would push for wholesale changes in the Court's approaches to cases involving rights, liberties, and justice. Most of this speculation centered on criminal law because one of the primary reasons President Richard Nixon appointed Burger was to turn back the Warren Court's liberal rulings in this area. But, as it turned out, the new chief justice had a strong interest in taking a leadership role in religion cases. In fact, Burger was so determined to exert influence over this area of the law that during his tenure on the Court (1969–1985 terms) he wrote 69 percent (eighteen of twenty-six) of the Court's majority opinions dealing with religion, a much higher percentage than his overall rate of 20 percent in all formally decided cases.[26]

What was Burger's "understanding" of the establishment clause? How did he seek to change the law?

---

26. Joseph F. Kobylka, "Leadership in the Supreme Court: Chief Justice Burger and Establishment Clause Litigation," *Western Political Quarterly* 42 (December 1989): 545.

BOX 4-3   CLASHING INTERESTS: SEPARATIONIST VERSUS ACCOMMODATIONIST INTEREST GROUPS IN RELIGIOUS ESTABLISHMENT LITIGATION

As the Supreme Court devoted more attention to issues involving religion, interest groups increased their level of participation in establishment clause litigation. These groups represent two points of view: the separationist groups want a strict separation of church and state, and the accommodationist groups support greater intermingling between political and religious institutions. Below we provide information about the major groups belonging to these competing coalitions.

Examples of Separationist Groups

GROUP	FOUNDING	PURPOSE
American Civil Liberties Union	1920	Formed to defend rights and liberties generally; religious establishment litigation is just one of its concerns.
American Jewish Congress	1918	Dedicated to protecting civil rights and liberties of all Americans, particularly Jewish Americans, whom it views as adversely affected by intermingling between church and state.
Americans United for Separation of Church and State	1947	Formed in response to *Everson* to revitalize the principle of separation between church and state.
CPEARL (Committee for Public Education and Religious Liberty)	1968	Formed after *Allen* to oppose the expansion of government funding of religious schools. A national coalition representing several other separationist groups.

Examples of Accommodationist Groups

GROUP	FOUNDING	PURPOSE
U.S. Catholic Conference	1966	Formed to speak for the American Catholic bishops on matters of social and educational policy. Litigates to bring about greater accommodation between church and state.
Christian Legal Society	1961	Dedicated to supporting state accommodation of religious beliefs.
COLPA (National Jewish Commission on Law and Public Affairs)	1965	Formed to represent the interests of Orthodox American Jews, whose interests are often divergent from those of other Jewish groups. Litigates to combat separatism.

SOURCES: Lee Epstein, "Interest Group Litigation during the Rehnquist Court Era," *Journal of Law and Politics* 4 (1993): 639–717; Frank J. Sorauf, *The Wall of Separation* (Princeton, NJ: Princeton University Press, 1976); and Leo Pfeffer, *Religion, State, and the Burger Court* (Buffalo, NY: Prometheus Books, 1984).

Was he successful? We address these questions by considering Burger's first two religious establishment cases, ***Walz v. Tax Commission of the City of New York*** (1970) and *Lemon v. Kurtzman* (1971).

Walz involved the property tax exemptions enjoyed by religious institutions. Frederick Walz bought a small, useless lot on Staten Island, New York, for the sole purpose of challenging the state's tax laws, which gave religious organizations exemptions from property taxes. Walz contended that the tax exemptions resulted in property owners making involuntary contributions to churches in violation of the establishment clause. After losing in the lower courts, Walz and his ACLU

attorneys appealed to the U.S. Supreme Court, arguing that "[t]he First Amendment's objective was to create a complete and permanent separation of the sphere of religious activity and civil authority by comprehensively . . . forbidding any form of . . . support for religion." New York pointed out that all fifty states had property tax exemptions for religious organizations and that religious groups carry out charitable functions of interest to the state.

Writing for a seven-person majority (only Douglas dissented), Burger found in favor of the state. The outcome was not surprising; after all, had the Court ruled the other way, the tax status of every religious institution in the United States would have been dramatically altered. The startling aspect of *Walz* was that Burger, in his first writing on the establishment clause, sought to usher in a major change. The opinion started traditionally enough, with an examination of the "purpose" prong of *Abington*:

The legislative purpose of property tax exemptions is neither the advancement nor the inhibition of religion; it is neither sponsorship nor hostility. New York, in common with the other States, has determined that certain entities that exist in a harmonious relationship to the community at large, and that foster its "moral or mental improvement," should not be inhibited in their activities by property taxation or the hazard of loss of those properties for nonpayment of taxes.

But, instead of exploring whether the effect of the legislation inhibited or advanced religion, as the *Abington* standard specified, Burger suggested the following:

Determining that the legislative purpose of tax exemption is not aimed at establishing, sponsoring, or supporting religion does not end the inquiry, however. We must also be sure that the end result—the effect—is not *an excessive government entanglement* with religion [emphasis added].

He went on to hold that property tax exemptions did not create an excessive entanglement with religion: to the contrary, even though tax exemptions to churches "necessarily operate to afford an indirect economic benefit," involvement with religion would be far greater if the exemptions did not exist. State officials might occasionally want to examine church records, or they might need to speak with clergy about expenditures, and so forth. As Burger concluded, the tax exemption "restricts the fiscal relationship between church and state, and tends to complement and reinforce the desired separation insulating each from the other."

In the end, *Walz* probably raised more questions about Burger and the fate of establishment clause litigation than it answered. Did Burger seek to redesign the *Abington* standard—through adoption of an "excessive entanglement" criterion—as a way to bring down the wall of separation between church and state? Would excessive entanglement now become a part of the Court's analytic tool bag for examining establishment claims? Or would the majority of the justices favor a return to a strict reading of *Abington*? Consider these questions as you read *Lemon v. Kurtzman* and its companion case, *Earley v. DiCenso*.

Lemon v. Kurtzman
Earley v. DiCenso

403 U.S. 602 (1971)
http://laws.findlaw.com/US/403/602.html
Oral arguments are available at http://www.oyez.org.
Vote (Lemon): 8 (Black, Blackmun, Brennan, Burger, Douglas,
Harlan, Stewart, White)
0

OPINION OF THE COURT: *Burger*
CONCURRING OPINIONS: *Brennan, White*

NOT PARTICIPATING: *Marshall*
Vote (DiCenso): 8 (Black, Blackmun, Brennan, Burger,
Douglas, Harlan, Marshall, Stewart)
1 (White)

OPINION OF THE COURT: *Burger*
CONCURRING OPINION: *Douglas*
DISSENTING OPINION: *White*

FACTS:

With the assistance of numerous organized interests, including the Pennsylvania Civil Liberties Union, the American Jewish Congress (AJC), the National Association for the Advancement of Colored People (NAACP), and the Pennsylvania Educational Association, Alton Lemon brought suit against David Kurtzman, state superintendent of schools. Lemon wanted the trial court to declare unconstitutional a Pennsylvania law that authorized Kurtzman to "purchase" secular educational services for nonpublic schools. Under this law, the superintendent would use state taxes levied on cigarettes to reimburse nonpublic schools for expenses incurred for teachers' salaries, textbooks, and instructional materials. The state authorized the funding with certain restrictions: it would pay for secular expenses only—that is, secular books and teachers' salaries for the same courses taught in public schools. To receive payments, schools had to keep separate records identifying secular and nonsecular expenses.

The act took effect in July 1968. Up to the time the Supreme Court heard the case, Pennsylvania had spent about $5 million annually. It reimbursed expenses at 1,181 nonpublic elementary and secondary schools, which accounted for about a half million students, around 20 percent of the school population. About 96 percent of the nonpublic school students attended religious schools, primarily Roman Catholic.

In *Earley v. DiCenso* the AJC challenged the Rhode Island Salary Supplement Act of 1969. Aimed at improving the quality of private education, this law supplemented the salaries of teachers of secular subjects in private elementary schools up to 15 percent of their current salaries with the restrictions that payments could be made only to those who agreed in writing not to teach religious subjects and salaries could not exceed the maximum salaries paid to public school instructors. The AJC argued that this law was a violation of the establishment clause, in part because 95 percent of the schools falling under the terms of the act were affiliated with the Roman Catholic Church. Moreover, all of the 250 teachers who had applied for salary supplements worked at Catholic schools. And, as evidence submitted at trial indicated, about two-thirds of them were Roman Catholic nuns.

The lower courts upheld the Pennsylvania funding statute but struck down the Rhode Island program.

ARGUMENTS:

For the appellants in the Pennsylvania case, Alton Lemon, et al., and appellees in the Rhode Island case, Joan DiCenso, et al.:

- The challenged aid programs violate the command of *Everson v. Board of Education* (1947) that no tax, large or small, can be used to support any religious activities or institutions.
- The aid programs had one purpose, to relieve the financial plight of the states' parochial school systems. This violates the secular purpose requirement established in *School District of Abington Township v. Schempp* (1963).
- These aid programs require government monitoring in violation of the excessive entanglement principle set in *Walz v. Tax Commission of the City of New York* (1970).

For the appellees in the Pennsylvania case, David Kurtzman, et al., and the appellants in the Rhode Island case, John R. Earley, et al.:

- Absolute separation of church and state is not practical or required. The appropriate test of the establishment clause should be government neutrality, not hostility.
- *Walz* recognized that interactions between state and church are inevitable in the modern world.
- The purpose of the challenged statute is decidedly secular—to improve secular subject education in the state's nonpublic schools.
- If for financial reasons the private schools fail, the state would not be able to meet the resulting demands on the public school system.

MR. CHIEF JUSTICE BURGER DELIVERED THE OPINION OF THE COURT.

These two appeals raise questions as to Pennsylvania and Rhode Island statutes providing state aid to church-related elementary and secondary schools. Both statutes are challenged as violative of the Establishment and Free Exercise Clauses of the First Amendment and the Due Process Clause of the Fourteenth Amendment. . . .

In *Everson v. Board of Education* (1947), this Court upheld a state statute that reimbursed the parents of parochial school children for bus transportation expenses. There MR. JUSTICE BLACK, writing for the majority, suggested that the decision carried to "the verge" of forbidden territory under the Religion Clauses. Candor compels acknowledgment, moreover, that we can only dimly perceive the lines of demarcation in this extraordinarily sensitive area of constitutional law.

The language of the Religion Clauses of the First Amendment is at best opaque, particularly when compared with other portions of the Amendment. Its authors did not simply prohibit the establishment of a state church or a state religion, an area history shows they regarded as very important and fraught with great dangers. Instead they commanded that there should be "no law respecting an establishment of religion." A law may be one "respecting" the forbidden objective while falling short of its total realization. A law "respecting" the proscribed result, that is, the establishment of religion, is not always easily identifiable as one violative of the Clause. A given law might not establish a state religion but nevertheless be one "respecting" that end in the sense of being a step that could lead to such establishment and hence offend the First Amendment.

In the absence of precisely stated constitutional prohibitions, we must draw lines with reference to the three main evils against which the Establishment Clause was intended to afford protection: "sponsorship, financial support, and active involvement of the sovereign in religious activity." *Walz v. Tax Commission* (1970).

Every analysis in this area must begin with consideration of the cumulative criteria developed by the Court over many years. Three such tests may be gleaned from our cases. First, the statute must have a secular legislative purpose; second, its principal or primary effect must be one that neither advances nor inhibits religion; finally, the statute must not foster "an excessive government entanglement with religion."

Inquiry into the legislative purposes of the Pennsylvania and Rhode Island statutes affords no basis for a conclusion that the legislative intent was to advance religion. On the contrary, the statutes themselves clearly state that they are intended to enhance the quality of the secular education in all schools covered by the compulsory attendance laws. There is no reason to believe the legislatures meant anything else. A State always has a legitimate concern for maintaining minimum standards in all schools it allows to operate. As in *[Board of Education v.] Allen*, [1968] we find nothing here that undermines the stated legislative intent; it must therefore be accorded appropriate deference.

In *Allen* the Court acknowledged that secular and religious teachings were not necessarily so intertwined that secular textbooks furnished to students by the State were in fact instrumental in the teaching of religion. The legislatures of Rhode Island and Pennsylvania have concluded that secular and religious education are identifiable and separable. In the abstract we have no quarrel with this conclusion.

The two legislatures, however, have also recognized that church-related elementary and secondary schools have a significant religious mission and that a substantial portion of their activities is religiously oriented. They have therefore sought to create statutory restrictions designed to guarantee the separation between secular and religious educational functions and to ensure that State financial aid supports only the former. All these provisions are precautions taken in candid recognition that these programs approached, even if they did not intrude upon, the forbidden areas under the Religion Clauses. We need not decide whether these legislative precautions restrict the principal or primary effect of the programs to the point where they do not offend the Religion Clauses, for we conclude that the cumulative impact of the entire relationship arising under the statutes in each State involves excessive entanglement between government and religion.

In *Walz v. Tax Commission*, the Court upheld state tax exemptions for real property owned by religious organizations and used for religious worship. That holding, however, tended to confine rather than enlarge the area of permissible state involvement with religious institutions by calling for close scrutiny of the degree of entanglement involved in the relationship. The objective is to prevent, as far as possible, the intrusion of either into the precincts of the other. . . .

In order to determine whether the government entanglement with religion is excessive, we must examine the character and purposes of the institutions that are benefited, the nature of the aid that the State provides, and the resulting relationship between the government and the religious authority. . . . Here we find that both statutes foster an impermissible degree of entanglement.

(a) Rhode Island program

The District Court made extensive findings on the grave potential for excessive entanglement that inheres in the religious character and purpose of the Roman Catholic elementary schools of Rhode Island, to date the sole beneficiaries of the Rhode Island Salary Supplement Act.

The church schools involved in the program are located close to parish churches. This understandably permits convenient access for religious exercises since instruction in faith and morals is part of the total educational process. The school buildings contain identifying religious symbols such as crosses on the exterior and crucifixes, and religious paintings and statues either in the classrooms or hallways. Although only approximately 30 minutes a day are devoted to direct religious instruction, there are religiously oriented extracurricular activities. Approximately two-thirds of the teachers in these schools are nuns of various religious orders. Their dedicated efforts provide an atmosphere in which religious instruction and religious vocations are natural and proper parts of life in such schools. Indeed, as the District Court found, the role of teaching nuns in enhancing the religious atmosphere has led the parochial school authorities to attempt to maintain a one-to-one ratio between nuns and lay teachers in all schools rather than to permit some to be staffed almost entirely by lay teachers.

On the basis of these findings the District Court concluded that the parochial schools constituted "an integral part of the religious mission of the Catholic Church." The various characteristics of the schools make them "a powerful vehicle for transmitting the Catholic faith to the next generation." This process of inculcating religious doctrine is, of course, enhanced by the impressionable age of the pupils, in primary schools particularly. In short, parochial schools involve substantial religious activity and purpose. . . .

The dangers and corresponding entanglements are enhanced by the particular form of aid that the Rhode Island Act provides. Our decisions from *Everson to Allen* have permitted the States to provide church-related schools with secular, neutral, or nonideological services, facilities, or materials. Bus transportation, school lunches, public health services, and secular textbooks supplied in common to all students were not thought to offend the Establishment Clause. We note that the dissenters in *Allen* seemed chiefly concerned with the pragmatic difficulties involved in ensuring the truly secular content of the textbooks provided at state expense. . . .

In our view the record shows these dangers are present to a substantial degree. The Rhode Island Roman Catholic elementary schools are under the general supervision of the Bishop of Providence and his appointed representative, the Diocesan Superintendent of Schools. In most cases, each individual parish, however, assumes the ultimate financial responsibility for the school, with the parish priest authorizing the allocation of parish funds. With only two exceptions, school principals are nuns appointed either by the Superintendent or the Mother Provincial of the order whose members staff the school. By 1969 lay teachers constituted more than a third of all teachers in the parochial elementary schools, and their number is growing. They are first interviewed by the superintendent's office and then by the school principal. The contracts are signed by the parish priest, and he retains some discretion in negotiating salary levels. Religious authority necessarily pervades the school system.

The schools are governed by the standards set forth in a "Handbook of School Regulations," which has the force of synodal law in the diocese. It emphasizes the role and importance of the teacher in parochial schools: "The prime factor for the success or the failure of the school is the spirit and personality, as well as the professional competency, of the teacher. . . ." The Handbook also states that: "Religious formation is not confined to formal courses; nor is it restricted to a single subject area." Finally, the Handbook advises teachers to stimulate interest in religious vocations and missionary work. Given the mission of the church school, these instructions are consistent and logical.

Several teachers testified, however, that they did not inject religion into their secular classes. And the District Court found that religious values did not necessarily affect the content of the secular instruction. But what has been recounted suggests the potential if not actual hazards of this form of state aid. The teacher is employed by a religious organization, subject to the direction and discipline of religious authorities, and works in a system dedicated to rearing children in a particular faith. These controls are not lessened by the fact that most of the lay teachers are of the Catholic faith. Inevitably some of a teacher's responsibilities hover on the border between secular and religious orientation. . . .

We do not assume, however, that parochial school teachers will be unsuccessful in their attempts to segregate their religious beliefs from their secular educational responsibilities. But the potential for impermissible fostering of religion is present. The Rhode Island Legislature has not, and could not, provide state aid on the basis of a mere assumption that secular teachers under religious discipline can avoid conflicts. The State must be certain, given the Religion Clauses, that subsidized teachers do not inculcate religion—indeed the State here has undertaken to do so. To ensure that no trespass occurs, the State has therefore carefully conditioned its aid with pervasive restrictions. An eligible recipient must teach only those courses that are offered in the public schools and use only those texts and materials that are found in the public schools. In addition the teacher must not engage in teaching any course in religion.

A comprehensive, discriminating, and continuing state surveillance will inevitably be required to ensure that these restrictions are obeyed and the First Amendment otherwise respected. Unlike a book, a teacher cannot be inspected once so as to determine the extent and intent of his or her personal beliefs and subjective acceptance of the limitations imposed by the First Amendment. These prophylactic contacts will involve excessive and enduring entanglement between state and church. . . .

(b) Pennsylvania program

The Pennsylvania statute also provides state aid to church-related schools for teachers' salaries. The complaint describes an educational system that is very similar to the one existing in Rhode Island. According to the allegations, the church-related elementary and secondary schools are controlled by religious organizations, have the purpose of propagating and promoting a particular religious faith, and conduct their operations to fulfill that purpose. . . .

As we noted earlier, the very restrictions and surveillance necessary to ensure that teachers play a strictly nonideological role give rise to entanglements between church and state. The Pennsylvania statute, like that of Rhode Island, fosters this kind of relationship. Reimbursement is not only limited to courses offered in the public schools and materials approved by state officials, but the statute excludes "any subject matter expressing religious teaching, or the morals or forms of worship of any sect." In addition, schools seeking reimbursements must maintain accounting procedures that require the State to establish the cost of the secular as distinguished from the religious instruction.

The Pennsylvania statute, moreover, has the further defect of providing state financial aid directly to the church-related schools. This factor distinguishes both *Everson* and *Allen,* for in both those cases the Court was careful to point out that state aid was provided to the student and his parents—not to the church-related school. . . .

The history of government grants of a continuing cash subsidy indicates that such programs have almost always been accompanied by varying measures of control and surveillance. The government cash grants before us now provide no basis for predicting that comprehensive measures of surveillance and controls will not follow. In particular the government's post-audit power to inspect and evaluate a church-related school's financial records and to determine which expenditures are religious and which are secular creates an intimate and continuing relationship between church and state. . . .

. . . The sole question is whether state aid to these schools can be squared with the dictates of the Religion Clauses. Under our system the choice has been made that government is to be entirely excluded from the area of religious instruction and churches excluded from the affairs of government. The Constitution decrees that religion must be a private matter for the individual, the family, and the institutions of private choice, and that while some involvement and entanglements are inevitable, lines must be drawn.

The judgment of the Rhode Island District Court . . . is affirmed. The judgment of the Pennsylvania District Court . . . is reversed, and the case is remanded for further proceedings consistent with this opinion.

MR. JUSTICE DOUGLAS, whom MR. JUSTICE BLACK joins, concurring.

We said in unequivocal words in *Everson v. Board of Education* [1947], "No tax in any amount, large or small, can be levied to support any religious activities or institutions, whatever they may be called, or whatever form they may adopt to teach or practice religion." We reiterated the same idea in *Zorach v. Clauson* [1952] and in *McGowan v. Maryland* [1961] and in *Torcaso v. Watkins* [1961]. We repeated the same idea in *McCollum v. Board of Education* [1948] and added that a State's tax-supported public schools could not be used "for the dissemination of religious doctrines" nor could a State provide the church "pupils for their religious classes through use of the State's compulsory public school machinery."

Yet in spite of this long and consistent history there are those who have the courage to announce that a

State may nonetheless finance the *secular* part of a sectarian school's educational program. That, however, makes a grave constitutional decision turn merely on cost accounting and bookkeeping entries. A history class, a literature class, or a science class in a parochial school is not a separate institute; it is part of the organic whole which the State subsidizes. The funds are used in these cases to pay or help pay the salaries of teachers in parochial schools; and the presence of teachers is critical to the essential purpose of the parochial school, *viz.*, to advance the religious endeavors of the particular church. It matters not that the teacher receiving taxpayers' money only teaches religion a fraction of the time. Nor does it matter that he or she teaches no religion. The school is an organism living on one budget. What the taxpayers give for salaries of those who teach only the humanities or science without any trace of proselytizing enables the school to use all of its own funds for religious training. . . .

In my view, the taxpayers' forced contribution to the parochial schools in the present cases violates the First Amendment.

The same day the Court handed down *Lemon*, it also decided **Tilton v. Richardson**, involving the constitutionality of the Higher Education Facilities Act. Passed by Congress in 1963, the law provided building grants to colleges and universities so long as the funded facility would not be "used for sectarian instruction or a place for religious worship" for twenty years. After the twenty-year period, a college or university receiving such aid was free to use the building for any purpose. A group of taxpayers from Connecticut brought suit against the secretary of the U.S. Department of Health, Education, and Welfare and four church-run colleges, claiming that federal aid to these religious institutions violated the establishment clause. The schools countered that this point was irrelevant as they had used government funding exclusively for secular purposes; for example, Sacred Heart College had built a library, and Fairfield University, a science building.

A three-judge panel of the federal district court upheld the validity of the funding program. The challengers appealed to the Supreme Court, asking the following question: Does federal aid to religious universities for secular purposes violate the establishment clause? Writing for a five-person majority, Burger held that it did not. He noted that the stated legislative purpose "expresses a legitimate secular objective to assist the nation's colleges and universities entirely appropriate for governmental action"; that its "provisions . . . will not advance religion"; and that there are sufficiently "significant differences between religious aspects of church-related institutions of higher learning and parochial elementary and secondary schools" to nullify complaints of excessive entanglement. The Court, however, struck down the provision allowing the colleges and universities to use their federally funded buildings for whatever purpose they wanted after twenty years.

What is the significance of *Lemon, DiCenso,* and *Tilton*? The cases cleared up some of the confusion created by *Walz* over legal standards governing establishment clause cases. It now seemed that the justices planned to adhere to a tripartite test, referred to as the Lemon test. First, to be constitutional the statute must have a *secular legislative purpose*; second, its principal or primary effect must be one that *neither advances nor inhibits religion*; and third,

the statute must not foster an *excessive government entanglement* with religion.

None of these prongs is new. As Box 4-4 illustrates, they had their genesis in earlier Supreme Court cases. In addition, because the Lemon test finds its roots in earlier Court decisions that were based on the belief that Madison and Jefferson envisioned a strict wall of separation between church and state, it seemed that the Court was not only following precedent but also reinforcing the historical understanding from which the precedent flowed. By adhering to history and precedent, the Court reached a separationist outcome in *Lemon* that it had not reached in *Everson* or *Allen*, the two major cases on aid to private schools.

If you are surprised that Chief Justice Burger, who, at least in *Walz*, seemed to want to lower the wall of separation, wrote these 1971 opinions, you are not alone. Members of separatist groups were surprised

BOX 4-4 THE ROOTS OF THE LEMON TEST

TEST	EVERSON (1947)	ABINGTON (1963)	WALZ (1970)	LEMON (1971)
Secular Purpose	The state has a legitimate, general interest in helping "parents get their children, regardless of their religion, safely and expeditiously to and from accredited schools."	"What [is] the purpose . . . of the enactment? If [it] is the advancement or inhibition of religion then the enactment exceeds the scope of legislative power. . . . That is to say that to withstand the strictures of the Establishment Clause there must be a secular legislative purpose."	"The legislative purpose of a property tax exemption is neither the advancement nor the inhibition of religion."	"The statute must have a secular legislative purpose."
Primary Effect	Governments cannot "pass laws which aid one religion, aid all religions, or prefer one religion over another."	"What [is] . . . the primary effect of the enactment? If [it] is the advancement or inhibition of religion then the enactment exceeds the scope of legislative power. . . . That is to say that to withstand the strictures of the Establishment Clause there must be a . . . primary effect that neither advances nor inhibits religion."		The statute's "principal or primary effect must be one that neither advances nor inhibits religion."
Excessive Entanglement			"We must . . . be sure that the end result— the effect—is not an excessive government entanglement with religion."	"The statute must not foster an excessive government entanglement with religion."

and overjoyed. After handing down major rulings upholding aid to religious schools, the Court finally had defined the constitutional line that government aid programs could not cross.

Applying the Lemon Test. The enunciation of a legal standard by which to judge religious establishment claims raises some questions: Would the justices of the Burger Court and their successors continue to apply the Lemon test? Would it stand the test of time?

Table 4-2 helps answer these questions. It summarizes the aid decisions the Court handed down after the 1971 adoption of the Lemon standard. The cases involve a wide variety of programs providing financial support to religious schools for expenses such as testing services, textbooks, building maintenance, instructional

TABLE 4-2 Aid to Religious Schools: Applying the Lemon Test

CASE	OUTCOME (OPINION TYPE)[a]	AID UPHELD	AID STRUCK	STANDARD USED
Levitt v. CPEARL (1973)	separation (majority, 8–1)		reimbursements for administering and grading tests and examinations required by state	*Lemon*
CPEARL v. Nyquist (1973)	separation (majority, 6–3)		grants for maintenance and building repair, tax benefits, tuition reimbursements	*Lemon*
Meek v. Pittenger (1975)	mixed (majority/judgment, 6–3)	textbook loans	counseling, testing, speech therapy; loans of "instructional materials and equipment"	*Lemon*
Roemer v. Maryland Public Works Bd. (1976)	accommodation (judgment, 5–4)	general-purpose funds to colleges and universities for secular purposes		*Lemon*
Wolman v. Walter (1977)	mixed (majority/judgment, 6–3)	diagnostic, health, therapeutic, and testing services; textbooks	instructional materials, equipment; field trips	*Lemon*
New York v. Cathedral Academy (1977)	separation (majority, 6–3)		direct reimbursement for record keeping and testing	*Lemon*
CPEARL v. Regan (1980)	accommodation (majority, 5–4)	reimbursements for meeting state requirements for regents examinations, "pupil attendance reporting," and so forth		*Lemon*
Mueller v. Allen (1983)	accommodation (majority, 5–4)	tax deductions for tuition, textbooks, transportation		*Lemon*
Grand Rapids School Dist. v. Ball (1985)	separation (majority, 7–2 and 5–4)		community education program offering courses (chess, home economics, languages) at end of school day; employing private school teachers and using public and private school facilities	*Lemon*
			shared time program offering secular classes to private school children in private school facilities (leased by the state) during regular school hours and taught by public school teachers	*Lemon*
Aguilar v. Felton (1985)	separation (majority, 5–4)		teacher/counselor salaries and supplies/materials for remedial instruction to private school students in private school facilities	*Lemon*

CASE	OUTCOME (OPINION TYPE)[a]	AID UPHELD	AID STRUCK	STANDARD USED
Witters v. Washington Serv. for the Blind (1986)	accommodation (majority, 9–0)	disabled student at Christian college cannot be denied state vocational rehabilitation assistance		*Lemon*
Zobrest v. Catalina Foothills School Dist. (1993)	accommodation (majority, 5–4)	disabled student at Roman Catholic high school can be furnished with a state-funded sign-language interpreter		neutrality; child benefit
Bd. of Ed. of Kiryas Joel Village School Dist. v. Grumet (1994)	separation (majority, 6–3)		school district created to accommodate handicapped children of particular sect	neutrality
Agostini v. Felton (1997)	accommodation (majority, 5–4)	special education classes taught in parochial schools; overruled *Aguilar v. Felton, Grand Rapids School District v. Ball* (in part)		accommodationist interpretation of *Lemon*
Mitchell v. Helms (2000)	accommodation (judgment, 6–3)	library services and materials, computer hardware and software, curricular materials; *Meek v. Pittenger, Wolman v. Walter* overruled		*Agostini*, neutrality
Zelman v. Simmons-Harris (2002)	accommodation (majority, 5–4)	vouchers to attend private schools		*Agostini*, neutrality, private choice

a. A judgment represents the views of a plurality, not a majority, of the Court's members. Unlike a majority opinion, a judgment lacks precedential value.

materials, and salaries. Between 1971 and 1986 the justices uniformly decided these cases by applying the Lemon test. Their solutions, however, show little consistency. The Court appeared just as likely to strike down these programs as to conclude that they were consistent with the requirements of the establishment clause. In each case the Court seemed to interpret the Lemon test differently—the justices were unable to reach consensus. Often these cases were decided by 5–4 or 6–3 votes, and frequently the Court was unable to construct a majority opinion that attracted the endorsement of at least five justices. The result was an area of the law that lacked consistency and predictability.

In 1986 the complexion of the Court changed, as Rehnquist became chief justice by replacing the retiring Burger, and Antonin Scalia joined the Court as an associate justice. Rehnquist had a consistent record of supporting the accommodationist position. Scalia, too, was a strong opponent of the strict separation of church and state. As a result, the balance of the Court shifted in the conservative direction.

As Table 4-2 illustrates, after 1986 the Court began to approve some programs that offered government aid to religious institutions, sometimes overruling separationist precedents in the process. At the same time, open and often harsh criticism of the Lemon test was showing up in opinions in the aid cases and in other establishment clause areas. For example, in *Lamb's Chapel v. Center Moriches Union Free School District* (1993), a dispute over the after-hours use of public school rooms by a religious group, Justice Scalia wrote:

Like some ghoul in a late-night horror movie that repeatedly sits up in its grave and shuffles abroad, after being repeatedly killed and buried, *Lemon* stalks our Establishment Clause jurisprudence once again, frightening the little children and school attorneys. . . . Over the years, however, no fewer than five of the currently sitting Justices [Kennedy, O'Connor, Rehnquist, Scalia, and White] have, in their own opinions, personally driven pencils through the creature's heart (the author of today's opinion repeatedly), and a sixth [Thomas] has joined an opinion doing so.

Individual justices have written opinions expressing a preference for a standard other than the Lemon test. Table 4-3 describes four of the suggested substitutes. The

TABLE 4-3 Religious Establishment Standards Offered as Alternatives to the Lemon Test

STANDARD	DEFINITION	CHIEF SUPPORTER
Nonpreferentialism	"The Framers intended the Establishment Clause to prohibit the designation of any church as a 'national' one. The Clause was also designed to stop the Federal Government from asserting a preference for one religious denomination or sect over others." (Rehnquist, dissenting in *Wallace v. Jaffree*)	Rehnquist
Endorsement	"The Establishment Clause prohibits government from making adherence to a religion relevant in any person's standing in the political community. Government can run afoul of that prohibition in two principal ways. One is excessive entanglement with religious institutions.... The second and more direct infringement is government endorsement or disapproval of religion."	O'Connor
	"Under this view, *Lemon*'s inquiry as to the purpose and effect of a statute requires courts to examine whether government's purpose is to endorse religion and whether the statute actually conveys a message of endorsement." (O'Connor, concurring in *Lynch v. Donnelly* and in *Wallace v. Jaffree*)	
Coercion	"Our cases disclose two limiting principles: government may not coerce anyone to support or participate in any religion or its exercise; and it may not, in the guise of avoiding hostility or callous indifference, give direct benefits to a religion in such a degree that it in fact 'establishes a religion or religious faith, or tends to do so.'" (Kennedy, concurring and dissenting in *County of Allegheny v. American Civil Liberties Union*)	Kennedy
Social Conflict	"In a society composed of many different religious creeds, I fear that this present departure from the Court's earlier understanding risks creating a form of religiously based conflict potentially harmful to the Nation's social fabric. Because I believe the Establishment Clause was written in part to avoid this kind of conflict . . . I respectfully dissent." (Breyer, dissenting in *Zelman v. Simmons-Harris*)	Breyer

Lemon test has survived, however, because a majority of the justices have yet to coalesce behind any of the alternative standards. Although the Lemon standard remains the Court's official position, justices are not always loyal to it. Sometimes the test is used, but sometimes it is downplayed, reinterpreted, or even ignored.

Agostini v. Felton (1997) illustrates the new way the justices used the Lemon test. The case required the Court to reexamine its 1985 decision in **Aguilar v. Felton**, which many consider the high-water mark for separationist rulings. A 5–4 Court in *Aguilar* applied the Lemon test to strike down a New York program that allowed state-supported remedial instruction of students in private schools. As you read *Agostini*, pay careful attention to the way the justices apply the Lemon test.

Agostini v. Felton

521 U.S. 203 (1997)
http://laws.findlaw.com/US/521/203.html
Oral arguments are available at http://www.oyez.org.
Vote: 5 (Kennedy, O'Connor, Rehnquist, Scalia, Thomas)
    4 (Breyer, Ginsburg, Souter, Stevens)

OPINION OF THE COURT: *O'Connor*
DISSENTING OPINIONS: *Ginsburg, Souter*

FACTS:

Aguilar v. Felton tested the constitutionality of New York City's provision of educational assistance under Title I of the Elementary and Secondary Education Act of 1965. Congress passed Title I to fund services for students at risk of academic failure—regardless of whether they attended public or private schools. Eligible under the program were all students who lived in low-income areas and were failing or at risk of failing at school. Local school systems received federal money to implement remedial education, guidance, and counseling programs for these students. New York received its first Title I funds in 1966. About 10 percent of the eligible students attended private, mostly religious, schools, and initially the city transported these students to public schools for the funded services. When this system proved unworkable, the city allowed public school employees to work at the private schools, with strict instructions to maintain the secular purposes of the programs. In *Aguilar* the Court found this program in violation of the establishment clause. Crucial to its decision was the fact that the public school teachers provided the services inside the religious school buildings. At the same time, in *School District of*

Grand Rapids v. Ball (1985), the Court struck down a similar "shared time" program in Michigan.

In response to *Aguilar,* New York revised its program by leasing more than one hundred vans to transport public school teachers to the private schools. The teachers would then use the vans, which were parked in public areas near the private schools, as places to provide services for the eligible students. Between 1986 and 1993, New York estimated that it spent more than $100 million to operate these mobile instructional units.

In 1995 parents of private school students and New York City went into federal court requesting that they be released from complying with the *Aguilar* decision. They argued that compliance was unreasonably expensive. They also claimed that the Supreme Court's establishment clause jurisprudence had so significantly changed since 1985 as to make *Aguilar* no longer good law. As evidence, they cited the accommodationist decisions the Supreme Court was handing down. They also pointed to **Board of Education of Kiryas Joel Village School District v. Grumet** (1994), in which five justices had called for the reconsideration or overruling of *Aguilar*. In fact, by 1997 Justice Stevens was the sole remaining member of the five-justice *Aguilar* majority. The district judge refused the request, noting, "There may be good reason to conclude that *Aguilar*'s demise is imminent, but it has not yet occurred." The court of appeals affirmed.

ARGUMENTS:

For the petitioners, Rachel Agostini, et al.:

- The remedial services program provides purely secular benefits on a religiously neutral basis.
- Providing remedial services does not fund religious activity, endorse anyone's religion, or coerce participation in any religious exercise.
- Providing remedial services on private school grounds does not constitute excessive government entanglement with religion.
- Supreme Court rulings subsequent to *Aguilar* have undermined the legal basis on which it rests. *Aguilar* should now be overruled.

For the respondents, Betty-Louise Felton, et al.:

- Allowing government services to be provided inside parochial schools would be a violation of the establishment clause under a number of Court precedents that have never been called into question.
- Providing services inside parochial schools may be perceived as an endorsement of religion or a symbolic union of church and state.

- Prohibiting state employees from providing services inside parochial schools prevents them from engaging in conduct supportive of the religious mission of the school.
- Providing secular services to religious schools may indirectly subsidize the religious activities of the schools.

JUSTICE O'CONNOR DELIVERED THE OPINION OF THE COURT.

In *Aguilar v. Felton* (1985), this Court held that the Establishment Clause of the First Amendment barred the city of New York from sending public school teachers into parochial schools to provide remedial education to disadvantaged children pursuant to a congressionally mandated program. . . .

. . . [P]etitioners' ability to satisfy the [requirements for relief] hinges on whether our later Establishment Clause cases have so undermined *Aguilar* that it is no longer good law. We now turn to that inquiry.

In order to evaluate whether *Aguilar* has been eroded by our subsequent Establishment Clause cases, it is necessary to understand the rationale upon which *Aguilar*, as well as its companion case, *School Dist. of Grand Rapids v. Ball* (1985), rested.

In *Ball*, the Court evaluated two programs implemented by the School District of Grand Rapids, Michigan. The district's Shared Time program, the one most analogous to Title I, provided remedial and "enrichment" classes, at public expense, to students attending nonpublic schools. The classes were taught during regular school hours by publicly employed teachers, using materials purchased with public funds, on the premises of nonpublic schools. The Shared Time courses were in subjects designed to supplement the "core curriculum" of the nonpublic schools. Of the 41 nonpublic schools eligible for the program, 40 were " 'pervasively sectarian' " in character—that is, "the purpos[e] of [those] schools [was] to advance their particular religions."

The Court conducted its analysis by applying the three part test set forth in *Lemon v. Kurtzman* (1971):

"First, the statute must have a secular legislative purpose; second, its principal or primary effect must be one that neither advances nor inhibits religion; finally, the statute must not foster an excessive government entanglement with religion."

The Court acknowledged that the Shared Time program served a purely secular purpose, thereby satisfying the first part of the so called *Lemon* test. Nevertheless, it ultimately concluded that the program had the impermissible effect of advancing religion.

The Court found that the program violated the Establishment Clause's prohibition against "government financed or government sponsored indoctrination into the beliefs of a particular religious faith" in at least three ways. First, drawing upon the analysis in *Meek v. Pittenger* (1975), the Court observed that "the teachers participating in the programs may become involved in intentionally or inadvertently inculcating particular religious tenets or beliefs." . . .

The presence of public teachers on parochial school grounds had a second, related impermissible effect: It created a "graphic symbol of the 'concert or union or dependency' of church and state," especially when perceived by "children in their formative years." The Court feared that this perception of a symbolic union between church and state would "convey] a message of government endorsement . . . of religion" and thereby violate a "core purpose" of the Establishment Clause.

Third, the Court found that the Shared Time program impermissibly financed religious indoctrination by subsidizing "the primary religious mission of the institutions affected." . . .

The New York City Title I program challenged in *Aguilar* closely resembled the Shared Time program struck down in *Ball*, but the Court found fault with an aspect of the Title I program not present in *Ball*: The Board had "adopted a system for monitoring the religious content of publicly funded Title I classes in the religious schools." Even though this monitoring system might prevent the Title I program from being used to inculcate religion, the Court concluded, as it had in *Lemon* and *Meek*, that the level of monitoring necessary to be "certain" that the program had an exclusively secular effect would "inevitably resul[t] in the excessive entanglement of church and state," thereby running afoul of *Lemon*'s third prong. . . .

Distilled to essentials, the Court's conclusion that the Shared Time program in *Ball* had the impermissible effect of advancing religion rested on three assumptions: (i) any public employee who works on the premises of a religious school is presumed to inculcate religion in her work; (ii) the presence of public employees on private school premises creates a symbolic union between church and state; and (iii) any and all public aid that directly aids the educational function of religious schools impermissibly finances religious indoctrination, even if the aid reaches such schools as a consequence of private decisionmaking. Additionally, in *Aguilar* there was a

fourth assumption: that New York City's Title I program necessitated an excessive government entanglement with religion because public employees who teach on the premises of religious schools must be closely monitored to ensure that they do not inculcate religion.

Our more recent cases have undermined the assumptions upon which *Ball* and *Aguilar* relied. To be sure, the general principles we use to evaluate whether government aid violates the Establishment Clause have not changed since *Aguilar* was decided. For example, we continue to ask whether the government acted with the purpose of advancing or inhibiting religion, and the nature of that inquiry has remained largely unchanged. Likewise, we continue to explore whether the aid has the "effect" of advancing or inhibiting religion. What has changed since we decided *Ball* and *Aguilar* is our understanding of the criteria used to assess whether aid to religion has an impermissible effect.

As we have repeatedly recognized, government inculcation of religious beliefs has the impermissible effect of advancing religion. Our cases subsequent to *Aguilar* have, however, modified in two significant respects the approach we use to assess indoctrination. First, we have abandoned the presumption erected in *Meek* and *Ball* that the placement of public employees on parochial school grounds inevitably results in the impermissible effect of state sponsored indoctrination or constitutes a symbolic union between government and religion. In *Zobrest v. Catalina Foothills School Dist.* (1993), we . . . expressly disavow[ed] the notion that "the Establishment Clause [laid] down [an] absolute bar to the placing of a public employee in a sectarian school." . . .

Second, we have departed from the rule relied on in *Ball* that all government aid that directly aids the educational function of religious schools is invalid. In *Witters v. Washington Dept. of Servs. for Blind* (1986), we held that the Establishment Clause did not bar a State from issuing a vocational tuition grant to a blind person who wished to use the grant to attend a Christian college and become a pastor, missionary, or youth director. Even though the grant recipient clearly would use the money to obtain religious education, we observed that the tuition grants were "'made available generally without regard to the sectarian-nonsectarian, or public-nonpublic nature of the institution benefited.'" . . .

Zobrest and *Witters* make clear that, under current law, the Shared Time program in *Ball* and New York City's Title I program in *Aguilar* will not, as a matter of law, be deemed to have the effect of advancing religion through indoctrination. Indeed, each of the premises upon which we relied in *Ball* to reach a contrary conclusion is no longer valid. First, there is no reason to presume that, simply because she enters a parochial school classroom, a full time public employee such as a Title I teacher will depart from her assigned duties and instructions and embark on religious indoctrination, any more than there was a reason in *Zobrest* to think an interpreter would inculcate religion by altering her translation of classroom lectures. Certainly, no evidence has ever shown that any New York City Title I instructor teaching on parochial school premises attempted to inculcate religion in students. Thus, both our precedent and our experience require us to reject respondents' remarkable argument that we must presume Title I instructors to be "uncontrollable and sometimes very unprofessional."

. . . *Zobrest* also repudiates *Ball*'s assumption that the presence of Title I teachers in parochial school classrooms will, without more, create the impression of a "symbolic union" between church and state. . . . We do not see any perceptible (let alone dispositive) difference in the degree of symbolic union between a student receiving remedial instruction in a classroom on his sectarian school's campus and one receiving instruction in a van parked just at the school's curbside. To draw this line based solely on the location of the public employee is neither "sensible" nor "sound," and the Court in *Zobrest* rejected it.

Nor under current law can we conclude that a program placing full time public employees on parochial campuses to provide Title I instruction would impermissibly finance religious indoctrination. . . . Moreover, as in *Zobrest*, Title I services are by law supplemental to the regular curricula. These services do not, therefore, "reliev[e] sectarian schools of costs they otherwise would have borne in educating their students." . . .

What is most fatal to the argument that New York City's Title I program directly subsidizes religion is that it applies with equal force when those services are provided off campus, and *Aguilar* implied that providing the services off campus is entirely consistent with the Establishment Clause. . . . Because the incentive is the same either way, we find no logical basis upon which to conclude that Title I services are an impermissible subsidy of religion when offered on campus, but not when offered off campus. Accordingly, contrary to our conclusion in *Aguilar*, placing full time employees on parochial school campuses does not as a matter of law have the impermissible effect of advancing religion through indoctrination. . . .

. . . Title I services are allocated on the basis of criteria that neither favor nor disfavor religion. The services are available to all children who meet the Act's eligibility requirements, no matter what their religious beliefs or where they go to school. The Board's program does not, therefore, give aid recipients any incentive to modify their religious beliefs or practices in order to obtain those services.

We turn now to *Aguilar*'s conclusion that New York City's Title I program resulted in an excessive entanglement between church and state. Whether a government aid program results in such an entanglement has consistently been an aspect of our Establishment Clause analysis. We have considered entanglement both in the course of assessing whether an aid program has an impermissible effect of advancing religion, and as a factor separate and apart from "effect," *Lemon v. Kurtzman*. . . .

Not all entanglements, of course, have the effect of advancing or inhibiting religion. Interaction between church and state is inevitable, and we have always tolerated some level of involvement between the two. Entanglement must be "excessive" before it runs afoul of the Establishment Clause.

The pre-*Aguilar* Title I program does not result in an "excessive" entanglement that advances or inhibits religion. As discussed previously, the Court's finding of "excessive" entanglement in *Aguilar* rested on three grounds: (i) the program would require "pervasive monitoring by public authorities" to ensure that Title I employees did not inculcate religion; (ii) the program required "administrative cooperation" between the Board and parochial schools; and (iii) the program might increase the dangers of "political divisiveness." Under our current understanding of the Establishment Clause, the last two considerations are insufficient by themselves to create an "excessive" entanglement. They are present no matter where Title I services are offered, and no court has held that Title I services cannot be offered off campus. Further, the assumption underlying the first consideration has been undermined. In *Aguilar*, the Court presumed that full time public employees on parochial school grounds would be tempted to inculcate religion, despite the ethical standards they were required to uphold. Because of this risk *pervasive* monitoring would be required. But after *Zobrest* we no longer presume that public employees will inculcate religion simply because they happen to be in a sectarian environment. Since we have abandoned the assumption that properly instructed public employees will fail to discharge their duties faithfully, we must also discard the assumption that *pervasive* monitoring of Title I teachers is required. There is no suggestion in the record before us that unannounced monthly visits of public supervisors are insufficient to prevent or to detect inculcation of religion by public employees. Moreover, we have not found excessive entanglement in cases in which States imposed far more onerous burdens on religious institutions than the monitoring system at issue here.

To summarize, New York City's Title I program does not run afoul of any of three primary criteria we currently use to evaluate whether government aid has the effect of advancing religion: it does not result in governmental indoctrination; define its recipients by reference to religion; or create an excessive entanglement. We therefore hold that a federally funded program providing supplemental, remedial instruction to disadvantaged children on a neutral basis is not invalid under the Establishment Clause when such instruction is given on the premises of sectarian schools by government employees pursuant to a program containing safeguards such as those present here. The same considerations that justify this holding require us to conclude that this carefully constrained program also cannot reasonably be viewed as an endorsement of religion. Accordingly, we must acknowledge that *Aguilar*, as well as the portion of *Ball* addressing Grand Rapids' Shared Time program, are no longer good law.

The doctrine of *stare decisis* does not preclude us from recognizing the change in our law and overruling *Aguilar* and those portions of *Ball* inconsistent with our more recent decisions. As we have often noted, *"[s]tare decisis* is not an inexorable command," but instead reflects a policy judgment that "in most matters it is more important that the applicable rule of law be settled than that it be settled right." That policy is at its weakest when we interpret the Constitution because our interpretation can be altered only by constitutional amendment or by overruling our prior decisions. Thus, we have held in several cases that *stare decisis* does not prevent us from overruling a previous decision where there has been a significant change in or subsequent development of our constitutional law. As discussed above, our Establishment Clause jurisprudence has changed significantly since we decided *Ball* and *Aguilar,* so our decision to overturn those cases rests on far more than "a present doctrinal disposition to come out differently from the Court of [1985]." We therefore overrule *Ball* and *Aguilar* to the extent those decisions are inconsistent with our current understanding of the Establishment Clause. . . .

For these reasons, we reverse the judgment of the Court of Appeals and remand to the District Court with instructions to vacate its September 26, 1985, order.

It is so ordered.

JUSTICE SOUTER, with whom JUSTICE STEVENS and JUSTICE GINSBURG join, and with whom JUSTICE BREYER joins as to Part II, dissenting.

I

In both *Aguilar* and *Ball,* we held that supplemental instruction by public school teachers on the premises of religious schools during regular school hours violated the Establishment Clause. . . .

. . . I believe *Aguilar* was a correct and sensible decision, and my only reservation about its opinion is that the emphasis on the excessive entanglement produced by monitoring religious instructional content obscured those facts that independently called for the application of two central tenets of Establishment Clause jurisprudence. The State is forbidden to subsidize religion directly and is just as surely forbidden to act in any way that could reasonably be viewed as religious endorsement.

. . . [T]he flat ban on subsidization antedates the Bill of Rights and has been an unwavering rule in Establishment Clause cases, qualified only by the conclusion two Terms ago that state exactions from college students are not the sort of public revenues subject to the ban. See *Rosenberger v. Rector and Visitors of Univ. of Va.* (1995). The rule expresses the hard lesson learned over and over again in the American past and in the experiences of the countries from which we have come, that religions supported by governments are compromised just as surely as the religious freedom of dissenters is burdened when the government supports religion. . . . The human tendency, of course, is to forget the hard lessons, and to overlook the history of governmental partnership with religion when a cause is worthy, and bureaucrats have programs. That tendency to forget is the reason for having the Establishment Clause (along with the Constitution's other structural and libertarian guarantees), in the hope of stopping the corrosion before it starts. . . .

What was true of the Title I scheme as struck down in *Aguilar* will be just as true when New York reverts to the old practices with the Court's approval after today. . . . If a State may constitutionally enter the schools to teach in the manner in question, it must in constitutional principle be free to assume, or assume payment for, the entire cost of instruction provided in any ostensibly secular subject in any religious school. . . .

In sum, if a line is to be drawn short of barring all state aid to religious schools for teaching standard subjects, the *Aguilar-Ball* line was a sensible one capable of principled adherence. It is no less sound, and no less necessary, today.

II

The Court today ignores this doctrine and claims that recent cases rejected the elemental assumptions underlying *Aguilar* and much of *Ball.* But the Court errs. Its holding that *Aguilar* and the portion of *Ball* addressing the Shared Time program are "no longer good law," rests on mistaken reading. . . .

In *Zobrest* the Court did indeed recognize that the Establishment Clause lays down no absolute bar to placing public employees in a sectarian school, but the rejection of such a *per se* rule was hinged expressly on the nature of the employee's job, sign language interpretation (or signing) and the circumscribed role of the signer. On this point (and without reference to the facts that the benefited student had received the same aid before enrolling in the religious school and the employee was to be assigned to the student not to the school) the Court explained itself this way: "[T]he task of a sign language interpreter seems to us quite different from that of a teacher or guidance counselor. . . . Nothing in this record suggests that a sign language interpreter would do more than accurately interpret whatever material is presented to the class as a whole. In fact, ethical guidelines require interpreters to 'transmit everything that is said in exactly the same way it was intended.'" The signer could thus be seen as more like a hearing aid than a teacher, and the signing could not be understood as an opportunity to inject religious content in what was supposed to be secular instruction. *Zobrest* accordingly holds only that in these limited circumstances where a public employee simply translates for one student the material presented to the class for the benefit of all students, the employee's presence in the sectarian school does not violate the Establishment Clause.

The Court, however, ignores the careful distinction drawn in *Zobrest* and insists that a full time public employee such as a Title I teacher is just like the signer, asserting that "there is no reason to presume that, simply because she enters a parochial school classroom, . . . [this] teacher will depart from her assigned duties and instructions and embark on religious indoctrination. . . ." Whatever may be the merits of this position (and I find it short on merit), it does not enjoy the authority of *Zobrest.* The Court may disagree with *Ball*'s assertion that a publicly employed teacher working in a sectarian school is apt to reinforce the pervasive inculcation of religious beliefs, but its disagreement is fresh law. . . .

Finally, instead of aid that comes to the religious school indirectly in the sense that its distribution results from private decisionmaking, a public educational agency distributes Title I aid in the form of programs and services directly to the religious schools. In *Zobrest* and *Witters*, it was fair to say that individual students were themselves applicants for individual benefits on a scale that could not amount to a systemic supplement. But under Title I, a local educational agency (which in New York City is the Board of Education) may receive federal funding by proposing programs approved to serve individual students who meet the criteria of need, which it then uses to provide such programs at the religious schools; students eligible for such programs may not apply directly for Title I funds. The aid, accordingly, is not even formally aid to the individual students (and even formally individual aid must be seen as aid to a school system when so many individuals receive it that it becomes a significant feature of the system).

In sum, nothing since *Ball and Aguilar* and before this case has eroded the distinction between "direct and substantial" and "indirect and incidental." That principled line is being breached only here and now. . . .

III

Finally, there is the issue of precedent. *Stare decisis* is no barrier in the Court's eyes because it reads *Aguilar* and *Ball* for exaggerated propositions that *Witters* and *Zobrest* are supposed to have limited to the point of abandoned doctrine. The Court's dispensation from *stare decisis* is, accordingly, no more convincing than its reading of those cases. Since *Aguilar* came down, no case has held that there need be no concern about a risk that publicly paid school teachers may further religious doctrine; no case has repudiated the distinction between direct and substantial aid and aid that is indirect and incidental; no case has held that fusing public and private faculties in one religious school does not create an impermissible union or carry an impermissible endorsement; and no case has held that direct subsidization of religious education is constitutional or that the assumption of a portion of a religious school's teaching responsibility is not direct subsidization. . . .

. . . [T]he object of Title I is worthy without doubt, and the cost of compliance is high. In the short run there is much that is genuinely unfortunate about the administration of the scheme under *Aguilar*'s rule. But constitutional lines have to be drawn, and on one side of every one of them is an otherwise sympathetic case that provokes impatience with the Constitution and with the line. But constitutional lines are the price of constitutional government.

For those who expected the Court finally to resolve the issue of aid to religious schools, *Agostini* was a disappointment. Once again, the Court split 5–4. *Lemon* was cited as the prevailing standard for deciding establishment clause cases, but Justice O'Connor acknowledged that the Court's use of that standard had evolved over the years. Compared with the past, the justices were now using a more accommodationist view of what constitutes an impermissible advancement of religion, and they were no longer categorically opposed to funding that directly supports the educational function of private schools.

Agostini's tilt toward the accommodationist position on parochial school aid, combined with the overruling of *Aguilar v. Felton* and *Grand Rapids School District v. Ball*, sent a strong signal. The justices may have had differences over the most appropriate test to use, but the Court's majority was generally sympathetic to government aid for religious schools. That position was solidified when the justices announced their decision three years later in **Mitchell v. Helms** (2000).

In *Mitchell* the Court responded to a legal challenge to Chapter 2 of the Education Consolidation and Improvement Act of 1981, a law allowing federal aid to public and private schools for educational materials, library holdings, and computer resources. The case focused on the program's distribution of federal funds in Jefferson Parish, Louisiana. Thirty percent of the allocated funds supported programs in accredited private schools; the remaining aid went to local public schools. Of the forty-six private schools benefiting from the aid, thirty-four were Roman Catholic, seven were otherwise religiously affiliated, and five were not affiliated with any church. The federal funds went first to state and local school officials, who then reallocated the support on the basis of the number of students served by the various schools. Public school authorities purchased the educational materials and equipment, which were then loaned to the individual schools.

The continuing divisions among the justices prevented them from arriving at a majority opinion deciding the case. Six of the justices, however, concluded that Chapter 2 was a constitutionally valid program. In the process of reaching that decision, the Court overruled two important precedents that had invalidated earlier aid programs, *Meek v. Pittenger* (1975) and *Wolman v. Walter* (1977).

In the plurality opinion Justice Clarence Thomas, joined by Kennedy, Rehnquist, and Scalia, concluded that *Mitchell* was controlled by the modified interpretation of the Lemon test established in *Agostini v. Felton*. The main question was whether the government aid in question advanced religion. According to the plurality opinion, such advancement occurs (1) if any religious indoctrination is attributable to the government aid; (2) if the aid program defines its recipients with reference to religion; or (3) if the aid creates an excessive government entanglement with religion. Of particular relevance is the program's neutrality. If the aid is allocated on the basis of secular criteria that neither favor nor disfavor religion and is made available to both religious and public schools on a nondiscriminatory basis, then the program is neutral in nature and is likely to be constitutionally valid.

The plurality rejected two major arguments advanced by the law's challengers: that it is always constitutionally impermissible to give aid directly to religious schools and that aid that can be diverted to religious use is always unconstitutional. Taking this approach, the plurality had little difficulty deciding that the challenged program was neutral and there was no evidence of religious indoctrination attributable to the government.

The three dissenters, Justices Souter, Stevens, and Ginsburg, decried the Court's willingness to approve aid given directly to sectarian institutions. They claimed that under the approach endorsed by the plurality, almost any aid program for religious schools would be permissible. The dissenters' position may or may not be supported by fact, but it is reasonably clear that the decisions in *Agostini* and *Mitchell*, and their overruling of four separationist precedents, cleared away many legal barriers to government programs that aid religious schools.

Neutrality and Private Choice. The *Mitchell* decision not only reinforced *Agostini*'s use of *Lemon* with an accommodationist twist but also revealed that the justices were beginning to emphasize different constitutional values. The plurality stressed neutrality as an important component in any valid aid program. That government aid programs should be neutral with respect to religion had been mentioned in numerous previous decisions, but here the Court placed greater reliance on it. Because educational materials and computer equipment were made available to all public and private schools without respect to religious affiliation, the accommodation-oriented justices ruled that the program was acceptable.

Two years later, the Court confronted the question of school vouchers, one of the most controversial issues in education policy. The response of the Court's majority again stresses the significance of neutrality, but it also highlights another value: private choice.

Voucher programs allow parents to remove their children from their assigned public schools and use state tuition assistance to enroll them in private schools or in other public schools. Proponents of voucher programs argue that they provide opportunities for children from low-income families to leave underperforming public schools and receive a higher-quality education at other institutions. Proponents also argue that such programs foster a spirit of competition that will ultimately force the public schools to improve themselves. Opponents claim that voucher programs undermine public education because the best students are attracted to private schools, leaving the public schools with even greater academic and disciplinary problems, as well as decreased funds to cope with them. The better approach, voucher opponents argue, is to use available money to improve the public schools rather than to encourage students to leave them. In addition to these public policy debates, there is the serious constitutional question: Do voucher programs that allow parents to use state money to pay tuition at religious schools violate the establishment clause? The Court addressed this question in *Zelman v. Simmons-Harris* (2002). As you read Chief Justice Rehnquist's majority opinion, pay attention to the emphasis he places on neutrality and individual private choice and the lack of reliance on the Lemon test.

Zelman v. Simmons-Harris

536 U.S. 639 (2002)
http://laws.findlaw.com/US/536/639.html
Oral arguments are available at http://www.oyez.org.
Vote: 5 (Kennedy, O'Connor, Rehnquist, Scalia, Thomas)
        4 (Breyer, Ginsburg, Souter, Stevens)
OPINION OF THE COURT: Rehnquist
CONCURRING OPINIONS: O'Connor, Thomas
DISSENTING OPINIONS: Breyer, Souter, Stevens

FACTS:

In the 1990s the Cleveland school district faced a crisis. The district served some seventy-five thousand children, most of them from low-income, minority families. Evaluation studies found it to be one of the worst-performing school districts in the nation. The district failed to meet any of the eighteen state standards for minimal acceptable performance. Only 10 percent of ninth graders could pass basic proficiency examinations. More than two-thirds of high school students either failed or dropped out before graduation. In 1995 the state assumed control over the district.

To improve performance, the state enacted its Pilot Project Scholarship Program. This program allowed parents to choose among the following alternatives:

1. Continue in Cleveland public schools as before.

2. Receive a scholarship (up to $2,250 per year) to attend an accredited, private, nonreligious school.

3. Receive a scholarship (up to $2,250 per year) to attend an accredited, private, religious school.

4. Remain in the Cleveland public schools and receive up to $500 in tutorial assistance.

5. Attend a public school outside the district. Other public school districts accepting Cleveland students would receive $2,250 from the Cleveland district as well as normal state funding for each student enrolled.

Scholarship levels were adjusted according to family income levels. Tuition assistance checks went directly to the parents, who then endorsed the checks to the participating private schools that accepted their children. Parents were required to pay a small portion of the private school tuition expense. Private schools participating in the program could not charge more than $2,500 for tuition. These schools retained their own admissions standards, although they were prohibited from discriminating on the basis of race, religion, or ethnic background. In separate actions the state created two additional educational alternatives: magnet public schools that specialized in certain subject areas and community schools that were governed by local boards independent of the regular public school district.

Although no public schools from adjacent districts opted to participate in the program, fifty-six private schools, 80 percent of them religious, did. Religious schools were the choice of 96.7 percent of the students who used tuition vouchers to attend private schools. A majority of students who used the scholarship program to attend religious schools were not of the same faith as the schools' sponsoring religious organizations.

Doris Simmons-Harris and other local citizens filed suit against Susan Tave Zelman, Ohio's superintendent of public instruction, charging that the voucher program violated the First Amendment's establishment clause. Both the federal district court and the court of appeals struck down the program. The state asked for Supreme Court review.

For the petitioner, Susan Tave Zelman,
Superintendent of Public Instruction:

- The Ohio voucher program is constitutional because it is religiously neutral and affords true private choice to parents.
- The program provides no financial incentives to choose religious schooling over other alternatives.
- The program in no way endorses any religion.

For the respondents, Doris Simmons-Harris, et al.:

- The Ohio voucher program is unconstitutional because it finances religious education.
- The program creates a public perception that the state is endorsing religious practices and beliefs.
- The options available to parents are heavily skewed toward religious schools.

 CHIEF JUSTICE REHNQUIST DELIVERED THE OPINION OF THE COURT.

The State of Ohio has established a pilot program designed to provide educational choices to families with children who reside in the Cleveland City School District. The question presented is whether this program offends the Establishment Clause of the United States Constitution. We hold that it does not. . . .

The Establishment Clause of the First Amendment, applied to the States through the Fourteenth Amendment, prevents a State from enacting laws that have the "purpose" or "effect" of advancing or inhibiting religion. *Agostini v. Felton* (1997). There is no dispute that the program challenged here was enacted for the valid secular purpose of providing educational assistance to poor children in a demonstrably failing public school system. Thus, the question presented is whether the Ohio program nonetheless has the forbidden "effect" of advancing or inhibiting religion.

To answer that question, our decisions have drawn a consistent distinction between government programs

Roberta Kitchen, right, and Rosa-Linda Demore-Brown, executive director of Cleveland Parents for School Choice, celebrate the Supreme Court's ruling in favor of school voucher programs that endorsed a six-year pilot program in inner-city Cleveland and provided parents tax-supported education stipends.

that provide aid directly to religious schools, *Mitchell v. Helms* (2000) (plurality opinion); *Agostini; Rosenberger v. Rector and Visitors of Univ. of Va.* (1995), and programs of true private choice, in which government aid reaches religious schools only as a result of the genuine and independent choices of private individuals, *Mueller v. Allen* (1983); *Witters v. Washington Dept. of Servs. for Blind* (1986); *Zobrest v. Catalina Foothills School Dist.* (1993). While our jurisprudence with respect to the constitutionality of direct aid programs has "changed significantly" over the past two decades, *Agostini*, our jurisprudence with respect to true private choice programs has remained consistent and unbroken. Three times we have confronted Establishment Clause challenges to neutral government programs that provide aid directly to a broad class of individuals, who, in turn, direct the aid to religious schools or institutions of their own choosing. Three times we have rejected such challenges.

In *Mueller,* we rejected an Establishment Clause challenge to a Minnesota program authorizing tax deductions for various educational expenses, including private school tuition costs, even though the great majority of the program's beneficiaries (96%) were parents of children in religious schools. We began by focusing on the class of beneficiaries, finding that because the class included "*all* parents," including parents with "children [who] attend nonsectarian private schools or sectarian private schools," (emphasis in original), the program was "not readily subject to challenge under the Establishment Clause." Then, viewing the program as a whole, we emphasized the principle of private choice, noting that public funds were made available to religious schools "only as a result of numerous, private choices of individual parents of school-age children." This, we said, ensured that "'no imprimatur of state approval' can be deemed to have been conferred on any particular religion, or on religion generally." We thus found it irrelevant to the constitutional inquiry that the vast majority of beneficiaries were parents of children in religious schools. . . . That the program was one of true private choice, with no evidence that the State deliberately skewed incentives toward religious schools, was sufficient for the program to survive scrutiny under the Establishment Clause.

In *Witters,* we used identical reasoning to reject an Establishment Clause challenge to a vocational scholarship program that provided tuition aid to a student studying at a religious institution to become a pastor. . . . We further remarked that, as in *Mueller,* "[the] program is made available generally without regard to the

sectarian-nonsectarian, or public-nonpublic nature of the institution benefited." In light of these factors, we held that the program was not inconsistent with the Establishment Clause. . . .

Finally, in *Zobrest,* we applied *Mueller* and *Witters* to reject an Establishment Clause challenge to a federal program that permitted sign-language interpreters to assist deaf children enrolled in religious schools. Reviewing our earlier decisions, we stated that "government programs that neutrally provide benefits to a broad class of citizens defined without reference to religion are not readily subject to an Establishment Clause challenge." Looking once again to the challenged program as a whole, we observed that the program "distributes benefits neutrally to any child qualifying as 'disabled.'" Its "primary beneficiaries," we said, were "disabled children, not sectarian schools."

We further observed that "[b]y according parents freedom to select a school of their choice, the statute ensures that a government-paid interpreter will be present in a sectarian school only as a result of the private decision of individual parents." Our focus again was on neutrality and the principle of private choice, not on the number of program beneficiaries attending religious schools. Because the program ensured that parents were the ones to select a religious school as the best learning environment for their handicapped child, the circuit between government and religion was broken, and the Establishment Clause was not implicated.

Mueller, Witters, and *Zobrest* thus make clear that where a government aid program is neutral with respect to religion, and provides assistance directly to a broad class of citizens who, in turn, direct government aid to religious schools wholly as a result of their own genuine and independent private choice, the program is not readily subject to challenge under the Establishment Clause. A program that shares these features permits government aid to reach religious institutions only by way of the deliberate choices of numerous individual recipients. The incidental advancement of a religious mission, or the perceived endorsement of a religious message, is reasonably attributable to the individual recipient, not to the government, whose role ends with the disbursement of benefits. . . .

We believe that the program challenged here is a program of true private choice, consistent with *Mueller, Witters,* and *Zobrest,* and thus constitutional. As was true in those cases, the Ohio program is neutral in all respects toward religion. It is part of a general and multifaceted undertaking by the State of Ohio to provide educational opportunities to the children of a failed school district. It confers educational assistance directly to a broad class of individuals defined without reference to religion, *i.e.*, any parent of a school-age child who resides in the Cleveland City School District. The program permits the participation of *all* schools within the district, religious or nonreligious. Adjacent public schools also may participate and have a financial incentive to do so. Program benefits are available to participating families on neutral terms, with no reference to religion. The only preference stated anywhere in the program is a preference for low-income families, who receive greater assistance and are given priority for admission at participating schools.

There are no "financial incentive[s]" that "ske[w]" the program toward religious schools. . . . The program here in fact creates financial *dis*incentives for religious schools, with private schools receiving only half the government assistance given to community schools and one-third the assistance given to magnet schools. Adjacent public schools, should any choose to accept program students, are also eligible to receive two to three times the state funding of a private religious school. Families too have a financial disincentive to choose a private religious school over other schools. Parents that choose to participate in the scholarship program and then to enroll their children in a private school (religious or nonreligious) must copay a portion of the school's tuition. Families that choose a community school, magnet school, or traditional public school pay nothing. Although such features of the program are not necessary to its constitutionality, they clearly dispel the claim that the program "creates . . . financial incentive[s] for parents to choose a sectarian school." *Zobrest.*

Respondents suggest that even without a financial incentive for parents to choose a religious school, the program creates a "public perception that the State is endorsing religious practices and beliefs." But we have repeatedly recognized that no reasonable observer would think a neutral program of private choice, where state aid reaches religious schools solely as a result of the numerous independent decisions of private individuals, carries with it the *imprimatur* of government endorsement. . . .

There also is no evidence that the program fails to provide genuine opportunities for Cleveland parents to select secular educational options for their school-age children. . . . That 46 of the 56 private schools now participating in the program are religious schools does not condemn it as a violation of the Establishment Clause. The Establishment Clause question is whether Ohio is coercing parents into sending their children to religious schools, and that question must be answered by evaluating *all* options Ohio provides Cleveland schoolchildren, only one of which is to obtain a program scholarship and then choose a religious school. . . .

Respondents . . . claim that even if we do not focus on the number of participating schools that are religious schools, we should attach constitutional significance to the fact that 96% of scholarship recipients have enrolled in religious schools. They claim that this alone proves parents lack genuine choice, even if no parent has ever said so. We need not consider this argument in detail, since it was flatly rejected in *Mueller,* where we found it irrelevant that 96% of parents taking deductions for tuition expenses paid tuition at religious schools. Indeed, we have recently found it irrelevant even to the constitutionality of a direct aid program that a vast majority of program benefits went to religious schools. See *Agostini.* The constitutionality of a neutral educational aid program simply does not turn on whether and why, in a particular area, at a particular time, most private schools are run by religious organizations, or most recipients choose to use the aid at a religious school. . . .

This point is aptly illustrated here. The 96% figure upon which the respondents . . . rely discounts entirely (1) the more than 1,900 Cleveland children enrolled in alternative community schools, (2) the more than 13,000 children enrolled in alternative magnet schools, and (3) the more than 1,400 children enrolled in traditional public schools with tutorial assistance. Including some or all of these children in the denominator of children enrolled in nontraditional schools during the 1999–2000 school year drops the percentage enrolled in religious schools from 96% to under 20%. . . .

In sum, the Ohio program is entirely neutral with respect to religion. It provides benefits directly to a wide spectrum of individuals, defined only by financial need and residence in a particular school district. It permits such individuals to exercise genuine choice among options public and private, secular and religious. The program is therefore a program of true private choice. In keeping with an unbroken line of decisions rejecting challenges to similar programs, we hold that the program does not offend the Establishment Clause.

The judgment of the Court of Appeals is reversed.

It is so ordered.

JUSTICE THOMAS, *concurring.*

Ten States have enacted some form of publicly funded private school choice as one means of raising the quality of education provided to underprivileged urban children. These programs address the root of the problem with failing urban public schools that disproportionately affect minority students. Society's other solution to these educational failures is often to provide racial preferences in higher education. Such preferences, however, run afoul of the Fourteenth Amendment's prohibition against distinctions based on race. By contrast, school choice programs that involve religious schools appear unconstitutional only to those who would twist the Fourteenth Amendment against itself by expansively incorporating the Establishment Clause. Converting the Fourteenth Amendment from a guarantee of opportunity to an obstacle against education reform distorts our constitutional values and disserves those in the greatest need. . . .

JUSTICE O'CONNOR, concurring.

[T]oday's decision [does not] signal a major departure from this Court's prior Establishment Clause jurisprudence. A central tool in our analysis of cases in this area has been the *Lemon* test. As originally formulated, a statute passed this test only if it had "a secular legislative purpose," if its "principal or primary effect" was one that "neither advance[d] nor inhibit[ed] religion," and if it did "not foster an excessive government entanglement with religion." *Lemon v. Kurtzman* (1971). In *Agostini v. Felton* (1997), we folded the entanglement inquiry into the primary effect inquiry. This made sense because both inquiries rely on the same evidence, and the degree of entanglement has implications for whether a statute advances or inhibits religion. The test today is basically the same as that set forth in *School Dist. of Abington Township v. Schempp* (1963) over 40 years ago.

The Court's opinion in these cases focuses on a narrow question related to the *Lemon* test: how to apply the primary effects prong in indirect aid cases? Specifically, it clarifies the basic inquiry when trying to determine whether a program that distributes aid to beneficiaries, rather than directly to service providers, has the primary effect of advancing or inhibiting religion or, as I have put it, of "endors[ing] or disapprov[ing] . . . religion." Courts are instructed to consider two factors: first, whether the program administers aid in a neutral fashion, without differentiation based on the religious status of beneficiaries or providers of services; second, and more importantly, whether beneficiaries of indirect aid have a genuine choice among religious and nonreligious organizations when determining the organization to which they will direct that aid. If the answer to either query is "no," the

program should be struck down under the Establishment Clause. . . .

In my view the . . . significant finding in these cases is that Cleveland parents who use vouchers to send their children to religious private schools do so as a result of true private choice. The Court rejects, correctly, the notion that the high percentage of voucher recipients who enroll in religious private schools necessarily demonstrates that parents do not actually have the option to send their children to nonreligious schools. . . .

Based on the reasoning in the Court's opinion, which is consistent with the realities of the Cleveland educational system, I am persuaded that the Cleveland voucher program affords parents of eligible children genuine nonreligious options and is consistent with the Establishment Clause.

JUSTICE BREYER, with whom JUSTICE STEVENS and JUSTICE SOUTER join, dissenting.

I write separately . . . to emphasize the risk that publicly financed voucher programs pose in terms of religiously based social conflict. I do so because I believe that the Establishment Clause concern for protecting the Nation's social fabric from religious conflict poses an overriding obstacle to the implementation of this well-intentioned school voucher program. . . .

. . . [T]he Court's 20th century Establishment Clause cases—both those limiting the practice of religion in public schools and those limiting the public funding of private religious education—focused directly upon social conflict, potentially created when government becomes involved in religious education. . . .

School voucher programs differ . . . in both kind and degree from aid programs upheld in the past. They differ in kind because they direct financing to a core function of the church: the teaching of religious truths to young children. For that reason the constitutional demand for "separation" is of particular constitutional concern. . . .

Vouchers also differ in degree. The aid programs recently upheld by the Court involved limited amounts of aid to religion. But the majority's analysis here appears to permit a considerable shift of taxpayer dollars from public secular schools to private religious schools. . . .

I do not believe that the "parental choice" aspect of the voucher program sufficiently offsets the concerns I have mentioned. Parental choice cannot help the taxpayer who does not want to finance the religious education of children. It will not always help the parent who may see little real choice between inadequate nonsectarian public education and adequate education at a school whose religious teachings are contrary to his own. It will not satisfy religious minorities unable to participate because they are too few in number to support the creation of their own private schools. It will not satisfy groups whose religious beliefs preclude them from participating in a government-sponsored program, and who may well feel ignored as government funds primarily support the education of children in the doctrines of the dominant religions. And it does little to ameliorate the entanglement problems or the related problems of social division. . . . Consequently, the fact that the parent may choose which school can cash the government's voucher check does not alleviate the Establishment Clause concerns associated with voucher programs.

. . . In a society composed of many different religious creeds, I fear that this present departure from the Court's earlier understanding risks creating a form of religiously based conflict potentially harmful to the Nation's social fabric. Because I believe the Establishment Clause was written in part to avoid this kind of conflict, and for reasons set forth by JUSTICE SOUTER and JUSTICE STEVENS, I respectfully dissent.

JUSTICE SOUTER, with whom JUSTICE STEVENS, JUSTICE GINSBURG, and JUSTICE BREYER join, dissenting.

The applicability of the Establishment Clause to public funding of benefits to religious schools was settled in *Everson v. Board of Ed. of Ewing* (1947), which inaugurated the modern era of establishment doctrine. The Court stated the principle in words from which there was no dissent:

"No tax in any amount, large or small, can be levied to support any religious activities or institutions, whatever they may be called, or whatever form they may adopt to teach or practice religion."

The Court has never in so many words repudiated this statement, let alone, in so many words, overruled *Everson*.

Today, however, the majority holds that the Establishment Clause is not offended by Ohio's Pilot Project Scholarship Program, under which students may be eligible to receive as much as $2,250 in the form of tuition vouchers transferable to religious schools. In the city of Cleveland the overwhelming proportion of large appropriations for voucher money must be spent on religious schools if it is to be spent at all, and will

be spent in amounts that cover almost all of tuition. The money will thus pay for eligible students' instruction not only in secular subjects but in religion as well, in schools that can fairly be characterized as founded to teach religious doctrine and to imbue teaching in all subjects with a religious dimension. Public tax money will pay at a systemic level for teaching the covenant with Israel and Mosaic law in Jewish schools, the primacy of the Apostle Peter and the Papacy in Catholic schools, the truth of reformed Christianity in Protestant schools, and the revelation to the Prophet in Muslim schools, to speak only of major religious groupings in the Republic.

How can a Court consistently leave *Everson* on the books and approve the Ohio vouchers? The answer is that it cannot. It is only by ignoring *Everson* that the majority can claim to rest on traditional law in its invocation of neutral aid provisions and private choice to sanction the Ohio law. It is, moreover, only by ignoring the meaning of neutrality and private choice themselves that the majority can even pretend to rest today's decision on those criteria. . . .

. . . *Everson*'s statement is still the touchstone of sound law, even though the reality is that in the matter of educational aid the Establishment Clause has largely been read away. True, the majority has not approved vouchers for religious schools alone, or aid earmarked for religious instruction. But no scheme so clumsy will ever get before us, and in the cases that we may see, like these, the Establishment Clause is largely silenced. I do not have the option to leave it silent, and I hope that a future Court will reconsider today's dramatic departure from basic Establishment Clause principle.

JUSTICE STEVENS, dissenting.

For the reasons stated by JUSTICE SOUTER and JUSTICE BREYER, I am convinced that the Court's decision is profoundly misguided. Admittedly, in reaching that conclusion I have been influenced by my understanding of the impact of religious strife on the decisions of our forbears to migrate to this continent, and on the decisions of neighbors in the Balkans, Northern Ireland, and the Middle East to mistrust one another. Whenever we remove a brick from the wall that was designed to separate religion and government, we increase the risk of religious strife and weaken the foundation of our democracy.

I respectfully dissent.

Along with *Agostini v. Felton* (1997) and *Mitchell v. Helms* (2000), the *Zelman* decision marked a significant shift in the direction of accommodation. Chief Justice Rehnquist's opinion for the Court ignored *Lemon* altogether. Instead, he stressed that the Cleveland voucher program was neutral with respect to religion. The government offered aid equally to students attending public and private schools, both religious and nonreligious. Furthermore, the way the government funds were spent was a result of the genuine and independent choices of private individuals. The program did not provide incentives that skewed those choices toward religious schools.

Although Justice O'Connor's concurring opinion claimed that *Zelman* did not represent a major departure from past establishment clause jurisprudence, the four dissenters disagreed. They emphasized that for the first time the Court permitted tax dollars to pay the tuition of primary and secondary students attending religious schools. In addition, Justice Breyer contended that the voucher program posed a significant risk of promoting religiously based social conflict, a danger the establishment clause was designed to prevent.

Although *Zelman* validated the Cleveland voucher program, it did not remove the confusion over the meaning of the establishment clause. As the Court's 5–4 vote and multiple opinions demonstrate, the justices remained badly divided. Moreover, the majority did not overrule *Lemon,* even though they ignored it. *Lemon* remains the Court's official standard for evaluating establishment clause claims.

We have seen the conflict over an appropriate establishment clause standard fought out in cases challenging government programs that fund religious activities. We now turn our attention to other areas where establishment clause disputes have arisen. As you read the cases and commentary that follow, ask yourself whether the Court has been any more successful in reaching a consistent interpretation of the First Amendment than it has with the religious aid cases.

Public Facilities and Funds

The justices have settled a number of cases involving access by religious groups to public facilities, most often public school buildings and resources. Initially, the justices took a firm position against allowing religious teaching or other activities in public buildings. As early as 1948, in *Illinois ex rel. McCollum v. Board of Education,* the Court struck down a so-called

released-time program in which public schools cooperated with local churches to provide religious education to students. The program was found to violate the establishment clause in large measure because the religious instruction took place in public school buildings.

In response, some school districts developed programs that allowed students, with parental permission, to be released from normal classes to receive instruction at religious centers located off-campus. In ***Zorach v. Clausen*** (1952) the Court approved such a program operating in New York. Writing for the majority, Justice Douglas, who normally advocated strong separationist positions, concluded that the revised programs corrected the fundamental defect of the old one; no longer would religious instruction occur on public school premises. But Douglas went further. He noted that the prohibition against religious establishment "does not say that in every and all respects there shall be separation of Church and State." If it did, according to Douglas, state and religion would be "hostile, suspicious, and even unfriendly" toward each other. This state of affairs would be out of line with the spirit of the First Amendment and the desires of the American people. For, as Douglas wrote in one of the most often quoted passages in this area of the law,

[w]e are a religious people whose institutions presuppose a Supreme Being. We guarantee the freedom to worship as one chooses. We make room for as wide a variety of beliefs and creeds as the spiritual needs of man deem. . . . When the state encourages religious instruction or cooperates with religious authorities by adjusting the schedule of public events to sectarian needs, it follows the best of our traditions. For it then respects the religious nature of our people and accommodates the public service to their spiritual needs. To hold that it may not would be to find callous indifference to religious groups. That would be preferring those who believe in no religion over those who do believe.

Justice Black, who wrote the Court's opinion in *McCollum,* dissented. He could find no significant difference between the invalid Illinois program and the revised policy challenged in *Zorach.* In his view, the *McCollum* program was unconstitutional not simply because it took place on school grounds but because it gave "invaluable aid to religion," a characteristic of all released-time programs, as well.

With *Zorach* the Court closed the released-time issue. So long as instruction takes place off school premises, it is constitutionally permissible. Beginning in the 1980s, however, the Court was confronted with another kind of question: May public schools deny religious groups the use of their facilities for meetings or other programs? This new generation of suits was different from the early released-time cases. Now public schools were denying religious groups access to their buildings, rather than seeking to facilitate the teaching of religion on or off their premises. Keep in mind that when these cases came up, the Court had a standard of law, the Lemon test, that it did not have at the time of *McCollum* and *Zorach*. How would the Court resolve this new kind of access case?

In the first of these cases, *Widmar v. Vincent* (1981), the Court struck down a University of Missouri at Kansas City policy that denied a student religious group the use of meeting rooms to which nonreligious groups were granted access. In doing so, the justices rejected the school's position that allowing the group to conduct religious activities in campus rooms would cross the constitutional line between church and state. Writing for the majority, Justice Lewis F. Powell applied the Lemon rule to find in favor of the students. He said that equal access policies have the secular purpose of encouraging the exchange of ideas. Further, he asserted that if the university retained its closed access policy, it would risk excessive entanglement with religion, as it would have to determine whether groups seeking access were engaging in religious speech or worship. Finally, Powell claimed that equal access policies do not have the primary effect of advancing religion; rather, they encourage "all forms of discourse."

Widmar dealt exclusively with colleges and universities, asserting that equal access policies at these institutions would not violate the establishment clause. In 1984, with passage of the Equal Access Act, Congress built on *Widmar*. The act required all public secondary schools with "limited open forum" policies to give equal access to "any students who wish to conduct a meeting within that limited open forum," regardless of the "religious, political, philosophical, or content of the speech at such meetings." A limited open forum is in effect if a school permits "one or more noncurriculum related student groups to meet in school premises during noninstructional times."

Some observers speculated that the Court would strike down the Equal Access Act as a violation of the religious establishment clause because the justices might be reluctant to apply a university policy to less mature secondary school students. In *Board of Education of Westside Community School v. Mergens* (1990), however,

a divided Court voted to uphold the law. In a plurality opinion (fully endorsed by only four members) Justice O'Connor held that the law did not have the primary effect of advancing religion. In her argument, O'Connor adopted the logic of the endorsement test, which itself built on *Lemon* (see Table 4-3): religion was not advanced because the speech endorsing it was private, not governmental. Private endorsements of religion (such as those that might occur during a group meeting), she asserted, were protected by the free speech and free exercise clauses of the First Amendment, but government endorsements violated the establishment clause.

Justices Kennedy and Scalia agreed that the act was constitutional, but they took issue with O'Connor's endorsement approach. They advocated a standard emphasizing the relative "coercive" nature of government policies. Kennedy wrote:

[N]o constitutional violation occurs if the school's action is based upon a recognition of the fact that membership in a religious club is one of many permissible ways for a student to further his or her own personal enrichment. The inquiry with respect to coercion must be whether the government imposes pressure upon a student to participate in a religious activity. This inquiry, of course, must be undertaken with sensitivity to the special circumstances that exist in a secondary school where the line between voluntary and coerced participation may be difficult to draw. No such coercion . . . has been shown to exist as a necessary result of this statute.

Mergens indicates the Court's willingness to uphold government policies that allow religious groups equal access to school facilities. It also shows the Court's lack of unity over the appropriate standard by which to adjudicate religious establishment cases. That is why observers anxiously awaited the decision in ***Lamb's Chapel v. Center Moriches Union Free School District*** (1993). Some thought that by 1993 the justices would coalesce around a particular test, but the Court's decision revealed only continued division.

Lamb's Chapel concerned the policies of Long Island's Center Moriches school district with respect to the after-school use of school property by outside groups and/or its use for purposes other than education. Consistent with state law, the school board issued rules allowing use of school property only for social, civic, or recreational purposes or by political organizations. Its rules prohibited use by groups for religious purposes.

Lamb's Chapel, an evangelical church located in the Center Moriches community, twice asked the school board for permission to show a six-part film series in school buildings after normal school hours. The series featured lectures by a psychologist on "the undermining influences of the media [which] could only be counterbalanced by returning to traditional, Christian family values instilled at an early age." Believing that the films were church related, the school district denied both requests.

Lamb's Chapel took the school district to court, asserting that the denial violated the church's First Amendment guarantees of free speech and religious liberty. After the lower courts rejected its claims, the church appealed to the U.S. Supreme Court, which struck down the school board's policy. Writing for a unanimous Court, Justice White found that the school board's denial of permission to show the films violated the free speech provisions of the First Amendment. Refusing access based on the religious content of the films constituted government regulation of speech "in ways that favor some viewpoints or ideas at the expense of others." White also rejected the school board's defense that its policies were required by the *Lemon* decision, arguing that there was no ground to conclude that the school district was endorsing the religious group by allowing it to hold a public meeting in a classroom after school hours.

Although the vote was unanimous, disagreements over the appropriate standard to use continued to divide the justices, and their rhetoric became more extreme. Three justices (Scalia, Kennedy, and Thomas) harshly criticized the Court's use of the Lemon test and the endorsement standard.

In 2001, however, the Court demonstrated a consistency unusual for establishment clause litigation when it reinforced its position on access to public school buildings in *Good News Club v. Milford Central School.* This dispute began when a private Christian children's organization requested the use of classrooms for weekly meetings. The school allowed outside groups to use school facilities after hours but excluded those whose purpose was to conduct religious instruction or services. Good News Club leaders acknowledged that the meetings were primarily for the singing of religious songs, Bible lessons, prayer, and Scripture recitations. Consequently, the request for access was denied.

The Supreme Court held that the denial violated the Good News Club's First Amendment rights because school officials had engaged in impermissible viewpoint discrimination. Upon creating a limited public forum, the school could deny access based on subject matter, but it could not discriminate on the basis of

Ronald Rosenberger, right, cofounder of the religious newspaper Wide Awake, holds a copy outside the Supreme Court after oral arguments in Rosenberger v. University of Virginia. *At left is cofounder Robert Prince.*

viewpoint. Other groups interested in promoting good character and values had been granted access; the Good News Club was also involved in character and moral development but promoted it from a distinctly Christian perspective. Therefore, viewpoint, not subject matter, impermissibly dictated the school's decision. Once again, the Court emphasized that there was no realistic danger that members of the community would believe that the school was endorsing religion or any particular creed; nor was there any evidence that any child would feel coerced into attending a Good News Club meeting.

But what about access to school funds? Are students in religious groups entitled to funds from a state university to promote their activities if students from nonreligious organizations receive such support? Such was the issue presented in **Rosenberger v. University of Virginia** (1995). In this dispute, Ronald Rosenberger, a member of a recognized organization of Christian students at the University of Virginia, objected to a denial of student activity funds to support the printing of the group's newspaper, *Wide Awake: A Christian Perspective at the*

University of Virginia. Other student groups received funding to support their publications, but the university's rules prohibited support for religious activities.

A closely divided Supreme Court ruled in favor of Rosenberger. Relying on decisions such as *Lamb's Chapel,* Justice Kennedy, writing for the Court, found the university's policies to be an unconstitutional form of "viewpoint discrimination." He explained that "it does not violate the Establishment Clause for a public university to grant access to its facilities on a religion-neutral basis to a wide spectrum of student groups." Ruling otherwise, according to Kennedy, would require the university to scrutinize all student speech to ensure that it did not contain excessively religious content. Four justices dissented from this view, condemning the majority for approving for the first time direct government expenditures to support core religious activities.

Clearly, the *Rosenberger* decision did little to settle the disagreements within the Court over the governing standard to use in this line of establishment clause cases. Although many thought that the Court might use *Rosenberger* to overrule *Lemon,* that did not occur. In fact, the majority opinion largely avoided any direct mention of *Lemon,* although the opinion certainly rested on precedents based on that decision. The justices seemed to have left this battle for another day.

Teaching Religious Principles in Public Schools

Some public schools have tried to promote particular religions by slanting the curriculum to favor religious views about secular subjects. The best-known and most enduring example is the way teachers address the origin of human life. Did humankind evolve, as scientists suggest (evolutionary theory), or did it come about as a result of some divine intervention, as various religions argue (creationism)?

This debate received an unusual amount of attention in 1925 when the ACLU, represented in court by Clarence Darrow, sponsored a legal challenge to a Tennessee law that made it a crime to teach evolutionary principles or any theory denigrating the biblical version of creation. That case, popularized as the Scopes monkey trial, never made it to the Supreme Court *(see Box 4-5),* but two similar challenges did.

The first was ***Epperson v. Arkansas,*** a 1968 case in which the Court considered the constitutionality of a 1928 state law that was an adaptation of Tennessee's 1925 law. The Arkansas law made it a crime for any state

university or public school instructor "to teach the theory or doctrine that mankind ascended or descended from a lower order of animals" or to "adopt or use . . . a textbook that teaches" evolutionary theory. The history of the law's adoption makes it clear that its purpose was to further religious beliefs about the beginning of life. For example, an advertisement placed in an Arkansas newspaper to drum up support for the act said: "The Bible or atheism, which? All atheists favor evolution. . . . Shall conscientious church members be forced to pay taxes to support teachers to teach evolution which will undermine the faith of their children?"

Epperson began in the mid-1960s when the school system in Little Rock, Arkansas, decided to adopt a biology book that contained a chapter on evolutionary theory. Susan Epperson, a biology teacher in a Little Rock high school, wanted to use the new book but was afraid—in light of the 1928 law—that she could face criminal prosecution if she did so. She asked the Arkansas courts to nullify the law, and, when the Arkansas Supreme Court turned down her request, she appealed her case to the U.S. Supreme Court.

Writing for a unanimous Court, Justice Abe Fortas reversed the state supreme court's ruling. Relying heavily on *Everson* (the Lemon test had yet to be established), Fortas said, "The First Amendment mandates governmental neutrality between religion and religion, between religion and nonreligion." Under this standard the outcome was clear to the justices:

Arkansas' law cannot be defended as an act of religious neutrality. Arkansas did not seek to excise from the curricula of its schools . . . all discussion of the origin of man. The law's effort was confined to an attempt to blot out a particular theory because of its supposed conflict with the Biblical account, literally read. Plainly, the law is contrary to the mandate of the First . . . Amendment.

Despite the Court's clear statement about the constitutional violation posed by laws that banned teaching about evolution, some states devised other ways to teach creationism. In *Edwards v. Aguillard* (1987) the Court reviewed one of these attempts. This case was decided after the Lemon test had been established and during the chief justiceship of William Rehnquist, who—along with Antonin Scalia—sought greater accommodation between church and state. As you read this case, consider the difference between the Court's opinion and the dissent filed by Scalia and joined by Rehnquist.

BOX 4-5   THE SCOPES MONKEY TRIAL

"The law is a ass," observed Charles Dickens's character, Mr. Bumble, in *Oliver Twist*. In 1925 many Americans, watching with amazement the circus-like proceedings of the dramatic Scopes trial in Tennessee, found themselves echoing the same sentiments. "Isn't it difficult to realize that a trial of this kind is possible in the twentieth century in the United States of America?" demanded the lawyer for the defense, the famed Clarence Darrow. In truth, the case appeared a vestigial survival from an earlier day when people were prosecuted for witchcraft or for offenses like imagining the king's death. Headlined in the press as the Great Monkey Trial, it pitted the biblical version of creation against the teachings of Charles Darwin, and did so in a courtroom atmosphere more closely resembling that of a revival meeting than a hall of justice.

The defendant, John T. Scopes, was a twenty-four-year-old high school teacher in Dayton, Tennessee, who was prosecuted for teaching evolution in violation of a state statute that prohibited the teaching in any public school of "any theory that denies the story of the divine creation of man as taught in the Bible, and to teach instead that man has descended from a lower order of animals." Conducted in the heat of July, the trial was a parody of all that a legal proceeding should be. Dayton was ready for what it hoped would be the Waterloo of science. "One was hard put . . . ," an observer wrote, "to know whether Dayton was holding a camp meeting, a Chautauqua, a street fair, a carnival or a belated Fourth of July celebration. Literally, it was drunk on religious excitement."

The courtroom itself was decked with a large banner, exhorting everyone to "Read your Bible daily." Darrow finally got it removed by demanding equal space for a banner urging, "Read your Evolution." The stars of the trial were the lawyers: Clarence Darrow, perhaps the best known criminal lawyer in American history (Lincoln Steffens had called him "the attorney for the damned"), representing Scopes and, indirectly, Darwin and evolution, and, against him, William Jennings Bryan, the Great Commoner, orator of the famed "Cross of Gold" speech in 1896, three-time candidate for president, and secretary of state under Woodrow Wilson, who had volunteered to direct the prosecution. Aging and sanctimonious, Bryan was the leading Fundamentalist of the day. "I am more interested in the Rock of Ages than in the age of rocks," he proclaimed.

At the trial's beginning, Darrow said later, "the judge . . . with great solemnity and all the dignity possible announced that Brother Twitchell would invoke the Divine blessing. This was new to me. I had practiced law for more than forty years, and had never before heard God called in to referee a court trial." Darrow's objection to the blessing was overruled, and each day's session began with a prayer by a different preacher. The high point of the trial saw Darrow put Bryan himself on the stand as an expert on "religion." *The New York Times* described this as the most amazing court scene in history, and out-of-state reporters and observers like the iconoclast H. L. Mencken had a field day conveying the incongruous proceedings to the nation. Bryan stuck doggedly to his insistence on the literal truth of the Bible, refusing, in Darrow's phrase, "to choose between his crude beliefs and the common intelligence of modern times."

In the end, the local population felt it won a righteous victory when the jury found Scopes guilty. But the judge imposed only a $100 fine, and, on appeal, the Tennessee Supreme Court reversed the decision on a technicality: the court, rather than the jury, had set the fine. The case itself was more dramatic than significant—unless it deserved remembrance as an example of the law at its worst. "I think," said Darrow during the trial, "this case will be remembered because it is the first case of this sort since we stopped trying people in America for witchcraft." On another plane, Darrow's withering examination during the trial went far to discredit Fundamentalist dogma. Though anti-evolution laws remained on the books in what Mencken referred to as "the Bible Belt" of the South, they were never again enforced. And in 1968, the U.S. Supreme Court finally struck down an Arkansas anti-evolution law, though admitting that by then "the statute is presently more of a curiosity than a vital fact of life."

SOURCE: Bernard Schwartz, *The American Heritage History of the Law in America* (New York: McGraw-Hill, 1974), 224. Reprinted by permission of the author.

Edwards v. Aguillard

482 U.S. 578 (1987)
http://laws.findlaw.com/US/482/578.html
Oral arguments are available at http://www.oyez.org.
Vote: 7 (Blackmun, Brennan, Marshall, O'Connor, Powell, Stevens, White)
    2 (Rehnquist, Scalia)

OPINION OF THE COURT: *Brennan*
CONCURRING OPINIONS: *Powell, White*
DISSENTING OPINION: *Scalia*

FACTS:

After *Epperson,* organized interests—particularly religious groups—lobbied state legislatures to pass new laws. Louisiana enacted the Balanced Treatment for Creation-Science and Evolution-Science in Public School Instruction Act in 1981. This law differed from the one struck down in *Epperson* because it did not outlaw the teaching of evolution. Rather, it prohibited schools from teaching evolutionary principles unless theories of creationism also were taught.

The state and various organizations offered two major lines of argument in support of this legislation. One is that evolutionary theory is a religious tenet, and the religion is secular humanism. If evolution is taught, then so should creationism, which has its origin in a literal reading of Genesis. In other words, public school teachers must give equal time to the two primary "religious" views of the origin of humankind. The second argument states that creationism is a science just like evolutionary theory

Don Aguillard, assistant principal at Acadiana High School in Scott, Louisiana, filed suit against the state's creation science law in 1981. Six years later, in Edwards v. Aguillard, the Supreme Court found that law to be in violation of the establishment clause.

and, therefore, deserves equal treatment in public school curricula.

Represented by the ACLU, Assistant Principal Don Aguillard and several teachers, parents, and religious groups challenged the act as a violation of the establishment clause. Attorneys and amici attacked the argument that creationism is a science. As amicus curiae National Academy of Sciences put it: "The explanatory power of a scientific hypothesis or theory is, in effect, the medium of exchange by which the value of a scientific theory is determined in the marketplace of ideas that constitutes the scientific community. Creationists do not compete in the marketplace, and creation-science does not offer scientific value." What the legislature had done, according to the ACLU, was to give equal time to a particular religion's view of the origins of humankind, which, the ACLU argued, violated the establishment clause.

ARGUMENTS:

For the appellant, Edwin Edwards, Governor of Louisiana:

- Previous decisions by the Supreme Court allow public school references to a creator or God (e.g., *Lynch v. Donnelly, Zorach v. Clausen, Engel v. Vitale*).
- Creation science consists of scientific evidence, not religious concepts. It is no less scientific than is the theory of evolution.
- The Balanced Treatment Act is constitutional because it has a primary secular purpose of advancing academic freedom.

For the appellee, Don Aguillard:

- The Creationism Act expressly endorses a religious belief based on a biblical account of origin of life and was intended to do so.
- The Creationism Act lacks any legitimate secular purpose.
- Implementing the Creationism Act into the public school curriculum necessarily requires an excessive government entanglement with religion.

■ **JUSTICE BRENNAN DELIVERED THE OPINION OF THE COURT.**

The Establishment Clause forbids the enactment of any law "respecting an establishment of religion." The Court has applied a three-pronged test to determine whether legislation comports with the Establishment Clause.

First, the legislature must have adopted the law with a secular purpose. Second, the statute's principal or primary effect must be one that neither advances nor inhibits religion. Third, the statute must not result in an excessive entanglement of government with religion. State action violates the Establishment Clause if it fails to satisfy any of these prongs.

In this case, the Court must determine whether the Establishment Clause was violated in the special context of the public elementary and secondary school system. States and local school boards are generally afforded considerable discretion in operating public schools. . . .

The Court has been particularly vigilant in monitoring compliance with the Establishment Clause in elementary and secondary schools. Families entrust public schools with the education of their children, but condition their trust on the understanding that the classroom will not purposely be used to advance religious views that may conflict with the private beliefs of the student and his or her family. Students in such institutions are impressionable and their attendance is involuntary. The State exerts great authority and coercive power through mandatory attendance requirements, and because of the students' emulation of teachers as role models and the children's susceptibility to peer pressure. . . .

Therefore, in employing the three-pronged *Lemon* test, we must do so mindful of the particular concerns that arise in the context of public elementary and secondary schools. We now turn to the evaluation of the Act under the *Lemon* test.

Lemon's first prong focuses on the purpose that animated adoption of the Act. . . . If the law was enacted for the purpose of endorsing religion, "no consideration of the second or third criteria [of *Lemon*] is necessary." In this case, the petitioners have identified no clear secular purpose for the Louisiana Act.

True, the Act's stated purpose is to protect academic freedom. This phrase might, in common parlance, be understood as referring to enhancing the freedom of teachers to teach what they will. The Court of Appeals, however, correctly concluded that the Act was not designed to further that goal. We find no merit in the State's argument that the "legislature may not [have] use[d] the terms 'academic freedom' in the correct legal sense. They might have [had] in mind, instead, a basic concept of fairness; teaching all of the evidence." Even if "academic freedom" is read to mean "teaching all of the evidence" with respect to

the origin of human beings, the Act does not further this purpose. The goal of providing a more comprehensive science curriculum is not furthered either by outlawing the teaching of evolution or by requiring the teaching of creation science.

While the Court is normally deferential to a State's articulation of a secular purpose, it is required that the statement of such purpose be sincere and not a sham. . . .

It is clear from the legislative history that the purpose of the legislative sponsor, Senator Bill Keith, was to narrow the science curriculum. During the legislative hearings, Senator Keith stated: "My preference would be that neither [creationism nor evolution] be taught." Such a ban on teaching does not promote—indeed, it undermines—the provision of a comprehensive scientific education.

It is equally clear that requiring schools to teach creation science with evolution does not advance academic freedom. The Act does not grant teachers a flexibility that they did not already possess to supplant the present science curriculum with the presentation of theories, besides evolution, about the origin of life. Indeed, the Court of Appeals found that no law prohibited Louisiana public schoolteachers from teaching any scientific theory. As the president of the Louisiana Science Teachers Association testified, "[a]ny scientific concept that's based on established fact can be included in our curriculum already, and no legislation allowing this is necessary." The Act provides Louisiana schoolteachers with no new authority. Thus the stated purpose is not furthered by it. . . .

Furthermore, the goal of basic "fairness" is hardly furthered by the Act's discriminatory preference for the teaching of creation science and against the teaching of evolution. While requiring that curriculum guides be developed for creation science, the Act says nothing of comparable guides for evolution. Similarly, research services are supplied for creation science but not for evolution. Only "creation scientists" can serve on the panel that supplies the resource services. The Act forbids school boards to discriminate against anyone who "chooses to be a creation-scientist" or to teach "creationism," but fails to protect those who choose to teach evolution or any other non-creation science theory, or who refuse to teach creation science.

If the Louisiana legislature's purpose was solely to maximize the comprehensiveness and effectiveness of science instruction, it would have encouraged the teaching of all scientific theories about the origins of humankind. But under the Act's requirements, teachers who were once free to teach any and all facets of this subject are now unable to do so. Moreover, the Act fails even to ensure that creation science will be taught, but instead requires the teaching of this theory only when the theory of evolution is taught. Thus we agree with the Court of Appeals' conclusion that the Act does not serve to protect academic freedom, but has the distinctly different purpose of discrediting "evolution by counterbalancing its teaching at every turn with the teaching of creationism." . . .

. . . The preeminent purpose of the Louisiana legislature was clearly to advance the religious viewpoint that a supernatural being created humankind. The term "creation science" was defined as embracing this particular religious doctrine by those responsible for the passage of the Creationism Act. Senator Keith's leading expert on creation science, Edward Boudreaux, testified at the legislative hearings that the theory of creation science included belief in the existence of a supernatural creator. Senator Keith also cited testimony from other experts to support the creation science view that "a creator [was] responsible for the universe and everything in it." The legislative history therefore reveals that the term "creation science," as contemplated by the legislature that adopted this Act, embodies the religious belief that a supernatural creator was responsible for the creation of humankind.

Furthermore, it is not happenstance that the legislature required the teaching of a theory that coincided with this religious view. The legislative history documents that the Act's primary purpose was to change the science curriculum of public schools in order to provide persuasive advantage to a particular religious doctrine that rejects the factual basis of evolution in its entirety. The sponsor of the Creationism Act, Senator Keith, explained during the legislative hearings that his disdain for the theory of evolution resulted from the support that evolution supplied to views contrary to his own religious beliefs. . . . The legislation therefore sought to alter the science curriculum to reflect endorsement of a religious view that is antagonistic to the theory of evolution.

In this case, the purpose of the Creationism Act was to restructure the science curriculum to conform with a particular religious viewpoint. Out of many possible science subjects taught in the public schools, the legislature chose to affect the teaching of the one scientific theory that historically has been opposed by certain

religious sects. As in *Epperson [v. Arkansas, 1968]*, the legislature passed the Act to give preference to those religious groups which have as one of their tenets the creation of humankind by a divine creator. The "overriding fact" that confronted the Court in *Epperson* was "that Arkansas' law selects from the body of knowledge a particular segment which it proscribes for the sole reason that it is deemed to conflict with . . . a particular interpretation of the Book of Genesis by a particular religious group." Similarly, the Creationism Act is designed *either* to promote the theory of creation science which embodies a particular religious tenet by requiring that creation science is taught whenever evolution is taught *or* to prohibit the teaching of a scientific theory disfavored by certain religious sects by forbidding the teaching of evolution when creation science is not also taught. The Establishment Clause, however, "forbids alike the preference of a religious doctrine or the prohibition of theory which is deemed antagonistic to a particular dogma." Because the primary purpose of the Creationism Act is to advance a particular religious belief, the Act endorses religion in violation of the First Amendment. . . .

The Louisiana Creationism Act advances a religious doctrine by requiring either the banishment of the theory of evolution from public school classrooms or the presentation of a religious viewpoint that rejects evolution in its entirety. The Act violates the Establishment Clause of the First Amendment because it seeks to employ the symbolic and financial support of government to achieve a religious purpose. The judgment of the Court of Appeals therefore is

Affirmed.

**JUSTICE SCALIA, with whom
THE CHIEF JUSTICE joins, dissenting.**

It is important to stress that the purpose forbidden by *Lemon* is the purpose to "advance religion." . . . Our cases in no way imply that the Establishment Clause forbids legislators merely to act upon their religious convictions. We surely would not strike down a law providing money to feed the hungry or shelter the homeless if it could be demonstrated that, but for the religious beliefs of the legislators, the funds would not have been approved. Notwithstanding the majority's implication to the contrary, we do not presume that the sole purpose of a law is to advance religion merely because it was supported strongly by organized religions or by adherents of particular faiths. . . . To do so would deprive religious men and women of their right to participate in the political process. Today's religious activism may give us the Balanced Treatment Act, but yesterday's resulted in the abolition of slavery, and tomorrow's may bring relief for famine victims. . . .

With the foregoing in mind, I now turn to the purposes underlying adoption of the Balanced Treatment Act.

We have relatively little information upon which to judge the motives of those who supported the Act. About the only direct evidence is the statute itself and transcripts of the seven committee hearings at which it was considered. . . . Nevertheless, there is ample evidence that the majority is wrong in holding that the Balanced Treatment Act is without secular purpose.

At the outset, it is important to note that the Balanced Treatment Act did not fly through the Louisiana Legislature on wings of fundamentalist religious fervor—which would be unlikely, in any event, since only a small minority of the State's citizens belong to fundamentalist religious denominations. The Act had its genesis (so to speak) in legislation introduced by Senator Bill Keith in June 1980. . . .

Before summarizing the testimony of Senator Keith and his supporters, I wish to make clear that I by no means intend to endorse its accuracy. But my views (and the views of this Court) about creation science and evolution are (or should be) beside the point. Our task is not to judge the debate about teaching the origins of life, but to ascertain what the members of the Louisiana Legislature believed. The vast majority of them voted to approve a bill which explicitly stated a secular purpose; what is crucial is not their *wisdom* in believing that purpose would be achieved by the bill, but their *sincerity* in believing it would be.

Most of the testimony in support of Senator Keith's bill came from the Senator himself and from scientists and educators he presented, many of whom enjoyed academic credentials that may have been regarded as quite impressive by members of the Louisiana Legislature. . . .

Senator Keith and his witnesses testified essentially as set forth in the following numbered paragraphs:

(1) There are two and only two scientific explanations for the beginning of life—evolution and creation science. . . .

(2) The body of scientific evidence supporting creation science is as strong as that supporting evolution. . . .

(3) Creation science is educationally valuable. Students exposed to it better understand the current state of scientific evidence about the origin of life. . . .

(4) Although creation science is educationally valuable and strictly scientific, it is now being censored from or misrepresented in the public schools. Evolution, in turn, is misrepresented as an absolute truth. . . .

(5) The censorship of creation science has at least two harmful effects. First, it deprives students of knowledge of one of the two scientific explanations for the origin of life and leads them to believe that evolution is proven fact; thus, their education suffers and they are wrongly taught that science has proved their religious beliefs false. Second, it violates the Establishment Clause. The United States Supreme Court has held that secular humanism is a religion. . . .

We have no way of knowing, of course, how many legislators believed the testimony of Senator Keith and his witnesses. But in the absence of evidence to the contrary, we have to assume that many of them did. Given that assumption, the Court today plainly errs in holding that the Louisiana Legislature passed the Balanced Treatment Act for exclusively religious purposes. . . .

I have to this point assumed the validity of the *Lemon* "purpose" test. In fact, however, I think the pessimistic evaluation that THE CHIEF JUSTICE made of the totality of *Lemon* is particularly applicable to the "purpose" prong: it is "a constitutional theory [that] has no basis in the history of the amendment it seeks to interpret, is difficult to apply and yields unprincipled results. . . ." [*Wallace v. Jaffree*, Rehnquist, dissenting]

Our cases interpreting and applying the purpose test have made such a maze of the Establishment Clause that even the most conscientious governmental officials can only guess what motives will be held unconstitutional. We have said essentially the following: Government may not act with the purpose of advancing religion, except when forced to do so by the Free Exercise Clause (which is now and then); or when eliminating existing governmental hostility to religion (which exists sometimes); or even when merely accommodating governmentally uninhibited religious practices, except that at some point (it is unclear where) intentional accommodation results in the fostering of religion, which is of course unconstitutional.

But the difficulty of knowing what vitiating purpose one is looking for is as nothing compared with the difficulty of knowing how or where to find it. For while it is possible to discern the objective "purpose" of a statute (i.e., the public good at which its provisions appear to be directed), or even the formal motivation for a statute where that is explicitly set forth (as it was, to no avail, here), discerning the subjective motivation of those enacting the statute is, to be honest, almost always an impossible task. The number of possible motivations, to begin with, is not binary, or indeed even finite. In the present case, for example, a particular legislator need not have voted for the Act either because he wanted to foster religion or because he wanted to improve education. He may have thought the bill would provide jobs for his district, or may have wanted to make amends with a faction of his party he had alienated on another vote, or he may have been a close friend of the bill's sponsor, or he may have been repaying a favor he owed the Majority Leader, or he may have hoped the Governor would appreciate his vote and make a fundraising appearance for him, or he may have been pressured to vote for a bill he disliked by a wealthy contributor . . . or, of course, he may have had (and very likely did have) a combination of some of the above and many other motivations. To look for *the sole purpose* of even a single legislator is probably to look for something that does not exist.

Putting that problem aside, however, where ought we to look for the individual legislator's purpose? We cannot of course assume that every member present (if, as is unlikely, we know who or even how many they were) agreed with the motivation expressed in a particular legislator's pre-enactment floor or committee statement. Quite obviously, "[w]hat motivates one legislator to make a speech about a statute is not necessarily what motivates scores of others to enact it." . . . Can we assume, then, that they all agree with the motivation expressed in the staff-prepared committee reports they might have read—even though we are unwilling to assume that they agreed with the motivation expressed in the very statute that they voted for? Should we consider post-enactment floor statements? Or postenactment testimony from legislators, obtained expressly for the lawsuit? Should we consider media reports on the realities of the legislative bargaining? All of these sources, of course, are eminently manipulable. . . .

Given the many hazards involved in assessing the subjective intent of governmental decisionmakers, the first prong of *Lemon* is defensible, I think, only if the text of the Establishment Clause demands it. That is surely not the case. The Clause states that "Congress shall make no law respecting an establishment of religion." One could argue, I suppose, that any time Congress acts with the *intent* of advancing religion, it has enacted a "law respecting an establishment of religion"; but far from being an unavoidable reading, it is quite an unnatural one. . . . It is, in short, far from an inevitable reading of the Establishment Clause that it forbids all governmental action intended to advance religion; and if not inevitable, any reading with such untoward consequences must be wrong.

In the past we have attempted to justify our embarrassing Establishment Clause jurisprudence on the ground that it "sacrifices clarity and predictability for flexibility." . . . One commentator has aptly characterized this as "a euphemism . . . for . . . the absence of any principled rationale." I think it time that we sacrifice some "flexibility" for "clarity and predictability." Abandoning *Lemon's* purpose test—a test which exacerbates the tension between the Free Exercise and Establishment Clauses, has no basis in the language or history of the Amendment, and, as today's decision shows, has wonderfully flexible consequences—would be a good place to start.

Writing for the Court, Brennan had little trouble applying *Lemon* to rule against the state. The majority found that the law lacked a secular purpose; rather, its purpose was to "endorse a particular religious view." But Justice Scalia's dissent was a sign of things to come. Not only did Scalia adopt the state's argument that there is "ample uncontradicted testimony" to indicate that "creation science is a body of scientific knowledge rather than a revealed belief," but he also criticized the purpose prong of *Lemon* as "indefensible" and as a main contributor to the Court's "embarrassing Establishment Clause jurisprudence." This may have been Scalia's first attack on *Lemon,* but, as we know from *Lamb's Chapel,* it would not be his last. Since *Edwards v. Aguillard,* Scalia has become more adamant in his view that *Lemon* should be discarded in favor of a standard that would bring more "clarity and predictability" to this area of the law.

In spite of decisions by the Supreme Court, the drive to incorporate a biblical interpretation of the origins of humankind into public school classrooms has not subsided. Instead, campaigns to include "intelligent design," as it has become known, in public school science curricula are active today in more than twenty states.[27] Public opinion polls have found that about three-quarters of Americans believe that God created humans in their

---

27. "U.S. Evolution Battle Opens," BBC News, September 27, 2005.

present form or that humans evolved with God's guidance, and that about two-thirds favor teaching creationism along with evolution in the public schools.[28] Furthermore, such polling results have been remarkably stable for decades. As creationism supporters achieve success in local school districts, court challenges on establishment clause grounds are inevitable.

Prayer in School

Throughout most of the nation's history, almost all public schools engaged in religious practices of some kind: they may have held devotional services, distributed Bibles, or taught about religion. Particularly prevalent in school was prayer. As Table 4-4 indicates, in the 1960s the Bible was read regularly in most public schools in the South and East; in other schools, students recited state-written prayers. Separationist groups believed that these practices violated the establishment clause and set out to persuade the Court to eradicate them. Their initial suit, ***Engel v. Vitale*** (1962), challenged a New York requirement that teachers each morning lead public school children in reciting a prayer written by the state's board of regents: "Almighty God, we acknowledge our dependence upon Thee, and we beg Thy blessings upon us, our parents, our teachers and our country." New York representatives argued that this prayer was innocuous and purposefully drafted so that it would not favor one religion over another. They also argued that student recitation was voluntary: children who did not want to participate could remain silent or leave the room. The New York Civil Liberties Union, representing parents from a Long Island school district, claimed that the religious neutrality of the prayer and the voluntary aspect were irrelevant. What mattered was that the state had written the prayer and, therefore, it violated the establishment clause.

Writing for the Court, Justice Black adopted the separationist argument:

We think the constitutional prohibition against laws respecting the establishment of religion must at least mean that in this country it is no part of the business of government to compose official prayers for any group of the American people to recite as a part of a religious program carried out by the government.

TABLE 4-4 Incidence of Bible Reading in Public Schools by Region, 1960 and 1966

| | PERCENTAGE OF SCHOOLS REPORTING BIBLE READING | |
REGION	1960	1966
East	67.6	4.3
Midwest	18.3	5.2
South	76.8	49.5
West	11.0	2.3

SOURCE: Frank J. Sorauf, *The Wall of Separation* (Princeton, NJ: Princeton University Press, 1976), 297.

Only Justice Stewart dissented from the Court's opinion. After citing many examples of congressional approval of religion, including the legislation adding the words "In God We Trust" on currency, he quoted Justice Douglas's statement, written a decade before, in the released-time case: "We are a religious people whose institutions presuppose a Supreme Being." What New York "has done has been to recognize and to follow the deeply entrenched and highly cherished spiritual traditions of our Nation," Stewart wrote.

Despite the majority's strong words, the decision was not a complete victory for separationists. The Court failed to enunciate a strict legal definition of establishment` (it announced no standard), and it dealt with only one aspect of prayer in school—state-written prayers—and not the more widespread practice of Bible reading. Moreover, *Engel* generated a tremendous public backlash. Less than 20 percent of the public supported the Court's decision. Church leaders condemned it, and Congress considered constitutional amendments to overturn it. Most of the justices described themselves as "surprised and pained" by the negative reaction. Chief Justice Warren later wrote: "I vividly remember one bold newspaper headline, 'Court outlaws God.' Many religious leaders in this same spirit condemned the Court." Justice Clark defended the Court's opinion in a public address: "Here was a state-written prayer circulated by the school district to state-employed teachers with instructions to have their pupils recite it. [The Constitution] provides that both state and Federal governments shall take no part respecting the establishment of religion. . . . 'No' means 'No.' That was all the Court decided."[29]

28. Gallup Poll reported December 17, 2010; CNN/ORC poll reported September 15, 2011; Pew Research Center for the People and the Press polling report issued February 15, 2009.

29. The justices' quotations come from Bernard Schwartz, *Super Chief* (New York: New York University Press, 1983), 441–442.

With all this uproar, it is no wonder that separationist groups were concerned when the Court agreed to hear arguments in *School District of Abington Township v. Schempp* and its companion case, *Murray v. Curlett*, appeals involving the more prevalent practice of Bible reading in public schools. Would the justices cave in to public pressure and reverse their stance in *Engel*?

School District of Abington Township v. Schempp

Murray v. Curlett

374 U.S. 203 (1963)
http://laws.findlaw.com/US/374/203.html
Oral arguments are available at http://www.oyez.org.
Vote: 8 (Black, Brennan, Clark, Douglas, Goldberg, Harlan, Warren, White)
   1 (Stewart)

OPINION OF THE COURT: *Clark*
CONCURRING OPINIONS: *Brennan, Douglas, Goldberg*
DISSENTING OPINION: *Stewart*

FACTS:

Successful in persuading the Court to strike down the recitation of state-written prayers in school, separationist groups came back to challenge more common occurrences—reading from the Bible and the recitation of the Lord's Prayer—at the beginning of each day. These practices were most prevalent in the South, so separationists, fearing a negative outcome, decided to avoid litigating in that region. Instead, they found a Pennsylvania family that was willing to serve as plaintiffs.

This dispute began in 1956 when Ellery, the eldest of Edward and Sidney Schempp's three children, objected to the Bible readings that were conducted each day at Abington High School. This practice was mandated by a Pennsylvania law that required that "at least ten verses from the Holy Bible shall be read, without comment, at the opening of each public school on each school day." The required number of Bible verses were read by selected students over the school's public address system, and the reading was followed by a recitation of the Lord's Prayer, during which students stood and repeated the prayer in unison. Those students whose parents did not want them to participate could, under the law, leave the room.

One day Ellery was selected to do the reading, but the high school junior showed his opposition to the school's practice by reading from the Koran rather than the King James version of the Bible. Ellery's protest led to his suspension from school. Edward and

Sidney Schempp holds the Bible as her husband, Edward, and their younger children, Roger and Donna, look on at their home in Roslyn, Pennsylvania, on June 18, 1963, one day after the Supreme Court announced its decision in School District of Abington Township v. Schempp. *The Court agreed with the Schempps that compulsory Bible reading in public schools violates the establishment clause.*

Sidney supported their son's position and decided to take legal action. They received assistance from the American Civil Liberties Union, an organization of which they were members.

Edward and Sidney Schempp were not atheists; in fact, they were active members of a Unitarian church, where they regularly attended services. But they did not want Ellery or their younger children, Roger and Donna, to engage in Bible reading at their public school. To them, "specific religious doctrines purveyed by a literal reading of the Bible" were not in accord with their particular religious beliefs. If their children left their classrooms to avoid the daily prayer recitations, they argued, teachers and classmates would label them as "oddballs," or "atheists," a term with "very bad" connotations to the Schempps. Their children also would miss hearing morning announcements that were read after the religious readings; in addition, other students, seeing them in the halls, would think that the Schempp children were being punished for "bad conduct." Including Roger and Donna in the lawsuit allowed the legal action to remain alive even after Ellery graduated and was no long affected by the school's religious practices.

Separationist groups presented the Schempps' reasons to the trial court. They also brought in religious leaders and other religious experts to support the claim that Bible reading inherently favored some religions over others and violated principles of religious establishment. Attorneys for the school board, on the other hand, sought to frame the case in moral rather than religious terms. They also found their own expert witnesses to testify that the Bible was nonsectarian. By the time the case reached the Supreme Court, it was quite clear that they were asking the justices to overrule *Engel.*

Murray v. Curlett involved a similar challenge to a Maryland law that required daily readings from the Bible or the recitation of the Lord's Prayer in public schools. The suit was brought by prominent atheist Madalyn Murray on behalf of her son William J. Murray III *(see Box 4-6).*

In the *Schempp* case, the federal district court in Pennsylvania struck down the public school Bible reading and prayer recitation requirement, but the Maryland Court of Appeals upheld the practice in the *Murray* case. The Supreme Court consolidated the two appeals into a single ruling.

ARGUMENTS:

For the appellant, School District of Abington Township:

- Bible reading in the Pennsylvania public schools has always been conducted in a secular manner, devoid of any proselytizing, indoctrination, or instruction. It does not interfere with anyone's free exercise rights.
- No participatory act is required. Parents may have their children excused from Bible reading sessions if they wish.
- The practice is neutral because it neither adds to nor subtracts from the nation's religious traditions.

For the appellees, Edward and Sidney Schempp:

- The reading of the Holy Bible under this statute is a mandatory devotional or religious act. As such, it violates the establishment clause.
- The practice prefers Christianity to all other religions, but the mandatory reading of any religious text would be contrary to the Constitution.

- The practice violates free exercise of religion because it requires those with contrary religious views to take public action in order to excuse themselves from the Bible reading sessions.

MR. JUSTICE CLARK DELIVERED THE OPINION OF THE COURT.

[T]his Court has rejected unequivocally the contention that the Establishment Clause forbids only governmental preference of one religion over another. Almost 20 years ago in *Everson* the Court said that "[n]either a state nor the Federal Government can set up a church. Neither can pass laws which aid one religion, aid all religions, or prefer one religion over another." . . .

. . . In short, the Court held that the Amendment

"requires the state to be a neutral in its relations with groups of religious believers and non-believers; it does not require the state to be their adversary. State power is no more to be used so as to handicap religions than it is to favor them." . . .

The wholesome "neutrality" of which this Court's cases speak . . . stems from a recognition of the teachings of history that powerful sects or groups might bring about a fusion of governmental and religious functions or a concert or dependency of one upon the other to the end that official support of the State or Federal Government would be placed behind the tenets of one or of all orthodoxies. This the Establishment Clause prohibits. And a further reason for neutrality is found in the Free Exercise Clause, which recognizes the value of religious training, teaching and observance and, more particularly, the right of every person to freely choose his own course with reference thereto, free of any compulsion from the state. This the Free Exercise Clause guarantees. Thus, as we have seen, the two clauses may overlap. As we have indicated, the Establishment Clause has been directly considered by this Court eight times in the past score of years and, with only one Justice dissenting on the point, it has consistently held that the clause withdrew all legislative power respecting religious belief or the expression thereof. The test may be stated as follows: what are the purpose and the primary effect of the enactment? If either is the advancement or inhibition of religion then the enactment exceeds the scope of legislative power as circumscribed by the Constitution. That is to say that to withstand the strictures

BOX 4-6 AFTERMATH . . . MADALYN MURRAY O'HAIR

In 1963 the U.S. Supreme Court, in *School District of Abington Township v. Schempp* and its companion case, *Murray v. Curlett,* declared Bible reading and the recitation of the Lord's Prayer in public schools to be unconstitutional. *Murray v. Curlett* was a lawsuit brought by Madalyn Murray on behalf of her son William, then a fourteen-year-old student in Baltimore. Madalyn Murray O'Hair, as she became known after her marriage to Richard O'Hair, was no stranger to controversy or the courts. Dubbed by *Life* magazine in 1964 "the most hated woman in America," O'Hair initiated several lawsuits based on First Amendment claims, including legal actions to have the words "In God We Trust" removed from U.S. currency and to prohibit astronauts from praying in space. She described the Bible as "nauseating, historically inaccurate and replete with the ravings of madmen." O'Hair, an abrasive, profane woman, attempted to defect to the Soviet Union in 1960 and later became associated with Larry Flynt, the publisher of *Hustler* magazine. She is probably best known as the founder of American Atheists, Inc., a national organization devoted to advancing the interests of atheists, headquartered in Austin, Texas.

On August 28, 1995, O'Hair, seventy-six years old and in declining health, mysteriously vanished, along with her second son, Jon Murray, and granddaughter Robin. Nothing appeared to be missing from their house—clothes were in the closets and food on the table. Many thought that O'Hair and her family had fled from her organization's declining membership and troubled financial condition. Speculation was fueled by evidence that more than $500,000 of American Atheists funds, most in gold coins, were missing and allegations that O'Hair had hidden organization funds in bank accounts in New Zealand.

Law enforcement authorities, however, were convinced that O'Hair and the others were victims of foul play. The chief suspects were David Waters, Gary Karr, and Danny Fry. Waters, a former American Atheists employee, had pleaded guilty to stealing $54,000 from the organization and had a grudge against O'Hair. Karr and Fry were associates of Waters; all three had criminal records. Evidence mounted that the three suspects had kidnapped the O'Hair family members, held them hostage, and extorted $500,000 before murdering them. Fry was removed from the suspect list when a body discovered on the banks of the Trinity River was identified as his. The head and hands had been severed in an obvious attempt to block identification.

Madalyn Murray O'Hair with son Jon and granddaughter Robin

Police put continued pressure on Waters and Karr, both of whom had been imprisoned for crimes related to the O'Hair disappearance. Finally, in 2001 Waters agreed to cooperate with authorities as part of a plea bargain on the murder charges. He led police to a remote ranch west of San Antonio, where three dismembered and burned bodies were found in a shallow grave along with a head and hands presumed to be Fry's. The bodies were identified through dental records and O'Hair's metal artificial hip. Police believe that the three victims had been killed in a north Austin storage unit and the remains discarded at the burial site.

In February 2003 Waters died in prison of cancer. Karr continues to serve a life sentence.

Another twist to the O'Hair story involves her son William Murray. After being treated for alcoholism, Murray publicly rejected atheism in May 1980 and became a Southern Baptist. For many years he has chaired the Religious Freedom Coalition, a conservative organization that supports, among other things, the reintroduction of prayer in the public schools. He once described his mother as "an evil person who led many to hell." As might be expected, Murray and his mother had been estranged for many years before her disappearance.

SOURCES: *Arizona Republic,* May 15, 2000; *Atlanta Journal-Constitution,* June 3, 2000; *Houston Chronicle,* December 29, 1996, March 3, 2000, March 16, 2001, February 5, 2003; *Washington Post,* March 28 and August 16–17, 1999; *Buffalo News,* April 25, 1999; *San Diego Union-Tribune,* October 22, 1999; *New York Times,* December 8, 1999, March 16, 2001; and William J. Murray, "The Madalyn Murray O'Hair Murder," statement issued by the Religious Freedom Coalition, April 5, 2011.

of the Establishment Clause there must be a secular legislative purpose and a primary effect that neither advances nor inhibits religion. *Everson v. Board of Education.* . . . The Free Exercise Clause, likewise considered many times here, withdraws from legislative power, state and federal, the exertion of any restraint on the free exercise of religion. Its purpose is to secure religious liberty in the individual by prohibiting any invasions thereof by civil authority. Hence it is necessary in a free exercise case for one to show the coercive effect of the enactment as it operates against him in the practice of his religion. The distinction between the two clauses is apparent—a violation of the Free Exercise Clause is predicated on coercion while the Establishment Clause violation need not be so attended.

Applying the Establishment Clause principles to the cases at bar we find that the States are requiring the selection and reading at the opening of the school day of verses from the Holy Bible and the recitation of the Lord's Prayer by the students in unison. These exercises are prescribed as part of the curricular activities of students who are required by law to attend school. They are held in the school buildings under the supervision and with the participation of teachers employed in those schools. None of these factors, other than compulsory school attendance, was present in the program upheld in *Zorach v. Clauson.* The trial court in [*Schempp*] has found that such an opening exercise is a religious ceremony and was intended by the State to be so. We agree with the trial court's finding as to the religious character of the exercises. Given that finding, the exercises and the law requiring them are in violation of the Establishment Clause. . . .

The conclusion follows that . . . the [law] require[s] religious exercises and such exercises are being conducted in direct violation of the rights of the appellees and petitioners. Nor are these required exercises mitigated by the fact that individual students may absent themselves upon parental request, for that fact furnishes no defense to a claim of unconstitutionality under the Establishment Clause. Further, it is no defense to urge that the religious practices here may be relatively minor encroachments on the First Amendment. The breach of neutrality that is today a trickling stream may all too soon become a raging torrent and, in the words of Madison, "it is proper to take alarm at the first experiment on our liberties."

It is insisted that unless these religious exercises are permitted a "religion of secularism" is established in the schools. We agree of course that the State may not establish a "religion of secularism" in the sense of affirmatively opposing or showing hostility to religion, thus "preferring those who believe in no religion over those who do believe." . . . We do not agree, however, that this decision in any sense has that effect. In addition, it might well be said that one's education is not complete without a study of comparative religion or the history of religion and its relationship to the advancement of civilization. It certainly may be said that the Bible is worthy of study for its literary and historic qualities. Nothing we have said here indicates that such study of the Bible or of religion, when presented objectively as part of a secular program of education, may not be effected consistently with the First Amendment. But the exercises here do not fall into those categories. They are religious exercises, required by the States in violation of the command of the First Amendment that the Government maintain strict neutrality, neither aiding nor opposing religion.

Finally, we cannot accept that the concept of neutrality, which does not permit a State to require a religious exercise even with the consent of the majority of those affected, collides with the majority's right to free exercise of religion. While the Free Exercise Clause clearly prohibits the use of state action to deny the rights of free exercise to anyone, it has never meant that a majority could use the machinery of the State to practice its beliefs. . . .

The place of religion in our society is an exalted one, achieved through a long tradition of reliance on the home, the church and the inviolable citadel of the individual heart and mind. We have come to recognize through bitter experience that it is not within the power of government to invade that citadel, whether its purpose or effect be to aid or oppose, to advance or retard. In the relationship between man and religion, the State is firmly committed to a position of neutrality. Though the application of that rule requires interpretation of a delicate sort, the rule itself is clearly and concisely stated in the words of the First Amendment. Applying that rule to the facts of these cases, we affirm the judgment in [*Schempp*]. In [*Murray*] the judgment is reversed and the cause remanded to the Maryland Court of Appeals for further proceedings consistent with this opinion.

It is so ordered.

MR. JUSTICE DOUGLAS, concurring.

These regimes violate the Establishment Clause in two different ways. In each case, the State is conducting a religious exercise; and, as the Court holds, that cannot be done without violating the "neutrality" required of the State by the balance of power between individual, church and state that has been struck by the First Amendment. But the Establishment Clause is not limited to precluding the State itself from conducting religious exercises. It also forbids the State to employ its facilities or funds in a way that gives any church, or all churches, greater strength in our society than it would have by relying on its members alone. Thus, the present regimes must fall under that clause for the additional reason that public funds, though small in amount, are being used to promote a religious exercise. Through the mechanism of the State, all of the people are being required to finance a religious exercise that only some of the people want and that violates the sensibilities of others.

MR. JUSTICE BRENNAN, concurring.

I join fully in the opinion and the judgment of the Court. I see no escape from the conclusion that the exercises called in question in these two cases violate the constitutional mandate. The reasons we gave only last Term in *Engel v. Vitale* for finding in the New York Regents' prayer an impermissible establishment of religion compel the same judgment of the practices at bar. The involvement of the secular with the religious is no less intimate here; and it is constitutionally irrelevant that the State has not composed the material for the inspirational exercises presently involved. It should be unnecessary to observe that our holding does not declare that the First Amendment manifests hostility to the practice or teaching of religion, but only applies prohibitions incorporated in the Bill of Rights in recognition of historic needs shared by Church and State alike. While it is my view that not every involvement of religion in public life is unconstitutional, I consider the exercises at bar a form of involvement which clearly violates the Establishment Clause.

MR. JUSTICE GOLDBERG, with whom MR. JUSTICE HARLAN joins, concurring.

The practices here involved do not fall within any sensible or acceptable concept of compelled or permitted accommodation, and involve the state so significantly and directly in the realm of the sectarian as to give rise to those very divisive influences and inhibitions of freedom which both religion clauses of the First Amendment preclude. The state has ordained and has utilized its facilities to engage in unmistakably religious exercises—the devotional reading and recitation of the Holy Bible—in a manner having substantial and significant import and impact. That it has selected, rather than written, a particular devotional liturgy seems to me without constitutional import. The pervasive religiosity and direct governmental involvement inhering in the prescription of prayer and Bible reading in the public schools, during and as part of the curricular day, involving young impressionable children whose school attendance is statutorily compelled, and utilizing the prestige, power, and influence of school administration, staff, and authority, cannot realistically be termed simply accommodation, and must fall within the interdiction of the First Amendment.

MR. JUSTICE STEWART, dissenting.

. . . [I]t is important to stress that, strictly speaking, what is at issue here is a privilege rather than a right. In other words, the question presented is not whether exercises such as those at issue here are constitutionally compelled, but rather whether they are constitutionally invalid. And that issue, in my view, turns on the question of coercion.

It is clear that the dangers of coercion involved in the holding of religious exercises in a schoolroom differ qualitatively from those presented by the use of similar exercises or affirmations in ceremonies attended by adults. Even as to children, however, the duty laid upon government in connection with religious exercises in the public schools is that of refraining from so structuring the school environment as to put any kind of pressure on a child to participate in those exercises; it is not that of providing an atmosphere in which children are kept scrupulously insulated from any awareness that some of their fellows may want to open the school day with prayer, or of the fact that there exist in our pluralistic society differences of religious belief. . . .

Viewed in this light, it seems to me clear that the records in both of the cases before us are wholly inadequate to support an informed or responsible decision. Both cases involve provisions which explicitly permit any student who wishes, to be excused from participation in the exercises. There is no evidence . . . as to whether there would exist any coercion of any kind upon a student who did not want to participate. . . . In the *Schempp* case the record shows no more than a subjective prophecy by a parent of what he thought would happen if a request were made to be excused from participation in the exercises under the amended statute. No such request was ever made, and there is no evidence whatever as to what might or would actually happen, nor of what administrative arrangements the school actually might or could make to free from pressure of any kind those who do not want to participate in the exercises. . . .

What our Constitution indispensably protects is the freedom of each of us, be he Jew or Agnostic, Christian or Atheist, Buddhist or Freethinker, to believe or disbelieve, to worship or not worship, to pray or keep silent, according to his own conscience, uncoerced and unrestrained by government. It is conceivable that these school boards, or even all school boards, might eventually find it impossible to administer a system of religious exercises during school hours in such a way as to meet this constitutional standard—in such a way as completely to free from any kind of official coercion those who do not affirmatively want to participate. But I think we must not assume that school boards so lack the qualities of inventiveness and good will as to make impossible the achievement of that goal.

I would remand both cases for further hearings.

These two cases, following on the heels of *Engel v. Vitale,* set firmly in American jurisprudence the principle that state-sponsored prayers in public schools violate the establishment clause. In addition, these decisions set out a standard of law, a two-pronged test that served as the forerunner of *Lemon.* But take note of Justice Stewart's dissent: his coercion approach provided fodder for justices of the Rehnquist Court—particularly Anthony Kennedy—who would later attempt to etch some version of it into law. In 1963 it represented the position of only one justice.

If the justices thought that *Abington* would quell the prayer-in-school controversy they had ignited in *Engel,* they could not have been more wrong. Opinion polls taken immediately after *Abington* indicated that only 24 percent of the public supported the Court's decision. The proportion of the public that endorsed the Court's prayer decisions gradually increased during the two decades following *Abington.* By 1983 about 40 percent of Americans supported the Court, and subsequent polling has found that level to have remained relatively constant since that

time.[30] Given the public antipathy for *Engel* and *Abington,* it is not surprising to find widespread noncompliance with the Court's decisions. Note the data in Table 4-4 showing that, contrary to other regions, almost half of the schools in the South continued to allow Bible reading three years after the Court's decision in *Abington.*

The American public's support for prayer in school and the determination of many local school systems to maintain voluntary prayer programs run contrary to the general trend among nations of the world *(see Box 4-7).* While other countries and their constitutional courts have grappled with the school prayer problem, the overwhelming majority have eliminated prayer programs from public education.

In the United States, in spite of the Court's rulings in *Engel, Abington,* and *Murray,* the school prayer issue was far from settled. Responding to public opposition to these decisions, over the years members of Congress have introduced close to 150 constitutional amendments to return prayer to the nation's classrooms. None has been successful.

With the constitutional amendment alternative proving unsuccessful, supporters of prayer in school returned their attention to the Supreme Court. The Warren era had now given way to the Burger Court, which had given signs of being sympathetic to the use of prayer in public places. This signal occurred in *Marsh v. Chambers* (1983), in which the Court found nothing unconstitutional about the Nebraska legislature hiring a Presbyterian minister to say a public prayer before each daily session. Chief Justice Burger's opinion for the Court rested primarily on original intent, as demonstrated by the long tradition of American legislatures, starting with the First Congress in 1789, of beginning their sessions with a prayer. The Court largely ignored the precedents set in the school prayer cases and did not apply the Lemon test, which quite probably would have led to a different result. Because of the *Marsh* ruling, when the Court agreed to hear **Wallace v. Jaffree** (1985) there was speculation that the justices might be on the verge of overruling precedents such as *Engel* and *Abington.*

Wallace v. Jaffree involved a challenge to an Alabama law authorizing, among other things, a daily period of

---

30. A review of public opinion data on the school prayer issue can be found in Lee Epstein, Jeffrey A. Segal, Harold J. Spaeth, and Thomas G. Walker, *The Supreme Court Compendium: Data, Decisions, and Developments,* 5th ed. (Washington, DC: CQ Press, 2012), Table 8-26.

BOX 4-7   SCHOOL PRAYER IN GLOBAL PERSPECTIVE

In what may be the only existing inventory of international practices regarding state-sanctioned school prayer, the American Civil Liberties Union concluded that "the major countries of the world, including Western Europe, Central America, and Asia, have rejected state-sponsored prayer in their public school systems." Indeed, only eleven of the seventy-two countries included in the study continue to permit the sort of state-sanctioned prayer that the U.S. Supreme Court rejected in *Engel v. Vitale* (1962)—and many of the eleven (including Finland, Greece, Libya, Nepal, Pakistan, Romania, Saudi Arabia, and Thailand) are countries that have state religions or are religiously homogeneous. Yet, according to the study, even nations that meet those criteria, such as Italy and Israel, have "steered a careful course around imposing prayer in the schools."

On the other hand, some religiously diverse countries—Great Britain and Sweden, for example—permit government-sponsored prayer or some form of voluntary prayer, even in the face of court challenges. In the *School Prayer Case* (1979) the Federal Constitutional Court of Germany took the position that voluntary prayer in public schools was constitutionally permissible so long as schools "guarantee the dissenting pupil the right to decide freely and without compulsion whether to participate in the prayer." The court justified its position in the following terms:

[Germany's constitutional document] grants not only freedom of belief but also the external freedom publicly to acknowledge one's belief. In this sense Articles 4 (1) and 4 (2) [guaranteeing freedom of religion and the right to practice religion free from harassment] guarantee a sphere in which to express these convictions actively. If the state permits school prayer in interdenominational state schools, then it does nothing more than exercise its right to establish a school system so that pupils who wish to do so may acknowledge their religious beliefs, even if only in the limited form of a universal and transdenominational appeal to God. . . .

To be sure, the state must balance this affirmative freedom to worship as expressed by permitting school prayer with the negative freedom of confession of other parents and pupils opposed to school prayer. Basically [schools] may achieve this balance by guaranteeing that participation be voluntary for pupils and teachers.

This decision stands in marked contrast to *School District of Abington Township v. Schempp* (1963). There, the Schempps' attorney impressed on the justices the ridicule the couple's children would face when they left the room to avoid religious readings. For this and other reasons, the Supreme Court ruled that even voluntary prayer violated the U.S. Constitution.

The German justices also were sensitive to the problem *Schempp* had raised: "Admittedly," the Constitutional Court wrote, "whenever the class prays, [the failure to participate] will have the effect of distinguishing the pupil in question from the praying pupils—especially if only one pupil professes other beliefs." Nonetheless, the court concluded that "one cannot assume that abstaining from school prayer will generally or even in a substantial number of cases force a dissenting pupil into an unbearable position as an outsider."

SOURCES: Donald Kommers, *The Constitutional Jurisprudence of the Federal Republic of Germany* (Durham, NC: Duke University Press, 1997); Allan Parachini et al., *Prayer in School: An International Survey* (Los Angeles: American Civil Liberties Union, May 1995), available at http://www.eric.ed.gov/PDFS/ED393711.pdf.

---

silence in all public schools "for meditation or voluntary prayer." Ishmael Jaffree, a lawyer for the Legal Services Administration, objected when the provisions of the law were implemented in his son's kindergarten class. When local school officials did not act on his protests, Jaffree filed suit.

Jaffree and other opponents of the Alabama law argued that it was unconstitutional because it lacked a secular purpose as required by *Lemon,* and because its legislative sponsors clearly viewed the required moment of silence as a way to return prayer to schools. The state countered that the law did not in any way offend the Constitution because it did not affirm religious belief or coerce participation in any prayer. The Reagan administration supported this position. In an amicus curiae brief, Solicitor General Rex Lee argued that the law was "perfectly neutral with respect to religious practices. It neither favors one religion over another nor conveys endorsement of religion."

Despite public opinion and political pressure, the Court did not overturn *Engel* or *Abington.* To the contrary, by invoking the Lemon test to strike down the Alabama law, the Court reaffirmed its commitment to those decisions and to the standards of law on which they were based. Specifically, the Court found that the Alabama law's primary purpose was not secular. In fact, the law, according to the Court, had no secular purpose at all.

Wallace was the Burger Court's last major religious establishment case; a year after the opinion was handed down, the chief justice retired. As we noted at the beginning of this section, Burger had sought to influence this area of the law, first by establishing the Lemon test and then, after realizing that *Lemon* might lead to a stronger wall of separation than he envisioned, through the adoption of a framers' intent approach (used in *Marsh*) or of a softened version of *Lemon*.

As the new chief justice, Rehnquist continued Burger's efforts to lead the Court closer to the accommodationist position. It is no secret that Rehnquist favored the Court overruling *Lemon*. The problem he faced was that his colleagues did not agree on a standard of law by which to adjudicate these cases.

In 1992 the Rehnquist Court heard its first major school prayer case, *Lee v. Weisman*. Some observers thought the Court would overturn *Lemon,* a position advocated by the Bush administration. Did the Court take this step? Note, too, how fractured the Court was. How did the dissenters' and concurrers' positions differ from that proposed by the majority?

Lee v. Weisman

505 U.S. 577 (1992)
http://laws.findlaw.com/US/505/577.html
Oral arguments are available at http://www.oyez.org.
Vote: 5 (Blackmun, Kennedy, O'Connor, Souter, Stevens)
   4 (Rehnquist, Scalia, Thomas, White)

OPINION OF THE COURT: *Kennedy*
CONCURRING OPINIONS: *Blackmun, Souter*
DISSENTING OPINION: *Scalia*

FACTS:

Each June, Nathan Bishop Middle School, a public school in Providence, Rhode Island, holds formal graduation exercises on school grounds. Attendance is voluntary. The principals of all Providence public middle schools and high schools are permitted to invite clergy to give invocations and benedictions at their schools' graduation ceremonies. Typically, what happens is

this: a school principal contacts a member of the clergy and asks him or her to give an invocation/benediction; if the clergyperson agrees, the principal gives him or her a copy of a pamphlet titled *Guidelines for Civic Occasions*. Prepared by the National Conference of Christians and Jews, the guidelines stress "inclusiveness and sensitivity" in writing nonsectarian prayers.

For the June 1989 graduation at Nathan Bishop Middle School, Principal Robert E. Lee followed this procedure. He invited Rabbi Leslie Gutterman to give the invocation and benediction and gave him a copy of the guidelines. Lee also advised Rabbi Gutterman that any prayers should be nonsectarian.

At the graduation the rabbi gave the following invocation:

God of the Free, Hope of the Brave:
   For the legacy of America where diversity is celebrated and the rights of minorities are protected, we thank You. May these young men and women grow up to enrich it.
   For the liberty of America, we thank You. May these new graduates grow up to guard it.
   For the political process of America in which all its citizens may participate, for its court system where all may seek justice, we thank You. May those we honor this morning always turn to it in trust.
   For the destiny of America, we thank You. May the graduates of Nathan Bishop Middle School so live that they might help to share it.
   May our aspirations for our country and for these young people, who are our hope for the future, be richly fulfilled.
   Amen.

In his benediction, the rabbi said:

O God, we are grateful to You for having endowed us with the capacity for learning which we have celebrated on this joyous commencement.
   Happy families give thanks for seeing their children achieve an important milestone. Send Your blessings upon the teachers and administrators who helped prepare them.
   The graduates now need strength and guidance for the future. Help them to understand that we are not complete with academic knowledge alone. We must each strive to fulfill what You require from all of us: To do justly, to love mercy, to walk humbly.
   We give thanks to You, Lord, for keeping us alive, sustaining us, and allowing us to reach this special, happy occasion.
   Amen.

Daniel Weisman, whose fourteen-year-old daughter, Deborah, was in the graduating class, complained about the prayer prior to the graduation, but the issue was not resolved. After the ceremony, which the family attended, Weisman filed suit challenging the school's policy allowing invocations and benedictions at graduation exercises as a violation of the First Amendment. Because there was little a court could do about a graduation ceremony already held, Weisman faced a "standing to sue" problem. To avoid this obstacle, he argued that unless the practice was stopped, his daughter inevitably would be faced with similar prayers when she graduated from high school. He asked a federal trial court to issue an order to Lee and other Providence officials prohibiting them from continuing this practice. The trial court found for Weisman, and a federal appellate court affirmed. As a result, Lee and the school board appealed to the U.S. Supreme Court. Joined by Kenneth W. Starr, the Bush administration's solicitor general, as an amicus curiae, they argued, as one justice later put it, "that these short prayers . . . are of profound meaning to many students and parents throughout this country who consider that due respect and acknowledgment for divine guidance and for the deepest spiritual aspirations of our people ought to be expressed at an event as important in life as a graduation." The school board and the solicitor general also asked the Supreme

Court to reconsider the Lemon test, which the district court had used to find against Principal Lee.

For the petitioners, Robert E. Lee and other Providence school officials:

- The graduation prayer involved no government coercion of religious conformity, a necessary element of an establishment clause violation.
- Attendance at the graduation ceremony is voluntary.
- Invocations and benedictions are traditional ceremonial practices in America. They were common and accepted at the time the First Amendment was proposed and ratified.

For the respondent, Daniel Weisman:

- Arranging to have a member of the clergy offer a prayer at a public school event is a violation of the establishment clause under any criteria used by the Court.
- The graduation prayer necessarily is an endorsement of religion and impermissibly entangles government with religion.
- Although coercion has never been a necessary element for an establishment clause violation, the challenged practice is nevertheless coercive. Students are faced with the choice of participating in the practice or not attending their own graduations.

JUSTICE KENNEDY DELIVERED THE OPINION OF THE COURT.

These dominant facts mark and control the confines of our decision: State officials direct the performance of a formal religious exercise at promotional and graduation ceremonies for secondary schools. Even for those students who object to the religious exercise, their attendance and participation in the state-sponsored religious activity are in a fair and real sense obligatory, though the school district does not require attendance as a condition for receipt of the diploma.

. . . [T]he controlling precedents as they relate to prayer and religious exercise in primary and secondary public schools compel the holding here that the policy of the city of Providence is an unconstitutional one. We can decide the case without reconsidering the general constitutional framework by which public schools' efforts to accommodate religion are measured. Thus we do not accept the invitation of petitioners and amicus the United States to reconsider our decision in *Lemon v. Kurtzman*. The government involvement with religious activity in this

When a Baptist minister was invited to offer an invocation during the middle school graduation of Merith Weisman, left, in 1986, her father, Daniel Weisman, objected to the school administration without success. Three years later, when the same Providence, Rhode Island, public school arranged for a local rabbi to deliver a nonsectarian invocation at the graduation of daughter Deborah, right, Weisman filed a lawsuit that led to the Supreme Court declaring that such prayer practices violate the establishment clause.

case is pervasive, to the point of creating a state-sponsored and state-directed religious exercise in a public school. Conducting this formal religious observance conflicts with settled rules pertaining to prayer exercises for students, and that suffices to determine the question before us.

The principle that government may accommodate the free exercise of religion does not supersede the fundamental limitations imposed by the Establishment Clause. It is beyond dispute that, at a minimum, the Constitution guarantees that government may not coerce anyone to support or participate in religion or its exercise, or otherwise act in a way which "establishes a [state] religion or religious faith, or tends to do so." . . . The State's involvement in the school prayers challenged today violates these central principles.

That involvement is as troubling as it is undenied. A school official, the principal, decided that an invocation and a benediction should be given; this is a choice attributable to the State, and from a constitutional perspective it is as if a state statute decreed that the prayers must occur. The principal chose the religious participant, here a rabbi, and that choice is also attributable to the State. The reason for the choice of a rabbi is not disclosed by the record, but the potential for divisiveness over the choice of a particular member of the clergy to conduct the ceremony is apparent. . . .

The State's role did not end with the decision to include a prayer and with the choice of clergyman. Principal Lee provided Rabbi Gutterman with a copy of the "Guidelines for Civic Occasions" and advised him that his prayers should be nonsectarian. Through these means, the principal directed and controlled the content of the prayer. . . . It is a cornerstone principle of our Establishment Clause jurisprudence that it is "no part of the business of government to compose official prayers for any group of the American people to recite as a part of a religious program carried on by government," *Engel v. Vitale* (1962), and that is what the school officials attempted to do.

Petitioners argue, and we find nothing in the case to refute it, that the directions for the content of the prayers were a good-faith attempt by the school to ensure that the sectarianism which is so often the flashpoint for religious animosity be removed from the graduation ceremony. The concern is understandable, as a prayer which uses ideas or images identified with a particular religion may foster a different sort of sectarian rivalry than an invocation or benediction in terms more neutral. The school's explanation, however, does not resolve the

dilemma caused by its participation. The question is not the good faith of the school in attempting to make the prayer acceptable to most persons, but the legitimacy of its undertaking that enterprise at all when the object is to produce a prayer to be used in a formal religious exercise which students, for all practical purposes, are obliged to attend. . . .

These concerns have particular application in the case of school officials, whose effort to monitor prayer will be perceived by the students as inducing a participation they might otherwise reject. Though the efforts of the school officials in this case to find common ground appear to have been a good-faith attempt to recognize the common aspects of religions and not the divisive ones, our precedents do not permit school officials to assist in composing prayers as an incident to a formal exercise for their students. *Engel v. Vitale.* And these same precedents caution us to measure the idea of a civic religion against the central meaning of the Religion Clauses of the First Amendment, which is that all creeds must be tolerated and none favored. The suggestion that government may establish an official or civic religion as a means of avoiding the establishment of a religion with more specific creeds strikes us as a contradiction that cannot be accepted.

The degree of school involvement here made it clear that the graduation prayers bore the imprint of the State and thus put school-age children who objected in an untenable position. We turn our attention now to consider the position of the students, both those who desired the prayer and she who did not. . . .

As we have observed before, there are heightened concerns with protecting freedom of conscience from subtle coercive pressure in the elementary and secondary public schools. . . . Our decisions in *Engel v. Vitale* and *Abington School District* recognize, among other things, that prayer exercises in public schools carry a particular risk of indirect coercion. The concern may not be limited to the context of schools, but it is most pronounced there. . . . What to most believers may seem nothing more than a reasonable request that the nonbeliever respect their religious practices, in a school context may appear to the nonbeliever or dissenter to be an attempt to employ the machinery of the State to enforce a religious orthodoxy.

We need not look beyond the circumstances of this case to see the phenomenon at work. The undeniable fact is that the school district's supervision and control of a high school graduation ceremony places public pressure, as well as peer pressure, on attending students to stand as a group or, at least, maintain respectful silence during the Invocation and Benediction. This pressure, though subtle and indirect, can be as real as any overt compulsion. Of course, in our culture standing or remaining silent can signify adherence to a view or simple respect for the views of others. And no doubt some persons who have no desire to join a prayer have little objection to standing as a sign of respect for those who do. But for the dissenter of high school age, who has a reasonable perception that she is being forced by the State to pray in a manner her conscience will not allow, the injury is no less real. There can be no doubt that for many, if not most, of the students at the graduation, the act of standing or remaining silent was an expression of participation in the rabbi's prayer. That was the very point of the religious exercise. It is of little comfort to a dissenter, then, to be told that for her the act of standing or remaining in silence signifies mere respect, rather than participation. What matters is that, given our social conventions, a reasonable dissenter in this milieu could believe that the group exercise signified her own participation or approval of it.

Finding no violation under these circumstances would place objectors in the dilemma of participating, with all that implies, or protesting. We do not address whether that choice is acceptable if the affected citizens are mature adults, but we think the State may not, consistent with the Establishment Clause, place primary and secondary school children in this position. Research in psychology supports the common assumption that adolescents are often susceptible to pressure from their peers towards conformity, and that the influence is strongest in matters of social convention. . . . To recognize that the choice imposed by the State constitutes an unacceptable constraint only acknowledges that the government may no more use social pressure to enforce orthodoxy than it may use more direct means. . . .

. . . [T]o say a teenage student has a real choice not to attend her high school graduation is formalistic in the extreme. True, Deborah could elect not to attend commencement without renouncing her diploma; but we shall not allow the case to turn on this point. Everyone knows that, in our society and in our culture, high school graduation is one of life's most significant occasions. A school rule which excuses attendance is beside the point. Attendance may not be required by official decree, yet it is apparent that a student is not free to absent herself from the graduation exercise in any real sense of the term "voluntary," for absence would require forfeiture of those intangible benefits which have motivated the student through youth and all her high school years. Graduation is a time for family and those closest to the student to celebrate success and express mutual wishes of gratitude and respect, all to the end of impressing upon the young person the role that it is his or her right and duty to assume in the community and all of its diverse parts.

The importance of the event is the point the school district and the United States rely upon to argue that a formal prayer ought to be permitted, but it becomes one of the principal reasons why their argument must fail. Their contention, one of considerable force were it not for the constitutional constraints applied to state action, is that the prayers are an essential part of these ceremonies because for many persons an occasion of this significance lacks meaning if there is no recognition, however brief, that human achievements cannot be understood apart from their spiritual essence. We think the Government's position that this interest suffices to force students to choose between compliance or forfeiture demonstrates fundamental inconsistency in its argumentation. It fails to acknowledge that what for many of Deborah's classmates and their parents was a spiritual imperative was for Daniel and Deborah Weisman religious conformance compelled by the State. While in some societies the wishes of the majority might prevail, the Establishment Clause of the First Amendment is addressed to this contingency and rejects the balance urged upon us. The Constitution forbids the State to exact religious conformity from a student as the price of attending her own high school graduation. This is the calculus the Constitution commands. . . .

. . . [B]y any reading of our cases, the conformity required of the student in this case was too high an exaction to withstand the test of the Establishment Clause. The prayer exercises in this case are especially improper because the State has in every practical sense compelled attendance and participation in an explicit religious exercise at an event of singular importance to every student, one the objecting student had no real alternative to avoid. . . .

. . . No holding by this Court suggests that a school can persuade or compel a student to participate in a religious exercise. That is being done here, and it is forbidden by the Establishment Clause of the First Amendment.

For the reasons we have stated, the judgment of the Court of Appeals is

Affirmed.

JUSTICE BLACKMUN, with whom JUSTICE STEVENS and JUSTICE O'CONNOR join, concurring.

There can be "no doubt" that the "invocation of God's blessings" delivered at Nathan Bishop Middle School "is a religious activity." . . . The question then is whether the government has "placed its official stamp of approval" on the prayer. As the Court ably demonstrates, when the government "compose[s] official prayers," selects the member of the clergy to deliver the prayer, has the prayer delivered at a public school event that is planned, supervised, and given by school officials, and pressures students to attend and participate in the prayer, there can be no doubt that the government is advancing and promoting religion. As our prior decisions teach us, it is this that the Constitution prohibits.

. . . The Court holds that the graduation prayer is unconstitutional because the State "in effect required participation in a religious exercise." Although our precedents make clear that proof of government coercion is not necessary to prove an Establishment Clause violation, it is sufficient. Government pressure to participate in a religious activity is an obvious indication that the government is endorsing or promoting religion.

But it is not enough that the government restrain from compelling religious practices: it must not engage in them either. . . . The Court repeatedly has recognized that a violation of the Establishment Clause is not predicated on coercion. . . . The Establishment Clause proscribes public schools from "conveying or attempting to convey a message that religion or a particular religious belief is favored or preferred," *County of Allegheny v. ACLU* (1989), even if the schools do not actually "impos[e] pressure upon a student to participate in a religious activity."

JUSTICE SOUTER, with whom JUSTICE STEVENS and JUSTICE O'CONNOR join, concurring.

Forty-five years ago, this Court announced a basic principle of constitutional law from which it has not strayed: the Establishment Clause forbids not only state practices that "aid one religion . . . or prefer one religion over another," but also those that "aid all religions." *Everson v. Board of Education of Ewing* (1947). Today we reaffirm that principle, holding that the Establishment Clause forbids state-sponsored prayers in public school settings no matter how nondenominational the prayers may be. In barring the State from sponsoring generically theistic prayers where it could not sponsor sectarian ones, we hold true to a line of precedent from which there is no adequate historical case to depart. . . .

Some have challenged this precedent by reading the Establishment Clause to permit "nonpreferential" state promotion of religion. The challengers argue that, as originally understood by the Framers, "the Establishment Clause did not require government neutrality between religion and irreligion, nor did it prohibit the Federal Government from providing nondiscriminatory aid to religion." *Wallace* (REHNQUIST, J., dissenting). While a case has been made for this position, it is not so convincing as to warrant reconsideration of our settled law; indeed, I find in the history of the Clause's textual development a more powerful argument supporting the Court's jurisprudence following *Everson.* . . .

Petitioners rest most of their argument on a theory that, whether or not the Establishment Clause permits extensive nonsectarian support for religion, it does not forbid the state to sponsor affirmations of religious belief that coerce neither support for religion nor participation in religious observance. . . . But we could not adopt that reading without abandoning our settled law, a course that, in my view, the text of the Clause would not readily permit. . . .

Over the years, this Court has declared the invalidity of many noncoercive state laws and practices conveying a message of religious endorsement. For example, in *Allegheny County* we forbade the prominent display of a nativity scene on public property; without contesting the dissent's observation that the crèche coerced no one into accepting or supporting whatever message it proclaimed, five Members of the Court found its display unconstitutional as a state endorsement of Christianity. Likewise, in *Wallace v. Jaffree* (1985), we struck down a state law requiring a moment of silence in public classrooms not because the statute coerced students to participate in prayer (for it did not), but because the manner of its enactment "conveyed a message of state approval of prayer activities in the public schools." . . .

Our precedents may not always have drawn perfectly straight lines. They simply cannot, however, support the position that a showing of coercion is necessary to a successful Establishment Clause claim. . . .

While the Establishment Clause's concept of neutrality is not self-revealing, our recent cases have invested it with specific content: the state may not favor or endorse either religion generally over nonreligion or one religion over others. . . . This principle against favoritism and endorsement has become the foundation of Establishment Clause jurisprudence, ensuring that religious belief is irrelevant to every citizen's standing in the political community. . . . Our aspiration to religious liberty, embodied in the First Amendment, permits no other standard.

JUSTICE SCALIA, with whom THE CHIEF JUSTICE, JUSTICE WHITE, and JUSTICE THOMAS join, dissenting.

Today's opinion shows more forcefully than volumes of argumentation why our Nation's protection, that fortress which is our Constitution, cannot possibly rest upon the changeable philosophical predilections of the Justices of this Court, but must have deep foundations in the historic practices of our people. . . .

The history and tradition of our Nation are replete with public ceremonies featuring prayers of thanksgiving and petition. . . .

Most recently, President Bush, continuing the tradition established by President Washington, asked those attending his inauguration to bow their heads, and made a prayer his first official act as President. . . .

The Court presumably would separate graduation invocations and benedictions from other instances of public "preservation and transmission of religious beliefs" on the ground that they involve "psychological coercion." . . . A few citations of "[r]esearch in psychology" that have no particular bearing upon the precise issue here cannot disguise the fact that the Court has gone beyond the realm where judges know what they are doing. The Court's argument that state officials have "coerced" students to take part in the invocation and benediction at graduation ceremonies is, not to put too fine a point on it, incoherent. . . .

. . . [W]hile I have no quarrel with the Court's general proposition that the Establishment Clause "guarantees that government may not coerce anyone to support or participate in religion or its exercise," I see no warrant for expanding the concept of coercion beyond acts backed by threat of penalty—a brand of coercion that, happily, is readily discernible to those of us who have made a career of reading the disciples of Blackstone rather than of Freud. The Framers were indeed opposed to coercion of religious worship by the National Government; but, as their own sponsorship of nonsectarian prayer in public events demonstrates, they understood that "[s]peech is not coercive; the listener may do as he likes." . . .

Our Religion Clause jurisprudence has become bedeviled (so to speak) by reliance on formulaic abstractions that are not derived from, but positively conflict with, our long-accepted constitutional traditions. Foremost among these has been the so-called *Lemon* test, see *Lemon v. Kurtzman* (1971), which has received

well-earned criticism from many members of this Court. . . . The Court today demonstrates the irrelevance of *Lemon* by essentially ignoring it, and the interment of that case may be the one happy byproduct of the Court's otherwise lamentable decision. Unfortunately, however, the Court has replaced *Lemon* with its psychocoercion test, which suffers the double disability of having no roots whatever in our people's historic practice, and being as infinitely expandable as the reasons for psychotherapy itself.

Another happy aspect of the case is that it is only a jurisprudential disaster and not a practical one. Given the odd basis for the Court's decision, invocations and benedictions will be able to be given at public-school graduations next June, as they have for the past century and a half, so long as school authorities make clear that anyone who abstains from screaming in protest does not necessarily participate in the prayers. All that is seemingly needed is an announcement, or perhaps a written insertion at the beginning of the graduation Program, to the effect that, while all are asked to rise for the invocation and benediction, none is compelled to join in them, nor will be assumed, by rising, to have done so. That obvious fact recited, the graduates and their parents may proceed to thank God, as Americans have always done, for the blessings He has generously bestowed on them and on their country. . . .

For the foregoing reasons, I dissent.

Justice Kennedy did not apply *Lemon* to resolve *Weisman*, but neither did he overturn it. To the contrary, he specifically declined to revisit *Lemon* on the ground that the Court's previous cases on prayer in school established clear and ample precedent for this decision. Applying a coercion standard, Kennedy noted that *Engel* and *Abington* recognized that "prayer exercises in public schools carry a particular risk of indirect coercion." It was this coercion, however subtle, at which Kennedy took offense. The concurrers, on the other hand, argued in favor of alternative standards: Stevens, Blackmun, and O'Connor continued to advocate an endorsement approach to *Lemon*. Souter, joined by Stevens and O'Connor, explicitly rejected Kennedy's coercion standard and Rehnquist's nonpreferentialism in favor of the endorsement approach. Souter also stressed that the Court should not abandon precedent governing religious establishment cases, yet he had little to say about *Lemon* in particular.

Youth group members from the Santa Fe and Bayou Drive Baptist Churches conduct a prayer circle under a stadium scoreboard. A student's prayer delivered over the loudspeaker prior to the kickoff of a high school football game became the subject of a Supreme Court case.

Most interesting of all may be Scalia's dissent. Joined by Rehnquist, White, and Thomas, Scalia lambasted the Court for ignoring America's historical traditions and engaging in amateur psychology by paying more attention to Freud than to the framers. About the only thing the dissenters found redeemable in *Weisman* was that the majority opinion ignored *Lemon* altogether.

It took eight years for the school prayer issue to find its way to the Supreme Court once again. In ***Santa Fe Independent School District v. Doe*** (2000) the justices faced a tradition of long standing in many communities: public prayer at high school football games. At issue was the policy of a Texas public school district that allowed student-led invocations to be delivered on the public address system during pregame ceremonies. To ensure continuing support for this practice, the school district required an annual vote of students, by secret ballot, on whether they wanted public prayers at the games. If the vote favored the invocations, a second election took place to select a single student who would deliver the prayers at all home games for that season. The school required that the prayers be consistent with the district's policy goals: to solemnize the event, to promote sportsmanship and safety, and to establish the appropriate environment for competition. Otherwise the content of the message was left to the discretion of the student delivering it.

Two families, one Mormon and the other Catholic, challenged the district's policy. Local sentiment strongly supported the pregame prayers, and as a consequence the lower courts allowed the individuals filing the challenge to proceed anonymously to protect them from intimidation and harassment.

The school district defended its policy on several grounds. First, it argued that because the invocations were controlled by the students and not by the district administration, the prayers constituted private expression, not government-mandated expression. Second, the two-stage election system ensured that the prayers would not be said without the support of the majority of the students. Third, the school district only permitted the process to take place—it was not in any way involved in the writing or presentation of the prayers. Finally, the prayers were said at a completely voluntary, extracurricular event. Attendance was not required, nor was participation in the recitation of the prayers. There was no coercion to participate.

Based on precedents such as *Weisman* and *Lemon*, a six-justice majority struck down the district's prayer practices as violations of the establishment clause. In an uncommon expression of unity, all six members of the majority subscribed to a single opinion written by Justice Stevens. No concurring opinions were issued. The majority found the district policy unconstitutional on several grounds. First, the practice constituted an endorsement of religion. The invocations were authorized by a government policy and took place on government property at a government-sponsored, school-related event. The school district clearly invited and encouraged the religious activity. The prayers sent a constitutionally impermissible message that nonadherents are "outsiders, not full members of the political community, and an accompanying message to adherents that they are insiders, favored members of the political community."

Second, the policy contained an element of coercion. Although generally voluntary, for some students (players, cheerleaders, and band members) attendance was not optional. In addition, in many communities high school football games are important social events with strong peer pressure to attend. The majority found it constitutionally unacceptable to force students to forgo attending such school-sponsored events to avoid conforming with a state-sponsored religious practice.

Third, the majority found the district's policy to be in direct violation of the Lemon test's requirement that government policies have a secular purpose. In spite of the district's arguments to the contrary, the Court concluded that the primary purpose of the prayers was religious.

Chief Justice Rehnquist, joined by Justices Scalia and Thomas, dissented. They objected not only to the outcome but also to the tone of the Court's opinion, which, Rehnquist said, "bristles with hostility to all things religious in public life." According to the minority, the country's traditions allow voluntary religious expressions by private individuals at public events such as football games.

The *Santa Fe* decision is the most recent in a long line of decisions in which the justices have found various forms of school prayer constitutionally impermissible. In an area of the law that is characterized by inconsistencies, the school prayer decisions stand out as remarkably stable. Although justices have squabbled over the most appropriate test to apply, the outcomes have never been in serious doubt—prayer in public schools is unconstitutional.

Religious Displays

Government-supported religious displays have led to objections on establishment clause grounds. Such displays occur most often during the Christmas season, when local governments decorate their main streets and municipal buildings to encourage the holiday spirit.

Lynch v. Donnelly (1984) was the Court's first significant ruling on this issue. The case involved a holiday display in Pawtucket, Rhode Island, that the Retail Merchants Association had been erecting every Christmas for four decades in a park owned by a non-profit organization. The display featured many different elements, including a Santa Claus house, reindeer, a Christmas tree, a clown, colored lights, a "Season's Greetings" banner, and a crèche (nativity scene) with the Christ child, Mary and Joseph, angels, animals, and so forth. The city had purchased the crèche for $1,365 in 1973, and the city spent about $20 annually to set it up and take it down. Believing these expenditures to constitute a violation of the establishment clause, the ACLU of Rhode Island sued the city. City officials and area businesspeople countered that the display had a secular purpose: to attract customers to the city's downtown shopping area.

Chief Justice Burger, speaking for a five-person majority, found that the display was not an impermissible breach of the establishment clause. In one of his more strongly worded accommodationist opinions, he pointed to many examples indicating "an unbroken history of official acknowledgment by all three branches of government of the role of religion in American life": executive orders proclaiming Christmas and Thanksgiving as national holidays, "In God We Trust" on currency, and publicly supported art galleries full of religious paintings.

Of special importance to the majority was the fact that the crèche was only one part of the display. It was one passive symbol, along with several other scenes, depicting American traditions during the winter holiday season. In short, Burger implied that Christmas was so much a part of our heritage that it came close to representing a national, nonsectarian celebration, rather than a religious holiday.

Five years later, the Court revisited the holiday display issue. ***County of Allegheny v. ACLU*** (1989) presented a challenge to two public holiday displays in Pittsburgh, Pennsylvania. The first was a crèche that belonged to a Roman Catholic group, the Holy Name Society. Beginning with the Christmas season of 1981, the city allowed the society to place the crèche on the grand staircase of the county courthouse, which is, by all accounts, the "main," "most beautiful," and "most public" part of the courthouse. The second challenged display was a Hanukkah menorah located outside of the City-County Building, where the mayor and other city officials have their offices. For much of its history, the city erected only a Christmas tree outside this building, but beginning in the 1980s it included the menorah. By 1986 the entire display included a forty-five-foot Christmas tree complete with lights and ornaments and an eighteen-foot Hanukkah menorah, owned by a Jewish group but stored and erected by the city.

Did these displays violate the establishment clause? This question gave the Court a good deal of trouble: a majority of justices could not agree over the appropriate standard by which to answer it. In the end, the Court issued a judgment written by Justice Blackmun, who began by outlining the approach he would take to the case:

Our ... decisions [subsequent to *Lemon*] further have refined the definition of governmental action that unconstitutionally advances religion. In recent years, we have paid particularly close attention to whether the challenged governmental practice either has the purpose or effect of "endorsing" religion, a concern that has long had a place in our Establishment Clause jurisprudence.

Applying these principles to the case at hand, Blackmun concluded that given its physical setting, the display of the crèche violated the establishment clause. It stood alone, in a place of particular prominence, communicating the unmistakable message that the county supported and promoted all that the nativity scene represented. But the Court found that the Christmas tree and menorah did not run afoul of the Constitution. Because the display included side-by-side symbols of two religious traditions celebrated during the winter holiday period, there was little to indicate government endorsement of a particular religious message.

Controversies over religious displays are, however, not confined to holiday symbols; they have also erupted over public exhibition of the Ten Commandments. In *Stone v. Graham* (1980) the Court struck down a Kentucky law that required the Ten Commandments to be posted in every public school classroom. A five-justice majority concluded that the law had a religious purpose, violating the first prong of the Lemon test. In 2005 the Ten Commandments issue returned to the Court in two cases.

The first was ***McCreary County, Kentucky v. American Civil Liberties Union of Kentucky*** (2005), which concerned a lingering dispute over a local ordinance requiring that the Ten Commandments be publicly posted in the county courthouse. When the ACLU filed a lawsuit to have the display removed, the county responded by expanding the exhibit. Along with the Ten Commandments, the county posted other documents, all with a religious flavor and all of smaller size than the Ten Commandments. Included among the expanded offerings were the national motto ("In God We Trust"), a proclamation by President Reagan declaring 1983 the Year of the Bible, and the religious passages of the Declaration of Independence. The ACLU pressed its suit against the county, and the district court, applying the Lemon test, found the county to be in violation of the establishment clause. The county responded by once again changing the display. This time the more overtly religious exhibits were replaced with nine displays of equal size. Among those joining the Ten Commandments were the Bill of Rights, the Preamble to the Kentucky Constitution, Lady Justice, and the Mayflower Compact. The overall exhibit was titled "The Foundations of American Law and Government." The ACLU was not satisfied. The district court and the court of appeals both held the county's actions to be at odds with the Constitution.

The county argued that the revised display met the Court's expectations as expressed in *Lynch v. Donnelly* and *County of Allegheny v. ACLU*. The Ten Commandments were now just one part of a display of many documents with secular significance. The Supreme Court, in a 5–4 vote, rejected the county's plea. In an opinion by Justice Souter, the Court held that the Ten Commandments is a document of both religious and secular importance. The county's actions, however, supported the conclusion that the placing of the Ten Commandments had a religious purpose. The county had expanded the display, after being sued, only in an attempt to keep the Ten Commandments in the courthouse.

The second case, *Van Orden v. Perry* (2005), focused on a large Ten Commandments monument erected on the grounds of the Texas state capitol. As you read this opinion, pay attention not only to how the majority treats the issue of a religious display on public property but also to how the justices treat the ongoing controversy over the appropriate standard to use in establishment clause cases.

This six-foot-tall stone slab bearing the Ten Commandments was the focal point of the Supreme Court's decision in Van Orden v. Perry (2005). *The justices ruled that the placement of this monument on the state capitol grounds in Austin, Texas, did not violate the First Amendment's establishment clause.*

Van Orden v. Perry

545 U.S. 677 (2005)
http://laws.findlaw.com/US/000/03-1500.html
Oral arguments are available at http://www.oyez.org.
Vote: 5 (Breyer, Kennedy, Rehnquist, Scalia, Thomas)
4 (Ginsburg, O'Connor, Souter, Stevens)

OPINION OF THE COURT: *Rehnquist*
CONCURRING OPINIONS: *Scalia, Thomas*
OPINION CONCURRING IN JUDGMENT: *Breyer*
DISSENTING OPINIONS: *O'Connor, Souter, Stevens*

FACTS:

The twenty-two-acre park surrounding the Texas capitol contains seventeen monuments and twenty-one historical markers commemorating the "people, ideals, and events that compose Texan identity." One of these is a six-foot-high monument displaying the text of the Ten Commandments. The Fraternal Order of Eagles gave the monument to the people of Texas in 1961. The Eagles also paid for the construction of the monument and its dedication.

Thomas Van Orden, a lawyer by training and a resident of Austin, frequently saw the monument on his walks through the capitol grounds. After doing so for about six years, he filed suit against Governor Rick Perry and other state officials asking the court to order the removal of the monument because its presence on the capitol grounds violated the establishment clause. The trial court judge rejected Van Orden's request, finding that the monument had a secular purpose and that no reasonable observer would conclude that the state was endorsing religion by allowing this passive monument to be placed on state property. The court of appeals affirmed, and the Supreme Court granted review.

ARGUMENTS:

For the petitioner, Thomas Van Orden:
- The Ten Commandments monument expresses a religious message and is a religious symbol.
- The prominent placement of the monument on the grounds of the state capitol violates the establishment clause because it favors one religion over others, has no secular purpose, and has the effect of endorsing religion.

For the respondent, Rick Perry, Governor of Texas:
- The Ten Commandments monument does not constitute state endorsement of religion nor does it have any element of coercion. The monument is smaller and less prominently located than several others on the capitol grounds.
- The Ten Commandments is an ancient legal code. The monument's placement between the state legislature and the state supreme court emphasizes its civic importance.

- The monument underscores the influence of the Ten Commandments on law and culture. No one would assume the words are an expression of state policy.

CHIEF JUSTICE REHNQUIST ANNOUNCED THE JUDGMENT OF THE COURT AND DELIVERED AN OPINION, IN WHICH JUSTICE SCALIA, JUSTICE KENNEDY, AND JUSTICE THOMAS JOIN.

The question here is whether the Establishment Clause of the First Amendment allows the display of a monument inscribed with the Ten Commandments on the Texas State Capitol grounds. We hold that it does. . . .

Our cases, Janus-like, point in two directions in applying the Establishment Clause. One face looks toward the strong role played by religion and religious traditions throughout our Nation's history. . . .

The other face looks toward the principle that governmental intervention in religious matters can itself endanger religious freedom.

This case, like all Establishment Clause challenges, presents us with the difficulty of respecting both faces. Our institutions presuppose a Supreme Being, yet these institutions must not press religious observances upon their citizens. One face looks to the past in acknowledgment of our Nation's heritage, while the other looks to the present in demanding a separation between church and state. Reconciling these two faces requires that we neither abdicate our responsibility to maintain a division between church and state nor evince a hostility to religion by disabling the government from in some ways recognizing our religious heritage. . . .

These two faces are evident in representative cases both upholding and invalidating laws under the Establishment Clause. Over the last 25 years, we have sometimes pointed to *Lemon v. Kurtzman* (1971) as providing the governing test in Establishment Clause challenges. Yet, just two years after *Lemon* was decided, we noted that the factors identified in *Lemon* serve as "no more than helpful signposts." *Hunt v. McNair* (1973). Many of our recent cases simply have not applied the *Lemon* test. See, *e.g., Zelman v. Simmons-Harris* (2002); *Good News Club v. Milford Central School* (2001). Others have applied it only after concluding that the challenged practice was invalid under a different Establishment Clause test.

Whatever may be the fate of the *Lemon* test in the larger scheme of Establishment Clause jurisprudence, we think it not useful in dealing with the sort of passive monument that Texas has erected on its Capitol grounds. Instead, our analysis is driven both by the nature of the monument and by our Nation's history.

As we explained in *Lynch v. Donnelly* (1984): "There is an unbroken history of official acknowledgment by all three branches of government of the role of religion in American life from at least 1789." . . .

Recognition of the role of God in our Nation's heritage has also been reflected in our decisions. We have acknowledged, for example, that "religion has been closely identified with our history and government," *School Dist. of Abington Township v. Schempp* [1963], and that "[t]he history of man is inseparable from the history of religion," *Engel v. Vitale* (1962). This recognition has led us to hold that the Establishment Clause permits a state legislature to open its daily sessions with a prayer by a chaplain paid by the State. *Marsh v. Chambers* [1983]. . . . With similar reasoning, we have upheld laws, which originated from one of the Ten Commandments, that prohibited the sale of merchandise on Sunday. *McGowan v. Maryland* (1961).

In this case we are faced with a display of the Ten Commandments on government property outside the Texas State Capitol. Such acknowledgments of the role played by the Ten Commandments in our Nation's heritage are common throughout America. We need only look within our own Courtroom. Since 1935, Moses has stood, holding two tablets that reveal portions of the Ten Commandments written in Hebrew, among other lawgivers in the south frieze. Representations of the Ten Commandments adorn the metal gates lining the north and south sides of the Courtroom as well as the doors leading into the Courtroom. Moses also sits on the exterior east facade of the building holding the Ten Commandments tablets.

Similar acknowledgments can be seen throughout a visitor's tour of our Nation's Capital. . . .

Of course, the Ten Commandments are religious—they were so viewed at their inception and so remain. The monument, therefore, has religious significance. According to Judeo-Christian belief, the Ten Commandments were given to Moses by God on Mt. Sinai. But Moses was a lawgiver as well as a religious leader. And the Ten Commandments have an undeniable historical meaning. . . . Simply having religious content or promoting a message consistent with a religious doctrine does not run afoul of the Establishment Clause.

There are, of course, limits to the display of religious messages or symbols. For example, we held unconstitutional a Kentucky statute requiring the posting of the Ten Commandments in every public schoolroom. *Stone v. Graham* (1980). In the classroom context, we found that the Kentucky statute had an improper and plainly religious purpose. As evidenced by *Stone*'s almost exclusive reliance upon two of our school prayer cases, *School Dist. of Abington Township v. Schempp* (1963) and *Engel v. Vitale* (1962), it stands as an example of the fact that we have "been particularly vigilant in monitoring compliance with the Establishment Clause in elementary and secondary schools," *Edwards v. Aguillard* (1987). Indeed, *Edwards v. Aguillard* recognized that *Stone*— along with *Schempp* and *Engel*—was a consequence of the "particular concerns that arise in the context of public elementary and secondary schools." Neither *Stone* itself nor subsequent opinions have indicated that *Stone*'s holding would extend to a legislative chamber or to capitol grounds.

The placement of the Ten Commandments monument on the Texas State Capitol grounds is a far more passive use of those texts than was the case in *Stone*, where the text confronted elementary school students every day. Indeed, Van Orden, the petitioner here, apparently walked by the monument for a number of years before bringing this lawsuit. The monument is therefore also quite different from the prayers involved in *Schempp* and *Lee v. Weisman* [1992]. Texas has treated her Capitol grounds monuments as representing the several strands in the State's political and legal history. The inclusion of the Ten Commandments monument in this group has a dual significance, partaking of both religion and government. We cannot say that Texas' display of this monument violates the Establishment Clause of the First Amendment.

The judgment of the Court of Appeals is affirmed.

It is so ordered.

JUSTICE SCALIA, concurring.

I join the opinion of the Chief Justice because I think it accurately reflects our current Establishment Clause jurisprudence—or at least the Establishment Clause jurisprudence we currently apply some of the time. I would prefer to reach the same result by adopting an Establishment Clause jurisprudence that is in accord with our Nation's past and present practices, and that can be consistently applied—the central relevant feature of which is that there is nothing unconstitutional in a State's favoring religion generally, honoring God through public prayer and acknowledgment, or,

in a nonproselytizing manner, venerating the Ten Commandments.

JUSTICE THOMAS, concurring.

The Court holds that the Ten Commandments monument found on the Texas State Capitol grounds does not violate the Establishment Clause. Rather than trying to suggest meaninglessness where there is meaning, the Chief Justice rightly recognizes that the monument has "religious significance." He properly recognizes the role of religion in this Nation's history and the permissibility of government displays acknowledging that history. For those reasons, I join the Chief Justice's opinion in full.

This case would be easy if the Court were willing to abandon the inconsistent guideposts it has adopted for addressing Establishment Clause challenges, and return to the original meaning of the Clause. I have previously suggested that the Clause's text and history "resis[t] incorporation" against the States. See *Elk Grove Unified School Dist. v. Newdow* (2004) (opinion concurring in judgment). If the Establishment Clause does not restrain the States, then it has no application here, where only state action is at issue.

Even if the Clause is incorporated, or if the Free Exercise Clause limits the power of States to establish religions, our task would be far simpler if we returned to the original meaning of the word "establishment" than it is under the various approaches this Court now uses. The Framers understood an establishment "necessarily [to] involve actual legal coercion." "In other words, establishment at the founding involved, for example, mandatory observance or mandatory payment of taxes supporting ministers." And "government practices that have nothing to do with creating or maintaining . . . coercive state establishments" simply do not "implicate the possible liberty interest of being free from coercive state establishments."

JUSTICE BREYER, concurring in the judgment.

The case before us is a borderline case. It concerns a large granite monument bearing the text of the Ten Commandments located on the grounds of the Texas State Capitol. On the one hand, the Commandments' text undeniably has a religious message, invoking, indeed emphasizing, the Diety. On the other hand, focusing on the text of the Commandments alone cannot conclusively resolve this case. Rather, to determine the message that the text here conveys, we must examine how the text is used. And that inquiry requires us to consider the context of the display. . . .

Here the tablets have been used as part of a display that communicates not simply a religious message, but a secular message as well. The circumstances surrounding the display's placement on the capitol grounds and its physical setting suggest that the State itself intended the latter, nonreligious aspects of the tablets' message to predominate. And the monument's 40-year history on the Texas state grounds indicates that that has been its effect. . . .

The physical setting of the monument, moreover, suggests little or nothing of the sacred. The monument sits in a large park containing 17 monuments and 21 historical markers, all designed to illustrate the "ideals" of those who settled in Texas and of those who have lived there since that time. The setting does not readily lend itself to meditation or any other religious activity. But it does provide a context of history and moral ideals. It (together with the display's inscription about its origin) communicates to visitors that the State sought to reflect moral principles, illustrating a relation between ethics and law that the State's citizens, historically speaking, have endorsed. That is to say, the context suggests that the State intended the display's moral message—an illustrative message reflecting the historical "ideals" of Texans—to predominate. . . .

For these reasons, I believe that the Texas display—serving a mixed but primarily nonreligious purpose, not primarily "advanc[ing]" or "inhibit[ing]" religion," and not creating an "excessive government entanglement with religion,"—might satisfy this Court's more formal Establishment Clause tests. But, as I have said, in reaching the conclusion that the Texas display falls on the permissible side of the constitutional line, I rely less upon a literal application of any particular test than upon consideration of the basic purposes of the First Amendment's Religion Clauses themselves. This display has stood apparently uncontested for nearly two generations. That experience helps us understand that as a practical matter of degree this display is unlikely to prove divisive. And this matter of degree is, I believe, critical in a borderline case such as this one.

At the same time, to reach a contrary conclusion here, based primarily upon on the religious nature of the tablets' text would, I fear, lead the law to exhibit a hostility toward religion that has no place in our Establishment Clause traditions. Such a holding might well encourage disputes concerning the removal of longstanding depictions of the Ten Commandments from public buildings across the Nation. And it could thereby create the very kind of religiously based divisiveness that the Establishment Clause seeks to avoid. . . .

I concur in the judgment of the Court.

JUSTICE STEVENS, with whom JUSTICE GINSBURG joins, dissenting.

Government's obligation to avoid divisiveness and exclusion in the religious sphere is compelled by the Establishment and Free Exercise Clauses, which together erect a wall of separation between church and state. This metaphorical wall protects principles long recognized and often recited in this Court's cases. The first and most fundamental of these principles, one that a majority of this Court today affirms, is that the Establishment Clause demands religious neutrality—government may not exercise a preference for one religious faith over another. This essential command, however, is not merely a prohibition against the government's differentiation among religious sects. We have repeatedly reaffirmed that neither a State nor the Federal Government "can constitutionally pass laws or impose requirements which aid all religions as against non-believers, and neither can aid those religions based on a belief in the existence of God as against those religions founded on different beliefs." *Torcaso v. Watkins* (1961). This principle is based on the straightforward notion that governmental promotion of orthodoxy is not saved by the aggregation of several orthodoxies under the State's banner. . . .

The monolith displayed on Texas Capitol grounds cannot be discounted as a passive acknowledgment of religion, nor can the State's refusal to remove it upon objection be explained as a simple desire to preserve a historic relic. This Nation's resolute commitment to neutrality with respect to religion is flatly inconsistent with the plurality's wholehearted validation of an official state endorsement of the message that there is one, and only one, God. . . .

The judgment of the Court in this case stands for the proposition that the Constitution permits governmental displays of sacred religious texts. This makes a mockery of the constitutional ideal that government must remain neutral between religion and irreligion. If a State may endorse a particular deity's command to "have no other gods before me," it is difficult to conceive of any textual display that would run afoul of the Establishment Clause. . . .

I respectfully dissent.

JUSTICE SOUTER, with whom JUSTICE STEVENS and JUSTICE GINSBURG join, dissenting.[31]

. . . [A] pedestrian happening upon the monument at issue here needs no training in religious doctrine to realize that the statement of the Commandments, quoting God himself, proclaims that the will of the divine being is the source of obligation to obey the rules, including the facially secular ones. In this case, moreover, the text is presented to give particular prominence to the Commandments' first sectarian reference, "I am the Lord thy God." That proclamation is centered on the stone and written in slightly larger letters than the subsequent recitation. To ensure that the religious nature of the monument is clear to even the most casual passerby, the word "Lord" appears in all capital letters (as does the word "am"), so that the most eye-catching segment of the quotation is the declaration "I AM the LORD thy God." What follows, of course, are the rules against other gods, graven images, vain swearing, and Sabbath breaking. And the full text of the fifth Commandment puts forward filial respect as a condition of long life in the land "which the Lord thy God giveth thee." These "[w]ords . . . make [the] . . . religious meaning unmistakably clear." *County of Allegheny v. American Civil Liberties Union, Greater Pittsburgh Chapter* (1989).

To drive the religious point home, and identify the message as religious to any viewer who failed to read the text, the engraved quotation is framed by religious symbols: two tablets with what appears to be ancient script on them, two Stars of David, and the superimposed Greek letters Chi and Rho as the familiar monogram of Christ. Nothing on the monument, in fact, detracts from its religious nature, and the plurality does not suggest otherwise. It would therefore be difficult to miss the point that the government of Texas is telling everyone who sees the monument to live up to a moral code because God requires it, with both code and conception of God being rightly understood as the inheritances specifically of Jews and Christians. . . .

. . . Texas . . . says that the Capitol grounds are like a museum for a collection of exhibits, the kind of setting that several Members of the Court have said can render the exhibition of religious artifacts permissible, even though in other circumstances their display would be seen as meant to convey a religious message forbidden to the State. . . .

But 17 monuments with no common appearance, history, or esthetic role scattered over 22 acres is not a museum, and anyone strolling around the lawn would surely take each memorial on its own terms without any dawning sense that some purpose held the miscellany together more coherently than fortuity and the edge of the grass. One monument expresses admiration for pioneer women. One pays respect to the fighters of World War II. And one quotes the God of Abraham whose command is the sanction for moral law. The themes are individual grit, patriotic courage, and God as the source of Jewish and Christian morality; there is no common denominator. . . .

. . . The monument in this case sits on the grounds of the Texas State Capitol. There is something significant in the common term "statehouse" to refer to a state capitol building: it is the civic home of every one of the State's citizens. If neutrality in religion means something, any citizen should be able to visit that civic home without having to confront religious expressions clearly meant to convey an official religious position that may be at odds with his own religion, or with rejection of religion. . . .

I would reverse the judgment of the Court of Appeals.

Van Orden, the Court's most recent extensive treatment of the establishment clause, illustrates the continuing divisions among the justices.[32] Chief Justice Rehnquist's plurality opinion again belittles the importance of *Lemon.* He argues that *Lemon* is no more than a "helpful signpost" and that the Court has often ignored it or applied different tests in its place. Justices Breyer, Scalia, and Thomas offer concurring views. Breyer concludes that the Texas display was just one of many monuments on the capitol grounds and that there was no evidence that the state was emphasizing the religious

---

31. In a separate statement, Justice O'Connor also expressed agreement with Souter's opinion.

32. More recently the Court decided another religious display case, but not on establishment clause grounds. ***Pleasant Grove City v. Summum*** (2009) involved a city's denial of a religious sect's request to erect a monument to the Seven Aphorisms of Summum and place it in a public park that contained eleven permanent monuments and displays, including the Ten Commandments. The city explained that the other monuments were either donated by local groups of long standing or were of historical significance to the city. The proposed Seven Aphorisms monument, the city said, would not be consistent with park's theme. Without dissent, the Supreme Court rejected the organization's claim that its free speech rights had been violated. The justices held that the issue was not the government's restriction of private speech. Rather, the monuments in the city park are a form of government speech, and the government is entitled to select the views it wants to express.

(over the secular) nature of the Ten Commandments. Scalia posits that there is nothing unconstitutional about venerating the Ten Commandments in a nonproselytizing manner. Thomas offers the most extreme position: he questions the validity of incorporating the establishment clause and making it applicable to the states.

The dissenters focus on the religious nature of the Ten Commandments. They claim that there is no place under the U.S. Constitution for the state to erect a monument to a divinely given code of law. Neutrality means not only that one denomination cannot be favored over another but also that believers cannot be favored over nonbelievers. Here the state endorsed a specific religious text. In Justice Stevens's words, this makes a "mockery of the constitutional ideal that government must remain neutral."

Government Involvement in the Affairs of Religious Organizations

The establishment clause issues discussed thus far have involved government aiding or accommodating religion through such means as granting financial support or permitting prayer and other religious exercises at government-sponsored functions or facilities. But government can also run afoul of the First Amendment when it becomes involved in the internal operations of religious organizations. Such intrusions into religious affairs also may give rise to free exercise issues. The "excessive government entanglement" prong of the Lemon test was adopted, in part, as a response to these dangers. As Chief Justice Burger noted in *Lemon*, "active involvement of the sovereign in religious activity" was one of the evils against which the Establishment Clause was intended to afford protection.

Religious institutions, along with many other entities of American society, have evolved significantly over the course of the nation's history. No longer are religious activities confined to simple, local places of worship. Many faith groups are involved in a host of social, political, and commercial activities. Some administer large educational or health care efforts, requiring massive budgets and significant numbers of employees. Others have wide-ranging ministries that extend well beyond the confines of their home communities. Megachurches have become common in many metropolitan areas. Religious groups use mass media to extend the reach of their messages to national and even international audiences.

This expansion in the size and scope of religious organizations has occurred along with the growth of

regulatory activity by state and federal governments. Many public activities in which churches are engaged are subject to this regulatory power. For example, church-owned hospitals and universities must conform to government-established standards for the operation of health care facilities and educational institutions.

But what about the internal affairs of a religious organization? Does the government have the authority to tell a religious institution how it must conduct its internal business? This question was presented to the Court in the case of *Hosanna-Tabor Evangelical Lutheran Church and School v. Equal Employment Opportunity Commission* (2012). The dispute began when a Lutheran church in Michigan fired a woman employed as a teacher in the church elementary school. The dismissed teacher maintained that she was the victim of illegal disability discrimination. After examining her claim, the U.S. Equal Employment Opportunity Commission (EEOC) agreed and took legal action against the church. Can the federal government constitutionally tell a church who it must hire or who it may fire? If the government dictates such personnel conditions, is the establishment clause violated? And do such government regulations conflict with the free exercise rights of the church members?

Hosanna-Tabor Evangelical Lutheran Church and School v. Equal Employment Opportunity Commission

565 U.S. ___ (2012)
http://laws.findlaw.com/us/000/10-553.html
Oral arguments are available at http://www.oyez.org.
Vote: 9 (Alito, Breyer, Ginsburg, Kagan, Kennedy,
     Roberts, Scalia, Sotomayor, Thomas)
     0

OPINION OF THE COURT: *Roberts*
CONCURRING OPINIONS: *Alito, Thomas*

FACTS:

Hosanna-Tabor Evangelical Lutheran Church of Redford, Michigan, is a member of the Missouri Synod of the Lutheran Church. In addition to the normal activities of a Lutheran congregation, the church operates a small school offering a "Christ-centered education" for children in kindergarten through eighth grade.

The Missouri Synod classifies teachers into two categories: called and lay. Called teachers are considered to have been invited to their vocation by God through a congregation. To be designated as called, a teacher must complete a special academic program offered by a Lutheran college or university, obtain the endorsement of a local synod district, and pass an oral examination by a faculty committee. A teacher who meets these qualifications may be "called" by a local congregation and receive the title "minister of religion—commissioned." Congregations employ called teachers for open-ended terms, and the teachers can have their calls rescinded only for cause. Lay or contract teachers are not required to complete the special Lutheran academic training and are hired for one-year renewable terms. Called and lay teachers have similar duties, but Lutheran congregations prefer to hire called teachers when they are available.

Cheryl Perich began working at Hosanna-Tabor in 1999 as a lay teacher, but within that first year she completed the required training and was elevated to called teacher status. She taught kindergarten and fourth grade, instructing students in typical secular subjects. She also taught religion class four days a week, led students in daily prayer and devotional exercises, and occasionally led the school's chapel service.

In 2004 Perich went on disability leave because she was experiencing symptoms of narcolepsy, a condition that caused her to enter sudden and deep sleeps from which she could not be roused. In January 2005 she informed the school that she would be ready to return to the classroom the following month. Hosanna-Tabor officials expressed concern that Perich would not be able to handle the physical demands of the job and informed her that a lay teacher had already been hired to take her place. The congregation offered to release her from her call and to subsidize her health insurance costs in return for her resignation. Perich refused to resign and provided documentation from her doctor stating that she would be ready to return to work in February. When the church refused to take her back at that time, Perich threatened a lawsuit. In response, the church terminated her employment. One reason given for the termination was that Perich's threat to take legal action violated a Lutheran principle that any disputes within the church should be settled internally.

Perich filed a complaint with the U.S. Equal Employment Opportunity Commission. The EEOC investigated and concluded that Hosanna-Tabor had violated the Americans with Disabilities Act (ADA) by firing Perich in retaliation for her threatened legal action, and the commission joined with Perich in a suit against the church. The district court ruled in favor of Hosanna-Tabor, holding that the First Amendment prohibited the government from dictating to a church who its ministers must be. The court of appeals reversed, concluding that Perich was not a "minister."

ARGUMENTS:

For the petitioner, Hosanna-Tabor Evangelical Lutheran Church and School:

- The establishment clause limits the government's authority to appoint ministers and resolve religious questions.
- The free exercise clause protects the right of religious organizations to choose who will perform important religious functions.
- Granting Perich's claim would impose an unwanted minister on the church and entangle the government in religious questions and affairs.

For the respondents, Equal Employment Opportunity Commission and Cheryl Perich:

- The government has a compelling interest in eradicating discrimination in the workplace. Religious employers, like other employers, cannot be permitted to retaliate against employees who report illegal conduct to the government.
- The free exercise clause does not prevent the application of neutral, generally applicable, antidiscrimination laws that incidentally burden religious practice.
- The application of the ADA in this case does not amount to government appointment of clergy in violation of the establishment clause, nor does it constitute excessive government entanglement with religion.

The Hosanna-Tabor Evangelical Lutheran Church and School in Redford, Michigan.

Certain employment discrimination laws authorize employees who have been wrongfully terminated to sue their employers for reinstatement and damages. The question presented is whether the Establishment and Free Exercise Clauses of the First Amendment bar such an action when the employer is a religious group and the employee is one of the group's ministers. . . .

The First Amendment provides, in part, that "Congress shall make no law respecting an establishment of religion, or prohibiting the free exercise thereof." We have said that these two Clauses "often exert conflicting pressures," *Cutter v. Wilkinson* (2005), and that there can be "internal tension . . . between the Establishment Clause and the Free Exercise Clause," *Tilton v. Richardson* (1971) (plurality opinion). Not so here. Both Religion Clauses bar the government from interfering with the decision of a religious group to fire one of its ministers. . . .

. . . Familiar with life under the established Church of England, the founding generation sought to foreclose the possibility of a national church. By forbidding the "establishment of religion" and guaranteeing the "free exercise thereof," the Religion Clauses ensured that the new Federal Government—unlike the English Crown—would have no role in filling ecclesiastical offices. The Establishment Clause prevents the Government from appointing ministers, and the Free Exercise Clause prevents it from interfering with the freedom of religious groups to select their own. . . .

Given this understanding of the Religion Clauses—and the absence of government employment regulation generally—it was some time before questions about government interference with a church's ability to select its own ministers came before the courts. This Court touched upon the issue indirectly, however, in the context of disputes over church property. Our decisions in that area confirm that it is impermissible for the government to contradict a church's determination of who can act as its ministers.

In *Watson v. Jones* (1872), the Court considered a dispute between antislavery and proslavery factions over who controlled the property of the Walnut Street Presbyterian Church in Louisville, Kentucky. The General Assembly of the Presbyterian Church had recognized the antislavery faction, and this Court—applying not the Constitution but a "broad and sound view of the relations of church and state under our system of laws"—declined to question that determination. We explained

that "whenever the questions of discipline, or of faith, or ecclesiastical rule, custom, or law have been decided by the highest of [the] church judicatories to which the matter has been carried, the legal tribunals must accept such decisions as final, and as binding on them." As we would put it later, our opinion in *Watson* "radiates . . . a spirit of freedom for religious organizations, an independence from secular control or manipulation—in short, power to decide for themselves, free from state interference, matters of church government as well as those of faith and doctrine." *Kedroff v. Saint Nicholas Cathedral of Russian Orthodox Church in North America* (1952). . . .

. . . The members of a religious group put their faith in the hands of their ministers. Requiring a church to accept or retain an unwanted minister, or punishing a church for failing to do so, intrudes upon more than a mere employment decision. Such action interferes with the internal governance of the church, depriving the church of control over the selection of those who will personify its beliefs. By imposing an unwanted minister, the state infringes the Free Exercise Clause, which protects a religious group's right to shape its own faith and mission through its appointments. According the state the power to determine which individuals will minister to the faithful also violates the Establishment Clause, which prohibits government involvement in such ecclesiastical decisions.

The EEOC and Perich acknowledge that employment discrimination laws would be unconstitutional as applied to religious groups in certain circumstances. They grant, for example, that it would violate the First Amendment for courts to apply such laws to compel the ordination of women by the Catholic Church or by an Orthodox Jewish seminary. According to the EEOC and Perich, religious organizations could successfully defend against employment discrimination claims in those circumstances by invoking the constitutional right to freedom of association—a right "implicit" in the First Amendment. *Roberts v. United States Jaycees* (1984). The EEOC and Perich thus see no need—and no basis—for a special rule for ministers grounded in the Religion Clauses themselves.

We find this position untenable. The right to freedom of association is a right enjoyed by religious and secular groups alike. It follows under the EEOC's and Perich's view that the First Amendment analysis should be the same, whether the association in question is the Lutheran Church, a labor union, or a social club. That result is hard to square with the text of the First Amendment itself, which gives special solicitude to the rights of religious organizations. We cannot accept the remarkable view that the Religion Clauses have nothing to say about a religious organization's freedom to select its own ministers.

The EEOC and Perich also contend that our decision in *Employment Div., Dept. of Human Resources of Ore. v. Smith* (1990) precludes recognition of a ministerial exception. In *Smith,* two members of the Native American Church were denied state unemployment benefits after it was determined that they had been fired from their jobs for ingesting peyote, a crime under Oregon law. We held that this did not violate the Free Exercise Clause, even though the peyote had been ingested for sacramental purposes, because the "right of free exercise does not relieve an individual of the obligation to comply with a valid and neutral law of general applicability on the ground that the law proscribes (or prescribes) conduct that his religion prescribes (or proscribes)."

It is true that the ADA's prohibition on retaliation, like Oregon's prohibition on peyote use, is a valid and neutral law of general applicability. But a church's selection of its ministers is unlike an individual's ingestion of peyote. *Smith* involved government regulation of only outward physical acts. The present case, in contrast, concerns government interference with an internal church decision that affects the faith and mission of the church itself. The contention that *Smith* forecloses recognition of a ministerial exception rooted in the Religion Clauses has no merit.

Having concluded that there is a ministerial exception grounded in the Religion Clauses of the First Amendment, we consider whether the exception applies in this case. We hold that it does. . . .

To begin with, Hosanna-Tabor held Perich out as a minister, with a role distinct from that of most of its members. When Hosanna-Tabor extended her a call, it issued her a "diploma of vocation" according her the title "Minister of Religion, Commissioned." She was tasked with performing that office "according to the Word of God and the confessional standards of the Evangelical Lutheran Church as drawn from the Sacred Scriptures." . . .

Perich's title as a minister reflected a significant degree of religious training followed by a formal process of commissioning. . . . It took Perich six years to fulfill these requirements. And when she eventually did, she was commissioned as a minister only upon election by the congregation, which recognized God's call to her to teach. At that point, her call could be rescinded only upon a supermajority vote of the congregation—a

protection designed to allow her to "preach the Word of God boldly."

Perich held herself out as a minister of the Church by accepting the formal call to religious service. . . . [S]he claimed a special housing allowance on her taxes that was available only to employees earning their compensation " 'in the exercise of the ministry.'" . . . In a form she submitted to the Synod following her termination, Perich again indicated that she regarded herself as a minister at Hosanna-Tabor, stating: "I feel that God is leading me to serve in the teaching ministry . . . . I am anxious to be in the teaching ministry again soon."

Perich's job duties reflected a role in conveying the Church's message and carrying out its mission. Hosanna-Tabor expressly charged her with "lead[ing] others toward Christian maturity" and "teach[ing] faithfully the Word of God, the Sacred Scriptures, in its truth and purity and as set forth in all the symbolical books of the Evangelical Lutheran Church." . . .

In light of these considerations—the formal title given Perich by the Church, the substance reflected in that title, her own use of that title, and the important religious functions she performed for the Church—we conclude that Perich was a minister covered by the ministerial exception. . . .

Because Perich was a minister within the meaning of the exception, the First Amendment requires dismissal of this employment discrimination suit against her religious employer. The EEOC and Perich originally sought an order reinstating Perich to her former position as a called teacher. By requiring the Church to accept a minister it did not want, such an order would have plainly violated the Church's freedom under the Religion Clauses to select its own ministers. . . .

The EEOC and Perich suggest that Hosanna-Tabor's asserted religious reason for firing Perich—that she violated the Synod's commitment to internal dispute resolution—was pretextual. That suggestion misses the point of the ministerial exception. The purpose of the exception is not to safeguard a church's decision to fire a minister only when it is made for a religious reason. The exception instead ensures that the authority to select and control who will minister to the faithful—a matter "strictly ecclesiastical," *Kedroff*—is the church's alone. . . .

The case before us is an employment discrimination suit brought on behalf of a minister, challenging her church's decision to fire her. Today we hold only that the ministerial exception bars such a suit. We express no view on whether the exception bars other types of suits, including actions by employees alleging breach of contract or tortious conduct by their religious employers. There will be time enough to address the applicability of the exception to other circumstances if and when they arise.

The interest of society in the enforcement of employment discrimination statutes is undoubtedly important. But so too is the interest of religious groups in choosing who will preach their beliefs, teach their faith, and carry out their mission. When a minister who has been fired sues her church alleging that her termination was discriminatory, the First Amendment has struck the balance for us. The church must be free to choose those who will guide it on its way.

The judgment of the Court of Appeals for the Sixth Circuit is reversed.

It is so ordered.

JUSTICE THOMAS, concurring.

I join the Court's opinion. I write separately to note that, in my view, the Religion Clauses require civil courts to apply the ministerial exception and to defer to a religious organization's good-faith understanding of who qualifies as its minister. As the Court explains, the Religion Clauses guarantee religious organizations autonomy in matters of internal governance, including the selection of those who will minister the faith. A religious organization's right to choose its ministers would be hollow, however, if secular courts could second-guess the organization's sincere determination that a given employee is a "minister" under the organization's theological tenets.

JUSTICE ALITO, with whom JUSTICE KAGAN joins, concurring.

I join the Court's opinion, but I write separately to clarify my understanding of the significance of formal ordination and designation as a "minister" in determining whether an "employee" of a religious group falls within the so-called "ministerial" exception. The term "minister" is commonly used by many Protestant denominations to refer to members of their clergy, but the term is rarely if ever used in this way by Catholics, Jews, Muslims, Hindus, or Buddhists. In addition, the concept of ordination as understood by most Christian churches and by Judaism has no clear counterpart in some Christian denominations and some other religions. Because virtually every religion in the world is represented in the population of the United States, it would be a mistake if the term "minister" or the concept of ordination were viewed

as central to the important issue of religious autonomy that is presented in cases like this one. Instead, courts should focus on the function performed by persons who work for religious bodies.

The First Amendment protects the freedom of religious groups to engage in certain key religious activities, including the conducting of worship services and other religious ceremonies and rituals, as well as the critical process of communicating the faith. Accordingly, religious groups must be free to choose the personnel who are essential to the performance of these functions.

The "ministerial" exception should be tailored to this purpose. It should apply to any "employee" who leads a religious organization, conducts worship services or important religious ceremonies or rituals, or serves as a messenger or teacher of its faith. If a religious group believes that the ability of such an employee to perform these key functions has been compromised, then the constitutional guarantee of religious freedom protects the group's right to remove the employee from his or her position.

In *Hosanna-Tabor* the justices concluded that the government could not impose its antidiscrimination laws on the decision of a religious group to terminate one of its ministers. The ruling on this central issue was unanimous—a rarity when the justices interpret the religion clauses. There were, however, some disagreements over the criteria for determining who is a minister, including an implication raised by Justice Thomas that the federal courts have no constitutional authority to define for a church who qualifies as a minister of its faith.

Chief Justice Roberts cautioned that the Court's decision was a narrow one, applying only to discrimination suits brought by a minister against the church attempting to fire her. As such, the decision tells us little about the extent of the constitutional protection religious organizations enjoy against government intrusion into their internal affairs. As Roberts noted, "There will be time enough to address the applicability of the exception to other circumstances if and when they arise."

What can we conclude about the Court's handling of establishment clause litigation in general? At the very least, we can say that this area of the law is unstable, with the justices sharply divided and taking very different approaches to resolving the cases. As we have observed each time the Court seems on the verge of eliminating the Lemon test, it reappears, as Justice

Scalia put it in *Lamb's Chapel*, "like some ghoul in a late-night horror movie." Whether the Court rejects *Lemon* once and for all seems to hinge on the justices' ability to agree on a replacement standard, which so far they have been unable to do.

Establishment clause cases are rife with contradictions and inconsistencies, and the justices fully acknowledge the problems they have had in this area. As Chief Justice Burger admitted, "[W]e can only dimly perceive the lines of demarcation in this extraordinarily sensitive area of constitutional law." Scalia characterized the Court's record as "embarrassing," Kennedy labeled the decisions as "tangled," and Thomas described the Court's establishment clause jurisprudence as "in hopeless disarray."

Will the Court seek to resolve the law's inconsistencies in the religious establishment area? What standard or test will it invoke to do so? Will *Lemon* survive or be modified, overruled, or simply ignored? Will the Court adopt any of the competing standards, such as coercion, endorsement, or nonpreferentialism, or will a new standard emerge? Now that you have read about many of the significant cases of the past, you probably realize that there are no easy answers.

ANNOTATED READINGS

Much scholarship has been devoted to general reviews of the religion clauses and the various means the Supreme Court has used to interpret them. Representative works include the following: Robert S. Alley, *The Supreme Court on Church and State* (New York: Oxford University Press, 1988); Jesse H. Choper, *Securing Religious Liberty: Principles for Judicial Interpretation of the Religion Clauses* (Chicago: University of Chicago Press, 1995); Catharine Cookson, *Regulating Religion: The Courts and the Free Exercise Clause* (New York: Oxford University Press, 2001); Louis Fisher, *Religious Liberty in America: Political Safeguards* (Lawrence: University Press of Kansas, 2002); Philip Hamburger, *Separation of Church and State* (Cambridge, MA: Harvard University Press, 2002); William Lee Miller, *The First Liberty: America's Foundation in Religious Freedom* (Washington, DC: Georgetown University Press, 2003); Stephen V. Monsma, *When Sacred and Secular Mix* (Lanham, MD: Rowman & Littlefield, 1996); John T. Noonan Jr., *The Lustre of Our Country: The American Experience of Religious Freedom* (Berkeley: University of California Press, 1998); Frank S. Ravitch, *Masters of Illusion: The Supreme Court and the Religion Clauses* (New York: New York University Press, 2007); Martin S. Sheffer, *God versus Caesar: Belief, Worship, and Proselytizing under the First Amendment* (Albany: State University of New York Press, 1999); Steven D. Smith, *Foreordained Failure: The Quest for a Constitutional Principle of Religious Freedom* (New York: Oxford University Press, 1995); and Garry Wills, *Under God* (New York: Simon & Schuster, 1990).

Other works have examined the influence of the nation's founders on religious liberties and the use of original intent in interpreting the First Amendment. These include Thomas J. Currey, *The First Amendment Freedoms: Church and State in America to the Passage of the First Amendment* (New York: Oxford University Press, 1986); Donald L. Drakeman, *Church, State and Original Intent* (New York: Cambridge University Press, 2009); Daniel L. Dreisbach, *Thomas Jefferson and the Wall of Separation between Church and State* (New York: New York University Press, 2002); Mark Douglas McGarvie, *One Nation under Law: America's Early National Struggles to Separate Church and State* (DeKalb: Northern Illinois University Press, 2004); Vincent Phillip Muñoz, *God and the Founders: Madison, Washington, and Jefferson* (New York: Cambridge University Press, 2009).

Also available are a number of excellent studies that delve deeply into specific landmark cases. Examples of these are Paula Abrams, *Cross Purposes: Pierce v. Society of Sisters and the Struggle over Compulsory Education* (Ann Arbor: University of Michigan Press, 2009); Bruce J. Dierenfield, *The Battle over School Prayer: How* Engel v. Vitale *Changed America* (Lawrence: University Press of Kansas, 2007); Garrett Epps, *Peyote vs. the State: Religious Freedom on Trial* (Norman: University of Oklahoma Press, 2009); Peter Irons, *God on Trial: Dispatches from America's Religious Battlefields* (New York: Viking/Penguin, 2007); Carolyn N. Long, *Religious Freedom and Indian Rights: The Case of* Oregon v. Smith (Lawrence: University Press of Kansas, 2000); David B. Manwaring, *Render unto Caesar: The Flag Salute Controversy* (Chicago: University of Chicago Press, 1962); David M. O'Brien, *Animal Sacrifice and Religious Freedom:* Church of Lukumi Babalu Aye v. City of Hialeah (Lawrence: University Press of Kansas, 2004); Shawn Francis Peters, *The* Yoder *Case: Religious Freedom, Education, and Parental Rights* (Lawrence: University Press of Kansas, 2003); and Stephen D. Solomon, *Ellery's Protest: How One Young Man Defied Tradition and Sparked the Battle over School Prayer* (Ann Arbor: University of Michigan Press, 2007).

5 Freedom of Speech, Assembly, and Association

AT ONE TIME or another, everyone has criticized a political official or complained about a government policy. Sometimes we express such grievances privately, to friends or relatives. At other times we may join with like-minded people and communicate our opinions collectively. Recall, for example, the "tea party" protesters prior to the 2010 congressional elections and the Occupy Wall Street demonstrations that preceded the 2012 presidential campaign. Speaking our minds is a privilege we enjoy in the United States, a privilege guaranteed by the First Amendment.

While the Bill of Rights was making its way through Congress and state legislatures, the First Amendment's freedom of expression provisions were hardly debated. The framers had a fundamental commitment to speech and press freedoms, especially as they related to the public discussion of political and social issues. After all, vigorous public oratory had fueled the Revolution and helped shape the contours of the new government.

The First Amendment's language is very bold: "Congress shall make no law . . . abridging the freedom of speech, or of the press; or the right of the people peaceably to assemble, and to petition the Government for a redress of grievances." These words seem to provide an impregnable shield against government actions that would restrict any of the four components of freedom of expression: speech, press, assembly, and

petition. But to what extent *does* the Constitution protect these rights? May mischievous patrons stand up in a crowded movie theater and shout, "Fire!" when they know there is no fire? May a publisher knowingly print lies about a member of the community to destroy that person's reputation? May a political group attempt to spread its message by driving sound trucks through residential neighborhoods at all hours? May an antimilitary activist burn his draft registration card in protest?

Despite the clear wording of the First Amendment, the answer to each of these questions is no. The Supreme Court never has adhered to a literal interpretation of the expression guarantees; rather, it has ruled that certain expressions, whether communicated verbally, in print, or by actions, may be restricted because of their possible effects.

This chapter is the first of four dealing with the right of expression. Here we first examine the development of constitutional standards for freedom of expression and then address the application of those standards to various kinds of expression. In the next three chapters we look at issues specific to the freedom of the press and discuss forms of expression that traditionally have been considered outside First Amendment protection, after which we examine the difficult First Amendment issues surrounding the Internet and other newly developed media forms.

THE DEVELOPMENT OF LEGAL STANDARDS: THE EMERGENCE OF LAW IN TIMES OF CRISIS

In the period following the September 11, 2001, terrorist attacks on the World Trade Center in New York City and the Pentagon just outside Washington, D.C., the balance between security and freedom shifted. The government placed a high priority on identifying possible terrorists and preventing future assaults. Although the reasons for taking such actions may seem logical, the price was the restriction of personal liberties. Among other actions, the government restricted the right of persons to move about freely by increasing security precautions at airports, expanded its authority to monitor telephone and Internet usage, and asserted greater powers of search and seizure.

Such actions should not be surprising. History teaches that governments everywhere tend to respond to national crises in a particular way, whether the emergencies stem from war, economic collapse, natural catastrophe, or internal rebellion. During such times the government may be unstable, political dissent and opposition to the government may increase, and the nation's very survival may be at stake. The response of political leaders is predictable: they place a priority on national security and unity and take firm action against subversive groups and opposition criticism. Often these reactions take the form of policies that restrict the right of the people to speak, publish, and organize.

The United States is no exception to this rule. In times of peace and general prosperity, the government has little reason to restrict freedom of expression. The nation is secure, and the people are relatively content. In times of crisis, however, the president and Congress may react harshly, contending that some forms of expression must be curtailed to protect national security.

This tendency demonstrated itself shortly after the nation's founding. In its early years the U.S. government was weak and vulnerable. The economy remained in disarray, Europe continued to pose a threat, and the ruling Federalist Party was the target of much political criticism. In response, Congress passed one of the most restrictive laws in American history, the Sedition Act of 1798. This statute made it a crime to write, print, utter, or publish malicious material that would defame the federal government, the president, or the members of Congress; that would bring them into disrepute; or that could excite the hatred of the people against them. Violations of the act were punishable by imprisonment of up to two years. The act expired in 1801 without any court challenges to its validity. It stands today as an important lesson that threatened regimes, even in nations with a fundamental commitment to political freedom, are capable of repressive measures.

The justices of the Supreme Court ultimately must decide where constitutional protections end and the government's authority to restrict expression begins. Because expression rights are most severely threatened during times of war and national crisis, the Court often has found itself searching for an appropriate constitutional standard in response to conflicts over government policies designed to protect national security. For this reason we turn to national security cases in the first part of this chapter to see how the justices have developed general theories of the freedom of expression. In later sections we address the ways the Court has responded to more specific expression controversies.

Clear and Present Danger Test

The Supreme Court faced no significant freedom of expression disputes during the nation's first century. Certainly, there were periods of national emergency, most notably the Civil War, and during these periods of stress the government took oppressive actions. For example, President Abraham Lincoln pursued a number of policies to suppress "treacherous" behavior, believing that "the nation must be able to protect itself against utterances which actually cause insubordination."[1] But the Supreme Court had no opportunity to rule on the constitutionality of the president's actions, at least on First Amendment grounds.

Significant changes occurred, however, with the outbreak of war in Europe in 1914 and the Russian Revolution in 1917. The United States turned its attention away from domestic programs and toward defense of the American system of government. The growing threats of socialism and communism touched off a wave of nationalism that led to many attacks against suspected subversives.

The patriotic fervor unleashed by World War I was strong and pervasive. No American was immune, not even Supreme Court justices. Consider Chief Justice

---

1. Zechariah Chafee Jr., *Free Speech in the United States* (Cambridge, MA: Harvard University Press, 1941), 266.

Government officers and clerks load a police ambulance with literature seized at the Communist Party headquarters in Cambridge, Massachusetts, in 1919. Such raids against communist organizations were not uncommon during the red scare era.

Edward D. White's response to an attorney who argued that the selective draft, enacted by Congress in 1917, lacked public support: "I don't think your statement has anything to do with legal arguments and should not have been said in this Court. It is a very unpatriotic statement to make."[2] Members of Congress, too, were caught up in the patriotic fervor gripping the nation. They, like the founders, felt it necessary to enact legislation to ensure that Americans presented a unified front to the world. The Espionage Act of 1917 prohibited any attempt to "interfere with the operation or success of the military or naval forces of the United States . . . to cause insubordination . . . in the military or naval forces . . . or willfully obstruct the recruiting or enlistment service of the United States." A year later, Congress passed the Sedition Act, which prohibited the uttering of, writing, or publishing of anything disloyal to the government, flag, or military forces of the United States.

Although the majority of Americans probably supported these laws, some groups and individuals thought they constituted intolerable infringements on civil liberties guarantees contained in the

First Amendment. Dissenters, however, were not of one political voice: some, most notably the American Union Against Militarism (a predecessor of the American Civil Liberties Union), were openly pacifist; others, primarily leaders of the Progressive Movement, were pure civil libertarians, opposed to any government intrusion into free expression; finally, there were the radicals—individuals who hoped to see the United States undergo a socialist or communist revolution. Regardless of their motivation, these individuals and groups brought legal challenges to the repressive laws and pushed the Supreme Court into freedom of expression cases for the first time. The Court decided the first of the World War I cases, *Schenck v. United States,* in 1919 and then three others the same year.

While reading *Schenck,* keep in mind the circumstances surrounding the Court's decision. The United States had just successfully completed a war effort in which more than 4 million Americans were in uniform and more than 1 million troops had been sent to fight in Europe. The number of Americans killed or seriously wounded exceeded 300,000. The national fervor and support for the war effort had been tremendous. In the face of this national unity, a socialist had engaged in active opposition to America's participation in the war. His appeal of an espionage conviction

---

2. Quoted by John R. Schmidhauser in *Constitutional Law in American Politics* (Monterey, CA: Brooks/Cole, 1984), 325.

allowed the Supreme Court to make its first major doctrinal statement on freedom of expression. What did the Court decide? What standard did it develop to adjudicate future claims?

Schenck v. United States

249 U.S. 47 (1919)
http://laws.findlaw.com/US/249/47.html
Vote: 9 (Brandeis, Clarke, Day, Holmes, McKenna,
        McReynolds, Pitney, Van Devanter, White)
        0

OPINION OF THE COURT: *Holmes*

FACTS:

In 1917 Charles Schenck, the general secretary of the Socialist Party of Philadelphia, printed fifteen thousand pamphlets urging resistance to the draft. He mailed these leaflets, described by the government's case as "frank, bitter, passionate appeal[s] for resistance to the Selective Service Law," to men listed in a local newspaper as having been called and accepted for military service. Federal authorities charged him with violating the Espionage Act; specifically, the United States alleged that Schenck conspired to obstruct military recruitment and illegally used the mail to do so. Schenck was convicted in federal district court, and he appealed on First Amendment grounds.

ARGUMENTS:

For the plaintiff-in-error, Charles T. Schenck:
- The law's harsh penalties have a chilling effect on anyone who contemplates criticizing the government. Severe punishment stops political discussion as effectively as censorship. The law imposes criminal penalties on the mere expression of opposition to a government policy.
- There is a constitutional distinction between words and actions. The First Amendment does not protect a man who violates the draft law by refusing to serve, but it does protect a man who says the draft law is wrong and ought to be repealed.

For the appellee, United States:
- The First Amendment does not license the distribution of materials that tend to influence persons to obstruct the draft. Schenck was found guilty of conspiring to cause lawfully drafted men to refuse military duty. This is an illegal act, not legitimate political agitation for a change in federal law.

 MR. JUSTICE HOLMES DELIVERED THE OPINION OF THE COURT.

The document in question upon its first printed side recited the first section of the Thirteenth Amendment, said that the idea embodied in it was violated by the Conscription Act and that a conscript is little better than a convict. In impassioned language it intimated that conscription was despotism in its worst form and a monstrous wrong against humanity in the interest of Wall Street's chosen few. It said "Do not submit to intimidation," but in form at least confined itself to peaceful measures such as a petition for the repeal of the act. The other and later printed side of the sheet was headed "Assert Your Rights." It stated reasons for alleging that any one violated the Constitution when he refused to recognize "your right to assert your opposition to the draft," and went on "If you do not assert and support your rights, you are helping to deny or disparage rights which it is the solemn duty of all citizens and residents of the United States to retain." It described the arguments on the other side as coming from cunning politicians and a mercenary capitalist press, and even silent consent to the conscription law as helping to support an infamous conspiracy. It denied the power to send our citizens away to foreign shores to shoot up the people of other lands, and added that words could not express the condemnation such cold-blooded ruthlessness deserves, &c., &c., winding up "You must do your share to maintain, support and uphold the rights of the people of this country." Of course the document would not have been sent unless it had been intended to have some effect, and we do not see what effect it could be expected to have upon persons subject to the draft except to influence them to obstruct the carrying of it out. The defendants do not deny that the jury might find against them on this point.

But it is said, suppose that that was the tendency of this circular, it is protected by the First Amendment to the Constitution. Two of the strongest expressions are said to be quoted respectively from well-known public men. It may well be that the prohibition of laws abridging the freedom of speech is not confined to previous restraints, although to prevent them may have been the main purpose. We admit that in many places and in ordinary times the defendants in saying all that was said in the circular would have been within their constitutional rights. But the character of every act depends upon the circumstances in which it is done. The most stringent protection of free speech would not protect a man in falsely shouting fire in a theatre and causing a panic. It does not even protect a man from an injunction against uttering words that may have all the effect of force. The question in every case is whether the words used are used in such circumstances and are of such a nature as to create a clear and present danger that they will bring about the substantive evils that Congress has a right to prevent. It is a question of proximity and degree. When a nation is at war many things that might be said in time of peace are such a hindrance to its effort that their utterance will not be endured so long as men fight and that no Court could regard them as protected by any constitutional right. It seems to be admitted that if an actual obstruction of the recruiting service were proved, liability for words that produced that effect might be enforced. The statute of 1917 in §4 punishes conspiracies to obstruct as well as actual obstruction. If the act, (speaking, or circulating a paper), its tendency and the intent with which it is done are the same, we perceive no ground for saying that success alone warrants making the act a crime. *Goldman v. United States* (1918). Indeed that case might be said to dispose of the present contention if the precedent covers all *media concludendi* [the steps of an argument]. But as the right to free speech was not referred to specifically, we have thought fit to add a few words.

It was not argued that a conspiracy to obstruct the draft was not within the words of the Act of 1917. The words are "obstruct the recruiting or enlistment service," and it might be suggested that they refer only to making it hard to get volunteers. Recruiting heretofore usually having been accomplished by getting volunteers the word is apt to call up that method only in our minds. But recruiting is gaining fresh supplies for the forces, as well by draft as otherwise. It is put as an alternative to enlistment or voluntary enrollment in this act. . . .

Judgments affirmed.

Oliver Wendell Holmes's opinion in *Schenck* represents the first important and substantial explication of free speech. Holmes provided the Court with a mechanism, known as the clear and present danger test, for framing such cases and a standard by which to adjudicate future claims:

The question in every case is whether the words used are used in such circumstances and are of such a nature as to create a clear and present danger that they will bring about the substantive evils that Congress has a right to prevent.

This test requires consideration not only of the content of the expression but also of the context in which the words are uttered, the consequences of those words, and when those consequences may occur.

In addition, Holmes's opinion was a politically astute compromise. On one hand, the clear and present danger test was a rather liberal interpretation of expression rights. On the other, the justices recognized that free speech rights were not absolute, and they found room within the clear and present danger test to uphold the conviction of an unpopular opponent of the war effort. In *Schenck*, Holmes was able to write into law a test favorable to expression rights that was acceptable to his colleagues and did not arouse the ire of Congress. As for Charles Schenck, although the crime for which he was convicted carried a sentence of up to ten years in prison for each count, he served a sentence of only six months.

One week after *Schenck*, Holmes applied his clear and present danger standard to two other challenges to the Espionage Act. In *Frohwerk v. United States*, a newspaper editor and an editorial writer for the *Missouri Staats Zeitung* urged the Court to overturn their convictions for publishing a series of articles accusing the United States of pursuing an imperialistic policy toward Germany. In *Frohwerk*'s companion case, *Debs v. United States*, Eugene V. Debs, a leader of the Socialist Party in the United States, had been convicted of violating the Espionage Act with a speech he delivered in Canton, Ohio. Extolling the virtues of socialism and praising the Bolshevik Revolution, Debs said:

The Socialist has a great idea. An expanding philosophy. It is spreading over the face of the earth. It is as useless to resist it as it is to resist the rising sunrise. . . . What a privilege it is to serve it. I have regretted a thousand times I can do so little for the movement that has done so much for me. . . . Do not worry over the charge of treason to your masters, but be concerned about the treason that involves yourself. This year we are going to sweep into power . . . and we are going to destroy capitalistic institutions and recreate them.

Federal authorities arrested Debs, charging him with attempting to incite insubordination, a violation of the Espionage Act. They cited as "evidence" not only his words but the timing of his speech, which he delivered just after Congress passed the Selective Service Act. Writing for the Court in both cases, Justice Holmes relied on the clear and present danger test to uphold the Debs and Frohwerk convictions. In fact, his only new statement of any significance was "that the First Amendment while prohibiting legislation against free speech as such cannot have been, and obviously was not intended to give immunity for every possible use of language."

Such an assertion again underscores the Court's unwillingness to read First Amendment guarantees literally and absolutely. Moreover, because Holmes wrote for the majority in both cases, the future vitality of the clear and present danger test seemed assured; the Court apparently agreed that the test provided a reasonable vehicle for judging First Amendment claims.

Bad Tendency Test

The perceived permanence of the clear and present danger test proved to be an illusion. Just eight months after the *Debs* and *Frohwerk* decisions, a majority of justices banished this test to a legal exile that would last for almost two decades. The first hint of their disaffection came in *Abrams v. United States,* the last of the 1919 quartet. As you read the *Abrams* decision, notice how Justice John H. Clarke's majority opinion moves away from the clear and present danger language and instead emphasizes the defendants' intentions and the tendency of the expression to cause illegal actions. Holmes's dissent, on the other hand, uses the clear and present danger philosophy to defend the right of political expression.

Abrams v. United States

250 U.S. 616 (1919)
http://laws.findlaw.com/US/250/616.html
Vote: 7 (Clarke, Day, McKenna, McReynolds, Pitney, Van Devanter, White)
*   2 (Brandeis, Holmes)*

OPINION OF THE COURT: *Clarke*
DISSENTING OPINION: *Holmes*

FACTS:

In October 1918, just weeks before the end of World War I, Jacob Abrams and four others were convicted of violating the Espionage Act. The defendants, well-educated Russian immigrants, all professed revolutionary, anarchist, or socialist political views. They had been residents of the United States for between five and fifteen years, but none had applied for naturalization. The conspirators had published and distributed leaflets, written in English and Yiddish, criticizing President Woodrow Wilson's decision to send U.S. troops into Russia and calling for a general strike to protest that policy. The leaflets were written in language characteristic of the rhetoric of the Russian Revolution: "Workers of the World! Awake! Rise! Put down your enemy and mine!" and "Yes! friends, there is only one enemy of the workers of the world and that is CAPITALISM." They

described the government of the United States as a "hypocritical," "cowardly," and "capitalistic" enemy. The protesters branded President Wilson a "Kaiser." The government charged Abrams and the others with intent to "cripple or hinder the United States in the prosecution of the war." The trial court sentenced the defendants to prison terms of fifteen to twenty years.

ARGUMENTS:

For the plaintiffs-in-error, Jacob Abrams, et al.:
- Denunciation of government policy, even in time of war, is constitutionally protected.
- If the government can restrict expression in wartime on the pretext of public welfare, it can do so in peacetime as well.
- The defendants are not alone in the positions they have expressed. Many others, whose patriotism is beyond question, have expressed similar views.

For the defendant-in-error, United States:
- Congress has the constitutional authority to legislate against acts of disloyalty in time of war.
- The regulation is justified under the government's power of self-preservation.
- The First Amendment was not intended to protect seditious libel, especially in wartime.

Samuel Lipman, Hyman Lychowsky, Mollie Steimer, and Jacob Abrams, World War I–era anarchists and revolutionaries, were found guilty of attempting to hinder the war effort. The Supreme Court upheld the conviction in Abrams v. United States.

MR. JUSTICE CLARKE DELIVERED THE OPINION OF THE COURT.

It was admitted on the trial that the defendants had united to print and distribute the described circulars and that five thousand of them had been printed and distributed about the 22d day of August, 1918. The group had a meeting place in New York City, in rooms rented by defendant Abrams, under an assumed name, and there the subject of printing the circulars was discussed about two weeks before the defendants were arrested. The defendant Abrams, although not a printer, on July 27, 1918, purchased the printing outfit with which the circulars were printed and installed it in a basement room where the work was done at night. The circulars were distributed, some by throwing them from a window of a building where one of the defendants was employed and others secretly, in New York City.

The defendants pleaded "not guilty," and the case of the Government consisted in showing the facts we have stated, and in introducing in evidence copies of the two printed circulars attached to the indictment, a sheet entitled "Revolutionists Unite for Action," written by the defendant Lipman, and found on him when he was arrested, and another paper, found at the headquarters of the group, and for which Abrams assumed responsibility. . . .

The claim chiefly elaborated upon by the defendants in the oral argument and in their brief is that there is no substantial evidence in the record to support the judgment upon the verdict of guilty and that the motion of the defendants for an instructed verdict in their favor was erroneously denied. A question of law is thus presented, which calls for an examination of the record, not for the purpose of weighing conflicting testimony, but only to determine whether there was some evidence, competent and substantial, before the jury, fairly tending to sustain the verdict. . . .

It will not do to say, as is now argued, that the only intent of these defendants was to prevent injury to the Russian cause. Men must be held to have intended, and to be accountable for, the effects which their acts were likely to produce. Even if their primary purpose and intent was to aid the cause of the Russian Revolution, the plan of action which they adopted necessarily involved, before it could be realized, defeat of the war program of the United States, for the obvious effect of this appeal, if it should become effective, as they hoped it might, would be to persuade persons of character such as those whom they regarded themselves as addressing, not to aid government loans and not to work in ammunition factories, where their work would produce "bullets, bayonets, cannon" and other munitions of war, the use of which would cause the "murder" of Germans and Russians. . . .

This is not an attempt to bring about a change of administration by candid discussion, for no matter what may have incited the outbreak on the part of the defendant anarchists, the manifest purpose of such a publication was to create an attempt to defeat the war plans of the Government of the United States, by bringing upon the country the paralysis of a general strike, thereby arresting the production of all munitions and other things essential to the conduct of the war. . . .

That the interpretation we have put upon these articles, circulated in the greatest port of our land, from which great numbers of soldiers were at the time taking ship daily, and in which great quantities of war supplies of every kind were at the time being manufactured for transportation overseas, is not only the fair interpretation of them, but that it is the meaning which their authors consciously intended should be conveyed by them to others is further shown by the additional writings found in the meeting place of the defendant group and on the person of one of them. . . .

Thus was again avowed the purpose to throw the country into a state of revolution if possible and to thereby frustrate the military program of the Government. . . .

. . . [T]he immediate occasion for this particular outbreak of lawlessness, on the part of the defendant alien anarchists, may have been resentment caused by our Government sending troops into Russia as a strategic operation against the Germans on the eastern battle front, yet the plain purpose of their propaganda was to excite, at the supreme crisis of the war, disaffection, sedition, riots, and, as they hoped, revolution, in this country for the purpose of embarrassing and if possible defeating the military plans of the Government in Europe. A technical distinction may perhaps be taken between disloyal and abusive language applied to the *form* of our government or language intended to bring the *form* of our government into contempt and disrepute, and language of like character and intended to produce like results directed against the President and Congress, the agencies through which that form of government must function in time of war. But it is not necessary to a decision of this case to consider whether such distinction is vital or merely formal, for the language of these circulars was obviously intended to provoke and to encourage resistance to the United States in the war, as the third count runs, and, the defendants, in terms, plainly urged and advocated a resort to a general strike of workers in ammunition factories for the purpose of curtailing the production of ordnance and munitions necessary and essential to the prosecution of the war as is charged in the fourth count. Thus it is clear not only that some evidence but that much persuasive evidence was before the jury tending to prove that the defendants were guilty as charged in both the third and fourth counts of the indictment and under the long established rule of law hereinbefore stated the judgment of the District Court must be.

Affirmed.

MR. JUSTICE HOLMES, dissenting.

I never have seen any reason to doubt that the questions of law that alone were before this Court in the cases of *Schenck, Frohwerk* and *Debs* were rightly decided. I do not doubt for a moment that by the same reasoning that would justify punishing persuasion to murder, the United States constitutionally may punish speech that produces or is intended to produce a clear and imminent danger that it will bring about forthwith certain substantive evils that the United States constitutionally may seek to prevent. The power undoubtedly is greater in time of war than in time of peace because war opens dangers that do not exist at other times.

But as against dangers peculiar to war, as against others, the principle of the right to free speech is always the same. It is only the present danger of immediate evil or an intent to bring it about that warrants Congress in setting a limit to the expression of opinion where private rights are not concerned. Congress certainly cannot forbid all effort to change the mind of the country. Now nobody can suppose that the surreptitious publishing of a silly leaflet by an unknown man, without more, would present any immediate danger that its opinions would hinder the success of the government arms or have any appreciable tendency to do so. Publishing those opinions for the very purpose of obstructing however, might indicate a greater danger and at any rate would have the quality of an attempt. So I assume that the second leaflet if published for the purposes alleged in the fourth count might be punishable. But it seems pretty clear to me that nothing less than that would bring these papers within the scope of this law. An actual intent in the sense that I have explained is necessary to constitute an attempt, where a further act of the same individual is required to complete the substantive crime. . . . It is necessary where the success of the attempt depends upon others because if that

intent is not present the actor's aim may be accomplished without bringing about the evils sought to be checked. An intent to prevent interference with the revolution in Russia might have been satisfied without any hindrance to carrying on the war in which we were engaged.

I do not see how anyone can find the intent required by the statute in any of the defendants' words. . . .

In this case sentences of twenty years imprisonment have been imposed for the publishing of two leaflets that I believe the defendants had as much right to publish as the Government has to publish the Constitution of the United States now vainly invoked by them. Even if I am technically wrong, and enough can be squeezed from these poor and puny anonymities to turn the color of legal litmus paper, I will add, even if what I think the necessary intent were shown, the most nominal punishment seems to me all that possibly could be inflicted, unless the defendants are to be made to suffer not for what the indictment alleges, but for the creed that they avow—a creed that I believe to be the creed of ignorance and immaturity when honestly held, as I see no reason to doubt that it was held here, but which, although made the subject of examination at the trial, no one has a right even to consider in dealing with the charges before the Court.

Persecution for the expression of opinions seems to me perfectly logical. If you have no doubt of your premises or your power and want a certain result with all your heart, you naturally express your wishes in law and sweep away all opposition. To allow opposition by speech seems to indicate that you think the speech impotent, as when a man says that he has squared the circle, or that you do not care whole-heartedly for the result, or that you doubt either your power or your premises. But when men have realized that time has upset many fighting faiths, they may come to believe even more than they believe the very foundations of their own conduct that the ultimate good desired is better reached by free trade in ideas—that the best test of truth is the power of the thought to get itself accepted in the competition of the market, and that truth is the only ground upon which their wishes safely can be carried out. That at any rate is the theory of our Constitution. It is an experiment, as all life is an experiment. Every year if not every day we have to wager our salvation upon some prophecy based upon imperfect knowledge. While that experiment is part of our system I think that we should be eternally vigilant against attempts to check the expression of opinions that we loathe and believe to be fraught with death, unless they so imminently threaten immediate interference with the lawful and pressing purposes of the law that an immediate check is required to save the country. I wholly disagree with the argument of the Government that the First Amendment left the common law as to seditious libel in force. History seems to me against the notion. I had conceived that the United States through many years had shown its repentance for the Sedition Act of 1798, by repaying fines that it imposed. Only the emergency that makes it immediately dangerous to leave the correction of evil counsels to time warrants making any exception to the sweeping command, "Congress shall make no law . . . abridging the freedom of speech." Of course, I am speaking only of expressions of opinion and exhortations, which were all that were uttered here, but I regret that I cannot put into more impressive words my belief that in their conviction upon this indictment the defendants were deprived of their rights under the Constitution of the United States.

MR. JUSTICE BRANDEIS concurs with the foregoing opinion.

It was evident to Holmes that the *Abrams* decision marked a turning away from the clear and present danger standard. In his dissent he tried to refine the test to show how the *Schenck* rationale could work in a variety of contexts.

But in *Abrams* Holmes failed to convince his colleagues. Instead, Clarke's majority opinion used a standard known as the bad tendency test, an approach derived from English common law. It asks, "Do the words have a *tendency* to bring about evil consequences?" rather than "Do the words bring about an immediate substantive evil?" Why the majority shifted constitutional standards is a mystery. We cannot say that the clear and present danger test produced results markedly different from the bad tendency standard. After all, Holmes had used the clear and present danger test in *Schenck, Debs,* and *Frohwerk* to uphold convictions, not to overturn them.

Regardless of the motivation, by the early 1920s it was obvious that a majority of justices rejected the clear and present danger standard in favor of more stringent constitutional interpretations, such as the bad tendency test. Two cases, *Gitlow v. New York* (1925) and **Whitney v. California** (1927), exemplify this shift, but with a slightly different twist. *Gitlow* and *Whitney* involved state prosecutions. Just as the federal government wanted to foster patriotism during wartime, the states also felt the need to promulgate their own versions of nationalism. The result was

passage of so-called state criminal syndicalism laws, which made it a crime to advocate, teach, aid, or abet in any activity designed to bring about the overthrow of the government by force or violence. The actual effect of such laws was to outlaw any association with views "abhorrent" to the interests of the United States, such as communism and socialism. Would the Court be willing to tolerate state intrusions into free speech?

Gitlow v. New York

268 U.S. 652 (1925)
http://laws.findlaw.com/US/268/652.html
Vote: 7 (Butler, Reynolds, Sanford, Stone, Sutherland, Taft, Van Devanter)
2 (Brandeis, Holmes)

OPINION OF THE COURT: *Sanford*

DISSENTING OPINION: *Holmes*

FACTS:

The issues in *Gitlow v. New York* arose during the early part of the twentieth century, when fear of communist subversion gripped the United States. To combat the

William Foster, left, and Benjamin Gitlow, presidential and vice presidential candidates for the Workers (Communist) Party, at Madison Square Garden in 1928. Gitlow's publication of the Left Wing Manifesto *led to his arrest and conviction under New York's criminal anarchy act. The Supreme Court upheld the conviction but ruled that states were bound by the freedom of speech provision of the First Amendment.*

so-called red menace, several states, including New York, created commissions to investigate subversive organizations. In 1919 and 1920 New York's commission ordered raids on the leaders of socialist and communist groups and seized their materials. Among those arrested was Benjamin Gitlow, a socialist charged with distributing a pamphlet titled the *Left Wing Manifesto*, which called for mass action to overthrow the capitalist system in the United States. Gitlow was prosecuted in a New York trial court for violating the state's criminal anarchy law. Under the leadership of Clarence Darrow, Gitlow's defense attorneys alleged that the statute violated the First Amendment's guarantee of freedom of expression. The defense was unsuccessful, and Gitlow appealed.

ARGUMENTS:

For the plaintiff-in-error, Benjamin Gitlow:

- The "liberty" identified in the Fourteenth Amendment due process clause includes the liberty of speech and press.
- The New York law is an unconstitutional restraint on liberty of expression because it is not restricted to circumstances under which expression causes an immediate substantive evil.

For the defendant-in-error, State of New York:

- Advocacy of the doctrine of criminal anarchy can be distinguished from expressing political beliefs.
- The Fourteenth Amendment does not prevent the states from limiting the freedom of speech or press.
- A state may punish expression that endangers the government, and it need not wait until the danger becomes immediate.

 MR. JUSTICE SANFORD DELIVERED THE OPINION OF THE COURT.

The sole contention here is, essentially, that as there was no evidence of any concrete result flowing from the publication of the Manifesto or of circumstances showing the likelihood of such result, the statute as construed and applied by the trial court penalizes the mere utterance, as such, of "doctrine" having no quality of incitement, without regard either to the circumstances of its utterance or to the likelihood of unlawful sequences; and that, as the exercise of the right of free expression with relation to government is only punishable "in circumstances involving likelihood of substantive evil," the statute contravenes the due process clause of the Fourteenth Amendment. The argument in support of this contention rests primarily upon the following propositions: 1st, That the "liberty" protected by the Fourteenth Amendment includes the liberty of speech and of the press; and 2d, That while liberty of expression "is not absolute," it may be restrained "only in circumstances where its exercise bears a causal relation with some substantive evil, consummated, attempted or likely," and as the statute "takes no account of circumstances," it unduly restrains this liberty and is therefore unconstitutional.

The precise question presented, and the only question which we can consider under this writ of error, then is whether the statute, as construed and applied in this case by the State courts, deprived the defendant of his liberty of expression in violation of the due process clause of the Fourteenth Amendment.

The statute does not penalize the utterance or publication of abstract "doctrine" or academic discussion having no quality of incitement to any concrete action. It is not aimed against mere historical or philosophical essays. It does not restrain the advocacy of changes in the form of government by constitutional and lawful means. What it prohibits is language advocating, advising or teaching the overthrow of organized government by unlawful means. These words imply urging to action. Advocacy is defined in the Century Dictionary as: "1. The act of pleading for, supporting, or recommending; active espousal." It is not the abstract "doctrine" of overthrowing organized government by unlawful means which is denounced by the statute, but the advocacy of action for the accomplishment of that purpose. . . .

The *Manifesto*, plainly, is neither the statement of abstract doctrine nor, as suggested by counsel, mere prediction that industrial disturbances and revolutionary mass strikes will result spontaneously in an inevitable process of evolution in the economic system. It advocates and urges in fervent language mass action which shall progressively foment industrial disturbances and through political mass strikes and revolutionary mass action overthrow and destroy organized parliamentary government. It concludes with a call to action in these words:

"The proletariat revolution and the Communist reconstruction of society—*the struggle for these*—is now indispensable. . . . The Communist International calls the proletariat of the world to the final struggle!"

This is not the expression of philosophical abstraction, the mere prediction of future events; it is the language of direct incitement.

The means advocated for bringing about the destruction of organized parliamentary government, namely, mass industrial revolts usurping the functions of municipal government, political mass strikes directed against the parliamentary state, and revolutionary mass action for its final destruction, necessarily imply the use of force and violence, and in their essential nature are inherently unlawful in a constitutional government of law and order. That the jury were warranted in finding that the Manifesto advocated not merely the abstract doctrine of overthrowing organized government by force, violence and unlawful means, but action to that end, is clear.

For present purposes we may and do assume that freedom of speech and of the press—which are protected by the First Amendment from abridgment by Congress—are among the fundamental personal rights and 'liberties' protected by the due process clause of the Fourteenth Amendment from impairment by the States. . . . It is a fundamental principle, long established, that the freedom of speech and of the press which is secured by the Constitution, does not confer an absolute right to speak or publish, without responsibility, whatever one may choose, or an unrestricted and unbridled license that gives immunity for every possible use of language and prevents the punishment of those who abuse this freedom. Reasonably limited . . . this freedom is an inestimable privilege in a free government; without such limitation, it might become the scourge of the republic.

That a State in the exercise of its police power may punish those who abuse this freedom by utterances inimical to the public welfare, tending to corrupt public morals, incite to crime, or disturb the public peace, is not open to question. . . .

And, for yet more imperative reasons, a State may punish utterances endangering the foundations of organized government and threatening its overthrow by unlawful means. These imperil its own existence as a constitutional State. Freedom of speech and press . . . does not protect disturbances to the public peace or the attempt to subvert the government. It does not protect publications or teachings which tend to subvert or imperil the government or to impede or hinder it in the performance of its governmental duties. It does not protect publications prompting the overthrow of

government by force; the punishment of those who publish articles which tend to destroy organized society being essential to the security of freedom and the stability of the State. And a State may penalize utterances which openly advocate the overthrow of the representative and constitutional form of government of the United States and the several States, by violence or other unlawful means. In short this freedom does not deprive a State of the primary and essential right of self-preservation; which, so long as human governments endure, they cannot be denied. . . .

By enacting the present statute the State has determined, through its legislative body, that utterances advocating the overthrow of organized government by force, violence and unlawful means, are so inimical to the general welfare and involve such danger of substantive evil that they may be penalized in the exercise of its police power. That determination must be given great weight. Every presumption is to be indulged in favor of the validity of the statute. And the case is to be considered "in the light of the principle that the State is primarily the judge of regulations required in the interest of public safety and welfare"; and that its police "statutes may only be declared unconstitutional where they are arbitrary or unreasonable attempts to exercise authority vested in the State in the public interest." That utterances inciting to the overthrow of organized government by unlawful means, present a sufficient danger of substantive evil to bring their punishment within the range of legislative discretion, is clear. Such utterances, by their very nature, involve danger to the public peace and to the security of the State. They threaten breaches of the peace and ultimate revolution. And the immediate danger is none the less real and substantial, because the effect of a given utterance cannot be accurately foreseen. The State cannot reasonably be required to measure the danger from every such utterance in the nice balance of a jeweler's scale. A single revolutionary spark may kindle a fire that, smouldering for a time, may burst into a sweeping and destructive conflagration. It cannot be said that the State is acting arbitrarily or unreasonably when in the exercise of its judgment as to the measures necessary to protect the public peace and safety, it seeks to extinguish the spark without waiting until it has enkindled the flame or blazed into the conflagration. It cannot reasonably be required to defer the adoption of measures for its own peace and safety until the revolutionary utterances lead to actual disturbances of the public peace or imminent and immediate danger of its own destruction; but it may, in the exercise of its judgment, suppress the threatened danger in its incipiency. . . .

We cannot hold that the present statute is an arbitrary or unreasonable exercise of the police power of the State unwarrantably infringing the freedom of speech or press; and we must and do sustain its constitutionality.

This being so, it may be applied to every utterance—not too trivial to be beneath the notice of the law—which is of such a character and used with such intent and purpose as to bring it within the prohibition of the statute. In other words, when the legislative body has determined generally, in the constitutional exercise of its discretion, that utterances of a certain kind involve such danger of substantive evil that they may be punished, the question whether any specific utterance coming within the prohibited class is likely, in and of itself, to bring about the substantive evil, is not open to consideration. It is sufficient that the statute itself be constitutional and that the use of the language comes within its prohibition.

It is clear that the question in such cases is entirely different from that involved in those cases where the statute merely prohibits certain acts involving the danger of substantive evil, without any reference to language itself, and it is sought to apply its provisions to language used by the defendant for the purpose of bringing about the prohibited results. There, if it be contended that the statute cannot be applied to the language used by the defendant because of its protection by the freedom of speech or press, it must necessarily be found, as an original question, without any previous determination by the legislative body, whether the specific language used involved such likelihood of bringing about the substantive evil as to deprive it of the constitutional protection. In such case it has been held that the general provisions of the statute may be constitutionally applied to the specific utterance of the defendant if its natural tendency and probable effect was to bring about the substantive evil which the legislative body might prevent. And the general statement in the Schenck Case, that the "question in every case is whether the words used are used in such circumstances and are of such a nature as to create a clear and present danger that they will bring about the substantive evils,"—upon which great reliance is placed in the defendant's argument—was manifestly intended, as shown by the context, to apply only in cases of this class, and has no application to those like the present, where the legislative body itself has previously determined the danger of substantive evil arising from utterances of a specified character.

The defendant's brief does not separately discuss any of the rulings of the trial court. It is only necessary to say that, applying the general rules already stated, we find that none of them involved any invasion of the constitutional rights of the defendant. It was not necessary, within the meaning of the statute, that the defendant should have advocated "some definite or immediate act or acts" of force, violence or unlawfulness. It was sufficient if such acts were advocated in general terms; and it was not essential that their immediate execution should have been advocated. Nor was it necessary that the language should have been "reasonably and ordinarily calculated to incite certain persons" to acts of force, violence or unlawfulness. The advocacy need not be addressed to specific persons. . . .

And finding, for the reasons stated, that the statute is not in itself unconstitutional, and that it has not been applied in the present case in derogation of any constitutional right, the judgment of the Court of Appeals is

Affirmed.

MR. JUSTICE HOLMES, dissenting.

MR. JUSTICE BRANDEIS and I are of opinion that this judgment should be reversed. The general principle of free speech, it seems to me, must be taken to be included in the Fourteenth Amendment, in view of the scope that has been given to the word "liberty" as there used, although perhaps it may be accepted with a somewhat larger latitude of interpretation than is allowed to Congress by the sweeping language that governs or ought to govern the laws of the United States. If I am right, then I think that the criterion sanctioned by the full Court in *Schenck v. United States* applies. "The question in every case is whether the words used are used in such circumstances and are of such a nature as to create a clear and present danger that they will bring about the substantive evils that [the State] has a right to prevent." It is true that in my opinion this criterion was departed from in *Abrams v. United States*, but the convictions that I expressed in that case are too deep for it to be possible for me as yet to believe that it and *Schaefer v. United States* [1920] have settled the law. If what I think the correct test is applied, it is manifest that there was no present danger of an attempt to overthrow the government by force on the part of the admittedly small minority who shared the defendant's views. It is said that this manifesto was more than a theory, that it was an incitement. Every idea is an incitement. It offers itself for belief and if believed it is acted on unless some other belief outweighs it or some failure of energy stifles the movement at its birth. The only difference between the expression of an opinion and an incitement in the narrower sense is the speaker's enthusiasm for the result. Eloquence may set fire to reason. But whatever may be thought of the redundant discourse before us it had no chance of starting a present conflagration. If in the long run the beliefs expressed in proletarian dictatorship are destined to be accepted by the dominant forces of the community, the only meaning of free speech is that they should be given their chance and have their way.

If the publication of this document had been laid as an attempt to induce an uprising against government at once and not at some indefinite time in the future it would have presented a different question. The object would have been one with which the law might deal, subject to the doubt whether there was any danger that the publication could produce any result, or in other words, whether it was not futile and too remote from possible consequences. But the indictment alleges the publication and nothing more.

Gitlow's effects on the development of civil liberties law are somewhat mixed. Perhaps the most enduring contribution of *Gitlow* is the statement that for "present purposes we may and do assume that freedom of speech and of the press—which are protected by the First Amendment from abridgment by Congress—are among the fundamental personal rights and 'liberties' protected by the due process clause of the Fourteenth Amendment from impairment by the States." This sweeping incorporation vastly expanded constitutional guarantees for freedom of expression. The prohibition against infringing on the freedoms of speech and press now applied to state and local governments as well as the federal government.

But the Court in *Gitlow* also limited personal freedom by moving further away from the clear and present

At a 1930 meeting, members of the Washington Communist Society plan a demonstration in front of the White House. The protest activities of such organizations frequently led to arrests and charges of First Amendment violations.

danger approach and embracing the bad tendency test. Look carefully at Justice Edward Sanford's majority opinion. He emphasizes that the possible danger resulting from speech need not be immediate to justify regulation: "A single revolutionary spark may kindle a fire that, smouldering for a time, may burst into a sweeping and destructive conflagration." In addition, the Court held that great deference should be given to the legislature's determination of what dangers warrant regulation and that "every presumption is to be indulged in favor of the validity of the statute."

In dissent, Holmes continued to press his clear and present danger standard, arguing that Gitlow's actions posed no obvious and immediate danger. He challenged the majority's view that speech can be regulated for evil effects that might occur sometime in the future by arguing that "every idea is an incitement." For Holmes, whatever danger Gitlow's message might pose, it was too inconsequential and too remote to justify government repression of expression rights.

Whitney v. California involved Charlotte Whitney, a well-known California heiress and a niece of Stephen J. Field, a former Supreme Court justice. She was an active member of the Oakland branch of the Socialist Party and voted for delegates sent by the chapter to a national party meeting held in 1919 in Chicago. At that convention the party ejected its more radical members, including the Oakland delegates, who in turn formed the Communist Labor Party of the United States. Local party chapters from California then held a state meeting in Oakland, where they created the Communist Labor Party of California.

Although Whitney had opposed the radical platform "urging a revolutionary class struggle" offered at the national convention, she nevertheless served as one of her chapter's delegates to the local meeting and, in fact, became chair of the credentials committee. Based on her association with this group and its predecessor, California authorities charged Whitney with violating the state's syndicalism law. In 1920 she was found guilty of organizing and associating with a party dedicated to overthrowing the U.S. government and sentenced to one to fourteen years in San Quentin State Prison.

On appeal to the Supreme Court, Whitney was represented by attorneys Walter Pollak and Walter Nelles from the newly formed American Civil Liberties Union (*see Box 5-1*). Pollak and Nelles had previously handled Benjamin Gitlow's appeal to the Supreme Court.

They argued that the California act violated the free speech clause of the First Amendment, but the justices upheld Whitney's conviction. They treated her claim just as they had Gitlow's, relying on the bad tendency test. The majority in *Whitney* asserted:

That the freedom of speech which is secured by the Constitution does not confer an absolute right to speak . . . whatever one may choose . . . and that a State in the exercise of its police power may punish those who abuse this freedom by utterances inimical to the public welfare, tending to incite crime, disturb the public peace, or endanger the foundations of organized government and threaten its overthrow by unlawful means, is not open to question.

The Court's ruling allowed the punishment of mere membership in a subversive organization without requiring proof of any concrete criminal actions to overthrow the government by illegal means.

Louis D. Brandeis and Holmes filed a concurrence in *Whitney*. They favored a return to the clear and present danger standard, but with this modification: that the evil take the form of behavior. Justice Brandeis wrote, "No danger flowing from speech can be deemed clear and present, unless the incidence of evil apprehended is so imminent that it may befall before there is opportunity for full discussions." What is even more curious (and a matter of some scholarly interest) is why these two justices concurred rather than dissented. It seems clear that Whitney's behavior did not meet the standard they articulated, making the question all the more intriguing. One reasonable hypothesis is that Brandeis wanted to demonstrate that the clear and present danger test was not necessarily a vehicle created to overturn convictions but merely a more equitable way to analyze First Amendment claims.

Regardless of the philosophical debates triggered by the series of cases from *Schenck* to *Whitney*, one fact remains clear: the justices seemed swept away by the wave of nationalism and patriotism in the aftermath of World War I. With but one exception, they acceded to the wishes of Congress and the states, which centered on the complementary goals of promoting nationalism and suppressing radicalism.[3]

---

3. The exception was *Fiske v. Kansas* (1927), decided the same day as *Whitney*. The justices concluded that there was insufficient evidence to sustain Fiske's conviction, and the Court for the first time overturned a conviction under a state syndicalism law.

BOX 5-1   THE AMERICAN CIVIL LIBERTIES UNION

By almost every measure the American Civil Liberties Union (ACLU) is the largest and most complex organization dedicated to public interest litigation in the United States. It claims 500,000 members and has organizations in every state, the District of Columbia, and Puerto Rico. It employs more than 200 staff attorneys and enjoys the services of thousands of volunteer lawyers.

Given its current form, the humble origins of the ACLU may come as a surprise. The ACLU's roots lie in a small organization called the Henry Street

Roger Baldwin, founder of the ACLU

Group, which was started by several leaders of the Progressive Movement to combat growing militarism. One year later, this group united with another to become the American Union Against Militarism (AUAM).

Between 1915 and 1917 the AUAM tried to lobby against any legislation designed to stimulate the U.S. "war machine." But in 1917, when Germany announced "its intention to resume unrestricted warfare," the AUAM turned its attention to the draft. The organization sought to defend those who had conscientious objections to serving in the military. This goal was handled primarily by an agency within the AUAM, the Bureau of Conscientious Objectors (BCO).

Under the leadership of the young, charismatic Roger Baldwin, the BCO eventually dominated the AUAM. Baldwin's BCO doubled the size of AUAM's membership and spent more than 50 percent of its funds. Clearly, Baldwin was an effective leader, but the AUAM's old-line Progressive leaders disliked his strategy of providing direct assistance to conscientious objectors, and they threatened to resign. To save the AUAM and to show solidarity with its "greater" agenda, Baldwin changed the name of the BCO to the Civil Liberties Bureau (CLB). This last-ditch effort failed, however, and in 1917 the new National CLB split from its parent organization, which expired shortly thereafter.

Between 1917 and 1919, the NCLB continued to defend conscientious objectors, but it could not prevent Baldwin's imprisonment for draft violations in 1918. Ironically, during Baldwin's jail term the seed was planted

for what is now known as the American Civil Liberties Union. In prison, Baldwin became acquainted with the activities of a radical labor union, the Industrial Workers of the World (IWW), an organization that made no secret of its use of violence and sabotage to achieve its policy needs.

After 1920 the newly formed ACLU would never again be a single-purpose organization; by 1925 it was speaking out for labor, pacifists, and persons who had been caught up by government raids during the "red scare." Defending the right of free speech eventually became the ACLU's major trademark as the organization moved into the 1930s, 1940s, and 1950s. While cultivating expertise in this area, ACLU leaders also realized that they had to "nationalize" the group. They took steps that included fuller recognition of the growing chain of ACLU affiliates throughout the United States and provision of more information to their membership, which increased by almost 5,000 annually.

The ACLU's efforts to build and regroup during the 1950s were quite timely, because the 1960s turned out to be critical years for the organization. Not only was the decade meaningful in the development of law governing civil rights and liberties, but also the ACLU itself seemed to embody the goals of the nation. The union's stance against the Vietnam War, President Richard Nixon, and racism and its defense of draft dodgers and student protesters proved to be highly popular. Between 1966 and 1973 the ACLU's membership skyrocketed from 77,200 to 222,000, and its litigation activities exploded.

To deal with its increasing caseload and to focus its energies on specific areas of the law, the ACLU established the ACLU Foundation in 1967. This foundation, in turn, established special national projects, including the National Prison, Women's Rights, and Reproductive Freedom Projects. The ACLU handles approximately six thousand cases each year.

SOURCES: Karen O'Connor and Lee Epstein, *Public Interest Law Groups* (Westport, CT: Greenwood Press, 1989); *Encyclopedia of Associations*, 2nd ed. (Farmington Mills, MI: Thomson/Gale Group, 2005); and ACLU Web site, http://www.aclu.org.

Preferred Freedoms Doctrine

As the anxieties of World War I and its aftermath faded, the debate over seditious speech was argued in calmer voices. As part of this general trend, the Supreme Court began to reevaluate its decisions from *Schenck* to *Whitney*.

The Court's greater willingness to consider the message of civil liberties advocates was first signaled in **Stromberg v. California** (1931). Yetta Stromberg, a nineteen-year-old member of the Young Communist League, served as a counselor at a summer camp for children ages ten to fifteen. She regularly introduced her campers to Marxist theory. In addition, she would raise a red banner and lead the children in reciting a workers' pledge of allegiance. She was convicted of violating a state statute that made it a crime to raise a red flag or banner publicly as a symbol of opposition to organized government or in support of anarchy. The Supreme Court reversed the conviction, holding that the California statute was excessively broad, applying not only to those who advocated violent overthrow of the government but also those who supported political change by orderly and peaceful means. Such vagueness and ambiguity do not comport with the demands of the First Amendment.

Stromberg was followed six years later by **DeJonge v. Oregon** (1937). As a member of the Communist Party in Portland, Oregon, Dirk DeJonge distributed handbills throughout the city calling for a meeting of all members and other interested parties. The purpose of the gathering was to protest police raids of members' houses. DeJonge held the meeting on July 27, 1934, and between 160 and 200 people attended, only a small percentage of whom belonged to the party. Although the members tried to sell copies of the party's newspaper, the *Daily Worker,* the agenda of the meeting was quite general, with all proceeding in an orderly fashion until the police raided it. They arrested DeJonge for violating Oregon's criminal syndicalism law, which prohibited the organization of the Communist Party.

The justices unanimously overturned DeJonge's conviction on this charge, holding that the state violated the First Amendment. The meeting had been peaceful and orderly, and DeJonge had not engaged in any "forcible subversion." According to the opinion by Chief Justice Charles Evans Hughes, written in language closely resembling the clear and present danger test, "peaceful assembly for lawful discussion cannot be made a crime."

Even more dramatic was a seemingly insignificant bit of writing—a footnote contained in Justice Harlan F. Stone's opinion in **United States v. Carolene Products** (1938). This case dealt with a federal ban on the shipment of a certain kind of milk—an economic, not a First Amendment, issue. But Stone's fourth footnote in this opinion includes the following:

There may be narrower scope for operation of the presumption of constitutionality when legislation appears on its face to be within a specific prohibition of the Constitution, such as those of the first ten Amendments, which are deemed equally specific when held to be embraced by the Fourteenth Amendment. . . .

It is unnecessary to consider now whether legislation which restricts those political processes which can ordinarily be expected to bring about repeal of undesirable legislation, is to be subjected to more exacting judicial scrutiny under the general prohibitions of the Fourteenth Amendment than are most other types of legislation. . . .

Nor need we enquire whether similar considerations enter into the review of statutes directed at particular religious, or national, or racial minorities; whether prejudice against discrete and insular minorities may be a special condition, which tends seriously to curtail the operation of those political processes ordinarily to be relied upon to protect minorities, and which may call for a correspondingly more searching judicial inquiry.

What appeared to be an obscure footnote in a relatively insignificant case took on tremendous importance for civil liberties claims, especially those based on First Amendment expression rights. As Alpheus Thomas Mason and Donald Grier Stephenson explain, each of the footnote's three paragraphs contains powerful ideas regarding the status of constitutional rights.[4] The first paragraph holds that whenever a government regulation appears on its face to be in conflict with the Bill of Rights, the usual presumption that laws are constitutional should be reduced or waived altogether. The second hints that the judiciary has a special responsibility to defend those rights essential to the effective functioning of the political process, a class of liberties that clearly includes freedom of expression rights. The third paragraph suggests a special role for the Court in protecting the rights of minorities and unpopular groups.

---

4. Alpheus Thomas Mason and Donald Grier Stephenson Jr., *American Constitutional Law,* 10th ed. (Englewood Cliffs, NJ: Prentice Hall, 1993), 279.

BOX 5-2 AFTERMATH ... CHARLOTTE ANITA WHITNEY

Charlotte Anita Whitney was born into a wealthy and influential California family in 1867. She graduated from Wellesley College and subsequently became a social worker in the slums of Oakland.

Following her 1920 conviction for organizing and associating with a party dedicated to the overthrow of the government, Whitney was incarcerated. She spent only a few days in jail, however, before she was released pending the outcome of her appeal.

When the Supreme Court upheld her conviction in 1927, clergy, intellectuals, labor leaders, and even some prominent businessmen mounted an effort to convince California's Republican governor, Clement C. Young, to pardon her. They argued that the syndicalism statute was enacted to punish those who engaged in terrorism and sabotage, not to imprison

Charlotte Anita Whitney

nonviolent activists such as Whitney. Young issued a full pardon one month after the Court's decision.

Whitney remained fully immersed in left-wing activism until her death in 1955. She served as a Communist Party officer and was the party's nominee for state treasurer in 1934, state comptroller in 1938, and U.S. Senate in 1940. In 1935 she was convicted of perjury for filing false petitions on behalf of Communist candidates for public office and sentenced to a $600 fine or three hundred days in jail. Whitney chose jail, but a nephew paid the fine on her behalf. During the course of her activism, Whitney contributed almost all of her considerable inheritance to radical causes.

The Supreme Court overruled *Whitney v. California* in 1969, fourteen years after Whitney's death.

The standard expressed in Footnote Four has become known as the preferred freedoms doctrine. This doctrine has notable significance for First Amendment claims because it means that the judiciary will apply special scrutiny to laws that appear to restrict freedom of expression, especially as those laws may relate to the articulation of unpopular political views. Put another way, "Laws restricting fundamental rights . . . would be regarded as suspect and potentially dangerous to the functioning of democracy."[5]

The importance of Justice Stone's footnote goes beyond its obvious declaration of a new standard for evaluating First Amendment claims. In *Carolene Products* Stone announces a modification in the fundamental role of the Court. He declares that the Court will assume a special responsibility for protecting civil rights and civil liberties and be particularly vigilant in guarding the rights of minorities and the politically unpopular. Although the groundwork for his position had been laid by earlier justices *(see Box 5-3)*, Stone's statement marked a major change in course for an

institution that had, for its entire history, been tilted toward settling private economic disputes and wrestling with questions of government power. From this point forward the civil liberties docket began to grow, and the Court rapidly began to evolve into an institution with a primary focus on civil liberties issues.[6]

But would the majority of the justices adopt Stone's preferred freedoms approach to First Amendment claims? Moreover, how would such an approach square with the clear and present danger standard to which several of them seemed to want to return? Attorneys, states, and civil libertarians had to wait only a year until the Court addressed these questions in **Schneider v. State of New Jersey (Town of Irvington)** (1939). *Schneider* was one of four cases the Court grouped together for a single decision. These cases involved municipal ordinances from New Jersey, Wisconsin, California, and Massachusetts that limited free expression. The Wisconsin, California, and Massachusetts laws restricted public handbill distribution to keep the streets uncluttered and

---

5. Stanley I. Kutler, ed., *The Supreme Court and the Constitution* (New York: W. W. Norton, 1984), 429.

6. Richard L. Pacelle, *The Transformation of the Supreme Court's Agenda: From the New Deal to the Reagan Administration* (Boulder, CO: Westview Press, 1991).

BOX 5-3   THE PREFERRED FREEDOMS DOCTRINE

Justice Harlan Fiske Stone's famous Footnote Four in *United States v. Carolene Products* (1938) gave birth to the preferred freedoms doctrine. This doctrine holds that some constitutional rights, particularly those protected by the First Amendment, are so fundamental to a free society that they deserve an especially high degree of judicial protection.

Stone's position built on theories advanced by earlier justices. Oliver Wendell Holmes Jr., for example, contended in several cases that government regulation of the economy required only a rational basis to establish its constitutionality, but that regulation of speech could take place only if a "clear and present danger" could be shown. Justice Benjamin Cardozo argued in *Palko v. Connecticut* (1937) that certain rights are so fundamental as to be indispensable for our system of liberty. Stone expanded these arguments to enlarge the role of the judiciary as a protector of freedom and to carve out a special responsibility for the protection of minority rights.

The preferred freedoms doctrine became more prominent in the years immediately after *Carolene Products.* Several judges who wanted expanded protection for First Amendment rights based their argument on the doctrine. In *Murdock v. Pennsylvania* (1943), Justice William O. Douglas declared, "Freedom of press, freedom of speech, freedom of religion are in a preferred position." Justice Hugo Black frequently stated that the rights contained in the First Amendment are the very heart of our government.

In contemporary times, the preferred freedoms doctrine is rarely applied in its original form, but its spirit lives on in subsequently adopted rules of judicial interpretation. The Court today often distinguishes between fundamental rights and other liberties, designating certain rights as deserving "strict scrutiny." Government may restrict such rights only if there is a compelling reason to do so. These doctrines directly flow from Stone's assertion in 1938 that the rights most central to our system of liberty deserve special status and protection.

SOURCE: C. Herman Pritchett, "Preferred Freedoms Doctrine," in *The Oxford Companion to the Supreme Court of the United States,* ed. Kermit L. Hall (New York: Oxford University Press, 1992), 663–664. Reprinted with permission of Oxford University Press.

---

free of litter. The New Jersey law required the approval of a police official before an individual or group could solicit, canvass, or distribute printed materials door-to-door. The law was designed to reduce incidents of fraud. In an 8–1 decision, the Court struck down each municipal regulation as an unconstitutional burden on free speech. Justice Owen Roberts stated:

We are of the opinion that the purpose to keep the streets clean [is] insufficient to justify an ordinance which prohibits a person rightfully on a public street from handing literature to one willing to receive it. Any burden imposed upon the city authorities in cleaning . . . the streets . . . results from the constitutional protection of the freedom of speech.

And

. . . a municipality cannot . . . require all who wish to disseminate ideas to present them first to police authorities for their consideration and approval, with a discretion in the police to say some ideas may, while others may not, be carried to the homes of citizens; some persons may, while others may not, disseminate information from house to house.

The Court's decision demonstrated that the justices were beginning to favor a preferred freedoms approach. They were giving priority to First Amendment expression rights over otherwise legitimate government interests.

Six years later, in ***Thomas v. Collins*** (1945), the Court moved even closer to embracing the preferred freedoms test. The case arose when R. J. Thomas, president of the United Automobile, Aircraft and Agricultural Workers (UAW) and vice president of the Congress of Industrial Organizations (CIO), arrived in Houston, Texas, to deliver a speech to a group of workers the CIO wanted to organize. Six hours before Thomas was to speak, Texas authorities served him with a restraining order, prohibiting him from making his scheduled address. Believing that the order constituted a violation of his free speech guarantees, Thomas delivered his speech anyway to an audience of about three hundred people. The meeting was described as "peaceful and orderly," but authorities arrested Thomas. He was sentenced to three days in jail and a $100 fine. On appeal to the U.S. Supreme Court, Thomas's claim of a free speech infringement received reinforcement from several civil liberties organizations, including the National Federation for Constitutional Liberties, which argued, "The activities of labor organizations involve the exercise of peaceful assembly, freedom of speech and freedom of the press."

In a 6–3 opinion, the Supreme Court agreed, ruling against the state, and what is most significant, using a preferred freedoms approach to reach that conclusion. Justice Wiley Rutledge, writing for the majority, asserted:

[This] case confronts us again with the duty our system places on this Court to say where the individual's freedom ends and the State's power begins. Choice of that border, now as always delicate, is perhaps more so where the usual presumptive supporting legislation is balanced *by the preferred place given in our scheme to the great, the indispensable democratic freedoms secured by the First Amendment.* . . . For [this] reason any attempt to restrict those liberties must be justified by clear public interest, threatened not . . . remotely, but by *a clear and present danger* [emphasis added].

Constitutional experts claim that this decision represents another major breakthrough in the area of freedom of speech. But why? First, it reinforces the majority view in *Schneider* that the preferred freedoms doctrine provides an appropriate solution to First Amendment problems. Second, Rutledge's language, "Any attempt to restrict the liberties of speech and assembly must be justified . . . by a clear and present danger," indicates that the Court, instead of abandoning Holmes's standard, had combined the clear and present danger standard with the preferred freedoms framework. The preferred freedoms "concept was never a repudiation of the notion of clear and present danger, but was seen as giving its purposes a firmer base and texture—incorporating it much as Einsteinian physics incorporates Newtonian."[7]

Aftermath of World War II: Competing Tests and a Divided Court

As *Thomas v. Collins* indicates, by the mid-1940s it seemed as if the Court had finally settled on an approach to solve First Amendment problems. Stone's preferred freedoms doctrine had gained acceptance among the justices, even though it served as a vehicle by which to overturn many laws restricting speech.

Like previous tests, however, the preferred freedoms doctrine was short-lived. In the early 1950s the Court began to turn back toward more conservative interpretations of the First Amendment. What caused this sudden change in direction? Three factors may explain it.

First, several changes in Court personnel occurred between 1945 and 1952. Chief Justice Frederick M. Vinson replaced Stone, the author of Footnote Four. Two relatively conservative justices, Tom C. Clark and Sherman Minton, took the place of two liberals, Frank Murphy and Wiley Rutledge. As we have seen in other areas of the law, such changes can have a substantial impact on Court outcomes.

Second, by 1949 it became evident that some of the justices were not satisfied with the preferred freedoms framework. Keep in mind that several had dissented in *Thomas,* but at the time they offered no alternative standard. This situation changed dramatically in 1949 with *Kovacs v. Cooper,* when the Court applied the preferred freedoms approach to approve a local ordinance prohibiting the use of sound and amplifying devices on city streets. In a long concurring opinion, Justice Felix Frankfurter agreed with the outcome in *Kovacs* but not with the Court's reasoning. Calling "preferred freedoms" a "mischievous phrase," Frankfurter articulated a new standard by which to review First Amendment claims. He argued that a "wise accommodation between liberty and order always has been, and ever will be, indispensable for a democratic society" and urged the Court to strike a "wise balance" between the two.

This standard, often called the ad hoc balancing test, urges the justices to balance, on a case-by-case basis, the individual free speech claim versus the government's reason for regulating the behavior. But, in Frankfurter's judgment, these competing claims were not of equal merit; the latter should be taken more seriously because legislators had already determined that the law in question met a compelling government interest. In Frankfurter's words:

So long as a legislature does not prescribe what ideas may be . . . expressed and what may not be, nor discriminate among those who would make inroads upon the public peace, it is not for us to supervise the limits the legislature may impose.

The balancing approach appealed to other justices, who began advocating it. Consider, for example, Justice Harlan's opinion for the Court in *Barenblatt v.*

---

7. Malcolm M. Feeley and Samuel Krislov, *Constitutional Law* (Boston: Little, Brown, 1985), 427.

During the anticommunist hysteria of post–World War II America, the House Un-American Activities Committee investigated alleged communist influence in the movie industry. Jack L. Warner, vice president of Warner Bros. Pictures, took the witness chair in 1947. Committee members included future president Richard Nixon, second from right.

United States (1959), in which he presents his support of ad hoc balancing in forthright terms: "Where First Amendment rights are asserted . . . resolution of the issue always involves a balancing by the courts of the competing private and public interests at stake in the particular circumstances shown."

A third reason for the Court's dramatic turnaround in the 1950s was the change in its external environment. After World War II the United States entered into a cold war with the Soviet Union. This period was characterized by an intense fear of communism, not unlike the time following World War I. Led by Senator Joseph McCarthy, R-Wis. (1947–1957), some politicians fed the fear by alleging that Communist Party sympathizers had infiltrated the upper echelons of the U.S. government. Others asserted that the Communist Party of the United States was growing in strength and numbers and spreading its message through motion pictures and plays.

Reflecting this fear of communism, Congress enacted legislation designed to suppress communist and other forms of subversive activity in the United States. For example, a section of the Labor-Management Relations Act of 1947 required union leaders to file affidavits proclaiming nonaffiliation with the Communist Party before they could attain National Labor Relations Board recognition of their unions. Congress passed this law in recognition of Marxist-Leninist theory, which assumes that it will be the "workers" who lead the "Revolution." In ***American Communications***

Association v. Douds (1950) union leaders mounted a First Amendment challenge to the law. Because this was one of the earliest of the cold war cases, many eagerly awaited the Court's decision: Would the justices, now under the leadership of Chief Justice Vinson, use the preferred freedoms approach, or would they adopt Frankfurter's ad hoc balancing test?

Apparently not immune to the pressures of the day, the Court adopted Frankfurter's approach. Writing for the Court, Vinson rejected the clear and present danger standard—the heart of the preferred freedoms approach—noting, "It is the considerations that gave birth to the phrase clear and present danger, not the phrase itself, that are vital in our decisions of questions involving . . . the First Amendment." In his view, the ad hoc balancing approach fully encapsulated that genesis: because Congress has determined that communism constitutes harmful conduct carried on by people, Congress may regulate such conduct in the public interest.

Vinson's standard is akin to the bad tendency test of the 1920s. Both operate under the assumption that the First Amendment protects the public good, as defined by legislatures, rather than individual expression. But just one year after *Douds,* in *Dennis v. United States,* the Court adopted yet another standard: the clear and probable danger test. At issue in *Dennis* was the Smith Act. Enacted in 1940, this statute prohibited anyone from knowingly or willfully advocating or teaching the overthrow of any government of the United States by force; from organizing any society to teach, advocate, or encourage the overthrow of the United States by force; or from becoming a member of any such society. By covering so many kinds of activities, the law provided authorities with a significant weapon to stop the spread of communism in the United States.

While reading *Dennis,* keep in mind the environment in which the justices operated. Remember that tremendous political pressures influenced the Court just as they did many other sectors of American life.

Dennis v. United States

341 U.S. 494 (1951)
http://laws.findlaw.com/US/341/494.html
Vote: 6 (Burton, Frankfurter, Jackson, Minton, Reed, Vinson)
    2 (Black, Douglas)

OPINION ANNOUNCING THE JUDGMENT OF THE COURT: *Vinson*
CONCURRING OPINIONS: *Frankfurter, Jackson*
DISSENTING OPINIONS: *Black, Douglas*
NOT PARTICIPATING: *Clark*

FACTS:

On July 20, 1948, eleven leaders of the National Board of the Communist Party were indicted for conspiring to teach and advocate the overthrow of the government by force and violence and to organize the Communist Party for that purpose in violation of the Smith Act. Their trial was a protracted affair, lasting nine months and generating sixteen thousand pages of evidence. A great deal of the testimony on both sides involved Marxist-Leninist theory and the inner workings of the Communist Party. The prosecutor's case read like a spy novel, full of international conspiracies, secret passwords and codebooks, aliases, and plots to overthrow the U.S. government. The defense was a bit more philosophical as it attempted to demonstrate that the leaders of this particular branch of the party wanted "to work for the improvement of conditions under capitalism and not for chaos and depression."

Not sympathetic to this line of reasoning, the trial court sentenced each defendant to five years in prison and a $10,000 fine. After their convictions were sustained by the court of appeals, Dennis and the others appealed to the U.S. Supreme Court, asking it to overturn their convictions and strike down the Smith Act as an unconstitutional infringement on free speech. They said, "The statute and the convictions which are here for review cannot be validated without at the same time destroying the constitutional foundations of American democracy."

Eleven leaders of the American Communist Party, including Eugene Dennis, second from left, were sentenced to prison in 1949 for conspiring to teach and advocate the overthrow of the U.S. government, a violation of the Smith Act. In Dennis v. United States *(1951), the Court upheld the law on the grounds that the threat of communism was grave enough to justify restricting free speech.*

ARGUMENTS:

For the petitioners, Eugene Dennis, et al.:

- The Smith Act, as written and applied in this case, unconstitutionally makes it a crime to teach or advocate an outlawed doctrine or to organize a group to teach or advocate that outlawed doctrine without regard to circumstances.

- The conspiracy provisions of the Smith Act make it a crime merely to agree to speak, distribute materials, or organize a political party to advance certain political ideas. No overt illegal act need be committed.

- The petitioners' intent does not justify a denial of constitutional protections. Rather, the government must show that the advocacy created a clear, present, and imminent danger of a substantive evil.

For the respondent, United States:

- The Smith Act in this case was applied not to abstract discussions by isolated agitators, but to American leaders of a worldwide totalitarian political movement.

- The Smith Act is a valid exercise of congressional authority to preserve democratic government and military security.

- The First Amendment does not protect the petitioners in their preparation for an attempt to establish by force in the United States a communist dictatorship whenever it may seem to them that circumstances favor such action.

MR. CHIEF JUSTICE VINSON ANNOUNCED THE JUDGMENT OF THE COURT.

The obvious purpose of the statute is to protect existing Government, not from change by peaceable, lawful and constitutional means, but from change by violence, revolution and terrorism. That it is within the *power* of the Congress to protect the Government of the United States from armed rebellion is a proposition which requires little discussion. Whatever theoretical merit there may be to the argument that there is a "right" to rebellion against dictatorial governments is without force where the existing structure of the government provides for peaceful and orderly change. We reject any principle of governmental helplessness in the face of preparation for revolution, which principle, carried to its logical conclusion, must lead to anarchy. No one could conceive that it is not within the power of Congress to prohibit acts intended to overthrow the Government by force and violence. The question with which we are concerned here is not whether Congress has such *power*, but whether the *means* which it has employed conflict with the First and Fifth Amendments to the Constitution. . . .

The very language of the Smith Act negates the interpretation which petitioners would have us impose on that Act. It is directed at advocacy, not discussion. Thus, the trial judge properly charged the jury that they could not convict if they found that petitioners did "no more than pursue peaceful studies and discussions or teaching and advocacy in the realm of ideas." He further charged that it was not unlawful "to conduct in an American college and university a course explaining the philosophical theories set forth in the books which have been placed in evidence." Such a charge is in strict accord with the statutory language, and illustrates the meaning to be placed on those words. Congress did not intend to eradicate the free discussion of political theories, to destroy the traditional rights of Americans to discuss and evaluate ideas without fear of governmental sanction. Rather Congress was concerned with the very kind of activity in which the evidence showed these petitioners engaged.

But although the statute is not directed at the hypothetical cases which petitioners have conjured, its application in this case has resulted in convictions for the teaching and advocacy of the overthrow of the Government by force and violence, which, even though coupled with the intent to accomplish that overthrow, contains an element of speech. For this reason, we must pay special heed to the demands of the First Amendment marking out the boundaries of speech. . . .

In this case we are squarely presented with the application of the "clear and present danger" test, and must decide what that phrase imports. We first note that many of the cases in which this Court has reversed convictions by use of this or similar tests have been based on the fact that the interest which the State was attempting to protect was itself too insubstantial to warrant restriction of speech. Overthrow of the Government by force and violence is certainly a substantial enough interest for the Government to limit speech. Indeed, this is the ultimate value of any society, for if a society cannot protect its very structure from armed internal attack, it must follow that no subordinate value can be protected. If, then, this interest may be protected, the literal problem which is presented is what has been meant by the use of the phrase "clear and present danger" of the utterances bringing about the evil within the power of Congress to punish.

Obviously, the words cannot mean that before the Government may act, it must wait until the *putsch* is about to be executed, the plans have been laid and the signal is awaited. If Government is aware that a group aiming at its overthrow is attempting to indoctrinate its members and to commit them to a course whereby they will strike when the leaders feel the circumstances permit, action by the Government is required. The argument that there is no need for Government to concern itself, for Government is strong, it possesses ample powers to put down a rebellion, it may defeat the revolution with ease needs no answer. For that is not the question. Certainly an attempt to overthrow the Government by force, even though doomed from the outset because of inadequate numbers or power of the revolutionists, is a sufficient evil for Congress to prevent. The damage which such attempts create both physically and politically to a nation makes it impossible to measure the validity in terms of the probability of success, or the immediacy of a successful attempt. In the instant case the trial judge charged the jury that they could not convict unless they found that petitioners intended to overthrow the Government "as speedily as circumstances would permit." This does not mean, and could not properly mean, that they would not strike until there was certainty of success. What was meant was that the revolutionists would strike when they thought the time was ripe. We must therefore reject the contention that success or probability of success is the criterion.

The situation with which Justices Holmes and Brandeis were concerned in *Gitlow* [*v. New York*, 1925] was a comparatively isolated event, bearing little relation in their minds to any substantial threat to the safety of the community. They were not confronted with any situation comparable to the instant one—the development of an apparatus designed and dedicated to the overthrow of the Government, in the context of world crisis after crisis.

Chief Judge Learned Hand, writing for the majority below, interpreted the phrase as follows: "In each case [courts] must ask whether the gravity of the 'evil,' discounted by its improbability, justifies such invasion of free speech as is necessary to avoid the danger." We adopt this statement of the rule. As articulated by Chief Judge Hand, it is as succinct and inclusive as any other we might devise at this time. It takes into consideration those factors which we deem relevant, and relates their significances. More we cannot expect from words. . . .

We hold that . . . the Smith Act do[es] not inherently, or as construed or applied in the instant case, violate the First Amendment and other provisions of the Bill of Rights. . . . Petitioners intended to overthrow the Government of the United States as speedily as the circumstances would permit. Their conspiracy to organize the Communist Party and to teach and advocate the overthrow of the Government of the United States by force and violence created a "clear and present danger" of an attempt to overthrow the Government by force and violence. They were properly and constitutionally convicted for violation of the Smith Act. The judgments of conviction are

Affirmed.

MR. JUSTICE FRANKFURTER, concurring in affirmance of the judgment.

Primary responsibility for adjusting the interests which compete in the situation before us of necessity belongs to the Congress. . . .

It is not for us to decide how we would adjust the clash of interests which this case presents were the primary responsibility for reconciling it ours. Congress has determined that the danger created by advocacy of overthrow justifies the ensuing restriction on freedom of speech. The determination was made after due deliberation,

and the seriousness of the congressional purpose is attested by the volume of legislation passed to effectuate the same ends.

Can we then say that the judgment Congress exercised was denied it by the Constitution? Can we establish a constitutional doctrine which forbids the elected representatives of the people to make this choice? Can we hold that the First Amendment deprives Congress of what it deemed necessary for the Government's protection?

To make validity of legislation depend on judicial reading of events still in the womb of time—a forecast, that is, of the outcome of forces at best appreciated only with knowledge of the topmost secrets of nations—is to charge the judiciary with duties beyond its equipment.

MR. JUSTICE BLACK, dissenting.

At the outset I want to emphasize what the crime involved in this case is, and what it is not. These petitioners were not charged with an attempt to overthrow the Government. They were not charged with overt acts of any kind designed to overthrow the Government. They were not even charged with saying anything or writing anything designed to overthrow the Government. The charge was that they agreed to assemble and to talk and publish certain ideas at a later date: The indictment is that they conspired to organize the Communist Party and to use speech or newspapers and other publications in the future to teach and advocate the forcible overthrow of the Government. No matter how it is worded, this is a virulent form of prior censorship of speech and press, which I believe the First Amendment forbids. I would hold §3 of the Smith Act authorizing this prior restraint unconstitutional on its face and as applied.

. . . To the Founders of this Nation . . . the benefits derived from free expression were worth the risk. They embodied this philosophy in the First Amendment's command that "Congress shall make no law . . . abridging the freedom of speech, or of the press. . . ." I have always believed that the First Amendment is the keystone of our Government, that the freedoms it guarantees provide the best insurance against destruction of all freedom. At least as to speech in the realm of public matters, I believe that the "clear and present danger" test does not "mark the furthermost constitutional boundaries of protected expression" but does "no more than recognize a minimum compulsion of the Bill of Rights." *Bridges v. California* [1941].

So long as this Court exercises the power of judicial review of legislation, I cannot agree that the First Amendment permits us to sustain laws suppressing freedom of speech and press on the basis of Congress' or our own notions of mere "reasonableness." Such a doctrine waters down the First Amendment so that it amounts to little more than an admonition to Congress. The Amendment as so construed is not likely to protect any but those "safe" or orthodox views which rarely need its protection. . . .

MR. JUSTICE DOUGLAS, dissenting.

Free speech has occupied an exalted position because of the high service it has given our society. Its protection is essential to the very existence of a democracy. The airing of ideas releases pressures which otherwise might become destructive. When ideas compete in the market for acceptance, full and free discussion exposes the false and they gain few adherents. Full and free discussion even of ideas we hate encourages the testing of our own prejudices and preconceptions. Full and free discussion keeps a society from becoming stagnant and unprepared for the stresses and strains that work to tear all civilizations apart.

Full and free discussion has indeed been the first article of our faith. We have founded our political system on it. It has been the safeguard of every religious, political, philosophical, economic, and racial group amongst us. We have counted on it to keep us from embracing what is cheap and false; we have trusted the common sense of our people to choose the doctrine true to our genius and to reject the rest. This has been the one single outstanding tenet that has made our institutions the symbol of freedom and equality. We have deemed it more costly to liberty to suppress a despised minority than to let them vent their spleen. We have above all else feared the political censor. We have wanted a land where our people can be exposed to all the diverse creeds and cultures of the world.

There comes a time when even speech loses its constitutional immunity. Speech innocuous one year may at another time fan such destructive flames that it must be halted in the interests of the safety of the Republic. That is the meaning of the clear and present danger test. When conditions are so critical that there will be no time to avoid the evil that the speech threatens, it is time to call a halt. Otherwise, free speech which is the strength of the Nation will be the cause of its destruction.

Yet free speech is the rule, not the exception. The restraint to be constitutional must be based on more than fear, on more than passionate opposition against the speech, on more than a revolted dislike for its contents. There must be some immediate injury to society that is likely if speech is allowed. . . .

. . . Free speech—the glory of our system of government—should not be sacrificed on anything less than plain and objective proof of danger that the evil advocated is imminent. On this record no one can say that petitioners and their converts are in such a strategic position as to have even the slightest chance of achieving their aims.

The First Amendment provides that "Congress shall make no law . . . abridging the freedom of speech." The Constitution provides no exception. This does not mean, however, that the Nation need hold its hand until it is in such weakened condition that there is no time to protect itself from incitement to revolution. Seditious conduct can always be punished. But the command of the First Amendment is so clear that we should not allow Congress to call a halt to free speech except in the extreme case of peril from the speech itself. The First Amendment makes confidence in the common sense of our people and in their maturity of judgment the great postulate of our democracy. Its philosophy is that violence is rarely, if ever, stopped by denying civil liberties to those advocating resort to force. The First Amendment reflects the philosophy of Jefferson "that it is time enough for the rightful purposes of civil government, for its officers to interfere when principles break out into overt acts against peace and good order." The political censor has no place in our public debates. Unless and until extreme and necessitous circumstances are shown, our aim should be to keep speech unfettered and to allow the processes of law to be invoked only when the provocateurs among us move from speech to action.

The *Dennis* decision illustrates the differing approaches advocated by members of the Court at that time. A plurality of the Court accepted Vinson's clear and probable danger test. Quoting appeals court judge Learned Hand, Vinson writes: "In each case courts must ask whether the gravity of the 'evil,' discounted by its improbability, justifies such invasion of free speech as is necessary to avoid the danger." But is this a reasonable interpretation of the test emanating from *Schenck*? That is, would Holmes have agreed with this language? Or does it more closely resemble the bad tendency standard, with which Holmes disagreed?

BOX 5-4   AFTERMATH . . . EUGENE DENNIS

Eugene Dennis was the most prominent of the eleven members of the Communist Party tried in 1949 for violating the Smith Act, criminal accusations that ultimately resulted in the Supreme Court's decision in *Dennis v. United States* (1951).

Born Francis X. Waldron August 10, 1905, in Seattle, Dennis became involved in Communist Party activities in his early twenties. In 1931, faced with the prospect of being indicted on charges of inciting a riot, he changed his name to Tim Ryan and fled to Russia with his wife, Peggy, and their two-year-old son. He returned to the United States in 1935, leaving his son in the Soviet Union to be raised as a Russian Communist. Assuming the name Eugene Dennis, he quickly moved up in the hierarchy of the American Communist Party. During World War II Dennis cooperated with the Russian KGB on intelligence activities and helped infiltrate the U.S. Office of Strategic Services. Following the war, he became general secretary of the party.

Dennis's legal problems began to mount in 1947 when he was sentenced to a year in prison for contempt of Congress as the result of his refusal to answer questions about his background. In 1949 he was tried for violating the Smith Act. When the Supreme Court upheld his conviction, he and his fellow defendants planned to jump bail and go underground. His plan miscarried, and Dennis went to prison in July 1951. After his release in 1955, Dennis resumed his activities with the party. Stricken with cancer, he gave up his leadership position in 1959 and died two years later.

Dennis's son, known as Timur Timofeev, became a Soviet citizen and directed the World Labor Movement in Moscow. Peggy Dennis continued her work with leftist causes after her husband's death. She died in 1993 and was buried next to her husband in the German Waldheim Cemetery in Chicago in a section reserved for Communist leaders.

SOURCES: *San Francisco Chronicle,* September 28, 1993; *New York Times,* October 12, 1993; Bernard K. Johnpoll and Harvey Klehr, *Biographical Dictionary of the American Left* (New York: Greenwood Press, 1986); and John Earl Haynes and Harvey Klehr, *Venona* (New Haven, CT: Yale University Press, 1999).

Justice Frankfurter, concurring in *Dennis,* continued to articulate a balancing approach, with its clear bias toward supporting government action. For Frankfurter, Congress had decided, after due deliberation, that communism was a significant threat, and the courts should restrain themselves from intervening.

In dissent, Justice Hugo Black expressed support for the preferred freedoms position and the clear and present danger test. "I have always believed," Black wrote, "that the First Amendment is the keystone of our Government, that the freedoms it guarantees provide the best insurance against the destruction of all freedom."

Finally, Justice William O. Douglas, in dissent, advocated an entirely different approach. He argued that the First Amendment prohibits Congress from abridging the freedom of speech, and it "provides no exception." This argument is often referred to as the "absolute freedoms" test because it applies the language of the First Amendment literally. The words "Congress shall make no law" impose an absolute prohibition against government regulation of freedom of speech.

As we shall see, Black and Douglas, the Court's strongest civil libertarians, remained in relative isolation during the early 1950s, but the Warren Court of the late 1950s and 1960s adopted many of their views.

In spite of the divided Court, *Dennis* is an important precedent: between 1951 and 1956 the justices used Vinson's clear and probable danger standard to uphold a number of loyalty programs.[8] Moreover, *Dennis* served as a benchmark in other areas of the law in which the federal government asked the Court for sweeping powers to investigate the Communist Party, other subversive groups, and their alleged adherents.

In sum, once again we see the Supreme Court responding to perceived threats to national security. As was the case during the 1920s, when the justices moved from a clear and present danger test to a bad

---

8. See, for example, *Adler v. Board of Education* (1952), in which the Court upheld a New York law (the so-called Feinberg Act) disqualifying from teaching positions persons affiliated with subversive groups.

tendency standard, in the 1950s they moved from a preferred freedoms approach to a revisionist interpretation of the Holmes standard, clear and probable danger.

Free Speech during the Warren Court Era

In his dissenting opinion in *Dennis*, Justice Black wrote the following:

Public opinion being what it now is, few will protest the conviction of these Communist petitioners. There is hope, however, that in calmer times, when present pressures, passions and fears subside, this or some later Court will restore the First Amendment liberties to the high preferred place where they belong in a free society.

Black's words were indeed prophetic. As the 1950s drew to a close, the high emotions of the anticommunist postwar period dissipated. Senator McCarthy, whose campaign against domestic communism had fueled much of the repressive legislation, was discredited and censured by the Senate. While the nation remained concerned about the communist threat and the possibility of nuclear war, the hysteria died down.

Once the red scare was over, the Supreme Court, now under the leadership of Chief Justice Earl Warren, began taking positions defending freedom of expression and association against the repressive legislation passed during the McCarthy era. It handed down a series of decisions upholding the constitutional rights of communists and other so-called subversives. For example, in *Albertson v. Subversive Activities Control Board* (1965) the justices repudiated federal laws requiring communist organizations to register with the government. In *Elfbrandt v. Russell* (1966) and *Whitehill v. Elkins* (1967) loyalty oath requirements directed at subversives were found constitutionally defective. The Court also struck down laws and enforcement actions barring communists from holding office in labor unions (*United States v. Brown,* 1965), prohibiting communists from working in defense plants (*United States v. Robel,* 1967), and stripping passports from Communist Party leaders (*Aptheker v. Secretary of State,* 1964). Clearly, these decisions and others handed down during more tranquil years would have been unheard of during the times of anticommunist hysteria.

By the end of the 1960s, then, the Court had turned away from many of its cold war rulings. It struck down as being in violation of the freedom to speak, publish, or associate much of the federal and state anticommunist legislation still on the books. An important representative of this era was *Brandenburg v. Ohio* (1969), one of the Warren Court's last major rulings. Ironically, the *Brandenburg* decision had nothing to do with the Communist Party or other groups dedicated to violent overthrow of the U.S. government. Instead, the dispute involved a group with a much different purpose, the racist Ku Klux Klan.

Brandenburg v. Ohio

395 U.S. 444 (1969)
http://laws.findlaw.com/US/395/444.html
Oral arguments are available at http://www.oyez.org.
Vote: 8 (Black, Brennan, Douglas, Harlan, Marshall, Stewart, Warren, White)
    0

PER CURIAM OPINION
CONCURRING OPINIONS: *Black, Douglas*

FACTS:

Clarence Brandenburg was the leader of an Ohio affiliate of the Ku Klux Klan, an organization dedicated to white supremacy. To obtain publicity for the KKK's goals, he invited a Cincinnati reporter and camera crew to attend a rally. Subsequently, local and national television stations aired footage of some of the events that occurred at this gathering. One film showed twelve hooded figures, some of whom carried firearms, gathered around a large wooden cross, which they burned. Brandenburg, in Klan regalia, spoke the following words: "We're not a revengent organization, but if our President, our Congress, our Supreme Court, continues to suppress the white, Caucasian race, it's possible that there might have to be some revengeance taken. We are marching on Congress July the Fourth, four hundred thousand strong. From there we are dividing into two groups, one group to march on St. Augustine, Florida, the other group to march into Mississippi." In another film, Brandenburg delivered a speech to the group in which he said, "Personally I believe the nigger should be returned to Africa, the Jew returned to Israel." Based on these films, Ohio authorities arrested Brandenburg for violating the Ohio Criminal Syndicalism law, passed in 1919 to prevent the spread of unpatriotic views. Similar to many other state laws of the sort upheld in

Gitlow, the Ohio act prohibited "advocat[ing] . . . the duty, necessity, or propriety of crime, sabotage, violence, or unlawful methods of terrorism as a means of accomplishing industrial or political reform," as well as voluntarily assembling with any group of persons formed to teach or advocate the doctrines of criminal syndicalism.

For the appellant, Clarence Brandenburg:

- Advocacy of illegal acts is constitutionally protected where the advocacy falls short of incitement and there is nothing to indicate that it will immediately lead to criminal behavior.
- The Ohio law fails to recognize the necessary constitutional distinction between "advocacy of abstract doctrine and advocacy directed at promoting unlawful action."

- The Ohio law fails to acknowledge the constitutional requirement that freedoms of speech and assembly cannot be restricted without showing a clear and present danger that the prohibited activities will bring about a punishable substantive evil.

For the appellee, State of Ohio:

- The Ohio law and the conviction of the defendant are based on an advocacy of action, not a discussion of an abstract doctrine.
- The Ohio law is similar to the New York statute upheld in *Gitlow v. New York* and the California statute approved in *Whitney v. California.*
- Freedom of expression is not absolute. A state cannot be reasonably required to delay restricting advocacy of illegal acts until actual disturbances of the peace take place or other illegal acts occur.

A Ku Klux Klan demonstration in Washington, D.C., in 1926. In 1969 the Supreme Court struck down an Ohio law that punished the advocacy of criminal activities.

PER CURIAM.

The appellant, a leader of a Ku Klux Klan group, was convicted under the Ohio Criminal Syndicalism statute. . . .

The . . . statute was enacted in 1919. From 1917 to 1920, identical or quite similar laws were adopted by 20 States and two territories. In 1927, this Court sustained the constitutionality of California's Criminal Syndicalism Act, the text of which is quite similar to that of the laws of Ohio. *Whitney v. California* (1927). The Court upheld the statute on the ground that, without more, "advocating" violent means to effect political and economic change involves such danger to the security of the State that the State may outlaw it. But *Whitney* has been thoroughly discredited by later decisions. See *Dennis v. United States* (1951). These later decisions have fashioned the principle that the constitutional guarantees of free speech and free press do not permit a State to forbid or proscribe advocacy of the use of force or of law violation except where such advocacy is directed to inciting or producing imminent lawless action and is likely to incite or produce such action. As we said in *Noto v. United States* (1961), "the mere abstract teaching . . . of the moral propriety or even moral necessity for a resort to force and violence, is not the same as preparing a group for violent action and steeling it to such action." A statute which fails to draw this distinction impermissibly intrudes upon the freedoms guaranteed by the First and Fourteenth Amendments. It sweeps within its condemnation speech which our Constitution has immunized from governmental control.

Measured by this test, Ohio's Criminal Syndicalism Act cannot be sustained. The Act punishes persons who "advocate or teach the duty, necessity, or propriety" of violence "as a means of accomplishing industrial or political reform"; or who publish or circulate or display any book or paper containing such advocacy; or who "justify" the commission of violent acts "with intent to exemplify, spread or advocate the propriety of the doctrines of criminal syndicalism"; or who "voluntarily assemble" with a group formed "to teach or advocate the doctrines of criminal syndicalism." Neither the indictment nor the trial judge's instructions to the jury in any way refined the statute's bald definition of the crime in terms of mere advocacy not distinguished from incitement to imminent lawless action.

Accordingly, we are here confronted with a statute which, by its own words and as applied, purports to punish mere advocacy and to forbid, on pain of criminal punishment, assembly with others merely to advocate the described type of action. Such a statute falls within the condemnation of the First and Fourteenth Amendments. The contrary teaching of *Whitney v. California* cannot be supported, and that decision is therefore overruled.

Reversed.

The Court in *Brandenburg* claimed that "the constitutional guarantees of free speech and free press do not permit a State to forbid or proscribe advocacy of the use of force or of law violation except where such advocacy is directed to inciting or producing imminent lawless action and is likely to incite or produce such action." Measured by this test, the Ohio law could not be sustained. By so ruling, the justices closed the door on the long series of repressive expression rulings.

Vietnam, the Civil Rights Movement, and the War on Terrorism

As the nation's fear of communist infiltration ebbed, a new international crisis was brewing in Vietnam. Although U.S. involvement in that conflict dated back to the Truman administration, it grew significantly in 1964, when President Lyndon Johnson announced that the North Vietnamese had attacked U.S. ships in the Gulf of Tonkin. Johnson launched a massive military buildup: by 1968, 541,000 U.S. troops had been sent to Vietnam. Initially, many Americans approved of Johnson's pursuit of the war, but by the late 1960s approval had turned to criticism. A peace movement, initially centered on college campuses, arose throughout the country.

In addition, another cause was gathering strength. The civil rights movement, which in the 1950s was isolated in the South, by the 1960s had taken hold in all major urban centers of the United States. Because of these two social currents, and the resistance to them, the decade was marked by domestic upheaval and turmoil. Although Congress did not respond with any legislation like the Smith Act, these protest movements generated many free expression cases. Some raised constitutional questions about mass demonstrations, the chief weapon of the civil rights and peace movements. Others involved the issues of political expression associated with that period—flag desecration, draft card burning, and so forth. Subsequent sections of this chapter will examine the questions that naturally flowed from these expressive actions.

The United States is not alone in facing conflicts between the principle of free expression and the exercise of that right in a manner the government views as undesirable. Box 5-5 provides examples of the way expression rights have been incorporated into the constitutions of several nations. Many of these countries have adopted democratic regimes quite recently, following histories of authoritarian rule. Like the United States before them, these nations must develop ways to apply constitutional principles to actual disputes. It is the application of abstract doctrine to real situations that will ultimately determine the level of openness and freedom the citizens of those nations will enjoy.

The history of freedom of expression demonstrates great variation in the government's responses to unpopular and opposition opinion, but it also reveals a pattern. When the nation is secure and prosperous, the government tends to be tolerant of dissenting views; in times of crisis, the regulation of expression veers toward the restrictive. As repressive policies are enforced and people object, the judiciary is called upon to determine how far the government may go in restricting free speech.

The events of the recent past show that this cyclical pattern of tolerance and restriction continues to operate. From the end of the Vietnam War to the turn of the century, Americans enjoyed relative peace and prosperity. As a consequence, few new government restrictions were placed on expression rights. All of that ended with the September 2001 terrorist attacks on the World Trade Center and the Pentagon.

President George W. Bush and Congress, with strong public support at that time, responded with the "war on terror," which included legislation designed to protect national security against future terrorist attacks. At the forefront of this effort was the USA Patriot Act of 2001. This statute, among other things, expanded the power of the government to monitor and intercept telephone, face-to-face, and electronic communications. It also broadened the government's authority to conduct searches and seizures, arrests, and detentions.

The Patriot Act was followed by the creation of the Department of Homeland Security in 2002. Twenty-two federal agencies with more than 170,000 employees were consolidated to make up the new cabinet-level department. It was given primary responsibility for protecting the nation's ports, borders, airports, and infrastructure—including utilities, the Internet, telecommunications, and financial networks—from terrorist attacks. Homeland Security assumed the duties of the Immigration and Naturalization Service. It also took on primary responsibility for emergency preparedness when it incorporated the Federal Emergency Management Agency. The department was given broad intelligence-gathering authority to help it carry out its mission.

Civil libertarians criticized the Patriot Act and the powers of the Department of Homeland Security for jeopardizing privacy and other fundamental rights, and for the chilling effect they had on the expression of opposition viewpoints. As subsequent years unfolded without additional terrorist attacks on the United States, public and government support for heightened restrictions on civil liberties began to wane. The 2008 election of President Barack Obama was in part reflective of the nation's perspective that the war on terror restrictions were no longer as necessary as they were in 2001. Nevertheless, history teaches that should a similar attack occur in the future, the government will respond with the same kinds of restrictive legislation that followed the September 11 tragedy.

CONTEMPORARY TESTS AND CONSTITUTIONAL GUIDELINES

Starting in the 1960s, the nation witnessed an explosion in both the variety and the volume of expressive activity—artistic, political, and otherwise—that was arguably protected under the First Amendment. Federal, state, and local governments often reacted by enforcing rules that curtailed free speech rights. In resolving the ensuing disputes, the Court was called upon to adjudicate a perennial conflict between the preservation of individual liberty and the imperatives of an ordered society. The justices developed an approach to First Amendment issues that sought to reconcile the philosophy of the framers with contemporary modes of expression and the needs of a modern society.

The modern Court has borrowed elements from several tests that arose out of the internal security cases *(see Table 5-1)*. Consistent with the preferred freedoms doctrine, the Court has placed a high priority on the

BOX 5-5   FREEDOM OF EXPRESSION IN GLOBAL PERSPECTIVE

As the following quotations from constitutional documents indicate, the United States is not the only country to guarantee its citizens freedom of expression. Many others protect the right as well.

Belgium—Constitution (Article 19)

"Freedom of worship, its public practice and freedom to demonstrate one's opinions on all matters are guaranteed, but offences committed when this freedom is used may be punished."

Bulgaria—Constitution (Article 39)

"Everyone shall be entitled to express an opinion or to promote it through words, written or oral, sound, or image, or in any other way."

Ireland—Constitution (Article 40)

"The State guarantees...the right of the citizens to express freely their convictions and opinions."

Germany—Basic Law (Article 5)

"Everyone has the right freely to express and to disseminate his opinion by speech, writing and pictures and freely to inform himself from generally accessible sources."

Japan—Constitution (Article 21)

"Freedom of assembly and association as well as speech, press, and all other forms of expression are guaranteed."

New Zealand—Bill of Rights Act (Section 14)

"Everyone has the right to freedom of expression, including the freedom to seek, receive, and impart information and opinions of any kind in any form."

Russian Federation—Constitution (Article 29)

"Everyone shall have the right to freedom of thought and speech."

South Africa—Constitution (Section 16)

"Everyone has the right to freedom of expression, which includes...the freedom of the press and other media."

The presence of a right in the constitution, however, does not guarantee that citizens can exercise it. For example, the former Soviet Union—by all accounts, a highly repressive society—guaranteed its citizens the "freedom of speech, of the press, and of assembly, meetings, street processions, and demonstrations," but these rights were without meaning.

Moreover, courts do not always interpret the words of constitutional documents in literal or absolute fashion. Consider, for example, the Canadian Charter of Rights and Freedoms, which reads: "Everyone has the following fundamental freedoms: freedom of thought, belief, opinion, and expression, including freedom of the press and other media of communication." These words would seem to work to the advantage of James Keegstra, a high school teacher who promoted anti-Semitism in his classroom. Keegstra described Jews to his students as "subversive," "money-loving," and "child killers."

But the Canadian Supreme Court did not rule in Keegstra's favor when he was found guilty of violating the criminal code by "unlawfully promoting hatred against an identifiable group." Rather, in a 1990 decision, the Court held:

[G]iven the unparalleled vigour with which hate propaganda repudiates and undermines democratic values, and in particular its condemnation of the view that all citizens need be treated with equal respect and dignity so as to make participation in the political process meaningful, [we are] unable to see the protection of such expression as integral to the democratic ideal.

How did the Court hurdle the Charter's freedom of expression provision? It did so, in part, by pointing to another provision—a provision unlike any in the U.S. Constitution: "This Charter shall be interpreted in a manner consistent with the preservation and enhancement of the multicultural heritage of Canadians."

Similar provisions are not unusual in newer constitutional documents, as South Africa's illustrates. After guaranteeing "everyone" the right to freedom of expression, the Constitution specifically states that this right does not extend to "advocacy of hatred that is based on race, ethnicity, gender or religion, and that constitutes incitement to cause harm." Such provisions, at least on their face, seem to give courts great latitude in punishing those who engage in "hate speech," even though, as we have seen in the United States, they are not necessarily required to do so.

SOURCE: Links to the constitutional documents of the world's nations are available at http://confinder.richmond.edu.

TABLE 5-1   Summary of Legal Standards Governing Free Speech

STANDARD	MAJOR PROPONENTS	EXAMPLE
Clear and Present Danger test "Whether the words are used in such circumstances and are of such a nature as to create a clear and present danger that they will bring about substantive evils that Congress has a right to prevent."	Holmes, Brandeis	*Schenck v. United States*, 1919
Bad Tendency test Do the words have a tendency to bring about something evil?	Clarke, Sanford	*Abrams v. United States*, 1919
Preferred Freedoms "There may be a narrower scope for operation of the presumption of constitutionality when legislation appears on its face to be within a specific prohibition of the Constitution, such as those of the first ten Amendments."	Douglas, Stone, Rutledge	*United States v. Carolene Products*, 1938; *Thomas v. Collins*, 1945
Absolutism "The First Amendment, its prohibition in terms absolute, was designed to preclude courts as well as legislatures from weighing values of speech against silence."	Black, Douglas	Never adopted. See Douglas's dissent in *Dennis v. United States*, 1951; Douglas and Black dissenting in *Roth v. United States*, 1957
Ad Hoc Balancing "On a case by case basis, the government's interest in regulation is weighed against the individual's interest in expression. Because the legislative process naturally involves a consideration of a wide range of societal interests, the courts normally defer to the government and presume that the regulation is valid."	Frankfurter, Harlan	Frankfurter's concurrence in *Kovacs v. Cooper*, 1949; Harlan's opinion in *Barenblatt v. United States*, 1959
Clear and Probable Danger "Whether the gravity of the "evil," discounted by its improbability, justifies such an invasion of free speech as is necessary to avoid danger."	Vinson	*Dennis v. United States*, 1951

First Amendment's expression rights, recognizing the fundamental position those freedoms hold in an open society. The justices, however, have never gone so far as to hold that freedom of speech is absolute. As Justice Holmes argued in the clear and present danger test, expression can be regulated. Government's constitutional ability to regulate expression depends not only on the words uttered but also on the circumstances under which the expression takes place and whether the speech results in substantive evils that the government has authority to prevent. Flowing from this, the justices have taken the position that the degree of protection offered by the First Amendment varies according to the nature of the speech, the place in which the expression occurs, the interests the government is pursuing by its restrictions, and the kind of regulation the government imposes.

The Court gives the highest priority to expression that focuses on political and social issues. This is consistent with the framers' reasons for adopting the First Amendment. In contrast, the government has greater authority to regulate less exalted forms of expression, such as advertising and commercial speech.

The setting in which the expression occurs is also important. The justices give a high priority to speech that takes place in a "traditional public forum." Streets, sidewalks, parks, and other areas where the public freely congregates and traditionally exchanges views fall into this category. A slightly lower degree of protection is accorded speech that occurs in a "designated or limited public forum." This includes areas that the government has dedicated to expression, such as city auditoriums and public meeting rooms. And the lowest level of protection is given to speech that occurs in a "nonpublic forum." This category encompasses government facilities that traditionally have not been locations for public discourse (jails, defense plants, polling places, nuclear facilities, and so on) and private property where the owner has not given consent.

Since the 1970s justices have also made sharp distinctions between content-based and content-neutral speech regulations. Content-based regulations are those that discriminate based on subject matter of the expression or the message conveyed. A good example is provided by *Chicago Police Department v. Mosley* (1972), where the Court unanimously struck down an ordinance that prohibited picketing within 150 feet of a school during school hours but made an exception for peaceful labor picketing. Justice Thurgood Marshall stated the Court's position clearly: "But, above all else, the First Amendment means that government has no power to restrict expression because of its message, its ideas, its subject matter, or its content. . . . Once a forum is opened up to assembly or speaking by some groups, government may not prohibit others from assembling or speaking on the basis of what they intend to say." Government may have a legitimate reason to limit expression at certain locations or certain times, but it must apply the restriction to all speech rather than making distinctions based on the content of the expression.

The Court has adopted the policy that content-based regulations can survive constitutional attack only if the interests pursued by the government are compelling ones and the constraints are narrowly tailored to achieve those interests. That is, the law should impose the least restriction of expression necessary for the government to attain its compelling goals. The Court, therefore, gives strict scrutiny to content-based regulations, the highest and most exacting standard used by the justices.

Content-neutral regulations, on the other hand, do not take into account the subject matter of the expression or the viewpoint expressed. A local ordinance, for example, that prohibits all door-to-door solicitation in residential areas between 8:00 P.M. and 8:00 A.M. is content neutral. The ban applies to religious proselytizers, political campaign workers, and even youngsters selling Girl Scout cookies. Here the government is pursuing the legitimate interest of ensuring a peaceful atmosphere at a time when most residents are resting. There is no government censorship based on the content of the views expressed. The Court takes a more lenient position on content-neutral regulations, permitting governments to impose reasonable time, place, and manner restrictions if these are designed to meet legitimate government goals.

In pursuit of this general approach to expression rights, the Supreme Court has designated legitimate interests that justify government regulation as well as forms of regulation that are inconsistent with First Amendment commands.

Government Interests and Speech Regulation

Under what conditions, then, may the government restrict expression? From the Court's decisions we can distill general categories of expressive behavior that concern legitimate government interests and may trigger valid government regulation.

Forms of Expression outside First Amendment Scope. Certain classes of expression have always been considered unprotected by the Constitution. Chief among these are obscenity and libel. As we shall see in Chapter 7, if expression meets the Court's rather strict definitions of libel or obscenity, the First Amendment imposes no barrier to government regulation.

Violence. The government has authority to protect citizens from personal injury. If expression takes a violent form or incites others to violence, the government may regulate it.

Property Damage. The government has a legitimate interest in protecting private and public property from being destroyed or damaged. Antiwar protesters, for example, who express themselves by setting fire to a National Guard armory have gone beyond their First Amendment guarantees and can be arrested for their conduct.

Criminal Speech. Some forms of expression are crimes by their very nature. For example, the Constitution does not protect those who might give military secrets to the enemy in time of war, engage in conspiracies to violate valid criminal laws, or lie under oath.

Encroaching on the Rights of Others. Freedom of expression does not provide a license to infringe on the rights of others. If animal rights protesters block an entrance to a zoo or pro-life groups prevent access to an abortion clinic, the government may intervene. In both cases, the protesters have curtailed the right of the public to move about without interference.

Burdens on Government Functions. Regulation is permissible if expression places a burden on a legitimate government function. If, for example, environmentalists lie down in front of bulldozers to prevent the construction of a dam by the U.S. Army Corps of Engineers, the government may remove them.

Trespass. The freedom of expression does not include the right to speak anywhere one wishes. A campaign worker, for example, does not have the right to come into your home without permission to promote the candidate's cause. Similarly, some public facilities are not legitimate places for groups of demonstrators to congregate. The government may, for example, prohibit antiwar activists from conducting a rally on a military base or demonstrators from entering a Veterans Administration hospital to protest the quality of medical care provided.

Time, Place, and Manner Restrictions. The recognition of legitimate reasons for regulation has given rise to the Court's time, place, and manner doctrine. By this standard the Court acknowledges that government has the general authority to impose reasonable time, place, and manner restrictions on the freedom of expression. Therefore, the Court would certainly uphold the arrest of demonstrators who gathered in the middle of an expressway or of political zealots who promoted their candidate by driving a sound truck through a residential area at 2:00 A.M.

Restraints on Government Power

Although the Court has been sympathetic to the government's need to regulate expression under certain carefully defined conditions, the justices also have been careful to place restraints on the government to prevent abuse. The Court has constructed generally accepted criteria to hold the government's power within acceptable bounds.

Appropriate Purpose. Any government restriction on freedom of expression must have a clearly defined, valid government purpose. A law that makes inciting to riot a crime, for example, would rest on the legitimate government purpose of curtailing violence. A law prohibiting criticism of the president, motivated by an interest in keeping incumbents in power, would clearly fail this test. In some areas the Court has demanded that the government's purpose be legitimate; in others, the justices have required a higher standard—that the purpose be a compelling one.

Prior Restraint. Government may prosecute individuals who violate legitimate restrictions on expression but, absent extraordinary circumstances, may not intervene before the fact. For example, the government may not constitutionally require a speaker to submit for review a copy of his or her speech before its delivery to ensure that nothing in it may incite the audience to violence.

Content and Viewpoint Discrimination. Laws regulating expression should be content and viewpoint neutral. It is not the government's role to evaluate expression based on the positions taken by the speaker. For example, a local ordinance that allows public gatherings for all groups except political organizations would be guilty of content discrimination. Viewpoint discrimination is an even more serious form of content-based regulation. An ordinance, for example, that permits demonstrations by prowar groups but not antiwar organizations would violate the principle against viewpoint discrimination. Restrictions based on content or viewpoint are subject to strict judicial scrutiny and are unlikely to survive a court challenge.

Overbreadth. Any regulation of expression must be narrowly tailored to meet the government's objectives. If a legislature, concerned with protests that cause violence, passes a law prohibiting all public demonstrations, the statute would fail the narrow construction requirement. This regulatory scheme would be overbroad, going far beyond what is necessary to deal with the legislature's legitimate concern by restricting constitutionally protected expression along with unprotected speech.

Vagueness. Legislatures must draft laws restricting freedom of expression with sufficient precision to give fair notice as to what is being regulated. If normally intelligent people have to guess what a statute means and are likely to come to different conclusions about what is prohibited by it, the statute is unconstitutionally vague.

Chilling Effect. A law intended to regulate certain forms of illegitimate expression cannot be written so as to make people fearful of engaging in legitimate activity. Often such a chilling effect stems from statutes that are vague or overbroad. Assume that a state legislature, concerned about sexual activity at nightclubs, passes a law making it illegal to serve alcohol in any establishment featuring nude entertainment. In response to that law, museum officials might be fearful of sponsoring a gathering at which patrons would sip wine while viewing an exhibition of paintings that includes nude figures. Here a statute intended to curb obscenity and indecent behavior creates a chilling effect on the exercise of legitimate activities.

CONTENT AND CONTEXTS

As you read the cases and commentary in the rest of this chapter and the three that follow, keep in mind the principles discussed in the previous section. You will observe many examples of the justices debating whether the expression in question merits regulation and whether the methods of regulation are constitutionally proper. You will witness the flexibility of these standards as the Court adjusts them to different contexts. Finally, you will see how individual justices differ in the ways they apply these standards based on their own ideologies and preferences.

Symbolic Speech

The First Amendment specifically protects the freedoms of speech and press, two forms of expression with which the framers were thoroughly familiar. In the days of the Revolution, political protest customarily took the form of eloquent addresses, sharply worded editorials, and fiery pamphlets. Verbal expression and published communication were the methods of political debate, and the founders unambiguously sought to protect them from government encroachment by drafting and ratifying the First Amendment.

But much has changed since then. The breadth and complexity of political and social views held by Americans have increased exponentially since the Revolution. The development of modern technology has multiplied the ways Americans can express those views, both individually and collectively. Many of these new methods go well beyond the traditional spoken and printed word.

Since the early 1960s, protest movements of all kinds have shown their opposition to government policies by expressive actions such as mass demonstrations, picketing, effigy burnings, and even flag desecration. But if a point is made by such actions rather than by verbal expression, does the First Amendment still grant immunity from government regulation? This question deals with symbolic speech and whether expressive conduct qualifies as speech under the meaning of the First Amendment. The Supreme Court has a long history of dealing with such issues.

Most of the symbolic speech cases have occurred in the modern period, but the debate over expressive conduct began much earlier. Recall the discussion of *Stromberg v. California* (1931), in which a camp counselor was convicted not because of anything she said but because she raised a red flag, an expressive act that

conflicted with California law. In reversing Stromberg's conviction on First Amendment grounds, the Supreme Court acknowledged that at least some forms of symbolic speech merit constitutional protection. Similarly, ***Thornhill v. Alabama*** (1940) struck down state laws that prohibited labor union picketing. For the Court, Justice Murphy concluded, "In the circumstances of our times the dissemination of information concerning the facts of a labor dispute must be regarded as within that area of free discussion that is guaranteed by the Constitution."

Decisions such as these established the principle that symbolic actions can qualify as speech and be accorded First Amendment protection. This principle does not mean, however, that the First Amendment shields from government regulation *any* act committed to express an idea or opinion. No one, for example, would seriously claim that assassination is a protected form of expressing political opposition. Perhaps even more than verbal expression, symbolic speech presents especially difficult questions of drawing constitutional boundaries, and the issue grows in complexity when expression combines speech and nonspeech elements.

The turbulence of the late 1960s brought a number of vexing symbolic expression issues before the Court. The first of these cases was *United States v. O'Brien* (1968), in which the defendants had expressed their opposition to the war in Southeast Asia by publicly and illegally burning their draft cards. The case presents a clash of values. The Warren Court had demonstrated a growing tolerance for First Amendment expression claims, but would this trend continue? Or would the fact that thousands of American troops were engaged in combat abroad influence the Court?

United States v. O'Brien

391 U.S. 367 (1968)
http://laws.findlaw.com/US/391/367.html
Oral arguments are available at http://www.oyez.org.
Vote: 7 (Black, Brennan, Fortas, Harlan, Stewart, Warren, White)
  1 (Douglas)

OPINION OF THE COURT: Warren
CONCURRING OPINION: Harlan
DISSENTING OPINION: Douglas
NOT PARTICIPATING: Marshall

FACTS:

On March 31, 1966, David O'Brien and three others burned their draft cards on the steps of a South Boston courthouse. A sizable, hostile crowd gathered. Agents of the Federal Bureau of Investigation took the four into

On March 31, 1966, David O'Brien and three other antiwar protesters demonstrated their opposition to U.S. military action in Vietnam by burning their draft cards on the steps of the South Boston courthouse. Their convictions for violating the Selective Service Act were affirmed in United States v. O'Brien.

the courthouse to protect them and to question them. The agents told O'Brien that he had violated a 1965 amendment to the Selective Service Act of 1948, making it illegal to "destroy or mutilate" draft cards. O'Brien replied that he understood but had burned his card anyway because he was "a pacifist and as such [could not] kill." After a federal court ruled that O'Brien had acted within the bounds of the Constitution, the United States asked the Supreme Court to hear the case.

ARGUMENTS:

For the petitioner, United States:
- Draft card burning is conduct, not speech.
- The burning of a document which plays a valid and important role in the operation of the Selective Service System does not qualify as constitutionally protected symbolic speech.
- Requiring the possession of draft cards is a reasonable congressional action supporting the effective administration of the Selective Service Act.

For the respondent, David Paul O'Brien:
- Congress passed the 1965 amendment to the Selective Service Act with the intent to stifle dissent. The law does not serve any rational legislative purpose.
- The law unconstitutionally restricts freedom of symbolic expression recognized in *Stromberg v.*

California and *West Virginia State Board of Education v. Barnette.*
- The clear and present danger test should be used to decide this case.

MR. CHIEF JUSTICE WARREN DELIVERED THE OPINION OF THE COURT.

O'Brien . . . argues that the 1965 Amendment is unconstitutional as applied to him because his act of burning his registration certificate was protected "symbolic speech" within the First Amendment. His argument is that the freedom of expression which the First Amendment guarantees includes all modes of "communication of ideas by conduct," and that his conduct is within this definition because he did it in "demonstration against the war and against the draft."

We cannot accept the view that an apparently limitless variety of conduct can be labeled "speech" whenever the person engaging in the conduct intends thereby to express an idea. However, even on the assumption that the alleged communicative element in O'Brien's conduct is sufficient to bring into play the First Amendment, it does not necessarily follow that the destruction of a registration certificate is constitutionally protected activity. This Court has held that when "speech" and "nonspeech" elements are combined in the same course of conduct, a sufficiently important governmental interest in regulating the nonspeech element can justify incidental limitations on First Amendment freedoms. To characterize the quality of the governmental interest which must appear, the Court has employed a variety of descriptive terms: compelling; substantial; subordinating; paramount; cogent; strong. Whatever imprecision inheres in these terms, we think it clear that a government regulation is sufficiently justified if it is within the constitutional power of the Government; if it furthers an important or substantial governmental interest; if the governmental interest is unrelated to the suppression of free expression; and if the incidental restriction on alleged First Amendment freedoms is no greater than is essential to the furtherance of that interest. We find that the 1965 Amendment to §12(b)(3) of the Universal Military Training and Service Act meets all of these requirements, and consequently that O'Brien can be constitutionally convicted for violating it.

The constitutional power of Congress to raise and support armies and to make all laws necessary and proper to that end is broad and sweeping. The power of Congress to classify and conscript manpower for military service is "beyond question." Pursuant to this power, Congress may establish a system of registration for individuals liable for training and service, and may require such individuals within reason to cooperate in the registration system. The issuance of certificates indicating the registration and eligibility classification of individuals is a legitimate and substantial administrative aid in the functioning of this system. And legislation to insure the continuing availability of issued certificates serves a legitimate and substantial purpose in the system's administration.

O'Brien's argument to the contrary is necessarily premised upon his unrealistic characterization of Selective Service certificates. He essentially adopts the position that such certificates are so many pieces of paper designed to notify registrants of their registration or classification, to be retained or tossed in the wastebasket according to the convenience or taste of the registrant. Once the registrant has received notification, according to this view, there is no reason for him to retain the certificates. O'Brien notes that most of the information on a registration certificate serves no notification purpose at all; the registrant hardly needs to be told his address and physical characteristics. We agree that the registration certificate contains much information of which the registrant needs no notification. This circumstance, however, does not lead to the conclusion

that the certificate serves no purpose, but that, like the classification certificate, it serves purposes in addition to initial notification. Many of these purposes would be defeated by the certificates' destruction or mutilation. Among these are:

1. The registration certificate serves as proof that the individual described thereon has registered for the draft. The classification certificate shows the eligibility classification of a named but undescribed individual. Voluntarily displaying the two certificates is an easy and painless way for a young man to dispel a question as to whether he might be delinquent in his Selective Service obligations. . . . Additionally, in a time of national crisis, reasonable availability to each registrant of the two small cards assures a rapid and uncomplicated means for determining his fitness for immediate induction, no matter how distant in our mobile society he may be from his local board.

2. The information supplied on the certificates facilitates communication between registrants and local boards, simplifying the system and benefiting all concerned. To begin with, each certificate bears the address of the registrant's local board, an item unlikely to be committed to memory. Further, each card bears the registrant's Selective Service number, and a registrant who has his number readily available so that he can communicate it to his local board can make simpler the board's task in locating his file. Finally, a registrant's inquiry, particularly through a local board other than his own, concerning his eligibility status is frequently answerable simply on the basis of his classification certificate; whereas, if the certificate were not reasonably available and the registrants were uncertain of his classification, the task of answering his questions would be considerably complicated.

3. Both certificates carry continual reminders that the registrant must notify his local board of any change of address, and other specified changes in his status. The smooth functioning of the system requires that local boards be continually aware of the status and whereabouts of registrants, and the destruction of certificates deprives the system of a potentially useful notice device.

4. The regulatory scheme involving Selective Service certificates includes clearly valid prohibitions against the alteration, forgery, or similar deceptive misuse of certificates. The destruction or mutilation of certificates obviously increases the difficulty of detecting and tracing

abuses such as these. Further, a mutilated certificate might itself be used for deceptive purposes.

The many functions performed by Selective Service certificates establish beyond doubt that Congress has a legitimate and substantial interest in preventing their wanton and unrestrained destruction and assuring their continuing availability by punishing people who knowingly and willfully destroy or mutilate them. . . .

We think it apparent that the continuing availability to each registrant of his Selective Service certificates substantially furthers the smooth and proper functioning of the system that Congress has established to raise armies. We think it also apparent that the Nation has a vital interest in having a system for raising armies that functions with maximum efficiency and is capable of easily and quickly responding to continually changing circumstances. For these reasons, the Government has a substantial interest in assuring the continuing availability of issued Selective Service certificates.

It is equally clear that the 1965 Amendment specifically protects this substantial government interest. We perceive no alternative means that would more precisely and narrowly assure the continuing availability of issued Selective Service certificates than a law which prohibits their willful mutilation or destruction. The 1965 Amendment prohibits such conduct and does nothing more. In other words, both the governmental interest and the operation of the 1965 Amendment are limited to the noncommunicative aspect of O'Brien's conduct. The governmental interest and the scope of the 1965 Amendment are limited to preventing harm to the smooth and efficient functioning of the Selective Service System. When O'Brien deliberately rendered unavailable his registration certificate, he willfully frustrated this governmental interest. For this noncommunicative impact of his conduct, and for nothing else, he was convicted. . . .

In conclusion, we find that because of the Government's substantial interest in assuring the continuing availability of issued Selective Service certificates, because amended §462(b) is an appropriately narrow means of protecting this interest and condemns only the independent noncommunicative impact of conduct within its reach, and because the noncommunicative impact of O'Brien's act of burning his registration certificate frustrated the Government's interest, a sufficient governmental interest has been shown to justify O'Brien's conviction.

Warren's opinion explicitly rejects the position that conduct used to express an idea automatically merits First Amendment protection. The Court held that whenever "speech" and "nonspeech" elements are combined, a sufficiently important government interest in regulating the nonspeech element can justify limitations on First Amendment rights. As applied in this case, the Court found that O'Brien's conduct (burning the draft card) placed a burden on a legitimate government activity (the power to raise and support armies). The government had a substantial interest in exercising its military authority, and the draft registration system was a reasonable means of achieving that end. Consequently, the government had the constitutional power to prosecute individuals who violated the Selective Service laws even if the acts in question communicated a message of political protest.

Among all symbolic expression issues, none has given the Court greater difficulty than flag desecration. As a national symbol, the American flag can evoke strong feelings, especially among people who have a history of public service, as do most members of the Supreme Court. Even those justices most committed to freedom of expression have indicated their discomfort in extending First Amendment protection to someone who destroys the flag as a method of political expression.

During the civil rights and Vietnam War protest years, the Court took two cases involving mistreatment of the flag. In the first, *Street v. New York* (1969), the justices heard the appeal of a civil rights protester who had verbally insulted the flag and set it on fire. The justices held that the pure speech elements of the protest were protected under the First Amendment, but they deadlocked, 4–4, on the issue of whether the burning of the flag enjoyed a similar constitutional privilege. In the second case, *Spence v. Washington* (1974), the Court again took up the physical desecration issue. Here an antiwar protester displayed an American flag with a large peace symbol taped to both sides. The justices ruled that the protester's actions constituted symbolic speech constitutionally immune from government regulation.

As the war in Vietnam abated, so did the protest cases. *Spence* had given constitutional protection to one fairly mild version of flag desecration, but would the justices come to the same conclusion with respect to more extreme forms of abusing the flag? That question was not answered until 1989, when the Court heard *Texas v. Johnson*.

Texas v. Johnson

491 U.S. 397 (1989)
http://laws.findlaw.com/US/491/397.html
Oral arguments are available at http://www.oyez.org.
Vote: 5 (Blackmun, Brennan, Kennedy, Marshall, Scalia)
    4 (O'Connor, Rehnquist, Stevens, White)

OPINION OF THE COURT: *Brennan*
CONCURRING OPINION: *Kennedy*
DISSENTING OPINIONS: *Rehnquist, Stevens*

FACTS:

In the summer of 1984 the Republican Party held its national convention in Dallas, Texas, and overwhelmingly supported President Ronald Reagan's reelection bid. While the party was meeting, a group of seventy-five to one hundred demonstrators marched through the city to protest the Reagan administration's policies. One of the demonstrators removed an American flag hanging in front of a bank building and gave it to Gregory Lee Johnson, one of the leaders of the march. As the march ended, Johnson unfurled the flag, doused it with kerosene, and set it on fire. As it burned, the protesters chanted, "America, the red, white, and blue, we spit on you." Authorities arrested Johnson, charging him with violating the Texas flag desecration law. He was convicted and sentenced to a one-year prison term and a $2,000 fine. A state court of appeals affirmed, but the Texas Court of Criminal Appeals reversed that holding.

ARGUMENTS:

For the petitioner, State of Texas:

- The First Amendment is not absolute, and expressive conduct demands less constitutional protection than pure speech.
- The Texas flag desecration statute advances two substantial interests: (1) protection of the flag as an important symbol of nationhood and unity, and (2) prevention of a breach of the peace.
- The Texas law is a valid "time, place, and manner" restriction on demonstrations.

For the respondent, Gregory Lee Johnson:

- The Texas statute is a viewpoint-based restriction on political expression because the state seeks to protect one view—that the flag is a symbol of nationhood and national unity.
- Because the state law singles out conduct that will "seriously offend one or more persons," the statute violates the First Amendment's prohibition on content-based discrimination.

- Johnson peacefully burned the flag in an obvious act of political expression that merits First Amendment protection.

 JUSTICE BRENNAN DELIVERED THE OPINION OF THE COURT.

Johnson was convicted of flag desecration for burning the flag rather than for uttering insulting words. This fact somewhat complicates our consideration of his conviction under the First Amendment. We must first determine whether Johnson's burning of the flag constituted expressive conduct, permitting him to invoke the First Amendment in challenging his conviction. If his conduct was expressive, we next decide whether the State's regulation is related to the suppression of free expression. If the State's regulation is not related to expression, then the less stringent standard we announced in *United States v. O'Brien* for regulations of noncommunicative conduct controls. If it is, then we are outside of *O'Brien*'s test, and we must ask whether this interest justifies Johnson's conviction under a more demanding standard. A third possibility is that the State's asserted interest is simply not implicated on these facts, and in that event the interest drops out of the picture.

The First Amendment literally forbids the abridgement only of 'speech,' but we have long recognized that its protection does not end at the spoken or written word. While we have rejected "the view that an apparently limitless variety of conduct can be labeled "speech" whenever the person engaging in the conduct intends thereby to express an idea," we have acknowledged that conduct may be "sufficiently imbued with elements of communication to fall within the scope of the First and Fourteenth Amendments."

In deciding whether particular conduct possesses sufficient communicative elements to bring the First Amendment into play, we have asked whether "[a]n intent to convey a particularized message was present, and [whether] the likelihood was great that the message would be understood by those who viewed it." Hence, we have recognized the expressive nature of students' wearing of black armbands to protest American military involvement in Vietnam. . . .

Especially pertinent to this case are our decisions recognizing the communicative nature of conduct relating to flags. Attaching a peace sign to the flag, saluting the flag, and displaying a red flag, we have held, all may find shelter under the First Amendment. That we have had little difficulty identifying an expressive element in

Gregory Johnson on June 28, 1989, holding an American flag given to him by a well-wisher. One week earlier the U.S. Supreme Court had reversed his conviction for violating the Texas flag desecration statute.

conduct relating to flags should not be surprising. The very purpose of a national flag is to serve as a symbol of our country; it is, one might say, "the one visible manifestation of two hundred years of nationhood." . . .

We have not automatically concluded, however, that any action taken with respect to our flag is expressive. Instead, in characterizing such action for First Amendment purposes, we have considered the context in which it occurred. . . .

. . . Johnson burned an American flag as part—indeed, as the culmination—of a political demonstration that coincided with the convening of the Republican Party and its renomination of Ronald Reagan for President. . . . In these circumstances, Johnson's burning of the flag was conduct "sufficiently imbued with elements of communication" to implicate the First Amendment.

The Government generally has a freer hand in restricting expressive conduct than it has in restricting the written or spoken word. . . . "A law *directed at* communicative nature of conduct must, like a law directed at speech itself, be justified by the substantial showing of need that the First Amendment requires." It is, in short, not simply the verbal or nonverbal nature of the expression, but the governmental interest at stake, that helps to determine whether a restriction on that expression is valid.

Thus, although we have recognized that where "'speech' and 'nonspeech' elements are combined in the same course of conduct, a sufficiently important governmental interest in regulating the nonspeech element can justify incidental limitations on First Amendment freedoms," we have limited the applicability of *O'Brien*'s relatively lenient standard to those cases in which "the governmental interest is unrelated to the suppression of free expression." In stating, moreover, that *O'Brien*'s test "in the last analysis is little, if any, different from the standard applied to time, place, or manner restrictions," we have highlighted the requirement that the governmental interest in question be unconnected to expression in order to come under *O'Brien*'s less demanding rule.

In order to decide whether *O'Brien*'s test applies here, therefore, we must decide whether Texas has asserted an interest in support of Johnson's conviction that is unrelated to the suppression of expression. If we find that an interest asserted by the State is simply not implicated on the facts before us, we need not ask whether *O'Brien*'s test applies. The State offers two separate interests to justify this conviction: preventing breaches of the peace, and preserving the flag as a symbol of nationhood and national unity. We hold that the first interest is not implicated on this record and that the second is related to the suppression of expression.

Texas claims that its interest in preventing breaches of the peace justifies Johnson's conviction for flag desecration. However, no disturbance of the peace actually occurred or threatened to occur because of Johnson's burning of the flag. . . .

The State's position, therefore, amounts to a claim that an audience that takes serious offense at particular expression is necessarily likely to disturb the peace and that the expression may be prohibited on this basis. Our precedents do not countenance such a presumption. On the contrary, they recognize that a principal "function of free speech under our system of government is to invite dispute. It may indeed best serve its high purpose when it induces a condition of unrest, creates dissatisfaction with conditions as they are, or even stirs people to anger." . . .

Nor does Johnson's expressive conduct fall within that small class of "fighting words" that are "likely to provoke the average person to retaliation, and thereby cause a breach of the peace." No reasonable onlooker would have regarded Johnson's generalized expression of dissatisfaction with the policies of the Federal Government as a direct personal insult or an invitation to exchange fisticuffs.

We thus conclude that the State's interest in maintaining order is not implicated on these facts. The State need not worry that our holding will disable it from preserving the peace. We do not suggest that the First Amendment forbids a State to prevent "imminent lawless action." . . .

The State also asserts an interest in preserving the flag as a symbol of nationhood and national unity. In *Spence* [*v. Washington,* 1974], we acknowledged that the Government's interest in preserving the flag's special symbolic value "is directly related to expression in the context of activity" such as affixing a peace symbol to a flag. We are equally persuaded that this interest is related to expression in the case of Johnson's burning of the flag. The State, apparently, is concerned that such conduct will lead people to believe either that the flag does not stand for nationhood and national unity, but instead reflects other, less positive concepts, or that the concepts reflected in the flag do not in fact exist, that is, we do not enjoy unity as a Nation. These concerns blossom only when a person's treatment of the flag communicates some message, and thus are related "to the suppression of free expression" within the meaning of *O'Brien.* We are thus outside of *O'Brien*'s test altogether.

It remains to consider whether the State's interest in preserving the flag as a symbol of nationhood and national unity justifies Johnson's conviction. . . .

. . . Johnson's political expression was restricted because of the content of the message he conveyed. We must therefore subject the State's asserted interest in preserving the special symbolic character of the flag to "the most exacting scrutiny."

Texas argues that its interest in preserving the flag as a symbol of nationhood and national unity survives this close analysis. Quoting extensively from the writings of this Court chronicling the flag's historic and symbolic role in our society, the State emphasizes the "'special place'" reserved for the flag in our Nation. The State's argument is not that it has an interest simply in maintaining the flag as a symbol of *something,* no matter what it symbolizes; indeed, if that were the State's position, it would be difficult to see how that interest is endangered by highly symbolic conduct such as Johnson's. Rather, the State's claim is that it has an interest

in preserving the flag as a symbol of *nationhood* and *national unity,* a symbol with a determinate range of meanings. According to Texas, if one physically treats the flag in a way that would tend to cast doubt on either the idea that nationhood and national unity are the flag's referents or that national unity actually exists, the message conveyed thereby is a harmful one and therefore may be prohibited.

If there is a bedrock principle underlying the First Amendment, it is that the Government may not prohibit the expression of an idea simply because society finds the idea itself offensive or disagreeable.

We have not recognized an exception to this principle even where our flag has been involved. In *Street v. New York* we held that a State may not criminally punish a person for uttering words critical of the flag. . . .

In short, nothing in our precedents suggests that a State may foster its own view of the flag by prohibiting expressive conduct relating to it. To bring its argument outside our precedents, Texas attempts to convince us that even if its interest in preserving the flag's symbolic role does not allow it to prohibit words or some expressive conduct critical of the flag, it does permit it to forbid the outright destruction of the flag. The State's argument cannot depend here on the distinction between written or spoken words and nonverbal conduct. That distinction, we have shown, is of no moment where the nonverbal conduct is expressive, as it is here, and where the regulation of that conduct is related to expression, as it is here. . . .

Texas' focus on the precise nature of Johnson's expression, moreover, misses the point of our prior decisions: their enduring lesson, that the Government may not prohibit expression simply because it disagrees with its message, is not dependent on the particular mode in which one chooses to express an idea. . . .

There is, moreover, no indication—either in the text of the Constitution or in our cases interpreting it—that a separate juridical category exists for the American flag alone. Indeed, we would not be surprised to learn that the persons who framed our Constitution and wrote the Amendment that we now construe were not known for their reverence for the Union Jack. The First Amendment does not guarantee that other concepts virtually sacred to our Nation as a whole—such as the principle that discrimination on the basis of race is odious and destructive—will go unquestioned in the marketplace of ideas. We decline, therefore, to create for the flag an exception to the joust of principles protected by the First Amendment. . . .

The way to preserve the flag's special role is not to punish those who feel differently about these matters. It is to persuade them that they are wrong. . . . And, precisely because it is our flag that is involved, one's response to the flag-burner may exploit the uniquely persuasive power of the flag itself. We can imagine no more appropriate response to burning a flag than waving one's own, no better way to counter a flag-burner's message than by saluting the flag that burns, no surer means of preserving the dignity even of the flag that burned than by—as one witness here did—according its remains a respectful burial. We do not consecrate the flag by punishing its desecration, for in doing so we dilute the freedom that this cherished emblem represents.

Johnson was convicted for engaging in expressive conduct. The State's interest in preventing breaches of the peace does not support his conviction because Johnson's conduct did not threaten to disturb the peace. Nor does the State's interest in preserving the flag as a symbol of nationhood and national unity justify his criminal conviction for engaging in political expression. The judgment of the Texas Court of Criminal Appeals is therefore

Affirmed.

JUSTICE KENNEDY, concurring.

I write not to qualify the words JUSTICE BRENNAN chooses so well, for he says with power all that is necessary to explain our ruling. I join his opinion without reservation, but with a keen sense that this case, like others before us from time to time, exacts its personal toll. . . .

The hard fact is that sometimes we must make decisions we do not like. We make them because they are right, right in the sense that the law and the Constitution, as we see them, compel the result. And so great is our commitment to the process that, except in the rare case, we do not pause to express distaste for the result, perhaps for fear of undermining a valued principle that dictates the decision. This is one of those rare cases.

CHIEF JUSTICE REHNQUIST, with whom JUSTICE WHITE and JUSTICE O'CONNOR join, dissenting.

In holding this Texas statute unconstitutional, the Court ignores Justice Holmes' familiar aphorism that "a page of history is worth a volume of logic." *New York Trust Co. v. Eisner* (1921). For more than 200 years, the American flag has occupied a unique position as the symbol of our Nation, a uniqueness that justifies a governmental

prohibition against flag burning in the way respondent Johnson did here. . . .

The American flag . . . has come to be the visible symbol embodying our Nation. It does not represent the views of any particular political party, and it does not represent any particular political philosophy. The flag is not simply another "idea" or "point of view" competing for recognition in the marketplace of ideas. Millions and millions of Americans regard it with an almost mystical reverence regardless of what sort of social, political, or philosophical beliefs they may have. I cannot agree that the First Amendment invalidates the Act of Congress, and the laws of 48 of the 50 States, which make criminal the public burning of the flag. . . .

. . . [T]he public burning of the American flag by Johnson was no essential part of any exposition of ideas, and at the same time it had a tendency to incite a breach of the peace. Johnson was free to make any verbal denunciation of the flag that he wished; indeed, he was free to burn the flag in private. He could publicly burn other symbols of the Government or effigies of political leaders. He did lead a march through the streets of Dallas, and conducted a rally in front of the Dallas City Hall. He engaged in a "die-in" to protest nuclear weapons. He shouted out various slogans during the march, including: "Reagan, Mondale which will it be? Either one means World War III"; "Ronald Reagan, killer of the hour, Perfect example of U.S. power"; and "red, white and blue, we spit on you, you stand for plunder, you will go under." For none of these acts was he arrested or prosecuted; it was only when he proceeded to burn publicly an American flag stolen from its rightful owner that he violated the Texas statute. . . .

. . . The Texas statute deprived Johnson of only one rather inarticulate symbolic form of protest—a form of protest that was profoundly offensive to many—and left him with a full panoply of other symbols and every conceivable form of verbal expression to express his deep disapproval of national policy. Thus, in no way can it be said that Texas is punishing him because his hearers—or any other group of people—were profoundly opposed to the message that he sought to convey. Such opposition is no proper basis for restricting speech or expression under the First Amendment. It was Johnson's use of this particular symbol, and not the idea that he sought to convey by it or by his many other expressions, for which he was punished. . . .

. . . Uncritical extension of constitutional protection to the burning of the flag risks the frustration of the very purpose for which organized governments are instituted. The Court decides that the American flag is just another symbol, about which not only must opinions pro and con be tolerated, but for which the most minimal public respect may not be enjoined. The government may conscript men into the Armed Forces where they must fight and perhaps die for the flag, but the government may not prohibit the public burning of the banner under which they fight. I would uphold the Texas statute as applied in this case.

JUSTICE STEVENS, dissenting.

As the Court analyzes this case, it presents the question whether the State of Texas, or indeed the Federal Government, has the power to prohibit the public desecration of the American flag. The question is unique. In my judgment, rules that apply to a host of other symbols, such as state flags, armbands, or various privately promoted emblems of political or commercial identity, are not necessarily controlling. Even if flag burning could be considered just another species of symbolic speech under the logical application of the rules that the Court has developed in its interpretation of the First Amendment in other contexts, this case has an intangible dimension that makes those rules inapplicable. . . .

The value of the flag as a symbol cannot be measured. Even so, I have no doubt that the interest in preserving that value for the future is both significant and legitimate. Conceivably, that value will be enhanced by the Court's conclusion that our national commitment to free expression is so strong that even the United States, as ultimate guarantor of that freedom, is without power to prohibit the desecration of its unique symbol. But I am unpersuaded. The creation of a federal right to post bulletin boards and graffiti on the Washington Monument might enlarge the market for free expression, but at a cost I would not pay. Similarly, in my considered judgment, sanctioning the public desecration of the flag will tarnish its value—both for those who cherish the ideas for which it waves and for those who desire to don the robes of martyrdom by burning it. That tarnish is not justified by the trivial burden on free expression occasioned by requiring that an available, alternative mode of expression—including uttering words critical of the flag, see Street v. New York (1969)—be employed. . . .

I respectfully dissent.

The Court's decision in *Johnson* is intriguing for a number of reasons. Note, for example, the rather odd alignments: the conservative Antonin Scalia and the usually conservative Anthony Kennedy voted with the majority; John Paul Stevens, almost always found with the liberal wing of the Court, dissented.

Perhaps most important was the tremendous—and, to some, surprising—uproar created by the Court's ruling. President George H. W. Bush immediately condemned it, and public opinion polls indicated that Americans generally favored a constitutional amendment overturning *Johnson.* But, after some politicking by civil liberties groups, senators, and representatives, Congress did not propose an amendment. Instead, it passed the Flag Protection Act of 1989, which penalized by a one-year jail sentence and a $1,000 fine anyone who "knowingly mutilates, defaces, physically defiles, burns, maintains on the floor or ground, or tramples upon any flag of the United States."

Because the federal act differed from the Texas law at issue in *Johnson*—it banned flag desecration regardless of the motivation of the burner, whereas the Texas law did so only if a jury found the activity to be offensive—some thought it would meet approval in the Supreme Court. Others saw this difference as relatively insignificant, and they were correct. In *United States v. Eichman* (1990) the Court, using the same reasoning expressed in *Johnson* and by the same vote, struck down this law as a violation of the First Amendment. *(See Box 5-6.)*

Public Forums and the Preservation of Order

Preserving public order and protecting citizens from injury caused by violence are among the essential duties of government. The Preamble to the Constitution includes ensuring "domestic Tranquility" among the six basic purposes for which the new government was formed. On some occasions, free expression can threaten order, especially when the expression takes place in a public forum or when it takes the form of a mass demonstration. If order breaks down, results may include bodily injury, property destruction, and the inability of the public to move freely. The government may not be able to carry out its duties. In any of these situations, a conflict arises between the nation's commitment to freedom of expression and the government's duty to maintain order. At what point is government constitutionally justified in repressing expression to stop or prevent violence?

BOX 5-6 AFTERMATH . . . GREGORY LEE JOHNSON

Shortly after the Supreme Court decided that Gregory Lee Johnson's burning of the American flag during the 1984 Republican National Convention was political expression protected by the First Amendment, Congress responded by passing the Flag Protection Act of 1989.

On October 30, two days after the new law took effect, a small group of demonstrators gathered on the steps of the Capitol in Washington to protest. Because the press had been informed that the protesters would burn flags, reporters, police, and curious passersby crowded the area. Suddenly four men separated themselves from the crowd and began to set fire to American flags.

The police reacted quickly—too quickly for one of the protesters. Gregory Lee Johnson was stopped before he could ignite his flag. Authorities arrested and prosecuted the other three demonstrators but ignored Johnson.

Represented by William Kunstler, an attorney well known for defending radical causes, the three protesters argued that the new flag desecration law was just as constitutionally flawed as the Texas statute struck down earlier. When the justices issued their opinion in *United States v. Eichman,* the protesters prevailed, defeating the government's case presented by Solicitor General Kenneth Starr. (Starr later gained notoriety as the independent counsel whose investigation into the activities of President Bill Clinton led to Clinton's impeachment by the House of Representatives.) In the end, it was Shawn Eichman's name, not Johnson's, that was attached to the Supreme Court's decision. Johnson, who had hoped to win another place in legal history, sharply criticized the police and prosecutors, claiming that his failure to be prosecuted with the others was a "gross miscarriage of justice."

SOURCES: *Washington Post,* October 31 and November 1, 1989; *New York Times,* April 11, 1990.

To deal with such expression, the justices have promulgated legal criteria distinct from those they use to adjudicate pure speech cases. The Court began to develop these standards in 1942 with *Chaplinsky v. New Hampshire.* As you read Justice Murphy's opinion in *Chaplinsky,* try to identify the legal standard he articulates and remember it as we look at later Court decisions in these areas. Did Murphy's approach continue to animate the Court's decisions during the civil rights and Vietnam War movements, or did the Court revise it to fit changing times?

Chaplinsky v. New Hampshire

315 U.S. 568 (1942)
http://laws.findlaw.com/US/315/568.html
Vote: 9 (Black, Byrnes, Douglas, Frankfurter,
       Jackson, Murphy, Reed, Roberts, Stone)
       0

OPINION OF THE COURT: *Murphy*

FACTS:

On April 6, 1940, Jehovah's Witness member Walter Chaplinsky was selling biblical pamphlets and literature, including *Watchtower* and *Consolation,* on a public street in New Hampshire. While he was announcing

the sale of his pamphlets, a crowd of about fifty people began to gather. Several took offense at Chaplinsky's comments about organized religion and "racketeer" priests and complained to the city marshal. The marshal warned Chaplinsky that the people were getting into an ugly mood, but Chaplinsky continued to express his religious views and distribute his literature. After one person tried to attack Chaplinsky, the marshal and three of his men intervened and forcibly began to take Chaplinsky to city hall. When a very agitated Chaplinsky demanded to know why they had arrested him and not the mob, one of the officers replied, "Shut up, you damn bastard," and Chaplinsky in turn called the officer a "damned fascist" and "a God damned racketeer." For those words, the state charged him with breaking a law prohibiting the use of "any offensive, derisive, or annoying word to any other person who is lawfully in the street." Chaplinsky was convicted and received a fine. He appealed.

ARGUMENTS:

For the appellant, Walter Chaplinsky:

- The police unlawfully arrested Chaplinsky and violently removed him even though he was peacefully exercising his right to freedom of expression. The police should have arrested those who were taunting and assaulting him.

- Rather than physically resist his unlawful arrest, Chaplinsky chose to speak, boldly expressing his righteous indignation about the government's wrongful conduct toward him.

- The fact that speech is likely to cause violence is no grounds for suppressing it. Here, in any event, there is no reason to believe that Chaplinsky's words would lead to violence by the police officers to whom the words were directed.

For the appellee, State of New Hampshire:

- The challenged law is a reasonable regulation to promote public order.

- The statute does not violate the appellant's right to the free exposition of his ideas, because the verbal conduct it prohibits bears no relationship to the process of attaining and disseminating truth.

MR. JUSTICE MURPHY DELIVERED THE OPINION OF THE COURT.

Allowing the broadest scope to the language and purpose of the Fourteenth Amendment, it is well understood that the right of free speech is not absolute at all times and under all circumstances. There are certain well-defined and narrowly limited classes of speech, the prevention and punishment of which have never been thought to raise any Constitutional problem. These include the lewd and obscene, the profane, the libelous, and the insulting or "fighting" words—those which by their very utterance inflict injury or tend to incite an immediate breach of the peace. It has been well observed that such utterances are no essential part of any exposition of ideas, and are of such slight social value as a step to truth that any benefit that may be derived from them is clearly outweighed by the social interest in order and morality. . . .

The state statute here challenged comes to us authoritatively construed by the highest court of New Hampshire. It has two provisions—the first relates to words or names addressed to another in a public place; the second refers to noises and exclamations. . . .

On the authority of its earlier decisions, the state court declared that the state's purpose was to preserve the public peace, no words being "forbidden except such as have a direct tendency to cause acts of violence by the persons to whom, individually, the remark is

addressed." It was further said: "The word 'offensive' is not to be defined in terms of what a particular addressee thinks. . . . The test is what men of common intelligence would understand would be words likely to cause an average addressee to fight. . . . The English language has a number of words and expressions which by general consent are 'fighting words' when said without a disarming smile. . . . Such words, as ordinary men know, are likely to cause a fight. So are threatening, profane or obscene revilings. Derisive and annoying words can be taken as coming within the purview of the statute as heretofore interpreted only when they have this characteristic of plainly tending to excite the addressee to a breach of the peace. . . . The statute, as construed, does no more than prohibit the face-to-face words plainly likely to cause a breach of the peace by the addressee, words whose speaking constitutes a breach of the peace by the speaker—including 'classical fighting words,' words in current use less 'classical' but equally likely to cause violence, and other disorderly words, including profanity, obscenity and threats."

We are unable to say that the limited scope of the statute as thus construed contravenes the Constitutional right of free expression. It is a statute narrowly drawn and limited to define and punish specific conduct lying within the domain of state power, the use in a public place of words likely to cause a breach of the peace. . . .

Nor can we say that the application of the statute to the facts disclosed by the record substantially or unreasonably impinges upon the privilege of free speech. Argument is unnecessary to demonstrate that the appellations "damned racketeer" and "damned Fascist" are epithets likely to provoke the average person to retaliation, and thereby cause a breach of the peace.

Affirmed.

In unanimously affirming Chaplinsky's conviction, the Court agreed with Murphy's enunciation of the so-called fighting words doctrine: that the government may regulate words "which by their very utterance inflict injury or tend to incite an immediate breach of peace."

Not all public order cases involve individuals shouting words that may prompt violent responses from the persons to whom they are directed. Sometimes a small group or even a single individual uses public property as a place of political protest. Occasionally, such expression occurs quite silently, such as in *Cohen v. California* (1971). Here the justices examined the use of a county courthouse as a forum for expression where the message is communicated in a way that many may find offensive.

Cohen v. California

403 U.S. 15 (1971)
http://laws.findlaw.com/US/403/15.html
Oral arguments are available at http://www.oyez.org.
Vote: 5 (Brennan, Douglas, Harlan, Marshall, Stewart)
    4 (Black, Blackmun, Burger, White)

OPINION OF THE COURT: *Harlan*
DISSENTING OPINION: *Blackmun*

FACTS:

In April 1968, at the height of the protest against the Vietnam War, Paul Cohen visited some friends in Los Angeles, his hometown. While they were discussing their opposition to the war, someone scrawled on Cohen's jacket the words *Fuck the Draft* and *Stop the War.* The following morning, Cohen wore his jacket in the corridors of a Los Angeles County courthouse, where men, women, and children were present, knowing it bore these messages.

Although Cohen took off the jacket before entering the courtroom, a police sergeant had observed it in the corridor. The officer asked the judge to cite Cohen for contempt of court. The judge refused, but the officer arrested Cohen, charging him with "willfully and unlawfully and maliciously disturbing the peace and quiet by engaging in tumultuous and offensive conduct."

Given the nature of Cohen's alleged offense, this case could have ended where it started, in a California trial court. No violence occurred, nor were large groups of people or spectators involved. But that was not to be. By the time of Cohen's trial in September, his cause had attracted the attention of the ACLU. Its Southern California affiliate decided that Cohen's case presented a significant issue—that the message on his jacket represented a form of protected expression—and it offered to finance Cohen's case.

Affirming Cohen's municipal court conviction, the California Court of Appeal found that it was "reasonably foreseeable that such conduct might cause others to rise up to commit a violent act." The California Supreme Court declined to review that decision, but Cohen's ACLU lawyers successfully petitioned the

U.S. Supreme Court to consider the First Amendment issues at stake.[9]

ARGUMENTS:

For the appellant, Paul Robert Cohen:
- There was no threat of violence from Cohen or from anyone who observed Cohen's expression.
- Cohen's expression was not obscene.
- The First Amendment protects offensive and nonoffensive speech equally.
- Profanity is a part of language in contemporary society and an indispensable ingredient in democratic dialogue.

For the appellee, State of California:
- The First Amendment is not absolute. It must be balanced against other public interests.
- Children, women, and men in the courthouse were forced to observe the offensive message on the jacket.
- Appellant's form of protest was so inherently inflammatory as to come within the class of words that are likely to provoke the average person to retaliation and thereby cause a breach of the peace.
- A person may commit a breach of the peace by making statements that are likely to provoke violence and disturbance of good order, even if that is not the intended effect.

MR. JUSTICE HARLAN DELIVERED THE OPINION OF THE COURT.

In order to lay hands on the precise issue which this case involves, it is useful first to canvass various matters which this record does *not* present.

The conviction quite clearly rests upon the asserted offensiveness of the *words* Cohen used to convey his message to the public. The only "conduct" which the State sought to punish is the fact of communication. . . . Further, the State certainly lacks power to punish Cohen for the

---

9. In addition to its constitutional ramifications, *Cohen* provides a unique opportunity to view intraorganizational politics. As Richard Cortner reports, the Southern California affiliate of the ACLU always felt the "key issue . . . and the one that arguments before the Court should focus on was the free expression issue." At the Supreme Court level, however, the ACLU's Northern California affiliate "urged the Court not to decide the case on the freedom of expression issue." The Southern California affiliate refused to give its consent to the filing of the brief, but the justices granted permission. See Richard C. Cortner, *The Supreme Court and Civil Liberties Policy* (Palo Alto, CA: Mayfield, 1975), 128–129.

underlying content of the message the inscription conveyed. At least so long as there is no showing of an intent to incite disobedience to or disruption of the draft, Cohen could not, consistently with the First and Fourteenth Amendments, be punished for asserting the evident position on the inutility or immorality of the draft his jacket reflected. *Yates v. United States.*

Appellant's conviction, then, rests squarely upon his exercise of the "freedom of speech" protected from arbitrary governmental interference by the Constitution and can be justified, if at all, only as a valid regulation of the manner in which he exercised that freedom, not as a permissible prohibition on the substantive message it conveys. This does not end the inquiry, of course, for the First and Fourteenth Amendments have never been thought to give absolute protection to every individual to speak whenever or wherever he pleases or to use any form of address in any circumstances that he chooses. In this vein, too, however, we think it important to note that several issues typically associated with such problems are not presented here.

In the first place, Cohen was tried under a statute applicable throughout the entire State. Any attempt to support this conviction on the ground that the statute seeks to preserve an appropriately decorous atmosphere in the courthouse where Cohen was arrested must fail in the absence of any language in the statute that would have put appellant on notice that certain kinds of otherwise permissible speech or conduct would nevertheless, under California law, not be tolerated in certain places. No fair reading of the phrase "offensive conduct" can be said sufficiently to inform the ordinary person that distinctions between certain locations are thereby created.

In the second place, as it comes to us, this case cannot be said to fall within those relatively few categories of instances where prior decisions have established the power of government to deal more comprehensively with certain forms of individual expression simply upon a showing that such a form was employed. This is not, for example, an obscenity case. Whatever else may be necessary to give rise to the States' broader power to prohibit obscene expression, such expression must be, in some significant way, erotic. It cannot plausibly be maintained that this vulgar allusion to the Selective Service System would conjure up such psychic stimulation in anyone likely to be confronted with Cohen's crudely defaced jacket.

This Court has also held that the States are free to ban the simple use, without a demonstration of additional justifying circumstances, of so-called "fighting words," those personally abusive epithets which, when addressed to the ordinary citizens, are, as a matter of common knowledge, inherently likely to provoke violent reaction. *Chaplinsky v. New Hampshire* (1942). While the four-letter word displayed by Cohen in relation to the draft is not uncommonly employed in a personally provocative fashion, in this instance it was clearly not "directed to the person of the hearer." *Cantwell v. Connecticut* (1940). No individual actually or likely to be present could reasonably have regarded the words on appellant's jacket as a direct personal insult. Nor do we have here an instance of the exercise of the State's police power to prevent a speaker from intentionally provoking a given group to hostile reaction. *Feiner v. New York* (1951); *Terminiello v. Chicago* (1949). There is, as noted above, no showing that anyone who saw Cohen was in fact violently aroused or that appellant intended such a result.

Finally, in arguments before this Court much has been made of the claim that Cohen's distasteful mode of expression was thrust upon unwilling or unsuspecting viewers, and that the State might therefore legitimately act as it did in order to protect the sensitive from otherwise unavoidable exposure to appellant's crude form of protest. Of course, the mere presumed presence of unwitting listeners or viewers does not serve automatically to justify curtailing all speech capable of giving offense. While this Court has recognized that government may properly act in many situations to prohibit intrusion into the privacy of the home of unwelcome views and ideas which cannot be totally banned from the public dialogue, we have at the same time consistently stressed that "we are often 'captives' outside the sanctuary of the home and subject to objectionable speech." The ability of government, consonant with the Constitution, to shut off discourse solely to protect others from hearing it is, in other words, dependent upon a showing that substantial privacy interests are being invaded in an essentially intolerable manner. Any broader view of this authority would effectively empower a majority to silence dissidents simply as a matter of personal predilections.

In this regard, persons confronted with Cohen's jacket were in a quite different posture than, say, those subjected to the raucous emissions of sound trucks blaring outside their residences. Those in the Los Angeles courthouse could effectively avoid further bombardment of their sensibilities simply by averting their eyes. And, while it may be that one has a more substantial claim to a recognizable privacy interest when walking through a courthouse corridor than, for example, strolling through Central Park, surely it is nothing like the interest in being free from unwanted expression in the confines of one's own home. Given the subtlety and complexity of the factors involved, if Cohen's "speech" was otherwise entitled to constitutional protection, we do not think the fact that some unwilling "listeners" in a public building may have been briefly exposed to it can serve to justify this breach of the peace conviction where, as here, there was no evidence that persons powerless to avoid appellant's conduct did in fact object to it, and where that portion of the statute upon which Cohen's conviction rests evinces no concern, either on its face or as construed by the California courts, with the special plight of the captive auditor, but, instead, indiscriminately sweeps within its prohibitions all "offensive conduct" that disturbs "any neighborhood or person."

Against this background, the issue flushed by this case stands out in bold relief. It is whether California can excise, as "offensive conduct," one particular scurrilous epithet from the public discourse, either upon the theory of the court below that its use is inherently likely to cause violent reaction or upon a more general assertion that the States, acting as guardians of public morality, may properly remove this offensive word from the public vocabulary.

The rationale of the California court is plainly untenable. At most it reflects an "undifferentiated fear or apprehension of disturbance which is not enough to overcome the right to freedom of expression." We have been shown no evidence that substantial numbers of citizens are standing ready to strike out physically at whoever may assault their sensibilities with execrations like that uttered by Cohen. There may be some persons about with such lawless and violent proclivities, but that is an insufficient base upon which to erect, consistently with constitutional values, a governmental power to force persons who wish to ventilate their dissident views into avoiding particular forms of expression. The argument amounts to little more than the self-defeating proposition that to avoid physical censorship of one who has not sought to provoke such a response by a hypothetical coterie of the violent and lawless, the States may more appropriately effectuate that censorship themselves.

Admittedly, it is not so obvious that the First and Fourteenth Amendments must be taken to disable the States from punishing public utterance of this unseemly expletive in order to maintain what they regard as a suitable level of discourse within the body politic. We think,

however, that examination and reflection will reveal the shortcomings of a contrary viewpoint.

At the outset, we cannot overemphasize that, in our judgment, most situations where the State has a justifiable interest in regulating speech will fall within one or more of the various established exceptions, discussed above but not applicable here, to the usual rule that governmental bodies may not prescribe the form or content of individual expression. Equally important to our conclusion is the constitutional backdrop against which our decision must be made. The constitutional right of free expression is powerful medicine in a society as diverse and populous as ours. It is designed and intended to remove governmental restraints from the arena of public discussion, putting the decision as to what views shall be voiced largely into the hands of each of us, in the hope that use of such freedom will ultimately produce a more capable citizenry and more perfect polity and in the belief that no other approach would comport with the premise of individual dignity and choice upon which our political system rests.

To many, the immediate consequence of this freedom may often appear to be only verbal tumult, discord, and even offensive utterance. These are, however, within established limits, in truth necessary side effects of the broader enduring values which the process of open debate permits us to achieve. That the air may at times seem filled with verbal cacophony is, in this sense not a sign of weakness but of strength. We cannot lose sight of the fact that, in what otherwise might seem a trifling and annoying instance of individual distasteful abuse of a privilege, these fundamental societal values are truly implicated. . . .

Against this perception of the constitutional policies involved, we discern certain more particularized considerations that peculiarly call for reversal of this conviction. First, the principle contended for by the State seems inherently boundless. How is one to distinguish this from any other offensive word? Surely the State has no right to cleanse public debate to the point where it is grammatically palatable to the most squeamish among us. Yet no readily ascertainable general principle exists for stopping short of that result were we to affirm the judgment below. For, while the particular four-letter word being litigated here is perhaps more distasteful than most others of its genre, it is nevertheless often true that one man's vulgarity is another's lyric. Indeed, we think it is largely because governmental officials cannot make principled distinctions in this area that the Constitution leaves matters of taste and style so largely to the individual.

Additionally, we cannot overlook the fact, because it is well illustrated by the episode involved here, that much linguistic expression serves a dual communicative function: it conveys not only ideas capable of relatively precise, detached explication, but otherwise inexpressible emotions as well. In fact, words are often chosen as much for their emotive as their cognitive force. We cannot sanction the view that the Constitution, while solicitous of the cognitive content of individual speech, has little or no regard for that emotive function which, practically speaking, may often be the more important element of the overall message sought to be communicated. . . .

Finally, and in the same vein, we cannot indulge the facile assumption that one can forbid particular words without also running a substantial risk of suppressing ideas in the process. Indeed, governments might soon seize upon the censorship of particular words as a convenient guise for banning the expression of unpopular views. We have been able, as noted above, to discern little social benefit that might result from running the risk of opening the door to such grave results.

It is, in sum, our judgment that, absent a more particularized and compelling reason for its actions, the State may not, consistently with the First and Fourteenth Amendments, make the simple public display here involved of this single four-letter expletive a criminal offense. Because that is the only arguably sustainable rationale for the conviction here at issue, the judgment below must be

Reversed.

MR. JUSTICE BLACKMUN, with whom THE CHIEF JUSTICE and MR. JUSTICE BLACK join, dissenting.
Cohen's absurd and immature antic, in my view, was mainly conduct and little speech. The California Court of Appeal appears so to have described it, and I cannot characterize it otherwise. Further, the case appears to me to be well within the sphere of *Chaplinsky v. New Hampshire* (1942), where Justice Murphy, a known champion of First Amendment freedoms, wrote for a unanimous bench. As a consequence, this Court's agonizing over First Amendment values seems misplaced and unnecessary.

Chaplinsky and *Cohen* involved individuals who expressed themselves in a way that caused local officials

to be concerned about a breakdown in order. Public safety interests become even more acute when the expression takes the form of a mass demonstration rather than individual speech. In addition to the hostility the group's message may provoke, the presence of a crowd makes it more likely that injuries or property damage will occur. Large crowds may interfere with free movement along streets, sidewalks, or other public areas. A demonstration that occurs near a government facility may place a burden on legitimate government activity. For these reasons, local police tend to watch such a gathering with great care. If the police, believing that a breakdown in order is about to occur, move to end the demonstration, the protesters may feel that their First Amendment rights are being violated. This scenario was replayed time after time during the civil rights and antiwar protest era and often recurs during political demonstrations today.

To help maintain public order, local governments may require permits to hold mass demonstrations, protests, and parades. Permits cannot be denied based on the content of the group's message. Instead, the permit procedure must rest on legitimate time, place, and manner considerations. The permitting process gives local officials advance notice of mass gatherings, enabling them to ensure that adequate police protection is in place. It also allows a local government to make sure that public facilities are properly used, that unlawful activities are not planned, and that financially responsible parties are identified should damages occur during the event.[10]

Additionally, local governments may place certain restrictions on the conduct of public gatherings. Again, these restraints must be content neutral and narrowly tailored to serve a sufficiently significant government interest. For example, in ***Ward v. Rock Against Racism*** (1989), the justices upheld a New York regulation that required groups performing in the Central Park band shell to use city-supplied amplification equipment supervised by a city-authorized sound technician. The purpose of the regulation was to ensure that the volume of the concert music would not unreasonably disturb local residents. The Court concluded that this was a valid time, place, and manner restriction.

Once public gatherings are in progress, local officials may intervene if unlawful activity takes place. Numerous such disputes worked their way to the

---

10. See *Thomas v. Chicago Park District* (2002).

Civil rights demonstrators conduct a sit-down at an all-white lunch counter in Portsmouth, Virginia, in 1960. Such protests against racial segregation laws were common forms of political expression during the civil rights movement.

Supreme Court and gave the justices opportunities to develop coherent rules of constitutional law governing public demonstrations. Comparing two cases, ***Edwards v. South Carolina*** (1963) and ***Adderley v. Florida*** (1966), provides insight into the ways the justices responded to these disputes.

Edwards v. South Carolina involved an appeal by 187 black high school and college students who were arrested for breach of peace during a 1961 civil rights protest. These students had joined with others to march from a Baptist church to the state capitol building "to submit a protest to the citizens of South Carolina to show their feelings and dissatisfaction with the present condition of discriminatory actions against Negroes." The students peacefully marched to the capitol grounds, where they were met by about thirty law enforcement officials, who informed them that as long as they stayed peaceful they could remain in the public area. For the next hour the group marched in an orderly fashion carrying signs with messages such as "I am proud to be a Negro." A crowd of onlookers, numbering two hundred to three hundred, watched the activities. There were no signs of imminent violence. The police then informed the students that they had fifteen more minutes to protest, after which they should disperse or face arrest. Holding hands and singing

"We shall not be moved," large numbers of students refused to go. Police arrested the students who refused to comply with the order.

The Supreme Court, 8–1, reversed the students' convictions. Important to the justices were the following points: First, the protesters had come to the seat of the government to present their views, and what better place to exercise the First Amendment right "to petition the Government for a redress of grievances"? Second, the students did not engage in violence, and the onlookers made no meaningful threat of violence. Third, no damage was done to public or private property. Fourth, the students stayed in a traditional public forum area, placing no burden on the administration of lawful government activities or the free movement of the public. Based on these facts, the Court said it was contrary to the First Amendment for the police to order the students to stop their protest and to arrest the students who did not comply.

Adderley v. Florida, also based on a civil rights demonstration, presents a different situation. Approximately two hundred Florida A&M students marched from the university to the county jail to protest an earlier arrest of several schoolmates. The group assembled outside the jailhouse entrance and engaged in singing, clapping, and dancing to express their opposition to the county's segregation policies. A deputy sheriff asked them to move back, claiming that they were blocking entry to the building. They partially complied by moving away from the door but not pulling back as far as the deputy requested. In their new location, the students blocked a driveway used for deliveries and the transportation of inmates. The sheriff then told the protesters that because they were trespassing on jail property, they would be arrested if they did not disperse within ten minutes. Some of the students left, but most remained. After a second warning, the sheriff arrested 107 students for trespass. Following a jury trial, Harriett Louise Adderley and 31 other persons were convicted of "trespass with a malicious and mischievous intent."

Although no violence had occurred, a five-justice majority found sufficient justification for the arrests. Unlike the state capitol grounds in *Edwards,* a jail is not a traditional public forum. A jail is a government facility dedicated to securing prisoners. In such a location, security interests must be given high priority, and these interests are incompatible with a gathering of protesters. "The State, no less than a private owner of property," Justice Black explained, "has power to preserve the property under its control for the use to which it is lawfully dedicated." In addition, blocking the driveway and the jailhouse entry placed a burden on the execution of government business and restricted the access of people who had business at the jail.

Edwards and *Adderley* are typical public forum disputes. Each involved large numbers of people collectively expressing their political opinions by assembling in a public place. Although the 1960s may have been the heyday for such activity, disputes over government regulation of public gatherings have not disappeared and are likely to continue. Table 5-2 provides

TABLE 5-2 Examples of Public Forum Cases Decided by the Supreme Court since 1988

CASE	FACTS	OUTCOME
Boos v. Barry (1988)	Challenge to a District of Columbia ordinance prohibiting the display of any sign within 500 feet of a foreign embassy that brings that foreign government into public disrepute, and prohibiting the congregation of three or more persons within 500 feet of an embassy.	The sign-display provision is an unconstitutional, content-based restriction on political expression. The congregation provision is a constitutional manner and place restriction.
Frisby v. Schultz (1988)	Challenge to a city ordinance prohibiting picketing before a residence of an individual.	Ordinance serves a legitimate governmental interest. It does not violate the First Amendment.
Ward v. Rock Against Racism (1989)	Challenge to a city regulation requiring bands playing in a city park to use sound-amplification equipment and sound technician provided by the city.	Ordinance is valid under the First Amendment as a reasonable regulation of place and manner of speech.
United States v. Kokinda (1990)	Challenge to a postal service regulation prohibiting the solicitation of contributions on sidewalks outside a post office.	Sidewalk outside a post office is not a traditional public forum. The regulation does not violate the First Amendment.
International Society for Krishna Consciousness v. Lee (1992)	Challenge to a New York Port Authority regulation forbidding the repetitive solicitation of money or distribution of literature in airport terminals.	An airport terminal is not a public forum. Repetitive, face-to-face solicitation may be disruptive, impede the normal flow of the public, and be fraudulent. The regulation is reasonable. The ban on the distribution of literature violates the First Amendment.
Forsyth County, Georgia v. Nationalist Movement (1992)	Challenge to a county ordinance allowing an official to fix the cost of a parade permit based on the estimated cost of providing sufficient security to maintain public order during the gathering.	The ordinance is unconstitutional because it gives excessive discretion to the official and allows the fee to be fixed on the content of the message and the projected public response to it.
Bray v. Alexandria Women's Health Clinic (1993)	An abortion clinic and its supporters sued to enjoin pro-life protesters from demonstrating at clinics in the Washington, D.C., area, claiming that such protests are in violation of the Civil Rights Act of 1871 because they reflect an "animus" against women and restrict freedom of interstate travel.	The protests were not directed at women as a class, but were intended to protect victims of abortion, stop its practice, and reverse its legalization. Although many women travel interstate to obtain abortion services, the right to interstate travel was not the focus of the protesters' activity.

CASE	FACTS	OUTCOME
Madsen v. Women's Health Center, Inc. (1994)	Pro-life groups challenged a state court injunction prohibiting them from protesting within 36 feet of an abortion clinic, restricting noise levels during times abortion surgeries were being conducted, prohibiting protesters from physically approaching clinic clients within 300 feet of the facility, and prohibiting protests within 300 feet of the residences of clinic workers.	The injunction against protests within 36 feet of clinic is generally upheld, as are the noise level restrictions. Banning protest activity within 300 feet of clinic or private residences is unconstitutional.
Schenck v. Pro-Choice Network of Western New York (1997)	Injunction issued to protect access rights of abortion clinic patients by (1) creating a fixed 15-foot buffer zone around clinic entrances and driveways, and (2) creating a floating 15-foot buffer zone around all individuals and vehicles entering and leaving the clinic.	Floating buffer zone violates First Amendment as excessively regulating the speech rights of the protesters, but fixed buffer zone is a valid restriction to protect access rights of clinic patients.
Thomas v. Chicago (2002)	City requirement that groups holding mass gatherings must apply for and be issued a meeting permit. Ordinance contains thirteen grounds for denial of the permit.	The ordinance is a content-neutral time, place, and manner regulation of the use of a public forum and includes adequate procedural safeguards.

the facts of ten such disputes since 1988, their outcomes, and synopses of the Court's reasoning. As you can see, the Court continues to face questions of how far the government may go in restricting the manner and place of protests. We also see that civil rights, religion, and foreign policy protests still dominate First Amendment litigation. More recent mass demonstration cases, however, are frequently more complex than those that arose during the height of the civil rights movement. They often involve multiple rights and interests. The protests that have occurred at abortion clinics illustrate this phenomenon. These cases usually involve clashes between pro-life advocates who protest at women's clinics and pro-choice groups that want the government to curtail the demonstrations. Two constitutional rights come into conflict. The demonstrators see the issue as freedom of speech; their opponents see it as needing to guarantee free access to legal abortion services without undue interference.

The decision in *Hill v. Colorado* (2000) illustrates both the issue and the Court's reaction to it. As you read the facts and opinions in this case, compare it to the Court's decisions on the antiwar and civil rights protest disputes. Is the Court applying the same standards it did in the earlier conflicts? Or does the abortion controversy involve interests and concerns that distinguish it from the civil rights and antiwar protests? Finally, to what extent do you think the justices' views on abortion rights influenced their individual votes in this freedom of expression case?

Hill v. Colorado

530 U.S. 703 (2000)
http://laws.findlaw.com/US/530/703.html
Oral arguments are available at http://www.oyez.org.
Vote: 6 (Breyer, Ginsburg, O'Connor, Rehnquist, Souter, Stevens)
3 (Kennedy, Scalia, Thomas)

OPINION OF THE COURT: *Stevens*
CONCURRING OPINION: *Souter*
DISSENTING OPINIONS: *Kennedy, Scalia*

FACTS:

In 1993 the Colorado legislature, concerned about protest activity occurring at abortion clinics, enacted a law placing restrictions on protesters within a radius of one hundred feet of the entrance to any "health care facility." Within that zone, the law prohibited any person from approaching within eight feet of any other person, without that person's consent, for the purpose of distributing literature, displaying a sign, or engaging in oral protest, education, or counseling. A violation of the law was a misdemeanor punishable by a fine of between $50 and $750 and/or up to six months' imprisonment.

Shortly after the statute was passed, Leila Jeanne Hill, Audrey Himmelmann, and Everitt W. Simpson Jr. filed suit claiming that the law on its face violates the First and Fourteenth Amendments. The challengers described themselves as sidewalk counselors who urge women seeking abortions to reconsider their decisions. Their activities at abortion clinics include verbal communication with women and their escorts, display of pro-life signs, and distribution of pro-life literature.

Protesters gather at a Denver Planned Parenthood clinic on June 28, 2000, the day the Supreme Court decided Hill v. Colorado. *The justices upheld a state statute prohibiting protesters at medical facilities from approaching within eight feet of any person.*

ARGUMENTS:

For the petitioners, Leila Jeanne Hill, Audrey Himmelmann, and Everitt W. Simpson Jr.:

- Speaking, displaying signs, and leafleting are constitutionally protected ways of disseminating information and viewpoints.
- Streets and sidewalks are traditional public forums.
- Because permission to speak is required, the law constitutes a prior restraint.
- The law is unconstitutionally content based, overbroad, and vague.

For the respondent, State of Colorado:

- The statute operates with precision to protect access to health care, public safety, and pedestrian and traffic movement while burdening as little expressive activity as possible.
- The law is a reasonable "time, place, and manner" regulation.
- Because permission from a government official is not required, the law does not meet the definition of an unconstitutional prior restraint.

JUSTICE STEVENS DELIVERED THE OPINION OF THE COURT.

Before confronting the question whether the Colorado statute reflects an acceptable balance between the constitutionally protected rights of law-abiding speakers and the interests of unwilling listeners, it is appropriate to examine the competing interests at stake. A brief review of both sides of the dispute reveals that each has legitimate and important concerns.

The First Amendment interests of petitioners are clear and undisputed. As a preface to their legal challenge, petitioners emphasize three propositions. First, they accurately explain that the areas protected by the statute encompass all the public ways within 100 feet of every entrance to every health care facility everywhere in the State of Colorado. There is no disagreement on this point, even though the legislative history makes it clear that its enactment was primarily motivated by activities in the vicinity of abortion clinics. Second, they correctly state that their leafletting, sign displays, and oral communications are protected by the First Amendment. The fact that the messages conveyed by those communications may be offensive to their recipients does not deprive them of constitutional protection. Third, the public sidewalks, streets, and ways affected by the statute are "quintessential" public forums for free speech. Finally, although there is debate about the magnitude of the statutory impediment to their ability to communicate effectively with persons in the regulated zones, that ability, particularly the ability to distribute leaflets, is unquestionably lessened by this statute.

On the other hand, petitioners do not challenge the legitimacy of the state interests that the statute is intended to serve. It is a traditional exercise of the States' "police powers to protect the health and safety of their citizens." *Medtronic, Inc. v. Lohr* (1996). That interest may justify a special focus on unimpeded access to health care facilities and the avoidance of potential trauma to patients associated with confrontational protests. See *Madsen v. Women's Health Center, Inc.* (1994); *NLRB v. Baptist Hospital, Inc.* (1979). . . .

It is also important when conducting this interest analysis to recognize the significant difference between state restrictions on a speaker's right to address a willing audience and those that protect listeners from unwanted communication. This statute deals only with the latter.

The right to free speech, of course, includes the right to attempt to persuade others to change their views, and may not be curtailed simply because the speaker's message may be offensive to his audience. But the protection afforded to offensive messages does not always embrace offensive speech that is so intrusive that the unwilling audience cannot avoid it. . . .

We have . . . recognized that the "right to persuade" . . . is protected by the First Amendment, *Thornhill v. Alabama* (1940), as well as by federal statutes. Yet we have continued to maintain that "no one has a right to press even 'good' ideas on an unwilling recipient." None of our decisions has minimized the enduring importance of "the right to be free" from persistent "importunity, following and dogging" after an offer to communicate has been declined. While the freedom to communicate is substantial, "the right of every person 'to be let alone' must be placed in the scales with the right of others to communicate." It is that right, as well as the right of "passage without obstruction," that the Colorado statute legitimately seeks to protect. The restrictions imposed by the Colorado statute only apply to communications that interfere with these rights rather than those that involve willing listeners. . . .

All four of the state court opinions upholding the validity of this statute concluded that it is a content-neutral

time, place, and manner regulation. Moreover, they all found support for their analysis in *Ward v. Rock Against Racism* (1989). It is therefore appropriate to comment on the "content neutrality" of the statute. As we explained in *Ward:*

"The principal inquiry in determining content neutrality, in speech cases generally and in time, place, or manner cases in particular, is whether the government has adopted a regulation of speech because of disagreement with the message it conveys."

The Colorado statute passes that test for three independent reasons. First, it is not a "regulation of speech." Rather, it is a regulation of the places where some speech may occur. Second, it was not adopted "because of disagreement with the message it conveys." This conclusion is supported not just by the Colorado courts' interpretation of legislative history, but more importantly by the State Supreme Court's unequivocal holding that the statute's "restrictions apply equally to all demonstrators, regardless of viewpoint, and the statutory language makes no reference to the content of the speech." Third, the State's interests in protecting access and privacy, and providing the police with clear guidelines, are unrelated to the content of the demonstrators' speech. As we have repeatedly explained, government regulation of expressive activity is "content neutral" if it is justified without reference to the content of regulated speech. . . .

The Colorado statute's regulation of the location of protests, education, and counseling . . . places no restrictions on—and clearly does not prohibit—either a particular viewpoint or any subject matter that may be discussed by a speaker. Rather, it simply establishes a minor place restriction on an extremely broad category of communications with unwilling listeners. Instead of drawing distinctions based on the subject that the approaching speaker may wish to address, the statute applies equally to used car salesmen, animal rights activists, fundraisers, environmentalists, and missionaries. Each can attempt to educate unwilling listeners on any subject, but without consent may not approach within eight feet to do so. . . .

. . . [T]he statute's restriction seeks to protect those who enter a health care facility from the harassment, the nuisance, the persistent importuning, the following, the dogging, and the implied threat of physical touching that can accompany an unwelcome approach within eight feet of a patient by a person wishing to argue vociferously face-to-face and perhaps thrust an undesired handbill upon her. The statutory phrases, "oral protest, education, or counseling," distinguish speech activities likely to have those consequences from speech activities . . . that are most unlikely to have those consequences. . . .

Similarly, the contention that a statute is "viewpoint based" simply because its enactment was motivated by the conduct of the partisans on one side of a debate is without support. . . . *Frisby v. Schultz* (1988). . . .

We also agree with the state courts' conclusion that [the statute] is a valid time, place, and manner regulation under the test applied in *Ward* because it is "narrowly tailored." We already have noted that the statute serves governmental interests that are significant and legitimate and that the restrictions are content neutral. We are likewise persuaded that the statute is "narrowly tailored" to serve those interests and that it leaves open ample alternative channels for communication. As we have emphasized on more than one occasion, when a content-neutral regulation does not entirely foreclose any means of communication, it may satisfy the tailoring requirement even though it is not the least restrictive or least intrusive means of serving the statutory goal.

The three types of communication regulated . . . are the display of signs, leafletting, and oral speech. The 8-foot separation between the speaker and the audience should not have any adverse impact on the readers' ability to read signs displayed by demonstrators. In fact, the separation might actually aid the pedestrians' ability to see the signs by preventing others from surrounding them and impeding their view. Furthermore, the statute places no limitations on the number, size, text, or images of the placards. And, as with all of the restrictions, the 8-foot zone does not affect demonstrators with signs who remain in place.

With respect to oral statements, the distance certainly can make it more difficult for a speaker to be heard, particularly if the level of background noise is high and other speakers are competing for the pedestrian's attention. Notably, the statute places no limitation on the number of speakers or the noise level, including the use of amplification equipment, although we have upheld such restrictions in past cases. . . . Unlike the 15-foot zone in *Schenck* [*v. Pro-Choice Network of Western New York,* 1997], this 8-foot zone allows the speaker to communicate at a "normal conversational distance." Additionally, the statute allows the speaker to remain in

one place, and other individuals can pass within eight feet of the protester without causing the protester to violate the statute. Finally, here there is a "knowing" requirement that protects speakers "who thought they were keeping pace with the targeted individual" at the proscribed distance from inadvertently violating the statute. . . .

The burden on the ability to distribute handbills is more serious because it seems possible that an 8-foot interval could hinder the ability of a leafletter to deliver handbills to some unwilling recipients. The statute does not, however, prevent a leafletter from simply standing near the path of oncoming pedestrians and proffering his or her material, which the pedestrians can easily accept. And, as in all leafletting situations, pedestrians continue to be free to decline the tender. . . .

Finally, in determining whether a statute is narrowly tailored, we have noted that "[w]e must, of course, take account of the place to which the regulations apply in determining whether these restrictions burden more speech than necessary." *Madsen.* . . .

Persons who are attempting to enter health care facilities—for any purpose—are often in particularly vulnerable physical and emotional conditions. The State of Colorado has responded to its substantial and legitimate interest in protecting these persons from unwanted encounters, confrontations, and even assaults by enacting an exceedingly modest restriction on the speakers' ability to approach. . . .

This restriction is thus reasonable and narrowly tailored. . . .

Finally, petitioners argue that [the statute's] consent requirement is invalid because it imposes an unconstitutional "prior restraint" on speech. We rejected this argument previously in *Schenck* and *Madsen.* . . . Under this statute, absolutely no channel of communication is foreclosed. No speaker is silenced. And no message is prohibited. Petitioners are simply wrong when they assert that "[t]he statute compels speakers to obtain consent to speak and it authorizes private citizens to deny petitioners' requests to engage in expressive activities." To the contrary, this statute does not provide for a "heckler's veto" but rather allows every speaker to engage freely in any expressive activity communicating all messages and viewpoints subject only to the narrow place requirement imbedded within the "approach" restriction.

Furthermore, our concerns about "prior restraints" relate to restrictions imposed by official censorship. The regulations in this case, however, only apply if the pedestrian does not consent to the approach. Private citizens have always retained the power to decide for themselves what they wish to read, and within limits, what oral messages they want to consider. This statute simply empowers private citizens entering a health care facility with the ability to prevent a speaker, who is within eight feet and advancing, from communicating a message they do not wish to hear. Further, the statute does not authorize the pedestrian to affect any other activity at any other location or relating to any other person. These restrictions thus do not constitute an unlawful prior restraint.

The judgment of the Colorado Supreme Court is affirmed.

It is so ordered.

JUSTICE SOUTER, with whom JUSTICE O'CONNOR, JUSTICE GINSBURG, and JUSTICE BREYER join, concurring.

. . . [The law] simply does not forbid the statement of any position on any subject. It does not declare any view as unfit for expression within the 100-foot zone or beyond it. What it forbids, and all it forbids, is approaching another person closer than eight feet (absent permission) to deliver the message. Anyone (let him be called protester, counselor, or educator) may take a stationary position within the regulated area and address any message to any person within sight or hearing. The stationary protester may be quiet and ingratiating, or loud and offensive; the law does not touch him. . . .

JUSTICE SCALIA, with whom JUSTICE THOMAS joins, dissenting.

The Court today concludes that a regulation requiring speakers on the public thoroughfares bordering medical facilities to speak from a distance of eight feet is "not a 'regulation of speech,'" but "a regulation of the places where some speech may occur," and that a regulation directed to only certain categories of speech (protest, education, and counseling) is not "content-based." For these reasons, it says, the regulation is immune from the exacting scrutiny we apply to content-based suppression of speech in the public forum. The Court then determines that the regulation survives the less rigorous scrutiny afforded content-neutral time, place, and manner restrictions because it is narrowly tailored to serve a government interest—protection of citizens' "right to be let alone." . . .

None of these remarkable conclusions should come as a surprise. What is before us, after all, is a speech regulation directed against the opponents of abortion, and it therefore enjoys the benefit of the "ad hoc nullification machine" that the Court has set in motion to push aside whatever doctrines of constitutional law stand in the way of that highly favored practice. Having deprived abortion opponents of the political right to persuade the electorate that abortion should be restricted by law, the Court today continues and expands its assault upon their individual right to persuade women contemplating abortion that what they are doing is wrong. Because, like the rest of our abortion jurisprudence, today's decision is in stark contradiction of the constitutional principles we apply in all other contexts, I dissent.

. . . Whatever may be said about the restrictions on the other types of expressive activity, the regulation as it applies to oral communications is obviously and undeniably content-based. A speaker wishing to approach another for the purpose of communicating *any* message except one of protest, education, or counseling may do so without first securing the other's consent. Whether a speaker must obtain permission before approaching within eight feet—and whether he will be sent to prison for failing to do so—depends entirely on *what he intends to say* when he gets there. I have no doubt that this regulation would be deemed content-based *in an instant* if the case before us involved antiwar protesters, or union members seeking to "educate" the public about the reasons for their strike. "[I]t is," we would say, "the content of the speech that determines whether it is within or without the statute's blunt prohibition," *Carey v. Brown* (1980). But the jurisprudence of this Court has a way of changing when abortion is involved. . . .

. . . [I]t blinks reality to regard this statute, in its application to oral communications, as anything other than a content-based restriction upon speech in the public forum. As such, it must survive that stringent mode of constitutional analysis our cases refer to as "strict scrutiny," which requires that the restriction be narrowly tailored to serve a compelling state interest. . . . Suffice it to say that if protecting people from unwelcome communications (the governmental interest the Court posits) is a compelling state interest, the First Amendment is a dead letter. And if . . . forbidding peaceful, nonthreatening, but uninvited speech from a distance closer than eight feet is a "narrowly tailored" means of preventing the obstruction of entrance to medical facilities (the governmental interest the State asserts) narrow tailoring must refer not to the standards of Versace, but to those of Omar the tentmaker. . . .

. . . [T]he 8-foot buffer zone attaches to *every* person on the public way or sidewalk within 100 feet of the entrance of a medical facility, regardless of whether that person is seeking to enter or exit the facility. In fact, the State acknowledged at oral argument that the buffer zone would attach to any person within 100 feet of the entrance door of a skyscraper in which a single doctor occupied an office on the 18th floor. And even with respect to those who *are* seeking to enter or exit the facilities, the statute does not protect them only from speech that is so intimidating or threatening as to impede access. Rather, it covers *all* unconsented-to approaches for the purpose of oral protest, education, or counseling (including those made for the purpose of the most peaceful appeals) and, perhaps even more significantly, *every* approach made for the purposes of leafletting or handbilling, which we have never considered, standing alone, obstructive or unduly intrusive. The sweep of this prohibition is breathtaking. . . .

Those whose concern is for the physical safety and security of clinic patients, workers, and doctors should take no comfort from today's decision. Individuals or groups intent on bullying or frightening women out of an abortion, or doctors out of performing that procedure, will not be deterred by Colorado's statute; bullhorns and screaming from eight feet away will serve their purposes well. But those who would accomplish their moral and religious objectives by peaceful and civil means, by trying to persuade individual women of the rightness of their cause, will be deterred; and that is not a good thing in a democracy. This Court once recognized, as the Framers surely did, that the freedom to speak and persuade is inseparable from, and antecedent to, the survival of self-government. The Court today rotates that essential safety valve on our democracy one-half turn to the right, and no one who seeks safe access to health care facilities in Colorado or elsewhere should feel that her security has by this decision been enhanced. . . .

Does the deck seem stacked? You bet. As I have suggested throughout this opinion, today's decision is not an isolated distortion of our traditional constitutional principles, but is one of many aggressively proabortion novelties announced by the Court in recent years. Today's distortions, however, are particularly blatant. Restrictive views of the First Amendment that have been in dissent since the 1930's suddenly find themselves in the majority. "Uninhibited, robust, and wide open" debate is replaced by the power of the state to protect an unheard-of "right to be let alone" on the public streets. I dissent.

JUSTICE KENNEDY, dissenting.

The Court's holding contradicts more than a half century of well-established First Amendment principles. For the first time, the Court approves a law which bars a private citizen from passing a message, in a peaceful manner and on a profound moral issue, to a fellow citizen on a public sidewalk. If from this time forward the Court repeats its grave errors of analysis, we shall have no longer the proud tradition of free and open discourse in a public forum. In my view, JUSTICE SCALIA'S First Amendment analysis is correct and mandates outright reversal. . . .

. . . The law imposes content-based restrictions on speech by reason of the terms it uses, the categories it employs, and the conditions for its enforcement. It is content based, too, by its predictable and intended operation. Whether particular messages violate the statute is determined by their substance. The law is a prime example of a statute inviting screening and censoring of individual speech; and it is serious error to hold otherwise. . . .

The statute is content based for an additional reason: It restricts speech on particular topics. Of course, the enactment restricts "oral protest, education, or counseling" on any subject; but a statute of broad application is not content neutral if its terms control the substance of a speaker's message. If oral protest, education, or counseling on every subject within an 8-foot zone present a danger to the public, the statute should apply to every building entrance in the State. It does not. It applies only to a special class of locations: entrances to buildings with health care facilities. We would close our eyes to reality were we to deny that "oral protest, education, or counseling" outside the entrances to medical facilities concern a narrow range of topics—indeed, one topic in particular. By confining the law's application to the specific locations where the prohibited discourse occurs, the State has made a content-based determination. The Court ought to so acknowledge. Clever content-based restrictions are no less offensive than censoring on the basis of content. If, just a few decades ago, a State with a history of enforcing racial discrimination had enacted a statute like this one, regulating "oral protest, education, or counseling" within 100 feet of the entrance to any lunch counter, our predecessors would not have hesitated to hold it was content based or viewpoint based. It should be a profound disappointment to defenders of the First Amendment that the Court today refuses to apply the same structural analysis when the speech involved is less palatable to it. . . .

. . . Here the citizens who claim First Amendment protection seek it for speech which, if it is to be effective, must take place at the very time and place a grievous moral wrong, in their view, is about to occur. The Court tears away from the protesters the guarantees of the First Amendment when they most need it. So committed is the Court to its course that it denies these protesters, in the face of what they consider to be one of life's gravest moral crises, even the opportunity to try to offer a fellow citizen a little pamphlet, a handheld paper seeking to reach a higher law.

I dissent.

Offensive and Hateful Speech

The cases we have discussed so far demonstrate a great diversity in the content and method of communication. Individuals in some of these cases have used conventional forms of protest, such as speeches, parades, and published documents; others have used unconventional methods that are offensive to many, such as Paul Cohen's wearing a jacket with crude words written on it or Gregory Johnson's burning of the American flag. Their expressions have included a wide array of philosophies and causes—communism, socialism, civil rights, religious beliefs, and opposition to war or abortion. In spite of this diversity, these cases share some common elements. Each has involved an individual or group communicating a political or social message, usually expressing dissatisfaction with certain government policies. This speech is the traditional form of political expression that the framers sought to protect when they approved the First Amendment.

Since the mid-1970s another form of communication has come before the Court, one that differs markedly from the traditional. Expression based on hatred goes well beyond offending the standards of appropriateness or good taste. It arises from hostile, discriminatory, and prejudicial attitudes toward another person's innate characteristics: sex, race, ethnicity, religion, or sexual orientation. When directed at a member of a targeted group, such expression is demeaning and hurtful. Hate speech tends to be devoid of traditional commentary on political issues or on the need for changes in public policy. Instead, its central theme is hostility toward individuals belonging

to the target group. May hate speech be banned, or does the First Amendment protect it? If regulation of such speech is permissible, under what conditions is it permissible? And what standard should control when it is regulated?

In responding to legal disputes over offensive and hateful speech, the Supreme Court has, on one hand, generally remained true to its core freedom of expression principles. The justices have emphasized, for example, that the government cannot suppress expression simply because of a fear that a breakdown in order might result. *National Socialist Party v. Skokie* (1977) is illustrative. In this case a township with a high percentage Jewish residents attempted to block a planned march by members of the Nazi Party, dressed in full regalia. The party claimed that Skokie's actions violated the First Amendment, and the Supreme Court agreed. In spite of the hateful nature of the Nazis' intended expression, denying the party the right to march was a form of censorship that the Constitution does not permit. The town could legitimately take action if the parade caused a breakdown in order, but it could not stop the event in advance.

The Supreme Court's ruling opened the door for the Nazis to march in Skokie, but the demonstration never took place. Shortly after the Supreme Court ruled, the party chose instead to march in Chicago.

In the *Skokie* case, and in *Brandenburg* before it, the justices struck down government regulation of racially based hate speech. In both cases, however, the Court's decision rested on defects in the way the government attempted to block the unacceptable expression. In *Brandenburg* the Court found constitutional problems with Ohio's Criminal Syndicalism Act, upon which the prosecution of a Klan leader was based. In *Skokie* the Court found that the local government was unconstitutionally attempting to repress speech before it occurred, a form of prior restraint. In neither case did the Court directly confront the question of whether the First Amendment allows government to punish expression based on hatred.

In response to an increase in hate speech incidents, in the 1990s many state and local governments, as well as colleges and universities, passed ordinances making hate speech punishable. Even though most Americans consider hate-based expression reprehensible, a deep division of opinion exists over whether it can be constitutionally banned. Individuals concerned with minority rights and elimination of bigotry have argued that laws making hate speech illegal are both necessary and constitutionally permissible. Free speech advocates, however, contend that such laws directly contradict the First Amend- ment. This issue often divides groups that are traditional allies in the attempt to expand personal rights and liberties *(see Box 5-7)*. The issue first found its way to the Supreme Court in the case of *R.A.V. v. City of St. Paul, Minnesota* (1992).

BOX 5-7   HATE SPEECH AND THE CIVIL LIBERTIES COMMUNITY

Regulating hate speech is an issue that divides the civil liberties community. Groups that historically have worked together to advance civil liberties and civil rights have found themselves in the uncomfortable position of fighting against each other over the issue of hate speech. Listed below are short excerpts from amicus curiae briefs submitted by traditionally liberal groups in the case of *R.A.V. v. City of St. Paul* (1992). Notice how the briefs emphasize different values. Those in favor of striking down the St. Paul ordinance stress the primacy of the First Amendment. Supporters of the law focus on the significance of equality considerations.

IN SUPPORT OF R.A.V.:

[T]he antibias ordinance cannot be defended on the ground that the State has a compelling interest in banning messages of racial and religious bigotry and intolerance. Although these messages are inconsistent with the Nation's highest aspirations, the Court has repeatedly held that the First Amendment does not permit a State to prohibit the communication of ideas simply because they are offensive or at odds with national policies.

—Center for Individual Rights

It is quite clear from the Court's First Amendment jurisprudence that government cannot criminalize such speech simply because it arouses anger, alarm and resentment.

—Association of American Publishers and the Freedom to Read Foundation

This society has rested its faith on the proposition that "the remedy [for speech] is more speech, not enforced silence" [Justice Brandeis concurring in *Whitney v. California*]. Accordingly, our constitutional tradition demands that even a message of racial supremacy is entitled to be heard so long as it remains in the realm of advocacy. Those who articulated this faith in public debate were not naive about the power of words or symbols. To the contrary, they believed that pernicious ideas were more dangerous when suppressed than when exposed.

—American Civil Liberties Union, Minnesota Civil Liberties Union, and the American Jewish Congress

IN SUPPORT OF THE ST. PAUL ORDINANCE:

Cross burnings, of which defendant R.A.V. is accused, should be recognized as a terrorist hate practice of intimidation and harassment, which, contrary to the purposes of the Fourteenth Amendment, works to institutionalize the civil inequality of protected groups. . . . [T]he statute in question does not violate the First Amendment because social inequality, including through expressive conduct, is a harm for which states are entitled leeway in regulation.

—National Black Women's Health Project

When not used in a personally threatening or assaultive manner, these symbols [burning cross and Nazi swastika] are part of the marketplace of ideas of which our society is justifiably tolerant; however, when used as a form of a bias-motivated personal attack, they cease to symbolize ideas and become violent tools that inflict injury. This Court has consistently recognized that this type of "expression" should not be afforded First Amendment protection.

—Anti-Defamation League of B'nai B'rith

Cross burning is an especially invidious act. A burning cross is an insult and a threat; it carries with it the historical baggage of past terrorism and physical attacks. When a cross burning is targeted against an individual and his family, it is more than just expression; it is a form of violence itself— symbolic violence.

—Asian American Legal Defense and Education Fund, the Asian Law Caucus, the Asian Pacific American Legal Center, and the National Asian Pacific American Bar Association

In his brief, [R.A.V.] intones principles of freedom of speech with which, in the abstract, no one will disagree. But the State of Minnesota was not indulging in theory when it charged [him] with a violation of the ordinance in controversy. It was dealing with what can only fairly be described as an act of terrorism. This conduct cannot rationally be viewed as protected by the First Amendment.

—National Association for the Advancement of Colored People and the Clarendon Foundation

R.A.V. v. City of St. Paul, Minnesota

505 U.S. 377 (1992)
http://laws.findlaw.com/US/505/377.html
Oral arguments are available at http://www.oyez.org.
Vote: 9 (Blackmun, Kennedy, O'Connor, Rehnquist,
     Scalia, Souter, Stevens, Thomas, White)
    0

OPINION OF THE COURT: *Scalia*
CONCURRING OPINIONS: *Blackmun, Stevens, White*

FACTS:

The city of St. Paul alleged that between 1:00 A.M. and 3:00 A.M. on June 21, 1990, Robert A. Viktora, a seventeen-year-old high school dropout, and several other teenagers "assembled a crudely made cross by taping together broken chair legs" and then burned the cross inside the fenced backyard of a black family that lived across the street from Viktora.[11] St. Paul could have prosecuted him under several criminal laws—for example, arson, which carries a maximum penalty of five years in prison and a $10,000 fine. Instead, it charged him with violating two laws, including the St. Paul Bias-Motivated Crime Ordinance. This law stated:

Whoever places on public or private property a symbol, object, appellation, characterization or graffiti, including, but not limited to, a burning cross or Nazi swastika, which one knows or has reasonable grounds to know arouses anger, alarm, or resentment in others on the basis of race, color, creed, religion, or gender commits disorderly conduct and shall be guilty of a misdemeanor.

Before Viktora's trial, his lawyer asked the judge to dismiss the charge, arguing that the ordinance violated the First Amendment because it was "substantially overbroad and impermissibly content-based." The trial court judge granted the motion, and the city appealed to the Minnesota Supreme Court.

The state supreme court reversed the trial court's decision, holding that the ordinance did not violate freedom of expression guarantees contained in the First Amendment. The court found that the ordinance prohibits conduct equivalent to "fighting words," unprotected expression under the First Amendment. It also ruled that the ordinance was not impermissibly content based because it was "a narrowly tailored means toward accomplishing the compelling governmental interest

---

11. Because of his age at the time, Viktora was identified in court proceedings only by his initials.

in protecting the community against bias-motivated threats to public safety and order."

ARGUMENTS:

For the petitioner, R.A.V.:
- The First Amendment protects expression even if it is offensive, insulting, outrageous, or intolerant.
- The law is overbroad, applying to any symbol or other means of expression that takes place in any private or public place and that could arouse anger, alarm or resentment in others on the basis of race, color, creed, religion, or gender.
- The law's specific mentioning of swastikas and burning crosses indicates viewpoint discrimination.
- The law must satisfy the highest level of judicial scrutiny, and it does not meet this test.

For the respondent, City of St. Paul:
- The Minnesota Supreme Court was correct that the ordinance is not overbroad or vague. It applies to fighting words and expression directed toward inciting or producing imminent lawless action.
- The ordinance is constitutional under the Supreme Court's ruling in *Chaplinsky v. New Hampshire* and subsequent decisions that have relied on *Chaplinsky*.
- The purpose of the ordinance is not to restrict expression, but to protect people who are uniquely vulnerable because they belong to a group that historically has been discriminated against.

JUSTICE SCALIA DELIVERED THE OPINION OF THE COURT.

In construing the St. Paul ordinance, we are bound by the construction given to it by the Minnesota court. Accordingly, we accept the Minnesota Supreme Court's authoritative statement that the ordinance reaches only those expressions that constitute "fighting words" within the meaning of *Chaplinsky* [*v. New Hampshire*, 1942]. . . . Assuming, *arguendo*, that all of the expression reached by the ordinance is proscribable under the "fighting words" doctrine, we nonetheless conclude that the ordinance is facially unconstitutional in that it prohibits otherwise permitted speech solely on the basis of the subjects the speech addresses. . . .

. . . Although the phrase in the ordinance, "arouses anger, alarm or resentment in others," has been limited by the Minnesota Supreme Court's construction to reach only those symbols or displays that amount to "fighting words," the remaining, unmodified terms make clear that the ordinance applies only to "fighting words" that insult, or provoke violence, "on the basis of race, color, creed, religion or gender." Displays containing abusive invective, no matter how vicious or severe, are permissible unless they are addressed to one of the specified disfavored topics. Those who wish to use "fighting words" in connection with other ideas—to express hostility, for example, on the basis of political affiliation, union membership, or homosexuality—are not covered. The First Amendment does not permit St. Paul to impose special prohibitions on those speakers who express views on disfavored subjects.

In its practical operation, moreover, the ordinance goes even beyond mere content discrimination, to actual viewpoint discrimination. Displays containing some words—odious racial epithets, for example—would be prohibited to proponents of all views. But "fighting words" that do not themselves invoke race, color, creed, religion, or gender—aspersions upon a person's mother, for example—would seemingly be usable *ad libitum* [as one wishes] in the placards of those arguing *in favor* of racial, color, etc. tolerance and equality, but could not be used by that speaker's opponents. One could hold up a sign saying, for example, that all "anti-Catholic bigots" are misbegotten; but not that all "papists" are, for that would insult and provoke violence "on the basis of religion." St. Paul has no such authority to license one side of a debate to fight freestyle, while requiring the other to follow Marquis of Queensbury Rules.

What we have here, it must be emphasized, is not a prohibition of fighting words that are directed at certain persons or groups (which would be *facially* valid if it met the requirements of the Equal Protection Clause); but rather, a prohibition of fighting words that contain (as the Minnesota Supreme Court repeatedly emphasized) messages of "bias-motivated" hatred and in particular, as applied to this case, messages "based on virulent notions of racial supremacy." One must wholeheartedly agree with the Minnesota Supreme Court that "[i]t is the responsibility, even the obligation, of diverse communities to confront such notions in whatever form they appear," but the manner of that confrontation cannot consist of selective limitations upon speech. St. Paul's brief asserts that a general "fighting words" law would not meet the city's needs because only a content-specific measure can communicate to minority groups that the "group hatred" aspect of such speech "is not condoned by the majority." The point of the First Amendment is that majority preferences must be expressed in

some fashion other than silencing speech on the basis of its content. . . .

. . . [T]he reason why fighting words are categorically excluded from the protection of the First Amendment is not that their content communicates any particular idea, but that their content embodies a particularly intolerable (and socially unnecessary) *mode* of expressing *whatever* idea the speaker wishes to convey. St. Paul has not singled out an especially offensive mode of expression—it has not, for example, selected for prohibition only those fighting words that communicate ideas in a threatening (as opposed to a merely obnoxious) manner. Rather, it has proscribed fighting words of whatever manner that communicate messages of racial, gender, or religious intolerance. Selectivity of this sort creates the possibility that the city is seeking to handicap the expression of particular ideas. That possibility would alone be enough to render the ordinance presumptively invalid, but St. Paul's comments and concessions in this case elevate the possibility to a certainty. . . .

Finally, St. Paul . . . defend[s] the conclusion of the Minnesota Supreme Court that, even if the ordinance regulates expression based on hostility towards its protected ideological content, this discrimination is nonetheless justified because it is narrowly tailored to serve compelling state interests. Specifically, they assert that the ordinance helps to ensure the basic human rights of members of groups that have historically been subjected to discrimination, including the right of such group members to live in peace where they wish. We do not doubt that these interests are compelling, and that the ordinance can be said to promote them. But the "danger of censorship" presented by a facially content-based statute requires that that weapon be employed only where it is "*necessary* to serve the asserted [compelling] interest." . . . The dispositive question in this case, therefore, is whether content discrimination is reasonably necessary to achieve St. Paul's compelling interests; it plainly is not. An ordinance not limited to the favored topics, for example, would have precisely the same beneficial effect. In fact the only interest distinctively served by the content limitation is that of displaying the city council's special hostility towards the particular biases thus singled out. That is precisely what the First Amendment forbids. The politicians of St. Paul are entitled to express that hostility—but not through the means of imposing unique limitations upon speakers who (however benightedly) disagree.

Russell and Laura Jones and their children. The Jones family awoke in the middle of the night to find a cross burning in their yard. The incident led to the Supreme Court decision in R.A.V. v. City of St. Paul.

Let there be no mistake about our belief that burning a cross in someone's front yard is reprehensible. But St. Paul has sufficient means at its disposal to prevent such behavior without adding the First Amendment to the fire.

The judgment of the Minnesota Supreme Court is reversed, and the case is remanded for proceedings not inconsistent with this opinion.

It is so ordered.

JUSTICE WHITE, with whom JUSTICE BLACKMUN, JUSTICE O'CONNOR, and . . . JUSTICE STEVENS join . . . concurring in the judgment.
I agree with the majority that the judgment of the Minnesota Supreme Court should be reversed. However, our agreement ends there. . . .

This Court's decisions have plainly stated that expression falling within certain limited categories so lacks the values the First Amendment was designed to protect that the Constitution affords no protection to that expression. . . .

. . . [T]his Court has long held certain discrete categories of expression to be proscribable on the basis of their content. For instance, the Court has held that the individual who falsely shouts "fire" in a crowded theater may not claim the protection of the First Amendment. *Schenck v. United States* (1919). The Court has concluded that neither child pornography nor obscenity is protected by the First Amendment. *New York v. Ferber* (1982); *Miller v. California* (1973); *Roth v. United States* (1957). And the Court has observed that, "[l]eaving aside the special considerations when public officials [and public figures] are the target, a libelous publication is not protected by the Constitution." *Ferber.*

All of these categories are content-based. But the Court has held that the First Amendment does not apply to them, because their expressive content is worthless or of *de minimis* value to society. . . .

. . . Nevertheless, the majority holds that the First Amendment protects those narrow categories of expression long held to be undeserving of First Amendment protection—at least to the extent that lawmakers may not regulate some fighting words more strictly than others because of their content. The Court announces that such content-based distinctions violate the First Amendment because "[t]he government may not regulate use based on hostility—or favoritism—towards the underlying message expressed." Should the government want to criminalize certain fighting words, the Court now requires it to criminalize all fighting words.

To borrow a phrase: "Such a simplistic, all-or-nothing-at-all approach to First Amendment protection is at odds with common sense, and with our jurisprudence as well." It is inconsistent to hold that the government may proscribe an entire category of speech because the content of that speech is evil, but that the government may not treat a subset of that category differently without violating the First Amendment; the content of the subset is, by definition, worthless and undeserving of constitutional protection.

. . . Fighting words are not a means of exchanging views, rallying supporters, or registering a protest; they are directed against individuals to provoke violence or to inflict injury. Therefore, a ban on all fighting words or on a subset of the fighting words category would restrict only the social evil of hate speech, without creating the danger of driving viewpoints from the marketplace. . . .

Any contribution of this holding to First Amendment jurisprudence is surely a negative one, since it necessarily signals that expressions of violence, such as the message of intimidation and racial hatred conveyed by burning a cross on someone's lawn, are of sufficient value to outweigh the social interest in order and morality that has traditionally placed such fighting words outside the First Amendment. Indeed, by characterizing fighting words as a form of "debate," the majority legitimates hate speech as a form of public discussion.

Furthermore, the Court obscures the line between speech that could be regulated freely on the basis of content (i.e., the narrow categories of expression falling outside the First Amendment) and that which could be regulated on the basis of content only upon a showing of a compelling state interest (i.e., all remaining expression). By placing fighting words, which the Court has long held to be valueless, on at least equal constitutional footing with political discourse and other forms of speech that we have deemed to have the greatest social value, the majority devalues the latter category. . . .

Although I disagree with the Court's analysis, I do agree with its conclusion: The St. Paul ordinance is unconstitutional. However, I would decide the case on overbreadth grounds.

The Supreme Court declared the St. Paul hate speech ordinance to be unconstitutional. The justices found the law defective because it singled out a particular kind of hate speech. The ordinance, therefore, violated the principle that laws regulating expression must not discriminate on the basis of content. The four concurring justices also found the law unacceptable, but they preferred to strike it down for being unconstitutionally vague and overbroad.

More recently, in the case of *Snyder v. Phelps,* the justices considered the right of demonstrators to express hateful and offensive messages while engaged in public picketing. In reading Chief Justice Roberts's opinion for the Court, pay close attention to his review of many of the topics we have discussed in this chapter—the importance of political expression, the Constitution's treatment of offensive and hateful speech, and the use of traditional public forums. Do you find his argument more compelling than Justice Samuel Alito's dissenting opinion that would allow

the government to protect innocent people from the severe emotional distress that may be caused by exposure to such hateful communications?

Snyder v. Phelps

562 U.S. ___ (2011)
http://laws.findlaw.com/US/000/09-751.html
Oral arguments are available at http://www.oyez.org.
Vote: 8 (Breyer, Ginsburg, Kagan, Kennedy, Roberts, Scalia, Sotomayor, Thomas)
    1 (Alito)

OPINION OF THE COURT: Roberts
CONCURRING OPINION: Breyer
DISSENTING OPINION: Alito

FACTS:

Marine Lance Corporal Matthew Snyder of Westminster, Maryland, died on March 3, 2006, while serving in Iraq. His funeral, which took place at his family's church, St. John's Catholic Church in Westminster, was the occasion for a protest staged by the members of Westboro Baptist Church of Topeka, Kansas.

Frank W. Phelps Sr. founded Westboro Baptist Church in 1955 and has been its only pastor since that time. The church, which otherwise subscribes to fundamentalist Protestant Christianity, teaches that God hates homosexuality and punishes the United States and its military for being tolerant of gays. The church often expresses its opposition to the Catholic Church and to what its members see as the general moral decline of the nation. For twenty years, members of the church have picketed military funerals to express these beliefs. Over the years they have engaged in almost 45,000 pickets in 816 cities; about 600 of these protests have been at military funerals. In order to spread its views, the church maintains a Web site, www.godhatesfags.com. Phelps is a retired attorney who specialized in criminal defense and the rights of minorities. Eleven of his thirteen children are also lawyers.

The church decided to picket Matthew Snyder's funeral and notified local authorities of its intent to do so. The protesters (Phelps and six of his relatives) complied with all local ordinances and police directions. The picketing took place one thousand feet from the church entrance in a fenced-in area on public land. None of protesters approached the mourners. There was no obstruction of those attending the funeral. The protesters held homemade signs indicating their opposition to the military, homosexuals, and the Catholic Church (e.g.,

Westboro Baptist Church members protest outside the Baltimore federal courthouse in 2007 while the jury deliberates over a lawsuit filed against the church by Albert Snyder. Left to right: Margie M. Phelps, her husband, Pastor Fred Phelps, and their daughter Margie J. Phelps.

"God Hates the USA," "Pope in Hell," "Fag Troops," "God Hates You," "Priests Rape Boys," "Thank God for IEDs," "God Hates Fags," "Thank You God for Dead Soldiers"). Church members sang hymns and recited Bible verses during their thirty-minute demonstration. (Later the church placed additional materials related to the funeral on its Web site, but that action is not relevant to this particular appeal.) Albert Snyder, Matthew's father, did not observe the demonstrators at the funeral, but he did see a television news program that night showing the protest.

In June of 2006, Albert Snyder filed a civil lawsuit against Phelps and Westboro Baptist Church claiming, among other things, intentional infliction of emotional distress, an unlawful act under Maryland law. Snyder claimed that he received severe and lasting emotional injury as a result of the church's actions, making him often tearful and angry and causing him to vomit. He also alleged that he could no longer think of his son without visualizing the protest signs. According to his medical experts, exposure to the protest worsened Snyder's diabetes and depression. One of Phelps's daughters, Margie J. Phelps, represented her father and the church in this legal dispute. She argued that the protesters' words were expressions of opinion on public issues and hyperbole rather than factual statements, and thus were protected by the First Amendment.

A federal district court jury ruled in favor of Snyder and awarded him $2.9 million in compensatory damages and $8 million in punitive damages. The Fourth Circuit Court of Appeals, however, reversed, holding that the protest consisted of expressions of opinion protected by the First Amendment, which therefore could not be the basis for civil liability. Snyder sought Supreme Court review.

ARGUMENTS:

For the petitioner, Albert Snyder:

- Westboro's speech had no rational connection to matters of public concern. Snyder did nothing to attach himself to any public event or controversy.
- The Court has never extended absolute protection to rhetorical hyperbole that cannot reasonably be interpreted as stating actual facts.
- A survivor has the right to privacy in protecting the memory of the dead.
- Westboro's expression restricted Snyder's ability to enjoy his First Amendment right to free exercise of religion and peaceful assembly.

For the respondent, Fred Phelps, Sr., Westboro Baptist Church, et al.:

- Westboro's expression concerned public issues. The language used was loose, figurative, and hyperbolic, which no reasonable person would interpret as stating actual facts.

- Snyder made himself a limited purpose public figure by speaking to the press about his son.
- Westboro's expression occurred well outside any zone of privacy that might reasonably be accorded to a funeral.
- Westboro's speech in no way curtailed the right of Snyder and others to engage in the religious rituals associated with the funeral.

CHIEF JUSTICE ROBERTS DELIVERED THE OPINION OF THE COURT.

To succeed on a claim for intentional infliction of emotional distress in Maryland, a plaintiff must demonstrate that the defendant intentionally or recklessly engaged in extreme and outrageous conduct that caused the plaintiff to suffer severe emotional distress. The Free Speech Clause of the First Amendment—"Congress shall make no law . . . abridging the freedom of speech"—can serve as a defense. . . . See, e.g., *Hustler Magazine, Inc. v. Falwell* (1988).

Whether the First Amendment prohibits holding Westboro liable for its speech in this case turns largely on whether that speech is of public or private concern, as determined by all the circumstances of the case. "[S]peech on 'matters of public concern' . . . is 'at the heart of the First Amendment's protection.'" *Dun & Bradstreet, Inc. v. Greenmoss Builders, Inc.* (1985) (opinion of Powell, J.). The First Amendment reflects "a profound national commitment to the principle that debate on public issues should be uninhibited, robust, and wide-open." *New York Times Co. v. Sullivan* (1964). That is because "speech concerning public affairs is more than self-expression; it is the essence of self-government." *Garrison v. Louisiana* (1964). Accordingly, "speech on public issues occupies the highest rung of the hierarchy of First Amendment values, and is entitled to special protection." *Connick v. Myers* (1983).

"[N]ot all speech is of equal First Amendment importance,'" however, and where matters of purely private significance are at issue, First Amendment protections are often less rigorous. That is because restricting speech on purely private matters does not implicate the same constitutional concerns as limiting speech on matters of public interest: "[T]here is no threat to the free and robust debate of public issues; there is no potential interference with a meaningful dialogue of ideas"; and the "threat of liability" does not pose the risk of "a reaction of self-censorship" on matters of public import.

. . . Speech deals with matters of public concern when it can "be fairly considered as relating to any matter of political, social, or other concern to the community," *Connick*, or when it "is a subject of legitimate news interest; that is, a subject of general interest and of value and concern to the public," *San Diego* [v. *Roe* (2004)]. The arguably "inappropriate or controversial character of a statement is irrelevant to the question whether it deals with a matter of public concern." *Rankin v. McPherson* (1987). . . .

Deciding whether speech is of public or private concern requires us to examine the content, form, and context of that speech, as revealed by the whole record. *Dun & Bradstreet, Connick.* . . . In considering content, form, and context, no factor is dispositive, and it is necessary to evaluate all the circumstances of the speech, including what was said, where it was said, and how it was said.

The "content" of Westboro's signs plainly relates to broad issues of interest to society at large, rather than matters of "purely private concern." The placards read "God Hates the USA/Thank God for 9/11," "America is Doomed," "Don't Pray for the USA," "Thank God for IEDs," "Fag Troops," "Semper Fi Fags," "God Hates Fags," "Maryland Taliban," "Fags Doom Nations," "Not Blessed Just Cursed," "Thank God for Dead Soldiers," "Pope in Hell," "Priests Rape Boys," "You're Going to Hell," and "God Hates You." While these messages may fall short of refined social or political commentary, the issues they highlight—the political and moral conduct of the United States and its citizens, the fate of our Nation, homosexuality in the military, and scandals involving the Catholic clergy—are matters of public import. The signs certainly convey Westboro's position on those issues, in a manner designed . . . to reach as broad a public audience as possible. And even if a few of the signs—such as "You're Going to Hell" and "God Hates You"—were viewed as containing messages related to Matthew Snyder or the Snyders specifically, that would not change the fact that the overall thrust and dominant theme of Westboro's demonstration spoke to broader public issues.

Apart from the content of Westboro's signs, Snyder contends that the "context" of the speech—its connection with his son's funeral—makes the speech a matter of private rather than public concern. The fact that Westboro spoke in connection with a funeral, however, cannot by itself transform the nature of Westboro's speech. Westboro's signs, displayed on public land next to a public street, reflect the fact that the church finds much to condemn in modern society. Its speech is "fairly characterized as constituting speech on a matter of public concern," and the funeral setting does not alter that conclusion. . . .

Westboro's choice to convey its views in conjunction with Matthew Snyder's funeral made the expression of those views particularly hurtful to many, especially to Matthew's father. The record makes clear that the applicable legal term—"emotional distress"—fails to capture fully the anguish Westboro's choice added to Mr. Snyder's already incalculable grief. But Westboro conducted its picketing peacefully on matters of public concern at a public place adjacent to a public street. Such space occupies a "special position in terms of First Amendment protection." *United States v. Grace* (1983). "[W]e have repeatedly referred to public streets as the archetype of a traditional public forum," noting that "'[t]ime out of mind' public streets and sidewalks have been used for public assembly and debate." *Frisby v. Schultz* (1988).

That said, "[e]ven protected speech is not equally permissible in all places and at all times." Id. Westboro's choice of where and when to conduct its picketing is not beyond the Government's regulatory reach—it is "subject to reasonable time, place, or manner restrictions" that are consistent with the standards announced in this Court's precedents. . . .

[T]he church members had the right to be where they were. Westboro alerted local authorities to its funeral protest and fully complied with police guidance on where the picketing could be staged. The picketing was conducted under police supervision some 1,000 feet from the church, out of the sight of those at the church. The protest was not unruly; there was no shouting, profanity, or violence.

The record confirms that any distress occasioned by Westboro's picketing turned on the content and viewpoint of the message conveyed, rather than any interference with the funeral itself. A group of parishioners standing at the very spot where Westboro stood, holding signs that said "God Bless America" and "God Loves You," would not have been subjected to liability. It was what Westboro said that exposed it to tort damages.

Given that Westboro's speech was at a public place on a matter of public concern, that speech is entitled to "special protection" under the First Amendment. Such speech cannot be restricted simply because it is upsetting or arouses contempt. "If there is a bedrock principle underlying the First Amendment, it is that the government may not prohibit the expression of an idea simply because society finds the idea itself offensive or disagreeable." *Texas v. Johnson* (1989). Indeed, "the point of all speech protection . . . is to shield just those choices of content that in someone's eyes are misguided, or even hurtful." *Hurley v. Irish-American Gay, Lesbian and Bisexual Group of Boston, Inc.* (1995).

The jury here was instructed that it could hold Westboro liable for intentional infliction of emotional distress based on a finding that Westboro's picketing was "outrageous." "Outrageousness," however, is a highly malleable standard with "an inherent subjectiveness about it which would allow a jury to impose liability on the basis of the jurors' tastes or views, or perhaps on the basis of their dislike of a particular expression." *Hustler.* In a case such as this, a jury is "unlikely to be neutral with respect to the content of [the] speech," posing "a real danger of becoming an instrument for the suppression of . . . 'vehement, caustic, and sometimes unpleasan[t]'" expression. *Bose Corp.* Such a risk is unacceptable; "in public debate [we] must tolerate insulting, and even outrageous, speech in order to provide adequate 'breathing space' to the freedoms protected by the First Amendment." *Boos v. Barry* (1988). What Westboro said, in the whole context of how and where it chose to say it, is entitled to "special protection" under the First Amendment, and that protection cannot be overcome by a jury finding that the picketing was outrageous. . . .

Westboro believes that America is morally flawed; many Americans might feel the same about Westboro. Westboro's funeral picketing is certainly hurtful and its contribution to public discourse may be negligible. But Westboro addressed matters of public import on public property, in a peaceful manner, in full compliance with the guidance of local officials. The speech was indeed planned to coincide with Matthew Snyder's funeral, but did not itself disrupt that funeral, and Westboro's choice to conduct its picketing at that time and place did not alter the nature of its speech.

Speech is powerful. It can stir people to action, move them to tears of both joy and sorrow, and—as it did here—inflict great pain. On the facts before us, we cannot react to that pain by punishing the speaker. As a Nation we have chosen a different course—to protect even hurtful speech on public issues to ensure that we do not stifle public debate. That choice requires that we shield Westboro from tort liability for its picketing in this case.

The judgment of the United States Court of Appeals for the Fourth Circuit is affirmed.

It is so ordered.

JUSTICE ALITO, dissenting.

Our profound national commitment to free and open debate is not a license for the vicious verbal assault that occurred in this case.

Petitioner Albert Snyder is not a public figure. He is simply a parent whose son, Marine Lance Corporal Matthew Snyder, was killed in Iraq. Mr. Snyder wanted what is surely the right of any parent who experiences such an incalculable loss: to bury his son in peace. But respondents, members of the Westboro Baptist Church, deprived him of that elementary right. They first issued a press release and thus turned Matthew's funeral into a tumultuous media event. They then appeared at the church, approached as closely as they could without trespassing, and launched a malevolent verbal attack on Matthew and his family at a time of acute emotional vulnerability. As a result, Albert Snyder suffered severe and lasting emotional injury. . . .

Respondents and other members of their church have strong opinions on certain moral, religious, and political issues, and the First Amendment ensures that they have almost limitless opportunities to express their views. They may write and distribute books, articles, and other texts; they may create and disseminate video and audio recordings; they may circulate petitions; they may speak to individuals and groups in public forums and in any private venue that wishes to accommodate them; they may picket peacefully in countless locations; they may appear on television and speak on the radio; they may post messages on the Internet and send out e-mails. And they may express their views in terms that are "uninhibited," "vehement," and "caustic." *New York Times Co. v. Sullivan* (1964).

It does not follow, however, that they may intentionally inflict severe emotional injury on private persons at a time of intense emotional sensitivity by launching vicious verbal attacks that make no contribution to public debate. . . .

. . . [T]hey maintained that the First Amendment gave them a license to engage in such conduct. They are wrong. . . .

This Court has recognized that words may "by their very utterance inflict injury" and that the First Amendment does not shield utterances that form "no essential part of any exposition of ideas, and are of such slight social value as a step to truth that any benefit that may be derived from them is clearly outweighed by the social interest in order and morality." *Chaplinsky v. New Hampshire* (1942). When grave injury is intentionally inflicted by means of an attack like the one at issue here, the First Amendment should not interfere with recovery.

In this case, respondents brutally attacked Matthew Snyder, and this attack, which was almost certain to inflict injury, was central to respondents' well-practiced strategy for attracting public attention.

On the morning of Matthew Snyder's funeral, respondents could have chosen to stage their protest at countless locations. They could have picketed the United States Capitol, the White House, the Supreme Court, the Pentagon, or any of the more than 5,600 military recruiting stations in this country. They could have returned to the Maryland State House or the United States Naval Academy, where they had been the day before. They could have selected any public road where pedestrians are allowed. (There are more than 4,000,000 miles of public roads in the United States.) They could have staged their protest in a public park. (There are more than 20,000 public parks in this country.) They could have chosen any Catholic church where no funeral was taking place. (There are nearly 19,000 Catholic churches in the United States.) But of course, a small group picketing at any of these locations would have probably gone unnoticed.

The Westboro Baptist Church, however, has devised a strategy that remedies this problem. As the Court notes, church members have protested at nearly 600 military funerals. They have also picketed the funerals of police officers, firefighters, and the victims of natural disasters, accidents, and shocking crimes. And in advance of these protests, they issue press releases to ensure that their protests will attract public attention.

This strategy works because it is expected that respondents' verbal assaults will wound the family and friends of the deceased and because the media is irresistibly drawn to the sight of persons who are visibly in grief. The more outrageous the funeral protest, the more publicity the Westboro Baptist Church is able to obtain. Thus, when the church recently announced its intention to picket the funeral of a 9-year-old girl killed in the shooting spree in Tucson—proclaiming that she was "better off dead"—their announcement was national news, and the church was able to obtain free air time on the radio in exchange for canceling its protest. Similarly, in 2006, the church got air time on a talk radio show in exchange for canceling its threatened protest at the funeral of five Amish girls killed by a crazed gunman.

In this case, respondents implemented the Westboro Baptist Church's publicity-seeking strategy. Their press release stated that they were going "to picket the funeral of Lance Cpl. Matthew A. Snyder" because "God Almighty killed Lance Cpl. Snyder. He died in shame, not honor—for a fag nation cursed by God . . . .Now in Hell—sine die." This announcement guaranteed that Matthew's funeral would be transformed into a raucous media event and began the wounding process. It is well known that anticipation may heighten the effect of a painful event.

On the day of the funeral, respondents, true to their word, displayed placards that conveyed the message promised in their press release. Signs stating "God Hates You" and "Thank God for Dead Soldiers" reiterated the message that God had caused Matthew's death in retribution for his sins. Others, stating "You're Going to Hell" and "Not Blessed Just Cursed," conveyed the message that Matthew was "in Hell—sine die."

. . . Moreover, since a church funeral is an event that naturally brings to mind thoughts about the afterlife, some of respondents' signs—e.g., "God Hates You," "Not Blessed Just Cursed," and "You're Going to Hell"— would have likely been interpreted as referring to God's judgment of the deceased.

Other signs would most naturally have been understood as suggesting—falsely—that Matthew was gay. Homosexuality was the theme of many of the signs. There were signs reading "God Hates Fags," "Semper Fi Fags," "Fags Doom Nations," and "Fag Troops." Another placard depicted two men engaging in anal intercourse. . . .

In light of this evidence, it is abundantly clear that respondents, going far beyond commentary on matters of public concern, specifically attacked Matthew Snyder because (1) he was a Catholic and (2) he was a member of the United States military. Both Matthew and petitioner were private figures, and this attack was not speech on a matter of public concern. While commentary on the Catholic Church or the United States military constitutes speech on matters of public concern, speech regarding Matthew Snyder's purely private conduct does not. . . .

Respondents' outrageous conduct caused petitioner great injury, and the Court now compounds that injury by depriving petitioner of a judgment that acknowledges the wrong he suffered.

In order to have a society in which public issues can be openly and vigorously debated, it is not necessary to allow the brutalization of innocent victims like petitioner. I therefore respectfully dissent.

Snyder v. Phelps is an example of the Court's general position that the First Amendment protects even obnoxious and hateful utterances—as long as they remain within the realm of expression. The justices' tolerance, however, ends when hateful speech is associated with criminal acts. Since the 1980s it has been common for states to pass legislation designed to combat "hate crimes." These laws make individuals convicted of bias-motivated crimes eligible to receive more severe sentences than if the crimes had been committed for other reasons. Often, evidence of a discriminatory motive comes in the form of the defendant's own statements.

The justices ruled on the constitutionality of such laws in ***Wisconsin v. Mitchell*** (1993). The state law in question allowed judges to impose an enhanced penalty if the convicted defendant targeted the victim because of the person's race, religion, color, disability, sexual orientation, national origin, or ancestry. In this instance, Todd Mitchell, then nineteen, had been convicted of aggravated battery for leading a group of young African American men to attack a fourteen-year-old white boy, beating him severely. It was clear from Mitchell's comments immediately before initiating the attack that the victim was picked for racial reasons alone. Under Wisconsin law, aggravated battery would normally carry a two-year maximum sentence, but because there was evidence of racial motivation, Mitchell received an enhanced sentence of four years in prison.

On appeal, Mitchell claimed that the sentencing judge violated the First Amendment by imposing a penalty based on his biased beliefs and statements rather than on the crime itself. The Supreme Court, however, rejected this argument, holding that it was within the power of the state to take motive into account when authorizing sentences. Furthermore, the justices ruled that it was reasonable for the legislature to conclude that bias-motivated crimes should be treated more harshly than other offenses because they are more likely to inflict greater individual and societal harm.

R.A.V., Snyder, and *Mitchell* do not settle the hate speech issue. Supporters of broad First Amendment protection and those who favor restricting discriminatory expression both can find encouragement in the Court's opinions. As a result, the battle over hateful and harassing expression continues on college campuses, in workplaces, and in legislatures, and the Court certainly has not seen its last appeal in this area.

Student Speech

Freedom of speech issues are not confined to questions about the content of the expression. Also important is the context in which the words are uttered and who is doing the speaking. What may be said freely in one setting might be subject to regulation in another.

Considerable controversy has arisen over freedom of speech in the public schools. Do the schools constitute a special setting that permits an elevated degree of speech regulation? Do minors have the same expression rights as adults? The debate over these questions began with *Tinker v. Des Moines Independent Community School District* in 1969.

Tinker v. Des Moines Independent Community School District

393 U.S. 503 (1969)
http://laws.findlaw.com/US/393/503.html
Oral arguments are available at http://www.oyez.org.
Vote: 7 (Brennan, Douglas, Fortas, Marshall, Stewart, Warren, White)
　　2 (Black, Harlan)
OPINION OF THE COURT: *Fortas*
CONCURRING OPINIONS: *Stewart, White*
DISSENTING OPINIONS: *Black, Harlan*

FACTS:

In December 1965 a group of adults and secondary school students in Des Moines, Iowa, devised two strategies to demonstrate their opposition to the Vietnam War: they would fast on December 16 and New Year's Day, and they would wear black armbands every day in between. Principals of the students' schools learned of the plan and feared the demonstration would be disruptive. As a consequence, they announced that students wearing the armbands to school would be suspended. Of the eighteen thousand children in the school district, all but five complied with the policy. Among those five were John Tinker, Mary Beth Tinker, and Christopher Eckhardt, whose parents allowed them to wear black armbands to school. The three students had a history of participating in other civil rights and antiwar protests. All three were suspended. ACLU attorneys representing the students argued that the armbands constituted legitimate symbolic speech and that, by suppressing such expression, the school officials had engaged in unconstitutional prior restraint.

ARGUMENTS:

For the petitioners, John and Mary Beth Tinker and Christopher Eckhardt:
- The First Amendment protects the right of public school students to free speech in their schools and classrooms.
- The prohibition against wearing the armbands was an unconstitutional prior restraint on freedom of speech.
- Wearing the armbands caused no disturbance or disruption of the school day.

Mary Beth Tinker, pictured here with her mother, Lorena Tinker, and younger brother Paul, took part in a Vietnam War protest by wearing a black armband in school—an action that got Mary Beth and her older brother, John, suspended in 1965. In Tinker v. Des Moines (1969) the Supreme Court ruled that the suspensions violated the students' First Amendment rights.

***For the respondent, Des Moines
Independent Community School District:***

- School officials should be given wide discretion to carry out their responsibility to maintain a scholarly, disciplined atmosphere in the classroom. The school policy at issue here was reasonably calculated to promote that goal.
- Des Moines school officials properly allowed full classroom discussion of public issues, such as the Vietnam War, but demonstrations are inappropriate inside the school.
- Disturbances at school cannot be measured by the same standards used for adults in other environments.

MR. JUSTICE FORTAS DELIVERED THE OPINION OF THE COURT.

. . . [T]he wearing of armbands in the circumstances of this case was entirely divorced from actually or potentially disruptive conduct by those participating in it. It was closely akin to "pure speech" which, we have repeatedly held, is entitled to comprehensive protection under the First Amendment.

First Amendment rights, applied in light of the special characteristics of the school environment, are available to teachers and students. It can hardly be argued that either students or teachers shed their constitutional rights to freedom of speech or expression at the schoolhouse gate. This has been the unmistakable holding of this Court for almost 50 years. . . .

In *West Virginia State Board of Education v. Barnette*, this Court held that under the First Amendment, the student in public school may not be compelled to salute the flag. . . .

On the other hand, the Court has repeatedly emphasized the need for affirming the comprehensive authority of the States and of school officials, consistent with fundamental constitutional safeguards, to prescribe and control conduct in the schools. Our problem lies in the area where students in the exercise of First Amendment rights collide with the rules of the school authorities.

The problem posed by the present case does not relate to regulation of the length of skirts or the type of clothing, to hair style, or deportment. It does not concern aggressive, disruptive action or even group demonstrations. Our problem involves direct, primary First Amendment rights akin to "pure speech."

The school officials banned and sought to punish petitioners for a silent, passive expression of opinion,

unaccompanied by any disorder or disturbance on the part of petitioners. There is here no evidence whatever of petitioners' interference, actual or nascent, with the schools' work or of collision with the rights of other students to be secure and to be let alone. Accordingly, this case does not concern speech or action that intrudes upon the work of the schools or the rights of other students.

Only a few of the 18,000 students in the school system wore the black armbands. Only five students were suspended for wearing them. There is no indication that the work of the schools or any class was disrupted. Outside the classrooms, a few students made hostile remarks to the children wearing armbands, but there were no threats or acts of violence on school premises.

. . . [I]n our system, undifferentiated fear or apprehension of disturbance is not enough to overcome the right to freedom of expression. Any departure from absolute regimentation may cause trouble. Any variation from the majority's opinion may inspire fear. Any word spoken, in class, in the lunchroom, or on the campus, that deviates from the views of another person may start an argument or cause a disturbance. But our Constitution says we must take this risk, and our history says that it is this sort of hazardous freedom—this kind of openness—that is the basis of our national strength and of the independence and vigor of Americans who grow up and live in this relatively permissive, often disputatious, society.

In order for the State in the person of school officials to justify prohibition of a particular expression of opinion, it must be able to show that its action was caused by something more than a mere desire to avoid the discomfort and unpleasantness that always accompany an unpopular viewpoint. Certainly where there is no finding and no showing that engaging in the forbidden conduct would "materially and substantially interfere with the requirements of appropriate discipline in the operation of the school," the prohibition cannot be sustained. . . .

It is also relevant that the school authorities did not purport to prohibit the wearing of all symbols of political or controversial significance. The record shows that students in some of the schools wore buttons relating to national political campaigns, and some even wore the Iron Cross, traditionally a symbol of Nazism. The order prohibiting the wearing of armbands did not extend to these. Instead, a particular symbol—black armbands worn to exhibit opposition to this Nation's involvement in Vietnam—was singled out for prohibition. Clearly, the prohibition of expression of one particular opinion, at least without evidence that it is necessary to avoid material and substantial interference with schoolwork or discipline, is not constitutionally permissible.

In our system, state-operated schools may not be enclaves of totalitarianism. School officials do not possess absolute authority over their students. Students in school as well as out of school are "persons" under our Constitution. They are possessed of fundamental rights which the State must respect, just as they themselves must respect their obligations to the State. In our system, students may not be regarded as closed-circuit recipients of only that which the State chooses to communicate. They may not be confined to the expression of those sentiments that are officially approved. In the absence of a specific showing of constitutionally valid reasons to regulate their speech, students are entitled to freedom of expression of their views. . . .

. . . The principal use to which the schools are dedicated is to accommodate students during prescribed hours for the purpose of certain types of activities. Among those activities is personal intercommunication among the students. This is not only an inevitable part of the process of attending school; it is also an important part of the educational process. A student's rights, therefore, do not embrace merely the classroom hours. When he is in the cafeteria, or on the playing field, or on the campus during the authorized hours, he may express his opinions, even on controversial subjects like the conflict in Vietnam, if he does so without "materially and substantially interfer[ing] with the requirements of appropriate discipline in the operation of the school" and without colliding with the rights of others. But conduct by the student, in class or out of it, which for any reason—whether it stems from time, place, or type of behavior—materially disrupts classwork or involves substantial disorder or invasion of the rights of others is, of course, not immunized by the constitutional guarantee of freedom of speech. . . .

As we have discussed, the record does not demonstrate any facts which might reasonably have led school authorities to forecast substantial disruption of or material interference with school activities, and no disturbances or disorders on the school premises in fact occurred. These petitioners merely went about their ordained rounds in school. Their deviation consisted only in wearing on their sleeve a band of black cloth, not more than two inches wide. They wore it to exhibit their disapproval of the Vietnam hostilities and their advocacy of a truce, to make their views known, and, by their example, to influence others to adopt them. They neither interrupted

school activities nor sought to intrude in the school affairs or the lives of others. They caused discussion outside of the classrooms, but no interference with work and no disorder. In the circumstances, our Constitution does not permit officials of the State to deny their form of expression. . . .

Reversed and remanded.

MR. JUSTICE BLACK, *dissenting.*

As I read the Court's opinion it relies upon the following grounds for holding unconstitutional the judgment of the Des Moines school officials and the two courts below. First, the Court concludes that the wearing of armbands is "symbolic speech" which is "akin to 'pure speech'" and therefore protected by the First and Fourteenth Amendments. Secondly, the Court decides that the public schools are an appropriate place to exercise "symbolic speech" as long as normal school functions are not "unreasonably" disrupted. Finally, the Court arrogates to itself, rather than to the State's elected officials charged with running the schools, the decision as to which school disciplinary regulations are "reasonable."

Assuming that the Court is correct in holding that the conduct of wearing armbands for the purpose of conveying political ideas is protected by the First Amendment, the crucial remaining questions are whether students and teachers may use the schools at their whim as a platform for the exercise of free speech—"symbolic" or "pure"—and whether the courts will allocate to themselves the function of deciding how the pupils' school day will be spent. While I have always believed that under the First and Fourteenth Amendments neither the State nor the Federal Government has any authority to regulate or censor the content of speech, I have never believed that any person has a right to give speeches or engage in demonstrations where he pleases and when he pleases. . . .

While the record does not show that any of these armband students shouted, used profane language, or were violent in any manner, detailed testimony by some of them shows their armbands caused comments, warnings by other students, the poking of fun at them, and a warning by an older football player that other, nonprotesting students had better let them alone. There is also evidence that a teacher of mathematics had his lesson period practically "wrecked" chiefly by disputes with Mary Beth Tinker, who wore her armband for her "demonstration." . . .

I deny . . . that it has been the "unmistakable holding of this Court for almost 50 years" that "students" and "teachers" take with them into the "schoolhouse gate" constitutional rights to "freedom of speech or expression." . . . The truth is that a teacher of kindergarten, grammar school, or high school pupils no more carries into a school with him a complete right to freedom of speech and expression than an anti-Catholic or anti-Semite carries with him a complete freedom of speech and religion into a Catholic church or Jewish synagogue. Nor does a person carry with him into the United States Senate or House, or into the Supreme Court, or any other court, a complete constitutional right to go into those places contrary to their rules and speak his mind on any subject he pleases. It is a myth to say that any person has a constitutional right to say what he pleases, where he pleases, and when he pleases. Our Court has decided precisely the opposite. . . .

. . . Here a very small number of students have crisply and summarily refused to obey a school order designed to give pupils who want to learn the opportunity to do so. One does not need to be a prophet or the son of a prophet to know that after the Court's holding today some students in Iowa schools and indeed in all schools will be ready, able, and willing to defy their teachers on practically all orders. This is the more unfortunate for the schools since groups of students all over the land are already running loose, conducting break-ins, sit-ins, lie-ins, and smash-ins. . . . Students engaged in such activities are apparently confident that they know far more about how to operate public school systems than do their parents, teachers, and elected school officials. . . . This case, therefore, wholly without constitutional reasons in my judgment, subjects all the public schools in the country to the whims and caprices of their loudest-mouthed, but may be not their brightest, students. I, for one, am not fully persuaded that school pupils are wise enough, even with this Court's expert help from Washington, to run the 23,390 public school systems in our 50 States. I wish, therefore, wholly to disclaim any purpose on my part to hold that the Federal Constitution compels the teachers, parents, and elected school officials to surrender control of the American public school system to public school students. I dissent.

Justice Fortas's majority opinion is a strong endorsement of constitutional protection for expression that takes place in the classroom. Teachers and students, he declared, do not shed their constitutional rights at the schoolhouse gate. As long as the speech does not disrupt the educational process, government has no authority to proscribe it.

Tinker, however, was not the last Court ruling on public school speech. In 1986 the justices confronted *Bethel School District No. 403 v. Fraser,* a dispute over a speech presented to a high school assembly. Matthew Fraser's remarks were in support of a classmate who was running for a student government position. The speech, however, was laced with sexual innuendo. Fraser, a senior with an excellent school record, had discussed the speech with two of his teachers, but he ignored their warnings that he might suffer serious consequences if he went ahead with his plans. The day after he gave the speech, he was suspended for three days for violating the school policy against "the use of obscene, profane language or gestures."

By a 7–2 vote, the justices upheld the suspension. Chief Justice Burger's opinion concluded that "the First Amendment does not prevent the school officials from determining that to permit a vulgar and lewd speech such as respondent's would undermine the school's basic educational mission." Unlike the *Tinker* case, Matthew Fraser was not being punished for the political content of his expression.

More recently, the Court returned to the public school expression issue in *Morse v. Frederick* (2007). As you read the *Morse* decision, notice the wide array of views expressed by the justices. Justice Stevens's dissenting opinion strongly supports the *Tinker* precedent; he would protect almost all student expression. At the other extreme, Justice Thomas believes that students have no constitutionally protected expression rights. He thinks *Tinker* should be overruled. The majority of the justices, however, take a more moderate position.

Morse v. Frederick

551 U. S. 393 (2007)
http://laws.findlaw.com/US/000/06-278.html
Oral arguments are available at http://www.oyez.org.
Vote: 5 (Alito, Kennedy, Roberts, Scalia, Thomas)
    4 (Breyer, Ginsburg, Souter, Stephens)

OPINION OF THE COURT: *Roberts*

CONCURRING OPINION: *Alito, Thomas*

**OPINION CONCURRING IN JUDGMENT IN PART
   AND DISSENTING IN PART: *Breyer***

DISSENTING OPINION: *Stevens*

In Morse v. Frederick the Supreme Court upheld the Juneau School District's suspension of Joseph Frederick for displaying a banner perceived as supportive of illegal drug use. Here Frederick's attorney stands alongside the banner that ignited the dispute.

FACTS:

On January 24, 2002, the Olympic Torch Relay passed through Juneau, Alaska, on its way to the Winter Games in Salt Lake City. The event was scheduled to pass along a street in front of Juneau-Douglas High School (JDHS). Principal Deborah Morse decided to have the school's staff and students observe the event as part of an approved school activity. Students were allowed to leave class and watch the relay from either side of the street. The school's cheerleaders and band performed during the event.

Joseph Frederick, a senior at the high school, joined some friends across the street from the school. As the torchbearers and television camera crews passed by, Frederick and his friends unfurled a fourteen-foot banner bearing the words "BONG HiTS 4 JESUS" in large letters. Morse immediately crossed the street and ordered the students to lower the banner. All complied except Frederick. Morse suspended Frederick for ten days on the grounds that he violated school policy pertaining to the advocacy of illegal drugs.

The school superintendent upheld the suspension, holding that it was an appropriate enforcement of school policy at a school-sponsored event. The message portrayed on the banner was not political expression and could be reasonably interpreted as supportive of illegal drug use. Frederick sued in federal district court for unspecified monetary damages, claiming that his First Amendment rights had been violated. The district judge held that "Morse had the authority, if not the obligation, to stop such messages at a school-sanctioned activity." The Court of Appeals for the Ninth Circuit, however, reversed on the grounds that student speech cannot be restricted without a showing that it poses a substantial risk of disruption. The school system requested Supreme Court review.

ARGUMENTS:

For the petitioners, Deborah Morse and the Juneau School Board:

- *Tinker v. Des Moines* and *Bethel School District No. 403 v. Fraser* allow regulation of student speech that disrupts or undermines the school's educational mission.
- Discouraging use of illegal substances is part of the school's mission.
- Frederick's pro-drug banner interfered with decorum by radically changing the focus of the school activity.
- Principal Morse properly disassociated the school from Frederick's pro-drug banner.

For the respondent, Joseph Frederick:

- Frederick's banner was displayed off school property. The Olympic Torch event was not school sponsored.
- Schools cannot punish nondisruptive student speech just because they disagree with the ideas expressed.
- The record does not show that Frederick's banner caused substantial disruption of the educational mission as required in *Tinker,* nor was the banner offensive within the meaning of *Fraser.*

At the outset, we reject Frederick's argument that this is not a school speech case—as has every other authority to address the question. . . . [W]e agree with the superintendent that Frederick cannot "stand in the midst of his fellow students, during school hours, at a school-sanctioned activity and claim he is not at school." . . .

The message on Frederick's banner is cryptic. It is no doubt offensive to some, perhaps amusing to others. To still others, it probably means nothing at all. Frederick himself claimed "that the words were just nonsense meant to attract television cameras." But Principal Morse thought the banner would be interpreted by those viewing it as promoting illegal drug use, and that interpretation is plainly a reasonable one. . . .

We agree with Morse. . . .

The pro-drug interpretation of the banner gains further plausibility given the paucity of alternative meanings the banner might bear. The best Frederick can come up with is that the banner is "meaningless and funny." . . . Gibberish is surely a possible interpretation of the words on the banner, but it is not the only one, and dismissing the banner as meaningless ignores its undeniable reference to illegal drugs.

The dissent mentions Frederick's "credible and uncontradicted explanation for the message—he just wanted to get on television." But that is a description of Frederick's motive for displaying the banner; it is not an interpretation of what the banner says. The way Frederick was going to fulfill his ambition of appearing on television was by unfurling a pro-drug banner at a school event, in the presence of teachers and fellow students.

. . . [T]his is plainly not a case about political debate over the criminalization of drug use or possession.

The question thus becomes whether a principal may, consistent with the First Amendment, restrict student speech at a school event, when that speech is reasonably viewed as promoting illegal drug use. We hold that she may. . . .

Tinker [v. Des Moines Independent Community School District (1969)] held that student expression may not be suppressed unless school officials reasonably conclude that it will "materially and substantially disrupt the work and discipline of the school." The essential facts of *Tinker* are quite stark, implicating concerns at the heart of the First Amendment. The students sought to engage in political speech, using the armbands to express their "disapproval of the Vietnam hostilities and their advocacy

of a truce, to make their views known, and, by their example, to influence others to adopt them." Political speech, of course, is "at the core of what the First Amendment is designed to protect." *Virginia v. Black* (2003). The only interest the Court discerned underlying the school's actions was the "mere desire to avoid the discomfort and unpleasantness that always accompany an unpopular viewpoint," or "an urgent wish to avoid the controversy which might result from the expression." *Tinker*. That interest was not enough to justify banning "a silent, passive expression of opinion, unaccompanied by any disorder or disturbance."

This Court's next student speech case was [*Bethel School District No. 403 v.] Fraser* [1986]. Matthew Fraser was suspended for delivering a speech before a high school assembly in which he employed what this Court called "an elaborate, graphic, and explicit sexual metaphor." . . . This Court [held] that the "School District acted entirely within its permissible authority in imposing sanctions upon Fraser in response to his offensively lewd and indecent speech." . . .

. . . For present purposes, it is enough to distill from *Fraser* two basic principles. First, Fraser's holding demonstrates that "the constitutional rights of students in public school are not automatically coextensive with the rights of adults in other settings." Had Fraser delivered the same speech in a public forum outside the school context, it would have been protected. In school, however, Fraser's First Amendment rights were circumscribed "in light of the special characteristics of the school environment." Second, *Fraser* established that the mode of analysis set forth in *Tinker* is not absolute. Whatever approach *Fraser* employed, it certainly did not conduct the "substantial disruption" analysis prescribed by *Tinker*. . . .

Drawing on the principles applied in our student speech cases, we have held in the Fourth Amendment context that "while children assuredly do not 'shed their constitutional rights . . . at the schoolhouse gate,' . . . the nature of those rights is what is appropriate for children in school." *Vernonia School Dist. 47J v. Acton* (1995). In particular, "the school setting requires some easing of the restrictions to which searches by public authorities are ordinarily subject." *New Jersey v. T. L. O.* (1985). . . .

Even more to the point, these cases also recognize that deterring drug use by schoolchildren is an "important—indeed, perhaps compelling" interest. Drug abuse can cause severe and permanent damage to the health and well-being of young people. . . .

Congress has declared that part of a school's job is educating students about the dangers of illegal drug use. It has provided billions of dollars to support state and local drug-prevention programs. . . .

Thousands of school boards throughout the country—including JDHS—have adopted policies aimed at effectuating this message. Those school boards know that peer pressure is perhaps "the single most important factor leading schoolchildren to take drugs," and that students are more likely to use drugs when the norms in school appear to tolerate such behavior. Student speech celebrating illegal drug use at a school event, in the presence of school administrators and teachers, thus poses a particular challenge for school officials working to protect those entrusted to their care from the dangers of drug abuse.

The "special characteristics of the school environment" and the governmental interest in stopping student drug abuse—reflected in the policies of Congress and myriad school boards, including JDHS—allow schools to restrict student expression that they reasonably regard as promoting illegal drug use. . . .

Petitioners urge us to adopt the broader rule that Frederick's speech is proscribable because it is plainly "offensive" as that term is used in *Fraser*. We think this stretches *Fraser* too far; that case should not be read to encompass any speech that could fit under some definition of "offensive." After all, much political and religious speech might be perceived as offensive to some. The concern here is not that Frederick's speech was offensive, but that it was reasonably viewed as promoting illegal drug use. . . .

School principals have a difficult job, and a vitally important one. When Frederick suddenly and unexpectedly unfurled his banner, Morse had to decide to act—or not act—on the spot. It was reasonable for her to conclude that the banner promoted illegal drug use—in violation of established school policy—and that failing to act would send a powerful message to the students in her charge, including Frederick, about how serious the school was about the dangers of illegal drug use. The First Amendment does not require schools to tolerate at school events student expression that contributes to those dangers.

The judgment of the United States Court of Appeals for the Ninth Circuit is reversed, and the case is remanded for further proceedings consistent with this opinion.

It is so ordered.

JUSTICE THOMAS, concurring.

The Court today decides that a public school may prohibit speech advocating illegal drug use. I agree and therefore join its opinion in full. I write separately to state my view that the standard set forth in *Tinker v. Des Moines Independent Community School Dist.* (1969), is without basis in the Constitution. . . .

. . . In my view, the history of public education suggests that the First Amendment, as originally understood, does not protect student speech in public schools. . . .

. . . [W]hen States developed public education systems in the early 1800's, no one doubted the government's ability to educate and discipline children as private schools did. Like their private counterparts, early public schools were not places for freewheeling debates or exploration of competing ideas. Rather, teachers instilled "a core of common values" in students and taught them self-control.

Teachers instilled these values not only by presenting ideas but also through strict discipline. Schools punished students for behavior the school considered disrespectful or wrong. Rules of etiquette were enforced, and courteous behavior was demanded. To meet their educational objectives, schools required absolute obedience.

In short, in the earliest public schools, teachers taught, and students listened. Teachers commanded, and students obeyed. Teachers did not rely solely on the power of ideas to persuade; they relied on discipline to maintain order. . . .

Tinker effected a sea change in students' speech rights, extending them well beyond traditional bounds. . . .

Accordingly, unless a student's speech would disrupt the educational process, students had a fundamental right to speak their minds (or wear their armbands)—even on matters the school disagreed with or found objectionable.

Justice Black dissented, criticizing the Court for "subject[ing] all the public schools in the country to the whims and caprices of their loudest-mouthed, but maybe not their brightest, students." He emphasized the instructive purpose of schools: "[T]axpayers send children to school on the premise that at their age they need to learn, not teach." In his view, the Court's decision "surrender[ed] control of the American public school system to public school students." . . .

. . . I see no constitutional imperative requiring public schools to allow all student speech. Parents decide whether to send their children to public schools. If parents do not like the rules imposed by those schools, they can seek redress in school boards or legislatures; they can send their children to private schools or home school them; or they can simply move. Whatever rules apply to student speech in public schools, those rules can be challenged by parents in the political process.

In place of that democratic regime, *Tinker* substituted judicial oversight of the day-to-day affairs of public schools. The Tinker Court made little attempt to ground its holding in the history of education or in the original understanding of the First Amendment. . . .

Justice Black may not have been "a prophet or the son of a prophet," but his dissent in *Tinker* has proved prophetic. In the name of the First Amendment, *Tinker* has undermined the traditional authority of teachers to maintain order in public schools. "Once a society that generally respected the authority of teachers, deferred to their judgment, and trusted them to act in the best interest of school children, we now accept defiance, disrespect, and disorder as daily occurrences in many of our public schools." We need look no further than this case for an example: Frederick asserts a constitutional right to utter at a school event what is either "[g]ibberish" or an open call to use illegal drugs. To elevate such impertinence to the status of constitutional protection would be farcical and would indeed be to "surrender control of the American public school system to public school students."

I join the Court's opinion because it erodes *Tinker's* hold in the realm of student speech, even though it does so by adding to the patchwork of exceptions to the *Tinker* standard. I think the better approach is to dispense with *Tinker* altogether, and given the opportunity, I would do so.

JUSTICE ALITO, with whom JUSTICE KENNEDY joins, concurring.

I join the opinion of the Court on the understanding that (a) it goes no further than to hold that a public school may restrict speech that a reasonable observer would interpret as advocating illegal drug use and (b) it provides no support for any restriction of speech that can plausibly be interpreted as commenting on any political or social issue, including speech on issues such as "the wisdom of the war on drugs or of legalizing marijuana for medicinal use."

JUSTICE STEVENS, with whom JUSTICE SOUTER and JUSTICE GINSBURG join, dissenting.

. . . I would hold . . . that the school's interest in protecting its students from exposure to speech "reasonably regarded as promoting illegal drug use" cannot justify disciplining Frederick for his attempt to make an ambiguous statement to a television audience simply because it contained an oblique reference to drugs. The First Amendment demands more, indeed, much more. . . .

Two cardinal First Amendment principles animate . . . the Court's opinion in *Tinker [v. Des Moines Independent Community School Dist.* (1969)]. . . . First, censorship based on the content of speech, particularly censorship that depends on the view point of the speaker, is subject to the most rigorous burden of justification. . . .

Second, punishing someone for advocating illegal conduct is constitutional only when the advocacy is likely to provoke the harm that the government seeks to avoid.

However necessary it may be to modify those principles in the school setting, *Tinker* affirmed their continuing vitality. . . .

Yet today the Court fashions a test that trivializes the two cardinal principles upon which *Tinker* rests. The Court's test invites stark viewpoint discrimination. In this case, for example, the principal has unabashedly acknowledged that she disciplined Frederick because she disagreed with the pro-drug viewpoint she ascribed to the message on the banner. . . . [T]he Court's holding in this case strikes at "the heart of the First Amendment" because it upholds a punishment meted out on the basis of a listener's disagreement with her understanding (or, more likely, misunderstanding) of the speaker's viewpoint. "If there is a bedrock principle underlying the First Amendment, it is that the Government may not prohibit the expression of an idea simply because society finds the idea itself offensive or disagreeable." *Texas v. Johnson* (1989).

It is also perfectly clear that "promoting illegal drug use" comes nowhere close to proscribable "incitement to imminent lawless action." Encouraging drug use might well increase the likelihood that a listener will try an illegal drug, but that hardly justifies censorship. . . .

No one seriously maintains that drug advocacy (much less Frederick's ridiculous sign) comes within the vanishingly small category of speech that can be prohibited because of its feared consequences. . . .

. . . [I]t is one thing to restrict speech that advocates drug use. It is another thing entirely to prohibit an obscure message with a drug theme that a third party subjectively—and not very reasonably—thinks is tantamount to express advocacy. . . .

There is absolutely no evidence that Frederick's banner's reference to drug paraphernalia "willful[ly]" infringed on anyone's rights or interfered with any of the school's educational programs. . . . Therefore, just as we insisted in *Tinker* that the school establish some likely connection between the armbands and their feared consequences, so too JDHS must show that Frederick's supposed advocacy stands a meaningful chance of making otherwise-abstemious students try marijuana. . . .

To the extent the Court defers to the principal's ostensibly reasonable judgment, it abdicates its constitutional responsibility. The beliefs of third parties, reasonable or otherwise, have never dictated which messages amount to proscribable advocacy. Indeed, it would be a strange constitutional doctrine that would allow the prohibition of only the narrowest category of speech advocating unlawful conduct, yet would permit a listener's perceptions to determine which speech deserved constitutional protection. . . .

Even in high school, a rule that permits only one point of view to be expressed is less likely to produce correct answers than the open discussion of countervailing views. In the national debate about a serious issue, it is the expression of the minority's viewpoint that most demands the protection of the First Amendment. . . .

I respectfully dissent.

The Right Not to Speak

The most common type of freedom of speech lawsuit involves a claim that the government has unconstitutionally prohibited, limited, or punished expression. While curtailing speech is the most prevalent form of government regulation, there are situations in which the government requires us to speak or write. For example, we may be ordered to appear as witnesses before courts, grand juries, or legislative investigating committees. The government compels us to provide information when we file our tax returns. We may be required to take oaths when we become citizens, provide court testimony, or assume public office. Americans generally consider these regulations to be reasonable

requirements relevant to legitimate government functions. But what if an individual does not want to comply with a government regulation that requires expression? Other than the Fifth Amendment's protection against the government compelling self-incriminating testimony, is there any restraint on the government's authority to coerce expression? To put it another way, does the First Amendment's guarantee of freedom of speech carry with it the freedom *not* to speak?

To understand this issue, we need to turn our attention once again to the flag salute cases discussed in Chapter 4. As you recall, in 1940 the Court in **Minersville School District v. Gobitis** upheld flag salute regulations against claims that the school system was violating the children's right to free exercise of religion. Just three years later, in *West Virginia State Board of Education v. Barnette,* the Court again considered the constitutionality of the compulsory flag salute laws in another suit brought by the Jehovah's Witnesses.

By this time, however, some conditions had changed. First, public opinion, so feverishly patriotic at the beginning of World War II, had calmed somewhat following a series of important American military victories. As a consequence, public pressure on the government to impose mandatory expressions of patriotism had moderated. Second, the Court had undergone some personnel changes that strengthened its civil libertarian wing. Third, the *Gobitis* decision had been roundly criticized in legal circles. These circumstances encouraged the Witnesses to be more optimistic about their chances of winning.

But one additional factor distinguished *Gobitis* from *Barnette.* Lawyers for the Witnesses decided to base the attack primarily on the freedom of speech rather than on religious liberty. As you read Justice Jackson's majority opinion in *Barnette,* notice how he weaves religion and expression rights into his explanation for striking down the flag salute laws.

West Virginia State Board of Education v. Barnette

319 U.S. 624 (1943)
http://laws.findlaw.com/US/319/624.html
Vote: 6 (Black, Douglas, Jackson, Murphy, Rutledge, Stone)
    3 (Frankfurter, Reed, Roberts)
OPINION OF THE COURT: *Jackson*
CONCURRING OPINIONS: *Black and Douglas (joint), Murphy*
DISSENTING OPINIONS: *Frankfurter, Reed and Roberts (joint)*

FACTS:

Following the *Gobitis* decision, the West Virginia legislature amended its laws to require that all public schools teach courses to increase students' knowledge of the American system of government and to foster patriotism. In support of this policy, the state board of education required that the American flag be saluted and the Pledge of Allegiance recited each day. Students who refused to participate could be charged with insubordination and expelled. Not attending school because of such an expulsion was grounds for a child to be declared delinquent. Parents of delinquent children were subject to fines and jail penalties of up to thirty days. In some cases officials threatened noncomplying students with reform school.

The Jehovah's Witnesses challenged these regulations in the name of the Barnette family, church members who had been harassed by the school system for failure to participate in the flag salute ritual. One of the Barnette children had, in fact, been expelled.

Despite the Supreme Court's decision in *Gobitis*, a three-judge district court sympathized with the Barnette family's plight. According to the well-respected circuit court judge John J. Parker: "The salute to the United States' flag is an expression of the homage of the soul. To force it upon one who has conscientious scruples against giving it is petty tyranny unworthy of the spirit of the Republic, and forbidden, we think, by the United States Constitution." After the decision, the West Virginia School Board appealed to the U.S. Supreme Court.

ARGUMENTS:

For the appellant, West Virginia State Board of Education:

- All questions presented in this case have already been authoritatively answered by the Court in *Minersville School District v. Gobitis.*
- No relevant changes in federal law have occurred since *Gobitis.*
- The case should be settled by applying the *Gobitis* precedent and upholding the state's flag salute law.

For the appellees, Walter Barnette, et al.:

- The challenged regulations abridge freedom of speech, freedom to worship, and freedom of conscience.
- The conduct of the appellees does not constitute a clear and present danger of a substantive evil that the government has a right to prevent.

- The advantages said to flow from compulsory flag saluting are not so great as to justify depriving children of an education merely because they refuse to salute the flag.
- The *Gobitis* decision has encouraged widespread, violent attacks on Jehovah's Witnesses.

MR. JUSTICE JACKSON DELIVERED THE OPINION OF THE COURT.

Here . . . we are dealing with a compulsion of students to declare a belief. They are not merely made acquainted with the flag salute so that they may be informed as to what it is or even what it means. The issue here is whether this slow and easily neglected route to aroused loyalties constitutionally may be short-cut by substituting a compulsory salute and slogan. . . .

There is no doubt that, in connection with the pledges, the flag salute is a form of utterance. Symbolism is a primitive but effective way of communicating ideas. The use of an emblem or flag to symbolize some system, idea, institution, or personality, is a short cut from mind to mind. Causes and nations, political parties, lodges and ecclesiastical groups seek to knit the loyalty of their following to a flag or banner, a color or design. The State announces rank, function, and authority through crowns and maces, uniforms and black robes; the church speaks through the Cross, the Crucifix, the altar and shrine, and clerical raiment. Symbols of State often convey political ideas just as religious symbols come to convey theological ones. Associated with many of these symbols are appropriate gestures of acceptance or respect: a salute, a bowed or bared head, a bended knee. A person gets from a symbol the meaning he puts into it, and what is one man's comfort and inspiration is another's jest and scorn.

Over a decade ago Chief Justice Hughes led this Court in holding that the display of a red flag as a symbol of opposition by peaceful and legal means to organized government was protected by the free speech guaranties of the Constitution. *Stromberg v. California* [1931]. Here it is the State that employs a flag as a symbol of adherence to government as presently organized. It requires the individual to communicate by word and sign his acceptance of the political ideas it thus bespeaks. Objection to this form of communication when coerced is an old one, well known to the framers of the Bill of Rights.

It is also to be noted that the compulsory flag salute and pledge requires affirmation of a belief and an attitude of mind. . . . [H]ere the power of compulsion is invoked without any allegation that remaining passive during a flag salute ritual creates a clear and present danger that would justify an effort even to muffle expression. To sustain the compulsory flag salute we are required to say that a Bill of Rights which guards the individual's right to speak his own mind, left it open to public authorities to compel him to utter what is not in his mind.

Whether the First Amendment to the Constitution will permit officials to order observance of ritual of this nature does not depend upon whether as a voluntary exercise we would think it to be good, bad or merely innocuous. . . .

Nor does the issue as we see it turn on one's possession of particular religious views or the sincerity with which they are held. While religion supplies appellees' motive for enduring the discomforts of making the issue in this case, many citizens who do not share these religious views hold such a compulsory rite to infringe constitutional liberty of the individual. It is not necessary to inquire whether non-conformist beliefs will exempt from the duty to salute unless we first find power to make the salute a legal duty.

The *Gobitis* decision, however, *assumed* as did the argument in that case and in this, that power exists in the State to impose the flag salute discipline upon school children in general. The Court only examined and rejected a claim based on religious beliefs of immunity from an unquestioned general rule. The question which underlies the flag salute controversy is whether such a ceremony so touching matters of opinion and political attitude may be imposed upon the individual by official authority under powers committed to any political organization under our Constitution. We examine rather than assume existence of this power and, against this broader definition of issues in this case, re-examine specific grounds assigned for the *Gobitis* decision.

1. It was said that the flag-salute controversy confronted the Court with "the problem which Lincoln cast in memorable dilemma: 'Must a government of necessity be too *strong* for the liberties of its people, or too *weak* to maintain its own existence?'" and that the answer must be in favor of strength. *Minersville School District v. Gobitis.*

We think these issues may be examined free of pressure or restraint growing out of such considerations.

It may be doubted whether Mr. Lincoln would have thought that the strength of government to maintain itself would be impressively vindicated by our confirming power of the state to expel a handful of children from school. Such oversimplification, so handy in political debate, often lacks the precision necessary to postulates of judicial reasoning. If validly applied to this problem, the utterance cited would resolve every issue of power in favor of those in authority and would require us to override every liberty thought to weaken or delay execution of their policies.

Government of limited power need not be anemic government. Assurance that rights are secure tends to diminish fear and jealousy of strong government, and by making us feel safe to live under it makes for its better support. Without promise of a limiting Bill of Rights it is doubtful if our Constitution could have mustered enough strength to enable its ratification. To enforce those rights today is not to choose weak government over strong government. It is only to adhere as a means of strength to individual freedom of mind in preference to officially disciplined uniformity for which history indicates a disappointing and disastrous end.

The subject now before us exemplifies this principle. Free public education, if faithful to the ideal of secular instruction and political neutrality, will not be partisan or enemy of any class, creed, party, or faction. If it is to impose any ideological discipline, however, each party or denomination must seek to control, or failing that, to weaken the influence of the educational system. Observance of the limitations of the Constitution will not weaken government in the field appropriate for its exercise.

2. It was also considered in the *Gobitis* case that functions of educational officers in states, counties and school districts were such that to interfere with their authority "would in effect make us the school board for the country."

The Fourteenth Amendment, as now applied to the States, protects the citizen against the State itself and all of its creatures—Boards of Education not excepted. These have, of course, important, delicate, and highly discretionary functions, but none that they may not perform within the limits of the Bill of Rights. That they are educating the young for citizenship is reason for scrupulous protection of Constitutional freedoms of the individual, if we are not to strangle the free mind at its source and teach youth to discount important principles of our government as mere platitudes.

Such Boards are numerous and their territorial juris-diction often small. But small and local authority may feel less sense of responsibility to the Constitution, and agencies of publicity may be less vigilant in calling it to account. The action of Congress in making flag obser-vance voluntary and respecting the conscience of the objector in a matter so vital as raising the Army con-trasts sharply with these local regulations in matters relatively trivial to the welfare of the nation. There are village tyrants as well as village Hampdens, but none who acts under color of law is beyond reach of the Constitution.

3. The *Gobitis* opinion reasoned that this is a field "where courts possess no marked and certainly no con-trolling competence," that it is committed to the legisla-tures as well as the courts to guard cherished liberties and that it is constitutionally appropriate to "fight out the wise use of legislative authority in the forum of pub-lic opinion and before legislative assemblies rather than to transfer such a contest to the judicial arena," since all the "effective means of inducing political changes are left free."

The very purpose of a Bill of Rights was to withdraw certain subjects from the vicissitudes of political contro-versy, to place them beyond the reach of majorities and officials and to establish them as legal principles to be applied by the courts. One's right to life, liberty, and property, to free speech, a free press, freedom of worship and assembly, and other fundamental rights may not be submitted to vote; they depend on the outcome of no elections.

In weighing arguments of the parties it is important to distinguish between the due process clause of the Four-teenth Amendment as an instrument for transmitting the principles of the First Amendment and those cases in which it is applied for its own sake. The test of legislation which collides with the Fourteenth Amendment, because it also collides with the principles of the First, is much more definite than the test when only the Fourteenth is involved. Much of the vagueness of the due process clause disap-pears when the specific prohibitions of the First become its standard. The right of a State to regulate, for example, a public utility may well include, so far as the due process test is concerned, power to impose all of the restrictions which a legislature may have a "rational basis" for adopt-ing. But freedoms of speech and of press, of assembly, and of worship may not be infringed on such slender grounds. They are susceptible of restriction only to prevent grave and immediate danger to interests which the state may

lawfully protect. It is important to note that while it is the Fourteenth Amendment which bears directly upon the State it is the more specific limiting principles of the First Amendment that finally govern this case. . . .

4. Lastly, and this is the very heart of the *Gobitis* opinion, it reasons that "National unity is the basis of national security," that the authorities have "the right to select appropriate means for its attainment," and hence reaches the conclusion that such compulsory measures toward "national unity" are constitutional. Upon the verity of this assumption depends our answer in this case.

National unity as an end which officials may foster by persuasion and example is not in question. The problem is whether under our Constitution compulsion as here employed is a permissible means for its achievement.

Struggles to coerce uniformity of sentiment in support of some end thought essential to their time and country have been waged by many good as well as by evil men. Nationalism is a relatively recent phenomenon but at other times and places the ends have been racial or ter-ritorial security, support of a dynasty or regime, and par-ticular plans for saving souls. As first and moderate methods to attain unity have failed, those bent on its accomplishment must resort to an ever-increasing sever-ity. . . . Those who begin coercive elimination of dissent soon find themselves exterminating dissenters. Compul-sory unification of opinion achieves only the unanimity of the graveyard.

It seems trite but necessary to say that the First Amendment to our Constitution was designed to avoid these ends by avoiding these beginnings. There is no mysticism in the American concept of the State or of the nature or origin of its authority. We set up government by consent of the governed, and the Bill of Rights denies those in power any legal opportunity to coerce that con-sent. Authority here is to be controlled by public opin-ion, not public opinion by authority.

The case is made difficult not because the principles of its decision are obscure but because the flag involved is our own. Nevertheless, we apply the limitations of the Constitution with no fear that freedom to be intel-lectually and spiritually diverse or even contrary will disintegrate the social organization. To believe that patriotism will not flourish if patriotic ceremonies are voluntary and spontaneous instead of a compulsory routine is to make an unflattering estimate of the appeal of our institutions to free minds. We can have intellec-tual individualism and the rich cultural diversity that we owe to exceptional minds only at the price of occasional eccentricity and abnormal attitudes. When they are so harmless to others or to the State as those we deal with here, the price is not too great. But freedom to differ is not limited to things that do not matter much. That would be a mere shadow of freedom. The test of its substance is the right to differ as to things that touch the heart of the existing order.

If there is any fixed star in our constitutional constellation, it is that no official, high or petty, can prescribe what shall be orthodox in politics, nationalism, religion, or other matters of opinion or force citizens to confess by word or act their faith therein. If there are any circumstances which permit an exception, they do not now occur to us.

We think the action of the local authorities in compelling the flag salute and pledge transcends constitutional limitations on their power and invades the sphere of intellect and spirit which it is the purpose of the First Amendment to our Constitution to reserve from all official control.

The decision of this Court in *Minersville School District v. Gobitis* and the holdings of those few per curiam decisions which preceded and foreshadowed it are overruled, and the judgment enjoining enforcement of the West Virginia Regulation is affirmed.

Affirmed.

MR. JUSTICE FRANKFURTER, dissenting.

One who belongs to the most vilified and persecuted minority in history is not likely to be insensible to the freedoms guaranteed by our Constitution. Were my purely personal attitude relevant I should wholeheartedly associate myself with the general libertarian views in the Court's opinion, representing as they do the thought and action of a lifetime. But as judges we are neither Jew nor Gentile, neither Catholic nor agnostic. We owe equal attachment to the Constitution and are equally bound by our judicial obligations whether we derive our citizenship from the earliest or latest immigrants to these shores. As a member of this Court I am not justified in writing my private notions of policy into the Constitution, no matter how deeply I may cherish them or how mischievous I may deem their disregard. The duty of a judge who must decide which of two claims before the Court shall prevail, that of a State to enact and enforce laws within its general competence or that of an individual to refuse obedience because of

the demands of his conscience, is not that of the ordinary person. It can never be emphasized too much that one's own opinion about the wisdom or evil of a law should be excluded altogether when one is doing one's duty on the bench. . . . [I]t would require more daring than I possess to deny that reasonable legislators could have taken the action which is before us for review. Most unwillingly, therefore, I must differ from my brethren with regard to legislation like this. I cannot bring my mind to believe that the "liberty" secured by the Due Process Clause gives this Court authority to deny to the State of West Virginia the attainment of that which we all recognize as a legitimate legislative end, namely, the promotion of good citizenship, by employment of the means here chosen.

In striking down the West Virginia compulsory flag salute law, the Court ruled that the individual has at least a qualified right to be free of government coercion to express views he or she disavows. This decision does not go so far as to hold that an individual's First Amendment right can be used to avoid obligations such as testifying in a court case or providing information on a tax return, but it precludes certain forms of coerced expression.

For another example of this principle, consider the plight of George and Maxine Maynard of Lebanon, New Hampshire. Like the Gobitas and Barnette families, the Maynards were Jehovah's Witnesses. Their entanglement with the law stemmed from a statute mandating that the state slogan "Live Free or Die" appear on all vehicle license plates. The Maynards considered the slogan repugnant to their moral, religious, and political beliefs. To disassociate himself from the slogan, George Maynard cut a portion of the slogan from the plates on his cars and covered the remaining words with tape, but he did not conceal the identifying letters or numbers. This resulted in repeated arrests of the Maynards for driving their vehicle in violation of state law. The Maynards sued, challenging the constitutionality of the law. They won, and the state appealed.

The case of **Wooley v. Maynard** (1977) presented the justices with a classic conflict between individual and state interests. The Maynards argued that their First Amendment rights protected them from state compulsion. George Maynard filed a statement saying, "I refuse to be coerced by the State into advertising a slogan which I find morally, ethically, religiously, and politically abhorrent." The state responded by contending that its interest in promoting an appreciation of history, individualism, and state pride outweighed the narrow interests of the Maynards.

Speaking for the Court, Chief Justice Burger ruled in favor of the Maynards. He explained:

We begin with the proposition that the right of freedom of thought protected by the First Amendment against state action includes both the right to speak freely and the right to refrain from speaking at all. A system which secures the right to proselytize religious, political, and ideological causes must also guarantee the concomitant right to decline to foster such concepts. The right to speak and the right to refrain from speaking are complementary components of the broader concept of "individual freedom of mind."

The justices concluded that the countervailing interests of the state were insufficiently compelling to outweigh the First Amendment liberties at stake. The state slogan was not ideologically neutral but proclaimed an official view of history, state pride, and individualism. While the state may have an interest in promoting these beliefs, such an interest cannot outweigh an individual's First Amendment right to avoid becoming an unwilling spokesperson for that message.

More than two decades later, the Court once again faced the issue of compelled speech. In **Board of Regents of the University of Wisconsin System v. Southworth** (2000), a group of students at the University of Wisconsin–Madison claimed that the university's funding policies violated their constitutional right not to speak. Like many colleges, the University of Wisconsin collects a student activity fee from each student in addition to tuition charges. Significant portions of the funds thus collected are used to support student organizations. The complaining students objected to their funds being spent to subsidize groups whose purposes they opposed—specifically, gay, socialist, labor, women's, and other liberal causes. They argued that the mandatory activity fee compelled them to provide financial support for messages they found offensive.

A unanimous Supreme Court rejected this claim. The justices held that the university was pursuing a legitimate educational policy of encouraging a free and open exchange of ideas among students and that a mandatory fee—which funded student health services and other activities in addition to supporting

speakers—was a reasonable way to promote this goal. The Court emphasized that the Constitution requires that such programs be administered in a viewpoint-neutral fashion. Because registered student groups of all types were eligible to receive student activity funds, the Wisconsin program satisfied this requirement and was therefore constitutionally acceptable.

A related question reached the Court in 2006. In **Rumsfeld v. Forum for Academic and Institutional Rights** the justices were presented with the claim that a federal law requiring universities to treat military recruiters on campus the same way they treat other job recruiters violated the First Amendment principle that the government cannot compel speech. As you read the opinion of Chief Justice John Roberts for a unanimous Court, note how he uses precedent to explain the Court's conclusion and how he distinguishes relevant precedents from those he believes do not apply to the case before the Court.

Rumsfeld v. Forum for Academic and Institutional Rights, Inc.

547 U.S. 47 (2006)
http://laws.findlaw.com/US/000/04-1152.html
Oral arguments are available at http://www.oyez.org.
Vote: 8 (Breyer, Ginsburg, Kennedy, Roberts, Scalia, Souter, Stevens, Thomas)
0

OPINION OF THE COURT: *Roberts*

DID NOT PARTICIPATE: *Alito*

FACTS:

At issue in this case is the Solomon Amendment, which says that if any part of a college or university denies military recruiters the same access granted to other employers, the entire institution may lose certain federal funds (10 USC, § 983). Congress passed the law after some colleges and universities began protesting the government's policy about homosexuals in the military by refusing to allow armed forces recruiters on campus. The schools objected to a provision in federal law (10 USC, § 654) that allowed the military to dismiss members who engaged in homosexual acts, stated that they were homosexual, or married persons known to be of the same biological sex.

The Forum for Academic and Institutional Rights (FAIR) is an association of law schools and law faculties with a declared mission "to promote academic freedom, support educational institutions in opposing discrimination, and vindicate the rights of institutions of higher education." FAIR members have adopted policies against discrimination based on, among other factors, sexual orientation. FAIR opposed the military's policy on sexual orientation and, as a consequence, also opposed the military's recruitment efforts on law school campuses.

As part of a campaign to keep military recruiters off campus, FAIR filed suit to have the Solomon Amendment declared unconstitutional. The organization argued that forced inclusion and equal treatment of military recruiters violated its members' First Amendment freedoms of speech and association. The district court upheld the Solomon Amendment, but the court of appeals reversed, holding that the statute forced a law school to choose between surrendering First Amendment rights and losing federal funding for its university. The Supreme Court granted review.

ARGUMENTS:

For the petitioner, Donald Rumsfeld,
Secretary of Defense, et al.:

- The Solomon Amendment is a carefully tailored exercise of congressional authority to raise and support the armed forces.
- The Solomon Amendment does not interfere with a law school's right to associate for expressive purposes, force a law school to take a position with which it does not agree, or affect the internal composition of a law school.
- Law schools can avoid the equal access requirement by declining federal funds.

For the respondent, Forum for Academic
and Institutional Rights, Inc.:

- The Solomon Amendment effectively forces law schools to disseminate military recruiting messages.
- The Solomon Amendment prohibits law schools from teaching their lessons of nondiscrimination in the most effective way.
- The Solomon Amendment forces law schools to associate with military recruiters.
- The penalty for not complying, the loss of federal funds, is the same as a command.

CHIEF JUSTICE ROBERTS DELIVERED THE OPINION OF THE COURT.

The Constitution grants Congress the power to "provide for the common Defence," "[t]o raise and support Armies," and "[t]o provide and maintain a Navy." Art. I, § 8, cls. 1,

12–13. Congress' power in this area "is broad and sweeping" [*United States v.*] *O'Brien* [1968], and there is no dispute in this case that it includes the authority to require campus access for military recruiters. That is, of course, unless Congress exceeds constitutional limitations on its power in enacting such legislation. See *Rostker v. Goldberg* (1981). But the fact that legislation that raises armies is subject to First Amendment constraints does not mean that we ignore the purpose of this legislation when determining its constitutionality; as we recognized in *Rostker*, "judicial deference . . . is at its apogee" when Congress legislates under its authority to raise and support armies. . . .

The Solomon Amendment neither limits what law schools may say nor requires them to say anything. Law schools remain free under the statute to express whatever views they may have on the military's congressionally mandated employment policy, all the while retaining eligibility for federal funds. As a general matter, the Solomon Amendment regulates conduct, not speech. It affects what law schools must *do*—afford equal access to military recruiters—not what they may or may not *say*.

Nevertheless, the Third Circuit concluded that the Solomon Amendment violates law schools' freedom of speech in a number of ways. First, in assisting military recruiters, law schools provide some services, such as sending e-mails and distributing flyers, that clearly involve speech. The Court of Appeals held that in supplying these services law schools are unconstitutionally compelled to speak the Government's message. Second, military recruiters are, to some extent, speaking while they are on campus. The Court of Appeals held that, by forcing law schools to permit the military on campus to express its message, the Solomon Amendment unconstitutionally requires law schools to host or accommodate the military's speech. Third, although the Court of Appeals thought that the Solomon Amendment regulated speech, it held in the alternative that, if the statute regulates conduct, this conduct is expressive and regulating it unconstitutionally infringes law schools' right to engage in expressive conduct. We consider each issue in turn.

Some of this Court's leading First Amendment precedents have established the principle that freedom of speech prohibits the government from telling people what they must say. In *West Virginia Bd. of Ed. v. Barnette* (1943), we held unconstitutional a state law requiring schoolchildren to recite the Pledge of Allegiance and to salute the flag. And in *Wooley v. Maynard* (1977), we held unconstitutional another that required New Hampshire motorists to display the state motto—"Live Free or Die"—on their license plates.

The Solomon Amendment does not require any similar expression by law schools. Nonetheless, recruiting assistance provided by the schools often includes elements of speech. For example, schools may send e-mails or post notices on bulletin boards on an employer's behalf. Law schools offering such services to other recruiters must also send e-mails and post notices on behalf of the military to comply with the Solomon Amendment. As FAIR points out, these compelled statements of fact ("The U.S. Army recruiter will meet interested students in Room 123 at 11 A.M."), like compelled statements of opinion, are subject to First Amendment scrutiny.

This sort of recruiting assistance, however, is a far cry from the compelled speech in *Barnette* and *Wooley*. The Solomon Amendment, unlike the laws at issue in those cases, does not dictate the content of the speech at all, which is only "compelled" if, and to the extent, the school provides such speech for other recruiters. There is nothing in this case approaching a Government-mandated pledge or motto that the school must endorse.

The compelled speech to which the law schools point is plainly incidental to the Solomon Amendment's regulation of conduct, and "it has never been deemed an abridgment of freedom of speech or press to make a course of conduct illegal merely because the conduct was in part initiated, evidenced, or carried out by means of language, either spoken, written, or printed." *Giboney v. Empire Storage & Ice Co.* (1949). Congress, for example, can prohibit employers from discriminating in hiring on the basis of race. The fact that this will require an employer to take down a sign reading "White Applicants Only" hardly means that the law should be analyzed as one regulating the employer's speech rather than conduct. Compelling a law school that sends scheduling e-mails for other recruiters to send one for a military recruiter is simply not the same as forcing a student to pledge allegiance, or forcing a Jehovah's Witness to display the motto "Live Free or Die," and it trivializes the freedom protected in *Barnette* and *Wooley* to suggest that it is.

Our compelled-speech cases are not limited to the situation in which an individual must personally speak the government's message. We have also in a number of instances limited the government's ability to force one speaker to host or accommodate another speaker's message. See *Hurley v. Irish-American Gay, Lesbian and Bisexual Group of Boston, Inc.* (1995) (state law cannot require a parade to include a group whose message the parade's organizer does not wish to send); . . . *Miami Herald Publishing Co. v. Tornillo* (1974) (right-of-reply statute violates editors' right to determine the content of their newspapers). Relying on these precedents, the Third Circuit concluded that the Solomon Amendment unconstitutionally compels law schools to accommodate the military's message "[b]y requiring schools to include military recruiters in the interviews and recruiting receptions the schools arrange."

The compelled-speech violation in each of our prior cases, however, resulted from the fact that the complaining speaker's own message was affected by the speech it was forced to accommodate. The expressive nature of a parade was central to our holding in *Hurley*. We concluded that because "every participating unit affects the message conveyed by the [parade's] private organizers," a law dictating that a particular group must be included in the parade "alter[s] the expressive content of th[e] parade." As a result, we held that the State's public accommodation law, as applied to a private parade, "violates the fundamental rule of protection under the First Amendment, that a speaker has the autonomy to choose the content of his own message."

. . . In *Tornillo*, we recognized that "the compelled printing of a reply . . . tak[es] up space that could be devoted to other material the newspaper may have preferred to print," and therefore concluded that this right-of-reply statute infringed the newspaper editors' freedom of speech by altering the message the paper wished to express. . . .

In this case, accommodating the military's message does not affect the law schools' speech, because the schools are not speaking when they host interviews and recruiting receptions. Unlike a parade organizer's choice of parade contingents, a law school's decision to allow recruiters on campus is not inherently expressive. Law schools facilitate recruiting to assist their students in obtaining jobs. A law school's recruiting services lack the expressive quality of a parade, a newsletter, or the editorial page of a newspaper; its accommodation of a military recruiter's message is not compelled speech because the accommodation does not sufficiently interfere with any message of the school.

The schools respond that if they treat military and nonmilitary recruiters alike in order to comply with the Solomon Amendment, they could be viewed as sending the message that they see nothing wrong with the military's policies, when they do. . . .

. . . Nothing about recruiting suggests that law schools agree with any speech by recruiters, and nothing in the Solomon Amendment restricts what the law schools may say about the military's policies. . . .

Having rejected the view that the Solomon Amendment impermissibly regulates *speech,* we must still consider whether the expressive nature of the *conduct* regulated by the statute brings that conduct within the First Amendment's protection. In *O'Brien,* we recognized that some forms of "'symbolic speech'" were deserving of First Amendment protection. But we rejected the view that "conduct can be labeled 'speech' whenever the person engaging in the conduct intends thereby to express an idea." Instead, we have extended First Amendment protection only to conduct that is inherently expressive. In *Texas v. Johnson* (1989), for example, we applied *O'Brien* and held that burning the American flag was sufficiently expressive to warrant First Amendment protection.

Unlike flag burning, the conduct regulated by the Solomon Amendment is not inherently expressive. Prior to the adoption of the Solomon Amendment's equal-access requirement, law schools "expressed" their disagreement with the military by treating military recruiters differently from other recruiters. But these actions were expressive only because the law schools accompanied their conduct with speech explaining it. For example, the point of requiring military interviews to be conducted on the undergraduate campus is not "overwhelmingly apparent." An observer who sees military recruiters interviewing away from the law school has no way of knowing whether the law school is expressing its disapproval of the military, all the law school's interview rooms are full, or the military recruiters decided for reasons of their own that they would rather interview someplace else.

The expressive component of a law school's actions is not created by the conduct itself but by the speech that accompanies it. The fact that such explanatory speech is necessary is strong evidence that the conduct at issue here is not so inherently expressive that it warrants protection under *O'Brien.* If combining speech and conduct were enough to create expressive conduct, a regulated party could always transform conduct into "speech" simply by talking about it. For instance, if an individual announces that he intends to express his disapproval of the Internal Revenue Service by refusing to pay his income taxes, we would have to apply *O'Brien* to determine whether the Tax Code violates the First Amendment. Neither *O'Brien* nor its progeny supports such a result.

. . . [T]he Third Circuit . . . concluded that . . . the Solomon Amendment does not pass muster under *O'Brien* because the Government failed to produce evidence establishing that the Solomon Amendment was necessary and effective. The Court of Appeals surmised that "the military has ample resources to recruit through alternative means," suggesting "loan repayment programs" and "television and radio advertisements." As a result, the Government—according to the Third Circuit—failed to establish that the statute's burden on speech is no greater than essential to furthering its interest in military recruiting.

We disagree with the Court of Appeals' reasoning and result. We have held that "an incidental burden on speech is no greater than is essential, and therefore is permissible under *O'Brien,* so long as the neutral regulation promotes a substantial government interest that would be achieved less effectively absent the regulation." *United States v. Albertini* (1985). The Solomon Amendment clearly satisfies this requirement. Military recruiting promotes the substantial Government interest in raising and supporting the Armed Forces—an objective that would be achieved less effectively if the military were forced to recruit on less favorable terms than other employers. The Court of Appeals' proposed alternative methods of recruiting are beside the point. The issue is not whether other means of raising an army and providing for a navy might be adequate. That is a judgment for Congress, not the courts. It suffices that the means chosen by Congress add to the effectiveness of military recruitment. Accordingly, even if the Solomon Amendment were regarded as regulating expressive conduct, it would not violate the First Amendment under *O'Brien.*

The Solomon Amendment does not violate law schools' freedom of speech, but the First Amendment's protection extends beyond the right to speak. We have recognized a First Amendment right to associate for the purpose of speaking, which we have termed a "right of expressive association." See, e.g., *Boy Scouts of America v. Dale* (2000). The reason we have extended First Amendment protection in this way is clear: The right to speak is often exercised most effectively by combining one's voice with the voices of others. See *Roberts v. United States Jaycees* (1984). If the government were free to restrict individuals' ability to join together and speak, it could essentially silence views that the First Amendment is intended to protect. . . .

. . . Law schools therefore "associate" with military recruiters in the sense that they interact with them. But recruiters are not part of the law school. Recruiters are, by definition, outsiders who come onto campus for the limited purpose of trying to hire students—not to become members of the school's expressive association. This distinction is critical. Unlike the public accommodations law in *Dale*, the Solomon Amendment does not force a law school "'to accept members it does not desire.'" The law schools say that allowing military recruiters equal access impairs their own expression by requiring them to associate with the recruiters, but just as saying conduct is undertaken for expressive purposes cannot make it symbolic speech, so too a speaker cannot "erect a shield" against laws requiring access "simply by asserting" that mere association "would impair its message." . . .

. . . Students and faculty are free to associate to voice their disapproval of the military's message; nothing about the statute affects the composition of the group by making group membership less desirable. The Solomon Amendment therefore does not violate a law school's First Amendment rights. A military recruiter's mere presence on campus does not violate a law school's right to associate, regardless of how repugnant the law school considers the recruiter's message.

In this case, *FAIR* has attempted to stretch a number of First Amendment doctrines well beyond the sort of activities these doctrines protect. The law schools object to having to treat military recruiters like other recruiters, but that regulation of conduct does not violate the First Amendment. To the extent that the Solomon Amendment incidentally affects expression, the law schools' effort to cast themselves as just like the schoolchildren in *Barnette*, the parade organizers in *Hurley*, and the Boy Scouts in *Dale* plainly overstates the expressive nature of their activity and the impact of the Solomon Amendment on it, while exaggerating the reach of our First Amendment precedents.

. . . We therefore reverse the judgment of the Third Circuit and remand the case for further proceedings consistent with this opinion.

It is so ordered.

In December 2010 Congress repealed 10 USC, § 654, and over the next twelve months more tolerant policies regarding gays in the military were implemented. In spite of these changes, the Court's decision in *Rumsfeld v. FAIR* remains relevant. Chief Justice Roberts's opinion for a unanimous Court explains well the justices' approach to compelled speech and how the First Amendment relates to it. The decision also provides an example of the Court's traditional deference to the needs of the military and how Congress often places conditions on the appropriation of federal funds in order to attain its policy goals.

Commercial Speech

As consumers of all sorts of goods and services, we are constantly bombarded with commercial speech advertisements. Open a newspaper, turn on a television or radio, or log on to the Internet and you are bound to find hundreds of ads aimed at communicating all kinds of messages. Although we see ads every day, we probably do not think about them in terms of the First Amendment. Does the First Amendment apply to this form of expression? If so, does it deserve the same constitutional protection as more traditional, equally commonplace, forms of speech?

Historically, courts have viewed commercial expression as more closely related to commerce than to speech. Government has an interest in regulating fraudulent or deceptive messages that may be found in advertisements. In addition, the subject matter of commercial expression is substantially different from the political and social speech at the heart of First Amendment protections. For these reasons, the courts have allowed more extensive government regulation of commercial expression than of other forms of speech. This principle was articulated in *Valentine v. Chrestensen* (1942), in which the Court upheld a law banning the distribution of handbills that advertised commercial goods and services. The Court concluded that the First Amendment does not protect "purely commercial advertising."

In the mid-1970s, however, the justices handed down four decisions that indicated a reconsideration of the constitutional status of commercial expression. The cases involved the advertising of abortion services, pharmaceutical prices, legal fees, and real estate.

The first of these decisions was ***Bigelow v. Virginia*** (1975). The dispute began when Jeffrey C. Bigelow, the managing editor of the *Virginia Weekly,* a Charlottesville newspaper focusing on the University of Virginia community, approved for publication the advertisement reproduced below. The ad promoted a service that made arrangements for women in Virginia (where

UNWANTED PREGNANCY
LET US HELP YOU
Abortions are now legal in New York.
There are no residency requirements.
FOR IMMEDIATE PLACEMENT IN
ACCREDITED HOSPITALS AND
CLINICS AT LOW COST
Contact
WOMEN'S PAVILION
515 Madison Avenue
New York, N.Y. 10022
or call anytime
(212) 371-6670 or (212) 371-6650
AVAILABLE 7 DAYS A WEEK

STRICTLY CONFIDENTIAL. We
will make all arrangements for you
and help you with information and
counseling.

abortions were illegal) to obtain abortions in New York (where abortions were legal). It ran on February 8, 1971, two years before the Supreme Court's decision in *Roe v. Wade,* which legalized abortions nationwide. Three months later, the state of Virginia charged Bigelow with violating an 1878 state law that said "if any person, by publication, lecture, [or] advertisement . . . encourage[s] or prompt[s] the procuring of [an] abortion . . . he shall be guilty of a misdemeanor." Bigelow was the first person ever accused of violating the law, despite its nearly hundred-year-old history.

Throughout his trial and appeals, Bigelow's attorneys argued that the First Amendment protected commercial speech and as a consequence Virginia's law was unconstitutional. Several judicial bodies, including the Supreme Court of Virginia, rejected this line of reasoning, saying that the free speech clause does not apply to paid commercial advertisements.

The U.S. Supreme Court reversed, finding that the lower courts interpreted *Valentine* much too broadly. For a majority of seven, Justice Blackmun explained, "The fact that the particular advertisement . . . had commercial aspects . . . did not negate all First Amendment

guarantees. . . . The existence of 'commercial activity, in itself, is no justification for narrowing the protection of expression secured by the First Amendment.'" Bigelow was advertising a legal service. There was no evidence that the advertisement was deceptive or fraudulent. The ad provided information about a service that existed in another state. If the state could restrict advertisements about such activities, it would violate the spirit of the First Amendment, which favors the widespread dissemination of information and opinion.

Although the justices ruled that Virginia could not apply its law to Bigelow's advertisement, they failed to provide a comprehensive response to the issue of First Amendment protection of commercial speech. Blackmun noted that the First Amendment protected commercial expression to "some degree," but the justices refused to decide "the precise extent to which the First Amendment permits regulation of advertising that is related to activities the State may legitimately regulate or even prohibit." Although *Bigelow* extended First Amendment protection to commercial speech, it also implied that certain ads, under certain circumstances, may be subject to state limitations. Commercial speech does not equal political speech in the eyes of the Constitution.

It did not take long for the Court to address some of the questions left unanswered in *Bigelow.* Its first opportunity came the very next year in ***Virginia State Board of Pharmacy v. Virginia Citizens Consumer Council, Inc.*** (1976). This litigation centered on a constitutional challenge to a Virginia regulation making it unlawful for a pharmacy to advertise the prices of its prescription medications. A pharmacist who violated the rule risked being cited for unprofessional conduct and possible monetary fines or license suspension. The state justified its regulation as protecting the public from deceptive advertising and maintaining the professionalism of the state's pharmacists. Further, it argued that advertising prices is pure commercial expression that (unlike Bigelow's advertisement) carries no political or social information. Such advertising, the state claimed, deserves no First Amendment protection and is fully subject to state regulation. In response, the Consumer Council claimed that drug pricing information is socially relevant and the public has the right to a free flow of information without state interference.

The Court struck down the Virginia regulation as inconsistent with the First Amendment. Again speaking for the Court, Justice Blackmun explained that the purely economic content of the advertisement does not disqualify it from First Amendment protection. The public has the right to receive truthful information about lawful products and services. Likewise, the pharmacist has the right to communicate that information. The state could achieve its legitimate goals of promoting professionalism and protecting the public from misleading advertising by methods less severe than banning commercial expression altogether.

Taken together, the decisions in *Bigelow* and *Virginia State Board of Pharmacy* indicated that the Court was expanding constitutional protections for commercial speech. Only Justice Rehnquist voted to uphold the state restrictions in both cases. Yet certain factors made it unclear how far the Court would go. First, Blackmun's opinion in the pharmacy decision said only that advertising is not "wholly outside" First Amendment protections. He acknowledged that "some forms of commercial speech regulation are surely permissible." Second, the justices who concurred in the pharmacy case also expressed some uneasiness. Justice Potter Stewart's concurring opinion, for example, emphasized that the Court's opinion should not be interpreted as removing the distinction between product and price advertising on one hand and ideological expression on the other. Chief Justice Burger cautioned against applying the Court's decision to other professions. After all, he explained, today's pharmacists deal primarily in standardized products. They are not like physicians and lawyers, whose services are not standardized and whose fees, therefore, cannot be directly compared.

Burger may have written his concurring opinion with one eye on the Court's docket, because the very next year the justices considered *Bates v. State Bar of Arizona* (1977), a challenge to a law prohibiting lawyers from advertising the prices for their services. Would the Court back away from its trend of expanding protections for commercial expression? Or would it continue along the road it started in *Bigelow*?

Bates v. State Bar of Arizona

433 U.S. 350 (1977)
http://laws.findlaw.com/US/433/350.html
Oral arguments are available at http://www.oyez.org.
Vote: 5 (Blackmun, Brennan, Marshall, Stevens, White)
    4 (Burger, Powell, Rehnquist, Stewart)
OPINION OF THE COURT: Blackmun
OPINIONS DISSENTING IN PART AND CONCURRING IN PART:
  Burger, Powell, Rehnquist

John Bates and Van O'Steen graduated from Arizona State University College of Law in 1972 and took jobs at a state legal aid society. After two years, they developed what was then a unique idea—they would open a legal clinic to provide "legal services at modest fees to persons of moderate income who did not qualify for government aid." In March 1974 they opened their clinic in Phoenix, but two years later they were barely surviving. The pair decided to take a risky step: they placed an ad in an Arizona newspaper (shown on previous page).

Why was their ad risky? Today, attorney advertisements are commonplace. From the 1910s through the 1970s, however, most state bar associations explicitly prohibited such activity. Arizona's rules contained this provision: "A lawyer shall not publicize himself . . . as a lawyer through newspaper or magazine advertisements, radio or television announcements, display advertisements in the city or telephone directories or other means of commercial publicity." So, after Bates and O'Steen published the advertisement, the state bar association initiated proceedings against them. They were found guilty and given the rather mild sentence of a one-week suspension from legal practice. Nevertheless, with the help of the ACLU, they decided to appeal the judgment, claiming that the ban constituted a violation of their First Amendment guarantee, under the Court's decision in *Virginia Pharmacy.*

ARGUMENTS:

For the appellants, John Bates and Van O'Steen:
- The appellants' advertisement is protected expression. The ban on it amounts to content discrimination in violation of the First Amendment.
- The appellants' expression is supported by the consumers' constitutional right to legal representation.
- The disciplinary ban on advertising serves no important state interests.

For the appellee, State Bar of Arizona:
- Since commercial advertising enjoys the lowest level of free speech protection, the ban against advertising legal services is constitutional.
- There has long been a professional tradition forbidding such advertising.
- Advertising legal services tends to encourage unnecessary litigation.

- The ban protects against fraud and deception and preserves the pride and dignity of the profession.
- Because legal skills vary from attorney to attorney, the advertising of fees for legal services is inevitably misleading.

◆ MR. JUSTICE BLACKMUN DELIVERED THE OPINION OF THE COURT.

Last Term, in *Virginia Pharmacy Board v. Virginia Consumer Council* (1976), the Court considered the validity under the First Amendment of a Virginia statute declaring that a pharmacist was guilty of "unprofessional conduct" if he advertised prescription drug prices. . . . [W]e held that commercial speech of that kind was entitled to the protection of the First Amendment. . . .

The heart of the dispute before us today is whether lawyers also may constitutionally advertise the *prices* at which certain routine services will be performed. Numerous justifications are proffered for the restriction of such price advertising. We consider each in turn:

1. *The Adverse Effect on Professionalism.* Appellee places particular emphasis on the adverse effects that it feels price advertising will have on the legal profession. The key to professionalism, it is argued, is the sense of pride that involvement in the discipline generates. It is claimed that price advertising will bring about commercialization, which will undermine the attorney's sense of dignity and self-worth. The hustle of the marketplace will adversely affect the profession's service orientation, and irreparably damage the delicate balance between the lawyer's need to earn and his obligation selflessly to serve. Advertising is also said to erode the client's trust in his attorney: Once the client perceives that the lawyer is motivated by profit, his confidence that the attorney is acting out of a commitment to the client's welfare is jeopardized. And advertising is said to tarnish the dignified public image of the profession.

We recognize, of course, and commend the spirit of public service with which the profession of law is practiced and to which it is dedicated. The present Members of this Court, licensed attorneys all, could not feel otherwise. And we would have reason to pause if we felt that our decision today would undercut that spirit. But we find the postulated connection between advertising and the erosion of true professionalism to be severely strained. At its core, the argument presumes that attorneys must conceal from themselves and from their clients the real-life fact that lawyers earn their livelihood at the bar. We suspect that few attorneys engage in such self-deception. And rare is the client, moreover, even one of the modest means, who enlists the aid of an attorney with the expectation that his services will be rendered free of charge. In fact, the American Bar Association advises that an attorney should reach "a clear agreement with his client as to the basis of the fee charges to be made," and that this is to be done "[a]s soon as feasible after a lawyer has been employed." If the commercial basis of the relationship is to be promptly disclosed on ethical grounds, once the client is in the office, it seems inconsistent to condemn the candid revelation of the same information before he arrives at that office.

Moreover, the assertion that advertising will diminish the attorney's reputation in the community is open to question. Bankers and engineers advertise, and yet these professions are not regarded as undignified. In fact, it has been suggested that the failure of lawyers to advertise creates public disillusionment with the profession. The absence of advertising may be seen to reflect the profession's failure to reach out and serve the community: Studies reveal that many persons do not obtain counsel even when they perceive a need because of the feared price of services or because of an inability to locate a competent attorney. . . .

It appears that the ban on advertising originated as a rule of etiquette and not as a rule of ethics. Early lawyers in Great Britain viewed the law as a form of public service, rather than as a means of earning a living, and they looked down on "trade" as unseemly. Eventually, the attitude toward advertising fostered by this view evolved into an aspect of the ethics of the profession. But habit and tradition are not in themselves an adequate answer to a constitutional challenge. In this day, we do not belittle the person who earns his living by the strength of his arm or the force of his mind. Since the belief that lawyers are somehow "above" trade has become an anachronism, the historical foundation for the advertising restraint has crumbled.

2. *The Inherently Misleading Nature of Attorney Advertising.* It is argued that advertising of legal services inevitably will be misleading (a) because such services are so individualized with regard to content and quality as to prevent informed comparison on the basis of an advertisement, (b) because the consumer of legal services is unable to determine in advance just what services he needs, and (c) because advertising by attorneys will highlight irrelevant factors and fail to show the relevant factor of skill.

We are not persuaded that restrained professional advertising by lawyers inevitably will be misleading. Although many services performed by attorneys are indeed unique, it is doubtful that any attorney would or could advertise fixed prices for services of that type. The only services that lend themselves to advertising are the routine ones: the uncontested divorce, the simple adoption, the uncontested personal bankruptcy, the change of name, and the like—the very services advertised by appellants. Although the precise service demanded in each task may vary slightly, and although legal services are not fungible, these facts do not make advertising misleading so long as the attorney does the necessary work at the advertised price. . . .

The second component of the argument—that advertising ignores the diagnostic role—fares little better. It is unlikely that many people go to an attorney merely to ascertain if they have a clean bill of legal health. Rather, attorneys are likely to be employed to perform specific tasks. Although the client may not know the detail involved in performing the task, he no doubt is able to identify the service he desires at the level of generality to which advertising lends itself.

The third component is not without merit: Advertising does not provide a complete foundation on which to select an attorney. But it seems peculiar to deny the consumer, on the ground that the information is incomplete, at least some of the relevant information needed to reach an informed decision. The alternative—the prohibition of advertising—serves only to restrict the information that flows to consumers. Moreover, the argument assumes that the public is not sophisticated enough to realize the limitations of advertising, and that the public is better kept in ignorance than trusted with correct but incomplete information. We suspect the argument rests on an underestimation of the public. In any event, we view as dubious any justification that is based on the benefits of public ignorance. See *Virginia Pharmacy Board v. Virginia Consumer Council.* Although, of course, the bar retains the power to correct omissions that have the effect of presenting an inaccurate picture, the preferred remedy is more disclosure, rather than less. If the naivete of the public will cause advertising by attorneys to be misleading, then it is the bar's role to assure that the populace is sufficiently informed as to enable it to place advertising in its proper perspective.

3. *The Adverse Effect on the Administration of Justice.* Advertising is said to have the undesirable effect of stirring up litigation. The judicial machinery is designed to serve those who feel sufficiently aggrieved to bring forward their claims. Advertising, it is argued, serves to encourage the assertion of legal rights in the courts, thereby undesirably unsettling societal repose. There is even a suggestion of barratry.

But advertising by attorneys is not an unmitigated source of harm to the administration of justice. It may offer great benefits. Although advertising might increase the use of the judicial machinery, we cannot accept the notion that it is always better for a person to suffer a wrong silently than to redress it by legal action. . . .

4. *The Undesirable Economic Effects of Advertising.* It is claimed that advertising will increase the overhead costs of the profession, and that these costs then will be passed along to consumers in the form of increased fees. Moreover, it is claimed that the additional cost of practice will create a substantial entry barrier, deterring or preventing young attorneys from penetrating the market and entrenching the position of the bar's established members.

These two arguments seem dubious at best. Neither distinguishes lawyers from others, and neither appears relevant to the First Amendment. The ban on advertising serves to increase the difficulty of discovering the lowest cost seller of acceptable ability. As a result, to this extent attorneys are isolated from competition, and the incentive to price competitively is reduced. Although it is true that the effect of advertising on the price of services has not been demonstrated, there is revealing evidence with regard to products: where consumers have the benefit of price advertising, retail prices often are dramatically lower than they would be without advertising. It is entirely possible that advertising will serve to reduce, not advance, the cost of legal services to the consumer.

The entry-barrier argument is equally unpersuasive. In the absence of advertising, an attorney must rely on his contacts with the community to generate a flow of business. In view of the time necessary to develop such contacts, the ban in fact serves to perpetuate the market position of established attorneys. Consideration of entry-barrier problems would urge that advertising be allowed so as to aid the new competitor in penetrating the market.

5. *The Adverse Effect of Advertising on the Quality of Service.* It is argued that the attorney may advertise a given "package" of service at a set price, and will be inclined to provide, by indiscriminate use, the standard package regardless of whether it fits the client's needs.

Restraints on advertising, however, are an ineffective way of deterring shoddy work. An attorney who is inclined to cut quality will do so regardless of the rule on advertising. And the advertisement of a standardized fee does not necessarily mean that the services offered are undesirably standardized. Indeed, the assertion that an attorney who advertises a standard fee will cut quality is substantially undermined by the fixed-fee schedule of appellee's own prepaid Legal Services Program. Even if advertising leads to the creation of "legal clinics" like that of appellants'— clinics that emphasize standardized procedures for routine problems—it is possible that such clinics will improve service by reducing the likelihood of error.

6. *The Difficulties of Enforcement.* Finally, it is argued that the wholesale restriction is justified by the problems of enforcement if any other course is taken. Because the public lacks sophistication in legal matters, it may be particularly susceptible to misleading or deceptive advertising by lawyers. After-the-fact action by the consumer lured by such advertising may not provide a realistic restraint because of the inability of the layman to assess whether the service he has received meets professional standards. Thus, the vigilance of a regulatory agency will be required. But because of the numerous purveyors of services, the overseeing of advertising will be burdensome.

It is at least somewhat incongruous for the opponents of advertising to extol the virtues and altruism of the legal profession at one point, and, at another, to assert that its members will seize the opportunity to mislead and distort. We suspect that, with advertising, most lawyers will behave as they always have: They will abide by their solemn oaths to uphold the integrity and honor of their profession and of the legal system. For every attorney who overreaches through advertising, there will be thousands of others who will be candid and honest and straightforward. And, of course, it will be in the latter's interest, as in other cases of misconduct at the bar, to assist in weeding out those few who abuse their trust.

In sum, we are not persuaded that any of the proffered justifications rise to the level of an acceptable reason for the suppression of all advertising by attorneys. . . .

In holding that advertising by attorneys may not be subjected to blanket suppression, and that the advertisement at issue is protected, we, of course, do not hold that advertising by attorneys may not be regulated in any way. We mention some of the clearly permissible limitations on advertising not foreclosed by our holding.

Advertising that is false, deceptive, or misleading of course is subject to restraint. Since the advertiser knows his product and has a commercial interest in its dissemination, we have little worry that regulation to assure truthfulness will discourage protected speech. And any concern that strict requirements for truthfulness will undesirably inhibit spontaneity seems inapplicable because commercial speech generally is calculated. Indeed, the public and private benefits from commercial speech derive from confidence in its accuracy and reliability. Thus, the leeway for untruthful or misleading expression that has been allowed in other contexts has little force in the commercial arena. In fact, because the public lacks sophistication concerning legal services, misstatements that might be overlooked or deemed unimportant in other advertising may be found quite inappropriate in legal advertising. . . . In sum, we recognize that many of the problems in defining the boundary between deceptive and nondeceptive advertising remain to be resolved, and we expect that the bar will have a special role to play in assuring that advertising by attorneys flows both freely and cleanly.

As with other varieties of speech, it follows as well that there may be reasonable restrictions on the time, place, and manner of advertising. Advertising concerning transactions that are themselves illegal obviously may be suppressed. And the special problems of advertising on the electronic broadcast media will warrant special consideration.

The constitutional issue in this case is only whether the State may prevent the publication in a newspaper of appellants' truthful advertisement concerning the availability and terms of routine legal services. We rule simply that the flow of such information may not be restrained, and we therefore hold the present application of the disciplinary rule against appellants to be violative of the First Amendment.

The judgment of the Supreme Court of Arizona is therefore affirmed in part and reversed in part.

It is so ordered.

MR. JUSTICE REHNQUIST, *dissenting in part.*

I continue to believe that the First Amendment speech provision, long regarded by this Court as a sanctuary for expressions of public importance or intellectual interest, is demeaned by invocation to protect advertisements of goods and services. I would hold quite simply that the appellants' advertisement, however truthful or reasonable it may be, is not the sort of expression that the Amendment was adopted to protect.

. . . [T]he Court's opinion offers very little guidance as to the extent or nature of permissible state regulation of professions such as law and medicine. . . . [O]nce the Court took the first step down the "slippery slope" in *Virginia Pharmacy Board*, the possibility of understandable and workable differentiations between protected speech and unprotected speech in the field of advertising largely evaporated. Once the exception of commercial speech from the protection of the First Amendment which had been established by *Valentine v. Chrestensen* was abandoned, the shift to case-by-case adjudication of First Amendment claims of advertisers was a predictable consequence.

. . . The *Valentine* distinction was constitutionally sound and practically workable, and I am still unwilling to take even one step down the "slippery slope" away from it.

In *Bates* the Court provided one of its clearest statements on the issue of advertising. While refuting the bar association's arguments, Justice Blackmun also listed the conditions under which attorneys may or may not advertise; for example, he stressed that Bates and O'Steen's ad mentioned only simple legal services, which any attorney could perform. Many have surmised from this distinction that bar associations probably could limit advertisements for complex legal work.

In the years following *Bates*, the judiciary has wrestled with questions of how much regulation of legal advertising is constitutionally permissible and under what circumstances.[12] Many lawyers and law firms have taken advantage of the ruling to advertise their services and fees. State bar associations have required only that the advertisements be truthful and not degrade the profession. Despite widespread

12. See, for example, *Ohralik v. Ohio State Bar* (1978) and *In re Primus* (1978).

advertising of legal services, studies have shown that a majority of the nation's attorneys oppose advertising and feel that it detracts from the dignity of the profession.[13]

The final important commercial advertising case of the mid-1970s was *Linmark Associates v. Township of Willingboro* (1977). Here, the Court dealt with posted signs, not printed ads; but more important, it addressed a form of suppressed expression that appeared to have not economic but social and political ends. *Linmark Associates* arose in March 1974, when the town of Willingboro, New Jersey, passed an ordinance outlawing the posting of For Sale signs on most property. Enacted at the urging of property owners, the statute attempted to halt certain economic and social trends within the town. Located near Fort Dix, McGuire Air Force Base, and several major corporations, the town was a natural for suburban development. By the 1960s the white population of the town had increased 350 percent. But, as suburban growth stabilized during the 1970s, so did Willingboro's. By the early 1970s the town's white population had declined by 5 percent, and the black population had grown from 11.7 percent in the 1960s to 18.2 percent. To stop what some called panic selling by whites and to maintain property values, which had been dropping steadily in the face of "white flight," the town passed the ordinance banning For Sale signs.

A real estate agency that wanted to erect a For Sale sign challenged the ordinance as a violation of its free expression guarantees. Backed by an amicus curiae brief from the ACLU, the agency argued that For Sale signs were not distinguishable from advertisements for drugs, abortions, or attorney services. The town countered with two sets of arguments. First, the law was limited, restricting one method of communication and leaving ample alternative channels available. Second, it claimed that the statute sought to achieve a legitimate and, in fact, vital government objective—to promote racial integration. This last argument attracted the attention of the NAACP Legal Defense Fund (LDF), which filed a supporting amicus curiae brief. By the time this case appeared before the Court, the stage was set for high

drama: *Linmark Associates* was one of only a handful of occasions when two powerful allies, the ACLU and the LDF, opposed each other.

Writing for a unanimous Court, Justice Thurgood Marshall, a former LDF attorney, agreed with the ACLU and struck down the town's ordinance. He acknowledged that although it had important objectives, in the final analysis the ordinance was no different from the law at issue in *Virginia Pharmacy*: it prevented "residents from obtaining certain information" without providing sufficient justification. As Marshall asserted, "If dissemination of this information can be restricted, then every locality in the country can suppress any facts that reflect poorly on it, so long as a plausible claim can be made that disclosure would cause recipients of the information to act 'irrationally.'"

The years 1975 through 1977 were important for commercial speech. The Court's decisions in *Bigelow*, *Virginia Pharmacy*, *Bates*, and *Linmark Associates* signaled a major change by elevating the degree of constitutional protection enjoyed by commercial expression. In the years that followed, the justices continued in that policy direction, although they never raised commercial advertising to the level enjoyed by political and social speech. For example, the Court struck down laws prohibiting the erection of advertising billboards (*Metromedia, Inc. v. San Diego*, 1981), banning the advertising of contraceptives by mail (*Bolger v. Youngs Drug Products Corporation*, 1983), and blocking a public utility from sending, with its monthly bills, statements that expressed the company's position on issues of public policy (*Consolidated Edison Company of New York, Inc. v. Public Service Commission of New York*, 1980). For the most part, the Court's decisions in the commercial expression cases were by substantial majorities, with only Justice Rehnquist consistently supporting the position of government regulators.

Because the Court acknowledged that advertising merits a lower level of protection than political or social speech, some confusion remained over the appropriate test to use in commercial expression cases. The justices remedied this situation in *Central Hudson Gas and Electric Corporation v. Public Service Commission of New York* (1980), a dispute over an energy conservation law prohibiting utility companies from advertising to promote the sale of their products.

---

13. Lauren Bowen, "Do Court Decisions Matter?" in *Contemplating Courts*, ed. Lee Epstein (Washington, DC: CQ Press, 1995), 376–389.

Central Hudson Gas and Electric Corporation v. Public Service Commission of New York

447 U.S. 557 (1980)
http://laws.findlaw.com/US/447/557.html
Oral arguments are available at http://www.oyez.org.
*Vote: 8 (Blackmun, Brennan, Burger, Marshall, Powell, Stevens,
        Stewart, White)*
      1 (Rehnquist)

OPINION OF THE COURT: *Powell*
CONCURRING OPINIONS: *Blackmun, Brennan, Stevens*
DISSENTING OPINION: *Rehnquist*

FACTS:

Facing an energy shortage during the winter of 1973 and 1974, the New York Public Service Commission ordered state public utility companies to stop all advertising that promoted the use of electricity. Three years later, when the shortage had eased, the commission requested public comments on a proposal to continue the ban on promotional advertising. Central Hudson Gas and Electric Corporation opposed the ban on First Amendment grounds. Declaring all advertising promoting the use of electricity to be contrary to the national policy of conserving energy, the commission extended the ban. Central Hudson challenged the regulation in state court. The New York Court of Appeals, upholding lower court rulings, concluded that government interests outweighed the limited constitutional value of the commercial speech at issue. Central Hudson appealed to the Supreme Court.

ARGUMENTS:

For the appellant, Central Hudson
Gas & Electric Corporation:

- This kind of advertising was found to be protected speech in decisions such as *Virginia State Board of Pharmacy v. Virginia Citizens Consumer Council* and *Bates v. State Bar of Arizona*. Those decisions should control this case.
- The state regulations are overbroad and vague.
- Central Hudson is being discriminated against because its nonutility competitors are not subject to the Commission's advertising ban.

For the appellee, Public Service
Commission of New York:

- Although protection for commercial speech has expanded, advertising remains subject to much greater regulation than noncommercial expression.

- The ban on promotional advertising advances the state's important interest in conserving energy.
- The Commission's regulations are clear, precise, and confined to the state interests sought to be achieved.
- The Commission has jurisdiction only over electric utilities. Therefore, it has no authority to extend its advertising ban to Central Hudson's nonutility competitors.

MR. JUSTICE POWELL DELIVERED THE OPINION OF THE COURT.

The case presents the question whether a regulation of the Public Service Commission of the State of New York violates the First and Fourteenth Amendments because it completely bans promotional advertising by an electrical utility. . . .

The Commission's order restricts only commercial speech, that is, expression related solely to the economic interests of the speaker and its audience. The First Amendment, as applied to the States through the Fourteenth Amendment, protects commercial speech from unwarranted governmental regulation. Commercial expression not only serves the economic interest of the speaker, but also assists consumers and furthers the societal interest in the fullest possible dissemination of information. In applying the First Amendment to this area, we have rejected the "highly paternalistic" view that government has complete power to suppress or regulate commercial speech. . . . Even when advertising communicates only an incomplete version of the relevant facts, the First Amendment presumes that some accurate information is better than no information at all.

Nevertheless, our decisions have recognized "the 'commonsense' distinction between speech proposing a commercial transaction, which occurs in an area traditionally subject to government regulation, and other varieties of speech." The Constitution therefore accords a lesser protection to commercial speech than to other constitutionally guaranteed expression. The protection available for particular commercial expression turns on the nature both of the expression and of the governmental interests served by its regulation.

The First Amendment's concern for commercial speech is based on the informational function of advertising. Consequently, there can be no constitutional objection to the suppression of commercial messages that do not accurately inform the public about lawful activity. The government may ban forms of communication more likely to deceive the public than to inform it, or commercial speech related to illegal activity. . . .

In commercial speech cases, . . . a four-part analysis has developed. At the outset, we must determine whether the expression is protected by the First Amendment. For commercial speech to come within that provision, it at least must concern lawful activity and not be misleading. Next, we ask whether the asserted governmental interest is substantial. If both inquiries yield positive answers, we must determine whether the regulation directly advances the governmental interest asserted, and whether it is not more extensive than is necessary to serve that interest.

We now apply this four-step analysis for commercial speech to the Commission's arguments in support of its ban on promotional advertising.

The Commission does not claim that the expression at issue either is inaccurate or relates to unlawful activity. . . .

The Commission offers [energy conservation as a major state interest justifying] the ban on promotional advertising. . . . Any increase in demand for electricity—during peak or off-peak periods—means greater consumption of energy. The Commission argues, and the New York court agreed, that the State's interest in conserving energy is sufficient to support suppression of advertising designed to increase consumption of electricity. In view of our country's dependence on energy resources beyond our control, no one can doubt the importance of energy conservation. Plainly, therefore, the state interest asserted is substantial. . . .

Next, we focus on the relationship between the State's interests and the advertising ban. . . .

. . . [T]he State's interest in energy conservation is directly advanced by the Commission order at issue here. There is an immediate connection between advertising and demand for electricity. Central Hudson would not contest the advertising ban unless it believed that promotion would increase its sales. Thus, we find a direct link between the state interest in conservation and the Commission's order.

We come finally to the critical inquiry in this case: whether the Commission's complete suppression of speech ordinarily protected by the First Amendment is no more extensive than necessary to further the State's interest in energy conservation. The Commission's

order reaches all promotional advertising, regardless of the impact of the touted service on overall energy use. But the energy conservation rationale, as important as it is, cannot justify suppressing information about electric devices or services that would cause no net increase in total energy use. In addition, no showing has been made that a more limited restriction on the content of promotional advertising would not serve adequately the State's interests. . . .

The Commission's order prevents appellant from promoting electric services that would reduce energy use by diverting demand from less efficient sources, or that would consume roughly the same amount of energy as do alternative sources. In neither situation would the utility's advertising endanger conservation or mislead the public. To the extent that the Commission's order suppresses speech that in no way impairs the State's interest in energy conservation, the Commission's order violates the First and Fourteenth Amendments, and must be invalidated.

The Commission also has not demonstrated that its interest in conservation cannot be protected adequately by more limited regulation of appellant's commercial expression. To further its policy of conservation, the Commission could attempt to restrict the format and content of Central Hudson's advertising. It might, for example, require that the advertisements include information about the relative efficiency and expense of the offered service, both under current conditions and for the foreseeable future. In the absence of a showing that more limited speech regulation would be ineffective, we cannot approve the complete suppression of Central Hudson's advertising. . . .

Accordingly, the judgment of the New York Court of Appeals is

Reversed.

MR. JUSTICE REHNQUIST, dissenting.

The Court's analysis, in my view, is wrong in several respects. Initially, I disagree with the Court's conclusion that the speech of a state-created monopoly, which is the subject of a comprehensive regulatory scheme, is entitled to protection under the First Amendment. I also think that the Court errs here in failing to recognize that the state law is most accurately viewed as an economic regulation, and that the speech involved (if it falls within the scope of the First Amendment at all) occupies a significantly more subordinate position in the hierarchy of First Amendment values than the Court gives it today. Finally, the Court, in reaching its decision, improperly substitutes its own judgment for that of the State in deciding how a proper ban on promotional advertising should be drafted. With regard to this latter point, the Court adopts as its final part of a four-part test a "no more extensive than necessary" analysis that will unduly impair a state legislature's ability to adopt legislation reasonably designed to promote interests that have always been rightly thought to be of great importance to the State.

The *Central Hudson* decision provided a welcome explanation of how the Court approaches commercial expression cases. If the commercial expression concerns a lawful activity and is not misleading, it merits First Amendment protection. The state may still regulate that expression, however, if the regulation serves a substantial government interest, directly advances that interest, and is no more extensive than necessary to achieve it.

The Court has applied the *Central Hudson* test in subsequent cases. In **City of Cincinnati v. Discovery Network** (1993) the justices struck down the enforcement of a city ordinance ordering the removal of news racks used for the distribution of free magazines and advertisements. In **44 Liquormart, Inc. v. Rhode Island** (1996) the justices by unanimous vote declared unconstitutional a state law that prohibited the advertising of alcoholic beverage prices. Although the justices did not agree as to rationale, *44 Liquormart* is especially significant because the justices voided the regulation in spite of the Twenty-first Amendment, which gives states strong authority to control alcoholic beverages. Decisions such as these indicate that governments have difficult standards to meet when they attempt to regulate nondeceptive commercial speech that concerns a lawful product or service. And in *Thompson v. Western States Medical Center* (2002) the Court struck down federal legislation that banned the advertising of compounded drugs—medicines created through the mixing or combining of ingredients by a doctor or pharmacist. In doing so, the Court reaffirmed the position of *Central Hudson* as the guiding authority on commercial expression issues.

In spite of its expansion of First Amendment protection for commercial speech, the Court has remained supportive of government actions against those who would abuse their rights. In *Illinois ex rel. Madigan v. Telemarketing Associates* (2003), for example, the justices unanimously ruled that the First Amendment does not bar states from taking actions against professional fund-raisers who make false or misleading representations. Clearly, commercial expression continues to receive less constitutional protection than does political or social speech. Election campaign commercials, for example, are allowed greater latitude regarding the accuracy of the information provided and the claims made than are ads for commercial products and services.

Freedom of Association

Essential to the exercise of political and social expression is the ability to join with like-minded individuals to advance mutual goals. The Supreme Court has long recognized that the right of association is implicit in the First Amendment's freedoms of speech, press, assembly, and petition.[14]

Protecting the right of individuals to form groups for political or social purposes often means extending constitutional guarantees to organizations that hold unpopular or even dangerous views. For example, in the 1960s the justices struck down government attempts to regulate the Communist Party by requiring membership registration (*Albertson v. Subversive Activities Control Board*, 1965), by penalizing individuals for party membership (*United States v. Robel*, 1967), and by removing from party members privileges other citizens enjoy (*Aptheker v. Secretary of State*, 1964).

Similarly, the Court intervened when southern states opposed to the goals of civil rights groups took actions to restrict the associational rights of their members. In **NAACP v. Alabama** (1958) the justices unanimously invalidated a state requirement that civil rights groups submit their membership rolls to state authorities, and in *NAACP v. Button* (1963) the Court blocked a Virginia action designed to cripple the use of litigation by civil rights organizations.

---

14. In addition, the Court has invoked the relevance of association rights to the protection of intimate human relationships (marriage, family, childbearing). We discuss these issues at length in Chapter 10.

In more recent times, conflicts have arisen between groups asserting First Amendment association rights and states enforcing legislation to reduce discrimination. Most frequently at issue are the policies of private organizations that restrict membership or services based on characteristics such as race, sex, sexual orientation, or religion. Country clubs, businessmen's clubs, fraternal organizations, and civic groups often have such membership restrictions. Do the members of private organizations have the constitutional right to impose whatever membership qualifications they desire? Or may the state, concerned that the exclusion of certain persons could deprive those individuals of opportunities for business and professional networking and advancement, enforce antidiscrimination statutes that make such membership restrictions unlawful?

The justices addressed this question in **Roberts v. United States Jaycees** (1984). The Jaycees, established in 1920 as the Junior Chamber of Commerce, is a private civic organization that helps young men participate in the affairs of their community. This dispute centered on the Jaycees' policy of restricting regular membership to men between the ages of eighteen and thirty-five. The Minnesota Department of Human Rights claimed that the organization's exclusion of women violated a state law prohibiting sex-based discrimination in public accommodations. The United States Jaycees argued that applying the Minnesota antidiscrimination law to its membership policies was a violation of the First Amendment's right to freedom of association.

In a 7–0 decision, the Supreme Court ruled against the Jaycees. The justices acknowledged that freedom of association is a necessary component of the First Amendment, but, they said, the right is not absolute and it does not apply equally to all private organizations. The greatest degree of protection goes to small, intimate relationships, such as marriage and family, and to those organizations expressing sincerely held political or ideological messages. Large groups with nonideological or commercial purposes and nonselective membership policies are less deserving. The Jaycees, according to the Court, is a large, national organization with no firm ideological views and membership selectivity based only on age and sex. As such, the group merited a level of First Amendment protection inferior to the state's interest in reducing arbitrary discrimination.

The Court in *Roberts* considered not only the nature of the organization itself but also the relationship between the expressive activities of the group and the effect of the government regulation. Two important questions must be asked: Is the group an expressive organization that attempts to communicate its viewpoints either publicly or privately? And, does the state regulation significantly burden the expression of those viewpoints?

The scheme adopted in the Jaycees' case was applied subsequently in two similar disputes. First, in *Board of Directors of Rotary International v. Rotary Club of Duarte* (1987) the Court approved the enforcement of California's antidiscrimination laws against Rotary Club chapters that excluded women as regular members. And in *New York State Club Association v. City of New York* (1988) the justices upheld a New York ordinance that applied antidiscrimination regulations to organizations having more than four hundred members, providing regular meal service, and receiving payment from nonmembers for services or facilities for the furtherance of business interests. These decisions emphasized factors such as the size of the group, the commercial activities of the group, and the low level of selectivity exercised in conferring membership. Both decisions concluded that the application of the nondiscrimination law would not significantly burden the group's expressive activities.

Roberts, Rotary, and *New York State Club Association* were unanimous rulings, creating the impression that the law was relatively settled: freedom of association rights must give way to state interests in combating discrimination. This impression was weakened in 1995, however, when the justices decided **Hurley v. Irish-American Gay, Lesbian and Bisexual Group of Boston.** This dispute arose when a private association organizing a Saint Patrick's Day parade in Boston rejected the application of a gay rights group to march in the celebration. The gay rights group sued, claiming that its exclusion from the parade violated the Massachusetts antidiscrimination statute. The Supreme Court unanimously ruled in favor of the parade organizers. The justices held that the First Amendment is violated by a state law requiring private sponsors of a parade to include among the marchers a group imparting a message that the organizers do not wish to convey. The Court applied the principles set in *Roberts* but came to quite a different result. Here the forced inclusion of the gay rights group was found to place a significant burden on the expression rights of the parade organizers.

This decision set the stage for the next major freedom of association dispute, *Boy Scouts of America v. Dale* (2000), a challenge to the dismissal of a scout leader on sexual orientation grounds. Would the Court find the facts in this case similar to the exclusion of women in *Roberts, Rotary,* and *New York State Club Association,* or would the justices conclude that the Boy Scouts' membership policies were protected by the First Amendment's freedom of association?

Boy Scouts of America v. Dale

530 U.S. 640 (2000)
http://laws.findlaw.com/US/530/640.html
Oral arguments are available at http://www.oyez.org.
Vote: 5 (Kennedy, O'Connor, Rehnquist, Scalia, Thomas)
     4 (Breyer, Ginsburg, Souter, Stevens)
OPINION OF THE COURT: *Rehnquist*
DISSENTING OPINIONS: *Souter, Stevens*

FACTS:

James Dale began his involvement in the Boy Scouts organization in 1978, when, at the age of eight, he joined Cub Scout Pack 142 in Monmouth, New Jersey. He became a Boy Scout in 1981 and remained an active scout until he turned eighteen. Dale was an exemplary member of the organization, being admitted to the prestigious Order of the Arrow and achieving the rank of Eagle Scout, scouting's highest honor. In 1989 he became an adult member of the organization and was an assistant scoutmaster.

Around the same time, Dale left home to attend Rutgers University. At college, Dale first acknowledged to himself and to others that he was gay. He joined and later became copresident of the Rutgers University Gay/Lesbian Alliance. After attending a seminar devoted to gay/lesbian health issues in 1990, he was interviewed and photographed for a newspaper story in which he discussed the need for gay teenagers to have appropriate role models.

Shortly after the newspaper article appeared, Dale received a letter from the Monmouth Council of the Boy Scouts of America revoking his adult membership in the Boy Scouts. When he requested a reason for this action, the council informed him that the Scouts "specifically forbid membership to

The Boy Scouts revoked the adult membership of James Dale because of his admitted homosexuality. In Boy Scouts of America v. Dale, *the Court determined that the organization had the right to exclude him.*

homosexuals." In 1992 Dale filed a complaint against the Boy Scouts claiming that the revocation of his membership violated a New Jersey law prohibiting discrimination based on sexual orientation in public accommodations. The Boy Scouts countered that as a private, nonprofit organization it had the right under the freedom of association guarantees of the First Amendment to deny membership to individuals whose views are not consistent with the group's values. The New Jersey Supreme Court ruled in favor of Dale, and the Boy Scouts asked for review by the U.S. Supreme Court.

ARGUMENTS:

For the petitioner, Boy Scouts of America:
- Requiring a Boy Scout troop to appoint an adult leader who opposes the organization's moral code violates freedom of speech and expressive association.

- *Hurley v. Irish-American Gay, Lesbian and Bisexual Group of Boston* controls this case.
- As intimate associations, Boy Scout troops have the constitutional right to decide for themselves whom to select to supervise other people's children.
- No state interest justifies these infringements on the First Amendment.

For the respondent, James Dale:

- The Boy Scouts is a large, national, relatively unselective organization with significant commercial activities. As such, it is not an intimate private group that is immune from government regulation.
- *Hurley* does not apply. This case involves identity-based exclusion, not compelled speech.
- Pluralism and diversity characterize the ideology of the scouting movement, not a condemnation of homosexuality.
- Reinstating Dale would have no significant effect on the Boy Scouts carrying out its expressive purposes.

CHIEF JUSTICE REHNQUIST DELIVERED THE OPINION OF THE COURT.

In *Roberts v. United States Jaycees* (1984), we observed that "implicit in the right to engage in activities protected by the First Amendment" is "a corresponding right to associate with others in pursuit of a wide variety of political, social, economic, educational, religious, and cultural ends." This right is crucial in preventing the majority from imposing its views on groups that would rather express other, perhaps unpopular, ideas. Government actions that may unconstitutionally burden this freedom may take many forms, one of which is "intrusion into the internal structure or affairs of an association" like a "regulation that forces the group to accept members it does not desire." Forcing a group to accept certain members may impair the ability of the group to express those views, and only those views, that it intends to express. Thus, "[f]reedom of association . . . plainly presupposes a freedom not to associate."

The forced inclusion of an unwanted person in a group infringes the group's freedom of expressive association if the presence of that person affects in a significant way the group's ability to advocate public or private viewpoints. *New York State Club Assn., Inc. v. City of New York* (1988). But the freedom of expressive association, like many freedoms, is not absolute. We have held that the freedom could be overridden "by regulations adopted to serve compelling state interests, unrelated to the suppression of ideas, that cannot be achieved through means significantly less restrictive of associational freedoms." *Roberts.*

To determine whether a group is protected by the First Amendment's expressive associational right, we must determine whether the group engages in "expressive association." The First Amendment's protection of expressive association is not reserved for advocacy groups. But to come within its ambit, a group must engage in some form of expression, whether it be public or private. . . .

. . . [T]he general mission of the Boy Scouts is clear: "[T]o instill values in young people." The Boy Scouts seeks to instill these values by having its adult leaders spend time with the youth members, instructing and engaging them in activities like camping, archery, and fishing. During the time spent with the youth members, the scoutmasters and assistant scoutmasters inculcate them with the Boy Scouts' values—both expressly and by example. It seems indisputable that an association that seeks to transmit such a system of values engages in expressive activity.

Given that the Boy Scouts engages in expressive activity, we must determine whether the forced inclusion of Dale as an assistant scoutmaster would significantly affect the Boy Scouts' ability to advocate public or private viewpoints. This inquiry necessarily requires us first to explore, to a limited extent, the nature of the Boy Scouts' view of homosexuality.

The values the Boy Scouts seeks to instill are "based on" those listed in the Scout Oath and Law. The Boy Scouts explains that the Scout Oath and Law provide "a positive moral code for living; they are a list of 'do's' rather than 'don'ts.'" The Boy Scouts asserts that homosexual conduct is inconsistent with the values embodied in the Scout Oath and Law, particularly with the values represented by the terms "morally straight" and "clean."

Obviously, the Scout Oath and Law do not expressly mention sexuality or sexual orientation. And the terms "morally straight" and "clean" are by no means self-defining. Different people would attribute to those terms very different meanings. For example, some people may believe that engaging in homosexual conduct is not at odds with being "morally straight" and "clean." And others may believe that engaging in homosexual conduct is contrary to being "morally straight" and "clean." The Boy Scouts says it falls within the latter category.

The New Jersey Supreme Court analyzed the Boy Scouts' beliefs and found that the "exclusion of members solely on the basis of their sexual orientation is inconsistent with Boy Scouts' commitment to a diverse and 'representative' membership . . . [and] contradicts Boy Scouts' overarching objective to reach 'all eligible youth.'" The court concluded that the exclusion of members like Dale "appears antithetical to the organization's goals and philosophy." But our cases reject this sort of inquiry; it is not the role of the courts to reject a group's expressed values because they disagree with those values or find them internally inconsistent.

The Boy Scouts asserts that it "teach[es] that homosexual conduct is not morally straight," and that it does "not want to promote homosexual conduct as a legitimate form of behavior." We accept the Boy Scouts' assertion. We need not inquire further to determine the nature of the Boy Scouts' expression with respect to homosexuality. But because the record before us contains written evidence of the Boy Scouts' viewpoint, we look to it as instructive, if only on the question of the sincerity of the professed beliefs.

A 1978 position statement to the Boy Scouts' Executive Committee . . . expresses the Boy Scouts' "official position" with regard to "homosexuality and Scouting":

". . . The Boy Scouts of America is a private, membership organization and leadership therein is a privilege and not a right. We do not believe that homosexuality and leadership in Scouting are appropriate. We will continue to select only those who in our judgment meet our standards and qualifications for leadership."

Thus, at least as of 1978—the year James Dale entered Scouting—the official position of the Boy Scouts was that avowed homosexuals were not to be Scout leaders.

A position statement promulgated by the Boy Scouts in 1991 (after Dale's membership was revoked but before this litigation was filed) also supports its current view:

"We believe that homosexual conduct is inconsistent with the requirement in the Scout Oath that a Scout be morally straight and in the Scout Law that a Scout be clean in word and deed, and that homosexuals do not provide a desirable role model for Scouts."

This position statement was redrafted numerous times but its core message remained consistent. . . .

. . . We cannot doubt that the Boy Scouts sincerely holds this view.

We must then determine whether Dale's presence as an assistant scoutmaster would significantly burden the Boy Scouts' desire to not "promote homosexual conduct as a legitimate form of behavior." As we give deference to an association's assertions regarding the nature of its expression, we must also give deference to an association's view of what would impair its expression. That is not to say that an expressive association can erect a shield against antidiscrimination laws simply by asserting that mere acceptance of a member from a particular group would impair its message. But here Dale, by his own admission, is one of a group of gay Scouts who have "become leaders in their community and are open and honest about their sexual orientation." Dale was the copresident of a gay and lesbian organization at college and remains a gay rights activist. Dale's presence in the Boy Scouts would, at the very least, force the organization to send a message, both to the youth members and the world, that the Boy Scouts accepts homosexual conduct as a legitimate form of behavior. . . .

The New Jersey Supreme Court determined that the Boy Scouts' ability to disseminate its message was not significantly affected by the forced inclusion of Dale as an assistant scoutmaster. . . .

We disagree with the New Jersey Supreme Court's conclusion. . . .

First, associations do not have to associate for the "purpose" of disseminating a certain message in order to be entitled to the protections of the First Amendment. An association must merely engage in expressive activity that could be impaired in order to be entitled to protection. . . .

Second, even if the Boy Scouts discourages Scout leaders from disseminating views on sexual issues—a fact that the Boy Scouts disputes with contrary evidence—the First Amendment protects the Boy Scouts' method of expression. If the Boy Scouts wishes Scout leaders to avoid questions of sexuality and teach only by example, this fact does not negate the sincerity of its belief discussed above.

Third, the First Amendment simply does not require that every member of a group agree on every issue in order for the group's policy to be "expressive association." The Boy Scouts takes an official position with respect to homosexual conduct, and that is sufficient for First Amendment purposes. . . . The fact that the organization does not trumpet its views from the housetops, or that it tolerates dissent within its ranks, does not mean that its views receive no First Amendment protection.

Having determined that the Boy Scouts is an expressive association and that the forced inclusion of Dale would significantly affect its expression, we inquire whether the application of New Jersey's public accommodations law to require that the Boy Scouts accept Dale as an assistant scoutmaster runs afoul of the Scouts' freedom of expressive association. We conclude that it does. . . .

. . . The state interests embodied in New Jersey's public accommodations law do not justify such a severe intrusion on the Boy Scouts' rights to freedom of expressive association. That being the case, we hold that the First Amendment prohibits the State from imposing such a requirement through the application of its public accommodations law. . . .

We are not, as we must not be, guided by our views of whether the Boy Scouts' teachings with respect to homosexual conduct are right or wrong; public or judicial disapproval of a tenet of an organization's expression does not justify the State's effort to compel the organization to accept members where such acceptance would derogate from the organization's expressive message. . . .

The judgment of the New Jersey Supreme Court is reversed, and the cause remanded for further proceedings not inconsistent with this opinion.

It is so ordered.

JUSTICE STEVENS, with whom JUSTICE SOUTER, JUSTICE GINSBURG, and JUSTICE BREYER join, dissenting.
The majority holds that New Jersey's law violates BSA's [Boy Scouts of America's] right to associate and its right to free speech. But that law does not "impos[e] any serious burdens" on BSA's "collective effort on behalf of [its] shared goals," *Roberts v. United States Jaycees* (1984), nor does it force BSA to communicate any message that it does not wish to endorse. New Jersey's law, therefore, abridges no constitutional right of the Boy Scouts. . . .

In this case, Boy Scouts of America contends that it teaches the young boys who are Scouts that homosexuality is immoral. Consequently, it argues, it would violate its right to associate to force it to admit homosexuals as members, as doing so would be at odds with its own shared goals and values. This contention, quite

plainly, requires us to look at what, exactly, are the values that BSA actually teaches.

. . . BSA describes itself as having a "representative membership," which it defines as "boy membership [that] reflects proportionately the characteristics of the boy population of its service area." In particular, the group emphasizes that "[n]either the charter nor the bylaws of the Boy Scouts of America permits the exclusion of any boy. . . . To meet these responsibilities we have made a commitment that our membership shall be representative of *all* the population in every community, district, and council." . . .

To bolster its claim that its shared goals include teaching that homosexuality is wrong, BSA directs our attention to two terms appearing in the Scout Oath and Law. The first is the phrase "morally straight," which appears in the Oath ("On my honor I will do my best . . . To keep myself . . . morally straight"); the second term is the word "clean," which appears in a list of 12 characteristics together comprising the Scout Law. . . .

It is plain as the light of day that neither one of these principles—"morally straight" and "clean"—says the slightest thing about homosexuality. Indeed, neither term in the Boy Scouts' Law and Oath expresses any position whatsoever on sexual matters.

BSA's published guidance on that topic underscores this point. Scouts, for example, are directed to receive their sex education at home or in school, but not from the organization. . . . In light of BSA's self-proclaimed ecumenism, furthermore, it is even more difficult to discern any shared goals or common moral stance on homosexuality. . . .

BSA's claim finds no support in our cases. We have recognized "a right to associate for the purpose of engaging in those activities protected by the First Amendment—speech, assembly, petition for the redress of grievances, and the exercise of religion." *Roberts.* And we have acknowledged that "when the State interferes with individuals' selection of those with whom they wish to join in a common endeavor, freedom of association . . . may be implicated." But "[t]he right to associate for expressive purposes is not . . . absolute"; rather, "the nature and degree of constitutional protection afforded freedom of association may vary depending on the extent to which . . . the constitutionally protected liberty is at stake in a given case." Indeed, the right to associate does not mean "that in every setting in which individuals exercise some discrimination in choosing associates, their selective process of inclusion and exclusion is protected by the Constitution." *New York State Club Assn., Inc. v. City of New York* (1988). . . .

. . . [T]he majority insists that we must "give deference to an association's assertions regarding the nature of its expression" and "we must also give deference to an association's view of what would impair its expression." . . .

This is an astounding view of the law. I am unaware of any previous instance in which our analysis of the scope of a constitutional right was determined by looking at what a litigant asserts in his or her brief and inquiring no further. . . . But the majority insists that our inquiry must be "limited" because "it is not the role of the courts to reject a group's expressed values because they disagree with those values or find them internally inconsistent."

But nothing in our cases calls for this Court to do any such thing. An organization can adopt the message of its choice, and it is not this Court's place to disagree with it. But we must inquire whether the group is, in fact, expressing a message (whatever it may be) and whether that message (if one is expressed) is significantly affected by a State's antidiscrimination law. More critically, that inquiry requires our *independent* analysis, rather than deference to a group's litigating posture. . . .

There is, of course, a valid concern that a court's independent review may run the risk of paying too little heed to an organization's sincerely held views. But unless one is prepared to turn the right to associate into a free pass out of antidiscrimination laws, an independent inquiry is a necessity. . . .

In this case, no such concern is warranted. It is entirely clear that BSA in fact expresses no clear, unequivocal message burdened by New Jersey's law. . . .

. . . Over the years, BSA has generously welcomed over 87 million young Americans into its ranks. In 1992 over one million adults were active BSA members. The notion that an organization of that size and enormous prestige implicitly endorses the views that each of those adults may express in a non-Scouting context is simply mind boggling. . . .

Unfavorable opinions about homosexuals "have ancient roots." *Bowers v. Hardwick* (1986). . . .

That such prejudices are still prevalent and that they have caused serious and tangible harm to countless members of the class New Jersey seeks to protect are established matters of fact that neither the Boy Scouts

nor the Court disputes. That harm can only be aggravated by the creation of a constitutional shield for a policy that is itself the product of a habitual way of thinking about strangers. As Justice Brandeis so wisely advised, "we must be ever on our guard, lest we erect our prejudices into legal principles."

If we would guide by the light of reason, we must let our minds be bold. I respectfully dissent.

ANNOTATED READINGS

A number of works provide good general explorations of the Constitution's freedom of expression guarantees. Among them are Zechariah Chafee, Jr., *Free Speech in the United States* (Cambridge, MA: Harvard University Press, 1941); Daniel A. Farber, *The First Amendment* (New York: Foundation Press, 1998); Stephen M. Feldman, *Free Expression and Democracy in America: A History* (Chicago: University of Chicago Press, 2008); Stanley Fish, *There's No Such Thing as Free Speech, and It's a Good Thing, Too* (New York: Oxford University Press, 1994); Karla K. Gower, *Liberty and Authority in Free Expression Law: The United States and Canada* (New York: LFB Scholarly Publishing, 2002); Mark A. Graber, *Transforming Free Speech* (Berkeley: University of California Press, 1991); Ken I. Kersch, *Freedom of Speech: Rights and Liberties under the Law* (Santa Barbara, CA: ABC-CLIO, 2003); Howard Schweber, *Speech, Conduct, and the First Amendment* (New York: Peter Lang, 2003); and Cass A. Sunstein, *Democracy and the Problem of Free Speech* (New York: Free Press, 1993).

The potential conflicts between freedom of expression and national security are explored in works such as Bruce Ackerman, *Before the Next Attack: Preserving Civil Liberties in an Age of Terrorism* (New Haven, CT: Yale University Press, 2006); Lee Epstein, Daniel E. Ho, Gary King, and Jeffrey A. Segal, "The Supreme Court during Crisis: How War Affects Only Nonwar Cases," *New York University Law Review* 80 (April 2005): 1–116; Ernest Freeberg, *Democracy's Prisoner: Eugene V. Debs, the Great War, and the Right to Dissent* (Cambridge, MA: Harvard University Press, 2009); Eric A. Posner and Adrian Vermeule, *Terror in the Balance: Security, Liberty, and the Courts* (New York: Oxford University Press, 2007); Richard A. Posner, *Not a Suicide Pact: The Constitution in a Time of National Emergency* (New York: Oxford University Press, 2006); Geoffrey R. Stone, *Perilous Times: Free Speech in*

Wartime from the Sedition Act of 1798 to the War on Terrorism (New York: W. W. Norton, 2004); Geoffrey R. Stone, *War and Liberty: An American Dilemma: 1790 to the Present* (New York: W. W. Norton, 2007); and Patrick S. Washburn, *A Question of Sedition* (New York: Oxford University Press, 1986).

Offensive and hateful speech gives rise to the inevitable tension between the Constitution's commitment to liberty of expression and its commitment to the equality of all persons. Works that address these issues include Jennine Bell, *Policing Hatred: Law Enforcement, Civil Rights, and Hate Crime* (New York: New York University Press, 2002); Edward J. Cleary, *Beyond the Burning Cross: The First Amendment and the Landmark* R.A.V. *Case* (New York: Random House, 1994); Jon B. Gould, *Speak No Evil: The Triumph of Hate Speech Regulation* (Chicago: University of Chicago Press, 2005); Frederick M. Lawrence, *Punishing Hate: Bias Crimes under American Law* (Cambridge, MA: Harvard University Press, 2002). Catherine A. MacKinnon, *Only Words* (Cambridge, MA: Harvard University Press, 1993); Laura Beth Nielsen, *License to Harass: Law, Hierarchy, and Offensive Public Speech* (Princeton, NJ: Princeton University Press, 2004); Philippa Strum, *When the Nazis Came to Skokie: Freedom for Speech We Hate* (Lawrence: University Press of Kansas, 1999); and Nicholas Wolfson, *Hate Speech, Sex Speech, Free Speech* (Westport, CT: Praeger, 1997).

The First Amendment's implications for the right of individuals not to speak is the subject of Haig Bosmajian, *The Freedom Not to Speak* (New York: New York University Press, 1999).

On the controversial issue of flag burning as a constitutionally protected means of expression, see Robert Justin Goldstein, *Burning the Flag: The Great 1989–1990 American Flag Desecration Controversy* (Kent, OH: Kent State University Press, 1996).

Examples of in-depth examinations of key cases dealing with the rights of students to express themselves freely in the public schools include James C. Foster, *Bong Hits 4 Jesus: A Perfect Constitutional Storm in Alaska's Capital* (Fairbanks: University of Alaska Press, 2010); and John W. Johnson, *The Struggle for Student Rights:* Tinker v. Des Moines *and the 1960s* (Lawrence: University Press of Kansas, 1997).

6

Freedom of the Press

FREEDOM OF THE Press is perhaps the most visible manifestation of Americans exercising their expression rights. Each day the print, broadcast, and electronic media blanket the nation with news, commentaries, and entertainment from varied perspectives. Newsstands, bookstores, and online booksellers flourish by offering periodicals and books devoted to every imaginable interest. Interactive media, such as talk radio, op-ed pages, letters to the editor, and blogs, allow citizens to become participants in the press rather than just consumers. The result is a robust exchange of information and opinion.

Much of what appears in the media is critical of government and government policies. Unlike the situation in some other countries, in the United States those who criticize officials can do so without government censorship or fear of retaliation. They enjoy protection provided by the First Amendment's stipulation that "Congress shall make no law . . . abridging the freedom . . . of the press."

This constitutional provision may seem quaint in this day and age of the Internet. After all, it seems nearly implausible to think that the government could physically prevent journalists from posting material online (though the same may not hold for publishing material in newspapers, as the cases to come reveal). But it's hardly implausible to believe that government officials might try to pass laws, or take other action, that would punish journalists after the material appeared. And this, among other reasons, is why the guarantee of a free press remains crucial today. It continues to reflect the framers' strong commitment to the importance of robust reporting. The framers saw the right to publish freely as important not only for its own sake but also because it acts as a significant protection against the government's denying other political and personal liberties. The founders believed that the rights of speech and religion would be meaningless without a free press, the watchdog that sounds a warning when other rights are threatened. Thomas Jefferson was so certain of this precept that in 1816 he proclaimed, "When the press is free, and every man is able to read, all is safe."

As British colonists, the framers were well schooled in the values of a free press, and history had also taught them that this right could not be taken for granted. England had controlled the press from the fifteenth through the seventeenth centuries, and the government's repressive measures became well entrenched. Following the introduction of printing into England in the 1400s, Britain developed a licensing system under which nothing could be printed without prior approval from the government.[1] When these licensing laws expired in 1695, the right to publish materials free from censorship became recognized under common law, which led English jurist William Blackstone to write, "The liberty of the press consists in laying no previous restraint upon publications and not

---

1. See Thomas I. Emerson, *The System of Freedom of Expression* (New York: Vintage Books, 1970), 504.

in freedom from censure for criminal matter when published."[2]

Although not fully embraced by the U.S. Supreme Court, Blackstone's words convey a significant message about freedom of the press, a message that the framers of the Constitution understood. They recognized that for a society to remain free, it must allow for the emergence of divergent views and opinions, which can be formed only through the open exchange of ideas. By censoring the press, government takes away a major mechanism (indeed, *the* major one during the eighteenth and nineteenth centuries) through which ideas can be openly shared, and the people know only what the government wants them to know. Under such circumstances, the press becomes an extension of government, not an independent observer, a check, or even a reliable source of information.

Why is this state of affairs so dangerous? Consider one of the most heinous regimes in the history of the world—Nazi Germany. How the Nazis came to power and carried out their deeds is still being debated, but certainly their ability to control the press and to use it as a propaganda tool is part of the explanation. The danger of government control of the press also can be seen closer to home. The Watergate scandal involved political manipulation and illegal behavior at the highest levels of government and led to the resignation of President Richard Nixon in 1974. We should remember that it was the press that first discovered the wrongdoing and brought it to light. If we allowed government to place prior restraints on the press—to censor it—the Watergate story would never have been published.

In the first part of this chapter, we examine the development of doctrine dealing with prior restraints. Does the Court today permit any censorship of the press (and other media), or is the press free to publish all the news it sees fit to print? But prior restraints are not the only limits government has tried to place on the press. In the second part of the chapter, we explore a less obvious constraint—government control of press content. Rather than questioning whether the government can completely prohibit the publication of certain items, the cases presented here asked the Court to determine whether the government has

any say in regulating the content of the items the press chooses to print. We conclude the chapter with a discussion of the special privileges claimed by the media. Reporters argue that they should enjoy a unique set of guarantees to perform their jobs. How has the Court reacted to these claims?

Taken together, these three issues—prior restraint, government control of press content, and the special rights of reporters—form the heart of freedom of the press questions. But the Court's decisions also distinguish the type of "press" in question. In general, the justices have treated printed matter (newspapers, magazines, and books) differently from the broadcast media (radio and television) and, more recently, have struggled with questions related to the Internet. Why? How have those differences manifested themselves? Are they justified? We take up these questions in the pages that follow, and we return to some of them in Chapter 8, where we consider unique legal problems raised by the Internet and other electronic media.

PRIOR RESTRAINT

No concept is more important to an understanding of freedom of the press than prior restraint, which occurs when the government reviews material to determine whether its publication will be allowed. Prior restraint is government censorship and antithetical to freedom of the press. If the First Amendment means anything, it means that no government has the authority to decide what may be published. The government may punish press activity that violates legitimate criminal laws, but such government sanctions may take place only *after* publication, not before.

Establishing a Standard

The principle that prior restraint runs contrary to the Constitution was established in the formative case *Near v. Minnesota* (1931). The justices took a strong stance against censorship, but does their decision imply that the government may never block the publication of material it considers inappropriate or harmful? Are there exceptions to the constitutional prohibition against prior restraint? Consider these questions as you read Chief Justice Charles Evans Hughes's opinion in *Near.*

---

2. Blackstone's *Commentaries on the Laws of England,* vol. 4 (London, 1765–1769), 151–152.

Near v. Minnesota

283 U.S. 697 (1931)
http://laws.findlaw.com/US/283/697.html
Vote: 5 (Brandeis, Holmes, Hughes, Roberts, Stone)
    4 (Butler, McReynolds, Sutherland, Van Devanter)

OPINION OF THE COURT: *Hughes*
DISSENTING OPINION: *Butler*

FACTS:

A 1925 Minnesota law provided for "the abatement, as a public nuisance, of a 'malicious, scandalous, and defamatory newspaper, magazine, or other periodical.'" In the fall of 1927 a county attorney asked a state judge to issue a restraining order banning publication of the *Saturday Press*. In the attorney's view, the newspaper, partly owned by Jay Near, was the epitome of a malicious, scandalous, and defamatory publication.[3] The *Saturday Press* committed itself to exposing corruption, bribery, gambling, and prostitution in Minneapolis, which Near often connected to Jews. The paper attacked specific city officials for being in league with gangsters and chided the established press for refusing to uncover the corruption. These attacks were colored by Near's racist, anti-Semitic attitudes. In one issue, Near wrote:

I simply state a fact when I say that ninety per cent of the crimes committed against society in this city are committed by Jew gangsters. . . . It is Jew, Jew, Jew, as long as one cares to comb over the records. I am launching no attack against the Jewish people AS A RACE. I am merely calling attention to a FACT. And if people of that race and faith wish to rid themselves of the odium and stigma THE RODENTS OF THEIR OWN RACE HAVE BROUGHT UPON THEM, they need only to step to the front and help the decent citizens of Minneapolis rid the city of these criminal Jews.

In a piece attacking establishment journalism, Near proclaimed: "Journalism today isn't prostituted so much as it is disgustingly flabby. I'd rather be a louse in the cotton shirt of a nigger than be a journalistic prostitute." Based on the paper's past record, a judge issued a temporary restraining order prohibiting the sale of printed and future editions. Believing that this action violated his rights, Near contacted the American Civil Liberties Union, which agreed to take his case. He

The only known photo of Saturday Press *editor Jay Near appeared April 19, 1936, in the* Minneapolis Tribune. *Near's successful appeal to the Supreme Court in 1931 marked the first time the Court enforced the First Amendment's guarantee of freedom of the press to strike a state law that imposed a prior restraint on a newspaper.*

grew uncomfortable with the organization, however, and instead obtained assistance from the publisher of the *Chicago Tribune.* Together, they challenged the Minnesota law as a violation of the First Amendment freedom of press guarantee, arguing that the law was tantamount to censorship.

ARGUMENTS:

For the appellant, Jay Near:

- The Minnesota law violates freedom of the press by imposing restraints prior to publication. Prior restraints violate traditional notions of free press, which allow publication of any material, regardless of its nature. Any abuses should be punished only after publication.

- The state does not have the power to prevent publication of any material, unless it advocates violent overthrow of the government or breach of law. General concern for the public welfare is insufficient to overcome the right to free press.

For the appellee, State of Minnesota:

- The right to free press does not extend to press that is obscene, scandalous, or defamatory. The Minnesota law is narrow, applying only to irresponsible press that is "malicious, scandalous, or defamatory," and therefore not protected by the First Amendment.

- The state has the power to restrict press that is injurious to public health, safety, and morals; the law promotes public peace by prohibiting dangerous press.

---

3. For an in-depth account of this case, see Fred W. Friendly, *Minnesota Rag* (New York: Random House, 1981). The quotes in this and the next paragraph come from this account.

- Publications can demonstrate that the material to be published is true and published in good faith, therefore lawful publications will not be affected by the statute.

MR. CHIEF JUSTICE HUGHES DELIVERED THE OPINION OF THE COURT.

[The Minnesota] statute, for the suppression as a public nuisance of a newspaper or periodical, is unusual, if not unique, and raises questions of grave importance transcending the local interests involved in the particular action. It is no longer open to doubt that the liberty of the press and of speech is within the liberty safeguarded by the due process clause of the Fourteenth Amendment from invasion by state action. It was found impossible to conclude that this essential personal liberty of the citizen was left unprotected by the general guaranty of fundamental rights of person and property. *Gitlow v. New York, Whitney v. California, Fiske v. Kansas.* . . .

. . . The object of the statute is not punishment, in the ordinary sense, but suppression of the offending newspaper or periodical. The reason for the enactment, as the state court has said, is that prosecutions to enforce penal statutes for libel do not result in "efficient repression or suppression of the evils of scandal." Describing the business of publication as a public nuisance does not obscure the substance of the proceeding which the statute authorizes. It is the continued publication of scandalous and defamatory matter that constitutes the business and the declared nuisance. In the case of public officers, it is the reiteration of charges of official misconduct, and the fact that the newspaper or periodical is principally devoted to that purpose, that exposes it to suppression. . . .

This suppression is accomplished by enjoining publication, and that restraint is the object and effect of the statute.

. . . The statute not only operates to suppress the offending newspaper or periodical, but to put the publisher under an effective censorship. When a newspaper or periodical is found to be "malicious, scandalous and defamatory," and is suppressed as such, resumption of publication is punishable as a contempt of court by fine or imprisonment. Thus, where a newspaper or periodical has been suppressed because of the circulation of charges against public officers of official misconduct, it would seem to be clear that the renewal of the publication of such charges would constitute a contempt, and that the judgment would lay a permanent restraint upon the publisher, to escape which he must satisfy the court as to the character of a new publication. Whether he would be permitted again to publish matter deemed to be derogatory to the same or other public officers would depend upon the court's ruling. . . .

If we cut through mere details of procedure, the operation and effect of the statute in substance is that public authorities may bring the owner or publisher of a newspaper or periodical before a judge upon a charge of conducting a business of publishing scandalous and defamatory matter—in particular that the matter consists of charges against public officers of official dereliction—and, unless the owner or publisher is able and disposed to bring competent evidence to satisfy the judge that the charges are true and are published with good motives and for justifiable ends, his newspaper or periodical is suppressed and further publication is made punishable as a contempt. This is of the essence of censorship.

The question is whether a statute authorizing such proceedings in restraint of publication is consistent with the conception of the liberty of the press as historically conceived and guaranteed. In determining the extent of the constitutional protection, it has been generally, if not universally, considered that it is the chief purpose of the guaranty to prevent previous restraints upon publication. The struggle in England, directed against the legislative power of the licenser, resulted in renunciation of the censorship of the press. The liberty deemed to be established was thus described by Blackstone: "The liberty of the press is indeed essential to the nature of a free state; but this consists in laying no *previous* restraints upon publications, and not in freedom from censure for criminal matter when published." . . .

The criticism upon Blackstone's statement has not been because immunity from previous restraint upon publication has not been regarded as deserving of special emphasis, but chiefly because that immunity cannot be deemed to exhaust the conception of the liberty guaranteed by State and Federal Constitutions. . . .

The objection has also been made that the principle as to immunity from previous restraint is stated too broadly, if every such restraint is deemed to be prohibited. That is undoubtedly true; the protection even as to previous restraint is not absolutely unlimited. But the limitation has been recognized only in exceptional cases. "When a nation is at war many things that might be said in time of peace are such a hindrance to its effort that their utterance will not be endured so long as men fight and that no Court could regard them as protected by any constitutional right." No one would question but that a government might prevent actual obstruction to its recruiting service or the publication of the sailing dates of transports or the number and location of troops. On similar grounds, the primary requirements of decency may be enforced against obscene publications. The security of the community life may be protected against incitements to acts of violence and the overthrow by force of orderly government. The constitutional guaranty of free speech does not "protect a man from an injunction against uttering words that may have all the effect of force." These limitations are not applicable here. . . .

The fact that for approximately one hundred and fifty years there has been almost an entire absence of attempts to impose previous restraints upon publications relating to the malfeasance of public officers is significant of the deep-seated conviction that such restraints would violate constitutional right. Public officers, whose character and conduct remains open to debate and free discussion in the press, find their remedies for false accusations in actions under libel laws providing for redress and punishment, and not in proceedings to restrain the publication of newspapers and periodicals. . . .

. . . The fact that the liberty of the press may be abused by miscreant purveyors of scandal does not make any the less necessary the immunity of the press from previous restraint in dealing with official misconduct. Subsequent punishment for such abuses as may exist is the appropriate remedy, consistent with constitutional privilege. . . .

The statute in question cannot be justified by reason of the fact that the publisher is permitted to show, before injunction issues, that the matter published is true and is published with good motives and for justifiable ends. If such a statute, authorizing suppression and injunction on such a basis, is constitutionally valid, it would be equally permissible for the Legislature to provide that at any time the publisher of any newspaper could be brought before a court, or even an administrative officer (as the constitutional protection may not be regarded as resting on mere procedural details), and required to produce proof of the truth of his publication, or of what he intended to publish and of his motives, or stand enjoined. If this can be done, the Legislature may provide machinery for determining in the complete exercise of its discretion what are justifiable ends and restrain publication accordingly. And it would be but a step to a complete system of censorship. . . .

Equally unavailing is the insistence that the statute is designed to prevent the circulation of scandal which tends to disturb the public peace and to provoke assaults and the commission of crime. Charges of reprehensible conduct, and in particular of official malfeasance, unquestionably create a public scandal, but the theory of the constitutional guaranty is that even a more serious public evil would be caused by authority to prevent publication. . . . There is nothing new in the fact that charges of reprehensible conduct may create resentment and the disposition to resort to violent means of redress, but this well-understood tendency did not alter the determination to protect the press against censorship and restraint upon publication. As was said in *New Yorker Staats-Zeitung v. Nolan,* "If the township may prevent the circulation of a newspaper for no reason other than that some of its inhabitants may violently disagree with it, and resent its circulation by resorting to physical violence, there is no limit to what may be prohibited." The danger of violent reactions becomes greater with effective organization of defiant groups resenting exposure, and, if this consideration warranted legislative interference with the initial freedom of publication, the constitutional protection would be reduced to a mere form of words.

For these reasons we hold the statute, so far as it authorized the proceedings in this action . . . , to be an infringement of the liberty of the press. . . .

Judgment reversed.

Chief Justice Hughes's opinion appears to take a definitive position against prior censorship. He wrote, "The statute not only seeks to suppress the offending newspaper . . . but to put the publisher under an effective censorship." But he acknowledged that the protection against "previous restraint is not absolutely unlimited." There may be exceptional circumstances under which government restraint is necessary. Hughes cited three vital interests that may justify government censorship: the protection of national security, the regulation of obscenity, and the prohibition of expression that would incite acts of violence. In Chapter 5 we discussed the Court's rulings on expression and violence, and we examine the question of obscenity in Chapter 7. Here, we turn our attention to the national security exception and then to an exception that Hughes did not consider: the authority of educators to control the content of student publications.

Prior Restraint and National Security

In *Near* Hughes explained that the government may legitimately prohibit the publication of certain material in times of war that it might not constitutionally regulate in times of peace. To see the Court's logic, suppose that during the war in Iraq a major newspaper received classified information about a planned U.S.-led military effort in the northern part of that country and announced that it would publish the information so the American people would be fully informed about the war effort. The military would understandably be concerned because publication would give the enemy advance knowledge of the operation. Could the government take action to prohibit publication, or would it be confined to pursuing criminal charges against the paper for illegal dissemination of classified documents after publication? According to *Near,* the courts would likely rule in favor of the government.

This issue has rarely come before the Supreme Court, with the exception of *New York Times v. United States* (1971). The continuing war on terrorism in the aftermath of September 11, 2001, and other militarized disputes may well give rise to new cases. Does the Court's decision in *New York Times,* in which the government attempted to stop two prominent newspapers from publishing classified documents pertaining to the Vietnam War, hold any lessons for the press and the government in the current environment?

New York Times v. United States

403 U.S. 713 (1971)
http://laws.findlaw.com/US/403/713.html
Oral arguments are available at http://www.oyez.org.
Vote: 6 (Black, Brennan, Douglas, Marshall, Stewart, White)
      3 (Blackmun, Burger, Harlan)

PER CURIAM OPINION

CONCURRING OPINIONS: Black, Brennan, Douglas, Marshall, Stewart, White

DISSENTING OPINIONS: Blackmun, Burger, Harlan

FACTS:

In June 1971 the *New York Times* and the *Washington Post* began publishing articles based on two government documents: a 1965 Defense Department depiction of the Gulf of Tonkin incident and the 1968 "History of U.S. Decision-Making Process on Viet Nam Policy," a seven-thousand-page, forty-seven-volume secret study undertaken by the Pentagon but photocopied and presented to the press by a Defense Department employee, Daniel Ellsberg. Known as the Pentagon Papers, the documents constituted a history of U.S. involvement in the war in Indochina, a subject of acute interest in the early 1970s.

After the newspapers published several installments, the U.S. government brought a motion in federal district court asking the court to order the papers to refrain from publishing any more installments. The government argued that the articles would cause "irreparable injury" to the country's national security. To support this assertion, the government said that the entire 1968 study was top secret, a classification "applied only to that information or material the defense aspect of which is paramount, and the unauthorized disclosure of which could result in exceptionally grave damage to the Nation." The newspapers disagreed, arguing that the material was largely of historical, not current, interest, and that nothing in the documents related to a time period after 1968. As such, the government's attempt to enjoin publication amounted to nothing less than prior restraint.

Because the issues in this case were so important and the public controversy so intense, the judicial system responded to the dispute in a very unusual manner. The government's request to the district court was dated June 15, 1971, and the lower courts handled the case in an expedited fashion, so that only nine days later the issue was before the Supreme Court. By then the justices had completed their work for the term and were about to go into their summer recess. To accommodate the case, the Court extended its session and heard arguments on June 26. Four days later, the Court issued a short "per curiam" opinion announcing that the majority rejected the government's demands. Then each of the justices submitted an opinion expressing his view. Six supported the newspapers, and three sided with the government.

ARGUMENTS:

For the petitioner, New York Times:

- The government must meet a heavy burden of proof to overcome the well-established presumption that prior restraint violates freedom of the press.

- In order to meet *Near*'s national security exception, it must be shown that publication of the material would cause an unavoidable, disastrous outcome. The publication of the articles in question does not meet this standard.

- Although there may be some circumstances that justify prior restraint, the executive branch does not have the inherent power to limit freedom of the press. At a minimum, there must be a clear mandate from the legislative branch.

Signaling a victory for the Washington Post *and the* New York Times, *the chief of presses at the* Post *holds the first edition of the paper announcing the Court's decision in* New York Times v. United States, *also known as the Pentagon Papers case, June 30, 1971.*

For the respondent, United States:

- Publication of the material in question poses irreparable and grave danger to the United States, and so the government is justified in imposing prior restraint. Secrecy and confidentiality are critical to the successful conduct of foreign affairs.

- The Court should defer to the executive branch because, as the controlling branch for foreign affairs and commander in chief of the military, it is in the best position to judge the effects of publication.

- In order to impose prior restraint, the government only needs to show a likelihood of harm, because it is impossible to predict the exact consequences of publication.

PER CURIAM.

We granted certiorari in these cases in which the United States seeks to enjoin the *New York Times* and the *Washington Post* from publishing the contents of a classified study entitled "History of U.S. Decision-Making Process on Viet Nam Policy."

"Any system of prior restraints of expression comes to this Court bearing a heavy presumption against its constitutional validity." The Government "thus carries a heavy burden of showing justification for the imposition of such a restraint." The District Court for the Southern District of New York in the *New York Times* case held that the Government had not met that burden. We agree.

. . . The order of the Court of Appeals for the Second Circuit is reversed, and the case is remanded with directions to enter a judgment affirming the judgment of the District Court for the Southern District of New York. The stays entered . . . by the Court are vacated. The judgments shall issue forthwith.

MR. JUSTICE BLACK, with whom MR. JUSTICE DOUGLAS joins, concurring.

I adhere to the view that the Government's case against the *Washington Post* should have been dismissed and that the injunction against the *New York Times* should have been vacated without oral argument when the cases were first presented to this Court. I believe that every moment's continuance of the injunctions against these newspapers amounts to a flagrant, indefensible, and continuing violation of the First Amendment. . . . In my view it is unfortunate that some of my Brethren are apparently willing to hold that the publication of news may sometimes be enjoined. Such a holding would make a shambles of the First Amendment.

Our Government was launched in 1789 with the adoption of the Constitution. The Bill of Rights, including the First Amendment, followed in 1791. Now, for the first time in the 182 years since the founding of the Republic, the federal courts are asked to hold that the First Amendment does not mean what it says, but rather means that the Government can halt the publication of current news of vital importance to the people of this country.

In seeking injunctions against these newspapers and in its presentation to the Court, the Executive Branch seems to have forgotten the essential purpose and history of the First Amendment. When the Constitution was adopted, many people strongly opposed it because the document contained no Bill of Rights to safeguard certain basic freedoms. They especially feared that the new powers granted to a central government might be interpreted to permit the government to curtail freedom of religion, press, assembly, and speech. In response to an overwhelming public clamor, James Madison offered a series of amendments to satisfy citizens that these great liberties would remain safe and beyond the power of government to abridge. Madison proposed what later became the First Amendment in three parts, two of which are set out below, and one of which proclaimed: "The people shall not be deprived or abridged of their right to speak, to write, or to publish their sentiments; *and the freedom of the press, as one of the great bulwarks of liberty, shall be inviolable."* The amendments were offered to curtail and restrict the general powers granted in the Executive, Legislative, and Judicial Branches two years before in the original Constitution. The Bill of Rights changed the original Constitution into a new charter under which no branch of government could abridge the people's freedoms of press, speech, religion, and assembly. Yet the Solicitor General argues and some members of the Court appear to agree that the general powers of the Government adopted in the original Constitution should be interpreted to limit and restrict the specific and emphatic guarantees of the Bill of Rights adopted later. I can imagine no greater perversion of history. . . .

In the First Amendment the Founding Fathers gave the free press the protection it must have to fulfill its essential role in our democracy. The press was to serve the governed, not the governors. The Government's power to censor the press was abolished so that the press would remain forever free to censure the Government. The press was protected so that it could bare the secrets of government and inform the people. Only a free and unrestrained press can effectively expose deception in government. And paramount among the responsibilities of a free press is the duty to prevent any part of the government from deceiving the people and sending them off to distant lands to die of foreign fevers and foreign shot and shell. In my view, far from deserving condemnation for their courageous reporting, the *New York Times,* the *Washington Post,* and other newspapers should be commended for serving the purpose that the Founding Fathers saw so clearly. In revealing the workings of government that led to the Vietnam war, the newspapers nobly did precisely that which the Founders hoped and trusted they would do.

The Government's case here is based on premises entirely different from those that guided the Framers of the First Amendment. . . .

. . . [T]he Government argues in its brief that in spite of the First Amendment, "[t]he authority of the Executive Department to protect the nation against publication of information whose disclosure would endanger the national security stems from two interrelated sources: the constitutional power of the President over the conduct of foreign affairs and his authority as Commander-in-Chief."

In other words, we are asked to hold that despite the First Amendment's emphatic command, the Executive Branch, the Congress, and the Judiciary can make laws enjoining publication of current news and abridging freedom of the press in the name of "national security." The Government does not even attempt to rely on any act of Congress. Instead, it makes the bold and dangerously far-reaching contention that the courts should take it upon themselves to "make" a law abridging freedom of the press in the name of equity, presidential power and national security, even when the representatives of the people in Congress have adhered to the command of the First Amendment and refused to make such a law. To find that the President has "inherent power" to halt the publication of news by resort to the courts would wipe out the First Amendment and destroy the fundamental liberty and security of the very people the Government hopes to make "secure." No one can read the history of the adoption of the First Amendment without being convinced beyond any doubt that it was injunctions like those sought here that Madison and his collaborators intended to outlaw in this Nation for all time.

The word "security" is a broad, vague generality whose contours should not be invoked to abrogate the fundamental law embodied in the First Amendment. The guarding of military and diplomatic secrets at the expense of informed representative government provides no real security for our Republic. The Framers of the First Amendment, fully aware of both the need to defend a new nation and the abuses of the English and Colonial Governments, sought to give this new society strength and security by providing that freedom of speech, press, religion, and assembly should not be abridged.

MR. JUSTICE DOUGLAS with whom MR. JUSTICE BLACK joins, concurring.

It should be noted at the outset that the First Amendment provides that "Congress shall make no law . . . abridging the freedom of speech, or of the press." That leaves, in my view, no room for governmental restraint on the press. . . .

The dominant purpose of the First Amendment was to prohibit the widespread practice of governmental suppression of embarrassing information. It is common knowledge that the First Amendment was adopted against the widespread use of the common law of seditious libel to punish the dissemination of material that is embarrassing to the powers-that-be. The present cases will, I think, go down in history as the most dramatic illustration of that principle. A debate of large proportions goes on in the Nation over our posture in Vietnam. That debate antedated the disclosure of the contents of the present documents. The latter are highly relevant to the debate in progress.

Secrecy in government is fundamentally anti-democratic, perpetuating bureaucratic errors. Open debate and discussion of public issues are vital to our national health. On public questions there should be "uninhibited, robust, and wide-open" debate.

MR. JUSTICE BRENNAN, concurring.

The entire thrust of the Government's claim throughout these cases has been that publication of the material sought to be enjoined "could," or "might," or "may" prejudice the national interest in various ways. But the First Amendment tolerates absolutely no prior judicial restraints of the press predicated upon surmise or conjecture that untoward consequences may result. Our cases, it is true, have indicated that there is a single, extremely narrow class of cases in which the First Amendment's ban on prior judicial restraint may be overridden. Our cases have thus far indicated that such cases may arise only when the Nation "is at war," during which times "[n]o one would question but that a government might prevent actual obstruction to its recruiting service or the publication of the sailing dates of transports or the number and location of troops." Even if the present world situation were assumed to be tantamount to a time of war, or if the power of presently available armaments would justify even in peacetime the suppression of information that would set in motion a nuclear holocaust, in neither of these actions has the Government presented or even alleged that publication of items from or based upon the material at issue would cause the happening of an event of that nature. "[T]he chief purpose of [the First Amendment's] guaranty [is] to prevent previous restraints upon publication." Thus, only governmental allegation and proof that publication must inevitably, directly, and immediately cause the occurrence of an event kindred to imperiling the safety of a transport already at sea can support even the issuance of an interim restraining order. In no event may mere conclusions be sufficient: for if the Executive Branch seeks judicial aid in preventing publication, it must inevitably submit the basis upon which that aid is sought to scrutiny by the judiciary. And therefore, every restraint issued in this case, whatever its form, has violated the First Amendment—and not less so because that restraint was justified as necessary to afford the courts an opportunity to examine the claim more thoroughly. Unless and until the Government has clearly made out its case, the First Amendment commands that no injunction may issue.

MR. JUSTICE STEWART, with whom
MR. JUSTICE WHITE joins, concurring.

In the governmental structure created by our Constitution, the Executive is endowed with enormous power in the two related areas of national defense and international relations. This power, largely unchecked by the Legislative and Judicial branches, has been pressed to the very hilt since the advent of the nuclear missile age. For better or for worse, the simple fact is that a President of the United States possesses vastly greater constitutional independence in these two vital areas of power than does, say, a prime minister of a country with a parliamentary form of government.

In the absence of the governmental checks and balances present in other areas of our national life, the only effective restraint upon executive policy and power in the areas of national defense and international affairs may lie in an enlightened citizenry—in an informed and critical public opinion which alone can here protect the values of democratic government. For this reason, it is perhaps here that a press that is alert, aware, and free most vitally serves the basic purpose of the First Amendment. For without an informed and free press there cannot be an enlightened people.

Yet it is elementary that the successful conduct of international diplomacy and the maintenance of an effective national defense require both confidentiality and secrecy. Other nations can hardly deal with this Nation in an atmosphere of mutual trust unless they can be assured that their confidences will be kept. And within our own executive departments, the development of considered and intelligent international policies would be impossible if those charged with their formulation could not communicate with each other freely, frankly, and in confidence. In the area of basic national defense the frequent need for absolute secrecy is, of course, self-evident.

I think there can be but one answer to this dilemma, if dilemma it be. The responsibility must be where the power is. If the Constitution gives the Executive a large degree of unshared power in the conduct of foreign affairs and the maintenance of our national defense, then under the Constitution the Executive must have the largely unshared duty to determine and preserve the degree of internal security necessary to exercise that power successfully. It is an awesome responsibility, requiring judgment and wisdom of a high order. I should suppose that moral, political, and practical considerations would dictate that a very first principle of that wisdom would be an insistence upon avoiding secrecy for its own sake. For when everything is classified, then nothing is classified, and the system becomes one to be disregarded by the cynical or the careless, and to be manipulated by those intent on self-protection or self-promotion. I should suppose, in short, that the hallmark of a truly effective internal security system would be the maximum possible disclosure, recognizing that secrecy can best be preserved only when credibility is truly maintained. But be that as it may, it is clear to me that it is the constitutional duty of the Executive—as a matter of sovereign prerogative and not as a matter of law as the courts know law—through the promulgation and enforcement of executive regulations, to protect the confidentiality necessary to carry out its responsibilities in the fields of international relations and national defense.

This is not to say that Congress and the courts have no role to play. Undoubtedly Congress has the power to enact specific and appropriate criminal laws to protect government property and preserve government secrets. Congress has passed such laws, and several of them are of very colorable relevance to the apparent circumstances of these cases. And if a criminal prosecution is instituted, it will be the responsibility of the courts to decide the applicability of the criminal law under which the charge is brought. Moreover, if Congress should pass a specific law authorizing civil proceedings in this field, the courts would likewise have the duty to decide the constitutionality of such a law as well as its applicability to the facts proved.

But in the cases before us we are asked neither to construe specific regulations nor to apply specific laws. We are asked, instead, to perform a function that the Constitution gave to the Executive, not the Judiciary. We are asked, quite simply, to prevent the publication by two newspapers of material that the Executive Branch insists should not, in the national interest, be published. I am convinced that the Executive is correct with respect to some of the documents involved. But I cannot say that disclosure of any of them will surely result in direct, immediate, and irreparable damage to our Nation or its people. That being so, there can under the First Amendment be but one judicial resolution of the issues before us. I join the judgments of the Court.

MR. JUSTICE WHITE, with whom MR. JUSTICE STEWART joins, concurring.

I concur in today's judgments, but only because of the concededly extraordinary protection against prior restraints enjoyed by the press under our constitutional system. I do not say that in no circumstances would the First Amendment permit an injunction against publishing information about government plans or operations.

Nor, after examining the materials the Government characterizes as the most sensitive and destructive, can I deny that revelation of these documents will do substantial damage to public interests. Indeed, I am confident that their disclosure will have that result. But I nevertheless agree that the United States has not satisfied the very heavy burden that it must meet to warrant an injunction against publication in these cases, at least in the absence of express and appropriately limited congressional authorization for prior restraints in circumstances such as these. . . .

It is not easy to reject the proposition urged by the United States and to deny relief on its good-faith claims in these cases that publication will work serious damage to the country. But that discomfiture is considerably dispelled by the infrequency of prior-restraint cases. Normally, publication will occur and the damage be done before the Government has either opportunity or grounds for suppression. So here, publication has already begun and a substantial part of the threatened damage has already occurred. The fact of a massive breakdown in security is known, access to the documents by many unauthorized people is undeniable, and the efficacy of equitable relief against these or other newspapers to avert anticipated damage is doubtful at best.

MR. CHIEF JUSTICE BURGER, dissenting.

So clear are the constitutional limitations on prior restraint against expression, that from the time of *Near v. Minnesota* we have had little occasion to be concerned with cases involving prior restraints against news reporting on matters of public interest. There is, therefore, little variation among the members of the Court in terms of resistance to prior restraints against publication. Adherence to this basic constitutional principle, however, does not make these cases simple ones. In these cases, the imperative of a free and unfettered press comes into collision with another imperative, the effective functioning of a complex modern government and specifically the effective exercise of certain constitutional powers of the Executive. Only those who view the First Amendment as an absolute in all circumstances—a view I respect, but reject—can find such cases as these to be simple or easy.

These cases are not simple for another and more immediate reason. We do not know the facts of the cases. No District Judge knew all the facts. No Court of Appeals Judge knew all the facts. No member of this Court knows all the facts.

Why are we in this posture, in which only those judges to whom the First Amendment is absolute and permits of no restraint in any circumstances or for any reason, are really in a position to act?

I suggest we are in this posture because these cases have been conducted in unseemly haste. . . . The prompt settling of these cases reflects our universal abhorrence of prior restraint. But prompt judicial action does not mean unjudicial haste.

Here, moreover, the frenetic haste is due in large part to the manner in which the *Times* proceeded from the date it obtained the purloined documents. It seems reasonably clear now that the haste precluded reasonable and deliberate judicial treatment of these cases and was not warranted. The precipitate action of this Court aborting trials not yet completed is not the kind of judicial conduct that ought to attend the disposition of a great issue.

MR. JUSTICE HARLAN, with whom THE CHIEF JUSTICE and MR. JUSTICE BLACKMUN join, dissenting.

With all respect, I consider that the Court has been almost irresponsibly feverish in dealing with these cases.

Both the Court of Appeals for the Second Circuit and the Court of Appeals for the District of Columbia Circuit rendered judgment on June 23. The *New York Times*'s petition for certiorari, its motion for accelerated consideration thereof, and its application for interim relief were filed in this Court on June 24 at about 11 A.M. The application of the United States for interim relief in the *Post* case was also filed here on June 24 at about 7:15 P.M. This Court's order setting a hearing before us on June 26 at 11 A.M., a course which I joined only to avoid the possibility of an even more peremptory action by the Court, was issued less than 24 hours before. The record in the *Post* case was filed with the Clerk shortly before 1 P.M. on June 25; the record in the *Times* case did not arrive until 7 or 8 o'clock that same night. The briefs of the parties were received less than two hours before argument on June 26.

This frenzied train of events took place in the name of the presumption against prior restraints created by the First Amendment. Due regard for the extraordinarily important and difficult questions involved in these litigations should have led the Court to shun such a precipitate timetable. In order to decide the merits of these cases properly, some or all of the following questions should have been faced:

1. Whether the Attorney General is authorized to bring these suits in the name of the United States. . . .

2. Whether the First Amendment permits the federal courts to enjoin publication of stories which would present a serious threat to national security.

3. Whether the threat to publish highly secret documents is of itself a sufficient implication of national security to justify an injunction on the theory that regardless of the contents of the documents harm enough results simply from the demonstration of such a breach of secrecy.

4. Whether the unauthorized disclosure of any of these particular documents would seriously impair the national security.

5. What weight should be given to the opinion of high officers in the Executive Branch of the Government with respect to questions 3 and 4.

6. Whether the newspapers are entitled to retain and use the documents notwithstanding the seemingly uncontested facts that the documents, or the originals of which they are duplicates, were purloined from the Government's possession and that the newspapers received them with knowledge that they had been feloniously acquired.

7. Whether the threatened harm to the national security or the Government's possessory interest in the documents justifies the issuance of an injunction against publication in light of—

   a. The strong First Amendment policy against prior restraints on publication;

   b. The doctrine against enjoining conduct in violation of criminal statutes; and

   c. The extent to which the materials at issue have apparently already been otherwise disseminated.

These are difficult questions of fact, of law, and of judgment; the potential consequences of erroneous decision are enormous. The time which has been available to us, to the lower courts, and to the parties has been wholly inadequate for giving these cases the kind of consideration they deserve. It is a reflection on the stability of the judicial process that these great issues—as important as any that have arisen during my time on the Court—should have been decided under the pressures engendered by the torrent of publicity that has attended these litigations from their inception.

Forced as I am to reach the merits of these cases, I dissent from the opinion and judgments of the Court. Within the severe limitations imposed by the time constraints under which I have been required to operate, I can only state my reasons in telescoped form, even though in different circumstances I would have felt constrained to deal with the cases in the fuller sweep indicated above. . . .

. . . It is plain to me that the scope of the judicial function in passing upon the activities of the Executive Branch of the Government in the field of foreign affairs is very narrowly restricted. This view is, I think, dictated by the concept of separation of powers upon which our constitutional system rests.

In a speech on the floor of the House of Representatives, Chief Justice John Marshall, then a member of that body, stated:

"The President is the sole organ of the nation in its external relations, and its sole representative with foreign nations."

From that time, shortly after the founding of the Nation, to this, there has been no substantial challenge to this description of the scope of executive power. . . .

The power to evaluate the "pernicious influence" of premature disclosure is not, however, lodged in the Executive alone. I agree that, in performance of its duty to protect the values of the First Amendment against political pressures, the judiciary must review the initial Executive determination to the point of satisfying itself that the subject matter of the dispute does lie within the proper compass of the President's foreign relations power. . . .

But in my judgment the judiciary may not properly go beyond these . . . inquiries and redetermine for itself the probable impact of disclosure on the national security. . . .

Even if there is some room for the judiciary to override the executive determination, it is plain that the scope of review must be exceedingly narrow. I can see no indication in the opinions of either the District Court or the Court of Appeals in the *Post* litigation that the conclusions of the Executive were given even the deference owing to an administrative agency, much less that owing to a co-equal branch of the Government operating within the field of its constitutional prerogative.

Accordingly, I would vacate the judgment of the Court of Appeals for the District of Columbia Circuit on this ground and remand the case for further proceedings in the District Court.

MR. JUSTICE BLACKMUN, dissenting.

The First Amendment . . . is only one part of an entire Constitution. Article II of the great document vests in the Executive Branch primary power over the conduct of foreign affairs, and places in that branch the responsibility for the Nation's safety. Each provision of the Constitution is important, and I cannot subscribe to a doctrine of unlimited absolutism for the First Amendment at the cost of downgrading other provisions. First Amendment absolutism has never commanded a majority of this Court. See, for example, *Near v. Minnesota*. What is needed here is a weighing, upon properly developed standards, of the broad right of the press to print and of the very narrow right of the Government to prevent. Such standards are not yet developed.

From start to finish, it took the federal judiciary only two weeks to decide this major constitutional dispute, but legal scholars continue to debate *New York Times*. Some suggest that it was the Court's, or at least the individual justices', strongest statement to date on freedom of the press, that the justices virtually eradicated Chief Justice Hughes's national security exception to prior restraint. These observers say that the justices were telling the government that there are few—if any—compelling reasons to justify government censorship of the press. Others disagree, noting that even though the result was clear, the individual opinions were not a resounding defense of the free press guarantee because the justices were divided in their views. Compare, for example, Justice Byron White's opinion with Justice Hugo Black's; one could hardly imagine greater divergence of thought between two individuals voting for the same outcome.

Prior Restraint and the War on Terrorism

Since *New York Times* the Court has had no other important cases dealing with prior restraint and national security concerns. Nevertheless, during military efforts the government has not hesitated to impose constraints on the media. Depending on one's point of view, the 1991 Gulf War marked either a high point or a low point in government-media relations: the government simply circumvented the need to censor the press by limiting its access to certain information.[4] During the war in Iraq that began in March 2003, six hundred "embedded" journalists were granted considerably more freedom, but it was far from absolute. For example, the Department of Defense requested that journalists refrain from publishing information that could harm America's national security and did not rule out the possibility that the department could demand to review reports before they were published or aired. Moreover, the George W. Bush administration asked the media to use "caution" in broadcasting videotapes from Osama bin Laden and others associated with the

---

4. See, for example, Kevin A. Smith, "The Media at the Tip of the Spear," *Michigan Law Review* 102 (2004): 1329–1372.

al-Qaeda organization. Still, in this age of the Internet, it can be difficult for the government to control public access to sensitive information. To see this, we need only consider WikiLeaks, "a not-for-profit" media organization that has posted on its Web site numerous secret and classified military and State Department documents. Some journalists have defended the actions of WikiLeaks, as has Daniel Ellsberg, who has claimed that "every attack now made on WikiLeaks . . . was made against me and the release of the Pentagon Papers at the time." But the Obama administration has not taken kindly to some of WikiLeaks's efforts, suggesting that they could be damaging to the United States. As of this writing, WikiLeaks remains under investigation by the administration.

Whatever you think of these efforts, it is worth knowing that the United States has not been alone in attempting to rein in the press since September 11, 2001. Following are some recent examples reported by Freedom House, a nonpartisan "advocate for democracy and human rights worldwide":[5]

- In France, counterterrorism authorities detained a *Le Monde* reporter for forty-eight hours after searching his Paris apartment. They believed that the journalist had published state secrets about terrorist attacks and wanted him to reveal his sources.
- Groups in the Philippines have expressed concern that a new antiterror law will allow the government to wiretap members of the media based on mere suspicion of involvement in terrorism.
- Australia's Security Intelligence Act provides for a five-year prison sentence for journalists who fail to produce their sources or to pass on information they receive about potential terrorist acts.

Clearly, as Freedom House suggests, "there is an international consensus that terrorism must be rooted out wherever possible." But there also is agreement, at least in many countries, on the importance of a free, independent press. Striking an appropriate balance between these two goals represents a challenge for courts all over the world. Based on the cases you have read so far, how do you think the justices would rule should a dispute presenting these issues reach the Court?

---

5. Freedom House has, since 1972, evaluated levels of political rights and civil liberties in nations throughout the world. For more information, visit the organization's Web site at http://www.freedomhouse.org.

Prior Restraint and the Student Press

Chief Justice Hughes's opinion in *Near,* as we have noted, articulated three possible exceptions to the general rule against government censorship of the press: protecting national security, regulating obscenity, and prohibiting expression that would incite acts of violence. *Hazelwood School District v. Kuhlmeier* (1988) asked the Court to consider another exception: allowing school administrators to impose certain standards on public school newspapers. As you read Justice White's opinion, ask yourself these questions: What importance do the justices place on the fact that the newspaper was run by students? Does the case have any implications beyond the student press? Is the decision an isolated exception, or does it significantly dilute the prior restraint doctrine that the justices have supported since *Near?*

Hazelwood School District v. Kuhlmeier

484 U.S. 260 (1988)
http://laws.findlaw.com/US/484/260.html
Oral arguments are available at http://www.oyez.org.
Vote: 5 (O'Connor, Rehnquist, Scalia, Stevens, White)
    3 (Blackmun, Brennan, Marshall)
OPINION OF THE COURT: *White*
DISSENTING OPINION: *Brennan*

FACTS:

In May 1983 the editors of the *Spectrum,* Hazelwood East High School's student newspaper, planned to publish articles on divorce and teenage pregnancy *(see Box 6-1).* Principal Robert E. Reynolds decided to excise two pages the newspaper's staff had produced because, in his view, "The students and families in the articles were described in such a way that the readers could tell who they were. When it became clear that [they] were going to tread on the right to privacy of students and their parents, I stepped in to stop the process."[6]

The *Spectrum* staff objected to the principal's decision. Believing it amounted to the same kind of prior censorship that the Court had condemned in *Near,* the student editors hired a lawyer and challenged the decision in court. A federal district court ruled for the principal, holding that no First Amendment violation had occurred. The court of appeals, however, reversed. In its view, the *Spectrum* was a public forum *(see page 227)* because it "was intended to be operated as a conduit for student viewpoint." Its status as a public forum,

---

6. Quoted in Mark A. Uhlig, "From Hazelwood to the High Court," *New York Times Magazine,* September 13, 1987, 102.

therefore, prevented the principal from censoring its contents except, according to the Supreme Court's ruling in *Tinker v. Des Moines* (1969) *(see pages 264–267),* when "necessary to avoid material and substantial interference with school work or discipline . . . or the rights of others." The court could find no such evidence in the record.

ARGUMENTS:

For the petitioner, Hazelwood School District:

- The school newspaper is not a public forum but part of an educational curriculum. Therefore, the newspaper is subject to reasonable teacher supervision and editorial control.
- Because of educational concerns, the constitutional rights of students in public school are more limited than those of adults in other settings. The Court should defer to the judgment of educators in controlling their curricula.
- The decision to censor the articles should be judged by a reasonableness standard. In this case the decision to censor was reasonable because of concerns about the privacy of the subjects and the appropriateness of the material.

For the respondent, Cathy Kuhlmeier:

- The school newspaper is a limited public forum created for students to share ideas openly, as evidenced by the School Board's own Curriculum Guide. Therefore, the publication has all the protections of free press afforded by the First Amendment.
- Allowing free press in educational institutions promotes democracy by encouraging the open sharing of ideas among young citizens.
- Censorship of the articles was unreasonable, because they did not violate any legal privacy rights. The appropriateness of the articles is not a proper measure of the school's right to censor them.

JUSTICE WHITE DELIVERED THE OPINION OF THE COURT.

This case concerns the extent to which educators may exercise editorial control over the contents of a high school newspaper produced as part of the school's journalism curriculum. . . .

Students in the public schools do not "shed their constitutional rights to freedom of speech or expression at the schoolhouse gate." They cannot be punished merely for expressing their personal views on the school premises—whether "in the cafeteria, or on the playing field,

or on the campus during the authorized hours"—unless school authorities have reason to believe that such expression will "substantially interfere with the work of the school or impinge upon the rights of other students."

We have nonetheless recognized that the First Amendment rights of students in the public schools "are not automatically coextensive with the rights of adults in other settings" and must be "applied in light of the special characteristics of the school environment." A school need not tolerate student speech that is inconsistent with its "basic educational mission," even though the government could not censor similar speech outside the school. Accordingly, we held in [*Bethel School District No. 403 v.*] *Fraser* [1986] that a student could be disciplined for having delivered a speech that was "sexually explicit" but not legally obscene at an official school assembly, because the school was entitled to "disassociate itself" from the speech in a manner that would demonstrate to others that such vulgarity is "wholly inconsistent with the 'fundamental values' of public school education." We thus recognized that "[t]he determination of what manner of speech in the classroom or in school assembly is inappropriate properly rests with the school board," rather than with the federal courts. It is in this context that respondents' First Amendment claims must be considered.

We deal first with the question whether Spectrum may appropriately be characterized as a forum for public expression. The public schools do not possess all of the attributes of streets, parks, and other traditional public forums that "time out of mind, have been used for purposes of assembly, communicating thoughts between citizens, and discussing public questions." Hence, school facilities may be deemed to be public forums only if school authorities have "by policy or by practice" opened those facilities "for indiscriminate use by the general public," or by some segment of the public, such as student organizations. If the facilities have instead been reserved for other intended purposes, "communicative or otherwise," then no public forum has been created, and school officials may impose reasonable restrictions on the speech of students, teachers, and other members of the school community. . . .

The evidence relied upon by the Court of Appeals in finding Spectrum to be a public forum, is equivocal, at best. For example, Board Policy 348.51, which stated in part that "[s]chool sponsored student publications will not restrict free expression or diverse viewpoints within the rules of responsible journalism," also stated that

BOX 6-1   CENSORED HIGH SCHOOL NEWSPAPER ARTICLE

The following is a reproduction of the uncorrected page proof of part of one of the two stories censored from the May 13, 1983, issue of the Hazelwood East High School *Spectrum*. Student editors took their objections all the way to the Supreme Court.

Divorce's impact on kids may have lifelong effect

by Shari Gordon

In the United States one marriage ends for every two that begin. The North County percentage of divorce is three marriages end out of four marriages that start.

There are more than two central characters in the painful drama of divorce. Children of divorced parents, literally million os them, are torn by the end of their parents' marriage.

"In the beginning I thought I caused the problem, but now I realize it wasn't me."

What causes divorce? According to Mr. Ken Kerkhoff, social studies teacher some of the causes are:

- Poor dating habits that lead to marriage.
- Not enough variables in common.
- Lack f communication.
- Lack of desire or effort to make the relationship work.

Figures aren't the whole story. The fact is that divorce has a psychological and sociological change on the child.

One junior commented on how the divorce occurred, "My dad dian't make any money, so my mother divorced him."

"My father was an alcoholic and he always came home drunk and my mom really couldn't stand it any longer," said another junior.

Diana Herbert, freshman, said "My dad wasn't spending enough time with my mom, my sister and I. He was always out of town or out late playing cards with the guys. My parents always argued about everything."

"In the beginning I thought I caused the problem, but now I realize it wasn't me," added Diana.

"I was only five when my parents got divorced," said Susan Kiefer, junior. "I didn't quite understand what the divorce really meant until about the age of seven. I understood that divorce meant my mother and father wouldn't be together again."

"It stinks!" exclaimed Jill Viola, junior. "They can, afterwards, remarry and start their lives over again, but their kids will always be caught in between."

Out of the 25 students interviewe 17 f them have parents that have remarried.

The feelings of divorce affects the kids for the rest of their lives, according to Mr. Kerckhoff. The effects of divorce on the kids lead to the following:

- Higher not of absenteeism in school.
- Higher rate of trouble with school, officials and police.
- Higher rate of depression and insecurity.
- Run a higher risk of divorce themselves.

All of these are the latest findings in research on single parent homes.

such publications were "developed within the adopted curriculum and its educational implications." One might reasonably infer from the full text of Policy 348.51 that school officials retained ultimate control over what constituted "responsible journalism" in a school-sponsored newspaper. Although the Statement of Policy published in the September 14, 1982, issue of Spectrum declared that "Spectrum, as a student-press publication, accepts all rights implied by the First Amendment," this statement, understood in the context of the paper's role in the school's curriculum, suggests, at most, that the administration will not interfere with the students' exercise of those First Amendment rights that attend the publication of a school-sponsored newspaper. It does not reflect an intent to expand those rights by converting a curricular newspaper into a public forum. . . . In sum, the evidence relied upon by the Court of Appeals fails to demonstrate the "clear intent to create a public forum" that existed in cases in which we found public forums to have been created. School officials did not evince either "by policy or by practice," any intent to open the pages of Spectrum to "indiscriminate use" by its student reporters and editors, or by the student body generally. Instead, they "reserve[d] the forum for its intended purpos[e]" as a supervised learning experience for journalism students. Accordingly, school officials were entitled to regulate the contents of Spectrum in any reasonable manner. It is this standard, rather than our decision in Tinker [v. Des Moines, 1969], that governs this case.

The question whether the First Amendment requires a school to tolerate particular student speech—the question that we addressed in Tinker—is different from the question whether the First Amendment requires a school affirmatively to promote particular student speech. The former question addresses educators' ability to silence a student's personal expression that happens to occur on the school premises. The latter question concerns educators' authority over school-sponsored publications, theatrical productions, and other expressive activities that students, parents, and members of the public might reasonably perceive to bear the imprimatur of the school. These activities may fairly be characterized as part of the school curriculum, whether or not they occur in a traditional classroom setting, so long as they are supervised by faculty members and designed to impart particular knowledge or skills to student participants and audiences.

Educators are entitled to exercise greater control over this second form of student expression to assure that participants learn whatever lessons the activity is designed to teach, that readers or listeners are not

exposed to material that may be inappropriate for their level of maturity, and that the views of the individual speakers are not erroneously attributed to the school. Hence, a school may in its capacity as publisher of a school newspaper or producer of a school play "disassociate itself" not only from speech that would "substantially interfere with [its] work . . . or impinge upon the rights of other students," but also from speech that is, for example, ungrammatical, poorly written, inadequately researched, biased or prejudiced, vulgar or profane, or unsuitable for immature audiences. A school must be able to set high standards for the student speech that is disseminated under its auspices—standards that may be higher than those demanded by some newspaper publishers or theatrical producers in the "real" world—and may refuse to disseminate student speech that does not meet those standards. In addition, a school must be able to take into account the emotional maturity of the intended audience in determining whether to disseminate student speech on potentially sensitive topics, which might range from the existence of Santa Claus in an elementary school setting to the particulars of teenage sexual activity in a high school setting. . . .

Accordingly, we conclude that the standard articulated in Tinker for determining when a school may punish student expression need not also be the standard for determining when a school may refuse to lend its name and resources to the dissemination of student expression. Instead, we hold that educators do not offend the First Amendment by exercising editorial control over the style and content of student speech in school-sponsored expressive activities so long as their actions are reasonably related to legitimate pedagogical concerns.

This standard is consistent with our oft-expressed view that the education of the Nation's youth is primarily the responsibility of parents, teachers, and state and local school officials, and not of federal judges. It is only when the decision to censor a school-sponsored publication, theatrical production, or other vehicle of student expression has no valid educational purpose that the First Amendment is so "directly and sharply implicate[d]" as to require judicial intervention to protect students' constitutional rights.

We also conclude that Principal Reynolds acted reasonably in requiring the deletion from the May 13 issue of Spectrum of the pregnancy article, the divorce article, and the remaining articles that were to appear on the same pages of the newspaper.

The initial paragraph of the pregnancy article declared that "[a]ll names have been changed to keep the identity of these girls a secret." The principal concluded that the students' anonymity was not adequately protected, however, given the other identifying information in the article and the small number of pregnant students at the school. Indeed, a teacher at the school credibly testified that she could positively identify at least one of the girls and possibly all three. It is likely that many students at Hazelwood East would have been at least as successful in identifying the girls. Reynolds therefore could reasonably have feared that the article violated whatever pledge of anonymity had been given to the pregnant students. In addition, he could reasonably have been concerned that the article was not sufficiently sensitive to the privacy interests of the students' boyfriends and parents, who were discussed in the article but who were given no opportunity to consent to its publication or to offer a response. The article did not contain graphic accounts of sexual activity. The girls did comment in the article, however, concerning their sexual histories and their use or nonuse of birth control. It was not unreasonable for the principal to have concluded that such frank talk was inappropriate in a school-sponsored publication distributed to 14-year-old freshmen and presumably taken home to be read by students' even younger brothers and sisters.

The student who was quoted by name in the version of the divorce article seen by Principal Reynolds made comments sharply critical of her father. The principal could reasonably have concluded that an individual publicly identified as an inattentive parent—indeed, as one who chose "playing cards with the guys" over home and family—was entitled to an opportunity to defend himself as a matter of journalistic fairness. These concerns were shared by both of Spectrum's faculty advisers for the 1982–1983 school year, who testified that they would not have allowed the article to be printed without deletion of the student's name. . . .

In sum, we cannot reject as unreasonable Principal Reynolds' conclusion that neither the pregnancy article nor the divorce article was suitable for publication in Spectrum. Reynolds could reasonably have concluded that the students who had written and edited these articles had not sufficiently mastered those portions of the Journalism II curriculum that pertained to the treatment of controversial issues and personal attacks, the need to protect the privacy of individuals whose most intimate concerns are to be revealed in the newspaper, and "the legal, moral, and ethical restrictions imposed upon journalists within a school community" that includes adolescent subjects and readers. Finally, we conclude that

the principal's decision to delete two pages of Spectrum, rather than to delete only the offending articles or to require that they be modified, was reasonable under the circumstances as he understood them. Accordingly, no violation of First Amendment rights occurred.

The judgment of the Court of Appeals for the Eighth Circuit is therefore

Reversed.

JUSTICE BRENNAN, with whom JUSTICE MARSHALL and JUSTICE BLACKMUN join, dissenting.

When the young men and women of Hazelwood East High School registered for Journalism II, they expected a civics lesson. Spectrum, the newspaper they were to publish, "was not just a class exercise in which students learned to prepare papers and hone writing skills, it was a . . . forum established to give students an opportunity to express their views while gaining an appreciation of their rights and responsibilities under the First Amendment to the United States Constitution. . . ." [T]he student journalists published a Statement of Policy—tacitly approved each year by school authorities—announcing their expectation that "Spectrum, as a student-press publication, accepts all rights implied by the First Amendment. . . . Only speech that 'materially and substantially interferes with the requirements of appropriate discipline' can be found unacceptable and therefore prohibited." The school board itself affirmatively guaranteed the students of Journalism II an atmosphere conducive to fostering such an appreciation and exercising the full panoply of rights associated with a free student press. "School sponsored student publications," it vowed, "will not restrict free expression or diverse viewpoints within the rules of responsible journalism."

This case arose when the Hazelwood East administration breached its own promise, dashing its students' expectations. The school principal, without prior consultation or explanation, excised six articles—comprising two full pages—of the May 13, 1983, issue of Spectrum. He did so not because any of the articles would "materially and substantially interfere with the requirements of appropriate discipline," but simply because he considered two of the six "inappropriate, personal, sensitive, and unsuitable" for student consumption.

In my view the principal broke more than just a promise. He violated the First Amendment's prohibitions against censorship of any student expression that neither disrupts classwork nor invades the rights of others, and against any censorship that is not narrowly tailored to serve its purpose. . . .

The Court opens its analysis in this case by purporting to reaffirm *Tinker*'s time-tested proposition that public school students "do not 'shed their constitutional rights to freedom of speech or expression at the schoolhouse gate.'" That is an ironic introduction to an opinion that denudes high school students of much of the First Amendment protection that *Tinker* itself prescribed. . . . The young men and women of Hazelwood East expected a civics lesson, but not the one the Court teaches them today.

I dissent.

When you consider whether *Hazelwood* can be reconciled with the rule announced in *Near*, keep this caveat in mind: the Court generally has recognized more limits on the First Amendment rights of students and juveniles than on those of adults. White sought to make this point clear in his opinion, but how convincing is his argument? For example, how did he distinguish this case from *Tinker*?

We will revisit the prior restraint controversy in the next chapter, when we take up the issue of government regulation of indecent and obscene expression. For now, let us turn to a related topic: government control of the content of messages from the press.

GOVERNMENT CONTROL OF PRESS CONTENT

Prior restraints of the media may constitute the most obvious way a government can control what its citizens see, hear, and read, but it is not the only way. Beyond preventing dissemination, governments can try to control the content of media messages. This practice may be less overt than imposing prior restraints, but it is no less dangerous. To see why, we only have to think again about the Nazi government in Germany. By controlling the press, the Nazi regime was able to disseminate the message that it wanted to get across to the public.

But why, in the United States, a country founded on democratic ideals, would questions of government control of the media ever come up? After all, such practices contradict values that Americans hold dear. The answer is that the government may have a good reason for seeking to control the media, such as the protection of the best interests of its citizens and of the democratic process. In the cases we review next, involving regulations on what the media must *exclude* on one hand and must *include* on the other, the government made just that argument—that the greater interests of society justified the government's decision to dictate what the media could or could not publish. Does the argument convince you that government should be allowed to place controls on the freedom of the press? Does the Court go along with this rationale?

Regulating the Press by Prohibiting Content

To begin to answer these questions, let us consider **Cox Broadcasting Corporation v. Cohn** (1975). At issue was a Georgia statute making it a crime for "any news media" to publish or broadcast "the name or identity of any female who may have been raped or upon whom an assault with intent to commit rape may have been made." The law was passed with the best of intentions. The victims of such brutal crimes have already suffered a great deal, and publicizing their names would only add to their anguish. Because rape, unlike other crimes, often carries with it an unfortunate and undeserved stigma, the privacy of the victims of rape should be protected.

The circumstances of *Cox Broadcasting* illustrate the point. The case began with events that took place in August 1971, when seventeen-year-old Cynthia Cohn attended a party with a large number of other high school students. A great deal of drinking took place. At the party six teenage boys raped Cohn, and, at some point during the assault, she was suffocated and died. The six boys were indicted for rape and murder.

Eight months later, five of the six boys pleaded guilty to the rape charge after the murder accusation was dropped. The sixth boy pleaded not guilty. While covering this story, a reporter for a television station owned by Cox Broadcasting found the name of the victim in the indictments. Because indictments are public documents, the reporter violated no law by inspecting them, but, in a news broadcast later that day, the reporter included Cynthia Cohn's name in his story. Martin Cohn, Cynthia's father, filed suit against Cox Broadcasting, claiming that the news reports containing the name of his daughter violated his right to privacy. His case was bolstered by the fact that Georgia law makes such reports unlawful. Cox Broadcasting claimed that the reports were protected under the First Amendment. The issue is straightforward: May a state constitutionally prohibit the press from reporting the names of rape victims?

With only Justice William Rehnquist dissenting, the Court held that a state may not, consistent with the First and Fourteenth Amendments, impose sanctions on the accurate publication of the name of a rape victim obtained from judicial records that are open to public inspection. Furthermore, the Court ruled that the publication of accurate reports of judicial proceedings merits special constitutional protection. Criminal activities and the way that courts manage criminal prosecutions are legitimate matters of public concern and, therefore, subjects the press is entitled to cover.

In *Cox Broadcasting* the Court developed a general principle of law: it would be loath to allow states to prohibit publication, in a truthful way, of public information. Indeed, since 1975 it has clung to this general principle. The next year, in *Nebraska Press Association v. Stuart* (1976), for example, the Court refused to allow a trial court judge to place a gag order on press coverage of pretrial proceedings, even though the order was designed to protect the defendant from prejudicial publicity. Three years later, in *Smith v. Daily Mail Publishing Co.* (1979), it struck down a law prohibiting the publication of the identity of juvenile offenders.

Regulating the Press by Mandating Content

What these cases show is that the Court generally is unwilling to support laws that prohibit the press from publishing otherwise legitimate information or punish the press for publishing such information. But that is not the only way governments try to control the press. Another is to *require* that it disseminate certain information. Totalitarian regimes have used this method to convert the press into a propaganda arm of the government. In the United States, government regulations requiring the press to carry specific information or publish particular stories have been motivated, some suggest, by more worthy purposes. **Miami Herald v. Tornillo** (1974) is an appropriate example. This suit challenged a Florida law that compelled newspapers to publish articles by candidates for political office when the paper criticized or attacked those candidates' records. The goal of the legislation was to ensure that full and fair information was available to the voters. The *Miami Herald* refused to comply, arguing that the government had no constitutional authority to order the newspaper to publish anything.

In a 9–0 decision the justices agreed; indeed, they were no more sympathetic to the government trying to

compel the press to publish stories than they were to the government prohibiting the press from disseminating certain information. As Chief Justice Warren Burger put it for the Court:

A responsible press is an undoubtedly desirable goal, but press responsibility is not mandated by the Constitution and like many other virtues it cannot be legislated.

Appellee's argument that the Florida statute does not amount to a restriction of appellant's right to speak because "the statute in question here has not prevented the *Miami Herald* from saying anything it wished" begs the core question. Compelling editors or publishers to publish that which "'reason' tells them should not be published" is what is at issue in this case. The Florida statute operates as a command in the same sense as a statute or regulation forbidding appellant to publish specified matter. Governmental restraint on publishing need not fall into familiar or traditional patterns to be subject to constitutional limitations on governmental powers. The Florida statute exacts a penalty on the basis of the content of a newspaper. The first phase of the penalty resulting from the compelled printing of a reply is exacted in terms of the cost in printing and composing time and materials and in taking up space that could be devoted to other material the newspaper may have preferred to print. . . .

Faced with the penalties that would accrue to any newspaper that published news or commentary arguably within the reach of the right-of-access statute, editors might well conclude that the safe course is to avoid controversy. Therefore, under the operation of the Florida statute, political and electoral coverage would be blunted or reduced. Government-enforced right of access inescapably 'dampens the vigor and limits the variety of public debate.' . . .

Even if a newspaper would face no additional costs to comply with a compulsory access law and would not be forced to forgo publication of news or opinion by the inclusion of a reply, the Florida statute fails to clear the barriers of the First Amendment because of its intrusion into the function of editors. A newspaper is more than a passive receptacle or conduit for news, comment, and advertising. The choice of material to go into a newspaper, and the decisions made as to limitations on the size and content of the paper, and treatment of public issues and public officials—whether fair or unfair—constitute the exercise of editorial control and judgment. It has yet to be demonstrated how governmental regulation of this crucial process can be exercised consistent with First Amendment guarantees of a free press as they have evolved to this time.

BOX 6-2   FREE PRESS IN GLOBAL PERSPECTIVE

Since 1972 Freedom House has evaluated levels of political rights and civil liberties in nations throughout the world. The data and graph presented here are from its 2011 survey on press freedom practices.[1] Countries were evaluated on three criteria: (1) laws and regulations that influence media content, (2) political pressures and controls on media content, and (3) economic influences over media content. Countries were rated on a scale from 0 to 100, with 0 representing the greatest degree of press freedom. Countries scoring 0 to 30 are regarded as having "free" media; 31 to 60, "partly free" media; and 61 to 100, "not free" media.

Ratings by Country

Overall, in 68 of the 196 countries (35 percent) the press is free, and in 65 countries (33 percent) it is partly free. This means that the press is not free in 63 countries (32 percent).

The six countries scoring highest (meaning the press is free) on Freedom House's index are Finland, Norway, Sweden, Belgium, Iceland, and Luxembourg. The six scoring lowest (the press is not free) are North Korea, Turkmenistan, Uzbekistan, Libya, Eritrea, and Burma. Freedom House rates the press as free in the United States, with a ranking of 17 (out of 196 countries).

Ratings by Population

The above data are useful for observing regional patterns, but they obscure other features, such as the numbers of people living in countries with or without free press. For example, the press is not free in 32 percent of the 196 countries, but 43 percent of the world's population lives in such countries.

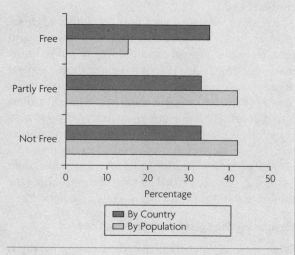

[1] The full Freedom House survey results, as well as the accompanying report, are available at http://www.freedomhouse.org.

Once again, we see that the Court has little tolerance for content-based regulations of the printed media. Indeed, over time, *Tornillo* has come to stand for the principle that governments in the United States should keep their "hands off" newspapers.[7]

The same cannot be said of governments elsewhere. Box 6-2 offers data from Freedom House's 2011 press freedom survey. Overall, only 35 percent of the 196 nations in the survey were found to have a truly free press—that is, a press free from serious legal, economic, and political influences on press content. To put it another way, only 15 percent of the world's people (with worldwide population now at about 7 billion) live in nations where the press is free from government intrusion.

Beyond Newspapers: Regulating the Broadcast Media and the Internet

Tornillo and most of the cases we have examined so far involve the print media, but over time, Americans have come to rely quite heavily on broadcast media and the Internet for political information. These days, far more people turn on their televisions than open their newspapers to learn about current events (66 percent versus 31 percent), and use of the Internet as a source of news continues to skyrocket. A 2010 survey found that nearly four out of every ten Americans "got most of their news about national and international issues" from online sources.[8] Should these sources enjoy the same degree of protection as newspapers? The Court addressed this question as it

---

7. See, for example, C. Edwin Baker, "Turner Broadcasting: Content-Based Regulation of Persons and Presses," *Supreme Court Review* (1994): 58–59.

8. Pew Research Center, *The State of the News Media, 2011,* at http://stateofthemedia.org.

pertained to the broadcast media in the 1969 case of ***Red Lion Broadcasting v. FCC.***

This question was of great interest to Congress, which regulates the broadcast industry through its power over interstate commerce. The legislature establishes general regulatory policy for the broadcast industry, and the Federal Communications Commission (FCC), which Congress created, implements those policies and carries out the day-to-day regulatory activity. The regulation is comprehensive. The federal government issues licenses to broadcast, requires that public interest programming be included, and prohibits certain kinds of language on the air. Radio and television stations must adhere to strict codes of operation and conform to regulations that are designed to promote the public interest. A station that does not conform to these rules may lose its license to broadcast, essentially putting the operation out of business.

Although the degree of regulation imposed by Congress has varied over the years, the federal government has always maintained that the electronic media may be regulated in ways that would not be allowed for the print media. The broadcast industry is different because, unlike the print media, radio and television stations operate by using the public airways. As the public airways can accommodate only a limited number of stations, the government must regulate the broadcast industry to ensure that it can operate effectively and for the public good. Does this argument have merit?

The Supreme Court has suggested that it does. In *Red Lion Broadcasting v. FCC* (1969), the justices heard a challenge to an FCC policy requiring radio and television broadcasters to discuss public issues on their stations and to provide fair coverage to each side of those issues. This policy was widely known as the fairness doctrine. The government thought it was necessary to ensure that all viewpoints could be expressed in light of the limited number of broadcast frequencies. The government also argued that the policy did not violate the First Amendment because it did not prohibit speech; it only guaranteed that the broadcast medium remain open to all viewpoints.

Red Lion Broadcasting, which challenged the policy, disagreed on both scores. Its lawyers argued that the policy cannot be justified by the fact that a limited number of broadcast frequencies exist because the same holds for daily newspapers: they too are small in number. They also claimed that by requiring broadcasters to

provide response time, the FCC was in fact dictating the content of programming.

The Court disagreed. Writing for a 7–0 majority, Justice White acknowledged that "the First Amendment is [not] irrelevant to public broadcasting. On the contrary, it has a major role to play as the Congress itself recognized in [the Federal Communications Act], which forbids FCC interference with 'the right of free speech by means of radio communication.'" But, he went on to write:

Although broadcasting is clearly a medium affected by a First Amendment interest, differences in the characteristics of new media justify differences in the First Amendment standards applied to them. . . . Where there are substantially more individuals who want to broadcast than there are frequencies to allocate, it is idle to posit an unabridgeable First Amendment right to broadcast comparable to the right of every individual to speak, write, or publish. If 100 persons want broadcast licenses but there are only 10 frequencies to allocate, all of them may have the same "right" to a license; but if there is to be any effective communication by radio, only a few can be licensed and the rest must be barred from the airwaves. It would be strange if the First Amendment, aimed at protecting and furthering communications, prevented the Government from making radio communication possible by requiring licenses to broadcast and by limiting the number of licenses so as not to overcrowd the spectrum. . . .

Interestingly enough, in 1987, nineteen years after *Red Lion*, the fairness doctrine was repealed. Yet *Red Lion* remains good law. It establishes that although the First Amendment applies to electronic media, the amendment is no barrier to reasonable government control and that Congress may treat broadcasting differently from the print media. In other words, for the reasons it gave in *Red Lion*, the Court holds regulations aimed at the electronic media to a less rigorous standard of First Amendment scrutiny than it does those intended for the print media.[9] To see this point, we need only compare the right-to-reply requirement at issue in *Tornillo* with the fairness doctrine. With but one exception, the regulations were identical: the first was geared to newspapers and the second to the broadcast media. The Court unanimously struck down the right-to-reply requirement but unanimously upheld the fairness doctrine.

---

9. This is the interpretation that commentators and the Court have adopted. It is interesting to note, however, that neither *Tornillo* nor *Red Lion* made reference to standards or levels of scrutiny. For more on this point, see Baker, "Turner Broadcasting."

FCC v. Pacifica Foundation (1978) and *FCC v. Fox Television Stations* (2009) provide other interesting examples of how the Court treats the electronic and print media differently. *Pacifica Foundation* began when a radio station owned by the Pacifica Foundation one afternoon broadcast a recorded monologue by humorist George Carlin titled "Filthy Words." In it Carlin recites a litany of words and phrases that, although not obscene, are considered indecent and offensive by many. In response to this broadcast, a man wrote a letter of complaint to the FCC, claiming that he heard the monologue on his car radio while he was driving with his young son. After an investigation, the FCC issued an order declaring the broadcast to have been in violation of a federal statute that prohibits the transmission of indecent language on the public airways. Pacifica appealed and was initially successful, but the Supreme Court reversed. In a 5–4 vote the justices held that of all forms of communication, broadcasting has the most limited First Amendment protection. The electronic media, the majority held, differ from the print media because they have a pervasive presence that can invade the privacy of the home and because they are uniquely available to children. Clearly, the regulation of indecent language upheld here would never be sustained by the Court if it were applied to the print media.

We could say the same of the FCC policy at issue in *Fox Television.* For decades after the Court's decision in *Pacifica Foundation,* the FCC followed a policy, as it explained, of pursuing indecency enforcement action only for the "repetitive occurrence of the indecent words"—as in Carlin's monologue. Fleeting or isolated expletives were not apparently deemed indecent. In 2004, however, the FCC seemed to change in course. After a live broadcast in which the singer Bono used the "F word," the FCC announced that it would treat even a single, isolated word as indecent. It did not, however, punish the offenders because, it wrote, "existing precedent would have permitted this broadcast."

Fox and other broadcasters challenged the new indecency policy as "arbitrary and capricious," but a divided Supreme Court disagreed. Writing for a plurality of the justices, Justice Scalia held that the new policy was neither arbitrary nor capricious under the laws that govern the FCC's use of its power. And while Scalia did not address whether the policy violated the Constitution—noting instead that those matters would be "determined soon enough"—he did write that "any chilled references to excretory and sexual material

'surely lie at the periphery of First Amendment concern,' *Pacifica* (plurality opinion of STEVENS, J.)."

Where does the Internet, the fastest-growing form of global communication, fall in this discussion? We take up this and related questions in Chapter 8. For now, consider the majority opinion in *Reno v. ACLU* (1997), in which the Court considered the constitutionality of a congressional act, the Communications Decency Act of 1996 (CDA), prohibiting communication to minors that is "indecent" or "obscene":

We [have] observed that "[e]ach medium of expression . . . may present its own problems." Thus, some of our cases have recognized special justifications for regulation of the broadcast media that are not applicable to other speakers, see *Red Lion Broadcasting Co. v. FCC* (1969). In [Red Lion and other cases], the Court relied on the history of extensive government regulation of the broadcast medium; the scarcity of available frequencies at its inception; and its "invasive" nature. These factors are not present in cyberspace. Neither before nor after the enactment of the CDA have the vast democratic fora of the Internet been subject to the type of government supervision and regulation that has attended the broadcast industry. Moreover, the Internet is not as "invasive" as radio or television. . . . Users seldom encounter content [on the Internet] "by accident." . . .

Finally, unlike the conditions that prevailed when Congress first authorized regulation of the broadcast spectrum, the Internet can hardly be considered a "scarce" expressive commodity. It provides relatively unlimited, low cost capacity for communications of all kinds. . . . As the District Court found, "The content on the Internet is as diverse as human thought." We agree with its conclusion that our cases provide no basis for qualifying the level of First Amendment scrutiny that should be applied to this medium.

Do you agree with the Court's logic? In your opinion, is the Internet more akin to the printed press, as the justices seem to think, than to the broadcast media? Whatever your belief, the answer supplied by the Court indicates that the federal government will have a more difficult time regulating the Internet than, say, broadcast television.

NEWS GATHERING AND SPECIAL RIGHTS

Challenging restraints on First Amendment rights is not the only battle the media have fought. For many years, the news media have asked courts for "special rights" not normally accorded average citizens but that journalists consider necessary if they are to provide "full and robust" coverage of local, national, and world events. In this section, we discuss two of these rights—reporters' privilege and access. While reading about them, ask yourself this question: Should the media enjoy a special legal status? With the 2005 imprisonment for eighty-five days of *New York Times* reporter Judith Miller for refusing to testify before a grand jury, this question once again became relevant. Also consider the extent to which the Court's rulings on these issues are consistent with those centering on government control of press content.

Reporters' Privilege

Judith Miller was hardly the first journalist to face serious consequences for refusing to reveal information desired by the government—information that any other citizen would be compelled to provide. As far back as 1840 reporters asserted the need for unusual legal privileges. That year the Senate held a secret meeting to debate a proposed treaty to end the Mexican-American War. John Nugent, a reporter for the *New York Herald,* managed to obtain a copy of the proposed draft and mailed it to his editor. The Senate subpoenaed Nugent, who refused to reveal his source of information. The Senate held him in contempt. Nugent was later sent to prison for protecting his source.[10]

From time to time others faced the same fate as Nugent, but during the 1960s and 1970s claims of reporters' privilege increased. Some credit this growth to the trial of the Chicago Seven, in which the government charged individuals with starting a riot in the streets outside the arena where the Democratic National Convention was taking place in 1968. The United States served subpoenas on the major networks, newspapers, and magazines to obtain any information they had on the disturbances. Others suggest that it was the Nixon administration's disdain for the press that led to the increase, and still others argue that the rise in investigative reporting ushered in by the Watergate scandal led reporters to assert their right to protect sources absolutely and unconditionally.

Whatever the cause, the debate over reporters' privilege reached new heights in 1972, when the Supreme Court agreed to hear several cases involving such claims. The cases presented somewhat different issues, but the points of view were clear on both sides. The government asserted that reporters were entitled to no special rights and privileges: if ordinary citizens were forced to testify upon subpoena, then so should those working for the media. In response, the media pointed to other privileged relationships. Attorneys, for example, cannot be forced to reveal information about their clients. Reporters also argued that if they were forced to answer questions about their sources, those sources would dry up, which would have a chilling effect on their ability to do their jobs and violate their free press guarantee.

Branzburg v. Hayes

408 U.S. 665 (1972)
http://laws.findlaw.com/US/408/665.html
Oral arguments are available at http://www.oyez.org.
Vote: 5 (Blackmun, Burger, Powell, Rehnquist, White)
     4 (Brennan, Douglas, Marshall, Stewart)

OPINION OF THE COURT: White
CONCURRING OPINION: Powell
DISSENTING OPINIONS: Douglas, Stewart

FACTS:

This case involved two articles written by Paul M. Branzburg, a reporter for the Louisville, Kentucky, *Courier-Journal*.[11] In the first article, Branzburg detailed his observations of two individuals "synthesizing hashish from Marijuana, an activity which they asserted earned them about $5,000 in three weeks." The article contained the following passage:

"I don't know why I am letting you do this story," [one of the individuals] said quietly. "To make the narcs mad I guess. That's the main reason." However, [the two individuals] *asked for and received a promise that their names would be changed* [emphasis added].

The second piece contained interviews Branzburg conducted with drug users in Frankfort, Kentucky. Branzburg was subpoenaed by a grand jury. He appeared but refused to answer the following questions:

1. Who was the person or persons you observed in possession of marijuana, about which you wrote an article?

---

10. This paragraph and the next draw heavily on Mark Neubauer, "The Newsmen's Privilege after *Branzburg*," *UCLA Law Review* 24 (1976): 160–192.

11. Also decided with *Branzburg* were *In re Pappas* and *United States v. Caldwell*.

2. Who was the person or persons you observed compounding marijuana, producing same to a compound known as hashish?

State trial court judge J. Miles Pound ordered Branzburg to answer the grand jury's questions. Branzburg again refused on First Amendment grounds and initiated legal action to stop the trial court from taking any action against him. The Kentucky Court of Appeals rejected Branzburg's reporter's privilege claim, and he sought Supreme Court review. During the course of these proceedings, John P. Hayes replaced Judge Pound in office and also as respondent on the appeal.

ARGUMENTS:

For the petitioner, Paul Branzburg:

• Forcing reporters to reveal confidential sources stifles their news-gathering capacity, because future sources will be deterred from providing information. This inhibits the ability of reporters to do their jobs and violates the First Amendment's protection of free press.

• In order to compel a reporter's testimony, the state has the heavy burden of showing that the testimony is absolutely necessary to prevent "direct, immediate, and irreparable" damage, a burden not met in this case.

For the respondent, John Hayes:

• A special privilege for reporters is not included in the First Amendment's right to free press. The only recognized privilege is the Fifth Amendment's right to avoid self-incrimination, which applies to all citizens.

• Reporters have the same obligation as ordinary citizens to testify regarding what they have witnessed.

 MR. JUSTICE WHITE DELIVERED THE OPINION OF THE COURT.

The issue in these cases is whether requiring newsmen to appear and testify before state or federal grand juries abridges the freedom of speech and press guaranteed by the First Amendment. We hold that it does not. . . .

We do not question the significance of free speech, press, or assembly to the country's welfare. Nor is it suggested that news gathering does not qualify for First Amendment protection; without some protection for seeking out the news, freedom of the press could be eviscerated. But these cases involve no intrusions upon speech or assembly, no prior restraint or restriction on what the press may publish, and no express or implied command that the press publish what it prefers to withhold. No exaction or tax for the privilege of publishing, and no penalty, civil or criminal, related to the content of published material is at issue here. The use of confidential sources by the press is not forbidden or restricted; reporters remain free to seek news from any source by means within the law. No attempt is made to require the press to publish its sources of information or indiscriminately to disclose them on request.

The sole issue before us is the obligation of reporters to respond to grand jury subpoenas as other citizens do and to answer questions relevant to an investigation into the commission of crime. Citizens generally are not constitutionally immune from grand jury subpoenas; and neither the First Amendment nor any other constitutional provision protects the average citizen from disclosing to a grand jury information that he has received in confidence. The claim is, however, that reporters are exempt from these obligations because if forced to respond to subpoenas and identify their sources or disclose other confidences, their informants will refuse or be reluctant to furnish newsworthy information in the future. This asserted burden on news gathering is said to make compelled testimony from newsmen constitutionally suspect and to require a privileged position for them.

It is clear that the First Amendment does not invalidate every incidental burdening of the press that may result from the enforcement of civil or criminal statutes of general applicability. Under prior cases, otherwise valid laws serving substantial public interests may be enforced against the press as against others, despite the possible burden that may be imposed. The Court has emphasized that "[t]he publisher of a newspaper has no special immunity from the application of general laws. He has no special privilege to invade the rights and liberties of others." . . .

A number of States have provided newsmen a statutory privilege of varying breadth, but the majority have not done so, and none has been provided by federal statute. Until now the only testimonial privilege for unofficial witnesses that is rooted in the Federal Constitution is the Fifth Amendment privilege against compelled self-incrimination. We are asked to create another by interpreting the First Amendment to grant newsmen a testimonial privilege that other citizens do not enjoy. This we decline to do. Fair and effective law enforcement aimed at providing security for the person and property of the individual is a fundamental function of government, and the grand jury plays an important, constitutionally mandated role in this process. On the records now before us, we perceive no basis for holding that the public interest in law enforcement and in ensuring effective grand jury proceedings is insufficient to override the consequential, but uncertain, burden on news gathering that is said to result from insisting that reporters, like other citizens, respond to relevant questions put to them in the course of a valid grand jury investigation or criminal trial. . . .

This conclusion itself involves no restraint on what newspapers may publish or on the type or quality of information reporters may seek to acquire, nor does it threaten the vast bulk of confidential relationships between reporters and their sources. Grand juries address themselves to the issues of whether crimes have been committed and who committed them. Only where news sources themselves are implicated in crime or possess information relevant to the grand jury's task need they or the reporter be concerned about grand jury subpoenas. Nothing before us indicates that a large number or percentage of all confidential news sources falls into either category and would in any way be deterred by our holding that the Constitution does not, as it never has, exempt the newsman from performing the citizen's normal duty of appearing and furnishing information relevant to the grand jury's task.

The preference for anonymity of those confidential informants involved in actual criminal conduct is presumably a product of their desire to escape criminal prosecution, and this preference, while understandable, is hardly deserving of constitutional protection. It would be frivolous to assert—and no one does in these cases—that the First Amendment, in the interest of securing news or otherwise, confers a license on either the reporter or his news sources to violate valid criminal laws. . . .

The argument that the flow of news will be diminished by compelling reporters to aid the grand jury in a criminal investigation is not irrational, nor are the records before us silent on the matter. But we remain unclear how often and to what extent informers are actually deterred from furnishing information when newsmen are forced to testify before a grand jury. The available data indicate that some newsmen rely a great deal on confidential sources and that some informants are particularly sensitive to the threat of exposure and may be silenced if it is held by this Court that, ordinarily, newsmen must testify pursuant to subpoenas, but the evidence fails to demonstrate that there would be a significant constriction of the flow of news to the public if this Court reaffirms the prior common-law and constitutional rule regarding the testimonial obligations of newsmen. Estimates of the inhibiting effect of such subpoenas on the willingness of informants to make disclosures to newsmen are widely divergent and to a great extent speculative. . . .

Accepting the fact, however, that an undetermined number of informants not themselves implicated in crime will nevertheless, for whatever reason, refuse to talk to newsmen if they fear identification by a reporter in an official investigation, we cannot accept the argument that the public interest in possible future news about crime from undisclosed, unverified sources must take precedence over the public interest in pursuing and prosecuting those crimes reported to the press by informants and in thus deterring the commission of such crimes in the future. . . .

At the federal level, Congress has freedom to determine whether a statutory newsman's privilege is necessary and desirable and to fashion standards and rules as narrow or broad as deemed necessary to deal with the evil discerned and, equally important, to refashion those rules as experience from time to time may dictate. There is also merit in leaving state legislatures free, within First Amendment limits, to fashion their own standards in light of the conditions and problems with respect to the relations between law enforcement officials and press in their own areas. It goes without saying, of course, that we are powerless to bar state courts from responding in their own way and construing their own constitutions so as to recognize a newsman's privilege, either qualified or absolute. . . .

The decision . . . in *Branzburg v. Hayes* . . . must be affirmed. Here, petitioner refused to answer questions that directly related to criminal conduct that he had observed and written about. The Kentucky Court of Appeals noted that marijuana is defined as a narcotic drug by statute and that unlicensed possession or compounding of it is a felony punishable by both fine and imprisonment. It held that petitioner "saw the commission of the statutory felonies of unlawful possession of marijuana and the unlawful conversion of it into hashish." . . . [I]f what the petitioner wrote was true, he had direct information to provide the grand jury concerning the commission of serious crimes.

[Affirmed.]

MR. JUSTICE DOUGLAS, *dissenting*.

Today's decision will impede the wide-open and robust dissemination of ideas and counterthought which a free press both fosters and protects and which is essential to the success of intelligent self-government. Forcing a reporter before a grand jury will have two retarding effects upon the ear and the pen of the press. Fear of exposure will cause dissidents to communicate less openly to trusted reporters. And, fear of accountability will cause editors and critics to write with more restrained pens. . . .

A reporter is no better than his source of information. Unless he has a privilege to withhold the identity of his source, he will be the victim of governmental intrigue or aggression. If he can be summoned to testify in secret before a grand jury, his sources will dry up and the attempted exposure, the effort to enlighten the public, will be ended. If what the Court sanctions today becomes settled law, then the reporter's main function in American society will be to pass on to the public the press releases which the various departments of government issue. . . .

MR. JUSTICE STEWART, with whom MR. JUSTICE BRENNAN and MR. JUSTICE MARSHALL join, dissenting.
The Court's crabbed view of the First Amendment reflects a disturbing insensitivity to the critical role of an independent press in our society. The question whether a reporter has a constitutional right to a confidential relationship with his source is of first impression here, but the principles that should guide our decision are as basic as any to be found in the Constitution. . . . [T]he Court . . . holds that a newsman has no First Amendment right to protect his sources when called before a grand jury. The Court thus invites state and federal authorities to undermine the historic independence of the press by attempting to annex the journalistic profession as an investigative arm of government. Not only will this decision impair performance of the press' constitutionally protected functions, but it will, I am convinced, in the long run harm rather than help the administration of justice. . . .

Accordingly, when a reporter is asked to appear before a grand jury and reveal confidences, I would hold that the government must (1) show that there is probable cause to believe that the newsman has information that is clearly relevant to a specific probable violation of law; (2) demonstrate that the information sought cannot be obtained by alternative means less destructive of First Amendment rights; and (3) demonstrate a compelling and overriding interest in the information.

In *Branzburg* the majority emphatically denied the existence of reporters' privilege. The dissenters were distraught: Justice Potter Stewart, who in his youth

had worked as a reporter for a Cincinnati newspaper and edited the *Yale Daily News* while in college, condemned the "Court's crabbed view of the First Amendment." Some legal scholars later criticized the Court for invoking contradictory premises about the role of the press. In *Branzburg* the majority refused to recognize the reporters' privilege even against arguments that its absence would hamper the ability of the press to cover events of public concern because it would deter informants from speaking with reporters. But recall that in *Tornillo* the Court struck down the right-to-reply regulation at least in part because it would "blunt or reduce" political coverage.[12]

The reaction of the media was even more vehement, with an outpouring of condemnation of *Branzburg* and calls for federal and state statutes that would shield reporters from revealing their sources. The states responded to these calls, with forty passing laws that recognize a privilege for reporters to refuse to divulge information about certain news-gathering activities.[13] But because these shield laws often limit protections to specific circumstances, they may not be particularly effective. Kentucky already had a shield law on the books at the time of Branzburg's grand jury proceedings. Unfortunately for the reporter, it covered only sources of information and not personal observation. Journalists still face the threat of imprisonment if they refuse to answer questions pertaining to their stories—as Branzburg himself learned only a few months after the Supreme Court handed down the decision in his case *(see Box 6-3)*. In addition, Congress has yet to enact a federal shield law, despite immense pressure from the public at the time when Judith Miller chose prison over divulging her sources.

The ability to shield sources is not the only privilege reporters claim, but their assertions of privilege in other areas also have not fared particularly well. ***Zurcher v. Stanford Daily*** (1978), in which student journalists pressed for special treatment under the Fourth Amendment, illustrates the point. In April 1971 the *Daily*, a Stanford University student newspaper, published a special edition devoted to an incident that had occurred at the university's hospital. A group of

---

12. For more on this point, see William P. Marshall and Susan Gilles, "The Supreme Court, the First Amendment, and Bad Journalism," *Supreme Court Review* (1994): 169–208.

13. For more details, see "Number of States with Shield Law Climbs to 40," Reporters Committee for Freedom of the Press, http://www.rcfp.org/browse-media-law-resources/news-media-law/news-media-law-summer-2011/number-states-shield-law-climbs.

> **BOX 6-3   AFTERMATH . . . PAUL BRANZBURG**

Paul Branzburg

Between 1969 and 1971 Paul M. Branzburg, an investigative reporter for the *Louisville Courier-Journal*, wrote a series of articles on illegal drug activities in central Kentucky. He was subpoenaed by two different grand juries and asked to provide information about his sources. When he refused to answer, contempt citations were issued. He appealed to the United States Supreme Court, which ruled on June 29, 1972, that the First Amendment confers no special privilege on reporters who do not answer grand jury questions.

In the aftermath of the Supreme Court ruling, Kentucky prosecutors again sought information from Branzburg concerning the drug users and dealers he had observed while researching his stories. Branzburg, who by this time had moved to Michigan to do investigative reporting for the *Detroit Free Press*, again declined to answer questions about his sources. On September 1, 1972, Branzburg was found in contempt of the Jefferson County court and was sentenced to six months in prison. When Branzburg refused to return to Kentucky voluntarily, state officials requested that Michigan authorities extradite him. Michigan's governor, William G. Milliken, denied the request, and Branzburg never served the six-month sentence.

SOURCES: *Louisville Courier-Journal*, June 30, 1972; Contemporary Authors On Line, Gale Group, 2000.

---

demonstrators had seized the hospital's administrative offices and barricaded the doors. When police forced their way in, a riot broke out, resulting in injuries to the officers. They could not identify their assailants, but one officer claimed to have seen a photographer in the building. In fact, the *Daily* published several pictures of the incident, none of which fully revealed the identities of the demonstrators. Because it was reasonable to think that the newspaper's photographer had more pictures, the day after the special edition was published, police obtained a warrant to search the *Daily*'s office for the pictures. They found none.

The *Daily* initiated a civil action against all those involved in issuing and executing the warrant. Its lawyers rejected the argument that the case involved only Fourth Amendment issues and argued that the First Amendment, together with the Fourth Amendment, forbade such searches. The attorneys suggested that a search of a newspaper's offices was not necessarily unconstitutional, but that it should be based on a subpoena rather than a warrant. This distinction, in their view, would eliminate "police scrutiny [of] unrelated material, which may be highly confidential and sensitive, retained in the newspaper's files." The government responded that the warrant had been properly obtained and executed and that newspapers were undeserving of special Fourth Amendment protection.

Writing for a divided Court, Justice White agreed with the government. He relied on the intent of the framers, noting that they "did not forbid warrants where the press was involved." He also suggested there was no reason to believe that those authorizing search warrants could not "guard against searches of the type, scope, and intrusiveness that would actually interfere with the timely publication of a newspaper." The Court dismissed the *Stanford Daily*'s claim, with the justices aligning themselves much as they had in *Branzburg*. White reiterated the *Branzburg* position that the press is not above the law, and Stewart reasserted his dissenting view in no uncertain terms: "It seems to me self-evident that police searches of newspapers burden the freedom of the press."[14]

The Right of Access

Several months after *Zurcher*, the Court decided ***Houchins v. KQED*** (1978), which raised another claim of privilege asserted by the press. Of concern in *Houchins* was the right of reporters to have access to inmates in a county jail, access that ordinarily would

---

14. Congress responded to these decisions by passing the Privacy Protection Act, which prohibits government officials from conducting searches and seizures of materials related to the journalism enterprise unless authorities believe that the writer has committed a crime or a life-threatening situation exists.

be denied to other individuals. Although this case is different from *Zurcher,* it poses a similar question: Should the justices accord the press rights and privileges beyond those enjoyed by average citizens?

A divided Court once again ruled against the press. As Chief Justice Burger explained in his plurality opinion:

The media are not a substitute for or an adjunct of the government, and like the courts, are "ill equipped" to deal with the problems of prison administration. We must not confuse the role of the media with that of government; each has special, crucial functions, each complementing—and sometimes conflicting with—the other.

Burger also said that the Court would be no more amenable to special access claims than it was to reporters' privilege; indeed, relying on past decisions such as *Branzburg,* Burger called the media's arguments "flawed." He held that the First Amendment did not mandate "a right of access to government information or sources of information within the government's control." This was strong language, which could be understood to limit press access to a wide range of state and federal proceedings.

In cases following *Houchins,* however, the Court has not gone so far as Burger's words suggested. In *Richmond Newspapers v. Virginia* (1980) *(see Chapter 12),* for example, it overruled a trial court judge who had denied the press access to a highly publicized murder trial, and Burger wrote the opinion: "The right to attend criminal trials is implicit within the guarantees of the First Amendment," and, if such access were denied, "important aspects of freedom of speech and of the press could be eviscerated."

On the other hand, consider *North Jersey Media Group v. Ashcroft,* involving a challenge to a memo issued by the chief U.S. immigration judge directing immigration judges to close deportation proceedings to the press and public in any case involving "special" circumstances—in other words, related to terrorism. The U.S. Court of Appeals for the Third Circuit upheld the policy, declaring that "the press and public possess no First Amendment right of access," and the Supreme Court denied certiorari. But suppose the justices had agreed to hear *North Jersey Media Group.* How do you think the Court would have ruled?

We leave this, as well as the other questions we have raised in this chapter, for you to answer. What cannot be gainsaid, however, is the important role the Court has played in setting the parameters of journalistic practice in the United States, a role it will undoubtedly continue to fill in the future.

ANNOTATED READINGS

There is no shortage of interesting studies of the freedom of the press (broadly defined). Books containing histories of the free press clause, seminal cases, or both include Fred W. Friendly, *Minnesota Rag* (New York: Random House, 1981); Peter Charles Hoffer, *The Free Press Crisis of 1800: Thomas Cooper's Trial for Seditious* Libel (Lawrence: University Press of Kansas, 2011); Leonard W. Levy, *Emergence of a Free Press* (New York: Oxford University Press, 1985), and Levy's edited book, *Freedom of Press from Zenger to Jefferson* (Durham, NC: Carolina Academic Press, 1996); Robert W. T. Martin, *The Founding of American Press Liberty, 1640–1880* (New York: New York University Press, 2001); Lucas A. Powe Jr., *The Fourth Estate and the Constitution* (Berkeley: University of California Press, 1991); John Prados and Margaret Pratt Porter, eds. *Inside the Pentagon Papers* (Lawrence: University Press of Kansas, 2004); David Rudenstine, *The Day the Presses Stopped: A History of the Pentagon Papers Case* (Berkeley: University of California Press, 1996); Mark R. Scherer, *Rights in the Balance: Free Press, Fair Trial, and Nebraska Press Association v. Stuart* (Lubbock: Texas Tech Press, 2008); Martin Shapiro, *The Pentagon Papers and the Courts* (San Francisco: Chandler, 1972); Jeffery Alan Smith, *War and Press Freedom: The Problem of Prerogative Power* (New York: Oxford University Press, 1999).

On evolving concepts of freedom of the press and new media, see Lee C. Bollinger, *Images of a Free Press* (Chicago: University of Chicago Press, 1991); Scott Gant, *We're All Journalists Now: The Transformation of the Press and the Reshaping of the Law in the Internet Age* (New York: Simon & Schuster, 2007); Mike Godwin, *Cyber Rights: Defending Free Speech in the Digital Age* (Cambridge: MIT Press, 2003); Richard Reeves, *What the People Know: Freedom and the Press* (Cambridge, MA: Harvard University Press, 1999); Joshua Rozenberg, *Privacy and the Press* (New York: Oxford University Press, 2004). For comparative analyses of the role of a free press, see Joseph Chappell, *Building the Fourth Estate: Democratization and the Rise of a Free Press* (Berkeley: University of California Press, 2002); Judith Lichtenberg, *Democracy and the Mass Media* (New York: Cambridge University Press, 1990); B. R. Sharma, *Freedom of Press under the Indian Constitution.* (Columbia, MO: South Asia Books, 1993).

7

The Boundaries of Free Expression: Libel, Obscenity, and Emerging Areas of Government Regulation

O NE OF THE Supreme Court's consistent teachings is that the First Amendment is not absolute despite its seeming absolute language ("Congress shall make no law . . ."). This lesson began in 1919, when Justice Oliver Wendell Holmes noted that the First Amendment would not protect a person who falsely yelled "Fire!" in a crowded theater, and it continues today. Put simply, some varieties of expression are illegitimate and may be punished. Many examples come to mind. One may not communicate military secrets to the enemy or make terrorist threats. One may not provide fraudulent information in commercial transactions or engage in discussions that amount to criminal conspiracies. One may not lie under oath or exchange insider information in securities transactions. In each of these cases the expression falls outside the boundaries of First Amendment protection.

This chapter explores the limits of First Amendment protection by examining two types of expression that have presented the justices with perplexing constitutional questions: libel and obscenity. Agreement is almost universal that the framers considered neither to be legitimate expression and did not intend the First Amendment to protect them from government regulation. Accepting this proposition, however, does not settle the matter, because other questions remain. How do we define libel and obscenity? What distinguishes libelous and obscene expression from protected speech and press? What standards of evidence should be

imposed? How can government regulate obscenity and libel without creating a "chilling effect" on protected expression?

We end the chapter with a section on more recent attempts by the government to create new categories of unprotected speech—cruelty and violence. In both areas the government crafted laws that borrowed from the Court's obscenity cases, but in both the justices invalidated the laws. Based on the cases in this chapter, along with those you read in Chapter 5, do you think the Court was correct in declining the government's invitation to regulate speech in these areas?

LIBEL

On any given day in the United States, we can buy a newspaper, navigate to a Web site, or turn on the television and find information on the activities of public officials, well-known figures, and even private citizens who have made news for various reasons. Sometimes the reports imply criticism—for example, a newspaper article about a public official accused of wrongdoing. In other cases, the reports are blatantly false. To see this phenomenon we need go no farther than to a supermarket checkout line and read the tabloid headlines about the alleged doings of celebrities.

As we know from our readings on freedom of the press, individuals or even governments generally cannot prohibit the media from disseminating such information—true or false. But once stories are published or televised, do the subjects of the stories have any recourse? Under U.S. law they do: they can bring *libel* actions against the offenders. If individuals believe that falsehoods in published or televised stories have resulted in the defamation of their character, they can ask the courts to hold the media responsible for their actions. They have this recourse because, like obscenity, libelous statements fall outside the scope of First Amendment protections.

Public Officials and Libel

The lack of First Amendment protection does not, however, mean that libel is a simple area of law. In fact, the Supreme Court has had a difficult time developing standards for its application. One reason for the Court's problem is that before 1964 libel was an undeveloped area of law.

Recall that in 1798 the Federalist Congress enacted the Sedition Act, which outlawed seditious libel, defined as criticism of the government and of government officials. Under this act, the government could bring criminal charges against those who made "false, scandalous, and malicious" statements that brought the United States or its representatives into "contempt or disrepute." Because President Thomas Jefferson later pardoned all those who had been convicted under the act, the Supreme Court never had an opportunity to rule on its constitutionality. For most of the nation's history, it was unclear whether seditious libel was protected or unprotected speech.[1]

What is clear is that, until the Court decided a landmark case in 1964, its position was that the states were free to determine their own standards for the most common form of libel—civil actions brought by individuals against other individuals, such as those running a newspaper. Some variation existed among state laws, but most allowed defamed individuals to seek two kinds of monetary damages: compensatory, for actual financial loss (e.g., an individual loses his or her job because of the story), and punitive, to punish the offender. To collect such damages, all the plaintiff generally had to demonstrate was that the story was false (truth is always a defense against claims of libel) and damaging.

These criteria might sound like simple standards for plaintiffs to meet, but the simplicity further compounded the Court's problems. Many newspapers, television stations, and other media argued that the traditional standard had a chilling effect on their First Amendment guarantee of a free press. They feared printing anything critical of government or public officials, in particular, because if a story contained even the smallest factual error, they could face a costly lawsuit. They felt constrained in their reporting of news. In *New York Times v. Sullivan* the Court radically departed from its former position. What standard did the Court articulate? How did it alter existing libel law?

New York Times v. Sullivan

376 U.S. 254 (1964)
http://laws.findlaw.com/US/376/254.html
Oral arguments are available at http://www.oyez.org.
Vote: 9 (Black, Brennan, Clark, Douglas, Goldberg,
  Harlan, Stewart, Warren, White)
  0

OPINION OF THE COURT: *Brennan*
CONCURRING OPINIONS: *Black, Goldberg*

FACTS:

The March 29, 1960, edition of the *New York Times* ran a full-page advertisement (reprinted here) to publicize the struggle for civil rights and to raise money for the cause. L. B. Sullivan, the police commissioner of the city of Montgomery, Alabama, took offense at the ad. It did not mention his name, but it gave an account of a civil rights demonstration in Montgomery and suggested that in putting down the demonstration, the police, who were under Sullivan's command, had engaged in wrongdoing.

Sullivan brought a libel action against the paper, alleging that the ad contained falsehoods—which, in fact, it did. For example, it claimed that demonstrating students sang "My Country, 'Tis of Thee," when they actually sang the "Star-Spangled Banner." In his charge to the jury, the judge said that the ad was "libelous per se," meaning that because it contained falsehoods, it was unprotected speech. In addition, he said, if the jury found that the statements were made "of and concerning" Sullivan, it could hold the *Times* liable. Taking these words to heart, the jury awarded Sullivan $500,000 in damages.

---

1. See Zechariah Chafee Jr., *Free Speech in the United States* (Cambridge, MA: Harvard University Press, 1941); and Leonard W. Levy, *Legacy of Suppression* (Cambridge, MA: Harvard University Press, 1960). See also Levy's revised and enlarged edition, *Emergence of a Free Press* (New York: Oxford University Press, 1985).

THE NEW YORK TIMES, TUESDAY, MARCH 29, 1960

> **"** *The growing movement of peaceful mass demonstrations by Negroes is something new in the South, something understandable. . . . Let Congress heed their rising voices, for they will be heard.***"**
>
> —*New York Times* editorial
> *Saturday, March 19, 1960*

Heed Their Rising Voices

As the whole world knows by now, thousands of Southern Negro students are engaged in widespread non-violent demonstrations in positive affirmation of the right to live in human dignity as guaranteed by the U. S. Constitution and the Bill of Rights. In their efforts to uphold these guarantees, they are being met by an unprecedented wave of terror by those who would deny and negate that document which the whole world looks upon as setting the pattern for modern freedom...

In Orangeburg, South Carolina, when 400 students peacefully sought to buy doughnuts and coffee at lunch counters in the business district, they were forcibly ejected, tear-gassed, soaked to the skin in freezing weather with fire hoses, arrested en masse and herded into an open barbed-wire stockade to stand for hours in the bitter cold.

In Montgomery, Alabama, after students sang "My Country, 'Tis of Thee" on the State Capitol steps, their leaders were expelled from school, and truckloads of police armed with shotguns and tear-gas ringed the Alabama State College Campus. When the entire student body protested to state authorities by refusing to re-register, their dining hall was padlocked in an attempt to starve them into submission.

In Tallahassee, Atlanta, Nashville, Savannah, Greensboro, Memphis, Richmond, Charlotte, and a host of other cities in the South, young American teenagers, in face of the entire weight of official state apparatus and police power, have boldly stepped forth as protagonists of democracy. Their courage and amazing restraint have inspired millions and given a new dignity to the cause of freedom.

Small wonder that the Southern violators of the Constitution fear this new, non-violent brand of freedom fighter... even as they fear the upswelling right-to-vote movement. Small wonder that they are determined to destroy the one man who, more than any other, symbolizes the new spirit now sweeping the South—the Rev. Dr. Martin Luther King, Jr., world-famous leader of the Montgomery Bus Protest. For it is his doctrine of non-violence which has inspired and guided the students in their widening wave of sit-ins; and it is this same Dr. King who founded and is president of the Southern Christian Leadership Conference—the organization which is spearheading the surging right-to-vote movement. Under Dr. King's direction the Leadership Conference conducts Student Workshops and Seminars in the philosophy and techniques of non-violent resistance.

Again and again the Southern violators have answered Dr. King's peaceful protests with intimidation and violence. They have bombed his home almost killing his wife and child. They have assaulted his person. They have arrested him seven times—for "speeding," "loitering" and similar "offenses." And now they have charged him with "perjury"—*a felony* under which they could imprison him for *ten years*. Obviously, their real purpose is to remove him physically as the leader to whom the students and millions of others—look for guidance and support, and thereby to intimidate *all* leaders who may rise in the South. Their strategy is to behead this affirmative movement, and thus to demoralize Negro Americans and weaken their will to struggle. The defense of Martin Luther King, spiritual leader of the student sit-in movement, clearly, therefore, is an integral part of the total struggle for freedom in the South.

Decent-minded Americans cannot help but applaud the creative daring of the students and the quiet heroism of Dr. King. But this is one of those moments in the stormy history of Freedom when men and women of good will must do more than applaud the rising-to-glory of others. The America whose good name hangs in the balance before a watchful world, the America whose heritage of Liberty these Southern Upholders of the Constitution are defending, is *our* America as well as theirs...

We must heed their rising voices—yes—but we must add our own.

We must extend ourselves above and beyond moral support and render the material help so urgently needed by those who are taking the risks, facing jail, and even death in a glorious re-affirmation of our Constitution and its Bill of Rights.

We urge you to join hands with our fellow Americans in the South by supporting, with your dollars, this combined appeal for all three needs—the defense of Martin Luther King—the support of the embattled students—and the struggle for the right-to-vote.

Your Help Is Urgently Needed . . . NOW!!

Stella Adler	Dr. Alan Knight Chalmers	Anthony Franciosa	John Killens	L. Joseph Overton	Maureen Stapleton
Raymond Pace Alexander	Richard Coe	Lorraine Hansbury	Eartha Kitt	Clarence Pickett	Frank Silvera
Harry Van Arsdale	Nat King Cole	Rev. Donald Harrington	Rabbi Edward Klein	Shad Polier	Hope Stevens
Harry Belafonte	Cheryl Crawford	Nat Hentoff	Hope Lange	Sidney Poitier	George Tabor
Julie Belafonte	Dorothy Dandridge	James Hicks	John Lewis	A. Philip Randolph	Rev. Gardner C.
Dr. Algernon Black	Ossie Davis	Mary Hinkson	Viveca Lindfors	John Raitt	Taylor
Marc Blitzstein	Sammy Davis, Jr.	Van Heflin	Carl Murphy	Elmer Rice	Norman Thomas
William Branch	Ruby Dee	Langston Hughes	Don Murray	Jackie Robinson	Kenneth Tynan
Marlon Brando	Dr. Philip Elliott	Morris Iushewitz	John Murray	Mrs. Eleanor Roosevelt	Charles White
Mrs. Ralph Bunche	Dr. Harry Emerson	Mahalia Jackson	A. J. Muste	Bayard Rustin	Shelley Winters
Diahann Carroll	Fosdick	Mordecai Johnson	Frederick O'Neal	Robert Ryan	Max Youngstein

We in the south who are struggling daily for dignity and freedom warmly endorse this appeal

Rev. Ralph D. Abernathy *(Montgomery, Ala.)*	Rev. Matthew D. McCollom *(Orangeburg, S.C.)*	Rev. Walter L. Hamilton *(Norfolk, Va.)*
Rev. Fred L. Shuttlesworth *(Birmingham, Ala.)*		I. S. Levy *(Columbia, S.C.)*
	Rev. William Holmes Borders *(Atlanta, Ga.)*	Rev. Martin Luther King, Sr. *(Atlanta, Ga.)*
Rev. Kelley Miller Smith *(Nashville, Tenn.)*		Rev. Henry C. Bunton *(Memphis, Tenn.)*
Rev. W. A. Dennis *(Chattanooga, Tenn.)*	Rev. Douglas Moore *(Durham, N.C.)*	Rev. S.S. Seay, Sr. *(Montgomery, Ala.)*
Rev. C. K. Steele *(Tallahassee, Fla.)*	Rev. Wyatt Tee Walker *(Petersburg, Va.)*	Rev. Samuel W. Williams *(Atlanta, Ga.)*

Rev. A. L. Davis *(New Orleans, La.)*
Mrs. Katie E. Whickham *(New Orleans, La.)*
Rev. W. H. Hall *(Hattiesburg, Miss.)*
Rev. J. E. Lowery *(Mobile, Ala.)*
Rev. T. J. Jemison *(Baton Rouge, La.)*

COMMITTEE TO DEFEND MARTIN LUTHER KING AND THE STRUGGLE FOR FREEDOM IN THE SOUTH

312 West 125th Street, New York 27, N.Y. UNiversity 6-1700

Chairmen: A. Philip Randolph, Dr. Gardner C. Taylor; *Chairmen of Cultural Division:* Harry Belafonte, Sidney Poitier; *Treasurer:* Nat King Cole; *Executive Director:* Bayard Rustin; *Chairmen of Church Division:* Father George B. Ford, Rev. Harry Emerson Fosdick, Rev. Thomas Kilgore, Jr., Rabbi Edward E. Klein; *Chairman of Labor Division:* Morris Iushewitz

Please mail this coupon TODAY!

Committee To Defend Martin Luther King
and
The Struggle For Freedom in The South
312 West 125th Street, New York 27, N.Y.
UNiversity 6-1700

I am enclosing my contribution of $_____
for the work of the Committee.

Name _____

Address _____

City _____ Zone ____ State ____

☐ I want to help   ☐ Please send further information

Please make checks payable to:
Committee to Defend Martin Luther King

The Supreme Court of Alabama affirmed this judgment. It specified that words are libelous per se when they "tend to injure a person libeled by them in his reputation, profession, trade or business, or charge him with an indictable offense, or tend to bring the individual into public contempt." This definition was fairly typical. The *New York Times* challenged the decision, arguing that the libel standard "presumes malice and falsity. . . . Such a rule of liability works an abridgment of the free press." The paper's attorneys added, "It is implicit in this Court's decisions that speech which is critical of governmental action may not be repressed upon the ground that it diminishes the reputation of those officers whose conduct it deplores."

ARGUMENTS:

For the petitioner, The New York Times Company:

- Political expression is protected by the First Amendment and is not subject to a truth test. Moreover, the First Amendment does not support punishment for criticism of government officials merely because such criticism may harm their official reputations.
- In balancing the state's interest in protecting the reputations of its officials against the Constitution's protection of political expression, libel should be found only where a public official proves that falsehoods were published with knowledge of their falsity, or "actual malice."

For the respondent, L. B. Sullivan:

- Libel is outside the realm of constitutionally protected speech.
- Commercial advertisements are not protected by the First Amendment guarantees of speech and the press.
- The doctrine of libel per se is a common-law doctrine, used in many other states, and does not violate the First Amendment.

 MR. JUSTICE BRENNAN DELIVERED THE OPINION OF THE COURT.

We are required in this case to determine for the first time the extent to which the constitutional protections for speech and press limit a State's power to award damages in a libel action brought by a public official against critics of his official conduct. . . .

Because of the importance of the constitutional issues involved, we granted the separate petitions for certiorari of the individual petitioners and of the *Times*. We reverse the judgment. We hold that the rule of law applied by the Alabama courts is constitutionally deficient for failure to provide the safeguards for freedom of speech and of the press that are required by the First and Fourteenth Amendments in a libel action brought by a public official against critics of his official conduct. We further hold that under the proper safeguards the evidence presented in this case is constitutionally insufficient to support the judgment for respondent.

L. B. Sullivan, second from right, poses with his attorneys after winning his libel suit against the New York Times. *The Supreme Court overturned the decision in 1964. Justice Brennan's opinion stated that in proving libel, public officials are held to a higher standard than private citizens.*

We may dispose at the outset of [t]he . . . contention . . . that the constitutional guarantees of freedom of speech and of the press are inapplicable here, at least so far as the *Times* is concerned, because the allegedly libelous statements were published as part of a paid, "commercial" advertisement. . . .

The publication here was not a "commercial" advertisement in the sense in which the word was used in [*Valentine v.*] *Chrestensen* [1942]. It communicated information, expressed opinion, recited grievances, protested claimed abuses, and sought financial support on behalf of a movement whose existence and objectives are matters of the highest public interest and concern. That the *Times* was paid for publishing the advertisement is as immaterial in this connection as is the fact that newspapers and books are sold. Any other conclusion would discourage newspapers from carrying "editorial advertisements" of this type, and so might shut off an important outlet for the promulgation of information and ideas by persons who do not themselves have access to publishing facilities—who wish to exercise their freedom of speech even though they are not members of the press. The effect would be to shackle the First Amendment in its attempt to secure "the widest possible dissemination of information from diverse and antagonistic sources." To avoid placing such a handicap upon the freedoms of expression, we hold that if the allegedly libelous statements would otherwise be constitutionally protected from the present judgment, they do not forfeit that protection because they were published in the form of a paid advertisement.

Under Alabama law as applied in this case, a publication is "libelous per se" if the words "tend to injure a person . . . in his reputation" or to "bring [him] into public contempt"; the trial court stated that the standard was met if the words are such as to "injure him in his public office, or impute misconduct to him in his office, or want of official integrity, or want of fidelity to a public trust. . . . " The jury must find that the words were published "of and concerning" the plaintiff, but where the plaintiff is a public official his place in the governmental hierarchy is sufficient evidence to support a finding that his reputation has been affected by statements that reflect upon the agency of which he is in charge. Once "libel per se" has been established, the defendant has no defense as to stated facts unless he can persuade the jury that they were true in all their particulars. His privilege of "fair comment" for expressions of opinion depends on the truth of the facts upon which the comment is based. Unless he can discharge the burden of

proving truth, general damages are presumed, and may be awarded without proof of pecuniary injury. A showing of actual malice is apparently a prerequisite to recovery of punitive damages, and the defendant may in any event forestall a punitive award by a retraction meeting the statutory requirements. Good motives and belief in truth do not negate an inference of malice, but are relevant only in mitigation of punitive damages if the jury chooses to accord them weight.

The question before us is whether this rule of liability, as applied to an action brought by a public official against critics of his official conduct, abridges the freedom of speech and of the press that is guaranteed by the First and Fourteenth Amendments.

Respondent relies heavily, as did the Alabama courts, on statements of this Court to the effect that the Constitution does not protect libelous publications. Those statements do not foreclose our inquiry here. None of the cases sustained the use of libel laws to impose sanctions upon expression critical of the official conduct of public officials. . . . In deciding the question now, we are compelled by neither precedent nor policy to give any more weight to the epithet "libel" than we have to other "mere labels" of state law. Like insurrection, contempt, advocacy of unlawful acts, breach of the peace, obscenity, solicitation of legal business, and the various other formulae for the repression of expression that have been challenged in this Court, libel can claim no talismanic immunity from constitutional limitations. It must be measured by standards that satisfy the First Amendment. . . .

. . . [W]e consider this case against the background of a profound national commitment to the principle that debate on public issues should be uninhibited, robust, and wide open, and that it may well include vehement, caustic, and sometimes unpleasantly sharp attacks on government and public officials. The present advertisement, as an expression of grievance and protest on one of the major public issues of our time, would seem clearly to qualify for the constitutional protection. The question is whether it forfeits that protection by the falsity of some of its factual statements and by its alleged defamation of respondent.

Authoritative interpretations of the First Amendment guarantees have consistently refused to recognize an exception for any test of truth—whether administered by judges, juries, or administrative officials—and especially one that puts the burden of proving truth on the speaker. The constitutional protection does not turn upon "the truth, popularity, or social utility of the ideas and beliefs which are offered." . . . That erroneous statement is inevitable in free debate, and that it must be protected if the freedoms of expression are to have the "breathing space" that they "need . . . to survive," was . . . recognized by the Court of Appeals for the District of Columbia Circuit in *Sweeney v. Patterson* [1942]. . . .

Injury to official reputation error affords no more warrant for repressing speech that would otherwise be free than does factual error. Where judicial officers are involved, this Court has held that concern for the dignity and reputation of the courts does not justify the punishment as criminal contempt of criticism of the judge or his decision. This is true even though the utterance contains "half-truths" and "misinformation." Such repression can be justified, if at all, only by a clear and present danger of the obstruction of justice. If judges are to be treated as "men of fortitude, able to thrive in a hardy climate," surely the same must be true of other government officials, such as elected city commissioners. Criticism of their official conduct does not lose its constitutional protection merely because it is effective criticism and hence diminishes their official reputations.

If neither factual error nor defamatory content suffices to remove the constitutional shield from criticism of official conduct, the combination of the two elements is no less inadequate. This is the lesson to be drawn from the great controversy over the Sedition Act of 1798, which first crystallized a national awareness of the central meaning of the First Amendment. That statute made it a crime, punishable by a $5,000 fine and five years in prison, "if any person shall write, print, utter or publish . . . any false, scandalous and malicious writing or writings against the government of the United States, or either House of the Congress . . . or the President . . . , with intent to defame . . . or to bring them, or either of them, into contempt or disrepute; or to excite against them, or either or any of them, the hatred of the good people of the United States." . . .

Although the Sedition Act was never tested in this Court, the attack upon its validity has carried the day in the court of history. Fines levied in its prosecution were repaid by Act of Congress on the ground that it was unconstitutional. Calhoun, reporting to the Senate on February 4, 1836, assumed that its invalidity was a matter "which no one now doubts." Jefferson, as President, pardoned those who had been convicted and sentenced under the Act and remitted their fines, stating: "I discharged every person under punishment or prosecution under the sedition law, because I considered, and now consider, that law to be a nullity, as absolute and as palpable as if Congress had ordered us to fall down and worship a golden image." The invalidity of the Act has also been assumed by Justices of this Court. These views reflect a broad consensus that the Act, because of the restraint it imposed upon criticism of government and public officials, was inconsistent with the First Amendment.

There is no force in respondent's argument that the constitutional limitations implicit in the history of the Sedition Act apply only to Congress and not to the States. It is true that the First Amendment was originally addressed only to action by the Federal Government, and that Jefferson, for one, while denying the power of Congress "to controul the freedom of the press," recognized such a power in the States. But this distinction was eliminated with the adoption of the Fourteenth Amendment and the application to the States of the First Amendment's restrictions.

What a State may not constitutionally bring about by means of a criminal statute is likewise beyond the reach of its civil law of libel. The fear of damage awards under a rule such as that invoked by the Alabama courts here may be markedly more inhibiting than the fear of prosecution under a criminal statute. Alabama, for example, has a criminal libel law which subjects to prosecution "any person who speaks, writes, or prints of and concerning another any accusation falsely and maliciously importing the commission by such person of a felony, or any other indictable offense involving moral turpitude," and which allows as punishment upon conviction a fine not exceeding $500 and a prison sentence of six months. Presumably a person charged with violation of this statute enjoys ordinary criminal-law safeguards such as the requirements of an indictment and of proof beyond a reasonable doubt. These safeguards are not available to the defendant in a civil action. The judgment awarded in this case—without the need for any proof of actual pecuniary loss—was one thousand times greater than the maximum fine provided by the Alabama criminal statute, and one hundred times greater than that provided by the Sedition Act. And since there is no double-jeopardy limitation applicable to civil lawsuits, this is not the only judgment that may be awarded against petitioners for the same publication. Whether or not a newspaper can survive a succession of such judgments, the pall of fear and timidity imposed upon those who would give voice to public criticism is an atmosphere in which the First Amendment freedoms cannot survive. Plainly the Alabama law of civil libel is "a form of regulation that creates hazards to protected freedoms markedly greater than those that attend reliance upon the criminal law."

The state rule of law is not saved by its allowance of the defense of truth. A defense for erroneous statements honestly made is no less essential here than was the requirement of proof of guilty knowledge which we held indispensable to a valid conviction of a bookseller for possessing obscene writings for sale. . . . A rule compelling the critic of official conduct to guarantee the truth of all his factual assertions—and to do so on pain of libel judgments virtually unlimited in amount—leads to a comparable "self-censorship." Allowance of the defense of truth, with the burden of proving it on the defendant, does not mean that only false speech will be deterred. Even courts accepting this defense as an adequate safeguard have recognized the difficulties of adducing legal proofs that the alleged libel was true in all its factual particulars. Under such a rule, would-be critics of official conduct may be deterred from voicing their criticism, even though it is believed to be true and even though it is in fact true, because of doubt whether it can be proved in court or fear of the expense of having to do so. They tend to make only statements which "steer far wider of the unlawful zone." The rule thus dampens the vigor and limits the variety of public debate. It is inconsistent with the First and Fourteenth Amendments.

The constitutional guarantees require, we think, a federal rule that prohibits a public official from recovering damages for a defamatory falsehood relating to his official conduct unless he proves that the statement was made with "actual malice"—that is, with knowledge that it was false or with reckless disregard of whether it was false or not. . . .

. . . [A] privilege for criticism of official conduct is appropriately analogous to the protection accorded a public official when he is sued for libel by a private citizen. . . . The reason for the official privilege is said to be that the threat of damage suits would otherwise "inhibit the fearless, vigorous, and effective administration of policies of government" and "dampen the ardor of all but the most resolute, or the most irresponsible, in the unflinching discharge of their duties." Analogous considerations support the privilege for the citizen-critic of government. It is as much his duty to criticize as it is the official's duty to administer. As Madison said, "the censorial power is in the people over the Government, and not in the Government over the people." It would give public servants an unjustified preference over the public they serve, if critics of official conduct did not have a fair equivalent of the immunity granted to the officials themselves.

We conclude that such a privilege is required by the First and Fourteenth Amendments.

We hold today that the Constitution delimits a State's power to award damages for libel in actions brought by public officials against critics of their official conduct. Since this is such an action, the rule requiring proof of actual malice is applicable. While Alabama law apparently requires proof of actual malice for an award of punitive damages, where general damages are concerned malice is "presumed." Such a presumption is inconsistent with the federal rule. . . . Since the trial judge did not instruct the jury to differentiate between general and punitive damages, it may be that the verdict was wholly an award of one or the other. But it is impossible to know, in view of the general verdict returned. Because of this uncertainty, the judgment must be reversed and the case remanded.

Since respondent may seek a new trial, we deem that considerations of effective judicial administration require us to review the evidence in the present record to determine whether it could constitutionally support a judgment for respondent. This Court's duty is not limited to the elaboration of constitutional principles; we must also in proper cases review the evidence to make certain that those principles have been constitutionally applied. This is such a case, particularly since the question is one of alleged trespass across "the line between speech unconditionally guaranteed and speech which may legitimately be regulated." In cases where that line must be drawn, the rule is that we "examine for ourselves the statements in issue and the circumstances under which they were made to see . . . whether they are of a character which the principles of the First Amendment, as adopted by the Due Process Clause of the Fourteenth Amendment, protect." We must "make an independent examination of the whole record," so as to assure ourselves that the judgment does not constitute a forbidden intrusion on the field of free expression.

Applying these standards, we consider that the proof presented to show actual malice lacks the convincing clarity which the constitutional standard demands, and hence that it would not constitutionally sustain the judgment for respondent under the proper rule of law. The case of the individual petitioners requires little discussion. Even assuming that they could constitutionally be found to have authorized the use of their names on the advertisement, there was no evidence whatever that they were aware of any erroneous statements or were in any way reckless in that regard. The judgment against them is thus without constitutional support.

As to the *Times,* we similarly conclude that the facts do not support a finding of actual malice. The statement by the *Times*' Secretary that . . . he thought the advertisement was "substantially correct" affords no constitutional warrant for the Alabama Supreme Court's conclusion that it was a "cavalier ignoring of the falsity of the advertisement from which, the jury could not have but been impressed with the bad faith of the *Times,* and its maliciousness inferable therefrom." The statement does not indicate malice at the time of the publication; even if the advertisement was not "substantially correct"—although respondent's own proofs tend to show that it was—that opinion was at least a reasonable one, and there was no evidence to impeach the witness' good faith in holding it. . . .

We also think the evidence was constitutionally defective in another respect: it was incapable of supporting the jury's finding that the allegedly libelous statements were made "of and concerning" respondent. Respondent relies on the words of the advertisement and the testimony of six witnesses to establish a connection between it and himself. . . . There was no reference to respondent in the advertisement, either by name or official position. A number of the allegedly libelous statements—the charges that the dining hall was padlocked and that Dr. King's home was bombed, his person assaulted, and a perjury prosecution instituted against him—did not even concern the police; despite the ingenuity of the arguments which would attach this significance to the word "They," it is plain that these statements could not reasonably be read as accusing respondent of personal involvement in the acts in question. . . .

The judgment of the Supreme Court of Alabama is reversed and the case is remanded to that court for further proceedings not inconsistent with this opinion.

Reversed and remanded.

MR. JUSTICE BLACK, with whom
MR. JUSTICE DOUGLAS joins, concurring.

I concur in reversing this half-million-dollar judgment against the New York Times Company and the four individual defendants. In reversing the Court holds that "the Constitution delimits a State's power to award damages for libel in actions brought by public officials against critics of their official conduct." I base my vote to reverse on the belief that the First and Fourteenth Amendments not merely "delimit" a State's power to award damages to "public officials against critics of their official conduct" but completely prohibit a State from exercising such a power. The Court goes on to hold that a State can subject such critics to damages if "actual malice" can be proved against them. "Malice," even as defined by the Court, is an elusive, abstract concept, hard to prove and hard to disprove. The requirement that malice be proved provides at best an evanescent protection for the right critically to discuss public affairs and certainly does not measure up to the sturdy safeguard embodied in the First Amendment. Unlike the Court, therefore, I vote to reverse exclusively on the ground that the Times and the individual defendants had an absolute, unconditional constitutional right to publish in the Times advertisement their criticisms of the Montgomery agencies and officials.

Many consider Brennan's opinion a tour de force on the subject of libel. By holding the Sedition Act of 1798 unconstitutional, however belatedly, Brennan said that the First Amendment protects seditious libel, that the government may not criminally punish individuals who speak out against government, in a true or false manner. But more important was the part of the opinion that dealt with civil actions. The concurrers argued that the press had an absolute and unconditional right to criticize government officials and that states could not permit civil actions in such cases. Brennan did not go that far, but he radically altered the standards that public officials acting in a public capacity had to meet before they could prove libel and receive damages. Calling previous rules of falsehood and defamation "constitutionally deficient," Brennan asserted that if plaintiffs were public officials, they had to demonstrate that the statement was false, damaging, and "made with 'actual malice'—that is, with knowledge that it was false or with reckless disregard of whether it was false or not." In his view, such an exacting standard—now called the *New York Times* test—was necessary because of a "profound national commitment to the principle that debate on public issues should be uninhibited, robust, and wide open." It is interesting to note that although other democratic countries might agree with this sentiment, at least some have not made it as difficult for public officials to sue for libel as the U.S. Supreme Court did in *Sullivan (see Box 7-1).*

Expanding the *New York Times* Test

Brennan's opinion in *New York Times v. Sullivan* significantly altered the course of libel law, making it more difficult for public officials to bring actions against the media. But the decision raised further questions—for example,

BOX 7-1   LIBEL IN GLOBAL PERSPECTIVE

According to some scholars, the U.S. Supreme Court has adopted rules that, compared with practices elsewhere, make it difficult for plaintiffs (the persons alleging misconduct) to prevail in libel lawsuits— especially if they are public officials and figures. For example, in the United States it is up to the plaintiff to prove that allegedly libelous statements are false, whereas under British law it is the defendant who must prove that the statements are true.

Moreover, in most countries plaintiffs do not have to meet the kind of "actual malice" standard that the Court adopted in *New York Times v. Sullivan*. The Canadian Supreme Court, in fact, explicitly declined to adopt this standard, saying in *Hill v. Church of Scientology* that democracies need to take reputation as seriously as freedom of expression. Germany's Constitutional Court has expressed similar sentiments, suggesting in several cases that no matter how important speech about politics is, it may be unwise to elevate it to the detriment of other societal interests, such as truth and human dignity. This attitude may reflect differences in American and German political experiences: Germany paid a steep price for tolerating unbridled political communication and does not want to make the same mistake again.

The sweep of U.S. protection has some interesting implications. First and most obvious, the likelihood of recovering damages in libel suits—even those involving public officials and figures—is far greater in other nations than in the United States. According to the media in some countries, this has a chilling effect on the press. In Ireland, for example, where libel law heavily favors plaintiffs and large awards are far from infrequent, the newspapers say they must exercise care in publishing controversial material and in encouraging aggressive reporting. In response, scholars and courts have suggested that societies must protect values such as reputation, dignity, and truth, in addition to a free press.

A second implication is less obvious: as more and more allegedly libelous material appears on the Internet, variation in nations' practices may encourage "country shopping" among plaintiffs. We have more to say on this point in Chapter 8.

SOURCES: Charles Tingley, "Reputation, Freedom of Expression and the Tort of Defamation in the United States and Canada: A Deceptive Polarity," *Alberta Law Review* 37 (1999): 620; Sarah Frazier, "Liberty of Expression in Ireland and the Need for a Constitutional Law of Defamation," *Vanderbilt Journal of Transnational Law* 32 (1999): 391; and Vicki C. Jackson and Mark Tushnet, *Comparative Constitutional Law,* 2nd ed. (New York: Foundation Press, 2003).

who is considered a public official? In footnote 23 Brennan wrote, "We have no occasion here to determine how far down into lower ranks of government employees the 'public official' designation would extend." When an appropriate case presented itself, the Court would have to draw some distinctions. How it did so would have significant ramifications because, under the *New York Times* test, only public officials had to prove actual malice; other plaintiffs were required only to show that published statements about them were false and damaging. Equally difficult were other questions raised by the decision: Did this new standard apply only to public officials engaged in their official duties? How could a public official prove actual malice? What did that term encompass?

In 1967 the Court decided two cases, **Curtis Publishing Company v. Butts** and **Associated Press v. Walker**, in hopes of clarifying its *New York Times* ruling. At issue in *Curtis* was a *Saturday Evening Post* article titled "The Story of a College Football Fix." The

writer asserted that Wally Butts, the athletic director at the University of Georgia, had given Paul Bryant, the football coach at the University of Alabama, "the plays, defensive patterns, and all the significant secrets Georgia's football team possessed." According to the article, Butts was attempting to fix a 1962 game between the two schools. The author claimed he had obtained this information from an Atlanta insurance salesman, who accidentally overheard the conversation between Butts and Bryant. Butts initiated a libel suit against the publishing company, arguing that the article was false and damaging.[2] And, although the Court had yet to hand down the *New York Times* decision, Butts's suit also alleged that actual malice

---

2. Up to this point, Butts had been a respected figure in coaching ranks and had been negotiating for a coaching position with a professional team. After the *Saturday Evening Post* published the story, he resigned from the University of Georgia for "health" reasons.

had occurred because the *Saturday Evening Post* "had departed greatly from the standards of good investigation and reporting." Evidence introduced at the trial showed that the *Saturday Evening Post* had done little to verify the insurance salesman's story. The magazine's attorneys "were aware of the progress" of the *New York Times* case but offered only a defense of truth. A jury awarded Butts $3,060,000 in damages, but the judge reduced the award to $460,000. The magazine asked for a new trial on *New York Times* grounds—that Butts was a public figure and should have to prove actual malice. The judge refused, asserting that Butts was not a public official and, even if he were, there was sufficient evidence to conclude that the magazine had acted with "reckless disregard for the truth."

Associated Press v. Walker concerned a 1962 Associated Press story, an eyewitness account of the riots at the University of Mississippi triggered by the government-ordered admission to the university of James Meredith, a black student. According to the story, retired army general Edwin Walker "took command of the violent crowd and . . . led a charge against federal marshals," who were in Mississippi to oversee the desegregation process. It also alleged that Walker gave the segregationists instructions on how to combat the effects of tear gas. Walker sued the Associated Press for $2 million in compensatory and punitive damages, arguing that the article was false and damaging. The jury awarded $500,000 in compensatory damages and $300,000 in punitive damages, but the judge set aside the latter on the grounds that Walker, while not a public official, was a public figure; his views on integration were well-known and, as such, he had to prove actual malice under the *New York Times* standard.

Both cases reached the Supreme Court during its 1966 term, and the Court decided the cases together. The justices were unable to agree on an opinion, but a majority (although for different reasons, which we review below) ruled in favor of Butts's claim and against Walker's. Seven justices (Brennan, Clark, Fortas, Harlan, Stewart, Warren, and White) agreed that Walker and Butts were public figures, but beyond that point they expressed substantial differences. Five (Black, Brennan, Douglas, Warren, and White) ruled that the *New York Times* standard applies also to public *figures* and not just public *officials*. In other words, even though Walker and Butts were not officials of the government, they would have to meet the *New York*

Times test to win their suits because they were individuals in the public eye. The remaining four (Clark, Fortas, Harlan, and Stewart) argued that a lesser standard of "highly unreasonable conduct constituting extreme departure from standards of investigating and reporting" should apply to public figures. Five justices (Clark, Fortas, Harlan, Stewart, and Warren) ruled in favor of Butts, upholding the lower court's decision, on the ground that Butts had demonstrated that the magazine had abandoned professional standards (Harlan, joined by Clark, Fortas, and Stewart) or exhibited a reckless disregard for the truth (Warren). The other four justices would have held against Butts. Brennan (joined by White) agreed with Warren that the *New York Times* standard could be met by evidence presented, but he argued that a new trial was needed because the jury was not properly instructed in this regard. Black (joined by Douglas) argued for complete reversal. All nine justices rejected Walker's claim. They said that Walker had failed to prove press improprieties, but they differed on what constituted journalistic impropriety. Harlan (joined by Clark, Fortas, and Stewart) argued that Walker had not met the "unreasonable conduct" standard; Black, Brennan, Douglas, Warren, and White asserted that he had not met the *New York Times* standard.[3] Still, amid all this disagreement, one principle emerged: those in the public eye would have to meet the *New York Times* test to win their libel cases.

If *Butts* and *Walker* helped clarify some aspects of *New York Times,* they also focused attention on this question: For purposes of libel law, how far does the "public figure" definition stretch? This is an important question because private individuals remained covered by traditional libel rules. A person who does not qualify as a public official or public figure must only prove that the published statements were false and caused damage. A showing of malice is not required. Drawing a line between public and private persons is not easy, and the Court itself has had a difficult time doing so.

Initially, in ***Rosenbloom v. Metromedia*** (1971), a plurality, led by Justice Brennan, held that the primary emphasis of the *New York Times* test "derives not so much from whether the plaintiff is a 'public official,'

---

3. Black and Douglas claimed that they did so only to obtain a majority; otherwise they would have adhered to their view that the First Amendment protects the press from all libel claims.

'public figure,'" or "'private individual' as it derives from the question whether the allegedly defamatory publication concerns a matter of public or general interest." In writing these words, Brennan claimed that the *New York Times* test applied to all stories of public interest regardless of the public status of the individual.

Naturally, the media were delighted: it would now be extremely difficult for any individual mentioned in a story of public interest to prove libel. Others were quick to criticize: Justice Marshall, usually an ally of Brennan, thought the opinion went much too far in shielding the press from libel suits by "millions of Americans who live their lives in obscurity." Others argued that it put a heavy burden on lower court judges to determine what is in the public's interest.

The Court, apparently siding with some of the critics, largely abandoned the *Rosenbloom* approach just three years later in *Gertz v. Welch* (1974). After a jury found a police officer guilty of murder, the victim's family retained Elmer Gertz, a Chicago attorney, to bring a civil action against the officer. In a story written for *American Opinion,* an outlet for the views of the John Birch Society, a far-right, anticommunist organization, Robert Welch suggested that Gertz was a "Communist-fronter" engaged in a plot to disgrace and frame the police. Gertz sued Welch for libel, arguing that the story was false and damaging to his career. Welch argued that Gertz was covered by the *New York Times* test under any standard adopted by the court—that is, whether Gertz was considered a public figure, a public official, or a person involved in a matter of public interest. Gertz, on the other hand, took the position that he was a private figure who had not voluntarily thrust himself into the public sphere.

The Court sided with Gertz. Writing for the majority, Justice Powell explained that Welch's

characterization of [Gertz] as a public figure . . . may rest on either of two alternative bases. In some instances an individual may achieve such pervasive fame or notoriety that he becomes a public figure for all purposes and in all contexts. More commonly, an individual voluntarily injects himself or is drawn into a particular public controversy and thereby becomes a public figure for a limited range of issues. In either case such persons assume special prominence in the resolution of public questions.

Powell continued: "Although petitioner was consequently well known in some circles, he had achieved no general fame or notoriety in the community. None of the prospective jurors called at the trial had ever heard of petitioner prior to this litigation. . . . In this context it is plain that petitioner was not a public figure. . . . He plainly did not thrust himself into the vortex of this public issue, nor did he engage the public's attention in an attempt to influence its outcome."

Perhaps to reinforce its approach in *Gertz,* just two years later, in ***Time, Inc. v. Firestone*** (1976), the Court dealt with a similar issue. In 1961 Mary Alice Sullivan married Russell Firestone, "the scion of one of America's wealthier industrial families." Three years later she filed for separation, and he countered with a plea for a divorce. The trial was a protracted, well-publicized affair, owing to the notoriety of the Firestones and the details of their relationship. In granting the divorce, the trial judge noted that each of the parties had accused the other of outrageous extramarital affairs, but that he found the testimony to be unreliable. After the divorce was final, *Time* magazine ran the following story in its "Milestones" section:

DIVORCED. By Russell A. Firestone Jr., 41, heir to the tire fortune: Mary Alice Sullivan Firestone, 32, his third wife; a onetime Palm Beach schoolteacher; on grounds of extreme cruelty and adultery; after six years of marriage, one son; in West Palm Beach, Fla. The 17-month intermittent trial produced enough testimony of extramarital adventures on both sides, said the judge, "to make Dr. Freud's hair curl."

Because the magazine reported as true material the judge explicitly discounted as unreliable, Mary Alice Firestone requested a printed retraction. When *Time* refused, she sued on the ground that the story was "false, malicious, and defamatory." *Time* argued that she was a public figure and, therefore, had to prove "actual malice." Relying on its ruling in *Gertz,* the Supreme Court disagreed, stating that Mary Alice Firestone

did not assume any role of especial prominence in the affairs of society, other than perhaps Palm Beach society, and did not thrust herself to the forefront of any particular public controversy in order to influence the resolution of the issues involved in it.

Although some commentators (including Justice White in a dissent in *Gertz*) did not think the Court went far enough to protect private citizens, there is general agreement that the combination of *Gertz* and *Firestone* excised *Rosenbloom* to the point of virtually overruling it. Under *Gertz* and *Firestone,* the focus moved back to the individual's status and away from the nature of the story or event. To the majority, both Gertz and Firestone were essentially private figures who came into public view only because of the defamation itself. Under these circumstances, the *New York Times* test is not applicable; in other words, private citizens need not prove actual malice to win a libel case.

Have *Gertz* and *Firestone* made it easier for plaintiffs to prove libel? Certainly, they eased the burden carried by private citizens, but, because the *New York Times* test remains, it can be quite difficult for public officials and public figures to meet the legal standards. Some have gone even further, suggesting that the *Times* test makes it virtually impossible for public figures to win libel judgments against the press, even when stories contain falsehoods.

Libel in the Republican Court Era

The Court's treatment of claims raised in *Gertz* and *Firestone* led many commentators to suggest that it would further narrow the scope of *New York Times.* Indeed, when the justices agreed to hear arguments in *Hustler Magazine v. Falwell,* some looked for a decision that would run counter to, if not overrule, *New York Times.* Did the Court deliver such a decision?

Hustler Magazine v. Falwell

485 U.S. 46 (1988)
http://laws.findlaw.com/US/485/46.html
Oral arguments are available at http://www.oyez.org.
Vote: 8 (Blackmun, Brennan, Marshall, O'Connor,
      Rehnquist, Scalia, Stevens, White)
      0

OPINION OF THE COURT: *Rehnquist*
CONCURRING OPINION: *White*
NOT PARTICIPATING: *Kennedy*

FACTS:

In the November 1983 issue of *Hustler* magazine, publisher Larry Flynt printed a parody of an advertisement for Campari Liqueur. The advertisement mimicked a Campari promotional campaign based on interviews with various celebrities in which they described their "first time." Although these interviews were laced with sexual double entendres, it always became clear by the end of the ads that the celebrities

were actually referring to the first time they tasted Campari. The *Hustler* magazine advertisement used the same format and layout as the real Campari ads. It was headlined "Jerry Falwell talks about his first time." Falwell was a nationally prominent Protestant minister, a leading political conservative, and the head of the now-defunct Moral Majority organization. The interview portion of the advertisement featured a fictional Falwell discussing his "first time"—an incestuous sexual encounter with his mother in an outhouse while both were intoxicated from drinking Campari. The advertisement portrayed Falwell as drunk, immoral, and hypocritical. At the bottom of the ad the following words appeared in small print: "Ad parody—not to be taken seriously." The magazine's

Thomas Nast's 1871 cartoon depicting "Boss" Tweed and his cronies was typical of the artist's hard-hitting depictions of public figures. In the Court's decision in Hustler Magazine v. Falwell, *Chief Justice Rehnquist refers directly to Nast's work as well as to several other examples of satirical political cartoons and caricatures.*

table of contents listed the item as "Fiction: Ad and Personality Parody."

Shortly after the issue was available for public purchase, Falwell sued the magazine and its publisher for libel, invasion of privacy, and intentional infliction of emotional distress. The trial judge dismissed the privacy claim before sending the case to the jury. The jury decided in favor of the magazine on the libel issue, concluding that the advertisement could not reasonably be understood as describing actual facts about Falwell or actual events in which he participated. However, the jury awarded Falwell $150,000 on the claim that the publisher of *Hustler* intentionally inflicted emotional distress.

At the Supreme Court level, there was no question as to whether Falwell was a public figure—he clearly was and, as such, had to prove malicious intent. Rather, the issue was whether Falwell could even bring a suit against a parody that did not purport to be factually accurate.

ARGUMENTS:

For the petitioners, Hustler
Magazine and Larry C. Flynt:

- The First Amendment protects the publication of "rhetorical hyperbole and opinion" as long as such statements are published without "knowing or reckless falsity."
- The parody of public figures "has a long tradition in American political and social commentary," and "questions of good taste are irrelevant" to the issue of First Amendment protection.
- The actual malice component of the *New York Times* test requires the publication of a false statement of fact, so if there is no false statement the publication is entitled to First Amendment protection.

For the respondent, Jerry Falwell:

- First Amendment protection requires a balancing test between state and constitutional interests. The state's interest in protecting its citizens from intentional infliction of emotional distress outweighs any free speech protections *Hustler*'s "deliberate character assassination" might have.
- The proper constitutional test for intentional infliction of emotional distress should be intentional conduct, not actual malice, because false statements of fact are irrelevant to intentional infliction of emotional distress.

CHIEF JUSTICE REHNQUIST DELIVERED THE OPINION OF THE COURT.

Petitioner Hustler Magazine, Inc., is a magazine of nationwide circulation. Respondent Jerry Falwell, a nationally known minister who has been active as a commentator on politics and public affairs, sued petitioner and its publisher, petitioner Larry Flynt, to recover damages for invasion of privacy, libel, and intentional infliction of emotional distress. The District Court directed a verdict against respondent on the privacy claim, and submitted the other two claims to a jury. The jury found for petitioners on the defamation claim, but found for respondent on the claim for intentional infliction of emotional distress and awarded damages. We now consider whether this award is consistent with the First and Fourteenth Amendments of the United States Constitution. . . .

This case presents us with a novel question involving First Amendment limitations upon a State's authority to protect its citizens from the intentional infliction of emotional distress. We must decide whether a public figure may recover damages for emotional harm caused by the publication of an ad parody offensive to him, and doubtless gross and repugnant in the eyes of most. Respondent would have us find that a State's interest in protecting public figures from emotional distress is sufficient to deny First Amendment protection to speech that is patently offensive and is intended to inflict emotional injury, even when that speech could not reasonably have been interpreted as stating actual facts about the public figure involved. This we decline to do.

At the heart of the First Amendment is the recognition of the fundamental importance of the free flow of ideas and opinions on matters of public interest and concern. . . . We have therefore been particularly vigilant to ensure that individual expressions of ideas remain free from governmentally imposed sanctions. The First Amendment recognizes no such thing as a "false" idea. . . .

The sort of robust political debate encouraged by the First Amendment is bound to produce speech that is critical of those who hold public office or those public figures who are "intimately involved in the resolution of important public questions or, by reason of their fame, shape events in areas of concern to society at large." Such criticism, inevitably, will not always be reasoned or moderate; public figures as well as public officials will be subject to "vehement, caustic, and sometimes unpleasantly sharp attacks." . . .

Of course, this does not mean that any speech about a public figure is immune from sanction in the form of damages. Since *New York Times v. Sullivan,* we have consistently ruled that a public figure may hold a speaker liable for the damage to reputation caused by publication of a defamatory falsehood, but only if the statement was made "with knowledge that it was false or with reckless disregard of whether it was false or not." False statements of fact are particularly valueless; they interfere with the truth-seeking function of the marketplace of ideas, and they cause damage to an individual's reputation that cannot easily be repaired by counterspeech, however persuasive or effective. But even though falsehoods have little value in and of themselves, they are "nevertheless inevitable in free debate," and a rule that would impose strict liability on a publisher for false factual assertions would have an undoubted "chilling" effect on speech relating to public figures that does have constitutional value. "Freedoms of expression require 'breathing space.'" This breathing space is provided by a constitutional rule that allows public figures to recover for libel or defamation only when they can prove *both* that the statement was false and that the statement was made with the requisite level of culpability.

Respondent argues, however, that a different standard should apply in this case because here the State seeks to prevent not reputational damage, but the severe emotional distress suffered by the person who is the subject of an offensive publication. In respondent's view, and in the view of the Court of Appeals, so long as the utterance was intended to inflict emotional distress, was outrageous, and did in fact inflict serious emotional distress, it is of no constitutional import whether the statement was a fact or an opinion, or whether it was true or false. It is the intent to cause injury that is the gravamen of the tort, and the State's interest in preventing emotional harm simply outweighs whatever interest a speaker may have in speech of this type.

Generally speaking the law does not regard the intent to inflict emotional distress as one which should receive much solicitude, and it is quite understandable that most if not all jurisdictions have chosen to make it civilly culpable where the conduct in question is sufficiently "outrageous." But in the world of debate about public affairs, many things done with motives that are less than admirable are protected by the First Amendment. In *Garrison v. Louisiana* (1964) we held that even when a speaker or writer is motivated by hatred or ill-will his expression was protected by the First Amendment:

"Debate on public issues will not be uninhibited if the speaker must run the risk that it will be proved in court that he spoke out of hatred; even if he did speak out of hatred, utterances honestly believed contribute to the free interchange of ideas and the ascertainment of truth."

Thus while such a bad motive may be deemed controlling for purposes of tort liability in other areas of the law, we think the First Amendment prohibits such a result in the area of public debate about public figures.

Were we to hold otherwise, there can be little doubt that political cartoonists and satirists would be subjected to damages awards without any showing that their work falsely defamed its subject. Webster's defines a caricature as "the deliberately distorted picturing or imitating of a person, literary style, etc. by exaggerating features or mannerisms for satirical effect." The appeal of the political cartoon or caricature is often based on exploration of unfortunate physical traits or politically embarrassing events—an exploration often calculated to injure the feelings of the subject of the portrayal. The art of the cartoonist is often not reasoned or even-handed, but slashing and one-sided. One cartoonist expressed the nature of the art in these words:

"The political cartoon is a weapon of attack, of scorn and ridicule and satire; it is least effective when it tries to pat some politician on the back. It is usually as welcome as a bee sting and is always controversial in some quarters."

Several famous examples of this type of intentionally injurious speech were drawn by Thomas Nast, probably the greatest American cartoonist to date, who was associated for many years during the post–Civil War era with *Harper's Weekly.* In the pages of that publication Nast conducted a graphic vendetta against William M. "Boss" Tweed and his corrupt associates in New York City's "Tweed Ring." It has been described by one historian of the subject as "a sustained attack which in its passion and effectiveness stands alone in the history of American graphic art." Another writer explains that the success of the Nast cartoon was achieved "because of the emotional impact of its presentation. It continuously goes beyond the bounds of good taste and conventional manners."

Despite their sometimes caustic nature, from the early cartoon portraying George Washington as an ass down to the present day, graphic depictions and satirical cartoons have played a prominent role in public and political debate. Nast's castigation of the Tweed Ring, Walt McDougall's characterization of presidential candidate James G. Blaine's banquet with the millionaires at Delmonico's as "The Royal Feast of Belshazzar," and numerous other efforts have undoubtedly had an effect on the course and outcome of contemporaneous debate. Lincoln's tall, gangling posture, Teddy Roosevelt's glasses and teeth, and Franklin D. Roosevelt's jutting jaw and cigarette holder have been memorialized by political cartoons with an effect that could not have been obtained by the photographer or the portrait artist. From the viewpoint of history it is clear that our political discourse would have been considerably poorer without them.

Respondent contends, however, that the caricature in question here was so "outrageous" as to distinguish it from more traditional political cartoons. There is no doubt that the caricature of respondent and his mother published in *Hustler* is at best a distant cousin of the political cartoons described above, and a rather poor relation at that. If it were possible by laying down a principled standard to separate the one from the other, public discourse would probably suffer little or no harm. But we doubt that there is any such standard, and we are quite sure that the pejorative description "outrageous" does not supply one. "Outrageousness" in the area of political and social discourse has an inherent subjectiveness about it which would allow a jury to impose liability on the basis of the jurors' tastes or views, or perhaps on the basis of their dislike of a particular expression. An "outrageousness" standard thus runs afoul of our longstanding refusal to allow damages to be awarded because the speech in question may have an adverse emotional impact on the audience. . . .

Admittedly . . . First Amendment principles, like other principles, are subject to limitations. We recognized that speech that is "'vulgar,' 'offensive,' and 'shocking'" is "not entitled to absolute constitutional protection under all circumstances." In *Chaplinsky v. New Hampshire* (1942), we held that a state could lawfully punish an individual for the use of insulting "'fighting' words—those which by their very utterance inflict injury or tend to incite an immediate breach of the peace." These limitations are but recognition . . . that this Court has "long recognized that not all speech is of equal First Amendment importance." But the sort of

expression involved in this case does not seem to us to be governed by any exception to the general First Amendment principles stated above.

We conclude that public figures and public officials may not recover for the tort of intentional infliction of emotional distress by reason of publications such as the one here at issue without showing in addition that the publication contains a false statement of fact which was made with "actual malice," *i.e.,* with knowledge that the statement was false or with reckless disregard as to whether or not it was true. This is not merely a "blind application" of the *New York Times* standard; it reflects our considered judgment that such a standard is necessary to give adequate "breathing space" to the freedoms protected by the First Amendment.

Here it is clear that respondent Falwell is a "public figure" for purposes of First Amendment law. The jury found against respondent on his libel claim when it decided that the *Hustler* ad parody could not "reasonably be understood as describing actual facts about [respondent] or actual events in which [he] participated." The Court of Appeals interpreted the jury's finding to be that the ad parody "was not reasonably believable," and in accordance with our custom we accept this finding. Respondent is thus relegated to his claim for damages awarded by the jury for the intentional infliction of emotional distress by "outrageous" conduct. But for reasons heretofore stated this claim cannot, consistently with the First Amendment, form a basis for the award of damages when the conduct in question is the publication of a caricature such as the ad parody involved here. The judgment of the Court of Appeals is accordingly

Reversed.

The opinion surprised some Court observers: after all, it was written by Chief Justice Rehnquist, who was not particularly well-known for supporting free press claims, and it was unanimous, a rarity in libel law. The media applauded the opinion, while Falwell fumed that "the Supreme Court has given the green light to Larry Flynt and his ilk to print what they wish about any public figure at any time with no fear of reprisal."[4] A green light it may be, but it is one Flynt went through at considerable cost *(see Box 7-2).*

---

4. Quoted in Stuart Taylor Jr., "Court 8–0, Extends Right to Criticize Those in Public Eye," *New York Times,* February 25, 1988, 1, 14.

BOX 7-2   AFTERMATH . . . LARRY FLYNT

Hustler Magazine V. Falwell (1988) was just one skirmish in a long series of legal battles fought by magazine publisher Larry Flynt. After introducing *Hustler* in 1974, Flynt frequently found himself in court defending the magazine against obscenity charges, usually stemming from its portrayals of women, sexual activities, and violence. Flynt claims he has spent almost $50 million in legal fees over a thirty-year period. While standing trial in Georgia in 1978, he was shot by a sniper and sustained injuries that left him partially paralyzed.

Larry Flynt holds the ad parody that was the cause of a libel suit brought by Jerry Falwell against Hustler *magazine.*

Ever flamboyant, Flynt uses a gold-plated wheelchair. He has always unabashedly promoted his cause. Prior to the Supreme Court's decision in the *Falwell* case, Flynt sent complementary *Hustler* magazine subscriptions to each of the nine justices.

In 1977, at the urging of President Jimmy Carter's sister Ruth, Flynt became a born-again Christian. He left the faith one year later.

Flynt continued to engage in controversial activities. In 1988 accusations were made that he had paid $1 million to a hit man to kill *Playboy* founder Hugh Hefner, singer Frank Sinatra, publisher Walter Annenberg, and *Penthouse* publisher Bob Guccione. Nothing came of those charges, but rumors of murder plots have persisted concerning Flynt and individuals closely associated with him.

In 1996 Flynt's daughter Tonya publicly accused him of sexually molesting her from the age of ten until she was eighteen. Flynt denied the charges, claiming that his estranged daughter had "serious mental problems" and was a "habitual liar." That same year, Oliver Stone produced a feature film on Flynt's life, *The People vs. Larry Flynt*. The movie, directed by Milos Forman, became a commercial and critical success, despite the fact that it was attacked by feminists and antipornography organizations for portraying Flynt as a champion of the First Amendment rather than as a dangerous purveyor of obscenity.

In 1998 Flynt, a fiercely partisan Democrat, entered the controversy surrounding the impeachment of President Bill Clinton by offering up to $1 million for information about members of Congress who had engaged in illicit sexual activities. Flynt's threat to release the information he gathered is said to have prompted the resignation of Representative Robert Livingston, R-La., who was slated to become Speaker of the House. Livingston publicly admitted to an extramarital affair. In 2003 Flynt, who operates his businesses from California, ran for governor of that state, claiming to be a "smut peddler who cares." He placed seventh in a field of 135 candidates.

Flynt publishes more than twenty magazines, but *Hustler*, with a circulation of 500,000 (down from its peak of 3 million), remains the centerpiece of his publishing empire. He has also entered the video and Internet markets. As to his legal battles, Flynt has said, "If the law protects a scumbag like me, then it protects all of us."

SOURCES: *Louisville Courier-Journal,* October 28, 1988; *New Orleans Times-Picayune,* May 25, 1996; *USA Today,* May 24, 1996; and *Washington Post,* March 20, 1979, February 10, 1997, December 19, 1998, and January 11, 1999.

The *Hustler Magazine* decision, then, not only failed to reverse *New York Times* but actually reinforced it. In *Hustler Magazine* the Court continued the trend set by *New York Times* to extend First Amendment protections to the press when it covers public officials and public figures. To sue successfully for damages, well-known persons must prove actual malice as well as falsity.

Libel and the Internet

The *Hustler* case reveals that even though the Court has steadfastly adhered to the *New York Times* test for public figures, the justices have spent decades fleshing out the details of that test. It may take the Court even longer to resolve the new problems cropping up as a result of the rapid expansion of the Internet.

Suppose Student X enters an online discussion on a university network about professors and writes falsely that "Professor John Smith is a fraud. He says he has a Ph.D. but really doesn't."[5] Even this very simple example raises extremely complex questions. Let us deal with one: Would the *New York Times* test apply? The answer, you may think, is that it would not because Smith is not a public figure. But one of the Court's most important ways of differentiating public from private figures is that public figures have access to the media and can easily refute charges against them. Could Professor Smith not do the same? He can tell his side of the story through the Internet. Moreover, because his university's computer system could probably determine all the users who had read Student X's comment, the professor could target his response, a luxury not afforded to public officials. Does this mean that all Internet users should be treated as public figures for purposes of libel suits?

The Supreme Court has yet to address this question and the many others relating to libel on the Internet that we address in the next chapter. For now, consider how you think the justices should resolve the case of Professor Smith.

OBSCENITY

However difficult it was for the Court to settle on a framework for libel, obscenity presented even more vexing problems. According to Justice John Marshall Harlan (II), "The subject of obscenity has produced a variety of views among the members of the Court unmatched in any other course of constitutional interpretation."[6] An even more candid statement came from Justice William J. Brennan, the member of the Court most associated with the subject. Discussing service on the Court, Brennan noted, "It takes a while before you can become even calm about approaching

a job like this. Which is not to say you do not make mistakes. In my case, there has been the obscenity area."[7]

What is it about obscenity that has produced such extraordinary statements? After all, the Court uniformly has held that obscenity is not entitled to First Amendment protection. The problem is determining what makes a work obscene. In other words, how should we define the term? The answer is important because how we differentiate protected expression from unprotected expression has broad implications for what we see, read, and hear. Consider the movie industry: in the not-so-distant past, strict definitions of obscenity required an actor to keep one foot on the floor when performing a bedroom scene. Imagine the number of modern-day films the courts would ban under such a standard. Today, the issues are no less salient: groups throughout the country try to bar certain books from public schools, to prohibit the sale of some music to minors, to stop libraries from subscribing to certain magazines, and to ban the transmission of some material on the Internet—all on obscenity grounds.

Given the importance of the task, one might think the Court has set definitive policy in this area. Perhaps that is now the case, but for more than four decades the Court grappled with the issue, particularly with fashioning a definition of obscenity. Why did this subject cause such problems? Has the Court come up with a reasonable solution? Or does it still face difficulty, floundering among competing schools of thought?

Obscenity in Perspective: Origins

The adjudication of obscenity claims is a modern phenomenon. Before the 1950s the Court generally avoided the issue by adopting the British definition of obscenity. In *Regina v. Hicklin* (1868), which involved a pamphlet questioning the morals of Catholic priests, a British court promulgated the following test: "whether the tendency of the matter charged as obscenity is to deprave and corrupt those whose minds are open to such immoral influences and into whose hands a publication of this sort might fall."

Under this standard, commonly referred to as the *Hicklin* test, the British court found the pamphlet

---

5. We have adapted the material in this section from material found on the Web site of the Cyberspace Law Institute (now available at http://web.archive.org/web/19961031234622/http://www.cli.org/default.html).

6. *Interstate Circuit v. Dallas* (1968).

7. Quoted in Nat Hentoff, "Profiles—The Constitutionalists," *New Yorker*, March 12, 1990, 54.

obscene. That it did so is not surprising: three aspects of the *Hicklin* test make it particularly difficult to overcome. First, the test targets "those whose minds are open to such immoral influences and into whose hands a publication of this sort might fall." Although this standard is vague, in practice, prosecutors often asked, What if this material were to fall into the hands of a child? In other words, the *Hicklin* test used a stringent level of acceptability—whether the material would be appropriate if a child were exposed to it. Second, the *Hicklin* test did not require that the publication be considered as a whole. Instead, a work could be declared obscene based on one of its parts. Third, the *Hicklin* test did not direct the courts to consider the social value of the work; rather, it provided only that the effect of the offensive sections be examined. As a result, the *Hicklin* standard left a wide range of expression unprotected.

The U.S. Supreme Court not only adopted the *Hicklin* standard but also strengthened it. In *Ex parte Jackson* (1878) the Court upheld the Comstock Act, which made it a crime to send obscene materials, including information on abortion and birth control, through the U.S. mail. The justices applied the *Hicklin* test and extended its coverage to include materials discussing reproduction.

While the Supreme Court clung to *Hicklin*, some U.S. lower courts were attempting to liberalize it or even reject it. A well-known example is *United States v. One Book Entitled "Ulysses" by James Joyce* (1934), in which Judge Augustus Hand argued that the proper standard should be whether the author *intended* to produce obscene materials. The diverse rulings from the lower courts, coupled with the Supreme Court's silence on the issue, began to have an effect. By the 1950s the pornography business was flourishing in the United States, with little restriction on who could buy or view such material. This situation led to a backlash, with irate citizens clamoring for tighter controls. Others, particularly attorneys with the American Civil Liberties Union, pressured courts to move in precisely the opposite direction—to rule that the First Amendment covers all materials, including those previously adjudged obscene. By the late 1950s these different interests were sending the same message to the justices: the time had come to deal with the issue.

In ***Butler v. Michigan*** (1957) the Court responded by declaring unconstitutional a state statute that defined obscenity along *Hicklin* test lines. The law made it a crime to distribute material "found to have a potentially deleterious influence on youth." The justices struck down the statute, finding fault with the child standard. It is incompatible with the First Amendment, the justices said, to reduce the reading material available to adults to that which is fit for children. To do so, according to Justice Felix Frankfurter's opinion, is "to burn the house to roast the pig."

The *Butler* decision mortally wounded the *Hicklin* test, but the justices had not provided an alternative. Later that year, however, the Court took its first stab at creating a contemporary American obscenity standard. The case was *Roth v. United States,* decided with a companion case, *Alberts v. California*. While reading *Roth,* consider the critical issue of standards: Justice Brennan continued to find fault with *Hicklin,* but what did he propose as a replacement?

Roth v. United States

354 U.S. 476 (1957)
http://laws.findlaw.com/US/354/476.html
Oral arguments are available at http://www.oyez.org.
Vote: 6 (Brennan, Burton, Clark, Frankfurter, Warren, Whittaker)
*   3 (Black, Douglas, Harlan)*

OPINION OF THE COURT: *Brennan*
CONCURRING OPINION: *Warren*
DISSENTING OPINIONS: *Douglas, Harlan*[8]

FACTS:

In 1955 the U.S. government obtained a twenty-six-count indictment against Samuel Roth, a New Yorker who published and sold books, photographs, and magazines, for violating a federal obscenity law. The government alleged that Roth had sent "obscene, indecent, and filthy matter" through the mail. Among those materials was a circular advertising *Photo and Body, Good Times,* and *American Aphrodite Number Thirteen*.

At Roth's trial the judge instructed the jury with this definition of obscenity: the material "must be calculated to debauch the minds and morals of those into whose hands it may fall and that the test in each case is the effect of the book, picture or publication considered as a whole, not upon any particular class, but upon all those whom it is likely to reach. In other

---

8. Harlan dissented in *Roth* but concurred in the companion case, *Alberts v. California.*

words, you determine its impact upon the average person in the community." The jury found Roth guilty on four of the counts, and the judge sentenced him to the maximum punishment of five years in prison and a $5,000 fine.

ARGUMENTS:

For the petitioner, Samuel Roth:

- With the sweeping language that "Congress shall make no law . . . abridging the freedom of speech, or of the press" the framers did not intend to make an obscenity exception to the First Amendment.
- Obscenity does not fit narrow exceptions to the First Amendment, such as Justice Holmes's "clear and present danger" test, because there is no evidence that it has an appreciable effect on people's conduct.
- Because the federal obscenity law is vague and relies on local standards, a person could not tell with "reasonable certainty" whether he or she has violated it.

For the respondent, United States:

- The First Amendment is not an absolute right and must be weighed against competing societal interests.
- Obscenity has little social value in the "marketplace of ideas," and it is apparent from history and earlier decisions that it lies outside First Amendment protection.
- The protection of public morals is important enough to justify this restraint on the freedom of speech.

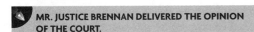

MR. JUSTICE BRENNAN DELIVERED THE OPINION OF THE COURT.

In *Roth,* the primary constitutional question is whether the federal obscenity statute violates the provision of the First Amendment that "Congress shall make no law . . . abridging the freedom of speech, or of the press. . . . "

The dispositive question is whether obscenity is utterance within the area of protected speech and press. Although this is the first time the question has been squarely presented to this Court, either under the First Amendment or under the Fourteenth Amendment, expressions found in numerous opinions indicate that this Court has always assumed that obscenity is not protected by the freedom of speech and press.

The guaranties of freedom of expression in effect in 10 of the 14 States which by 1792 had ratified the Constitution, gave no absolute protection for every utterance. Thirteen of the 14 States provided for the prosecution of libel, and all of those States made either blasphemy or profanity, or both, statutory crimes. As early as 1712, Massachusetts made it criminal to publish "any filthy, obscene, or profane song, pamphlet, libel or mock sermon" in imitation or mimicking of religious services. Thus, profanity and obscenity were related offenses.

In light of this history, it is apparent that the unconditional phrasing of the First Amendment was not intended to protect every utterance. This phrasing did not prevent this Court from concluding that libelous utterances are not within the area of constitutionally protected speech. At the time of the adoption of the First Amendment, obscenity law was not as fully developed as libel law, but there is sufficiently contemporaneous evidence to show that obscenity, too, was outside the protection intended for speech and press.

The protection given speech and press was fashioned to assure unfettered interchange of ideas for the bringing about of political and social changes desired by the people. . . .

All ideas having even the slightest redeeming social importance—unorthodox ideas, controversial ideas, even ideas hateful to the prevailing climate of opinion—have the full protection of the guaranties, unless excludable because they encroach upon the limited area of more important interests. But implicit in the history of the First Amendment is the rejection of obscenity as utterly without redeeming social importance. This rejection for that reason is mirrored in the universal judgment that obscenity should be restrained, reflected in the international agreement of over 50 nations, in the obscenity laws of all of the 48 States, and in the 20 obscenity laws enacted by the Congress from 1842 to 1956. This is the same judgment expressed by this Court in *Chaplinsky v. New Hampshire.* . . . We hold that obscenity is not within the area of constitutionally protected speech or press.

It is strenuously urged that these obscenity statutes offend the constitutional guaranties because they punish incitation to impure sexual *thoughts*, not shown to be related to any overt antisocial conduct which is or may be incited in the persons stimulated to such *thoughts.* In *Roth*, the trial judge instructed the jury: "The words 'obscene, lewd and lascivious' as used in the law, signify that form of immorality which has relation to sexual impurity and has a tendency to excite lustful *thoughts.*" . . . It is insisted that the constitutional guaranties are violated because convictions may be had without proof either that obscene material will perceptibly create a clear and present danger of antisocial conduct, or will probably induce its recipients to such conduct. . . .

However, sex and obscenity are not synonymous. Obscene material is material which deals with sex in a manner appealing to prurient interest. The portrayal of sex, *e.g.,* in art, literature and scientific works, is not itself sufficient reason to deny material the constitutional protection of freedom of speech and press. Sex, a great and mysterious motive force in human life, has indisputably been a subject of absorbing interest to mankind through the ages; it is one of the vital problems of human interest and public concern. . . .

The fundamental freedoms of speech and press have contributed greatly to the development and well-being of our free society and are indispensable to its continued growth. Ceaseless vigilance is the watchword to prevent their erosion by Congress or by the States. The door barring federal and state intrusion into this area cannot be left ajar; it must be kept tightly closed and opened only the slightest crack necessary to prevent encroachment upon more important interests. It is therefore vital that the standards for judging obscenity safeguard the protection of freedom of speech and press for material which does not treat sex in a manner appealing to prurient interest.

The early leading standard of obscenity allowed material to be judged merely by the effect of an isolated excerpt upon particularly susceptible persons. *Regina v. Hicklin.* Some American courts adopted this standard but later decisions have rejected it and substituted this test: whether to the average person, applying contemporary community standards, the dominant theme of the material taken as a whole appeals to prurient interest. The *Hicklin* test, judging obscenity by the effect of isolated passages upon the most susceptible persons, might well encompass material legitimately treating with sex, and so it must be rejected as unconstitutionally restrictive of the freedoms of speech and press. On the other hand, the substituted standard provides safeguards adequate to withstand the charge of constitutional infirmity.

Both trial courts below sufficiently followed the proper standard. Both courts used the proper definition of obscenity. . . . [I]n *Roth,* the trial judge instructed the jury as follows:

. . . The test is not whether it would arouse sexual desires or sexual impure thoughts in those comprising a particular segment of the community, the young, the immature or the highly prudish or would leave another segment, the scientific or highly educated or the so-called worldly-wise and sophisticated indifferent and unmoved. . . .

"The test in each case is the effect of the book, picture or publication considered as a whole, not upon any particular class, but upon all those whom it is likely to reach. In other words, you determine its impact upon the average person in the community. The books, pictures and circulars must be judged as a whole, in their entire context, and you are not to consider detached or separate portions in reaching a conclusion. You judge the circulars, pictures and publications which have been put in evidence by present-day standards of the community. You may ask yourselves does it offend the common conscience of the community by present-day standards.

"In this case, ladies and gentlemen of the jury, you and you alone are the exclusive judges of what the common conscience of the community is, and in determining that conscience you are to consider the community as a whole, young and old, educated and uneducated, the religious and the irreligious—men, women and children." . . .

In summary, then, we hold that these statutes, applied according to the proper standard for judging obscenity, do not offend constitutional safeguards against convictions based upon protected material, or fail to give men in acting adequate notice of what is prohibited. . . .

The judgment [is] affirmed.

MR. CHIEF JUSTICE WARREN, concurring in the result.

I agree with the result reached by the Court in these cases, but, because we are operating in a field of expression and because broad language used here may eventually be applied to the arts and sciences and freedom of communication generally, I would limit our decision to the facts before us and to the validity of the statutes in question as applied. . . .

The line dividing the salacious or pornographic from literature or science is not straight and unwavering. Present laws depend largely upon the effect that the materials may have upon those who receive them. It is manifest that the same object may have a different impact, varying according to the part of the community it reached. But there is more to these cases. It is not the book that is on trial; it is a person. The conduct of the defendant is the central issue, not the obscenity of a book or picture. The nature of the materials is, of course, relevant as an attribute of the defendant's conduct, but the materials are thus placed in context from which they draw color and character. A wholly different result might be reached in a different setting.

MR. JUSTICE HARLAN, concurring [in part] and dissenting [in part].

Proceeding from the premise that "no issue is presented in either case, concerning the obscenity of the material involved," the Court finds the "dispositive question" to be "whether obscenity is utterance within the area of protected speech and press," and then holds that "obscenity" is not so protected because it is "utterly without redeeming social importance." This sweeping formula appears to me to beg the very question before us. The Court seems to assume that "obscenity" is a peculiar *genus* of "speech and press," which is as distinct, recognizable, and classifiable as poison ivy is among other plants. On this basis the *constitutional* question before us simply becomes, as the Court says, whether "obscenity," as an abstraction, is protected by the First and Fourteenth amendments, and the question whether a *particular* book may be suppressed becomes a mere matter of classification, of "fact," to be entrusted to a fact-finder and insulated from independent constitutional judgment. But surely the problem cannot be solved in such a generalized fashion. Every communication has an individuality and "value" of its own. The suppression of a particular writing or other tangible form of expression is, therefore, an *individual* matter, and in the nature of things every such suppression raises an individual constitutional problem, in which a reviewing court must determine for *itself* whether the attacked expression is suppressible within constitutional standards. Since those standards do not readily lend themselves to generalized definitions, the constitutional problem in the last analysis becomes one of particularized judgments which appellate courts must make for themselves.

MR. JUSTICE DOUGLAS, with whom MR. JUSTICE BLACK concurs, dissenting.

When we sustain these convictions, we make the legality of a publication turn on the purity of thought which a book or tract instills in the mind of the reader. I do not think we can approve that standard and be faithful to the command of the First Amendment, which by its terms is a restraint on Congress and which by the Fourteenth is a restraint on the states. . . .

I do not think that the problem can be resolved by the Court's statement that "obscenity is not expression protected by the First Amendment." With the exception of *Beauharnais v. Illinois,* none of our cases has resolved problems of free speech and free press by placing any form of expression beyond the pale of the absolute prohibition of the First Amendment. . . . I reject too the implication that problems of freedom of speech and of the press are to be resolved by weighing against the values of free expression, the judgment of the Court that a particular form of that expression has "no redeeming social importance." The First Amendment, its prohibition in terms absolute, was designed to preclude courts as well as legislatures from weighing the values of speech against silence. The First Amendment puts free speech in the preferred position. . . .

I would give the broad sweep of the First Amendment full support. I have the same confidence in the ability of our people to reject noxious literature as I have in their capacity to sort out the true from the false in theology, economics, politics, or any other field.

Although they were badly divided, a majority of the justices in *Roth* supported a new standard articulated by Justice Brennan in his opinion of the Court. Now known as the *Roth* test, Brennan's obscenity standard posed the following: "Whether to the average person applying contemporary community standards, the dominant theme of the material, taken as a whole, appeals to prurient interests."

At first glance, Brennan's opinion seems to forge a compromise between competing views. On one hand, he appeased "decency" advocates by rejecting the view that nothing is obscene; on the other, he set a new standard of obscenity that was far less restrictive than *Hicklin.* The new *Roth* test was a significant departure from the *Hicklin* standard. First, *Roth* imposed an "average person" test, replacing *Hicklin*'s child standard with that of an adult. Second, the "contemporary community standards" criterion recognized the evolving nature of society's views of sexual morality. Third, the "dominant theme of the material taken as a whole" approach rejected *Hicklin*'s notion that a work can be declared obscene based on the content of a single part. And finally, the "prurient interests" element ensured that only material with sexual content would potentially fall under the obscenity rubric.

A majority of the Court supported Brennan's opinion, but the Court remained deeply divided over the proper way to handle the obscenity issue. In the ensuing years, the Court confronted several appeals that provided opportunities for the justices to improve upon *Roth*. Attempts to replace *Roth* were unsuccessful. The justices simply could not agree on an acceptable substitute.

Although *Roth* survived, the justices did amplify and build upon its meaning. Perhaps the most significant of the post-*Roth* decisions were **Jacobellis v. Ohio** (1964) and **Memoirs v. Massachusetts** (1966). In *Jacobellis* the Court considered the appeal of Nico Jacobellis, the manager of a movie theater, who had been charged by Ohio authorities with showing an obscene film. Called *Les Amants* (*The Lovers*), the movie depicts a love affair between an archaeologist and a woman who leaves her husband and child for him. *Les Amants* contains one "explicit love scene."

Brennan's opinion in *Jacobellis* is noteworthy for several reasons. First, Brennan refined his *Roth* test by stating that contemporary community standards were those of the nation, not of a local community. In doing so, he not only held the film to be protected speech but also substantially liberalized *Roth*. It is bound to be the case that individual communities seeking to ban obscenity have stricter standards than those of the

country at large. Under Brennan's refinement, Tulsa, Oklahoma, would be bound by the same obscenity standards as New York City. Second, Brennan added a new provision to the *Roth* test: not only must material meet all of the provisions of the test to be legally obscene, but it also must be found to be "utterly without redeeming social importance."

In *Memoirs v. Massachusetts* the Court further explained what was required under its new social importance standard. This case reviewed the attempts of Massachusetts to declare obscene John Cleland's *Memoirs of a Woman of Pleasure*. This book, popularly known as *Fanny Hill,* dated from 1749. A concededly erotic novel, *Memoirs* traces the escapades of a London prostitute. The Massachusetts Supreme Court held that a book need not be "unqualifiedly worthless before it could be deemed obscene"; that is, just because *Memoirs* contained some nonerotic passages did not mean that it had redeeming value. Although divided (*see Box 7-3*), the U.S. Supreme Court disagreed. In his judgment for the Court, Brennan expanded the parameters of *Roth*. If a work had a "modicum of social value" it could not be adjudged obscene.

By 1966, then, the justices, though hardly united, had substantially altered *Roth,* as shown in Box 7-3, which compares the test in 1957 to that articulated in 1966. Would anything be defined as obscene under the *Roth-Jacobellis-Memoirs* test? We might think that hard-core pornography would fall outside the test, but could not a clever moviemaker, author, or publisher circumvent it? If a short passage of some merit appears in the middle of an erotic book or pornographic movie, does the product have redeeming value?

 BOX 7-3 *ROTH, JACOBELLIS,* **AND** *MEMOIRS* **COMPARED**

Roth: "Whether to the average person, applying contemporary community standards, the dominant theme of the material taken as a whole appeals to prurient interest."

Roth and *Jacobellis:* "Whether to the average person applying" standards of "the society at large," the "dominant theme of the material taken as a whole appeals to

prurient interest" and is "utterly without redeeming social importance."

Roth, Jacobellis, and *Memoirs:* "Whether to the average person applying standards of the society at large," the "dominant theme of the material taken as a whole appeals to prurient interest" and "is utterly without redeeming social importance," possessing not "a modicum of social value."

Indeed, the Court's decisions had the effect of eliminating most works from the obscene category; the majority of the obscenity convictions that made it to the Court during the late 1960s were reversed. Nevertheless, prosecutors remained uncertain about what the Court was doing with the issue because the Court did not provide them with much guidance. Rather than write majority opinions with detailed rationales, the Court often issued only short per curiam opinions that simply announced its decisions. Moreover, because these opinions occasionally revealed serious disagreements among the justices, they increased confusion in legal communities. For example, in *Redrup v. New York* (1967) the Court reversed Robert Redrup's pandering conviction under a New York state law. In its per curiam opinion the Court stated:

Two members of this Court have consistently adhered to the view that a State is utterly without power to suppress, control, or punish the distribution of any writings or pictures upon the ground of their "obscenity." A third has held to the opinion that a State's power in this area is narrowly limited to a distinct and clearly identifiable class of material. Others have subscribed to a not dissimilar standard, holding that a State may not constitutionally inhibit the distribution of literary material as obscene unless "(a) the dominant theme of the material taken as a whole appeals to a prurient interest in sex; (b) the material is patently offensive because it affronts contemporary community standards relating to the description or representation of sexual matters; and (c) the material is utterly without redeeming social value," emphasizing that the "three elements must coalesce," and that no such material can "be proscribed unless it is found to be utterly without redeeming social value." Another justice has not viewed the "social value" element as an independent factor in the judgment of obscenity.

Whichever of these constitutional views is brought to bear upon the cases before us, it is clear the judgments cannot stand.

The only point of agreement in *Redrup* was that under various tests the material in question was not obscene. Otherwise, the opinion smacked of resignation; apparently, some of the justices had given up on the issue, and the rest were fractionalized. In fact, by 1967 the members of the Court had adopted so many different views of obscenity that state prosecutors and

legislators had no firm guidelines *(see Box 7-4)*. Should they adopt the principles set forth in *Roth* when many of the justices now rejected that standard? If not, what could they substitute for it?

The justices' inability to define obscenity in turn crippled enforcement efforts. After 1967 the Court summarily reversed thirty-two cases by citing *Redrup*.[9] This move led many scholars to suggest that by the end of the 1960s obscenity prosecutions were almost impossible to obtain. In other words, after *Redrup* it appeared that the Court was protecting almost any kind of expression. The country was approaching the "end of obscenity." Expanded First Amendment protection prompted an explosion in sexually oriented materials. Adult movies, magazines, and books were more widely distributed than ever before.

The Political Environment and the "Nixon" Court

The reaction to these developments was also predictable. A backlash developed primarily among more conservative citizens who were not pleased with the increasing numbers of adult bookstores, theaters, and nightclubs and were disturbed that sexually explicit materials had become so widely available.

In the presidential election of 1968, the Republican candidate Richard Nixon delivered a campaign message that was quite critical of the Supreme Court. His expressed discontent with the justices covered a wide array of decisions, but the Court's obscenity decisions were primary targets for his campaign rhetoric. He promised the voters that if he became president he would appoint justices to the Court who were more conservative in their orientation. When he took office he kept his promise. He had the opportunity to appoint four new justices to the Court, including a new chief justice, Warren Burger. Nixon's appointments turned the Court in a more conservative direction, and observers knew that eventually the justices would reconsider the line of liberal obscenity rulings that had begun with *Roth*. The anticipated change became apparent on June 21, 1973, when the justices announced their decision in *Miller v. California*.

9. Joseph F. Kobylka, *The Politics of Obscenity* (Westport, CT: Greenwood Press, 1991), 6.

BOX 7-4 WHAT IS OBSCENE?

JUSTICE	CASE	STANDARD
Brennan	*Roth v. United States*, 1957 (as modified by *Jacobellis v. Ohio*, 1964, and *Memoirs v. Massachusetts*, 1966)	"[W]hether to the average person, applying contemporary community standards, the dominant theme of the material taken as a whole appeals to the prurient interest." "Contemporary community standards" means national standards. The material must be utterly without redeeming social value.
Warren	*Jacobellis*	"For all the sound and fury that the Roth test has generated, it has not been proved unsound, and I believe that we should try to live with it—at least until a more satisfactory definition is evolved.... It is my belief that when the Court said in Roth that obscenity is to be defined by reference to 'community standards' it meant community standards—not a national standard...."
Harlan	*Jacobellis*	"[T]he states are constitutionally permitted greater latitude in determining what is bannable on the score of obscenity than is so with the Federal Government.... I would not prohibit [the states] from banning any material which, taken as a whole, has been reasonably found in state judicial proceedings to treat sex in a fundamentally offensive manner, under rationally established criteria for judging such material."
Douglas, Black	*Roth, Jacobellis, Memoirs*	"[I]f the First Amendment guarantee of freedom of speech and press is to mean anything in this field, it must allow protests even against the moral code that the standard of the day sets for the community." "[T]he First Amendment leaves no power in government to regulate expression of ideas."
Stewart	*Jacobellis*	"Under the First and Fourteenth Amendments criminal laws in this area are constitutionally limited to hard-core pornography. I shall not today attempt further to define [hard-core pornography].... But I know it when I see it."
Clark	*Memoirs*	"I [believe that today's decision] rejects the basic holding of Roth.... I understand [the obscenity test] to include only two constitutional requirements: (1) the [material] must be judged as a whole, not by its parts; and (2) it must be judged in terms of its appeal to the prurient interest of the average person, applying contemporary community standards.... [S]ocial importance does not constitute a separate and distinct constitutional test. Such evidence must be considered together with evidence that the material in question appeals to the prurient interest and is patently offensive."

NOTE: Warren joined Brennan's *Memoirs* opinion; therefore, he also adopted the "utterly without redeeming social value" standard.

Miller v. California

413 U.S. 15 (1973)
http://laws.findlaw.com/US/413/15.html
Oral arguments are available at http://www.oyez.org.
Vote: 5 (Blackmun, Burger, Powell, Rehnquist, White)
    4 (Brennan, Douglas, Marshall, Stewart)

OPINION OF THE COURT: *Burger*
DISSENTING OPINIONS: *Douglas, Brennan*

FACTS:

Marvin Miller, a vendor of so-called adult material, conducted a mass-mail campaign to drum up sales for his books. The pamphlets were fairly explicit, containing pictures of men and women engaging in various sexual activities, often with their genitals prominently displayed.

Had Miller sent the brochures to interested individuals only, he might not have been caught. But because he did a mass mailing, some pamphlets ended up in the hands of people who did not want them. Miller was arrested when the manager of a restaurant and his mother opened one of the envelopes and complained to the police.

ARGUMENTS:

For the appellant, Marvin Miller:

- California's use of a statewide decency standard as the "contemporary community standards" test required under *Roth* is a violation of the First Amendment.

- The proper standard is a national standard. A national standard best serves both the state's interest in protecting morals and the constitutional interest in promoting free expression.
- The brochures were not obscene because they were not "utterly without redeeming social value."

For the appellee, State of California:

- A statewide standard for contemporary community standards is proper because the brochures being regulated are matters of local concern. Further, Miller presents no evidence that California's standards differed substantially from national ones.
- The brochures depict hard-core pornography and are obscene as a matter of law.

MR. CHIEF JUSTICE BURGER DELIVERED THE OPINION OF THE COURT.

This is one of a group of "obscenity-pornography" cases being reviewed by the Court in a re-examination of standards enunciated in earlier cases involving what Mr. Justice Harlan called "the intractable obscenity problem." . . .

This case involves the application of a State's criminal obscenity statute to a situation in which sexually explicit materials have been thrust by aggressive sales action upon unwilling recipients who had in no way indicated any desire to receive such materials. This Court has recognized that the States have a legitimate interest in prohibiting dissemination or exhibition of obscene material when the mode of dissemination carries with it a significant danger of offending the sensibilities of unwilling recipients or of exposure to juveniles. It is in this context that we are called on to define the standards which must be used to identify obscene material that a State may regulate without infringing on the First Amendment as applicable to the States through the Fourteenth Amendment. . . .

. . . [O]bscene material is unprotected by the First Amendment. We acknowledge, however, the inherent dangers of undertaking to regulate any form of expression. State statutes designed to regulate obscene materials must be carefully limited. As a result, we now confine the permissible scope of such regulation to works which depict or describe sexual conduct. That conduct must be specifically defined by the applicable state law, as written or authoritatively construed. A state offense must also be limited to works which, taken as a whole, appeal to the prurient interest in sex, which portray sexual conduct in a patently offensive way, and which, taken as a whole, do not have serious literary, artistic, political, or scientific value.

The basic guidelines for the trier of fact must be: (a) whether "the average person, applying contemporary community standards" would find that the work, taken as a whole, appeals to the prurient interest; (b) whether the work depicts or describes, in a patently offensive way, sexual conduct specifically defined by the applicable state law; and (c) whether the work, taken as a whole, lacks serious literary, artistic, political, or scientific value. We do not adopt as a constitutional standard the *"utterly without redeeming social value"* test of *Memoirs v. Massachusetts*; that concept has never commanded the adherence of more than three Justices at one time. If a state law that regulates obscene material is thus limited, as written or construed, the First Amendment values applicable to the States through the Fourteenth Amendment are adequately protected by the ultimate power of appellate courts to conduct an independent review of constitutional claims when necessary.

We emphasize that it is not our function to propose regulatory schemes for the States. That must await their concrete legislative efforts. It is possible, however, to give a few plain examples of what a state statute could define for regulation under part (b) of the standard announced in this opinion.

(a) Patently offensive representations or descriptions of ultimate sexual acts, normal or perverted, actual or simulated.

(b) Patently offensive representation or descriptions of masturbation, excretory functions, and lewd exhibition of the genitals.

Sex and nudity may not be exploited without limit by films or pictures exhibited or sold in places of public accommodation any more than live sex and nudity can be exhibited or sold without limit in such public places. At a minimum, prurient, patently offensive depiction or description of sexual conduct must have serious literary, artistic, political, or scientific value to merit First Amendment protection. . . .

Under the holdings announced today, no one will be subject to prosecution for the sale or exposure of obscene materials unless these materials depict or describe patently offensive "hard core" sexual conduct specifically defined by the regulating state law, as written or construed. We are satisfied that these specific prerequisites will provide fair notice to a dealer in such materials that his public and commercial activities may bring prosecution.

If the inability to define regulated materials with ultimate, god-like precision altogether removes the power of the States or the Congress to regulate, then "hard core" pornography may be exposed without limit to the juvenile, the passerby, and the consenting adult alike. . . .

It is certainly true that the absence, since *Roth,* of a single majority view of this Court as to proper standards for testing obscenity has placed a strain on both state and federal courts. But today, for the first time since *Roth* was decided in 1957, a majority of this Court has agreed on concrete guidelines to isolate "hard core" pornography from expression protected by the First Amendment. Now we . . . attempt to provide positive guidance to federal and state courts alike.

This may not be an easy road, free from difficulty. But no amount of "fatigue" should lead us to adopt a convenient "institutional" rationale—an absolutist, "anything goes" view of the First Amendment—because it will lighten our burdens. "Such an abnegation of judicial supervision in this field would be inconsistent with our duty to uphold the constitutional guarantees." Nor should we remedy "tension between state and federal courts" by arbitrarily depriving the States of a power reserved to them under the Constitution, a power which they have enjoyed and exercised continuously from before the adoption of the First Amendment to this day. "Our duty admits of no 'substitute for facing up to the tough individual problems of constitutional judgment involved in every obscenity case.'"

Under a National Constitution, fundamental First Amendment limitations on the powers of the States do not vary from community to community, but this does not mean that there are, or should or can be, fixed, uniform national standards of precisely what appeals to the "prurient interest" or is "patently offensive." These are essentially questions of fact, and our Nation is simply too big and too diverse for this Court to reasonably expect that such standards could be articulated for all 50 States in a single formulation, even assuming the prerequisite consensus exists. When triers of fact are asked to decide whether "the average person, applying contemporary community standards" would consider certain materials "prurient," it would be unrealistic to require that the answer be based on some abstract formulation. The adversary system, with lay jurors as the usual ultimate fact-finders in criminal prosecutions, has historically permitted triers of fact to draw on the standards of their community, guided always by limiting instructions on the law. To require a State to structure obscenity proceedings around evidence of a *national* "community standard" would be an exercise in futility.

. . . [T]his case was tried on the theory that the California obscenity statute sought to incorporate the tripartite test of *Memoirs.* This, a "national" standard of First Amendment protection enumerated by a plurality of this Court, was correctly regarded at the time of trial as limiting state prosecution under the controlling case law. The jury, however, was explicitly instructed that, in determining whether the "dominant theme of the material as a whole . . . appeals to the prurient interest" and in determining whether the material "goes substantially beyond customary limits of candor and affronts contemporary community standards of decency," it was to apply "contemporary community standards of the State of California." . . .

We conclude that neither the State's alleged failure to offer evidence of "national standards," nor the trial court's charge that the jury consider state community standards, were constitutional errors. Nothing in the First Amendment requires that a jury must consider hypothetical and unascertainable "national standards" when attempting to determine whether certain materials are obscene as a matter of fact. . . . It is neither realistic nor constitutionally sound to read the First Amendment as requiring that the people of Maine or Mississippi accept public depiction of conduct found tolerable in Las Vegas or New York City. People in different States vary in their tastes and attitudes, and this diversity is not to be strangled by the absolutism of imposed uniformity. . . . We hold that the requirement that the jury evaluate the materials with reference to "contemporary standards of the State of California" serves this protective purpose and is constitutionally adequate.

The dissenting Justices sound the alarm of repression. But, in our view, to equate the free and robust exchange of ideas and political debate with commercial exploitation of obscene material demeans the grand conception of the First Amendment and its high purposes in the historic struggle for freedom. It is a "misuse of the great guarantees of free speech and free press. . . ." The First Amendment protects works which, taken as a whole, have serious literary, artistic, political, or scientific value, regardless of whether the government or a majority of the people approve of the ideas these works represent. . . . But the public portrayal of hard-core sexual conduct for its own sake, and for the ensuing commercial gain, is a different matter. . . .

In sum, we (a) reaffirm the *Roth* holding that obscene material is not protected by the First Amendment; (b) hold that such material can be regulated by the States, subject to the specific safeguards enunciated above, without a showing that the material is *"utterly* without redeeming social value"; and (c) hold that obscenity is to be determined by applying "contemporary community standards," not "national standards." . . .

Vacated and remanded.

MR. JUSTICE DOUGLAS, dissenting.

Today we leave open the way for California to send a man to prison for distributing brochures that advertise books and a movie under freshly written standards defining obscenity which until today's decision were never the part of any law. . . .

Today the Court retreats from the earlier formulations of the constitutional test and undertakes to make new definitions. This effort, like the earlier ones, is earnest and well intentioned. The difficulty is that we do not deal with constitutional terms, since "obscenity" is not mentioned in the Constitution or Bill of Rights. And the First Amendment makes no such exception from "the press" which it undertakes to protect nor, as I have said on other occasions, is an exception necessarily implied for there was no recognized exception to the free press at the time the Bill of Rights was adopted which treated "obscene" publications differently from other types of papers, magazines, and books. So there are no constitutional guidelines for deciding what is and what is not "obscene." The Court is at large because we deal with tastes and standards of literature. What shocks me may be sustenance for my neighbor. What causes one person to boil up in rage over one pamphlet or movie may reflect only his neurosis, not shared by others. We deal here with a regime of censorship which, if adopted, should be done by constitutional amendment after full debate by the people. . . .

We deal with highly emotional, not rational, questions. To many the Song of Solomon is obscene. I do not think we, the judges, were ever given the constitutional power to make definitions of obscenity. If it is to be defined, let the people debate and decide by a constitutional amendment what they want to ban as obscene and what standards they want the legislatures and the courts to apply. Perhaps the people will decide that the path towards a mature, integrated society requires that all ideas competing for acceptance must have no censor. Perhaps they will decide otherwise. Whatever the choice, the courts will have some guidelines. Now we have none except our own predilections.

MR. JUSTICE BRENNAN, with whom MR. JUSTICE STEWART and MR. JUSTICE MARSHALL join, dissenting.[10]

In the case before us, appellant was convicted of distributing obscene matter in violation of California Penal Code §311.2, on the basis of evidence that he had caused to be mailed unsolicited brochures advertising various books and a movie. I need not now decide whether a statute might be drawn to impose, within the requirements of the First Amendment, criminal penalties for the precise conduct at issue here. For it is clear that . . . the statute under which the prosecution was brought is unconstitutionally overbroad, and therefore invalid on its face.

The same day, the Court also handed down a decision in *Paris Adult Theatre I v. Slaton,* which involved a 1970 complaint filed by Atlanta, Georgia, against the Paris Adult Theatre. The complaint asserted that the theater was showing obscene films. During the trial, the judge viewed two of the offending films, which depicted simulated fellatio, cunnilingus, and group sexual intercourse. The judge ruled in favor of the theater, mainly because the owners limited admission to the theater to persons who were at least twenty-one years old. After the Georgia Supreme Court reversed, the owners appealed to the U.S. Supreme Court. The justices, however, affirmed the ruling, refusing to extend the theater First Amendment protection, even though only consenting adults could see the films.

Miller (and *Paris Adult Theatre I*) substantially changed the constitutional definition of obscenity. In Table 7-1 we compare the *Roth* test and its expansions with the new *Miller* standard. Although the Court retained three important elements of the *Roth* test—the adult standard, the work taken as a whole, and the restriction of obscenity to sexually oriented materials—two major changes stand out. First, the *Miller* test specifically gives the states the authority to define what is obscene. The Court, therefore, emphasized local values rather than the national standard suggested in *Jacobellis.* Second, the Court did away with the notion that a work merited protection as long as it did not meet the "utterly without redeeming social value" criterion. Instead, the justices held that to receive First Amendment protection, sexually oriented materials had to have serious literary, artistic,

---

10. *Authors' note:* Brennan filed a more pointed dissent in *Paris Adult Theatre I v. Slaton,* decided on the same day as *Miller.* See excerpt, page 354.

TABLE 7-1 *Roth-Jacobellis-Memoirs* and *Miller* Compared

	ROTH-JACOBELLIS-MEMOIRS (THE WARREN COURT)	*MILLER* (THE BURGER COURT)
Relevant audience	Average person	Average person
Scope of consideration	Work taken as a whole	Work taken as a whole
Standard	Sexual material found patently offensive by the national standards of society at large	Sexual conduct found patently offensive by contemporary community standards as specifically defined by applicable state law
Value of the work	Utterly without redeeming social importance	Lacks serious literary, artistic, political, or scientific value

political, or scientific value. As a consequence, the new *Miller* test permitted much greater regulation of sexually explicit materials than did the *Roth* standard.

In addition to the significant change in obscenity law ushered in by *Miller* and its companion case, *Paris Adult Theatre I*, liberals from the Warren Court era also noted the change in approach. Justice Brennan wrote in his dissenting opinion in *Paris Adult Theatre I*:

Our experience since *Roth* requires us not only to abandon the effort to pick out obscene materials on a case-by-case basis, but also to reconsider a fundamental postulate of *Roth*: that there exists a definable class of sexually oriented expression that may be totally suppressed by the Federal and State Governments. Assuming that such a class of expression does in fact exist, I am forced to conclude that the concept of "obscenity" cannot be defined with sufficient specificity and clarity to provide fair notice to persons who create and distribute sexually oriented materials, to prevent substantial erosion of protected speech as a by-product of the attempt to suppress unprotected speech, and to avoid very costly institutional harms. Given these inevitable side effects of state efforts to suppress what is assumed to be *unprotected* speech, we must scrutinize with care the state interest that is asserted to justify the suppression. For in the absence of some very substantial interest in suppressing such speech, we can hardly condone the ill effects that seem to flow inevitably from the effort. . . .

In short, while I cannot say that the interests of the State—apart from the question of juveniles and unconsenting adults—are trivial or nonexistent, I am compelled to conclude that these interests cannot justify the substantial damage to constitutional rights and to this Nation's judicial machinery that inevitably results from state efforts to bar the distribution even of unprotected material to consenting adults. . . . I would hold, therefore, that at least in the absence of distribution to juveniles or obtrusive exposure to unconsenting adults, the First and Fourteenth Amendments

prohibit the State and Federal Governments from attempting wholly to suppress sexually oriented materials on the basis of their allegedly "obscene" contents.

Brennan's opinion, which was joined by Justices Thurgood Marshall and Potter Stewart, is remarkable for three reasons. First, after almost two decades of leading the Court in attempts to define obscenity, the author of *Roth* finally decided that it could not be done. Second, the three liberals argued that efforts to regulate "obscene" material inevitably led to unacceptable restrictions on protected expression. Third, Brennan and the others concluded that state and federal authorities should be banned from regulating sexually oriented expression altogether, except to protect juveniles and unconsenting adults.

It would be difficult to imagine two more different positions than those taken by the majority and the dissenters in these obscenity cases, but they are alike in this respect: both sides wanted to extricate the Court from the obscenity business. Brennan and the other dissenters advocated an almost total end to government regulation of obscenity, while the *Miller* majority wanted to put an end to federal obscenity cases by shifting authority to the states.

Miller in Action: Children, Obscenity, and the Internet

The Warren Court's message to prosecutors had been that obscenity convictions would not stand, but the Nixon justices signaled encouragement. Law enforcement officials, state legislators, and prosecutors now recognized that they could enforce obscenity laws with some hope of obtaining solid convictions. And in the Supreme Court they were not wrong. Between 1957 and 1969—the heyday of the *Roth* test—the justices supported First Amendment claims in about 70 percent

BOX 7-5   ENFORCING OBSCENITY STATUTES

Controversies involving pornography mainly have centered on defining what is obscene, but legal battles also have been fought over the methods of enforcing antiobscenity statutes. Here we consider the weapons governments possess to combat obscenity.

Distribution. If a book, magazine, or film meets the legal definition of obscenity, the federal government has three types of laws to block its distribution. The first prohibits the importation of pornography. Customs officials may intercept shipments of obscene films and publications produced abroad and intended for U.S. distribution. The second prohibits the interstate shipment of obscene materials and allows federal officials to take legal action against individuals who transport materials across state lines to sell them. The third prohibits use of the U.S. mail to distribute obscene goods and brings federal postal officials into the fight against obscenity.

State authorities regulate local activities such as pornographic bookstores and adult movie theaters. Under the *Miller* test, states and localities have broad authority to define what is patently offensive and to enforce laws against selling obscene materials or commercially showing obscene films. Individuals who knowingly sell or otherwise distribute legally obscene materials may be prosecuted under state criminal laws or be subject to other state legal action.

Zoning. To combat the effects of adult theaters, nightclubs, and bookstores, local governments can use their zoning powers. In *City of Renton v. Playtime Theatres, Inc.* (1986) the Court examined the question of zoning restrictions on such establishments. Renton, Washington, had passed a zoning ordinance that prohibited adult theaters within a thousand feet of any residential area, church, school, or park. The Court upheld the ordinance in spite of arguments by the theater company that it constituted content-based discrimination. Because the ordinance did not prohibit adult theaters but only regulated their placement, the Court treated the law as a "time, place, or manner" restriction. The Court found that the law was not aimed at the content of the expression but was designed to control the secondary effects of such establishments on the surrounding community. This ruling strongly reinforces the authority of local governments to use their zoning powers to regulate for public decency.

Racketeering Statutes. As part of a strategy to combat obscenity, some jurisdictions have employed RICO (Racketeer Influenced and Corrupt Organizations) laws. RICO statutes are commonly used to prosecute organized crime and apply when a party engages in a demonstrable pattern of repeated criminal violations. RICO laws impose severe penalties, including seizures of property that may have been acquired with the profits from criminal acts. Some booksellers have alleged that the RICO laws place an unconstitutional burden on freedom of expression, that they force booksellers to practice self-censorship rather than risk prosecution. But in the case of *Fort Wayne Books, Inc. v. Indiana* (1989) the Court disagreed and upheld the authority of the state to use RICO laws to combat obscenity. It concluded that the "deterrence of the sale of obscene materials is a legitimate end of state anti-obscenity laws" and that the Constitution did not forbid enhancing penalties through the use of a RICO statute. It also rejected the chilling effect argument, holding, "The mere assertion of some possible self-censorship resulting from a statute is not enough to render an anti-obscenity law unconstitutional under our precedents."

Government Funding. The government also has dealt with the obscenity "problem" by withholding funds for material it deems obscene. Some funding decisions by the National Endowment for the Arts (NEA) came under intense public scrutiny because they were thought to support works of art that many in the public and Congress believed to be obscene. In response to the public outcry over these decisions, Congress in 1990 revised the NEA funding law to require the head of the agency to take into consideration "general standards of decency and respect for the diverse beliefs and values of the American public." So far, only one Supreme Court case has challenged the provision. In *National Endowment for the Arts v. Finley* (1998) the Court took up the issue of whether the government could set standards for public support that take into consideration factors that would be illegitimate in a regulatory statute. The 8–1 majority said that Congress has a "wide latitude to set spending priorities" and that the admonition to take decency and respect into account did not silence speakers by censoring their ideas.

of their obscenity decisions; that number dropped to 28 percent after *Miller*.[11] The Court did not side with government in every obscenity case it heard, but, as these percentages indicate, the shift in jurisprudence from *Roth* to *Miller* was significant.

On the other hand, if the justices in the majority in *Miller* thought that they could free the Court from obscenity cases by shifting from a national to a local focus, they were not completely correct. The number of cases dropped, but they did not disappear from the Court's docket. In fact, between 1974 and 2010 the Court decided thirty-seven cases touching on matters of obscenity and pornography.[12] Many of the early disputes centered on how far governments could go to combat traditional print materials and films that are legally obscene. In Box 7-5, we highlight some of the weapons government officials have deployed, along with the Court's reactions.

We devote the balance of this section to a question that has come to dominate the Court's obscenity docket: To what lengths may government go to protect children from obscenity and pornography? In the post-*Miller* era, state and federal governments have attempted to protect children from obscene—and perhaps legal, but sexually oriented—materials by *eliminating child pornography* and *minimizing children's access to such materials.*

Child Pornography

We begin with child pornography, a subject many now associate with the Internet, even though the Court first took it up years before use of the Web became widespread, in the important case of *New York v. Ferber* (1982).

New York v. Ferber

458 U.S. 747 (1982)
http://laws.findlaw.com/US/458/747.html
Oral arguments are available at http://www.oyez.org.
Vote: 9 (Blackmun, Brennan, Burger, Marshall, O'Connor,
    Powell, Rehnquist, Stevens, White)
    0

OPINION OF THE COURT: *White*

CONCURRING OPINIONS: *Brennan, O'Connor, Stevens*

---

11. Data are from the U.S. Supreme Court Judicial Database, http://supremecourtdatabase.org. The post-*Miller* data run through the 2010 term.

12. We calculated this figure from data available on the U.S. Supreme Court Judicial Database.

FACTS:

In efforts to combat the exploitation of children for the production of pornography, forty-seven states and the federal government passed various laws designed to curtail the production of child pornography. Twenty of the states (including New York) prohibited the distribution of material depicting children engaged in sexual conduct without requiring that the material be legally obscene.

Bookstore owner Paul Ferber was charged with violating this law when he sold two movies to an undercover police officer. The films were "devoted almost exclusively to depicting two young boys masturbating." In his defense, Ferber argued that the law "works serious and substantial violation of the First Amendment by measures and means unnecessary to accomplish its legislative objectives." State attorneys acknowledged the potential ramifications of closing an entire area to constitutional protection, but they suggested that the state had a compelling and overriding interest "in protecting children from sexual abuse."

ARGUMENTS:

For the petitioner, State of New York:

- The prohibition of all "material depicting children . . . engaged in sexual conduct" furthers the compelling state interest of protecting children from sexual abuse in the least restrictive manner possible.
- There is no effective alternative to protect children from sexual abuse short of prohibiting all materials regardless of whether they are legally obscene.

For the respondent, Paul Ira Ferber:

- By prohibiting material "regardless of whether it is obscene," the New York statute violates *Miller*'s holding that only sexually obscene material falls outside the protection of the First Amendment.
- The statute is overly broad and prohibits legitimate and socially valuable forms of expression, in addition to obscene material.

JUSTICE WHITE DELIVERED THE OPINION OF THE COURT.

At issue in this case is the constitutionality of a New York criminal statute which prohibits persons from knowingly promoting sexual performances by children under the age of 16 by distributing material which depicts such performances. . . .

In *Miller v. California* a majority of the Court agreed that a "state offense must . . . be limited to works which, taken as a whole, appeal to the prurient interest in sex, which portray sexual conduct in a patently offensive way, and which, taken as a whole, do not have serious literary, artistic, political, or scientific value." Over the past decade, we have adhered to the guidelines expressed in *Miller*, which subsequently has been followed in the regulatory schemes of most States.

The *Miller* standard, like its predecessors, was an accommodation between the State's interests in protecting the "sensibilities of unwilling recipients" from exposure to pornographic material and the dangers of censorship inherent in unabashedly content-based laws. Like obscenity statutes, laws directed at the dissemination of child pornography run the risk of suppressing protected expression by allowing the hand of the censor to become unduly heavy. For the following reasons, however, we are persuaded that the States are entitled to greater leeway in the regulation of pornographic depictions of children.

First. It is evident beyond the need for elaboration that a State's interest in "safeguarding the physical and psychological well-being of a minor" is "compelling." . . .

The prevention of sexual exploitation and abuse of children constitutes a government objective of surpassing importance. The legislative findings accompanying passage of the New York laws reflect this concern:

"[T]here has been a proliferation of exploitation of children as subjects in sexual performances. The care of children is a sacred trust and should not be abused by those who seek to profit through a commercial network based upon the exploitation of children. The public policy of the state demands the protection of children from exploitation through sexual performances."

We shall not second-guess this legislative judgment. Respondent has not intimated that we do so. Suffice it to say that virtually all of the States and the United States have passed legislation proscribing the production of or otherwise combating "child pornography." The legislative judgment, as well as the judgment found in the relevant literature, is that the use of children as subjects of pornographic materials is harmful to the physiological, emotional, and mental health of the child. That judgment, we think, easily passes muster under the First Amendment.

Second. The distribution of photographs and films depicting sexual activity by juveniles is intrinsically related to the sexual abuse of children in at least two ways. First, the materials produced are a permanent record of the children's participation and the harm to the child is exacerbated by their circulation. Second, the distribution network for child pornography must be closed if the production of material which requires the sexual exploitation of children is to be effectively controlled. Indeed, there is no serious contention that the legislature was unjustified in believing that it is difficult, if not impossible, to halt the exploitation of children by pursuing only those who produce the photographs and movies. While the production of pornographic materials is a low-profile, clandestine industry, the need to market the resulting products requires a visible apparatus of distribution. The most expeditious if not the only practical method of law enforcement may be to dry up the market for this material by imposing severe criminal penalties on persons selling, advertising, or otherwise promoting the product. Thirty-five States and Congress have concluded that restraints on the distribution of pornographic materials are required in order to effectively combat the problem, and there is a body of literature and testimony to support these legislative conclusions.

Respondent does not contend that the State is unjustified in pursuing those who distribute child pornography. Rather, he argues that it is enough for the State to prohibit the distribution of materials that are legally obscene under the *Miller* test. While some States may find that this approach properly accommodates its interests, it does not follow that the First Amendment prohibits a State from going further. The *Miller* standard, like all general definitions of what may be banned as obscene, does not reflect the State's particular and more compelling interest in prosecuting those who promote the sexual exploitation of children. Thus, the question under the *Miller* test of whether a work, taken as a whole, appeals to the prurient interest of the average person bears no connection to the issue of whether a child has been physically or psychologically harmed in the production of the work. Similarly, a sexually explicit depiction need not be "patently offensive" in order to have required the sexual exploitation of a child for its production. In addition, a work which, taken on the whole, contains serious literary, artistic, political, or scientific value may nevertheless embody the hardest core of child pornography. "It is irrelevant to the child [who has been abused] whether or not the material . . . has a literary, artistic, political, or social value." We therefore cannot conclude that the *Miller* standard is a satisfactory solution to the child pornography problem.

Third. The advertising and selling of child pornography provide an economic motive for and are thus an integral part of the production of such materials, an activity illegal throughout the Nation. "It rarely has been suggested that the constitutional freedom for speech and press extends its immunity to speech or writing used as an integral part of conduct in violation of a valid criminal statute." We note that were the statutes outlawing the employment of children in these films and photographs fully effective, and the constitutionality of these laws has not been questioned, the First Amendment implications would be no greater than that presented by laws against distribution: enforceable production laws would leave no child pornography to be marketed.

Fourth. The value of permitting live performances and photographic reproductions of children engaged in lewd sexual conduct is exceedingly modest, if not *de minimis.* We consider it unlikely that visual depictions of children performing sexual acts or lewdly exhibiting their genitals would often constitute an important and necessary part of a literary performance or scientific or educational work. As a state judge in this case observed, if it were necessary for literary or artistic value, a person over the statutory age who perhaps looked younger could be utilized. Simulation outside of the prohibition of the statute could provide another alternative. Nor is there any question here of censoring a particular literary theme or portrayal of sexual activity. The First Amendment interest is limited to that of rendering the portrayal somewhat more "realistic" by utilizing or photographing children.

Fifth. Recognizing and classifying child pornography as a category of material outside the protection of the First Amendment is not incompatible with our earlier decisions. . . .

There are, of course, limits on the category of child pornography which, like obscenity, is unprotected by the First Amendment. As with all legislation in this sensitive area, the conduct to be prohibited must be adequately defined by the applicable state law, as written or authoritatively construed. Here the nature of the harm to be combated requires that the state offense be limited to works that *visually* depict sexual conduct by children below a specified age. The category of "sexual conduct" proscribed must also be suitably limited and described.

The test for child pornography is separate from the obscenity standard enunciated in *Miller,* but may be compared to it for the purpose of clarity. The *Miller* formulation is adjusted in the following respects: A trier of fact need not find that the material appeals to the prurient interest of the average person; it is not required that sexual conduct portrayed be done so in a patently offensive manner; and the material at issue need not be considered as a whole. We note that the distribution of descriptions or other depictions of sexual conduct, not otherwise obscene, which do not involve live performance or photographic or other visual reproduction of live performances, retains First Amendment protection. As with obscenity laws, criminal responsibility may not be imposed without some element of scienter on the part of the defendant. . . .

Judgment is reversed and the case remanded.

JUSTICE BRENNAN, with whom JUSTICE MARSHALL JOINS, concurring in the judgment.

I agree with much of what is said in the Court's opinion. As I made clear in the opinion I delivered for the Court in *Ginsberg v. New York* (1968), the State has a special interest in protecting the well-being of its youth. This special and compelling interest, and the particular vulnerability of children, afford the State the leeway to regulate pornographic material, the promotion of which is harmful to children, even though the State does not have such leeway when it seeks only to protect consenting adults from exposure to such material. . . .

But, in my view, application of [the New York law] or any similar statute to depictions of children that, in themselves, do have serious literary, artistic, scientific, or medical value would violate the First Amendment. As the Court recognizes, the limited classes of speech the suppression of which does not raise serious First Amendment concerns have two attributes. They are of exceedingly "slight social value," and the State has a compelling interest in their regulation. The First Amendment value of depictions of children that are, in themselves, serious contributions to art, literature, or science is, by definition, simply not "*de minimis.*" At the same time, the State's interest in suppression of such materials is likely to be far less compelling. For the Court's assumption of harm to the child resulting from the "permanent record" and "circulation" of the child's "participation," lacks much of its force where the depiction is a serious contribution to art or science. The production of materials of serious value is not the "low profile, clandestine industry" that, according to the Court, produces purely pornographic materials. In short, it is inconceivable how a depiction of a child that is itself a serious contribution to the world of art or literature or science can be deemed "material outside the protection of the First Amendment."

I, of course, adhere to my view that, in the absence of exposure, or particular harm, to juveniles or unconsenting adults, the State lacks power to suppress sexually oriented materials. See, *e.g., Paris Adult Theatre I v. Slaton* (1973) (BRENNAN, J., dissenting). With this understanding, I concur in the Court's judgment in this case.

Child pornography hit a nerve with the Court: even the most liberal justices agreed with the *Ferber* resolution. But *Ferber* concerned film, a rather traditional medium. What about the use of the newer medium of the Internet for the spread of child pornography and other types of obscenity? Few would contest that the Internet can provide easy access to materials that constitute child pornography.[13] An online search on as innocent a word as "dollhouse" could yield hits to scores of pornographic sites. Accordingly, many groups pressured Congress and the states to regulate expression on the Internet, often with controversial results. Lawmakers responded with legislation designed to curtail the electronic dissemination of sexually explicit images of children or that appear to be of children.[14] Opponents of these laws contended that, however well-intentioned, they restricted legitimate and protected expression. Indeed, the passage of each state or federal law limiting expression on the Internet was met with immediate legal challenges. Newly formed organizations devoted to keeping the Internet free from regulation joined with traditional civil liberties groups, such as the ACLU, to attack these restrictions as violations of the First Amendment.

In the next chapter we provide a detailed look at how the Court has dealt with efforts to regulate various forms of expression on the Internet. For now, it is worth noting that the justices have given Congress some (but not complete) leeway in regulating the electronic dissemination of child pornography. In *United States v. Williams* (2008) *(excerpted on pages 380–384),* for example, they upheld a law that prohibited anyone from knowingly advertising, promoting, presenting,

distributing, or soliciting "any material or purported material that reflects the belief, or that is intended to cause another to believe, that the material or purported material" contains illegal child pornography. Writing for the Court, Justice Scalia noted, "The statute's definition of the material or purported material that may not be pandered or solicited precisely tracks the material held constitutionally proscribable in *Ferber* and *Miller*: obscene material depicting (actual or virtual) children engaged in sexually explicit conduct, and any other material depicting actual children engaged in sexually explicit conduct."

Shielding Children from Access to Sexually Explicit Material

The government's efforts to control the dissemination of child pornography—whether via traditional or new media—represent only one side of the equation. The other is the government's attempts to prevent children from gaining *access* to sexually explicit material.

These are not new efforts. In the 1968 case of *Ginsberg v. New York,* the Court heard a challenge to a New York law that made it illegal to sell to a minor under the age of seventeen any picture "which depicts nudity . . . and which is harmful to minors," and "any . . . magazine . . . which contains [such pictures] and which, taken as a whole, is harmful to minors." Even though the material would not have been classified as obscene for adults, the Court upheld the law. It reasoned that the "well-being of its children is of course a subject within the State's constitutional power to regulate," and that law advanced two interests relating to the state's power:

First of all, constitutional interpretation has consistently recognized that the parents' claim to authority in their own household to direct the rearing of their children is basic in the structure of our society. . . . The legislature could properly conclude that parents and others, teachers for example, who have this primary responsibility for children's well-being are entitled to the support of laws designed to aid discharge of that responsibility. . . . Moreover, the prohibition against sales to minors does not bar parents who so desire from purchasing the magazines for their children.

[Next] the State . . . has an independent interest in the well-being of its youth. "While the supervision of children's reading may best be left to their parents, the knowledge that parental control or guidance cannot always be provided and society's transcendent interest in protecting the welfare of children justify reasonable regulation of the sale of material to them."

---

13. Recent polls indicate that obscenity on the Internet is a concern of more than 80 percent of Americans.

14. They also responded with legislation designed to curtail electronic dissemination of sexually oriented material that is inappropriate for children to view. We consider these laws in the next section, as well as in Chapter 8.

As we shall see, the State of California made use of *Ginsberg* in its (unsuccessful) attempt to convince the Court to uphold its law prohibiting the sale of violent video games to minors.

Ginsberg was not the only early case touching on access to sexually explicit material. In fact, in response to two Court decisions in the 1960s holding that nothing in the Constitution necessarily prohibited state or local governments from requiring film exhibitors to submit films before showing them commercially, the Motion Picture Association of America and the International Film Importers and Distributors of America devised a system for rating and labeling movies.[15] The industry informs the public of the "general suitability" of a film by assigning it one of the following ratings:

G: General Audiences (all ages admitted)
PG: Parental Guidance Suggested (some material may not be suitable for children)
PG-13: Parents Strongly Cautioned (some material may be inappropriate for children under 13)
R: Restricted (children under 17 require accompanying parent or adult guardian)
NC-17: No One 17 and Under Admitted[16]

This system of voluntary rating has been successful: state and local governments have generally deferred to the ratings system and ceased their prior submission programs. The film industry is more comfortable with self-regulation than with the scrutiny of state and local censorship boards. The system has worked so well that the recording industry, pressured by criticism from various parent groups about explicit lyrics, developed a voluntary labeling system to avoid government regulation, as did the television industry *(see Box 7-6)*. The producers of video games followed suit, but their ratings system did not stop several states from passing laws that prohibited the sale of violent video games to minors. In *Brown v. Entertainment Merchants Association* (2011), however, the Supreme Court invalidated these laws as violations of the First Amendment, as we shall see at the end of the chapter.

Regulating children's access to sexually explicit material on the Internet has also moved to the fore.

Perhaps because there is no one association that speaks for (and can regulate) the entire Web, Congress has stepped in. Over the last decade or so, it has enacted two kinds of laws. One type, represented by the Communications Decency Act of 1996 (CDA) and the Child Online Protection Act of 1998 (COPA, sometimes called CDA II), generally attempts to regulate the transmission of certain kinds of material or messages to people under the age of eighteen. The second type involves the use of filtering devices to block minors from viewing certain material. Because we consider both in Chapter 8, suffice it to note here that laws falling into the first category have received a somewhat unenthusiastic reception in the Court, but the justices have been more open to the second type of regulation. In the next chapter, we explore explanations for the differences in treatment.

Reframing the Obscenity Debate

Clearly, the Burger and Rehnquist Courts' efforts to end the obscenity battle were not a complete success. The questions of what constitutes obscenity, to what degree the dissemination of sexually explicit materials merits constitutional protection, and what weapons governments may use to combat such materials—not to mention the multitude of challenges raised by the tremendous growth of the Internet—remain stubbornly difficult to resolve. Yet the Court's basic approach to resolving them stayed the same: as we now know, since *Roth* the justices have viewed obscenity as largely a First Amendment question.

For decades now, however, groups of feminist scholars have been trying to frame the matter in different terms.[17] The issue of obscenity, they argue, should not focus on the rights of the author, producer, or distributor. Instead, society should look at the negative impacts pornographic materials have on women. Sexually explicit material does not merit First Amendment protection if it objectifies and demeans women. It is discriminatory on the basis of sex. According to this argument, the courts should view obscenity as a sexual equality issue, not a freedom of expression question.

---

15. The two cases were ***Times Film Corporation v. Chicago*** (1961) and ***Freedman v. Maryland*** (1965).

16. Originally, NC-17 was the X rating.

17. See, for example, Catharine MacKinnon, *Only Words* (Cambridge, MA: Harvard University Press, 1993). Not all feminists subscribe to MacKinnon's position, as Nadine Strossen makes clear in her *Defending Pornography: Free Speech, Sex, and the Fight for Women's Rights* (New York: New York University Press, 2000).

BOX 7-6 INDUSTRY WARNING LABELS

Recording Industry

In a move designed to head off government regulation, in May 1990 the recording industry introduced a uniform, voluntary warning label to go on recordings that have explicit lyrics.

Whether to apply the label, which reads "Parental Advisory—Explicit Lyrics," was at the discretion of record companies and individual artists. The system was intended to alert consumers to recordings that could be deemed objectionable because of explicit lyrics dealing with sex, violence, suicide, and substance abuse.

Television

In December 1996 the television industry, under heavy public pressure, also adopted a ratings system. The following is a summary of the seven categories now in use:

Y: All Children. This program is designed to be appropriate for all children.

Y-7: Directed to Older Children. This program is designed for children age 7 and above.

Y7-FV: Directed to Older Children—Fantasy Violence.

TV-G: General Audience. Most parents would find this program suitable for all ages.

TV-PG: Parental Guidance Suggested. This program contains material that parents may find unsuitable for younger children.

TV-14: Parents Strongly Cautioned. This program contains some material that many parents would find unsuitable for children under 14 years of age.

TV-M: Mature Audience Only. This program is specifically designed to be viewed by adults and therefore may be unsuitable for children under 17.

Computer and Video Games

In 1994 the major association representing companies that publish computer and video games created the Entertainment Software Rating Board to rate computer and video game content using the following system:

Early childhood: Content may be suitable for ages 3 and older.

Everyone: Content may be suitable for ages 6 and older.

Everyone 10+: Content may be suitable for ages 10 and older.

Teen: Content may be suitable for ages 13 and older.

Mature: Content may be suitable for ages 17 and older.

Adults only: Content should only be played by persons 18 years and older.

Adopting this view would allow government to regulate sexually oriented materials as part of an effort to bring about greater equality between the sexes. Support for this position divides the liberal community, which traditionally has fought to defeat conservative efforts to restrict freedom of expression—including recent efforts to regulate the Internet.

So far the Supreme Court has seen only one case that framed obscenity as an issue of sexual equality. *American Booksellers Association, Inc. v. Hudnut* (1986) concerned an Indianapolis ordinance that, in accord with a model statute offered by feminist scholars, defined pornography as "the graphic sexually explicit subordination of women." The U.S. Court of Appeals for the Seventh Circuit ruled the ordinance unconstitutional, and the Supreme Court summarily agreed. The court of appeals reasoned as follows:

The Indianapolis ordinance does not refer to the prurient interest, the offensiveness, or to the standards of the community. It demands attention to particular depictions, not to the work judged as a whole. It is irrelevant under the ordinance whether the work has literary, artistic, political, or scientific value....

We do not try to balance the arguments for and against an ordinance such as this. The ordinance discriminates on the ground of the content of speech. Speech treating women in the approved way—in sexual encounters "premised on equality"—is lawful no matter how sexually explicit. Speech treating women in the disapproved way—as submissive in matters sexual or as enjoying humiliation—is unlawful no matter how significant the literary, artistic, or political qualities of the work taken as a whole. The state may not ordain preferred viewpoints in this way. The Constitution forbids the state to declare one perspective right and silence opponents.

Because the Court did not issue an opinion on the merits in this dispute, we can say that it continues to treat obscenity as a First Amendment issue, not as a matter of sexual equality. In contrast, in 1992 the Supreme Court of Canada essentially adopted the approach urged by feminist groups there and in the United States. In the eyes of that court, "The message of obscenity which degrades and dehumanizes is analogous to that of hate propaganda."

Free speech advocates have criticized the Canadian court's decision, and some feminists have applauded it. As such, the debate over the reframing of obscenity provides an interesting example of a point we made in the introduction to this section of the book: that traditional definitions of the terms *liberal* and *conservative* are perhaps becoming less useful, particularly in the First Amendment context.

CRUELTY AND VIOLENCE

Perhaps the same could be said about the Court's most recent forays into First Amendment boundaries. In two cases, **United States v. Stevens** (2010) and *Brown v. Entertainment Merchants Association* (2011), the justices of the Roberts Court considered arguments by the federal and state governments to prohibit certain kinds of seemingly distasteful expression in the name of protecting vulnerable interests—in *Stevens* the sale of videos depicting cruelty to animals and in *Brown* the sale of violent video games to children. That is, the government asked the Court to treat these relatively new forms of expression as it does obscenity and place them beyond full First Amendment protection. In both cases, the justices declined.

Stevens involved a 1999 federal law that criminalized the commercial creation, sale, or possession of certain depictions of animal cruelty. The statute addressed only portrayals of harmful acts, not the underlying conduct. It applied to any visual or auditory depiction "in which a living animal is intentionally maimed, mutilated, tortured, wounded, or killed," if that conduct violates federal or state law where "the creation, sale, or possession takes place." Another clause,

following from the Court's obscenity cases, exempted depictions with "serious religious, political, scientific, educational, journalistic, historical, or artistic value."

In debating the law, Congress focused primarily on "crush videos," which feature the torture and killing of helpless animals.[18] Moreover, because he was concerned about its constitutionality under the First Amendment, President Clinton, when he signed the law, told the Justice Department to focus on "wanton cruelty to animals designed to appeal to a prurient interest in sex." According to the president of the Humane Society of the United States, this had the effect of "almost immediately dr[ying] up the crush video industry."

Prosecutions continued, however, mostly against those compiling or selling videos depicting dogfights. Robert Stevens was among those indicted, and upon conviction he was sentenced to thirty-seven months in prison. Stevens argued that the law violated his free speech rights under the First Amendment. The government responded with a proposed balancing test to determine whether the First Amendment applies to a particular form of expression: "Whether a given category of speech enjoys First Amendment protection depends upon a categorical balancing of the value of the speech against its societal costs." Because depictions of "illegal acts of animal cruelty" necessarily "lack expressive value," the government reasoned that they should "be regulated as *unprotected* speech." In other words, depictions of animal cruelty should be added to the list of types of unprotected expression that, as we know, includes libel and obscenity (along with other categories described in Chapter 5, such as incitement).

In an 8–1 decision (with Justice Alito dissenting), the Court rejected the government's claims. Writing for the majority, Chief Justice Roberts began by skewering the government's proposed balancing test:

When we have identified categories of speech as fully outside the protection of the First Amendment, it has not been on the basis of a simple cost-benefit analysis. In [*New York v.*] *Ferber* [1982], for example, we classified child pornography as such a category. We noted that the State of New York had a compelling interest in protecting children from abuse, and

---

18. We derive the information in this paragraph from Adam Liptak, "Justices Reject Ban on Videos of Animal Cruelty," *New York Times*, April 20, 2010, A1.

that the value of using children in these works (as opposed to simulated conduct or adult actors) was *de minimis*. But our decision did not rest on this "balance of competing interests" alone. We made clear that *Ferber* presented a special case: The market for child pornography was "intrinsically related" to the underlying abuse, and was therefore "an integral part of the production of such materials, an activity illegal throughout the Nation."

Our decisions in *Ferber* and other cases cannot be taken as establishing a freewheeling authority to declare new categories of speech outside the scope of the First Amendment. Maybe there are some categories of speech that have been historically unprotected, but have not yet been specifically identified or discussed as such in our case law. But if so, there is no evidence that "depictions of animal cruelty" is among them. We need not foreclose the future recognition of such additional categories to reject the Government's highly manipulable balancing test as a means of identifying them.

Roberts went on to invalidate the statute based on existing First Amendment doctrine. In particular, he found that the law, as it was written, was "alarming" in its breadth *(see Chapter 5)*. He provided the following example:

In the District of Columbia . . . all hunting is unlawful. Other jurisdictions permit or encourage hunting, and there is an enormous national market for hunting-related depictions in which a living animal is intentionally killed. Hunting periodicals have circulations in the hundreds of thousands or millions. . . . Nonetheless, because the statute allows each jurisdiction to export its laws to the rest of the country, [the law] extends to *any* magazine or video depicting lawful hunting, so long as that depiction is sold within the Nation's Capital.

The chief justice did leave open the possibility that a new law limited to extreme animal cruelty or crush videos, which seemed to be the government's priorities, could pass constitutional muster.

In some ways, *Brown v. Entertainment Merchants Association,* excerpted below, is a broader decision. Not only did the Court reject the state of California's request to remove the sale of violent video games to minors from First Amendment protection, the majority informed the state that all laws prohibiting the sale of such games would be subject to strict scrutiny (meaning that they could be very unlikely to survive; see Chapter 5). Why? And why did Justice Alito's concurring opinion, not to mention the dissenters' commentary, take issue with this approach?

Brown v. Entertainment Merchants Association

564 U.S. ___ (2011)
http://laws.findlaw.com/us/000/08-1448.html
Oral arguments are available at http://www.oyez.org.
Vote: 7 (Alito, Ginsburg, Kagan, Kennedy, Roberts, Scalia, Sotomayor)
    2 (Breyer, Thomas)
OPINION OF THE COURT: *Scalia*
CONCURRING OPINION: *Alito*

FACTS:

In 2005 the California assembly passed Bill 1179, prohibiting the sale of violent video games to minors and requiring such games to be appropriately labeled. The act was designed to aid parents in restricting their children's access to increasingly gruesome video games. The legislative goals were to prevent violent, aggressive, and antisocial behavior, and to prevent psychological or neurological harm to minors who play violent video games. The legislature relied on social scientific studies that reported a link between playing violent video games and an increase in aggressive thoughts and behavior, antisocial behavior, and a desensitization to violence. Violators of the law were subject to a $1,000 fine for each count.

Borrowing directly from the Supreme Court's obscenity precedents, the statute defined violent video games as those games in which "the range of options available to a player includes killing, maiming, dismembering, or sexually assaulting an image of a human being, if those acts are depicted in a manner that a reasonable person, considering the game as a whole, would find appeals to a deviant or morbid interest of minors, that is patently offensive to prevailing standards in the community as to what is suitable for minors, and that causes the game, as a whole to lack serious literary, artistic, political, or scientific value for minors." Also coming under the provisions of this law were games that enable a player virtually to inflict serious injury upon images of human beings or characters with substantially human characteristics in a manner that is especially heinous, cruel, or depraved in that it involves torture or serious physical abuse to the victim.

The Entertainment Merchants Association, a not-for-profit international trade association dedicated to advancing the interests of the home entertainment industry, filed suit against the state in the name of the governor claiming that Bill 1179 violated the freedom of speech clause of the First Amendment. The federal district court struck down the law, and the U.S. Court of Appeals for the Ninth Circuit affirmed.

ARGUMENTS:

For the petitioner, Edmund G. Brown, Jr., Governor of the State of California:

- In *Ginsberg v. New York* (1968), the Court held that states may properly restrict minors' access to sexually explicit material that is fully protected as to adults because the law helped parents to discharge their responsibility and because of the government's "independent interest in the well-being of its youth." There is no sound basis in logic or policy for treating offensively violent, harmful material with no redeeming value for children any differently from sexually explicit material.

- The state has a vital interest in reinforcing parents' authority to direct the upbringing of children in order to protect their physical and psychological welfare, as well as their ethical and moral development, thus restrictions on minors' access to offensively violent material are constitutionally permissible.

- The law also serves to eliminate the perceived societal approval of minors purchasing and playing offensively violent video games—a distinct harm to the development of minors. Modern social science shows that consumption of video games is significantly linked to increases in aggressive behavior.

For the respondent, Entertainment Merchants Association

- The California law is the latest in a long history of overreactions to new expressive media. In the past, comic books, true-crime novels, movies, rock music, and other new media have all been accused of harming our youth. In each case, the perceived threat later proved unfounded. Video games are no different. They are a widely popular form of expression enjoyed by millions of people. As such, under the First Amendment, they cannot be censored absent the most compelling justification.

- California argues that "offensively violent" video games should be placed outside the protection of the First Amendment, at least as to minors. The Court recently rejected a similar argument in *United States v. Stevens* (2010), emphatically refusing the government's proposal that it should use a balancing test to decide whether portrayals of animal cruelty are constitutionally unprotected.

- Nothing in *Ginsberg* or the Court's school speech or broadcasting cases supports California's sweeping argument for a new category of unprotected speech subject to content-based censorship. Unlike the explicit sexuality at issue in *Ginsberg,* violence is not and never has been a taboo subject for children.

⬤ JUSTICE SCALIA DELIVERED THE OPINION OF THE COURT.

California correctly acknowledges that video games qualify for First Amendment protection. The Free Speech Clause exists principally to protect discourse on public matters, but we have long recognized that it is difficult to distinguish politics from entertainment, and dangerous to try. . . . Like the protected books, plays, and movies that preceded them, video games communicate ideas—and even social messages—through many familiar literary devices (such as characters, dialogue, plot, and music) and through features distinctive to the medium (such as the player's interaction with the virtual world). That suffices to confer First Amendment protection. Under our Constitution, "esthetic and moral judgments about art and literature . . . are for the individual to make, not for the Government to decree, even with the mandate or approval of a majority." *United States v. Playboy Entertainment Group, Inc.* (2000). And whatever the challenges of applying the Constitution to ever-advancing technology, "the basic principles of freedom of speech and the press, like the First Amendment's command, do not vary" when a new and different medium for communication appears.

The most basic of those principles is this: "[A]s a general matter, . . . government has no power to restrict expression because of its message, its ideas, its subject matter, or its content." *Ashcroft v. American Civil Liberties Union* (2002). There are of course exceptions. "'From 1791 to the present,' . . . the First Amendment has 'permitted restrictions upon the content of speech in a few limited areas,' and has never 'include[d] a freedom to disregard these traditional limitations.'" *United States v. Stevens* (2010). These limited areas—such as obscenity, *Roth v. United States* (1957), incitement, *Brandenburg v. Ohio* (1969), and fighting words, *Chaplinsky v. New Hampshire* (1942)—represent "well-defined and narrowly limited classes of speech, the prevention and punishment of which have never been thought to raise any Constitutional problem."

Last Term, in *Stevens,* we held that new categories of unprotected speech may not be added to the list by a legislature that concludes certain speech is too harmful to be tolerated. *Stevens* concerned a federal statute purporting to criminalize the creation, sale, or possession of certain depictions of animal cruelty. The statute covered depictions "in which a living animal is intentionally maimed, mutilated, tortured, wounded, or killed" if that harm to the animal was illegal where the "the creation, sale, or possession t[ook] place." A saving clause largely borrowed from our obscenity jurisprudence, see *Miller v. California* (1973), exempted depictions with "serious religious, political, scientific, educational, journalistic, historical, or artistic value." We held that statute to be an impermissible content-based restriction on speech. There was no American tradition of forbidding the *depiction of* animal cruelty—though States have long had laws against *committing* it.

The Government argued in *Stevens* that lack of a historical warrant did not matter; that it could create new categories of unprotected speech by applying a "simple balancing test" that weighs the value of a particular category of speech against its social costs and then punishes that category of speech if it fails the test. We emphatically rejected that "startling and dangerous" proposition. . . . [W]ithout persuasive evidence that a novel restriction on content is part of a long (if heretofore unrecognized) tradition of proscription, a legislature may not revise the "judgment [of] the American people," embodied in the First Amendment, "that the benefits of its restrictions on the Government outweigh the costs."

That holding controls this case. As in *Stevens,* California has tried to make violent-speech regulation look like obscenity regulation by appending a saving clause required for the latter. That does not suffice. Our cases have been clear that the obscenity exception to the First Amendment does not cover whatever a legislature finds shocking, but only depictions of "sexual conduct," *Miller.* . . .

. . . California . . . wishes to create a wholly new category of content-based regulation that is permissible only for speech directed at children.

That is unprecedented and mistaken. "[M]inors are entitled to a significant measure of First Amendment protection, and only in relatively narrow and well-defined circumstances may government bar public dissemination of protected materials to them." No doubt a State possesses legitimate power to protect children from harm, *Ginsberg* [v. *New York*, 1968], but that does not include a free-floating power to restrict the ideas to which children may be exposed. "Speech that is neither obscene as to youths nor subject to some other legitimate proscription cannot be suppressed solely to protect the young from ideas or images that a legislative body thinks unsuitable for them."

California's argument would fare better if there were a longstanding tradition in this country of specially restricting children's access to depictions of violence, but there is none. Certainly the *books* we give children to read—or read to them when they are younger—contain no shortage of gore. Grimm's Fairy Tales, for example, are grim indeed. As her just deserts for trying to poison Snow White, the wicked queen is made to dance in red hot slippers "till she fell dead on the floor, a sad example of envy and jealousy." Cinderella's evil stepsisters have their eyes pecked out by doves. And Hansel and Gretel (children!) kill their captor by baking her in an oven.

High-school reading lists are full of similar fare. Homer's Odysseus blinds Polyphemus the Cyclops by grinding out his eye with a heated stake. In the *Inferno,* Dante and Virgil watch corrupt politicians struggle to stay submerged beneath a lake of boiling pitch, lest they be skewered by devils above the surface. And Golding's *Lord of the Flies* recounts how a schoolboy called Piggy is savagely murdered *by other children* while marooned on an island. . . .

California claims that video games present special problems because they are "interactive," in that the player participates in the violent action on screen and determines its outcome. The latter feature is nothing new: Since at least the publication of *The Adventures of You: Sugarcane Island* in 1969, young readers of choose-your-own-adventure stories have been able to make decisions that determine the plot by following instructions about which page to turn to. As for the argument that video games enable participation in the violent action, that seems to us more a matter of degree than of kind. . . .

Because the Act imposes a restriction on the content of protected speech, it is invalid unless California can demonstrate that it passes strict scrutiny—that is, unless it is justified by a compelling government interest and is narrowly drawn to serve that interest. The State must specifically identify an "actual problem" in need of solving, and the curtailment of free speech must be actually necessary to the solution. That is a demanding standard. "It is rare that a regulation restricting speech because of its content will ever be permissible."

California cannot meet that standard. At the outset, it acknowledges that it cannot show a direct causal link between violent video games and harm to minors. Rather, relying upon our decision in *Turner Broadcasting System, Inc. v. FCC* (1994), the State claims that it need not produce such proof because the legislature can make a predictive judgment that such a link exists, based on competing psychological studies. But reliance on *Turner Broadcasting* is misplaced. That decision applied *intermediate scrutiny* to a content-neutral regulation. California's burden is much higher, and because it bears the risk of uncertainty, ambiguous proof will not suffice.

The State's evidence is not compelling. California relies primarily on the research of Dr. Craig Anderson and a few other research psychologists whose studies purport to show a connection between exposure to violent video games and harmful effects on children. These studies have been rejected by every court to consider them, and with good reason: They do not prove that violent video games *cause* minors to *act* aggressively (which would at least be a beginning). Instead, "[n]early all of the research is based on correlation, not evidence of causation, and most of the studies suffer from significant, admitted flaws in methodology." They show at best some correlation between exposure to violent entertainment and minuscule real-world effects, such as children's feeling more aggressive or making louder noises in the few minutes after playing a violent game than after playing a nonviolent game.

Even taking for granted Dr. Anderson's conclusions that violent video games produce some effect on children's feelings of aggression, those effects are both small and indistinguishable from effects produced by other media. . . .

Of course, California has (wisely) declined to restrict Saturday morning cartoons, the sale of games rated for young children, or the distribution of pictures of guns. The consequence is that its regulation is wildly underinclusive when judged against its asserted justification, which in our view is alone enough to defeat it. Underinclusiveness raises serious doubts about whether the government is in fact pursuing the interest it invokes, rather than disfavoring a particular speaker or viewpoint. Here, California has singled out the purveyors of video games for disfavored treatment—at least when compared to booksellers, cartoonists, and movie producers—and has given no persuasive reason why.

The Act is also seriously underinclusive in another respect—and a respect that renders irrelevant the contentions of the concurrence and the dissents that video games are qualitatively different from other portrayals of violence. The California Legislature is perfectly willing to leave this dangerous, mind-altering material in the hands of children so long as one parent (or even an aunt or uncle) says it's OK. And there are not even any requirements as to how this parental or avuncular relationship is to be verified; apparently the child's or putative parent's, aunt's, or uncle's say-so suffices. That is not how one addresses a serious social problem. . . .

. . . California cannot show that the Act's restrictions meet a substantial need of parents who wish to restrict their children's access to violent video games but cannot do so. The video-game industry has in place a voluntary rating system designed to inform consumers about the content of games. . . . This system does much to ensure that minors cannot purchase seriously violent games on their own, and that parents who care about the matter can readily evaluate the games their children bring home. Filling the remaining modest gap in concerned-parents' control can hardly be a compelling state interest.

And finally, the Act's purported aid to parental authority is vastly overinclusive. Not all of the children who are forbidden to purchase violent video games on their own have parents who care whether they purchase violent video games. While some of the legislation's effect may indeed be in support of what some parents of the restricted children actually want, its entire effect is only in support of what the State thinks parents *ought* to want. This is not the narrow tailoring to "assisting parents" that restriction of First Amendment rights requires.

California's effort to regulate violent video games is the latest episode in a long series of failed attempts to censor violent entertainment for minors. While we have pointed out above that some of the evidence brought forward to support the harmfulness of video games is unpersuasive, we do not mean to demean or disparage the concerns that underlie the attempt to regulate them—concerns that may and doubtless do prompt a good deal of parental oversight. We have no business passing judgment on the view of the California Legislature that violent video games (or, for that matter, any other forms of speech) corrupt the young or harm their moral development. Our task is only to say whether or not such works constitute a "well-defined and narrowly limited clas[s] of speech, the prevention and punishment of which have never been thought to raise any Constitutional problem," *Chaplinsky* (the answer plainly is no); and if not, whether the regulation of such works is justified by that high degree of necessity we have described as a compelling state interest (it is not). Even where the protection of children is the object, the constitutional limits on governmental action apply. . . .

We affirm the judgment below.

It is so ordered.

JUSTICE ALITO, with whom THE CHIEF JUSTICE joins, concurring in the judgment.

. . . Although the California statute is well intentioned, its terms are not framed with the precision that the Constitution demands, and I therefore agree with the Court that this particular law cannot be sustained.

I disagree, however, with the approach taken in the Court's opinion. In considering the application of unchanging constitutional principles to new and rapidly evolving technology, this Court should proceed with caution. We should make every effort to understand the new technology. We should take into account the possibility that developing technology may have important societal implications that will become apparent only with time. We should not jump to the conclusion that new technology is fundamentally the same as some older thing with which we are familiar. And we should not hastily dismiss the judgment of legislators, who may be in a better position than we are to assess the implications of new technology. The opinion of the Court exhibits none of this caution. . . .

Respondents in this case, representing the video-game industry, ask us to strike down the California law on two grounds: The broad ground adopted by the Court and the narrower ground that the law's definition of "violent video game" is impermissibly vague. Because I agree with the latter argument, I see no need to reach the broader First Amendment issues addressed by the Court.

. . . Vague laws force potential speakers to "'steer far wider of the unlawful zone' . . . than if the boundaries of the forbidden areas were clearly marked." While "perfect clarity and precise guidance have never been required even of regulations that restrict expressive activity," *Ward v. Rock Against Racism* (1989), "government may regulate in the area" of First Amendment freedoms "only with narrow specificity," *NAACP v. Button* [1963]. These principles apply to laws that regulate expression for the purpose of protecting children. . . .

Here, the California law does not define "violent video games" with the "narrow specificity" that the

Constitution demands. In an effort to avoid First Amendment problems, the California Legislature modeled its violent video game statute on the New York law that this Court upheld in *Ginsberg v. New York* (1968)—a law that prohibited the sale of certain sexually related materials to minors. But the California Legislature departed from the *Ginsberg* model in an important respect, and the legislature overlooked important differences between the materials falling within the scope of the two statutes. . . .

There is a critical difference . . . between obscenity laws and laws regulating violence in entertainment. By the time of this Court's landmark obscenity cases in the 1960's, obscenity had long been prohibited, see *Roth,* and this experience had helped to shape certain generally accepted norms concerning expression related to sex.

There is no similar history regarding expression related to violence. As the Court notes, classic literature contains descriptions of great violence, and even children's stories sometimes depict very violent scenes.

Although our society does not generally regard all depictions of violence as suitable for children or adolescents, the prevalence of violent depictions in children's literature and entertainment creates numerous opportunities for reasonable people to disagree about which depictions may excite "deviant" or "morbid" impulses.

Finally, the difficulty of ascertaining the community standards incorporated into the California law is compounded by the legislature's decision to lump all minors together. The California law draws no distinction between young children and adolescents who are nearing the age of majority. . . .

For these reasons, I conclude that the California violent video game law fails to provide the fair notice that the Constitution requires. And I would go no further. I would not express any view on whether a properly drawn statute would or would not survive First Amendment scrutiny. We should address that question only if and when it is necessary to do so.

JUSTICE THOMAS, dissenting.

The Court's decision today does not comport with the original public understanding of the First Amendment. The majority strikes down, as facially unconstitutional, a state law that prohibits the direct sale or rental of certain video games to minors because the law "abridg[es] the freedom of speech." But I do not think the First Amendment stretches that far. The practices and beliefs of the founding generation establish that "the freedom of speech," as originally understood, does not include a right to speak to minors (or a right of minors to access speech) without going through the minors' parents or guardians. I would hold that the law at issue is not facially unconstitutional under the First Amendment, and reverse and remand for further proceedings.

JUSTICE BREYER, dissenting.

California's law imposes no more than a modest restriction on expression. The statute prevents no one from playing a video game, it prevents no adult from buying a video game, and it prevents no child or adolescent from obtaining a game provided a parent is willing to help. All it prevents is a child or adolescent from buying, without a parent's assistance, a gruesomely violent video game of a kind that the industry *itself* tells us it wants to keep out of the hands of those under the age of 17.

Nor is the statute, if upheld, likely to create a precedent that would adversely affect other media, say films, or videos, or books. A typical video game involves a significant amount of physical activity. And pushing buttons that achieve an interactive, virtual form of target practice (using images of human beings as targets), while containing an expressive component, is not just like watching a typical movie.

The interest that California advances in support of the statute is compelling. As this Court has previously described that interest, it consists of both (1) the "basic" parental claim "to authority in their own household to direct the rearing of their children," which makes it proper to enact "laws designed to aid discharge of [parental] responsibility," and (2) the State's "independent interest in the well-being of its youth." *Ginsberg.* And where these interests work in tandem, it is not fatally "underinclusive" for a State to advance its interests in protecting children against the special harms present in an interactive video game medium through a default rule that still allows parents to provide their children with what their parents wish.

Both interests are present here. As to the need to help parents guide their children, the Court noted in 1968 that "'parental control or guidance cannot always be provided.'" Today, 5.3 million grade-school-age children of working parents are routinely home alone. Thus, it has, if anything, become more important to supplement parents' authority to guide their children's development. . . .

. . . In particular, extremely violent games can harm children by rewarding them for being violently aggressive in play, and thereby often teaching them to be violently aggressive in life. And video games can cause more harm in this respect than can typically passive media, such as books or films or television programs.

There are many scientific studies that support California's views. Social scientists, for example, have found *causal* evidence that playing these games results in harm. Longitudinal studies, which measure changes over time, have found that increased exposure to violent video games causes an increase in aggression over the same period. . . .

And "meta-analyses," *i.e.,* studies of all the studies, have concluded that exposure to violent video games "was positively associated with aggressive behavior, aggressive cognition, and aggressive affect," and that "playing violent video games is a *causal* risk factor for long-term harmful outcomes." Anderson et al., Violent Video Game Effects on Aggression, Empathy, and Prosocial Behavior in Eastern and Western Countries: A Meta-Analytic Review, 136 *Psychological Bulletin* (2010).

Some of these studies take care to explain in a common-sense way why video games are potentially more harmful than, say, films or books or television. In essence, they say that the closer a child's behavior comes, not to watching, but to *acting* out horrific violence, the greater the potential psychological harm. . . .

Unlike the majority, I would find sufficient grounds in these studies and expert opinions for this Court to defer to an elected legislature's conclusion that the video games in question are particularly likely to harm children. This Court has always thought it owed an elected legislature some degree of deference in respect to legislative facts of this kind, particularly when they involve technical matters that are beyond our competence, and even in First Amendment cases. The majority, in reaching its own, opposite conclusion about the validity of the relevant studies, grants the legislature no deference at all. . . .

The upshot is that California's statute, as applied to its heartland of applications (*i.e.,* buyers under 17; extremely violent, realistic video games), imposes a restriction on speech that is modest at most. That restriction is justified by a compelling interest (supplementing parents' efforts to prevent their children from purchasing potentially harmful violent, interactive material). And there is no equally effective, less restrictive alternative. California's statute is consequently constitutional on its face—though litigants remain free to challenge the statute as applied in particular instances, including any effort by the State to apply it to minors aged 17.

I add that the majority's different conclusion creates a serious anomaly in First Amendment law. *Ginsberg* makes clear that a State can prohibit the sale to minors of depictions of nudity; today the Court makes clear that a State cannot prohibit the sale to minors of the most violent interactive video games. But what sense does it make to forbid selling to a 13-year-old boy a magazine with an image of a nude woman, while protecting a sale to that 13-year-old of an interactive video game in which he actively, but virtually, binds and gags the woman, then tortures and kills her? What kind of First Amendment would permit the government to protect children by restricting sales of that extremely violent video game *only* when the woman—bound, gagged, tortured, and killed—is also topless?

This anomaly is not compelled by the First Amendment. It disappears once one recognizes that extreme violence, where interactive, and *without literary, artistic, or similar justification,* can prove at least as, if not more, harmful to children as photographs of nudity. And the record here is more than adequate to support such a view. That is why I believe that *Ginsberg* controls the outcome here *a fortiori.* And it is why I believe California's law is constitutional on its face.

. . . Sometimes, children need to learn by making choices for themselves. Other times, choices are made for children—by their parents, by their teachers, and by the people acting democratically through their governments. In my view, the First Amendment does not disable government from helping parents make such a choice here—a choice not to have their children buy extremely violent, interactive video games, which they more than reasonably fear pose only the risk of harm to those children.

Although the vote in *Brown* was not especially divided, the range of opinions expressed by the justices was nearly as diverse as in the pre-*Miller* obscenity cases. To Justice Scalia, video games are more akin to fairy tales, which "contain no shortage of gore," than they are to sexually explicit material. They deserve full First Amendment protection, meaning that the law can survive only if the state presents a compelling government interest and is narrowly drawn to serve that interest *(see Chapter 5).* To Justice Scalia, the social science evidence was not sufficiently compelling. In his concurring opinion, Justice Alito took issue with the majority's

broad ruling. He would have struck down the law as unconstitutionally vague, leaving open the possibility that the state could rewrite it (as the Court did in *Stevens*). Alito too thought the Court should not have necessarily treated video games as "the same as some older thing with which we are familiar." As he put it, "We should take into account the possibility that developing technology may have important societal implications that will become apparent only with time." Even the dissenters expressed divergent reasons for their disagreement with the majority. In accord with his version of originalism, Justice Thomas rejected the idea that the First Amendment included "a right to speak to minors (or a right of minors to access speech) without going through the minors' parents or guardians." Justice Breyer, in contrast, argued that the Court should have deferred to the state's findings about the potential harm associated with violent video games.

No doubt *Stevens* and *Brown* represent the first of what will be many cases generated by new technology. At this point, whether the Court will stick to its position of defining only a limited number of categories of expression as beyond the reach of the First Amendment—notably, obscenity and libel—is anyone's guess.

ANNOTATED READINGS

Books on the Supreme Court's treatment of obscenity and libel abound. Here we focus on traditional media. See Chapter 8 for reading suggestions regarding the Court and electronic media.

Books on obscenity and pornography include Brenda Cossman, Shannon Bell, Becki Ross, and Lise Gotell, *Bad Attitudes on Trial: Pornography, Feminism, and the* Butler *Decision* (Toronto: University of Toronto Press, 1997); Donald Alexander Downs, *The New Politics of Pornography* (Chicago: University of Chicago Press, 1989); Susan Gubar, *For Adult Use Only: The Dilemmas of Violent Pornography* (Bloomington: Indiana University Press, 1989); Steven J. Heyman, *Free Speech and Human Dignity* (New Haven, CT: Yale University Press, 2008); Richard F. Hixson, *Pornography and the Justices: The Supreme Court and the Intractable Obscenity Problem* (Carbondale: Southern Illinois University Press, 1996); Joseph F. Kobylka, *The Politics of Obscenity: Group Litigation in a Time of Legal Change* (New York: Greenwood Press, 1991); Catharine MacKinnon, *Only Words* (Cambridge, MA: Harvard

University Press, 1993); Charles Rembar, *The End of Obscenity* (New York: Bantam Books, 1968); Kevin W. Saunders, *Degradation: What the History of Obscenity Tells Us about Hate* Speech (New York: New York University Press, 2011); Nadine Strossen, *Defending Pornography: Free Speech, Sex, and the Fight for Women's Rights.* (New York: New York University Press, 2000); L. W. Sumner, *The Hateful and the Obscene: Studies in the Limits of Free Expression* (Toronto: University of Toronto Press, 2004); James Weinstein, *Hate Speech, Pornography, and the Radical Attack on Free Speech Doctrine* (Boulder, CO: Westview Press, 1999); Laura Wittern-Keller and Raymond Haberski Jr., *The Miracle Case: Film Censorship and the Supreme Court* (Lawrence: University Press of Kansas, 2008); Franklin E. Zimring and Gordon J. Hawkins, *Pornography in a Free Society* (New York: Cambridge University Press, 1991).

For studies of libel law, see Renata Adler, *Reckless Disregard:* Westmoreland v. CBS et al., Sharon v. Time (New York: Vintage Books, 1986); Elmer Gertz, Gertz v. Robert Welch, Inc.: *The Story of a Landmark Libel Case* (Carbondale: Southern Illinois University Press, 1992); Donald M. Gillmor, *Power, Publicity, and the Abuse of Libel Law* (New York: Oxford University Press, 1992); Kermit L. Hall and Melvin I. Urofsky, New York Times v. Sullivan: *Civil Rights, Libel Law, and the Free* Press (University Press of Kansas, 2011); Peter E. Kane, *Errors, Lies, and Libel* (Carbondale: Southern Illinois University Press, 1992); James Kirby, *Fumble: Bear Bryant, Wally Butts, and the Great College Football Scandal.* (San Diego, CA: Harcourt Brace Jovanovich, 1986); Anthony Lewis, *Make No Law: The Sullivan Case and the First Amendment* (New York: Random House, 1991); Rodney A. Smolla, *Jerry Falwell v. Larry Flynt: The First Amendment on Trial* (Champaign: University of Illinois Press, 1990); Russell L. Weaver, Andrew T. Kenyon, David F. Partlett, and Clive P. Walker, *The Right to Speak Ill: Defamation, Reputation, and Free Speech* (Durham, NC: Carolina Academic Press, 2006).

8 The First Amendment and the Internet

ANY OF THE CASES we considered in Chapters 5, 6, and 7 involved forms of expression that would have been familiar to the framers of the Constitution. Speech critical of the government, gatherings aimed at producing legal change, and newspapers reporting on the day's events were all part of their world. Electronic communication, of course, was not. The rise of personal computing, but especially the development of the Internet, has created entirely new methods of communication. What began in 1969 as a military project has grown into an international network of interconnected computers. Internet communication is instantaneous and interactive. Unlike radio, electronic media can carry text, graphics, and sound. Unlike a television station, the Internet does not reside in a single location but is a network of communicators not confined by state or national boundaries. Unlike the broadcast media, which are restricted by the number of frequencies available, the Internet can accommodate communication by perhaps an infinite number of people. And unlike many other forms of expression, participating in electronic speech does not require a large expenditure of money. These factors make electronic communication potentially the most effective and participatory method of expression yet devised. The Internet carries the promise of creating a truly robust, free marketplace of ideas.

But electronic expression also carries certain dangers. Readily available computers allow children access to materials that might be inappropriate for them. Participation in electronic chat rooms has led to cases of abduction, sex crimes, and even murder. Moreover, the potential for fraud and deception is perhaps even greater in electronic communication than in more traditional forms of expression. The ability to collect and catalog huge amounts of data allows for invasions of privacy. Open access to the Internet means that no supervising authority ensures the veracity of posted messages. Harassment based on sex, race, ethnicity, or sexual orientation can easily occur in an electronic world. Groups with political or social messages repugnant to the majority have an equal voice with mainstream organizations in spite of their small numbers and minimal funds.

Confronting the darker side of the Internet is providing challenges to government regulators at all levels. Congress and the state legislatures have already passed many laws in their attempts to reduce electronic wrongdoing. Courts are now interpreting these laws, and law schools have responded with courses dedicated to computers and Internet law. For the most part, however, the court decisions and law school courses address areas outside the constitutional realm, such as patents on computer software, electronic transactions, and identity theft.

Within constitutional law, the questions that have moved to the fore tend to implicate free expression—in particular, the extent to which Congress can regulate indecent material and child pornography on the Web without violating First Amendment rights. That the government has tried to regulate in this area is none too surprising. "Cyberporn" is now a worldwide business, generating, by some estimates, $100 billion in annual revenue. Child pornography, which is illegal in most countries, may now account for as much as 20 percent of pornographic sites on the Web. Total federal prosecutions in child pornography cases increased by more than 450 percent over the last decade.

Appropriately alarmed by the growth of this illegal industry, as well as the possible ill effects of other types of indecent material on children, beginning in the 1990s Congress enacted laws of two flavors: shielding children from sexually explicit material and prohibiting child pornography on the Internet. But with the passage of each new law came an immediate legal challenge. Newly formed organizations devoted to keeping the Internet free have joined with traditional civil liberties groups, such as the ACLU, to attack these regulations as violations of the First Amendment. While these organizations are hardly proponents of child pornography, they contend that the federal laws are too burdensome, suppressing legitimate and protected expression.

Initial lower court decisions overwhelmingly supported First Amendment claims against the laws, but how has the Supreme Court responded? As we shall see, the answer is mixed, with the Court striking down some congressional efforts and upholding others.

No doubt the jostling between Congress and the justices over regulating expression on the Internet will continue. But a number of other thorny questions relating to the Web are making their way into the courts as well. At the end of this chapter we consider these emerging areas of law—some of which will likely be prominent features of the Court's agenda in the decade to come.

SHIELDING CHILDREN FROM ACCESS TO SEXUALLY EXPLICIT MATERIAL

Preventing children from gaining access to sexually explicit material is not a new issue, as we noted in Chapter 7. Amid pressure from governments and various interest groups, the film, music, television, and gaming industries have adopted various rating and labeling systems (see Box 7-6, page 361).

Perhaps because no one industry represents the worldwide Internet, Congress has stepped in and passed two types of laws. One, represented by the Communications Decency Act of 1996 (CDA) and the Child Online Protection Act of 1998 (COPA, sometimes called CDA II), generally attempts to regulate the transmission of certain kinds of material or messages to people under the age of eighteen. The second type involves the use of filtering devices to block minors from viewing certain material.

Regulating Access to Internet Sites

Reno v. American Civil Liberties Union (1997) presented a challenge to the first CDA, the Communications Decency Act of 1996. It is noteworthy not only because it provides some indication of the Court's thinking on regulating Internet access but also because it presented the justices' first opportunity to consider the legal status of the Internet. Would the justices characterize the Web as a medium akin to newspapers, or would they liken it to other more modern-day media, such as television and radio? This is an important question because, as we learned in Chapter 6, the press enjoys higher First Amendment protection than do the broadcast media.

Reno v. American Civil Liberties Union

521 U.S. 844 (1997)
http://laws.findlaw.com/US/521/844.html
Oral arguments are available at http://www.oyez.org.
Vote: 7 (Breyer, Ginsburg, Kennedy, Scalia, Souter, Stevens, Thomas)
  2 (O'Connor, Rehnquist)

OPINION OF THE COURT: *Stevens*
OPINION CONCURRING IN PART AND DISSENTING IN PART:
  O'Connor

FACTS:

Passed in 1996 by large majorities in both houses of Congress and signed into law by President Bill Clinton, the Communications Decency Act—part of a larger legislative package regulating the telecommunications industry—sought to control children's access to sexually explicit material transmitted electronically, especially via the Internet. As soon as the law was passed, a coalition of about fifty organizations and businesses, led by the ACLU, filed suit, asserting that it violated the First Amendment.

Specifically, the lawsuit challenged two provisions of the act, known as the indecent transmission provision and the patently offensive display provision. The indecent transmission section prohibited online communication to minors that is indecent or obscene, "regardless of whether the user of such service placed the call or initiated the communication." The patently offensive display provision prohibited the transmission of messages that depict or describe, "in terms patently offensive as measured by community standards, sexual or excretory activities or organs" in a manner that "is available to a person under the age of eighteen." Violators of these provisions could be fined or imprisoned for two years, or both. The law recognized as a legitimate defense "good faith, reasonable, effective, and appropriate actions" to restrict access by minors to the prohibited communications.

A three-judge district court, although divided over the rationale, held that the law was unconstitutionally vague. Attorney General Janet Reno, representing the United States, appealed to the Supreme Court.

For the appellants, Janet Reno, Attorney General of the United States, et al.:

- The Internet's potential as an educational and informational resource will be wasted if people are reluctant to use it for fear of exposing their children to sexually explicit material.
- The display provision is constitutional under *FCC v. Pacifica*. Just as it was constitutional for the FCC to dictate the time of day when indecent material could be broadcast on the radio, Congress can channel indecent communications to places on the Internet where children are unlikely to see them.
- There is no less burdensome way to achieve this legitimate governmental interest. Its impositions on adult-to-adult communication are justified by the protection afforded to children by the act.
- The CDA is no more vague than the obscenity standard established in *Miller v. California* (1973) *(excerpted in Chapter 7)*.

For the appellees, ACLU, et al.:

- The CDA criminalizes a broad range of constitutionally protected "indecent" speech (not only commercial pornography) that may have serious value.
- The law is not narrowly tailored to accomplish the goal of protecting minors because it also restricts adult access to sexually explicit communications.
- Terms such as *indecent* and *patently offensive* are unconstitutionally vague. It is impossible to determine exactly what speech the CDA criminalizes.

JUSTICE STEVENS DELIVERED THE OPINION OF THE COURT.

In *Southeastern Promotions, Ltd. v. Conrad* (1975), we observed that "each medium of expression . . . may present its own problems." Thus, some of our cases have recognized special justifications for regulation of the broadcast media that are not applicable to other speakers. In these cases, the Court relied on the history of extensive government regulation of the broadcast medium; the scarcity of available frequencies at its inception; and its "invasive" nature.

Those factors are not present in cyberspace. Neither before nor after the enactment of the CDA [Communications Decency Act] have the vast democratic fora of the Internet been subject to the type of government supervision and regulation that has attended the broadcast industry. Moreover, the Internet is not as "invasive" as radio or television. The District Court specifically found that "communications over the Internet do not 'invade' an individual's home or appear on one's computer screen unbidden. Users seldom encounter content 'by accident.'" . . .

. . . [U]nlike the conditions that prevailed when Congress first authorized regulation of the broadcast spectrum, the Internet can hardly be considered a "scarce" expressive commodity. It provides relatively unlimited, low-cost capacity for communication of all kinds. The Government estimates that "as many as 40 million people use the Internet today [1997], and that figure is expected to grow to 200 million by 1999." This dynamic, multifaceted category of communication includes not only traditional print and news services, but also audio, video, and still images, as well as interactive, real-time dialogue. Through the use of chat rooms, any person with a phone line can become a town crier with a voice that resonates farther than it could from any soapbox. Through the use of Web pages, mail exploders, and newsgroups, the same individual can become a pamphleteer. As the District Court found, "the content on the Internet is as diverse as human thought." We agree with its conclusion that our cases provide no basis for qualifying the level of First Amendment scrutiny that should be applied to this medium.

. . . [T]he many ambiguities [of the CDA] concerning the scope of its coverage render it problematic for purposes of the First Amendment. For instance, each of the two parts of the CDA uses a different linguistic form. The first uses the word "indecent," while the second speaks of material that "in context, depicts or describes, in terms patently offensive as measured by contemporary community standards, sexual or excretory activities or organs." Given the absence of a definition of either term, this difference in language will provoke uncertainty among speakers about how the two standards relate to each other and just what they mean. Could a speaker confidently assume that a serious discussion about birth control practices, homosexuality . . . or the consequences of prison rape would not violate the CDA? This uncertainty undermines the likelihood that the CDA has been carefully tailored to the congressional goal of protecting minors from potentially harmful materials.

The vagueness of the CDA is a matter of special concern for two reasons. First, the CDA is a content-based regulation of speech. The vagueness of such a regulation raises special First Amendment concerns because of its obvious chilling effect on free speech. Second, the CDA is a criminal statute. In addition to the opprobrium and stigma of a criminal conviction, the CDA threatens violators with penalties including up to two years in prison for each act of violation. The severity of criminal sanctions may well cause speakers to remain silent rather than communicate even arguably unlawful words, ideas, and images. . . .

The Government argues that the statute is no more vague than the obscenity standard this Court established in *Miller v. California* (1973). But that is not so. In *Miller,* this Court reviewed a criminal conviction against a commercial vendor who mailed brochures containing pictures of sexually explicit activities to individuals who had not requested such materials. Having struggled for some time to establish a definition of obscenity, we set forth in *Miller* the test for obscenity that controls to this day:

(a) whether the average person, applying contemporary community standards would find that the work, taken as a whole, appeals to the prurient interest; (b) whether the work depicts or describes, in a patently offensive way, sexual conduct specifically defined by the applicable state law; and (c) whether the work, taken as a whole, lacks serious literary, artistic, political, or scientific value.

Because the CDA's "patently offensive" standard (and, we assume *arguendo,* its synonymous "indecent" standard) is one part of the three-prong *Miller* test, the Government reasons, it cannot be unconstitutionally vague.

The Government's assertion is incorrect as a matter of fact. The second prong of the *Miller* test—the purportedly analogous standard—contains a critical requirement that is omitted from the CDA: that the proscribed material be "specifically defined by the applicable state law." This requirement reduces the vagueness inherent in the open ended term "patently offensive" as used in the CDA. Moreover, the *Miller* definition is limited to "sexual conduct," whereas the CDA extends also to include (1) "excretory activities" as well as (2) "organs" of both a sexual and excretory nature.

The Government's reasoning is also flawed. Just because a definition including three limitations is not vague, it does not follow that one of those limitations, standing by itself, is not vague. Each of *Miller*'s additional two prongs—(1) that, taken as a whole, the material appeal to the "prurient" interest, and (2) that it "lack serious literary, artistic, political, or scientific value"—critically limits the uncertain sweep of the obscenity definition. The second requirement is particularly important because, unlike the "patently offensive" and "prurient interest" criteria, it is not judged by contemporary community standards. This "societal value" requirement, absent in the CDA, allows appellate courts to impose some limitations and regularity on the definition by setting, as a matter of law, a national floor for socially redeeming value. The Government's contention that courts will be able to give such legal limitations to the CDA's standards is belied by *Miller*'s own rationale for having juries determine whether material is "patently offensive" according to community standards: that such questions are essentially ones of *fact*.

In contrast to *Miller* and our other previous cases, the CDA thus presents a greater threat of censoring speech that, in fact, falls outside the statute's scope. Given the vague contours of the coverage of the statute, it unquestionably silences some speakers whose messages would be entitled to constitutional protection. That danger provides further reason for insisting that the statute not be overly broad. The CDA's burden on protected speech cannot be justified if it could be avoided by a more carefully drafted statute.

We are persuaded that the CDA lacks the precision that the First Amendment requires when a statute regulates the content of speech. In order to deny minors access to potentially harmful speech, the CDA effectively suppresses a large amount of speech that adults have a constitutional right to receive and to address to one another. That burden on adult speech is unacceptable if less restrictive alternatives would be at least as effective in achieving the legitimate purpose that the statute was enacted to serve.

In evaluating the free speech rights of adults, we have made it perfectly clear that "sexual expression which is indecent but not obscene is protected by the First Amendment." Indeed, [we have] admonished that "the fact that society may find speech offensive is not a sufficient reason for suppressing it."

It is true that we have repeatedly recognized the governmental interest in protecting children from harmful materials. See *Ginsberg* [*v. New York,* 1968]. But that interest does not justify an unnecessarily broad suppression of speech addressed to adults. As we have explained, the Government may not "reduce the adult population . . . to . . . only what is fit for children." . . .

In arguing that the CDA does not so diminish adult communication, the Government relies on the incorrect factual premise that prohibiting a transmission whenever it is known that one of its recipients is a minor would not interfere with adult-to-adult communication. The findings of the District Court make clear that this premise is untenable.

Given the size of the potential audience for most messages, in the absence of a viable age verification process, the sender must be charged with knowing that one or more minors will likely view it. Knowledge that, for instance, one or more members of a 100-person chat group will be minor—and therefore that it would be a crime to send the group an indecent message—would surely burden communication among adults.

The District Court found that at the time of trial existing technology did not include any effective method for a sender to prevent minors from obtaining access to its communications on the Internet without also denying access to adults. The Court found no effective way to determine the age of a user who is accessing material through e-mail, mail exploders, newsgroups, or chat rooms. As a practical matter, the Court also found that it would be prohibitively expensive for noncommercial—as well as some commercial—speakers who have Web sites to verify that their users are adults. These limitations must inevitably curtail a significant amount of adult communication on the Internet. By contrast, the District Court found that "despite its limitations, currently available *user-based* software suggests that a reasonably effective method by which *parents* can prevent their children from accessing sexually explicit and other material which *parents* may believe is inappropriate for their children will soon be widely available" (emphases added).

The breadth of the CDA's coverage is wholly unprecedented. Unlike the regulations upheld in *Ginsberg* and [*FCC v.*] *Pacifica* [1978], the scope of the CDA is not limited to commercial speech or commercial entities. Its open ended prohibitions embrace all nonprofit entities and individuals posting indecent messages or displaying them on their own computers in the presence of minors. The general, undefined terms "indecent" and "patently offensive" cover large amounts of nonpornographic material with serious educational or other value. Moreover, the "community standards" criterion as applied to the Internet means that any communication available to a nationwide audience will be judged by the standards of the community most likely to be offended by the message. The regulated subject matter . . . may also extend to discussions about prison rape or safe sexual practices, artistic images that include nude subjects, and arguably the card catalogue of the Carnegie Library. . . .

In this Court, though not in the District Court, the Government asserts that—in addition to its interest in protecting children—its "equally significant" interest in fostering the growth of the Internet provides an independent basis for upholding the constitutionality of the CDA. The Government apparently assumes that the unregulated availability of "indecent" and "patently offensive" material on the Internet is driving countless citizens away from the medium because of the risk of exposing themselves or their children to harmful material.

We find this argument singularly unpersuasive. The dramatic expansion of this new marketplace of ideas contradicts the factual basis of this contention. The record demonstrates that the growth of the Internet has been and continues to be phenomenal. As a matter of constitutional tradition, in the absence of evidence to the contrary, we presume that governmental regulation of the content of speech is more likely to interfere with the free exchange of ideas than to encourage it. The interest in encouraging freedom of expression in a democratic society outweighs any theoretical but unproven benefit of censorship.

For the foregoing reasons, the judgment of the district court is affirmed.

It is so ordered.

JUSTICE O'CONNOR, with whom THE CHIEF JUSTICE joins, concurring in the judgment in part and dissenting in part.

I write separately to explain why I view the Communications Decency Act of 1996 (CDA) as little more than an attempt by Congress to create "adult zones" on the Internet. Our precedent indicates that the creation of such zones can be constitutionally sound. Despite the soundness of its purpose, however, portions of the CDA are unconstitutional because they stray from the blueprint our prior cases have developed for constructing a "zoning law" that passes constitutional muster. . . .

Our cases make clear that a "zoning" law is valid only if adults are still able to obtain the regulated speech. If they cannot, the law does more than simply keep children away from speech they have no right to obtain—it interferes with the rights of adults to obtain constitutionally protected speech and effectively "reduces the adult population . . . to reading only what is fit for children." The electronic world is fundamentally different. Because it is no more than the interconnection of electronic pathways, cyberspace allows speakers and listeners to mask their identities. Cyberspace undeniably reflects some form of geography; chat rooms and Web sites, for example, exist at fixed "locations" on the Internet. Since users can transmit and receive messages on the Internet without revealing anything about their identities or ages, however, it is not currently possible to exclude persons from accessing certain messages on the basis of their identity. . . .

Although the prospects for the eventual zoning of the Internet appear promising, I agree with the Court that we must evaluate the constitutionality of the CDA as it applies to the Internet as it exists today. Given the present state of cyberspace, I agree with the Court that the "display" provision cannot pass muster . . . .

The "indecency transmission" and "specific person" provisions present a closer issue, for they are not unconstitutional in all of their applications. . . . [T]he "indecency transmission" provision makes it a crime to transmit knowingly an indecent message to a person the sender knows is under 18 years of age. The "specific person" provision proscribes the same conduct, although it does not as explicitly require the sender to know that the intended recipient of his indecent message is a minor. Appellant urges the Court to construe the provision to impose such a knowledge requirement, and I would do so.

So construed, both provisions are constitutional as applied to a conversation involving only an adult and one or more minors—*e.g.* when an adult speaker sends an e-mail knowing the addressee is a minor, or when an adult and minor converse by themselves or with other minors in a chat room. . . .

Thus, the constitutionality of the CDA as a zoning law hinges on the extent to which it substantially interferes with the First Amendment rights of adults. Because the rights of adults are infringed only by the "display" provision and by the "indecency transmission" and the "specific person" provisions as applied to communications involving more than one adult, I would invalidate the CDA only to that extent. Insofar as the "indecency transmission" and "specific person" provisions prohibit the use of indecent speech in communications between an adult and one or more minors, however, they can and should be sustained. The Court reaches a contrary conclusion, and from that holding I respectfully dissent.

In *Reno*, the Supreme Court agreed with the district court—the CDA was constitutionally defective. It did, however, "save" the CDA in one respect:

Appellees do not challenge the application of the statute to obscene speech, which, they acknowledge, can be banned totally because it enjoys no First Amendment protection. See *Miller*. As set forth by the statute, the restriction of "obscene" material enjoys a textual manifestation separate from that for "indecent" material, which we have held unconstitutional. Therefore, we will sever the term "or indecent" from the statute. . . . In no other respect, however, can [the law] be saved by such a textual surgery.

For at least two reasons, *Reno* is an interesting decision. First, it seems to provide an early indication of the Court's thinking about the Internet: that it is closer in kind to the printed press than it is to broadcast media. It might follow that Internet speech will enjoy a higher level of protection than broadcast speech. This does not mean the justices will strike down all attempts to regulate the Web, only that they may hold such laws to a higher standard of First Amendment scrutiny than they apply to regulations on television and other broadcast media.

Then there's the Court's ruling itself, which struck down the CDA's prohibition against sending "indecent" or "patently offensive" communications to minors. In general, the Court found these terms too vague to pass muster under the First Amendment: "The CDA fails to provide us with any definition of the term 'indecent' . . . and, importantly, omits any requirement that the 'patently offensive' material . . . lack serious literary, artistic, political, or scientific value."

Reaction to the Court's decision, at least among the act's congressional supporters, was harsh. As Senator Christopher Bond, R-Mo., put it, the ruling was "an unfortunate blow to those of us who want to protect our children from sexual predators using the Internet. . . . I believe Congress will try again, and that we'll get it right next time."[1]

Congress did try again. In 1998 it passed the Child Online Protection Act, which prohibited distribution of "any communication for commercial purposes that is available to any minor and that includes any material that is harmful to minors" (in distinction to the CDA, which prohibited "indecent" and "patently offensive" communications in a manner accessible to minors).[2] Violators could face criminal prosecution, with fines of up to $50,000 a day.

To determine whether material is "harmful to minors," the act relied on the *Miller* test, including the "community standards" measure. A federal district court struck down COPA on much the same grounds as the Supreme Court used in *Reno*. A U.S. court of appeals agreed, concluding that the Supreme Court's community standards jurisprudence "has no applicability to the Internet and the Web" because Web publishers are currently without the ability to control the geographic scope of the recipients of their communications. This logic seems to reflect the Court's words in *Reno* that "the 'community standards' criterion as applied to the Internet means that any communication available to a nationwide audience will be judged by the standards of the community most likely to be offended by the message."

In *Ashcroft v. American Civil Liberties Union [I]* (2002), the Court disagreed. Writing for the majority (or plurality, depending on the section of the opinion), Justice Clarence Thomas declared that the use of COPA's "community standards" to identify material harmful to children did not render the statute facially

invalid in part because COPA applied to a narrower class of material than did the CDA.

But the decision did not settle the matter. By its own reckoning, *Ashcroft* was "quite limited," stating only that the community standards criterion itself does not necessarily run afoul of the First Amendment. Indeed, the Court did not express an opinion on other questions (such as whether the law is unconstitutionally vague or would fail to pass a strict scrutiny analysis) and instead sent the case back to the court of appeals.

Once again the court of appeals held that COPA violated the First Amendment, this time on the ground that it was not the "least restrictive" alternative available to accomplish Congress's goal of shielding children from harmful materials. Writing for a five-person majority in *Ashcroft v. American Civil Liberties Union [II]* (2004), Justice Kennedy agreed. He began by explaining the least restrictive test used by the lower court:

When plaintiffs challenge a content-based speech restriction, the burden is on the Government to prove that the proposed alternatives will not be as effective as the challenged statute.

In considering this question, a court assumes that certain protected speech may be regulated, and then asks what is the least restrictive alternative that can be used to achieve [the government's] goal. The purpose of the test is not to consider whether the challenged restriction has some effect in achieving Congress' goal, regardless of the restriction it imposes. The purpose of the test is to ensure that speech is restricted no further than necessary to achieve the goal, for it is important to assure that legitimate speech is not chilled or punished. For that reason, the test does not begin with the status quo of existing regulations, then ask whether the challenged restriction has some additional ability to achieve Congress' legitimate interest. Any restriction on speech could be justified under that analysis. Instead, the court should ask whether the challenged regulation is the least restrictive means among available, effective alternatives.

To Kennedy, the answer was straightforward: the government had not made its case that COPA was the least restrictive alternative. In particular, he pointed to blocking and filtering software that is "less restrictive than COPA. They impose selective restrictions on speech at the receiving end, not universal restrictions at the source. . . . Above all, promoting the use of filters does not condemn as criminal any category of speech, and so the potential chilling effect is eliminated, or at least much diminished." He further

---

1. Quoted in the *St. Louis Post Dispatch*, June 27, 1997, A16.

2. CDA II defines material that is "harmful to minors" as "any communication, picture, image, graphic image file, article, recording, writing, or other matter of any kind that is obscene or that (A) the average person, applying contemporary community standards, would find, taking the material as a whole and with respect to minors, is designed to appeal to, or is designed to pander to, the prurient interest; (B) depicts, describes, or represents, in a manner patently offensive with respect to minors, an actual or simulated sexual act or sexual contact, an actual or simulated normal or perverted sexual act, or a lewd exhibition of the genitals or postpubescent female breast; and (C) taken as a whole, lacks serious literary, artistic, political, or scientific value for minors."

argued that filters "also may well be more effective than COPA [because] they can prevent minors from seeing all pornography, not just pornography posted to the Web from America."

Filtering Software

Kennedy's emphasis on filtering software was hardly coincidental. Just the year before *Ashcroft II*, the Court had issued a decision in *United States v. American Library Association* (2003). At issue in this case was the constitutionality of yet another congressional attempt to prevent children from visiting certain Internet sites: the Children's Internet Protection Act of 2000, which withholds federal financial aid to libraries that do not use "filtering" software to block "visual depictions" that are harmful to minors. Six of the justices voted to uphold the law, but Chief Justice William Rehnquist failed to obtain a majority for his view that restricting the ability of adult library users to access certain Internet sites was no more in violation of the First Amendment than placing limits on their ability to borrow books that librarians did not use their discretion to purchase. Two of the six, Justices Kennedy and Stephen Breyer, were a bit more circumspect. They agreed that the law was constitutional on its face, but they both expressed some concerns about how it may work in practice. Kennedy wrote:

If, on the request of an adult user, a librarian will unblock filtered material or disable the Internet software filter without significant delay, there is little to this case. The Government represents this is indeed the fact. . . . If some libraries do not have the capacity to unblock specific Web sites or to disable the filter or if it is shown that an adult user's election to view constitutionally protected Internet material is burdened in some other substantial way, that would be the subject for an as-applied challenge, not the facial challenge made in this case.

PROHIBITING CHILD PORNOGRAPHY

In light of *American Library Association*, yet another fractured decision, and the Court's failure to issue a decisive ruling on COPA, it is likely that we have not seen the last of congressional efforts to shield children, followed by the inevitable court challenges. We could say the same about the second area of congressional regulation—prohibiting child pornography on the Internet. Recall that in *New York v. Ferber* (1982) *(excerpted in Chapter 7)*, the justices—even the Court's most liberal members—showed strong support for legislative prohibitions against producing and distributing materials depicting children engaged in sexual activity.

The computer-generated image of Dr. Aki Ross, a character from Final Fantasy, *a popular computer game and science-fiction film, demonstrates the technology that antipornography groups say can also be used to create "virtual child porn" on computer screens.*

But *Ferber* concerned film, a rather traditional medium. Would they give government similar leeway to regulate the spread of child pornography on the Internet? The Court's initial answer to this question came in ***Ashcroft v. Free Speech Coalition*** (2002), a challenge to the Child Pornography Prevention Act of 1996 (CPPA).

Prior to passage of the CPPA, Congress defined child pornography as the type of depictions at issue in *New York v. Ferber*—those using actual minors. With passage of the CPPA, Congress retained that prohibition and added several others. Of particular relevance in *Ashcroft* was §2256(8)(B), which forbade "any visual depiction, including any photograph, film, video, picture, or computer or computer-generated image or picture" that "is, or appears to be, of a minor engaging in sexually explicit conduct." The prohibition did not depend on how the image was produced. The section captured a range of depictions, sometimes called "virtual child pornography," which included computer-generated images as well as images produced by more traditional means. Even though no actual children participated in making these products, Congress found that simulated child pornography nevertheless posed a significant threat to children because pedophiles could use the pornographic images to encourage children to participate in sexual activity or to "whet their own sexual appetites," "thereby increasing the creation and distribution of child pornography and the sexual abuse and exploitation of actual children." Under these rationales, harm flows from the *content* of the images, not from the means of their production.

Congress identified yet another problem created by computer-generated images: their existence could make it harder to prosecute pornographers who use actual minors. As imaging technology improves, Congress found, it becomes more difficult to prove that a particular picture was produced using a particular individual or even a real adult or child. To ensure that defendants possessing child pornography using real minors could not evade prosecution, Congress extended the ban to virtual child pornography even if the virtual pornography did not meet the *Miller* definition of obscenity.

The Free Speech Coalition, a California trade association for the adult-entertainment industry, challenged the statute in U.S. district court, alleging that its members did not use minors in its sexually explicit works. It admitted, however, that some of these materials could fall within the CPPA's expanded definition of child pornography. The coalition argued that the "appears to be" and "conveys the impression" provisions were overbroad and vague, discouraging it from producing works protected by the First Amendment. The district court disagreed and ruled in favor of the government. But in 1999 the U.S. Court of Appeals for the Ninth Circuit reversed this decision, reasoning that the federal government could not prohibit speech based on a danger that it could encourage viewers to commit illegal acts. The court held the CPPA to be substantially overbroad, because it bans materials that are neither obscene under *Miller* nor produced by the exploitation of real children, as was the case in *Ferber*. The Ninth Circuit's ruling was directly at odds with the rulings of four other federal courts of appeals, each of which had upheld the constitutionality of the CPPA.

The Supreme Court, however, agreed with the Ninth Circuit. Writing for a six-member majority, Justice Kennedy began by stating the crux of the matter: Is the CPPA constitutional "where it proscribes a significant universe of speech that is neither obscene under *Miller* nor child pornography under *Ferber*"? His answer was that it is not.

While recognizing that "the sexual abuse of a child is a most serious crime and an act repugnant to the moral instincts of a decent people" and that "Congress may pass valid laws to protect children from abuse," he also noted that "the CPPA is much more than a supplement to the existing federal prohibition on obscenity." It has the potential to prohibit speech that may have serious literary, artistic, political, or scientific value. In Kennedy's words:

The statute proscribes the visual depiction of an idea—that of teenagers engaging in sexual activity—that is a fact of modern society and has been a theme in art and literature throughout the ages. Under the CPPA, images are prohibited so long as the persons appear to be under 18 years of age. This is higher than the legal age for marriage in many States, as well as the age at which persons may consent to sexual relations. It is, of course, undeniable that some youths engage in sexual activity before the legal age, either on their own inclination or because they are victims of sexual abuse.

Both themes—teenage sexual activity and the sexual abuse of children—have inspired countless literary works. William Shakespeare created the most famous pair of teenage lovers, one of whom is just 13 years of age. See *Romeo and Juliet*. In the drama, Shakespeare portrays the relationship as something splendid and innocent, but not juvenile. The work has inspired no less than 40 motion pictures, some of which suggest that the teenagers consummated their relationship.

> ### BOX 8-1   CONGRESS AND THE COURTS: A CONTINUING DIALOGUE OVER THE REGULATION OF THE INTERNET
>
> **Attempts to Regulate Access**
>
> | CONGRESS | THE SUPREME COURT'S RESPONSE |
> | --- | --- |
> | Communications Decency Act of 1996 (CDA) | Strikes down in *Reno v. American Civil Liberties Union* (1997) |
> | Responds to Reno with the Child Online Protection Act of 1998 (COPA, sometimes called CDA II) | Strikes down in *Ashcroft v. American Civil Liberties Union* (2004) |
> | Children's Internet Protection Act of 2000 | Upholds in *United States v. American Library Association* (2003) |
>
> **Attempts to Prohibit Child Pornography (including Virtual Pornography)**
>
> | CONGRESS | THE SUPREME COURT'S RESPONSE |
> | --- | --- |
> | Child Pornography Prevention Act of 1996 (CPPA) | Strikes down in *Ashcroft v. Free Speech Coalition* (2002) |
> | Responds to Free Speech Coalition with PROTECT Act of 2003 | Upholds in *United States v. Williams* (2008) |

Shakespeare may not have written sexually explicit scenes for the Elizabethan audience, but were modern directors to adopt a less conventional approach, that fact alone would not compel the conclusion that the work was obscene....

At the end of the day, the Court held that the use of child actors engaged in real or simulated sexual activity is a crime of sexual abuse that Congress may punish. But similar activity involving adult actors is not a crime. Unless the material is legally obscene or purposefully marketed to children, such regulation crosses the First Amendment boundaries. As Kennedy concluded:

[The Act] covers materials beyond the categories recognized in *Ferber* and *Miller,* and the reasons the Government offers in support of limiting the freedom of speech have no justification in our precedents or in the law of the First Amendment. The provision abridges the freedom to engage in a substantial amount of lawful speech. For this reason, it is overbroad and unconstitutional.

A year after the Court struck down the Communications Decency Act in *Reno,* Congress passed another version of the CDA, which fared no better than the first *(see Box 8-1).* Likewise, in response to the ruling in *Free Speech Coalition,* Congress "went back to the drawing board," as Justice Scalia put it, and enacted the PROTECT Act of 2003. This time, however, in *United States v. Williams,* the Court upheld the congressional revision. While two justices in the majority in *Free Speech Coalition,* Souter and Ginsburg, argued that the new law

was just as problematic as the old one, the majority disagreed. Do you agree with Justices Souter and Ginsburg? Or does the majority have the better argument?

United States v. Williams

553 U.S. 285 (2008)
http://laws.findlaw.com/US/000/06-694.html
Oral arguments are available at http://www.oyez.org.
Vote: 7 (Alito, Breyer, Kennedy, Roberts, Scalia, Stevens, Thomas)
    2 (Ginsburg, Souter)

OPINION OF THE COURT: *Scalia*
CONCURRING OPINION: *Stevens*
DISSENTING OPINION: *Souter*

FACTS:

In *Ashcroft v. Free Speech Coalition* (2002) the Supreme Court held that Congress could ban child pornography only if it featured real children. Concerned, however, that the Internet and other technology would enable many child pornographers to evade conviction, Congress responded with the Prosecutorial Remedies and Other Tools to end the Exploitation of Children Today Act of 2003 (PROTECT). Congress attempted to rectify the defects of the law struck down in *Free Speech Coalition* by limiting the commission of crime to the "pandering" and solicitation of child pornography. That is, PROTECT targets the actual attempt at selling such materials and prohibits "knowingly advertis[ing], promot[ing], present[ing], distribut[ing] or solicit[ing] any material or purported material in a manner that reflects the belief, or that is intended to cause another to believe, that the material or purported material" is illegal child pornography.

In April 2004, using a sexually explicit screen name, Michael Williams signed on to the same public Internet chat room that a Secret Service agent had also joined. Williams posted a message that read, "Dad of toddler has 'good' pics of her an [sic] me for swap of your toddler pics, or live cam," and a hyperlink that led to pictures of actual children (between ages five and fifteen) engaging in sexual conduct. After obtaining a search warrant for Williams's home, authorities seized hard drives containing additional images of real children engaged in sexually explicit conduct, some of it sadomasochistic. Williams pleaded guilty to charges of pandering and possessing child pornography under the new law, but reserved the right to challenge the constitutionality of the law. The district court rejected his challenge, but the U.S. Court of Appeals for the Eleventh Circuit reversed the pandering conviction, finding that the statute was overbroad under the First Amendment and impermissibly vague under the due process clause of the Fifth Amendment.

ARGUMENTS:

For the petitioner, United States:
- The act attempts to remedy the precise constitutional defects identified by the Court in *Free Speech Coalition.* Congress found that simulated child pornography fuels the market for real child pornography material, thus causing harm to real children. Nothing in the Constitution prevents Congress from banning such conduct.
- A statute is not overbroad unless it not only infringes constitutionally protected speech but also does so to an impermissible degree. The court of appeals made no effort to apply that test. Rather, it relied on hypotheticals to conclude that the law is overbroad. Here, the law applies almost exclusively to speech that is clearly not protected under the First Amendment.
- The law is not impermissibly vague. A criminal statute need only put people on notice of what is unlawful and allow law enforcement agents to recognize violations when they occur. Here, only pandering or soliciting of apparent child pornography is targeted. The kind of material forbidden by the law is consistent with what the Court has defined as child pornography.

For the respondent, Michael Williams:
- Under the overbreadth doctrine, a statute that prohibits a substantial amount of constitutionally protected speech is invalid on its face. PROTECT is overbroad because, among other things, it would criminalize a person who merely brags that he or she intends to offer or solicit child pornography.
- PROTECT is also overbroad because it captures noncommercial, noninciting speech. Under the law, if someone merely asks a person with whom he is engaged in a casual conversation, "Would you happen to have any child pornography that I can look at?" and the person says, "No," he would be in violation of the law.
- PROTECT is impermissibly vague because it has no objective measure by which the public can anticipate what conduct is forbidden. For that very reason, it gives law enforcement agents too much power to make subjective decisions about what speech is illegal.

JUSTICE SCALIA DELIVERED THE OPINION OF THE COURT.

[Prosecutorial Remedies and Other Tools to end the Exploitation of Children Today Act of 2003] criminalizes, in certain specified circumstances, the pandering or solicitation of child pornography. This case presents the question whether that statute is overbroad under the First Amendment or impermissibly vague under the Due Process Clause of the Fifth Amendment. . . .

According to our First Amendment overbreadth doctrine, a statute is facially invalid if it prohibits a substantial amount of protected speech. The doctrine seeks to strike a balance between competing social costs. On the one hand, the threat of enforcement of an overbroad law deters people from engaging in constitutionally protected speech, inhibiting the free exchange of ideas. On the other hand, invalidating a law that in some of its applications is perfectly constitutional—particularly a law directed at conduct so antisocial that it has been made criminal—has obvious harmful effects. In order to maintain an appropriate balance, we have vigorously enforced the requirement that a statute's overbreadth be *substantial,* not only in an absolute sense, but also relative to the statute's plainly legitimate sweep.

The first step in overbreadth analysis is to construe the challenged statute; it is impossible to determine whether a statute reaches too far without first knowing what the statute covers. Generally speaking, the Act prohibits offers to provide and requests to obtain child pornography. The statute does not require the actual existence of child pornography. In this respect, it differs from the statutes in [*New York v.*] *Ferber* [1982], *Osborne* [*v. Ohio,* 1990], and [*Ashcroft v.*] *Free Speech Coalition* [2002], which prohibited the possession or distribution of child pornography. Rather than targeting the underlying material, this statute bans the collateral speech that introduces such material into the child-pornography distribution network. Thus, an Internet user who solicits child pornography from an undercover agent violates the statute, even if the officer possesses no child pornography. Likewise, a person who advertises virtual child pornography as depicting actual children also falls within the reach of the statute.

The statute's definition of the material or purported material that may not be pandered or solicited precisely tracks the material held constitutionally proscribable in *Ferber* and *Miller* [*v. California,* 1973]: obscene material depicting (actual or virtual) children engaged in sexually explicit conduct, and any other material depicting actual children engaged in sexually explicit conduct. . . .

We now turn to whether the statute, as we have construed it, criminalizes a substantial amount of protected expressive activity.

Offers to engage in illegal transactions are categorically excluded from First Amendment protection. . . . The Eleventh Circuit, however, believed that the exclusion of First Amendment protection extended only to *commercial* offers to provide or receive contraband: "Because [the statute] is not limited to commercial speech but extends also to non-commercial promotion, presentation, distribution, and solicitation, we must subject the content-based restriction of the PROTECT Act pandering provision to strict scrutiny. . . ."

This mistakes the rationale for the categorical exclusion. It is based not on the less privileged First Amendment status of commercial speech, but on the principle that offers to give or receive what it is unlawful to possess have no social value and thus, like obscenity, enjoy no First Amendment protection. . . . It would be an odd constitutional principle that permitted the government to prohibit offers to sell illegal drugs, but not offers to give them away for free.

To be sure, there remains an important distinction between a proposal to engage in illegal activity and the abstract advocacy of illegality. The Act before us does not prohibit advocacy of child pornography, but only offers to provide or requests to obtain it. There is no

doubt that this prohibition falls well within constitutional bounds. . . .

In sum, we hold that offers to provide or requests to obtain child pornography are categorically excluded from the First Amendment. . . .

The Eleventh Circuit believed it a constitutional difficulty that no child pornography need exist to trigger the statute. In its view, the fact that the statute could punish a "braggart, exaggerator, or outright liar" rendered it unconstitutional. That seems to us a strange constitutional calculus. Although we have held that the government can ban *both* fraudulent offers, *and* offers to provide illegal products, the Eleventh Circuit would forbid the government from punishing *fraudulent offers to provide illegal products.* We see no logic in that position; if anything, such statements are doubly excluded from the First Amendment. . . .

The Eleventh Circuit found "particularly objectionable" the fact that the "reflects the belief" prong of the statute could ensnare a person who mistakenly believes that material is child pornography. . . . The Eleventh Circuit thought that it would be unconstitutional to punish someone for mistakenly distributing virtual child pornography as real child pornography. We disagree. Offers to deal in illegal products or otherwise engage in illegal activity do not acquire First Amendment protection when the offeror is mistaken about the factual predicate of his offer. The pandering and solicitation made unlawful by the Act are sorts of inchoate crimes—acts looking toward the commission of another crime, the delivery of child pornography. As with other inchoate crimes—attempt and conspiracy, for example—impossibility of completing the crime because the facts were not as the defendant believed is not a defense. . . .

Amici contend that some advertisements for mainstream Hollywood movies that depict underage characters having sex violate the statute. We think it implausible that a reputable distributor of Hollywood movies, such as Amazon.com, believes that one of these films contains *actual* children engaging in *actual or simulated* sex on camera; and even more implausible that Amazon.com would *intend* to make its customers believe such a thing. The average person understands that sex scenes in mainstream movies use nonchild actors, depict sexual activity in a way that would not rise to the explicit level necessary under the statute, or, in most cases, both. . . .

. . . [T]he dissent accuses us of silently overruling our prior decisions in *Ferber* and *Free Speech Coalition.* According to the dissent, Congress has made an end-run around the First Amendment's protection of virtual child pornography by prohibiting proposals to transact in such images rather than prohibiting the images themselves. But an offer to provide or request to receive virtual child pornography is not prohibited by the statute. A crime is committed only when the speaker believes or intends the listener to believe that the subject of the proposed transaction depicts *real* children. It is simply not true that this means "a protected category of expression [will] inevitably be suppressed." Simulated child pornography will be as available as ever, so long as it is offered and sought *as such,* and not as real child pornography. The dissent would require an exception from the statute's prohibition when, unbeknownst to one or both of the parties to the proposal, the completed transaction would not have been unlawful because it is (we have said) protected by the First Amendment. We fail to see what First Amendment interest would be served by drawing a distinction between two defendants who attempt to acquire contraband, one of whom happens to be mistaken about the contraband nature of what he would acquire. Is Congress forbidden from punishing those who attempt to acquire what they believe to be national-security documents, but which are actually fakes? To ask is to answer. There is no First Amendment exception from the general principle of criminal law that a person attempting to commit a crime need not be exonerated because he has a mistaken view of the facts.

As an alternative ground for facial invalidation, the Eleventh Circuit held that [the statute] is void for vagueness. Vagueness doctrine is an outgrowth not of the First Amendment, but of the Due Process Clause of the Fifth Amendment. A conviction fails to comport with due process if the statute under which it is obtained fails to provide a person of ordinary intelligence fair notice of what is prohibited, or is so standardless that it authorizes or encourages seriously discriminatory enforcement. . . .

The Eleventh Circuit believed that the phrases "'in a manner that reflects the belief'" and "'in a manner . . . that is intended to cause another to believe'" are "so vague and standardless as to what may not be said that the public is left with no objective measure to which behavior can be conformed." The court gave two examples. First, an email claiming to contain photograph attachments and including a message that says "'little Janie in the bath—hubba, hubba!'" According to the Eleventh Circuit, given that the statute does not require the actual existence of illegal material, the Government would have "virtually unbounded discretion"

to deem such a statement in violation of the "'reflects the belief'" prong. The court's second example was an e-mail entitled "'Good pics of kids in bed'" with a photograph attachment of toddlers in pajamas asleep in their beds. The court described three hypothetical senders: a proud grandparent, a "chronic forwarder of cute photos with racy tongue-in-cheek subject lines," and a child molester who seeks to trade the photographs for more graphic material. . . .

We think that neither of these hypotheticals, without further facts, would enable a reasonable juror to find, beyond a reasonable doubt, that the speaker believed and spoke in a manner that reflected the belief, or spoke in a manner intended to cause another to believe, that the pictures displayed actual children engaged in "sexually explicit conduct" as defined in the Act. The prosecutions would be thrown out at the threshold.

But the Eleventh Circuit's error is more fundamental than merely its selection of unproblematic hypotheticals. Its basic mistake lies in the belief that the mere fact that close cases can be envisioned renders a statute vague. That is not so. Close cases can be imagined under virtually any statute. The problem that poses is addressed, not by the doctrine of vagueness, but by the requirement of proof beyond a reasonable doubt.

What renders a statute vague is not the possibility that it will sometimes be difficult to determine whether the incriminating fact it establishes has been proved; but rather the indeterminacy of precisely what that fact is. Thus, we have struck down statutes that tied criminal culpability to whether the defendant's conduct was "annoying" or "indecent"—wholly subjective judgments without statutory definitions, narrowing context, or settled legal meanings.

There is no such indeterminacy here. The statute requires that the defendant hold, and make a statement that reflects, the belief that the material is child pornography; or that he communicate in a manner intended to cause another so to believe. Those are clear questions of fact. Whether someone held a belief or had an intent is a true-or-false determination, not a subjective judgment such as whether conduct is "annoying" or "indecent." . . .

Child pornography harms and debases the most defenseless of our citizens. Both the State and Federal Governments have sought to suppress it for many years, only to find it proliferating through the new medium of the Internet. This Court held unconstitutional Congress's previous attempt to meet this new threat, and Congress responded with a carefully crafted attempt to eliminate the First Amendment problems we identified. As far as the provision at issue in this case is concerned, that effort was successful.

The judgment of the Eleventh Circuit is reversed.

It is so ordered.

JUSTICE STEVENS, with whom JUSTICE BREYER joins, concurring.

The dissent argues that the statute impermissibly undermines our First Amendment precedents insofar as it covers proposals to transact in constitutionally protected material. It is true that proof that a pornographic but not obscene representation did not depict real children would place that representation on the protected side of the line. But any constitutional concerns that might arise on that score are surely answered by the construction the Court gives the statute's operative provisions; that is, proposing a transaction in such material would not give rise to criminal liability under the statute unless the defendant actually believed, or intended to induce another to believe, that the material in question depicted real children.

Accordingly, when material which is protected— particularly if it possesses serious literary, artistic, political, or scientific value—is advertised, promoted, presented, distributed, or solicited for some lawful and non-lascivious purpose, such conduct is not captured by the statutory prohibition.

JUSTICE SOUTER, with whom JUSTICE GINSBURG joins, dissenting.

. . . [T]he Act requires no finding that an actual child be shown in the pornographic setting in order to prove a violation. And the fair assumption (apparently made by Congress) is that in some instances, the child pornography in question will be fake, with the picture showing only a simulation of a child, for example, or a very young-looking adult convincingly passed off as a child; in those cases the proposal is for a transaction that could not itself be made criminal, because the absence of a child model means that the image is constitutionally protected. But under the Act, that is irrelevant. What matters is not the inclusion of an actual child in the image, or the validity of forbidding the transaction proposed; what counts is simply the manifest belief or intent to cause a belief that a true minor is shown in the pornographic depiction referred to.

The tension with existing constitutional law is obvious. *Free Speech Coalition* reaffirmed that non-obscene virtual pornographic images are protected, because they fail to trigger the concern for child safety that disentitles child pornography to First Amendment protection. The case thus held that pictures without real minors (but only simulations, or young-looking adults) may not be the subject of a non-obscenity pornography crime. . . . The Act, however, punishes proposals regarding images when the inclusion of actual children is not established by the prosecution, as well as images that show no real children at all; and this, despite the fact that, under *Free Speech Coalition,* the first proposed transfer could not be punished without the very proof the Act is meant to dispense with, and the second could not be made criminal at all.

What justification can there be for making independent crimes of proposals to engage in transactions that may include protected materials? . . .

. . . No one can seriously assume that after today's decision the Government will go on prosecuting defendants for selling child pornography; it will prosecute for merely proposing a pornography transaction manifesting or inducing the belief that a photo is real child pornography, free of any need to demonstrate that any extant underlying photo does show a real child. If the Act can be enforced, it will function just as it was meant to do, by merging the whole subject of child pornography into the offense of proposing a transaction, dispensing with the real-child element in the underlying subject. And eliminating the need to prove a real child will be a loss of some consequence. This is so not because there will possibly be less pornography available owing to the greater ease of prosecuting, but simply because there must be a line between what the Government may suppress and what it may not, and a segment of that line will be gone. This Court went to great pains to draw it in *Ferber* and *Free Speech Coalition*; it was worth drawing and it is worth respecting now in facing the attempt to end-run that line through the provisions of the Act. . . .

. . . [I]n practical terms *Ferber* and *Free Speech Coalition* fall. They are left as empty as if the Court overruled them formally, and when a case as well considered and as recently decided as *Free Speech Coalition* is put aside (after a mere six years) there ought to be a very good reason. . . .

The Court may have upheld PROTECT, but debate over how to regulate the flow of pornography on the Internet will undoubtedly continue. It has become an issue in political campaigns, with some candidates complaining about the lack of regulation of pornography on the Internet, and it will undoubtedly reappear in future elections. Moreover, states continue to pass laws—mini-CDAs—that ban the communication of indecent material to minors. Given the decisions in *Reno v. ACLU* and *Ashcroft v. ACLU,* the lower courts have been loath to uphold such laws, but that tendency could change should yet another version of the federal CDA pass constitutional muster. If it does not, the question of how to frame legislation will continue to loom large at least in part because the Internet is a form of communication unlike others government has sought to regulate in the past.

EMERGING ISSUES

As American courts and legislatures ponder these issues, other nations are beginning to take serious steps to regulate the flow of pornography on the Internet *(see Box 8-2)*. At the same time, parents and libraries throughout the United States are taking matters into their own hands through the use of filtering software and other mechanisms. And their actions, too, are generating lawsuits. Across the country, parents have filed lawsuits against Internet service providers (such as Yahoo!, Inc. and AOL) for failing to monitor their sites properly. In one case, *Doe v. Bates,* the parents of a minor child alleged that Yahoo! knowingly hosted illegal child pornography on the "Candyman" Yahoo! Group.

A district court dismissed the case, ruling that Yahoo! was immune from such suits. How the Supreme Court will rule on these and other matters as they make their way up the judicial ladder remains to be seen, but surely we have not heard the last word from the Court or Congress on attempts to shield children from pornography.

What is more, pornography is hardly the only constitutional issue that will occupy the Court's attention in the coming years. In Chapter 6, we noted that many states now grant special privileges to reporters. But what happens now that the Internet has enabled all of us to

---

BOX 8-2   INTERNET PORNOGRAPHY IN GLOBAL PERSPECTIVE

As the cases and materials in this chapter indicate, the U.S. Congress has passed various laws designed to regulate pornography—especially child pornography—and other indecent material on the Internet. That the Supreme Court has struck down some of the laws on First Amendment grounds is only one of the obstacles Congress faces in curtailing the flow of pornography. Another is that the Internet transcends national boundaries—more than two billion people, in more than two hundred countries, are now online.[1] Therefore, the effectiveness of any one law will depend not on the efforts of a single nation but on a far-reaching worldwide effort.

To date, many countries have made individual and cooperative efforts. Germany, for example, has been especially "aggressive," with the federal government keeping lists of and cracking down on illegal Web sites. The European Union has established "an alert platform" that enables authorities in member states to share information about child pornography sites. In addition, the members of the Association of Southeast Asian Nations (which includes Brunei, Indonesia, Malaysia, Philippines, Singapore, Thailand, and Vietnam, among others) have agreed to block access to Internet sites that run counter to "Asian values." This last step may reflect more than an attempt to protect citizens from obscenity; it may represent a fear of an "'Americanized' Internet culture." The French government has worked out an agreement with Internet service providers to block sites containing child pornography (as well as racial hatred and those linked to terrorism). If a site carries such content, its maintainers could be subject to prosecution. Canada, New Zealand, and several of the Scandinavian countries have worked out similar arrangements. Japan, a leading source of Internet child pornography, prohibits its distribution, but not its possession. It is now considering a law that would criminalize possession as well, but to date simple possession remains legal.

Keep in mind that many of these regulations, at least in some nations, will be subject to judicial review. Inevitably, some will fail to satisfy various constitutional requirements, just as has been the case in the United States *(see Box 8-1)*.

---

[1] Data on Internet usage are available at http://www.internetworldstats.com/stats.htm.

be "journalists" via online journals, blogs, and personal Web sites?[3] Should all "reporters" enjoy the same privileges? If not, how might the courts draw distinctions between journalists working for traditional media outlets and writers for online journals and blogs? Likewise, in Chapter 7, we raised a set of questions relating to libel on the Internet, which the Supreme Court has yet to resolve.

Finally, the right to privacy—a subject we cover in considerable detail in Chapter 10—is an underdeveloped legal area in this age of information. These days, we tend to associate privacy with reproductive freedom or perhaps right-to-die issues. But we live in an era when even the most intimate details of our lives can be easily disseminated on the Internet. Justice Scalia may have learned this the hard way when a professor teaching a law class on Internet privacy asked his students to create a "dossier" on the justice from information gleaned entirely from online sources. The students were able to generate a fifteen-page document that included Scalia's home phone number, his wife's e-mail address, lists of his favorite foods and television shows, and so on.[4]

Justice Scalia was apparently not amused. "It is not a rare phenomenon that what is legal may also be quite irresponsible," he wrote. "That appears in the First Amendment context all the time. What can be said often should not be said. [The professor's] exercise is an example of perfectly legal, abominably poor judgment."[5] But how he and the rest of the Court will deal with privacy and the Internet in the context of specific cases we can only speculate. What we can say is that you will have the opportunity to consider some of the emerging questions and possible answers when you read about the right to privacy in Chapter 10.

ANNOTATED READINGS

In the last decade, scholars and other commentators have published numerous books relating to the Internet and the First Amendment. Those focusing, in part or in full, on pornography include Yaman Akdeniz, *Internet Child Pornography and the Law: National and International Responses* (Burlington, VT: Ashgate, 2008); Mike Godwin, *Cyber Rights: Defending Free Speech in the Digital Age* (Cambridge: MIT Press, 2003); Philip Jenkins, *Beyond Tolerance: Child Pornography Online* (New York: New York University Press, 2001). Other treatments include Scott Gant, *We're All Journalists Now: The Transformation of the Press and the Reshaping of the Law in the Internet Age* (New York: Simon & Schuster, 2007); Jack Goldsmith and Tim Wu, *Who Controls the Internet?* (New York: Oxford University Press, 2006); Jeremy Harris Lipschultz, *Free Expression in the Age of the Internet* (Boulder, CO: Westview Press, 2000); Daniel J. Solove, *The Future of Reputation: Gossip, Rumor, and Privacy on the Internet* (New Haven, CT: Yale University Press, 2007).

---

3. For more on this point, see Scott Gant, *We're All Journalists Now: The Transformation of the Press and the Reshaping of the Law in the Internet Age* (New York: Simon & Schuster, 2007).

4. Reported in Noam Cohen, "Law Students Teach Scalia about Privacy and the Web," *New York Times*, May 18, 2009, B3.

5. Quoted in Kashmir Hill, "Update: Fordham's Dossier on Justice Scalia," Above the Law Web site, http://abovethelaw.com/?s=Reidenberg.

9   The Right to Keep and Bear Arms

PROMINENTLY DISPLAYED in the literature distributed by the National Rifle Association (NRA) and similar groups are statements invoking the Second Amendment. Advocates of gun ownership rights assert that this amendment protects the fundamental right of individuals to keep and bear arms. But supporters of gun control legislation claim that the amendment guarantees no such thing. The conflict between these two points of view has continued without interruption since the earliest government attempts to limit gun ownership rights. In large measure the controversy rests on the ambiguity of the amendment's wording.

The Second Amendment states in full, "A well regulated Militia, being necessary to the security of a free State, the right of the people to keep and bear arms shall not be infringed." The form of this amendment makes it somewhat of an oddity compared to the other provisions of the Bill of Rights, because it comes with its own preamble. The structure gives rise to the question of the extent to which the preamble conditions the right itself.

As a result, two distinctly different interpretations of the amendment have been advanced. The first, often expressed by those who favor government restrictions on private gun ownership, emphasizes the first half of the amendment. According to this view, the amendment guarantees only a *collective* right of the states to arm their militias. No individual right to own firearms exists unless it is in conjunction with a state militia. This position, therefore, interprets the amendment's prefatory clause as significantly controlling the meaning of the right to keep and bear arms.

If, as gun control supporters argue, the amendment was intended as a barrier against the federal government disarming state militias, then the amendment has little relevance today. In the nation's early years, the states, with no standing armies in place, responded to emergencies by calling private persons to serve in their militias. When called into service, these individuals were often expected to bring their own weapons with them. But states no longer call on citizen militias. Whatever roles the state militias played in the nation's first century are now carried out by other institutions, such as the states' National Guard units.

The second interpretation, advocated by pro-gun interests, emphasizes the second half of the amendment. It concludes that the Constitution guarantees an *individual* right to keep and bear arms. The preamble's reference to well-regulated state militias does not in any way limit the amendment's operative clause that explicitly guarantees "the right of the people" to own and carry weapons. The freedom to keep and bear arms, among other purposes, supports the inalienable right of individuals to engage in self-defensive behavior when necessary. As such, the Second Amendment is no less relevant today than it was when it was ratified in 1791.

The wording of the Second Amendment provides significant obstacles to understanding its meaning. Further complicating matters is the fact that historical records allow different interpretations of what Congress intended by proposing the amendment and what the state legislatures thought it meant when they ratified it. Until recently the Supreme Court has not offered much assistance, rarely accepting cases that call for an interpretation of gun ownership rights.

All the while, of course, the freedom to own and carry guns has been a significant political and social issue. Gun control supporters cite the social costs associated with the irresponsible use of firearms. These include gun-related crimes of violence and domestic abuse, as well as accidental injuries and deaths, often involving children. On the other side, advocates of gun ownership rights argue that the frequency of violent crime only underscores the need for responsible citizens to arm themselves for their personal protection.

Additionally, the subject of gun rights is not just a legal one. It has always been associated with strong political views. As Table 9-1 illustrates, almost equal numbers of Americans support each side of the debate. The resulting political controversy also sharply divides the nation along partisan, gender, and regional lines.

INITIAL INTERPRETATIONS

Congress did little to regulate firearms prior to the twentieth century, and as a consequence the Supreme Court on only rare occasions had need to interpret the Second Amendment.[1] Support for federal weapons restrictions, however, began to grow in the 1920s, largely fueled by the increases in organized crime that occurred during Prohibition and into the Great Depression. Particularly significant in raising public awareness of the misuse of guns was a violent confrontation between warring criminal organizations in Chicago in the infamous 1929 St. Valentine's Day Massacre. Congress responded by first imposing a ban on the use of the postal service to transport certain weapons and then by passing the National Firearms Act of 1934 (NFA), the first significant piece of federal gun control legislation.

The NFA was not a direct regulation of weapons. Because federal authority over possession of firearms was constitutionally suspect, Congress instead used its power to levy taxes and regulate interstate commerce to justify the legislation. The law imposed an excise tax on certain particularly lethal weapons and required their registration. It further prohibited the interstate transportation of any unregistered firearm covered by the act.

With respect to its compatibility with the Constitution, the NFA was controversial. Many thought

---

1. For example, *United States v. Cruikshank* (1876), *Presser v. Illinois* (1886), *Miller v. Texas* (1894).

TABLE 9-1   Public Opinion and Gun Ownership, 2010

Question: "What do you think is more important—to protect the right of Americans to own guns, OR to control gun ownership?"

	PROTECT GUN OWNERSHIP RIGHTS %	CONTROL GUN OWNERSHIP %
Total	46	50
Sex		
Men	57	40
Women	37	58
Race		
White	54	42
Black	30	66
Hispanic	21	75
Education		
College graduate	44	53
Some college	52	44
High school or less	45	51
Political affiliation		
Republican	70	26
Democrat	30	67
Independent	46	50
Region		
East	36	60
Midwest	52	44
South	49	48
West	44	50

SOURCE: Pew Research Center. National poll taken September, 2010. Respondents who answered "Don't Know" are not included. See "Views of Gun Control—A Detailed Demographic Breakdown," http://pewresearch.org/pubs/1858/gun-control-rights-division-demographics-party-ideology-religion-region-tea-party. © 2011 Pew Research Center for the People & the Press. Reprinted with permission.

its provisions violated the Second Amendment. The legitimacy of the 1934 law was tested in ***United States v. Miller*** (1939). To decide this case the justices were required to determine if the right to keep and bear arms was a personal liberty or only a collective right tied to the need for state militias.

The case began when Jack Miller and Frank Layton, two relatively insignificant career criminals, were indicted for transporting from Oklahoma to Arkansas a "shotgun having a barrel of less than eighteen inches in length"—that is, a sawed-off shotgun.[2] A tax had not been paid on the weapon and it was unregistered, both violations of the NFA. Miller and Layton challenged

---

2. For an interesting analysis of this case, see Brian L. Frye, "The Peculiar Story of *United States v. Miller*," *NYU Journal of Law and Liberty* 3 (2008): 48–82.

BOX 9-1   AFTERMATH . . . JACK MILLER AND FRANK LAYTON

Jack Miller was associated with the O'Malley Gang, an Oklahoma criminal organization that specialized in bank robberies. In 1934 he was indicted and jailed with other members of the gang for robbing two Oklahoma banks. Miller, a 240-pound Native American, decided to cooperate with the authorities. The evidence he provided helped convict four gang members, and in return he was released from jail. When the convicted robbers successfully escaped in a violent jailbreak in December 1935, Miller became a marked man. Fortunately for him, within a week police recaptured two of the escapees and killed the remaining two.

On April 3, 1939, just weeks before the Supreme Court would hand down its ruling in *United States v. Miller*, Jack Miller, Robert "Major" Taylor, and an accomplice, armed with shotguns, held up the Route 66 Club, a bar in Miami, Oklahoma. Their take was $80. The next day, Miller's body was found on the bank of Little Spencer Creek, just southwest of Chelsea, Oklahoma. Miller had been shot four times with a .38-caliber weapon. Found at his side was his .45-caliber automatic pistol. It had been fired three times. Miller was forty years old. Two days later, Miller's stripped and torched automobile was discovered. Police arrested Taylor for the murder, but homicide charges were dropped for lack of evidence. Taylor, however, pleaded guilty to armed robbery and was sentenced to ten years in prison.

Frank Layton, Miller's codefendant in the Supreme Court case, pleaded guilty in 1940 to the reinstated firearms charge. He was sentenced to five years' probation. Layton died in 1967. Miller and Layton are both buried in Woodlawn Cemetery in Claremore, Oklahoma.

SOURCES: Brian L. Frye, "The Peculiar Story of *United States v. Miller*," *NYU Journal of Law and Liberty* 3 (2008): 48–82; "Oklahoma Gangster's Impact on U.S. Gun Laws," News at 6, KOTV, Tulsa, Oklahoma, January 29, 2008; *United States v. Miller* (1939): Gun Law News, http://www.gunlawnews.org/Miller.html.

---

the criminal charges against them by claiming that the NFA violated the Second Amendment's right to keep and bear arms. The district court ruled in their favor in a short, memorandum opinion, providing no legal reasoning or comprehensive justification for the decision.

The United States appealed the decision to the Supreme Court, urging the justices to uphold the law. When the appeal reached the Court, only the federal government's position was argued. No one appeared to represent Miller and Layton. Therefore, the position that the NFA violated the Second Amendment was not defended by briefs or oral arguments before the Supreme Court or by a coherent opinion from the lower court. One could hardly imagine more favorable conditions for the federal government's position to prevail.

The justices unanimously supported the federal government's position, holding that the NFA did not violate the Constitution. The Court's opinion by Justice James Clark McReynolds explicitly interpreted the Second Amendment in light of its preamble. McReynolds wrote:

In the absence of any evidence tending to show that possession or use of a "shotgun having a barrel of less than eighteen inches in length" at this time has some reasonable relationship to the preservation or efficiency of a well regulated militia, we cannot say that the Second Amendment guarantees the right to keep and bear such an instrument. Certainly it is not within judicial notice that this weapon is any part of the ordinary military equipment or that its use could contribute to the common defense. . . .

With obvious purpose to assure the continuation and render possible the effectiveness of [state militias] the declaration and guarantee of the Second Amendment were made. It must be interpreted and applied with that end in view.

Miller has been viewed as generally supporting the collective right theory of the Second Amendment—that is, the position that the right to keep and bear arms was guaranteed only as a means of supporting the state militias. Gun rights advocates, however, see the *Miller* decision much differently. They argue that the nation's early reliance on citizen soldiers to staff the state militias was predicated on private gun ownership.

THE SECOND AMENDMENT REVISITED

The *Miller* decision certainly did not end the controversy over the Second Amendment. Gun rights groups continued to argue that a correct reading of the historical record proves that the Supreme Court got it wrong. And gun control advocates, citing the high rate of violent crime and numerous incidents of shootings stemming from the irresponsible or accidental use of firearms, pushed for increased state and federal weapons restrictions.

In the interim, lawyers and historians began to reexamine the meaning of the Second Amendment. Earlier generations of scholars generally sided with the position that the Second Amendment guarantees only the collective right to keep and bear arms. Analyzing additional historical records, however, led several contemporary scholars to conclude that the NRA and its allies may have a stronger legal argument than previously thought.[3] As Justice Clarence Thomas put it in a footnote to his concurring opinion in *Printz v. United States* (1997): "Marshalling an impressive array of historical evidence, a growing body of scholarly commentary indicates that the 'right to keep and bear arms' is, as the amendment's text suggests, a personal right."

For decades the Supreme Court avoided cases that presented difficult Second Amendment issues. The lower courts, however, did rule on such cases and often reached contradictory conclusions on the amendment's meaning.[4] In *District of Columbia v. Heller* (2008) the Court finally addressed these differing interpretations. As you read the opinions in this case, pay close attention to the justices' reasoning, especially their attempts to use historical analyses to establish what was understood to be the meaning of the amendment at the time it was proposed and ratified.

District of Columbia v. Heller

554 U.S. 570 (2008)
http://laws.findlaw.com/us/000/07-290.html
Oral arguments are available at http://www.oyez.org.
Vote: 5 (Alito, Kennedy, Roberts, Scalia, Thomas)
        4 (Breyer, Ginsburg, Souter, Stevens)

OPINION OF THE COURT: *Scalia*
DISSENTING OPINIONS: *Stevens, Breyer*

---

3. See, for example, Joyce Lee Malcolm, *To Keep and Bear Arms: The Origins of an Anglo-American Right* (Cambridge, MA: Harvard University Press, 1996); Stephen P. Halbrook, *That Every Man Be Armed: The Evolution of a Constitutional Right,* 2d ed. (Oakland, CA: Independent Institute, 1994); William Van Alstyne, "The Second Amendment and the Personal Right to Arms," *Duke Law Journal* 43 (1994): 1236–1255; Sanford Levinson, "The Embarrassing Second Amendment," *Yale Law Journal* 99 (1989): 637–659; Don B. Kates, "Handgun Prohibition and the Original Meaning of the Second Amendment," *Michigan Law Review* 82 (1983): 204–273.

4. For example, the Fifth Circuit Court of Appeals endorsed the individual right interpretation of the Second Amendment in *United States v. Emerson* (270 F.3d 203, 5th Cir. 2001), but the Ninth Circuit Court of Appeals adopted the collective right approach in *Silveira v. Lockyer* (312 F.3d 1052, 9th Cir. 2003).

FACTS:

In 1976 the District of Columbia, concerned with the high levels of gun-related crime, passed the nation's most restrictive gun control ordinance. The law essentially banned the private possession of handguns. Individuals could own shotguns and rifles, but only if the weapons were registered, kept unloaded, and disassembled or restricted by trigger locks. The law allowed the chief of police, under certain circumstances, to issue a one-year certificate permitting an individual to carry a handgun.

Dick Anthony Heller, a Washington, D.C., security officer, had been granted a license to carry a handgun while on duty providing security at the Federal Judicial Center. Heller applied for permission to own a handgun for self-defense, but he was refused. Claiming that the D.C. statute violated his Second Amendment right to bear arms, Heller brought a suit against the city. The district court dismissed his case, but the U.S. Court of Appeals for the District of Columbia reversed, holding that the Second Amendment protected Heller's right to possess a firearm for self-defense.

Heller's case did not occur spontaneously; instead it was planned and sponsored by attorney Robert Levy, who wanted to test the constitutionality of the District's gun control law. Levy had become a wealthy man in his first career in the financial information industry. At age forty-nine, he entered George Mason Law School and graduated first in his class. After clerking for two federal judges, he devoted his professional life to libertarian causes. Levy, who had never owned a gun, saw the District's law as a violation of personal freedom and private property rights. He recruited six possible plaintiffs to challenge the law, but only Heller met the strict standing requirements to pursue legal action. To eliminate any possible influence over the case by the National Rifle Association or any other gun rights group, Levy funded the litigation out of his own pocket.

ARGUMENTS:

For the petitioner, District of Columbia:

- Consistent with *United States v. Miller,* the Second Amendment protects the right to keep and bear arms only as it relates to service in a government-sponsored militia. The ratification debates provide little evidence that the purpose of the amendment was to protect private use of arms.

- The amendment was created in response to fears that a tyrannical federal government might attempt to disarm the state militias. Furthermore, because the

Dick Heller leaves police headquarters in Washington, D.C., on August 18, 2008, with his newly issued gun registration. Two months earlier, in District of Columbia v. Heller, *the Supreme Court declared the District's handgun ban unconstitutional.*

District of Columbia is not a state, this rationale does not apply.

- If the Court concludes that the amendment protects private ownership, it should nevertheless allow reasonable government regulations because of the dangers posed by guns.

For the respondent, Dick Heller:

- The Second Amendment protects an individual right that existed before the Constitution was adopted. The Court's rationale in *Miller* presumes that individuals in the eighteenth century had the right to own the weapons they brought with them when they were called to militia service.
- The preamble to the Second Amendment provides but one justification for protecting gun ownership. It in no way limits the primary right that the amendment protects.
- The Second Amendment protects arms that civilians would reasonably possess for lawful purposes (e.g., self-defense) or that could be used in militia service.

JUSTICE SCALIA DELIVERED THE OPINION OF THE COURT.

The Second Amendment is naturally divided into two parts: its prefatory clause and its operative clause. The former does not limit the latter grammatically, but rather announces a purpose. The Amendment could be rephrased, "Because a well regulated Militia is necessary to the security of a free State, the right of the people to keep and bear Arms shall not be infringed." . . .[O]ther legal documents of the founding era . . . commonly included a prefatory statement of purpose.

Logic demands that there be a link between the stated purpose and the command. The Second Amendment would be nonsensical if it read, "A well regulated Militia, being necessary to the security of a free State, the right of the people to petition for redress of grievances shall not be infringed." That requirement of logical connection may cause a prefatory clause to resolve an ambiguity in the operative clause. . . . But apart from that clarifying function, a prefatory clause does not limit or expand the scope of the operative clause. . . .

1. Operative Clause

a. "Right of the People." The first salient feature of the operative clause is that it codifies a "right of the people." The unamended Constitution and the Bill of Rights use the phrase "right of the people" two other times, in the First Amendment's Assembly-and-Petition Clause and in the Fourth Amendment's Search-and-Seizure Clause. . . . All . . . of these instances unambiguously refer to individual rights, not "collective" rights, or rights that may be exercised only through participation in some corporate body. . . .

This contrasts markedly with the phrase "the militia" in the prefatory clause. As we will describe below, the "militia" in colonial America consisted of a subset of "the people"—those who were male, able bodied, and within a certain age range. Reading the Second Amendment as protecting only the right to "keep and bear Arms" in an organized militia therefore fits poorly with the operative clause's description of the holder of that right as "the people."

We start therefore with a strong presumption that the Second Amendment right is exercised individually and belongs to all Americans.

b. "Keep and bear Arms." We move now from the holder of the right—"the people"—to the substance of the right: "to keep and bear Arms."

Before addressing the verbs "keep" and "bear," we interpret their object: "Arms." The 18th-century meaning is no different from the meaning today. . . .

The term was applied, then as now, to weapons that were not specifically designed for military use and were not employed in a military capacity. . . .

. . . We turn to the phrases "keep arms" and "bear arms." [Dictionaries] defined "keep" as, most relevantly, "[t]o retain; not to lose," and "[t]o have in custody." Webster defined it as "[t]o hold; to retain in one's power or possession." No party has apprised us of an idiomatic meaning of "keep Arms." Thus, the most natural reading of "keep Arms" in the Second Amendment is to "have weapons." . . .

At the time of the founding, as now, to "bear" meant to "carry." When used with "arms," however, the term has a meaning that refers to carrying for a particular purpose—confrontation. In *Muscarello v. United States* (1998), in the course of analyzing the meaning of "carries a firearm" in a federal criminal statute, Justice Ginsburg wrote that "[s]urely a most familiar meaning is, as the Constitution's Second Amendment . . . indicate[s]: 'wear, bear, or carry . . . upon the person or in the clothing or in a pocket, for the purpose . . . of being armed and ready for offensive or defensive action in a case of conflict with another person.' " . . . Although the phrase implies that the carrying of the weapon is for the purpose of "offensive or defensive action," it in no way connotes participation in a structured military organization.

. . . In numerous instances, "bear arms" was unambiguously used to refer to the carrying of weapons outside of an organized militia. The most prominent examples are those most relevant to the Second Amendment: Nine state constitutional provisions written in the 18th century or the first two decades of the 19th, which enshrined a right of citizens to "bear arms in defense of themselves and the state" or "bear arms in defense of himself and the state." It is clear from those formulations that "bear arms" did not refer only to carrying a weapon in an organized military

unit. . . . These provisions demonstrate—again, in the most analogous linguistic context—that "bear arms" was not limited to the carrying of arms in a militia. . . .

In any event, the meaning of "bear arms" that petitioners and Justice Stevens propose is *not even* the (sometimes) idiomatic meaning. Rather, they manufacture a hybrid definition, whereby "bear arms" connotes the actual carrying of arms (and therefore is not really an idiom) but only in the service of an organized militia. . . . Giving "bear Arms" its idiomatic meaning would cause the protected right to consist of the right to be a soldier or to wage war—an absurdity that no commentator has ever endorsed. Worse still, the phrase "keep and bear Arms" would be incoherent. The word "Arms" would have two different meanings at once: "weapons" (as the object of "keep") and (as the object of "bear") one-half of an idiom. It would be rather like saying "He filled and kicked the bucket" to mean "He filled the bucket and died." Grotesque. . . .

c. Meaning of the Operative Clause. Putting all of these textual elements together, we find that they guarantee the individual right to possess and carry weapons in case of confrontation. This meaning is strongly confirmed by the historical background of the Second Amendment. We look to this because it has always been widely understood that the Second Amendment, like the First and Fourth Amendments, codified a *pre-existing* right. . . .

There seems to us no doubt, on the basis of both text and history, that the Second Amendment conferred an individual right to keep and bear arms. . . .

2. Prefatory Clause

The prefatory clause reads: "A well regulated Militia, being necessary to the security of a free State. . . ."

a. "Well-Regulated Militia." In *United States v. Miller* (1939), we explained that "the Militia comprised all males physically capable of acting in concert for the common defense." That definition comports with founding-era sources.

Petitioners take a seemingly narrower view of the militia, stating that "[m]ilitias are the state- and congressionally-regulated military forces described in the Militia Clauses. Although we agree with petitioners' interpretive assumption that "militia" means the same thing in Article I and the Second Amendment, we believe that petitioners identify the wrong thing, namely, the organized militia. Unlike armies and navies, which Congress is given the power to create, the militia is assumed by Article I already to be *in existence*. . . .

3. Relationship between Prefatory Clause and Operative Clause

We reach the question, then: Does the preface fit with an operative clause that creates an individual right to keep and bear arms? It fits perfectly, once one knows the history that the founding generation knew and that we have described above. That history showed that the way tyrants had eliminated a militia consisting of all the able-bodied men was not by banning the militia but simply by taking away the people's arms, enabling a select militia or standing army to suppress political opponents. . . .

The debate with respect to the right to keep and bear arms, as with other guarantees in the Bill of Rights, was not over whether it was desirable (all agreed that it was) but over whether it needed to be codified in the Constitution. During the 1788 ratification debates, the fear that the federal government would disarm the people in order to impose rule through a standing army or select militia was pervasive in Antifederalist rhetoric. . . . Federalists responded that because Congress was given no power to abridge the ancient right of individuals to keep and bear arms, such a force could never oppress the people. It was understood across the political spectrum that the right helped to secure the ideal of a citizen militia, which might be necessary to oppose an oppressive military force if the constitutional order broke down. . . .

. . . If, as the [petitioners] believe, the Second Amendment right is no more than the right to keep and use weapons as a member of an organized militia—if, that is, the *organized* militia is the sole institutional beneficiary of the Second Amendment's guarantee—it does not assure the existence of a "citizens' militia" as a safeguard against tyranny. For Congress retains plenary authority to organize the militia, which must include the authority to say who will belong to the organized force. . . . Thus, if petitioners are correct, the Second Amendment protects citizens' right to use a gun in an organization from which Congress has plenary authority to exclude them. . . .

Our interpretation is confirmed by analogous arms-bearing rights in state constitutions that preceded and immediately followed adoption of the Second Amendment. Four States adopted analogues to the Federal Second Amendment in the period between independence and the ratification of the Bill of Rights. . . .

We therefore believe that the most likely reading of [some] pre-Second Amendment state constitutional provisions is that they secured an individual right to bear arms for defensive purposes. Other States did not include rights to bear arms in their pre-1789 constitutions. . . .

The historical narrative that petitioners must endorse would thus treat the Federal Second Amendment as an odd outlier, protecting a right unknown in state constitutions or at English common law, based on little more than an overreading of the prefatory clause.

We conclude that nothing in our precedents forecloses our adoption of the original understanding of the Second Amendment. It should be unsurprising that such a significant matter has been for so long judicially unresolved. For most of our history, the Bill of Rights was not thought applicable to the States, and the Federal Government did not significantly regulate the possession of firearms by law-abiding citizens. Other provisions of the Bill of Rights have similarly remained unilluminated for lengthy periods. . . .

Like most rights, the right secured by the Second Amendment is not unlimited. From Blackstone through the 19th-century cases, commentators and courts routinely explained that the right was not a right to keep and carry any weapon whatsoever in any manner whatsoever and for whatever purpose. . . . Although we do not undertake an exhaustive historical analysis today of the full scope of the Second Amendment, nothing in our opinion should be taken to cast doubt on longstanding prohibitions on the possession of firearms by felons and the mentally ill, or laws forbidding the carrying of firearms in sensitive places such as schools and government buildings, or laws imposing conditions and qualifications on the commercial sale of arms.

We also recognize another important limitation on the right to keep and carry arms. *Miller* said, as we have explained, that the sorts of weapons protected were those "in common use at the time." We think that limitation is fairly supported by the historical tradition of prohibiting the carrying of "dangerous and unusual weapons." . . .

. . . [T]he inherent right of self-defense has been central to the Second Amendment right. The handgun ban amounts to a prohibition of an entire class of "arms" that is overwhelmingly chosen by American society for that lawful purpose. The prohibition extends, moreover, to the home, where the need for defense of self, family, and property is most acute. Under any of the standards of scrutiny that we have applied to enumerated constitutional rights, banning from the home "the most preferred firearm in the nation to 'keep' and use for protection of one's home and family," would fail constitutional muster.

Few laws in the history of our Nation have come close to the severe restriction of the District's handgun ban. And some of those few have been struck down. . . .

. . . [T]he American people have considered the handgun to be the quintessential self-defense weapon. There are many reasons that a citizen may prefer a handgun for home defense: It is easier to store in a location that is readily accessible in an emergency; it cannot easily be redirected or wrestled away by an attacker; it is easier to use for those without the upper-body strength to lift and aim a long gun; it can be pointed at a burglar with one hand while the other hand dials the police. Whatever the reason, handguns are the most popular weapon chosen by Americans for self-defense in the home, and a complete prohibition of their use is invalid.

We must also address the District's requirement (as applied to respondent's handgun) that firearms in the home be rendered and kept inoperable at all times. This makes it impossible for citizens to use them for the core lawful purpose of self-defense and is hence unconstitutional. The District argues that we should interpret this element of the statute to contain an exception for self-defense. But we think that is precluded by the unequivocal text, and by the presence of certain other enumerated exceptions: "Except for law enforcement personnel . . . , each registrant shall keep any firearm in his possession unloaded and disassembled or bound by a trigger lock or similar device unless such firearm is kept at his place of business, or while being used for lawful recreational purposes within the District of Columbia." The nonexistence of a self-defense exception is also suggested by the D.C. Court of Appeals' statement that the statute forbids residents to use firearms to stop intruders. . . .

We know of no other enumerated constitutional right whose core protection has been subjected to a free-standing "interest-balancing" approach. The very enumeration of the right takes out of the hands of government—even the Third Branch of Government—the power to decide on a case-by-case basis whether the right is *really worth* insisting upon. A constitutional guarantee subject to future judges' assessments of its usefulness is no constitutional guarantee at all. Constitutional rights are enshrined with the scope they were understood to have when the people adopted them, whether or not future legislatures or (yes) even future judges think that scope too broad. We would not apply an "interest-balancing" approach to the prohibition of a peaceful neo-Nazi march through Skokie. The First Amendment contains the freedom-of-speech guarantee that the people ratified, which included exceptions for obscenity, libel, and disclosure of state secrets, but not for the expression of extremely unpopular and wrong-headed views. The Second Amendment is no different. Like the First, it is the very *product* of an interest-balancing by the people. . . .

In sum, we hold that the District's ban on handgun possession in the home violates the Second Amendment, as does its prohibition against rendering any lawful firearm in the home operable for the purpose of immediate self-defense. Assuming that Heller is not disqualified from the exercise of Second Amendment rights, the District must permit him to register his handgun and must issue him a license to carry it in the home.

We are aware of the problem of handgun violence in this country, and we take seriously the concerns raised by the many *amici* who believe that prohibition of handgun ownership is a solution. The Constitution leaves the District of Columbia a variety of tools for combating that problem, including some measures regulating handguns. But the enshrinement of constitutional rights necessarily takes certain policy choices off the table. These include the absolute prohibition of handguns held and used for self-defense in the home. Undoubtedly some think that the Second Amendment is outmoded in a society where our standing army is the pride of our Nation, where well-trained police forces provide personal security, and where gun violence is a serious problem. That is perhaps debatable, but what is not debatable is that it is not the role of this Court to pronounce the Second Amendment extinct.

We affirm the judgment of the Court of Appeals.

It is so ordered.

JUSTICE STEVENS, with whom JUSTICE SOUTER, JUSTICE GINSBURG, and JUSTICE BREYER join, dissenting.

The Second Amendment was adopted to protect the right of the people of each of the several States to maintain a well-regulated militia. It was a response to concerns raised during the ratification of the Constitution that the power of Congress to disarm the state militias and create a national standing army posed an intolerable threat to the sovereignty of the several States. Neither the text of the Amendment nor the arguments advanced by its proponents evidenced the slightest interest in limiting any legislature's authority to regulate private civilian uses of firearms. Specifically, there is no indication that the Framers of the Amendment intended to enshrine the common-law right of self-defense in the Constitution.

. . . The view of the Amendment we took in *Miller*—that it protects the right to keep and bear arms for certain military purposes, but that it does not curtail the Legislature's power to regulate the nonmilitary use and ownership of weapons—is both the most natural reading of the Amendment's text and the interpretation most faithful to the history of its adoption.

Since our decision in *Miller,* hundreds of judges have relied on the view of the Amendment we endorsed there. . . . No new evidence has surfaced . . . supporting the view that the Amendment was intended to curtail the power of Congress to regulate civilian use or misuse of weapons. Indeed, a review of the drafting history of the Amendment demonstrates that its Framers *rejected* proposals that would have broadened its coverage to include such uses.

The opinion the Court announces today fails to identify any new evidence supporting the view that the Amendment was intended to limit the power of Congress to regulate civilian uses of weapons. . . .

Even if the textual and historical arguments on both sides of the issue were evenly balanced, respect for the well-settled views of all of our predecessors on this Court, and for the rule of law itself would prevent most jurists from endorsing such a dramatic upheaval in the law. . . .

Until today, it has been understood that legislatures may regulate the civilian use and misuse of firearms so long as they do not interfere with the preservation of a well-regulated militia. The Court's announcement of a new constitutional right to own and use firearms for private purposes upsets that settled understanding, but leaves for future cases the formidable task of defining the scope of permissible regulations. Today judicial craftsmen have confidently asserted that a policy choice that denies a "law-abiding, responsible citize[n]" the right to keep and use weapons in the home for self-defense is "off the table." Given the presumption that most citizens are law abiding, and the reality that the need to defend oneself may suddenly arise in a host of locations outside the home, I fear that the District's policy choice may well be just the first of an unknown number of dominoes to be knocked off the table. . . .

The Court properly disclaims any interest in evaluating the wisdom of the specific policy choice challenged in this case, but it fails to pay heed to a far more important policy choice—the choice made by the Framers themselves. The Court would have us believe that over 200 years ago, the Framers made a choice to limit the tools available to elected officials wishing to regulate civilian uses of weapons, and to authorize this Court to use the common-law process of case-by-case judicial lawmaking to define the contours of acceptable gun control policy. Absent compelling evidence that is nowhere to be found in the Court's opinion, I could not possibly conclude that the Framers made such a choice.

For these reasons, I respectfully dissent.

JUSTICE BREYER, with whom JUSTICE STEVENS, JUSTICE SOUTER, and JUSTICE GINSBURG join, dissenting.

. . . [T]he protection the [Second] Amendment provides is not absolute. The Amendment permits government to regulate the interests that it serves. Thus, irrespective of what those interests are—whether they do or do not include an independent interest in self-defense—the majority's view cannot be correct unless it can show that the District's regulation is unreasonable or inappropriate in Second Amendment terms. This the majority cannot do. . . .

. . . The law is tailored to the urban crime problem in that it is local in scope and thus affects only a geographic area both limited in size and entirely urban; the law concerns handguns, which are specially linked to urban gun deaths and injuries, and which are the overwhelmingly favorite weapon of armed criminals; and at the same time, the law imposes a burden upon gun owners that seems proportionately no greater than restrictions in existence at the time the Second Amendment was adopted. In these circumstances, the District's law falls within the zone that the Second Amendment leaves open to regulation by legislatures.

The majority in *Heller* rejected the collective right interpretation of the Second Amendment and held that the Constitution guarantees an individual right to keep and bear arms. Importantly, however, Justice Scalia's majority opinion clearly stated that the personal right to possess weapons is not unlimited. Historical tradition, he suggested, would support prohibiting felons and the mentally ill from possessing firearms, banning especially dangerous or unusual weapons, forbidding weapons in sensitive locations such as schools and government buildings, and regulating the commercial sale of guns.[5] Although the majority declined to establish a test by which to evaluate gun control laws, Scalia concluded that under any standard of scrutiny a ban on handguns, the most popular weapon for personal and family defense, would constitutionally fail.

HELLER AND THE STATES

The Court's position in *Heller* was a sharp break from the past. We should be mindful, however, that the case dealt only with the very restrictive gun control ordinance in

---

5. The Court underscored this point one year later in *United States v. Hayes* (2009), when, without explicitly citing *Heller,* it upheld a 1996 amendment to the federal Gun Control Act that prohibits anyone convicted of a misdemeanor domestic violence charge from possessing a firearm.

Washington, D.C. The District of Columbia is not a state; it is ultimately controlled by the federal government.

This distinction is important. At the time the Court issued *Heller,* the Second Amendment was one of the few provisions of the Bill of Rights that had not been incorporated. *(See Chapter 3, and especially Table 3-1.)* Therefore, the amendment restricted the legislative power of the federal government, but not the authority of state or local governments. The Supreme Court reminded us of this fact as early as 1875 in *United States v. Cruikshank,* in which Chief Justice Morrison Waite for the majority wrote, "This is one of the amendments that has no other effect than to restrict the powers of the national government." And again in *Presser v. Illinois* (1886), the Court held that "the amendment is a limitation only upon the power of congress and the national government, and not upon that of the state."

The Court's interpretation of the Second Amendment in *Heller* had no direct effect on the authority of the states to regulate firearms as they saw fit. Instead, the states were bound primarily by the gun ownership and usage provisions of their own constitutions and laws. This, of course, begged the question of whether the justices ultimately would see fit to find that the right to keep and bear arms is a "fundamental" right and therefore applicable to the states through the due process clause of the Fourteenth Amendment.

It took little time for the Court to answer this question. Just two years after *Heller,* in *McDonald v. City of Chicago, Illinois* (2010), the justices heard a challenge to laws enacted by the city of Chicago and the village of Oak Park, Illinois, that effectively banned handgun possession by almost all private citizens. Writing for a five-justice majority, Samuel Alito left no doubt about the Second Amendment's application to the states: "We have previously held that most of the provisions of the Bill of Rights apply with full force to both the Federal Government and the States. Applying the standard that is well established in our case law, we hold that the Second Amendment right is fully applicable to the States."

But even *McDonald* does not fully settle the matter. It is clear that the restrictive handgun laws at issue in *Heller* and *McDonald* were inconsistent with the Constitution, but as the Court acknowledged, "Like most rights, the right secured by the Second Amendment is not unlimited." In *Heller,* Justice Scalia noted some of those limits, such as "long-standing prohibitions on the possession of firearms by felons and the mentally ill." What other legitimate restrictions there may be remains for the Court to determine in future cases.

ANNOTATED READINGS

The debate over the original meaning of the Second Amendment has generated a significant body of literature based on the studies and analyses of legal scholars, political scientists, and historians. Examples of some of the contributions to the discussion of this controversial issue are Randy E. Barnett and Don B. Kates, "Under Fire: The New Consensus on the Second Amendment," *Emory Law Journal* 45 (1996): 1140–1259; Saul Cornell, *Whose Right to Bear Arms Did the Second Amendment Protect?* (New York: St. Martin's Press, 2000); Stephen P. Halbrook, "The Right of the People or the Power of the State: Bearing Arms, Arming Militias, and the Second Amendment," *Valparaiso University Law Review* 26 (1991): 131–207; Don B. Kates, "Handgun Prohibition and the Original Meaning of the Second Amendment," *Michigan Law Review* 82 (1983): 204–273; Sanford Levinson, "The Embarrassing Second Amendment," *Yale Law Journal* 99 (1989): 637–659; Glenn Harlan Reynolds, "A Critical Guide to the Second Amendment," *Tennessee Law Review* 62 (1995): 461–512; Robert E. Shalhope, "The Ideological Origins of the Second Amendment," *Journal of American History* 6 (1982): 599–614; William Van Alstyne, "The Second Amendment and the Personal Right to Arms," *Duke Law Journal* 43 (1994): 1236–1255; Eugene Volokh, "The Amazing Vanishing Second Amendment," *New York University Law Review* 73 (1998): 831–840; Eugene Volokh, "The Commonplace Second Amendment," *New York University Law Review* 73 (1998): 793–821.

Some scholars have arrived at conclusions about the Second Amendment based on historical analyses that have traced the development of the right and the conditions surrounding it. See, for example, Joyce Lee Malcolm, *To Keep and Bear Arms: The Origins of an Anglo-American Right* (Cambridge, MA: Harvard University Press, 1996); and H. Richard Uviller and William G. Merkel, *Militia and the Right to Arms: Or How the Second Amendment Fell Silent* (Durham, NC: Duke University Press, 2002).

Others have examined the right to keep and bear arms from a public policy perspective. See James B. Jacobs, *Can Gun Control Work?* (New York: Oxford University Press, 2002); and John R. Lott, *More Guns, Less Crime: Understanding Crime and Gun-Control Laws* (Chicago: University of Chicago Press, 2010).

For an interesting look at the National Rifle Association and other such groups, see Osha Gray Davidson, *Under Fire: The NRA and the Battle for Gun Control* (Iowa City: University of Iowa Press, 1998).

10 The Right to Privacy

SUPPOSE THE SEMESTER is coming to an end and final examinations are only a week away. Two roommates plan to spend the week studying in their dorm room. For many, studying is a solitary activity carried on behind closed doors. Assume the roommates go to their room, close the door, and place a Do Not Disturb sign outside. They expect others to leave them alone and respect their privacy.

But is that expectation reasonable? The answer seems obvious: people have a right to be let alone. To many Americans, privacy is a basic and fundamental part of civil liberties and rights. But the issue is far more complicated than that, primarily because the Constitution makes no explicit mention of this right. The word *privacy* appears neither in the text of the charter nor in the Bill of Rights. This omission has led to questions about this presumed guarantee that the Supreme Court has had difficulty answering.

Do Americans have a constitutional right to privacy, and, if so, where does this right originate? For the past five decades, the Court has responded affirmatively to the first part of the query, but individual justices have offered different answers to the second. As we shall see, some assert that the right emanates from the overlap of several specific constitutional guarantees, most notably:

1. The First Amendment's right of association

2. The Third Amendment's prohibition against quartering soldiers

3. The Fourth Amendment's search and seizure clause

4. The Fifth Amendment guarantees against self-incrimination

5. The Ninth Amendment

Other justices argue they need look only at the Ninth Amendment, which says that the "enumeration in the Constitution, of certain rights, shall not be construed to deny or disparage others retained by the people." Finally, most modern-day justices find that the Fourteenth Amendment's due process clause prohibits government intrusion in ways that infringe upon liberties of citizens.

Another question concerns the areas the right covers. Today, many Americans equate the right to privacy with reproductive freedom, and, indeed, the Court has used privacy as a basis for legalizing contraception and abortion. But suppose the two studious roommates, in the privacy of their room, decide to use some cocaine. Possession of this drug is illegal, so does someone have the right to use it—engage in criminal activity—in private? Or does the government have the right to invade that privacy? In short, where do we draw the line? To what extent should the state limit the right to privacy?

In the end, we are left with many questions concerning the amorphous right to privacy. In addition, while reading this chapter, consider these: Have approaches to privacy and the rights encompassed in privacy, such as abortion, changed substantially over the years? If so, why? Have alterations in the membership of the Court generated changes in the reach of the right to privacy? Or has the Court responded to pressure from the larger political environment?

THE RIGHT TO PRIVACY: FOUNDATIONS

In today's legal and political context, the right to privacy has become almost synonymous with reproductive freedom. The reason may be that the case in which the Court first articulated a constitutional right to privacy, *Griswold v. Connecticut* (1965), involved birth control, and *Roe v. Wade* (1973), a decision that depended on *Griswold,* legalized abortion.

Prior to these decisions, the Court had contemplated privacy in somewhat different contexts. Following the common-law dictates that "a man's home is his castle" and all "have the right to be let alone," Louis Brandeis, a future Supreme Court justice, coauthored an 1890 *Harvard Law Review* article asserting that privacy rights should be applied to civil law cases of libel.[1] The article had enormous long-term influence, in no small part because it created a new legal "wrong"—the invasion of privacy.

After Brandeis joined the Court, he continued his quest to see a right to privacy etched into law. Among his best-known attempts was a dissent in **Olmstead v. United States** (1928), which involved the ability of federal agents to wiretap telephones without warrants. The majority of the justices ruled that neither the Fifth Amendment's protection against self-incrimination nor the Fourth Amendment's search and seizure provision protected individuals against wiretaps. Brandeis dissented, saying that the Fourth and Fifth Amendments prohibited such activity:

The makers of our Constitution undertook to secure conditions favorable to the pursuit of happiness. They recognized the significance of man's spiritual nature, of his feelings and of his intellect. They knew that only a part of the pain, pleasure and satisfactions of life are to be found in material things. They sought to protect Americans in their beliefs, their thoughts, their emotions and their sensations. They

conferred, as against the Government, the right to be let alone—the most comprehensive of rights and the right most valued by civilized men. To protect that right, every unjustifiable intrusion by the Government upon the privacy of the individual, whatever the means employed, must be deemed a violation of the Fourth Amendment. And the use, as evidence in a criminal proceeding, of facts ascertained by such intrusion must be deemed a violation of the Fifth.

However persuasive Brandeis's words might appear, they stood for nearly thirty years as the Court's only serious mention of a right to privacy. Court after Court ignored this dissent.

Justices of earlier eras, however, had paid attention to a concept that would later become associated with privacy—the concept of liberty. The word *liberty* appears in the due process clauses of the Fifth and Fourteenth Amendments. The Fifth Amendment states that Congress shall not deprive any person of "life, liberty, or property, without due process of law," and the Fourteenth Amendment uses the same wording to apply to the states. In the early 1900s the Supreme Court created a doctrine known as substantive due process to guide its interpretation of some government policies challenged as violations of the guarantees contained in the due process clauses.

Under the doctrine of substantive due process, the Court stressed the word *liberty* in the due process clauses to prevent governments from enacting certain kinds of laws, particularly those that would regulate business practices. **Lochner v. New York** (1905) illustrates the point. In this case, the Court reviewed an 1897 New York law that prohibited employees of bakeries from working more than ten hours per day and sixty hours per week. Joseph Lochner, the owner of a New York bakery, was convicted of violating the law, and he challenged it on Fourteenth Amendment due process grounds. He argued that the due process clause gives employers and employees the liberty to enter into contracts specifying the number of hours employees could work. By interfering with that contractual arrangement, the New York law, in his view, violated this guarantee. Five of the nine justices agreed. Writing for the majority, Justice Rufus W. Peckham noted:

The statute necessarily interferes with the right of contract between the employer and employees, concerning the number of hours in which the latter may labor in the bakery of the employer. The general right to make a contract in relation to

---

1. Louis Brandeis and Samuel Warren, "The Right of Privacy," *Harvard Law Review* 4 (1890): 193. William L. Prosser notes that Brandeis and Warren wrote this piece in response to the yellow journalism of the day. See William L. Prosser, "Privacy," *California Law Review* 48 (1960): 383–423.

his business is part of the liberty of the individual protected by the 14th Amendment of the Federal Constitution. Under that provision no state can deprive any person of life, liberty, or property without due process of law. The right to purchase or to sell labor is part of the liberty protected by this amendment, unless there are circumstances which exclude the right. There are, however, certain powers, existing in the sovereignty of each state in the Union, somewhat vaguely termed police powers, the exact description and limitation of which have not been attempted by the courts. Those powers, broadly stated, and without, at present, any attempt at a more specific limitation, relate to the safety, health, morals, and general welfare of the public. Both property and liberty are held on such reasonable conditions as may be imposed by the governing power of the state in the exercise of those powers, and with such conditions the 14th Amendment was not designed to interfere.

The Court struck down the law on the ground that it was a "meddlesome" and "unreasonable interference with an employer's right of contract protected in the liberty guarantee of the 14th Amendment."

The Court also applied the doctrine of substantive due process to regulations outside business. In **Meyer v. Nebraska** (1923) the justices considered a state law, enacted after World War I, that forbade schools from teaching German and other foreign languages to students below the eighth grade. They invoked a substantive due process approach to strike down the law, reasoning that the word *liberty* in the Fourteenth Amendment protects more than the right to contract. It also covers "the right of the individual . . . to engage in any of the common occupations of life, to acquire useful knowledge, to marry, establish a home and bring up children, to worship God according to the dictates of his own conscience, and generally to enjoy those privileges long recognized at common law as essential to the orderly pursuit of happiness by free men." According to the Court, government cannot interfere with these liberties, "under the guise of protecting the public interest, by legislative action which is arbitrary or without reasonable relation to some purpose within the competency of the State to that effect."

Meyer and *Lochner* are examples of substantive due process in action. Under this approach, the Court struck down legislation interfering with liberty unless governments could demonstrate that they were seeking to achieve ends that were not "arbitrary," "capricious," or "unreasonable." To some analysts, this doctrine was

the epitome of judicial activism because it allowed the Court to function as "superlegislature," the ultimate decider of what governments can and cannot do.

Through the 1930s the Court used the doctrine of substantive due process to nullify many laws, particularly those—as in *Lochner*—that sought to regulate businesses. The members of the Court were laissez-faire–oriented justices who believed that the government should not interfere with the business of business. During the New Deal, however, substantive due process fell into disrepute because the public demanded government involvement to straighten out the economy. The Court changed its approach: the justices would allow states to adopt whatever economic policies they desired if the policies were reasonably related to legitimate government interests. Known as the rational basis approach to the Fourteenth Amendment, it differs significantly from substantive due process because, under it, courts generally defer to governments and presume the validity of their policies.

Application of the rational basis test led the Court to uphold legislation such as minimum-wage and maximum-hours laws, which it had previously struck down on liberty grounds, even if the laws did not necessarily seem reasonable to the justices. In one case, in fact, the justices characterized a particular state's economic policy as "needless" and "wasteful." They upheld the law anyway, proclaiming, "The day is gone when this Court uses the Due Process Clause of the Fourteenth Amendment to strike down state laws, regulatory of business and industrial conditions, because they may be unwise, improvident, or out of harmony with a particular school of thought."[2] The majority added that if the people did not like the legislation their governments passed, they should "resort to the polls, not to the courts." With this declaration, the Court seemed to strike the death knell for substantive due process. It would no longer substitute its "social and economic beliefs for the judgment of legislative bodies, who are elected to pass laws."[3]

What does the discredited doctrine of substantive due process have to do with the right to privacy? Justice John Marshall Harlan (II) tied these two concepts

2. The case was *Williamson v. Lee Optical Company* (1955). The law at issue prohibited persons other than ophthalmologists and optometrists from fitting, adjusting, adapting, or applying eyeglass lenses and frames.

3. *Ferguson v. Skrupa* (1963).

together. Harlan was not an activist justice, and he was certainly no liberal, but he took great offense at the Court's handling of a 1961 case, **Poe v. Ullman.** At issue in *Poe* was the constitutionality of an 1879 Connecticut law prohibiting the use of birth control, even by married couples. A physician challenged the act on behalf of two women who wanted to use contraceptives for health reasons.

The majority of the Court voted to dismiss the case on procedural grounds. Several other justices disagreed with this holding, but Harlan's dissent was memorable. He argued that the Fourteenth Amendment's due process clause could be used to strike the law:

I consider that this Connecticut legislation . . . violates the Fourteenth Amendment. . . . [It] involves what, by common understanding throughout the English-speaking world, must be granted to be the fundamental aspect of "liberty," the privacy of the home in its most basic sense, and it is this which requires that the statute be subjected to "strict scrutiny."

In making this claim, Harlan sought to demonstrate that the concepts of liberty and privacy were constitutionally bound together, that the word *liberty,* as used in the due process clauses, "embraced" a right to privacy. And, because that right was fundamental, laws that touched on liberty/privacy interests, such as the one at issue in *Poe,* must be subjected to "strict scrutiny," meaning that the Court should presume that laws infringing on liberty/privacy were unconstitutional unless the state could show that the policies were the least restrictive means to accomplish a compelling interest.

Harlan's opinion was extraordinary in two ways. First, some scholars have pointed out that it resurrected the long-dead (and discredited) doctrine of substantive due process, which the Court had buried in the 1930s. Now Harlan wanted to reinject some substance into the word *liberty,* but with a twist. In his view, rather than protecting economic rights, due process protects fundamental rights, those the Court believes to be important in the concept of ordered liberty. One of these fundamental liberties—privacy—provides the second novel aspect of Harlan's opinion. As we have indicated, he was not writing on a blank slate; Brandeis had written about a right to privacy in the contexts of libel and search and seizure. In fact, Harlan cited—with approval—Brandeis's dissent in *Olmstead.* Still, Harlan's application of the doctrine to marital sexual relations was bold. As he wrote, "It is

difficult to imagine what is more private or more intimate than a husband and wife's marital relations."

Harlan's assertion (and that by William O. Douglas, another dissenter in *Poe*)[4] of a constitutional right to privacy proved too much, too soon for the Court; the majority of the justices were not yet willing to adopt it. But just four years later, in *Griswold v. Connecticut,* a dramatic change took place when the justices suddenly altered their views. More important is what they said about the right to privacy: the majority agreed that it existed, even if they disagreed over where it resides in the Constitution.

Griswold v. Connecticut

381 U.S. 479 (1965)
http://laws.findlaw.com/US/381/479.html
Oral arguments are available at http://www.oyez.org.
Vote: 7 (Brennan, Clark, Douglas, Goldberg, Harlan, Warren, White)
    2 (Black, Stewart)

OPINION OF THE COURT: *Douglas*
CONCURRING OPINIONS: *Goldberg, Harlan, White*
DISSENTING OPINIONS: *Black, Stewart*

FACTS:

In *Poe v. Ullman,* physician C. Lee Buxton tested Connecticut's 1879 law banning contraceptives on behalf of two of his patients. The majority of the Court voted to dismiss the case on procedural grounds, with the opinion for the Court pointing out that no prosecutions under the law had been recorded even though contraceptives were apparently "commonly and notoriously sold in Connecticut drug stores."

Griswold v. Connecticut was virtually a carbon copy of *Poe,* with but a few differences designed to meet some of the shortcomings of the earlier case.[5] Estelle

---

4. *In Poe,* Douglas wrote: "Though I believe that 'due process' as used in the Fourteenth Amendment includes all of the first eight Amendments, I do not think it is restricted . . . to them. The right 'to marry, establish a home and bring up children' was said in *Meyer v. State of Nebraska* to come within the 'liberty' of the person protected by the Due Process Clause of the Fourteenth Amendment . . . 'liberty' within the purview of the Fifth Amendment includes the right of 'privacy.' . . . This notion of privacy is not drawn from the blue. It emanates from the totality of the constitutional scheme under which we live."

5. For interesting accounts of *Griswold,* see Fred W. Friendly and Martha J. H. Elliot, *The Constitution: That Delicate Balance* (New York: Random House, 1984); and Bernard Schwartz, *The Unpublished Opinions of the Warren Court* (New York: Oxford University Press, 1985).

Dr. C. Lee Buxton, center, medical director for the Planned Parenthood League of Connecticut, and Estelle Griswold, right, executive director of the Planned Parenthood League of Connecticut, appear at police headquarters after their arrest. The two were held for violating the state's anticontraception law.

Griswold, the executive director of the Planned Parenthood League of Connecticut, and Buxton opened a birth control clinic in 1961 with the intent of being arrested for violating the same Connecticut law at issue in *Poe*. Three days later, Griswold was arrested for dispensing contraceptives to a married couple.

In the U.S. Supreme Court, Griswold's attorney, Yale Law School professor Thomas Emerson, challenged the Connecticut law on some of the same grounds set forth in the *Poe* dissent. Emerson took a substantive due process approach to the Fourteenth Amendment, arguing that the law infringed on individual liberty. He strengthened the privacy argument by asserting that it could be found in five amendments: the First, Third, Fourth, Ninth, and Fourteenth.

ARGUMENTS:

For the appellants, Estelle T. Griswold and C. Lee Buxton:

- The Connecticut anticontraceptive statutes deny appellants the right to liberty and property without due process of law in violation of the Fourteenth Amendment.
- The rights involved are fundamental, rather than commercial, and the legislative objectives sought by the Connecticut statutes have never been clearly enunciated. Therefore, the Court owes only a minimal deference to the legislature.

- The statute considered as a public health or moral regulation is overbroad and arbitrary; other potential objectives, such as population control or restricting sexual intercourse to the propagation of children, are inappropriate legislative purposes.
- The statutes violate due process in that they constitute an unwarranted invasion of privacy as recognized by the Court. Regardless of whether one finds the right to privacy in the Third, Fourth, Fifth, Ninth, or Fourteenth Amendment, or some combination thereof, the right to privacy protects, at least, the sanctity of the home and the intimacies of the sexual relationship in marriage (the core elements of this case).

For the appellee, State of Connecticut:

- The ban on contraceptives is a proper exercise of the police power of the state. Other states have similar regulations that have been upheld, and the legislature has left open other birth control options, such as the rhythm method and withdrawal.
- There is no invasion of privacy, because the proof of the offense was obtained legally and without coercion from voluntary witnesses.

MR. JUSTICE DOUGLAS DELIVERED THE OPINION OF THE COURT.

. . . [W]e are met with a wide range of questions that implicate the Due Process Clause of the Fourteenth Amendment. . . . We do not sit as a super-legislature to determine the wisdom, need, and propriety of laws that touch economic problems, business affairs, or social conditions. This law, however, operates directly on an intimate relation of husband and wife and their physician's role in one aspect of that relation.

The association of people is not mentioned in the Constitution nor in the Bill of Rights. The right to educate a child in a school of the parents' choice—whether public or private or parochial—is also not mentioned. Nor is the right to study any particular subject or any foreign language. Yet the First Amendment has been construed to include certain of those rights.

By *Pierce v. Society of Sisters* [1925], the right to educate one's children as one chooses is made applicable to the States by the force of the First and Fourteenth Amendments. By *Meyer v. Nebraska* [1923], the same dignity is given the right to study the German language in a private school. In other words, the State may not, consistently with the spirit of the First Amendment, contract the spectrum of available knowledge.

. . . Without those peripheral rights the specific rights would be less secure. . . .

. . . [Previous] cases suggest that specific guarantees in the Bill of Rights have penumbras, formed by emanations from those guarantees that help give them life and substance. Various guarantees create zones of privacy. The right of association contained in the penumbra of the First Amendment is one. . . . The Third Amendment in its prohibition against the quartering of soldiers "in any house" in time of peace without the consent of the owner is another facet of that privacy. The Fourth Amendment explicitly affirms the "right of the people to be secure in their persons, houses, papers, and effects, against unreasonable searches and seizures." The Fifth Amendment in its Self-Incrimination Clause enables the citizen to create a zone of privacy which government may not force him to surrender to his detriment. The Ninth Amendment provides: "The enumeration in the Constitution, of certain rights, shall not be construed to deny or disparage others retained by the people."

The Fourth and Fifth Amendments were described in *Boyd v. United States* as protection against all governmental invasions "of the sanctity of a man's home and the privacies of life." We recently referred to the Fourth Amendment as creating a "right to privacy, no less important than any other right carefully and particularly reserved to the people."

We have had many controversies over these penumbral rights of "privacy and repose." These cases bear witness that the right of privacy which presses for recognition here is a legitimate one.

The present case, then, concerns a relationship lying within the zone of privacy created by several fundamental constitutional guarantees. And it concerns a law which, in forbidding the *use* of contraceptives rather than regulating their manufacture or sale, seeks to achieve its goals by means having a maximum destructive impact upon that relationship. Such a law cannot stand in light of the familiar principle, so often applied by this Court, that a "governmental purpose to control or prevent activities constitutionally subject to state regulation may not be achieved by means which sweep unnecessarily broadly and thereby invade the area of protected freedoms." Would we allow the police to search the sacred precincts of marital bedrooms for telltale signs of the use of contraceptives? The very idea is repulsive to the notions of privacy surrounding the marriage relationship.

We deal with a right of privacy older than the Bill of Rights—older than our political parties, older than our school system. Marriage is a coming together for better or for worse, hopefully enduring, and intimate to the degree of being sacred. It is an association that promotes a way of life, not causes; harmony in living, not political faiths; bilateral loyalty, not commercial or social projects. Yet it is an association for as noble a purpose as any involved in our prior decisions.

Reversed.

MR. JUSTICE GOLDBERG, whom THE CHIEF JUSTICE and MR. JUSTICE BRENNAN join, concurring.

I agree with the Court that Connecticut's birth-control law unconstitutionally intrudes upon the right of marital privacy, and I join in its opinion and judgment. Although I have not accepted the view that "due process" as used in the Fourteenth Amendment includes all of the first eight Amendments, I do agree that the concept of liberty protects those personal rights that are fundamental, and is not confined to the specific terms of the Bill of Rights. My conclusion that the concept of liberty is not so restricted and that it embraces the right of marital privacy though that right is not mentioned explicitly in the Constitution is supported both by numerous decisions of this Court, referred to in the Court's opinion, and by the language and history of the Ninth Amendment. In reaching the conclusion that the right of marital privacy is protected, as being within the protected penumbra of specific guarantees of the Bill of Rights, the Court refers to the Ninth Amendment. . . .

While this Court has had little occasion to interpret the Ninth Amendment, "it cannot be presumed that any clause in the constitution is intended to be without effect." The Ninth Amendment to the Constitution may be regarded by some as a recent discovery and may be forgotten by others, but since 1791 it has been a basic part of the Constitution which we are sworn to uphold. To hold that a right so basic and fundamental and so deep-rooted in our society as the right of privacy in marriage may be infringed because that right is not guaranteed in so many words by the first eight amendments to the Constitution is to ignore the Ninth Amendment and to give it no effect whatsoever. Moreover, a judicial construction that this fundamental right is not protected by the Constitution because it is not mentioned in explicit terms by one of the first eight amendments or elsewhere in the Constitution would violate the Ninth Amendment, which specifically states that "the enumeration in the Constitution, of certain rights shall not be *construed* to deny or disparage others retained by the people." (Emphasis added.) . . .

Nor am I turning somersaults with history in arguing that the Ninth Amendment is relevant in a case dealing with a State's infringement of a fundamental right. While the Ninth Amendment—and indeed the entire Bill of Rights—originally concerned restrictions upon federal power, the subsequently enacted Fourteenth Amendment prohibits the States as well from abridging fundamental personal liberties. And, the Ninth Amendment, in indicating that not all such liberties are specifically mentioned in the first eight amendments, is surely relevant in showing the existence of other fundamental personal rights, now protected from state, as well as federal, infringement. . . .

In sum, I believe that the right of privacy in the marital relation is fundamental and basic—a personal right "retained by the people" within the meaning of the Ninth Amendment. Connecticut cannot constitutionally abridge this fundamental right, which is protected by the Fourteenth Amendment from infringement by the States. I agree with the Court that petitioners' convictions must therefore be reversed.

MR. JUSTICE HARLAN, concurring in the judgment.
I fully agree with the judgment of reversal, but find myself unable to join the Court's opinion. . . .

In my view, the proper constitutional inquiry in this case is whether this Connecticut statute infringes the Due Process Clause of the Fourteenth Amendment because the enactment violates basic values "implicit in the concept of ordered liberty." For reasons stated at length in my dissenting opinion in *Poe v. Ullman,* I believe that it does. While the relevant inquiry may be aided by resort to one or more of the provisions of the Bill of Rights, it is not dependent on them or any of their radiations. The Due Process Clause of the Fourteenth Amendment stands, in my opinion, on its own bottom.

MR. JUSTICE WHITE, concurring in the judgment.
In my view, this Connecticut law, as applied to married couples, deprives them of "liberty" without due process of law, as that concept is used in the Fourteenth Amendment. . . .

. . . There is no serious contention that Connecticut thinks the use of artificial or external methods of contraception immoral or unwise in itself, or that the anti-use statute is founded upon any policy of promoting population expansion. Rather, the statute is said to serve the State's policy against all forms of promiscuous or illicit sexual relationships, be they premarital or extramarital, concededly a permissible and legitimate legislative goal.

Without taking issue with the premise that the fear of conception operates as a deterrent to such relationships in addition to the criminal proscriptions Connecticut has against such conduct, I wholly fail to see how the ban on the use of contraceptives by married couples in any way reinforces the State's ban on illicit sexual relationships. Connecticut does not bar the importation or possession of contraceptive devices; they are not considered contraband material under state law, and their availability in that State is not seriously disputed. The only way Connecticut seeks to limit or control the availability of such devices is through its general aiding and abetting statute, whose operation in this context has been quite obviously ineffective, and whose most serious use has been against birth control clinics rendering advice to married, rather than unmarried, persons. Indeed, after over 80 years of the State's proscription of use, the legality of the sale of such devices to prevent disease has never been expressly passed upon, although it appears that sales have long occurred and have only infrequently been challenged. . . . Moreover, it would appear that the sale of contraceptives to prevent disease is plainly legal under Connecticut law.

In these circumstances, one is rather hard pressed to explain how the ban on use by married persons in any way prevents use of such devices by persons engaging in illicit sexual relations, and thereby contributes to the State's policy against such relationships. Neither the state courts nor the State before the bar of this Court has tendered such an explanation. It is purely fanciful to believe that the broad proscription on use facilitates discovery of use by persons engaging in a prohibited relationship, or for some other reason makes such use more unlikely, and thus can be supported by any sort of administrative consideration.

MR. JUSTICE BLACK, with whom MR. JUSTICE STEWART joins, dissenting.
The Court talks about a constitutional "right of privacy" as though there is some constitutional provision or provisions forbidding any law ever to be passed which

might abridge the "privacy" of individuals. But there is not. There are, of course, guarantees in certain specific constitutional provisions which are designed in part to protect privacy at certain times and places with respect to certain activities. Such, for example, is the Fourth Amendment's guarantee against "unreasonable searches and seizures." But I think it belittles that Amendment to talk about it as though it protects nothing but "privacy." To treat it that way is to give it a niggardly interpretation, not the kind of liberal reading I think any Bill of Rights provision should be given. . . .

One of the most effective ways of diluting or expanding a constitutionally guaranteed right is to substitute for the crucial word or words of a constitutional guarantee another word or words, more or less flexible and more or less restricted in meaning. This fact is well illustrated by the use of the term "right of privacy" as a comprehensive substitute for the Fourth Amendment's guarantee against "unreasonable searches and seizures." "Privacy" is a broad, abstract and ambiguous concept which can easily be shrunken in meaning but which can also, on the other hand, easily be interpreted as a constitutional ban against many things other than searches and seizures. . . . For these reasons I get nowhere in this case by talk about a constitutional "right of privacy" as an emanation from one or more constitutional provisions. I like my privacy as well as the next one, but I am nevertheless compelled to admit that government has a right to invade it unless prohibited by some specific constitutional provision. For these reasons I cannot agree with the Court's judgment and the reasons it gives for holding this Connecticut law unconstitutional.

. . . I think that if properly construed neither the Due Process Clause nor the Ninth Amendment, nor both together, could under any circumstances be a proper basis for invalidating the Connecticut law. I discuss the due process and Ninth Amendment arguments together because on analysis they turn out to be the same thing—merely using different words to claim for this Court and the federal judiciary power to invalidate any legislative act which the judges find irrational, unreasonable or offensive.

The due process argument which my Brothers Harlan and White adopt here is based, as their opinions indicate, on the premise that this Court is vested with power to invalidate all state laws that it considers to be arbitrary, capricious, unreasonable, or oppressive, or on this Court's belief that a particular state law under scrutiny has no "rational or justifying" purpose, or is offensive to a "sense of fairness and justice." If these formulas based on "natural justice," or others which mean the same thing, are to prevail, they require judges to determine what is or is not constitutional on the basis of their own appraisal of what laws are unwise or unnecessary. The power to make such decisions is of course that of a legislative body. Surely it has to be admitted that no provision of the Constitution specifically gives such blanket power to courts to exercise such a supervisory veto over the wisdom and value of legislative policies and to hold unconstitutional those laws which they believe unwise or dangerous. I readily admit that no legislative body, state or national, should pass laws that can justly be given any of the invidious labels invoked as constitutional excuses to strike down state laws. But perhaps it is not too much to say that no legislative body ever does pass laws without believing that they will accomplish a sane, rational, wise and justifiable purpose. While . . . our Court has constitutional power to strike down statutes, state or federal, that violate commands of the Federal Constitution, I do not believe that we are granted power by the Due Process Clause or any other constitutional provision or provisions to measure constitutionality by our belief that legislation is arbitrary, capricious or unreasonable, or accomplishes no justifiable purpose, or is offensive to our own notions of "civilized standards of conduct." Such an appraisal of the wisdom of legislation is an attribute of the power to make laws, not of the power to interpret them. The use by federal courts of such a formula or doctrine or whatnot to veto federal or state laws simply takes away from Congress and States the power to make laws based on their own judgment of fairness and wisdom and transfers that power to this Court for ultimate determination—a power which was specifically denied to federal courts by the convention that framed the Constitution. . . .

My Brother Goldberg has adopted the recent discovery that the Ninth Amendment as well as the Due Process Clause can be used by this Court as authority to strike down all state legislation which this Court thinks violates "fundamental principles of liberty and justice," or is contrary to the "traditions and [collective] conscience of our people." He also states, without proof satisfactory to me, that in making decisions on this basis judges will not consider "their personal and private notions." One may ask how they can avoid considering them. Our Court certainly has no machinery with which to take a Gallup Poll. And the scientific miracles of this age have not yet produced a gadget which the Court can use to determine what traditions are rooted in the "[collective] conscience of our people." Moreover, one would certainly have to look far beyond the language of the Ninth Amendment to find that the Framers vested in this Court any such awesome veto powers over lawmaking, either by the States or by the Congress. . . . If any broad, unlimited power to hold laws unconstitutional because they offend what this Court conceives to be the "[collective] conscience of our people" is vested in this Court by the Ninth Amendment, the Fourteenth Amendment, or any other provision of the Constitution, it was not given by the Framers, but rather has been bestowed on the Court by the Court. This fact is perhaps responsible for the peculiar phenomenon that for a period of a century and a half no serious suggestion was ever made that the Ninth Amendment, enacted to protect state powers against federal invasion, could be used as a weapon of federal power to prevent state legislatures from passing laws they consider appropriate to govern local affairs. Use of any such broad, unbounded judicial authority would make of this Court's members a day-to-day constitutional convention. . . .

I realize that many good and able men have eloquently spoken and written, sometimes in rhapsodical strains, about the duty of this Court to keep the Constitution in tune with the times. The idea is that the Constitution must be changed from time to time and that this Court is charged with a duty to make those changes. For myself, I must with all deference reject that philosophy. The Constitution makers knew the need for change and provided for it. Amendments suggested by the people's elected representatives can be submitted to the people or their selected agents for ratification. That method of change was good for our Fathers, and being somewhat old-fashioned I must add it is good enough for me. And so, I cannot rely on the Due Process Clause or the Ninth Amendment or any mysterious and uncertain natural law concept as a reason for striking down this state law. The Due Process Clause with an "arbitrary and capricious" . . . formula was liberally used by this Court to strike down economic legislation in the early decades of this century, threatening, many people thought, the tranquility and stability of the Nation. See, e.g., *Lochner v. New York*. That formula, based on subjective considerations of "natural justice," is no less dangerous when used to enforce this Court's views about personal rights than those about economic rights. I had thought that we

had laid that formula, as a means for striking down state legislation, to rest once and for all.

MR. JUSTICE STEWART, whom MR. JUSTICE BLACK joins, dissenting.

Since 1879 Connecticut has had on its books a law which forbids the use of contraceptives by anyone. I think this is an uncommonly silly law. As a practical matter, the law is obviously unenforceable, except in the oblique context of the present case. As a philosophical matter, I believe the use of contraceptives in the relationship of marriage should be left to personal and private choice, based upon each individual's moral, ethical, and religious beliefs. As a matter of social policy, I think professional counsel about methods of birth control should be available to all, so that each individual's choice can be meaningfully made. But we are not asked in this case to say whether we think this law is unwise, or even asinine. We are asked to hold that it violates the United States Constitution. And that I cannot do. . . .

What provision of the Constitution. . . does make this state law invalid? The Court says it is the right of privacy "created by several fundamental constitutional guarantees." With all deference, I can find no such general right of privacy in the Bill of Rights, in any other part of the Constitution, or in any case ever before decided by this Court. . . .

It is the essence of judicial duty to subordinate our own personal views, our own ideas of what legislation is wise and what is not. If, as I should surely hope, the law before us does not reflect the standards of the people of Connecticut, the people of Connecticut can freely exercise their true Ninth and Tenth Amendment rights to persuade their elected representatives to repeal it. That is the constitutional way to take this law off the books.

Griswold was a landmark decision because it created a constitutional right to privacy and deemed that right fundamental (for how the decision affected the appellants, Griswold and Buxton, see Box 10-1). Under *Griswold*, governments may place limits on the right to privacy only if those limits survive "strict" constitutional scrutiny, which means that the government must demonstrate that its restrictions are necessary and narrowly tailored to serve a compelling government interest. The justices, however, disagreed about where that right exists within the Constitution *(see Table 10-1)*. Douglas's opinion for the Court asserted that specific guarantees in the

BOX 10-1 AFTERMATH . . . ESTELLE GRISWOLD AND C. LEE BUXTON

After the Supreme Court ruled in their favor, it took Estelle Griswold and Lee Buxton a little more than three months to reopen the New Haven Planned Parenthood birth control clinic. On September 20, 1965, the clinic conducted its first birth control counseling session since its short-lived, ten-day stint in November 1961. This time, however, its activities were legal. Prior to the Supreme Court's ruling, Planned Parenthood legally could offer only transportation services from New Haven to birth control counselors in the neighboring states of Rhode Island and New York, where such counseling was permitted. Because its counseling services were in demand and little opposition was raised, Planned Parenthood soon opened additional clinics in other Connecticut communities. Physicians and staff working in these clinics no longer had to face arrest for dispensing contraceptive devices or information.

Lee Buxton, who served as medical director for the New Haven Clinic as well as chair of the Department of Obstetrics and Gynecology at the Yale University School of Medicine, had fallen into poor health by the time the Supreme Court issued its ruling. Plagued by depression and alcoholism, Buxton took a leave of absence from Yale in 1965. He was hospitalized several times over the next three years and died in July 1969.

Estelle Griswold turned sixty-five years old the day after the Court issued its opinion. She remained in her position as executive director of the Planned Parenthood League of Connecticut, but her tenure there was not a happy one. She had experienced long-standing disagreements with other birth control activists related both to policy issues and to her assertive leadership style. In the summer of 1965, shortly after the Court's ruling, she announced her intention to step down. By the end of that year she had severed her relationship with the

Estelle Griswold, left, and Cornelia D. Jahncke, president of the Planned Parenthood League of Connecticut, Inc., read a newspaper account of the 1965 Supreme Court decision establishing the constitutional right to privacy and striking down a Connecticut law banning the distribution of contraceptives.

organization. Shortly after she retired, Griswold's husband, Richard, died after a long battle with emphysema. She moved to Fort Myers, Florida, where she devoted her time to campaigning for the legalization of abortion and promoting the rights of senior citizens. Griswold died in 1981 at the age of eighty-one.

SOURCES: Lori Ann Brass, "An Arrest in New Haven, Contraception and the Right to Privacy," *Yale Medicine* 41, no. 3 (Spring 2007); John W. Johnson, Griswold v. Connecticut: *Birth Control and the Constitutional Right to Privacy* (Lawrence: University Press of Kansas, 2005; Ernest Kohom, "The Department of Obstetrics and Gynecology at Yale: The First One Hundred Fifty Years, from Nathan Smith to Lee Buxton," *Yale Journal of Biology and Medicine* 66 (1993): 85–105; Susan Ware, ed., *Notable American Women: A Biographical Dictionary Completing the Twentieth Century* (Cambridge, MA: Belknap Press, 2004).

Bill of Rights have penumbras, formed by emanations from First, Third, Fourth, Fifth, and Ninth Amendment guarantees "that help give them life and substance." In other words, Douglas claimed that even though the Constitution fails to mention privacy, clauses within the document create zones that give rise to the right. In making this argument, Douglas avoided reliance on the Fourteenth Amendment's due process clause. He apparently believed that grounding privacy in that clause

would hark back to the days of *Lochner* and substantive due process, a doctrine he explicitly rejected.

Arthur J. Goldberg, writing for Earl Warren and William J. Brennan Jr., did not dispute Douglas's penumbra theory but chose to emphasize the relevance of the Ninth Amendment. In Goldberg's view, that amendment could be read to contain a right to privacy. His logic was simple: the wording of the amendment, coupled with its history, suggested that it was "proffered

TABLE 10-1   Where Is the Right to Privacy Located in the Constitution? The Splits in Griswold

LOCATION OF THE PRIVACY RIGHT	JUSTICES
First, Third, Fourth, Fifth, and Ninth Amendments	Douglas, Clark
Ninth Amendment	Goldberg, Brennan, Warren
Fourteenth Amendment (due process clause)	Harlan, White
No general right to privacy in the Constitution	Black, Stewart

to quiet expressed fears that a bill of specifically enumerated rights could not be sufficiently broad to cover all essential rights," including the right to privacy. Harlan reiterated his stance in *Poe* that the due process clause of the Fourteenth Amendment prohibits such legislation. In holding to his *Poe* opinion, however, Harlan went one step beyond the Goldberg concurrers. He rejected Douglas's penumbra theory and asserted, "While the relevant inquiry may be aided by resort to one or more of the provisions of the Bill of Rights, it is not dependent on them or any of their radiations." Byron White also filed a concurring opinion lending support to Harlan's due process view of privacy.

The *Griswold* opinions make clear that the justices did not speak with one voice. Seven agreed, more or less, that a right to privacy existed, but they located that right in three distinct constitutional spheres. The other two—Hugo L. Black and Potter Stewart—argued that the Constitution does not contain a general right to privacy, but they did more than that. They took their colleagues to task for, in their view, reverting to the days of *Lochner* and substantive due process. Black and Stewart maintained that the people, not the courts, should pressure legislatures to change "unwise" laws.

Whether a right to privacy existed and where the right was located, however, were not the only questions raised by *Griswold*. Another issue concerned what this newly found right covered. Clearly, it protected "notions of privacy surrounding the marriage relationship," but beyond that observers could only speculate.

In this chapter we examine the other areas where the Court has applied *Griswold*. We look first at *Griswold*'s role in the issue of abortion and then into its extensions into other private activities. Keep the *Griswold* precedent in mind. To which interpretation of the right to privacy has the Court subscribed in the cases

that follow? Has the Court's approach changed with its increasing conservatism? Or do the majority of justices continue to adopt *Griswold*'s basic tenets?

REPRODUCTIVE FREEDOM AND THE RIGHT TO PRIVACY: ABORTION

Many of the issues flowing from *Griswold*—such as drug testing and the right to die—are hotly debated, as we shall see in the next sections, but those discussions are comparatively mild compared to the controversy stirred up by the Court's use of the right to privacy doctrine to legalize abortion in *Roe v. Wade* (1973). Since this decision, abortion has taken center stage in public discourse. It has affected the outcomes of many political races; occupied preeminent places on legislative, executive, and judicial agendas; and become a heated topic for discussion in the nomination proceedings for Supreme Court and lower federal court judges.

What is particularly intriguing about the issue is that the furor was generated by the Court. Prior to the decision in *Roe*, abortion was not an important political issue. As Figure 10-1 shows, many states had on their books laws enacted in the late 1800s that permitted abortion only to save the life of the mother. Other states had reformed their legislation in the 1960s to include legal abortion for pregnancies resulting from rape or incest or those in which there was a high likelihood of a deformed baby. The majority of states defined performing or obtaining an abortion, under all other circumstances, as criminal offenses. These conditions did not mean that states were under no pressure to change their laws. During the 1960s a growing pro-choice movement, consisting of groups such as the American Civil Liberties Union and the National Association for the Repeal of Abortion Laws (NARAL; later renamed the National Abortion Rights Action League and today known as NARAL Pro-Choice America), sought to persuade states to legalize the procedure fully—that is, allow abortion on demand.

When only a handful of states even considered taking such action, attorneys and leaders of the pro-choice movement supplemented their legislative lobbying with litigation, initiating dozens of suits in federal and state courts. These cases challenged restrictive abortion laws on several grounds, including the First Amendment's freedoms of association and speech for doctors (and patients) and the Fourteenth

FIGURE 10-1   Legislative Action on Abortion through the Early 1970s

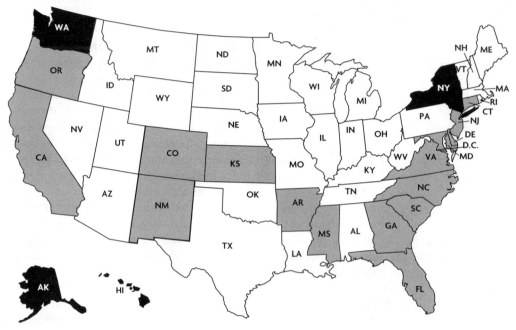

Key:

States in white: Retained existing law, which generally permitted abortions to save the life of the mother only.

States in grey: Altered existing abortion law, between 1966 and 1970, to permit abortion under certain circumstances, such as pregnancies resulting from rape or incest.

States in black: Repealed existing abortion law to allow for some form of "abortion on demand."

Amendment's equal protection clause (discrimination against women). But the most commonly invoked legal ground was *Griswold*'s right to privacy. Because it was unclear to attorneys which clause of the Constitution generated the right to privacy, in many cases, pro-choice lawyers covered their bases by arguing on all three specific grounds. Their larger point was clear: the right to privacy was broad enough to encompass the right to obtain an abortion. Moreover, because the right to privacy was "fundamental," logic would hold that the right to obtain an abortion was also fundamental, meaning that states could proscribe the procedure only with a compelling interest. Such an interest, pro-choice attorneys asserted, did not exist.

The result of this legal activity was an avalanche of litigation. Pro-choice groups had flooded the U.S. courts with lawsuits—some on behalf of doctors, some for women—challenging both major kinds of abortion laws: those that permitted abortion only to save the life of the mother and those that allowed abortion in cases

of rape or incest or to save the life of the mother. They were hoping that the Supreme Court would hear at least one.

Their wish was granted when the Court agreed to hear arguments in December of 1971 in two cases, *Roe v. Wade,* a challenge to a Texas law representing the most restrictive kinds of abortion laws, and *Doe v. Bolton,* a challenge to a Georgia law representing the newer, less restrictive laws. Because the Court had problems resolving these cases, they were reargued at the beginning of the next term.

In the meantime, the justices handed down a decision that had some bearing on the debate. In 1972 the Court struck down a Massachusetts law that prohibited the sale of contraceptives to unmarried people. Writing for a six-person majority (with only Chief Justice Warren Burger dissenting) in *Eisenstadt v. Baird,* Justice Brennan asserted that the law violated the "rights of single people" under the Fourteenth Amendment's equal protection clause. But, in dicta, he went much further:

If under *Griswold* the distribution of contraceptives to married persons cannot be prohibited, a ban on distribution to unmarried persons would be equally impermissible. It is true that in *Griswold* the right of privacy in question inhered in the marital relationship. Yet the marital couple is not an independent entity with a mind and heart of its own, but an association of two individuals each with separate intellectual and emotional makeup. If the right of privacy means anything, it is the right of the individual, married or single, to be free from unwarranted governmental intrusion into matters so fundamentally affecting a person as the decision whether to bear or beget a child.

Whether Brennan wrote this with *Roe* and *Doe* in mind we do not know, but clearly *Eisenstadt* heartened pro-choice forces. Their optimism was not misplaced, for, on January 22, 1973, when the Court handed down its decisions in *Roe* and *Doe,* they had won. As you read *Roe,* pay particular attention to the Court's logic. On what grounds did it strike down the Texas law?

Roe v. Wade

410 U.S. 113 (1973)
http://laws.findlaw.com/US/410/113.html
Oral arguments are available at http://www.oyez.org.
Vote: 7 (Blackmun, Brennan, Burger, Douglas, Marshall, Powell, Stewart)
     2 (Rehnquist, White)

OPINION OF THE COURT: *Blackmun*
CONCURRING OPINIONS: *Burger, Douglas, Stewart*
DISSENTING OPINIONS: *Rehnquist, White*

FACTS:

In August 1969 Norma McCorvey, a twenty-one-year-old carnival worker living in Texas, claimed to have been raped and to be pregnant as a result of that rape.[6] Her doctor refused to perform an abortion, citing an 1857 Texas law, revised in 1879, that made it a crime to "procure an abortion" unless it was necessary to save the life of a mother. He provided her with the name of a lawyer who handled adoptions. The lawyer, in turn,

6. We draw this discussion from the papers of William J. Brennan Jr., Manuscript Division, Library of Congress; Lee Epstein and Joseph F. Kobylka, *The Supreme Court and Legal Change* (Chapel Hill: University of North Carolina Press, 1992); Lee Epstein and Jack Knight, *The Choices Justices Make* (Washington, DC: CQ Press, 1998); and Marion Faux, *Roe v. Wade* (New York: Macmillan, 1988). For other accounts, see Eva Rubin, *Abortion, Politics, and the Courts* (Westport, CT: Greenwood Press, 1987); and Richard C. Cortner, *The Supreme Court and Civil Liberties Policy* (Palo Alto, CA: Mayfield, 1975).

sent her to two other attorneys, Linda Coffee and Sarah Weddington, who he knew were interested in challenging the Texas law.

Coffee and Weddington went after the Texas law with a vengeance, challenging it on all possible grounds: privacy, women's rights, due process, and so forth. Their efforts paid off: a three-judge district court panel ruled in their favor, mostly on Ninth Amendment privacy grounds. But because the district court ruling did not overturn the state law, McCorvey, using the pseudonym Jane Roe, and her attorneys appealed to the U.S. Supreme Court.

Once the Court agreed to hear the case, pro-choice and pro-life forces mobilized. On the pro-choice side, the ACLU and other groups helped Weddington and Coffee, who had never appeared before the Court, prepare their briefs and arguments. These groups also lined up numerous amici, ranging from the American College of Obstetricians and Gynecologists to the Planned Parenthood Federation to the American Association of University Women. In general, the pro-choice side wanted to convince the Court that abortion was a fundamental right under the *Griswold* doctrine. Unless Texas could provide a compelling and narrowly drawn interest, the law should fall. It also presented a mass of data indicating that physical and mental health risks are associated with restrictive abortion laws.

The state countered with arguments concerning the rights of fetuses. In its brief, it devoted twenty-four pages, along with nine photographs of fetuses at various stages of development, to depict the "humanness" of the unborn and to support its argument that a state has a compelling interest in protecting human life. The state's position was supported by several pro-life organizations, including the National Right to Life Committee and the League for Infants, Fetuses, and the Elderly, as well as by groups of doctors and nurses.

On December 13, 1971, the Supreme Court heard oral arguments, and three days later it met to decide the abortion cases. Only seven justices were present because President Richard Nixon's newest appointees, Lewis F. Powell Jr. and William H. Rehnquist, had not participated in oral arguments. Of the seven participating justices, a four-person majority (Brennan, Douglas, Thurgood Marshall, and Stewart) thought the abortion laws should be stricken, although for somewhat different reasons. Moreover, they were unsure about the "time problem"—whether a woman should be able to obtain an abortion any time during her pregnancy or over a more limited period, such as the first six months. White came down most definitively in favor of the pro-life position. Burger and Harry A. Blackmun, who had joined the Court in 1969 and 1970, respectively, were less decisive; the chief justice leaned toward upholding laws prohibiting abortion, and Blackmun leaned toward the pro-choice camp. Although there was disagreement over the reasons the laws were unconstitutional and over the time frame for abortions, the result was clear: the pro-choice side would win by a 5–2 or 4–3 vote, depending on how Blackmun voted. Burger assigned the opinion to Blackmun, whom he had known since grade school.

This (mis)assignment triggered a series of events. The first was an irate letter from Douglas to Burger, in which Douglas had two bones to pick: first, as the senior member of the majority, he should have assigned the opinion; second, Blackmun should not have received the assignment in any event because Douglas's vote tallies put him in the minority. Burger responded that he would not change the assignment. He said: "At the close of discussion of this case, I remarked to the Conference that there were, literally, not enough columns to mark up an accurate reflection of the voting. . . . I therefore marked down no votes and said this was a case that would have to stand or fall on the writing, when it was done. . . . This is still my view of how to handle . . . this sensitive case."

Still uncertain of how Blackmun would dispose of the case and of what rationale he would use, some of the justices began preparing opinions. Indeed, it took Douglas only a few weeks to circulate a memorandum to Brennan, who responded with some suggestions for revision and the admonition that Douglas hold on to the opinion until Blackmun circulated his.

It was a long wait. In mid-May 1972 Blackmun sent around his first draft in *Roe*—a draft that came to the "right" result in Brennan's and Douglas's minds but did so for the wrong (that is, narrowest possible) reason: that the restrictive Texas abortion law was void because it was vague, not because it interfered with any fundamental right. The four pro-choicers were disappointed and urged Blackmun to recast his draft. In so doing, they raised the opinion assignment issue again. Douglas wrote to Blackmun:

In *Roe v. Wade,* my notes confirm what Bill Brennan wrote yesterday in his memo to you—that abortion statutes were invalid save as they required that an abortion be performed by a licensed physician within a limited time after conception.

That was the clear view of a majority of the seven who heard argument. My notes also indicate that the Chief had the opposed view, which made it puzzling as to why he made the assignment at all except that he indicated he might affirm on vagueness. My notes indicate that Byron [White] was not firmly settled and that you might join the majority of four. So I think we should meet what Bill Brennan calls the "core constitutional issue."

At the same time, Douglas and the others were ready to sign Blackmun's draft, believing that it represented the best they could do.

They were happier with Blackmun's effort in *Doe v. Bolton,* the Georgia abortion case, because it adopted much of Douglas's and Brennan's beliefs about the importance of privacy and women's rights. Where they thought Blackmun went astray was in exploring the state's interest in protecting life. In this version, he stressed the point that somewhere around quickening (the point in pregnancy when fetal movement is first felt), a woman's right to privacy is no longer "unlimited. It must be balanced against the state. We cannot automatically strike down . . . features of the Georgia statute simply because they restrict any right on the part of the woman to have an abortion at will." Despite the qualms Brennan and Douglas had over such a balancing approach, they planned to sign the opinion; it led Blackmun to the "right" result. Douglas went so far as to "congratulate" Blackmun on his "fine job" and expressed the hope that "we can agree to get the cases down this Term, so that we can spend our energies next Term on other matters."[7]

Just when it appeared that a five-person majority would coalesce around Blackmun's opinion, on May 31 Burger initiated efforts to have the case reargued. Ostensibly, his reason was that "[t]hese cases . . . are not as simple for me as they appear for the others." He also "complained that part of his problem . . . resulted from the poor quality of oral argument." Brennan, Douglas, Stewart, and Marshall disagreed. In their view, Burger pushed for reargument because he was displeased with Blackmun's opinion in *Doe* and thought his side would stand a better chance of victory next term when Powell and Rehnquist would participate in oral arguments. Douglas later suggested that Burger believed the *Doe* opinion would prove embarrassing to President Nixon's reelection campaign and sought to minimize

---

7. This memo was, in part, a response to Burger's (and Blackmun's) suggestion that the cases be reargued.

the damage. The same day Burger issued his memo, Blackmun also suggested that the cases be reargued. In a memo to conference, he wrote: "Although it would prove costly to me personally, in the light of energy and hours expended, I have now concluded, somewhat reluctantly, that reargument in both cases at an early date in the next term, would perhaps be advisable." Despite Brennan's and Douglas's attempts to thwart this action, after White and the two new appointees voted with Burger, on the last day of the 1971 term the Court ordered rearguments in both *Roe* and *Doe*.[8]

ARGUMENTS:

For the appellants, Jane Roe, et al.:

- The Texas statute infringes fundamental personal rights, namely the right to medical care and the right to marital and personal privacy—of which the right to abortion is a part—secured by the First, Fourth, Ninth, and Fourteenth Amendments.
- The statute is not rationally related to any legitimate public health concern, any legitimate interest in regulating private sexual conduct, or any interest in protecting human life.

For the appellee, Henry Wade, District Attorney of Dallas County, Texas:

- The Constitution does not guarantee women the right to abortion.
- Personal and marital privacy are not absolute rights.
- Modern science clearly establishes that life begins at conception. Therefore, the state has a compelling interest in preserving the life of a fetus, even if this abridges some privacy right of the mother.

MR. JUSTICE BLACKMUN DELIVERED THE OPINION OF THE COURT.

We forthwith acknowledge our awareness of the sensitive and emotional nature of the abortion controversy, of the vigorous opposing views, even among physicians,

---

8. Both Brennan and Douglas wrote letters to Blackmun attempting to convince him that the cases should not be reargued. When Blackmun did not agree, Douglas warned Burger: "If the vote of Conference is to reargue, then I will file a statement telling what is happening to us and the tragedy it entails." He also accused Burger, in a memo to conference, of trying "to bend the Court to his will" and imperiling "the integrity of the institution." Douglas never carried through on his threat to take the matter public, but the *Washington Post* carried a story about it.

and of the deep and seemingly absolute convictions that the subject inspires. One's philosophy, one's experiences, one's exposure to the raw edges of human existence, one's religious training, one's attitudes toward life and family and their values, and the moral standards one establishes and seeks to observe, are all likely to influence and to color one's thinking and conclusions about abortion.

In addition, population growth, pollution, poverty, and racial overtones tend to complicate and not to simplify the problem.

Our task, of course, is to resolve the issue by constitutional measurement, free of emotion and of predilection. We seek earnestly to do this, and, because we do, we have inquired into, and in this opinion place some emphasis upon, medical and medical-legal history and what that history reveals about man's attitudes toward the abortion procedure over the centuries. . . .

The principal thrust of appellant's attack on the Texas statutes is that they improperly invade a right, said to be possessed by the pregnant woman, to choose to terminate her pregnancy. Appellant would discover this right in the concept of personal "liberty" embodied in the Fourteenth Amendment's Due Process Clause in personal, marital, familial, and sexual privacy said to be protected by the Bill of Rights or its penumbras, see *Griswold v. Connecticut* (1965), or among those rights reserved to the people by the Ninth Amendment, *Griswold v. Connecticut*. . . .

It perhaps is not generally appreciated that the restrictive criminal abortion laws in effect in a majority of States today are of relatively recent vintage. Those laws, generally proscribing abortion or its attempt at any time during pregnancy except when necessary to preserve the pregnant woman's life, are not of ancient or even of common-law origin. Instead, they derive from statutory changes effected, for the most part, in the latter half of the 19th century. . . .

Three reasons have been advanced to explain historically the enactment of criminal abortion laws in the 19th century and to justify their continued existence.

It has been argued occasionally that these laws were the product of a Victorian social concern to discourage illicit sexual conduct. Texas, however, does not advance this justification in the present case, and it appears that no court or commentator has taken the argument seriously. . . .

A second reason is concerned with abortion as a medical procedure. When most criminal abortion laws were first enacted, the procedure was a hazardous one for the woman. This was particularly true prior to the development of antisepsis. . . . Thus, it has been argued that a State's real concern in enacting a criminal abortion law was to protect the pregnant woman, that is, to restrain her from submitting to a procedure that placed her life in serious jeopardy.

Modern medical techniques have altered this situation. . . . Consequently, any interest of the State in protecting the woman from an inherently hazardous procedure, except when it would be equally dangerous for her to forgo it, has largely disappeared. Of course, important state interests in the areas of health and medical standards do remain. The State has a legitimate interest in seeing to it that abortion, like any other medical procedure, is performed under circumstances that insure maximum safety for the patient. . . . Moreover, the risk to the woman increases as her pregnancy continues. Thus, the State retains a definite interest in protecting the woman's own health and safety when an abortion is proposed at a late stage of pregnancy.

The third reason is the State's interest—some phrase it in terms of duty—in protecting prenatal life. Some of the argument for this justification rests on the theory that a new human life is present from the moment of conception. The State's interest and general obligation to protect life then extends, it is argued, to prenatal life. Only when the life of the pregnant mother herself is at stake, balanced against the life she carries within her, should the interest of the embryo or fetus not prevail. Logically, of course, a legitimate state interest in this area need not stand or fall on acceptance of the belief that life begins at conception or at some other point prior to live birth. In assessing the State's interest, recognition may be given to the less rigid claim that as long as at least *potential* life is involved, the State may assert interests beyond the protection of the pregnant woman alone. . . .

It is with these interests, and the weight to be attached to them, that this case is concerned.

The Constitution does not explicitly mention any right of privacy. In a line of decisions, however, the Court has recognized that a right of personal privacy, or a guarantee of certain areas or zones of privacy, does exist under the Constitution. In varying contexts, the Court or individual Justices have, indeed, found at least the roots of that right in the First Amendment, in the Fourth and Fifth Amendments, in the penumbras of the Bill of Rights, in the Ninth Amendment, or in the concept of liberty guaranteed by the first section of the Fourteenth Amendment. These decisions make it clear that only personal rights that can be deemed "fundamental" or "implicit in the concept of ordered liberty" are included in this guarantee of personal privacy. They also make it clear that the right has some extension to activities relating to marriage, procreation, family relationships, and child rearing and education.

This right of privacy, whether it be founded in the Fourteenth Amendment's concept of personal liberty and restrictions upon state action, as we feel it is, or, as the District Court determined, in the Ninth Amendment's reservation of rights to the people, is broad enough to encompass a woman's decision whether or not to terminate her pregnancy. The detriment that the State would impose upon the pregnant woman by denying this choice altogether is apparent. Specific and direct harm medically diagnosable even in early pregnancy may be involved. Maternity, or additional offspring, may force upon the woman a distressful life and future. Psychological harm may be imminent. Mental and physical health may be taxed by child care. There is also the distress, for all concerned, associated with the unwanted child, and there is the problem of bringing a child into a family already unable, psychologically and otherwise, to care for it. In other cases, as in this one, the additional difficulties and continuing stigma of unwed motherhood may be involved. All these are factors the woman and her responsible physician necessarily will consider in consultation.

On the basis of elements such as these, appellant and some *amici* argue that the woman's right is absolute and that she is entitled to terminate her pregnancy at whatever time, in whatever way, and for whatever reason she alone chooses. With this we do not agree. Appellant's arguments that Texas either has no valid interest at all in regulating the abortion decision, or no interest strong enough to support any limitation upon the woman's sole determination, are unpersuasive. The Court's decisions recognizing a right of privacy also acknowledge that some state regulation in areas protected by that right is appropriate. As noted above, a State may properly assert important interests in safeguarding health, in maintaining medical standards, and in protecting potential life. At some point in pregnancy, these respective interests become sufficiently compelling to sustain regulation of the factors that govern the abortion decision. The privacy right involved, therefore, cannot be said to be absolute. . . .

We, therefore, conclude that the right of personal privacy includes the abortion decision, but that this right is not unqualified and must be considered against important state interests in regulation. . . .

The District Court held that the appellee failed to meet his burden of demonstrating that the Texas statute's infringement upon Roe's rights was necessary to support a compelling state interest, and that, although the appellee presented "several compelling justifications for state presence in the area of abortions," the statutes outstripped these justifications and swept "far beyond any areas of compelling state interest." Appellant and appellee both contest that holding. Appellant, as has been indicated, claims an absolute right that bars any state imposition of criminal penalties in the area. Appellee argues that the State's determination to recognize and protect prenatal life from and after conception constitutes a compelling state interest. As noted above, we do not agree fully with either formulation.

A. The appellee and certain *amici* argue that the fetus is a "person" within the language and meaning of the Fourteenth Amendment. . . .

The Constitution does not define "person" in so many words. Section 1 of the Fourteenth Amendment contains three references to "person." The first, in defining "citizens," speaks of "persons born or naturalized in the United States." The word also appears both in the Due Process Clause and in the Equal Protection Clause. "Person" is used in other places in the Constitution: in the listing of qualifications for Representatives and Senators, Art. I, §2, cl. 2, and §3, cl. 3; in the Apportionment Clause, Art. I, §2, §3. . . . But in nearly all these instances, the use of the word is such that it has application only postnatally. None indicates, with any assurance, that it has any possible prenatal application.

All this, together with our observation that throughout the major portion of the 19th century prevailing legal abortion practices were far freer than they are today, persuades us that the word "person," as used in the Fourteenth Amendment, does not include the unborn. . . .

This conclusion, however, does not of itself fully answer the contentions raised by Texas, and we pass on to other considerations.

B. The pregnant woman cannot be isolated in her privacy. She carries an embryo and, later, a fetus, if one accepts the medical definitions of the developing young in the human uterus. The situation therefore is inherently different from marital intimacy, or bedroom possession of obscene material, or marriage, or procreation. . . . As we have intimated above, it is reasonable and appropriate for a State to decide that at some point in time another interest, that of health of the mother or that of potential human life, becomes significantly involved. The woman's privacy is no longer sole and any right of privacy she possesses must be measured accordingly.

Texas urges that, apart from the Fourteenth Amendment, life begins at conception and is present throughout pregnancy, and that, therefore, the State has a compelling interest in protecting that life from and after conception. We need not resolve the difficult question of when life begins. When those trained in the respective disciplines of medicine, philosophy, and theology are unable to arrive at any consensus, the judiciary, at this point in the development of man's knowledge, is not in a position to speculate as to the answer. . . .

In view of all this, we do not agree that, by adopting one theory of life, Texas may override the rights of the pregnant woman that are at stake. We repeat, however, that the State does have an important and legitimate interest in preserving and protecting the health of the pregnant woman, whether she be a resident of the State or a non-resident who seeks medical consultation and treatment there, and that it has still another important and legitimate interest in protecting the potentiality of human life. These interests are separate and distinct. Each grows in substantiality as the woman approaches term and, at a point during pregnancy, each becomes "compelling."

With respect to the State's important and legitimate interest in the health of the mother, the "compelling" point, in the light of present medical knowledge, is at approximately the end of the first trimester. This is so because of the now-established medical fact . . . that until the end of the first trimester mortality in abortion may be less than mortality in normal childbirth. It follows that, from and after this point, a State may regulate the abortion procedure to the extent that the regulation reasonably relates to the preservation and protection of maternal health. Examples of permissible state regulation in this area are requirements as to the qualifications of the person who is to perform the abortion; as to the licensure of that person; as to the facility in which the procedure is to be performed, that is, whether it must be a hospital or may be a clinic or some other place of less-than-hospital status; as to the licensing of the facility; and the like.

This means, on the other hand, that, for the period of pregnancy prior to this "compelling" point, the attending physician, in consultation with his patient, is free to determine, without regulation by the State, that, in his medical judgment, the patient's pregnancy should be terminated. If that decision is reached, the judgment may be effectuated by an abortion free of interference by the State.

With respect to the State's important and legitimate interest in potential life, the "compelling" point is at viability. This is so because the fetus then presumably has the capability of meaningful life outside the mother's womb. State regulation protective of fetal life after viability thus has both logical and biological justifications. If the State is interested in protecting fetal life after viability, it may go so far as to proscribe abortion during that period, except when it is necessary to preserve the life or health of the mother.

Measured against these standards, . . . the Texas [law] . . . , in restricting legal abortions to those "procured or attempted by medical advice for the purpose of saving the life of the mother," sweeps too broadly. The statute makes no distinction between abortions performed early in pregnancy and those performed later, and it limits to a single reason, "saving" the mother's life, the legal justification for the procedure. The statute, therefore, cannot survive the constitutional attack made upon it here. . . .

To summarize and to repeat:

1. A state criminal abortion statute of the current Texas type, that excepts from criminality only a *life-saving* procedure on behalf of the mother, without regard to pregnancy stage and without recognition of the other interests involved, is violative of the Due Process Clause of the Fourteenth Amendment.

(a) For the stage prior to approximately the end of the first trimester, the abortion decision and its effectuation must be left to the medical judgment of the pregnant woman's attending physician.

(b) For the stage subsequent to approximately the end of the first trimester, the State, in promoting its interest in the health of the mother, may, if it chooses, regulate the abortion procedure in ways that are reasonably related to maternal health.

(c) For the stage subsequent to viability, the State in promoting its interest in the potentiality of human life may, if it chooses, regulate, and even proscribe, abortion except where it is necessary, in appropriate medical judgment, for the preservation of the life or health of the mother. . . .

This holding, we feel, is consistent with the relative weights of the respective interests involved, with the lessons and examples of medical and legal history, with the lenity of the common law, and with the demands of the profound problems of the present day. The decision leaves the State free to place increasing restrictions on abortion as the period of pregnancy lengthens, so long as those restrictions are tailored to the recognized state interests. The decision vindicates the right of the physician to administer medical treatment according to his professional judgment up to the points where important state interests provide compelling justifications for intervention. Up to those points, the abortion decision in all its aspects is inherently, and primarily, a medical decision, and basic responsibility for it must rest with the physician. If an individual practitioner abuses the privilege of exercising proper medical judgment, the usual remedies, judicial and intra-professional, are available.[9]

Affirmed in part and reversed in part.

MR. JUSTICE REHNQUIST, dissenting.

. . . I have difficulty in concluding, as the Court does, that the right of "privacy" is involved in this case. Texas, by the statute here challenged, bars the performance of a medical abortion by a licensed physician on a plaintiff such as Roe. A transaction resulting in an operation such as this is not "private" in the ordinary usage of that word. Nor is the "privacy" that the Court finds here even a distant relative of the freedom from searches and seizures protected by the Fourth Amendment to the Constitution, which the Court has referred to as embodying a right to privacy.

If the Court means by the term "privacy" no more than that the claim of a person to be free from unwanted

9. *Authors' note:* In *Doe*, decided the same day as *Roe*, the Court reviewed a challenge to the newer abortion laws, enacted by some states in the 1960s. While Texas permitted abortion only to save a mother's life, Georgia allowed it under the following circumstances: (1) when a "duly licensed Georgia physician" determined in "his best clinical judgment" that carrying the baby to term would injure the mother's life or health; (2) when a high likelihood existed that the fetus would be born with a serious deformity; and (3) when the pregnancy was the result of rape. The law contained other requirements, the most stringent of which was that two other doctors agree with the judgment of the one performing the abortion. Reiterating his opinion in *Roe*, Blackmun struck down the Georgia law as a violation of Fourteenth Amendment guarantees. Once again, six other members of the Court agreed with his conclusion.

state regulation of consensual transactions may be a form of "liberty" protected by the Fourteenth Amendment, there is no doubt that similar claims have been upheld in our earlier decisions on the basis of that liberty. I agree . . . that the "liberty," against deprivation of which without due process the Fourteenth Amendment protects, embraces more than the rights found in the Bill of Rights. But that liberty is not guaranteed absolutely against deprivation, only against deprivation without due process of law. The test traditionally applied in the area of social and economic legislation is whether or not a law such as that challenged has a rational relation to a valid state objective. . . . The Due Process Clause of the Fourteenth Amendment undoubtedly does place a limit, albeit a broad one, on legislative power to enact laws such as this. If the Texas statute were to prohibit an abortion even where the mother's life is in jeopardy, I have little doubt that such a statute would lack a rational relation to a valid state objective. . . . But the Court's sweeping invalidation of any restrictions on abortion during the first trimester is impossible to justify under that standard, and the conscious weighing of competing factors that the Court's opinion apparently substitutes for the established test is far more appropriate to a legislative judgment than to a judicial one.

The Court eschews the history of the Fourteenth Amendment in its reliance on the "compelling state interest" test. . . . But the Court adds a new wrinkle to this test by transposing it from the legal considerations associated with the Equal Protection Clause of the Fourteenth Amendment to this case arising under the Due Process Clause of the Fourteenth Amendment. Unless I misapprehend the consequences of this transplanting of the "compelling state interest test," the Court's opinion will accomplish the seemingly impossible feat of leaving this area of the law more confused than it found it.

While the Court's opinion quotes from the dissent of Mr. Justice Holmes in *Lochner v. New York* (1905), the result it reaches is more closely attuned to the majority opinion . . . in that case. As in *Lochner* and similar cases applying substantive due process standards to economic and social welfare legislation, the adoption of the compelling state interest standard will inevitably require this Court to examine the legislative policies and pass on the wisdom of these policies in the very process of deciding whether a particular state interest put forward may or may not be "compelling." The decision here to break pregnancy into three distinct terms and to outline the permissible restrictions the State may impose in each one, for example, partakes more of judicial legislation than it does of a determination of the intent of the drafters of the Fourteenth Amendment.

The fact that a majority of the States reflecting, after all, the majority sentiment in those States, have had restrictions on abortions for at least a century is a strong indication, it seems to me, that the asserted right to an abortion is not "so rooted in the traditions and conscience of our people as to be ranked as fundamental." . . . Even today, when society's views on abortion are changing, the very existence of the debate is evidence that the "right" to an abortion is not so universally accepted as the appellant would have us believe.

To reach its result, the Court necessarily has had to find within the scope of the Fourteenth Amendment a right that was apparently completely unknown to the drafters of the Amendment. As early as 1821, the first state law dealing directly with abortion was enacted by the Connecticut Legislature. By the time of the adoption of the Fourteenth Amendment in 1868, there were at least 36 laws enacted by state or territorial legislatures limiting abortion. While many States have amended or updated their laws, 21 of the laws on the books in 1868 remain in effect today. Indeed, the Texas statute struck down today was, as the majority notes, first enacted in 1857 and "has remained substantially unchanged to the present time."

There apparently was no question concerning the validity of this provision or of any of the other state statutes when the Fourteenth Amendment was adopted. The only conclusion possible from this history is that the drafters did not intend to have the Fourteenth Amendment withdraw from the States the power to legislate with respect to this matter. . . .

For all of the foregoing reasons, I respectfully dissent.

MR. JUSTICE WHITE, with whom MR. JUSTICE REHNQUIST joins, dissenting.

With all due respect, I dissent. I find nothing in the language or history of the Constitution to support the Court's judgment. The Court simply fashions and announces a new constitutional right for pregnant women and, with scarcely any reason or authority for its action, invests that right with sufficient substance to override most existing state abortion statutes. The upshot is that the people and the legislatures of the 50 States are constitutionally disentitled to weigh the relative importance of the continued existence and development of the fetus, on the one hand, against a spectrum of possible impacts on the mother, on the other hand. As an exercise of raw judicial power, the Court perhaps has authority to do what it does today; but in my view its judgment is an improvident and extravagant exercise of the power of judicial review that the Constitution extends to this Court.

The Court apparently values the convenience of the pregnant mother more than the continued existence and development of the life or potential life that she carries. Whether or not I might agree with that marshaling of values, I can in no event join the Court's judgment because I find no constitutional warrant for imposing such an order of priorities on the people and legislatures of the States. In a sensitive area such as this, involving as it does issues over which reasonable men may easily and heatedly differ, I cannot accept the Court's exercise of its clear power of choice by interposing a constitutional barrier to state efforts to protect human life and by investing mothers and doctors with the constitutionally protected right to exterminate it. This issue, for the most part, should be left with the people and to the political processes the people have devised to govern their affairs.

Chief Justice Burger had initiated the campaign to have *Roe* and *Doe* reargued in part because he believed that the new Nixon appointees would strengthen the pro-life side. This assumption, as we now know, turned out to be only half right. Justice Rehnquist dissented, but Justice Powell placed his feet firmly in the pro-choice camp. Moreover, the second time around, Justice Blackmun wrote an opinion that was far broader than his original draft.

Indeed, Blackmun's decisions in *Roe* and *Doe* were a tour de force on the subject of abortion. They provided a comprehensive history of government regulation of abortion and reviewed in some detail arguments for and against the procedure.[10] Most important was his conclusion: the right to privacy "is broad enough to encompass a woman's decision whether or not to terminate a pregnancy." Behind this assertion are several ideas. First, the Court, while not rejecting a Ninth Amendment theory of privacy, preferred to

locate the right in the Fourteenth Amendment's due process clause, an approach suggested by Justices Harlan and White in their concurring opinions in *Griswold* (*see Table 10-1*). Second, the Court found the abortion right fundamental and, therefore, would use a compelling state interest test to assess the constitutionality of restrictions on that right—but with something of a twist. For the reasons Blackmun gave in his opinion, the state's interests in protecting the woman's health and in protecting the "potentiality of human life" grow "in substantiality as the woman approaches term and, at a point during pregnancy . . . become compelling." This point led the majority to adopt the trimester scheme (*see Table 10-2*). Under this scheme, the state's compelling interest arises at the point of fetal viability. It may, however, regulate second-trimester abortions in ways that "are reasonably related to the mother's health."

In their dissents, Justices White and Rehnquist lambasted the trimester scheme, as well as almost every other aspect of the opinion. They thought it relied on "raw judicial power" to reach an "extravagant" and "improvident" decision. Rehnquist found that the Court's use of a compelling state interest test to assess statutes under the Fourteenth Amendment's due process clause represented a return to the discredited doctrine of substantive due process as expressed in *Lochner v. New York,* a complaint that echoed Black's dissent in *Griswold.* Rehnquist would have preferred that the Court adopt a "rational basis" approach to the abortion right as it had to regulations challenged on due process grounds after the fall of substantive due process. Under this approach, the Court would have to decide only whether the government had acted reasonably to achieve a legitimate government objective. Using a rational basis approach, as you can imagine, the Court generally defers to the government and presumes the validity of the government's action. Had the Court adopted this approach to the abortion right, it would have upheld the Texas and Georgia restrictions. White, joined by Rehnquist, thought the Court had gone well beyond the scope of its powers and of the text and history of the Constitution to generate a policy statement that smacked of judicial activism. To White, it was up to the people and their elected officials to determine the fate of abortion, not the Court.

As Blackmun's opinion was nearly two years in the making, the other justices knew that it would be a comprehensive statement. Outsiders, however, were

---

10. Our excerpt omits the long history. For the full version see FindLaw at http://laws.findlaw.com/US/410/113.html.

shocked; few expected such an opinion from a Nixon appointee. But Blackmun's opinion was not the only surprise. Burger's decision to go along with the majority also startled many observers. Moreover, White and Stewart cast rather puzzling votes given their opinions in *Griswold*. Stewart had dissented in *Griswold*, asserting that the Constitution does not guarantee a general right to privacy. If he believed that, how could he agree to the creation of the right to obtain legal abortions, a right that rested on privacy? White, on the other hand, had been in the majority in *Griswold*. But for him, apparently, the right to privacy was not broad enough to cover abortion.

What explains the justices' positions in *Roe* and *Doe* are matters of speculation, for, as Blackmun once noted, it is always hard to predict how a new justice will come down on the abortion issue. What is not a matter of speculation is that the responses to *Roe*—both positive and negative—were (and still are) among the strongest in the Court's history.

TABLE 10-2   The *Roe v. Wade* Trimester Framework

STAGE OF PREGNANCY	DEGREE OF PERMISSIBLE STATE REGULATION OF THE DECISION TO TERMINATE PREGNANCY
Prior to the end of the first trimester (approximately months 1–3)	Almost none: "the abortion decision and its effectuation must be left to [the woman and] the medical judgment of the pregnant woman's attending physician."
The end of the first trimester through "viability" (approximately months 4–6)	Some: "the state, in promoting its interest in the health of the mother, may, if it chooses, regulate the abortion procedure in ways that are reasonably related to maternal health." But it may not prohibit abortions.
Subsequent to viability (approximately months 7–9)	High: "the state, in promoting its interest in the potentiality of human life, may, if it chooses, regulate, and even proscribe, abortion except where necessary, in appropriate medical judgment, for the preservation of the life or health of the mother."

FIGURE 10-2   Public Opinion and Abortion, 1975–2011

Circumstances Under Which Abortion Should Be Legal

Do you think abortions should be legal under any circumstances, legal only under certain circumstances, or illegal in all circumstances?

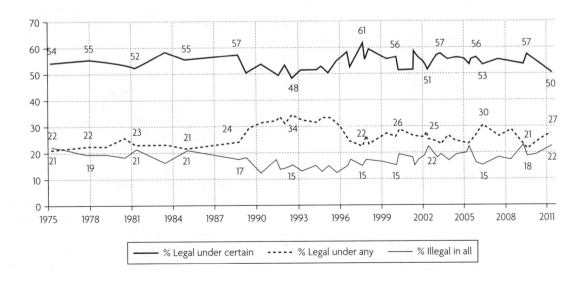

Reaction came from all quarters of American life. Some legal scholars applauded the *Roe* opinion, asserting that it indicated the Court's sensitivity to changing times. Others ripped it to shreds. They called the trimester scheme unworkable and said that, as medical technology advanced, viability would come earlier in pregnancy. Others attacked the decision's use of the Fourteenth Amendment, agreeing with Rehnquist that it was a retreat to pre–New Deal days. Still others claimed it usurped the intention of *Griswold.* Legal scholar John Hart Ely wrote that a right to privacy against "governmental snooping" is legitimate, but a general freedom of "autonomy"—"to live one's life without governmental interference"—goes beyond the scope of *Griswold.*[11]

Roe also divided the political community. Some legislators were relieved that the Court, and not they, had handled this political hot potato. Others were outraged on moral grounds (believing that abortion is murder) and still others on constitutional grounds (thinking that abortion rights should be a matter of public policy for legislators, not judges, to determine).

The public was split over its support for the Court's ruling, with about 50 percent of Americans supporting it and the rest either opposing it or offering no opinion. But, as Figure 10-2 shows, divisions over abortion rights did not come about as a result of *Roe.* Since the first public opinion polls taken on abortion in the aftermath of *Roe,* citizens have been of many different minds on the subject. For example, a 2010 Gallup Poll found that 52 percent of Americans believe that abortion should be legal under certain circumstances, such as if the pregnancy threatens a woman's life or health, 25 percent say it should be legal under any circumstances, and 19 percent think it should be illegal under all circumstances. Political scientists Charles Franklin and Liane Kosaki show that in the final analysis, all *Roe* did was intensify basic divisions over abortion: those who were pro-choice before the decision became even more so, and the same held true for those on the pro-life side.[12]

Although *Roe* may not have changed public opinion on abortion, it had the important effect of mobilizing the movement to oppose it. Before 1973, groups opposed to legalized abortion had lobbied successfully against efforts to liberalize state laws. When *Roe* nullified these legislative victories, these groups vowed to see the decision overturned; in short, *Roe* and *Doe* fanned the fire rather than extinguished it. As for Norma McCorvey, whose unwanted pregnancy started the conflict, she has changed her mind about abortion (*see Box 10-2*).

The Aftermath of *Roe*: Attempts to Limit the Decision

Pro-life groups are dedicated to the eradication of *Roe v. Wade,* a goal that they can best accomplish in one of two ways: by persuading Congress to propose an amendment to the Constitution or by persuading the Court to overrule its decision. In the immediate aftermath of *Roe,* neither of these options was viable. Despite the public's mixed view of abortion, during the 1970s only about one-third of Americans supported a constitutional amendment to proscribe it. The lack of support may explain why Congress, ever cognizant of the polls, did not pass any of the "human life" amendments it considered in the 1970s. And, given the 7–2 vote in *Roe,* many changes in the Court's membership would have to occur for the Court to reconsider its stance on abortion.

Faced with this situation, pro-life groups determined that their best course of action was to seek limitations on the ways in which women could obtain and pay for abortions. They lobbied legislatures to enact restrictions on the right to an abortion. Two types of restrictions predominated—those that required consent of a woman's husband or a minor's parents and those that limited government funding for abortion services. These efforts were quite successful. During the 1970s, eighteen states required some form of consent, and thirty (along with the federal government) restricted funding. To put it another way, by 1978 only about fifteen states had not enacted laws requiring consent or restricting funding.

As you might expect, pro-choice groups responded with legal challenges to these limits on the abortion right. But, for the most part, they failed. Consider the consent laws. The first major post-*Roe* battle, ***Planned Parenthood v. Danforth*** (1976), involved this subject—one the Court had not considered in *Roe.* The state of Missouri had passed legislation that required the written consent of the pregnant woman and her spouse or, for an unmarried minor, her parents, before an abortion could be performed.

---

11. John Hart Ely, "The Wages of Crying Wolf: A Comment on *Roe v. Wade*," *Yale Law Journal* 82 (1973): 920.

12. Charles H. Franklin and Liane C. Kosaki, "The Republican Schoolmaster: The Supreme Court, Public Opinion, and Abortion," *American Political Science Review* 83 (1989): 751–772.

BOX 10-2   AFTERMATH . . . NORMA MCCORVEY

The life of Norma Mccorvey, the pregnant carnival worker who, as Jane Roe, challenged Texas's abortion laws in the Supreme Court, took several interesting turns after *Roe v. Wade* was handed down.

At first, McCorvey's personal life was relatively untouched by the decision. She did not have an abortion, but gave her baby up for adoption. She remained anonymous, continuing to lead a life that included poverty, homelessness, drug and alcohol addiction, petty crimes, and attempted suicide. Then, in the 1980s, McCorvey went public and announced that she was the real "Jane Roe." She also confessed that she had lied at the time of her case when she claimed that her pregnancy was the result of rape.

McCorvey worked for several years in Dallas abortion clinics, using her wages to help support her drug habit. She also dabbled in New Age religions and the occult and had a romantic relationship with a store clerk who had caught her shoplifting.

In 1995, Operation Rescue, the Christian-based pro-life activist group, moved its headquarters to Dallas, taking office space next door to the abortion clinic where McCorvey worked. The Reverend Philip "Flip" Benham, an Operation Rescue leader, and other members of the group befriended McCorvey. Subsequently, she underwent a religious conversion, became an evangelical Christian, and joined Benham's nondenominational Hillcrest

Norma McCorvey stands with nine-year-old Meredith Champion at an Operation Rescue rally in downtown Dallas in January 1997. McCorvey, the real "Jane Roe" of Roe v. Wade (1973), is now pro-life and works with the pro-life group.

Church. Her 1995 baptism in a backyard swimming pool was nationally televised.

McCorvey left the abortion clinic and began working for Operation Rescue, proclaiming, "I don't have to go to the death camps anymore, to earn six bucks an hour." McCorvey also founded an organization, Roe No More Ministry, that provides information to groups opposing abortion. She experienced a second religious conversion in 1998 when she became a Roman Catholic. In 2000 McCorvey signed her name to a lawsuit asking the federal courts to declare that women seeking abortions have the right to be told that they are carrying a human being and to be shown a sonogram of the fetus. The suit was not successful.

Looking back at her participation in *Roe v. Wade*, McCorvey now says that she feels she was exploited by the pro-choice movement. She claims she met her lawyers in the case only twice, the first time over pizza and beer, and that she did not even know what the word *abortion* meant. "All I simply did was sign," she says. "I never appeared in any court. I never testified in front of any jury or judge."

SOURCES: *St. Louis Post Dispatch,* June 12, 1998; *Chicago Sun-Times,* July 27, 1998; *Boston Globe,* October 19, 1998; *Omaha World-Herald,* October 29 and 30, 1998; *Los Angeles Times,* December 8, 1999; *Houston Chronicle,* January 13, 2000; and *Independent* (London), March 16, 2000.

The Court found no constitutional violation in requiring a woman to give her own consent to the procedure, but it struck down spousal and parental consent provisions as violative of the Constitution and inconsistent with *Roe.* Blackmun's majority opinion, however, gave the pro-life movement a little hope. It struck down Missouri's parental consent requirement, but it also stated, "We emphasize that our holding that

parental consent is invalid does not suggest that every minor, regardless of age or maturity, may give effective consent for the termination of her pregnancy." With these words, Blackmun opened the door to the possibility of some form of required parental consent.

Pro-life forces took advantage of Blackmun's statement, persuading states to enact various parental and other consent requirements, many of which came before the Court. And, although the Court has continued to strike down laws forcing a woman to obtain the consent of or to notify her spouse/partner prior to obtaining an abortion, it has generally allowed states to require parental consent or notification, especially if the law allowed a minor to bypass the parent and instead to seek the consent of a judge. Moreover, in *Ayotte v. Planned Parenthood of Northern New England* (2006), the Court held that when states require parental notification they must include exceptions if the minor's life or health is in danger.

On funding for abortions, however, the Court's decisions are straightforward. In a trio of 1977 decisions, the Court upheld state or local restrictions on the funding of abortions.[13] Three years later, an even bigger battle erupted over the Hyde amendment, which limited federal Medicaid funding of abortions to those "where the life of the mother would be endangered if the fetus were carried to term." Pro-choice groups quickly challenged the regulation on three grounds: it violated due process because it impinged on a fundamental right; it denied equal protection because it discriminated against women, especially poor women; and it violated the First Amendment because it burdened religious exercise and constituted religious establishment guarantees. In **Harris v. McCrae** (1980), however, a 5–4 Court rejected all three arguments and upheld the regulation. Writing for the majority, Justice Stewart asserted that the Court "cannot overturn duly enacted statutes simply because they may be unwise, improvident or out of harmony with a particular school of thought." More important, however, was the opinion's legal rationale:

[R]egardless of whether the freedom of a woman to choose to terminate her pregnancy for health reasons lies at the core or the periphery of the due process liberty recognized in [*Roe v.*] *Wade*, it simply does not follow that a woman's freedom of choice carries with it a constitutional entitlement to the financial resources to avail herself of the full range of protected choices. . . . [A]lthough government may not place obstacles in the path of a woman's exercise of her freedom of choice, it need not remove those not of its own creation. Indigency falls in the latter category.

Attempts to Overturn *Roe*: *Akron*, *Webster*, and *Casey*

In the early 1980s, pro-life forces had several reasons to feel optimistic. First, they had achieved considerable success in the funding decisions. Second, the 1980 elections placed Ronald Reagan, the first presidential contender ever to support, unequivocally, the goals of the pro-life movement, in the White House. It was almost assured that Reagan's judicial appointees would also oppose abortion. And third, personnel changes on the Supreme Court that were damaging to the pro-choice position had already taken place. John Paul Stevens replaced William O. Douglas. Although Stevens appeared to lean toward the pro-choice position, he could hardly embrace that view more enthusiastically than the man he replaced. After all, Douglas had written the opinion in *Griswold* and supported the pro-choice position in every subsequent case. Sandra Day O'Connor, Reagan's first appointment, replaced Potter Stewart, who had voted with the *Roe* majority. O'Connor's position on abortion was far from clear. Some pro-life groups alleged that O'Connor supported the pro-choice side, basing their argument on votes she had cast in the Arizona state legislature. But during her confirmation proceedings, she refused to answer questions on abortion, saying only that it was "a practice in which I would not have engaged." But, she added, she was "over the hill" and "not going to be pregnant any more . . . so perhaps it's easy for me to speak."

Given the changing context, pro-life forces began mounting a more direct attack on *Roe*, still hoping to overturn it. The first major battle occurred in **Akron v. Akron Center for Reproductive Health** (1983). At issue was a 1978 ordinance passed by the city council of Akron, Ohio, that contained five restrictions on the abortion right: (1) all post–first-trimester abortions must be performed in a hospital; (2) minors under the age of fifteen must obtain written consent of a parent or a court prior to an abortion; (3) a woman must give informed consent (for example, a physician must tell her that the "unborn child is a

---

13. *Beal v. Doe* (upholding a Pennsylvania law limiting Medicaid funding "to those abortions that are certified by physicians as medically necessary"); *Maher v. Roe* (upholding a Connecticut Welfare Department regulation limiting state Medicaid "benefits for first trimester abortions [to those] . . . that are 'medically necessary'"); *Poelker v. Doe* (upholding a St. Louis policy directive that barred city-owned hospitals from performing abortions). In all three cases, the Court rejected constitutional claims that the restrictions at issue interfered with the fundamental right to obtain an abortion as articulated in *Roe* and that they discriminated on the basis of socioeconomic status and against those choosing abortion over childbirth.

BOX 10-3　PROPOSED APPROACHES TO RESTRICTIVE ABORTION LAWS

APPROACH	EXEMPLARY OPINIONS	DEFINITION
Strict scrutiny	Blackmun in *Roe*; Powell in *Akron*	The right to abortion is fundamental. So laws restricting that right must be the least restrictive means available to achieve a compelling state interest. In the abortion context, a state's interest grows more compelling as the pregnancy passes from the first to second to third trimesters.
Undue burden	O'Connor in *Akron*	The right to decide whether to terminate a pregnancy is fundamental. So laws placing an undue burden on the woman's decision to terminate her pregnancy may be subject to strict scrutiny; other kinds of laws need only be rationally related to a legitimate state interest (rational basis test).
Rational basis	Rehnquist in *Roe*	The right to abortion is no different from economic rights claimed under the Fourteenth Amendment due process clause. So the law must be a reasonable measure designed to achieve a legitimate state interest.

human life form from the moment of conception") prior to an abortion; (4) twenty-four hours must elapse between the time the pregnant woman signs the consent form and the abortion; and (5) doctors who perform abortions "shall insure that the remains of the unborn child are disposed of in a humane and sanitary manner."

Invoking the *Roe* precedent, the Court, in an opinion written by Powell and supported by five others (Brennan, Blackmun, Burger, Marshall, and Stevens) struck down the Akron law. The first four provisions were seen as unnecessary and unconstitutional impediments placed in the way of a woman's right to choose, and the fifth was struck down as unconstitutionally vague.

What is noteworthy, however, is that the prochoice side had lost a vote. The 7–2 *Roe* majority was now 6–3, with O'Connor writing a dissent in *Akron* that was signed by Rehnquist and White. O'Connor's opinion was a scathing critique of *Roe*. Citing medical advances, she wrote that at the time of *Roe*, "viability before 28 weeks was considered unusual," but newer studies indicated viability as early as twenty-five weeks. This proved, she said, that because it is inherently tied to ever-changing medical technology, "the *Roe* framework . . . is clearly on a collision course with itself," and because lines separating viability from nonviability are fading, compelling state interests exist throughout pregnancy. O'Connor urged that the trimester framework be abandoned and replaced with one that "protects the woman from *unduly burdensome* interference with her freedom to decide whether to terminate her pregnancy"

(emphasis added).[14] But what would O'Connor count as "unduly burdensome" regulation? Powell claimed that "the dissent would uphold virtually any abortion regulation under a rational-basis test," meaning that it would find constitutional any regulation that was reasonably related to a government interest. Such a standard, Powell noted, would gut *Roe*. O'Connor did not go that far. Rather, she suggested that if the law in question "unduly burdened" the fundamental right to seek an abortion, the Court should apply strict scrutiny; if the law does not "unduly burden" the abortion right, then the Court should apply a rational basis test.

Therefore, as shown in Box 10-3, by 1983 the justices had proposed three different approaches to restrictive abortion laws. Although the majority of the justices continued to support *Roe*'s strict scrutiny standard, O'Connor's dissent raised questions. Would she stick with her "undue burden" standard? If so, would she be able to persuade other justices to adopt it? And what exactly did she mean by an "undue burden?" Would she use it as a vehicle to overrule *Roe*?

These questions, but particularly the last one, were on the minds of observers when the Court agreed to

---

14. O'Connor's analysis paralleled the one that Reagan's solicitor general, Rex E. Lee, offered in an amicus curiae brief filed on behalf of the United States in *Akron*. Lee's reading of *Roe*'s progeny led him to conclude that from *Danforth* on, the justices had never really "applied" *Roe*'s "sweeping" language regarding first-trimester abortions but had made exceptions. He argued that the Court "has repeatedly adopted an 'unduly burdensome' analysis." That is, the Court had permitted state regulations of abortion as long as they did not "unduly burden" that decision.

hear ***Webster v. Reproductive Health Services*** (1989).[15] This case involved a Missouri law that, like the regulations at issue in *Akron,* sought to restrict the abortion right. Moreover, in the six years between *Akron* and *Webster,* additional personnel changes on the Court had weakened *Roe*'s prospects for survival. Rehnquist, a persistent *Roe* critic, replaced Burger as chief justice. Joining the Court were Antonin Scalia, who took Rehnquist's associate justice position, and Anthony Kennedy, who replaced Powell, who retired. Scalia and Kennedy, both Reagan appointees, were seen as two probable anti-*Roe* votes. Was *Roe* doomed? Blackmun thought so. He wondered out loud: "Will *Roe v. Wade* go down the drain? I think there's a very distinct possibility that it will, this term. You can count the votes."[16]

At issue in *Webster* was a Missouri law that prohibited state employees and public facilities from being used to perform an abortion unless the mother's life was in jeopardy; banned state employees from encouraging or counseling a woman to have an abortion not necessary to save her life; and required physicians, prior to performing an abortion, to conduct a viability test on the fetus of any woman thought to be pregnant twenty weeks or more. In addition, the statute's preamble declared that human life begins at conception.

The possibility that the justices would use *Webster* to reverse *Roe* was not lost on pro-choice and pro-life forces, who filed seventy-eight amicus curiae briefs (the largest number ever submitted to the Court in a single case), representing more than five thousand different groups and interests. The Bush administration not only filed a brief supporting state regulation of abortions but also participated in oral argument, again requesting the Court to overrule *Roe.* Would the newly configured Rehnquist Court accept this invitation? Was the ruling as much of a landmark as many Court watchers expected it to be?

The answer to both questions is a qualified no. On one hand, in a 5–4 vote, a badly fractured Court refused to strike down any of the law's provisions. The justices held that it was consistent with the Court's funding decisions for Missouri to ban public facilities from being used for abortions and state employees from performing or encouraging abortions. The state's interest in preserving viable human life was also judged as sufficient to justify the viability tests. The four justices in the minority—Blackmun, Brennan, Marshall, and Stevens—disagreed, expressing their support for the 1973 *Roe* precedent. (The justices did not rule on the declaration in the law's preamble that life begins at conception on the ground that the language amounted to little more than a statement of philosophy with no enforceable effect.)

On the other hand, although the pro-life forces were able to attract five votes to uphold the Missouri law, they did not persuade the Court to overturn *Roe.* Indeed, the Court explicitly declared that it would not revisit the issue. Moreover, the majority could not agree on a single opinion deciding the case. Rehnquist wrote the primary opinion and was joined by White and Kennedy. Scalia and O'Connor joined parts of Rehnquist's opinion but also staked out their own views. Scalia was the only justice to call for *Roe* to be overruled. O'Connor continued to push for her "undue burden" approach to abortion restrictions. In the end, it was her loyalty to this approach that kept *Roe* alive and kept *Webster* from being the landmark decision many had expected.

Even so, *Roe* seemed to be operating on borrowed time because President George H. W. Bush eventually would have the opportunity to appoint justices who could tip the balance against the abortion decision. It was not long before this view was tested. By the time the Court agreed to hear arguments in another major abortion case, *Planned Parenthood of Southeastern Pennsylvania v. Casey* (1992), Bush had appointed two justices. David Souter and Clarence Thomas replaced the pro-choice justices Brennan and Marshall, respectively. These membership changes seemed to confirm the greatest hope and fear of the pro-life and pro-choice movements: *Roe* would finally go. Or would it?

---

15. In between *Akron* and *Webster,* the Court decided *Thornburgh v. American College of Obstetricians and Gynecologists* (1986). At issue in *Thornburgh* was a Pennsylvania law similar to the one that the Court had struck down in *Akron.* Reiterating its position in *Akron,* a five-person Court invalidated the law. After thirteen years of generally supporting the abortion right, Chief Justice Burger joined *Roe*'s opponents and voted to uphold the law. Also dissenting were White, O'Connor, and Rehnquist.

16. Quoted in "Justice Fears for *Roe* Ruling," *New York Times,* September 14, 1988.

Planned Parenthood of Southeastern Pennsylvania v. Casey

505 U.S. 833 (1992)
http://laws.findlaw.com/US/505/833.html
Oral arguments are available at http://www.oyez.org.

OPINION ANNOUNCING THE JUDGMENT OF THE COURT AND DELIVERING THE OPINION OF THE COURT: *Kennedy, O'Connor, Souter*

CONCURRING IN PART: *Blackmun, Rehnquist, Scalia, Stevens, Thomas, White*

DISSENTING IN PART: *Blackmun, Rehnquist, Scalia, Stevens, Thomas, White*

OPINIONS CONCURRING IN PART AND DISSENTING IN PART: *Blackmun, Rehnquist, Scalia, Stevens*

FACTS:

After the Court's decision in *Webster v. Reproductive Health Services,* Pennsylvania revised its Abortion Control Act, which the Court had, by a 5–4 vote, struck down in *Thornburgh v. American College of Obstetricians and Gynecologists* (1986).[17] Given the membership changes on the Court and the *Webster* decision, the state thought the Court would now uphold the amended law. Pennsylvania's law required (1) informed consent and a twenty-four-hour waiting period before abortions could be performed; (2) parental (or judicial) consent for minors; (3) spousal notification; and (4) comprehensive record keeping and reporting of the following information for each abortion performed: the name of the physician, the woman's age, the number of prior pregnancies or abortions she had had, the weight and age of the aborted fetus, whether the woman was married, and, if relevant, the reason(s) the woman failed to notify her spouse.

Before these provisions went into effect, five women's clinics challenged their constitutionality. A federal district court generally agreed with the clinics, but the U.S. Court of Appeals for the Third Circuit reversed, using O'Connor's "undue burden" standard, which—based on its reading of *Webster*—was "the law of the land." In the appeals court's opinion, the provisions, with the exception of spousal consent, did not place an undue burden on the decision of whether to terminate a pregnancy. The court applied a rational basis test under which the three provisions easily passed constitutional muster. The spousal consent provision, in the court's view, placed an undue burden on the abortion decision by exposing women to spousal abuse and violence. It therefore applied the strict scrutiny test and concluded that the provision could not stand. Judge Samuel Alito, who now sits on the Supreme Court, disagreed with his appellate court colleagues on this portion of the decision. In a dissenting opinion, he wrote that he would have upheld the spousal consent provision: "The Pennsylvania legislature could have rationally believed that some married women are initially

_____

17. See note 15 for a discussion of *Thornburgh.*

inclined to obtain an abortion without their husbands' knowledge because of perceived problems—such as economic constraints, future plans or the husbands' previously expressed opposition—that may be obviated by discussion prior to the abortion."

As a result of this mixed opinion, the state and the clinics appealed to the Supreme Court. In a move designed to intensify the debate over abortion before the 1992 elections, Planned Parenthood asked the justices to issue a nonambiguous decision: either affirm or overturn *Roe.* The state, joined by the Bush administration's solicitor general, Kenneth Starr, also asked the Court "to end the current uncertainty" surrounding the abortion issue and overrule *Roe.* The state and the federal government wanted the Court to adopt a rational basis approach to abortion and to use that standard to uphold all of Pennsylvania's laws. Given the membership changes on the Court, many observers predicted the Court would do precisely that.

ARGUMENTS:

For the petitioners, Planned Parenthood of Southeastern Pennsylvania, et al.:

- The Court must strike down the statute and reaffirm the central holding of *Roe v. Wade* that the right to choose abortion is a fundamental right protected by the Constitution and must, therefore, apply strict scrutiny in reviewing the statute. The doctrine of stare decisis, the workability of the trimester framework, and the profound impact that *Roe* has had on the lives of American women support this decision.
- The "undue burden" test is vague and unworkable.
- The "rational basis" test is too deferential and encourages intolerable legislative interference with women's reproductive choices.
- The statute is invalid under any standard of review, because the various consent, delay, and counseling provisions violate the woman's rights of privacy, marital integrity, and equal protection while failing to further a legitimate state interest.

For the respondents, Casey, et al.:

- The Court should uphold the statute and revisit *Roe* only to the extent necessary to clarify the limits on the right to abortion. The right is subject to reasonable state regulation to safeguard important state interests, and the proper standard of review is the "undue burden" standard—under which this law passes constitutional muster.

- In the alternative, the Court should overrule *Roe v. Wade* and return the regulation of abortion to the democratic process.

> JUSTICE O'CONNOR, JUSTICE KENNEDY, AND JUSTICE SOUTER ANNOUNCED THE JUDGMENT OF THE COURT AND DELIVERED THE OPINION OF THE COURT WITH RESPECT TO PARTS I, II, III, V-A, V-C, AND VI, AN OPINION WITH RESPECT TO PART V-E, IN WHICH JUSTICE STEVENS JOINS, AND AN OPINION WITH RESPECT TO PARTS IV, V-B, AND V-D.

I

Liberty finds no refuge in a jurisprudence of doubt. Yet 19 years after our holding that the Constitution protects a woman's right to terminate her pregnancy in its early stages, *Roe v. Wade* (1973), that definition of liberty is still questioned. Joining the respondents as amicus curiae, the United States, as it has done in five other cases in the last decade, again asks us to overrule *Roe*. . . .

After considering the fundamental constitutional questions resolved by *Roe*, principles of institutional integrity, and the rule of *stare decisis*, we are led to conclude this: the essential holding of *Roe v. Wade* should be retained and once again reaffirmed.

It must be stated at the outset and with clarity that *Roe*'s essential holding, the holding we reaffirm, has three parts. First is a recognition of the right of the woman to choose to have an abortion before viability and to obtain it without undue interference from the State. Before viability, the State's interests are not strong enough to support a prohibition of abortion or the imposition of a substantial obstacle to the woman's effective right to elect the procedure. Second is a confirmation of the State's power to restrict abortions after fetal viability, if the law contains exceptions for pregnancies which endanger a woman's life or health. And third is the principle that the State has legitimate interests from the outset of the pregnancy in protecting the health of the woman and the life of the fetus that may become a child. These principles do not contradict one another; and we adhere to each.

II

. . . These considerations begin our analysis of the woman's interest in terminating her pregnancy but cannot end it, for this reason: though the abortion decision may originate within the zone of conscience and belief, it is more than a philosophic exercise. Abortion is a unique act. It is an act fraught with consequences for others: for the woman who must live with the implications of her decision; for the persons who perform and assist in the procedure; for the spouse, family, and society which must confront the knowledge that these procedures exist, procedures some deem nothing short of an act of violence against innocent human life; and, depending on one's beliefs, for the life or potential life that is aborted. Though abortion is conduct, it does not follow that the State is entitled to proscribe it in all instances. That is because the liberty of the woman is at stake in a sense unique to the human condition and so unique to the law. The mother who carries a child to full term is subject to anxieties, to physical constraints, to pain that only she must bear. That these sacrifices have from the beginning of the human race been endured by woman with a pride that ennobles her in the eyes of others and gives to the infant a bond of love cannot alone be grounds for the State to insist she make the sacrifice. Her suffering is too intimate and personal for the State to insist, without more, upon its own vision of the woman's role, however dominant that vision has been in the course of our history and our culture. The destiny of the woman must be shaped to a large extent on her own conception of her spiritual imperatives and her place in society. . . .

While we appreciate the weight of the arguments made on behalf of the State in the case before us, arguments which in their ultimate formulation conclude that *Roe* should be overruled, the reservations any of us may have in reaffirming the central holding of *Roe* are outweighed by the explication of individual liberty we have given combined with the force of *stare decisis*. We turn now to that doctrine.

III

Even when the decision to overrule a prior case is not, as in the rare, latter instance, virtually foreordained, it is common wisdom that the rule of *stare decisis* is not an "inexorable command," and certainly it is not such in every constitutional case.

So in this case we may inquire whether *Roe*'s central rule has been found unworkable; whether the rule's limitation on state power could be removed without serious inequity to those who have relied upon it or significant damage to the stability of the society governed by the rule in question; whether the law's growth in the intervening years has left *Roe*'s central rule a doctrinal anachronism discounted by society; and whether *Roe*'s premises of fact have so far changed in the ensuing two decades as to render its central holding somehow irrelevant or unjustifiable in dealing with the issue it addressed.

Although *Roe* has engendered opposition, it has in no sense proven "unworkable," representing as it does a simple limitation beyond which a state law is unenforceable. While *Roe* has, of course, required judicial assessment of state laws affecting the exercise of the choice guaranteed against government infringement, and although the need for such review will remain as a consequence of today's decision, the required determinations fall within judicial competence.

The inquiry into reliance counts the cost of a rule's repudiation as it would fall on those who have relied reasonably on the rule's continued application. Since the classic case for weighing reliance heavily in favor of following the earlier rule occurs in the commercial context, where advance planning of great precision is most obviously a necessity, it is no cause for surprise that some would find no reliance worthy of consideration in support of *Roe*. . . .

[One] can readily imagine an argument stressing . . . any reliance interest would be *de minimis*. This argument would be premised on the hypothesis that reproductive planning could take virtually immediate account of any sudden restoration of state authority to ban abortions.

To eliminate the issue of reliance that easily, however, one would need to limit cognizable reliance to specific instances of sexual activity. But to do this would be simply to refuse to face the fact that for two decades of economic and social developments, people have organized intimate relationships and made choices that define their views of themselves and their places in society, in reliance on the availability of abortion in the event that contraception should fail. The ability of women to participate equally in the economic and social life of the Nation has been facilitated by their ability to control their reproductive lives. The Constitution serves human values, and while the effect of reliance on *Roe* cannot be exactly measured, neither can the certain cost of overruling *Roe* for people who have ordered their thinking and living around that case be dismissed.

No evolution of legal principle has left *Roe*'s doctrinal footings weaker than they were in 1973. No development of constitutional law since the case was decided has implicitly or explicitly left *Roe* behind as a mere survivor of obsolete constitutional thinking. . . .

[T]ime has overtaken some of *Roe*'s factual assumptions: advances in maternal health care allow for abortions safe to the mother later in pregnancy than was true in 1973, and advances in neonatal care have advanced viability to a point somewhat earlier. But these facts go only to the scheme of time limits on the realization of competing interests, and the divergences from the factual premises of 1973 have no bearing on the validity of *Roe*'s central holding, that viability marks the earliest point at which the State's interest in fetal life is constitutionally adequate to justify a legislative ban on nontherapeutic abortions. The soundness or unsoundness of that constitutional judgment in no sense turns on whether viability occurs at approximately 28 weeks, as was usual at the time of *Roe,* at 23 to 24 weeks, as it sometimes does today, or at some moment even slightly earlier in pregnancy, as it may if fetal respiratory capacity can somehow be enhanced in the future. Whenever it may occur, the attainment of viability may continue to serve as the critical fact, just as it has done since *Roe* was decided; which is to say that no change in *Roe*'s factual underpinning has left its central holding obsolete, and none supports an argument for overruling it.

The sum of the precedential inquiry to this point shows *Roe*'s underpinnings unweakened in any way affecting its central holding. While it has engendered disapproval, it has not been unworkable. An entire generation has come of age free to assume *Roe*'s concept of liberty in defining the capacity of women to act in society, and to make reproductive decisions; no erosion of principle going to liberty or personal autonomy has left *Roe*'s central holding a doctrinal remnant; *Roe* portends no developments at odds with other precedent for the analysis of personal liberty; and no changes of fact have rendered viability more or less appropriate as the point at which the balance of interests tips. Within the bounds of normal *stare decisis* analysis, then, and subject to the considerations on which it customarily turns, the stronger argument is for affirming *Roe*'s central holding, with whatever degree of personal reluctance any of us may have, not for overruling it.

In a less significant case, *stare decisis* analysis could, and would, stop at the point we have reached. . . .

. . . Our analysis would not be complete, however, without explaining why overruling *Roe*'s central holding would not only reach an unjustifiable result under principles of *stare decisis,* but would seriously weaken the Court's capacity to exercise the judicial power and to function as the Supreme Court of a Nation dedicated to the rule of law. To understand why this would be so it is necessary to understand the source of this Court's authority, the conditions necessary for its preservation, and its relationship to the country's understanding of itself as a constitutional Republic.

The root of American governmental power is revealed most clearly in the instance of the power conferred by the Constitution upon the Judiciary of the United States and specifically upon this Court. As Americans of each succeeding generation are rightly told, the Court cannot buy support for its decisions by spending money and, except to a minor degree, it cannot independently coerce obedience to its decrees. The Court's power lies, rather, in its legitimacy, a product of substance and perception that shows itself in the people's acceptance of the Judiciary as fit to determine what the Nation's law means and to declare what it demands.

The underlying substance of this legitimacy is of course the warrant for the Court's decisions in the Constitution and the lesser sources of legal principle on which the Court draws. That substance is expressed in the Court's opinions, and our contemporary understanding is such that a decision without principled justification would be no judicial act at all. But even when justification is furnished by apposite legal principle, something more is required. Because not every conscientious claim of principled justification will be accepted as such, the justification claimed must be beyond dispute. The Court must take care to speak and act in ways that allow people to accept its decisions on the terms the Court claims for them, as grounded truly in principle, not as compromises with social and political pressures having, as such, no bearing on the principled choices that the Court is obliged to make. Thus, the Court's legitimacy depends on making legally principled decisions under circumstances in which their principled character is sufficiently plausible to be accepted by the Nation.

The need for principled action to be perceived as such is implicated to some degree whenever this, or any other appellate court, overrules a prior case. This is not to say, of course, that this Court cannot give a perfectly satisfactory explanation in most cases. People understand that some of the Constitution's language is hard to fathom and that the Court's Justices are sometimes able to perceive significant facts or to understand principles of law that eluded their predecessors and that justify departures from existing decisions. However upsetting it may be to those most directly affected when one judicially derived rule replaces another, the country can accept some correction of error without necessarily questioning the legitimacy of the Court.

In two circumstances, however, the Court would almost certainly fail to receive the benefit of the doubt in overruling prior cases. There is, first, a point beyond which frequent overruling would overtax the country's belief in the Court's good faith. Despite the variety of reasons that may inform and justify a decision to overrule, we cannot forget that such a decision is usually perceived (and perceived correctly) as, at the least, a statement that a prior decision was wrong. There is a limit to the amount of error that can plausibly be imputed to prior courts. If that limit should be exceeded, disturbance of prior rulings would be taken as evidence that justifiable reexamination of principle had given way to drives for particular results in the short term. The legitimacy of the Court would fade with the frequency of its vacillation.

That first circumstance can be described as hypothetical; the second is to the point here and now. Where, in the performance of its judicial duties, the Court decides a case in such a way as to resolve the sort of intensely divisive controversy reflected in *Roe* and those rare, comparable cases, its decision has a dimension that the resolution of the normal case does not carry. It is the dimension present whenever the Court's interpretation of the Constitution calls the contending sides of a national controversy to end their national division by accepting a common mandate rooted in the Constitution.

The Court is not asked to do this very often, having thus addressed the Nation only twice in our lifetime, in the decisions of *Brown* [*v. Board of Education*] and *Roe*. But when the Court does act in this way, its decision requires an equally rare precedential force to counter the inevitable efforts to overturn it and to thwart its implementation. Some of those efforts may be mere unprincipled emotional reactions; others may proceed from principles worthy of profound respect. But whatever the premises of opposition may be, only the most convincing justification under accepted standards of precedent could suffice to demonstrate that a later decision overruling the first was anything but a surrender to political pressure, and an unjustified repudiation of the principle on which the Court staked its authority in the first instance. So to overrule under fire in the absence of the most compelling reason to reexamine a watershed decision would subvert the Court's legitimacy beyond any serious question. . . .

The Court's duty in the present case is clear. In 1973, it confronted the already-divisive issue of governmental power to limit personal choice to undergo abortion, for which it provided a new resolution based on the due process guaranteed by the Fourteenth Amendment. Whether or not a new social consensus is developing on that issue, its divisiveness is no less today than in 1973, and pressure to overrule the decision, like pressure to retain it, has grown only more intense. A decision to overrule *Roe*'s essential holding under the existing circumstances would address error, if error there was, at the cost of both profound and unnecessary damage to the Court's legitimacy, and to the Nation's commitment to the rule of law. It is therefore imperative to adhere to the essence of *Roe*'s original decision, and we do so today.

IV

. . . The woman's right to terminate her pregnancy before viability is the most central principle of *Roe v. Wade.* It is a rule of law and a component of liberty we cannot renounce. . . .

[But] we reject . . . [*Roe*'s] trimester framework, which we do not consider to be part of the essential holding of *Roe.* . . . Measures aimed at ensuring that a woman's choice contemplates the consequences for the fetus do not necessarily interfere with the right recognized in *Roe,* although those measures have been found to be inconsistent with the rigid trimester framework announced in that case. A logical reading of the central holding in *Roe* itself, and a necessary reconciliation of the liberty of the woman and the interest of the State in promoting prenatal life, require, in our view, that we abandon the trimester framework as a rigid prohibition on all previability regulation aimed at the protection of fetal life. The trimester framework suffers from these basic flaws: in its formulation it misconceives the nature of the pregnant woman's interest; and in practice it undervalues the State's interest in potential life, as recognized in *Roe.* . . .

. . . Only where state regulation imposes an undue burden on a woman's ability to make this decision does the power of the State reach into the heart of the liberty protected by the Due Process Clause. . . .

The concept of an undue burden has been utilized by the Court as well as individual members of the Court, including two of us, in ways that could be considered inconsistent. . . . Because we set forth a standard of general application to which we intend to adhere, it is important to clarify what is meant by an undue burden.

A finding of an undue burden is a shorthand for the conclusion that a state regulation has the purpose or effect of placing a substantial obstacle in the path of a woman seeking an abortion of a nonviable fetus. A statute with this purpose is invalid because the means chosen by the State to further the interest in potential life must be calculated to inform the woman's free choice, not hinder it. And a statute which, while furthering the interest in potential life or some other valid state interest, has the effect of placing a substantial obstacle in the path of a woman's choice cannot be considered a permissible means of serving its legitimate ends. To the extent that the opinions of the Court or of individual Justices use the undue burden standard in a manner that is inconsistent with this analysis, we set out what in our view should be the controlling standard. . . . Understood another way, we answer the question, left open in previous opinions discussing the undue burden formulation, whether a law designed to further the State's interest in fetal life which imposes an undue burden on the woman's decision before fetal viability could be constitutional. See, *e.g., Akron I* (O'CONNOR, J., dissenting). The answer is no.

Some guiding principles should emerge. What is at stake is the woman's right to make the ultimate decision, not a right to be insulated from all others in doing so. Regulations which do no more than create a structural mechanism by which the State, or the parent or guardian of a minor, may express profound respect for the life of the unborn are permitted, if they are not a substantial obstacle to the woman's exercise of the right to choose. Unless it has that effect on her right of choice, a state measure designed to persuade her to choose childbirth over abortion will be upheld if reasonably related to that goal. Regulations designed to foster the health of a woman seeking an abortion are valid if they do not constitute an undue burden.

Even when jurists reason from shared premises, some disagreement is inevitable. That is to be expected in the application of any legal standard which must accommodate life's complexity. We do not expect it to be otherwise with respect to the undue burden standard. We give this summary:

(a) To protect the central right recognized by *Roe v. Wade* while at the same time accommodating the State's profound interest in potential life, we will employ the undue burden analysis as explained in this opinion. An undue burden exists, and therefore a provision of law is invalid, if its purpose or effect is to place a substantial obstacle in the path of a woman seeking an abortion before the fetus attains viability.

(b)   We reject the rigid trimester framework of *Roe v. Wade.* To promote the State's profound interest in potential life, throughout pregnancy the State may take measures to ensure that the woman's choice is informed, and measures designed to advance this interest will not be invalidated as long as their purpose is to persuade the woman to choose childbirth over abortion. These measures must not be an undue burden on the right.

(c)   As with any medical procedure, the State may enact regulations to further the health or safety of a woman seeking an abortion. Unnecessary health regulations that have the purpose or effect of presenting a substantial obstacle to a woman seeking an abortion impose an undue burden on the right.

(d)   Our adoption of the undue burden analysis does not disturb the central holding of *Roe v. Wade,* and we reaffirm that holding. Regardless of whether exceptions are made for particular circumstances, a State may not prohibit any woman from making the ultimate decision to terminate her pregnancy before viability.

(e)   We also reaffirm *Roe*'s holding that "subsequent to viability, the State in promoting its interest in the potentiality of human life may, if it chooses, regulate, and even proscribe, abortion except where it is necessary, in appropriate medical judgment, for the preservation of the life or health of the mother." *Roe v. Wade.*

These principles control our assessment of the Pennsylvania statute, and we now turn to the issue of the validity of its challenged provisions.

V

The Court of Appeals applied what it believed to be the undue burden standard and upheld each of the provisions except for the husband notification requirement. We agree generally with this conclusion, but refine the undue burden analysis in accordance with the principles articulated above. We now consider the separate statutory sections at issue. . . .

[In the remainder of this section of the opinion the Court ruled on the law. It upheld the following provisions on the ground that they do not place an undue burden on the abortion right:

1.   Informed Consent/24-hour waiting period (Part V-B); "Even the broadest reading of *Roe* . . . has not suggested that there is a constitutional right to abortion on demand. . . . Rather, the right protected by *Roe* is a right to decide to terminate a pregnancy free of undue interference by the State. Because the informed consent requirement facilitates the wise exercise of that right it cannot be classified as an interference with the right *Roe* protects. The informed consent requirement is not an undue burden on that right."

2.   Parental Consent (Part V-D): "We have been over most of this ground before. Our cases establish, and we reaffirm today, that a State may require a minor seeking an abortion to obtain the consent of a parent or guardian, provided that there is an adequate judicial bypass procedure. . . ."

3.   Recordkeeping and Reporting (Part V-E): "[A]ll the provisions at issue here except that relating to spousal notice are constitutional. The collection of information with respect to actual patients is a vital element of medical research, and so it cannot be said that the requirements serve no purpose other than to make abortions more difficult. Nor do we find that the requirements impose a substantial obstacle to a woman's choice. At most they might increase the cost of some abortions by a slight amount."

The Court struck the following provisions on the ground that they place an undue burden on the abortion right:

1.   Spousal notification (V-C): "The spousal notification requirement is thus likely to prevent a significant number of women from obtaining an abortion. It does not merely make abortions a little more difficult or expensive to obtain; for many women, it will impose a substantial obstacle. We must not blind ourselves to the fact that the significant number of women who fear for their safety and the safety of their children are likely to be deterred from procuring an abortion as surely as if the Commonwealth had outlawed abortion in all cases."

2.   Recordkeeping and Reporting (Part V-E): "Subsection (12) of the reporting provision requires the reporting of, among other things, a married woman's "reason for failure to provide notice" to her husband. This provision in effect requires women, as a condition of obtaining an abortion, to provide the Commonwealth with the precise information we have already recognized that many women have pressing reasons not to reveal. Like the spousal notice requirement itself, this provision places an undue burden on a woman's choice, and must be invalidated for that reason."]

VI

Our Constitution is a covenant running from the first generation of Americans to us and then to future generations. It is a coherent succession. Each generation must learn anew that the Constitution's written terms embody ideas and aspirations that must survive more ages than one. We accept our responsibility not to retreat from interpreting the full meaning of the covenant in light of all of our precedents. We invoke it once again to define the freedom guaranteed by the Constitution's own promise, the promise of liberty.

Affirmed in part, reversed in part, and remanded.

JUSTICE STEVENS, concurring in part and dissenting in part.

My disagreement with the joint opinion begins with its understanding of the trimester framework established in *Roe.* Contrary to the suggestion of the joint opinion, it is not a "contradiction" to recognize that the State may have a legitimate interest in potential human life and, at the same time, to conclude that interest does not justify the regulation of abortion before viability (although other interests, such as maternal health, may). The fact that the State's interest is legitimate does not tell us when, if ever, that interest outweighs the pregnant woman's interest in personal liberty. . . .

In my opinion, the principles established in this long line of cases and the wisdom reflected in Justice Powell's opinion for the Court in *Akron* (and followed by the Court just six years ago in *Thornburgh*) should govern our decision today. . . .

["Under these principles," Justice Stevens wrote, he disagreed with Parts IV, V-B, and V-D of the joint opinion, but joined the remainder. He was particularly concerned about the twenty-four-hour waiting period.]

In my opinion, a correct application of the "undue burden" standard leads to the same conclusion concerning the constitutionality of [this requirement]. A state-imposed burden on the exercise of a constitutional right is measured both by its effects and by its character: A burden may be "undue" either because the burden is too severe or because it lacks a legitimate, rational justification.

The 24-hour delay requirement fails both parts of this test. The findings of the District Court establish the severity of the burden that the 24-hour delay imposes on many pregnant women. Yet even in those cases in which the delay is not especially onerous, it is, in my opinion, "undue" because there is no evidence that such a delay serves a useful and legitimate purpose. As indicated above, there is no legitimate reason to require a woman who has agonized over her decision to leave the clinic or hospital and return again another day. While a general requirement that a physician notify her patients about the risks of a proposed medical procedure is appropriate, a rigid requirement that all patients wait 24 hours or (what is true in practice) much longer to evaluate the significance of information that is either common knowledge or irrelevant is an irrational and, therefore, "undue" burden.

JUSTICE BLACKMUN, concurring in part, concurring in the judgment in part, and dissenting in part.

I join parts I, II, III, V-A, V-C, and VI of the joint opinion of JUSTICES O'CONNOR, KENNEDY, and SOUTER. . . .

Make no mistake, the joint opinion of JUSTICES O'CONNOR, KENNEDY, and SOUTER is an act of personal courage and constitutional principle. In contrast to previous decisions in which JUSTICES O'CONNOR and KENNEDY postponed reconsideration of *Roe v. Wade* (1973), the authors of the joint opinion today join JUSTICE STEVENS and me in concluding that "the essential holding of *Roe* should be retained and once again reaffirmed." In brief, five Members of this Court today recognize that "the Constitution protects a woman's right to terminate her pregnancy in its early stages." . . .

[But] . . . *Roe*'s requirement of strict scrutiny as implemented through a trimester framework should not be disturbed. No other approach has gained a majority, and no other is more protective of the woman's fundamental right. Lastly, no other approach properly accommodates the woman's constitutional right with the State's legitimate interests. . . .

Application of the strict scrutiny standard results in the invalidation of all the challenged provisions. Indeed, as this Court has invalidated virtually identical provisions in prior cases, *stare decisis* requires that we again strike them down. . . .

In one sense, the Court's approach is worlds apart from that of THE CHIEF JUSTICE and JUSTICE SCALIA. And yet, in another sense, the distance between the two approaches is short—the distance is but a single vote.

I am 83 years old. I cannot remain on this Court forever, and when I do step down, the confirmation process for my successor well may focus on the issue before us today. That, I regret, may be exactly where the choice between the two worlds will be made.

CHIEF JUSTICE REHNQUIST, with whom JUSTICE WHITE, JUSTICE SCALIA, and JUSTICE THOMAS join, concurring in the judgment in part and dissenting in part.

The joint opinion, following its newly-minted variation on *stare decisis*, retains the outer shell of *Roe v. Wade* (1973), but beats a wholesale retreat from the substance of that case. We believe that *Roe* was wrongly decided, and that it can and should be overruled consistently with our traditional approach to *stare decisis* in constitutional cases. We would adopt the approach of the plurality in *Webster v. Reproductive Health Services* (1989), and uphold the challenged provisions of the Pennsylvania statute in their entirety. . . .

. . . [T]he joint opinion . . . state[s] that when the Court "resolve[s] the sort of intensely divisive controversy reflected in *Roe* and those rare, comparable cases," its decision is exempt from reconsideration under established principles of *stare decisis* in constitutional cases. This is so, the joint opinion contends, because in those "intensely divisive" cases the Court has "call[ed] the contending sides of a national controversy to end their national division by accepting a common mandate rooted in the Constitution," and must therefore take special care not to be perceived as "surrender[ing] to political pressure" and continued opposition. This is a truly novel principle, one which is contrary to both the Court's historical practice and to the Court's traditional willingness to tolerate criticism of its opinions. Under this principle, when the Court has ruled on a divisive issue, it is apparently prevented from overruling that decision for the sole reason that it was incorrect, unless opposition to the original decision has died away.

The . . . difficulty with this principle lies in its assumption that cases which are "intensely divisive" can be readily distinguished from those that are not. The question of whether a particular issue is "intensely divisive" enough to qualify for special protection is entirely subjective and dependent on the individual assumptions of the members of this Court. In addition, because the Court's duty is to ignore public opinion and criticism on issues that come before it, its members are in perhaps the worst position to judge whether a decision divides the Nation deeply enough to justify such uncommon protection. Although many of the Court's decisions divide the populace to a large degree, we have not previously on that account shied away from applying normal rules of *stare decisis* when urged to reconsider earlier decisions. Over the past 21 years, for example, the Court has overruled in whole or in part 34 of its previous constitutional decisions. . . .

The end result of the joint opinion's paeans of praise for legitimacy is the enunciation of a brand new standard for evaluating state regulation of a woman's right to abortion—the "undue burden" standard. As indicated above, *Roe v. Wade* adopted a "fundamental right" standard under which state regulations could survive only if they met the requirement of "strict scrutiny." While we disagree with that standard, it at least had a recognized basis in constitutional law at the time *Roe* was decided. The same cannot be said for the "undue burden" standard, which is created largely out of whole cloth by the authors of the joint opinion. It is a standard which even today does not command the support of a majority of this Court. And it will not, we believe, result in the sort of "simple limitation," easily applied, which the joint opinion anticipates. In sum, it is a standard which is not built to last.

. . . Accordingly, we think that the correct analysis is that . . . [a] woman's interest in having an abortion is a form of liberty protected by the Due Process Clause, but States may regulate abortion procedures in ways rationally related to a legitimate state interest. . . .

[Using this standard] we . . . would hold that each of the challenged provisions of the Pennsylvania statute is consistent with the Constitution. It bears emphasis that our conclusion in this regard does not carry with it any necessary approval of these regulations. Our task is, as always, to decide only whether the challenged provisions of a law comport with the United States Constitution. If, as we believe, these do, their wisdom as a matter of public policy is for the people of Pennsylvania to decide.

JUSTICE SCALIA, with whom THE CHIEF JUSTICE, JUSTICE WHITE, and JUSTICE THOMAS join, concurring in the judgment in part and dissenting in part.

My views on this matter are unchanged from those I set forth in my separate opinion . . . in *Webster v. Reproductive Health Services* (1989) (SCALIA, J., concurring in part and concurring in judgment). . . . The States may, if they wish, permit abortion-on-demand, but the Constitution does not *require* them to do so. The permissibility of abortion, and the limitations upon it, are to be resolved like most important questions in our democracy: by citizens trying to persuade one another and then voting. . . .

Beyond that brief summary of the essence of my position, I will not swell the United States Reports with repetition of what I have said before; and applying the rational basis test, I would uphold the Pennsylvania statute in its entirety. . . . The Court's reliance upon *stare decisis* can best be described as contrived. It insists upon the necessity of adhering not to all of *Roe,* but only to what it calls the "central holding." . . .

I am certainly not in a good position to dispute that the Court *has saved* the "central holding" of *Roe,* since to do that effectively I would have to know what the Court has saved, which in turn would require me to understand (as I do not) what the "undue burden" test means. I must confess, however, that I have always thought, and I think a lot of other people have always thought, that the arbitrary trimester framework, which the Court today discards, was quite as central to *Roe* as the arbitrary viability test, which the Court today retains. It seems particularly ungrateful to carve the trimester framework out of the core of *Roe,* since its very rigidity (in sharp contrast to the utter indeterminability of the "undue burden" test) is probably the only reason the Court is able to say, in urging *stare decisis,* that *Roe* "has in no sense proven 'unworkable.'" I suppose the Court is entitled to call a "central holding" whatever it wants to call a "central holding"—which is, come to think of it, perhaps one of the difficulties with this modified version of *stare decisis.* I thought I might note, however, that the following portions of *Roe* have not been saved:

- Under *Roe,* requiring that a woman seeking an abortion be provided truthful information about abortion before giving informed written consent is unconstitutional, if the information is designed to influence her choice, *Akron I.* Under the joint opinion's "undue burden" regime (as applied today, at least) such a requirement is constitutional.
- Under *Roe,* requiring that information be provided by a doctor, rather than by nonphysician counselors, is unconstitutional, *Akron I.* Under the "undue burden" regime (as applied today, at least) it is not.
- Under *Roe,* requiring a 24-hour waiting period between the time the woman gives her informed consent and the time of the abortion is unconstitutional, *Akron I.* Under the "undue burden" regime (as applied today, at least) it is not.
- Under *Roe,* requiring detailed reports that include demographic data about each woman who seeks an abortion and various information about each

abortion is unconstitutional, *Thornburgh.* Under the "undue burden" regime (as applied today, at least) it generally is not. . . .

The Imperial Judiciary lives. . . .

We should get out of this area, where we have no right to be, and where we do neither ourselves nor the country any good by remaining.

What are we to make of *Casey*? On one hand, reports of *Roe*'s demise were exaggerated. The Court did not overrule *Roe*; to the contrary, it reaffirmed the "central holding" of the 1973 decision that a woman should have "some" freedom to terminate a pregnancy. On the other, the "joint opinion" gutted the core of *Roe*. The trimester framework was gone. Under *Casey,* states may now enact laws—regulating the entire pregnancy—that further their interest in potential life so long as those laws are rationally related to that end and do not put an undue burden on the right to terminate a pregnancy. Laws that do not meet this standard will be subject to strict scrutiny, such as the spousal notification provision at issue in *Casey.*

In general, this undue burden approach, which O'Connor originally proposed in 1983 in her *Akron* dissent, could lead to very different outcomes in abortion cases. Justice Scalia's dissent indicates that many of the provisions at issue in *Casey* that the Court upheld under the undue burden standard would have been struck down under *Roe*'s strict scrutiny approach. Yet at least Stevens and Blackmun held out hope that the undue burden standard could be applied, in the future, to strike down restrictive laws.

The Roberts Court and the Future of *Roe v. Wade*

As we have seen, ever since the early 1980s abortion opponents have held out hope that the Court would overturn *Roe v. Wade.* The justices came close in *Webster,* only to reaffirm the abortion right in *Casey.*

Will the current Court, now under the leadership of George W. Bush's appointee, John Roberts, change course? Will *Roe* go? For pro-choice advocates, **Gonzales v. Carhart** (2007), the only major abortion case decided by the Roberts Court, offers some cause for concern. In *Gonzales,* the justices considered a federal law banning "partial-birth abortions"—a term often used to describe one of several different kinds of (controversial) procedures used to terminate pregnancies after four months. The law under consideration prohibited, among other things, "knowingly perform[ing] a partial-birth abortion . . . that is [not] necessary to save the life of a mother." It defines "partial-birth abortion" as a procedure in which the doctor "(A) deliberately and intentionally vaginally delivers a living fetus until, in the case of a head-first presentation, the entire fetal head is outside the [mother's] body . . . , or, in the case of breech presentation, any part of the fetal trunk past the navel is outside the [mother's] body . . . , for the purpose of performing an overt act that the person knows will kill the partially delivered living fetus"; and "(B) performs the overt act, other than completion of delivery, that kills the fetus."

Just seven years earlier, in **Stenberg v. Carhart** (2000), the Court had struck down a similar law passed in Nebraska. Writing for a five-person majority, Justice Stephen Breyer held that under the precedents established in *Roe v. Wade* (1973) and *Planned Parenthood of Southeastern Pennsylvania v. Casey* (1992), the state law placed an undue burden on the right to an abortion because it limited a woman's choice of abortion procedures.

The majority also noted several other defects in the Nebraska law—notably that it did not contain an exception to preserve the health of the woman—to which Congress attempted to respond when it passed the federal ban on partial-birth abortions three years after *Stenberg*. For example, Congress justified the lack of an inclusion of a health exception based on its own fact-finding that there is a moral, medical, and ethical consensus that partial-birth abortion is a gruesome and inhumane procedure that is never medically necessary and should be prohibited.

This was insufficient to convince two courts of appeals to uphold the law. The U.S. Court of Appeals for the Eighth Circuit found that a lack of consensus existed in the medical community as to the banned procedure's necessity, and therefore *Stenberg* required legislatures to err on the side of protecting women's health by including a health exception. In a separate suit, *Gonzales v. Planned Parenthood Federation of America*, in which the pro-choice organization Planned Parenthood challenged the act, a district court also struck it down as unconstitutional. It held that the law unduly burdened a woman's ability to choose a second-trimester abortion and lacked a health exception as required by *Stenberg*. The Ninth Circuit Court of Appeals agreed and affirmed. The Supreme Court

consolidated the two suits, with *Gonzales v. Carhart* as the lead case.

This time the Court upheld the law. Writing for another five-person majority, Justice Kennedy found that the challengers had failed to demonstrate that the law placed an undue burden on women. In so doing, he relied on congressional findings that the intact dilation and extraction procedure is never needed to protect the health of the woman, thus a health exception was unnecessary. In a further effort to distinguish *Stenberg*, he also held that the Nebraska state law was more ambiguous than its federal counterpart.

Writing in dissent, Justice Ginsburg chided the majority for ignoring abortion precedent and not reinforcing the "essential holding" of *Roe*. As she put it, "Today's decision is alarming. It refuses to take *Casey* and *Stenberg* seriously. It tolerates, indeed applauds, federal intervention to ban nationwide a procedure found necessary and proper in certain cases by the American College of Obstetricians and Gynecologists. . . . And, for the first time since *Roe,* the Court blesses a prohibition with no exception safeguarding a woman's health."

Even though the Court's retreat from *Stenberg* in *Carhart* alarmed pro-choice advocates, we might speculate that *Carhart* does not necessarily signal a retreat from *Casey*—at least not in the short term. First, as we show in Table 10-3, the Court has experienced many membership changes since 1973, and, even assuming that Roberts and Samuel Alito oppose *Roe* (and assuming Kagan and Sotomayor support it), it appears that the anti-*Roe* side still lacks a vote. This is not to say that the Court will retain its current approach to abortion—the undue burden standard. Actually, even among *Roe*'s supporters some divergence exists over the appropriate legal approach to abortion. It is not clear that any member of the current Court subscribes to *Roe*'s strict scrutiny approach. Breyer and perhaps even Ginsburg seem content with the O'Connor undue burden standard, although before her appointment to the Court, Ginsburg urged courts to use the equal protection clause to analyze abortion cases.[18] Kagan's and Sotomayor's approach(es) remains unknown.

Second is a point that the joint opinion in *Casey* underscores: the Court rarely overturns its own precedent. We

---

18. In a 1985 law review article, Ginsburg urged courts to acknowledge the "women's equality aspect" in the abortion issue. See Ruth Bader Ginsburg, "Some Thoughts on Autonomy and Equality in Relation to *Roe v. Wade*," *North Carolina Law Review* 63 (1985): 375–386.

TABLE 10-3   Support for *Roe V. Wade*

ROE V. WADE (1973)	AKRON V. AKRON CENTER (1983)	WEBSTER V. REPRODUCTIVE HEALTH SERVICES (1989)	PLANNED PARENTHOOD V. CASEY (1992)	CURRENT COURT (2011)
Blackmun	Blackmun	Blackmun	Blackmun	Breyer
Brennan	Brennan	Brennan	Souter	Sotomayor?
Burger	Burger	*Rehnquist*	*Rehnquist*	Roberts
Douglas	Stevens	Stevens	Stevens	Kagan?
Marshall	Marshall	Marshall	*Thomas*	*Thomas*
Powell	Powell	*Kennedy*	Kennedy	Kennedy
Rehnquist	*Rehnquist*	*Scalia*	*Scalia*	*Scalia*
Stewart	*O'Connor*	*O'Connor*	O'Connor	*Alito*
White	*White*	*White*	*White*	Ginsburg

KEY: Justices whose names appear in boldface support *Roe* or at least its central holding; justices whose names appear in italics either voiced concerns about *Roe* or would overturn it. Chief Justice Roberts and Justice Alito have yet to express their views on *Roe* explicitly in Supreme Court litigation; their names appear here in italics based on their votes in abortion-related litigation and on their writings prior to their ascension to the Court. Kagan and Sotomayor have yet to participate in an abortion case.

do not claim that *Roe*'s place in American jurisprudence is assured; that would be too strong a statement. What we do want to suggest is that *Roe*'s demise, if it comes, will likely occur through a gradual whittling-away process rather than through an explicit overruling. This approach is consistent with how the Court often treats precedents with which it disagrees but does not, for various reasons, wish to overturn.

Third, if the Court actually does pay some attention to public opinion, as some scholars suggest, then *Roe* may be on solid ground. Polls taken immediately after *Casey* found that a large majority of Americans (more than 80 percent) favor the right to abortion under at least some circumstances (such as when a woman's health is endangered by the pregnancy). Nearly fifteen years later, 56 percent surveyed in January 2006 said they would not be in favor of Samuel Alito's nomination to the Court if they were "convinced he would vote to overturn *Roe v. Wade*."[19] On the other hand, as we noted earlier, large numbers of Americans support restrictions on the abortion right (*see Figure 10-2*).

Whatever the fate of *Roe*, it seems inevitable that Americans (and the Court) will continue to debate the abortion issue, with no easy answers apparent. But Americans are not alone. As Box 10-4 describes, more than 60 percent of the world's population lives in the sixty-eight nations that now permit abortion without severe restrictions, but the issue continues to generate controversy all over the world.

PRIVATE ACTIVITIES AND THE APPLICATION OF *GRISWOLD*

Little doubt exists that many Americans now equate the right to privacy, first established in *Griswold v. Connecticut*, with reproductive freedom, especially the right to abortion, but the right to privacy has implications for many other activities, including those we cover below: private sexual activities, the right to die, drug testing, and various others following from the information age. In fact, one of the first important applications of *Griswold* came in a criminal procedure case, *Katz v. United States* (1967).[20] FBI agents suspected Charles Katz of engaging in illegal bookmaking activity; in particular, they thought he was "transmitting wagering information by telephone from Los Angeles to Miami and Boston." To gather evidence, they placed listening and recording devices outside the telephone booth where Katz made his calls and used the transcripts of his conversations to obtain an eight-count indictment.

---

19. Gallup Poll conducted January 6–8, 2006. The question was as follows: "Suppose that after his confirmation hearings you were convinced Samuel Alito would vote to overturn the *Roe v. Wade* decision on abortion. If that were the case, would you like to see the Senate vote in favor of Alito serving on the Supreme Court, or not?" Of those responding, 34 percent said they would vote in favor; 56 percent said they would not; 11 percent had no opinion.

20. An excerpt of *Katz* appears in Chapter 11.

BOX 10-4 ABORTION IN GLOBAL PERSPECTIVE

Prior to the U.S. Supreme Court's 1973 decision in *Roe v. Wade*, several nations—including China, India, the former Soviet Union, and the United Kingdom—already had liberalized their abortion laws. But the vast majority of change has come in the post-*Roe* period. Here is a breakdown of the laws concerning abortion in the 197 countries surveyed by the Guttmacher Institute:

- 32 of the 197 countries, home to about 6 percent of all women of childbearing age, do not allow abortion on any grounds. The vast majority of the 32 are developing countries in Africa (e.g., Angola, Congo, Senegal), Asia (e.g., Laos, the Philippines), and Latin America (e.g., Chile, Haiti, Nicaragua).
- 36 of the 197 countries (roughly 21 percent of all women of childbearing age) allow abortion only to save the life of the pregnant woman (though some allow abortion in cases of rape as well). Of these 36 countries, only Ireland is in a developed region. Mexico is also in this category but its states are free to devise their own laws. In 2007, the Mexican federal district, where Mexico City is located, legalized abortion during the first twelve weeks of pregnancy.
- 59 of the 197 countries permit abortion to save the woman's life and protect her physical health (36) or to save the woman's life and protect her physical *and* mental health (23). About 14 percent of all women of childbearing age live in one of these countries. But, as the Guttmacher Institute notes, "The abortion laws in

these 59 countries are subject to very wide variations in interpretation and implementation." For example, although there are restrictions on abortions in Hong Kong, Israel, New Zealand, South Korea, and Spain, in these locations abortion services are "available virtually on request."

- 14 of the 197 countries allow abortion for the reasons above, along with socioeconomic reasons. Some 22 percent of women of childbearing age live in one of these countries, but this figure is inflated by India (home to more than one billion people). Other countries falling into this category include smaller less developed nations (e.g., Barbados, Fiji) and the developed countries of Australia, Great Britain, and Japan.
- 56 of the 197 countries allow abortion without restriction as to reason. Approximately 39 percent of all women of childbearing age live in one of these countries, although this percentage is inflated because China falls into this category. It is also true that many of these 56 countries restrict abortions to the first trimester of pregnancy.
- Finally, in many countries—including Denmark, Greece, Italy, and the Slovak Republic—minors cannot obtain abortions without parental consent.

SOURCE: Susheela Sing, Deirdre Wulf, Rubina Hussain, Akinrinola Bankole, and Gilda Sedgh, *Abortion Worldwide: A Decade of Uneven Progress* (New York: Guttmacher Institute, 2009), http://www.guttmacher.org/pubs/Abortion-Worldwide.pdf.

Katz challenged the use of the transcripts as evidence against him, asserting that his conversations were private and that the government had violated his rights under the Fourth Amendment. The government argued that in previous Fourth Amendment search and seizure cases, the justices permitted the use of bugs and microphones so long as agents did not "physically penetrate" an individual's space. Because the FBI had attached listening devices to the *outside* of the phone booth, it claimed that it did not invade Katz's space.

The Court disagreed. In his majority opinion, Justice Stewart dealt primarily with existing precedent governing searches and seizures (a topic covered in Chapter 11), but he also touched on the privacy issue, asserting: "What a person knowingly exposes to the

public, even in his own home or office, is not a subject of Fourth Amendment protection. But what he seeks to preserve as private, even in an area accessible to the public, may be constitutionally protected." Justice Harlan, in a concurring opinion, put it in these terms: if a person has "exhibited an actual (subjective) expectation of privacy," and "the expectation . . . [is] one that society is prepared to recognize as 'reasonable,'" then he or she comes under the protection of the Fourth Amendment. In other words, the justices—even Stewart, who dissented in *Griswold*—were willing to apply the right to privacy to searches and seizures. If citizens expect privacy, as Katz did when he entered the telephone booth, then they are entitled to it. This position was not wholly different from what Justice Brandeis had advocated in *Olmstead v. United States* about forty years before *Katz.*

Two years later, in **Stanley v. Georgia** (1969), the Court had another occasion to examine the privacy doctrine and its relationship to searches and seizures. While police were investigating Robert Stanley for illegal bookmaking, they obtained a warrant to search his home. Authorities found little evidence of gambling activity, but they did find three reels of film. They watched the movies and arrested Stanley for possessing obscene material. Stanley's attorney challenged the seizure and arrest on the ground that the law should not "punish mere private possession of obscene material"—that his client had a right of privacy to view whatever he wished in his own home. The state argued that it had the right to seize obscene materials because they are illegal to possess. Indeed, in previous decisions, the Court had said that states could regulate the dissemination of obscene movies, magazines, and so forth.

In a unanimous opinion for the Court, Justice Marshall accepted Stanley's argument. Taking a lesson from Brandeis's dissent in *Olmstead,* he asserted: "If the First Amendment means anything, it means that a State has no business telling a man, sitting alone in his house, what books he may read or films he may watch." Put somewhat differently, states can regulate obscenity but cannot prohibit such activity inside someone's house. The First Amendment and privacy rights simply prohibit this kind of intrusion into the home.

This last point is important: *Stanley* hinged on a violation of a fundamental liberty—in this instance, the First Amendment. Marshall made this clear in a footnote to his opinion:

What we have said in no way infringes upon the power of the State or Federal Government to make possession of other items, such as narcotics, firearms, or stolen goods, a crime. Our holding in the present case turns upon the Georgia statute's infringement of fundamental liberties protected by the First Amendment. No First Amendment rights are involved in most statutes making mere possession a crime.

Private Sexual Activity

But would the Court apply *Stanley* to activities forbidden by the state that did not fall under the First Amendment? Of special concern was the question of whether laws criminalizing certain forms of sexual activity would now be unconstitutional given decisions such as *Katz* and *Stanley*—particularly if the activity in question took place in private and involved only consenting adults.

Bowers v. Hardwick (1986) raised this very question. This dispute began in 1982 when an Atlanta police officer arrived at Michael Hardwick's home to serve him with an arrest warrant for failure to keep a court date. According to the officer, one of Hardwick's housemates answered the door. He told the officer that he did not know if Hardwick was home, but that the officer was free to enter and look for him. As the officer walked down the hallway, he passed a partially open bedroom door and observed Hardwick engaged in sodomy with another man. The officer arrested Hardwick for violating a Georgia law that prohibited the practice of oral or anal sex.[21] The district attorney decided not to pursue the matter, but Hardwick and his ACLU attorneys challenged the law, asserting that it violated the fundamental right to privacy as articulated in *Griswold* and should be subject to strict constitutional scrutiny.[22] After the court of appeals ruled in Hardwick's favor, the state asked the Supreme Court to review the case.

At first the Supreme Court could not muster the necessary four votes to hear the case, but after Justice White circulated an opinion to his colleagues, dissenting from the denial of certiorari, a sufficient number of justices agreed to review it. In particular, they granted certiorari to address this question: Did the court of appeals err when it concluded that Georgia's sodomy statute infringes upon the fundamental rights of homosexuals and required the state to demonstrate a compelling interest to support the constitutionality of the statute?

Splitting 5 to 4, the Court upheld the Georgia law. Writing for himself and Burger, O'Connor, Powell, and Rehnquist, White said, "[F]undamental liberties . . . are characterized as those . . . that are 'deeply rooted in this Nation's history and tradition'"—a type of liberty that, according to White, homosexual sodomy was surely not:

Sodomy was a criminal offense at common law and was forbidden by the laws of the original thirteen States when they ratified the Bill of Rights. . . . In fact, until 1961, all 50 States outlawed sodomy, and today 24 States and the District of Columbia continue to provide criminal penalties for sodomy performed in private and between consenting adults. Against

---

21. The majority opinion dealt exclusively with "consensual homosexual sodomy," expressing "no opinion . . . on other acts of sodomy."

22. For more on this case, see Peter Irons, *The Courage of Their Convictions* (New York: Free Press, 1988).

this background, to claim that a right to engage in such conduct is "deeply rooted in this Nation's history and tradition" or "implicit in the concept of ordered liberty" is, at best, facetious.

In a concurring opinion, Chief Justice Burger also pointed to the "ancient roots" of proscriptions against sodomy:

Decisions of individuals relating to homosexual conduct have been subject to state intervention throughout the history of Western civilization. Condemnation of those practices is firmly rooted in Judeao-Christian moral and ethical standards. Homosexual sodomy was a capital crime under Roman law. During the English Reformation when powers of the ecclesiastical courts were transferred to the King's Courts, the first English statute criminalizing sodomy was passed. Blackstone described "the infamous crime against nature" as an offense of "deeper malignity" than rape, a heinous act "the very mention of which is a disgrace to human nature," and "a crime not fit to be named." The common law of England, including its prohibition of sodomy, became the received law of Georgia and the other Colonies. In 1816 the Georgia Legislature passed the statute at issue here, and that statute has been continuously in force in one form or another since that time. To hold that the act of homosexual sodomy is somehow protected as a fundamental right would be to cast aside millennia of moral teaching.

White's majority opinion also dismissed the importance of *Stanley,* giving it a rather narrow reading: it protected the performance of some otherwise illegal activity only if the First Amendment was implicated. Because *Bowers* did not raise a First Amendment objection to sodomy laws, *Stanley* was not applicable.

Led by Harry Blackmun, the dissenters, Brennan, Marshall, and Stevens, objected to the Court's characterization of the issue. It was not, Blackmun argued, a matter of right to engage in sodomy but instead a question of privacy rights. The dissenters also called White's interpretation of *Stanley* "unconvincing." In

Tyron Garner, left, and John Geddes Lawrence greet supporters at Houston City Hall who had gathered to celebrate the Court's landmark decision in Lawrence v. Texas. *The justices struck down a Texas sodomy law, a decision applauded by gay rights advocates as a historic ruling that overturned sodomy laws in thirteen states.*

their view, *Stanley* took its cues from Brandeis's dissent in *Olmstead* and, accordingly, rested as much on the Fourth Amendment as on the First.

Did the Burger Court in *Bowers* begin to dismantle the Warren Court's rulings in *Stanley* and *Griswold,* or did it merely draw sensible limits around them? For most Americans, the latter would have been true. In surveys conducted during the 1980s through the mid-1990s, about 75 percent of respondents said they believed "sexual relations between two adults of the same sex" are wrong. Note, however, that in *Bowers* the justices showed less consensus than the public: the case was decided by a one-vote margin, and, after he retired, Justice Powell said that he "probably made a mistake" in voting to uphold the Georgia laws. Blackmun, in his dissent, explicitly expressed his hope that the Court "will reconsider its analysis."

That reconsideration may not have come as quickly as Blackmun had wished, but it did come. In *Lawrence v. Texas* (2003), the justices overruled *Bowers*. As you read the excerpt below, consider why you think the Court took the rare step of overturning one of its own decisions. Also consider the meaning of *Lawrence* for the development of privacy law.

Lawrence v. Texas

539 U.S. 558 (2003)
http://laws.findlaw.com/US/539/558.html
Oral arguments are available at http://www.oyez.org.
Vote: 6 (Breyer, Ginsburg, Kennedy, O'Connor, Souter, Stevens)
*   3 (Rehnquist, Scalia, Thomas)*

OPINION OF THE COURT: *Kennedy*
OPINION CONCURRING IN THE JUDGMENT: *O'Connor*
DISSENTING OPINIONS: *Scalia, Thomas*

FACTS:

In many ways, *Lawrence* is quite similar to *Bowers*. Like *Bowers,* this case began with a police visit to a private residence. After receiving a phone call about a possible weapons disturbance, police officers in Houston, Texas, entered the apartment of John Geddes Lawrence, where they observed Lawrence and another man, Tyron Garner, engaging in a sexual act. The two men were arrested and eventually convicted of violating a Texas law that made it a crime for two persons of the same sex to engage in sodomy. This law, unlike the one at issue in *Bowers,* applied only to participants of the same sex.

Lawrence and Garner challenged the statute as a violation of the equal protection clause of the Fourteenth Amendment, a similar provision of the Texas constitution, and the due process clause of the Fourteenth Amendment. After Texas courts, relying on the Supreme Court's decision in *Bowers,* rejected these claims, the two appealed to the U.S. Supreme Court.

Once the Supreme Court granted certiorari in *Lawrence,* numerous amici entered the dispute, asking the Court to strike down the law. In some of the briefs, scholars criticized the historical premises on which the majority opinion and Chief Justice Burger's concurrence in *Bowers* relied. Others pointed to the changing circumstances of the two cases. For example, at the time the Court decided *Bowers,* half of the states outlawed sodomy; by 2003 that number was reduced to thirteen, of which four enforced their laws only against homosexual conduct.

ARGUMENTS:

For the petitioners, John Geddes Lawrence, et al.:

- The Texas law is an unjustified violation of privacy and liberty rights. All Americans, including homosexuals, have the right to privacy in the home, to bodily integrity, and to make their own choices about private, consensual sexual relations; Texas cannot justify abridging these rights.

- The principles of stare decisis do not require adherence to the *Bowers* precedent, because some of the assumptions underlying the *Bowers* decision, such as the belief that contemporary morals and tradition condemn homosexual sodomy, are no longer reliable.

- The Texas law denies homosexuals the equal protection of the law by singling out one group, homosexual men, for disadvantaged status without any legitimate legislative purpose.

For the respondent, the State of Texas:

- The Court should adhere to *Bowers* and reaffirm that the Fourteenth Amendment due process guarantee protects only those personal liberties that are deeply rooted in tradition—that is, fundamental. The historical prohibition of a variety of types of extramarital sexual conduct indicates that homosexual sodomy is not a fundamental right.

- The statute, because it neither infringes a fundamental right nor is based on suspect classification, needs only to implicate a legitimate legislative end to survive rational basis scrutiny. Two worthy governmental goals are served by the act: the implementation of public morality and the promotion of family values.

- The statute does not evince a discriminatory purpose because it is facially applicable not only to homosexuals but also to those regarding themselves as bisexual and heterosexual.

JUSTICE KENNEDY DELIVERED THE OPINION OF THE COURT.

Liberty protects the person from unwarranted government intrusions into a dwelling or other private places. In our tradition the State is not omnipresent in the home. And there are other spheres of our lives and existence, outside the home, where the State should not be a dominant presence. Freedom extends beyond spatial bounds. Liberty presumes an autonomy of self that includes freedom of thought, belief, expression, and certain intimate conduct. The instant case involves liberty of the person both in its spatial and more transcendent dimensions. . . .

We granted certiorari to consider three questions:

"1. Whether Petitioners' criminal convictions under the Texas 'Homosexual Conduct' law—which criminalizes sexual intimacy by same-sex couples, but not identical behavior by different-sex couples—violate the Fourteenth Amendment guarantee of equal protection of laws?

"2. Whether Petitioners' criminal convictions for adult consensual sexual intimacy in the home violate their vital interests in liberty and privacy protected by the Due Process Clause of the Fourteenth Amendment?

"3. Whether *Bowers v. Hardwick* (1986) should be overruled?"

The petitioners were adults at the time of the alleged offense. Their conduct was in private and consensual.

We conclude the case should be resolved by determining whether the petitioners were free as adults to engage in the private conduct in the exercise of their liberty under the Due Process Clause of the Fourteenth Amendment to the Constitution. For this inquiry we deem it necessary to reconsider the Court's holding in *Bowers*. . . .

The Court began its substantive discussion in *Bowers* as follows: "The issue presented is whether the Federal Constitution confers a fundamental right upon homosexuals to engage in sodomy and hence invalidates the laws of the many States that still make such

conduct illegal and have done so for a very long time." That statement, we now conclude, discloses the Court's own failure to appreciate the extent of the liberty at stake. To say that the issue in *Bowers* was simply the right to engage in certain sexual conduct demeans the claim the individual put forward, just as it would demean a married couple were it to be said marriage is simply about the right to have sexual intercourse. The laws involved in *Bowers* and here are, to be sure, statutes that purport to do no more than prohibit a particular sexual act. Their penalties and purposes, though, have more far-reaching consequences, touching upon the most private human conduct, sexual behavior, and in the most private of places, the home. The statutes do seek to control a personal relationship that, whether or not entitled to formal recognition in the law, is within the liberty of persons to choose without being punished as criminals.

This, as a general rule, should counsel against attempts by the State, or a court, to define the meaning of the relationship or to set its boundaries absent injury to a person or abuse of an institution the law protects. It suffices for us to acknowledge that adults may choose to enter upon this relationship in the confines of their homes and their own private lives and still retain their dignity as free persons. When sexuality finds overt expression in intimate conduct with another person, the conduct can be but one element in a personal bond that is more enduring. The liberty protected by the Constitution allows homosexual persons the right to make this choice.

Having misapprehended the claim of liberty there presented to it, and thus stating the claim to be whether there is a fundamental right to engage in consensual sodomy, the *Bowers* Court said: "Proscriptions against that conduct have ancient roots." In academic writings, and in many of the scholarly *amicus* briefs filed to assist the Court in this case, there are fundamental criticisms of the historical premises relied upon by the majority and concurring opinions in *Bowers*. We need not enter this debate in the attempt to reach a definitive historical judgment, but the following considerations counsel against adopting the definitive conclusions upon which *Bowers* placed such reliance.

At the outset it should be noted that there is no longstanding history in this country of laws directed at homosexual conduct as a distinct matter. Beginning in colonial times there were prohibitions of sodomy derived from the English criminal laws passed in the first instance by the Reformation Parliament of 1533. The English prohibition was understood to include relations between men and women as well as relations between men and men. The absence of legal prohibitions focusing on homosexual conduct may be explained in part by noting that according to some scholars the concept of the homosexual as a distinct category of person did not emerge until the late 19th century. Thus early American sodomy laws were not directed at homosexuals as such but instead sought to prohibit nonprocreative sexual activity more generally. This does not suggest approval of homosexual conduct. It does tend to show that this particular form of conduct was not thought of as a separate category from like conduct between heterosexual persons. . . .

. . . [F]ar from possessing "ancient roots," American laws targeting same-sex couples did not develop until the last third of the 20th century. The reported decisions concerning the prosecution of consensual, homosexual sodomy between adults for the years 1880–1995 are not always clear in the details, but a significant number involved conduct in a public place.

It was not until the 1970's that any State singled out same-sex relations for criminal prosecution, and only nine States have done so. . . .

In summary, the historical grounds relied upon in *Bowers* are more complex than the majority opinion and the concurring opinion by Chief Justice Burger indicate. Their historical premises are not without doubt and, at the very least, are overstated. . . .

Chief Justice Burger joined the opinion for the Court in *Bowers* and further explained his views as follows: "Decisions of individuals relating to homosexual conduct have been subject to state intervention throughout the history of Western civilization. Condemnation of those practices is firmly rooted in Judeao-Christian moral and ethical standards." As with Justice White's assumptions about history, scholarship casts some doubt on the sweeping nature of the statement by Chief Justice Burger as it pertains to private homosexual conduct between consenting adults. In all events we think that our laws and traditions in the past half century are of most relevance here. These references show an emerging awareness that liberty gives substantial protection to adult persons in deciding how to conduct their private lives in matters pertaining to sex.

This emerging recognition should have been apparent when *Bowers* was decided. In 1955 the American Law Institute promulgated the Model Penal Code and made clear that it did not recommend or provide for "criminal penalties for consensual sexual relations conducted in private." In 1961 Illinois changed its laws to conform to the Model Penal Code. Other States soon followed.

In *Bowers* the Court referred to the fact that before 1961 all 50 States had outlawed sodomy, and that at the time of the Court's decision 24 States and the District of Columbia had sodomy laws. Justice Powell pointed out that these prohibitions often were being ignored, however. Georgia, for instance, had not sought to enforce its law for decades. . . .

. . . [A]lmost five years before *Bowers* was decided the European Court of Human Rights considered a case with parallels to *Bowers* and to today's case. An adult male resident in Northern Ireland alleged he was a practicing homosexual who desired to engage in consensual homosexual conduct. The laws of Northern Ireland forbade him that right. He alleged that he had been questioned, his home had been searched, and he feared criminal prosecution. The court held that the laws proscribing the conduct were invalid under the European Convention on Human Rights. Authoritative in all countries that are members of the Council of Europe (21 nations then, 45 nations now), the decision is at odds with the premise in *Bowers* that the claim put forward was insubstantial in our Western civilization.

In our own constitutional system the deficiencies in *Bowers* became even more apparent in the years following its announcement. The 25 States with laws prohibiting the relevant conduct referenced in the *Bowers* decision are reduced now to 13, of which 4 enforce their laws only against homosexual conduct. In those States where sodomy is still proscribed, whether for same-sex or heterosexual conduct, there is a pattern of nonenforcement with respect to consenting adults acting in private. The State of Texas admitted in 1994 that as of that date it had not prosecuted anyone under those circumstances.

Two principal cases decided after *Bowers* cast its holding into even more doubt. In *Planned Parenthood of Southeastern Pa. v. Casey* (1992), the Court reaffirmed the substantive force of the liberty protected by the Due Process Clause. The *Casey* decision again confirmed that our laws and tradition afford constitutional protection to personal decisions relating to marriage, procreation, contraception, family relationships, child rearing, and education. . . .

Persons in a homosexual relationship may seek autonomy for these purposes, just as heterosexual persons do. The decision in *Bowers* would deny them this right.

The second post-*Bowers* case of principal relevance is *Romer v. Evans* (1996). There the Court struck down class-based legislation directed at homosexuals as a violation of the Equal Protection Clause.[23] *Romer* invalidated an amendment to Colorado's constitution which named as a solitary class persons who were homosexuals, lesbians, or bisexual either by "orientation, conduct, practices or relationships," and deprived them of protection under state antidiscrimination laws. . . .

As an alternative argument in this case, counsel for the petitioners and some *amici* contend that *Romer* provides the basis for declaring the Texas statute invalid under the Equal Protection Clause. That is a tenable argument, but we conclude the instant case requires us to address whether *Bowers* itself has continuing validity. Were we to hold the statute invalid under the Equal Protection Clause some might question whether a prohibition would be valid if drawn differently, say, to prohibit the conduct both between same-sex and different-sex participants.

Equality of treatment and the due process right to demand respect for conduct protected by the substantive guarantee of liberty are linked in important respects, and a decision on the latter point advances both interests. If protected conduct is made criminal and the law which does so remains unexamined for its substantive validity, its stigma might remain even if it were not enforceable as drawn for equal protection reasons. When homosexual conduct is made criminal by the law of the State, that declaration in and of itself is an invitation to subject homosexual persons to discrimination both in the public and in the private spheres. The central holding of *Bowers* has been brought in question by this case, and it should be addressed. Its continuance as precedent demeans the lives of homosexual persons. . . .

The foundations of *Bowers* have sustained serious erosion from our recent decisions in *Casey* and *Romer*. When our precedent has been thus weakened, criticism from other sources is of greater significance. In the United States criticism of *Bowers* has been substantial and continuing, disapproving of its reasoning in all respects, not just as to its historical assumptions. . . .

The doctrine of *stare decisis* is essential to the respect accorded to the judgments of the Court and to the stability of the law. It is not, however, an inexorable command. In *Casey* we noted that when a Court is asked to overrule

a precedent recognizing a constitutional liberty interest, individual or societal reliance on the existence of that liberty cautions with particular strength against reversing course. The holding in *Bowers,* however, has not induced detrimental reliance comparable to some instances where recognized individual rights are involved. Indeed, there has been no individual or societal reliance on *Bowers* of the sort that could counsel against overturning its holding once there are compelling reasons to do so. *Bowers* itself causes uncertainty, for the precedents before and after its issuance contradict its central holding. . . .

Bowers was not correct when it was decided, and it is not correct today. It ought not to remain binding precedent. *Bowers v. Hardwick* should be and now is overruled.

The present case does not involve minors. It does not involve persons who might be injured or coerced or who are situated in relationships where consent might not easily be refused. It does not involve public conduct or prostitution. It does not involve whether the government must give formal recognition to any relationship that homosexual persons seek to enter. The case involves two adults who, with full and mutual consent from each other, engaged in sexual practices common to a homosexual lifestyle. The petitioners are entitled to respect for their private lives. The State cannot demean their existence or control their destiny by making their private sexual conduct a crime. Their right to liberty under the Due Process Clause gives them the full right to engage in their conduct without intervention of the government. "It is a promise of the Constitution that there is a realm of personal liberty which the government may not enter." The Texas statute furthers no legitimate state interest which can justify its intrusion into the personal and private life of the individual.

Had those who drew and ratified the Due Process Clauses of the Fifth Amendment or the Fourteenth Amendment known the components of liberty in its manifold possibilities, they might have been more specific. They did not presume to have this insight. They knew times can blind us to certain truths and later generations can see that laws once thought necessary and proper in fact serve only to oppress. As the Constitution endures, persons in every generation can invoke its principles in their own search for greater freedom.

The judgment of the Court of Appeals for the Texas Fourteenth District is reversed, and the case is remanded for further proceedings not inconsistent with this opinion.

---

23. *Authors' note:* For an excerpt and discussion of *Romer,* see Chapter 13, pages 671–676.

It is so ordered.

JUSTICE O'CONNOR, concurring in the judgment.

The Court today overrules *Bowers v. Hardwick* (1986). I joined *Bowers,* and do not join the Court in overruling it. Nevertheless, I agree with the Court that Texas' statute banning same-sex sodomy is unconstitutional. Rather than relying on the substantive component of the Fourteenth Amendment's Due Process Clause, as the Court does, I base my conclusion on the Fourteenth Amendment's Equal Protection Clause.

The Equal Protection Clause of the Fourteenth Amendment "is essentially a direction that all persons similarly situated should be treated alike." Under our rational basis standard of review, "legislation is presumed to be valid and will be sustained if the classification drawn by the statute is rationally related to a legitimate state interest." . . .

Texas attempts to justify its law, and the effects of the law, by arguing that the statute satisfies rational basis review because it furthers the legitimate governmental interest of the promotion of morality. In *Bowers,* we held that a state law criminalizing sodomy as applied to homosexual couples did not violate substantive due process. We rejected the argument that no rational basis existed to justify the law, pointing to the government's interest in promoting morality. The only question in front of the Court in *Bowers* was whether the substantive component of the Due Process Clause protected a right to engage in homosexual sodomy. *Bowers* did not hold that moral disapproval of a group is a rational basis under the Equal Protection Clause to criminalize homosexual sodomy when heterosexual sodomy is not punished.

This case raises a different issue than *Bowers*: whether, under the Equal Protection Clause, moral disapproval is a legitimate state interest to justify by itself a statute that bans homosexual sodomy, but not heterosexual sodomy. It is not. Moral disapproval of this group, like a bare desire to harm the group, is an interest that is insufficient to satisfy rational basis review under the Equal Protection Clause. Indeed, we have never held that moral disapproval, without any other asserted state interest, is a sufficient rationale under the Equal Protection Clause to justify a law that discriminates among groups of persons. . . .

A law branding one class of persons as criminal solely based on the State's moral disapproval of that class and the conduct associated with that class runs contrary to the values of the Constitution and the Equal Protection Clause, under any standard of review. I therefore concur in the Court's judgment that Texas' sodomy law banning "deviate sexual intercourse" between consenting adults of the same sex, but not between consenting adults of different sexes, is unconstitutional.

JUSTICE SCALIA, with whom THE CHIEF JUSTICE and JUSTICE THOMAS join, dissenting.

I begin with the Court's surprising readiness to reconsider a decision rendered a mere 17 years ago in *Bowers v. Hardwick*. I do not myself believe in rigid adherence to *stare decisis* in constitutional cases; but I do believe that we should be consistent rather than manipulative in invoking the doctrine. Today's opinions in support of reversal do not bother to distinguish—or indeed, even bother to mention—the paean to *stare decisis* coauthored by three Members of today's majority in *Planned Parenthood v. Casey*. There, when *stare decisis* meant preservation of judicially invented abortion rights, the widespread criticism of *Roe* was strong reason to *reaffirm* it. . . .

Today, however, the widespread opposition to *Bowers,* a decision resolving an issue as "intensely divisive" as the issue in *Roe,* is offered as a reason in favor of *overruling* it. Gone, too, is any "enquiry" (of the sort conducted in *Casey*) into whether the decision sought to be overruled has "proven 'unworkable.'"

Today's approach to *stare decisis* invites us to overrule an erroneously decided precedent (including an "intensely divisive" decision) if: (1) its foundations have been "eroded" by subsequent decisions, (2) it has been subject to "substantial and continuing" criticism, and (3) it has not induced "individual or societal reliance" that counsels against overturning. The problem is that *Roe* itself—which today's majority surely has no disposition to overrule—satisfies these conditions to at least the same degree as *Bowers*.

(1) . . . I do not quarrel with the Court's claim that *Romer v. Evans* "eroded" the "foundations" of *Bowers*' rational-basis holding. But *Roe* and *Casey* have been equally "eroded" by *Washington v. Glucksberg* (1997), which held that *only* fundamental rights which are "'deeply rooted in this Nation's history and tradition'" qualify for anything other than rational basis scrutiny under the doctrine of "substantive due process." *Roe* and *Casey,* of course, subjected the restriction of abortion to heightened scrutiny without even attempting to establish that the freedom to abort *was* rooted in this Nation's tradition.

(2) *Bowers,* the Court says, has been subject to "substantial and continuing [criticism], disapproving of its reasoning in all respects, not just as to its historical assumptions." Exactly what those nonhistorical criticisms

are, and whether the Court even agrees with them, are left unsaid, although the Court does cite two books. Of course, *Roe* too (and by extension *Casey*) had been (and still is) subject to unrelenting criticism, including criticism from the two commentators cited by the Court today.

(3) That leaves, to distinguish the rock-solid, unamendable disposition of *Roe* from the readily overrulable *Bowers,* only the third factor. "[T]here has been," the Court says, "no individual or societal reliance on *Bowers* of the sort that could counsel against overturning its holding. . . ." It seems to me that the "societal reliance" on the principles confirmed in *Bowers* and discarded today has been overwhelming. Countless judicial decisions and legislative enactments have relied on the ancient proposition that a governing majority's belief that certain sexual behavior is "immoral and unacceptable" constitutes a rational basis for regulation. We ourselves relied extensively on *Bowers* when we concluded, in **Barnes v. Glen Theatre, Inc.,** (1991), that Indiana's public indecency statute furthered "a substantial government interest in protecting order and morality." State laws against bigamy, same-sex marriage, adult incest, prostitution, masturbation, adultery, fornication, bestiality, and obscenity are likewise sustainable only in light of *Bowers'* validation of laws based on moral choices. Every single one of these laws is called into question by today's decision; the Court makes no effort to cabin the scope of its decision to exclude them from its holding. The impossibility of distinguishing homosexuality from other traditional "morals" offenses is precisely why *Bowers* rejected the rational-basis challenge. . . .

What a massive disruption of the current social order, therefore, the overruling of *Bowers* entails. Not so the overruling of *Roe,* which would simply have restored the regime that existed for centuries before 1973, in which the permissibility of and restrictions upon abortion were determined legislatively State-by-State. . . .

To tell the truth, it does not surprise me, and should surprise no one, that the Court has chosen today to revise the standards of *stare decisis* set forth in *Casey.* It has thereby exposed *Casey's* extraordinary deference to precedent for the result-oriented expedient that it is.

Having decided that it need not adhere to *stare decisis,* the Court still must establish that *Bowers* was wrongly decided and that the Texas statute, as applied to petitioners, is unconstitutional.

[The Texas law] undoubtedly imposes constraints on liberty. So do laws prohibiting prostitution, recreational

use of heroin, and, for that matter, working more than 60 hours per week in a bakery. But there is no right to "liberty" under the Due Process Clause, though today's opinion repeatedly makes that claim. The Fourteenth Amendment *expressly allows* States to deprive their citizens of "liberty," *so long as "due process of law" is provided.* . . .

Our opinions applying the doctrine known as "substantive due process" hold that the Due Process Clause prohibits States from infringing *fundamental* liberty interests, unless the infringement is narrowly tailored to serve a compelling state interest. We have held repeatedly, in cases the Court today does not overrule, that *only* fundamental rights qualify for this so-called "heightened scrutiny" protection—that is, rights which are "'deeply rooted in this Nation's history and tradition.'" All other liberty interests may be abridged or abrogated pursuant to a validly enacted state law if that law is rationally related to a legitimate state interest.

Bowers held, first, that criminal prohibitions of homosexual sodomy are not subject to heightened scrutiny because they do not implicate a "fundamental right" under the Due Process Clause. Noting that "[p]roscriptions against that conduct have ancient roots," that "[s]odomy was a criminal offense at common law and was forbidden by the laws of the original 13 States when they ratified the Bill of Rights," and that many States had retained their bans on sodomy, *Bowers* concluded that a right to engage in homosexual sodomy was not "'deeply rooted in this Nation's history and tradition.'"

The Court today does not overrule this holding. Not once does it describe homosexual sodomy as a "fundamental right" or a "fundamental liberty interest," nor does it subject the Texas statute to strict scrutiny. Instead, having failed to establish that the right to homosexual sodomy is "'deeply rooted in this Nation's history and tradition,'" the Court concludes that the application of Texas's statute to petitioners' conduct fails the rational-basis test, and overrules *Bowers'* holding to the contrary. "The Texas statute furthers no legitimate state interest which can justify its intrusion into the personal and private life of the individual." . . .

. . . This proposition is so out of accord with our jurisprudence—indeed, with the jurisprudence of *any* society we know—that it requires little discussion.

The Texas statute undeniably seeks to further the belief of its citizens that certain forms of sexual behavior are "immoral and unacceptable"—the same interest furthered by criminal laws against fornication, bigamy, adultery, adult incest, bestiality, and obscenity. . . .

Today's opinion is the product of a Court, which is the product of a law-profession culture, that has largely signed on to the so-called homosexual agenda, by which I mean the agenda promoted by some homosexual activists directed at eliminating the moral opprobrium that has traditionally attached to homosexual conduct. I noted in an earlier opinion the fact that the American Association of Law Schools (to which any reputable law school *must* seek to belong) excludes from membership any school that refuses to ban from its job-interview facilities a law firm (no matter how small) that does not wish to hire as a prospective partner a person who openly engages in homosexual conduct. . . .

Let me be clear that I have nothing against homosexuals, or any other group, promoting their agenda through normal democratic means. Social perceptions of sexual and other morality change over time, and every group has the right to persuade its fellow citizens that its view of such matters is the best. That homosexuals have achieved some success in that enterprise is attested to by the fact that Texas is one of the few remaining States that criminalize private, consensual homosexual acts. But persuading one's fellow citizens is one thing, and imposing one's views in absence of democratic majority will is something else. I would no more *require* a State to criminalize homosexual acts—or, for that matter, display *any* moral disapprobation of them— than I would *forbid* it to do so. What Texas has chosen to do is well within the range of traditional democratic action, and its hand should not be stayed through the invention of a brand-new "constitutional right" by a Court that is impatient of democratic change. It is indeed true that "later generations can see that laws once thought necessary and proper in fact serve only to oppress"; and when that happens, later generations can repeal those laws. But it is the premise of our system that those judgments are to be made by the people, and not imposed by a governing caste that knows best.

One of the benefits of leaving regulation of this matter to the people rather than to the courts is that the people, unlike judges, need not carry things to their logical conclusion. The people may feel that their disapprobation of homosexual conduct is strong enough to disallow homosexual marriage, but not strong enough to criminalize private homosexual acts—and may legislate accordingly. The Court today pretends that it possesses a similar freedom of action, so that we need not fear judicial imposition of homosexual marriage, as has recently occurred in Canada (in a decision that the Canadian Government has chosen not to appeal). At the end of its opinion—after having laid waste the foundations of our rational-basis jurisprudence—the Court says that the present case "does not involve whether the government must give formal recognition to any relationship that homosexual persons seek to enter." Do not believe it. More illuminating than this bald, unreasoned disclaimer is the progression of thought displayed by an earlier passage in the Court's opinion, which notes the constitutional protections afforded to "personal decisions relating to *marriage,* procreation, contraception, family relationships, child rearing, and education," and then declares that "[p]ersons in a homosexual relationship may seek autonomy for these purposes, just as heterosexual persons do." Today's opinion dismantles the structure of constitutional law that has permitted a distinction to be made between heterosexual and homosexual unions, insofar as formal recognition in marriage is concerned. If moral disapprobation of homosexual conduct is "no legitimate state interest" for purposes of proscribing that conduct; and if, as the Court coos (casting aside all pretense of neutrality), "[w]hen sexuality finds overt expression in intimate conduct with another person, the conduct can be but one element in a personal bond that is more enduring," what justification could there possibly be for denying the benefits of marriage to homosexual couples exercising "[t]he liberty protected by the Constitution." Surely not the encouragement of procreation, since the sterile and the elderly are allowed to marry. This case "does not involve" the issue of homosexual marriage only if one entertains the belief that principle and logic have nothing to do with the decisions of this Court. Many will hope that, as the Court comfortingly assures us, this is so.

The matters appropriate for this Court's resolution are only three: Texas's prohibition of sodomy neither infringes a "fundamental right" (which the Court does not dispute), nor is unsupported by a rational relation to what the Constitution considers a legitimate state interest, nor denies the equal protection of the laws. I dissent.

JUSTICE THOMAS, dissenting.

I join JUSTICE SCALIA'S dissenting opinion. I write separately to note that the law before the Court today "is . . . uncommonly silly." *Griswold v. Connecticut* (1965) (Stewart, J., dissenting). If I were a member of the Texas Legislature, I would vote to repeal it. Punishing someone for expressing his sexual preference through noncommercial consensual conduct with another adult does not appear to be a worthy way to expend valuable law enforcement resources.

Notwithstanding this, I recognize that as a member of this Court I am not empowered to help petitioners and others similarly situated. My duty, rather, is to "decide cases 'agreeably to the Constitution and laws of the United States.'" And, just like Justice Stewart, I "can find [neither in the Bill of Rights nor any other part of the Constitution a] general right of privacy," or as the Court terms it today, the "liberty of the person both in its spatial and more transcendent dimensions."

As one astute observer put it, "While the political, social, and legal ramifications may take years to play out, there is no doubt that *Lawrence v. Texas* is a constitutional watershed."[24] The case is a constitutional watershed not only because of the majority's sympathetic treatment of gays and lesbians, a subject to which we return in Chapter 13, but also because it is rare for the Court to reverse itself. Moreover, it is perhaps even rarer for the justices to admit that the Court made a mistake, but here it did just that. Kennedy claimed that in *Bowers* the justices "overstated" the historical premises on which their analyses relied, that they failed "to appreciate the extent of the liberty interest at stake," and that they did not take into account contemporaneous developments regarding the liberty of adults to decide how to conduct their private lives.

Justice Scalia's dissent takes issue with many of the majority's claims: he even accuses the justices of bending to the whims of a "law-profession culture that has largely signed on to the so-called homosexual agenda." But Scalia's views did not carry the day; they attracted support from only two other justices. Finally, note the majority's continuing commitment to a right to privacy flowing from the Fourteenth Amendment's due process clause—and its reach to "personal decisions relating to marriage, procreation, contraception, family relationships, child rearing, and education." To be sure, it did not rely on *Stanley v. Georgia,* but it did make much use both of foundational cases in this area, such as *Griswold v. Connecticut,* and more contemporary cases, such as *Planned Parenthood v. Casey.*

Seen in this way *Lawrence* may be a watershed, but it is not the only one that recent Court decisions

24. Linda Greenhouse, "In Momentous Term, Supreme Court Justices Remake Both Law and Themselves," *New York Times,* July 1, 2003, A18.

Nancy Cruzan fell into a persistent vegetative state following a 1983 automobile accident. She was the central figure in the Supreme Court's 1990 right-to-die ruling. Adding to the family tragedy, Cruzan's father, Lester, was unable to cope with depression following his daughter's accident and took his own life in 1996.

touching on the right to privacy have established. During the Rehnquist Court years, the justices rendered important rulings in two troublesome privacy issues: the right to die and drug testing. And others are now reaching the Court's doorstep—namely, issues associated with the "information age," including terrorism. In what follows, we consider all three.

The Right to Die

Right-to-die cases present many different kinds of questions. The Court first examined whether and under what circumstances the family or guardian of an incapacitated individual can make the decision to end life. In the 1970s and 1980s, most state courts allowed various forms of what are called "substituted judgments"; that is, they permitted relatives or guardians to "surmise" what the patient would have wanted or to act in the "best interest" of the patient. A frequently cited example of the use of substituted judgment is the New Jersey Supreme Court's ruling in *In re Quinlan* (1976). As twenty-two-year-old

Karen Ann Quinlan lay in a coma, her parents sought to have the respirator that was sustaining her life removed. When Karen's doctors refused, the Quinlans went to court. The state supreme court decided that the right to privacy is broad enough to allow a patient to decline medical treatment under certain circumstances. Because Karen could not make that decision for herself, the "only practical way to prevent the destruction of the right [to privacy] is to permit the guardian and family of Karen to render their best judgment as to whether she would exercise it in these circumstances."

Under this decision, the Quinlans could (and did) have Karen's respirator removed without intervention from the state and its courts. Although most state courts endorsed *Quinlan,* the Missouri Supreme Court took a different stance.[25] Viewing the state's interest in preserving life as controlling, it asserted that the family must provide "clear and convincing" evidence that the patient would have wanted medical care terminated. This kind of standard is often difficult for families to meet because they must provide direct evidence about the patient's desires.

In any event, rules that permit patients and their families to end treatment have garnered public support. In the 1940s only about 37 percent of Americans agreed that doctors should be allowed to end a terminal patient's life if that patient or the family request it. More recent polls show that the number has grown to nearly 70 percent.

Would the Supreme Court agree with the public? Would it allow even competent patients to end their medical treatment? If so, would it also permit families to make these decisions? What kind of proof would it require? These were the questions the Court dealt with in its first right-to-die case.

Cruzan v. Director, Missouri Department of Health

497 U.S. 261 (1990)
http://laws.findlaw.com/US/497/261.html
Oral arguments are available at http://www.oyez.org.
Vote: 5 (Kennedy, O'Connor, Rehnquist, Scalia, White)
  4 (Blackmun, Brennan, Marshall, Stevens)

OPINION OF THE COURT: *Rehnquist*
CONCURRING OPINIONS: *O'Connor, Scalia*
DISSENTING OPINIONS: *Brennan, Stevens*

---

25. For a list of state right-to-die cases that predate *Cruzan,* see Henry R. Glick, "Policy Making and State Supreme Courts," in *The American Courts: A Critical Assessment,* ed. John B. Gates and Charles A. Johnson (Washington, DC: CQ Press, 1990), 108–110.

FACTS:

In January 1983, Nancy Beth Cruzan was in a serious car accident. When paramedics found her, she was "lying face down in a ditch without detectable respiratory or cardiac function." Although they were able to restore her breathing and heartbeat, Cruzan remained unconscious and was taken to a hospital. Both short- and long-term medical efforts failed, and, as a result, Cruzan degenerated to a persistent vegetative state, "a condition in which a person exhibits motor reflexes but evinces no indications of significant cognitive function." She required feeding and hydration tubes to stay alive. When Cruzan's case was presented before the Court, some experts suggested that she might live another thirty years, but no one predicted any improvement in her condition.

Her parents, Lester and Joyce Cruzan, asked doctors to remove her feeding tubes, a step that would lead to Nancy's death. The hospital staff refused, and the Cruzans sought permission from a state court. They argued that "a person in Nancy's condition had a fundamental right to refuse or direct the withdrawal of 'death prolonging procedures.'" The Cruzans presented as evidence that when Nancy was twenty-five, she had told a friend that "she would not wish to continue her life unless she could live it at least halfway normally."

The trial court ruled in their favor, but the state supreme court reversed. It found no support in common law for a right to die, and it refused to apply privacy doctrines to the Cruzan situation. It also held that because the state had a strong interest in preserving life, the Cruzans would have to provide "clear and convincing evidence" that their daughter would have wanted her feeding tubes withdrawn.

ARGUMENTS:

For the petitioner, Nancy Cruzan, by her parents and co-guardians, Lester and Joyce Cruzan:
- The due process clause protects individuals against unwarranted bodily intrusions by the state, including unwanted medical treatment.
- Family decision making is deeply rooted in this country's history. If a person is unable to exercise the right to refuse medical care directly due to incompetence, a loving family is much better positioned than the state to express the patient's desire to continue life in a vegetative state or not.

- The exclusion of the family from the decision-making process and the high standard of proof endorsed by the Missouri court deny virtually all incompetent persons, as a class, the right to refuse unwanted medical treatment, without serving a legitimate state end.

For the respondent, Director of Missouri Department of Health:

- The right to refuse medical treatment is rooted in the common law, not in the Constitution, so the Court should decline to extend the due process clause to include a right to refuse medical treatment.
- The right to refuse medical treatment is not absolute and does not include a "right to die." In fact, there is a long-standing tradition of public policy against suicide.
- The state's strong interest in preserving the life of its citizens justifies the imposition of a judicial decision maker and a high standard of proof.

CHIEF JUSTICE REHNQUIST DELIVERED THE OPINION OF THE COURT.

We granted certiorari to consider the question of whether Cruzan has a right under the United States Constitution which would require the hospital to withdraw life-sustaining treatment from her under these circumstances. . . .

The Fourteenth Amendment provides that no state shall "deprive any person of life, liberty, or property, without due process of law." The principle that a competent person has a constitutionally protected liberty interest in refusing unwanted medical treatment may be inferred from our prior decisions. . . .

But determining that a person has a "liberty interest" under the Due Process Clause does not end the inquiry; "whether respondent's constitutional rights have been violated must be determined by balancing his liberty interests against the relevant state interests."

Petitioners insist that under the general holdings of our cases, the forced administration of life-sustaining medical treatment, and even of artificially-delivered food and water essential to life, would implicate a competent person's liberty interest. Although we think the logic of the cases . . . would embrace such a liberty interest, the dramatic consequences involved in refusal of such treatment would inform the inquiry as to whether the deprivation of that interest is constitutionally permissible. But for purposes of this case, we assume that the United States Constitution would grant a competent person a constitutionally protected right to refuse lifesaving hydration and nutrition.

Petitioners go on to assert that an incompetent person should possess the same right in this respect as is possessed by a competent person. . . .

The difficulty with petitioners' claim is that in a sense it begs the question: an incompetent person is not able to make an informed and voluntary choice to exercise a hypothetical right to refuse treatment or any other right. Such a "right" must be exercised for her, if at all, by some sort of surrogate. Here, Missouri has in effect recognized that under certain circumstances a surrogate may act for the patient in electing to have hydration and nutrition withdrawn in such a way as to cause death, but it has established a procedural safeguard to assure that the action of the surrogate conforms as best it may to the wishes expressed by the patient while competent. Missouri requires that evidence of the incompetent's wishes as to the withdrawal of treatment be proved by clear and convincing evidence. The question, then, is whether the United States Constitution forbids the establishment of this procedural requirement by the State. We hold that it does not.

Whether or not Missouri's clear and convincing evidence requirement comports with the United States Constitution depends in part on what interests the State may properly seek to protect in this situation. Missouri relies on its interest in the protection and preservation of human life, and there can be no gainsaying this interest. As a general matter, the States—indeed, all civilized nations—demonstrate their commitment to life by treating homicide as a serious crime. Moreover, the majority of States in this country have laws imposing criminal penalties on one who assists another to commit suicide. We do not think a State is required to remain neutral in the face of an informed and voluntary decision by a physically-able adult to starve to death.

But in the context presented here, a State has more particular interests at stake. The choice between life and death is a deeply personal decision of obvious and overwhelming finality. We believe Missouri may legitimately seek to safeguard the personal element of this choice through the imposition of heightened evidentiary requirements. It cannot be disputed that the Due Process Clause protects an interest in life as well as an interest in refusing life-sustaining medical treatment. Not all incompetent patients will have loved ones available to serve as surrogate decision-makers. And even where family members are present, "there will, of course, be some unfortunate situations in which family members will not act to protect a patient." A State is entitled to guard against potential abuses in such situations. Similarly, a State is entitled to consider that a judicial proceeding to make a determination regarding an incompetent's wishes may very well not be an adversarial one, with the added guarantee of accurate factfinding that the adversary process brings with it. Finally, we think a State may properly decline to make judgments about the "quality" of life that a particular individual may enjoy, and simply assert an unqualified interest in the preservation of human life to be weighed against the constitutionally protected interests of the individual.

In our view, Missouri has permissibly sought to advance these interests through the adoption of . . . "an intermediate standard of proof—'clear and convincing evidence'—when the individual interests at stake in a state proceeding are both 'particularly important' and 'more substantial than mere loss of money.'"

We think it self-evident that the interests at stake in the instant proceedings are more substantial, both on an individual and societal level, than those involved in a run-of-the-mine civil dispute. But not only does the standard of proof reflect the importance of a particular adjudication, it also serves as "a societal judgment about how the risk of error should be distributed between the litigants." The more stringent the burden of proof a party must bear, the more that party bears the risk of an erroneous decision. We believe that Missouri may permissibly place an increased risk of an erroneous decision on those seeking to terminate an incompetent individual's life-sustaining treatment. An erroneous decision not to terminate results in a maintenance of the status quo; the possibility of subsequent developments such as advancements in medical science, the discovery of new evidence regarding the patient's intent, changes in the law, or simply the unexpected death of the patient despite the administration of life-sustaining treatment, at least create the potential that a wrong decision will eventually be corrected or its impact mitigated. An erroneous decision to withdraw life-sustaining treatment, however, is not susceptible of correction. . . .

It is also worth noting that most, if not all, States simply forbid oral testimony entirely in determining the wishes of parties in transactions which, while important, simply do not have the consequences that a decision to terminate a person's life does. At common law and by statute in most States, the parole evidence rule prevents the variations of the terms of a written contract by oral testimony. The statute of frauds makes unenforceable oral contracts to leave property by will, and statutes regulating the making of wills universally require that those instruments be in writing. There is no doubt that statutes requiring wills to be in writing, and statutes of frauds which require that a contract to make a will be in writing, on occasion frustrate the effectuation of the intent of a particular decedent, just as Missouri's requirement of proof in this case may have frustrated the effectuation of the not-fully-expressed desires of Nancy Cruzan. But the Constitution does not require general rules to work faultlessly; no general rule can.

In sum, we conclude that a State may apply a clear and convincing evidence standard in proceedings where a guardian seeks to discontinue nutrition and hydration of a person diagnosed to be in a persistent vegetative state. . . .

The Supreme Court of Missouri held that in this case the testimony adduced at trial did not amount to clear and convincing proof of the patient's desire to have hydration and nutrition withdrawn. In so doing, it reversed a decision of the Missouri trial court which had found that the evidence "suggest[ed]" Nancy Cruzan would not have desired to continue such measures, but which had not adopted the standard of "clear and convincing evidence" enunciated by the Supreme Court. The testimony adduced at trial consisted primarily of Nancy Cruzan's statements made to a housemate about a year before her accident that she would not want to live should she face life as a "vegetable," and other observations to the same effect. The observations did not deal in terms with withdrawal of medical treatment or of hydration and nutrition. We cannot say that the Supreme Court of Missouri committed constitutional error in reaching the conclusion that it did.

Petitioners alternatively contend that Missouri must accept the "substituted judgment" of close family members even in the absence of substantial proof that their views reflect the views of the patient. . . . Here again petitioners would seek to turn a decision which allowed a State to rely on family decisionmaking into a constitutional requirement that the State recognize such decisionmaking. But constitutional law does not work that way.

No doubt is engendered by anything in this record but that Nancy Cruzan's mother and father are loving and caring parents. If the State were required by the United States Constitution to repose a right of "substituted judgment" with anyone, the Cruzans would surely qualify. But we do not think the Due Process Clause requires the State to repose judgment on these matters with anyone but the patient herself. Close family members may have a strong feeling—a feeling not at all ignoble or unworthy, but not entirely disinterested, either—that they do not wish to witness the continuation of the life of a loved one which they regard as hopeless, meaningless, and even degrading. But there is no automatic assurance that the view of close family members will necessarily be the same as the patient's would have been had she been confronted with the prospect of her situation while competent. All of the reasons previously discussed for allowing Missouri to require clear and convincing evidence of the patient's wishes lead us to conclude that the State may choose to defer only to those wishes, rather than confide the decision to close family members.

The judgment of the Supreme Court of Missouri is

Affirmed.

JUSTICE O'CONNOR, concurring.

I agree that a protected liberty interest in refusing unwanted medical treatment may be inferred from our prior decisions . . . and that the refusal of artificially delivered food and water is encompassed within that liberty interest. . . .

I . . . write separately to emphasize that the Court does not today decide the issue whether a State must also give effect to the decisions of a surrogate decision-maker. In my view, such a duty may well be constitutionally required to protect the patient's liberty interest in refusing medical treatment. Few individuals provide explicit oral or written instructions regarding their intent to refuse medical treatment should they become incompetent. States which decline to consider any evidence other than such instructions may frequently fail to honor a patient's intent. Such failures might be avoided if the State considered an equally probative source of evidence: the patient's appointment of a proxy to make health care decisions on her behalf. Delegating the authority to make medical decisions to a family member or friend is becoming a common method of planning for the future. Several States have recognized the practical wisdom of such a procedure by enacting durable power of attorney statutes that specifically authorize an individual to appoint a surrogate to make medical treatment decisions. . . .

Today's decision, holding only that the Constitution permits a State to require clear and convincing evidence of Nancy Cruzan's desire to have artificial hydration and nutrition withdrawn, does not preclude a future determination that the Constitution requires the States to implement the decisions of a patient's duly appointed surrogate. Nor does it prevent States from developing other approaches for protecting an incompetent individual's liberty interest in refusing medical treatment. . . . [N]o national consensus has yet emerged on the best solution for this difficult and sensitive problem. Today we decide only that one State's practice does not violate the Constitution; the more challenging task of crafting appropriate procedures for safeguarding incompetents' liberty interests is entrusted to the "laboratory" of the States.

JUSTICE SCALIA, concurring.

The various opinions in this case portray quite clearly the difficult, indeed agonizing, questions that are presented by the constantly increasing power of science to keep the human body alive for longer than any reasonable person would want to inhabit it. The States have begun to grapple with these problems through legislation. I am concerned, from the tenor of today's opinions, that we are poised to confuse that enterprise as successfully as we have confused the enterprise of legislating concerning abortion—requiring it to be conducted against a background of federal constitutional imperatives that are unknown because they are being newly crafted from Term to Term. That would be a great misfortune.

While I agree with the Court's analysis today, and therefore join in its opinion, I would have preferred that we announce, clearly and promptly, that the federal courts have no business in this field; that American law has always accorded the State the power to prevent, by force if necessary, suicide—including suicide by refusing to take appropriate measures necessary to preserve one's life; that the point at which life becomes "worthless," and the point at which the means necessary to preserve it become "extraordinary" or "inappropriate," are neither set forth in the Constitution nor known to the nine Justices of this Court any better than they are known to nine people picked at random from the Kansas City telephone directory; and hence, that even when it is demonstrated by clear and convincing evidence that a patient no longer wishes certain measures to be taken to preserve her life, it is up to the citizens of Missouri to decide, through their elected representatives, whether that wish will be honored. . . .

. . . This Court need not, and has no authority to, inject itself into every field of human activity where irrationality and oppression may theoretically occur, and if it tries to do so it will destroy itself.

JUSTICE BRENNAN, with whom JUSTICE MARSHALL and JUSTICE BLACKMUN join, dissenting.

Today the Court, while tentatively accepting that there is some degree of constitutionally protected liberty interest in avoiding unwanted medical treatment, including life-sustaining medical treatment such as artificial nutrition and hydration, affirms the decision of the Missouri Supreme Court. The majority opinion, as I read it, would affirm that decision on the ground that a State may require "clear and convincing" evidence of Nancy Cruzan's prior decision to forgo life- sustaining treatment under circumstances such as hers in order to ensure that her actual wishes are honored. Because I believe that Nancy Cruzan has a fundamental right to be free of unwanted artificial nutrition and hydration, which right is not outweighed by any interests of the State, and because I find that the improperly biased procedural obstacles imposed by the Missouri Supreme Court impermissibly burden that right, I respectfully dissent. Nancy Cruzan is entitled to choose to die with dignity. . . .

The question before this Court is a relatively narrow one: whether the Due Process Clause allows Missouri to require a now-incompetent patient in an irreversible persistent vegetative state to remain on life-support absent rigorously clear and convincing evidence that avoiding the treatment represents the patient's prior, express choice. . . .

A State's inability to discern an incompetent patient's choice still need not mean that a State is rendered powerless to protect that choice. But I would find that the Due Process Clause prohibits a State from doing more than that. A State may ensure that the person who makes the decision on the patient's behalf is the one whom the patient himself would have selected to make that choice for him. And a State may exclude from consideration anyone having improper motives. But a State generally must either repose the choice with the person whom the patient himself would most likely have chosen as proxy or leave the decision to the patient's family.

As many as 10,000 patients are being maintained in persistent vegetative states in the United States, and the number is expected to increase significantly in the near future. . . . The 80% of Americans who die in hospitals are "likely to meet their end . . . 'in a sedated or comatose state; betubed nasally, abdominally and intravenously;

and far more like manipulated objects than like moral subjects.'" A fifth of all adults surviving to age 80 will suffer a progressive dementing disorder prior to death.

. . . The new medical technology can reclaim those who would have been irretrievably lost a few decades ago and restore them to active lives. For Nancy Cruzan, it failed, and for others with wasting incurable disease it may be doomed to failure. In these unfortunate situations, the bodies and preferences and memories of the victims do not escheat to the State; nor does our Constitution permit the State or any other government to commandeer them. No singularity of feeling exists upon which such a government might confidently rely as *parens patriae*. . . . Missouri and this Court have displaced Nancy's own assessment of the processes associated with dying. They have discarded evidence of her will, ignored her values, and deprived her of the right to a decision as closely approximating her own choice as humanly possible. They have done so disingenuously in her name, and openly in Missouri's own. That Missouri and this Court may truly be motivated only by concern for incompetent patients makes no matter. . . .

I respectfully dissent.

In August 1990, two months after the Court's decision, the Cruzans petitioned a Missouri court for a new hearing. At the hearing, three of Nancy's former coworkers testified that she had said she would not want to live "like a vegetable." Despite protests from pro-life groups, a state court judge ruled December 14 that the Cruzans could have Nancy's feeding tube removed. The tube was removed, and Nancy died on December 26.

For the Cruzans the battle was over, but, as Justice Brennan pointed out in his dissent, there were approximately ten thousand "Nancy Cruzans" in the United States at that time, a figure that could increase exponentially as medical technology advances. Does the Court's opinion provide guidance for them and their families? Yes and no. On one hand, the Court clearly ruled that the Fourteenth Amendment's due process clause permits a competent individual to terminate medical treatment. As to incompetent patients, the majority of the justices suggested that states may fashion their own standards, including those that require "clear and convincing evidence" of the patient's interests. Living wills, as O'Connor's concurrence suggests, may be the best form of such evidence (*see Box 10-5*).

BOX 10-5   LIVING WILLS

In 1976 California became the first state to adopt living will legislation. Since then, almost all the other states have followed suit. A living will permits an individual various types of control over the use of heroic, life-sustaining measures in his or her medical treatment in the event of a terminal illness. The demand for living will laws has been a product of increased social concern about the ability and tendency of modern medicine to keep elderly, terminally ill, and permanently comatose patients alive beyond what would be likely in the natural course of aging or infirmity. Respirators, cardiac resuscitation, artificial feeding and hydration, drug treatment, and other procedures may prevent what might have been a natural and relatively easy death, often from pneumonia, known widely in the past as the "old man's friend." Living will laws—and the broader issue of the right to die—affect all age and social groups, although the growing elderly population is disproportionately affected.

NATURAL DEATH ACT DECLARATION ("LIVING WILL")

Virginia's Natural Death Act was enacted in 1983 to permit Virginians to record their wishes regarding extraordinary care in the event of terminal illness. The declaration below is the suggested form developed by the state legislators to implement the Act. Fill out this form and give it to your physician and any relatives and friends you would like to have a copy. You must sign in the presence of two witnesses, and both witnesses must sign in your presence. Blood relatives or spouse may not be witnesses.

DECLARATION

In accordance with the Virginia Natural Death Act, this Declaration was made on _____.

Month/Day/Year

I, _____, willfully and voluntarily make known my desire and do here-by declare:

Name of person making declaration

You must choose between the following two paragraphs. PARAGRAPH ONE designates a person to make a decision for you. In PARAGRAPH TWO, you make the decision. Cross through the paragraph you do NOT want.

PARAGRAPH ONE:

If at any time I should have a terminal condition and I am comatose, incompetent or otherwise mentally or physically incapable of communication, I designate _____ to make a decision on my behalf as to whether life-prolonging procedures shall be withheld or withdrawn. In the event that my designee decides that such procedures should be withheld or withdrawn, I wish to be permitted to die naturally with only the administration of medication or the performance of any medical procedure deemed necessary to provide me with comfort care or to alleviate pain. (OPTION: I specifically direct that the following procedures or treatments be provided to me:

OR

PARAGRAPH TWO:

If at any time I should have a terminal condition where the application of life-prolonging procedures would serve only to artificially prolong the dying process, I direct that such procedures be withheld or withdrawn, and that I be permitted to die naturally with only the administration of medication or the performance of any medical procedure deemed necessary to provide me with comfort care or to alleviate pain. (OPTION: I specifically direct that the following procedures or treatments be provided to me:

_____.

_____.

On the other hand, the case did not call for the Court to address another dimension of the right-to-die question—suicides or "assisted suicides" for the terminally ill. May a person take his or her own life or arrange an assisted suicide when suffering from an incurable illness? In the 1990s this question took on unusual importance as the media were full of accounts of people with progressively debilitating diseases seeking to end their lives and of the assisted suicides conducted by Dr. Jack Kevorkian and others. Some of the justices' opinions provided hints as to how they would rule on "mercy killings," assisted suicides, and so forth. In a 1996 speech, Justice Scalia did more than provide a hint: he asserted his belief that the Constitution plainly provides "no right to die."[26]

Seven years after *Cruzan* the Court had the opportunity to consider whether the right to privacy or "liberty interest" is broad enough to encompass assisted suicides. That opportunity came in two 1997 cases, **Washington v. Glucksberg** and **Vacco v. Quill**, both involving state laws making it a crime to assist another to commit suicide. By 9–0 votes, the justices rejected claims that such statutes violate the due process and equal protection clauses. In addition to identifying long-standing traditions against suicide, the Court found that the states had legitimate interests in preserving human life, protecting the integrity and ethics of the medical profession, safeguarding the vulnerable from coercion, and ensuring the value of life, even of those who are ready to die.

What should we learn from these decisions? On one hand, the justices made it crystal clear that states may maintain their existing bans on assisted suicides. On the other, they did not foreclose the possibility of future constitutional claims. In a concurring opinion, Justice O'Connor, for example, left open the possibility that the Court might respond positively to the question of "whether a mentally competent person who is experiencing great suffering has a constitutionally cognizable interest in controlling the circumstances of his or her imminent death."

O'Connor turned out to be prophetic. In **Gonzales v. Oregon** (2006) the Court took up Oregon's Death with Dignity Act, which permits state-licensed physicians to dispense or prescribe a lethal dose of drugs upon the request of a terminally ill patient. Although the law had been in effect since 1994 and had survived a ballot initiative designed to repeal it, in 2001 Attorney General John Ashcroft issued a rule asserting that the statute was unlawful. He claimed that the Controlled Substances Act (CSA) of 1970, enacted by Congress to regulate the legitimate and illegitimate trafficking of drugs, criminalizes the use of controlled substances to assist suicide. Physicians dispensing drugs for this purpose, he declared, were not engaging in the legitimate practice of medicine and could lose their privilege to write prescriptions.

The state, a physician, a pharmacist, and some terminally ill state residents challenged the rule. By the time the case reached the Supreme Court, Ashcroft was no longer attorney general, but his successor, Alberto Gonzales, stood by Ashcroft's interpretation of the CSA.

In a 6–3 decision, the Supreme Court expressed its firm disagreement with the Gonzales/Ashcroft rule. Writing for the majority, Justice Kennedy explained:

In deciding whether the CSA can be read as prohibiting physician-assisted suicide, we look to the statute's text and design. The statute and our case law amply support the conclusion that Congress regulates medical practice insofar as it bars doctors from using their prescription-writing powers as a means to engage in illicit drug dealing and trafficking as conventionally understood. Beyond this, however, the statute manifests no intent to regulate the practice of medicine generally. The silence is understandable given the structure and limitations of federalism, which allow the States "'great latitude under their police powers to legislate as to the protection of the lives, limbs, health, comfort, and quiet of all persons.'"

Chief Justice Roberts did not write an opinion, but he joined a dissent by Justice Scalia (as did Justice Thomas). Scalia wrote that it was "easy to sympathize" with the position he thought the majority opinion reflected—"a feeling that the subject of assisted suicide is none of the Federal Government's business." But, unlike the majority, he believed that "unless we were to repudiate a long and well-established principle of our jurisprudence," it was well within Congress's power to prevent assisted suicide.

To be sure, *Gonzales v. Oregon* will not be the last word on this subject. Indeed, Chief Justice Rehnquist's words in *Glucksberg* remain as true today as when he wrote them: "Throughout the Nation, Americans are

26. Antonin Scalia, "A Theory of Constitutional Interpretation," remarks at the Catholic University Law School, Washington, D.C., October 18, 1996.

engaged in an earnest and profound debate about the morality, legality, and practicality of physician-assisted suicide." He further noted that the Court's decision "permits this debate to continue, as it should in a democratic society." We might say the same about *Gonzales.*

Drug Testing

As the Court and the public continue to wrestle with the right to die, another privacy-related issue has moved to the forefront: drug testing. Many public and private employers have initiated drug-screening or -testing programs for job applicants or employees; some schools have started them for students. Under many of these programs, individuals must have their urine tested even if the examiner has no reason to suspect illegal drug use.

Those who support drug testing assert that the nation has legitimate concerns regarding drug abuse and the social problems that flow from illegal drug operations. Drug testing, they argue, is an effective method of identifying individuals who have consumed illegal substances. Finally, proponents suggest that a urinalysis is a minor intrusion into an individual's privacy rights and a minor incursion into the body.

Opponents respond that, under *Katz v. United States,* employers may be intruding into their employees' reasonable privacy expectations. They assert that employers order tests without reason to believe that a specific employee has committed a crime. In other words, opponents allege that drug-testing programs violate the right to privacy.

Beginning in 1989 the Court began to sort through these competing claims. Note that the Court upheld the programs at issue in the first three of its major rulings *(see Table 10-4).* In those cases, the justices took the position that government interests outweigh individuals' expectations of privacy. Two of the Court's last three rulings, however, favored individual interests. In **Chandler v. Miller** (1997), the Court held that a Georgia law requiring drug screening of all candidates for public office went too far, that it "diminishes personal privacy for a symbol's sake." And in **Ferguson v. City of Charleston** (2001) the Court struck down a state hospital's policy of conducting drug tests on obstetrical patients and turning the results, if positive, over to law enforcement agents. In *Board of Education of Pottawatomie County v. Earls* (2002), however, the Court held that a school policy requiring students

to consent to urinalysis testing for drugs in order to participate in any extracurricular activity was insufficiently intrusive to violate the students' expectation of privacy. Given the Court's decision in **Vernonia School Dist. 47J v. Acton** (1995), this was not an entirely unexpected decision.

Privacy in the Information Age

Drug-testing programs touch on privacy issues related to the body. If you are required to submit to a urinalysis at your workplace, your employer obtains information about your physical state. What about other information, such as the petitions you sign, the amount of money you owe in school loans, the Web sites you visit, and the content of your e-mail messages and cell phone conversations? Do you have the right to privacy over what others can find out about you?

Some of these matters are not especially tied to the rise in electronic communication. In **Doe v. Reed** (2010), for example, the Court considered a challenge to the public release of petitions (including the signers' names and addresses) supporting a ballot referendum that would have overturned a state law expanding the rights of same-sex domestic partners. The Court held (8–1) that the release of the petitions did not violate the First Amendment rights of the signers because the state has an important interest in preserving the integrity of the electoral process. But several justices, notably Thomas in dissent, raised questions about the privacy interests of the petition's signers.

As for the other questions—about the Web sites you visit and the content of your e-mails—in the not-so-distant past no one would have raised them because communication devices such as e-mail and Web sites did not exist. Moreover, even a case such as *Doe* would have had less (potential) impact because publicizing the names of those who sign petitions would have been more difficult and expensive without the Web. With the growth of computerized record keeping and the Internet, information of all types is now readily available—and information about you may be available to those with whom you may not want to share it. This was the case for Michael A. Smyth, who, in an e-mail to a coworker, allegedly called his employers "back-stabbing bastards." Smyth's bosses at the Pillsbury Company fired him for transmitting inappropriate comments. Smyth brought suit claiming that

TABLE 10-4   The Supreme Court and Drug-Testing Programs

CASE	PROGRAM	COURT'S HOLDING
Skinner v. Railway Labor Executives' Association (1989)	Requirement of the Federal Railroad Administration that employees take a breath or urine test if they were involved in a train accident or other serious incident.	The justices ruled, 7–2, that although "federal regulations requiring employees of private railroads to produce urine samples for chemical testing implicate the Fourth Amendment, as those tests invade reasonable expectations of privacy," the program at issue was not unreasonable. The Court said the government has a strong interest in preventing train accidents, some of which had been caused by employees using drugs and alcohol.
National Treasury Union v. Von Raab (1989)	Requirement of the U.S. Customs Bureau that all job applicants be screened for drugs, as well as those seeking promotions to positions that (1) involve direct drug "interdiction," (2) require employees to carry weapons, and (3) require employees to handle classified material.	The justices upheld the program, 5–4, even though it was a suspicionless program that authorized drug testing without any evidence that a crime had been committed. The majority found the program reasonable because "[t]he Government's compelling interests in preventing the promotion of drug users to positions where they might endanger the integrity of our Nation's borders or the life of the citizenry outweigh the privacy interests of those who seek promotion to these positions, who enjoy a diminished expectation of privacy by virtue of the special, and obvious, physical and ethical demands of those positions."
Vernonia School District 47J v. Acton (1995)	School system requirement that students wishing to play sports sign a form giving consent to drug testing. The school tests all athletes at the beginning of each season of their sport and randomly thereafter.	The Court held, 6–3, that random, suspicionless drug testing of students by public school officials does not violate the Constitution. The Court said that students have reduced privacy expectations, and that "[l]egitimate privacy expectations are even less with regard to student athletes. School sports are not for the bashful. They require 'suiting up' before each practice or event, and showering and changing afterwards. . . ." Moreover, "[b]y choosing to 'go out for the team,' they voluntarily subject themselves to a degree of regulation even higher than that imposed on students generally."
Chandler v. Miller (1997)	Law passed by Georgia requiring all candidates for public office to take a urine test as a condition for appearing on the ballot.	The justices held, 8–1, that the law violated the Constitution. For the majority, Ginsburg noted that the Court had upheld drug-testing programs for which the government presented some "special need," such as the protection of public safety. Here, Georgia was seeking to protect its "image," which is insufficient to justify the law. "However well-meant, the candidate drug test Georgia has devised diminishes personal privacy for a symbol's sake. The Fourth Amendment shields society against that state action."
Ferguson v. City of Charleston (2001)	State hospital policy of conducting drug tests on obstetrical patients and turning the results (if positive) over to law enforcement agents.	The justices held, 6–3, that the policy violated the Constitution. According to the majority, "respondents argue in essence that their ultimate purpose—namely, protecting the health of both mother and child—is a beneficent one. In Chandler, however, we did not simply accept the State's invocation of a 'special need.' Instead, we carried out a 'close review' of the scheme at issue before concluding that the need in question was not 'special,' as that term has been defined in our cases. In this case, a review of the . . . policy plainly reveals that the purpose actually served by the [hospital] searches 'is ultimately indistinguishable from the general interest in crime control.'"
Board of Education of Pottawatomie County v. Earls (2002)	School district policy requiring all middle and high school students to consent to urinalysis testing for drugs in order to participate in any extracurricular activity.	The Court found, 5–4, that the school policy was a reasonable means of furthering the school's important interest in preventing and deterring drug use among its students, and that the invasion of the students' privacy was not significant.

his termination violated his right to privacy under state common law, but a district court dismissed his suit. The only U.S. Supreme Court case to take on this issue to date also went against the employee. In ***City of Ontario, California v. Quon*** (2010), the Court considered whether the city had infringed on police officers' privacy rights under the Fourth Amendment when it checked the text messages on their pagers. In a 9–0 ruling, it held that the search of public employees' pagers was reasonable, but it was quick to deem its decision "narrow," explicitly stating that a "broad holding concerning employees' privacy expectations vis-à-vis employer-provided technological equipment might have implications for future cases that cannot be predicted."

Not only individuals but also society as a whole may bear high costs for the ability to gather data quickly, as an experiment conducted by a Los Angeles television reporter vividly shows. Using the name of convicted child killer Richard Allen Davis, the reporter contacted one of the country's largest compilers of consumer data. For $277, the company sent her a list of more than five thousand children's names, ages, addresses, and phone numbers.[27]

The larger problem is that the law has fallen behind technology. To date, Congress has passed only a few laws to limit the dissemination of information.[28] In fact, these days the federal government and state legislatures all seem to be heading in the opposite direction. Every state now has on its books a "Megan's law," named for a child murdered by a convicted sex offender. Such laws typically require individuals convicted of sexual abuse to register with law enforcement authorities after they are released from jail or prison and authorize public disclosure of information about them. Quite often that information is posted on the Internet and may include the offenders' photographs and current addresses. Moreover, following the events of September 11, 2001, Congress passed the USA Patriot Act, which, among other provisions, augments the government's ability to conduct surveillance of electronic communications.

That legislative activity has been observed on some dimensions of privacy and inactivity on others may well reflect fundamental disagreements over possible remedies and even their desirability. On one hand, we as a society do not want the names and addresses of five thousand children to fall into the hands of a convicted killer, nor do we want those who pose serious threats to the security of the nation to go undetected. On the other hand, many individuals enjoy their unfettered freedom to use the Internet, e-mail, and so forth, and view government attempts at regulation of such communications with great skepticism.

The public is closely divided over these issues. For example, only about 50 percent of Americans say they would approve of the government examining their electronic communications as part of its war against terrorism, and 45 percent claim they would disapprove. These same matters may also divide the Supreme Court. Although it has yet to jump into this particular fray, it has upheld Megan's laws *(see Chapter 12)*.

Though *Quon* may provide some hints, it remains to be seen on which side of this debate the justices will fall. There is little doubt, however, that these and other issues relating to privacy in our age of information will eventually make their way up to the Court; some already have, as our discussion of *Ashcroft v. Free Speech Coalition* in Chapter 8 illustrates. Those rulings have tended to hinge on First Amendment concerns rather than on privacy, but it seems clear that cases centering on privacy and the Internet will follow and become a major part of the Court's docket.

ANNOTATED READINGS

On the foundations of the right to privacy and ensuing debates, see Thomas I. Emerson, "Nine Justices in Search of a Doctrine," *Michigan Law Review* 64 (1965): 219–234; James E. Fleming, *Securing Constitutional Democracy: The Case for Autonomy* (Chicago: University of Chicago Press, 2006); John W. Johnson, *Griswold v. Connecticut: Birth Control and the Constitutional Right of Privacy* (Lawrence: University Press of Kansas, 2005); Daniel J. Solove, *Understanding Privacy* (Cambridge, MA: Harvard University Press, 2008); Philippa Strum,

---

27. Children are not the only people at risk. Undoubtedly, if you have applied for a credit card, subscribed to a magazine, or made a purchase online, your name appears on some marketer's list, and that list is available to virtually anyone for a price.

28. The Video Protection Act of 1988, for example, makes it illegal to release information about the videos a person rents or buys. Congress passed this law in response to concerns that arose when the press published the titles of videos Robert Bork had rented while his 1987 nomination to the Supreme Court was pending in the Senate.

Privacy: The Debate in the United States since 1945 (Fort Worth, TX: Harcourt Brace College, 1998).

Roe v. Wade, abortion, and reproductive freedom have generated no shortage of volumes. See, for example, Judith A. Baer, *Historical and Multicultural Encyclopedia of Women's Reproductive Rights in the United States* (Westport, CT: Greenwood Press, 2001); Susan R. Burgess, *Contest for Constitutional Authority: The Abortion and War Powers Debate* (Lawrence: University Press of Kansas, 1992); John Hart Ely, "The Wages of Crying Wolf: A Comment on *Roe v. Wade*," *Yale Law Journal* 82 (1973): 920–949; Lee Epstein and Joseph F. Kobylka, *The Supreme Court and Legal Change: Abortion and the Death Penalty* (Chapel Hill: University of North Carolina Press, 1992); David. J. Garrow, *Liberty and Sexuality: The Right to Privacy and the Making of* Roe v. Wade (Berkeley: University of California Press, 1998); Mark A. Graber, *Rethinking Abortion: Equal Choice, the Constitution, and Reproductive Politics* (Princeton, NJ: Princeton University Press, 1996); Linda Greenhouse and Reva Siegel, *Before* Roe v. Wade: *Voices That Shaped the Abortion Debate before the Supreme Court Ruling* (New York: Kaplan, 2010); N. E. H. Hull and Peter Charles Hoffer, Roe v. Wade: *The Abortion Rights Controversy in American History* (Lawrence: University Press of Kansas, 2010); Eileen L. McDonagh, *Breaking the Abortion Deadlock* (New York: Oxford University Press, 1996); Richard L. Pacelle Jr., *Between Law and Politics: The Solicitor General and the Structuring of Race, Gender, and Reproductive Rights Litigation* (College Station: Texas A&M University Press, 2003); Leslie J. Reagan, *When Abortion Was a Crime: Women, Medicine, and Law in the United States, 1867–1973* (Berkeley: University of California Press, 1997); Laurence H. Tribe, *Abortion: The Clash of Absolutes* (New York: W. W. Norton, 1990); Barbara M. Yarnold, *Abortion Politics in the Federal Courts: Right versus Right* (Westport, CT: Praeger, 1995).

For studies centering on private sexual activities, see William N. Eskridge Jr., *Dishonorable Passions: Sodomy Laws in America, 1861–2003* (New York:

Viking, 2008); William N. Eskridge Jr., *Gaylaw: Challenging the Apartheid of the Closet* (Cambridge, MA: Harvard University Press, 1999); David A. J. Richards, *The Case for Gay Rights: From* Bowers *to* Lawrence *and Beyond* (Lawrence: University Press of Kansas, 2009). For more studies of gay rights, see Chapter 13.

On the issues related to the right to die, see Susan M. Behuniak and Arthur G. Svenson, *Physician-Assisted Suicide: The Anatomy of a Constitutional Law Issue* (Lanham, MD: Rowman & Littlefield, 2003); Elizabeth Price Foley, *The Law of Life and Death* (Cambridge, MA: Harvard University Press, 2011); Elizabeth Atwood Gailey, *Write to Death: News Framing of the Right-to-Die Conflict from Quinlan's Coma to Kevorkian's Conviction* (Westport, CT: Praeger, 2003); Henry R. Glick, *The Right to Die: Policy Innovation and Its Consequences* (New York: Columbia University Press, 1992); Jennifer M. Scherer and Rita J. Simon, *Euthanasia and the Right to Die: A Comparative View* (Lanham, MD: Rowman & Littlefield, 1999); Melvin I. Urofsky, *Lethal Judgments: Assisted Suicide and American Law* (Lawrence: University Press of Kansas, 2000); Raymond Whiting, *A Natural Right to Die: Twenty-three Centuries of Debate* (Westport, CT: Greenwood Press, 2002); Marjorie B. Zucker, *The Right to Die Debate: A Documentary History* (Westport, CT: Greenwood Press, 1999).

On drug testing, see John Gilliom, *Surveillance, Privacy, and the Law: Employee Drug Testing and the Politics of Social Control* (Ann Arbor: University of Michigan Press, 1994).

For discussion of the rights to privacy and the rise of electronic communication, see Colin J. Bennett and Rebecca Grant, eds., *Visions of Privacy: Policy Choices for the Digital Age* (Toronto: University of Toronto Press, 1999); Saul Levmore and Martha C. Nussbaum, eds., *The Offensive Internet: Speech, Privacy, and Reputation* (Cambridge, MA: Harvard University Press, 2011); Jon L. Mills, *Privacy: The Lost Right* (New York: Oxford University Press, 2008); Daniel J. Solove, *The Future of Reputation: Gossip, Rumor, and Privacy on the Internet* (New Haven, CT: Yale University Press, 2008).

The Rights of the Criminally Accused

PART III

The Criminal Justice System and Constitutional Rights

11. INVESTIGATIONS AND EVIDENCE

12. ATTORNEYS, TRIALS, AND PUNISHMENTS

The Criminal Justice System and Constitutional Rights

W E AMERICANS REGARD the Bill of Rights as an enumeration of our most cherished freedoms. The right to speak freely and to worship (or not) without undue interference from government are the guarantees to which politicians and citizens refer most often when they describe the unique character of the United States. We may need to be reminded, therefore, that four of the first eight amendments guarantee rights for the *criminally accused*. The framers of the Constitution placed great emphasis on criminal rights because they had grown to despise the abusive practices of British criminal procedure. They believed that agents of government should not enter private homes or search personal property without proper justification and that the accused should not be tried without the benefit of public scrutiny.

Consequently, the Fourth Amendment protects us from unreasonable searches and prescribes the procedures by which law enforcement officials can obtain search warrants. The Fifth Amendment prohibits self-incrimination and double jeopardy and provides for grand juries and due process of law. The Sixth Amendment governs trial proceedings. It calls for speedy and public jury trials during which defendants can call witnesses and face their accusers. It also provides for the assistance of counsel. The Eighth Amendment prohibits excessive bail and monetary fines and any punishments that are cruel and unusual.

The framers insisted on constitutional guarantees that would protect the guilty as well as the innocent against the potentially abusive prosecutorial powers of the government.

Just because these rights are not the first that come to mind when we think about the Bill of Rights does not mean that they are any less important or less relevant to society. At least once during your life, you are likely to participate in the criminal justice system. You may be the victim of a crime. You may serve as a juror in a criminal trial or become involved as a witness. You may even be accused of a crime. As citizens, we should understand the rights accorded us and the procedures that invoke such guarantees.

The two chapters that follow explore the constitutional rights of the criminally accused and the Supreme Court's interpretation of them. To appreciate their importance, however, we first take a brief look at the stages of the criminal justice process. Following that discussion, we describe trends in Supreme Court decision making in this area.

OVERVIEW OF THE CRIMINAL JUSTICE SYSTEM

Figure III-1 provides a general overview of the criminal justice system and the constitutional rights

FIGURE III-1   The American Criminal Justice System

STAGE	GOVERNING AMENDMENT[a]
Reported or suspected crime ↓	
Investigation by law enforcement officials ↓	Fourth Amendment search and seizure rights
	Fifth Amendment self-incrimination clause
Arrest ↓	Sixth Amendment right to counsel clause
Booking ↓	
Decision to prosecute ↓	
Pretrial hearings (initial appearance, bail hearing, preliminary hearing, arraignment) ↓	Fifth Amendment grand jury clause
	Sixth Amendment notification clause
	Eighth Amendment bail clause
Trial ↓	Fifth Amendment self-incrimination clause
	Sixth Amendment speedy and public trial, jury, confrontation, and compulsory process clauses
Sentencing ↓	Eighth Amendment cruel and unusual punishment clause
	Eighth Amendment excessive fines clause
Appeals, postconviction stages	Fifth Amendment double jeopardy clause

a. The right to due process of law is in effect throughout the process.

effective at each stage. Two points should be kept in mind. First, because the states have a degree of latitude in developing their criminal justice systems, these procedures vary from jurisdiction to jurisdiction. Second, less than 10 percent of all criminal cases actually proceed through every stage of the system. At some point during the process, most criminal defendants plead guilty, thereby waiving their right to a jury trial, and proceed directly to sentencing. Most of these guilty pleas are the result of plea-bargaining arrangements in which the accused agrees to admit guilt in exchange for reduced charges or a lenient sentence.

This qualification noted, the criminal process begins with the response of law enforcement officials to a suspected violation of a state or federal law. Many scholars and lawyers consider this part of the process to be of the utmost importance. The way police conduct their investigation and gather evidence affects all subsequent decisions made by lawyers, judges, and juries. The police are also significant actors because of the conflicting roles society asks them to play. We expect police officers to act lawfully, within the confines of the Constitution. We do not want them to break down our doors and search our houses without proper cause. But society also expects effective law enforcement, with the police using reasonable discretion to make arrests and apply the laws. We do not want a heinous crime to go unpunished because constitutional guarantees have unreasonably tied the hands of police. Law enforcement officers must understand the rules well enough to act without violating them, because when they make mistakes the consequences can be enormous.

Once police make an arrest and take an individual into custody, the prosecuting attorney joins the process. The prosecutor of state crimes, commonly known as the district attorney, is an elected official having jurisdiction over criminal matters in a given local jurisdiction, usually a county. Prosecutors of federal offenses, who are appointed by the president and confirmed by the Senate, are called United States attorneys. Their assignments correspond to the geographical jurisdictions of the federal district courts, and they serve at the president's pleasure. State and federal prosecutors decide whether the government will bring charges against the accused. Among other factors, a prosecutor considers whether police acted properly in gathering evidence and making the arrest. If the prosecutor decides not to press charges, the police must release the suspect, and the process ends. If prosecution is indicated, the government brings the individual before a judge, who ensures that the accused has legal representation and understands the charges. The judge also must verify that police had adequate justification for holding the accused. The judge may set bail, a monetary guarantee that the accused will appear for trial if he or she is released from custody, or deny bail.

The system next provides a step to ensure that the prosecutor is not abusing the power to charge persons with crimes. This check on prosecutorial discretion takes place in one of two ways. An individual accused of committing a federal offense or of violating the laws of some states will receive a grand jury hearing in accordance with the Fifth Amendment. Composed of laypersons, the grand jury, without the accused being present, examines the prosecutor's case to determine whether the government's evidence is strong enough to support formal charges. If the grand jury decides that the prosecutor has satisfied the legal requirements, it issues a formal document, known as an *indictment,* ordering the accused to stand trial on specified charges. If the grand jury concludes that the prosecutor's case is insufficient, the defendant is released.

Because the right to a grand jury hearing is not one of the incorporated provisions of the Bill of Rights, states are free to develop other methods of checking the prosecutor. Several states use preliminary hearings, which more closely resemble trials than does the grand jury process. At such a hearing, both prosecution and defense may present their cases to a judge who evaluates the adequacy of the government's evidence. If the judge agrees that the prosecutor's case justifies a trial, the prosecutor issues an *information.* Roughly the equivalent of an indictment, the information is a formal document that orders the accused to stand trial on certain specified violations of the criminal code. If the prosecutor's case is found inadequate to justify a trial, the judge may order the release of the defendant.

Once formally charged, the defendant proceeds to the arraignment stage. At arraignment, a judge reads the indictment or information to ensure that the defendant understands the charges and the applicable constitutional rights. The judge also asks if the defendant is represented by counsel. Because the specific criminal accusations may have changed in seriousness or number of counts since the defendant's initial appearance, the judge reviews and perhaps modifies the bail amount. Finally, the judge accepts the defendant's plea: guilty, nolo contendere (no contest), or not guilty. Should the defendant plead guilty or no contest, a trial is not necessary, and the accused proceeds to sentencing.

A plea of not guilty normally leads to a full trial governed by constitutional provisions found in the Fifth and Sixth Amendments. The accused is entitled to a fair, public, and speedy trial by jury. A judge presides over the trial, and the two opposing lawyers question witnesses and summarize case facts. When both sides have presented their cases, the jury deliberates to reach a verdict. If the individual is found guilty, the judge issues a sentence, which, under Eighth Amendment protections, may not be cruel and unusual.

If the defendant is found not guilty, the process ends. Fifth Amendment prohibition against double jeopardy bars the government from putting an acquitted defendant on trial a second time for the same offense. The prosecution has no right to appeal an acquittal verdict reached by the trial court. Should the verdict be guilty, however, the defendant has the right to appeal the conviction to a higher court. The appeals court reviews the trial procedures to determine whether any significant errors in law or procedure occurred. If dissatisfied with the findings of the appeals court, either side—the government or the defense—may try for a review by an even higher court. These requests may be denied, because the system generally provides for only one appeal as a matter of right. Subsequent appeals are left to the discretion of the appellate courts.

TRENDS IN COURT DECISION MAKING

In the next two chapters, we examine each stage in the criminal justice system vis-à-vis the constitutional rights of the criminally accused. While reading the narrative and opinions, keep in mind that the four amendments governing criminal proceedings do not work in isolation. Rather, they fit into a larger scheme that includes law, politics, local custom, and the practical necessities of coping with crime in a contemporary society.

The rights accorded the criminally accused by the four amendments set limits that, in tandem with the legal system, define the criminal justice process. The system depends heavily upon Supreme Court interpretation of the several clauses contained in those amendments. As we have seen in other legal areas, however, the way the Court interprets constitutional rights is not determined exclusively by traditional legal factors such as precedent, the plain language of the law, or the intent of the framers. Historical circumstances, ideological stances, and pressure from other institutions and private groups also affect the course of law, which explains why jurisprudence varies from one Supreme Court era to the next or even from term to term.

Perhaps no issue illustrates this intersection of law and politics better than criminal rights. In the 1960s, with Chief Justice Earl Warren at the helm, the Supreme Court revolutionized criminal law by expanding the protections accorded those charged with crimes. The extent to which the Warren Court altered existing law will become clear as you read the cases to come. For now, note the high percentage of decisions favoring the criminally accused during the 1960s, as depicted in Figure III-2.

The liberal trend did not go unnoticed. President Richard Nixon was among the first to recognize that expanded rights for the criminally accused upset a majority of Americans. During his presidential campaign of 1968 and once he was elected, Nixon emphasized a law-and-order theme, proclaiming to the voters that the liberal Warren Court had gone too far. In a 1968 speech Nixon said, "It's time for some honest talk about the problem of order in the United States. Let us always respect, as I do, our courts and those who serve on them, but let us also recognize that some of our courts in their decisions have gone too far in weakening the peace forces as against the criminal forces in this country." All who heard these words knew that Nixon was referring only to the Warren Court. Apparently, many voters agreed with the future president. Public opinion polls taken in 1968 showed that nearly two-thirds of Americans believed that the courts were not dealing with criminals harshly enough, compared with about 50 percent just three years earlier.[1] In short, Nixon had hit a nerve with U.S. citizens; he placed crime on the public agenda, where it remains.

Nixon also had the opportunity to keep his promise to restore law and order to American communities by changing the membership of the Supreme Court. One year before Nixon took office, Warren had resigned to give President Lyndon Johnson the chance to appoint his successor. When Johnson's choice for that position, Justice Abe Fortas, failed to obtain Senate confirmation, the chief justiceship remained vacant for Nixon to fill. His choice was Warren Burger, a court of appeals judge who agreed with Nixon's stance on criminal law.

---

1. Harold W. Stanley and Richard G. Niemi, *Vital Statistics on American Politics, 2005–2006* (Washington, DC: CQ Press, 2006), 164.

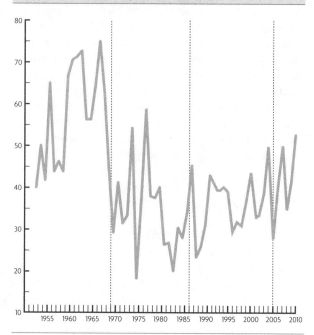

FIGURE III-2 Percentage of Supreme Court Criminal Rights Cases Decided in Favor of the Accused, 1953–2010 Terms

SOURCE: Calculated by the authors from data available on the U.S. Supreme Court Judicial Database (http://supremecourtdatabase.org).

NOTE: Reference lines indicate the Warren, Burger, Rehnquist, and Roberts Courts.

During the 1970s those who sympathized with the liberal decisions of the Warren Court watched in horror as Nixon appointed three more justices to the Court. The American Civil Liberties Union and various legal aid societies predicted that this new Court would not only stop any expansion of criminal rights but also begin to overturn Warren Court precedents. Figure III-2 shows there may be some truth to this view. The Court proved less supportive of criminal rights under Burger's leadership than under Warren's. This trend continued when William Rehnquist replaced Burger as chief justice in 1986. Whether it will persist during the Roberts Court years is unclear; John Roberts only took the helm in 2005. Nonetheless, the data so far are suggestive. When it comes to criminal procedure, the Roberts Court appears to be closer to its immediate predecessor, the Rehnquist Court, than to the earlier Warren Court. Over the first five terms with Roberts as chief justice, the Court ruled for the defendant in only about four of every ten cases (as did the Rehnquist Court), compared with about six of every ten during the Warren years. Some commentators have even suggested that the Roberts Court is continuing the Rehnquist Court's project of "stealth overruling" landmark Warren Court decisions, including *Miranda v. Arizona.*[2] If so, perhaps we should not be surprised. George W. Bush, a conservative Republican president, appointed Roberts and Samuel Alito, a former prosecutor. Both have turned out to give great deference to law enforcement officials. Roberts has supported the government in 73 percent of cases, and Alito in 83 percent. So far, Barack Obama's appointees, Elena Kagan and Sonia Sotomayor, have tended to vote in favor of defendants in criminal cases, but Sotomayor, also a former prosecutor, is no Earl Warren (or Thurgood Marshall or William Brennan). Her support of defendants' rights

has fallen more in the 50–60 percent range, rather than in the range of 70–80 percent.

Of course, you should keep in mind that the data depicted in Figure III-2 present only an aggregated view of Court behavior. To understand whether, in fact, the Burger and Rehnquist Courts managed to alter existing precedent, we must examine the changes in particular areas of criminal law and procedure. As you read the next two chapters, note the date of each decision. Cases decided between 1953 and 1969 are Warren Court decisions, those between 1970 and 1986 are Burger Court opinions, those decided through the 2004 term are Rehnquist Court cases, and all subsequent cases belong to the Roberts Court. Can you identify differences in interpretation? Did the Burger, Rehnquist, and now Roberts Courts weaken the pro-defendant precedents set by the Warren Court, as many civil libertarians predicted? If so, did this reaction impose a reasonable balance between effective law enforcement and the rights of the accused, or did it go too far in favoring the prosecution of criminal defendants?

---

2. See, for example, Barry Friedman, "The Wages of Stealth Overruling (with Particular Attention to *Miranda v. Arizona*)," *Georgetown Law Journal* 99 (2010): 1–62.

Investigations and Evidence

O N DECEMBER 21, 1911, police officers, acting on a tip, arrested Fremont Weeks at Union Station in Kansas City, where he worked for an express shipping company. They charged him with using the U.S. mails to transport lottery tickets, a violation of federal law. Simultaneously, other police officers went to the accused's house and learned from neighbors where Weeks hid his key. The officers obtained the key, entered the house, and conducted a search without a search warrant and without the owner's permission. They found various papers and articles, which they seized and turned over to the U.S. marshal.

Believing that additional investigation would yield more promising evidence, the marshal returned to the Weeks home later that day accompanied by police officers. A boarder who lived there allowed the officers to come in after they knocked. Once again, police entered the house without a search warrant. They removed books, letters, money, papers, notes, evidence of indebtedness, stock certificates, insurance policies, bonds, deeds, candy, and clothes. When federal authorities examined what had been seized, they found some letters, lottery tickets, and other written statements, which were used as evidence against Weeks, but most of the materials taken were not relevant to the criminal charges.

Over objections that the police had violated the search and seizure provisions of the Fourth Amendment, the government used the evidence against Weeks at his trial and obtained a conviction. Weeks was fined and sentenced to prison. He challenged the conviction on appeal, ultimately taking his case to the Supreme Court. The justices found that the police had violated the Fourth Amendment and that, because the evidence had been unconstitutionally obtained, it should not have been used in court to establish the defendant's guilt. The conviction was overturned, and Weeks went free.

How is it possible that Weeks could avoid criminal penalties? The evidence showed, without doubt, that he was guilty of the charges. The answer is simple: proof that a crime was committed is a necessary but insufficient condition for a successful prosecution. The government must also show that the proof (or evidence) was obtained in a way that respected the rights of the accused.

The decision in **Weeks v. United States** (1914) represents one of the Court's earliest attempts to grapple with issues related to constitutional violations committed by police while gathering evidence and what to do when such violations occur. This area of the law has not yielded easy answers. In each term of the modern Court, the justices have heard cases in which individuals convicted of crimes have claimed that police acted improperly in gathering evidence. The stakes in these cases are important. They not only affect law enforcement procedures and criminal punishments but also establish constitutional rules that protect all of us against unreasonable government intrusion into our lives.

Evidence presented in criminal cases can be categorized as either physical or testimonial. The gathering of physical evidence, such as the items at issue in the

Weeks case, is governed by the Fourth Amendment's prohibition against unreasonable searches and seizures. Testimonial evidence, such as statements made to police by criminal suspects, is limited by the Fifth Amendment's guarantee against self-incrimination. In this chapter we focus on these two rights and on how the Supreme Court has interpreted them.

SEARCHES AND SEIZURES

To build a case against a criminal suspect, a prosecutor often relies on physical evidence gathered by the police. This evidence may assume many different forms: the money or goods taken during a theft, the weapons or tools used to carry out the crime, the clothing worn during the offense, illegal drugs, hair or blood samples, and so forth. Physical evidence can be a powerful indicator of the guilt or innocence of a suspect. Given advances in technology (such as DNA testing), physical evidence today can yield much more information than was the case even in fairly recent times.

The founders recognized the importance of physical evidence to the criminal process, but they also understood that people's rights could be abused by overzealous law enforcement efforts to obtain such evidence. As a consequence, the Fourth Amendment, which deals exclusively with searches and seizures, became part of the Bill of Rights.

The Fourth Amendment has its genesis in the framers' resentment of an English institution, the writs of assistance. These writs were general search warrants that did not specify the places or things to be searched. They were authorized by the crown in England beginning in the mid-1600s; by the early 1700s they were used in the colonies primarily to allow customs officials to conduct unrestricted searches. By authorizing these searches, Britain hoped to discourage smuggling by colonial merchants and to enforce existing restrictions on colonial trade.[1]

As general searches grew more common, some colonists began to express their distaste for what they felt were major intrusions on their personal privacy and political liberty. In 1766 the House of Commons in England invalidated general search warrants. By

then, however, the damage in the colonies had been done. Right before the Declaration of Independence was issued, Samuel Adams said that opposition to the general searches was the "Commencement of the Controversy between Great Britain and America."[2] By the time Madison proposed the Bill of Rights to Congress, it was clear that most Americans shared a contempt for general search warrants. Almost all of the newly adopted state constitutions restricted government searches and seizures.

The Fourth Amendment contains two provisions, the first stating the basic right against unreasonable searches and seizures, and the second detailing the requirements for search warrants:

[1] The right of the people to be secure in their persons, houses, papers, and effects, against unreasonable searches and seizures, shall not be violated, and [2] no Warrants shall issue, but upon probable cause, supported by Oath or affirmation, and particularly describing the place to be searched, and the persons or things to be seized.

The amendment clearly balances the government's need to gather evidence with the citizen's right not to suffer unnecessary government intrusions. The amendment does not stop police from searching and seizing, it simply outlaws such activities as are deemed "unreasonable." But what distinguishes a reasonable from an unreasonable search and seizure? As in so many other areas, the task of applying important principles to concrete cases—that is, of giving meaning to the Constitution—has fallen to the Supreme Court.

What Does the Fourth Amendment Protect?

Just what the Fourth Amendment protects is a fundamental search and seizure question. Initially, the prevailing view was that the Fourth Amendment did not restrict police searches and seizures unless law enforcement physically intruded on a person's property. This approach emphasized that the Fourth Amendment protected individuals from government searches of their "person, houses, papers, and effects." If the government did not physically search through a person's belongings or trespass on a person's property, Fourth Amendment restrictions on law enforcement did not apply.

The Court articulated this position best in its 1928 ruling in *Olmstead v. United States*, the first major

1. For more on the writs of assistance, see Melvin I. Urofsky and Paul Finkelman, *A March of Liberty,* 2nd ed. (New York: Oxford University Press, 2002), 43–44.

2. Quoted in Ira Glasser, *Visions of Liberty: The Bill of Rights for All Americans* (New York: Arcade, 1991), 166.

electronic eavesdropping case to come before the justices. Federal agents had reason to believe that Roy Olmstead was importing and selling alcohol in violation of the National Prohibition Act. To collect evidence against him, the agents, without first obtaining a search warrant, placed wiretaps on Olmstead's telephone lines. They did so without setting foot on Olmstead's property. One tap was applied in the basement of a large office building in which Olmstead rented space, and the other on a telephone line on the street outside Olmstead's home. These taps allowed the agents to overhear conversations involving illegal activities.

Olmstead challenged the evidence. He claimed that even though the agents had not entered his home or office, they had, through the wiretaps, searched and seized his conversations in violation of the Fourth Amendment. The government maintained that because the agents had not trespassed onto Olmstead's property, the wiretapping was a procedure that need not comply with Fourth Amendment requirements.

The Court ruled in favor of the government. After reviewing the general history of the Fourth Amendment, the justices concluded that the Constitution did not protect Olmstead's conversations because it covers only searches of "material things—the person, the house, his papers or his effects." Therefore, "[t]he Amendment does not forbid what was done here. There was no searching. There was no seizure. The evidence was secured by the use of the sense of hearing and that only. There was no entry of the houses or offices of the defendants."

The Court's logic was lost on four justices, who wrote dissenting opinions. Of these, Justice Louis Brandeis's is the best remembered. Brandeis echoed the words of those who had fought against the general warrants when he wrote:

The makers of our Constitution undertook to secure conditions favorable to the pursuit of happiness. . . . They conferred, as against the Government, the right to be let alone—the most comprehensive of rights and the right most valued by civilized men. To protect that right, every unjustifiable intrusion by the Government upon the privacy of the individual, whatever the means employed, must be deemed a violation of the Fourth Amendment.

To Brandeis, it was immaterial that agents had not needed to enter Olmstead's home or office to place the wiretaps; it was equally unimportant that "the intrusion was in aid of law enforcement." He declared, "The greatest dangers to liberty lurk in insidious encroachment by men of zeal, well-meaning but without understanding."

The Brandeis position, however, did not prevail. Instead, borrowing from the legal concept of trespass, the majority interpreted the Fourth Amendment to protect only against physical intrusions into constitutionally protected areas. This line of reasoning became known as the "physical penetration" rule. As long as the police did not physically encroach on an individual's "person, houses, papers, or effects," evidence gathered without a search warrant could be used in court.

Over the next four decades the Court continued to use this trespass approach to the Fourth Amendment.[3] During this time, however, criticism was growing, especially within the legal community, that the physical penetration rule did not sufficiently protect individuals' rights. In response, the justices decided to reconsider their traditional approach to the question of when Fourth Amendment restrictions on searches and seizures apply. They did so in *Katz v. United States* (1967).

As you read this case, pay attention to the way the Court treats the conflict between the need of the people to be secure against unwanted government intrusions and law enforcement's need to have effective weapons to combat crime. Note also the dissenting opinion of Justice Hugo Black, in which he forcefully argues against judicial interpretations that stray too far from the original meaning of the words of the framers.

Katz v. United States

389 U.S. 347 (1967)
http://laws.findlaw.com/US/389/347.html
Oral arguments are available at http://www.oyez.org.
Vote: 7 (Brennan, Douglas, Fortas, Harlan, Stewart, Warren, White)
1 (Black)

OPINION OF THE COURT: *Stewart*

CONCURRING OPINIONS: *Douglas, Harlan, White*

DISSENTING OPINION: *Black*

NOT PARTICIPATING: *Marshall*

FACTS:

FBI agents suspected Charles Katz of engaging in illegal bookmaking activity; in particular, they thought he was placing bets and transmitting other wagering information by telephone from California to Miami and Boston. Based on surveillance, the agents learned

---

3. See, for example, ***Goldman v. United States*** (1942).

that Katz made daily calls from one of two adjacent public telephone booths located on Sunset Boulevard in Los Angeles. (Keep in mind that back then public telephones were often housed in glass booths.) To gather evidence, they attached a listening and recording device to the shared outside top of the telephone booths. No part of the listening device extended into either booth. The device was activated before Katz entered either booth, and his conversations were recorded. Agents repeated this process several times. Although the agents had a traditional search warrant to seize certain physical objects (gambling records, bet slips, and so on), they did not have judicial authorization to gather conversational evidence from a phone booth. Federal attorneys used the transcripts of the recorded conversations to obtain an eight-count indictment.

Believing that the Court would use the physical penetration test, Katz and the government both centered their arguments on the nature of the place where the conversations occurred. Katz challenged the use of the transcripts as evidence against him on the ground that the telephone booth was a "constitutionally protected area." In making this argument, which was not so different from Olmstead's nearly forty years earlier, Katz may have been on somewhat stronger ground than Olmstead had been. In the 1965 case of *Griswold v. Connecticut (see Chapter 10)*, the Supreme Court had created a constitutional right to privacy. Although *Griswold* involved birth control, some observers believed it was also applicable to Katz's situation. In other words, police could not invade his privacy unless they obtained a search warrant.

ARGUMENTS:

For the petitioner, Charles Katz:
- The primary purpose of the Fourth Amendment is to protect personal privacy, not property.
- Rapidly advancing technology has rendered ineffective the physical trespass approach to the Fourth Amendment, and it should be abandoned.
- The phone booth is a constitutionally protected area, and Katz had every expectation that what he said in that space would not be overheard by the government.

For the respondent, United States:
- Consistent with the law, the agents conducted no trespass or physical invasion of the interior of the phone booths.

- Because police had a strong basis for probable cause and because they limited the scope of the surveillance to the exact location where the crime was being committed, this search should be considered reasonable even if the Court abandons the physical penetration rule.
- A person in a public phone booth is normally visible to others, and the person's conversations can often be overheard by those in an adjoining phone booth. Consequently, the degree of privacy Katz could have reasonably expected in a public telephone booth is much less than he would expect in his home.

MR. JUSTICE STEWART DELIVERED THE OPINION OF THE COURT.

We granted certiorari in order to consider the constitutional questions thus presented.

The petitioner has phrased those questions as follows:

"A. Whether a public telephone booth is a constitutionally protected area so that evidence obtained by attaching an electronic listening recording device to the top of such a booth is obtained in violation of the right to privacy of the user of the booth.

"B. Whether physical penetration of a constitutionally protected area is necessary before a search and seizure can be said to be violative of the Fourth Amendment to the United States Constitution."

We decline to adopt this formulation of the issues. In the first place, the correct solution of Fourth Amendment problems is not necessarily promoted by incantation of the phrase "constitutionally protected area." Secondly, the Fourth Amendment cannot be translated into a general constitutional "right to privacy." That Amendment protects individual privacy against certain kinds of governmental intrusion, but its protections go further, and often have nothing to do with privacy at all. Other provisions of the Constitution protect personal privacy from other forms of governmental invasion. But the protection of a person's *general* right to privacy—his right to be let alone by other people—is, like the protection of his property and of his very life, left largely to the law of the individual States.

Because of the misleading way the issues have been formulated, the parties have attached great significance to the characterization of the telephone booth from which the petitioner placed his calls. The petitioner has strenuously argued that the booth was a "constitutionally protected area." The Government has maintained with equal vigor that it was not. But this effort to decide whether or not a given "area," viewed in the abstract, is "constitutionally protected" deflects attention from the problem presented by this case. For the Fourth Amendment protects people, not places. What a person knowingly exposes to the public, even in his own home or office, is not a subject of Fourth Amendment protection. But what he seeks to preserve as private, even in an area accessible to the public, may be constitutionally protected.

The Government stresses the fact that the telephone booth from which the petitioner made his calls was constructed partly of glass, so that he was as visible after he entered it as he would have been if he had remained outside. But what he sought to exclude when he entered the booth was not the intruding eye—it was the uninvited ear. He did not shed his right to do so simply because he made his calls from a place where he might be seen. No less than an individual in a business office, in a friend's apartment, or in a taxicab, a person in a telephone booth may rely upon the protection of the Fourth Amendment. One who occupies it, shuts the door behind him, and pays the toll that permits him to place a call is surely entitled to assume that the words he utters into the mouthpiece will not be broadcast to the world. To read the Constitution more narrowly is to ignore the vital role that the public telephone has come to play in private communication.

The Government contends, however, that the activities of its agents in this case should not be tested by Fourth Amendment requirements, for the surveillance technique they employed involved no physical penetration of the telephone booth from which the petitioner placed his calls. It is true that the absence of such penetration was at one time thought to foreclose further Fourth Amendment inquiry, *Olmstead v. United States; Goldman v. United States,* for that Amendment was thought to limit only searches and seizures of tangible property. But "the premise that property interests control the right of the Government to search and seize has been discredited." . . . Indeed, we have expressly held that the Fourth Amendment governs not only the seizure of tangible items, but extends as well to the recording of oral statements, overheard without any "technical trespass under . . . local property law." Once this much is acknowledged, and once it is recognized that the Fourth Amendment protects people—and not simply "areas"—against

unreasonable searches and seizures, it becomes clear that the reach of that Amendment cannot turn upon the presence or absence of a physical intrusion into any given enclosure.

We conclude that the underpinnings of *Olmstead* and *Goldman* have been so eroded . . . [that they] can no longer be regarded as controlling. The Government's activities in electronically listening to and recording the petitioner's words violated the privacy upon which he justifiably relied while using the telephone booth and thus constituted a "search and seizure" within the meaning of the Fourth Amendment. The fact that the electronic device employed to achieve that end did not happen to penetrate the wall of the booth can have no constitutional significance.

The question remaining for decision, then, is whether the search and seizure conducted in this case complied with constitutional standards. In that regard, the Government's position is that its agents acted in an entirely defensible manner: They did not begin their electronic surveillance until investigation of the petitioner's activities had established a strong probability that he was using the telephone in question to transmit gambling information to persons in other States, in violation of federal law. Moreover, the surveillance was limited, both in scope and in duration, to the specific purpose of establishing the contents of the petitioner's unlawful telephonic communications. The agents confined their surveillance to the brief periods during which he used the telephone booth, and they took great care to overhear only the conversations of the petitioner himself.

Accepting this account of the Government's actions as accurate, it is clear that this surveillance was so narrowly circumscribed that a duly authorized magistrate, properly notified of the need for such investigation, specifically informed of the basis on which it was to proceed, and clearly apprised of the precise intrusion it would entail, could constitutionally have authorized, with appropriate safeguards, the very limited search and seizure that the Government asserts in fact took place. Only last Term we sustained the validity of such an authorization, holding that, under sufficiently "precise and discriminate circumstances," a federal court may empower government agents to employ a concealed electronic device "for the narrow and particularized purpose of ascertaining the truth of the . . . allegations" of a "detailed factual affidavit alleging the commission of a specific criminal offense." . . . Here, too, a similar judicial order could have accommodated "the legitimate needs of law enforcement" by authorizing the carefully limited use of electronic surveillance.

The Government urges that, because its agents relied upon the decisions in *Olmstead* and *Goldman,* and because they did no more here than they might properly have done with prior judicial sanction, we should retroactively validate their conduct. That we cannot do. It is apparent that the agents in this case acted with restraint. Yet the inescapable fact is that this restraint was imposed by the agents themselves, not by a judicial officer. They were not required, before commencing the search, to present their estimate of probable cause for detached scrutiny by a neutral magistrate. They were not compelled, during the conduct of the search itself, to observe precise limits established in advance by a specific court order. Nor were they directed, after the search had been completed, to notify the authorizing magistrate in detail of all that had been seized. In the absence of such safeguards, this Court has never sustained a search upon the sole ground that officers reasonably expected to find evidence of a particular crime and voluntarily confined their activities to the least intrusive means consistent with that end. Searches conducted without warrants have been held unlawful "notwithstanding facts unquestionably showing probable cause," for the Constitution requires "that the deliberate, impartial judgment of a judicial officer . . . be interposed between the citizen and the police. . . . " "Over and again this Court has emphasized that the mandate of the [Fourth] Amendment requires adherence to judicial processes," and that searches conducted outside the judicial process, without prior approval by judge or magistrate, are per se unreasonable under the Fourth Amendment—subject only to a few specifically established and well-delineated exceptions.

It is difficult to imagine how any of those exceptions could ever apply to the sort of search and seizure involved in this case. Even electronic surveillance substantially contemporaneous with an individual's arrest could hardly be deemed an "incident" of that arrest. . . . And, of course, the very nature of electronic surveillance precludes its use pursuant to the suspect's consent.

The Government does not question these basic principles. Rather, it urges the creation of a new exception to cover this case. It argues that surveillance of a telephone booth should be exempted from the usual requirement of advance authorization by a magistrate upon a showing of probable cause. We cannot agree. Omission of such authorization "bypasses the safeguards provided by an objective predetermination of probable cause, and substitutes instead the far less reliable procedure of an after-the-event justification for the . . . search, too likely to be subtly influenced by the familiar shortcomings of hindsight judgment." And bypassing a neutral predetermination of the scope of a search leaves individuals secure from Fourth Amendment violations "only in the discretion of the police."

These considerations do not vanish when the search in question is transferred from the setting of a home, an office, or a hotel room to that of a telephone booth. Wherever a man may be, he is entitled to know that he will remain free from unreasonable searches and seizures. The government agents here ignored "the procedure of antecedent justification . . . that is central to the Fourth Amendment," a procedure that we hold to be a constitutional precondition of the kind of electronic surveillance involved in this case. Because the surveillance here failed to meet that condition, and because it led to the petitioner's conviction, the judgment must be reversed.

MR. JUSTICE HARLAN, concurring.

I join the opinion of the Court, which I read to hold only (a) that an enclosed telephone booth is an area where, like a home . . . a person has a constitutionally protected reasonable expectation of privacy; (b) that electronic as well as physical intrusion into a place that is in this sense private may constitute a violation of the Fourth Amendment; and (c) that the invasion of a constitutionally protected area by federal authorities is, as the Court has long held, presumptively unreasonable in the absence of a search warrant.

As the Court's opinion states, "the Fourth Amendment protects people, not places." The question, however, is what protection it affords to those people. Generally, as here, the answer to that question requires reference to a "place." My understanding of the rule that has emerged from prior decisions is that there is a twofold requirement, first that a person have exhibited an actual (subjective) expectation of privacy and, second, that the expectation be one that society is prepared to recognize as "reasonable." Thus a man's home is, for most purposes, a place where he expects privacy, but objects, activities, or statements that he exposes to the "plain view" of outsiders are not "protected" because no intention to keep them to himself has been exhibited. On the other hand, conversations in the open would not be protected against being overheard, for the expectation of privacy under the circumstances would be unreasonable.

The critical fact in this case is that "[o]ne who occupies it, [a telephone booth] shuts the door behind him, and pays the toll that permits him to place a call is surely entitled to assume" that his conversation is not being intercepted. The point is not that the booth is "accessible to the public" at other times, but that it is a temporarily private place whose momentary occupants' expectations of freedom from intrusion are recognized as reasonable. . . .

This case requires us to reconsider *Goldman,* and I agree that it should now be overruled. Its limitation on Fourth Amendment protection is, in the present day, bad physics as well as bad law, for reasonable expectations of privacy may be defeated by electronic as well as physical invasion.

Finally, I do not read the Court's opinion to declare that no interception of a conversation one-half of which occurs in a public telephone booth can be reasonable in the absence of a warrant. As elsewhere under the Fourth Amendment, warrants are the general rule, to which the legitimate needs of law enforcement may demand specific exceptions. It will be time enough to consider any such exceptions when an appropriate occasion presents itself, and I agree with the Court that this is not one.

MR. JUSTICE BLACK, dissenting.

While I realize that an argument based on the meaning of words lacks the scope, and no doubt the appeal, of broad policy discussions and philosophical discourses on such nebulous subjects as privacy, for me, the language of the Amendment is the crucial place to look in construing a written document such as our Constitution. The Fourth Amendment says that

The right of the people to be secure in their persons, houses, papers, and effects, against unreasonable searches and seizures, shall not be violated, and no Warrants shall issue, but upon probable cause, supported by Oath or affirmation, and particularly describing the place to be searched and the persons or things to be seized.

The first clause protects "persons, houses, papers, and effects against unreasonable searches and seizures. . . . " These words connote the idea of tangible things with size, form, and weight, things capable of being searched, seized, or both. The second clause of the Amendment still further establishes its Framers' purpose to limit its protection to tangible things by providing that no warrants shall issue but those "particularly describing the place to be searched, and the persons or things to

be seized." A conversation overheard by eavesdropping, whether by plain snooping or wiretapping, is not tangible and, under the normally accepted meanings of the words, can neither be searched nor seized. In addition the language of the second clause indicates that the Amendment refers not only to something tangible so it can be seized but to something already in existence so it can be described. Yet the Court's interpretation would have the Amendment apply to overhearing future conversations which by their very nature are nonexistent until they take place. How can one "describe" a future conversation, and, if one cannot, how can a magistrate issue a warrant to eavesdrop one in the future? It is argued that information showing what is expected to be said is sufficient to limit the boundaries of what later can be admitted into evidence; but does such general information really meet the specific language of the Amendment which says "particularly describing"? Rather than using language in a completely artificial way, I must conclude that the Fourth Amendment simply does not apply to eavesdropping.

Tapping telephone wires, of course, was an unknown possibility at the time the Fourth Amendment was adopted. But eavesdropping (and wiretapping is nothing more than eavesdropping by telephone) was . . . "an ancient practice which, at common law, was condemned as a nuisance." 4 Blackstone, Commentaries, 168. "In those days, the eavesdropper listened by naked ear under the eaves of houses or their windows, or beyond their walls seeking out private discourse." There can be no doubt that the Framers were aware of this practice, and, if they had desired to outlaw or restrict the use of evidence obtained by eavesdropping, I believe that they would have used the appropriate language to do so in the Fourth Amendment. They certainly would not have left such a task to the ingenuity of language-stretching judges. No one, it seems to me, can read the debates on the Bill of Rights without reaching the conclusion that its Framers and critics well knew the meaning of the words they used, what they would be understood to mean by others, their scope and their limitations. Under these circumstances it strikes me as a charge against their scholarship, their common sense and their candor to give to the Fourth Amendment's language the eavesdropping meaning the Court imputes to it today. . . .

Since I see no way in which the words of the Fourth Amendment can be construed to apply to eavesdropping, that closes the matter for me. In interpreting the Bill of Rights, I willingly go as far as a liberal construction of the language takes me, but I simply cannot in good conscience give a meaning to words which they have never before been thought to have and which they certainly do not have in common ordinary usage. I will not distort the words of the Amendment in order to "keep the Constitution up to date" or "to bring it into harmony with the times." It was never meant that this Court have such power, which, in effect, would make us a continuously functioning constitutional convention. . . .

The Fourth Amendment protects privacy only to the extent that it prohibits unreasonable searches and seizures of "persons, houses, papers, and effects." No general right is created by the Amendment so as to give this Court the unlimited power to hold unconstitutional everything which affects privacy. Certainly the Framers, well acquainted as they were with the excesses of governmental power, did not intend to grant this Court such omnipotent lawmaking authority as that. The history of governments proves that it is dangerous to freedom to repose such powers in courts.

For these reasons, I respectfully dissent.

Katz is an important, perhaps landmark, ruling for the following reasons. First, the Court applied the right of privacy to searches and seizures. If citizens have an "expectation of privacy" that "society is prepared to recognize as 'reasonable,'" as Justice John Marshall Harlan's concurrence noted, then they are entitled to it. Under such circumstances the Fourth Amendment applies, and police must conform to its requirements.

Second, the Fourth Amendment protects people and not places or things. The majority consequently rejected the physical penetration rule. A person's Fourth Amendment rights can be violated even if police never physically intrude on the individual's property or possessions. Furthermore, the protection against unreasonable seizures applies not only to tangible objects but also to intangible things, such as conversations. Brandeis had advocated this position in his *Olmstead* dissent forty years earlier.

Moreover, this new "expectation of privacy" approach to the Fourth Amendment applies not just to electronic surveillance but to all forms of searches and seizures. If an individual expects privacy, and society views that expectation as reasonable, then the Fourth Amendment governs any police searching or seizing activity.

An example of the Court applying the *Katz* approach can be seen in **Kyllo v. United States** (2001). Federal drug agents, suspecting that Danny Kyllo was growing marijuana in his Oregon home, set up a thermal imaging device across the street from his residence to measure the amount of heat leaving the house. Because the agents did not enter Kyllo's yard or home, they believed that no search warrant was necessary. The device revealed that an unusually large amount of heat was leaving the garage area, a finding consistent with the use of grow lights to encourage plant development. Armed with the results of the thermal imaging tests and the statements of informants, the agents obtained a warrant to search Kyllo's home, where they found more than one hundred marijuana plants. The Supreme Court held that the use of the thermal imaging device without a warrant violated the Fourth Amendment. Even though officers did not physically enter Kyllo's residence, through the use of modern technology they were able to detect activity inside. The government therefore had intruded where Kyllo had a reasonable expectation of privacy. Under such circumstances a warrant is required.

Katz, therefore, set a new standard for determining what is protected by the Fourth Amendment, one that has since guided our understandings of search and seizure law. Most constitutional scholars interpreted the Court's action in *Katz* as deserting any allegiance to the interpretation that Fourth Amendment protections rest on the foundation of physical trespass law. But had the Court fully repudiated the pre-*Katz* views of search and seizure protection? The decision in *United States v. Jones* answers this question.

United States v. Jones

565 U.S. ___ (2012)
http://laws.findlaw.com/us/000/10-1259.html
Oral arguments are available at http://www.oyez.org.
Vote: 9 (Alito, Breyer, Ginsburg, Kagan, Kennedy,
      Roberts, Scalia, Sotomayor, Thomas)
      0

OPINION OF THE COURT: *Scalia*
CONCURRING OPINION: *Sotomayor*
OPINION CONCURRING IN JUDGMENT: *Alito*

FACTS:

Antoine Jones was the owner of Levels, a nightclub in the District of Columbia. The FBI and the Metropolitan Police Department suspected Jones of cocaine trafficking, and as part of their investigation, law enforcement officers kept Jones and his nightclub under visual surveillance, installed a camera near the nightclub, used a device to register the phone numbers of anyone calling Jones or receiving phone calls from him, and installed a wiretap on Jones's cell phone. The telephone surveillance and tapping required a warrant, which the police obtained.

In addition, the officers secured a warrant authorizing them to install covertly and to monitor a GPS tracking device on a Jeep Grand Cherokee registered to Jones's wife but used exclusively by him. The warrant required that the GPS device be installed within a ten-day period and in the District of Columbia. Contrary to these requirements, the officers installed the device on the undercarriage of the Jeep on the eleventh day while the car was parked in Maryland. Later they changed batteries on the device while it was parked in another public parking lot in Maryland. For this reason, both sides to this dispute agreed that the use of the GPS device was technically "warrantless."

The GPS remained on the car for twenty-eight days, all the while tracking the Jeep's movement and locations. Over this four-week period the device transmitted to police computers more than two thousand pages of data on the car's movements, but the device could not tell police who was driving, if there were passengers, or what the driver and passengers did in the car or at their destination. The police were especially interested in the car's movement to a suspected drug stash house in Fort Washington, Maryland.

Antoine Jones successfully challenged his cocaine conviction because evidence used against him was collected by means of a GPS device placed on his vehicle by police who did not have a warrant to do so.

Based on intercepted phone calls, police learned that Jones was expecting a shipment of cocaine in October 2005. On October 24, police executed search warrants for a number of locations. They recovered a large amount of cash, cocaine, weapons, and drug paraphernalia from the car and the stash house that resulted in multiple criminal charges against Jones.

After an initial trial ending in an acquittal on some charges and a deadlocked jury on others, Jones was indicted on a new charge of conspiracy to distribute cocaine. Over Jones's objections, the judge allowed the information collected by the GPS device to be admitted as evidence. Jones was convicted and sentenced to life in prison. He also was ordered to forfeit $1 million in drug proceeds. The Court of Appeals for the District of Columbia, however, reversed the conviction on the grounds that the warrantless use of the GPS device to monitor the movement of the automobile for a month violated the search and seizure provisions of the Fourth Amendment. The United States requested Supreme Court review of that decision.

ARGUMENTS:

For the petitioner, United States:

- Fourth Amendment protections do not extend to matters knowingly exposed to the public.
- A person traveling in an automobile on public thoroughfares has no reasonable expectation of privacy in his movements from one place to another.
- The length of a particular surveillance does not determine whether it constitutes a search.
- The attachment of the GPS device yielded no information on its own (although it created the potential for information gathering), nor did it interfere with Jones's full use of the automobile. Therefore, it was neither a search nor a seizure.

For the respondent, Antoine Jones:

- Jones had a reasonable expectation of privacy that the government would not physically intrude on his private property to affix a GPS device without his knowledge or consent.
- Warrantless government GPS surveillance is a grave and novel threat to personal privacy and security.
- Although a person traveling on public thoroughfares knowingly exposes himself to visual observation, he does not knowingly offer GPS data to public viewing.

- Encroachment on Fourth Amendment rights is particularly serious when it occurs over a prolonged period of time.

JUSTICE SCALIA DELIVERED THE OPINION OF THE COURT.

We decide whether the attachment of a Global-Positioning-System (GPS) tracking device to an individual's vehicle, and subsequent use of that device to monitor the vehicle's movements on public streets, constitutes a search or seizure within the meaning of the Fourth Amendment. . . .

The Fourth Amendment provides in relevant part that "[t]he right of the people to be secure in their persons, houses, papers, and effects, against unreasonable searches and seizures, shall not be violated." It is beyond dispute that a vehicle is an "effect" as that term is used in the Amendment. We hold that the Government's installation of a GPS device on a target's vehicle, and its use of that device to monitor the vehicle's movements, constitutes a "search."

It is important to be clear about what occurred in this case: The Government physically occupied private property for the purpose of obtaining information. We have no doubt that such a physical intrusion would have been considered a "search" within the meaning of the Fourth Amendment when it was adopted. . . .

The text of the Fourth Amendment reflects its close connection to property, since otherwise it would have referred simply to "the right of the people to be secure against unreasonable searches and seizures"; the phrase "in their persons, houses, papers, and effects" would have been superfluous.

Consistent with this understanding, our Fourth Amendment jurisprudence was tied to common-law trespass, at least until the latter half of the 20th century. *Kyllo v. United States* (2001). Thus, in *Olmstead v. United States* (1928), we held that wiretaps attached to telephone wires on the public streets did not constitute a Fourth Amendment search because "[t]here was no entry of the houses or offices of the defendants."

Our later cases, of course, have deviated from that exclusively property-based approach. In *Katz v. United States* (1967), we said that "the Fourth Amendment protects people, not places," and found a violation in attachment of an eavesdropping device to a public telephone booth. Our later cases have applied the analysis of Justice Harlan's concurrence in that case, which said that a violation occurs when government officers violate a person's "reasonable expectation of privacy."

The Government contends that the Harlan standard shows that no search occurred here, since Jones had no "reasonable expectation of privacy" in the area of the Jeep accessed by Government agents (its underbody) and in the locations of the Jeep on the public roads, which were visible to all. But we need not address the Government's contentions, because Jones's Fourth Amendment rights do not rise or fall with the *Katz* formulation. At bottom, we must "assur[e] preservation of that degree of privacy against government that existed when the Fourth Amendment was adopted." *Kyllo.* . . .

. . . *Katz* . . . established that "property rights are not the sole measure of Fourth Amendment violations," but did not "snuf[f] out the previously recognized protection for property." As Justice Brennan explained in his concurrence in [*United States v.*] *Knotts* [1983], *Katz* did not erode the principle "that, when the Government does engage in physical intrusion of a constitutionally protected area in order to obtain information, that intrusion may constitute a violation of the Fourth Amendment." We have embodied that preservation of past rights in our very definition of "reasonable expectation of privacy" which we have said to be an expectation "that has a source outside of the Fourth Amendment, either by reference to concepts of real or personal property law or to understandings that are recognized and permitted by society." *Minnesota v. Carter* (1998). *Katz* did not narrow the Fourth Amendment's scope. . . .

. . . [T]he *Katz* reasonable-expectation-of-privacy test has been added to, not substituted for, the common-law trespassory test. . . .

The concurrence begins by accusing us of applying "18th-century tort law." That is a distortion. What we apply is an 18th-century guarantee against unreasonable searches, which we believe must provide *at a minimum* the degree of protection it afforded when it was adopted. The concurrence does not share that belief. It would apply *exclusively Katz*'s reasonable-expectation-of-privacy test, even when that eliminates rights that previously existed. . . .

. . . [U]nlike the concurrence, which would make *Katz* the exclusive test, we do not make trespass the exclusive test. Situations involving merely the transmission of electronic signals without trespass would remain subject to *Katz* analysis. . . .

The judgment of the Court of Appeals for the D.C. Circuit is affirmed.

It is so ordered.

JUSTICE SOTOMAYOR, concurring.

I join the Court's opinion because I agree that a search within the meaning of the Fourth Amendment occurs, at a minimum, "[w]here, as here, the Government obtains information by physically intruding on a constitutionally protected area." In this case, the Government installed a Global Positioning System (GPS) tracking device on respondent Antoine Jones' Jeep without a valid warrant and without Jones' consent, then used that device to monitor the Jeep's movements over the course of four weeks. The Government usurped Jones' property for the purpose of conducting surveillance on him, thereby invading privacy interests long afforded, and undoubtedly entitled to, Fourth Amendment protection. See, e.g., *Silverman v. United States* (1961).

Of course, the Fourth Amendment is not concerned only with trespassory intrusions on property. See, e.g., *Kyllo v. United States* (2001). Rather, even in the absence of a trespass, "a Fourth Amendment search occurs when the government violates a subjective expectation of privacy that society recognizes as reasonable." In *Katz,* this Court enlarged its then-prevailing focus on property rights by announcing that the reach of the Fourth Amendment does not "turn upon the presence or absence of a physical intrusion." As the majority's opinion makes clear, however, *Katz*'s reasonable-expectation-of-privacy test augmented, but did not displace or diminish, the common-law trespassory test that preceded it. Thus, "when the Government does engage in physical intrusion of a constitutionally protected area in order to obtain information, that intrusion may constitute a violation of the Fourth Amendment." *United States v. Knotts* (1983) (Brennan, J., concurring in judgment). Justice Alito's approach, which discounts altogether the constitutional relevance of the Government's physical intrusion on Jones' Jeep, erodes that longstanding protection for privacy expectations inherent in items of property that people possess or control. By contrast, the trespassory test applied in the majority's opinion reflects an irreducible constitutional minimum: When the Government physically invades personal property to gather information, a search occurs. The reaffirmation of that principle suffices to decide this case. . . .

. . . I therefore join the majority's opinion.

JUSTICE ALITO, with whom JUSTICE GINSBURG, JUSTICE BREYER, and JUSTICE KAGAN join, concurring in the judgment.

This case requires us to apply the Fourth Amendment's prohibition of unreasonable searches and seizures to a 21st-century surveillance technique, the use of a Global Positioning System (GPS) device to monitor a vehicle's movements for an extended period of time. Ironically, the Court has chosen to decide this case based on 18th-century tort law. . . .

This holding, in my judgment, is unwise. It strains the language of the Fourth Amendment; it has little if any support in current Fourth Amendment case law; and it is highly artificial.

I would analyze the question presented in this case by asking whether respondent's reasonable expectations of privacy were violated by the long-term monitoring of the movements of the vehicle he drove. . . .

The Court's reasoning in this case is very similar to that in the Court's early decisions involving wiretapping and electronic eavesdropping, namely, that a technical trespass followed by the gathering of evidence constitutes a search. In the early electronic surveillance cases, the Court concluded that a Fourth Amendment search occurred when private conversations were monitored as a result of an "unauthorized physical penetration into the premises occupied" by the defendant. *Silverman v. United States* (1961). . . .

By contrast, in cases in which there was no trespass, it was held that there was no search. Thus, in *Olmstead v. United States* (1928), the Court found that the Fourth Amendment did not apply because "[t]he taps from house lines were made in the streets near the houses." . . .

This trespass-based rule was repeatedly criticized. . . .

Katz v. United States (1967) finally did away with the old approach, holding that a trespass was not required for a Fourth Amendment violation. *Katz* involved the use of a listening device that was attached to the outside of a public telephone booth and that allowed police officers to eavesdrop on one end of the target's phone conversation. This procedure did not physically intrude on the area occupied by the target, but the *Katz* Court, "repudiate[ed]" the old doctrine, *Rakas v. Illinois* (1978), and held that "[t]he fact that the electronic device employed . . . did not happen to penetrate the wall of the booth can have no constitutional significance." What mattered, the Court now held, was whether the conduct at issue "violated the privacy upon which [the defendant] justifiably relied while using the telephone booth." *Katz.*

Under this approach, as the Court later put it when addressing the relevance of a technical trespass, "an actual trespass is neither necessary nor sufficient to establish a constitutional violation." *United States v. Karo* (1984). . . .

Recent years have seen the emergence of many new devices that permit the monitoring of a person's movements. In some locales, closed-circuit television video monitoring is becoming ubiquitous. On toll roads, automatic toll collection systems create a precise record of the movements of motorists who choose to make use of that convenience. Many motorists purchase cars that are equipped with devices that permit a central station to ascertain the car's location at any time so that roadside assistance may be provided if needed and the car may be found if it is stolen.

Perhaps most significant, cell phones and other wireless devices now permit wireless carriers to track and record the location of users. . . .

In the pre-computer age, the greatest protections of privacy were neither constitutional nor statutory, but practical. Traditional surveillance for any extended period of time was difficult and costly and therefore rarely undertaken. The surveillance at issue in this case—constant monitoring of the location of a vehicle for four weeks—would have required a large team of agents, multiple vehicles, and perhaps aerial assistance. Only an investigation of unusual importance could have justified such an expenditure of law enforcement resources. Devices like the one used in the present case, however, make long-term monitoring relatively easy and cheap. . . .

. . . The best that we can do in this case is to apply existing Fourth Amendment doctrine and to ask whether the use of GPS tracking in a particular case involved a degree of intrusion that a reasonable person would not have anticipated.

Under this approach, relatively short-term monitoring of a person's movements on public streets accords with expectations of privacy that our society has recognized as reasonable. But the use of longer term GPS monitoring in investigations of most offenses impinges on expectations of privacy. For such offenses, society's expectation has been that law enforcement agents and others would not—and indeed, in the main, simply could not—secretly monitor and catalogue every single movement of an individual's car for a very long period. In this case, for four weeks, law enforcement agents tracked every movement that respondent made in the vehicle he was driving. We need not identify with precision the point at which the tracking of this vehicle became a search, for the line was surely crossed before the 4-week mark. Other cases may present more difficult questions. But where uncertainty exists with respect to whether a certain period of GPS surveillance

is long enough to constitute a Fourth Amendment search, the police may always seek a warrant. We also need not consider whether prolonged GPS monitoring in the context of investigations involving extraordinary offenses would similarly intrude on a constitutionally protected sphere of privacy. In such cases, long-term tracking might have been mounted using previously available techniques.

For these reasons, I conclude that the lengthy monitoring that occurred in this case constituted a search under the Fourth Amendment. I therefore agree with the majority that the decision of the Court of Appeals must be affirmed.

Justice Scalia's opinion for the Court makes clear that the government violates the Fourth Amendment when it physically intrudes on a suspect's constitutionally protected space with the purpose of gathering information against the individual. *Katz* did not repudiate the trespass approach. Rather, the physical penetration standard and the reasonable expectation of privacy approach exist together. According to the majority in *Jones*, the combination of these two standard expands Fourth Amendment protections beyond what would be covered if just one of the two tests were to be used exclusively.

Searches and Search Warrants

If police wish to conduct a search that will intrude where an individual has a reasonable expectation of privacy, the search must be approved by a judge or qualify under a limited number of exceptions to the judicial authorization requirement. Otherwise it is deemed unreasonable and in violation of the Fourth Amendment.

The Constitution mentions only one search authorization method: the search warrant. Clause 2 of the Fourth Amendment outlines the steps police must follow to obtain a search warrant. A police officer must go before a judge or magistrate and swear under oath that he or she has reason to believe that a crime has been committed and that evidence of the crime is located in a particular place. This information often is presented in a sworn statement called an affidavit. The judge then determines whether there is probable cause to believe a crime has been committed and that evidence of it will be found in the area sought to be searched. If such cause is present, the judge authorizes a search by issuing a warrant that carefully describes the area to be searched and the items that may be seized. Police are then permitted to execute the search in a way that does not extend beyond the boundaries described in the warrant.

Although obtaining a search warrant sounds like a straightforward procedure, searches conducted with warrants occur less frequently than we might expect, and one reason is the elusive nature of probable cause. The rationale behind the probable cause requirement is easy to understand: individuals are deserving of security in their private lives, and government intrusion should not be allowed unless there is substantial reason for it. But what is probable cause, and how do police know when they have it?

In *Brinegar v. United States* (1949) the Supreme Court explained that when police, or even judges, deal "with probable cause . . . as the very name implies, [they] deal with probabilities. These are not technical; they are the factual and practical considerations of everyday life on which reasonable and prudent men, not legal technicians, act." But does this statement provide police with any guidance? For example, assume that a number of credible witnesses inform police that a certain man is operating as a fence, buying and reselling stolen goods out of a particular apartment. One of these witnesses claims to have purchased a stolen wristwatch at the apartment and gives it to the police. After placing the apartment under surveillance, the police see significant numbers of people entering or leaving the apartment carrying articles or packages. Under these conditions police clearly have probable cause to believe that crimes have been committed and a sufficient factual basis to persuade a judge to issue a warrant to search the apartment. Much police work, however, is not so simple. Many investigations are based on tips from anonymous informants, ambiguous witness statements, and other kinds of evidence that can be given sinister or innocent interpretations. When does evidence become incriminating enough to allow a judge to issue a search warrant?

In *Aguilar v. Texas* (1964) the Supreme Court, under Chief Justice Earl Warren's leadership, articulated a stringent two-pronged test to determine whether informants' tips or letters could be used as probable cause to obtain search warrants. First, the tip had to "reveal adequately" the informant's "basis of knowledge." How did the individual come to possess the information given to the police? Second, the tip "had to provide facts

sufficiently establishing either the veracity of the affiant's informant, or, alternatively, the 'reliability' of the informant's report." The Court later developed the test more fully in *Spinelli v. United States* (1969) and thereafter referred to it as the Aguilar-Spinelli test.

In the years following *Aguilar,* police and law enforcement organizations complained that this test made it extremely difficult for them to use any letter or tip as the basis for probable cause. These criticisms, coupled with changes in Supreme Court personnel, created an atmosphere in which the Court would reevaluate Aguilar-Spinelli. The opportunity came in *Illinois v. Gates* (1983). Justice William Rehnquist's opinion not only analyzes the concept of probable cause but also provides an interesting example of how the Court deals with precedent it no longer believes to be prudent policy.

Illinois v. Gates

462 U.S. 213 (1983)
http://laws.findlaw.com/US/462/213.html
Oral arguments are available at http://www.oyez.org.
Vote: 6 (Blackmun, Burger, O'Connor, Powell, Rehnquist, White)
    3 (Brennan, Marshall, Stevens)

OPINION OF THE COURT: Rehnquist
CONCURRING OPINION: White
DISSENTING OPINIONS: Brennan, Stevens

FACTS:

On May 3, 1978, police in the Chicago suburb of Bloomingdale received the following anonymous letter:

This letter is to inform you that you have a couple in your town who strictly make their living on selling drugs. They are Sue and Lance Gates, they live on Greenway, off Bloomingdale Rd. in the condominiums. Most of their buys are done in Florida. Sue his wife drives their car to Florida, where she leaves it to be loaded up with drugs, then Lance flies down and drives it back. Sue flies back after she drops the car off in Florida. May 3 she is driving down there again and Lance will be flying down in a few days to drive it back. At the time Lance drives the car back he has the trunk loaded with over $100,000.00 in drugs. Presently they have over $100,000.00 worth of drugs in their basement.

They brag about the fact they never have to work, and make their entire living on pushers.

I guarantee if you watch them carefully you will make a big catch. They are friends with some big drug dealers, who visit their house often.

Bloomingdale Police Department detective Charles Mader verified several points in the anonymous letter. He also discovered that a reservation for a flight from Chicago to West Palm Beach had been made in Lance Gates's name. The police arranged for Gates to be kept under surveillance while in Florida. This investigation revealed that Lance Gates had joined his wife in West Palm Beach and that the two were driving back to Illinois. At this point police obtained a warrant to search their car and home based on the anonymous tip and corroboration of the essential facts included in that tip. When the couple returned to Bloomingdale, police searched their car and found 350 pounds of marijuana. A search of the home uncovered additional evidence of drug trafficking.

The Gateses' attorney argued that the judge should exclude this evidence from trial because, under the Aguilar-Spinelli test, police lacked sufficient probable cause. Specifically, the letter failed to state how the writer came upon the information, a requirement mandated by Aguilar-Spinelli. At a pretrial hearing the judge agreed that the evidence could not be used at the trial. The prosecution appealed the ruling, but the Illinois Supreme Court affirmed it.

The U.S. Supreme Court accepted the case to address this question: May a judge issue a search warrant on the basis of a "partially corroborated anonymous informant's tip"?

ARGUMENTS:

For the petitioner, State of Illinois:
- The Aguilar-Spinelli test's requirement that an informant's basis of knowledge be revealed was satisfied by the detailed information contained in the letter.
- The Aguilar-Spinelli test's requirement that police establish the veracity of the informant's tip was satisfied by police corroboration of the facts stated in the letter and the fact that the informant had no apparent reason to lie.
- Although the requirements of Aguilar-Spinelli were met in this case, the test should be replaced by a new rule or a reinterpretation of precedent that imposes a simpler, more practical standard for the use of hearsay evidence to establish probable cause.

For the respondents, Lance and Susan Gates:
- The application for a search warrant did not adequately establish how the informant acquired his knowledge.

- The police did not satisfy the requirement that the credibility of the informant be established. Police did not know who the informant was, and they verified very few of the facts contained in the informant's letter.
- The lower court correctly ruled that under the Aguilar-Spinelli test probable cause was not sufficiently established and that the warrant should not have been issued.

JUSTICE REHNQUIST DELIVERED THE OPINION OF THE COURT.

The Illinois Supreme Court concluded—and we are inclined to agree—that standing alone, the anonymous letter sent to the Bloomingdale Police Department would not provide the basis for a magistrate's determination that there was probable cause to believe contraband would be found in the Gateses' car and home. The letter provides virtually nothing from which one might conclude that its author is either honest or his information reliable; likewise, the letter gives absolutely no indication of the basis for the writer's predictions regarding the Gateses' criminal activities. Something more was required, then, before a magistrate could conclude that there was probable cause to believe that contraband would be found in the Gateses' home and car.

The Illinois Supreme Court also properly recognized that Detective Mader's affidavit might be capable of supplementing the anonymous letter with information sufficient to permit a determination of probable cause. In holding that the affidavit in fact did not contain sufficient additional information to sustain a determination of probable cause, the Illinois court applied a "two-pronged test," derived from our decision in *Spinelli v. United States* (1969). The Illinois Supreme Court, like some others, apparently understood *Spinelli* as requiring that the anonymous letter satisfy each of two independent requirements before it could be relied on. According to this view, the letter, as supplemented by Mader's affidavit, first had to adequately reveal the "basis of knowledge" of the letterwriter—the particular means by which he came by the information given in his report. Second, it had to provide facts sufficiently establishing either the "veracity" of the affiant's informant, or, alternatively, the "reliability" of the informant's report in this particular case.

The Illinois court, alluding to an elaborate set of legal rules that have developed among various lower courts to enforce the "two-pronged test," found that the test had not been satisfied. . . . Thus, it concluded that no showing of probable cause had been made.

We agree with the Illinois Supreme Court that an informant's "veracity," "reliability," and "basis of knowledge" are all highly relevant in determining the value of his report. We do not agree, however, that these elements should be understood as entirely separate and independent requirements to be rigidly exacted in every case, which the opinion of the Supreme Court of Illinois would imply. Rather, as detailed below, they should be understood simply as closely intertwined issues that may usefully illuminate the commonsense, practical question whether there is "probable cause" to believe that contraband or evidence is located in a particular place.

This totality-of-the-circumstances approach is far more consistent with our prior treatment of probable cause than is any rigid demand that specific "tests" be satisfied by every informant's tip. Perhaps the central teaching of our decisions bearing on the probable-cause standard is that it is a "practical, nontechnical conception." "In dealing with probable cause, . . . as the very name implies, we deal with probabilities. These are not technical; they are the factual and practical considerations of everyday life on which reasonable and prudent men, not legal technicians, act." . . .

As these comments illustrate, probable cause is a fluid concept—turning on the assessment of probabilities in particular factual contexts—not readily, or even usefully, reduced to a neat set of legal rules. Informants' tips doubtless come in many shapes and sizes from many different types of persons. . . .

Moreover, the "two-pronged test" directs analysis into two largely independent channels—the informant's "veracity" or "reliability" and his "basis of knowledge." There are persuasive arguments against according these two elements such independent status. Instead, they are better understood as relevant considerations in the totality-of-the-circumstances analysis that traditionally has guided probable-cause determinations: a deficiency in one may be compensated for, in determining the overall reliability of a tip, by a strong showing as to the other, or by some other indicia of reliability. . . .

We . . . have recognized that affidavits "are normally drafted by nonlawyers in the midst and haste of a criminal investigation. Technical requirements of elaborate specificity once exacted under common law pleadings have no proper place in this area." . . . The rigorous inquiry into the *Spinelli* prongs and the complex superstructure of evidentiary and analytical rules that some have seen implicit in our *Spinelli* decision, cannot be

reconciled with the fact that many warrants are, quite properly, issued on the basis of nontechnical, commonsense judgments of laymen applying a standard less demanding than those used in more formal legal proceedings. Likewise, given the informal, often hurried context in which it must be applied, the "built-in subtleties" of the "two-pronged test" are particularly unlikely to assist magistrates in determining probable cause.

Similarly, we have repeatedly said that after-the-fact scrutiny by courts of the sufficiency of an affidavit should not take the form of *de novo* review. . . .

If the affidavits submitted by police officers are subjected to the type of scrutiny some courts have deemed appropriate, police might well resort to warrantless searches, with the hope of relying on consent or some other exception to the Warrant Clause that might develop at the time of the search. . . .

Finally, the direction taken by decisions following *Spinelli* poorly serves "the most basic function of any government": "to provide for the security of the individual and of his property." The strictures that inevitably accompany the "two-pronged test" cannot avoid seriously impeding the task of law enforcement. . . .

For all these reasons, we conclude that it is wiser to abandon the "two-pronged test" established by our decisions in *Aguilar* and *Spinelli*. In its place we reaffirm the totality-of-the-circumstances analysis that traditionally has informed probable-cause determinations. The task of the issuing magistrate is simply to make a practical, commonsense decision whether, given all the circumstances set forth in the affidavit before him, including the "veracity" and "basis of knowledge" of persons supplying hearsay information, there is a fair probability that contraband or evidence of a crime will be found in a particular place. And the duty of a reviewing court is simply to ensure that the magistrate had a "substantial basis for . . . concluding" that probable cause existed. We are convinced that this flexible, easily applied standard will better achieve the accommodation of public and private interests that the Fourth Amendment requires than does the approach that has developed from *Aguilar* and *Spinelli*. . . .

The showing of probable cause in the present case . . . [is] compelling. . . . Even standing alone, the facts obtained through the independent investigation of Mader and the DEA [Drug Enforcement Administration] at least suggested that the Gateses were involved in drug trafficking. In addition to being a popular vacation site, Florida is well-known as a source of narcotics and other illegal drugs. Lance Gates' flight to West Palm Beach, his brief, overnight stay in a motel, and apparent immediate return north to Chicago in the family car, conveniently awaiting him in West Palm Beach, is as suggestive of a prearranged drug run, as it is of an ordinary vacation trip.

In addition, the judge could rely on the anonymous letter, which had been corroborated in major part. . . . The corroboration of the letter's predictions that the Gateses' car would be in Florida, that Lance Gates would fly to Florida in the next day or so, and that he would drive the car north toward Bloomingdale all indicated, albeit not with certainty, that the informant's other assertions also were true. . . .

Finally, the anonymous letter contained a range of details relating not just to easily obtained facts and conditions existing at the time of the tip, but to future actions of third parties ordinarily not easily predicted. The letterwriter's accurate information as to the travel plans of each of the Gateses was of a character likely obtained only from the Gateses themselves, or from someone familiar with their not entirely ordinary travel plans. If the informant had access to accurate information of this type, a magistrate could properly conclude that it was not unlikely that he also had access to reliable information of the Gateses' alleged illegal activities. Of course, the Gateses' travel plans might have been learned from a talkative neighbor or travel agent; under the "two-pronged test" developed from *Spinelli,* the character of the details in the anonymous letter might well not permit a sufficiently clear inference regarding the letterwriter's "basis of knowledge." But, as discussed previously, probable cause does not demand the certainty we associate with formal trials. It is enough that there was a fair probability that the writer of the anonymous letter had obtained his entire story either from the Gateses or someone they trusted. And corroboration of major portions of the letter's predictions provides just this probability. It is apparent, therefore, that the judge issuing the warrant had a "substantial basis for . . . concluding" that probable cause to search the Gateses' home and car existed. The judgment of the Supreme Court of Illinois therefore must be

Reversed.

JUSTICE BRENNAN, with whom JUSTICE MARSHALL joins, dissenting.

I write separately to dissent from the Court's unjustified and ill-advised rejection of the two-prong test for evaluating the validity of a warrant based on hearsay announced in *Aguilar v. Texas* (1964) and refined in *Spinelli v. United States* (1969). . . .

The Court's complete failure to provide any persuasive reason for rejecting *Aguilar* and *Spinelli* doubtlessly reflects impatience with what it perceives to be "overly technical" rules governing searches and seizures under the Fourth Amendment. Words such as "practical," "nontechnical," and "common sense," as used in the Court's opinion, are but code words for an overly permissive attitude towards police practices in derogation of the rights secured by the Fourth Amendment. Everyone shares the Court's concern over the horrors of drug trafficking, but under our Constitution, only measures consistent with the Fourth Amendment may be employed by government to cure this evil. We must be ever mindful of Justice Stewart's admonition in *Coolidge v. New Hampshire* (1971): "[I]n times of unrest, whether caused by crime or racial conflict or fear of internal subversion, this basic law and the values that it represents may appear unrealistic or 'extravagant' to some. But the values were those of the authors of our fundamental constitutional concepts." . . .

Rights secured by the Fourth Amendment are particularly difficult to protect, because their "advocates are usually criminals." *Draper v. United States* [1959] (Douglas, J., dissenting). But the rules "we fashion [are] for the innocent and guilty alike." *Ibid.* By replacing *Aguilar* and *Spinelli* with a test that provides no assurance that magistrates, rather than the police, or informants, will make determinations of probable cause; imposes no structure on magistrates' probable-cause inquiries; and invites the possibility that intrusions may be justified on less than reliable information from an honest or credible person, today's decision threatens to "obliterate one of the most fundamental distinctions between our form of government, where officers are under the law, and the police-state, where they are the law." *Johnson v. United States* [1948].

The "totality-of-the-circumstances" standard established in *Illinois v. Gates* clearly facilitates police efforts to obtain search warrants. If convinced that probable cause to search exists, a judge may issue a warrant that specifically defines the area to be searched and the person or things to be seized. Police are authorized only to search the area described in the warrant. They may seize only things listed on the warrant, unless they find items whose very possession is a crime. Finally, police must execute the warrant in an orderly and timely fashion.[4] With these requirements met, the search and seizure are likely to be found reasonable.

---

4. See *Wilson v. Arkansas* (1995) and *Richards v. Wisconsin* (1997) for rules pertaining to the orderly execution of a search warrant.

Exceptions to the Warrant Requirement

Although warrants are the constitutionally preferred way for searches and seizures to be authorized, the search warrant procedure is cumbersome. It requires police to seek out and convince a judge that probable cause exists to justify a search and seizure. At times, adhering to such procedural requirements is not practical. The Supreme Court has recognized this fact and as a consequence has designated certain circumstances under which obtaining a warrant is not required. Here we discuss six such "exceptions" to the warrant requirement: (1) searches incident to a valid arrest, (2) searches to ensure that evidence is not lost, (3) searches based on consent, (4) searches to ensure the safety of the law enforcement official, (5) searches done in "hot pursuit," and (6) searches conducted under the plain view doctrine. Although these exceptions to the warrant requirement have expanded the authority of the police to search, the justices have placed constraints on each: the exceptions are limited in scope based on the initial justifications the Court used to create them.

As you read the material that follows, ask yourself these questions: Why did the Court create these exceptions to the warrant requirement? What are the limits placed on them? Do these exceptions maintain an appropriate balance between individual rights and the needs of law enforcement? And, most important, do these sometimes complex rules help define what constitutes a "reasonable" search? As Chief Justice John Roberts reminded us in **Brigham City v. Stuart** (2006), reasonableness is the "ultimate touchstone of the Fourth Amendment."

Searches Incident to a Valid Arrest. As a general principle of law, police may conduct a search when placing a suspect under a valid arrest. No search warrant is required. For example, if a law enforcement official checks a lawfully apprehended suspect for weapons, the officer is engaging in a search incident to a valid arrest. The Supreme Court has allowed such searches for two reasons: to remove weapons or other objects that might place the officer in danger or provide a means of escape, and to prevent the suspect from disposing of evidence.

The Court has imposed two types of limits—temporal and spatial—on searches incident to a valid arrest. The temporal limit means that police can conduct such a search only at the time of the arrest. If the

arresting officers forget to check something or someone at the time of arrest, they cannot later return to conduct a search unless they have some other authorization to do so. This rule makes sense in light of the original purposes for allowing searches incident to arrest: an individual can place a police officer in jeopardy or attempt escape at the time of an arrest, but these dangers do not exist once police remove the individual from the scene.

The spatial limitation means that searches made incident to a valid arrest may extend no farther than searching the arrested suspect and the area under the suspect's immediate control.[5] Such searches are allowed so that police can respond to any immediate threats to safety and security. They are not designed to be full, evidentiary searches such as those authorized by a warrant.

Loss of Evidence Searches. Police can conduct warrantless searches and seizures to prevent the loss of evidence. Frequently, officers come upon situations in which they must act quickly to preserve evidence that is in danger of being destroyed by, for example, a drug dealer about to flush narcotics down the toilet or an armed robber intent on throwing the weapon into the river. It would not be reasonable to require an officer faced with such a situation to find a judge to issue a search warrant. By the time the law enforcement official complied with this requirement, the evidence would be gone. Therefore, the Supreme Court has allowed police considerable latitude in acting without a warrant under such circumstances.

Like other searches and seizures, evidence-loss searches are limited: the search and seizure may extend no farther than necessary to preserve the evidence from loss or destruction. Searches justified under evidence-loss conditions may not be full evidence-seeking procedures; rather, they must focus exclusively on the evidence at risk.[6]

Consent Searches. As a rule, law enforcement officials can conduct warrantless searches upon consent. Like most general principles of law, however, the Court has placed constraints on such searches. To be considered valid, consent searches must satisfy two criteria. First, permission to search must be given freely and voluntarily. Second, the individual granting consent must have the authority to do so.

---

5. ***Chimel v. California*** (1969).

6. ***Cupp v. Murphy*** (1973).

The requirement that consent to a search be voluntary means that permission cannot be coerced. If police engage in actual or threatened physical violence to obtain permission, the search fails the voluntary consent requirement. In addition, consent is not considered valid if the police lie or use trickery to extract permission.[7] The second requirement restricts the number of people who are legally eligible to authorize a police search. The owner-occupant of a house, for example, has the authority to allow police to enter the home and search it. Similar authority extends to the person who leases an apartment, the proprietor of a shop, or the driver of an automobile. In each of these cases, the person has legal control over the area and can grant permission for a search.[8]

If consent is voluntarily given by a person with apparent authority, police may search without first obtaining a warrant. However, the search may extend only so far as the permission grant allows.

Safety Searches. The decisions of the Supreme Court have recognized that in the conduct of their duties police frequently find themselves in dangerous situations. What action may a police officer take in confronting a person who may pose a danger to the officer or the public? Suppose the officer believes that a suspicious person may be armed, but none of the conditions justifying a search and seizure is present—that is, no warrant, insufficient evidence to justify an arrest, no consent, and so on. The response of the Court has been to allow safety searches.

Under the Court's safety search rulings, a police officer may stop and pat down a suspect in a criminal case whom the police believe poses a danger in order to find and remove any weapons. According to the Court, for such searches to be valid, two conditions must be met. First, police must have reasonable suspicion to believe that the person is involved in criminal activity; and second, they must also have cause to believe the person is armed and dangerous. Such searches are

limited to removing the danger. As a consequence, the officer may not probe beyond a place where a hidden weapon is likely to be.[9]

Hot Pursuit. Suppose a police officer observes the robbery of a jewelry store and chases the fleeing robber.[10] The running suspect enters a house. Must the police officer pursuing the suspect obtain a warrant to enter the building? As a general rule of law, the answer is no, and the reason is that the Supreme Court has carved out yet another exception to the Fourth Amendment's warrant requirement: "hot pursuit." In other words, the Court has said that it would be reasonable for the police officer to enter the house without a search warrant because evidence could be destroyed and lives could be endangered. And if the officer were to find evidence of a crime—for example, jewelry that was taken from the store—under the hot pursuit exception, the evidence could be used against the defendant.

As with all other exceptions to the warrant requirement, the Court has placed limits on the hot pursuit exception—limits that, as always, reflect the original rationale for the exception. Granting police the power to engage in hot pursuit is based on the unusual circumstances the officers face: that the suspect will evade arrest, that evidence will be lost, and that the fleeing suspect will pose a threat to innocent people. These exigencies justify a warrantless search and seizure.[11] But the search must focus only on the apprehension of the fleeing suspect.

Plain View Doctrine. Our discussion so far has described circumstances under which police may search and the guidelines the Court has established to determine reasonableness. Under each justification for a search there are limitations: searches based on a warrant must be confined to the place specified in the document; consent searches may go no farther than the grant of permission stipulates; and safety searches can extend only far enough to discover or remove the possible danger. But what if, while conducting a valid search, police come upon incriminating evidence not covered by the search warrant? For example, suppose law enforcement officials have a warrant to search a

---

7. *Bumper v. North Carolina* (1968).

8. The Court has often dealt with issues arising from situations in which multiple individuals have legal authority over a residence. Generally the Court has held that a co-occupant or a person police reasonably believe to be a co-occupant may give consent to search the residence (*United States v. Matlock,* 1974; *Illinois v. Rodriguez,* 1990). That permission may be negated, however, if another co-occupant is physically present and expressly refuses to consent (**Georgia v. Randolph**, 2006).

9. *Terry v. Ohio* (1968); *Adams v. Williams* (1972).

10. We adopt this discussion from Marvin Zalman and Larry Siegel, *Criminal Procedure,* 2nd ed. (St. Paul, MN: West, 1997), 284–285.

11. **Warden v. Hayden** (1967).

house for stolen goods, and while executing the warrant they see illegal drugs in the house. What should they do? Must they ignore the contraband, or can they seize it? These questions are addressed by the plain view doctrine, a controversial rule that expands the powers of police to gather evidence. This doctrine holds that if police officers are lawfully present in a place and contraband is openly visible there, the officers may seize it without any additional authorization.

Some analysts refer to the plain view doctrine as yet another exception to the Fourth Amendment's warrant requirement. This interpretation is reasonable because the doctrine gives police freedom to seize contraband and other evidence of a crime without having a warrant authorizing them to seize those specific items. Nevertheless, police must first be acting lawfully when any seizable items come into plain view.[12] Accordingly, the plain view doctrine often comes into play when a warrant has been issued for other purposes or after some other warrant exception has first been invoked. Imagine that two officers come to a student's apartment door and the student allows them to enter. Walking into the living room, police spot marijuana on a table. Under the plain view doctrine, the officers could seize the marijuana because the student *consented* to the entry. Had the student denied the officers permission and they entered anyway, the plain view doctrine would not apply unless the officers had a search warrant or some other legitimate reason for entering the apartment.

Places Searched

Americans value their privacy, but in some areas of their lives they have greater objections to government intrusion than in others. Consequently, in the course of developing its search and seizure jurisprudence, the Supreme Court has recognized that not all places merit the same degree of constitutional protection. Undoubtedly we have the highest levels of privacy expectations over our bodies and our homes. Here we tolerate invasive government activity only when it is highly justified. The Court has acknowledged this societal value by applying the most exacting scrutiny to law enforcement searches of our persons and our residences.

At the other end of the continuum are certain contexts and places where our expectations of privacy are quite low. The Supreme Court has identified several of these and has developed rules that allow law enforcement much greater latitude by reducing the level of

justification necessary for a search or eliminating warrant requirements altogether. For example, the Court has long adhered to an "open field" exception, holding that police need little justification to search on tracts of undeveloped land, even if privately owned.[13] Prisoners and their cells may be searched without a warrant or other justification because of the nature of the institution and the need for tight security.[14] Police may examine discarded garbage without a warrant because the owner has given up any ownership rights over it.[15] In the remaining portions of this section, we give special attention to two of the places that merit lower levels of Fourth Amendment protection: automobiles and public schools.

From its very first car search case, ***Carroll v. United States (1925)***, the Court has held that automobiles do not deserve the same degree of protection as people and homes. In general, the Court has given the police broad authority to search cars without warrants because (1) cars are mobile, and thus evidence can quickly be removed from the area under investigation; (2) automobile windows allow outsiders to look in, and thus drivers have a lower expectation of privacy inside a car than they do in their homes; and (3) the government has a pervasive interest in regulating cars.

Even though the rule that automobiles deserve little constitutional protection from warrantless searches was well established, the Court was confronted with many car search questions beginning in the 1970s. How far may such searches extend? May police search only the area where driver and passengers sit? What about the glove compartment and trunk? Are luggage and other containers in a car fair game? What degree of justification or cause do law enforcement officials need before they can conduct warrantless searches of cars? If an automobile is impounded, may police search and inventory the contents? In general, the justices have been rather unsympathetic to claims of constitutional protection when automobiles are searched and evidence of a crime found.[16] Table 11-1 provides several examples of this "automobile exception."

---

12. ***Arizona v. Hicks*** (1987).

13. *Oliver v. United States* (1984).

14. *Hudson v. Palmer* (1984).

15. ***California v. Greenwood*** (1988).

16. This is not to say that the Court always decides in favor of law enforcement in automobile search cases. In *Knowles v. Iowa* (1998), for example, the justices held that a routine traffic stop culminating in the issuing of a citation is insufficient to justify a full search of the car. Prior to this decision, the laws of many states assumed that the "search incident to a lawful arrest" rules applied to traffic stops.

TABLE 11-1   Examples of the Automobile Exception

CASE	FACTS	RULING
Carroll v. United States (1925)	Federal agents suspect individuals are transporting illegal liquor. They stop and search car, finding evidence of the crime.	Automobiles merit low levels of protection. Their mobility often makes obtaining a search warrant impractical.
Chambers v. Maroney (1970)	Robbery suspects are pulled over and arrested. Their impounded automobile is searched and evidence is found in trunk.	To secure its contents, protect against liability claims, and remove any potential dangers, police may conduct an inventory search of an impounded automobile when its occupants have been arrested.
New York v. Belton (1981)	Police stop a car for speeding. The officer smells marijuana, arrests the suspects, and searches the car, finding cocaine in the zipped pocket of a jacket in the backseat.	After police have made a lawful arrest of an occupant of an automobile, they may search, incident to the arrest, the entire passenger compartment and the contents of any container therein.
United States v. Ross (1982)	Based on a reliable informant's tip that he sold drugs out of his car trunk, police stop Ross. They search the car, finding a pistol in the glove compartment and illegal drugs contained in a brown paper bag in the trunk.	With probable cause police may search every part of a vehicle and any contents that may conceal the object of the search.
Michigan State Police v. Sitz (1990)	Police stop all passing cars pursuant to a sobriety checkpoint program.	Brief stops, where police do not use discretion to determine who will be stopped, reasonably advance the state's interest in preventing drunk driving.
California v. Acevedo (1991)	Police observe a suspect leaving a house with a package they have reason to believe contains marijuana. The suspect places a package in the trunk of the car. The police stop the car, open the trunk, and seize the evidence.	Police may search an automobile and the containers within it where they have probable cause to believe contraband or evidence is contained.
Whren v. United States (1996)	After stopping a driver for a traffic violation, police observe and seize two plastic bags of what appears to be cocaine in the passenger's hands.	There was probable cause for the traffic stop, allowing the police to observe what appeared to be illegal drugs. Seizure is valid.
Wyoming v. Houghton (1999)	A police officer stops a car for a faulty brake light and sees a hypodermic syringe in the driver's pocket. The driver admits to drug use. The officer searches the car and finds illegal drugs in a passenger's purse.	If probable cause justifies a search of a lawfully stopped vehicle, it justifies the search of every part of the vehicle and every article or container therein that might conceal the object of the search.
United States v. Arvizu (2002)	A border patrol agent stops a vehicle with a driver acting suspiciously on a remote road commonly used by smugglers to avoid a border patrol checkpoint. A search of the vehicle yields more than one hundred pounds of marijuana.	The officer's reasonable suspicion of criminal activity was sufficient to justify the stop and search. The Court allows law enforcement greater latitude when they are protecting our national borders.
Illinois v. Lidster (2004)	Seeking an unknown hit-and-run driver, police set up a checkpoint to stop drivers and ask if they have any relevant information about the crime. One of those stopped is clearly driving under the influence of alcohol and is arrested.	Informational checkpoint stops do not violate the Fourth Amendment.

Cases involving car searches continue to appear on the Court's docket, and they present issues that tend to divide the justices. Consider, for example, the case of *Arizona v. Gant* (2009). As you read the opinions notice how the Court applies the "search incident to a valid arrest" exception to the warrant requirement along with the low levels of expected privacy that apply to automobiles. Note also the concerns expressed by the justices about creating a rule that can be effectively applied by police and lower court judges.

Arizona v. Gant

556 U.S. 332 (2009)
http://laws.findlaw.com/US/000/07-542.html
Vote: 5 (Ginsburg, Scalia, Souter, Stevens, Thomas)
    4 (Alito, Breyer, Kennedy, Roberts)
OPINION OF THE COURT: *Stevens*
CONCURRING OPINION: *Scalia*
DISSENTING OPINIONS: *Alito, Breyer*

FACTS:

On August 25, 1999, acting on an anonymous tip that a residence on North Walnut Avenue was being used to sell drugs, Tucson police officers Griffith and Reed went to the house. Rodney Gant answered their knock. He identified himself and told the officers that the owner was not present but was expected to return later. After leaving the house, Griffith and Reed checked police records and discovered that Gant had an outstanding warrant for driving with a suspended license.

The two officers, soon joined by a third, returned to the house that evening. They saw a man near the back of the house and a woman in a car parked in front of the house. They arrested the man for providing a false name and the woman for possession of drug paraphernalia. Both were handcuffed and secured in separate patrol cars. About that time, a car entered the house's driveway and the officers recognized Gant as the driver. As Gant got out of his car, Officer Griffith called out to him. Gant and Griffith walked toward each other and met about 10–12 feet away from Gant's parked car. Griffith immediately placed Gant under arrest on the suspended license violation and handcuffed him. Because the other two suspects were secured in the only two patrol cars available, Griffith called for backup. When two more officers arrived, they locked Gant in the backseat of their car.

After Gant was secured in the patrol car, two officers searched his car. One of the officers found a gun and the other discovered a bag of cocaine in the pocket of a jacket in the backseat. Gant was then charged with drug violations. Gant's attorneys claimed that the evidence should be suppressed because police had conducted a warrantless search in violation of the Fourth Amendment. The state maintained that the passenger compartment of a vehicle could be searched without a warrant "incident to the arrest" of the vehicle's recent occupant. The trial court judge agreed with the government and allowed the evidence to be used. Gant was convicted and sentenced to three years in prison, but the Arizona Supreme Court reversed.

ARGUMENTS:

For the petitioner, State of Arizona:

- *New York v. Belton* (1981) established a bright-line rule that police may search the passenger compartment of an automobile after arresting the automobile's occupant. Such searches do not require a demonstrated threat to officer safety or the need to preserve evidence.
- This rule was reaffirmed in *Thornton v. United States* (2004) and should not be disturbed.
- The *Belton* rule correctly balances the individual's privacy interests and the government's interest in officer safety and evidence preservation. *Belton* brings certainty and clarity to this difficult area of Fourth Amendment law. Police need bright-line rules to guide them in the field.

For the respondent, Rodney Joseph Gant:

- To be constitutional, warrantless searches incident to arrest can take place only if they are designed either to (1) preserve evidence of a crime or (2) remove any weapons the arrested person might use to resist or escape. These requirements were established in *Chimel v. California* (1969).
- Such searches are limited to the area under the suspect's immediate control. If at the time of the search the suspect cannot conceivably access the place to be searched, the area may not lawfully be searched.
- Gant was handcuffed and secured in the backseat of a patrol car when his own car was searched, so he could not have accessed a weapon or evidence located in his car. In addition, Gant was arrested for a driving offense for which no evidence needed to be secured.
- To the extent that *New York v. Belton* (1981) is interpreted as authorizing the police to search a car whenever the arrestee was a recent occupant, that interpretation should be reevaluated.

▶ JUSTICE STEVENS DELIVERED THE OPINION OF THE COURT.

Consistent with our precedent, our analysis begins, as it should in every case addressing the reasonableness of a warrantless search, with the basic rule that "searches conducted outside the judicial process, without prior approval by judge or magistrate, are *per se* unreasonable under the Fourth Amendment—subject only to a few specifically established and well-delineated exceptions." *Katz v. United States* (1967). Among the exceptions to the warrant requirement is a search incident to a lawful arrest. The exception derives from interests in officer safety and evidence preservation that are typically implicated in arrest situations. In *Chimel [v. California* (1969)], we held that a search incident to arrest may only include "the arrestee's person and the area 'within his immediate control'—construing that phrase to mean the area from within which he might gain possession of a weapon or destructible evidence." That limitation, which continues to define the boundaries of the exception, ensures that the scope of a search incident to arrest is commensurate with its purposes of protecting arresting officers and safeguarding any evidence of the offense of arrest that an arrestee might conceal or destroy. If there is no possibility that an arrestee could reach into the area that law enforcement officers seek to search, both justifications for the search-incident-to-arrest exception are absent and the rule does not apply.

In [*New York v.*] *Belton* (1981), we considered *Chimel*'s application to the automobile context. A lone police officer in that case stopped a speeding car in which Belton was one of four occupants. While asking for the driver's license and registration, the officer smelled burnt marijuana and observed an envelope on the car floor marked "Supergold"—a name he associated with marijuana. Thus having probable cause to believe the occupants had committed a drug offense, the officer ordered them out of the vehicle, placed them under arrest, and patted them down. Without handcuffing the arrestees, the officer "'split them up into four separate areas of the Thruway . . . so they would not be in physical touching area of each other'" and searched the vehicle, including the pocket of a jacket on the backseat, in which he found cocaine. . . .

. . . [W]e held that when an officer lawfully arrests "the occupant of an automobile, he may, as a contemporaneous incident of that arrest, search the passenger compartment of the automobile" and any containers therein. That holding was based in large part on our assumption "that articles inside the relatively narrow compass of the passenger compartment of an automobile are in fact generally, even if not inevitably, within 'the area into which an arrestee might reach.'"

The Arizona Supreme Court . . . concluded that the search of Gant's car was unreasonable because Gant clearly could not have accessed his car at the time of the search. It also found that no other exception to the warrant requirement applied in this case. . . .

Despite the textual and evidentiary support for the Arizona Supreme Court's reading of *Belton,* our opinion has been widely understood to allow a vehicle search incident to the arrest of a recent occupant even if there is no possibility the arrestee could gain access to the vehicle at the time of the search. This reading may be attributable to Justice Brennan's dissent in *Belton,* in which he characterized the Court's holding as resting on the "fiction . . . that the interior of a car is *always* within the immediate control of an arrestee who has recently been in the car." Under the majority's approach, he argued, "the result would presumably be the same even if [the officer] had handcuffed Belton and his companions in the patrol car" before conducting the search. Since we decided *Belton,* Courts of Appeals have given different answers to the question whether a vehicle must be within an arrestee's reach to justify a vehicle search incident to arrest, but Justice Brennan's reading of the Court's opinion has predominated. . . . Indeed, some courts have upheld searches under *Belton* "even when . . . the handcuffed arrestee has already left the scene."

Under this broad reading of *Belton,* a vehicle search would be authorized incident to every arrest of a recent occupant notwithstanding that in most cases the vehicle's passenger compartment will not be within the arrestee's reach at the time of the search. To read *Belton* as authorizing a vehicle search incident to every recent occupant's arrest would thus untether the rule from the justifications underlying the *Chimel* exception—a result clearly incompatible with our statement in *Belton* that it "in no way alters the fundamental principles established in the *Chimel* case regarding the basic scope of searches incident to lawful custodial arrests. Accordingly, we reject this reading of *Belton* and hold that the *Chimel* rationale authorizes police to search a vehicle incident to a recent occupant's arrest only when the arrestee is unsecured and within reaching distance of the passenger compartment at the time of the search.

Although it does not follow from *Chimel,* we also conclude that circumstances unique to the vehicle context justify a search incident to a lawful arrest when it is "reasonable to believe evidence relevant to the crime of arrest might be found in the vehicle." In many cases, as when a recent occupant is arrested for a traffic violation, there will be no reasonable basis to believe the vehicle contains relevant evidence. But in others, including *Belton* and *Thornton* [v. *United States* (2004)], the offense of arrest will supply a basis for searching the passenger compartment of an arrestee's vehicle and any containers therein.

Neither the possibility of access nor the likelihood of discovering offense-related evidence authorized the search in this case. Unlike in *Belton,* which involved a single officer confronted with four unsecured arrestees, the five officers in this case outnumbered the three arrestees, all of whom had been handcuffed and secured in separate patrol cars before the officers searched Gant's car. Under those circumstances, Gant clearly was not within reaching distance of his car at the time of the search. An evidentiary basis for the search was also lacking in this case. Whereas Belton and Thornton were arrested for drug offenses, Gant was arrested for driving with a suspended license—an offense for which police could not expect to find evidence in the passenger compartment of Gant's car. Because police could not reasonably have believed either that Gant could have accessed his car at the time of the search or that evidence of the offense for which he was arrested might have been found therein, the search in this case was unreasonable. . . .

We have never relied on *stare decisis* to justify the continuance of an unconstitutional police practice. And we would be particularly loath to uphold an unconstitutional result in a case that is so easily distinguished from the decisions that arguably compel it. The safety and evidentiary interests that supported the search in *Belton* simply are not present in this case. Indeed, it is hard to imagine two cases that are factually more distinct, as *Belton* involved one officer confronted by four unsecured arrestees suspected of committing a drug offense and this case involves several officers confronted with a securely detained arrestee apprehended for driving with a suspended license. This case is also distinguishable from *Thornton,* in which the petitioner was arrested for a drug offense. . . .

Police may search a vehicle incident to a recent occupant's arrest only if the arrestee is within reaching distance of the passenger compartment at the time of the search or it is reasonable to believe the vehicle contains evidence of the offense of arrest. When these justifications are absent, a search of an arrestee's vehicle will be unreasonable unless police obtain a warrant or show that another exception to the warrant requirement applies. The Arizona Supreme Court correctly held that this case involved an unreasonable search. Accordingly, the judgment of the State Supreme Court is affirmed.

It is so ordered.

JUSTICE SCALIA, concurring.

. . . It is abundantly clear that [traditional] standards [of reasonableness] do not justify what I take to be the rule set forth in *New York v. Belton* (1981), and *Thornton*: that arresting officers may always search an arrestee's vehicle in order to protect themselves from hidden weapons. When an arrest is made in connection with a roadside stop, police virtually always have a less intrusive and more effective means of ensuring their safety—and a means that is virtually always employed: ordering the arrestee away from the vehicle, patting him down in the open, handcuffing him, and placing him in the squad car.

Law enforcement officers face a risk of being shot whenever they pull a car over. But that risk is at its height at the time of the initial confrontation; and it is *not at all* reduced by allowing a search of the stopped vehicle after the driver has been arrested and placed in the squad car. . . .

. . . In my view we should simply abandon the *Belton-Thornton* charade of officer safety and overrule those cases. I would hold that a vehicle search incident to arrest is *ipso facto* "reasonable" only when the object of the search is evidence of the crime for which the arrest was made, or of another crime that the officer has probable cause to believe occurred. Because respondent was arrested for driving without a license (a crime for which no evidence could be expected to be found in the vehicle), I would hold in the present case that the search was unlawful. . . .

JUSTICE BREYER, dissenting.

I agree with JUSTICE ALITO that *New York v. Belton* (1981), is best read as setting forth a bright line rule that permits a warrantless search of the passenger compartment of an automobile incident to the lawful arrest of an occupant—regardless of the danger the arrested individual in fact poses. I also agree with JUSTICE STEVENS, however, that the rule can produce results divorced from its underlying Fourth Amendment rationale. For that reason I would look for a better rule—were the question before us one of first impression.

The matter, however, is not one of first impression, and that fact makes a substantial difference. The *Belton* rule has been followed not only by this Court in *Thornton v. United States* (2004), but also by numerous other courts. Principles of *stare decisis* must apply, and those who wish this Court to change a well-established legal precedent—where, as here, there has been considerable reliance on the legal rule in question—bear a heavy burden. I have not found that burden met. Nor do I believe that the other considerations ordinarily relevant when determining whether to overrule a case are satisfied. I consequently join JUSTICE ALITO's dissenting opinion. . . .

JUSTICE ALITO, with whom THE CHIEF JUSTICE and JUSTICE KENNEDY join, and with whom JUSTICE BREYER joins . . . .

Twenty-eight years ago, in *New York v. Belton* (1981), this Court held that "when a policeman has made a lawful custodial arrest of the occupant of an automobile, he may, as a contemporaneous incident of that arrest, search the passenger compartment of that automobile." Five years ago, in *Thornton v. United States* (2004)—a case involving a situation not materially distinguishable from the situation here—the Court not only reaffirmed but extended the holding of *Belton,* making it applicable to recent occupants. Today's decision effectively overrules those important decisions, even though respondent Gant has not asked us to do so.

To take the place of the overruled precedents, the Court adopts a new two-part rule under which a police officer who arrests a vehicle occupant or recent occupant may search the passenger compartment if (1) the arrestee is within reaching distance of the vehicle at the time of the search or (2) the officer has reason to believe that the vehicle contains evidence of the offense of arrest. The first part of this new rule may endanger arresting officers. . . . The second part of the new rule is taken from JUSTICE SCALIA's separate opinion in *Thornton* without any independent explanation of its origin or justification and is virtually certain to confuse law enforcement officers and judges for some time to come. The Court's decision will cause the suppression of evidence gathered in many searches carried out in good-faith reliance on well-settled case law, and although the Court purports to base its analysis on the landmark decision in *Chimel v. California* (1969), the Court's reasoning undermines *Chimel.* I would follow *Belton,* and I therefore respectfully dissent.

The majority opinion in *Gant* rigorously applies the requirement in *Chimel* that a search incident to a valid arrest can extend only to the area under the arrested suspect's immediate control. Therefore, once a suspect has been secured and placed in a patrol car, a search of his vehicle is no longer justified on that basis. However, the Court also recognizes the "circumstances unique to the vehicle context" by allowing searches of the automobile after arrest and without warrant, if it is reasonable to believe that the car contains evidence associated with the offense upon which the arrest is based.

Public schools are also places meriting low levels of constitutional protection. The main case in this area is *New Jersey v. T.L.O.* (1985), a case involving a fourteen-year-old high school freshman. T.L.O. (the full names of minors are frequently not used in court cases) and a friend were suspected of smoking in the girls' bathroom. T.L.O. was brought into the office of the assistant vice principal, where she denied the school offense. The vice principal demanded to see her purse, and when she gave it to him, he opened it and saw a packet of cigarettes inside. When he reached into the purse to remove the cigarettes, he found cigarette rolling papers, a pipe, a small amount of marijuana, and other items that suggested drug use and distribution. The case was turned over to the police. In juvenile court T.L.O. moved to suppress the evidence, claiming an unconstitutional search.

The U.S. Supreme Court ruled that the search was reasonable under the Fourth Amendment. In doing so the justices balanced the student's need for individual privacy against the school's interests in maintaining order, safety, and a proper educational environment. The Court concluded that in the public school context, warrantless searches do not require probable cause, but only a reasonable suspicion that the student is violating the law or school rules. However, the Court admonished that the reasonableness of school searches also depends on the age and gender of the student being searched. In subsequent cases, the Court used the *T.L.O.* rationale to uphold warrantless, suspicionless drug testing of high school athletes[17] as well as drug testing of students involved in other forms of extracurricular activities.[18]

In 2009 the question of student searches returned to the Court. This time a more controversial subject was the focus of the Court's attention. *Safford Unified School District #1 v. Redding* involved the strip searching of students suspected of possessing and distributing drugs. As you read this case, see how the justices apply reasonableness standards to school searches, express sympathy for bodily privacy concerns, and emphasize the age and gender of the student searched. Also, note the dissenting views of Justice Thomas, whose opinion supporting school discipline is similar

---

17. ***Vernonia School District 47J v. Acton*** (1995).

18. *Board of Education of Pottawatomie County v. Earls* (2002).

to his minority position in the "Bong Hits 4 Jesus" case of *Morse v. Frederick* discussed in Chapter 5.

Safford Unified School District #1 v. Redding

557 U.S. 364 (2009)
http://laws.findlaw.com/US/000/08-479.html
Vote: 8 (Alito, Breyer, Ginsburg, Kennedy, Roberts, Scalia, Souter, Stevens)
    1 (Thomas)

OPINION OF THE COURT: *Souter*
OPINIONS CONCURRING IN PART AND DISSENTING IN PART:
    Ginsburg, Stevens
OPINION CONCURRING IN JUDGMENT IN PART AND DISSENTING IN PART: *Thomas*

FACTS:

On October 8, 2003, Savana Redding, a thirteen-year-old student at Safford (Arizona) Middle School, was called away from her mathematics class by Assistant Principal Kerry Wilson. In Wilson's office Redding was shown an unzipped day planner containing several knives, lighters, a permanent marker, and a cigarette. Redding admitted that the day planner was hers but claimed that she had lent it to a friend, Marissa Glines, a few days earlier. Redding said that none of the articles belonged to her. Wilson then showed Redding four white prescription-strength ibuprofen pills and one over-the-counter blue naproxen pill and told her that he had received a report that she was giving pills to fellow students who were going to take them at lunchtime. Redding denied the

Savana Redding stands outside the Supreme Court on April 21, 2009, the day of oral arguments on her claim that six years earlier Arizona school officials violated her constitutional rights by subjecting her to a strip search for suspected drugs.

charge and agreed to let Wilson search her belongings. Wilson and administrative assistant Helen Romero searched Redding's backpack, finding nothing.

Wilson then instructed Romero to take Redding to the school nurse's office to search her clothes for pills. Romero and the nurse, Peggy Schwallier, asked Redding to remove her jacket, socks, and shoes, leaving her in stretch pants and a T-shirt (both without pockets), which she was then asked to remove. Finally, Redding was told to pull her bra out and to the side and shake it, and to pull out the elastic on her underpants, thus exposing her breasts and pelvic area to some degree. No pills were found.

April Redding, Savana's mother, filed suit against the school district, Wilson, Romero, and Schwallier. She requested monetary damages from the defendants for conducting a strip search of her daughter in violation of the Fourth Amendment. The federal district court found no constitutional violation. However, the Ninth Circuit Court of Appeals reversed, holding that Redding's right to personal privacy was unreasonably violated by the strip search. The Supreme Court considered the issue of the reasonableness of the search as well as the question of whether the individual school officials were immune from civil liability in such cases. The excerpt that appears below focuses on the question of the constitutionality of the search.

ARGUMENTS:

**For the petitioners, Safford Unified
School District #1, et al.:**

- Searches of students in public schools do not require probable cause, but only reasonable suspicion (*New Jersey v. T.L.O.*).
- The search was valid from its inception because there were reasonable grounds to believe that Redding was violating the school's drug policy.
- Given the places where pills can be hidden, the scope of the search was reasonable and extended no farther than necessary. The search was brief and conducted in private by female school officials. Redding was not touched during the search.
- The drugs that were the object of this search posed an immediate danger since officials had information that students were going to take the pills at lunchtime.

For the respondent, April Redding:

- The information available to school officials would not give them reasonable suspicion to believe that Redding was hiding pills in her undergarments.

- The student who supplied key information lacked credibility.
- The search was invasive, degrading, and traumatizing, and far more extensive in scope than the circumstances warranted.
- The amount of justification required for a student search should depend on the extensiveness of the search. Greater justification is necessary for a strip search than a backpack search.

JUSTICE SOUTER DELIVERED THE OPINION OF THE COURT.

The issue here is whether a 13-year-old student's Fourth Amendment right was violated when she was subjected to a search of her bra and underpants by school officials acting on reasonable suspicion that she had brought forbidden prescription and over-the-counter drugs to school. Because there were no reasons to suspect the drugs presented a danger or were concealed in her underwear, we hold that the search did violate the Constitution. . . .

The Fourth Amendment "right of the people to be secure in their persons . . . against unreasonable searches and seizures" generally requires a law enforcement officer to have probable cause for conducting a search. . . .

In [*New Jersey v.*] *T. L. O.* [1985], we recognized that the school setting "requires some modification of the level of suspicion of illicit activity needed to justify a search" and held that for searches by school officials "a careful balancing of governmental and private interests suggests that the public interest is best served by a Fourth Amendment standard of reasonableness that stops short of probable cause." We have thus applied a standard of reasonable suspicion to determine the legality of a school administrator's search of a student and have held that a school search "will be permissible in its scope when the measures adopted are reasonably related to the objectives of the search and not excessively intrusive in light of the age and sex of the student and the nature of the infraction."

A number of our cases on probable cause have an implicit bearing on the reliable knowledge element of reasonable suspicion. . . . At the end of the day, however, we have realized that these factors cannot rigidly control, *Illinois v. Gates* (1983), and we have come back to saying that the standards are "fluid concepts that take their substantive content from the particular contexts" in which they are being assessed.

Perhaps the best that can be said generally about the required knowledge component of probable cause for a law enforcement officer's evidence search is that it raise a "fair probability" or a "substantial chance" of discovering evidence of criminal activity. The lesser standard for school searches could as readily be described as a moderate chance of finding evidence of wrongdoing.

In this case, the school's policies strictly prohibit the nonmedical use, possession, or sale of any drug on school grounds, including "[a]ny prescription or over-the-counter drug, except those for which permission to use in school has been granted pursuant to Board policy." A week before Savana was searched, another student, Jordan Romero (no relation of the school's administrative assistant), told the principal and Assistant Principal Wilson that "certain students were bringing drugs and weapons on campus," and that he had been sick after taking some pills that "he got from a classmate." On the morning of October 8, the same boy handed Wilson a white pill that he said Marissa Glines had given him. He told Wilson that students were planning to take the pills at lunch.

Wilson learned from Peggy Schwallier, the school nurse, that the pill was Ibuprofen 400 mg, available only by prescription. Wilson then called Marissa out of class. Outside the classroom, Marissa's teacher handed Wilson the day planner, found within Marissa's reach, containing various contraband items. Wilson escorted Marissa back to his office.

In the presence of Helen Romero, Wilson requested Marissa to turn out her pockets and open her wallet. Marissa produced a blue pill, several white ones, and a razor blade. Wilson asked where the blue pill came from, and Marissa answered, "I guess it slipped in when she gave me the IBU 400s." When Wilson asked whom she meant, Marissa replied, "Savana Redding." Wilson then enquired about the day planner and its contents; Marissa denied knowing anything about them. Wilson did not ask Marissa any followup questions to determine whether there was any likelihood that Savana presently had pills: neither asking when Marissa received the pills from Savana nor where Savana might be hiding them.

Schwallier did not immediately recognize the blue pill, but information provided through a poison control hotline indicated that the pill was a 200-mg dose of an antiinflammatory drug, generically called naproxen, available over the counter. At Wilson's direction, Marissa was then subjected to a search of her bra and underpants by Romero and Schwallier, as Savana was later on. The search revealed no additional pills.

It was at this juncture that Wilson called Savana into his office and showed her the day planner. Their conversation established that Savana and Marissa were on friendly terms: while she denied knowledge of the contraband, Savana admitted that the day planner was hers and that she had lent it to Marissa. Wilson had other reports of their friendship from staff members, who had identified Savana and Marissa as part of an unusually rowdy group at the school's opening dance in August, during which alcohol and cigarettes were found in the girls' bathroom. Wilson had reason to connect the girls with this contraband, for Wilson knew that Jordan Romero had told the principal that before the dance, he had been at a party at Savana's house where alcohol was served. Marissa's statement that the pills came from Savana was thus sufficiently plausible to warrant suspicion that Savana was involved in pill distribution.

This suspicion of Wilson's was enough to justify a search of Savana's backpack and outer clothing. If a student is reasonably suspected of giving out contraband pills, she is reasonably suspected of carrying them on her person and in the carryall that has become an item of student uniform in most places today. If Wilson's reasonable suspicion of pill distribution were not understood to support searches of outer clothes and backpack, it would not justify any search worth making. And the look into Savana's bag, in her presence and in the relative privacy of Wilson's office, was not excessively intrusive, any more than Romero's subsequent search of her outer clothing.

Here it is that the parties part company, with Savana's claim that extending the search at Wilson's behest to the point of making her pull out her underwear was constitutionally unreasonable. The exact label for this final step in the intrusion is not important, though strip search is a fair way to speak of it. Romero and Schwallier directed Savana to remove her clothes down to her underwear, and then "pull out" her bra and the elastic band on her underpants. Although Romero and Schwallier stated that they did not see anything when Savana followed their instructions, we would not define strip search and its Fourth Amendment consequences in a way that would guarantee litigation about who was looking and how much was seen. The very fact of Savana's pulling her underwear away from her body in the presence of the two officials who were able to see her necessarily exposed her breasts and pelvic area to some degree, and both subjective and reasonable societal expectations of personal privacy support the treatment of such a search as categorically distinct, requiring distinct elements of justification on the part of school authorities for going beyond a search of outer clothing and belongings.

Savana's subjective expectation of privacy against such a search is inherent in her account of it as embarrassing, frightening, and humiliating. The reasonableness of her expectation (required by the Fourth Amendment standard) is indicated by the consistent experiences of other young people similarly searched, whose adolescent vulnerability intensifies the patent intrusiveness of the exposure. The common reaction of these adolescents simply registers the obviously different meaning of a search exposing the body from the experience of nakedness or near undress in other school circumstances. Changing for gym is getting ready for play; exposing for a search is responding to an accusation reserved for suspected wrongdoers and fairly understood as so degrading that a number of communities have decided that strip searches in schools are never reasonable and have banned them no matter what the facts may be.

The indignity of the search does not, of course, outlaw it, but it does implicate the rule of reasonableness as stated in *T. L. O.,* that "the search as actually conducted [be] reasonably related in scope to the circumstances which justified the interference in the first place." The scope will be permissible, that is, when it is "not excessively intrusive in light of the age and sex of the student and the nature of the infraction."

Here, the content of the suspicion failed to match the degree of intrusion. Wilson knew beforehand that the pills were prescription-strength ibuprofen and over-the-counter naproxen, common pain relievers equivalent to two Advil, or one Aleve. He must have been aware of the nature and limited threat of the specific drugs he was searching for, and while just about anything can be taken in quantities that will do real harm, Wilson had no reason to suspect that large amounts of the drugs were being passed around, or that individual students were receiving great numbers of pills.

Nor could Wilson have suspected that Savana was hiding common painkillers in her underwear. Petitioners suggest, as a truth universally acknowledged, that "students . . . hid[e] contraband in or under their clothing," and cite a smattering of cases of students with contraband in their underwear. But when the categorically extreme intrusiveness of a search down to the body of an adolescent requires some justification in suspected facts, general background possibilities fall short; a reasonable search that extensive calls for suspicion that it will pay off. But nondangerous school contraband does not raise the specter of stashes in intimate places, and there is no evidence in the record of any general practice among

Safford Middle School students of hiding that sort of thing in underwear; neither Jordan nor Marissa suggested to Wilson that Savana was doing that, and the preceding search of Marissa that Wilson ordered yielded nothing. Wilson never even determined when Marissa had received the pills from Savana; if it had been a few days before, that would weigh heavily against any reasonable conclusion that Savana presently had the pills on her person, much less in her underwear.

In sum, what was missing from the suspected facts that pointed to Savana was any indication of danger to the students from the power of the drugs or their quantity, and any reason to suppose that Savana was carrying pills in her underwear. We think that the combination of these deficiencies was fatal to finding the search reasonable.

In so holding, we mean to cast no ill reflection on the assistant principal, for the record raises no doubt that his motive throughout was to eliminate drugs from his school and protect students from what Jordan Romero had gone through. Parents are known to overreact to protect their children from danger, and a school official with responsibility for safety may tend to do the same. The difference is that the Fourth Amendment places limits on the official, even with the high degree of deference that courts must pay to the educator's professional judgment.

We do mean, though, to make it clear that the *T. L. O.* concern to limit a school search to reasonable scope requires the support of reasonable suspicion of danger or of resort to underwear for hiding evidence of wrongdoing before a search can reasonably make the quantum leap from outer clothes and backpacks to exposure of intimate parts. The meaning of such a search, and the degradation its subject may reasonably feel, place a search that intrusive in a category of its own demanding its own specific suspicions. . . .

. . . The judgment of the Ninth Circuit is therefore affirmed in part and reversed in part. . . .

It is so ordered.

JUSTICE THOMAS, concurring in the judgment in part and dissenting in part.

I would hold that the search of Savana Redding did not violate the Fourth Amendment. . . .

The analysis of whether the scope of the search here was permissible . . . is straightforward. Indeed, the majority . . . acknowledges that school officials had reasonable suspicion to look in Redding's backpack and outer clothing. . . . The majority nevertheless concludes that proceeding any further with the search was unreasonable.

But there is no support for this conclusion. The reasonable suspicion that Redding possessed the pills for distribution purposes did not dissipate simply because the search of her backpack turned up nothing. It was eminently reasonable to conclude that the backpack was empty because Redding was secreting the pills in a place she thought no one would look.

Redding would not have been the first person to conceal pills in her undergarments. Nor will she be the last after today's decision, which announces the safest place to secrete contraband in school. . . .

Judges are not qualified to second-guess the best manner for maintaining quiet and order in the school environment. Such institutional judgments . . . involve a host of policy choices that must be made by locally elected representatives, rather than by federal judges interpreting the basic charter of Government for the entire country. It is a mistake for judges to assume the responsibility for deciding which school rules are important enough to allow for invasive searches and which rules are not.

Even if this Court were authorized to second-guess the importance of school rules, the Court's assessment of the importance of this district's policy is flawed. It is a crime to possess or use prescription-strength Ibuprofen without a prescription. By prohibiting unauthorized prescription drugs on school grounds—and conducting a search to ensure students abide by that prohibition—the school rule here was consistent with a routine provision of the state criminal code. It hardly seems unreasonable for school officials to enforce a rule that, in effect, proscribes conduct that amounts to a crime. . . .

Admittedly, the Ibuprofen and Naproxen at issue in this case are not the prescription painkillers at the forefront of the prescription-drug-abuse problem. But they are not without their own dangers. . . .

If a student with a previously unknown intolerance to Ibuprofen or Naproxen were to take either drug and become ill, the public outrage would likely be directed toward the school for failing to take steps to prevent the unmonitored use of the drug. In light of the risks involved, a school's decision to establish and enforce a school prohibition on the possession of any unauthorized drug is thus a reasonable judgment.

In determining whether the search's scope was reasonable under the Fourth Amendment, it is therefore irrelevant whether officials suspected Redding of possessing prescription-strength Ibuprofen, nonprescription-strength Naproxen, or some harder street drug. Safford prohibited its possession on school property. Reasonable suspicion that Redding was in possession of drugs in violation of these policies, therefore, justified a search extending to any area where small pills could be concealed. . . .

In the end, the task of implementing and amending public school policies is beyond this Court's function. Parents, teachers, school administrators, local politicians, and state officials are all better suited than judges to determine the appropriate limits on searches conducted by school officials. Preservation of order, discipline, and safety in public schools is simply not the domain of the Constitution. And, common sense is not a judicial monopoly or a Constitutional imperative.

"[T]he nationwide drug epidemic makes the war against drugs a pressing concern in every school." And yet the Court has limited the authority of school officials to conduct searches for the drugs that the officials believe pose a serious safety risk to their students. By doing so, the majority has confirmed that a return to the doctrine of in loco parentis is required to keep the judiciary from essentially seizing control of public schools. Only then will teachers again be able to "govern the[ir] pupils, quicken the slothful, spur the indolent, restrain the impetuous, and control the stubborn" by making "rules, giv[ing] commands, and punish[ing] disobedience" without interference from judges [*Patterson v. Nutter,* 78 Me. 509 (1886)]. By deciding that it is better equipped to decide what behavior should be permitted in schools, the Court has undercut student safety and undermined the authority of school administrators and local officials. Even more troubling, it has done so in a case in which the underlying response by school administrators was reasonable and justified. I cannot join this regrettable decision. I, therefore, respectfully dissent from the Court's determination that this search violated the Fourth Amendment.

Savana Redding's age and gender undoubtedly influenced the Court's conclusion that her strip search was unreasonable. Outside the context of the public school setting, however, the justices have been more tolerant of such intrusive searches. This especially has been the case in the setting of a correctional facility. In ***Florence v. Board of Chosen Freeholders of the County of Burlington*** (2012) the justices held that routine strip searches of incoming detainees at a county jail are constitutionally permissible even when the new inmate faces minor charges and has not yet been convicted. The majority reasoned that jail officials have ample justification to check newly arriving detainees for infectious diseases, weapons, and drugs and other

contraband in order to secure the facility and protect other members of the inmate population.

Arrests and the Fourth Amendment

Discussions about constitutional protections against unreasonable searches and seizures usually focus on law enforcement's evidence-gathering activities. We often forget that the Fourth Amendment also applies to the seizure of persons, meaning that when police officers make arrests, they must meet Fourth Amendment requirements.

Although many Americans think of an arrest as police taking a person into custody, it is—for legal purposes—something less. Whenever a legal authority deprives an individual for some period of time of his or her freedom of movement and rights of personal privacy, that act is considered an arrest. The extent of the deprivation varies from case to case. At one extreme is a full, formal arrest, where a suspect is taken into custody in order to be charged with a crime. At the other is a routine stop during which a person is deprived of his or her freedom of movement briefly and minimally. This kind of arrest may occur when police see a person acting suspiciously on the street or when a driver is pulled over for a routine traffic violation. The degree to which the Fourth Amendment restricts police depends greatly on the extent of the deprivation.

Before police can make a formal arrest, they must satisfy the Fourth Amendment's probable cause requirement. One way to meet this requirement is to obtain an arrest warrant. For example, assume a woman calls police to report that she has been assaulted by an acquaintance. Police may go to a judge and request a warrant for the arrest of the suspect. They might present to the judge the woman's statement, documentation of the injuries she suffered, and other supporting evidence. The judge may determine that the probable cause requirement has been met and issue a warrant for the arrest of the suspect.

Police, however, do not always need a warrant to make an arrest. Take, for example, a situation in which police are called to a bar where a fight has been reported. Upon entering the bar, they find a man dead of stab wounds and witnesses who identify the person who stabbed him. Police at that point have probable cause to believe that a crime has been committed and that a particular person committed that crime; they can make an arrest. Also, a police officer who observes a crime being committed can make an arrest without the benefit of an arrest warrant. The direct observation of the criminal activity is enough.

A "stop," on the other hand, occurs when police temporarily restrain a person's mobility with no intention of taking the individual into full custody. Because of the minimal deprivation of freedom that occurs during a stop, courts have imposed a lower standard of justification. Full arrests must meet the probable cause requirement, but police need only reasonable suspicion to conduct a stop, or temporary detention. The reasonable suspicion requirement is, however, just as difficult to define as probable cause. Usually it is considered to include situations in which a police officer has a factual basis for suspecting that criminal activity has occurred or is about to occur. The officer may conduct a stop, which, depending on what the officer discovers on the basis of the stop, may lead to a full formal arrest.

Often a stop occurs when police officers have reason to suspect a person of a crime and also believe the person is armed and dangerous. Under such circumstances, the officer may stop the individual and frisk him or her for weapons. These actions are often referred to as "Terry stops," taking the name from the Supreme Court decision that approved them, *Terry v. Ohio* (1968).

As you read *Terry*, note how Chief Justice Warren distinguishes "formal arrests" from less intrusive "stops." See how the Court reaches the conclusion that a stop requires only reasonable suspicion and may be conducted absent the evidence necessary to establish probable cause. Compare Warren's views with those of Justice William O. Douglas, whose dissent rejects the position that under the Fourth Amendment stops can be distinguished from arrests. In his view, a "stop and frisk" procedure is a search and seizure requiring the same probable cause that the Fourth Amendment requires for custodial arrests.

Terry v. Ohio

392 U.S. 1 (1968)
http://laws.findlaw.com/US/392/1.html
Oral arguments are available at http://www.oyez.org.
Vote: 8 (Black, Brennan, Fortas, Harlan, Marshall, Stewart, Warren, White)
*   1 (Douglas)*

OPINION OF THE COURT: *Warren*
CONCURRING OPINIONS: *Black, Harlan, White*
DISSENTING OPINION: *Douglas*

FACTS:

As Detective Martin McFadden, a thirty-nine-year veteran of the Cleveland police force, was patrolling in plainclothes one afternoon, he observed John Terry and Richard Chilton, two men he had never seen before. He watched as the two paced along the street, "pausing to stare in the same store window roughly 24 times." After each pass by the window, Terry and Chilton conferred. McFadden then observed a third man, Carl Katz, join the two briefly and then depart. Terry and Chilton then met up with Katz several blocks away. Acting on his suspicion that the men were planning to rob the store, McFadden approached the trio, identified himself as a police officer, and asked them to identify themselves. The suspects began whispering to each other, and Terry mumbled a response. The officer then spun Terry around, patted down his outside clothing, and found a pistol in his overcoat pocket. He ordered the others to face the wall with their hands raised and patted them down as well. McFadden found a gun on another of the men and arrested them both on concealed weapons charges.

Terry challenged the validity of his initial detention and search. The trial court judge agreed that Officer McFadden lacked probable cause, but he held that officers have the right to stop and frisk when they believe their lives are in jeopardy.

ARGUMENTS:

For the petitioner, John Terry, et al.:

- Under the Fourth Amendment arrest requires probable cause, and Officer McFadden did not have probable cause to arrest Terry.
- It violates the Fourth Amendment to substitute a "stop and frisk" doctrine for traditional arrest requirements.
- Imposing a "reasonable suspicion" standard instead of probable cause violates the Fourth Amendment.

For the respondent, State of Ohio:

- The police have the right to stop and question a person engaged in suspicious behavior even absent probable cause.
- A police officer has the right to frisk a stopped individual for the protection of his own safety.
- A stop and frisk is less intrusive than a formal arrest or a full search. Therefore, it is reasonable to require a lower standard (reasonable suspicion) for a stop and frisk than that required for a formal arrest or a full search (probable cause).

MR. CHIEF JUSTICE WARREN DELIVERED THE OPINION OF THE COURT.

This case presents serious questions concerning the role of the Fourth Amendment in the confrontation on the street between the citizen and the policeman investigating suspicious circumstances. . . .

. . . We have recently held that "the Fourth Amendment protects people, not places," and wherever an individual may harbor a reasonable "expectation of privacy," he is entitled to be free from unreasonable governmental intrusion. . . .Unquestionably petitioner was entitled to the protection of the Fourth Amendment as he walked down the street in Cleveland. The question is whether in all the circumstances of this on-the-street encounter, his right to personal security was violated by an unreasonable search and seizure.

We would be less than candid if we did not acknowledge that this question thrusts to the fore difficult and troublesome issues regarding a sensitive area of police activity—issues which have never before been squarely presented to this Court. Reflective of the tensions involved are the practical and constitutional arguments pressed with great vigor on both sides of the public debate over the power of the police to "stop and frisk"—as it is sometimes euphemistically termed—suspicious persons.

On the one hand, it is frequently argued that in dealing with the rapidly unfolding and often dangerous situations on city streets the police are in need of an escalating set of flexible responses, graduated in relation to the amount of information they possess. For this purpose it is urged that distinctions should be made between a "stop" and an "arrest" (or a "seizure" of a person), and between a "frisk" and a "search." Thus, it is argued, the police should be allowed to "stop" a person and detain him briefly for questioning upon suspicion that he may be connected with criminal activity. Upon suspicion that the person may be armed, the police should have the power to "frisk" him for weapons. If the "stop" and the "frisk" give rise to probable cause to believe that the suspect has committed a crime, then the police should be empowered to make a formal "arrest," and a full incident "search" of the person. This scheme is justified in part upon the notion that a "stop" and a "frisk" amount to a mere "minor inconvenience and petty indignity," which can properly be imposed upon the citizen in the interest of effective law enforcement on the basis of a police officer's suspicion.

On the other side the argument is made that the authority of the police must be strictly circumscribed by the law of arrest and search as it has developed to date in the traditional jurisprudence of the Fourth Amendment. It is contended with some force that there is not—and cannot be—a variety of police activity which does not depend solely upon the voluntary cooperation of the citizen and yet which stops short of an arrest based upon probable cause to make such an arrest. The heart of the Fourth Amendment, the argument runs, is a severe requirement of specific justification for any intrusion upon protected personal security, coupled with a highly developed system of judicial controls to enforce upon the agents of the State the commands of the Constitution. Acquiescence by the courts in the compulsion inherent in the field interrogation practices at issue here, it is urged, would constitute an abdication of judicial control over, and indeed an encouragement of, substantial interference with liberty and personal security by police officers whose judgment is necessarily colored by their primary involvement in "the often competitive enterprise of ferreting out crime." This, it is argued, can only serve to exacerbate police-community tensions in the crowded centers of our Nation's cities. . . .

Having thus roughly sketched the perimeters of the constitutional debate over the limits on police investigative conduct in general and the background against which this case presents itself, we turn our attention to the quite narrow question posed by the facts before us: whether it is always unreasonable for a policeman to seize a person and subject him to a limited search for weapons unless there is probable cause for an arrest. Given the narrowness of this question, we have no occasion to canvass in detail the constitutional limitations upon the scope of a policeman's power when he confronts a citizen without probable cause to arrest him.

Our first task is to establish at what point in this encounter the Fourth Amendment becomes relevant. That is, we must decide whether and when Officer McFadden "seized" Terry and whether and when he conducted a "search." There is some suggestion in the use of such terms as "stop" and "frisk" that such police conduct is outside the purview of the Fourth Amendment because neither action rises to the level of a "search" or "seizure" within the meaning of the Constitution. We emphatically reject this notion. It is quite plain that the Fourth Amendment governs "seizures" of the person which do not eventuate in a trip to the station house and prosecution for crime—"arrests" in traditional terminology. It must be recognized that whenever a police officer accosts an individual and restrains his freedom to walk away, he has "seized" that person. And it is nothing less than sheer torture of the English language to suggest that a careful exploration of the outer surfaces of a person's clothing all over his or her body in an attempt to find weapons is not a "search." Moreover, it is simply fantastic to urge that such a procedure performed in public by a policeman while the citizen stands helpless, perhaps facing a wall with his hands raised, is a "petty indignity." It is a serious intrusion upon the sanctity of the person, which may inflict great indignity and arouse strong resentment, and it is not to be undertaken lightly.

The danger in the logic which proceeds upon distinctions between a "stop" and an "arrest," or "seizure" of the person, and between a "frisk" and a "search" is twofold. It seeks to isolate from constitutional scrutiny the initial stages of the contact between the policeman and the citizen. And by suggesting a rigid all-or-nothing model of justification and regulation under the Amendment, it obscures the utility of limitations upon the scope, as well as the initiation, of police action as a means of constitutional regulation. This Court has held in the past that a search which is reasonable at its inception may violate the Fourth Amendment by virtue of its intolerable intensity and scope. . . .

The distinctions of classical "stop-and-frisk" theory thus serve to divert attention from the central inquiry under the Fourth Amendment—the reasonableness in all the circumstances of the particular governmental invasion of a citizen's personal security. "Search" and "seizure" are not talismans. We therefore reject the notions that the Fourth Amendment does not come into play at all as a limitation upon police conduct if the officers stop short of something called a "technical arrest" or a "full-blown search."

In this case there can be no question, then, that Officer McFadden "seized" petitioner and subjected him to a "search" when he took hold of him and patted down the outer surfaces of his clothing. We must decide whether at that point it was reasonable for Officer McFadden to have interfered with petitioner's personal security as he did. . . .

. . . In order to assess the reasonableness of Officer McFadden's conduct as a general proposition, it is necessary "first to focus upon the governmental interest which allegedly justifies official intrusion upon the constitutionally protected interests of the private citizen," for there is "no ready test for determining reasonableness other than by balancing the need to search or seize against the invasion which the search or seizure entails." And in justifying the particular intrusion the police officer must be able to point to specific and articulable facts which, taken together with rational inferences from those facts,

reasonably warrant that intrusion. The scheme of the Fourth Amendment becomes meaningful only when it is assured that at some point the conduct of those charged with enforcing the laws can be subjected to the more detached, neutral scrutiny of a judge who must evaluate the reasonableness of a particular search or seizure in light of the particular circumstances. And in making that assessment it is imperative that the facts be judged against an objective standard: would the facts available to the officer at the moment of the seizure or the search "warrant a man of reasonable caution in the belief" that the action taken was appropriate? . . .

Applying these principles to this case, we consider first the nature and extent of the governmental interests involved. One general interest is of course that of effective crime prevention and detection; it is this interest which underlies the recognition that a police officer may in appropriate circumstances and in an appropriate manner approach a person for purposes of investigating possibly criminal behavior even though there is no probable cause to make an arrest. It was this legitimate investigative function Officer McFadden was discharging when he decided to approach petitioner and his companions. He had observed Terry, Chilton, and Katz go through a series of acts, each of them perhaps innocent in itself, but which taken together warranted further investigation. There is nothing unusual in two men standing together on a street corner, perhaps waiting for someone. Nor is there anything suspicious about people in such circumstances strolling up and down the street, singly or in pairs. Store windows, moreover, are made to be looked in. But the story is quite different where, as here, two men hover about a street corner for an extended period of time, at the end of which it becomes apparent that they are not waiting for anyone or anything; where these men pace alternately along an identical route, pausing to stare in the same store window roughly 24 times; where each completion of this route is followed immediately by a conference between the two men on the corner; where they are joined in one of these conferences by a third man who leaves swiftly; and where the two men finally follow the third and rejoin him a couple of blocks away. It would have been poor police work indeed for an officer of 30 years' experience in the detection of thievery from stores in this same neighborhood to have failed to investigate this behavior further.

The crux of this case, however, is not the propriety of Officer McFadden's taking steps to investigate petitioner's suspicious behavior, but rather, whether there was justification for McFadden's invasion of Terry's personal security by searching him for weapons in the course of that investigation. We are now concerned with more than the governmental interest in investigating crime; in addition, there is the more immediate interest of the police officer in taking steps to assure himself that the person with whom he is dealing is not armed with a weapon that could unexpectedly and fatally be used against him. Certainly it would be unreasonable to require that police officers take unnecessary risks in the performance of their duties. American criminals have a long tradition of armed violence, and every year in this country many law enforcement officers are killed in the line of duty, and thousands more are wounded. . . .

In view of these facts, we cannot blind ourselves to the need for law enforcement officers to protect themselves and other prospective victims of violence in situations where they may lack probable cause for an arrest. When an officer is justified in believing that the individual whose suspicious behavior he is investigating at close range is armed and presently dangerous to the officer or to others, it would appear to be clearly unreasonable to deny the officer the power to take necessary measures to determine whether the person is in fact carrying a weapon and to neutralize the threat of physical harm. . . .

We conclude that the revolver seized from Terry was properly admitted in evidence against him. At the time he seized petitioner and searched him for weapons, Officer McFadden had reasonable grounds to believe that petitioner was armed and dangerous, and it was necessary for the protection of himself and others to take swift measures to discover the true facts and neutralize the threat of harm if it materialized. The policeman carefully restricted his search to what was appropriate to the discovery of the particular items which he sought. Each case of this sort will, of course, have to be decided on its own facts. We merely hold today that where a police officer observes unusual conduct which leads him reasonably to conclude in light of his experience that criminal activity may be afoot and that the persons with whom he is dealing may be armed and presently dangerous, where in the course of investigating this behavior he identifies himself as a policeman and makes reasonable inquiries, and where nothing in the initial stages of the encounter serves to dispel his reasonable fear for his own or others' safety, he is entitled for the protection of himself and others in the area to conduct a carefully limited search of the outer clothing of such persons in an attempt to discover weapons which might be used to assault him.

Such a search is a reasonable search under the Fourth Amendment, and any weapons seized may properly be introduced in evidence against the person from whom they were taken.

Affirmed.

MR. JUSTICE DOUGLAS, dissenting.

The infringement on personal liberty of any "seizure" of a person can only be "reasonable" under the Fourth Amendment if we require the police to possess "probable cause" before they seize him. Only that line draws a meaningful distinction between an officer's mere inkling and the presence of facts within the officer's personal knowledge which would convince a reasonable man that the person seized has committed, is committing, or is about to commit a particular crime. . . .

To give the police greater power than a magistrate is to take a long step down the totalitarian path. Perhaps such a step is desirable to cope with modern forms of lawlessness. But if it is taken, it should be the deliberate choice of the people through a constitutional amendment. Until the Fourth Amendment, which is closely allied with the Fifth, is rewritten, the person and the effects of the individual are beyond the reach of all government agencies until there are reasonable grounds to believe (probable cause) that a criminal venture has been launched or is about to be launched.

There have been powerful hydraulic pressures throughout our history that bear heavily on the Court to water down constitutional guarantees and give the police the upper hand. That hydraulic pressure has probably never been greater than it is today.

Yet if the individual is no longer to be sovereign, if the police can pick him up whenever they do not like the cut of his jib, if they can "seize" and "search" him in their discretion, we enter a new regime. The decision to enter it should be made only after a full debate by the people of this country.

Terry v. Ohio expands the authority of police to investigate possible crimes. If an individual exhibits suspicious behavior that would lead a law enforcement official reasonably to suspect that criminal behavior is occurring or is about to occur, the officer can detain the person to investigate, and may also conduct a pat search of the person's outer clothing to search for weapons, provided there is cause to believe the person may be armed and currently dangerous.[19]

Scholars, lawyers, judges, and others concerned with the process of criminal justice regard *Terry v. Ohio* as one of the Supreme Court's more significant decisions. It is interesting to note that *Terry* was decided by the Warren Court, and it stands as one of the few exceptions to the Warren Court's generally liberal record in criminal procedures cases.

ENFORCING THE FOURTH AMENDMENT: THE EXCLUSIONARY RULE

So far, our discussion has focused on the constitutional rules governing searches and seizures. We have learned that the Court has carved out numerous exceptions to the general principle that police should obtain warrants to conduct searches. At the same time, we have seen that the Court has placed limits on those exceptions. For example, if police use the "incident to arrest" exception to conduct a warrantless search of an individual, they must conduct that search *at the time* the individual is arrested. As we discussed, the Court justified this exception on the ground that the suspect may be carrying weapons that could endanger the lives of police officers or provide a means of escape. If police returned to the crime scene after the suspect was removed and conducted a warrantless search, the Court would not allow them to use the "incident to arrest" exception to justify their search. After all, with the suspect in custody the danger of escape and the threat to police safety would no longer be present.

But suppose that is precisely what police did? They went back to the scene of the crime a day later, found evidence, and tried to justify the search under the incident to arrest exception. We know that this search and seizure would be illegal, but what is to prevent police from doing it anyway? In England, if police conduct an illegal search, the evidence they obtain *may* be used in court against the accused, but the person whose privacy rights have been violated can sue the police for damages. This system of police liability enables the British to enforce search and seizure rights.

The United States provides a different remedy for police infractions.[20] Violations of the Fourth Amendment are discouraged through application of the exclusionary rule, which excludes from being presented in court any evidence that was obtained by police actions that violated a suspect's right to be free from unreasonable government searches and seizures. This rule, created by judges, gives police and other government officials a strong incentive to adhere to constitutional standards while gathering evidence, since their work will be for naught if they obtain the evidence by violating the suspect's constitutional rights. Thus, even if police obtain highly incriminating evidence of guilt, if that evidence is obtained through means that violate a suspect's search and seizure rights, it may not be used by prosecutors to establish guilt. The rationale behind the rule is straightforward: if police know that evidence produced by an illegal search will be of no use, they have a strong motive not to violate the Constitution during criminal investigations.

Development of the Exclusionary Rule

At one time, law enforcement officials in the United States faced no federal punitive measures for conducting illegal searches and seizures. Unless the individual states imposed some form of redress, the police were not held liable for their activities. Unconstitutionally obtained evidence was not excluded from trials. The law began to change in 1914 when the Court handed down ***Weeks v. United States***, the case with which we began this chapter. Recall that police officers and a U.S. marshal went to Weeks's house and, without a warrant, carried off boxes of his papers, documents, and other possessions. These materials were not narrowly selected for their relevance; rather, they were voluminous business records and personal possessions that authorities could search in hopes of finding possible incriminating evidence. Should the documents be used as evidence against Weeks, even though they were gathered in an illegal manner? Writing for the Court, Justice William R. Day proclaimed:

If letters and private documents can thus be seized and held and used as evidence against a citizen accused of an offense, the protection of the Fourth Amendment declaring his right to be secure against such searches and seizures is of no value, and, so far as those thus placed are concerned, might as well be stricken from the Constitution.

---

19. See *Illinois v. Wardlow* (2000) and *Florida v. J.L.* (2000) for examples of the Court's application of the principles set forth in *Terry v. Ohio*.

20. It is true that in the United States, under certain circum-

stances, civil suits can be initiated for violations of Fourth Amendment rights, but our discussion focuses on the exclusionary rule, the major remedy used in criminal proceedings.

With this conclusion, the Court, through Justice Day, created the exclusionary rule: judges must exclude from trial any evidence gathered in violation of the Fourth Amendment.

Although *Weeks* constituted a major decision, it was limited in scope, applying only to *federal* agents and *federal* judges in *federal* criminal cases. It was clear, however, that eventually the Court would be asked to apply the exclusionary rule to the states, where most criminal prosecutions take place. But it was also the case that many states or their judges resisted adopting an exclusionary rule. *People v. Defore* (1926) is perhaps the best-known example. In that case, Benjamin Cardozo, then a judge on the New York Court of Appeals, rejected adoption of *Weeks* to New York. He wrote the now-famous lines disparaging the exclusionary rule: "The criminal is to go free because the constable has blundered. . . . A room is searched against the law, and the body of a murdered man is found. . . . The privacy of the home has been infringed, and the murderer goes free."

The issue first reached the Supreme Court in 1949 in **Wolf v. Colorado.** This case involved Julius Wolf, a Colorado physician who, along with others, was suspected of performing illegal abortions. In order to bolster the state's case against Dr. Wolf, a deputy sheriff took an appointment book from Wolf's office. Authorities followed up on the names in the book, gathering enough evidence to convict him. Wolf's attorney argued that because the case against his client rested on illegally obtained evidence, the Court should dismiss it. To implement his arguments, however, the justices first would have to apply or incorporate the Fourth Amendment and then impose the exclusionary rule on the states (*see Chapter 3*).

Writing for the Court, Justice Felix Frankfurter agreed to incorporate the Fourth Amendment. To be secure against unreasonable searches and seizures was deemed a fundamental right, "basic to a free society," and the provisions of the amendment applied to the states through the due process clause of the Fourteenth Amendment. The Court, however, refused to hold that the exclusionary rule was a necessary part of the Fourth Amendment and upheld Wolf's conviction. The rule was one method of enforcing search and seizure rights, but it was not the only one. In other words, although state law enforcement officials must abide by the guarantees contained in the Fourth Amendment, judges need not use a particular mechanism, such as the exclusionary rule, to ensure compliance. Frankfurter

noted that the law in England, where there was no exclusionary rule, and in the states, the majority of which rejected the rule, proved that justice could be served without this check on police behavior. States were left free to adopt whatever procedures they wished to enforce search and seizure rights. The exclusionary rule was not mandatory.

Growing conflicts between state and federal search and seizure rules, coupled with changes in Court personnel, caused the Court to reconsider the applicability of the exclusionary rule to states in *Mapp v. Ohio* (1961). As you read *Mapp,* can you discern why it is such a significant, yet controversial, opinion? Also, note the emphasis Justice Tom C. Clark's majority opinion places on privacy considerations, remarkable because the case was decided four years before the Court established the right to privacy in *Griswold v. Connecticut.* Finally, does Clark's opinion leave any room for exceptions? This question arose during the 1980s and continues into the current Supreme Court era.

Mapp v. Ohio

367 U.S. 643 (1961)
http://laws.findlaw.com/US/367/643.html
Oral arguments are available at http://www.oyez.org.
Vote: 6 (Black, Brennan, Clark, Douglas, Stewart, Warren)
    3 (Frankfurter, Harlan, Whittaker)

OPINION OF THE COURT: *Clark*
CONCURRING OPINIONS: *Black, Douglas, Stewart*
DISSENTING OPINION: *Harlan*

FACTS:

Dollree Mapp, a woman in her twenties, carried on a number of illegal activities in her Cleveland home. For several months the police had attempted to shut down her operations, but apparently Mapp was tipped off, because each time police planned a raid, she managed to elude them.

On May 23, 1957, police officers, led by Sergeant Carl Delau, tried to enter Mapp's house, this time on the ground that she was harboring a fugitive from justice. (The fugitive was suspected of bombing the house of an alleged Cleveland numbers racketeer, Don King, who later became a prominent boxing promoter.)[21] When the police arrived, Mapp refused to let them

---

21. See Fred W. Friendly and Martha J. H. Elliott, *The Constitution: That Delicate Balance* (New York: Random House, 1984), 128–133.

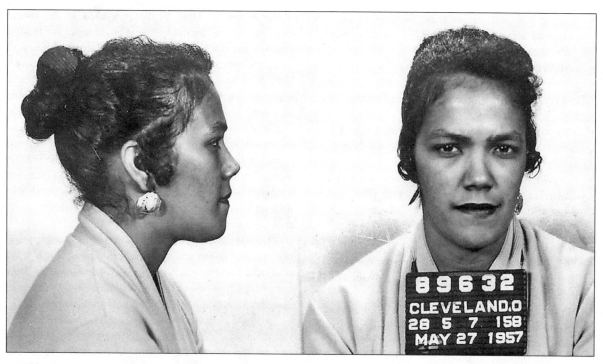

In 1957 Dollree Mapp was arrested for possession of obscene materials. The police seized vital evidence against her during an unconstitutional search. In Mapp v. Ohio *(1961) the Supreme Court reversed her conviction, holding that evidence obtained through an illegal search could not be admitted in court.*

in because they did not have a search warrant. Delau returned to his car, radioed for a search warrant, and kept the house under surveillance. Three hours later, and with additional police officers, Delau again tried to enter. This time Mapp did not come to the door, so police forced it open.

At this point several events occurred almost simultaneously. Mapp's attorney, whom she had called when police first appeared, arrived and tried to see her. Police would not let him in. Hearing the police break in, Mapp came downstairs and began arguing with them. Delau held up a piece of paper, which he claimed was a search warrant. Mapp grabbed it and stuffed it down her blouse. A fight broke out, during which police handcuffed Mapp, retrieved the paper, and searched the house. The police found no evidence of the fugitive, but they did seize some allegedly obscene books and pictures, which were illegal to possess under Ohio law. Mapp claimed that the materials belonged to a former roomer and were being kept by Mapp, along with other belongings, until the roomer could pick them up. At trial the prosecution did not produce the search warrant, and no explanation was offered for the failure to

do so. Mapp was found guilty of felony possession of obscene materials and sentenced to prison for a term of one to seven years. Her attorney appealed to the U.S. Supreme Court, primarily attacking the constitutionality of the Ohio obscenity law and the harsh sentence Mapp received. The justices, however, ignored several arguments advanced by both Mapp and the state, focusing instead on their interest in the search and seizure aspects of the case.[22]

ARGUMENTS:

For the appellant, Dollree Mapp:

- Mapp innocently acquired the materials, which did not belong to her. Had she destroyed them she would have violated a state law against damaging others' property, punishable by up to seven years in prison.

---

22. Interestingly, the attorney for Mapp, while claiming that the police entered Mapp's home illegally, did not argue the exclusionary rule issue. *Wolf v. Colorado* was not even cited in Mapp's brief. It was the ACLU, acting as an amicus in this case, that directly asked the justices in its brief and oral argument to reconsider *Wolf v. Colorado. Mapp,* therefore, provides an excellent illustration of how amicus curiae participation can influence the justices.

- A state law that makes mere possession of lewd materials a crime violates the First and Fourteenth Amendments.
- A state law exposing people to seven years in prison for the simple possession of lewd materials violates the cruel and unusual punishment provision of the Eighth Amendment.
- The police violated the Fourth Amendment by the extreme actions they took in entering the home and conducting the search.
- No evidence of a warrant issued for the search and seizure of obscene materials was ever produced by the state.

For the appellee, State of Ohio:

- The jury made the factual determination that Mapp knowingly and personally possessed the items in question.
- Obscenity is not protected by the First Amendment. To eradicate it the state's police powers must be broad enough to ban every aspect of obscenity, including possession.
- Mapp's sentence was a general one. The actual time to be spent in prison will be determined by the state parole commission according to established criteria. This sentence is not cruel and unusual.
- As the Constitution allows under *Wolf v. Colorado,* Ohio does not use an exclusionary rule. Therefore, even if police violated search and seizure laws the evidence obtained may still be used.

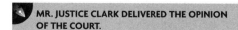

MR. JUSTICE CLARK DELIVERED THE OPINION OF THE COURT.

Seventy-five years ago, in *Boyd v. United States* . . . [t]he Court noted that

constitutional provisions for the security of person and property should be liberally construed. . . . It is the duty of courts to be watchful for the constitutional rights of the citizen, and against any stealthy encroachments thereon.

In this jealous regard for maintaining the integrity of individual rights, the Court gave life to Madison's prediction that "independent tribunals of justice . . . will be naturally led to resist every encroachment upon rights expressly stipulated for in the Constitution by the declaration of rights." . . .

Less than 30 years after *Boyd,* this Court, in *Weeks v. United States,* 1914, . . . stated that use of the seized evidence involved "a denial of the constitutional rights of the accused." Thus, in the year 1914, in the *Weeks* case, this Court "for the first time" held that "in a federal prosecution the Fourth Amendment barred the use of evidence secured through an illegal search and seizure." This Court has ever since required of federal law officers a strict adherence to that command which this Court has held to be a clear, specific, and constitutionally required—even if judicially implied—deterrent safeguard without insistence upon which the Fourth Amendment would have been reduced to "a form of words." It meant, quite simply, that "conviction by means of unlawful seizures and enforced confessions . . . should find no sanction in the judgments of the courts . . . ," that such evidence "shall not be used at all."

There are in the cases of this Court some passing references to the *Weeks* rule as being one of evidence. But the plain and unequivocal language of *Weeks*—and its later paraphrase in *Wolf*—to the effect that the *Weeks* rule is of constitutional origin, remains entirely undisturbed. . . .

In 1949, 35 years after *Weeks* was announced, this Court, in *Wolf v. Colorado,* again for the first time, discussed the effect of the Fourth Amendment upon the states through the operation of the Due Process Clause of the Fourteenth Amendment. It said:

[W]e have no hesitation in saying that were a State affirmatively to sanction such police incursion into privacy it would run counter to the guaranty of the Fourteenth Amendment.

Nevertheless, after declaring that the "security of one's privacy against arbitrary intrusion by the police" is "implicit in 'the concept of ordered liberty' and as such enforceable against the States through the Due Process Clause," and announcing that it "stoutly adhere[d]" to the *Weeks* decision, the Court decided that the *Weeks* exclusionary rule would not then be imposed upon the States as "an essential ingredient of the right." The Court's reasons for not considering essential to the right to privacy, as a curb imposed upon the States by the Due Process Clause, that which decades before had been posited as part and parcel of the Fourth Amendment's limitation upon federal encroachment of individual privacy, were bottomed on factual considerations.

While they are not basically relevant to a decision that the exclusionary rule is an essential ingredient of the Fourth Amendment as the right it embodies is vouchsafed against the States by the Due Process Clause, we will consider the current validity of the factual grounds upon which *Wolf* was based.

The Court in *Wolf* first stated that "[t]he contrariety of views of the States" on the adoption of the exclusionary rule of *Weeks* was "particularly impressive" and, in this connection that it could not "brush aside the experience of States which deem the incidence of such conduct by the police too slight to call for a deterrent remedy . . . by overriding the [States'] relevant rules of evidence." While in 1949, prior to the *Wolf* case, almost two-thirds of the States were opposed to the use of the exclusionary rule, now, despite the *Wolf* case, more than half of those since passing upon it, by their own legislative or judicial decision, have wholly or partly adopted or adhered to the *Weeks* rule. Significantly, among those now following the rule is California, which, according to its highest court, was "compelled to reach that conclusion because other remedies have completely failed to secure compliance with the constitutional provisions. . . . " In connection with this California case, we note that the second basis elaborated in *Wolf* in support of its failure to enforce the exclusionary doctrine against the States was that "other means of protection" have been afforded "the right to privacy." The experience of California that such other remedies have been worthless and futile is buttressed by the experience of other States. . . .

Likewise, time has set its face against . . . *Wolf*. . . . [T]he force of that reasoning has been largely vitiated by later decisions of this Court. These include the recent discarding of the "silver platter" doctrine which allowed federal judicial use of evidence seized in violation of the Constitution by state agents; the relaxation of the formerly strict requirements as to standing to challenge the use of evidence thus seized, so that now the procedure of exclusion, "ultimately referable to constitutional safeguards," is available to anyone even "legitimately on [the] premises" unlawfully searched; and finally, the formulation of a method to prevent state use of evidence unconstitutionally seized by federal agents. Because there can be no fixed formula, we are admittedly met with "recurring questions of the [r]easonableness of searches," but less is not to be expected when dealing with a Constitution, and, at any rate, "reasonableness is in the first instance for the [trial court] to determine."

It, therefore, plainly appears that the factual considerations supporting the failure of the *Wolf* Court to include the *Weeks* exclusionary rule when it recognized the enforceability of the right to privacy against the States in 1949, while not basically relevant to the constitutional consideration, could not, in any analysis, now be deemed controlling.

Some five years after *Wolf*, in answer to a plea made here Term after Term that we overturn its doctrine on applicability of the *Weeks* exclusionary rule, this Court indicated that such should not be done until the States had "adequate opportunity to adopt or reject the [*Weeks*] rule." . . . Today we once again examine *Wolf*'s constitutional documentation of the right to privacy free from unreasonable state intrusion, and, after its dozen years on our books, are led by it to close the only courtroom door remaining open to evidence secured by official lawlessness in flagrant abuse of that basic right, reserved to all persons as a specific guarantee against that very same unlawful conduct. We hold that all evidence obtained by searches and seizures in violation of the Constitution is, by that same authority, inadmissible in a state court.

Since the Fourth Amendment's right of privacy has been declared enforceable against the States through the Due Process Clause of the Fourteenth, it is enforceable against them by the same sanction of exclusion as is used against the Federal Government. Were it otherwise, then just as without the *Weeks* rule the assurance against unreasonable federal searches and seizures would be "a form of words," valueless and undeserving of mention in a perpetual charter of inestimable human liberties, so too, without that rule the freedom from state invasions of privacy would be so ephemeral and so neatly severed from its conceptual nexus with the freedom from all brutish means of coercing evidence as not to merit this Court's high regard as a freedom "implicit in 'the concept of ordered liberty.'" At the time that the Court held in *Wolf* that the Amendment was applicable to the States through the Due Process Clause, the cases of this Court, as we have seen, had steadfastly held that as to federal officers the Fourth Amendment included the exclusion of the evidence seized in violation of its provisions. Even *Wolf* "stoutly adhered" to that proposition. The right to privacy, when conceded operatively enforceable against the States, was not susceptible of destruction by avulsion of the sanction upon which its protection and enjoyment had always been deemed dependent. . . . Therefore, in extending the substantive protections of due process to all constitutionally unreasonable searches—state or federal—it was logically and constitutionally necessary that the exclusion doctrine—an essential part of the right to privacy—be also insisted upon as an essential ingredient of the right newly recognized by the *Wolf* case. In short, the admission of the new constitutional right by *Wolf* could not consistently tolerate denial of its most important constitutional privilege, namely, the exclusion of the evidence which an accused had been forced to give by reason of the unlawful seizure. To hold otherwise is to grant the right but in reality to withhold its privilege and enjoyment. Only last year the Court itself recognized that the purpose of the exclusionary rule "is to deter—to compel respect for the constitutional guaranty in the only effectively available way—by removing the incentive to disregard it." *Elkins v. United States* [1960].

Indeed, we are aware of no restraint, similar to that rejected today, conditioning the enforcement of any other basic constitutional right. The right to privacy, no less important than any other right carefully and particularly reserved to the people, would stand in marked contrast to all other rights declared as "basic to a free society." This Court has not hesitated to enforce as strictly against the States as it does against the Federal Government the rights of free speech and of a free press, the rights to notice and to a fair, public trial, including, as it does, the right not to be convicted by use of a coerced confession, however logically relevant it be, and without regard to its reliability. And nothing could be more certain than that when a coerced confession is involved, "the relevant rules of evidence" are overridden without regard to "the incidence of such conduct by the police," slight or frequent. Why should not the same rule apply to what is tantamount to coerced testimony by way of unconstitutional seizure of goods, papers, effects, documents, etc.? We find that, as to the Federal Government, the Fourth and Fifth Amendments and, as to the States, the freedom from unconscionable invasions of privacy and the freedom from convictions based upon coerced confessions do enjoy an "intimate relation" in their perpetuation of "principles of humanity and civil liberty [secured] . . . only after years of struggle." The philosophy of each Amendment and of each freedom is complementary to, although not dependent upon, that of the other in its sphere of influence—the very least that together they assure in either sphere is that no man is to be convicted on unconstitutional evidence.

Moreover, our holding that the exclusionary rule is an essential part of both the Fourth and Fourteenth Amendments is not only the logical dictate of prior cases, but it also makes very good sense. There is no war between the Constitution and common sense. Presently, a federal prosecutor may make no use of evidence illegally seized, but a State's attorney across the street may, although he supposedly is operating under the enforceable prohibitions of the same Amendment. Thus the State, by admitting evidence unlawfully seized, serves to encourage disobedience to the Federal Constitution which it is bound to uphold. Moreover, "[t]he very essence of a healthy federalism depends upon the avoidance of needless conflict between state and federal courts." Such a conflict, hereafter needless, arose this very Term, in *Wilson v. Schnettler,* in which . . . we gave full recognition to our practice in this regard by refusing to restrain a federal officer from testifying in a state court as to evidence unconstitutionally seized by him in the performance of his duties. Yet the double standard recognized until today hardly put such a thesis into practice. In nonexclusionary States, federal officers, being human, were by it invited to and did, as our cases indicate, step across the street to the State's attorney with their unconstitutionally seized evidence. Prosecution on the basis of that evidence was then had in a state court in utter disregard of the enforceable Fourth Amendment. If the fruits of an unconstitutional search had been inadmissible in both state and federal courts, this inducement to evasion would have been sooner eliminated. There would be no need to reconcile such cases as . . . *Schnettler,* pointing up the hazardous uncertainties of our heretofore ambivalent approach. . . .

There are those who say, as did Justice (then Judge) Cardozo, that under our constitutional exclusionary doctrine "[t]he criminal is to go free because the constable has blundered." *People v. Defore.* In some cases this will undoubtedly be the result. But . . . "there is another consideration—the imperative of judicial integrity." The criminal goes free, if he must, but it is the law that sets him free. Nothing can destroy a government more quickly than its failure to observe its own laws, or worse, its disregard of the character of its own existence. Nor can it lightly be assumed that, as a practical matter, adoption of the exclusionary rule fetters law enforcement. Only last year this Court expressly considered that contention and found that "pragmatic evidence of a sort" to the contrary was not wanting. . . . *Elkins v. United States.* The Court noted that

Moreover, the experience of the states is impressive. . . . The movement towards the rule of exclusion has been halting but seemingly inexorable.

The ignoble shortcut to conviction left open to the State tends to destroy the entire system of constitutional restraints on which the liberties of the people rest. Having once recognized that the right to privacy embodied in the Fourth Amendment is enforceable against the States, and that the right to be secure against rude invasions of privacy by state officers is, therefore, constitutional in origin, we can no longer permit that right to remain an empty promise. Because it is enforceable in the same manner and to like effect as other basic rights secured by the Due Process Clause, we can no longer permit it to be revocable at the whim of any police officer who, in the name of law enforcement itself, chooses to suspend its enjoyment. Our decision, founded on reason and truth, gives to the individual no more than that which the Constitution guarantees him, to the police officer no less than that to which honest law enforcement is entitled, and, to the courts, that judicial integrity so necessary in the true administration of justice.

The judgment of the Supreme Court of Ohio is reversed and the cause remanded for further proceedings not inconsistent with this opinion.

Reversed and remanded.

MR. JUSTICE BLACK, concurring.

I am still not persuaded that the Fourth Amendment, standing alone, would be enough to bar the introduction into evidence against an accused of papers and effects seized from him in violation of its commands. For the Fourth Amendment does not itself contain any provision expressly precluding the use of such evidence, and I am extremely doubtful that such a provision could properly be inferred from nothing more than the basic command against unreasonable searches and seizures. Reflection on the problem, however, in the light of cases coming before the Court since *Wolf,* has led me to conclude that when the Fourth Amendment's ban against unreasonable searches and seizures is considered together with the Fifth Amendment's ban against compelled self-incrimination, a constitutional basis emerges which not only justifies but actually requires the exclusionary rule.

The close interrelationship between the Fourth and Fifth amendments, as they apply to this problem, has long been recognized and, indeed, was expressly made the ground for this Court's holding in *Boyd v. United States* [1866]. There the Court fully discussed this relationship and declared itself "unable to perceive that the seizure of a man's private books and papers to be

used in evidence against him is substantially different from compelling him to be a witness against himself." It was upon this ground that Mr. Justice Rutledge largely relied in his dissenting opinion in the *Wolf* case. And, although I rejected the argument at that time, its force has, for me at least, become compelling with the more thorough understanding of the problem brought on by recent cases.

MR. JUSTICE DOUGLAS, concurring.

We held in *Wolf v. People of State of Colorado* that the Fourth Amendment was applicable to the states by reason of the due process clause of the Fourteenth Amendment. But a majority held that the exclusionary rule of the *Weeks* case was not required of the states, that they could apply such sanctions as they chose. That position had the necessary votes to carry the day. But with all respect it was not the voice of reason or principle.

As stated in the *Weeks* case, if evidence seized in violation of the Fourth Amendment can be used against an accused, "his right to be secure against such searches and seizures is of no value, and . . . might as well be stricken from the Constitution."

When we allowed States to give constitutional sanction to the "shabby business" of unlawful entry into a home (to use an expression of Mr. Justice Murphy), we did indeed rob the Fourth Amendment of much meaningful force.

MR. JUSTICE HARLAN, whom MR. JUSTICE FRANKFURTER and MR. JUSTICE WHITTAKER join, dissenting.

I would not impose upon the States this federal exclusionary remedy. The reasons given by the majority for now suddenly turning its back on *Wolf* seem to me notably unconvincing.

First, it is said that "the factual grounds upon which *Wolf* was based" have since changed, in that more States now follow the *Weeks* exclusionary rule than was so at the time *Wolf* was decided. While that is true, a recent survey indicates that at present one-half of the States still adhere to the common-law non-exclusionary rule, and one, Maryland, retains the rule as to felonies. . . .

The preservation of a proper balance between state and federal responsibility in the administration of criminal justice demands patience on the part of those who might like to see things move faster among the States in this respect. Problems of criminal law enforcement vary widely from State to State. One State, in considering the totality of its legal picture, may conclude that the need for embracing the *Weeks* rule is pressing because other remedies are unavailable or inadequate to secure compliance with the substantive Constitutional principle involved. Another, though equally solicitous of Constitutional rights, may choose to pursue one purpose at a time, allowing all evidence relevant to guilt to be brought into a criminal trial, and dealing with Constitutional infractions by other means. Still another may consider the exclusionary rule too rough-and-ready a remedy, in that it reaches only unconstitutional intrusions which eventuate in criminal prosecution of the victims. Further, a State after experimenting with the *Weeks* rule for a time may, because of unsatisfactory experience with it, decide to revert to a non-exclusionary rule. And so on. From the standpoint of Constitutional permissibility in pointing a State in one direction or another, I do not see at all why "time has set its face against" the considerations which led Mr. Justice Cardozo, then chief judge of the New York Court of Appeals, to reject for New York in *People v. Defore,* the *Weeks* exclusionary rule. For us the question remains, as it has always been, one of state power, not one of passing judgment on the wisdom of one state course or another. In my view this Court should continue to forbear from fettering the States with an adamant rule which may embarrass them in coping with their own peculiar problems in criminal law enforcement.

The application of the exclusionary rule provides yet another example of the Warren Court's revolutionary treatment of the rights of the criminally accused. It also illustrates the highly politicized nature of criminal law. Since 1961, when the Court informed states that they must adopt it, the exclusionary rule has been attacked and defended by scholars, lawyers, and judges. Opponents argue that letting a guilty person go free is too great a price for society to pay just because a police officer violated search and seizure guidelines. Supporters fear that if the exclusionary rule is eliminated, police will have no incentive to respect the law.

Exceptions to the Exclusionary Rule

The disagreement over the exclusionary rule expressed in academic circles and by the public was also evident among the justices. Six voted to overturn Mapp's conviction, but only five expressed full support for the exclusionary rule. Justice Stewart voted with the majority, but on other grounds. When Chief Justice Warren left the Court and was replaced by the law-and-order-minded Warren Burger in 1969, legal scholars predicted that the Court might well overrule *Mapp*. With each additional Court appointment by Republican presidents Richard Nixon, Gerald Ford, and Ronald Reagan, speculation about the end of the exclusionary rule increased.

At first, predictions of *Mapp*'s demise proved unfounded. Although some of the more conservative justices openly criticized the exclusionary rule,

---

BOX 11-1   AFTERMATH . . . DOLLREE MAPP

Dollree Mapp was a free woman following the Supreme Court's reversal of her obscenity conviction in 1961. As a consequence of the decision, state courts were obliged to use the exclusionary rule as a means of enforcing Fourth Amendment search and seizure rights.

In 1968 Mapp moved from Cleveland to New York City. She did not give up her life of crime. In November 1970 police arrested Mapp on charges of possession of and trafficking in stolen property. Pursuing the investigation, detectives obtained a warrant to search her home. They found stolen goods valued at more than $100,000 and 50,000 envelopes of heroin. Although she claimed

that the search warrant was defective, New York courts did not agree. After her trial she was sentenced to a term of twenty years to life in the New York Correctional Institution for Women.

On New Year's Eve 1980, Governor Hugh Carey of New York commuted Mapp's sentence to the nine years she had already served. As a consequence, Mapp, then forty-seven years old, became eligible for release on parole.

SOURCES: *New York Times,* May 27, 1971, December 15, 1975, January 1, 1981; and James A. Inciardi, *Criminal Justice,* 4th ed. (Fort Worth, TX: Harcourt Brace Jovanovich, 1993).

no significant changes were made.[23] But in 1974 the justices dealt a major blow to *Mapp* when they held in *United States v. Calandra* that the exclusionary rule did not apply to grand jury hearings. *Calandra* touched off another wave of predictions that the Court would overrule *Mapp*. Still, no major changes occurred immediately.

In the mid-1980s, however, the situation began to change, as conservative justices came to dominate the Court and the public also favored conservative positions. Significant political pressure was building to alter liberal, Warren Court rulings. The time seemed ripe for change, and in *United States v. Leon* (1984) the Court endorsed the most significant of the proposed modifications to *Mapp*: the good-faith exception to the exclusionary rule. Why did the Court authorize this exception? Justice Brennan, who dissented, was the sole remaining member of the five-person majority who agreed with Clark's opinion in *Mapp*. Why did he object to the Court's decision in *Leon*? Note that he pointed to *Calandra* as the beginning of the demise of the rule.

United States v. Leon

468 U.S. 897 (1984)
http://laws.findlaw.com/US/468/897.html
Oral arguments are available at http://www.oyez.org.
Vote: 6 (Blackmun, Burger, O'Connor, Powell, Rehnquist, White)
    3 (Brennan, Marshall, Stevens)

OPINION OF THE COURT: *White*
CONCURRING OPINION: *Blackmun*
DISSENTING OPINIONS: *Brennan, Stevens*

FACTS:

In 1981, police in Burbank, California, received a tip from a person of unproven reliability identifying Patsy Stewart and Armando Sanchez as drug dealers. According to the informant, the pair kept small quantities of drugs in their house on Price Drive in Burbank and a larger inventory at another residence in the same city. Police began a surveillance of the Price Drive house, where they spotted a car belonging to Ricardo Del Castillo, who had a history of drug possession. Del Castillo's probation records led police to Alberto Leon, a known drug dealer. Based on observation, continued surveillance of the residences, and information from a

second informant, Officer Cyril Rombach, a veteran detective, drew up an affidavit to obtain a search warrant, which a judge issued. With the warrant, police searched several residences and seized large quantities of drugs. Leon, Stewart, Sanchez, and Del Castillo were arrested.

At the trial stage, attorneys for the defendants argued that the search warrant was invalid. They claimed that because the original informant lacked established credibility, the judge did not have probable cause to issue the warrant. The government's lawyers admitted that the defendants had a valid point but argued that the courts should decline to throw out the entire case because of a defective warrant. They said that the officers had acted in "good faith," that the police believed they had a legitimate warrant and acted accordingly.

ARGUMENTS:

For the petitioner, United States:

- As a judicially created rule, the exclusionary rule may be modified by the Court in the light of experience.
- The only justification for the exclusionary rule is its presumed deterrent effect on unlawful police conduct. It should not be applied to situations where it would not have a deterrent effect on police misbehavior.
- The costs of the exclusionary rule outweigh its benefits when applied to evidence obtained from a search that a reasonably well-trained officer would not have recognized as violating the Fourth Amendment.
- The Court should apply a good-faith exception to the exclusionary rule in cases, like this one, where the police faithfully observe search and seizure rules.

For the respondents, Alberto Leon, Armando Sanchez, Patsy Ann Stewart, and Ricardo Del Castillo:

- A good-faith exception to the exclusionary rule applied to search warrants would bar any meaningful review of a magistrate's decision.
- The Fourth Amendment is not self-executing, and the exclusionary rule operates as a disincentive to violating the Constitution.
- The exclusionary rule results in the loss of very few convictions. In the vast majority of cases evidence gathered pursuant to a warrant is validly obtained.
- Fourth Amendment rights are too fundamental to be subjected to a cost-benefit analysis.

---

23. See, for example, Chief Justice Burger's dissenting opinion in *Bivens v. Six Unknown Fed. Narcotics Agents* (1971).

JUSTICE WHITE DELIVERED THE OPINION OF THE COURT.

This case presents the question whether the Fourth Amendment exclusionary rule should be modified so as not to bar the use in the prosecution's case-in-chief of evidence obtained by officers acting in reasonable reliance on a search warrant issued by a detached and neutral magistrate but ultimately found to be unsupported by probable cause. To resolve this question, we must consider once again the tension between the sometimes competing goals of, on the one hand, deterring official misconduct and removing inducements to unreasonable invasions of privacy and, on the other, establishing procedures under which criminal defendants are "acquitted or convicted on the basis of all the evidence which exposes the truth." . . .

The Fourth Amendment contains no provision expressly precluding the use of evidence obtained in violation of its commands, and an examination of its origin and purposes makes clear that the use of fruits of a past unlawful search or seizure "work[s] no new Fourth Amendment wrong." The wrong condemned by the Amendment is "fully accomplished" by the unlawful search or seizure itself, and the exclusionary rule is neither intended nor able to "cure the invasion of the defendant's rights which he has already suffered." The rule thus operates as "a judicially created remedy designed to safeguard Fourth Amendment rights generally through its deterrent effect, rather than a personal constitutional right of the person aggrieved."

Whether the exclusionary sanction is appropriately imposed in a particular case, our decisions make clear, is "an issue separate from the question whether the Fourth Amendment rights of the party seeking to invoke the rule were violated by police conduct." Only the former question is currently before us, and it must be resolved by weighing the costs and benefits of preventing the use in the prosecution's case-in-chief of inherently trustworthy tangible evidence obtained in reliance on a search warrant issued by a detached and neutral magistrate that ultimately is found to be defective.

The substantial social costs exacted by the exclusionary rule for the vindication of Fourth Amendment rights have long been a source of concern. "Our cases have consistently recognized that unbending application of the exclusionary sanction to enforce ideals of governmental rectitude would impede unacceptably the truth-finding functions of judge and jury." An objectionable collateral consequence of this interference with the criminal justice system's truth-finding function is that some guilty defendants may go free or receive reduced sentences as a result of favorable plea bargains. Particularly when law enforcement officers have acted in objective good faith or their transgressions have been minor, the magnitude of the benefit conferred on such guilty defendants offends basic concepts of the criminal justice system. Indiscriminate application of the exclusionary rule, therefore, may well "generat[e] disrespect for the law and the administration of justice." Accordingly, "[a]s with any remedial device, the application of the rule has been restricted to those areas where its remedial objectives are thought most efficaciously served."

Close attention to those remedial objectives has characterized our recent decisions concerning the scope of the Fourth Amendment exclusionary rule. The Court has, to be sure, not seriously questioned, "in the absence of a more efficacious sanction, the continued application of the rule to suppress evidence from the [prosecution's] case where a Fourth Amendment violation has been substantial and deliberate. . . . " Nevertheless, the balancing approach that has evolved in various contexts—including criminal trials—"forcefully suggest[s] that the exclusionary rule be more generally modified to permit the introduction of evidence obtained in the reasonable good-faith belief that a search or seizure was in accord with the Fourth Amendment." . . .

As yet, we have not recognized any form of good-faith exception to the Fourth Amendment exclusionary rule. But the balancing approach that has evolved during the years of experience with the rule provides strong support for the modification currently urged upon us. As we discuss below, our evaluation of the costs and benefits of suppressing reliable physical evidence seized by officers reasonably relying on a warrant issued by a detached and neutral magistrate leads to the conclusion that such evidence should be admissible in the prosecution's case-in-chief.

Because a search warrant "provides the detached scrutiny of a neutral magistrate, which is a more reliable safeguard against improper searches than the hurried judgment of a law enforcement officer 'engaged in the often competitive enterprise of ferreting out crime,'" we have expressed a strong preference for warrants and declared that "in a doubtful or marginal case a search under a warrant may be sustainable where without one it would fail." Reasonable minds frequently may differ on the question whether a particular affidavit establishes probable cause, and we have thus concluded that the preference for warrants is most appropriately effectuated by according "great deference" to a magistrate's determination.

Deference to the magistrate, however, is not boundless. It is clear, first, that the deference accorded to a magistrate's finding of probable cause does not preclude inquiry into the knowing or reckless falsity of the affidavit on which that determination was based. Second, the courts must also insist that the magistrate purport to "perform his 'neutral and detached' function and not serve merely as a rubber stamp for the police." . . .

Third, reviewing courts will not defer to a warrant based on an affidavit that does not "provide the magistrate with a substantial basis for determining the existence of probable cause." . . . Even if the warrant application was supported by more than a "bare bones" affidavit, a reviewing court may properly conclude that, notwithstanding the deference that magistrates deserve, the warrant was invalid because the magistrate's probable-cause determination reflected an improper analysis of the totality of the circumstances or because the form of the warrant was improper in some respect.

Only in the first of these three situations, however, has the Court set forth a rationale for suppressing evidence obtained pursuant to a search warrant; in the other areas, it has simply excluded such evidence without considering whether Fourth Amendment interests will be advanced. To the extent that proponents of exclusion rely on its behavioral effects on judges and magistrates in these areas, their reliance is misplaced. First, the exclusionary rule is designed to deter police misconduct rather than to punish the errors of judges and magistrates. Second, there exists no evidence suggesting that judges and magistrates are inclined to ignore or subvert the Fourth Amendment or that lawlessness among these actors requires application of the extreme sanction of exclusion.

Third, and most important, we discern no basis, and are offered none, for believing that exclusion of evidence seized pursuant to a warrant will have a significant deterrent effect on the issuing judge or magistrate. Many of the factors that indicate that the exclusionary rule cannot provide an effective "special" or "general" deterrent for individual offending law enforcement officers apply as well to judges or magistrates. And, to the extent that the rule is thought to operate as a "systemic" deterrent on a wider audience, it clearly can have no such effect on individuals empowered to issue search warrants. Judges and magistrates are not adjuncts to the law enforcement team; as neutral judicial officers, they have no stake in the outcome of particular criminal prosecutions. The threat of exclusion thus cannot be expected significantly to deter them. Imposition of the exclusionary sanction is not necessary meaningfully to inform judicial officers of their errors, and we cannot conclude that admitting evidence obtained pursuant to a warrant while at the same time declaring that the warrant was somehow defective will in any way reduce judicial officers' professional incentives to comply with the Fourth Amendment, encourage them to repeat their mistakes, or lead to the granting of all colorable warrant requests.

If exclusion of evidence obtained pursuant to a subsequently invalidated warrant is to have any deterrent effect, therefore, it must alter the behavior of individual law enforcement officers or the policies of their departments. One could argue that applying the exclusionary rule in cases where the police failed to demonstrate probable cause in the warrant application deters future inadequate presentations or "magistrate shopping" and thus promotes the ends of the Fourth Amendment. Suppressing evidence obtained pursuant to a technically defective warrant supported by probable cause also might encourage officers to scrutinize more closely the form of the warrant and to point out suspected judicial errors. We find such arguments speculative and conclude that suppression of evidence obtained pursuant to a warrant should be ordered only on a case-by-case basis and only in those unusual cases in which exclusion will further the purposes of the exclusionary rule.

We have frequently questioned whether the exclusionary rule can have any deterrent effect when the offending officers acted in the objectively reasonable belief that their conduct did not violate the Fourth Amendment. . . . But even assuming that the rule effectively deters some police misconduct and provides incentives for the law enforcement profession as a whole to conduct itself in accord with the Fourth Amendment, it cannot be expected, and should not be applied, to deter objectively reasonable law enforcement activity. . . .

We conclude that the marginal or nonexistent benefits produced by suppressing evidence obtained in objectively reasonable reliance on a subsequently invalidated search warrant cannot justify the substantial costs of exclusion. We do not suggest, however, that exclusion is always inappropriate in cases where an officer has obtained a warrant and abided by its terms. "[S]earches pursuant to a warrant will rarely require any deep inquiry into reasonableness," for "a warrant issued by a magistrate normally suffices to establish" that a law enforcement officer has "acted in good faith in conducting the search." Nevertheless, the officer's reliance on the magistrate's probable-cause determination and on the technical sufficiency of the warrant he issues must be objectively reasonable, and it is clear that in some circumstances the officer will have no reasonable grounds for believing that the warrant was properly issued.

Suppression therefore remains an appropriate remedy if the magistrate or judge in issuing a warrant was misled by information in an affidavit that the affiant knew was false or would have known was false except for his reckless disregard of the truth. The exception we recognize today will also not apply in cases where the issuing magistrate wholly abandoned his judicial role. . . . [I]n such circumstances, no reasonably well-trained officer should rely on the warrant. Nor would an officer manifest objective good faith in relying on a warrant based on an affidavit "so lacking in indicia of probable cause as to render official belief in its existence entirely unreasonable." Finally, depending on the circumstances of the particular case, a warrant may be so facially deficient—*i.e.,* in failing to particularize the place to be searched or the things to be seized—that the executing officers cannot reasonably presume it to be valid.

In so limiting the suppression remedy, we leave untouched the probable-cause standard and the various requirements for a valid warrant. Other objections to the modification of the Fourth Amendment exclusionary rule we consider to be insubstantial. The good-faith exception for searches conducted pursuant to warrants is not intended to signal our unwillingness strictly to enforce the requirements of the Fourth Amendment, and we do not believe that it will have this effect. As we have already suggested, the good-faith exception, turning as it does on objective reasonableness, should not be difficult to apply in practice. . . .

When the principles we have enunciated today are applied to the facts of this case, it is apparent that the judgment of the Court of Appeals cannot stand. The Court of Appeals applied the prevailing legal standards to Officer Rombach's warrant application and concluded that the application could not support the magistrate's probable-cause determination. In so doing, the court clearly informed the magistrate that he had erred in issuing the challenged warrant. This aspect of the court's judgment is not under attack in this proceeding. . . .

In the absence of an allegation that the magistrate abandoned his detached and neutral role, suppression is appropriate only if the officers were dishonest or reckless in preparing their affidavit or could not have harbored an objectively reasonable belief in the existence of probable cause. . . . Under these circumstances, the officers' reliance on the magistrate's determination of probable cause was objectively reasonable, and application of the extreme sanction of exclusion is inappropriate.

Accordingly, the judgment of the Court of Appeals is

Reversed.

JUSTICE BRENNAN, with whom JUSTICE MARSHALL joins, dissenting.

Ten years ago in *United States v. Calandra* (1974), I expressed the fear that the Court's decision "may signal that a majority of my colleagues have positioned themselves to reopen the door [to evidence secured by official lawlessness] still further and abandon altogether the exclusionary rule in search-and-seizure cases." (BRENNAN, J., dissenting.) Since then, in case after case, I have witnessed the Court's gradual but determined strangulation of the rule. It now appears that the Court's victory over the Fourth Amendment is complete. That today's decision represents the *pièce de resistance* of the Court's past efforts cannot be doubted, for today the Court sanctions the use in the prosecution's case-in-chief of illegally obtained evidence against the individual whose rights have been violated—a result that had previously been thought to be foreclosed.

The Court seeks to justify this result on the ground that the "costs" of adhering to the exclusionary rule in cases like those before us exceed the "benefits." But the language of deterrence and of cost/benefit analysis, if used indiscriminately, can have a narcotic effect. It creates an illusion of technical precision and ineluctability. It suggests that not only constitutional principle but also empirical data support the majority's result. When the Court's analysis is examined carefully, however, it is clear that we have not been treated to an honest assessment of the merits of the exclusionary rule, but have instead been drawn into a curious world where the "costs" of excluding illegally obtained evidence loom to exaggerated heights and where the "benefits" of such exclusion are made to disappear with a mere wave of the hand.

The majority ignores the fundamental constitutional importance of what is at stake here. While the machinery of law enforcement and indeed the nature of crime itself have changed dramatically since the Fourth Amendment became part of the Nation's fundamental law in 1791, what the Framers understood then remains true today—that the task of combating crime and convicting the guilty will in every era seem of such critical and pressing concern that we may be lured by the temptations of expediency into forsaking our commitment to protecting individual liberty and privacy. It was for that very reason that the Framers of the Bill of Rights insisted that law enforcement efforts be permanently and unambiguously restricted in order to preserve personal freedoms. In the constitutional scheme they ordained, the sometimes unpopular task of ensuring that the government's enforcement efforts remain within the strict boundaries fixed by the Fourth Amendment was entrusted to the courts. . . . If those independent tribunals lose their resolve, however, as the Court has done today, and give way to the seductive call of expediency, the vital guarantees of the Fourth Amendment are reduced to nothing more than a "form of words." . . .

At bottom, the Court's decision turns on the proposition that the exclusionary rule is merely a "'judicially created remedy designed to safeguard Fourth Amendment rights generally through its deterrent effect, rather than a personal constitutional right.'" . . . The germ of that idea is found in *Wolf v. Colorado* (1949), and although I had thought that such a narrow conception of the rule had been forever put to rest by our decision in *Mapp v. Ohio* (1961), it has been revived by the present Court and reaches full flower with today's decision. . . .

I submit that such a crabbed reading of the Fourth Amendment casts aside the teaching of those Justices who first formulated the exclusionary rule, and rests ultimately on an impoverished understanding of judicial responsibility in our constitutional scheme. For my part, "[t]he right of the people to be secure in their persons, houses, papers, and effects, against unreasonable searches and seizures" comprises a personal right to exclude all evidence secured by means of unreasonable searches and seizures. . . .

When the public, as it quite properly has done in the past as well as in the present, demands that those in government increase their efforts to combat crime, it is all too easy for those government officials to seek expedient solutions. . . . In the long run, however, we as a society pay a heavy price for such expediency, because as Justice Jackson observed, the rights guaranteed in the Fourth Amendment "are not mere second-class rights but belong in the catalog of indispensable freedoms." Once lost, such rights are difficult to recover. There is hope, however, that in time this or some later

Court will restore these precious freedoms to their rightful place as a primary protection for our citizens against overreaching officialdom.

I dissent.

As you can see, Justice White's opinion rests on the view that the purpose of the exclusionary rule is to serve as a deterrent against police misbehavior. When police act in good faith, as they did in this case, the punitive aspect of the exclusionary rule becomes irrelevant.

In his dissent, Justice Brennan called *Leon* the *pièce de resistance* for those opposed to the rule. Unlike White, he believed that *Leon* erodes the rule's deterrent function because it can lead to all sorts of illegal police behavior. For example, he predicted that police would attempt to secure warrants on only minimal information, knowing full well that if they can obtain one, whatever evidence is seized will stand up in court.

Brennan was expressing his fear that the Supreme Court would blunt the effectiveness of the exclusionary rule by creating exceptions to it. To him, the Court, while stating its allegiance to *Mapp*, weakened the precedent in decisions such as *Leon* and another 1984 case, *Nix v. Williams*. In *Nix* the Court established an additional exception to the exclusionary rule, the inevitable discovery exception. This ruling holds that evidence discovered as the result of an illegal search can still be introduced in court if it can be shown that the evidence would have been found anyway.

After 1984 the justices appeared to have reached a truce of sorts over the exclusionary rule. The liberal justices seemed pleased that the conservatives had not succeeded in overruling *Mapp* altogether, and the conservative justices were satisfied that they had introduced sufficient exceptions to make the exclusionary rule reasonable. As a consequence, the status of the exclusionary rule did not undergo significant change for the next two decades.

In 2006, however, the justices in **Hudson v. Michigan** once again faced an exclusionary rule dispute. The more conservative members of the Court, perhaps bolstered by the appointments of Chief Justice Roberts and Justice Alito, joined to approve the use of evidence gathered by police who entered a home without following proper procedures. Is Justice Scalia's opinion establishing another exception to the exclusionary rule convincing? Or is Justice Breyer's opinion for the four dissenters more compelling?

Hudson v. Michigan

547 U.S. 586 (2006)
http://laws.findlaw.com/us/000/04-1360.html
Oral arguments are available at http://www.oyez.org.
Vote: 5 (Alito, Kennedy, Roberts, Scalia, Thomas)
    4 (Breyer, Ginsburg, Souter, Stevens)

OPINION OF THE COURT: *Scalia*
OPINION CONCURRING IN PART AND CONCURRING IN JUDGMENT: *Kennedy*
DISSENTING OPINION: *Breyer*

FACTS:

Michigan police obtained a properly issued warrant to search the home of Booker T. Hudson for drugs and firearms. Upon arrival at the house, police knocked and announced their presence. The officers, however, did not wait a reasonable amount of time for Hudson to answer the door; three to five seconds after knocking, they entered the home. Inside, they found a surprised Booker Hudson sitting in a chair. They proceeded to search, finding a large quantity of illegal drugs, including cocaine rocks in Hudson's pocket and a loaded gun lodged between the cushion and armrest of his chair. Hudson was charged with unlawful possession of drugs and firearms.

Hudson's attorneys argued that the evidence should be excluded from the trial because police had failed to comply with the traditional "knock-and-announce" rule. That rule requires police executing a search warrant to wait a reasonable amount of time for the occupant to respond to a knock before entering a home. The trial court granted Hudson's motion to suppress the evidence, but the Michigan Court of Appeals reversed. Hudson was convicted of drug possession. He appealed, again raising the exclusionary rule argument. The Michigan Supreme Court affirmed the use of the evidence and the conviction. Hudson requested U.S. Supreme Court review.

ARGUMENTS:

For the petitioner, Booker T. Hudson Jr.:

- Evidence found inside the home following a knock-and-announce violation is the fruit of an illegal search because the violation renders the entry illegal. Evidence so gathered should be inadmissible.
- The inevitable discovery exception does not apply because there is no independent source for the evidence.
- The exclusionary rule is the only available deterrent to knock-and-announce violations.

For the respondent, State of Michigan:

- The exclusionary rule is premised on the existence of a causal relationship between the incriminating evidence and the constitutional violation that furnished it. That is, had police not engaged in unlawful conduct they would not have obtained the evidence.
- In the case of a knock-and-announce violation there is no such causal relationship: the same evidence would have been found if the officers had knocked and then waited longer than three to five seconds before entering the home.

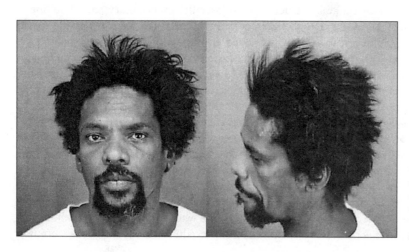

In 2006 the Supreme Court held that evidence gathered against Booker T. Hudson, shown here in 1998 Detroit Police Department photos, was admissible in spite of the failure of police to comply with traditional "knock-and-announce" procedures.

The common-law principle that law enforcement officers must announce their presence and provide residents an opportunity to open the door is an ancient one. See *Wilson v. Arkansas* (1995). Since 1917, when Congress passed the Espionage Act, this traditional protection has been part of federal statutory law. . . . We applied that statute in *Miller v. United States* (1958) and again in *Sabbath v. United States* (1968). Finally, in *Wilson,* we were asked whether the rule was also a command of the Fourth Amendment. Tracing its origins in our English legal heritage, we concluded that it was. . . .

. . . From the trial level onward, Michigan has conceded that the entry was a knock-and-announce violation. The issue here is remedy. *Wilson* specifically declined to decide whether the exclusionary rule is appropriate for violation of the knock-and-announce requirement. That question is squarely before us now.

In *Weeks v. United States* (1914), we adopted the federal exclusionary rule for evidence that was unlawfully seized from a home without a warrant in violation of the Fourth Amendment. We began applying the same rule to the States, through the Fourteenth Amendment, in *Mapp v. Ohio* (1961).

Suppression of evidence, however, has always been our last resort, not our first impulse. The exclusionary rule generates "substantial social costs," *United States v. Leon* (1984), which sometimes include setting the guilty free and the dangerous at large. We have therefore been "cautio[us] against expanding" it, *Colorado v. Connelly* (1986), and "have repeatedly emphasized that the rule's 'costly toll' upon truth-seeking and law enforcement objectives presents a high obstacle for those urging [its] application," *Pennsylvania Bd. of Probation and Parole v. Scott* (1998). We have rejected "[i]ndiscriminate application" of the rule, *Leon,* and have held it to be applicable only "where its remedial objectives are thought most efficaciously served," *United States v. Calandra* (1974)—that is, "where its deterrence benefits outweigh its 'substantial social costs,'" *Scott.*

We did not always speak so guardedly. Expansive dicta in *Mapp,* for example, suggested wide scope for the exclusionary rule. . . . But we have long since rejected that approach. . . . [I]n *Leon,* . . . we explained that "[w]hether the exclusionary sanction is appropriately imposed in a particular case . . . is 'an issue separate from the question whether the Fourth Amendment rights of the party seeking to invoke the rule were violated by police conduct.'"

In other words, exclusion may not be premised on the mere fact that a constitutional violation was a "but-for" cause of obtaining evidence. Our cases show that but-for causality is only a necessary, not a sufficient, condition for suppression. In this case, of course, the constitutional violation of an illegal manner of entry was not a but-for cause of obtaining the evidence. Whether that preliminary misstep had occurred or not, the police would have executed the warrant they had obtained, and would have discovered the gun and drugs inside the house. But even if the illegal entry here could be characterized as a but-for cause of discovering what was inside, we have "never held that evidence is 'fruit of the poisonous tree' simply because 'it would not have come to light but for the illegal actions of the police.'" *Segura v. United States* (1984). Rather, but-for cause, or "causation in the logical sense alone," *United States v. Ceccolini* (1978), can be too attenuated to justify exclusion. . . . of the primary taint.'" *Wong Sun v. United States* (1963) (quoting J. Maguire, Evidence of Guilt (1959)).

Attenuation can occur, of course, when the causal connection is remote. Attenuation also occurs when, even given a direct causal connection, the interest protected by the constitutional guarantee that has been violated would not be served by suppression of the evidence obtained. . . .

For this reason, cases excluding the fruits of unlawful warrantless searches, see, *e.g., Boyd v. United States* (1886); *Weeks; Silverthorne Lumber Co. v. United States* (1920); *Mapp,* say nothing about the appropriateness of exclusion to vindicate the interests protected by the knock-and-announce requirement. Until a valid warrant has issued, citizens are entitled to shield "their persons, houses, papers, and effects," from the government's scrutiny. Exclusion of the evidence obtained by a warrantless search vindicates that entitlement. The interests protected by the knock-and-announce requirement are quite different—and do not include the shielding of potential evidence from the government's eyes.

One of those interests is the protection of human life and limb, because an unannounced entry may provoke violence in supposed self-defense by the surprised resident. Another interest is the protection of property. . . . The knock-and-announce rule gives individuals "the opportunity to comply with the law and to avoid the destruction of property occasioned by a forcible entry." And thirdly, the knock-and-announce rule protects those elements of privacy and dignity that can be destroyed by a sudden entrance. It gives residents the "opportunity to prepare themselves for" the entry of the police. "The brief interlude between announcement and entry with a warrant may be the opportunity that an individual has to pull on clothes or get out of bed." In other words, it assures the opportunity to collect oneself before answering the door.

What the knock-and-announce rule has never protected, however, is one's interest in preventing the government from seeing or taking evidence described in a warrant. Since the interests that were violated in this case have nothing to do with the seizure of the evidence, the exclusionary rule is inapplicable.

Quite apart from the requirement of unattenuated causation, the exclusionary rule has never been applied except "where its deterrence benefits outweigh its 'substantial social costs,'" *Scott* (quoting *Leon*). The costs here are considerable. In addition to the grave adverse consequence that exclusion of relevant incriminating evidence always entails (viz., the risk of releasing dangerous criminals into society), imposing that massive remedy for a knock-and-announce violation would generate a constant flood of alleged failures to observe the rule. . . . The cost of entering this lottery would be small, but the jackpot enormous: suppression of all evidence, amounting in many cases to a get-out-of-jail-free card. Courts would experience as never before the reality that "[t]he exclusionary rule frequently requires extensive litigation to determine whether particular evidence must be excluded." *Scott*. . . .

Another consequence of the incongruent remedy *Hudson* proposes would be police officers' refraining from timely entry after knocking and announcing. As we have observed, the amount of time they must wait is necessarily uncertain. If the consequences of running afoul of the rule were so massive, officers would be inclined to wait longer than the law requires—producing preventable violence against officers in some cases, and the destruction of evidence in many others. . . .

Next to these "substantial social costs" we must consider the deterrence benefits, existence of which is a necessary condition for exclusion. To begin with, the value of deterrence depends upon the strength of the incentive to commit the forbidden act. Viewed from this perspective, deterrence of knock-and-announce violations is not worth a lot. Violation of the warrant requirement sometimes produces incriminating evidence that could not otherwise be obtained. But ignoring knock-and-announce can realistically be expected to achieve absolutely nothing except the prevention of destruction of evidence and the avoidance of life-threatening resistance by occupants of the premises—dangers which, if there is even "reasonable suspicion" of their existence, suspend the knock-and-announce requirement anyway. Massive deterrence is hardly required.

It seems to us not even true, as Hudson contends, that without suppression there will be no deterrence of knock-and-announce violations at all. . . . Assuming (as the assertion must) that civil suit is not an effective deterrent, one can think of many forms of police misconduct that are similarly "undeterred." When, for example, a confessed suspect in the killing of a police officer, arrested (along with incriminating evidence) in a lawful warranted search, is subjected to physical abuse at the station house, would it seriously be suggested that the evidence must be excluded, since that is the only "effective deterrent"? And what, other than civil suit, is the "effective deterrent" of police violation of an already-confessed suspect's Sixth Amendment rights by denying him prompt access to counsel? Many would regard these violated rights as more significant than the right not to be intruded upon in one's nightclothes—and yet nothing but "ineffective" civil suit is available as a deterrent. And the police incentive for those violations is arguably greater than the incentive for disregarding the knock-and-announce rule. . . .

Another development over the past half-century that deters civil-rights violations is the increasing professionalism of police forces, including a new emphasis on internal police discipline. Even as long ago as 1980 we felt it proper to "assume" that unlawful police behavior would "be dealt with appropriately" by the authorities, *United States v. Payner* (1980), but we now have increasing evidence that police forces across the United States take the constitutional rights of citizens seriously. . . . Failure to teach and enforce constitutional requirements exposes municipalities to financial liability. Moreover, modern police forces are staffed with professionals; it is not credible to assert that internal discipline, which can limit successful careers, will not have a deterrent effect. There is also evidence that the increasing use of various forms of citizen review can enhance police accountability.

In sum, the social costs of applying the exclusionary rule to knock-and-announce violations are considerable; the incentive to such violations is minimal to begin with, and the extant deterrences against them are substantial—incomparably greater than the factors deterring warrantless entries when *Mapp* was decided. Resort to the massive remedy of suppressing evidence of guilt is unjustified. . . .

For the foregoing reasons we affirm the judgment of the Michigan Court of Appeals.

It is so ordered.

JUSTICE KENNEDY, concurring in part and concurring in the judgment.

Two points should be underscored with respect to today's decision. First, the knock-and-announce requirement protects rights and expectations linked to ancient principles in our constitutional order. The Court's decision should not be interpreted as suggesting that violations of the requirement are trivial or beyond the law's concern. Second, the continued operation of the exclusionary rule, as settled and defined by our precedents, is not in doubt. Today's decision determines only that in the specific context of the knock-and-announce requirement, a violation is not sufficiently related to the later discovery of evidence to justify suppression. . . .

In this case the relevant evidence was discovered not because of a failure to knock-and-announce, but because of a subsequent search pursuant to a lawful warrant. The Court in my view is correct to hold that suppression was not required . . . I accordingly join those Parts and concur in the judgment.

JUSTICE BREYER, with whom JUSTICE STEVENS, JUSTICE SOUTER, and JUSTICE GINSBURG join, dissenting.

In *Wilson v. Arkansas* (1995), a unanimous Court held that the Fourth Amendment normally requires law enforcement officers to knock and announce their presence before entering a dwelling. Today's opinion holds that evidence seized from a home following a violation of this requirement need not be suppressed.

As a result, the Court destroys the strongest legal incentive to comply with the Constitution's knock-and-announce requirement. And the Court does so without significant support in precedent. At least I can find no such support in the many Fourth Amendment cases the Court has decided in the near century since it first set forth the exclusionary principle in *Weeks v. United States* (1914).

Today's opinion is thus doubly troubling. It represents a significant departure from the Court's precedents. And it weakens, perhaps destroys, much of the practical value of the Constitution's knock-and-announce protection. . . .

Reading our knock-and-announce cases, . . . it is clear that the exclusionary rule should apply. For one thing, elementary logic leads to that conclusion. We have held that a court must "conside[r]" whether officers complied with the knock-and-announce requirement "in assessing the reasonableness of a search or seizure." *Wilson.* The Fourth Amendment insists that an unreasonable search or seizure is, constitutionally speaking, an illegal search or seizure. And ever since *Weeks* (in respect to federal prosecutions) and *Mapp* (in respect to state prosecutions), "the use of evidence secured through an illegal search and seizure" is "barred" in criminal trials. . . .

There may be instances in the law where text or history or tradition leaves room for a judicial decision that rests upon little more than an unvarnished judicial instinct. But this is not one of them. Rather, our Fourth Amendment traditions place high value upon protecting privacy in the home. They emphasize the need to assure that its constitutional protections are effective, lest the Amendment "sound the word of promise to the ear but break it to the hope." They include an exclusionary principle, which since *Weeks* has formed the centerpiece of the criminal law's effort to ensure the practical reality of those promises. That is why the Court should assure itself that any departure from that principle is firmly grounded in logic, in history, in precedent, and in empirical fact. It has not done so. That is why, with respect, I dissent.

In the original good-faith exception decision of *United States v. Leon*, the Court held that the primary goal of the exclusionary rule is to deter police misbehavior. The rule was not designed to deter the misbehavior of others. Thus, in *Leon* the Court ruled that evidence gathered by police pursuant to an inappropriately issued search warrant is admissible if the law enforcement officials acted in good faith. The error was committed by the judge who issued the warrant and not by the police.

In *Hudson v. Michigan,* however, the Court failed to apply the exclusionary rule when the error was committed by the police. The majority reasoned that exclusion is appropriate only when the error directly contributes to the seizure of the evidence. Finding the illegal drugs in Hudson's home in no way was the result of the failure by police to comply fully with the knock-and-announce rule.

In *Herring v. United States* (2009), however, the justices confronted a situation where the error was committed by the police department *and* there was a direct causal relationship between the misbehavior and the gathering of the evidence. Would the justices hold that the evidence is inadmissible in such situations or would they add to the growing number of exceptions to the exclusionary rule?

Herring v. United States

555 U.S. 135 (2009)
http://laws.findlaw.com/US/000/07-513.html
Oral arguments are available at http://www.oyez.org.
Vote: 5 (Alito, Kennedy, Roberts, Scalia, Thomas)
    4 (Breyer, Ginsburg, Souter, Stevens)

OPINION OF THE COURT: *Roberts*
DISSENTING OPINIONS: *Breyer, Ginsburg*

FACTS:

On July 7, 2004, Investigator Mark Anderson learned that Bennie Dean Herring had driven to the Coffee County (Alabama) Sheriff's Department to reclaim some possessions from his impounded truck. Anderson knew that Herring had a history of criminal activity, and he asked Sandy Pope, the department's warrant clerk, to check county records for any outstanding arrest warrants for Herring. When Pope found none, Anderson requested that she contact neighboring Dale County. Dale authorities reported that their computer records listed an outstanding arrest warrant for Herring, for failure to appear on a felony charge. Pope asked Dale County to fax over a copy of the warrant for confirmation.

While waiting for confirmation of the arrest warrant, Anderson and Deputy Neil Bradley detained and arrested Herring when he drove out of the impoundment lot. A search incident to the arrest revealed methamphetamine in Herring's pocket and a pistol in his vehicle (which, as a convicted felon, Herring was prohibited from possessing). While the arrest was taking place, officials in Dale County contacted Sandy Pope to inform her that a mistake had been made. A search for the original arrest warrant revealed that it had been canceled five months earlier; the computer database had not been properly updated. All of this unfolded within about fifteen minutes, but not before Herring had already been arrested.

Herring was charged with violations of federal drug and weapons laws. His attorney moved to suppress the evidence, arguing that because Herring's arrest was based on erroneous information it was

unlawful, and the ensuing search was therefore invalid. The district and appeals courts ruled that the arresting officers did nothing illegal and had every reason to believe that there were ample grounds to make the arrest. The evidence, therefore, was admissible based on the good-faith exception to the exclusionary rule.

ARGUMENTS:

For the petitioner, Bennie Dean Herring:

- The Supreme Court has long held that evidence obtained from warrantless arrests without probable cause is inadmissible.
- The good-faith exception adopted in *United States v. Leon* applies to illegal searches resulting from judicial errors, not illegal searches caused by police errors.
- The exclusionary rule should apply when evidence is obtained because of negligent record keeping by police. There is no reason to create a new exception to the exclusionary rule to cover such situations.

For the respondent, United States:

- The exclusionary rule generates substantial costs to the criminal justice system by prohibiting judges and juries from considering otherwise valid and reliable evidence.
- The Court has wisely applied the exclusionary rule only to situations where the rule can deter police from violating the Fourth Amendment.
- The officers in this case acted reasonably and made an arrest based on what they had every reason to believe was reliable information. The exclusionary rule would not have deterred them from acting as they did.
- Suppression of evidence is not an appropriate remedy for deterrence of clerical record-keeping errors.

CHIEF JUSTICE ROBERTS DELIVERED THE OPINION OF THE COURT.

For purposes of deciding this case . . . we accept the parties' assumption that there was a Fourth Amendment violation. The issue is whether the exclusionary rule should be applied.

The Fourth Amendment protects "[t]he right of the people to be secure in their persons, houses, papers, and effects, against unreasonable searches and seizures," but "contains no provision expressly precluding the use of evidence obtained in violation of its commands," *Arizona v. Evans* (1995). Nonetheless, our decisions establish an exclusionary rule that, when applicable, forbids the use of improperly obtained evidence at trial. We have stated that this judicially created rule is "designed to safeguard Fourth Amendment rights generally through its deterrent effect." *United States v. Calandra* (1974).

In analyzing the applicability of the rule, [*United States v.*] *Leon* [1984] admonished that we must consider the actions of all the police officers involved. The Coffee County officers did nothing improper. Indeed, the error was noticed so quickly because Coffee County requested a faxed confirmation of the warrant.

The Eleventh Circuit concluded, however, that somebody in Dale County should have updated the computer database to reflect the recall of the arrest warrant. The court also concluded that this error was negligent, but did not find it to be reckless or deliberate. That fact is crucial to our holding that this error is not enough by itself to require "the extreme sanction of exclusion."

1. The fact that a Fourth Amendment violation occurred—i.e., that a search or arrest was unreasonable—does not necessarily mean that the exclusionary rule applies. Indeed, exclusion "has always been our last resort, not our first impulse," *Hudson v. Michigan* (2006), and our precedents establish important principles that constrain application of the exclusionary rule.

First, the exclusionary rule is not an individual right and applies only where it "result[s] in appreciable deterrence." *Leon.* We have repeatedly rejected the argument that exclusion is a necessary consequence of a Fourth Amendment violation. Instead we have focused on the efficacy of the rule in deterring Fourth Amendment violations in the future.

In addition, the benefits of deterrence must outweigh the costs. . . . The principal cost of applying the rule is, of course, letting guilty and possibly dangerous defendants go free—something that "offends basic concepts of the criminal justice system." *Leon.* . . .

These principles are reflected in the holding of *Leon*: When police act under a warrant that is invalid for lack of probable cause, the exclusionary rule does not apply if the police acted "in objectively reasonable reliance" on the subsequently invalidated search warrant. We (perhaps confusingly) called this objectively reasonable reliance "good faith." . . .

2. The extent to which the exclusionary rule is justified by these deterrence principles varies with the culpability of the law enforcement conduct. As we said in *Leon*, "an assessment of the flagrancy of the police misconduct constitutes an important step in the calculus" of applying the exclusionary rule. Similarly, in [*Illinois v.*] *Krull* [1987] we elaborated that "evidence should be suppressed 'only if it can be said that the law enforcement officer had knowledge, or may properly be charged with knowledge, that the search was unconstitutional under the Fourth Amendment.'" . . .

Indeed, the abuses that gave rise to the exclusionary rule featured intentional conduct that was patently unconstitutional. In *Weeks* [*v. United States* (1914)], a foundational exclusionary rule case, the officers had broken into the defendant's home (using a key shown to them by a neighbor), confiscated incriminating papers, then returned again with a U.S. Marshal to confiscate even more. Not only did they have no search warrant, which the Court held was required, but they could not have gotten one had they tried. They were so lacking in sworn and particularized information that "not even an order of court would have justified such procedure." *Silverthorne Lumber Co. v. United States* (1920) . . . was similar; federal officials "without a shadow of authority" went to the defendants' office and "made a clean sweep" of every paper they could find. Even the Government seemed to acknowledge that the "seizure was an outrage."

Equally flagrant conduct was at issue in *Mapp v. Ohio* (1961), which overruled *Wolf v. Colorado* (1949), and extended the exclusionary rule to the States. Officers forced open a door to Ms. Mapp's house, kept her lawyer from entering, brandished what the court concluded was a false warrant, then forced her into handcuffs and canvassed the house for obscenity. An error that arises from nonrecurring and attenuated negligence is thus far removed from the core concerns that led us to adopt the rule in the first place. And in fact since *Leon*, we have never applied the rule to exclude evidence obtained in violation of the Fourth Amendment, where the police conduct was no more intentional or culpable than this.

3. To trigger the exclusionary rule, police conduct must be sufficiently deliberate that exclusion can meaningfully deter it, and sufficiently culpable that such deterrence is worth the price paid by the justice system. As laid out in our cases, the exclusionary rule serves to deter deliberate, reckless, or grossly negligent conduct, or in

some circumstances recurring or systemic negligence. The error in this case does not rise to that level. . . .

. . . We have already held that "our good-faith inquiry is confined to the objectively ascertainable question whether a reasonably well trained officer would have known that the search was illegal" in light of "all of the circumstances." *Leon.* . . .

4. We do not suggest that all recordkeeping errors by the police are immune from the exclusionary rule. In this case, however, the conduct at issue was not so objectively culpable as to require exclusion. In *Leon* we held that "the marginal or nonexistent benefits produced by suppressing evidence obtained in objectively reasonable reliance on a subsequently invalidated search warrant cannot justify the substantial costs of exclusion." The same is true when evidence is obtained in objectively reasonable reliance on a subsequently recalled warrant.

If the police have been shown to be reckless in maintaining a warrant system, or to have knowingly made false entries to lay the groundwork for future false arrests, exclusion would certainly be justified under our cases should such misconduct cause a Fourth Amendment violation. . . .Petitioner's fears that our decision will cause police departments to deliberately keep their officers ignorant are thus unfounded. . . .

Petitioner's claim that police negligence automatically triggers suppression cannot be squared with the principles underlying the exclusionary rule, as they have been explained in our cases. In light of our repeated holdings that the deterrent effect of suppression must be substantial and outweigh any harm to the justice system, we conclude that when police mistakes are the result of negligence such as that described here, rather than systemic error or reckless disregard of constitutional requirements, any marginal deterrence does not "pay its way." In such a case, the criminal should not "go free because the constable has blundered." *People v. Defore* (1926) (opinion of the Court by Cardozo, J.).

The judgment of the Court of Appeals for the Eleventh Circuit is affirmed.

It is so ordered.

JUSTICE GINSBURG, with whom JUSTICE STEVENS, JUSTICE SOUTER, and JUSTICE BREYER join, dissenting.

The Court maintains that Herring's case is one in which the exclusionary rule could have scant deterrent effect and therefore would not "pay its way." I disagree. . . .

Is the potential deterrence here worth the costs it imposes? In light of the paramount importance of accurate recordkeeping in law enforcement, I would answer yes, and next explain why, as I see it, Herring's motion presents a particularly strong case for suppression.

Electronic databases form the nervous system of contemporary criminal justice operations. In recent years, their breadth and influence have dramatically expanded. Police today can access databases that include not only the updated National Crime Information Center (NCIC), but also terrorist watchlists, the Federal Government's employee eligibility system, and various commercial databases. Moreover, States are actively expanding information sharing between jurisdictions. As a result, law enforcement has an increasing supply of information within its easy electronic reach.

The risk of error stemming from these databases is not slim. Herring's amici warn that law enforcement databases are insufficiently monitored and often out of date. Government reports describe, for example, flaws in NCIC databases, terrorist watchlist databases, and databases associated with the Federal Government's employment eligibility verification system.

Inaccuracies in expansive, interconnected collections of electronic information raise grave concerns for individual liberty. "The offense to the dignity of the citizen who is arrested, handcuffed, and searched on a public street simply because some bureaucrat has failed to maintain an accurate computer data base" is evocative of the use of general warrants that so outraged the authors of our Bill of Rights.

The Court assures that "exclusion would certainly be justified" if "the police have been shown to be reckless in maintaining a warrant system, or to have knowingly made false entries to lay the groundwork for future false arrests." This concession provides little comfort.

First, by restricting suppression to bookkeeping errors that are deliberate or reckless, the majority leaves Herring, and others like him, with no remedy for violations of their constitutional rights. . . .

Second, I doubt that police forces already possess sufficient incentives to maintain up-to-date records. The Government argues that police have no desire to send officers out on arrests unnecessarily, because arrests consume resources and place officers in danger. The facts of this case do not fit that description of police motivation. Here the officer wanted to arrest Herring and consulted the Department's records to legitimate his predisposition.

Third, even when deliberate or reckless conduct is afoot, the Court's assurance will often be an empty promise: How is an impecunious defendant to make the required showing? If the answer is that a defendant is entitled to discovery (and if necessary, an audit of police databases), then the Court has imposed a considerable administrative burden on courts and law enforcement.

Negligent recordkeeping errors by law enforcement threaten individual liberty, are susceptible to deterrence by the exclusionary rule, and cannot be remedied effectively through other means. Such errors present no occasion to further erode the exclusionary rule. The rule "is needed to make the Fourth Amendment something real; a guarantee that does not carry with it the exclusion of evidence obtained by its violation is a chimera." In keeping with the rule's "core concerns," suppression should have attended the unconstitutional search in this case.

For the reasons stated, I would reverse the judgment of the Eleventh Circuit.

JUSTICE BREYER, with whom JUSTICE SOUTER joins, dissenting.

In *Arizona v. Evans* (1995), we held that recordkeeping errors made by a court clerk do not trigger the exclusionary rule, so long as the police reasonably relied upon the court clerk's recordkeeping. The rationale for our decision was premised on a distinction between judicial errors and police errors, and we gave several reasons for recognizing that distinction.

First, we noted that "the exclusionary rule was historically designed as a means of deterring police misconduct, not mistakes by court employees." Second, we found "no evidence that court employees are inclined to ignore or subvert the Fourth Amendment or that lawlessness among these actors requires application of the extreme sanction of exclusion." Third, we recognized that there was "no basis for believing that application of the exclusionary rule ... [would] have a significant effect on court employees responsible for informing the police that a warrant has been quashed. Because court clerks are not adjuncts to the law enforcement team engaged in the often competitive enterprise of ferreting out crime, they have no stake in the outcome of particular criminal prosecutions." Taken together, these reasons explain why police recordkeeping errors should be treated differently than judicial ones. . . .

Distinguishing between police recordkeeping errors and judicial ones not only is consistent with our precedent, but also is far easier for courts to administer than

the Chief Justice's case-by-case, multifactored inquiry into the degree of police culpability. I therefore would apply the exclusionary rule when police personnel are responsible for a recordkeeping error that results in a Fourth Amendment violation.

The need for a clear line, and the recognition of such a line in our precedent, are further reasons in support of the outcome that Justice Ginsburg's dissent would reach.

The Court's decisions in *Hudson* and *Herring* remind us of the controversial nature of exclusionary rule questions. In both cases the justices split, 5–4, with the conservative majority rejecting the position that exclusion is required. These decisions underscore the current Court's position that suppression of evidence, in Justice Scalia's words, is "our last resort, not our first impulse." Those who favor law enforcement interests believe that the Court's current view is a reasonable one that balances individual protections with the need to combat crime. Others, however, hold that decisions such as *Leon, Hudson,* and *Herring* are a far cry from the position advanced by the Warren Court in *Mapp v. Ohio* and wonder whether the Court will continue to chip away at the viability of the exclusionary rule.

THE FIFTH AMENDMENT AND SELF-INCRIMINATION

As we now know, the Fourth Amendment governs the procedures by which police obtain evidence—generally physical evidence. But evidence used in criminal investigations is not always physical or material. Arrests and, ultimately, convictions often hinge on verbal evidence—witness statements, confessions, and the like—the gathering of which is governed by the Fifth Amendment's self-incrimination clause: "No person . . . shall be compelled in any criminal case to be a witness against himself." Taken together, the Fourth (physical) and Fifth (verbal) Amendments dictate the procedures police use to gather most evidence against individuals.

The self-incrimination clause is violated if two elements are present: first, some form of testimonial evidence must be given that incriminates the person who provides it, and, second, the testimonial evidence must somehow be compelled by the government. Like the Fourth Amendment, the self-incrimination provision is enforced through the exclusion of evidence. If a person makes incriminating admissions as a result of government coercion, the statements cannot be introduced in court as evidence of a crime.

The Self-Incrimination Clause and Testimony

Perhaps the best-known application of the self-incrimination clause involves the protection it extends to individuals charged with criminal offenses. Stated simply, a defendant in a criminal case cannot be compelled to take the witness stand to give testimony. Demanding that a defendant do so in many cases would force the defendant to make a choice between admitting guilt or committing perjury. If the government is to obtain a criminal conviction it must do so on evidence other than compelled admissions from the defendant.

If a criminal defendant refuses to take the witness stand, no implication of guilt may be drawn. The judge is prohibited from telling the jury to consider the defendant's refusal to deny his or her guilt in evaluating the case. In fact, the jury is typically instructed not to draw any adverse inference from a defendant's failure to testify, or even to discuss it during deliberations. Nor may a prosecutor argue that a defendant's decision not to testify is evidence of wrongdoing. Such actions by judges or prosecutors would be clear violations of the Fifth Amendment. An individual's decision to invoke the Fifth Amendment privilege and not answer questions can be interpreted as nothing more than a decision to remain silent.

Furthermore, individuals must be free to exercise their Fifth Amendment rights. The government is prohibited from coercing a person to testify. Prosecutors, for example, may not threaten a defendant with a more severe sentence if he or she does not take the witness stand. Nor may the government use economic pressure to coerce an individual to waive the Fifth Amendment privilege. In *Garrity v. New Jersey* (1967) and *Gardner v. Broderick* (1968) the Supreme Court ruled that public employees could not be threatened with the loss of their jobs if they did not testify in government investigations of corruption and wrongdoing.

The right not to testify extends beyond the case of a defendant's own criminal trial. It applies to any government trial or hearing. Individuals who are called to testify in civil cases or in trials where others have been charged with crimes may refuse to do so if their truthful answers to questions might implicate them in criminal activity. The Fifth Amendment also protects individuals who are called to be witnesses in investigations conducted by grand juries, legislative bodies, and other government agencies.

History is full of important investigations during which witnesses refused to cooperate by asserting their Fifth Amendment privilege. During the red scare of the 1950s, Senator Joseph R. McCarthy, R-Wis., called many to testify before his Senate subcommittee investigating communist activities, and some refused to testify on constitutional grounds. In 1987 witnesses invoked the Fifth Amendment when Congress investigated the sale of arms to Iran in exchange for hostages. Several individuals directly involved in the scandal refused to testify on the grounds that their statements would implicate them. High-ranking officials from Enron, WorldCom, and Arthur Andersen invoked the privilege during the government's investigation of corporate wrongdoing that rocked the nation's financial markets in the early 2000s.

The protections witnesses enjoy under the Fifth Amendment are well established. As a consequence, the Supreme Court is rarely called upon to answer significant questions concerning the application of the self-incrimination clause to individuals providing testimony at trials and government hearings. Such has not been the case, however, with respect to the applicability of the Fifth Amendment to pretrial police interrogation of suspects. Here legal disputes have been persistent and divisive.

The Self-Incrimination Clause and Police Interrogations

Even before the 1960s, when the courts became more sensitive to defendants' rights, the Supreme Court had established certain guidelines for police interrogations. For the most part, these guidelines dealt with the concept of coercion. Principles of self-incrimination and due process of law are violated, the Court held, when confessions are coerced from a suspect. Such illegal coercion may be either physical or psychological.

The issue of the use of physical force to obtain confessions was raised at the Supreme Court as early as 1936 in **Brown v. Mississippi.**[24] Law enforcement officers, with the assistance of other racist citizens, stripped, whipped, hanged until near death, and otherwise physically tortured black suspects to force them into confessing to a murder. Writing for the Court, Chief Justice Charles Evans Hughes stated, "It would be difficult to conceive of methods more revolting to the sense of justice than those taken to procure the confessions of these petitioners."

More than twenty years later, in **Spano v. New York** (1959), the Court struck a blow against the use of psychological coercion. In this case, Vincent Joseph Spano, an Italian immigrant with little formal education and a history of emotional instability, was psychologically coerced by police into confessing to a murder. The justices unanimously agreed that the police violated Spano's rights: psychological coercion has no place in a modern criminal justice system. Three members of the Court felt that Chief Justice Warren's majority opinion did not go far enough toward protecting the privilege against self-incrimination. In their concurring opinion, Justices Brennan, Douglas, and Black argued that attorneys should be present during interrogations to protect unsuspecting and naive defendants from unscrupulous police tactics.

A few years later the Supreme Court was asked to address two new questions regarding police interrogations. First, in *Escobedo v. Illinois* (1964), the justices grappled with the issue raised by the concurring opinions in *Spano*: If a person under arrest wants an attorney to be present during police questioning, must that request be honored? And, because the Court answered this question affirmatively, how should this right be enforced? The Court answered that question in *Miranda v. Arizona* (1966).

The decisions in *Escobedo* and *Miranda* are two of the most important in criminal law. Consider the following questions as you read these decisions: First, and most critical, what position does the Court take on the privilege against self-incrimination? Second, how does the Court safeguard that right? Finally, why do scholars and lawyers consider these decisions and their progeny so important, and why are they so controversial?

---

24. For more details, see Richard C. Cortner, *A Scottsboro Case in Mississippi: The Supreme Court and* Brown v. Mississippi (Jackson: University of Mississippi Press, 1986).

Escobedo v. Illinois

378 U.S. 478 (1964)
http://laws.findlaw.com/US/378/478.html
Oral arguments are available at http://www.oyez.org.
Vote: 5 (Black, Brennan, Douglas, Goldberg, Warren)
    4 (Clark, Harlan, Stewart, White)

OPINION OF THE COURT: *Goldberg*
DISSENTING OPINIONS: *Harlan, Stewart, White*

FACTS:

At 2:30 A.M. on January 20, 1960, police arrested Danny Escobedo, a twenty-two-year-old man of Mexican extraction, for the murder of his brother-in-law, Manuel Valtierra. They attempted to interrogate him, but, on the advice of his lawyer, Escobedo refused to make any statements and was released. Subsequently, Escobedo's friend Benedict DiGerlando, who was in police custody and considered another suspect, told police that Escobedo had indeed shot Valtierra

Danny Escobedo's 1960 arrest and conviction for the murder of his brother-in-law led to a Supreme Court decision that expanded constitutional protections for criminal defendants during police interrogations. This photograph of Escobedo was taken as he awaited processing on charges of burglarizing a hot dog stand not long after the Supreme Court issued its landmark ruling in Escobedo v. Illinois *in 1964.*

because the victim had mistreated Escobedo's sister. On January 30, ten days after the murder, police again arrested Escobedo, as well as his sister Grace.

As police transported the pair to the station, they explained that DiGerlando had told them the whole story, so they might as well confess. Escobedo again declined. At the station, Escobedo asked to see his attorney, but the police refused. His attorney came to the police station and repeatedly asked to see his client, but he was refused access. Instead, police and prosecutors questioned Escobedo for fourteen and a half hours until he made damaging statements that were later used against him. DiGerlando and Escobedo subsequently were found guilty in the killing. Escobedo appealed, claiming that he was denied his right to counsel and that counsel should have been present during the interrogation.

ARGUMENTS:

For the petitioner, Danny Escobedo:
- The circumstances of his interrogation render Escobedo's statements involuntary. The objectionable conditions included the failure of police to advise him of his rights, his being held incommunicado, his youthfulness and minority status, the length of his interrogation, and the deliberate deception practiced by police.
- Escobedo was denied his right to counsel even though he asked to see his attorney and his attorney was available and wanted to see him.

For the respondent, State of Illinois:
- Escobedo's incriminating statements were voluntarily given. He had consulted with his attorney daily during the ten days following the murder. He had been advised to remain silent by his attorney. There was no reason to believe that he was less than normal in intelligence, maturity, and judgment.
- The Court has never held that the right to counsel begins at arrest or applies to questioning immediately after arrest.

MR. JUSTICE GOLDBERG DELIVERED THE OPINION OF THE COURT.

The critical question in this case is whether, under the circumstances, the refusal by the police to honor petitioner's request to consult with his lawyer during the course of an interrogation constitutes a denial of "the

Assistance of Counsel" in violation of the Sixth Amendment to the Constitution as "made obligatory upon the States by the Fourteenth Amendment," and thereby renders inadmissible in a state criminal trial any incriminating statement elicited by the police during the interrogation. . . .

. . . We granted a writ of certiorari to consider whether the petitioner's statement was constitutionally admissible at his trial. We conclude, for the reasons stated below, that it was not and, accordingly, we reverse the judgment of conviction. . . .

The interrogation here was conducted before petitioner was formally indicted. But in the context of this case, that fact should make no difference. When petitioner requested, and was denied, an opportunity to consult with his lawyer, the investigation had ceased to be a general investigation of "an unsolved crime." Petitioner had become the accused, and the purpose of the interrogation was to "get him" to confess his guilt despite his constitutional right not to do so. At the time of his arrest and throughout the course of the interrogation, the police told petitioner that they had convincing evidence that he had fired the fatal shots. Without informing him of his absolute right to remain silent in the face of this accusation, the police urged him to make a statement. . . .

Petitioner, a layman, was undoubtedly unaware that under Illinois law an admission of "mere" complicity in the murder plot was legally as damaging as an admission of firing of the fatal shots. The "guiding hand of counsel" was essential to advise petitioner of his rights in this delicate situation. This was the "stage when legal aid and advice" were most critical to petitioner. [I]t was a stage surely as critical as . . . arraignment and preliminary hearing. What happened at this interrogation could certainly "affect the whole trial," since rights "may be as irretrievably lost, if not then and there asserted, as they are when an accused represented by counsel waives a right for strategic purposes." It would exalt form over substance to make the right to counsel, under these circumstances, depend on whether at the time of the interrogation, the authorities had secured a formal indictment. Petitioner had, for all practical purposes, already been charged with murder. . . .

. . . In *Gideon v. Wainwright* [1963] we held that every person accused of a crime, whether state or federal, is entitled to a lawyer at trial. . . .

It is argued that if the right to counsel is afforded prior to indictment, the number of confessions obtained by the police will diminish significantly, because most confessions are obtained during the period between arrest and indictment, and "any lawyer worth his salt will tell the suspect in no uncertain terms to make no statement to police under any circumstances." This argument, of course, cuts two ways. The fact that many confessions are obtained during this period points up its critical nature as a "stage when legal aid and advice" are surely needed. The right to counsel would indeed be hollow if it began at a period when few confessions were obtained. There is necessarily a direct relationship between the importance of a stage to the police in their quest for a confession and the criticalness of that stage to the accused in his need for legal advice. Our Constitution, unlike some others, strikes the balance in favor of the right of the accused to be advised by his lawyer of his privilege against self-incrimination.

We have learned the lesson of history, ancient and modern, that a system of criminal law enforcement which comes to depend on the "confession" will, in the long run, be less reliable and more subject to abuses than a system which depends on extrinsic evidence independently secured through skillful investigation. . . . This Court also has recognized that "history amply shows that confessions have often been extorted to save law enforcement officials the trouble and effort of obtaining valid and independent evidence. . . . "

We have also learned the companion lesson of history that no system of criminal justice can, or should, survive if it comes to depend for its continued effectiveness on the citizens' abdication through unawareness of their constitutional rights. No system worth preserving should have to fear that if an accused is permitted to consult with a lawyer, he will become aware of, and exercise, these rights. If the exercise of constitutional rights will thwart the effectiveness of a system of law enforcement, then there is something very wrong with that system.

We hold, therefore, that where, as here, the investigation is no longer a general inquiry into an unsolved crime but has begun to focus on a particular suspect, the suspect has been taken into police custody, the police carry out a process of interrogations that lends itself to eliciting incriminating statements, the suspect has requested and been denied an opportunity to consult with his lawyer, and the police have not effectively warned him of his absolute constitutional right to remain silent, the accused has been denied "the Assistance of Counsel" in violation of the Sixth Amendment to the Constitution as "made obligatory upon the States by the Fourteenth Amendment," and that no statement elicited by the police during the interrogation may be used against him at a criminal trial. . . .

Nothing we have said today affects the powers of the police to investigate "an unsolved crime" by gathering information from witnesses and by other "proper investigative efforts." We hold only that when the process shifts from investigatory to accusatory—when its focus is on the accused and its purpose is to elicit a confession—our adversary system begins to operate, and, under the circumstances here, the accused must be permitted to consult with his lawyer.

The judgment of the Illinois Supreme Court is reversed and the case remanded for proceedings not inconsistent with this opinion.

Reversed and remanded.

MR. JUSTICE WHITE with whom
MR. JUSTICE CLARK and MR. JUSTICE STEWART
join, dissenting.
In *Massiah v. United States* [1964] the Court held that as of the date of the indictment the prosecution is disentitled to secure admissions from the accused. The Court now moves that date back to the time when the prosecution begins to "focus" on the accused. . . . At the very least the Court holds that once the accused becomes a suspect and, presumably, is arrested, any admission made to the police thereafter is inadmissible evidence unless the accused has waived his right to counsel. The decision is thus another major step in the direction of the goal which the Court seemingly has in mind—to bar from evidence all admissions obtained from an individual suspected of crime, whether involuntarily made or not. . . . I reject this step and the invitation to go farther which the Court has now issued. . . .

By abandoning the voluntary-involuntary test for admissibility of confessions, the Court seems driven by the notion that it is uncivilized law enforcement to use an accused's own admissions against him at his trial. It attempts to find a home for this new and nebulous rule of due process by attaching it to the right to counsel guaranteed in the federal system by the Sixth Amendment and binding upon the States by virtue of the due process guarantee of the Fourteenth Amendment. The right to counsel now not only entitles the accused to counsel's advice and aid in preparing for trial but stands as an impenetrable barrier to any interrogation once the accused has become a suspect. From that very moment apparently his right to counsel attaches, a rule wholly unworkable and impossible to administer unless police cars are equipped with public defenders and undercover agents and police informants have defense counsel at their side. I would not abandon the Court's prior cases defining with some care and analysis the circumstances requiring the presence or aid of counsel and substitute the amorphous and wholly unworkable principle that counsel is constitutionally required whenever he would or could be helpful. . . .

It is incongruous to assume that the provision for counsel in the Sixth Amendment was meant to amend or supersede the self-incrimination provision of the Fifth Amendment, which is now applicable to the States. *Malloy v. Hogan* [1964]. That amendment addresses itself to the very issue of incriminating admissions of an

accused and resolves it by proscribing only compelled statements. . . .

I do not suggest for a moment that law enforcement will be destroyed by the rule announced today. The need for peace and order is too insistent for that. But it will be crippled and its task made a great deal more difficult, all in my opinion, for unsound, unstated reasons, which can find no home in any of the provisions of the Constitution.

Danny Escobedo had been denied his right to counsel, and the majority found this right to be a primary defense against violations of the self-incrimination clause. If an attorney is present, it is unlikely that police would use even subtle methods to coerce a confession from a suspect. The *Escobedo* majority held

---

BOX 11-2   AFTERMATH . . . DANNY ESCOBEDO

Danny Escobedo's conviction for the murder of his brother-in-law, Manuel Valtierra, was neither his first nor his last encounter with the criminal justice system. In 1953 Escobedo, then sixteen, was incarcerated in a juvenile facility on theft charges. He was convicted of theft again in 1957 and of assault with a deadly weapon in 1958.

Escobedo had served four years of a twenty-year sentence for Valtierra's murder when the Supreme Court reversed his conviction in 1964. He then drifted from job to job in Chicago, at various times working as a plumber, a dockworker, a security guard, a carpenter, and a printer. He also had difficulty staying out of trouble with the law, a situation he blamed on police officers trying to advance their careers at his expense. Shortly after his release, he was arrested for weapons violations, selling drugs to an undercover police officer, and robbing a hot dog stand. Each of these cases ended with dropped charges or acquittal. In 1967, however, Escobedo was convicted on narcotics charges, for which he spent seven years in federal prisons.

Escobedo was arrested again in 1984 when his thirteen-year-old stepdaughter claimed that he had molested her six different times. Escobedo denied the charges, alleging that they stemmed from a bitter custody battle over the girl. He was convicted of two counts of taking indecent liberties with a minor and sentenced to twelve years in prison. He appealed his conviction, claiming that

after his arrest police handcuffed him to a wall for more than eight hours before allowing him to call his attorney.

While free on a $50,000 bond pending the appeal of his indecency conviction, Escobedo shot a man in a bar. He pleaded guilty to attempted murder and was sentenced to eleven years in prison.

In 1999, while on probation after his conviction for a federal weapons violation and also under investigation for the 1983 ice-pick stabbing of a Korean fur and leather dealer, Escobedo disappeared. He was placed on the U.S. Marshals Service's "fifteen most wanted fugitives" list. In 2001, a combined effort by the Marshals Service and Mexican police tracked Escobedo to a desolate rural area of Mexico, where the sixty-four-year-old fugitive was arrested. He was subsequently returned to the United States.

In 2003, Escobedo was convicted of the ice-pick murder and sentenced to forty years in prison. He had been arrested twenty-five times since his 1964 Supreme Court victory.

Escobedo's sister remarried after the famous decision of *Escobedo v. Illinois.* Her husband was later found shot to death by an unknown assailant.

SOURCES: *New York Times,* September 17 and October 29, 1984, September 27, 1985, June 22, 2001; *Washington Post,* September 28, 1985; *San Diego Union-Tribune,* October 22, 1985; *Chicago Tribune,* June 21, 2001; *Chicago Sun Times,* May 1 and August 28, 2003; and Rocco J. Tresolini, *These Liberties* (Philadelphia: J. B. Lippincott, 1968).

that the right to counsel begins at the accusatory stage of the process, defined as the point at which the investigation ceases to be general and focuses on a specific individual. The right is in effect for every critical stage of the process, which includes all interrogations. But once the Court ruled this way, it was faced, in *Miranda v. Arizona,* with a more difficult and far-reaching question: How should this new right be enforced?

Miranda v. Arizona

384 U.S. 436 (1966)
http://laws.findlaw.com/US/384/436.html
Oral arguments are available at http://www.oyez.org.
Vote: 5 (Black, Brennan, Douglas, Fortas, Warren)
    4 (Clark, Harlan, Stewart, White)
OPINION OF THE COURT: *Warren*
OPINION DISSENTING IN PART: *Clark*
DISSENTING OPINIONS: *Harlan, White*

FACTS:

Ernesto Miranda, a twenty-three-year-old indigent, uneducated truck driver, allegedly kidnapped and raped an eighteen-year-old woman outside of Phoenix, Arizona. Ten days after the incident, police arrested him, took him to the station, and interrogated him. After two hours of questioning, Miranda confessed. There was no evidence of any police misbehavior during the interrogation, and at no point during questioning did Miranda request an attorney. Because of the decision in *Gideon v. Wainwright* (1963) *(see Chapter 12),* which mandated that all indigent criminal defendants receive a defense attorney at government expense, the trial judge appointed a lawyer to defend Miranda against the charges. By most accounts, that attorney provided an inadequate defense—he hoped to prove Miranda mentally defective or insane—and Miranda was convicted and received a sentence of twenty to thirty years. The conviction was based not only on the confession but also on other evidence, including the victim's positive identification of Miranda during a lineup.

Miranda retained new attorneys, who presented wholly different arguments to the Supreme Court, where Miranda's appeal was combined with three others presenting similar issues. The attorneys claimed that because the entire interrogation process is so inherently coercive that any individual will eventually break down, the Court should affirmatively protect the right against self-incrimination by adding to those protections already extended in *Escobedo.*

ARGUMENTS:

For the petitioner, Ernesto A. Miranda:

- Under the Fifth and Sixth Amendments arrested persons have the right to counsel when interrogated by police.
- Providing counsel to suspects does not unduly handicap the police in doing their work.
- Skilled interrogators can easily compel confessions from ignorant individuals without legal representation. Providing legal assistance after a confession has been made is of little help to the suspect.
- In order to reduce the inherently coercive atmosphere of police interrogation, police should inform suspects of their right to counsel and their right to have the opportunity to consult counsel prior to being questioned.

Ernesto Miranda waits as the jury deliberates his case before finding him guilty of kidnapping and rape after he confessed to the crime while in police custody. In a landmark ruling, Miranda v. Arizona (1966), the Supreme Court reversed the conviction because Miranda had not been told he had the right to remain silent and to have an attorney present during questioning.

For the respondent, State of Arizona:

- Nothing in this case justifies a rule of the constitutional impact and proportions sought by the petitioner.
- Miranda's confession was not coerced. He had sufficient education and emotional stability to understand what he was doing. There was no brutality or other coercive police behavior. The questioning was of relatively short duration.
- Unlike Escobedo, Miranda did not have an attorney and did not request to see one, and the police did not deny him that right.

> **MR. CHIEF JUSTICE WARREN DELIVERED THE OPINION OF THE COURT.**

The cases before us raise questions which go to the roots of our concepts of American criminal jurisprudence: the restraints society must observe consistent with the Federal Constitution in prosecuting individuals for crime.[25] More specifically, we deal with the admissibility of statements obtained from an individual who is subjected to custodial police interrogation and the necessity for procedures which assure that the individual is accorded his privilege under the Fifth Amendment to the Constitution not to be compelled to incriminate himself.

We dealt with certain phases of this problem recently in *Escobedo v. State of Illinois* (1964). . . .

This case has been the subject of judicial interpretation and spirited legal debate since it was decided two years ago. Both state and federal courts, in assessing its implications, have arrived at varying conclusions. A wealth of scholarly material has been written tracing its ramifications and underpinnings. Police and prosecutor have speculated on its range and desirability. We granted certiorari in these cases in order further to explore some facets of the problems, thus exposed, of applying the privilege against self-incrimination to in-custody interrogation, and to give concrete constitutional guidelines for law enforcement agencies and courts to follow.

We start here, as we did in *Escobedo,* with the premise that our holding is not an innovation in our jurisprudence, but is an application of principles long recognized and applied in other settings. We have undertaken a thorough re-examination of the *Escobedo* decision and

25. *Authors' note:* Along with *Miranda*, the Court decided *Vignera v. New York, Westover v. United States,* and *California v. Stewart.*

the principles it announced, and we reaffirm it. That case was but an explication of basic rights that are enshrined in our Constitution—that "No person . . . shall be compelled in any criminal case to be a witness against himself," and that "the accused shall . . . have the Assistance of Counsel"—rights which were put in jeopardy in that case through official overbearing. . . .

It was necessary in *Escobedo,* as here, to insure that what was proclaimed in the Constitution had not become but a "form of words" in the hands of government officials. And it is in this spirit, consistent with our role as judges, that we adhere to the principles of *Escobedo* today.

Our holding will be spelled out with some specificity in the pages which follow but briefly stated it is this: the prosecution may not use statements, whether exculpatory or inculpatory, stemming from custodial interrogation of the defendant unless it demonstrates the use of procedural safeguards effective to secure the privilege against self-incrimination. By custodial interrogation, we mean questioning initiated by law enforcement officers after a person has been taken into custody or otherwise deprived of his freedom of action in any significant way. As for the procedural safeguards to be employed, unless other fully effective means are devised to inform accused persons of their right of silence and to assure a continuous opportunity to exercise it, the following measures are required. Prior to any questioning, the person must be warned that he has a right to remain silent, that any statement he does make may be used as evidence against him, and that he has a right to the presence of an attorney, either retained or appointed. The defendant may waive effectuation of these rights, provided the waiver is made voluntarily, knowingly and intelligently. If, however, he indicates in any manner and at any stage of the process that he wishes to consult with an attorney before speaking there can be no questioning. Likewise, if the individual is alone and indicates in any manner that he does not wish to be interrogated, the police may not question him. The mere fact that he may have answered some questions or volunteered some statements on his own does not deprive him of the right to refrain from answering any further inquiries until he has consulted with an attorney and thereafter consents to be questioned.

The constitutional issue we decide in each of these cases is the admissibility of statements obtained from a defendant questioned while in custody or otherwise deprived of his freedom of action in any significant way. . . .

An understanding of the nature and setting of this in-custody interrogation is essential to our decisions today. The difficulty in depicting what transpires at such interrogations stems from the fact that in this country they have largely taken place incommunicado. From extensive factual studies undertaken in the early 1930's, including the famous Wickersham Report to Congress by a Presidential Commission, it is clear that police violence and the "third degree" flourished at that time. In a series of cases decided by this Court long after these studies, the police resorted to physical brutality—beatings, hanging, whipping—and to sustained and protracted questioning incommunicado in order to extort confessions. The Commission on Civil Rights in 1961 found much evidence to indicate that "some policemen still resort to physical force to obtain confessions. . . . " Only recently in Kings County, New York, the police brutally beat, kicked and placed lighted cigarette butts on the back of a potential witness under interrogation for the purpose of securing a statement incriminating a third party.

The examples given above are undoubtedly the exception now, but they are sufficiently widespread to be the object of concern. Unless a proper limitation upon custodial interrogation is achieved—such as these decisions will advance—there can be no assurance that practices of this nature will be eradicated in the foreseeable future. . . .

Again we stress that the modern practice of in-custody interrogation is psychologically rather than physically oriented. As we have stated before, "[T]his Court has recognized that coercion can be mental as well as physical, and that the blood of the accused is not the only hallmark of an unconstitutional inquisition." *Blackburn v. State of Alabama* (1960). Interrogation still takes place in privacy. Privacy results in secrecy and this in turn results in a gap in our knowledge as to what in fact goes on in the interrogation rooms. A valuable source of information about present police practices, however, may be found in various police manuals and texts which document procedures employed with success in the past, and which recommend various other effective tactics. These texts are used by law enforcement agencies themselves as guides. It should be noted that these texts professedly present the most enlightened and effective means presently used to obtain statements through custodial interrogation. By considering these texts and other data, it is possible to describe the procedures observed and noted around the country.

The officers are told by the manuals that the "principal psychological factor contributing to a successful interrogation is privacy—being alone with the person under interrogation." . . .

To highlight the isolation and unfamiliar surroundings, the manuals instruct the police to display an air of confidence in the suspect's guilt and from outward appearance to maintain only an interest in confirming certain details. The guilt of the subject is to be posited as a fact. The interrogator should direct his comments toward the reasons why the subject committed the act, rather than court failure by asking the subject whether he did it. Like other men, perhaps the subject has had a bad family life, had an unhappy childhood, had too much to drink, had an unrequited desire for women. The officers are instructed to minimize the moral seriousness of the offense, to cast blame on the victim or on society. These tactics are designed to put the subject in a psychological state where his story is but an elaboration of what the police purport to know already—that he is guilty. Explanations to the contrary are dismissed and discouraged.

The texts thus stress that the major qualities an interrogator should possess are patience and perseverance. . . .

The manuals suggest that the suspect be offered legal excuses for his actions in order to obtain an initial admission of guilt. . . .

When the techniques described above prove unavailing, the texts recommend they be alternated with a show of some hostility. . . .

The interrogators sometimes are instructed to induce a confession out of trickery. . . .

Even without employing brutality, the "third degree" or the specific stratagems described above, the very fact of custodial interrogation exacts a heavy toll on individual liberty and trades on the weakness of individuals. . . .

In these cases, we might not find the defendants' statements to have been involuntary in traditional terms. Our concern for adequate safeguards to protect precious Fifth Amendment rights is, of course, not lessened in the slightest. In each of the cases, the defendant was thrust into an unfamiliar atmosphere and run through menacing police interrogation procedures. The potentiality for compulsion is forcefully apparent, for example, in *Miranda,* where the indigent Mexican defendant was a seriously disturbed individual with pronounced sexual fantasies. . . . To be sure, the records do not evince overt physical coercion or patent psychological ploys. The fact remains that in none of these cases did the officers undertake to afford appropriate safeguards at the outset of the interrogation to insure that the statements were truly the product of free choice.

It is obvious that such an interrogation environment is created for no purpose other than to subjugate the individual to the will of his examiner. This atmosphere carries its own badge of intimidation. To be sure, this is not physical intimidation, but it is equally destructive of human dignity. The current practice of incommunicado interrogation is at odds with one of our Nation's most cherished principles—that the individual may not be compelled to incriminate himself. Unless adequate protective devices are employed to dispel the compulsion inherent in custodial surroundings, no statement obtained from the defendant can truly be the product of his free choice.

From the foregoing, we can readily perceive an intimate connection between the privilege against self-incrimination and police custodial questioning. . . .

Today, then, there can be no doubt that the Fifth Amendment privilege is available outside of criminal court proceedings and serves to protect persons in all settings in which their freedom of action is curtailed in any significant way from being compelled to incriminate themselves. We have concluded that without proper safeguards the process of in-custody interrogation of persons suspected or accused of crime contains inherently compelling pressures which work to undermine the individual's will to resist and to compel him to speak where he would not otherwise do so freely. In order to combat these pressures and to permit a full opportunity to exercise the privilege against self-incrimination, the accused must be adequately and effectively apprised of his rights and the exercise of those rights must be fully honored. . . .

At the outset, if a person in custody is to be subjected to interrogation, he must first be informed in clear and unequivocal terms that he has the right to remain silent. For those unaware of the privilege, the warning is needed simply to make them aware of it—the threshold requirement for an intelligent decision as to its exercise. More important, such a warning is an absolute prerequisite in overcoming the inherent pressures of the interrogation atmosphere. . . . Further, the warning will show the individual that his interrogators are prepared to recognize his privilege should he choose to exercise it.

The Fifth Amendment privilege is so fundamental to our system of constitutional rule and the expedient of giving an adequate warning as to the availability of the privilege so simple, we will not pause to inquire in individual cases whether the defendant was aware of his rights without a warning being given. Assessments of the knowledge the defendant possessed, based on information as to his age, education, intelligence, or prior contact with authorities, can never be more than speculation; a warning is a clear-cut fact. More important, whatever the background of the person interrogated, a warning at the time of the interrogation is indispensable to overcome its pressures and to insure that the individual knows he is free to exercise the privilege at that point in time.

The warning of the right to remain silent must be accompanied by the explanation that anything said can and will be used against the individual in court. This warning is needed in order to make him aware not only of the privilege, but also of the consequences of forgoing it. It is only through an awareness of these consequences that there can be any assurance of real understanding and intelligent exercise of the privilege. Moreover, this warning may serve to make the individual more acutely aware that he is faced with a phase of the adversary system—that he is not in the presence of persons acting solely in his interest.

The circumstances surrounding in-custody interrogation can operate very quickly to overbear the will of one merely made aware of his privilege by his interrogators. Therefore, the right to have counsel present at the interrogation is indispensable to the protection of the Fifth Amendment privilege under the system we delineate today. Our aim is to assure that the individual's right to choose between silence and speech remains unfettered throughout the interrogation process. A once-stated warning, delivered by those who will conduct the interrogation, cannot itself suffice to that end among those who most require knowledge of their rights. A mere warning given by the interrogators is not alone sufficient to accomplish that end. Prosecutors themselves claim that the admonishment of the right to remain silent without more "will benefit only the recidivist and the professional." Even preliminary advice given to the accused by his own attorney can be swiftly overcome by the secret interrogation process. Thus, the need for counsel to protect the Fifth Amendment privilege comprehends not merely a right to consult with counsel prior to questioning, but also to have counsel present during any questioning if the defendant so desires.

The presence of counsel at the interrogation may serve several significant subsidiary functions as well. If the accused decides to talk to his interrogators, the assistance of counsel can mitigate the dangers of untrustworthiness. With a lawyer present the likelihood that the police will practice coercion is reduced, and if coercion is nevertheless exercised the lawyer can testify to it in court. The presence of a lawyer can also help to guarantee that the accused gives a fully accurate statement to the police and that the statement is rightly reported by the prosecution at trial.

An individual need not make a pre-interrogation request for a lawyer. While such request affirmatively secures his right to have one, his failure to ask for a lawyer does not constitute a waiver. No effective waiver of the right to counsel during interrogation can be recognized unless specifically made after the warnings we here delineate have been given. The accused who does not know his rights and therefore does not make a request may be the person who most needs counsel. . . .

Accordingly we hold that an individual held for interrogation must be clearly informed that he has the right to consult with a lawyer and to have the lawyer with him during interrogation under the system for protecting the privilege we delineate today. As with the warnings of the right to remain silent and that anything stated can be used in evidence against him, this warning is an absolute prerequisite to interrogation. No amount of circumstantial evidence that the person may have been aware of this right will suffice to stand in its stead. Only through such a warning is there ascertainable assurance that the accused was aware of this right.

If an individual indicates that he wishes the assistance of counsel before any interrogation occurs, the authorities cannot rationally ignore or deny his request on the basis that the individual does not have or cannot afford a retained attorney. The financial ability of the individual has no relationship to the scope of the rights involved here. The privilege against self-incrimination secured by the Constitution applies to all individuals. The need for counsel in order to protect the privilege exists for the indigent as well as the affluent. In fact, were we to limit these constitutional rights to those who can retain an attorney, our decisions today would be of little significance. The cases before us as well as the vast majority of confession cases with which we have dealt in the past involve those unable to retain counsel. While authorities are not required to relieve the accused of his poverty, they have the obligation not to take advantage of indigence in the administration of justice. Denial of counsel to the indigent at the time of interrogation while allowing an attorney to those who can afford one would be no more supportable by reason or logic than the similar situation at trial and on appeal struck down in *Gideon v. Wainwright* (1963).

In order fully to apprise a person interrogated of the extent of his rights under this system then, it is necessary to warn him not only that he has the right to consult with an attorney, but also that if he is indigent a lawyer will be appointed to represent him. Without this additional warning, the admonition of the right to consult with counsel would often be understood as meaning only that he can consult with a lawyer if he has one or has the funds to obtain one. The warning of a right to counsel would be hollow if not couched in terms that would convey to the indigent—the person most often subjected to interrogation—the knowledge that he too has a right to have counsel present. As with the warnings of the right to remain silent and of the general right to counsel, only by effective and express explanation to the indigent of this right can there be assurance that he was truly in a position to exercise it.

Once warnings have been given, the subsequent procedure is clear. If the individual indicates in any manner, at any time prior to or during questioning, that he wishes to remain silent, the interrogation must cease. At this point he has shown that he intends to exercise his Fifth Amendment privilege; any statement taken after the person invokes his privilege cannot be other than the product of compulsion, subtle or otherwise. Without the right to cut off questioning, the setting of in-custody interrogation operates on the individual to overcome free choice in producing a statement after the privilege has been once invoked. If the individual states that he wants an attorney, the interrogation must cease until an attorney is present. At that time, the individual must have an opportunity to confer with the attorney and to have him present during any subsequent questioning. If the individual cannot obtain an attorney and he indicates that he wants one before speaking to police, they must respect his decision to remain silent. . . .

If the interrogation continues without the presence of an attorney and a statement is taken, a heavy burden rests on the government to demonstrate that the defendant knowingly and intelligently waived his privilege against self-incrimination and his right to retained or appointed counsel. . . .

The warnings required and the waiver necessary in accordance with our opinion today are, in the absence of a fully effective equivalent, prerequisites to the admissibility of any statement made by a defendant. No distinction can be drawn between statements which are direct confessions and statements which amount to "admissions" of part or all of an offense. The privilege against self-incrimination protects the individual from being compelled to incriminate himself in any manner; it does not distinguish degrees of incrimination. . . .

To summarize, we hold that when an individual is taken into custody or otherwise deprived of his freedom by the authorities in any significant way and is subjected to questioning, the privilege against self-incrimination is jeopardized. Procedural safeguards must be employed to protect the privilege and unless other fully effective means are adopted to notify the person of his right of silence and to assure that the exercise of the right will be scrupulously honored, the following measures are required. He must be warned prior to any questioning that he has the right to remain silent, that anything he says can be used against him in a court of law, that he has the right to the presence of an attorney, and that if he cannot afford an attorney one will be appointed for him prior to any questioning if he so desires. Opportunity to exercise these rights must be afforded to him throughout the interrogation. After such warnings have been given, and such opportunity afforded him, the individual may knowingly and intelligently waive these rights and agree to answer questions or make a statement. But unless and until such warnings and waiver are demonstrated by the prosecution at trial, no evidence obtained as a result of interrogation can be used against him. . . .

In announcing these principles, we are not unmindful of the burdens which law enforcement officials must bear, often under trying circumstances. We also fully recognize the obligation of all citizens to aid in enforcing the criminal laws. This Court, while protecting individual rights, has always given ample latitude to law enforcement agencies in the legitimate exercise of their duties. The limits we have placed on the interrogation process should not constitute an undue interference with a proper system of law enforcement. . . . [O]ur decision does not in any way preclude police from carrying out their traditional investigatory functions. Although confessions may play an important role in some convictions, the cases before us present graphic examples of the overstatement of the "need" for confessions. . . .

Over the years the Federal Bureau of Investigation has compiled an exemplary record of effective law enforcement while advising any suspect or arrested person, at the outset of an interview, that he is not required to make a statement, that any statement may be used against him in court, that the individual may obtain the services of an attorney of his own choice and, more recently, that he has a right to free counsel if he is unable to pay. . . .

The practice of the FBI can readily be emulated by state and local enforcement agencies. The argument that the FBI deals with different crimes than are dealt with by state authorities does not mitigate the significance of the FBI experience. . . .

Judicial solutions to problems of constitutional dimension have evolved decade by decade. As courts have been presented with the need to enforce constitutional rights, they have found means of doing so. That was our responsibility when *Escobedo* was before us and it is our responsibility today. Where rights secured by the Constitution are involved, there can be no rule making or legislation which would abrogate them.

Reversed.

MR. JUSTICE WHITE, with whom MR. JUSTICE HARLAN and MR. JUSTICE STEWART join, dissenting.

The obvious underpinning of the Court's decision is a deep-seated distrust of all confessions. As the Court declares that the accused may not be interrogated without counsel present, absent a waiver of the right to counsel, and as the Court all but admonishes the lawyer to advise the accused to remain silent, the result adds up to a judicial judgment that evidence from the accused should not be used against him in any way, whether compelled or not. This is the not so subtle overtone of the opinion—that it is inherently wrong for the police to gather evidence from the accused himself. And this is precisely the nub of this dissent. I see nothing wrong or immoral, and certainly nothing unconstitutional, in the police's asking a suspect whom they have reasonable cause to arrest whether or not he killed his wife or in confronting him with the evidence on which the arrest was based, at least where he has been plainly advised that he may remain completely silent. Until today, "the admissions or confessions of the prisoner, when voluntarily and freely made, have always ranked high in the scale of incriminating evidence." Particularly when corroborated, as where the police have confirmed the accused's disclosure of the hiding place of implements or fruits of the crime, such confessions have the highest reliability and significantly contribute to the certitude with which we may believe the accused is guilty. Moreover, it is by no means certain that the process of confessing is injurious to the accused. To the contrary it may provide psychological relief and enhance the prospects for rehabilitation.

BOX 11-3   AFTERMATH . . . ERNESTO MIRANDA

In February 1967, following the Supreme Court's decision overturning his conviction on kidnapping and rape charges, Ernesto Miranda was retried, this time with his incriminating statements excluded. To mask his identity from the jurors, Miranda stood trial as "José Gomez." He was convicted and sentenced to twenty to thirty years in prison. Most damning was the testimony of his common-law wife, who claimed that Miranda had admitted to her that he had kidnapped and raped the victim. He was also convicted of an unrelated robbery of a woman at knifepoint and was sentenced to a concurrent term of twenty to twenty-five years.

In December 1972 Miranda was released on parole. Only two years later, he was arrested on drug and firearms charges after being stopped for a routine traffic violation. These charges were dropped because of Fourth Amendment violations and insufficient evidence. In 1975 he returned to prison for a short time on a parole violation.

Miranda's life ended in 1976. While drinking and playing cards in a Phoenix skid row bar, he became involved in a fight with two illegal aliens. Miranda got the best of the fight and went to the restroom to wash his bloodied hands. When he returned, the two attacked him with a knife. Miranda was stabbed once in the chest and once in the abdomen. He collapsed and died. Miranda was thirty-four years old. Upon arresting his assailants, police read them their Miranda warnings.

SOURCES: *New York Times*, October 12, 1974; *Atlanta Journal*, December 13, 1972, February 1, 1976, February 2, 1976; and James A. Inciardi, *Criminal Justice*, 4th ed. (Fort Worth, TX: Harcourt Brace Jovanovich, 1993).

This is not to say that the value of respect for the inviolability of the accused's individual personality should be accorded no weight or that all confessions should be indiscriminately admitted. This Court has long read the Constitution to proscribe compelled confessions, a salutary rule from which there should be no retreat. But I see no sound basis, factual or otherwise, and the Court gives none, for concluding that the present rule against the receipt of coerced confessions is inadequate for the task of sorting out inadmissible evidence and must be replaced by the *per se* rule which is now imposed. Even if the new concept can be said to have advantages of some sort over the present law, they are far outweighed by its likely undesirable impact on other very relevant and important interests. . . .

The rule announced today will measurably weaken the ability of the criminal law to perform these tasks. It is a deliberate calculus to prevent interrogations, to reduce the incidence of confessions and pleas of guilty and to increase the number of trials. Criminal trials, no matter how efficient the police are, are not sure bets for the prosecution, nor should they be if the evidence is not forthcoming. Under the present law, the prosecution fails to prove its case in about 30% of the criminal cases actually tried in the federal courts. But it is something else again to remove from the ordinary criminal case all those confessions which heretofore have been held to be free and voluntary acts of the accused and to thus establish a new constitutional barrier to the ascertainment of truth by the judicial process. There is, in my view, every reason to believe that a good many criminal defendants who otherwise would have been convicted on what this Court has previously thought to be the most satisfactory kind of evidence will now, under this new version of the Fifth Amendment, either not be tried at all or will be acquitted if the State's evidence, minus the confession, is put to the test of litigation.

I have no desire whatsoever to share the responsibility for any such impact on the present criminal process.

Chief Justice Warren's majority opinion in *Miranda* is a tour de force on self-incrimination, creating the so-called Miranda warnings that police must read to suspects before any custodial interrogation. But the opinion left open a number of questions. In fact, the majority of self-incrimination cases after 1966 are the fallout from *Miranda,* seeking to fill two gaps it left open: (1) What is custody? and (2) What constitutes interrogation?

These two questions are of utmost importance for police. The *Miranda* ruling provided little guidance to police questioning individuals outside the traditional interrogation room setting. Nor did the decision discuss situations in which police question individuals in a nonaccusatory fashion. Under such circumstances, must police advise individuals of their rights?

As you read about the Court's answers to these questions, keep another point in mind: immediately after *Miranda*, law enforcement officials condemned the decision. They—as did the dissenters—thought it would seriously hamper their ability to investigate and solve crimes. Some analysts thought Chief Justice Burger—who generally supported the government in criminal cases and whose Court was largely responsible for filling *Miranda*'s gaps—would be sympathetic to the concerns of law enforcement officials. Was he? Moreover, has *Miranda* created the burden on law enforcement that some suspected?

What Is Custody? The first post-*Miranda* case the justices reviewed dealt with custody. In **Orozco v. Texas** (1969) the Court determined that "custodial interrogations," regardless of where they occur, require Miranda warnings. In this instance, police questioned an alleged murderer in his boardinghouse room at 4:00 A.M., while he was in bed. They did not read him his rights, believing that they must do so only when they take individuals out of their environment, that is, into police headquarters. But, as Justice Black noted:

The State has argued here that since Orozco was interrogated on his own bed, in familiar surroundings, our *Miranda* holding should not apply. . . . But the opinion iterated and reiterated the absolute necessity for officers interrogating people "in custody" to give the described warnings. According to the officers' testimony, petitioner was under arrest and not free to leave. . . . The *Miranda* opinion declared that the warnings were required when the person being interrogated was in custody at the station *or otherwise deprived of his freedom of action in any significant way.*

Orozco v. Texas was the Warren Court's only major post-*Miranda* decision on custody. Although it sent a clear signal to law enforcement officials that they must provide the required warnings to all individuals deprived of their freedom, regardless of where that deprivation occurs, it created more gaps for the Burger Court to fill in. For example, must police warn an individual who voluntarily accedes to police questioning? Is interrogation of a person suspected of certain kinds of crimes exempt from *Miranda*?

In several cases, the Burger Court moved away from the spirit of the *Orozco* decision. In *Beckwith v. United States* (1976), for example, the Court held that Miranda warnings were not required when agents of the Internal Revenue Service questioned a man in a

---

PD 47
Rev. 8/73

METROPOLITAN POLICE DEPARTMENT WARNING AS TO YOUR RIGHTS

You are under arrest. Before we ask you any questions, you must understand what your rights are.

You have the right to remain silent. You are not required to say anything to us at any time or to answer any questions. Anything you say can be used against you in court.

You have the right to talk to a lawyer for advice before we question you and to have him with you during questioning.

If you cannot afford a lawyer and want one, a lawyer will be provided for you.

If you want to answer questions now without a lawyer present you will still have the right to stop answering at any time. You also have the right to stop answering at any time until you talk to a lawyer.

WAIVER

1. Have you read or had read to you the warning as to your rights?

2. Do you understand these rights?

3. Do you wish to answer any questions?

4. Are you willing to answer questions without having an attorney present?

5. Signature of defendant on line below.

   _____

6. Time _____   Date _____

7. Signature of Officer _____

8. Signature of Witness _____

congenial and noncoercive manner at the man's residence, even though the investigation later could lead to criminal tax fraud violations. In *Oregon v. Mathiason* (1977) the Court ruled that a noncoercive custodial interrogation, in which an individual voluntarily appears at a police station for questioning, does not require Miranda warnings. As the Burger Court gradually narrowed the circumstances under which police had to inform suspects of their rights, many thought that the Court would overrule *Miranda,* and **Berkemer v. McCarty** (1984) seemed the perfect vehicle.

This case had its beginnings when an Ohio highway patrol officer saw Richard McCarty's car weaving in and out of traffic lanes. The officer pulled McCarty over and asked him to step out of his car. McCarty had difficulty standing up. The officer asked McCarty if he had taken anything, and McCarty said he had consumed two beers and smoked two joints of marijuana. The officer arrested him and drove him to the police station. At no point was McCarty given full Miranda warnings. Even though McCarty's blood test showed no alcohol, police interrogated him further, and he made additional incriminating statements. McCarty was charged with driving while intoxicated, a misdemeanor, for which he received ten days in jail and a fine.

On appeal, the Supreme Court confronted two important questions. First, does the Miranda rule apply to minor infractions such as misdemeanor traffic offenses or only to more serious crimes? And second, if the Miranda rule does apply to minor crimes, at what point should McCarty have been advised of his rights—at the initial roadside stop or when he was formally arrested and taken to the station?

With a unanimous vote, the justices responded that Miranda rights apply to anyone accused of a crime, regardless of the nature or severity of the alleged offense. If an accused individual is taken into custody, he or she must be given Miranda warnings before any interrogation. The justices also held, however, that the common roadside stop of a motorist does not constitute "custody" for Miranda purposes. Unlike arrests for more significant charges, the roadside stop does not create an overwhelmingly coercive environment. The Court offered three justifications: First, the roadside stop is a routine procedure that almost every driver experiences sooner or later. Second, the common roadside stop is brief in duration. Third, the roadside stop takes place in public, where police could be observed abusing their authority. The justices ruled that because a roadside stop is

not a custodial situation for Miranda purposes, the officer had no obligation to provide Miranda warnings when he initially questioned McCarty, and McCarty's responses to those questions could be used as evidence. However, once the officer formally arrested McCarty and placed him in the patrol car for transport to the police station, the conditions of a routine roadside stop had changed and a custodial condition had begun. Miranda warnings, therefore, should have been given prior to any questioning from that point forward. As a result, McCarty's incriminating statements at the police station, made without the benefit of Miranda warnings, were inadmissible.

Although *Berkemer v. McCarty* may have reduced police confusion over the issue of custody, we must consider its compatibility with the Warren Court's mandate in *Miranda* and *Orozco.* Did *Berkemer* merely clarify those opinions, as some have suggested, or did it undermine their intent? If you believe the latter, how else could the Court have ruled? Would the reading of Miranda rights at all roadside stops, even for relatively minor offenses such as speeding, have been a viable alternative?

What Constitutes Interrogation? Based on *Escobedo* and *Miranda,* police must inform individuals of their rights before they question them in an accusatory fashion. But both of these decisions dealt with traditional interrogations, occurring within the confines of a police station and using a standard "question and answer" format. What about questioning in the guise of conversation? That is, must police read Miranda warnings before they engage in any dialogue with a suspect?

The Burger Court grappled with this question in ***Brewer v. Williams*** (1977). This case involved Robert Williams, a deeply religious man with severe psychological problems, who allegedly kidnapped and killed a ten-year-old girl in Des Moines, Iowa, on Christmas Eve, 1968. Two days later Williams turned himself in to police in Davenport, some 170 miles away, after apparently dumping the child's body somewhere along the way. Williams telephoned an attorney in Des Moines, who told him to remain silent, talking neither to the Davenport police nor to the Des Moines detectives who were to take him back to that city.

As the detectives drove Williams to Des Moines, they engaged the suspect in a wide-ranging conversation. At one point they began delivering what has become known as the "Christian burial speech." Recognizing Williams's religious convictions, one of the detectives addressed him as Reverend and said:

I want to give you something to think about while we're traveling down the road. . . . Number one, I want you to observe the weather conditions, it's raining, it's sleeting, it's freezing, driving is very treacherous, visibility is poor, it's going to be dark early this evening. They are predicting several inches of snow for tonight, and I feel that you yourself are the only person that knows where this little girl's body is, that you yourself have only been there once, and if you get a snow on top of it you yourself may be unable to find it. And, since we will be going right past the area on the way into Des Moines, I feel that we could stop and locate the body, that the parents of this little girl should be entitled to a Christian burial for the little girl who was snatched away from them on Christmas Eve and murdered. And I feel we should stop and locate it on the way in rather than waiting until morning and trying to come back out after a snow storm and possibly not being able to find it at all. . . . I do not want you to answer me. I don't want to discuss it any further. Just think about it as we're riding down the road.

Williams promptly directed police to the girl's body.

At his trial, Williams's attorney argued that the statements made by him in the car should be excluded as evidence, as should any evidence—the body—resulting from those statements. The statements, the attorney argued, were inadmissible because they had been obtained by illegal means. By playing on Williams's weaknesses, police had tricked him. Their conversation, therefore, amounted to an interrogation, immediately prior to which Williams should have been advised of his rights.

In a 5–4 vote the U.S. Supreme Court agreed. Writing for the majority, Justice Stewart said:

There can be no serious doubt . . . that [the detective] deliberately and designedly set out to elicit information from Williams just as surely as . . . if he had formally interrogated him. [He] was fully aware before departing . . . that Williams was being represented [by counsel]. Yet, he purposely sought during Williams' isolation from his lawyers to obtain as much incriminating evidence as possible.

The importance of the *Williams* case is the Court's acknowledgment that for Miranda purposes an interrogation may take many forms. It is not confined to a traditional question-and-answer session in a police interrogation room. Regardless of the form it takes, any attempt to obtain incriminating statements from a suspect in custody triggers the need to give Miranda warnings.

Exceptions to the Miranda Rule and Its Continuing Viability. The Warren Court premised its decision in *Miranda* on the inevitable power imbalance between the accused and the police during custodial interrogations. Without some procedure to safeguard the rights of the accused, suspects too often would forgo their privilege against self-incrimination under intense and ultimately coercive police questioning. Arguably, the justices operated under the assumption that incriminating statements made in the absence of Miranda warnings would automatically violate the Fifth Amendment and that such evidence should be excluded from court.

Beginning in 1971 and continuing into the twenty-first century, however, the Burger, Rehnquist, and Roberts Courts applied *Miranda* in a narrow fashion and even created exceptions to the rule. These holdings often stemmed from cases presenting unusual circumstances in which prosecutors argued that *Miranda*'s ban on the use of self-incriminating statements should not apply. Table 11-2 summarizes the rulings from a number of these cases. Some Court observers speculated that the cumulative effect of these various exceptions to *Miranda* had watered down the rule to the point that it lacked any real meaning. Others guessed that if this trend continued, a formal overruling of *Miranda* was inevitable.

Those who predicted that *Miranda* would be overturned have so far been wrong. Although the Court has continued to apply the precedent in a relatively narrow fashion, it has remained loyal to *Miranda*'s central principles. The justices vigorously rebuffed a full frontal attack on *Miranda* that accompanied ***Dickerson v. United States*** (2000). At issue in this case was a federal statute declaring that the administration of Miranda warnings was not required for a confession to be valid, but was just one of several elements that could be used to establish that a confession was given voluntarily. Upholding the statute would essentially convert Miranda warnings from a constitutional requirement to an optional practice.

With only Justices Scalia and Thomas dissenting, the Court reaffirmed the *Miranda* ruling. The majority held

TABLE 11-2   Exceptions to *Miranda:* Some Examples

CASE	FACTS	RULING
Harris v. New York (1971)	An arrested drug suspect made incriminating statements without the benefit of Miranda warnings. At trial he gave an alibi at odds with his earlier statements. To impeach his credibility, the prosecutor introduced the suspect's initial statements.	Statements made without Miranda warnings may be used for the narrow purpose of counteracting perjury.
Michigan v. Tucker (1974)	A rape suspect who had not been given Miranda warnings claimed he was with a friend at the time of the crime. Police questioned the friend, who did not corroborate the story, and his testimony was used as evidence.	Although police were led to the witness by the defendant's statements made without the required warnings, the reliability of the witness's testimony is not affected and the testimony may be used.
New York v. Quarles (1984)	A rape suspect was apprehended after a chase through a supermarket. Police discovered an empty holster and asked, "Where's the gun?" The suspect revealed where he dropped it. Police then read the suspect his Miranda warnings.	When there is a danger to public safety, police may ask questions to remove that danger prior to reading Miranda warnings. Answers to such questions may be used as evidence.
Oregon v. Elstad (1985)	A burglary suspect made an incriminating statement prior to receiving Miranda warnings. He later was given his warnings at the police station and confessed. The confession was used in court over his attorney's objection that the initial self-incriminating statement tainted all future interrogations.	The confession may be used as evidence because it was preceded by Miranda warnings. Initial statements made prior to warnings may not be used.
Moran v. Burbine (1986)	A murder suspect in custody made incriminating statements after receiving Miranda warnings and waiving his right to have an attorney present during questioning. The suspect's lawyer had previously contacted police and indicated a desire to advise his client. Police did not inform the suspect of his lawyer's wishes.	Statements may be used as evidence. The defendant knew he had a right to an attorney and a right to remain silent. His waiver of these rights was not coerced.
Illinois v. Perkins (1990)	An undercover police agent obtained incriminating statements from a prison inmate without first providing Miranda warnings.	Miranda warnings are not required when a suspect is unaware he or she is speaking to a law enforcement official and gives a voluntary statement.
New York v. Harris (1990)	Police unlawfully entered the home of a murder suspect without a warrant and without permission. They arrested the suspect and took him to the police station. He was read his Miranda warnings and subsequently signed a written confession.	The fact that police enter a home illegally to make an arrest does not taint a subsequent confession at the police station that takes place after Miranda warnings are given.
Davis v. United States (1994)	In the middle of an interrogation session a murder suspect, who had received proper Miranda warnings, commented, "Maybe I should talk to a lawyer." The questioning continued for about another hour, at which time the suspect said, "I think I want a lawyer before I say anything else." At that point the investigators terminated the interview.	*Miranda* does not require police to stop questioning when the suspect makes an ambiguous reference to an attorney.
United States v. Patane (2004)	An arrested suspect, who did not receive full Miranda warnings, was questioned at his home by police officers about a possible firearms violation. The suspect voluntarily admitted to having the pistol in question and gave the officers permission to retrieve it from his bedroom.	The failure to give full Miranda warnings does not require suppression of physical evidence obtained from information voluntarily supplied by the suspect in custody.

(Continued)

TABLE 11-2 (Continued)

CASE	FACTS	RULING
Montejo v. Louisiana (2009)	Although he remained silent and never requested a lawyer, an indigent charged with first-degree murder was automatically assigned counsel. After the appointment, but before the suspect ever consulted with his attorney, the suspect was read his Miranda warnings, cooperated in a police-initiated interrogation, and confessed to the crime.	Overruling *Michigan v. Jackson* (1986), the Court held that police are prevented from initiating custodial interrogations only after the defendant affirmatively asserts the right to counsel.
Howes v. Fields (2012)	Without first giving Miranda warnings, two armed sheriff's deputies interrogated an inmate in a jailhouse conference room concerning a crime unrelated to his incarceration. The inmate confessed.	Because the inmate was informed that he could terminate the interrogation at any time and return to his cell, he was not "in custody" for Miranda purposes and therefore no warnings were required.

that *Miranda* rested firmly on the Fifth Amendment and Congress had no authority to alter by statute the Court's interpretation. Furthermore, the justices rejected arguments to overrule *Miranda* on their own, describing the required warnings as having become part of the national culture. Chief Justice Rehnquist's majority opinion acknowledged that the justices had made certain exceptions to *Miranda* to ease its burdens on legitimate law enforcement efforts, but declared that the core of the decision remained unchanged: "unwarned statements may not be used as evidence" when the prosecution presents its case to establish the guilt of the defendant.[26] In a similar fashion the justices have rejected attempts by law enforcement agents to abuse the latitude provided by the Court's exceptions to *Miranda*. *Missouri v. Seibert* (2004) serves as a good illustration.

Seibert focuses on police interrogation practices that evolved in response to the Court's decision in *Oregon v. Elstad* (1985). Pursuing a tip provided by a neighbor during a burglary investigation, police came to the home of Michael Elstad, who made incriminating statements before the officers could advise him of his self-incrimination rights under *Miranda*. The officers arrested Elstad and took him to the police station, where they advised him of his Miranda rights and questioned him. Elstad made a full confession. The trial court judge disallowed the statements made in

Elstad's home but admitted the confession given later at police headquarters.

In a subsequent appeal to the Supreme Court, Elstad's attorneys argued that the confession also should be declared inadmissible because it flowed from the initial incriminating statements that were made without the benefit of Miranda warnings. The justices held, however, that the trial court had ruled correctly. The statements made in Elstad's home were inadmissible, but the Miranda warnings that preceded the interrogation at police headquarters made the formal confession voluntary and valid.

As demonstrated in *Seibert*, law enforcement seized upon *Elstad* as an opportunity to evade the spirit of the *Miranda* ruling. As you read the Court's decision, note how the justices reject the attempt by police to extend a Court-approved exception to *Miranda* beyond its original purpose.

Missouri v. Seibert

542 U.S. 600 (2004)
http://laws.findlaw.com/US/542/600.html
Oral arguments are available at http://www.oyez.org.
Vote: 5 (Breyer, Ginsburg, Kennedy, Souter, Stevens)
    4 (O'Connor, Rehnquist, Scalia, Thomas)

OPINION ANNOUNCING THE JUDGMENT OF THE COURT: *Souter*
CONCURRING OPINIONS: *Breyer, Kennedy*
DISSENTING OPINION: *O'Connor*

FACTS:

Patrice Seibert of Rolla, Missouri, had a twelve-year-old son, Jonathan, who suffered from cerebral palsy. When Jonathan died in his sleep, Seibert feared that

---

26. The Court, however, did not alter its earlier holding in *Harris v. New York* (1971) that allowed statements made without proper Miranda warnings to be introduced at the trial's rebuttal stage to discredit the defendant if he or she offered possibly perjured testimony.

she might be charged with child neglect because her son suffered a bad case of bedsores. To avoid such charges, Seibert, with her two teenage sons and two of their friends, devised a plan to conceal the facts. They decided to set Seibert's mobile home on fire to make it appear as if Jonathan had died in an accidental blaze. To guard against charges that Jonathan had been left unattended, they planned to leave Donald Rector, a mentally ill teenager living with the family, in the mobile home when the fire was set. Seibert's son Darian and a friend carried out the plan, and Rector died in the fire.

Five days later, Officer Kevin Clinton confronted Seibert at a local hospital, where Darian was recovering from burns. He took her into custody, but on instructions from Officer Richard Hanrahan, Clinton did not provide Seibert with Miranda warnings. At the police station Hanrahan interrogated Seibert for about forty minutes, during which time she made incrimi-

nating statements. After giving her a twenty-minute coffee and cigarette break, Hanrahan turned on a tape recorder and gave Seibert her Miranda warnings. Seibert waived her rights, and Hanrahan resumed the questioning. He asked Seibert to repeat her incriminating statements, and she did. Prosecutors charged Seibert with first-degree murder.

Officer Hanrahan admitted that withholding the Miranda warnings was a conscious decision. He claimed he was following an interrogation technique he was taught: question first, then give the Miranda warnings, and finally question again with the goal of getting the suspect to repeat the incriminating statements.

Defense attorneys moved to suppress both the prewarning and postwarning statements, but the trial court, following the precedent set in *Oregon v. Elstad*, held that the postwarning statements could be admitted. The state supreme court reversed, ruling that the two interrogation sessions were nearly continuous and the statements made in the second session were clearly a product of the first. The state requested review by the U.S. Supreme Court.

In Missouri v. Seibert *the Supreme Court declared inadmissible the self-incriminating statements that led to Patrice Seibert's conviction on murder charges. The police interrogation techniques that produced those statements violated the* Miranda *ruling.*

ARGUMENTS:

For the petitioner, State of Missouri:

- *Miranda* imposes only a narrow exclusionary rule governing the admissibility of unwarned statements made during custodial interrogations.
- *Oregon v. Elstad* established that voluntary statements made after Miranda warnings have been given are admissible even if similar statements were previously obtained without Miranda warnings.
- The Constitution is not violated when police ask questions without giving Miranda warnings. A constitutional violation occurs only when those statements are introduced as evidence in court. Statements made without Miranda warnings are already inadmissible. No other remedy is needed.

For the respondent, Patrice Seibert:

- All statements made following a willful and unreasonable refusal by police to give Miranda warnings should be inadmissible.
- If the Court approves the police strategy used here, it will encourage nationwide evasion of the spirit of *Miranda*.

- Unlike in *Elstad,* the "two-part" interrogation used here was essentially one long interrogation period with Miranda warnings intentionally not given until police extracted a confession. Under these circumstances, Seibert's restated confession was not voluntarily given.

JUSTICE SOUTER ANNOUNCED THE JUDGMENT OF THE COURT AND DELIVERED AN OPINION, IN WHICH JUSTICE STEVENS, JUSTICE GINSBURG, AND JUSTICE BREYER JOIN.

This case tests a police protocol for custodial interrogation that calls for giving no warnings of the rights to silence and counsel until interrogation has produced a confession. Although such a statement is generally inadmissible, since taken in violation of *Miranda v. Arizona* (1966), the interrogating officer follows it with *Miranda* warnings and then leads the suspect to cover the same ground a second time. The question here is the admissibility of the repeated statement. . . .

In *Miranda,* we explained that the "voluntariness doctrine in the state cases . . . encompasses all interrogation practices which are likely to exert such pressure upon an individual as to disable him from making a free and rational choice." We appreciated the difficulty of judicial enquiry *post hoc* into the circumstances of a police interrogation, *Dickerson v. United States* (2000), and recognized that "the coercion inherent in custodial interrogation blurs the line between voluntary and involuntary statements, and thus heightens the risk" that the privilege against self-incrimination will not be observed. Hence our concern that the "traditional totality-of-the-circumstances" test posed an "unacceptably great" risk that involuntary custodial confessions would escape detection.

Accordingly, "to reduce the risk of a coerced confession and to implement the Self-Incrimination Clause," this Court in *Miranda* concluded that "the accused must be adequately and effectively apprised of his rights and the exercise of those rights must be fully honored." *Miranda* conditioned the admissibility at trial of any custodial confession on warning a suspect of his rights: failure to give the prescribed warnings and obtain a waiver of rights before custodial questioning generally requires exclusion of any statements obtained. Conversely, giving the warnings and getting a waiver has generally produced a virtual ticket of admissibility. . . . [T]his common consequence would not be common at all were it not that *Miranda* warnings are customarily given under circumstances allowing for a real choice between talking and remaining silent. . . .

The technique of interrogating in successive, unwarned and warned phases raises a new challenge to *Miranda.* Although we have no statistics on the frequency of this practice, it is not confined to Rolla, Missouri. An officer of that police department testified that the strategy of withholding *Miranda* warnings until after interrogating and drawing out a confession was promoted not only by his own department, but by a national police training organization and other departments in which he had worked. . . .

When a confession so obtained is offered and challenged, attention must be paid to the conflicting objects of *Miranda* and question-first. *Miranda* addressed "interrogation practices . . . likely . . . to disable [an individual] from making a free and rational choice" about speaking, and held that a suspect must be "adequately and effectively" advised of the choice the Constitution guarantees. The object of question-first is to render *Miranda* warnings ineffective by waiting for a particularly opportune time to give them, after the suspect has already confessed.

. . . By any objective measure, applied to circumstances exemplified here, it is likely that if the interrogators employ the technique of withholding warnings until after interrogation succeeds in eliciting a confession, the warnings will be ineffective in preparing the suspect for successive interrogation, close in time and similar in content. After all, the reason that question-first is catching on is as obvious as its manifest purpose, which is to get a confession the suspect would not make if he understood his rights at the outset; the sensible underlying assumption is that with one confession in hand before the warnings, the interrogator can count on getting its duplicate, with trifling additional trouble. Upon hearing warnings only in the aftermath of interrogation and just after making a confession, a suspect would hardly think he had a genuine right to remain silent, let alone persist in so believing once the police began to lead him over the same ground again. . . . [T]elling a suspect that "anything you say can and will be used against you," without expressly excepting the statement just given, could lead to an entirely reasonable inference that what he has just said will be used, with subsequent silence being of no avail. Thus, when *Miranda* warnings are inserted in the midst of coordinated and continuing interrogation, they are likely to mislead and "depriv[e] a defendant of knowledge essential to his ability to understand the nature of his rights and the consequences of abandoning them." *Moran v. Burbine* (1986). . . .

Strategists dedicated to draining the substance out of *Miranda* cannot accomplish by training instructions what *Dickerson* held Congress could not do by statute. Because the question-first tactic effectively threatens to thwart *Miranda*'s purpose of reducing the risk that a coerced confession would be admitted, and because the facts here do not reasonably support a conclusion that the warnings given could have served their purpose, Seibert's postwarning statements are inadmissible. The judgment of the Supreme Court of Missouri is affirmed.

It is so ordered.

JUSTICE KENNEDY concurring in the judgment.

The police used a two-step questioning technique based on a deliberate violation of *Miranda*. The *Miranda* warning was withheld to obscure both the practical and legal significance of the admonition when finally given. As JUSTICE SOUTER points out, the two-step technique permits the accused to conclude that the right not to respond did not exist when the earlier incriminating statements were made. The strategy is based on the assumption that *Miranda* warnings will tend to mean less when recited midinterrogation, after inculpatory statements have already been obtained. This tactic relies on an intentional misrepresentation of the protection that *Miranda* offers and does not serve any legitimate objectives that might otherwise justify its use.

Further, the interrogating officer here relied on the defendant's prewarning statement to obtain the postwarning statement used against her at trial. The postwarning interview resembled a cross-examination. The officer confronted the defendant with her inadmissible prewarning statements and pushed her to acknowledge them. This shows the temptations for abuse inherent in the two-step technique. Reference to the prewarning statement was an implicit suggestion that the mere repetition of the earlier statement was not independently incriminating. The implicit suggestion was false.

The technique used in this case distorts the meaning of *Miranda* and furthers no legitimate countervailing interest. The *Miranda* rule would be frustrated were we to allow police to undermine its meaning and effect. The technique simply creates too high a risk that postwarning

statements will be obtained when a suspect was deprived of "knowledge essential to his ability to understand the nature of his rights and the consequences of abandoning them." *Moran v. Burbine* (1986). When an interrogator uses this deliberate, two-step strategy, predicated upon violating *Miranda* during an extended interview, postwarning statements that are related to the substance of prewarning statements must be excluded absent specific, curative steps. . . .

The admissibility of postwarning statements should continue to be governed by the principles of *Elstad* unless the deliberate two-step strategy was employed. If the deliberate two-step strategy has been used, postwarning statements that are related to the substance of prewarning statements must be excluded unless curative measures are taken before the postwarning statement is made. Curative measures should be designed to ensure that a reasonable person in the suspect's situation would understand the import and effect of the *Miranda* warning and of the *Miranda* waiver. For example, a substantial break in time and circumstances between the prewarning statement and the *Miranda* warning may suffice in most circumstances, as it allows the accused to distinguish the two contexts and appreciate that the interrogation has taken a new turn. Alternatively, an additional warning that explains the likely inadmissibility of the prewarning custodial statement may be sufficient. No curative steps were taken in this case, however, so the postwarning statements are inadmissible and the conviction cannot stand.

JUSTICE O'CONNOR, with whom THE CHIEF JUSTICE, JUSTICE SCALIA, and JUSTICE THOMAS join, dissenting.

I believe that we are bound by [*Oregon v.*] *Elstad* to reach a different result, and I would vacate the judgment of the Supreme Court of Missouri. . . .

I would analyze the two-step interrogation procedure under the voluntariness standards central to the Fifth Amendment and reiterated in *Elstad*. *Elstad* commands that if Seibert's first statement is shown to have been involuntary, the court must examine whether the taint dissipated through the passing of time or a change in circumstances: "When a prior statement is actually coerced, the time that passes between confessions, the change in place of interrogations, and the change in identity of the interrogators all bear on whether that coercion has carried over into the second confession." In addition, Seibert's second statement should be suppressed if she showed that it was involuntary despite the *Miranda* warnings. . . .

Because I believe that the plurality gives insufficient deference to *Elstad* and that JUSTICE KENNEDY places improper weight on subjective intent, I respectfully dissent.

With decisions such as *Dickerson* and *Seibert*, it appears that *Miranda*'s core principle is firmly in place and will not be overruled in the foreseeable future. Nevertheless, it is undoubtedly true that in the hands of a conservative majority the Court over time has whittled away at the scope of the rule, thereby significantly narrowing its applicability and leaving behind the broad interpretation initially fashioned by the more liberal Warren Court.

The issue of self-incriminating statements made by criminal suspects has commanded considerable attention from the Court. In fact, over the past few decades *Miranda v. Arizona* has been the justices' most frequently cited precedent. But the United States is not the only nation concerned with this issue. As Box 11-4 illustrates, other countries have also grappled with the problem of coerced confessions.

BOX 11-4   *MIRANDA* IN GLOBAL PERSPECTIVE

Although many Americans may think that Miranda warnings are a unique feature of the U.S. criminal justice system, this is not the case. Indeed, in his opinion for the Court in *Miranda*, Chief Justice Earl Warren noted that "Scottish judicial decisions bar use in evidence of most confessions obtained through police interrogation. In India, confessions made to police not in the presence of a magistrate have been excluded by rule of evidence since 1872, at a time when it operated under British law."

Warren also pointed to the Judges' Rules of 1912, operative in England at the time of *Miranda*:

II. As soon as a police officer has evidence which would afford reasonable grounds for suspecting that a person has committed an offence, he shall caution that person or cause him to be cautioned before putting to him any questions, or further questions, relating to that offence. The caution shall be in the following terms:

"You are not obliged to say anything unless you wish to do so but what you say may be put into writing and given in evidence."

When after being cautioned a person is being questioned, or elects to make a statement, a record shall be kept of the time and place at which any such questioning or statement began and ended and of the persons present.

The Judges' Rules also provided

[t]hat every person at any stage of an investigation should be able to communicate and to consult privately with a solicitor. This is so even if he is in custody provided that in such a case no unreasonable delay or hindrance is caused to the processes of investigation or the administration of justice by his doing so.

Some scholars claim that today British practice even more closely resembles *Miranda*. During the 1980s, Parliament passed several acts to safeguard the rights of the criminally accused, including a provision that allows suspects to have an attorney present during questioning. And under the 1994 Criminal Justice and Public Order Act, British police officers are required to read the following warning to suspects:

You do not have to say anything. But if you do not mention now something which you later use in your defence, the court may decide that your failure to mention it now strengthens the case against you. A record will be made of anything you say and it may be given in evidence if you are brought to trial.

Note the similarity to *Miranda*: police must tell suspects that they have the right to remain silent. The difference, however, is equally striking: whereas *Miranda* suggests that only statements suspects make can be used against them, the British rule indicates that silence may be invoked against them as well.

SOURCES: William E. Schmidt, "Silence May Speak against the Accused in Britain," *New York Times*, November 11, 1994, 10; Paul G. Cassell, "Miranda's Social Costs: An Empirical Reassessment," *Northwestern University Law Review* 90 (1996): 387–440.

Now that you have an understanding of the constitutional rights designed to protect the criminally accused during the evidence-gathering stages of the process, turn to Chapter 12, which deals with what the Constitution requires during the trial and punishment phases.

ANNOTATED READINGS

A number of works provide in-depth discussion of the American criminal court system and the procedures pertaining to the collection and use of evidence. Among them are Craig M. Bradley, *The Failure of the Criminal Procedure Revolution* (Philadelphia: University of Pennsylvania Press, 1993); James Eisenstein, Roy B. Fleming, and Peter F. Nardulli, *The Contours of Justice: Communities and Their Courts* (Boston: Little, Brown, 1988); James A. Inciardi, *Criminal Justice*, 9th ed. (Fort Worth, TX: Harcourt Brace, 2009); David W. Neubauer and Henry F. Fradella, *America's Courts and the Criminal Justice System*, 10th ed. (Belmont, CA: Wadsworth, 2011); Stuart Scheingold, *The Politics of Law and Order* (New York: Longman, 1984); Frank Schmalleger, *Criminal Justice Today*, 12th ed (Upper Saddle River, NJ: Pearson, 2012); and Jon R. Waltz, *Introduction to Criminal Evidence*, 4th ed. (Chicago: Nelson-Hall, 1997).

Excellent examples of literature covering the search and seizure provisions of the Fourth Amendment are Samuel Dash, *The Intruders: Unreasonable Searches and Seizures from King John to John Ashcroft* (New Brunswick, NJ: Rutgers University Press, 2004); Carolyn N. Long, Mapp v. Ohio: *Guarding against Unreasonable Searches and Seizures* (Lawrence: University Press of Kansas, 2006); Thomas N. McInis, *Evolution of the Fourth Amendment* (New York: Lexington Books, 2009); Darien A. McWhirter, *Search, Seizure, and Privacy: Exploring the Constitution* (Phoenix, AZ: Oryx Press, 1994); and Andrew E. Taslitz, *Reconstructing the Fourth Amendment: A History of Search and Seizure, 1789–1868* (New York: New York University Press, 2006).

The privilege against self-incrimination is explored in the following works: Liva Baker, *Miranda: Crime, Law, and Politics* (New York: Atheneum, 1983); R. H. Helmholz, Charles M. Gray, John H. Langbein, Eben Moglen, Henry E. Smith, and Albert W. Alschuler, *The Privilege against Self-Incrimination: Its Origins and Development* (Chicago: University of Chicago Press, 1997); Richard A. Leo and George C. Thomas III, *The Miranda Debate: Law, Justice, and Policing* (Boston: Northeastern University Press, 1998); Richard J. Medalie, *From* Escobedo *to* Miranda (Washington, DC: Lerner Law Books, 1966); and John B. Taylor, *The Right to Counsel and Privilege against Self-Incrimination: Rights and Liberties under the Law* (Santa Barbara, CA: ABC-CLIO, 2004).

12

Attorneys, Trials, and Punishments

THE FRAMERS CLEARLY understood the importance of fairness in evidence gathering; they also understood the need to ensure the integrity of the formal stages of the criminal process. Consequently, they included in the Bill of Rights specific guarantees to prohibit the government from abusing prosecuted defendants. These rights are among those we most value, such as the right to be represented by counsel, to be tried by an impartial jury of our peers, and to be protected against punishments that are cruel and unusual. Other guarantees, less well-known but no less important, also enjoy constitutional status: the rights to a speedy and public trial, to confront our accusers in open court, to have access to evidence favorable to our defense, and to have a reasonable opportunity for bail. Taken as a whole, these rights were designed to help achieve a universally valued goal—fundamentally fair criminal trials. In this chapter we discuss what the Constitution says about these important procedural guarantees and how they have evolved through Supreme Court interpretations over the years.

THE RIGHT TO COUNSEL

The Sixth Amendment states, "In all criminal prosecutions, the accused shall enjoy the right . . . to have the Assistance of Counsel for his defence." At the time these words were written, the law was relatively uncomplicated, and lawyers in the new nation were scarce. Some individuals charged with crimes sought the advice of counsel, but most handled their own cases. Still, the framers understood the importance of legal representation well enough to include the right to counsel in the Bill of Rights.

Today, perhaps no other right guaranteed to the criminally accused is more important than the right to counsel. Until relatively recently, a lawyer representing a criminal client could do the job by appearing at trial and dealing with well-established principles of evidence and procedure. Today, however, appearing at trial is only a small part of what a criminal defense attorney must do. As we saw in the Fifth Amendment cases reviewed in Chapter 11, the Supreme Court has repeatedly emphasized that the role of the defense attorney begins when police first interrogate a suspect. From arrest through appeal, there are critical and complicated stages during which a defendant's rights might be violated. It is counsel's responsibility to ensure that the interests of the defendant are not jeopardized. The defense attorney, therefore, is the primary guarantee that all of the other rights of criminal due process are observed.

The provisions of the Sixth Amendment are sufficiently clear that little controversy has arisen over the right of an individual to have legal representation throughout the various stages of the criminal justice process. Historically, however, it was always the responsibility of the accused to secure a lawyer and to pay for the lawyer's services. The most prolonged

The plight of the nine "Scottsboro boys," arrested in rural Alabama in 1931 for raping two white females, spawned numerous legal actions, including Powell v. Alabama *(1932), which expanded the rights of indigents to legal representation. Samuel Leibowitz, a prominent attorney and later a judge, handled the defendants' cases after their original convictions. He is shown here conferring with seven of his clients. Deputy Sheriff Charles McComb stands to the left.*

controversy over legal representation in criminal matters centered on the rights of those who cannot pay for legal assistance.

Indigents and the Right to Counsel: Foundations

As the complexity of the U.S. system of justice increased, greater numbers of people retained lawyers to handle their cases. But as soon as this practice took hold, people began to complain about economic discrimination. Civil libertarians and reformers throughout the country argued that only those who could afford it were guaranteed the right to counsel; indigent defendants were denied their constitutional guarantee. Reformers claimed that the only way to eliminate this injustice would be through a Supreme Court decision that would force governments to appoint free counsel for poor defendants.

In *Powell v. Alabama* (1932) the Supreme Court scrutinized this claim for the first time. Justice George Sutherland's opinion for the majority does not adopt the view that states must assign counsel to indigents in *all* cases, but does he completely shut the door on such an interpretation of the Constitution?

Powell v. Alabama (The Scottsboro Boys Case)

287 U.S. 45 (1932)
http://laws.findlaw.com/US/287/45.html
Vote: 7 (Brandeis, Cardozo, Hughes, Roberts, Stone, Sutherland, Van Devanter)
  2 (Butler, McReynolds)

OPINION OF THE COURT: *Sutherland*
DISSENTING OPINION: *Butler*

FACTS:

Riding in an open car on a freight train traveling from Chattanooga, Tennessee, through Alabama on March 25, 1931, were nine young black men, seven young white men, and two white women.[1] During the journey, the

---

1. For more on this case, see Dan T. Carter, *Scottsboro: A Tragedy of the American South* (New York: Oxford University Press, 1969).

young men got into a fight, which ended with the white youths being thrown off the train and the women claiming the black youths had raped them. Word of the alleged rapes spread, and when the train reached Paint Rock, a sheriff's posse arrested the black youths, who ranged in age from twelve to twenty, and jailed them in the county seat of Scottsboro, Alabama. A hostile, racist crowd subsequently gathered to harass the alleged assailants, and extra security personnel were needed to prevent a lynching.

When the youths appeared at the courthouse, it was obvious they were frightened. They were young, uneducated, and away from home, with no friends or family to help them. Because they were charged with a capital offense, the judge, according to Alabama law, was supposed to appoint counsel to assist them. Instead, he assigned all the town's members of the bar to represent the accused.[2] No single lawyer took responsibility for their defense. Moreover, the judge set their trial date for April 6, just six days after they were indicted.

On the morning of April 6, a Tennessee lawyer named Stephen R. Roddy appeared to represent the defendants. Sent by people interested in their plight, Roddy had not yet prepared a case and was not familiar with Alabama law and procedure. The judge authorized Milo Moody, a local attorney, to work with Roddy. In rapid succession the nine defendants were tried in a series of four trials. Given the hostile environment in which they were tried, it should come as no surprise that eight of the nine "Scottsboro boys" were found guilty and sentenced to death.

The main question emerging from this case was this: Do indigents have the right to counsel at government expense?

ARGUMENTS:

For the petitioners, Ozie Powell, Willie Roberson, Andy Wright, Olen Montgomery, Haywood Patterson, Charlie Weems, and Clarence Norris:

- Consultation with counsel and opportunity for preparation and presentation of proper defense at trial are rights included in the due process clause.
- Because there was no fair, impartial, and deliberate trial, the proceedings violated the due process clause.

---

2. Many states had laws mandating the appointment of counsel for capital crimes such as rape. In *Coker v. Georgia* (1977) the Supreme Court outlawed the use of the death penalty in rape cases.

For the respondent, State of Alabama:

- Petitioners' counsel had time to prepare their case and proceeded along proper lines for a week prior to trial.
- The trials were fair and impartial. No denial of due process of law in contravention of the Fourteenth Amendment took place.
- In the absence of showing that the extra security was actually needed to dispel mob violence, the extra security in Scottsboro cannot be taken as evidence of the fact that the trial was not fair and impartial.
- It is important to appreciate that "due process of law" is process according to the system of law in each state.

MR. JUSTICE SUTHERLAND DELIVERED THE OPINION OF THE COURT.

It is hardly necessary to say that the right to counsel being conceded, a defendant should be afforded a fair opportunity to secure counsel of his own choice. Not only was that not done here, but such designation of counsel as was attempted was either so indefinite or so close upon the trial as to amount to a denial of effective and substantial aid in that regard. . . .

. . . [U]ntil the very morning of the trial no lawyer had been named or definitely designated to represent the defendants. Prior to that time, the trial judge had "appointed all the members of the bar" for the limited "purpose of arraigning the defendants." Whether they would represent the defendants thereafter, if no counsel appeared in their behalf, was a matter of speculation only, or, as the judge indicated, of mere anticipation on the part of the court. Such a designation, even if made for all purposes, would, in our opinion, have fallen far short of meeting, in any proper sense, a requirement for the appointment of counsel. How many lawyers were members of the bar does not appear; but, in the very nature of things, whether many or few, they would not, thus collectively named, have been given that clear appreciation of responsibility or impressed with that individual sense of duty which should and naturally would accompany the appointment of a selected member of the bar, specifically named and assigned.

That this action of the trial judge in respect of appointment of counsel was little more than an expansive gesture, imposing no substantial or definite obligation upon any one, is borne out by the fact that prior to the calling of the case for trial on April 6, a leading member of the local bar accepted employment on the side of the prosecution and actively participated in the trial. . . . This the lawyer in question, of his own accord, frankly stated to the court; and no doubt he acted with the utmost good faith. Probably other members of the bar had a like understanding. In any event, the circumstance lends emphasis to the conclusion that during perhaps the most critical period of the proceedings against these defendants, that is to say, from the time of their arraignment until the beginning of their trial, when consultation, thoroughgoing investigation and preparation were vitally important, the defendants did not have the aid of counsel in any real sense, although they were as much entitled to such aid during that period as at the trial itself. . . .

The defendants, young, ignorant, illiterate, surrounded by hostile sentiment, haled back and forth under guard of soldiers, charged with an atrocious crime regarded with especial horror in the community where they were to be tried, were thus put in peril of their lives within a few moments after counsel for the first time charged with any degree of responsibility began to represent them.

It is not enough to assume that counsel thus precipitated into the case thought there was no defense, and exercised their best judgment in proceeding to trial without preparation. Neither they nor the court could say what a prompt and thoroughgoing investigation might disclose as to the facts. No attempt was made to investigate. No opportunity to do so was given. . . .

. . . [W]e think the failure of the trial court to give them reasonable time and opportunity to secure counsel was a clear denial of due process.

But passing that, and assuming their inability, even if opportunity had been given, to employ counsel, as the trial court evidently did assume, we are of opinion that, under the circumstances just stated, the necessity of counsel was so vital and imperative that the failure of the trial court to make an effective appointment of counsel was likewise a denial of due process within the meaning of the Fourteenth Amendment. Whether this would be so in other criminal prosecutions, or under other circumstances, we need not determine. All that is necessary now to decide, as we do decide, is that in a capital case, where the defendant is unable to employ counsel, and is incapable adequately of making his own defense because of ignorance, feeblemindedness, illiteracy, or the like, it is the duty of the court, whether requested or not, to assign counsel for him as a necessary requisite of due process of law; and that duty is not discharged by an assignment at

such a time or under such circumstances as to preclude the giving of effective aid in the preparation and trial of the case. To hold otherwise would be to ignore the fundamental postulate, already adverted to, "that there are certain immutable principles of justice which inhere in the very idea of free government which no member of the Union may disregard." In a case such as this, whatever may be the rule in other cases, the right to have counsel appointed, when necessary, is a logical corollary from the constitutional right to be heard by counsel.

Judgments reversed.

MR. JUSTICE BUTLER, dissenting.

The Court . . . grounds its opinion and judgment upon a single assertion of fact. It is that petitioners "were denied the right of counsel, with the accustomed incidents of consultation and opportunity of preparation for trial." If that is true, they were denied due process of law and are entitled to have the judgments against them reversed.

But no such denial is shown by the record.

Nine defendants . . . were accused in one indictment. . . . Instead of trying them *en masse,* the State gave four trials and so lessened the danger of mistake and injustice that inevitably attends an attempt in a single trial to ascertain the guilt or innocence of many accused. . . .

. . . It must be inferred from the record that Mr. Roddy at all times was in touch with the defendants and the people who procured him to act for them. Mr. Moody and others of the local bar also acted for defendants at the time of the first arraignment, and . . . thereafter proceeded in the discharge of their duty, including conferences with the defendants. There is not the slightest ground to suppose that Roddy or Moody were by fear or in any manner restrained from full performance of their duties. Indeed, it clearly appears that the State, by proper and adequate show of its purpose and power to preserve order, furnished adequate protection to them and the defendants.

When the first case was called for trial, defendants' attorneys had already prepared, and then submitted, a motion for change of venue, together with supporting papers. They were ready to, and did at once, introduce testimony of witnesses to sustain that demand. . . .

If there had been any lack of opportunity for preparation, trial counsel would have applied to the court for postponement. No such application was made. There was no suggestion, at the trial or in the motion for a new trial which they made, that Mr. Roddy or Mr. Moody was denied such opportunity, or that they were not, in fact, fully prepared. The amended motion for new trial, by counsel who succeeded them, contains the first suggestion that defendants were denied counsel or opportunity to prepare for trial. But neither Mr. Roddy nor Mr. Moody has given any support to that claim. Their silence requires a finding that the claim is groundless, for if it had any merit they would be bound to support it. And no one has come to suggest any lack of zeal or good faith on their part.

If correct, the ruling that the failure of the trial court to give petitioners time and opportunity to secure counsel was denial of due process is enough, and with this the opinion should end. But the Court goes on to declare that "the failure of the trial court to make an effective appointment of counsel was likewise a denial of due process within the meaning of the Fourteenth Amendment." This

is an extension of federal authority into a field hitherto occupied exclusively by the several States. Nothing before the Court calls for a consideration of the point. It was not suggested below, and petitioners do not ask for its decision here. The Court, without being called upon to consider it, adjudges without a hearing an important constitutional question concerning criminal procedure in state courts. . . .

The record wholly fails to reveal that petitioners have been deprived of any right guaranteed by the Federal Constitution, and I am of opinion that the judgment should be affirmed.

MR. JUSTICE MCREYNOLDS concurs in this opinion.

The Court declined to decide if the Constitution guarantees the right to counsel for every defendant. But, writing for the majority, Justice Sutherland recognized

---

BOX 12-1 AFTERMATH . . . THE SCOTTSBORO BOYS

Their convictions were reversed by the Supreme Court in 1932, but the subsequent lives of the nine defendants known as the "Scottsboro Boys" were filled with tragedy and additional criminal accusations. Even though one of the alleged rape victims later admitted that she had not been raped, the defendants were convicted following their second trial. This time the convictions were overturned by the Supreme Court in *Norris v. Alabama* (1935) because of racial discrimination in jury selection. Between 1936 and 1937, additional retrials took place, leading to the convictions of four of the original defendants, with sentences ranging from seventy-five years in prison to death.

In 1937 the rape charges were dropped against Olen Montgomery, Willie Roberson, and Eugene Williams. They subsequently fell into obscurity.

Charges against Roy Wright also were dismissed. In 1959 Wright stabbed his wife to death and then took his own life.

Rape charges against Ozie Powell were dropped. He was later convicted of shooting a law enforcement officer in the head. He received a long prison sentence but was paroled in 1946.

Charlie Weems, Andrew Wright, Haywood Patterson, and Clarence Norris were convicted of the rape charges on retrial. Weems and Patterson were sentenced to

seventy-five years in prison, Wright to a term of ninety-nine years, and Norris to death.

Three of the convicted men were subsequently released from prison, and one escaped. Weems was paroled in 1943. Wright was paroled in 1944 but was returned to prison three times for parole violations. In 1951 Wright was accused of raping a thirteen-year-old girl, but he was acquitted and released. Patterson escaped from prison and fled to Michigan. In 1951 he was convicted of manslaughter and sentenced to prison. Shortly thereafter he died of lung cancer.

Norris had his death sentence commuted to life in prison in 1938. He was paroled in 1944 but was sent back to prison for leaving the state in violation of his parole agreement. Norris was paroled again in 1946 and almost immediately fled the state in violation of parole a second time. He lived undercover in New York City for many years. In 1976 the attorney general of Alabama acknowledged that subsequent studies of the case had concluded that Norris was not guilty of the original rape charge, and Governor George Wallace pardoned him. A bill to compensate Norris for wrongful conviction was defeated in the Alabama legislature. Norris died in 1989 at the age of seventy-six.

SOURCE: James A. Inciardi, *Criminal Justice*, 4th ed. (Fort Worth, TX: Harcourt Brace Jovanovich, 1993), 372.

that cases involving unusual situations (capital offenses, intense public pressure, or young, uneducated, and inexperienced defendants) would necessitate lawyers' participation to secure fundamental fairness for defendants. Although the Court in *Powell* made no sweeping statements about the Sixth Amendment, it mandated for the first time the appointment of counsel.

Given the pervasive racism in the criminal justice systems in the American South at the time, the extent to which this ruling helped the defendants in *Powell* may have been negligible *(see Box 12-1)*. But, just six years after *Powell*, the Court went one step further. In *Johnson v. Zerbst* it ruled that indigent defendants involved in federal criminal prosecutions are entitled to be represented by counsel.

Although *Johnson* was a major ruling, like *Powell*, its scope was limited. As we saw with the line of cases leading to the universal application of the exclusionary rule, decisions applying only to the federal government affect an insignificant number of defendants because most prosecutions occur in the states. Criminal defense attorneys, therefore, pushed the Court to apply *Johnson* to the states in the same way they argued in *Wolf v. Colorado* (1949) that *Weeks v. United States* (1914), which established the exclusionary rule, ought to govern state investigations. But just as the *Wolf* attempt failed to convince a majority of the Court to apply certain Fourth Amendment guarantees to the states, so too did **Betts v. Brady** (1942), the first attempt after *Johnson*.

Indicted for robbery in Maryland, Smith Betts—a poor, uneducated, but literate, white man—wanted an attorney at government expense. Like many states, Maryland provided indigents with counsel only in rape and murder cases. Betts conducted his own defense and was convicted. On appeal he asked the Supreme Court to apply *Johnson* to the states, thereby incorporating the Sixth Amendment guarantee. The Court refused, 6–3. Writing for the majority, Justice Owen Roberts claimed that the framers never intended that the right to counsel be defined as a fundamental guarantee, just that it apply to extreme situations as in *Powell*. When Roberts compared Betts's claim to that of the Scottsboro defendants, he found that it came up short because Betts was not helpless or illiterate, and he was in no danger of the death penalty for his offense.

Justice Hugo L. Black dissented. He wrote:

Denial to the poor of the request for counsel in proceedings based on charges of serious crime has been long regarded as shocking to the "universal sense of justice" throughout this country. . . . Most . . . states have shown their agreement [and] assure that no man shall be deprived of counsel merely because of his poverty. Any other practice seems to me to defeat the promise of our democratic society to provide equal justice under law.

Twenty-one years later, a Court more sympathetic to the rights of the criminally accused reevaluated the wisdom of *Betts v. Brady*. As you read the famous case of *Gideon v. Wainwright*, think about these questions: Why did the Court extend the right to government-provided attorneys to indigents accused of state crimes? Did something distinguish *Gideon* from *Betts*, or did other factors come into play?

Gideon v. Wainwright

372 U.S. 335 (1963)
http://laws.findlaw.com/US/372/335.html
Oral arguments are available at http://www.oyez.org.
Vote: 9 (Black, Brennan, Clark, Douglas, Goldberg, Harlan, Stewart, Warren, White)
    0

OPINION OF THE COURT: *Black*
CONCURRING OPINIONS: *Clark, Douglas, Harlan*

FACTS:

Florida officials charged Clarence Earl Gideon with breaking and entering a poolroom. The trial court refused to appoint counsel for him because Florida did not provide free lawyers to those charged with anything less than a capital offense. Gideon, like Betts, a poor, uneducated, white man, tried to defend himself but failed. After studying the law in the prison library and attempting a number of lower court actions, Gideon filed a petition for a writ of certiorari with the U.S. Supreme Court.[3] The petition was handwritten on prison notepaper, but the justices granted it a review.

Because Gideon was without counsel, the Court appointed Abe Fortas, a well-known attorney (and future Supreme Court justice), to represent him. Twenty-two states filed an amicus curiae brief, which was written by Minnesota's attorney general, Walter Mondale (and future senator and U.S. vice president), supporting Gideon's argument. Clarence Gideon went from being a poor convict facing a lonely court battle to a man represented by some of the country's finest legal minds.

3. See Anthony Lewis, *Gideon's Trumpet* (New York: Vintage Books, 1964).

For the petitioner, Clarence Earl Gideon:

- The Fourteenth Amendment requires that counsel be appointed to represent an indigent defendant in every criminal case involving a serious offense.
- The great majority of the states now make provision for the appointment of counsel in all felony cases, either explicitly or as a matter of practice.

For the respondent, Louie L. Wainwright:

- The *Betts v. Brady* rule provides a clear and consistent standard for determining the right to counsel under the Fourteenth Amendment.
- Under our federal system, the states should not be required by constitutional mandate to provide counsel for indigent defendants in every case.
- The rights provided by states in appointing counsel have not been generally accepted as being fundamental or constitutional in character.
- Historically, there is no basis for requiring states to appoint counsel automatically in all cases.

MR. JUSTICE BLACK DELIVERED THE OPINION OF THE COURT.

Since 1942, when *Betts v. Brady* was decided by a divided Court, the problem of a defendant's federal constitutional right to counsel in a state court has been a continuing source of controversy and litigation in both state and federal courts. To give this problem another review here, we granted certiorari. Since Gideon was proceeding *in forma pauperis* [without the funds to pursue the normal cost of criminal defense], we appointed counsel to represent him and requested both sides to discuss in their briefs and oral arguments the following: "Should this Court's holding in *Betts v. Brady* be reconsidered?"

The facts upon which Betts claimed that he had been unconstitutionally denied the right to have counsel appointed to assist him are strikingly like the facts upon which Gideon here bases his federal constitutional claim. . . . Since the facts and circumstances of the two cases are so nearly indistinguishable, we think the *Betts v. Brady* holding if left standing would require us to reject Gideon's claim that the Constitution guarantees him the assistance of counsel. Upon full reconsideration we conclude that *Betts v. Brady* should be overruled.

The Sixth Amendment provides, "In all criminal prosecutions, the accused shall enjoy the right . . . to have the Assistance of Counsel for his defence." We have construed this to mean that in federal courts counsel must be provided for defendants unable to employ counsel unless the right is competently and intelligently waived. Betts argued that this right is extended to indigent defendants in state courts by the Fourteenth Amendment. In response the Court stated that, while the Sixth Amendment laid down "no rule for the conduct of the states, the question recurs whether the constraint laid by the amendment upon the national courts expresses a rule so fundamental and essential to a fair trial, and so, to due process of law, that it is made obligatory upon the states by the Fourteenth Amendment." In order to decide whether the Sixth Amendment's guarantee of counsel is of this fundamental nature, the Court in *Betts* set out and considered "[r]elevant data on the subject . . . afforded by constitutional and statutory provisions subsisting in the colonies and the states prior to the inclusion of the Bill of Rights in the national Constitution, and in the constitutional, legislative, and judicial history of the states to the present date." On the basis of this historical data the Court concluded that "appointment of counsel is not a fundamental right, essential to a fair trial." . . .

We accept *Betts v. Brady*'s assumption, based as it was on our prior cases, that a provision of the Bill of Rights which is "fundamental and essential to a fair trial" is made obligatory upon the States by the Fourteenth Amendment. We think the Court in *Betts* was wrong, however, in concluding that the Sixth Amendment's guarantee of counsel is not one of these fundamental rights. Ten years before *Betts v. Brady,* this Court, after full consideration of all the historical data examined in *Betts,* had unequivocally declared that "the right to the aid of counsel is of this fundamental character." *Powell v. Alabama* (1932). While the Court at the close of its *Powell* opinion did by its language, as this Court frequently does, limit its holding to the particular facts and circumstances of that case, its conclusions about the fundamental nature of the right to counsel are unmistakable. Several years later, in 1936, the Court reemphasized what it had said about the fundamental nature of the right to counsel in this language:

We concluded that certain fundamental rights, safeguarded by the first eight amendments against federal action, were also safeguarded against state action by the due process of law clause of the Fourteenth Amendment, and among them the fundamental right of the accused to the aid of counsel in a criminal prosecution." *Grosjean v. American Press Co.* (1936). . . .

. . . In light of these and many other prior decisions of the Court, it is not surprising that the *Betts* Court, when faced with the contention that "one charged with crime, who is unable to obtain counsel, must be furnished counsel by the state," conceded that "[e]xpressions in the opinions of this court lend color to the argument. . . ." The fact is that in deciding as it did—that "appointment of counsel is not a fundamental right, essential to a fair trial"—the Court in *Betts v. Brady* made an abrupt break with its own well considered precedents. In returning to these old precedents, sounder we believe than the new, we but restore constitutional principles established to achieve a fair system of justice. Not only these precedents but also reason and reflection require us to recognize that in our adversary system of criminal justice, any person haled into court, who is too poor to hire a lawyer, cannot be assured a fair trial unless counsel is provided for him. This seems to us to be an obvious truth. Governments, both state and federal, quite properly spend vast sums of money to establish machinery to try defendants accused of crime. Lawyers to prosecute are everywhere deemed essential to protect the public's interest in an orderly society. Similarly, there are few defendants charged with crime, few indeed, who fail to hire the best lawyers they can get to prepare and present their defenses. That government hires lawyers to prosecute and defendants who have the money hire lawyers to defend are the strongest indications of the widespread belief that lawyers in criminal courts are necessities, not luxuries. The right of one charged with crime to counsel may not be deemed fundamental and essential to fair trials in some countries, but it is in ours. From the very beginning, our state and national constitutions and laws have laid great emphasis on procedural and substantive safeguards designed to assure fair trials before impartial tribunals in which every defendant stands equal before the law. This noble ideal cannot be realized if the poor man charged with crime has to face his accusers without a lawyer to assist him. A defendant's need for a lawyer is nowhere better stated than [the Court's opinion in] *Powell v. Alabama*. . . .

The Court in *Betts v. Brady* departed from the sound wisdom upon which the Court's holding in *Powell v. Alabama* rested. Florida, supported by two other States, has asked that *Betts v. Brady* be left intact. Twenty-two States, as friends of the Court, argue that *Betts* was "an anachronism when handed down" and that it should now be overruled. We agree. The judgment is reversed and the cause is remanded to the

Supreme Court of Florida for further action not inconsistent with this opinion.

Reversed.

MR. JUSTICE HARLAN, concurring.

I agree that *Betts v. Brady* should be overruled, but consider it entitled to a more respectful burial than has been accorded. . . .

I cannot subscribe to the view that *Betts v. Brady* represented "an abrupt break with its own well-considered precedents." In 1932, in *Powell v. Alabama,* a capital case, this Court declared that under the particular facts there presented—"the ignorance and illiteracy of the defendants, their youth, the circumstances of public hostility . . . and above all that they stood in deadly peril of their lives"—the state court had a duty to assign counsel for the trial as a necessary requisite of due process of law. It is evident that these limiting facts were not added to the opinion as an afterthought; they were repeatedly emphasized and were clearly regarded as important to the result.

Thus when this Court, a decade later, decided *Betts v. Brady,* it did no more than to admit of the possible existence of special circumstances in noncapital as well as capital trials, while at the same time insisting that such circumstances be shown in order to establish a denial of due process. . . . The declaration that the right to appointed counsel in state prosecutions, as established in *Powell v. Alabama,* was not limited to capital cases was in truth not a departure from, but an extension of, existing precedent.

The principles declared in *Powell* and in *Betts,* however, have had a troubled journey throughout the years. . . .

In noncapital cases, the "special circumstances" rule has continued to exist in form while its substance has been substantially and steadily eroded. . . . The Court has come to recognize, in other words, that the mere existence of a serious criminal charge constituted in itself special circumstances requiring the services of counsel at trial. In truth the *Betts v. Brady* rule is no longer a reality. . . .

The special circumstances rule has been formally abandoned in capital cases, and the time has now come when it should be similarly abandoned in noncapital cases, at least as to offenses which, as the one involved here, carry the possibility of a substantial prison sentence. (Whether the rule should extend to *all* criminal cases need not now be decided.) This indeed does no more than to make explicit something that has long since been foreshadowed in our decisions. . . .

On these premises I join in the judgment of the Court.

Beyond its legal significance, *Gideon* is interesting for several reasons. First, the case provides another example of the Warren Court's revolution in criminal rights. The Court of 1963 took a carbon copy of *Betts* and came up with a radically different solution. *Gideon* completed a process of constitutional evolution in which the Court first applied a rule of law to the federal government, refused to extend that rule to the states, and then reversed its position and brought the states under the rule's applicability. As indicated in Table 12-1, this historical pattern is the same as in the battle over applicability of the exclusionary rule, considered in Chapter 11.

Second, *Gideon* is a classic example of the importance of dissents. In considering cases applying the Bill of Rights to the states, we saw how Justice John Marshall Harlan's minority views in the incorporation cases were adopted by later justices. Here, however, we see an even more unusual event: Justice Black, who wrote the dissenting opinion in *Betts,* wrote the majority opinion in *Gideon.*

Finally, *Gideon v. Wainwright* has had a tremendous impact on the U.S. criminal justice system, in which 80–90 percent of the criminally accused are eligible for indigent defense.[4] To comply with the Court's ruling, states had to alter their defender systems, creating mechanisms to provide lawyers for the accused. Many localities created public defender offices that mirrored their prosecuting attorneys' offices. In other words, the states hire lawyers to represent indigents. Other areas use court-appointed attorney systems in which judges assign members of the legal community to represent the underprivileged.

Applying Gideon

Despite its importance, *Gideon* left several questions unanswered—most of which were addressed not by the justices of the Warren Court but by the Burger, Rehnquist, and Roberts Courts. First, which crimes does the ruling cover? Does it cover only serious

offenses, felonies, such as the one Gideon was accused of committing? Or does it apply to minor crimes as well?[5] The Court provided answers in **Argersinger v. Hamlin** (1972) and **Scott v. Illinois** (1979). In these cases the justices developed the "loss of liberty" rule: an indigent charged with a crime that upon conviction will lead to incarceration for even one day is entitled to be represented by counsel at government expense. To put it another way, regardless of the range of penalties available to a judge, indigent criminal defendants may not be sentenced to incarceration unless they have been offered legal representation at government expense.

Twenty-three years after *Scott v. Illinois*, in **Alabama v. Shelton** (2002), the justices of the Rehnquist Court reinforced this basic premise. LeReed Shelton, convicted of third-degree assault, was sentenced to a jail term of thirty days, which the trial court immediately suspended, placing Shelton on probation for two years. The question the Court addressed was whether the Sixth Amendment right to appointed counsel, as delineated in *Argersinger* and *Scott,* applies to a defendant in Shelton's situation. The majority answered in the affirmative, holding that "a suspended sentence that may 'end up in the actual deprivation of a person's liberty' may not be imposed unless the defendant was accorded 'the guiding hand of counsel' in the prosecution for the

---

4. See National Center for State Courts, http://www.ncsconline.org/WC/CourTopics/FAQs.asp?topic=IndDef.

5. Questions have also arisen over whether the state must provide counsel at certain kinds of civil proceedings. Because the Court has limited the Sixth Amendment's coverage to criminal cases, litigants have turned to the Fourteenth Amendment's due process clause, with mixed success. In *In re Gault* (1967), for example, the Court held that the Fourteenth Amendment requires the state to pay for a lawyer in a civil "juvenile delinquency" proceeding that could lead to incarceration. But in *Gagon v. Scarpelli* (1973) it ruled that the state is not required to provide counsel at a probation revocation hearing to a person who was sent to prison after his probation was revoked. The Court's most recent decision in this area, **Turner v. Rogers** (2011), falls somewhere between the two. The question in *Turner* was whether the Fourteenth Amendment's due process clause requires the state to provide counsel at civil contempt proceedings to an indigent who is subject to a child support order and who potentially faces incarceration. Although the Court ruled that the due process clause does not *automatically* require counsel in these circumstances, it also held that there may be circumstances under which the state must appoint counsel to ensure that the proceedings are "fundamentally fair." The state must take into account (1) the nature of "the private interest that will be affected," (2) the comparative "risk" of an "erroneous deprivation" of that interest with and without "additional or substitute procedural safeguards," and (3) the nature and magnitude of any countervailing interest in not providing "additional or substitute procedural requirement[s]."

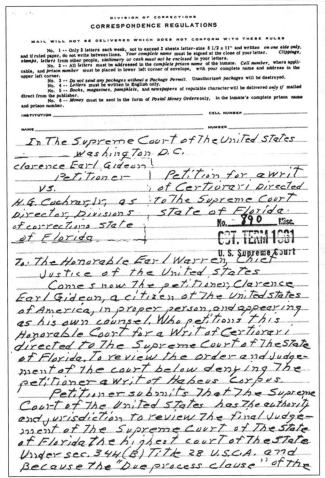

Above, Clarence Earl Gideon.

Left, Clarence Earl Gideon's handwritten petition to the Supreme Court.

TABLE 12-1 Comparison of the Development of the Exclusionary Rule and the Right to Counsel for Indigents

DOCTRINE	EXCLUSIONARY RULE	RIGHT TO COUNSEL FOR INDIGENTS
Establishment of right for federal prosecutions	*Weeks v. United States* (1918)	*Johnson v. Zerbst* (1938)
Refusal to apply to states	*Wolf v. Colorado* (1949)	*Betts v. Brady* (1942)
Application to states	*Mapp v. Ohio* (1961)	*Gideon v. Wainwright* (1963)

crime charged." To the four dissenters—Antonin Scalia, William Rehnquist, Anthony Kennedy, and Clarence Thomas—this logic turned *Argersinger* and *Scott* upside down: "Today's decision ignores this long and consistent jurisprudence, extending the misdemeanor right to counsel to cases bearing the mere threat of imprisonment," Scalia wrote. "Respondent's 30-day suspended sentence, and the accompanying 2-year term of probation, are invalidated for lack of appointed counsel even though respondent has not suffered, and may never suffer, a deprivation of liberty."

A second unanswered question flowing from *Gideon* was this: To which stages of the process does the right to government-provided counsel apply? In his opinion in *Gideon*, Black said that an indigent accused of a criminal offense must be represented by counsel at trial. What Black did not address was whether that right extended through the appellate process. And if so, did such a right apply only to obligatory appeals (usually the first appeal after a trial) or also to discretionary appeals (subsequent appeals that the appellate court—usually a state supreme court—may or may not agree to hear)?

In **Douglas v. California** (1963) the Court answered part of this question, holding that the right indeed extended through the first obligatory appeal. Eleven years later, however, in **Ross v. Moffitt** (1974), the Burger Court—while not reversing the Warren Court—refused to extend the right to state-provided counsel for indigents to subsequent appeals. Writing for the majority, Rehnquist concluded that the defendant was not "denied meaningful access" to his state supreme court "simply because the State does not appoint counsel to aid him in seeking review. At that stage he will have, at the very least, a transcript or other record of the trial proceedings, a brief on his behalf in the Court of Appeals . . . and in many cases an opinion by the Court of Appeals disposing of his case." Rehnquist went on to note: "We do not mean by this opinion to in any way discourage those States which have, as a matter of legislative choice, made counsel available . . . at all stages of judicial review. . . . Our reading of the Fourteenth Amendment leaves these choices to the State."

As it turned out, twenty years after *Ross* Michigan made a choice with regard to the availability of counsel, but not the one Rehnquist envisioned. His opinion in *Ross* allowed states, if they wished, to provide counsel at all stages in the appellate process. Michigan, however, removed the right to counsel for indigent defendants who pled guilty at trial and were trying to make a first appeal of their cases.

In **Halbert v. Michigan** (2005) the Supreme Court invalidated Michigan's law—a step, it said, necessitated by *Douglas* and *Ross*. Indeed, the majority made a point to note that Rehnquist's opinion in *Ross* rested heavily on the assumption that indigents would have access to an attorney during a first-tier review:

As the Court in *Ross* emphasized, . . . the attorney appointed to serve at the intermediate [first-tier] review level will have reviewed the trial court record, researched the legal issues, and prepared a brief reflecting that review and research. The defendant seeking second-tier review may also be armed with an opinion of the intermediate appellate court addressing the issues counsel raised. A first-tier review applicant, forced to act *pro se* [on his own], will face a record unreviewed by appellate counsel, and will be equipped with no attorney's brief prepared for, or reasoned opinion by, a court of review.

Money, Justice, and (Effective) Representation

Gideon, along with its progeny, is a decision of extraordinary importance. It brought legal representation to a class of defendants who previously had not enjoyed the services of attorneys. Yet, as significant as the case is, financial resources remain an important influence on how someone fares when charged with a crime.

Today, most poor people accused of crimes are represented by public defenders or by attorneys appointed by trial court judges. The services provided these defendants are certainly adequate in most cases, but *Gideon* cannot be said to have totally reduced the gap between rich and poor. Those individuals with substantial resources are still able to hire the best lawyers, investigators, and experts to advance their defenses against criminal charges.

Many people cite the 1994–1995 O. J. Simpson criminal trial as a case in point. Simpson, an actor and former professional football star, was accused of killing his ex-wife, Nicole Brown, and an acquaintance of hers, Ronald Goldman. The trial proceedings were televised nationwide and held the country's attention for months. Because Simpson was wealthy, he was able to assemble a group of defense lawyers more formidable perhaps than had been seen in any previous criminal trial. Dubbed the Dream Team, it included some of the nation's most prominent criminal lawyers: Johnnie Cochran, F. Lee Bailey, Robert Shapiro, Alan Dershowitz, and Barry Scheck. After months of legal maneuvering, the Simpson defense team successfully combated the prosecution's evidence and persuaded the jury to return a verdict of not guilty. To many commentators, money made the difference. An indigent facing similar charges and evidence would have been represented by a single public defender, and most experts agree that someone in that situation probably would be convicted.

This is not to say that defendants have no recourse if they believe that their attorneys have not effectively represented them. Indeed, the Court has recognized that "the right to counsel is the right to the effective assistance of counsel."[6] And it has laid out, in *Strickland*

---

6. *McMann v. Richardson* (1970).

v. Washington (1984), a test that defendants must meet if they desire to invoke that right:

A convicted defendant's claim that counsel's assistance was so defective as to require reversal of a conviction or death sentence has two components. First, the defendant must show that counsel's performance was deficient. This requires showing that counsel made errors so serious that counsel was not functioning as the "counsel" guaranteed the defendant by the Sixth Amendment. Second, the defendant must show that the deficient performance prejudiced the defense. This requires showing that counsel's errors were so serious as to deprive the defendant of a fair trial, a trial whose result is reliable. Unless a defendant makes both showings, it cannot be said that the conviction or death sentence resulted from a breakdown in the adversary process that renders the result unreliable.

In subsequent cases, the Court followed the *Strickland* approach, while also clinging to its command concerning the desirability of judicial deference:

Judicial scrutiny of counsel's performance must be highly deferential. It is all too tempting for a defendant to second-guess counsel's assistance after conviction or adverse sentence, and it is all too easy for a court, examining counsel's defense after it has proved unsuccessful, to conclude that a particular act or omission of counsel was unreasonable. . . . There are countless ways to provide effective assistance in any given case. Even the best criminal defense attorneys would not defend a particular client in the same way.

In fact, between 1984, when it articulated the *Strickland* standard, and 2011, the Court found in favor of a defendant asserting an ineffective counsel claim in only about a third of such cases.

THE PRETRIAL PERIOD AND THE RIGHT TO BAIL

The defense attorney must protect the accused's rights during every stage of the criminal process, starting with interrogation and investigation and the formal stages of the pretrial period. If already retained or appointed, counsel represents the accused at the initial appearance and is present at the arraignment and preliminary hearing. The defense attorney may negotiate with the prosecuting attorney over the exact charges to be brought. Pretrial motions may be made seeking judicial rulings on questions of evidence and procedure. The defense attorney also begins preparing the case to be presented to a jury should the defendant go to trial.

Of all the pretrial stages, the setting of bail is perhaps the most important to the defendant. Bail is a monetary guarantee ensuring that the accused, once released from custody, will show up for the trial. Defendants who are not eligible for bail and those who cannot raise the money must wait in jail until their trial dates. Defendants who can "make bail" are released pending their trials. A judge may also elect to release a criminal defendant on his or her own recognizance, which requires no bail, if the defendant is not a threat to community safety and seems likely to return to court for subsequent proceedings.

How does a judge decide who is eligible for release? How is the bail amount determined? Individuals charged with misdemeanors are automatically eligible for bail, and the amount is usually set according to a specific fee schedule. For those charged with felonies, a judge sets bail on a case-by-case basis. Among the factors the judge considers are the seriousness of the offense, the trustworthiness of the individual, and the Eighth Amendment's prohibition against excessive bail. Until 1987 the Supreme Court had not decided a major dispute over what factors a judge may appropriately consider in making bail determinations; that year **United States v. Salerno** challenged the Bail Reform Act of 1984.

Salerno stemmed from racketeering charges the Justice Department brought against Anthony Salerno, the boss of the Genovese crime family, in 1986. At Salerno's bail hearing, U.S. attorneys urged the judge to deny bail on the ground that the accused would continue to engage in criminal activity if released. Before 1984 judges probably would not have considered such a factor in their decision-making processes because bail had always been used only to ensure a defendant's presence at trial. But in 1984 Congress passed the Bail Reform Act, authorizing judges to deny bail to defendants to "assure . . . the safety of any other person and the community." After federal prosecutors presented evidence suggesting that Salerno would commit murder if let out, the judge denied bail. Salerno successfully appealed to the U.S. Court of Appeals, which declared the 1984 act unconstitutional. The federal government then asked the Supreme Court to reverse.

In a 6–3 decision the Court did just that. Writing for the majority, Chief Justice Rehnquist held that the 1984 act did not violate the Eighth Amendment's prohibition against excessive bail. Rehnquist agreed with Salerno's argument about the primary function of bail—to ensure that defendants appear at their trials and thus "safeguard the courts' role in adjudicating the guilt or innocence of defendants," but he rejected "the proposition that the Eighth Amendment categorically prohibits the government from pursuing other admittedly compelling interests through regulation of pretrial release." "Nothing in the text of the Bail Clause," he continued, "limits permissible government considerations solely to questions of flight." To Rehnquist and the majority,

The only arguable substantive limitation of the Bail Clause is that the government's proposed conditions of release or detention not be "excessive" in light of the perceived evil. Of course, to determine whether the government's response is excessive, we must compare that response against the interest the government seeks to protect by means of that response. Thus, when the government has admitted that its only interest is in preventing flight, bail must be set by a court at a sum designed to ensure that goal, and no more. We believe that when Congress has mandated detention on the basis of a compelling interest other than prevention of flight, as it has here, the Eighth Amendment does not require release on bail. . . .

We are unwilling to say that this congressional determination, based as it is upon that primary concern of every government—a concern for the safety and indeed the lives of its citizens—on its face violates . . . the Excessive Bail Clause of the Eighth Amendment.

Justice Thurgood Marshall, in a dissenting opinion, took issue with this analysis and instead expressed his agreement with a statement Chief Justice Fred Vinson had made nearly thirty years earlier in *Stack v. Boyle* (1951): "Unless th[e] right to bail before trial is preserved, the presumption of innocence, secured only after centuries of struggle, would lose its meaning."

By upholding the 1984 federal law, the majority gave implicit assent to the statutes of twenty-four states that allowed the denial of bail on similar bases.[7]

---

7. Similarly, in *Demore v. Kim* (2003), the Court upheld the 1996 Illegal Immigration Reform and Immigrant Responsibility Act, which states that aliens subject to deportation based on certain kinds of past criminal convictions must be detained without bail while a decision over their deportation is pending. Lawyers challenging the

Unlike Salerno, however, the majority of defendants are eligible for bail. The job of their attorneys is to convince the judges to set bail at affordable levels. Most criminal defendants cannot put up their entire bail amounts, even if they are set fairly low, so many seek the services of bail bondsmen. For a nonrefundable fee (normally set at around 10 percent of the bail amount), a bail bondsman files a bail bond with the court for the full amount of a defendant's bail. The bond substitutes for cash bail and allows the defendant to be free pending trial. Most bail bondsmen also require that a bail bond be secured with property as collateral in case the defendant fails to appear in court. In some jurisdictions, if the government believes that a defendant has paid cash bail from funds procured through the very criminal enterprise for which he or she is being prosecuted (for example, in an embezzlement or drug sales case), it may ask for a court hearing to inquire into the source of bail funds.

Because the bail procedure discriminates against the poor, and the bail bonding industry has often been linked to unsavory practices, many criminal justice experts regard the bail stage as one of the weakest links in the system. Many jurisdictions allow worthy defendants to be released on their own recognizance pending trial without putting up bail, but overall the support for bail reform is scant. Most citizens lack sympathy for those accused of crimes. Many law-and-order-minded Americans believe that even a person merely charged with a crime should not be released pending resolution of the case, notwithstanding the presumption of innocence. As a result, the bail system operates today much as it did a hundred years ago.

THE SIXTH AMENDMENT AND FAIR TRIALS

From a quantitative perspective, trials are insignificant, as less than 10 percent of all criminal prosecutions go to trial. In the other cases, the defendants plead guilty, usually after arriving at plea-bargaining

---

act claimed that detention must be based on individualized findings, such as whether the person is a danger to society or a flight risk—but, because detention is mandatory under the act, no such findings are required. In a 5–4 decision, the Court upheld the challenged portion of the act. In so ruling, the Court considered the numerical evidence in the government's brief indicating, among other things, that "once released, more than 20% of deportable criminal aliens failed to appear for their removal hearings."

agreements with the prosecutors. In such an arrangement, the defendant waives the right to a jury trial and agrees to plead guilty in return for certain concessions made by the prosecutor. These concessions normally involve a reduction in the seriousness of the crimes charged, a reduction in the number of counts, or a recommendation for a lenient sentence. Although many citizens look at such arrangements unfavorably, the Supreme Court has sanctioned the practice of plea bargaining, and it remains the most common way criminal prosecutions are settled.[8]

Qualitatively, however, trials are significant; the most serious crimes go to trial. In addition, trials serve a symbolic function and educate the public about crime and justice in the community. Further, they embody values that Americans treasure—openness and fundamental and objective fairness.

The framers clearly intended American trials to be the epitome of justice. They drafted the Sixth Amendment to correct the weaknesses they had observed in the English justice system, weaknesses that included closed proceedings, long delays, and few safeguards for defendants. Specifically, Sixth Amendment provisions governing trials state:

In all criminal prosecutions, the accused shall enjoy the right to a speedy and public trial, by an impartial jury of the State and district wherein the crime shall have been committed, . . . to be confronted with the witnesses against him; to have compulsory process for obtaining witnesses in his favor.

In short, the Sixth Amendment provides strict guidelines for trial proceedings. In the next pages we examine how the Supreme Court has interpreted each right specified in the amendment and the overall impact of its decisions on the trial process.

Speedy Trials

Individuals accused of crimes have the right to their day in court, and if justice is to be meaningful, trials must be scheduled in a timely fashion. The framers considered it unfair for the government to lay criminal charges against suspects and then postpone their trials for months or even years. Consequently, the Sixth Amendment states that trials must be speedy.

Before the late 1960s the speedy trial provision of the Sixth Amendment was seldom invoked because most cases proceeded from arrest to trial in a timely fashion. But then backlogs of cases began to build up at the trial court level. The Supreme Court was asked to interpret the speedy trial clause, and, as little legal doctrine existed, the cases coming to the Court raised basic issues about the clause's meaning.

Among the most important of these early cases was ***Barker v. Wingo*** (1972), in which the Court confronted this question: What criteria are to be used to determine if a postindictment delay is unreasonable? In this case, two individuals, Willie Barker and Silas Manning, were charged with beating an elderly Kentucky couple to death with a tire iron. The prosecutor had a strong case against Manning, but not against Barker. To convict Barker, the prosecutor needed Manning to testify, but Manning refused on Fifth Amendment grounds. The prosecutor devised the following strategy: he would put Manning on trial first, and, after obtaining a conviction against him, he would try Barker and call Manning as a major witness. Manning would no longer be able to refuse to testify on Fifth Amendment grounds because once he was convicted of murder he could not further incriminate himself.

This strategy was theoretically sound, but it ran into difficulties. Getting Manning convicted took longer than the prosecutor had anticipated. In fact, because of hung juries, successful appeals, and subsequent retrials, it took several years. Prosecutors had to ask the court to postpone Barker's trial sixteen times. When the twelfth continuance was requested, Barker's attorneys began to assert a violation of the speedy trial provision of the Sixth Amendment. Finally, five years after he was indicted for murder, Barker was tried, found guilty, and sentenced to life in prison.

Barker's attorneys appealed the conviction on the grounds that the five-year delay was a violation of the Sixth Amendment. A unanimous Supreme Court, through an opinion by Justice Lewis F. Powell, refused to designate a specific length of time that would constitute unreasonable delay. Instead, the justices recognized that this period could vary from case to case. The Court, however, established four criteria that should be considered in deciding questions of unreasonable delay: the length of the delay, the reason for the delay, the point at which the defendant begins asserting a Sixth Amendment violation, and whether the delay prejudiced the defendant's case.

8. See, for example, *North Carolina v. Alford* (1970).

As applied to Barker, the Court found no constitutional violation. Although the five-year delay was admittedly long, the reason for the delay—the unavailability of an important witness—was sound. Furthermore, the defendant did not register objections to the delay until well into the process. Finally, the Court was unable to see that the defendant suffered any prejudice caused by the delay. Under Powell's balancing test, defendants have a great deal to prove before the Court finds a violation of the speedy trial provision.

The general reaction to *Barker* was that criminal defendants deserved greater protections of the right to a speedy trial than the Court's interpretation of the Sixth Amendment allowed. Consequently, Congress and many state legislatures passed speedy trial laws that compel the prosecution to be ready to proceed with a trial within a specified number of days. For example, the federal Speedy Trial Act of 1974 requires indictment within thirty days of arrest, arraignment within ten days after indictment, and trial within sixty days after arraignment. Failure to meet the requirements of the speedy trial law can lead to the dismissal of charges against the defendant.

Nonetheless, questions over the application of *Barker* continue to emerge. In **Vermont v. Brillon** (2009), for example, the Court considered whether delays caused solely by an indigent defendant's public defender could violate the defendant's speedy trial rights and be charged against the state pursuant to the test in *Barker*. The defendant Brillon argued that the Court should answer in the affirmative because public defenders are paid by the state. Writing for a 7–2 Court, Justice Ginsburg held against Brillon. She noted that "assigned counsel generally are not state actors for purposes of a speedy-trial claim," and so in applying *Barker,* she attributed most of the delay to the defendant's counsel and not the state.

Jury Trials

As they had with many other aspects of law and procedure, the framers incorporated the British jury system into the U.S. Constitution. The Sixth Amendment states in part, "In all criminal prosecutions, the accused shall enjoy the right to a . . . trial, by an impartial jury." But what did the term *jury* mean to the framers? We can speculate that they thought the system they inherited from the British required that a jury be composed of the defendant's peers, that it consist of twelve persons, and that it reach unanimous verdicts. Today,

none of these meanings, as we shall see in the following pages, is fully operative in criminal proceedings.

Jury Members. Presumably, in England being tried by a jury of one's peers meant that one would face members of one's social class. In other words, a commoner would be tried by a jury of commoners and a nobleman by a jury of noblemen. In the United States such class distinctions are not recognized; rather, a jury of one's peers means a jury that represents a cross section of the community. To put together representative panels, many jurisdictions follow a procedure that works this way:

1. Individuals living within a specified geographical area are called for jury duty. Most localities randomly select names from voter registration, property tax, or driver's license lists.

2. Those selected form the jury pool, or venire, the group from which attorneys choose the jury.

3. The judge may conduct initial interviews and excuse certain classes of people (felons, illiterates, the mentally ill) and certain occupational groups, as allowed under the laws of the particular jurisdiction.

4. The remaining individuals are available to be chosen to serve on a trial (petit) jury. In the final selection phase, the opposing attorneys interview the prospective jurors in the process called voir dire. During voir dire, attorneys can dismiss those individuals they believe would not vote in the best interests of their clients. The attorneys, therefore, select the jury.

During voir dire, attorneys have available two means of eliminating potential jurors. When a prospective juror appears to be unqualified to carry out the obligations of service, attorneys can *challenge for cause.* To do so, they must explain to the judge their reasons for requesting the disqualification of that prospective juror (for example, because of a conflict of interest, a bias against the defendant or the prosecution, or a stated refusal to follow the law). The judge can grant or deny the challenge for cause. Challenges for cause are unlimited. Attorneys also have a fixed number of *peremptory challenges,* which they may use to excuse jurors without stating reasons.

The objective of this long-standing process is to form a petit jury representing a cross section of the community. Does the process work? This question has been the subject of numerous scholarly analyses and is still debated. Many argue that the system is the best among myriad inferior alternatives. Others claim that it is plagued with problems from beginning to end, resulting in unacceptable biases. For example, because most localities now draw their jury pools from voter registration lists, juries may reflect the "average" voter—white, middle-age, and middle-class. Additional criticism comes from the practice of "jury stacking." Lawyers have always tried to use their challenges to eliminate jurors likely to be unsympathetic to their side, but in the past they generally proceeded only on the basis of their personal experience, professional judgment, and idiosyncratic hunches. Today, some lawyers prefer to engage firms that sample public opinion in a community to map the backgrounds of ideal jurors. They also hire social psychologists to sit in the courtroom during the voir dire and observe potential jurors to predict their attitudes more accurately.

Another concern is that attorneys, specifically prosecutors, may use their peremptory challenges systematically to excuse African Americans and other ethnic minorities from juries. This action is based on the belief that black jurors are reluctant to convict black defendants. Although trial court judges have long recognized that prosecutors engaged in this practice, they could do little about it because peremptory challenges do not require the approval of the judge. Most courts refused to interfere with the traditional privilege of attorneys to excuse jurors for no specific reason, viewing it as part of a litigation strategy. The U.S. Supreme Court, in *Swain v. Alabama* (1965), reinforced this sentiment by making it difficult for judges to prohibit prosecutors from using the peremptory challenge to remove prospective jurors for reasons of race.

In *Batson v. Kentucky* (1986), however, the Court reevaluated *Swain* and startled the legal community by holding that even peremptory challenges are subject to court scrutiny. As you read this case, note that all but two of the Burger Court justices agreed with a ruling that clearly flew in the face of well-established custom and precedent. *Batson* is an interesting (and unusual) example of a decision in which the Burger Court modified a Warren Court precedent and replaced it with a decision more favorable to the rights of the criminally accused.

Batson v. Kentucky

476 U.S. 79 (1986)
http://laws.findlaw.com/US/476/79.html
Oral arguments are available at http://www.oyez.org.
Vote: 7 (Blackmun, Brennan, Marshall, O'Connor, Powell, Stevens, White)
    2 (Burger, Rehnquist)

OPINION OF THE COURT: *Powell*
CONCURRING OPINIONS: *Marshall, O'Connor, Stevens, White*
DISSENTING OPINIONS: *Burger, Rehnquist*

FACTS:

James Batson, a black man, was indicted for second-degree burglary. His venire included four African Americans, but the prosecutor used his peremptory challenges to eliminate them, leaving Batson with an all-white jury. Batson's attorney challenged this outcome, claiming that it denied his client equal protection of the laws and his Sixth Amendment right to an impartial jury representing a cross section of the community. The trial court and the Kentucky Supreme Court denied this claim in part because of the sanctity of peremptory challenges.

The U.S. Supreme Court was asked to address this question: May prosecutors use their peremptory challenges to eliminate prospective jurors of a specific racial group? Naturally, such an issue drew many opinions in the form of amicus curiae briefs from organized interest groups. The NAACP Legal Defense and Educational Fund, for example, argued, "The exclusion of Blacks from juries not only stigmatizes them and deprives them of their right . . . to participate in the criminal justice system. It destroys the appearance of justice." The National Legal Aid and Defender Association, representing the public defender offices and legal aid societies, framed its argument a bit differently: "No significant state interest exists in allowing unrestricted use of the peremptory challenge . . . because it is not essential to the ability of the prosecutor to select fair and impartial jurors."

ARGUMENTS:

For the petitioner, James Kirkland Batson:

- Using peremptory challenges to exclude members of a particular race or ethnic group denies the accused the right to a jury composed of a cross section of the community.
- The constitutional right to a representative jury should trump a state statute allowing peremptory challenges for no stated reason.

- At the very least, Batson should have been afforded a hearing on his claim and the state attorneys should be required to state the reasons for their challenges.

For the respondent, State of Kentucky:
- Justice is better served by the *Swain* approach than by engaging in burden shifting when a defendant believes a prosecutor has engaged in improper exclusion of jurors.
- The effect of peremptory challenges is not confined to the selection of a jury, but has an impact on the entire criminal trial.
- Petitioner failed to present proof in the trial court regarding the alleged constitutional violation.

JUSTICE POWELL DELIVERED THE OPINION OF THE COURT.

This case requires us to reexamine that portion of *Swain v. Alabama* concerning the evidentiary burden placed on a criminal defendant who claims that he has been denied equal protection through the State's use of peremptory challenges to exclude members of his race from the petit jury. . . .

In *Swain v. Alabama,* this Court recognized that a "State's purposeful or deliberate denial to Negroes on account of race of participation as jurors in the administration of justice violates the Equal Protection Clause." This principle has been "consistently and repeatedly" reaffirmed, in numerous decisions of this Court both preceding and following *Swain.* We reaffirm the principle today.

More than a century ago, the Court decided that the State denies a black defendant equal protection of the laws when it puts him on trial before a jury from which members of his race have been purposefully excluded. *Strauder v. West Virginia* (1880). That decision laid the foundation for the Court's unceasing efforts to eradicate racial discrimination in the procedures used to select the venire from which individual jurors are drawn. In *Strauder,* the Court explained that the central concern of the recently ratified Fourteenth Amendment was to put an end to governmental discrimination on account of race. Exclusion of black citizens from service as jurors constitutes a primary example of the evil the Fourteenth Amendment was designed to cure.

In holding that racial discrimination in jury selection offends the Equal Protection Clause, the Court in *Strauder* recognized, however, that a defendant has no right to a "petit jury composed in whole or in part of persons of his own race." But the defendant does have the right to be tried by a jury whose members are selected pursuant to nondiscriminatory criteria. The Equal Protection Clause guarantees the defendant that the State will not exclude members of his race from the jury venire on account of race or on the false assumption that members of his race as a group are not qualified to serve as jurors.

Purposeful racial discrimination in selection of the venire violates a defendant's right to equal protection because it denies him the protection that a trial by jury is intended to secure. "The very idea of a jury is a body . . . composed of the peers or equals of the person whose rights it is selected or summoned to determine; that is, of his neighbors, fellows, associates, persons having the same legal status in society as that which he holds." . . .

Racial discrimination in selection of jurors harms not only the accused whose life or liberty they are summoned to try. Competence to serve as a juror ultimately depends on an assessment of individual qualifications and ability impartially to consider evidence presented at a trial. A person's race simply "is unrelated to his fitness as a juror." As long ago as *Strauder,* therefore, the Court recognized that by denying a person participation in jury service on account of his race, the State unconstitutionally discriminated against the excluded juror. . . .

In *Strauder,* the Court invalidated a state statute that provided that only white men could serve as jurors. We can be confident that no state now has such a law. The Constitution requires, however, that we look beyond the face of the statute defining juror qualifications and also consider challenged selection practices to afford "protection against action of the State through its administrative officers in effecting the prohibited discrimination." . . .

Accordingly, the component of the jury selection process at issue here, the State's privilege to strike individual jurors through peremptory challenges, is subject to the commands of the Equal Protection Clause. Although a prosecutor ordinarily is entitled to exercise permitted peremptory challenges "for any reason at all, as long as that reason is related to his view concerning the outcome" of the case to be tried, the Equal Protection Clause forbids the prosecutor to challenge potential jurors solely on account of their race or on the assumption that black jurors as a group will be unable impartially to consider the State's case against a black defendant.

The principles announced in *Strauder* never have been questioned in any subsequent decision of this Court. Rather, the Court has been called upon repeatedly to review the application of those principles to particular facts. A recurring question in these cases, as in any case alleging a violation of the Equal Protection Clause, was whether the defendant had met his burden of proving purposeful discrimination on the part of the State. That question also was at the heart of the portion of *Swain v. Alabama* we reexamine today.

Swain required the Court to decide, among other issues, whether a black defendant was denied equal protection by the State's exercise of peremptory challenges to exclude members of his race from the petit jury. The record in *Swain* showed that the prosecutor had used the State's peremptory challenges to strike the six black persons included on the petit jury venire. While rejecting the defendant's claim for failure to prove purposeful discrimination, the Court nonetheless indicated that the Equal Protection Clause placed some limits on the State's exercise of peremptory challenges.

The Court sought to accommodate the prosecutor's historical privilege of peremptory challenge free of judicial control, and the constitutional prohibition on exclusion of persons from jury service on account of race. While the Constitution does not confer a right to peremptory challenges, those challenges traditionally have been viewed as one means of assuring the selection of a qualified and unbiased jury. To preserve the peremptory nature of the prosecutor's challenge, the Court in *Swain* declined to scrutinize his actions in a particular case by relying on a presumption that he properly exercised the State's challenges. . . .

The Court went on to observe, however, that a state may not exercise its challenges in contravention of the Equal Protection Clause. It was impermissible for a prosecutor to use his challenges to exclude blacks from the jury "for reasons wholly unrelated to the outcome of the particular case on trial" or to deny to blacks "the same right and opportunity to participate in the administration of justice enjoyed by the white population." Accordingly, a black defendant could make out a prima facie case of purposeful discrimination on proof that the peremptory challenge system was "being perverted" in that manner. For example, an inference of purposeful discrimination would be raised on evidence that a prosecutor, "in case after case, whatever the circumstances, whatever the crime and whoever the defendant or the victim may be, is responsible for the removal of Negroes who have been selected as qualified jurors by the jury commissioners and who have survived challenges for cause, with the result that no Negroes ever serve on

petit juries." Evidence offered by the defendant in *Swain* did not meet that standard. While the defendant showed that prosecutors in the jurisdiction had exercised their strikes to exclude blacks from the jury, he offered no proof of the circumstances under which prosecutors were responsible for striking black jurors beyond the facts of his own case.

A number of lower courts following the teaching of *Swain* reasoned that proof of repeated striking of blacks over a number of cases was necessary to establish a violation of the Equal Protection Clause. Since this interpretation of *Swain* has placed on defendants a crippling burden of proof, prosecutors' peremptory challenges are now largely immune from constitutional scrutiny. . . . [We] reject this evidentiary formulation as inconsistent with standards that have been developed since *Swain* for assessing a prima facie case under the Equal Protection Clause. . . .

The standards for assessing a prima facie case in the context of discriminatory selection of the venire have been fully articulated since *Swain*. These principles support our conclusion that a defendant may establish a prima facie case of purposeful discrimination in selection of the petit jury solely on evidence concerning the prosecutor's exercise of peremptory challenges at the defendant's trial. To establish such a case, the defendant first must show that he is a member of a cognizable racial group and that the prosecutor has exercised peremptory challenges to remove from the venire members of the defendant's race. Second, the defendant is entitled to rely on the fact, as to which there can be no dispute, that peremptory challenges constitute a jury selection practice that permits "those to discriminate who are of a mind to discriminate." Finally, the defendant must show that these facts and any other relevant circumstances raise an inference that the prosecutor used that practice to exclude the veniremen from the petit jury on account of their race. This combination of factors in the empanelling of the petit jury, as in the selection of the venire, raises the necessary inference of purposeful discrimination.

In deciding whether the defendant has made the requisite showing, the trial court should consider all relevant circumstances. For example, a "pattern" of strikes against black jurors included in the particular venire might give rise to an inference of discrimination. Similarly, the prosecutor's questions and statements during *voir dire* examination and in exercising his challenges may support or refute an inference of discriminatory purpose. These examples are merely illustrative. We have confidence that trial judges, experienced in supervising *voir dire,* will be able to decide if the circumstances concerning the prosecutor's use of peremptory challenges creates a prima facie case of discrimination against black jurors.

Once the defendant makes a prima facie showing, the burden shifts to the State to come forward with a neutral explanation for challenging black jurors. Though this requirement imposes a limitation in some cases on the full peremptory character of the historic challenge, we emphasize that the prosecutor's explanation need not rise to the level justifying exercise of a challenge for cause. But the prosecutor may not rebut the defendant's prima facie case of discrimination by stating merely that he challenged jurors of the defendant's race on the assumption—or his intuitive judgment—that they would be partial to the defendant because of their shared race. Just as the Equal Protection Clause forbids the States to exclude black persons from the venire on the assumption that blacks as a group are unqualified to serve as jurors, so it forbids the States to strike black veniremen on the assumption that they will be biased in a particular case simply because the defendant is black. The core guarantee of equal protection, ensuring citizens that their State will not discriminate on account of race, would be meaningless were we to approve the exclusion of jurors on the basis of such assumptions, which arise solely from the jurors' race. Nor may the prosecutor rebut the defendant's case merely by denying that he had a discriminatory motive or "affirming his good faith in individual selections." If these general assertions were accepted as rebutting a defendant's prima facie case, the Equal Protection Clause "would be but a vain and illusory requirement." The prosecutor therefore must articulate a neutral explanation related to the particular case to be tried. The trial court then will have the duty to determine if the defendant has established purposeful discrimination.

The State contends that our holding will eviscerate the fair trial values served by the peremptory challenge. Conceding that the Constitution does not guarantee a right to peremptory challenges and that *Swain* did state that their use ultimately is subject to the strictures of equal protection, the State argues that the privilege of unfettered exercise of the challenge is of vital importance to the criminal justice system.

While we recognize, of course, that the peremptory challenge occupies an important position in our trial procedures, we do not agree that our decision today will undermine the contribution the challenge generally makes to the administration of justice. The reality of practice, amply reflected in many state and federal court opinions, shows that the challenge may be, and unfortunately at times has been, used to discriminate against black jurors. By requiring trial courts to be sensitive to the racially discriminatory use of peremptory challenges, our decision enforces the mandate of equal protection and furthers the ends of justice. In view of the heterogeneous population of our nation, public respect for our criminal justice system and the rule of law will be strengthened if we ensure that no citizen is disqualified from jury service because of his race. . . .

In this case, petitioner made a timely objection to the prosecutor's removal of all black persons on the venire. Because the trial court flatly rejected the objection without requiring the prosecutor to give an explanation for his action, we remand this case for further proceedings. If the trial court decides that the facts establish, prima facie, purposeful discrimination and the prosecutor does not come forward with a neutral explanation for his action, our precedents require that petitioner's conviction be reversed.

It is so ordered.

JUSTICE MARSHALL, concurring.

I join JUSTICE POWELL's eloquent opinion for the Court, which takes a historic step toward eliminating the shameful practice of racial discrimination in the selection of juries. . . . I nonetheless write separately to express my views. The decision today will not end the racial discrimination that peremptories inject into the jury-selection process. That goal can be accomplished only by eliminating peremptory challenges entirely. . . .

Misuse of the peremptory challenge to exclude black jurors has become both common and flagrant. Black defendants rarely have been able to compile statistics showing the extent of that practice, but the few cases setting out such figures are instructive. See *United States v. Carter* (CA8 [Court of Appeals] 1975) (in 15 criminal cases in 1974 in the Western District of Missouri involving black defendants, prosecutors peremptorily challenged 81% of black jurors), cert. denied (1976); *United States v. McDaniels* (ED La. 1974) (in 53 criminal cases in 1972–1974 in the Eastern District of Louisiana involving black defendants, federal prosecutors used 68.9% of their peremptory challenges against black jurors, who made up less than one-quarter of the venire). . . . An instruction book used by the prosecutor's office in Dallas County, Texas, explicitly advised prosecutors that they conduct jury selection so as to eliminate "'any member of a minority group.'" In 100 felony trials in Dallas County in 1983–1984, prosecutors peremptorily struck 405 out of 467 eligible black jurors; the chance of a qualified black sitting on a jury was one-in-ten, compared to one-in-two for a white. . . .

Much ink has been spilled regarding the historic importance of defendants' peremptory challenges. . . . [T]he *Swain* Court emphasized the "very old credentials" of the peremptory challenge and cited the "long and widely held belief that peremptory challenge is a necessary part of trial by jury." But this Court has also repeatedly stated that the right of peremptory challenge is not of constitutional magnitude, and may be withheld altogether without impairing the constitutional guarantee of impartial jury and fair trial. The potential for racial prejudice, further, inheres in the defendant's challenge as well. If the prosecutor's peremptory challenge could be eliminated only at the cost of eliminating the defendant's challenge as well, I do not think that would be too great a price to pay.

I applaud the Court's holding that the racially discriminatory use of peremptory challenges violates the Equal Protection Clause, and I join the Court's opinion. However, only by banning peremptories entirely can such discrimination be ended.

JUSTICE REHNQUIST, with whom THE CHIEF JUSTICE joins, dissenting.

I cannot subscribe to the Court's unprecedented use of the Equal Protection Clause to restrict the historic scope of the peremptory challenge, which has been described as "a necessary part of trial by jury." *Swain.* In my view, there is simply nothing "unequal" about the State's using its peremptory challenges to strike blacks from the jury in cases involving black defendants, so long as such challenges are also used to exclude whites in cases involving white defendants, Hispanics in cases involving Hispanic defendants, Asians in cases involving Asian defendants, and so on. This case-specific use of peremptory challenges by the State does not single out blacks, or members of any other race for that matter, for discriminatory treatment. Such use of peremptories is at best based upon seat-of-the-pants instincts, which are undoubtedly crudely stereotypical and may in many cases be hopelessly mistaken. But as long as they are applied across the board to jurors of all races and nationalities, I do not see—and the Court most certainly has not explained—how their use violates the Equal Protection Clause.

Nor does such use of peremptory challenges by the State infringe upon any other constitutional interests. The Court does not suggest that exclusion of blacks from the jury through the State's use of peremptory challenges results in a violation of either the fair-cross-section or impartiality component of the Sixth Amendment. And because the case specific use of peremptory challenges by the State does not deny blacks the right to serve as jurors in cases involving nonblack defendants, it harms neither the excluded jurors nor the remainder of the community.

The use of group affiliations, such as age, race, or occupation, as a "proxy" for potential juror partiality, based on the assumption or belief that members of one group are more likely to favor defendants who belong to the same group, has long been accepted as a legitimate basis for the State's exercise of peremptory challenges. See Swain. Indeed, given the need for reasonable limitations on the time devoted to voir dire, the use of such "proxies" by both the State and the defendant may be extremely useful in eliminating from the jury persons who might be biased in one way or another. The Court today holds that the State may not use its peremptory challenges to strike black prospective jurors on this basis without violating the Constitution. But I do not believe there is anything in the Equal Protection Clause, or any other constitutional provision, that justifies such a departure from the substantive holding contained in Part II of Swain. Petitioner in the instant case failed to make a sufficient showing to overcome the presumption announced in Swain that the State's use of peremptory challenges was related to the context of the case. I would therefore affirm the judgment of the court below.

Batson represents an important turn in Supreme Court doctrine governing jury selection. Prior to this case, the justices *generally* refused to interfere with attorney exercise of peremptory challenges, even in the face of evidence that prosecutors often used them to exclude blacks from juries, as reported in Marshall's concurrence. In *Batson* the justices reevaluated their approach and established a framework by which defendants could challenge prosecutors who appeared to be using their peremptory challenges in a racially discriminatory way.

Batson, however, was just the beginning of the Court's reevaluation of the peremptory challenge system. In *Powers v. Ohio* (1991) it ruled that criminal defendants may object to race-based exclusion of jurors through peremptory challenges even where the defendant and the excluded juror belong to different racial groups. During the same term, in *Edmonson v. Leesville Concrete Co.,* it also applied the *Batson* framework to civil cases, holding that private litigants may not use their peremptory challenges in a racially biased manner. In *Georgia v. McCollum* (1992) the Court held that the *prosecution* can stop the *defense* from exercising its peremptories to eliminate blacks from a jury. In other words, it ruled that the *Batson* framework applies to both sides of criminal cases, the prosecution *and the defense.*

Then, just two years after *McCollum,* the justices were urged to extend this line of reasoning to jury challenges based on sex. In **J.E.B. v. Alabama ex rel. T.B.** (1994) they accepted this invitation and applied *Batson* to intentional sex discrimination in selecting jurors.

According to some observers, the decisions in these post-*Batson* cases were not unexpected; rather, they represent logical extensions of *Batson* and related Court decisions that opened up to judicial scrutiny the exercise of peremptory challenges. But others argue that the Court has gone too far, that it has moved perilously close to the position advocated by Justice Marshall in his *Batson* concurrence: the eradication of peremptory challenges altogether. As Justice Scalia, a critic of Court doctrine in this area, put it in his *McCollum* dissent:

Today's decision gives the lie once again to the belief that an activist, "evolutionary" constitutional jurisprudence always evolves in the direction of greater individual rights. In the interest of promoting the supposedly greater good of race relations in the society as a whole (make no mistake that that is what underlies all of this), we use the Constitution to destroy the ages-old right of criminal defendants to exercise peremptory challenges as they wish, to secure a jury that they consider fair.

Do you agree? Or do you think the Court has taken appropriate steps to ensure fairness in the jury selection process?

Jury Size. Another long-standing tradition Americans adopted from the British is jury size. Since the fourteenth century, all English juries have had twelve people, a number of disputed origin. Some suggest that it

represents the twelve apostles; others claim it emanates from the twelve tribes of Israel. A point on which all agree is that the framers accepted twelve as the proper number for a jury.

Beginning in the mid-1960s, however, many states began to abandon this practice, substituting six-person juries in noncapital cases. These states reasoned that six-person juries would be more economical, faster, and more likely to reach a verdict. Was the use of fewer than twelve people consistent with the demands of the Sixth Amendment? The Court answered this question in **Williams v. Florida**, a 1970 appeal from a robbery conviction. For the Court, Justice Byron White explained that the number twelve had no special constitutional significance. The traditional twelve-person jury was basically the result of historical accident. All the Constitution requires, according to the Court, is a jury sufficiently large to allow actual deliberation and to represent a cross section of the community. The six-person jury used to convict Williams was sufficiently large to meet these standards.

After *Williams,* a number of states followed Florida's lead and now use juries smaller than twelve for some offenses. Nevertheless, legal scholars have closely scrutinized White's reasoning, and numerous empirical investigations have tried to determine whether six-person juries reach conclusions significantly different from those reached by their twelve-person counterparts. Although the scholarly verdict is far from unanimous, many now agree that "research on the effects of panel size on jury performance indicates that the use of six-member juries does not result in significant differences in either trial outcome or deliberation quality."[9] On the other hand, studies have confirmed the obvious: the fewer the jurors, the less time it takes for the panel to reach a verdict.

Jury Verdicts. Following the English tradition, the framers thought juries should reach unanimous verdicts or none at all. If a jury cannot reach a unanimous verdict, the judge declares the jury "hung," and the prosecutor either schedules a retrial or releases the defendant. For the sake of efficient justice, some

---

9. Reid Hastie, Steven D. Penrod, and Nancy Pennington, *Inside the Jury* (Cambridge, MA: Harvard University Press, 1983), 38. Other scholars have found differences between large and small juries but agree that "regardless of which jury type is chosen some desirable features of the unchosen type are lost." Michael J. Saks, *Jury Verdicts* (Lexington, MA: Lexington Books, 1977), 107.

states altered the unanimity rule for twelve-person juries, requiring instead the agreement of nine or ten of the twelve.

Two cases, *Johnson v. Louisiana* and *Apodaca v. Oregon*, decided together in 1972, tested the constitutionality of nonunanimous juries. The side in support of nonunanimity claimed that the alternative was excessive and obsolete in modern society and that because hung juries occurred more frequently, the unanimity requirement often led to miscarriages of justice. The other side pointed out that the very essence of jury decision making is that verdicts are based on doubt. If no reasonable doubt exists about a person's guilt, the jury is supposed to reach a guilty verdict; if doubt is present, the jury should come to the opposite conclusion.

But if a jury is split 9–3 or 10–2, does that not indicate a reasonable doubt? According to Justice White, writing for the Court, a less than unanimous verdict does not violate the Sixth Amendment. A lack of unanimity is not the equivalent of doubt. He concluded:

[T]he fact of three dissenting votes to acquit raises no question of constitutional substance about either the integrity or the accuracy of the majority vote of guilt. . . .

[By obtaining] nine [votes] to convict, the State satisfied its burden of proving guilt beyond any reasonable doubt.

Impartial Juries

As we have seen, Supreme Court decisions have led to jury practices that differ substantially from the vision of the framers. These decisions have been controversial, but they pale in comparison to the furor over the notion of impartial juries.[10] Given the constitutional guarantees of a public trial and freedom of the press, how can judges see to it that defendants receive fair, impartial jury trials? This question has major constitutional importance because it forces courts to deal with conflicting rights. The Sixth Amendment requires judges to regulate trials, ensuring, among other things, that jury members have not prejudged the outcome. In a highly publicized case, the judge's task can become arduous. The judge must deal with the media exercising its constitutional guarantee of a free press. How can judges keep trials

fair without interfering with the rights of the press and the public?

The cases that follow deal with the controversies surrounding impartial juries. Has the Court struck a reasonable balance between competing constitutional rights? Is such a balance even possible?

Press v. Jury: The Warren Court. Before the mid-1960s, no balance existed between freedom of the press and the right to an impartial jury—the former far outweighed the latter. In cases involving well-known individuals or issues of great interest to the public, the press descended on courtrooms. Because there were no well-defined rules, reporters, accompanied by crews carrying bulky, noisy equipment, simply showed up and interviewed and photographed witnesses and other participants at will.

Not surprisingly, the Warren Court placed limitations on the media. Although this issue is not one that can be placed on an ideological continuum, the Warren Court clearly favored the rights of the criminally accused. *Sheppard v. Maxwell* (1966) is the Warren Court's strongest statement on this clash of rights. This case provided an excellent vehicle for the Court because it was the most widely publicized case of its day and illustrates the adverse effects media pressure can produce.[11]

Sheppard v. Maxwell

384 U.S. 333 (1966)
http://laws.findlaw.com/US/384/333.html
Oral arguments are available at http://www.oyez.org.
Vote: 8 (Brennan, Clark, Douglas, Fortas, Harlan, Stewart, Warren, White)
1 (Black)

OPINION OF THE COURT: *Clark*

FACTS:

On July 4, 1954, Marilyn Sheppard, the pregnant wife of Dr. Sam Sheppard, a well-known osteopath, was murdered. According to Sheppard, he and his wife had entertained friends and watched television in their lakefront Cleveland, Ohio, home the night before. He fell asleep on the couch, and Marilyn went upstairs to bed. In the early morning, he awoke to her screams. He ran upstairs, where he struggled with a "form" and

---

10. See *Patton v. Yount* (1984).

11. Several movies have been based on this case, including *The Lawyer* (1970) and *The Fugitive* (1993); a television series based on the case, also titled *The Fugitive,* ran from 1963 to 1967.

was knocked unconscious. Returning to consciousness, he heard noises outside, ran to the lake's edge, and unsuccessfully wrestled with this "form" on the beach. Then he went back into the house, found his wife dead, and called his neighbor, the village mayor. These events touched off a monthlong investigation, coupled with an avalanche of negative publicity, that culminated in Sheppard's arrest.

The negative publicity began on July 7, the day of Marilyn's funeral, when a newspaper story criticized the Sheppard family for refusing to cooperate with the investigation. It continued for the rest of the month. Accusations against Sheppard and demands that he be prosecuted for the murder appeared in the local press almost daily. The coroner's inquest became a media circus, swarming with print and broadcast journalists. Sheppard was denied access to his attorney at various critical stages of the process. He was arrested on the night of July 30, the same day a front-page editorial asked, "Why Isn't Sam Sheppard in Jail?" and portrayed him as a liar and an unfaithful husband. The arrest did not quiet the press; instead, the publicity onslaught continued.

Sheppard's trial began on October 18. Both the judge and the chief prosecutor were running for public office, and the election was just two weeks later. All three Cleveland newspapers published the names and addresses of people called for jury service. As a result, prospective jurors received numerous messages from people wanting to express their views on the case. During jury selection, a Cleveland newspaper ran a two-inch-high, front-page headline: "But Who Will Speak for Marilyn?"

Hundreds of reporters were in Cleveland to cover the trial. The courtroom, filled with journalists from all media and the equipment they needed to report on the trial, was so noisy that much of the testimony could not be heard despite a newly installed loudspeaker system. Photographs of the jury appeared more than forty times in Cleveland newspapers. Local officials failed to monitor the jurors, who made numerous telephone calls during deliberations, with no records kept regarding whom they called or what was said. After five days of deliberations, the jury returned a verdict of guilty.

Later, represented by defense attorney F. Lee Bailey (who would defend O. J. Simpson in another infamous murder trial), Sheppard filed for federal habeas corpus relief, claiming he was denied a fair trial due to the excessive activity by the news

media.[12] Unsuccessful in the lower courts, Sheppard appealed to the Supreme Court.

ARGUMENTS:

For the petitioner, Sam H. Sheppard:

- Sheppard was effectively tried and convicted by the news media, and a fair trial in the courtroom could not and in fact did not occur.
- The trial judge was not sufficiently impartial to preside at the proceeding and should have voluntarily recused himself.
- Unauthorized communications to the jurors during deliberations violated Sheppard's right to due process of law.

For the respondent, E. L. Maxwell:

- Sheppard does not show the actual existence of judge or juror prejudice.
- The newspaper publicity was not so unequivocal as to warrant a finding of pervasive prejudice.
- Transcripts of the jury selection process demonstrate fairness beyond due process of law requirements.
- The defense's failure to challenge the jury selection process, and its failure to suggest that the jury be sequestered, shows that an impartial jury was selected.

 MR. JUSTICE CLARK DELIVERED THE OPINION OF THE COURT.

The principle that justice cannot survive behind walls of silence has long been reflected in the "Anglo-American distrust for secret trials." A responsible press has always been regarded as the handmaiden of effective judicial administration, especially in the criminal field. Its function in this regard is documented by an impressive record of service over several centuries. The press does not simply publish information about trials but guards against the miscarriage of justice by subjecting the police, prosecutors, and judicial processes to extensive public scrutiny and criticism. This Court has, therefore, been unwilling to place any direct limitations on the freedom traditionally exercised by the news media for "[w]hat transpires in the court room is public property." . . .

---

12. Bailey credits the Sheppard case with launching his career. See F. Lee Bailey, *The Defense Never Rests* (New York: Signet, 1971), chap. 2. Also see Cynthia Cooper, *Mockery of Justice: The True Story of the Sheppard Murder Case* (Boston: Northeastern University Press, 1995).

But the Court has also pointed out that "[l]egal trials are not like elections, to be won through the use of the meeting-hall, the radio, and the newspaper." And the Court has insisted that no one be punished for a crime without "a charge fairly made and fairly tried in a public tribunal free of prejudice, passion, excitement, and tyrannical power." . . .

Only last Term in *Estes v. State of Texas* (1965) we set aside a conviction despite the absence of any showing of prejudice. We said there:

It is true that in most cases involving claims of due process deprivations we require a showing of identifiable prejudice to the accused. Nevertheless, at times a procedure employed by the State involves such a probability that prejudice will result that it is deemed inherently lacking in due process.

And we cited with approval the language of MR. JUSTICE BLACK . . . that "our system of law has always endeavored to prevent even the probability of unfairness."

It is clear that the totality of circumstances in this case also warrants such an approach. Unlike Estes, Sheppard was not granted a change of venue to a locale away from where the publicity originated; nor was his jury sequestered. . . . [T]he Sheppard jurors were subjected to newspaper, radio and television coverage of the trial while not taking part in the proceedings. They were allowed to go their separate ways outside of the courtroom, without adequate directions not to read or listen to anything concerning the case. . . . At intervals during the trial, the judge simply repeated his "suggestions" and "requests" that the jurors not expose themselves to comment upon the case. Moreover, the jurors were thrust into the role of celebrities by the judge's failure to insulate them from reporters and photographers. The numerous pictures of the jurors, with their addresses, which appeared in the newspapers before and during the trial itself, exposed them to expressions of opinion from both cranks and friends. The fact that anonymous letters had been received by prospective jurors should have made the judge aware that this publicity seriously threatened the jurors' privacy.

The press coverage of the Estes trial was not nearly as massive and pervasive as the attention given by the Cleveland newspapers and broadcasting stations to Sheppard's prosecution. Sheppard stood indicted for the murder of his wife; the State was demanding the death penalty. For months the virulent publicity about Sheppard and the murder had made the case notorious. Charges and countercharges were aired in the news media besides those for which Sheppard was called to trial. In addition, only three months before trial, Sheppard was examined for more than five hours without counsel during a three-day inquest which ended in a public brawl. The inquest was televised live from a high school gymnasium seating hundreds of people. Furthermore, the trial began two weeks before a hotly contested election at which both Chief Prosecutor Mahon and Judge Blythin were candidates for judgeships.

While we cannot say that Sheppard was denied due process by the judge's refusal to take precautions against the influence of pretrial publicity alone, the court's later rulings must be considered against the setting in which the trial was held. In light of this background, we believe that the arrangements made by the judge with the news media caused Sheppard to be deprived of that "judicial serenity and calm to which [he] was entitled." The fact is that bedlam reigned at the courthouse during the trial and newsmen took over practically the entire courtroom, hounding most of the participants in the trial, especially Sheppard. . . .

There can be no question about the nature of the publicity which surrounded Sheppard's trial. . . . Indeed, every court that has considered this case, save the court that tried it, has deplored the manner in which the news media inflamed and prejudiced the public. . . .

Nor is there doubt that this deluge of publicity reached at least some of the jury. On the only occasion that the jury was queried, two jurors admitted in open court to hearing the highly inflammatory charge that a prison inmate claimed Sheppard as the father of her illegitimate child. Despite the extent and nature of the publicity to which the jury was exposed during trial, the judge refused defense counsel's other requests that the jurors be asked whether they had read or heard specific prejudicial comment about the case, including the incidents we have previously summarized. In these circumstances, we can assume that some of this material reached members of the jury.

The court's fundamental error is compounded by the holding that it lacked power to control the publicity about the trial. From the very inception of the proceedings the judge announced that neither he nor anyone else could restrict prejudicial news accounts. And he reiterated this view on numerous occasions. Since he viewed the news media as his target, the judge never considered other means that are often utilized to reduce the appearance of prejudicial material and to protect the jury from outside influence. We conclude that these procedures would have been sufficient to guarantee Sheppard a fair trial and so do not consider what sanctions might be available against a recalcitrant press nor the charges of bias now made against the state trial judge.

The carnival atmosphere at trial could easily have been avoided since the courtroom and courthouse premises are subject to the control of the court. . . . [T]he presence of the press at judicial proceedings must be limited when it is apparent that the accused might otherwise be prejudiced or disadvantaged. Bearing in mind the massive pretrial publicity, the judge should have adopted stricter rules governing the use of the courtroom by newsmen, as Sheppard's counsel requested. The number of reporters in the courtroom itself could have been limited at the first sign that their presence would disrupt the trial. They certainly should not have been placed inside the bar. Furthermore, the judge should have more closely regulated the conduct of newsmen in the courtroom. For instance, the judge belatedly asked them not to handle and photograph trial exhibits lying on the counsel table during recesses.

. . . [T]he court should have insulated the witnesses. All of the newspapers and radio stations apparently interviewed prospective witnesses at will, and in many instances disclosed their testimony. . . .

. . . [T]he court should have made some effort to control the release of leads, information, and gossip to the press by police officers, witnesses, and the counsel for both sides. Much of the information thus disclosed was inaccurate, leading to groundless rumors and confusion. . . .

The fact that many of the prejudicial news items can be traced to the prosecution, as well as the defense, aggravates the judge's failure to take any action. Effective control of these sources—concededly within the court's power—might well have prevented the divulgence of inaccurate information, rumors, and accusations that made up much of the inflammatory publicity, at least after Sheppard's indictment.

More specifically, the trial court might well have proscribed extrajudicial statements by any lawyer, party, witness, or court official which divulged prejudicial matters, such as the refusal of Sheppard to submit to interrogation or take any lie detector tests; any statement made by Sheppard to officials; the identity of prospective witnesses or their probable testimony; any belief in guilt or innocence; or like statements concerning the merits of the case. . . .

From the cases coming here we note that unfair and prejudicial news comment on pending trials has become increasingly prevalent. Due process requires that the accused receive a trial by an impartial jury free from outside influences. Given the pervasiveness of modern communications and the difficulty of effacing prejudicial publicity from the minds of the jurors, the trial courts must take strong measures to ensure that the balance is never weighed against the accused. And appellate tribunals have the duty to make an independent evaluation of the circumstances. Of course, there is nothing that proscribes the press from reporting events that transpire in the courtroom. But where there is a reasonable likelihood that prejudicial news prior to trial will prevent a fair trial, the judge should continue the case until the threat abates, or transfer it to another county not so permeated with publicity. In addition, sequestration of the jury was something the judge should have raised *sua sponte* with counsel. If publicity during the proceedings threatens the fairness of the trial, a new trial should be ordered. But we must remember that reversals are but palliatives; the cure lies in those remedial measures that will prevent the prejudice at its inception. The courts must take such steps by rule and regulation that will protect their processes from prejudicial outside interferences. Neither prosecutors, counsel for defense, the accused, witnesses, court staff nor enforcement officers coming under the jurisdiction of the court should be permitted to frustrate its function. Collaboration between counsel and the press as to information affecting the fairness of a criminal trial is not only subject to regulation, but is highly censurable and worthy of disciplinary measures.

Since the state trial judge did not fulfill his duty to protect Sheppard from the inherently prejudicial publicity which saturated the community and to control disruptive influences in the courtroom, we must reverse the denial of the habeas petition. The case is remanded to the District Court with instructions to issue a writ and order that Sheppard be released from custody unless the State puts him to its charges again within a reasonable time.

It is so ordered.

BOX 12-2   AFTERMATH . . . SAM SHEPPARD

D r. Sam Sheppard was convicted for the 1954 murder of his wife, Marilyn, and spent ten years in an Ohio prison. Following the Supreme Court's reversal of the conviction in 1966, Sheppard was retried for the offense and found not guilty due to a lack of sufficient evidence. In spite of the acquittal, many people remained convinced that Sheppard was guilty. No other person was ever arrested for the crime. Unable to restart his medical career, Sheppard fell into a life of alcohol abuse and died of liver disease in 1970 at the age of forty-six. His son, Sam Reese Sheppard, who was seven years old at the time of the murder, spent much of his adult life attempting to clear his father's name.

An alternative suspect had surfaced in 1959 when Richard Eberling, who had worked at the Sheppard home as a window washer, was arrested for burglary. During the course of their investigation, police found a ring belonging to Marilyn Sheppard in Eberling's home. Eberling later was convicted of murdering a ninety-year-old widow, Ethel May Durdin, and sentenced to life in prison. A woman who had worked with Eberling claimed that he had boasted of killing Marilyn Sheppard. Eberling, who later denied any involvement in the Sheppard murder, died in prison in 1998.

Certain evidence at the Sheppard murder scene was never fully explained. Blood was spattered throughout the house. Given her wounds, it would have been nearly impossible for that blood to have come from Marilyn, and no cuts were found on Sam. This gave rise to the theory that a third person was there that night. Marilyn's two broken teeth allowed speculation that she had bitten her assailant, causing the blood loss.

Sam Reese Sheppard filed suit against the state of Ohio for the wrongful imprisonment of his father. To win the case and a subsequent damage award, he would have to convince a jury that his father was innocent. DNA evidence was taken from Eberling before his death, and the bodies of Sam and Marilyn Sheppard were exhumed for DNA samples. The DNA tests showed that the blood found at the crime scene was not from either Sam or

Sam Sheppard embraces his son and his second wife, Ariane, as they leave the courthouse following his acquittal in September 1966. At right is F. Lee Bailey, Sheppard's attorney.

Marilyn Sheppard, and that Eberling could not be excluded as the source of the blood.

The wrongful imprisonment trial took place in 2000. Sheppard's case was largely based on the DNA evidence. Attorneys for Ohio, who earlier made private statements hinting at Sheppard's probable innocence, aggressively defended against the lawsuit, claiming that the state had prosecuted the right man in the first place. They branded the DNA evidence as "mumbo jumbo" and portrayed Sam Sheppard as an adulterous playboy who killed his pregnant wife to get out of an unhappy marriage. After a trial taking two months, the jury returned a verdict in favor of the state. Sam Reese Sheppard had lost the battle to clear his father's name, but he continues his crusade and efforts to abolish capital punishment.

SOURCE: *New York Times,* March 26, 1996, February 5, 1997, April 13, 2000; and *USA Today,* April 13, 2000.

The Supreme Court's ruling ordered Sheppard, who had already spent ten years behind bars, released from prison. He was retried for the murder of his wife in 1966 and found not guilty. But even

that did not end the saga of Sam Sheppard, as Box 12-2 details.

As for other defendants, *Sheppard* provides lower court judges with real ammunition to combat the dangers of an overzealous press. In Justice Tom C. Clark's view, judges can take a variety of actions to prevent trials from becoming carnivals, mockeries of justice, as the Sheppard trial did.

Press v. Juries: After Sheppard. As trial court judges continued to limit the role and presence of the media at criminal proceedings, critics began to question the new balance between rights. This time the criticism was that the courts were excessively favoring the rights of the defendant. In a 1979 case, *Gannett Co. v. DePasquale,* the Burger Court had the opportunity to "rebalance" the scales. A newspaper company asked the Court to prohibit a judge from closing the pretrial hearings for a highly publicized case. Writing for a majority of the Court, however, Justice Potter Stewart declined to do so. Adopting the Warren Court's reasoning in *Sheppard,* he claimed that adverse publicity can endanger proceedings, a problem particularly acute at the pretrial stages. Stewart wrote:

This Court has long recognized that adverse publicity can endanger the ability of a defendant to receive a fair trial. . . . To safeguard the due process rights of the accused, a trial judge has an affirmative constitutional duty to minimize the effects of prejudicial pretrial publicity. . . . And because of the Constitution's pervasive concern for these due process rights, a trial judge may surely take protective measures even when they are not strictly and inescapably necessary.

He also dealt with Gannett's assertion of a First Amendment right by stating that "any denial of access in this case was not absolute but only temporary."

Indeed, a year later, in *Richmond Newspapers v. Virginia,* the Court ruled in favor of a First Amendment claim over a Sixth Amendment claim, modifying the balance between these rights. In this case, the justices addressed what some consider the bottom-line issue in this kind of dispute: May a judge completely close a trial? The justices ruled against such a practice, but why? What distinguishes trials from pretrial hearings?

Richmond Newspapers v. Virginia

448 U.S. 555 (1980)
http://laws.findlaw.com/US/448/555.html
Oral arguments are available at http://www.oyez.org.
Vote: 7 (Blackmun, Brennan, Burger, Marshall, Stevens, Stewart, White)
   1 (Rehnquist)

OPINION ANNOUNCING THE JUDGMENT OF THE COURT: *Burger*
CONCURRING OPINIONS: *Blackmun, Brennan, Stevens, Stewart, White*
DISSENTING OPINION: *Rehnquist*
NOT PARTICIPATING: *Powell*

FACTS:

In July 1976 a Virginia court convicted a man named John Paul Stevenson of stabbing a hotel manager to death. An appellate court reversed the conviction on a procedural error, and a new trial took place before the same court. But that proceeding and one other ended in mistrials. By the time the fourth trial date was set in 1978, the case had garnered a great deal of public and media interest. Because such attention could interfere with jury selection, Stevenson's attorney asked the judge to close the trial to the public. When the prosecutor voiced no objection, the judge granted the request, a privilege judges had under the Virginia closure law.

Reporters covering the case brought suit against the state, arguing that its law violated the First Amendment. This claim received legal support from numerous civil liberties and media organizations. They not only agreed with the appellants but also asked the Court to overrule *Gannett.* The Reporters Committee for Freedom of the Press, on behalf of several media associations, said, "Great confusion has arisen as to what *Gannett* means, and the case is being used as grounds for closing all types of criminal proceedings." The American Civil Liberties Union stated, "The public and press have a constitutionally protected right of access to criminal pretrial and trial proceedings."

ARGUMENTS:

For the appellant, Richmond Newspapers, Inc.:
- The U.S. Constitution guarantees the right to attend and observe criminal trials.
- The Virginia closure statute violates the Constitution's guarantees that criminal trials will be open to public attendance and observation.

For the appellee, Commonwealth of Virginia:
- The First Amendment does not afford the public or press a right to attend criminal trials.
- The Sixth Amendment embodies no public right of access to criminal trials.
- The First and Sixth Amendments, when taken in conjunction, do not support a public right of access to criminal trials.

MR. CHIEF JUSTICE BURGER ANNOUNCED THE JUDGMENT OF THE COURT.

The narrow question presented in this case is whether the right of the public and press to attend criminal trials is guaranteed under the United States Constitution. . . .

We begin consideration of this case by noting that the precise issue presented here has not previously been before this Court for decision. In *Gannett Co. v. DePasquale* [1979], the Court was not required to decide whether a right of access to *trials,* as distinguished from hearings on pretrial motions, was constitutionally guaranteed. The Court held that the Sixth Amendment's guarantee to the accused of a public trial gave neither the public nor the press an enforceable right of access to a pretrial suppression hearing. . . .

In prior cases the Court has treated questions involving conflicts between publicity and a defendant's right to a fair trial. But here for the first time the Court is asked to decide whether a criminal trial itself may be closed to the public upon the unopposed request of a defendant, without any demonstration that closure is required to protect the defendant's superior right to a fair trial, or that some other overriding consideration requires closure.

. . . [T]he historical evidence demonstrates conclusively that at the time when our organic laws were adopted, criminal trials both here and in England had long been presumptively open. This is no quirk of history; rather, it has long been recognized as an indispensable attribute to an Anglo-American trial. . . .

From this unbroken, uncontradicted history, supported by reasons as valid today as in centuries past, we are bound to conclude that a presumption of openness inheres in the very nature of a criminal trial under our system of justice. This conclusion is hardly novel; without a direct holding on the issue, the Court has voiced its recognition of it in a variety of contexts over the years. . . .

Despite the history of criminal trials being presumptively open since long before the Constitution, the State presses its contention that neither the Constitution nor the Bill of Rights contains any provision which by its terms guarantees to the public the right to attend criminal trials. Standing alone, this is correct, but there remains the question whether, absent an explicit provision, the Constitution affords protection against exclusion of the public from criminal trials.

The First Amendment, in conjunction with the Fourteenth, prohibits governments from "abridging the freedom of speech, or of the press; or the right of the people peaceably to assemble, and to petition the Government for a redress of grievances." These expressly guaranteed freedoms share a common core purpose of assuring freedom of communication on matters relating to the functioning of government. Plainly it would be difficult to single out any aspect of government of higher concern and importance to the people than the manner in which criminal trials are conducted; . . . recognition of this pervades the centuries-old history of open trials and the opinions of this Court.

The Bill of Rights was enacted against the backdrop of the long history of trials being presumptively open. Public access to trials was then regarded as an important aspect of the process itself; the conduct of trials "before as many of the people as chuse to attend" was regarded as one of "the inestimable advantages of a free English constitution of government." In guaranteeing freedoms such as those of speech and press, the First Amendment can be read as protecting the right of everyone to attend trials so as to give meaning to those explicit guarantees. . . . What this means in the context of trials is that the First Amendment guarantees of speech and press, standing alone, prohibit government from summarily closing courtroom doors which had long been open to the public at the time that Amendment was adopted. . . .

It is not crucial whether we describe this right to attend criminal trials to hear, see, and communicate observations concerning them as a "right of access" or a "right to gather information," for we have recognized that "without some protection for seeking out the news, freedom of the press could be eviscerated." The explicit, guaranteed rights to speak and to publish concerning what takes place at a trial would lose much meaning if access to observe the trial could, as it was here, be foreclosed arbitrarily. . . .

The State argues that the Constitution nowhere spells out a guarantee for the right of the public to attend trials, and that accordingly no such right is protected. The possibility that such a contention could be made did not escape the notice of the Constitution's draftsmen; they were concerned that some important rights might be thought disparaged because not specifically guaranteed. It was even argued that because of this danger no Bill of Rights should be adopted. . . .

But arguments such as the State makes have not precluded recognition of important rights not enumerated. Notwithstanding the appropriate caution against reading into the Constitution rights not explicitly defined, the Court has acknowledged that certain unarticulated rights are implicit in enumerated guarantees. For example, the rights of association and of privacy, the right to be presumed innocent, and the right to be judged by a standard of proof beyond a reasonable doubt in a criminal trial, as well as the right to travel, appear nowhere in the Constitution or Bill of Rights. Yet these important but unarticulated rights have nonetheless been found to share constitutional protection in common with explicit guarantees. . . .

We hold that the right to attend criminal trials is implicit in the guarantees of the First Amendment; without the freedom to attend such trials, which people have exercised for centuries, important aspects of freedom of speech and "of the press could be eviscerated."

Having concluded there was a guaranteed right of the public under the First and Fourteenth Amendments to attend the trial of Stevenson's case, we return to the closure order challenged by appellants. The Court in *Gannett* made clear that although the Sixth Amendment guarantees the accused a right to a public trial, it does not give a right to a private trial. Despite the fact that this was the fourth trial of the accused, the trial judge made no findings to support closure; no inquiry was made as to whether alternative solutions would have met the need to ensure fairness; there was no recognition of any right under the Constitution for the public or press to attend the trial. In contrast to the pretrial proceeding dealt with in *Gannett,* there exist in the context of the trial itself various tested alternatives to satisfy the constitutional demands of fairness. There was no suggestion that any problems with witnesses could not have been dealt with by their exclusion from the courtroom or their sequestration during the trial. Nor is there anything to indicate that sequestration of the jurors would not have guarded against their being subjected to any improper information. All of the alternatives admittedly present difficulties for trial courts, but none of the factors relied on here was beyond the realm of the manageable. Absent an overriding interest articulated in findings, the trial of a criminal case must be open to the public. Accordingly, the judgment under review is

Reversed.

MR. JUSTICE BRENNAN, with whom MR. JUSTICE MARSHALL joins, concurring in the judgment.

. . . [R]esolution of First Amendment public access claims in individual cases must be strongly influenced by the weight of historical practice and by an assessment of the specific structural value of public access in the circumstances. With regard to the case at hand, our ingrained tradition of public trials and the importance of public access to the broader purposes of the trial process, tip the balance strongly toward the rule that trials be open. What countervailing interests might be sufficiently compelling to reverse this presumption of openness need not concern us now, for the statute at stake here authorizes trial closures at the unfettered discretion of the judge and parties. Accordingly, Va. Code §19.2-266 (Supp. 1980) violates the First and Fourteenth Amendments, and the decision of the Virginia Supreme Court to the contrary should be reversed.

MR. JUSTICE REHNQUIST, dissenting.

For the reasons stated in my separate concurrence in *Gannett Co. v. DePasquale* (1979), I do not believe that either the First or Sixth Amendment, as made applicable to the States by the Fourteenth, requires that a State's reasons for denying public access to a trial, where both the prosecuting attorney and the defendant have consented to an order of closure approved by the judge, are subject to any additional constitutional review at our hands. And I most certainly do not believe that the Ninth Amendment confers upon us any such power to review orders of state trial judges closing trials in such situations.

We have, at present, 50 state judicial systems and one federal judicial system in the United States, and our authority to reverse a decision by the highest court of the State is limited to only those occasions when the state decision violates some provision of the United States Constitution. And that authority should be exercised with a full sense that the judges whose decisions we review are making the same effort as we to uphold the Constitution. As said by Mr. Justice Jackson, concurring in the result in *Brown v. Allen* (1953), "We are not final because we are infallible, but we are infallible only because we are final." . . .

The issue here is not whether the "right" to freedom of the press conferred by the First Amendment to the Constitution overrides the defendant's "right" to a fair trial conferred by other Amendments to the Constitution; it is, instead, whether any provision in the Constitution may fairly be read to prohibit what the trial judge in the Virginia state-court system did in this case. Being unable to find any such prohibition in the First, Sixth, Ninth, or any other Amendment to the United States Constitution, or in the Constitution itself, I dissent.

In finding the balance between defendants' rights and those of the press, the Court said that judges can pursue a variety of strategies to protect the accused, but they cannot completely close trial proceedings to the public and press. Today, judges are more lenient toward press coverage of criminal trials than in the past. One reason is that audio and video recording equipment is not as noisy and disruptive as it was when *Sheppard* was decided. The media can record or televise trials without violating the conditions necessary for the dispassionate consideration of evidence. In recent years, some new courtrooms have been constructed with video-recording facilities fully incorporated into the building plans.

TRIAL PROCEEDINGS

Once attorneys complete the voir dire and select the petit jury, the trial begins. Almost all trials follow the same format. First, the attorneys make opening statements. Each side (beginning with the prosecution because it has the burden of proof) presents an opening statement, typically setting forth the facts and a theory of the case or an explanation why the facts will support a verdict of either guilty or not guilty.

Next, each side presents its case, again beginning with the prosecution. At this point, attorneys call witnesses who testify for their side and then are cross-examined by the opposing attorney. This stage is the heart of the trial, and here, as in all other important parts of the criminal justice system, the Constitution affords defendants a great many rights. For example, the Sixth Amendment includes the defendant's right to "be confronted with the witnesses against him." This provision, often called the confrontation clause, includes several guarantees. First, defendants have the right to be present during their trials. Unlike some

countries, the United States generally does not permit trials in absentia.[13]

Second, the confrontation clause requires that prosecution witnesses appear in open court in the presence of the defendant to give their testimony under oath. As a consequence, the prosecution typically cannot obtain a conviction based on anonymous testimony or on information provided by witnesses who are unwilling to appear in court. Although this requirement appears to be both reasonable and necessary for most crimes, it has received considerable criticism for crimes such as rape and child abuse. Rape victims, for example, may refuse to report their rapes to the police because they know that if they do so they may be required to give their testimony in open court. Similarly, many fear that children who have been abused will be traumatized by having to tell their stories in court with the persons who abused them visibly present.

Although the justices have generally adhered to the requirement that prosecution witnesses appear in court, they have been sympathetic to the situation facing children who may have been the victims of abuse. In *Maryland v. Craig* (1990), for example, the Court upheld a Maryland procedure that allowed abused children to testify via closed-circuit television. This procedure permitted the defendant to see the testimony of the alleged victim but protected the child witness from the trauma of face-to-face interaction with her accused abuser. For the majority, Justice O'Connor outlined the Court's reasoning:

[W]e conclude that where necessary to protect a child witness from trauma that would be caused by testifying in the physical presence of the defendant, at least where such trauma would impair the child's ability to communicate, the Confrontation Clause does not prohibit use of a procedure that, despite the absence of face-to-face confrontation,

---

13. In *Illinois v. Allen* (1970), however, the Supreme Court considered the actions of a trial judge in response to a defendant's misbehavior in the courtroom. William Allen, on trial for armed robbery, verbally abused the judge and others in the courtroom, threw papers, continually talked loudly, and interrupted witnesses. After ample warning, the judge ordered Allen removed, and the trial continued in his absence. Allen was convicted, and he appealed on the grounds that he was not allowed to be present during his trial. A unanimous Court rejected his appeal. Justice Black's opinion explained that the right to confrontation can be waived by the defendant's own abusive behavior. Black indicated that in extreme cases a judge may order the defendant to be bound and gagged.

ensures the reliability of the evidence by subjecting it to rigorous adversarial testing and thereby preserves the essence of effective confrontation. Because there is no dispute that the child witnesses in this case testified under oath, were subject to full cross-examination, and were able to be observed by the judge, jury, and defendant as they testified, we conclude that, to the extent that a proper finding of necessity has been made, the admission of such testimony would be consonant with the Confrontation Clause.

A third component of the right to confrontation is cross-examination. Not only does the prosecution have to produce witnesses who testify under oath in open court before the defendant, but those witnesses are also subject to questioning by the defense. This requirement is based on the theory that a jury will best be able to discern the truth if testimony—*even out-of-court testimony,* in some instances—is tested by vigorous examination from the opposing side. Justice Scalia, typically no friend of criminal defendants,[14] made this point emphatically in ***Crawford v. Washington*** (2004). The defendant, Michael Crawford, was accused of stabbing a man who allegedly tried to rape his wife, Sylvia. At his trial, the state played for the jury a recorded statement that Sylvia made during a police interrogation suggesting that the stabbing was not committed while her husband was defending her against a rape. Sylvia did not testify because of the state's marital privilege, which generally bars the spouse of a defendant from testifying without the defendant spouse's consent. Crawford objected to Sylvia's tape-recorded statement on the ground that his attorney never had an opportunity to cross-examine his wife, and so admitting the evidence violated his Sixth Amendment right of confrontation.

The Court agreed with Michael Crawford. In a tour de force on the historical underpinnings of the confrontation clause, Scalia drew two inferences. "First, the principal evil at which the Confrontation Clause was directed was the use of *ex parte* examinations as evidence against the accused." To Scalia, writing for the majority, this meant that the clause applies not only to any in-court testimony but also to any out-of-court statements introduced at trial. As he put it, we "reject the view that the confrontation clause applies of its own force only to in-court testimony. . . . It applies to 'witnesses' against the accused—in other words, those who 'bear testimony.'" Thus, "Statements taken by police officers in the course of interrogations are . . . testimonial." Second, Scalia wrote that "the Framers would not have allowed admission of testimonial statements of a witness who did not appear at trial unless he was unavailable to testify, and the defendant had had a prior opportunity for cross-examination." Therefore, taken together, Crawford was denied the right to confrontation because the out-of-court statement amounted to testimony and Crawford's attorney never had a prior opportunity to cross-examine it.

The basic holding of *Crawford* seems simple enough. If witnesses providing testimonial evidence against the defendant cannot be cross-examined in open court, prosecutors can introduce their testimony only if the witnesses are unavailable and there was some prior opportunity for cross-examination. But what exactly is testimony? In *Crawford,* the majority wrote that the term "applies at a minimum to prior testimony at a preliminary hearing, before a grand jury, or at a former trial; and to police interrogations." Beyond that, it decided to "leave for another day any effort to spell out a comprehensive definition of 'testimonial.'"

Well, that day came soon enough. In three cases coming on the heels of *Crawford*, the Court sought to clarify the meaning of "testimony." In the first, ***Davis v. Washington*** (2006), the justices agreed that prosecutors could introduce victims' emergency phone calls to 911 even if the victims are not in court for cross-examination. In the same opinion, however, the Court refused to allow a victim's statement to police, given at the crime scene, to be used at trial unless the victim was willing to be cross-examined. The difference between the two, according to Justice Scalia's majority opinion, is that the phone call is not a "testimonial statement" covered by the confrontation clause, but the on-the-scene statement to police investigating a crime is.

At least to a majority of five, the second of the post-*Crawford* cases, ***Melendez-Diaz v. Massachusetts*** (2009), reaffirms this distinction. At Luis Melendez-Diaz's trial, the prosecution introduced sworn certificates of state laboratory analysts stating that material

---

14. Since the start of the Roberts Court (through 2011), Scalia has voted in favor of the defendant in only 32 percent of the Court's 126 cases. Only Thomas (22 percent), Roberts (27 percent), and Alito (17 percent) have lower percentages. By contrast, Stevens, Souter, Ginsburg, Sotomayor, and Kagan have all supported defendants at a rate of 60 percent or higher.

seized by police and connected to Melendez-Diaz was quite likely cocaine. Melendez-Diaz's attorney objected, claiming that under Supreme Court precedent, the analysts should testify in person and face cross-examination. The Supreme Court agreed. Writing for a majority of five, Justice Scalia—who, as *Crawford* and *Davis* suggest, was taking the lead in developing the Court's confrontation clause jurisprudence—held that because the certificates fell within the "core class of testimonial statements" they were covered by the confrontation clause. The defendant should have had the chance to cross-examine the analysts.

The dissenters, led by Justice Kennedy, disagreed. To them *Davis* and *Crawford* "stand for the proposition that formal statements made by a conventional witness—one who has personal knowledge of some aspect of the defendant's guilt—may not be admitted without the witness appearing at trial to meet the accused face to face. But *Davis* [does] not say . . . that anyone who makes a testimonial statement is a witness for purposes of the Confrontation Clause, even when that person has, in fact, witnessed nothing to give them personal knowledge of the defendant's guilt." In 2011, a majority of the Court in **Michigan v. Bryant** moved closer to the dissenters in *Melendez-Diaz*. With Justice Sotomayor writing for the majority, the Court held that a statement made to police by a victim at a crime scene was nontestimonial even though the victim died before the start of the trial. The Court's reasoning in this instance was that the statement was nontestimonial in nature because it was made with the purpose of assisting the police in an ongoing emergency situation. Scalia (along with Ginsburg) now found himself in dissent. He accused the Court of distorting and confusing the confrontation clause doctrine that he had worked to build. To Scalia, because the victim's purpose was to ensure the arrest and prosecution of the defendant, the victim's statement clearly amounted to testimony for purposes of the confrontation clause. "No framing-era confrontation case," Scalia wrote, "that I know of, neither here nor in England, took such an enfeebled view of the right to confrontation."

Undoubtedly the debate over the nature of testimony will continue. It is important to know, however, that in addition to specific Sixth Amendment guarantees, defendants facing trial have rights under the Fifth Amendment's due process and self-incrimination clauses. As we have seen, the rather vague term *due*

process has been used to ensure that police obtain evidence by fair means and as a way to apply constitutional guarantees to the states. The Court also has invoked it to guarantee that defendants receive fair treatment from prosecutors and courts.

One manifestation of due process in action in criminal proceedings came in **Sell v. United States** (2003). Here the Court addressed the question of whether the government can force mentally ill defendants to take antipsychotic drugs to render them competent to stand trial. The government argued that it had an interest in obtaining an adjudication of the defendant's guilt or innocence, and that the only way it could achieve that end in this case was to administer the drugs. The defendant's attorneys responded that "allowing the government to administer antipsychotic medication against his will solely to render him competent to stand trial" violated the Constitution by depriving him of liberty without due process. In a 6–3 decision, the Court sided with the United States. Writing for the majority, Justice Stephen Breyer concluded that "the Constitution permits the Government involuntarily to administer antipsychotic drugs to a mentally ill defendant facing serious criminal charges in order to render that defendant competent to stand trial." But the Court also said that the circumstances under which the government could do so are limited: if the treatment is medically appropriate; if it is substantially unlikely to have side effects that may undermine the fairness of the trial; and if, taking account of less intrusive alternatives, it is necessary in order to further important government trial-related interests.

FINAL TRIAL STAGE: AN OVERVIEW OF SENTENCING

Once both sides have presented their evidence through witness testimony, physical evidence, documents, and other exhibits, the attorneys make closing arguments in which they summarize their cases and try to convince the jury that the facts and the law logically require a particular verdict. Next, the judge makes a charge to the jury, providing jurors with instructions on the applicable law and guidelines on which to base a decision. The jury then deliberates in an attempt to reach a verdict. What goes on in the jury room is private and known only to the jurors. Once the jury reaches a verdict, it announces its decision in open court. If the jury finds the defendant not guilty, the accused goes free. If it finds the defendant guilty, the judge will typically set a future court date to determine and pronounce the appropriate sentence.[15]

Although this last step seems straightforward enough, it has engendered a good deal of debate. The primary concern, it seems, is that on any given day in the United States, defendants convicted of the same crime in different localities can receive vastly different sentences. Why do disparities exist? One reason is that judges consider a variety of information before pronouncing sentence, including the nature of the crime committed; the defendant's past convictions or lack thereof; the defendant's family situation and future prospects; the defendant's addictions to drugs and alcohol, if any; and the impact of the crime on any victims. This information is typically conveyed to the judge in presentence reports prepared by the probation department and through evidence presented by the attorneys. Judges maintain that by considering a broad array of information about convicted defendants, they can form a more complete picture and hand down appropriate sentences. Discretionary sentencing has its share of detractors, however. Some scholars argue that irrelevant factors enter the process. Just as partisanship and ideology play roles in Supreme Court decision making, they also influence trial court judges at sentencing. Another serious issue is that racial discrimination may influence sentencing decisions; some research has suggested that white judges are likely to deal more harshly with convicted blacks than with whites.[16]

Given these complaints, it is not surprising that Congress tried to limit judges' discretion by creating the United States Sentencing Commission. The commission's task is to establish sentencing guidelines that federal judges must follow. The guidelines are designed to reduce the likelihood that improper discrimination will affect a sentence while allowing judges some

flexibility to tailor a penalty to the individual defendant based on legally relevant criteria. The law identifies certain conditions that allow a judge to depart from the guidelines in an appropriate case.

In **United States v. Booker** (2005), however, the Supreme Court gave federal judges even greater flexibility. Freddie J. Booker was charged with possession with intent to distribute at least 50 grams of crack cocaine. Having heard evidence that he had 92.5 grams in his duffel bag, a jury found him guilty of violating a federal law that prescribes for that offense a minimum sentence of ten years in prison and a maximum sentence of life.

Based on Booker's criminal history and the quantity of drugs the jury had heard about, the Sentencing Guidelines required the district court judge to select a "base" sentence of not less than 210 nor more than 262 months in prison. After a posttrial sentencing hearing, the judge concluded that Booker had possessed an additional 566 grams of crack cocaine and that he was guilty of obstructing justice. Those findings mandated that the judge select a sentence between 360 months and life imprisonment; the judge imposed a sentence at the low end of the range. Therefore, instead of the sentence of twenty-one years and ten months that the judge could have imposed on the facts proved to the jury beyond a reasonable doubt, Booker received a thirty-year sentence.

The U.S. Court of Appeals for the Seventh Circuit held that this application of the Sentencing Guidelines conflicted with several recent Supreme Court decisions, which held that "[o]ther than the fact of a prior conviction, any fact that increases the penalty for a crime beyond the prescribed statutory maximum must be submitted to a jury, and proved beyond a reasonable doubt."[17] Otherwise, the defendant's Sixth Amendment right to a jury trial is violated.

---

15. In death penalty cases the Supreme Court has required that jurors participate in the sentencing process (*Ring v. Arizona*, 2002).

16. See Susan Welch, Michael Combs, and John Gruhl, "Do Black Judges Make a Difference?," *American Journal of Political Science* 32 (1988): 126–136. Other studies, however, have not found much evidence of racially based sentencing. In general, a reasonable conclusion is that "[d]iscrimination appears to exist in some places, for some types of crimes, and for some judges, but not universally." Lawrence Baum, *American Courts: Process and Policy,* 6th ed. (Boston: Houghton Mifflin, 2008), 186.

17. The quote is from the Court's decision in *Apprendi v. New Jersey* (2000). Charles C. Apprendi Jr. pled guilty to possessing a gun for unlawful purposes, and the prosecutor filed a motion to "enhance" (increase) the sentence because the crime was racially motivated. Under the state's hate crime statute, such enhancement can occur if a trial judge finds that the defendant committed the crime with the purpose of intimidating a person or group because of race. The judge found such evidence and sentenced Apprendi to twelve years in prison. Although the Court has held that states may enhance sentences for racially motivated crimes (e.g., in *Wisconsin v. Mitchell, 1993*), it invalidated New Jersey's law on the ground that the facts that led to the increased sentence had not been submitted to a jury.

The Supreme Court agreed with the lower court's interpretation of its precedent, noting that "the Sixth Amendment requires juries, not judges, to find facts relevant to sentencing."

Although a holding that bans judges from imposing a sentence higher than the maximum authorized by the jury's verdict seems to restrict judges, the Court's remedy may actually give them greater discretion. The majority ruled that federal judges cannot ignore the Sentencing Act's guidelines, but neither should they view them as mandatory and binding. As modified by the Court's decision, "the Federal Sentencing Act makes the Guidelines effectively advisory. It requires a sentencing court to consider Guidelines ranges, but it permits the court to tailor the sentence in light of other statutory concerns as well."

Whether federal judges will continue to follow the guidelines or view them as merely advisory remains to be seen. What we can say is that the Court continues to clarify the *Booker* decision. In **Kimbrough v. United States** (2007), for example, the justices held that when determining a sentencing range, trial court judges may consider the disparity in the guidelines' treatment of crack and powder cocaine. More recently, in *Oregon v. Ice* (2009), the Court ruled that the Sixth Amendment does not prohibit states from assigning to judges, rather than to juries, the task of finding facts necessary to impose consecutive, rather than concurrent, sentences for multiple offenses.

THE EIGHTH AMENDMENT

In addition to statutory attempts to limit judicial discretion in sentencing, there is an important constitutional limit: the clause in the Eighth Amendment that bans cruel and unusual punishments. The meaning of this clause has plagued generations of justices, with no issue more perplexing than the constitutionality and application of the death penalty. In what follows, we begin with the justices' attempts to define "cruel and usual," and then we turn to the perplexing issue of capital punishment.

Defining "Cruel and Unusual"

The meaning of "cruel and unusual" is open to interpretation. Has the Court provided us with any definition of that concept? Indeed, in **Solem v. Helm** (1983) it attempted to do just that. In 1979 Jerry Helm was convicted of writing a $100 bad check. He had been convicted six previous times of such crimes as obtaining money under false pretenses and driving while intoxicated. None of his crimes was violent, none was a crime against a person, and all were related to a history of alcohol abuse. The judge, believing Helm to be beyond rehabilitation, invoked the South Dakota recidivism law and sentenced him to life in prison without possibility of parole. After two years of trying to get the governor to commute his sentence, Helm turned to the courts, claiming that his punishment was cruel and unusual.

By a 5–4 vote, the Supreme Court found that the life sentence violated the cruel and unusual punishment clause. Justice Powell's majority opinion held that the Eighth Amendment proscribes not only barbaric punishments but also sentences that are *disproportionate to the crime committed*. To determine whether a sentence is so disproportionate that it violates the Eighth Amendment, the justices said that they would consider three factors: "(i) the gravity of the offense and the harshness of the penalty; (ii) the sentences imposed on other criminals in the same jurisdiction; and (iii) the sentences imposed for commission of the same crime in other jurisdictions." As applied in this case, life in prison without parole was out of proportion to the bad check charges.

To some, the *Solem* approach was simply the Court's adaptation of the old adage "Let the punishment fit the crime." But the use of the *Solem* proportionality concept has not been accepted by all the justices, and its application has not always been easy. In *Harmelin v. Michigan* (1991), for example, the justices rejected a convict's claim that a sentence of life in prison without possibility of parole for a first-time offense of cocaine possession violated the cruel and unusual punishment clause, but they could not agree on the reason this sentence was not grossly disproportionate. Justice Scalia wrote that the proportionality principle is "an aspect of our death penalty jurisprudence, rather than a generalizable aspect of Eighth Amendment law." As a result, he refused to apply proportionality principles except in cases involving capital punishment. Justice Kennedy asserted that the same principles apply in capital and noncapital cases, and he went on to identify them: "the primacy of the legislature, the variety of legitimate penological schemes, the nature of our federal system, and the requirement that proportionality review be guided by objective factors" that "inform the final one: The Eighth Amendment does not require strict proportionality between crime and sentence. Rather, it forbids only extreme sentences that are 'grossly disproportionate' to the crime."

In 2003 the issue returned to the Court in ***Ewing v. California***. In this case the Court addressed the constitutionality of sentencing statutes popularly known as "three strikes and you're out" laws. Under such a scheme, a defendant convicted of a felony who has twice previously been convicted of a serious or violent felony can be sentenced to a long prison term, including life in prison. Such laws are designed to deter crime and to protect the public from habitual criminals by imprisoning them for long periods of time. In 1993 Washington became the first state to enact a three-strikes law when its voters approved such a proposal by a 3–1 margin. Over the next two years, twenty-four states and the federal government adopted similar measures.

The *Ewing* case was a constitutional challenge to California's three-strikes law. Gary Ewing had previous convictions for three burglaries and a robbery when he was arrested in 2000 for shoplifting three expensive golf clubs. Under California law, the prosecutor had the option of charging Ewing with a felony or a misdemeanor. The prosecutor decided that a felony grand theft charge was the appropriate alternative. Ewing was convicted of the felony charge and therefore became eligible for sentencing under the state's three-strikes statute. The judge sentenced him to a term of twenty-five years to life in prison. Ewing appealed, claiming that the sentence was disproportionate to the triggering offense of stealing three golf clubs.

The Court upheld the state law. The plurality adopted Kennedy's approach in *Harmelin*, which emphasizes judicial deference to the legislature, particularly its determination that recidivism is a matter of great state concern and that interests of public safety justify this harsh sentencing option. In considering whether the specific punishment meted out to Ewing violated Kennedy's proportionality principles, Justice O'Connor explained that it did not, that the long prison term was not imposed because Ewing stole three golf clubs. Rather, the penalty was based on the grand theft violation as part of a long history of criminal activity. Consequently, the sentence was not grossly disproportionate and did not violate the Eighth Amendment's prohibition on cruel and unusual punishment.

In dissent, Justice Breyer (along with Justices John Paul Stevens, David Souter, and Ruth Bader Ginsburg) took issue with this analysis. Even under the *Harmelin*

framework, Breyer asserted, Ewing's punishment was "grossly disproportionate" to the crime. He then demonstrated that it was also disproportionate to sentencing practices in other jurisdictions and even in California.[18] The plurality in *Ewing* said this kind of comparative analysis was "not mandated."

Divisions on the Court remain. In the 2010 case of *Graham v. Florida*, for example, the Court considered whether the Constitution permits a juvenile offender to be sentenced to life in prison without parole for a nonhomicide crime. While on probation, Terrance Graham, a minor, was arrested for committing two robberies. Finding Graham in violation of his probation, the judge sentenced Graham to life. Since Florida had abolished its parole system, once sentenced to life imprisonment, Graham had no possibility of release. He challenged his sentence under the Eighth Amendment's cruel and unusual punishment clause.

Writing for the majority, Justice Kennedy began by claiming that the determination of whether a punishment is cruel and unusual embodies "a moral judgment" to be made by the Court, and is not always to be determined by practices elsewhere. Under this approach, he ruled that it was "grossly disproportionate" for a court to sentence a defendant under the age of eighteen to a sentence of life without the possibility of parole unless the defendant had committed a homicide. As Kennedy wrote:

Terrance Graham's sentence guarantees he will die in prison without any meaningful opportunity to obtain release, no matter what he might do to demonstrate that the bad acts he committed as a teenager are not representative of his true character, even if he spends the next half century attempting

---

18. Breyer wrote: "California has reserved, and still reserves, Ewing-type prison time, *i.e.*, at least 25 real years in prison, for criminals convicted of crimes far worse than was Ewing's. Statistics for the years 1945 to 1981, for example, indicate that typical (nonrecidivist) male first-degree murderers served between 10 and 15 real years in prison, with 90 percent of all such murderers serving less than 20 real years. Moreover, California, which has moved toward a real-time sentencing system (where the statutory punishment approximates the time served), still punishes far less harshly those who have engaged in far more serious conduct. It imposes, for example, upon nonrecidivists guilty of arson causing great bodily injury a maximum sentence of nine years in prison (prison term of 5, 7, or 9 years for arson that causes great bodily injury); it imposes upon those guilty of voluntary manslaughter a maximum sentence of 11 years (prison term of 3, 6, or 11 years for voluntary manslaughter). It reserves the sentence that it here imposes upon (former-burglar-now-golf-club-thief) Ewing, for nonrecidivist, first-degree murderers (sentence of 25 years to life for first-degree murder)."

to atone for his crimes and learn from his mistakes. The State has denied him any chance to later demonstrate that he is fit to rejoin society based solely on a nonhomicide crime that he committed while he was a child in the eyes of the law. This the Eighth Amendment does not permit.

The Court's decision was extraordinary because it held that a type of punishment—life without the possibility of parole—could not be imposed on an entire category of offenders—juveniles. This was the first time the justices ever took such a step in a noncapital Eighth Amendment case. (As we shall see in the next section, the Court has held that the state cannot impose the death penalty on certain categories of offenders, including juveniles and the mentally retarded.)

This drew a strong dissent from Justice Thomas (writing for Scalia and Alito, in part):

Until today, the Court has based its categorical proportionality rulings on the notion that the Constitution gives special protection to capital defendants because the death penalty is a uniquely severe punishment that must be reserved for only those who are "most deserving of execution." Of course, the Eighth Amendment itself makes no distinction between capital and noncapital sentencing, but the "bright line" the Court drew between the two penalties has for many years served as the principal justification for the Court's willingness to reject democratic choices regarding the death penalty.

Today's decision eviscerates that distinction.

Thomas also took issue with Kennedy's approach: "I am unwilling to assume that we, as members of this Court, are any more capable of making such moral judgments than our fellow citizens. Nothing in our training as judges qualifies us for that task, and nothing in Article III gives us that authority."

Even members of the majority vote coalition expressed disagreement with the majority opinion. Chief Justice Roberts, concurring in the judgment, agreed that Graham's sentence violated the Eighth Amendment but stated that he would not have announced a categorical rule disallowing such sentences under all circumstances. To him, previous precedents counsel courts to consider the "particular defendant and particular crime at issue."

Whatever you think of Kennedy's, Thomas's, and Roberts's approaches, one thing is clear: given the continuing fault lines on the Court over how to assess whether a punishment violates the Eighth Amendment, we have not yet heard the last word on this subject.

Capital Punishment: Foundations

From the line of cases beginning with *Solem* we see that the Court remains divided about the meaning of cruel and unusual punishment. But where does the death penalty fit on the spectrum of cruel and unusual punishments? By the time of *Solem* in 1983, the Court had already answered that question: since 1947 the Court has held that the death penalty is inherently neither cruel nor unusual.[19]

In fact, never have a *majority* of the justices agreed that the death penalty is cruel and unusual. But why not? The answer lies largely with the intent of the framers (at the time of ratification, death penalties were in use) and with the due process clauses of the Fifth and Fourteenth Amendments, which state that no person can be deprived of life without due process of law. Presumably, if due process is observed, a person *can* be deprived of life. Another answer may center on a phrase that Chief Justice Earl Warren once used in a noncapital case, *Trop v. Dulles* (1958). In deciding whether it constituted "cruel and unusual punishment" for the government to strip the petitioner, Albert Trop, of his citizenship for deserting the army, Warren reasoned that the "words of the [Eighth] Amendment are not precise . . . [but] their scope is not static." Accordingly, "the Amendment must draw its meaning from the *evolving standards of decency that mark the progress of a maturing society*" (emphasis added). Applying this approach to *Trop*, Warren said that the punishment of denationalization was cruel and unusual. But some argue that it is difficult to see how the punishment of death is not consistent with "evolving standards of decency" when so many Americans seem to support it. *(See Table 12-2.)*

Even so, many lawyers and interest groups have been working for years, even decades, to eliminate capital punishment on due process grounds. The NAACP Legal Defense and Educational Fund (commonly known as the Legal Defense Fund, or LDF) sponsored one of the first such attempts in **Furman v. Georgia** (1972). William Furman, a black man, was accused of murdering a white man, the father of five children. Under Georgia law, the jury determined whether a convicted murderer should be put to death. This system, the LDF argued, led to unacceptable disparities in sentencing: blacks convicted of murdering whites were

19. See *Louisiana ex rel. Frances v. Resweber* (1947).

far more likely to receive the death penalty than were whites convicted of the same crime.

A divided Supreme Court agreed with the LDF. In a short per curiam opinion deciding *Furman* and two companion cases, the justices said, "The Court holds that the imposition and carrying out of the death penalty in these cases constitutes cruel and unusual punishment." Following this terse statement, however, were nine separate opinions (five for the LDF and four against), running 243 pages (fifty thousand words)—the longest in Court history.[20]

The views presented in the opinions of the five-member majority varied considerably—three justices (Douglas, Stewart, and White) thought capital punishment, *as currently imposed*, violated the Constitution, and two (Brennan and Marshall) said it was unconstitutional in all circumstances. Beyond this, the five justices agreed on only one major point of law: that states that allowed capital punishment applied it in an arbitrary manner, particularly with regard to race. But they framed even this statement in divergent terms. Douglas said arbitrariness led to discriminatory sentencing. Brennan used arbitrariness as part of a four-part test designed to determine whether the death penalty is acceptable punishment. He found that it was degrading, arbitrary, unacceptable to contemporary society, and excessive. Marshall adopted a similar approach but explained that arbitrariness was but one reason capital punishment was cruel and unusual and "morally unacceptable." To Stewart, arbitrariness in sentencing meant that the death penalty was imposed in a "wanton" and "freak[ish] manner," akin to being struck by lightning. For White, arbitrariness led to the infrequency of imposition, which in turn made death a less-than-credible deterrent.

The dissenters, Blackmun, Burger, Powell, and Rehnquist (the four Nixon appointees), were more uniform in their critiques. To a lesser or greater extent, all expressed the view that the Court was encroaching on legislative turf and that Americans had not "repudiated" the death penalty. Blackmun also lambasted the majority for expressing views wholly inconsistent with past precedent. In particular, he noted that Stewart and White had previously found that it would be virtually impossible to create sentencing standards, but now

they were striking laws in part because of the absence of such standards.

Chief Justice Burger's opinion raised a unique issue: he noted that the plurality (Douglas, Stewart, and White) had not ruled that capital punishment under all circumstances was unconstitutional and that it may be possible for states to rewrite their laws to meet their objections. As he asserted: "It is clear that if state legislatures and the Congress wish to maintain the availability of capital punishment, significant statutory changes will have to be made. . . . [L]egislative bodies may seek to bring their laws into compliance with the Court's ruling by providing standards for juries and judges to follow . . . or by more narrowly defining crimes for which the penalty is imposed." Privately, however, Burger thought his suggestion futile, lamenting later, "There will never be another execution in this country."[21]

This view was echoed in many quarters. A University of Washington law professor wrote, "My hunch is that *Furman* spells the complete end of capital punishment in this country."[22] LDF attorneys were ecstatic. One called it "the biggest step forward criminal justice has taken in 1,000 years."[23]

As it turned out, the abolitionists celebrated a bit too soon, because the Supreme Court was not finished with the death penalty. Just three years after *Furman,* the Court agreed to hear *Gregg v. Georgia* to consider the constitutionality of a new breed of death penalty laws written to overcome the defects of the old laws. Did these new laws reduce the chance for "wanton and freakish" punishment of the sort the Court found so distasteful in *Furman*? Consider this question as you read the facts and opinions in *Gregg v. Georgia.*

Gregg v. Georgia

428 U.S. 153 (1976)

http://laws.findlaw.com/US/428/153.html

Oral arguments are available at http://www.oyez.org.

Vote: 7 (Blackmun, Burger, Powell, Rehnquist, Stevens, Stewart, White)

  2 (Brennan, Marshall)

OPINION ANNOUNCING THE JUDGMENT OF THE COURT: *Stewart*

CONCURRING OPINIONS: *Blackmun, Burger and Rehnquist, White*

DISSENTING OPINIONS: *Brennan, Marshall*

---

20. We adopt this discussion from Lee Epstein and Joseph F. Kobylka, *The Supreme Court and Legal Change: Abortion and the Death Penalty* (Chapel Hill: University of North Carolina Press, 1992), 78–80.

21. Quoted in Bob Woodward and Scott Armstrong, *The Brethren* (New York: Simon & Schuster, 1979), 219.

22. John M. Junker, "The Death Penalty Cases: A Preliminary Comment," *Washington Law Review* 48 (1972): 109.

23. Quoted in Frederick Mann, "Anthony Amsterdam," *Juris Doctor* 3 (1973): 31–32.

FACTS:

Taking cues from *Furman,* many states set out to revise their death penalty laws. Among the new plans was one proposed by Georgia (and other states). At the heart of this law was the "bifurcated trial," which consisted of two stages—the guilt phase and the penalty phase. Under such a system, the trial proceeds as usual, with a jury finding the defendant guilty or not guilty. If the verdict is guilty, the prosecution can seek the death penalty at the penalty stage, in which the defense attorney presents the mitigating facts and the prosecution presents the aggravating facts. Mitigating facts include the individual's record, family responsibility, psychiatric reports, chances for rehabilitation, and age.[24] These factors are not specified in law. The prosecution, however, has to demonstrate that at least one codified aggravating factor was present.

The Georgia law specified ten aggravating factors, including murders committed "while the offender was engaged in the commission of another capital offense," the murder of "a judicial officer . . . or . . . district attorney because of the exercise of his official duty," and murders that are "outrageously or wantonly vile, horrible, or inhumane." After hearing both sides, the jury determines whether the convicted individual receives the death penalty. By spelling out the conditions that must be present before a death penalty can be imposed, the law sought to reduce the jury's discretion and eliminate the arbitrary application of the death penalty that the Court found unacceptable in *Furman.* As a further safeguard, the Georgia Supreme Court was to review all jury determinations of death. This new law was applied to Troy Gregg and was quickly challenged by abolitionist interests.

Gregg and a friend were hitchhiking north in Florida. Two men picked them up, and the foursome was later joined by another passenger who rode with them as far as Atlanta, Georgia. The four then continued to a rest stop on the highway. The next day, the bodies of the two drivers were found in a nearby ditch. The individual let off in Atlanta identified Gregg and his friend as possible assailants. Gregg was tried under Georgia's new death penalty system. He was convicted of murder and sentenced to death, a penalty the state's highest court upheld.

ARGUMENTS:

For the petitioner, Troy Leon Gregg:
- The Georgia capital punishment law allows discretionary judgments that subject defendants to arbitrary imposition of the death penalty.
- No legitimate penal purpose of the state justifies the extreme cruelty of extinguishing human life.
- The Eighth Amendment prohibits arbitrary exceptions being made to limitations on the state's power to punish.
- The penalty of death is an unconstitutionally cruel and unusual punishment considering the "evolving standards of decency" of the last quarter of the twentieth century.

For the respondent, State of Georgia:
- The Georgia death penalty provisions are characterized by meaningful discretion.
- The death penalty is not per se cruel and unusual punishment condemned by the Eighth or Fourteenth Amendment of the Constitution.

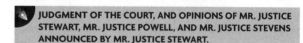

JUDGMENT OF THE COURT, AND OPINIONS OF MR. JUSTICE STEWART, MR. JUSTICE POWELL, AND MR. JUSTICE STEVENS ANNOUNCED BY MR. JUSTICE STEWART.

The issue in this case is whether the imposition of the sentence of death for the crime of murder under the law of Georgia violates the Eighth and Fourteenth Amendments. . . .

We address initially the basic contention that the punishment of death for the crime of murder is, under all circumstances, "cruel and unusual" in violation of the Eighth and Fourteenth Amendments of the Constitution. . . . [W]e . . . [also] consider the sentence of death imposed under the Georgia statutes at issue in this case.

The Court on a number of occasions has both assumed and asserted the constitutionality of capital punishment. In several cases that assumption provided a necessary foundation for the decision, as the Court was asked to decide whether a particular method of carrying out a capital sentence would be allowed to stand under the Eighth Amendment. But until *Furman v. Georgia* (1972), the Court never confronted squarely the fundamental claim that the punishment of death always, regardless of the enormity of the offense or the procedure followed in imposing the sentence, is cruel

---

24. In *Eddings v. Oklahoma* (1982) the Court agreed that age constituted a mitigating factor, which, at that point, meant that juries and judges may consider age before sentencing a minor to the death penalty. In fact, the Court has held that someone as young as sixteen at the time the crime was committed can be executed. See *Thompson v. Oklahoma* (1988) and *Stanford v. Kentucky* (1989). The Court overturned these decisions in 2005.

and unusual punishment in violation of the Constitution. Although this issue was presented and addressed in *Furman,* it was not resolved by the Court. Four Justices would have held that capital punishment is not unconstitutional *per se;* two Justices would have reached the opposite conclusion; and three Justices, while agreeing that the statutes then before the Court were invalid as applied, left open the question whether such punishment may ever be imposed. We now hold that the punishment of death does not invariably violate the Constitution.

. . . The phrase [cruel and unusual punishment] first appeared in the English Bill of Rights of 1689, which was drafted by Parliament at the accession of William and Mary. The English version appears to have been directed against punishments unauthorized by statute and beyond the jurisdiction of the sentencing court, as well as those disproportionate to the offense involved. The American draftsmen, who adopted the English phrasing in drafting the Eighth Amendment, were primarily concerned, however, with proscribing "tortures" and other "barbarous" methods of punishment.

In the earliest cases raising Eighth Amendment claims, the Court focused on particular methods of execution to determine whether they were too cruel to pass constitutional muster. The constitutionality of the sentence of death itself was not at issue, and the criterion used to evaluate the mode of execution was its similarity to "torture" and other "barbarous" methods.

But the Court has not confined the prohibition embodied in the Eighth Amendment to "barbarous" methods that were generally outlawed in the 18th century. Instead, the Amendment has been interpreted in a flexible and dynamic manner. The Court early recognized that "a principle to be vital must be capable of wider application than the mischief which gave it birth." *Weems v. United States* (1910). Thus the Clause forbidding "cruel and unusual" punishments "is not fastened to the obsolete but may acquire meaning as public opinion becomes enlightened by a humane justice." . . .

It is clear from . . . [these] precedents that the Eighth Amendment has not been regarded as a static concept. As Mr. Chief Justice Warren said, in an oft-quoted phrase, "[t]he Amendment must draw its meaning from the evolving standards of decency that mark the progress of a maturing society." Thus, an assessment of contemporary values concerning the infliction of a challenged sanction is relevant to the application of the Eighth Amendment. As we develop below more fully, this assessment does not call for a subjective judgment. It requires, rather, that we look to objective indicia that reflect the public attitude toward a given sanction.

But our cases also make clear that public perceptions of standards of decency with respect to criminal sanctions are not conclusive. A penalty also must accord with "the dignity of man," which is the "basic concept underlying the Eighth Amendment." This means, at least, that the punishment not be "excessive." When a form of punishment in the abstract (in this case, whether capital punishment may ever be imposed as a sanction for murder) rather than in the particular (the propriety of death as a penalty to be applied to a specific defendant for a specific crime) is under consideration, the inquiry into "excessiveness" has two aspects. First, the punishment must not involve the unnecessary and wanton infliction of pain. Second, the punishment must not be grossly out of proportion to the severity of the crime.

Of course, the requirements of the Eighth Amendment must be applied with an awareness of the limited role to be played by the courts. This does not mean that judges have no role to play, for the Eighth Amendment is a restraint upon the exercise of legislative power. . . .

But, while we have an obligation to insure that constitutional bounds are not overreached, we may not act as judges as we might as legislators. . . .

Therefore, in assessing a punishment selected by a democratically elected legislature against the constitutional measure, we presume its validity. We may not require the legislature to select the least severe penalty possible so long as the penalty selected is not cruelly inhumane or disproportionate to the crime involved. And a heavy burden rests on those who would attack the judgment of the representatives of the people. . . .

In the discussion to this point we have sought to identify the principles and considerations that guide a court in addressing an Eighth Amendment claim. We now consider specifically whether the sentence of death for the crime of murder is a *per se* violation of the Eighth and Fourteenth Amendments to the Constitution. We note first that history and precedent strongly support a negative answer to this question.

The imposition of the death penalty for the crime of murder has a long history of acceptance both in the United States and in England. . . .

It is apparent from the text of the Constitution itself that the existence of capital punishment was accepted by the Framers. At the time the Eighth Amendment was ratified, capital punishment was a common sanction in every State. . . . The Fifth Amendment, adopted at the same time as the Eighth, contemplated the continued existence of the capital sanction by imposing certain limits on the prosecution of capital cases:

No person shall be held to answer for a capital, or otherwise infamous crime, unless on a presentment or indictment of a Grand Jury . . . ; nor shall any person be subject for the same offense to be twice put in jeopardy of life or limb; . . . nor be deprived of life, liberty, or property, without due process of law. . . .

And the Fourteenth Amendment, adopted over three-quarters of a century later, similarly contemplates the existence of the capital sanction in providing that no State shall deprive any person of "life, liberty, or property" without due process of law.

For nearly two centuries, this Court, repeatedly and often expressly, has recognized that capital punishment is not invalid *per se*. . . .

Four years ago, the petitioners in *Furman* and its companion cases predicated their argument primarily upon the asserted proposition that standards of decency had evolved to the point where capital punishment no longer could be tolerated. The petitioners in those cases said, in effect, that the evolutionary process had come to an end, and that standards of decency required that the Eighth Amendment be construed finally as prohibiting capital punishment for any crime regardless of its depravity and impact on society. . . .

The petitioners in the capital cases before the Court today renew the "standards of decency" argument, but developments during the four years since *Furman* have undercut substantially the assumptions upon which their argument rested. Despite the continuing debate, dating back to the 19th century, over the morality and utility of capital punishment, it is now evident that a large proportion of American society continues to regard it as an appropriate and necessary criminal sanction.

The most marked indication of society's endorsement of the death penalty for murder is the legislative response to *Furman*. The legislatures of at least 35 States have enacted new statutes that provide for the death penalty for at least some crimes that result in the death of another person. And the Congress of the United States, in 1974, enacted a statute providing the death penalty for aircraft piracy that results in death. These recently adopted statutes have attempted to address the concerns expressed by the Court in *Furman* primarily (i) by specifying the factors to be weighed and the procedures to be followed in deciding when to impose a capital sentence, or (ii) by making the death penalty mandatory for specified crimes. But all of the post-*Furman* statutes make clear that capital punishment itself has not been rejected by the elected representatives of the people. . . .

The jury also is a significant and reliable objective index of contemporary values because it is so directly involved. . . . It may be true that evolving standards have influenced juries in recent decades to be more discriminating in imposing the sentence of death. But the relative infrequency of jury verdicts imposing the death sentence does not indicate rejection of capital punishment *per se*. Rather, the reluctance of juries in many cases to impose the sentence may well reflect the humane feeling that this most irrevocable of sanctions should be reserved for a small number of extreme cases. Indeed, the actions of juries in many States since *Furman* are fully compatible with the legislative judgments, reflected in the new statutes, as to the continued utility and necessity of capital punishment in appropriate cases. At the close of 1974 at least 254 persons had been sentenced to death since *Furman,* and by the end of March 1976, more than 460 persons were subject to death sentences.

As we have seen, however, the Eighth Amendment demands more than that a challenged punishment be acceptable to contemporary society. The Court also must ask whether it comports with the basic concept of human dignity at the core of the Amendment. Although we cannot "invalidate a category of penalties because we deem less severe penalties adequate to serve the ends of penology," the sanction imposed cannot be so totally without penological justification that it results in the gratuitous infliction of suffering.

The death penalty is said to serve two principal social purposes: retribution and deterrence of capital crimes by prospective offenders.

In part, capital punishment is an expression of society's moral outrage at particularly offensive conduct. This function may be unappealing to many, but it is essential in an ordered society that asks its citizens to rely on legal processes rather than self-help to vindicate their wrongs. . . . "Retribution is no longer the dominant objective of the criminal law," but neither is it a forbidden objective nor one inconsistent with our respect for the dignity of men. . . .

Statistical attempts to evaluate the worth of the death penalty as a deterrent to crimes by potential offenders have occasioned a great deal of debate. The results simply have been inconclusive. . . .

Although some of the studies suggest that the death penalty may not function as a significantly greater deterrent than lesser penalties, there is no convincing empirical evidence either supporting or refuting this view. We may nevertheless assume safely that there are murderers, such as those who act in passion, for whom the threat of death has little or no deterrent effect. But for many others, the death penalty undoubtedly is a significant deterrent. There are carefully contemplated murders, such as murder for hire, where the possible penalty of death may well enter into the cold calculus that precedes the decision to act. And there are some categories of murder, such as murder by a life prisoner, where other sanctions may not be adequate. . . .

Finally, we must consider whether the punishment of death is disproportionate in relation to the crime for which it is imposed. There is no question that death as a punishment is unique in its severity and irrevocability. When a defendant's life is at stake, the Court has been particularly sensitive to insure that every safeguard is observed. But we are concerned here only with the imposition of capital punishment for the crime of murder, and when a life has been taken deliberately by the offender, we cannot say that the punishment is invariably disproportionate to the crime. It is an extreme sanction, suitable to the most extreme of crimes.

We hold that the death penalty is not a form of punishment that may never be imposed, regardless of the circumstances of the offense, regardless of the character of the offender, and regardless of the procedure followed in reaching the decision to impose it.

We now consider whether Georgia may impose the death penalty on the petitioner in this case.

While *Furman* did not hold that the infliction of the death penalty *per se* violates the Constitution's ban on cruel and unusual punishments, it did recognize that the penalty of death is different in kind from any other punishment imposed under our system of criminal justice. Because of the uniqueness of the death penalty, *Furman* held that it could not be imposed under sentencing procedures that created a substantial risk that it would be inflicted in an arbitrary and capricious manner. . . .

Furman mandates that where discretion is afforded a sentencing body on a matter so grave as the determination of whether a human life should be taken or spared, that discretion must be suitably directed and limited so as to minimize the risk of wholly arbitrary and capricious action. . . .

Jury sentencing has been considered desirable in capital cases in order "to maintain a link between contemporary community values and the penal system—a link without which the determination of punishment could hardly reflect 'the evolving standards of decency that mark the progress of a maturing society.'" But it creates special problems. Much of the information that is relevant to the sentencing decision may have no relevance to the question of guilt, or may even be extremely prejudicial to a fair determination of that question. This problem, however, is scarcely insurmountable. Those who have studied the question suggest that a bifurcated procedure—one in which the question of sentence is not considered until the determination of guilt has been made—is the best answer. . . . When a human life is at stake and when the jury must have information prejudicial to the question of guilt but relevant to the question of penalty in order to impose a rational sentence, a bifurcated system is more likely to ensure elimination of the constitutional deficiencies identified in *Furman.*

But the provision of relevant information under fair procedural rules is not alone sufficient to guarantee that the information will be properly used in the imposition of punishment, especially if sentencing is performed by a jury. Since the members of a jury will have had little, if any, previous experience in sentencing, they are unlikely to be skilled in dealing with the information they are given. To the extent that this problem is inherent in jury sentencing, it may not be totally correctable. It seems clear, however, that the problem will be alleviated if the jury is given guidance regarding the factors about the crime and the defendant that the State, representing organized society, deems particularly relevant to the sentencing decision. . . .

While some have suggested that standards to guide a capital jury's sentencing deliberations are impossible to formulate, the fact is that such standards have been developed. . . . While such standards are by necessity somewhat general, they do provide guidance to the sentencing authority and thereby reduce the likelihood that it will impose a sentence that fairly can be called capricious or arbitrary. Where the sentencing authority is required to specify the factors it relied upon in reaching its decision, the further safeguard of meaningful appellate review is available to ensure that death sentences are not imposed capriciously or in a freakish manner.

In summary, the concerns expressed in *Furman* that the penalty of death not be imposed in an arbitrary or capricious manner can be met by a carefully drafted statute that ensures that the sentencing authority is given adequate information and guidance. As a general proposition these concerns are best met by a system that provides for a bifurcated proceeding at which the sentencing authority is apprised of the information relevant to the imposition of sentence and provided with standards to guide its use of the information. . . .

We now turn to consideration of the constitutionality of Georgia's capital-sentencing procedures. In the wake of *Furman*, Georgia amended its capital punishment statute but chose not to narrow the scope of its murder provisions. Thus, now as before *Furman*, in Georgia "[a] person commits murder when he unlawfully and with malice aforethought, either express or implied, causes the death of another human being." All persons convicted of murder "shall be punished by death or by imprisonment for life."

Georgia did act, however, to narrow the class of murderers subject to capital punishment by specifying 10 statutory aggravating circumstances, one of which must be found by the jury to exist beyond a reasonable doubt before a death sentence can ever be imposed. In addition, the jury is authorized to consider any other appropriate aggravating or mitigating circumstances. The jury is not required to find any mitigating circumstance in order to make a recommendation of mercy that is binding on the trial court, but it must find a *statutory* aggravating circumstance before recommending a sentence of death.

These procedures require the jury to consider the circumstances of the crime and the criminal before it recommends sentence. No longer can a Georgia jury do as *Furman*'s jury did: reach a finding of the defendant's guilt and then, without guidance or direction, decide whether he should live or die. Instead, the jury's attention is directed to the specific circumstances of the crime. . . . In addition, the jury's attention is focused on the characteristics of the person who committed the crime. . . . As a result, while some jury discretion still exists, "the discretion to be exercised is controlled by clear and objective standards so as to produce nondiscriminatory application."

As an important additional safeguard against arbitrariness and caprice, the Georgia statutory scheme provides for automatic appeal of all death sentences to the State's Supreme Court. That court is required by statute to review each sentence of death and determine whether it was imposed under the influence of passion or prejudice, whether the evidence supports the jury's finding of a statutory aggravating circumstance, and whether the sentence is disproportionate compared to those sentences imposed in similar cases.

In short, Georgia's new sentencing procedures require as a prerequisite to the imposition of the death penalty, specific jury findings as to the circumstances of the crime or the character of the defendant. Moreover, to guard further against a situation comparable to that presented in *Furman*, the Supreme Court of Georgia compares each death sentence with the sentences imposed on similarly situated defendants to ensure that the sentence of death in a particular case is not disproportionate. On their face these procedures seem to satisfy the concerns of *Furman*. No longer should there be "no meaningful basis for distinguishing the few cases in which [the death penalty] is imposed from the many cases in which it is not." . . .

The basic concern of *Furman* centered on those defendants who were being condemned to death capriciously and arbitrarily. Under the procedures before the Court in that case, sentencing authorities were not directed to give attention to the nature or circumstances of the crime committed or to the character or record of the defendant. Left unguided, juries imposed the death sentence in a way that could only be called freakish. The new Georgia sentencing procedures, by contrast, focus the jury's attention on the particularized nature of the crime and the particularized characteristics of the individual defendant. While the jury is permitted to consider any aggravating or mitigating circumstances, it must find and identify at least one statutory aggravating factor before it may impose a penalty of death. In this way the jury's discretion is channeled. No longer can a jury wantonly and freakishly impose the death sentence; it is always circumscribed by the legislative guidelines. In addition, the review function of the Supreme Court of Georgia affords additional assurance that the concerns that prompted our decision in *Furman* are not present to any significant degree in the Georgia procedure applied here.

For the reasons expressed in this opinion, we hold that the statutory system under which Gregg was sentenced to death does not violate the Constitution. Accordingly, the judgment of the Georgia Supreme Court is affirmed.

It is so ordered.

MR. JUSTICE WHITE, with whom THE CHIEF JUSTICE and MR. JUSTICE REHNQUIST join, concurring in the judgment. The Georgia legislature has plainly made an effort to guide the jury in the exercise of its discretion, while at the same time permitting the jury to dispense mercy on the basis of factors too intangible to write into a statute, and I cannot accept the naked assertion that the effort is bound to fail. As the types of murders for which the death penalty may be imposed become more narrowly defined and are limited to those which are particularly serious or for which the death penalty is peculiarly appropriate as they are in Georgia by reason of the aggravating-circumstance requirement, it becomes reasonable to expect that juries—even given discretion *not* to impose the death penalty—will impose the death penalty in a substantial portion of the cases so defined. If they do, it can no longer be said that the penalty is being imposed wantonly and freakishly or so infrequently that it loses its usefulness as a sentencing device. There is, therefore, reason to expect that Georgia's current system would escape the infirmities which invalidated its previous system under *Furman.* However, the Georgia Legislature was not satisfied with a system which might, but also might not, turn out in practice to result in death sentences being imposed with reasonable consistency for certain serious murders. Instead, it gave the Georgia Supreme Court the power and the obligation to perform precisely the task which three Justices of this Court, whose opinions were necessary to the result, performed in *Furman:* namely, the task of deciding whether in fact the death penalty was being administered for any given class of crime in a discriminatory, standardless, or rare fashion.

. . . Indeed, if the Georgia Supreme Court properly performs the task assigned to it under the Georgia statutes, death sentences imposed for discriminatory reasons or wantonly or freakishly for any given category of crime will be set aside. Petitioner has wholly failed to establish, and has not even attempted to establish, that the Georgia Supreme Court failed properly to perform its task in this case or that it is incapable of performing its task adequately in all cases; and this Court should not assume that it did not do so.

MR. JUSTICE BRENNAN, dissenting.
My opinion in *Furman v. Georgia* concluded that . . . the punishment of death, for whatever crime and under all circumstances, is "cruel and unusual" in violation of the Eighth and Fourteenth Amendments of the Constitution. . . .

The fatal constitutional infirmity in the punishment of death is that it treats

"members of the human race as nonhumans, as objects to be toyed with and discarded. [It is] thus inconsistent with the fundamental premise of the Clause that even the vilest criminal remains a human being possessed of common human dignity."

As such it is a penalty that "subjects the individual to a fate forbidden by the principle of civilized treatment guaranteed by the [Clause]." I therefore would hold, on that ground alone, that death is today a cruel and unusual punishment prohibited by the Clause.

MR. JUSTICE MARSHALL, dissenting.
In *Furman v. Georgia* (1972) (concurring opinion), I set forth at some length my views on the basic issue presented to the Court in these cases. The death penalty, I concluded, is a cruel and unusual punishment prohibited by the Eighth and Fourteenth Amendments. That continues to be my view. . . .

. . . An excessive penalty is invalid under the Cruel and Unusual Punishments Clause "even though popular sentiment may favor it." The inquiry here, then, is simply whether the death penalty is necessary to accomplish the legitimate legislative purposes in punishment, or whether a less severe penalty—life imprisonment—would do as well.

The two purposes that sustain the death penalty as nonexcessive in the Court's view are general deterrence and retribution. In *Furman,* I canvassed the relevant data on the deterrent effect of capital punishment. . . . The available evidence, I concluded in *Furman,* was convincing that "capital punishment is not necessary as a deterrent to crime in our society." . . .

The other principal purpose said to be served by the death penalty is retribution. The notion that retribution can serve as a moral justification for the sanction of death finds credence in the opinion of my Brothers STEWART, POWELL, and STEVENS, and that of my Brother WHITE. . . . It is this notion that I find to be the most disturbing aspect of today's unfortunate decisions.

The concept of retribution is a multifaceted one, and any discussion of its role in the criminal law must be undertaken with caution. On one level, it can be said that the notion of retribution or reprobation is the basis of our insistence that only those who have broken the law be punished, and in this sense the notion is quite obviously central to a just system of criminal sanctions. But our recognition that retribution plays a crucial role in determining who may be punished by no means requires approval of retribution as a general justification for punishment. It is the question whether retribution can provide a moral justification for punishment—in particular, capital punishment—that we must consider.

My Brothers STEWART, POWELL, and STEVENS, offer the following explanation of the retributive justification for capital punishment:

The instinct for retribution is part of the nature of man, and channeling that instinct in the administration of criminal justice serves an important purpose in promoting the stability of a society governed by law. When people begin to believe that organized society is unwilling or unable to impose upon criminal offenders the punishment they 'deserve,' then there are sown the seeds of anarchy—of self-help, vigilante justice, and lynch law.

This statement is wholly inadequate to justify the death penalty. As my Brother BRENNAN stated in *Furman*,

There is no evidence whatever that utilization of imprisonment rather than death encourages private blood feuds and other disorders.

It simply defies belief to suggest that the death penalty is necessary to prevent the American people from taking the law into their own hands. . . .

The death penalty, unnecessary to promote the goal of deterrence or to further any legitimate notion of retribution, is an excessive penalty forbidden by the Eighth and Fourteenth Amendments. I respectfully dissent from the Court's judgment upholding the sentences of death imposed upon the petitioners in these cases.

Despite the plethora of opinions in *Gregg*, the majority of justices agreed that the Georgia law was constitutional; indeed, some members of the Court referred to it as a model death penalty scheme. Interestingly, however, Gregg himself would not be executed under the law, though he did suffer a premature death *(see Box 12-3)*.

What accounts for the change in the law between *Furman* and *Gregg*? Given that some scholars and even

some justices thought that *Furman* had brought an end to capital punishment, this about-face is all the more puzzling. Analysts offer several explanations. Some point to the membership change on the Court that occurred between the two cases: William O. Douglas, who had voted with the five-person *Furman* majority, had been replaced by John Paul Stevens, who voted with the seven-person *Gregg* majority.

Other explanations center on the turn in the political environment between the early 1970s, when *Furman* was decided, and the mid-1970s. Gallup Polls and other surveys indicate that American public opinion was relatively divided on the issue of capital punishment in the early 1970s: around the time of the *Furman* decision, just slightly more than a majority of Americans polled responded that they favored the death penalty when asked if they favored or opposed it. When the same question was asked in 1974, however, public opinion in favor of capital punishment stood at roughly two-thirds of Americans (somewhat higher than where it stands today, at about 61 percent). Given this trend in public opinion, state legislators could hardly wait to reconvene after *Furman* and pass new laws designed to limit arbitrariness in sentencing. Indeed, almost every state that had a death penalty prior to *Furman* reinstated it by 1976. The national government even got into the act. The day after the *Furman* decision came down, President Richard Nixon seized on Burger's dissent in noting that the Court had not completely ruled out capital punishment. He subsequently sent to Congress a bill calling for the death penalty for certain federal crimes.

Some scholars suggest that the Court took seriously Warren's assertion in *Trop* that punishments should be judged by "evolving standards of decency," which, in light of public and government response to *Furman,* seemed to favor the retention of capital punishment; others, less charitably, assert that the Court simply succumbed to public pressure in this area. Americans wanted the death penalty and the justices caved in, the argument goes. Even Justice Marshall, in his *Gregg* dissent, acknowledged that post-*Furman* "developments have a significant bearing on a realistic assessment of the moral acceptability of the death penalty to the American people." Marshall, however, also maintained that "the American people are largely unaware of the information critical to a judgment on the morality of the death

BOX 12-3 AFTERMATH . . . TROY LEON GREGG

On July 2, 1976, the Supreme Court upheld Troy Leon Gregg's death sentence for the robbery and murders of Fred Simmons and Bob Moore, who had provided a ride to the hitchhiking Gregg. Although Gregg would suffer a premature death, it would not be at the hands of the state executioner.

On July 28, 1980, shortly before he was scheduled for execution, Gregg and three other death row inmates (Timothy McCorquodale, Johnny L. Johnson, and David Jarrell) escaped from the Georgia State Prison in Reidsville. Dressed in pajamas modified to look like guard uniforms and wearing forged identification badges, the four condemned prisoners hack-

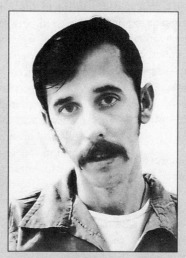

Convicted murderer Troy Leon Gregg

sawed through the bars of an exercise room window close to their fourth-floor cells. Under prison regulations this portion of the escape route was never to be left unattended by guards, but the four prisoners passed undetected. Once through the window, the inmates were able to gain access to fire escapes leading to the ground. After convincing an inquiring guard that they were doing a prison security check, the disguised escapees walked out of the prison unimpeded. Waiting for them outside was a car left by one of McCorquodale's relatives.

Shortly after the escape Gregg made a bragging telephone call to Charles Postell, a reporter for the *Albany Herald* who had written a number of articles based on interviews with death row inmates. At first Postell thought the call was a hoax, but he later became convinced when Gregg explained that the escapees would rather die than live one more day under the inhumane conditions on death row. Postell called the prison warden's office but initially was told, "Everyone is accounted for at this time. Gregg is in his cell. There has been no escape." Colonel William Lowe, deputy commissioner of the Department of Offender Rehabilitation, stated later that Postell's report of the escape "was the first time we knew about it."

Over the next two days, law enforcement tracked the fugitives to a house on North Carolina's Lake Wylie. Twenty local police and FBI agents surrounded the house. After spending six hours attempting to convince the escapees to give themselves up, the officers lobbed tear gas into the building, resulting in the peaceful arrest of McCorquodale, Johnson, and Jarrell. Also arrested was William Flamont, the renter of the house, who was charged with harboring the three.

Noticeably absent was Troy Gregg. Gregg had been beaten to death the previous day during a brawl in a North Carolina biker bar. His body was found by a group of swimmers at the bottom of Mountain Island Lake, located about twelve miles from the house in which the others were hiding.

Nine individuals subsequently were indicted for helping the four convicts escape. Among them were a corrections officer, other inmates, and the escapees' relatives. Also indicted were *Albany Herald* reporter Charles Postell and his wife, Judi, who were accused of buying ten hacksaw blades and delivering them to Minnie Hunter, an aunt of one of the escapees, who mailed them to the prison, where they were intercepted by corrections officials. Another set of hacksaw blades mailed by a cousin of one of the inmates, however, did reach the prisoners. The charges against Postell and his wife were subsequently dropped when a key prosecution witness's credibility was tainted after he was linked to an attempt to extort $15,000 from Postell in return for favorable testimony.

SOURCES: *Atlanta Daily World*, August 17, 1980; *Christian Science Monitor*, August 29 and November 18, 1980; *New York Times*, July 29, July 31, August 28, and November 14, 1980; Kevin Clarke, "Suspended Sentence: How the U.S. Almost Put Capital Punishment to Death," *Salt of the Earth*, March/April 1997; *Washington Post*, July 29, August 28, and November 10, 1980.

penalty, and . . . if they were better informed they would consider it shocking, unjust, and unacceptable." No one has compiled systematic evidence to support Marshall's claim, but we do know that Americans respond differently to questions depending on how they are worded. For example, when polls asked in 2011, "Which punishment do you prefer for people convicted of committing murder: the death penalty or life in prison with no chance of parole?" respondents' support for the death penalty dropped to 48 percent, with 50 percent favoring prison without parole.[25] *(For more on this point, see Table 12-2 and accompanying text below.)*

Yet another explanation centers on the new laws themselves and the way attorneys tried to challenge them. To put it simply, abolitionist lawyers may have overestimated the degree of their victory in *Furman*. In their arguments to the Court, they asserted that "death is different," but this view was held by only two justices in *Furman*—Brennan and Marshall. The others, especially Stewart and White, were more concerned with the arbitrariness of death penalty sentencing than with its constitutionality. In the end, as White's concurrence in *Gregg* indicates, abolitionist attorneys were unable to convince the majority that the new laws—which explicitly sought to eliminate arbitrariness in sentencing by limiting jury discretion—were unconstitutional.

Whatever the explanation for the Court's change of direction, the results were clear. Many states adopted a variation of Georgia's death penalty law (currently, thirty-three states have death penalty laws on their books), and executions increased accordingly. During the 1970s only 3 people were legally executed in the United States; in the 1990s that figure was 478. Between 2000 and May 2012, 697 people were executed. As of January 1, 2012, 3,189 individuals were on death rows.[26]

The Current State of the Death Penalty

In some ways, *Gregg* settled the death penalty issue: the Court asserted that capital punishment does not violate the Constitution, a position to which it still adheres. But opponents of the death penalty did not give up. In the immediate aftermath of *Gregg*, they continued to bring lawsuits, many of which were aimed at narrowing the application of capital punishment. In other words, this litigation challenged state procedures rather than the constitutionality of the death penalty.

A good number of these procedural cases involved this question: What factors should sentencers consider in their deliberations? Occasionally, the Court has ruled for defendants in these disputes. In *Eddings v. Oklahoma* (1982), for example, it held that a trial court judge could not refuse to hear mitigating evidence pointing to the defendant's youth, troubled childhood, and history of mental problems. But the Court generally has taken a pro–death penalty posture. A prime example is **McCleskey v. Kemp** (1987), one of the few constitutional attacks on capital punishment since *Gregg*. Despite statistical evidence showing that black defendants were 1.1 times more likely than other defendants to receive death sentences, the Court rejected arguments that the disparate application of death penalty laws violates the Constitution.[27]

Challenging the death penalty became even more difficult in 1996, when President Bill Clinton signed into law the Antiterrorism and Effective Death Penalty Act. This statute directed that habeas corpus petitions presenting claims that had already been presented in earlier petitions should be dismissed. It also directed that second or subsequent habeas corpus petitions that presented new claims should be dismissed unless the claims could not have been made previously because of a subsequent change in the law or the discovery of facts not knowable at the time of the earlier petition. This act severely restricted the opportunities for death row inmates to challenge their sentences in federal court. Shortly after passage of the act, the Supreme Court upheld its constitutionality in *Felker v. Turpin* (1996), denying relief to a Georgia death row inmate.

Should we conclude from these decisions that death penalty opponents have lost their cause? After all, public support for capital punishment seems to remain strong, politicians rarely take public stances against the death penalty (in fact, all of the most recent presidents have publicly supported capital punishment), and the justices of the Rehnquist Court and now the Roberts Court have typically ruled against the defendant in these cases. Of the twenty capital cases the Court heard

---

25. The remaining 2 percent had no opinion. CNN/ORC poll conducted September 23–25, 2011. The margin of effort was ±3 percent.

26. Data from the Death Penalty Information Center, http://www.deathpenaltyinfo.org.

---

27. Lewis Powell, who wrote the *McCleskey* opinion, was an important vote in capital punishment cases of the 1980s. Powell later expressed regret for supporting Georgia's claims in *McCleskey*.

from its 1994 term through its 2008 term, it ruled with the defendant in eight (that is, it ruled against the defendant 60 percent of the time). Moreover, even assuming that Chief Justice John G. Roberts Jr. sits squarely in the pro–death penalty wing of the Court (as did his predecessor, William Rehnquist) and that Justice Sonia Sotomayor is pro-defendant (as was her predecessor, David Souter), the Alito-for-O'Connor change may not bode particularly well for opponents of the death penalty. Although O'Connor was not as liberal in her decisions as Stevens or Ginsburg, she and Justice Kennedy occasionally joined them; so far, Alito almost always rules for the state.

Kansas v. Marsh (2006) may serve to make the point. The question confronting the justices was the constitutionality of a Kansas law that automatically imposed a death sentence if the jury decided that the aggravating circumstances equaled the mitigating circumstances. The case was originally argued in December 2005, while O'Connor was still on the Court. The Senate confirmed Alito, and the Court heard rearguments in April 2006 (probably because the justices were divided 4–4). Two months later, the Court upheld the law, 5–4. Naturally, many observers have speculated that it was Alito who made the difference between striking down and upholding the Kansas law. Two years later *Baze v. Rees* (2008) seemed to reinforce the fears of death penalty opponents. In *Baze*, the justices rejected a challenge to the use of lethal injection as a method for executing those convicted of a capital offense. Writing for a deeply divided Court, Chief Justice Roberts held, "Simply because an execution method may result in pain, either by accident or as an inescapable consequence of death, does not establish the sort of 'objectively intolerable risk of harm' that qualifies as cruel and unusual."

Yet the future may not be completely hopeless for abolitionists. In the 2000s—both before and after O'Connor left the Court—the justices issued several decisions that adopted arguments offered by death penalty opponents. The first came in *Atkins v. Virginia* (2002), in which the Court revisited its controversial ruling in *Penry v. Lynaugh* (1989) that the Eighth Amendment does not categorically prohibit the execution of a mentally retarded defendant convicted of capital murder. Notice, as you read the excerpt of *Atkins*, that the justices not only divided over the case outcome but also vigorously debated the proper methods of determining what constitutes cruel and unusual punishment given society's "evolving standards of decency."

Ralph Baze, the convicted murderer of two Kentucky law enforcement officers, was unsuccessful in his attempt to convince the Supreme Court that executions by lethal injection violate the cruel and unusual punishment provision of the Eighth Amendment.

Atkins v. Virginia

536 U.S. 304 (2002)
http://laws.findlaw.com/US/536/304.html
Oral arguments are available at http://www.oyez.org.
Vote: 6 (Breyer, Ginsburg, Kennedy, O'Connor, Souter, Stevens)
      3 (Rehnquist, Scalia, Thomas)
OPINION OF THE COURT: Stevens
DISSENTING OPINIONS: Rehnquist, Scalia

FACTS:

Close to midnight on August 16, 1996, Daryl Renard Atkins and William Jones, after a day spent drinking and smoking marijuana, walked to a convenience store intending to buy more alcohol. When they realized that they did not have enough money to make the purchase, they decided to rob a customer. Armed with a semiautomatic handgun, they abducted Eric Nesbitt, an airman from Langley Air Force Base. Atkins and Jones robbed Nesbitt of the money he was carrying and drove him to an automated teller machine, where they forced him to withdraw $200. That done, they drove Nesbitt to an isolated location, where he was shot eight times in the thorax, chest, abdomen, arms, and legs, resulting in his death.

Atkins and Jones were initially charged with capital murder, but prosecutors permitted Jones to plead guilty to first-degree murder in exchange for his testimony against Atkins. By pleading guilty, Jones was ineligible for the death penalty under Virginia law. At Atkins's trial, both men confirmed most of the details of the incident, with the important exception that each claimed that the other had shot Nesbitt. The jury believed Jones's account, convicting Atkins and sentencing him to death. The Virginia Supreme Court upheld the conviction but ordered a new penalty phase of the trial because the trial court had used an improper verdict form.

At the second hearing, the jury heard testimony from a forensic psychologist, hired by the defense, that Atkins was mildly retarded, with an IQ of 59 and an impaired capacity to interact successfully with his environment on a daily basis. A psychologist for the prosecution claimed, however, that although Atkins may have had an antisocial personality disorder, he was at least of average intelligence. The jury also heard about Atkins's sixteen prior felony convictions for robbery, attempted robbery, abduction, firearms violations, and maiming. After considering the evidence, the jurors sentenced Atkins to death.

Atkins's lawyers asked the Virginia Supreme Court to commute the sentence to life in prison on the ground that it is unconstitutional to execute an individual who is mentally retarded. The Virginia court rejected this argument, relying on the U.S. Supreme Court's ruling in *Penry v. Lynaugh*. The Supreme Court accepted the case in order to reconsider the *Penry* precedent.

ARGUMENTS:

For the petitioner, Daryl Atkins:

- Mental retardation impairs understanding and functioning in ways that substantially reduce personal culpability.
- A sentence of death is grossly disproportionate to the personal culpability of mentally retarded individuals.
- Executing the mentally retarded offends our society's "evolving standards of decency," requiring *Perry v. Lynaugh* to be overruled.

Daryl Renard Atkins glances over his shoulder in a Virginia courtroom in February 1998 before being sentenced to death for carjacking and killing an airman. Four years later the Supreme Court would use the Atkins case to strike down Virginia's law permitting the execution of mentally retarded defendants.

For the respondent, Commonwealth of Virginia:

- The Court correctly decided in *Perry v. Lynaugh* that the retarded should be treated as individuals, not as a homogeneous class. *Penry* should be reaffirmed.
- Not all retarded persons lack the capacity to act with the degree of culpability associated with the death penalty.
- There is insufficient evidence to establish the existence of national consensus for removing all retarded persons from execution eligibility.

JUSTICE STEVENS DELIVERED THE OPINION OF THE COURT.

Those mentally retarded persons who meet the law's requirements for criminal responsibility should be tried and punished when they commit crimes. Because of their disabilities in areas of reasoning, judgment, and control of their impulses, however, they do not act with the level of moral culpability that characterizes the most serious adult criminal conduct. Moreover, their impairments can jeopardize the reliability and fairness of capital proceedings against mentally retarded defendants.

Presumably for these reasons, in the 13 years since we decided *Penry v. Lynaugh* (1989), the American public, legislators, scholars, and judges have deliberated over the question whether the death penalty should ever be imposed on a mentally retarded criminal. The consensus reflected in those deliberations informs our answer to the question presented by this case: whether such executions are "cruel and unusual punishments" prohibited by the Eighth Amendment to the Federal Constitution. . . .

The Eighth Amendment succinctly prohibits "excessive" sanctions. It provides: "Excessive bail shall not be required, nor excessive fines imposed, nor cruel and unusual punishments inflicted." In *Weems v. United States* (1910), we held that a punishment of 12 years jailed in irons at hard and painful labor for the crime of falsifying records was excessive. We explained "that it is a precept of justice that punishment for crime should be graduated and proportioned to the offense." We have repeatedly applied this proportionality precept in later cases interpreting the Eighth Amendment. . . .

A claim that punishment is excessive is judged not by the standards that prevailed in 1685 when Lord Jeffreys presided over the "Bloody Assizes" or when the Bill of Rights was adopted, but rather by those that currently prevail. As Chief Justice Warren explained in his opinion in *Trop v. Dulles* (1958): "The basic concept underlying the Eighth Amendment is nothing less than the dignity of man. . . . The Amendment must draw its meaning from the evolving standards of decency that mark the progress of a maturing society."

Proportionality review under those evolving standards should be informed by "objective factors to the maximum possible extent." We have pinpointed that the "clearest and most reliable objective evidence of contemporary values is the legislation enacted by the country's legislatures." *Penry.* Relying in part on such legislative evidence, we have held that death is an impermissibly excessive punishment for the rape of an adult woman, *Coker v. Georgia* (1977), or for a defendant who neither took life, attempted to take life, nor intended to take life, *Enmund v. Florida* (1982). . . .

We also acknowledged in *Coker* that the objective evidence, though of great importance, did not "wholly determine" the controversy, "for the Constitution contemplates that in the end our own judgment will be brought to bear on the question of the acceptability of the death penalty under the Eighth Amendment." . . . Thus, in cases involving a consensus, our own judgment is "brought to bear," by asking whether there is reason to disagree with the judgment reached by the citizenry and its legislators.

Guided by our approach in these cases, we shall first review the judgment of legislatures that have addressed the suitability of imposing the death penalty on the mentally retarded and then consider reasons for agreeing or disagreeing with their judgment.

The parties have not called our attention to any state legislative consideration of the suitability of imposing the death penalty on mentally retarded offenders prior to 1986. In that year, the public reaction to the execution of a mentally retarded murderer [Jerome Bowden] in Georgia apparently led to the enactment of the first state statute prohibiting such executions. In 1988, when Congress enacted legislation reinstating the federal death penalty, it expressly provided that a "sentence of death shall not be carried out upon a person who is mentally retarded." In 1989, Maryland enacted a similar prohibition. It was in that year that we decided *Penry,* and concluded that those two state enactments, "even when added to the 14 States that have rejected capital punishment completely, do not provide sufficient evidence at present of a national consensus."

Much has changed since then. Responding to the national attention received by the Bowden execution and our decision in *Penry,* state legislatures across the country began to address the issue. In 1990 Kentucky and Tennessee enacted statutes similar to those in Georgia and Maryland, as did New Mexico in 1991, and Arkansas, Colorado, Washington, Indiana, and Kansas in 1993 and 1994. In 1995, when New York reinstated its death penalty, it emulated the Federal Government by expressly exempting the mentally retarded. Nebraska followed suit in 1998. There appear to have been no similar enactments during the next two years, but in 2000 and 2001 six more States—South Dakota, Arizona, Connecticut, Florida, Missouri, and North Carolina—joined the procession. The Texas Legislature unanimously adopted a similar bill, and bills have passed at least one house in other States, including Virginia and Nevada.

It is not so much the number of these States that is significant, but the consistency of the direction of change. Given the well-known fact that anticrime legislation is far more popular than legislation providing protections for persons guilty of violent crime, the large number of States prohibiting the execution of mentally retarded persons (and the complete absence of States passing legislation reinstating the power to conduct such executions) provides powerful evidence that today our society views mentally retarded offenders as categorically less culpable than the average criminal. The evidence carries even greater force when it is noted that the legislatures that have addressed the issue have voted overwhelmingly in favor of the prohibition. Moreover, even in those States that allow the execution of mentally retarded offenders, the practice is uncommon. Some States, for example New Hampshire and New Jersey, continue to authorize executions, but none have been carried out in decades. Thus there is little need to pursue legislation barring the execution of the mentally retarded in those States. And it appears that even among those States that regularly execute offenders and that have no prohibition with regard to the mentally retarded, only five have executed offenders possessing a known IQ less than 70 since we decided *Penry.* The practice, therefore, has become truly unusual, and it is fair to say that a national consensus has developed against it.*

---

*Additional evidence makes it clear that this legislative judgment reflects a much broader social and professional consensus. For example, several organizations with germane expertise have adopted official positions opposing the imposition of the death penalty upon a mentally retarded offender. See Brief for American Psychological Association et al. as *Amici Curiae*; Brief for AAMR et al. as *Amici Curiae*. In addition, representatives of widely diverse religious communities in the United States, reflecting Christian, Jewish, Muslim, and Buddhist traditions, have filed an amicus curiae brief explaining that even though their views about the death penalty differ, they all "share a conviction that the execution of persons with mental retardation cannot be morally justified." See Brief for United States Catholic Conference et al. as *Amici Curiae* in *McCarver v. North Carolina.* Moreover, within the world community, the imposition of the death penalty for crimes committed by mentally retarded offenders is overwhelmingly disapproved. Brief for The European Union as *Amicus Curiae* in *McCarver v. North Carolina.* Finally, polling data shows a widespread consensus among Americans, even those who support the death penalty, that executing the mentally retarded is wrong. R. Bonner & S. Rimer, "Executing the Mentally Retarded Even as Laws Begin to Shift," *N.Y. Times,* Aug. 7, 2000, p. A1; App. B to Brief for AAMR as *Amicus Curiae* in *McCarver v. North Carolina,* O.T. 2001, No. 00-8727 (appending approximately 20 state and national polls on the issue). Although these factors are by no means dispositive, their consistency with the legislative evidence lends further support to our conclusion that there is a consensus among those who have addressed the issue. See *Thompson v. Oklahoma* (1988) (considering the views of "respected professional organizations, by other nations that share our Anglo-American heritage, and by the leading members of the Western European community").

To the extent there is serious disagreement about the execution of mentally retarded offenders, it is in determining which offenders are in fact retarded. In this case, for instance, the Commonwealth of Virginia disputes that Atkins suffers from mental retardation. Not all people who claim to be mentally retarded will be so impaired as to fall within the range of mentally retarded offenders about whom there is a national consensus. As was our approach in *Ford v. Wainwright* [1986], with regard to insanity, "we leave to the State[s] the task of developing appropriate ways to enforce the constitutional restriction upon its execution of sentences." . . .

. . . [O]ur death penalty jurisprudence provides two reasons consistent with the legislative consensus that the mentally retarded should be categorically excluded from execution. First, there is a serious question as to whether either justification that we have recognized as a basis for the death penalty applies to mentally retarded offenders. *Gregg v. Georgia* (1976) identified "retribution and deterrence of capital crimes by prospective offenders" as the social purposes served by the death penalty. Unless the imposition of the death penalty on a mentally retarded person "measurably contributes to one or both of these goals, it 'is nothing more than the purposeless and needless imposition of pain and suffering,' and hence an unconstitutional punishment." *Enmund.*

With respect to retribution—the interest in seeing that the offender gets his "just deserts"—the severity of the appropriate punishment necessarily depends on the culpability of the offender. Since *Gregg,* our jurisprudence has consistently confined the imposition of the death penalty to a narrow category of the most serious crimes. For example, in *Godfrey v. Georgia* (1980), we set aside a death sentence because the petitioner's crimes did not reflect "a consciousness materially more 'depraved' than that of any person guilty of murder." If the culpability of the average murderer is insufficient to justify the most extreme sanction available to the State, the lesser culpability of the mentally retarded offender surely does not merit that form of retribution. Thus, pursuant to our narrowing jurisprudence, which seeks to ensure that only the most deserving of execution are put to death, an exclusion for the mentally retarded is appropriate.

With respect to deterrence—the interest in preventing capital crimes by prospective offenders—"it seems likely that 'capital punishment can serve as a deterrent only when murder is the result of premeditation and deliberation,'" *Enmund.* Exempting the mentally retarded from that punishment will not affect the "cold calculus that precedes the decision" of other potential murderers. Indeed, that sort of calculus is at the opposite end of the spectrum from behavior of mentally retarded offenders. . . . Nor will exempting the mentally retarded from execution lessen the deterrent effect of the death penalty with respect to offenders who are not mentally retarded. Such individuals are unprotected by the exemption and will continue to face the threat of execution. Thus, executing the mentally retarded will not measurably further the goal of deterrence.

The reduced capacity of mentally retarded offenders provides a second justification for a categorical rule making such offenders ineligible for the death penalty. The risk "that the death penalty will be imposed in spite of factors which may call for a less severe penalty," *Lockett v. Ohio* (1978), is enhanced, not only by the possibility of false confessions, but also by the lesser ability of mentally retarded defendants to make a persuasive showing of mitigation in the face of prosecutorial evidence of one or more aggravating factors. Mentally retarded defendants may be less able to give meaningful assistance to their counsel and are typically poor witnesses, and their demeanor may create an unwarranted impression of lack of remorse for their crimes. . . . Mentally retarded defendants in the aggregate face a special risk of wrongful execution.

Our independent evaluation of the issue reveals no reason to disagree with the judgment of "the legislatures that have recently addressed the matter" and concluded that death is not a suitable punishment for a mentally retarded criminal. We are not persuaded that the execution of mentally retarded criminals will measurably advance the deterrent or the retributive purpose of the death penalty. Construing and applying the Eighth Amendment in the light of our "evolving standards of decency," we therefore conclude that such punishment is excessive and that the Constitution "places a substantive restriction on the State's power to take the life" of a mentally retarded offender.

The judgment of the Virginia Supreme Court is reversed and the case is remanded for further proceedings not inconsistent with this opinion.

It is so ordered.

JUSTICE SCALIA, with whom THE CHIEF JUSTICE and JUSTICE THOMAS join, dissenting.

Today's decision is the pinnacle of our Eighth Amendment death-is-different jurisprudence. Not only does it, like all of that jurisprudence, find no support in the text or history of the Eighth Amendment; it does not even have support in current social attitudes regarding the conditions that render an otherwise just death penalty inappropriate. Seldom has an opinion of this Court rested so obviously upon nothing but the personal views of its members. . . .

. . . [The] petitioner's mental retardation was a *central issue* at sentencing. The jury concluded, however, that his alleged retardation was not a compelling reason to exempt him from the death penalty in light of the brutality of his crime and his long demonstrated propensity for violence. "In upsetting this particularized judgment on the basis of a constitutional absolute," the Court concludes that no one who is even slightly mentally retarded can have sufficient "moral responsibility to be subjected to capital punishment for any crime. As a sociological and moral conclusion that is implausible; and it is doubly implausible as an interpretation of the United States Constitution." *Thompson v. Oklahoma* (1988) (SCALIA, J., dissenting).

Under our Eighth Amendment jurisprudence, a punishment is "cruel and unusual" if it falls within one of two categories: "those modes or acts of punishment that had been considered cruel and unusual at the time that the Bill of Rights was adopted," and modes of punishment that are inconsistent with modern "standards of decency," as evinced by objective indicia, the most important of which is "legislation enacted by the country's legislatures," *Penry v. Lynaugh* (1989).

The Court makes no pretense that execution of the mildly mentally retarded would have been considered "cruel and unusual" in 1791. . . .

The Court is left to argue, therefore, that execution of the mildly retarded is inconsistent with the "evolving standards of decency that mark the progress of a maturing society." *Trop v. Dulles* (1958). Before today, our opinions consistently emphasized that Eighth Amendment judgments regarding the existence of social "standards" "should be informed by objective factors to the maximum possible extent" and "should not be, or appear to be, merely the subjective views of individual Justices." "First" among these objective factors are the "statutes passed by society's elected representatives," *Stanford v. Kentucky* (1989), because it "will rarely if ever be the case that the Members of this Court will have a better sense of the evolution in views of the American people than do their elected representatives," *Thompson* (SCALIA, J., dissenting).

The Court pays lip service to these precedents as it miraculously extracts a "national consensus" forbidding execution of the mentally retarded from the fact that 18 States—less than *half* (47%) of the 38 States that permit capital punishment (for whom the issue exists)—have very recently enacted legislation barring execution of the mentally retarded. . . .

. . . How is it possible that agreement among 47% of the death penalty jurisdictions amounts to "consensus"? Our prior cases have generally required a much higher degree of agreement before finding a punishment cruel and unusual on "evolving standards" grounds. In *Coker,* we proscribed the death penalty for rape of an adult woman after finding that only one jurisdiction, Georgia, authorized such a punishment. In *Enmund,* we invalidated the death penalty for mere participation in a robbery in which an accomplice took a life, a punishment not permitted in 28 of the death penalty States (78%). . . . What the Court calls evidence of "consensus" in the present case (a fudged 47%) more closely resembles evidence that we found *inadequate* to establish consensus in earlier cases. . . .

Moreover, a major factor that the Court entirely disregards is that the legislation of all 18 States it relies on is still in its infancy. The oldest of the statutes is only 14 years old; five were enacted last year; over half were enacted within the past eight years. Few, if any, of the States have had sufficient experience with these laws to know whether they are sensible in the long term. It is "myopic to base sweeping constitutional principles upon the narrow experience of [a few] years."

The Court attempts to bolster its embarrassingly feeble evidence of "consensus" with the following: "It is not so much the number of these States that is significant, but the *consistency* of the direction of change." But in what *other* direction *could we possibly* see change? Given that 14 years ago *all* the death penalty statutes included the mentally retarded, *any* change (except precipitate undoing of what had just been done) was *bound to be* in the one direction the Court finds significant enough to overcome the lack of real consensus. . . . In any event, reliance upon "trends," even those of much longer duration than a mere 14 years, is a perilous basis for constitutional adjudication. . . .

But the Prize for the Court's Most Feeble Effort to fabricate "national consensus" must go to its appeal (deservedly relegated to a footnote) to the views of assorted professional and religious organizations, members of the so-called "world community," and respondents to opinion polls. I agree with the Chief Justice that the views of professional and religious organizations and the results of opinion polls are irrelevant. Equally irrelevant are the practices of the "world community," whose notions of justice are (thankfully) not always those of our people. "We must never forget that it is a Constitution for the United States of America that we are expounding. . . . [W]here there is not first a settled consensus among our own people, the views of other nations, however enlightened the Justices of this Court may think them to be, cannot be imposed upon Americans through the Constitution." *Thompson* (SCALIA, J., dissenting).

Beyond the empty talk of a "national consensus," the Court gives us a brief glimpse of what really underlies today's decision: pretension to a power confined *neither* by the moral sentiments originally enshrined in the Eighth Amendment (its original meaning) *nor even* by the current moral sentiments of the American people. "'[T]he Constitution,'" the Court says, "'contemplates that in the end *our own judgment* will be brought to bear on the question of the acceptability of the death penalty under the Eighth Amendment.'" The arrogance of this assumption of power takes one's breath away. And it explains, of course, why the Court can be so cavalier about the evidence of consensus. It is just a game, after all. "[I]n the end," it is the *feelings* and *intuition* of a majority of the Justices that count—"the perceptions of decency, or of penology, or of mercy, entertained . . . by a majority of the small and unrepresentative segment of our society that sits on this Court." *Thompson* (SCALIA, J., dissenting). . . .

. . . [T]he Court gives two reasons why the death penalty is an excessive punishment for all mentally retarded offenders. First, the "diminished capacities" of the mentally retarded raise a "serious question" whether their execution contributes to the "social purposes" of the death penalty, viz., retribution and deterrence. (The Court conveniently ignores a third "social purpose" of the death penalty—"incapacitation of dangerous criminals and the consequent prevention of crimes that they may otherwise commit in the future," *Gregg v. Georgia* (1976) (joint opinion of STEWART, POWELL, and STEVENS, JJ.). But never mind; its discussion of even the other two does not bear analysis.) Retribution is not advanced, the argument goes, because the mentally retarded are *no more culpable* than the average murderer, whom we have already held lacks sufficient culpability to warrant the death penalty, see *Godfrey v. Georgia* (1980). Who says so? Is there an established correlation between mental acuity and the ability to conform one's conduct to the law in such a rudimentary matter as murder? Are the mentally retarded really more disposed (and hence more likely) to commit willfully cruel and serious crime than others? In my experience, the opposite is true: being childlike generally suggests innocence rather than brutality. . . .

. . . The fact that juries continue to sentence mentally retarded offenders to death for extreme crimes shows that society's moral outrage sometimes demands execution of retarded offenders. By what principle of law, science, or logic can the Court pronounce that this is wrong? There is none. Once the Court admits (as it does) that mental retardation does not render the offender morally *blameless,* there is no basis for saying that the death penalty is *never* appropriate retribution, no matter *how* heinous the crime. As long as a mentally retarded offender knows "the difference between right and wrong," only the sentencer can assess whether his retardation reduces his culpability enough to exempt him from the death penalty for the particular murder in question.

As for the other social purpose of the death penalty that the Court discusses, deterrence: That is not advanced, the Court tells us, because the mentally retarded are "less likely" than their non-retarded counterparts to "process the information of the possibility of execution as a penalty and . . . control their conduct based upon that information." . . . [T]he Court does not say that *all* mentally retarded individuals cannot "process the information of the possibility of execution as a penalty and . . . control their conduct based upon that information"; it merely asserts that they are "less likely" to be able to do so. But surely the deterrent effect of a penalty is adequately vindicated if it successfully deters many, but not all, of the target class. Virginia's death penalty, for example, does not fail of its deterrent effect simply because *some* criminals are unaware that Virginia *has* the death penalty. . . . I am not sure that a murderer is somehow less blameworthy if (though he knew his act was wrong) he did not fully appreciate that he could die for it; but if so, we should treat a mentally retarded murderer the way we treat an offender who may be "less likely" to respond to the death penalty because he was abused as a child. We do not hold him

immune from capital punishment, but require his background to be considered by the sentencer as a mitigating factor. *Eddings v. Oklahoma* (1982).

The Court throws one last factor into its grab bag of reasons why execution of the retarded is "excessive" in all cases: Mentally retarded offenders "face a special risk of wrongful execution" because they are less able "to make a persuasive showing of mitigation," "to give meaningful assistance to their counsel," and to be effective witnesses. "Special risk" is pretty flabby language (even flabbier than "less likely")—and I suppose a similar "special risk" could be said to exist for just plain stupid people, inarticulate people, even ugly people. If this unsupported claim has any substance to it (which I doubt) it might support a due process claim in all criminal prosecutions of the mentally retarded; but it is hard to see how it has anything to do with an Eighth Amendment claim that execution of the mentally retarded is cruel and unusual.

Atkins may not have been the end of the line for Daryl Atkins *(see Box 12-4),* but the Court's decision was clear: states cannot impose the death penalty on the mentally retarded. Coming on the heels of this decision were ***Roper v. Simmons*** (2005) and ***Kennedy v. Louisiana*** (2008), in which the Court also drew bright lines, exempting certain kinds of offenders (*Roper*) or crimes (*Kennedy*) from the death penalty. In 1993 Missouri charged seventeen-year-old Christopher Simmons with murdering Shirley Crook. About nine months later, after he had turned eighteen, he was convicted and sentenced to death. Executing a juvenile was, at the time, consistent with the Supreme Court's decision in *Stanford v. Kentucky* (1989) holding that the Constitution does not prohibit the execution of juvenile offenders over fifteen but under eighteen years of age at the time of the crime.

Nevertheless, after the Court handed down its decision in *Atkins,* Simmons asked the state supreme court to set aside his death sentence. He argued that under the reasoning of *Atkins* the Constitution prohibits the execution of a juvenile who was under eighteen when the crime was committed. Despite *Stanford,* the Missouri Supreme Court agreed and resentenced Simmons to "life imprisonment without eligibility for probation, parole, or release except by act of the Governor." It found that since *Stanford,* a national consensus had developed against the

BOX 12-4   AFTERMATH . . . DARYL ATKINS

tkins V. Virginia serves as a lesson that a Supreme
Court decision may answer a constitutional question
definitively, but it does not necessarily settle the underlying dispute.

Following the Supreme Court's ruling, the Virginia legislature revised the state's capital punishment laws to prohibit the execution of the mentally retarded. The law defined mental retardation and established procedures to be followed when an accused murderer claims to be retarded. The Supreme Court ruling and the statutory revisions enacted by Virginia, however, did not necessarily save Daryl Atkins from execution by lethal injection. Prosecutors continued to assert that Atkins was not retarded and therefore could be put to death for the murder of Eric Nesbitt.

A trial to determine Atkins's mental status began on July 25, 2005, and lasted two weeks. Prosecution and defense mental health experts presented conflicting opinions regarding Atkins's intelligence level. Multiple administrations of IQ tests were not definitive. Prosecution and defense attorneys vigorously debated whether Atkins's long record of academic failure in elementary school and high school was due to his lack of intelligence or his laziness and drug usage. The court heard from a parade of witnesses, including former teachers, friends, and family members, who recounted stories of how Atkins reacted to various life situations. A high school coach, for example, explained that he had to cut Atkins from the football team because Atkins could not learn the playbook—he confused left and right and also had difficulty distinguishing odd from even. A former classmate testified that he let Atkins copy a homework assignment with the warning not to rewrite it word for word, but Atkins copied it verbatim, including the classmate's name. Other testimony, however, revealed that Atkins knew that Lincoln was president during the Civil War, that Michelangelo painted the Sistine Chapel, and that Rome was the capital of Italy.

After two days of deliberation, the jury came to the unanimous decision that Atkins had failed to prove that he was mentally retarded. As a result, a date was set for his execution. Atkins's attorneys appealed, however, and the Virginia Supreme Court reversed, finding that the prosecution had used a psychologist who was not legally qualified to offer an opinion on the retardation question and that the trial court judge had erred by giving the jurors too much information about previous court rulings. The appellate judges ordered a second retardation trial.

On the eve of the second trial, a witness came forward with allegations that dramatically altered the case. The witness, a lawyer who had represented William Jones (Atkins's original codefendant), claimed that the prosecution had committed a major breach of procedure prior to Atkins's original trial in 1997 by failing to disclose to the defense information that could have brought into question the credibility of the prosecution's key witness. After a two-day hearing over these allegations, the trial court judge ruled on January 17, 2008, that prosecutorial misconduct had occurred. As a remedy the judge reduced Atkins's death sentence to life in prison without parole, an action later upheld by the Virginia Supreme Court.

Today Atkins is serving his sentence in Virginia's Wallens Ridge State Prison. The issue of his mental retardation was never officially resolved.

SOURCE: Thomas G. Walker, *Eligible for Execution: The Story of the Daryl Atkins Case* (Washington, DC: CQ Press, 2009).

execution of juvenile offenders. The court cited as evidence that eighteen states prohibit the execution of juveniles, that twelve other states bar executions altogether, that no state has lowered its age of execution below eighteen since *Stanford*, that five states have legislatively or by case law raised or established the minimum age for execution at eighteen, and that the imposition of the juvenile death penalty has become truly unusual over the last decade.

Writing for a five-person majority (the justices of the *Atkins* majority, except O'Connor), Justice Kennedy affirmed the Missouri court's decision.[28] Just as the Court did in *Atkins* and as the Missouri court did in *Roper*, Kennedy pointed to a growing national consensus against the execution of juveniles.

28. See also our discussion, earlier in this chapter, of Kennedy's opinion in *Graham v. Florida* (2010).

He, like Justice Stevens in *Atkins,* also turned to international opinion:

As [Simmons] and a number of *amici* emphasize, Article 37 of the United Nations Convention on the Rights of the Child, which every country in the world has ratified save for the United States and Somalia, contains an express prohibition on capital punishment for crimes committed by juveniles under 18. No ratifying country has entered a reservation to the provision prohibiting the execution of juvenile offenders. Parallel prohibitions are contained in other significant international covenants.

Respondent and his *amici* have submitted, and petitioner does not contest, that only seven countries other than the United States have executed juvenile offenders since 1990: Iran, Pakistan, Saudi Arabia, Yemen, Nigeria, the Democratic Republic of Congo, and China. Since then each of these countries has either abolished capital punishment for juveniles or made public disavowal of the practice. In sum, it is fair to say that the United States now stands alone in a world that has turned its face against the juvenile death penalty.

Justice Scalia's dissent tracked the one he wrote in *Atkins.* He contended that gauging the national consensus on juvenile executions should have no place in the Court's jurisprudence, and even if it did, only eighteen (or 47 percent) of the states that permit capital punishment prohibit the execution of offenders under the age of eighteen. "Words have no meaning," he wrote, "if the views of less than 50% of death penalty States can constitute a national consensus."

Justice Scalia (along with Justices Roberts, Thomas, and Alito) also dissented in *Kennedy*—a case that traces back to the Court's three-decade old opinion in *Coker v. Georgia* (1977). In *Coker,* the justices held that it is unconstitutional to execute a defendant who rapes an adult woman in part because the death penalty would be disproportionate to the crime, assuming the rape did not (or did not intend to) result in death. In *Kennedy,* the justices addressed a related question— whether the Eighth Amendment creates a constitutional bar to the death penalty for a person convicted of raping a child—and answered it as they did in *Coker.* In looking at its own precedents, the history of the Eighth Amendment, and evolving standards of decency (as measured by practices in the states, among other indicia), the Court concluded that the death penalty for the rape of a child is disproportionate to the crime and struck down Louisiana's law that allowed

it. Along the way, Kennedy, who once again wrote for the majority, pointed out that "44 states had not made child rape a capital offense."[29]

What should we make of *Atkins, Roper,* and *Kennedy*? Surely, they indicate that at least some members of the Court are willing to reconsider the application, if not the constitutionality, of the death penalty: *Atkins* overruled *Penry, Roper* reversed *Stanford,* and *Kennedy* reaffirmed *Coker.* They also indicate that the abolitionist cause is not wholly lost, including a point we made earlier: the public may not be as unified behind the death penalty as some of the less subtle polls show. When asked whether they support capital punishment, the majority of Americans answer that they do, as shown in Table 12-2. But when pollsters ask more nuanced questions, such as questions 2 and 3 in the table, the responses are murkier. Will information of this kind affect future Court decisions? We cannot know. We can only point out that contemporary justices have divided over the value of public opinion in their decision-making process—with Stevens in *Atkins* viewing public opinion as a reasonable measure of "evolving standards of decency" and Scalia claiming that it is not.

Another issue raised in *Atkins* that may favor the abolitionist position concerns practices in other societies. In their opinions for the Court in *Atkins* and *Roper,* Justices Stevens and Kennedy took note of a global consensus against the execution of the mentally retarded and juveniles. This consensus, it is worth noting, holds not just for executions at issue in *Atkins* and *Roper* but for all others as well. As we detail in Box 12-5, the Court's general position on the death penalty directly contradicts the practices adopted in many other democratic societies—some of which are now putting pressure on the United States to reevaluate its position. If *Atkins* and *Roper* are any indication, some Court members may be swayed by the growing world consensus (at least in democratic nations), but certainly not all. Justice Scalia is blunt on this point, writing in *Roper:* a "basic premise of the Court's argument—that American law should conform to the laws of the rest of the world—ought to be rejected out of hand. . . . In many significant respects the laws of

---

29. Justice Kennedy also noted that the federal government had not applied the death penalty to child rape. This statement turned out to be true for civilians, but it was in error for military personnel, who can be subjected to the death penalty for raping a child. The state asked the justices for a rehearing, but they denied the request.

TABLE 12-2	Responses to Questions on the Death Penalty

1. Are you in favor of the death penalty for a person convicted of murder?

Favor	61%
Oppose	35
No opinion	4

2. If you could choose between the following two approaches, which do you think is the better penalty for murder: the death penalty, or life imprisonment with absolutely no possibility of parole?

Death Penalty	48%
Life Imprisonment	50
No opinion	2

3. Do you [favor or oppose] the death penalty for persons convicted of murder when they were under the age of 18?

Strongly Favor/Favor	37%
Strongly Oppose/Oppose	54
No opinion	9

SOURCES: Question 1, Gallup Poll, October 6–9, 2011 (margin of error = ±4; question 2, CNN/ORC poll, September 23–25, 2011 (margin of error = ±3); question 3, Pew Research Center, July 7–17, 2005.

most other countries differ from our law—including not only such explicit provisions of our Constitution as the right to jury trial and grand jury indictment, but even many interpretations of the Constitution prescribed by this Court itself."

The debate between those justices who think it legitimate to examine practices elsewhere and those who do not will undoubtedly continue, whether in the context of the death penalty or in other legal areas. Also likely to get some play in the Court is yet another development that may work in the abolitionists' favor: the use of DNA test results and other forms of evidence to prove that some death row inmates were wrongfully convicted. As of 2011, 139 death row prisoners in the United States had been exonerated by new evidence. In Illinois alone, 20 on death row were proven innocent (5 by newly available DNA evidence), a situation so extreme that the governor called for a moratorium on executions. These findings generated calls for moratoriums elsewhere, and Maryland has now followed the lead of Illinois. Justice Ginsburg seems to support the move, citing her concern over the quality of legal care many defendants receive: "I have yet to see a death case among the dozens coming to the Supreme Court on eve of execution stay applications in which the defendant was well represented at trial."

Whether her newest colleagues, Justices Alito, Roberts, Sotomayor, and Kagan, will agree remains an

---

BOX 12-5   CAPITAL PUNISHMENT IN GLOBAL PERSPECTIVE

While the number of legal executions in the United States remains high, the numbers in other nations are declining markedly—primarily because more than two-thirds have abolished the death penalty in law or in practice. These countries include Australia, Canada, and most Western European democracies.

Many newly fledged democracies also have eradicated capital punishment. Estonia's parliament, for example, voted to ratify an international treaty that obliges the country to end its death penalty. The constitutional courts in Lithuania, South Africa, and the Ukraine have found their death penalties to be unconstitutional. The South African court's decision was particularly interesting because the justices reviewed but ultimately rejected U.S. Supreme Court doctrine and rationale.

Fifty-eight countries retain the death penalty for ordinary crimes,[1] but not many of them use it with any regularity. For example, 527 of the *known* executions that occurred in 2010 took place in only twenty-two countries, and more than 80 percent were in Iran (252), North Korea (60), Saudi Arabia (27), the United States (46), and Yemen (53). (These figures exclude a twenty-third country, China, where data on this subject are unreliable. Some believe that thousands of executions occurred in China in 2010.)

SOURCES: Data from the Death Penalty Information Center, http://www.deathpenaltyinfo.org; and Amnesty International, http://www.amnesty.org.

[1] Nine retain it for exceptional crimes only; thirty-five retain the death penalty but have not executed anyone in the past ten years.

open question. But some indication came in *House v. Bell* (2006), in which the justices for the first time considered whether the courts should take DNA results into account when deciding whether a defendant should have access to the federal courts (via habeas corpus)—access that would typically be barred. Writing for the majority, Justice Kennedy was persuaded that DNA testing conducted after the trial called into question "central forensic proof" connecting the defendant to the crime, and in fact may point to a different suspect altogether. Accordingly, the majority concluded, "This is the rare case where—had the jury heard all the conflicting testimony—it is more likely than not that no reasonable juror viewing the record as a whole would lack reasonable doubt." Justice Alito did not participate in the case, and Chief Justice Roberts dissented. Writing for Justices Scalia and Thomas, Roberts asserted:

The question is not whether House was prejudiced at his trial because the jurors were not aware of the new evidence, but whether all the evidence, considered together, proves that House was actually innocent, so that no reasonable juror would vote to convict him. Considering all the evidence, and giving due regard to the District Court's findings on whether House's new evidence was reliable, I do not find it probable that no reasonable juror would vote to convict him, and accordingly I dissent.

Despite the ruling in *House* and the other recent victories by foes of the death penalty,[30] we must keep in mind that for the present the Court remains committed to the position that the cruel and unusual punishments clause of the Eighth Amendment does not prohibit the death penalty, a stance that, in general, many Americans and their representatives support.

POSTTRIAL PROTECTIONS AND THE DOUBLE JEOPARDY CLAUSE

Individuals who have been fully prosecuted for criminal offenses retain certain procedural protections during the posttrial period. Convicted defendants have

the right to challenge the validity of their trials, usually through appeal. Under the concept of due process of law, a person convicted of a crime may ask a higher court to review what transpired during the trial to determine whether there was any significant procedural error. If the appeals court finds that a reversible error occurred—one significant enough to have affected the outcome of the trial—the conviction may be declared invalid or a new trial may be ordered. A convicted defendant has the right to have his or her case heard on appeal once; any subsequent appeals take place at the discretion of the appellate court.

Another way of challenging a conviction is to file a motion for a new trial. If new evidence comes to light that brings a trial's outcome into question, a convicted defendant may request a new trial. The defendant must then show that the new evidence could not have been known or presented at the first trial and that it is strong enough to cast serious doubt on the original verdict. Such motions are rarely granted.

An entirely different set of posttrial protections is accorded by the double jeopardy clause of the Fifth Amendment: "nor shall any person be subject for the same offence to be twice put in jeopardy of life or limb." The right against double jeopardy is one of the least understood provisions governing the criminal process. This lack of understanding stems from both the unusual wording of the clause and some confusing rulings by the Supreme Court.

The double jeopardy clause includes three basic protections. First, an individual tried for an offense and found not guilty cannot be prosecuted a second time for the same offense. This guarantee was designed to ensure that someone would not be subjected to multiple prosecutions for the same crime. Without this restraint, a powerful government could conduct prosecution after prosecution until a conviction was finally obtained. With each successive prosecution the defendant's resources would be decreased, leaving the individual more vulnerable in subsequent trials. It seemed only fair to the framers to restrict the government to one attempt to convict a defendant on a single offense. Furthermore, this right prohibits the government from appealing a trial court's verdict of not guilty. Once a not guilty verdict is announced, the defendant is forever free from criminal prosecutions based on that offense.

But what is meant by the term *same offense*? The Supreme Court answered part of this question in

---

30. On the other hand, in *District Attorney's Office for the Third Judicial District v. Osborne* (2009), the Court held that persons convicted of a crime do not enjoy a constitutional right to obtain access to the state's (here, Alaska's) DNA evidence. While this is an important decision, its practical implications may be rather limited. Today, Oklahoma is the only state that does not allow inmates access to their DNA tests, though in some states the laws are quite limited.

Ashe v. Swenson (1970). Bob Fred Ashe, along with others, was charged with breaking into a house and robbing its owner and five others who were playing poker. The prosecutor tried Ashe for robbing one of the poker players. That trial ended in a verdict of not guilty because of insufficient evidence. Six weeks later, the prosecutor charged Ashe with robbing another member of the poker party and this time got a conviction. Ashe claimed on appeal that the second trial violated his right to be protected from double jeopardy. The Supreme Court agreed, holding that the robbery was a single offense, although there were multiple victims. Except for the name of the victim, the second trial dealt with exactly the same incident and circumstances as the first. Therefore, to be found not guilty in the first trial precluded a second. In Justice Stewart's words, the Fifth Amendment "surely protects a man who has been acquitted from having to 'run the gauntlet' a second time."

The double jeopardy clause, however, does not bar separate governments from prosecuting an individual based on the same incident. In *Heath v. Alabama* (1985) the Court applied this dual sovereignty doctrine to Larry Gene Heath, who had arranged to have his wife, who was nine months pregnant, kidnapped and killed. The hired killers took Rebecca Heath from her home in Alabama and murdered her in Georgia. Heath was arrested in Georgia and pleaded guilty to murder charges as part of a plea-bargain arrangement to avoid the death penalty. Alabama authorities, independently investigating the crime, then indicted Heath for kidnapping and murder. Heath objected on double jeopardy grounds, but the Supreme Court held that the Fifth Amendment did not prohibit prosecution by Alabama. An act that offends the criminal laws of two jurisdictions may be punished by both.

The same doctrine can be applied to an action that violates both state and federal criminal codes. An example is the infamous 1992 Rodney King incident. A state jury acquitted Los Angeles police officers who had been accused of beating King following a high-speed chase. The verdict was reached despite a damaging and frequently televised videotape of the incident. Federal prosecutors later won convictions by convincing a different jury that the officers' actions constituted a criminal violation of King's civil rights.

A second protection of the double jeopardy clause is the ban against prosecuting someone a second time for an offense on which a guilty verdict has already been returned. Suppose a woman is convicted of killing a coworker and receives a long prison sentence. The prosecutors may consider the penalty too lenient, but the double jeopardy clause prohibits them from trying her a second time to obtain a more severe sentence. In *United States v. Ball* (1896), however, the Supreme Court held that a second trial is not necessarily prohibited if the defendant appeals the trial court decision and an appellate court reverses the conviction. Nor is a second trial prohibited if the first ends in a hung jury—that is, if the jurors are deadlocked and cannot reach a verdict. The justices came to this conclusion in the Court's first double jeopardy case, *United States v. Perez* (1824).

Third, the double jeopardy clause bars multiple punishments for the same offense, which was the central issue in two 1996 cases, *United States v. Ursery* and *United States v. $405,089.23*, which the Court decided together. These cases challenged the property forfeiture actions taken by the federal government against certain criminals. This aggressive law enforcement strategy allows the government to make a two-pronged attack on crime. The government not only charges the accused with criminal offenses but also institutes a separate legal action requesting the forfeiture of any property used in the crime or purchased with the fruits of the crime. Property forfeiture is a civil, not criminal, action. In the *Ursery* case, federal authorities found evidence of marijuana production in Guy Ursery's house and marijuana plants growing on adjacent land. The government prosecuted criminal drug charges against him and moved to have his house and land forfeited to the government. In *$404,089.23* the government charged two individuals with illegal drug distribution and in a separate legal action moved to seize cash, silver, boats, aircraft, and automobiles on the grounds that they were purchased with illegal money or used in the criminal activity.

The defendants in these cases claimed that the criminal prosecutions and the civil property forfeiture actions constituted double penalties for the same offenses in violation of the Fifth Amendment. In an 8–1 decision, the justices disagreed. The Court concluded that Congress in drafting the property forfeiture statutes intended such actions to be civil matters and not criminal punishment. Furthermore, the justices found that property forfeitures are not "so punitive in form or effect as to render them criminal in spite of Congress' intent to the contrary." The Court's decision was a major victory for law enforcement authorities. Property seizures, particularly against those engaged in highly profitable crimes such as drug dealing, allow the government to attack crime more vigorously than they can with using criminal sentences alone.

In *Kansas v. Hendricks* (1997) the justices continued to take a narrow view of the double jeopardy clause. This case involved a challenge to a statute that permitted the state to keep certain sexual offenders in custody even after they had served their sentences. According to the law, violent sexual predators who have mental abnormalities that prohibit them from controlling their unlawful sexual conduct may be committed to mental health facilities after completion of their criminal sentences. Such a civil commitment, involuntary and indeterminate in length, can take place only after strict procedural safeguards are observed, including a jury trial.

Leroy Hendricks was a pedophile with a forty-year history of sexually molesting young boys and girls. In 1984 he was convicted of sexually assaulting two teenage boys. As his prison sentence was about to be completed in 1994, Kansas authorities, who believed Hendricks was a danger to society, initiated proceedings to commit him to a mental institution. A jury found beyond a reasonable doubt that he should be committed. Hendricks appealed, claiming that the commitment constituted a second punishment for his offense in violation of the double jeopardy and due process clauses. A closely divided Supreme Court

upheld the law, finding that the civil commitment was not a second criminal punishment but a separate civil procedure allowing the state to protect the public from sexual predators who are unable to control their behavior. With double jeopardy doubts erased by the Court, lawmakers in several other states proposed adopting legislation modeled on the Kansas statute.

POSTRELEASE PROTECTIONS

Hendricks points to an interesting phenomenon: states occasionally attempt to develop ways to isolate convicted criminals from society even after those persons have served their prison sentences. In two cases handed down in 2003, *Connecticut Department of Public Safety v. Doe* and *Smith v. Doe,* the Court considered a variation on isolation: registration.

Although the legal challenges in these cases differed, the laws at issue—those requiring sex offenders to register their names and home addresses with local law enforcement authorities—are similar, and they bear the names of child victims. Eleven-year-old Jacob Wetterling was kidnapped at gunpoint in 1989 and has not been found. Unknown to local law enforcement, released sex offenders were living in community halfway houses (though no arrests were made). Megan Kanka, a seven-year-old New Jersey girl, was sexually assaulted and murdered in 1994 by a neighbor who,

In 1997 the Supreme Court rejected a double jeopardy challenge to the Kansas Sexually Violent Predator Act, which allowed the state to confine individuals diagnosed as pedophiles to mental institutions after they had served their criminal sentences. The state invoked the act for the first time to commit convicted child molester Leroy Hendricks, shown here with his attorney during his October 1994 trial.

unknown to the victim's family, had prior convictions for sex offenses against children. In 1994, Congress passed the Jacob Wetterling Crimes Against Children and Sexually Violent Offender Registration Act of 1994, which it amended in 1996; this act is now better known as Megan's law. The act called on the states to pass their own Megan's laws, which require convicted sex offenders to register with the state's department of corrections if they are incarcerated or with the local police if they are not. Under Megan's laws, sex offenders must provide various types of information, such as name, aliases, identifying features, address, place of employment, date of birth, conviction information, driver's license number, information about vehicles to which the individual has access, and postconviction treatment history. In a majority of states much of this information is in turn made available to the public via the Internet.

By 1996 every state, the District of Columbia, and the federal government had enacted some form of Megan's law, but the Supreme Court did not assess the constitutionality of such laws until 2003. In that year, it rejected claims that public disclosure violated the due process clause because officials did not afford sex offender registrants predeprivation hearings to determine whether they were likely to be "currently dangerous."[31] Writing for a 9–0 Court in *Connecticut Department of Public Safety v. Doe,* Chief Justice Rehnquist held that the government "has decided that the registry requirement shall be based on the fact of previous conviction, not the fact of current dangerousness. Indeed, the public registry explicitly states that officials have not determined that any registrant is currently dangerous. . . . [D]ue process does not require the opportunity to prove a fact that is not material to the State's statutory scheme."

In reaching this decision, the justices stated: "Sex offenders are a serious threat in this Nation. The victims of sex assault are most often juveniles," and "when convicted sex offenders reenter society, they are much more likely than any other type of offender to be re-arrested for a new rape or sex assault." Whether these facts influenced their decision, we do not know. What they said is that because the registries list offenders and their crimes and do not attempt to say or predict whether an individual is currently dangerous, states are not barred by principles of procedural due process from maintaining them.

ANNOTATED READINGS

Of the topics we cover in this chapter, two have received substantial attention: the jury system and the death penalty. On juries, see Reid Hastie, Steven D. Penrod, and Nancy Pennington, *Inside the Jury* (Cambridge, MA: Harvard University Press, 1983); Randolph N. Jonakait, *The American Jury System* (New Haven, CT: Yale University Press, 2003); Harry Kalven Jr. and Hans Zeisel, *The American Jury* (Boston: Little, Brown, 1966); Neil Vidmar and Valerie P. Hans, *America Juries: The Verdict* (New York: Prometheus Books, 2007).

Books on the death penalty include David C. Baldus, George G. Woodworth, and Charles A. Pulaski Jr., *Equal Justice and the Death Penalty* (Boston: Northeastern University Press, 1990); Stuart Banner, *The Death Penalty: An American History* (Cambridge, MA: Harvard University Press, 2002); Frank R. Baumgartner, Suzanna L. DeBoef, and Amber E. Boydstun, *The Decline of the Death Penalty and the Discovery of Innocence* (New York: Cambridge University Press, 2008); Jennifer L. Culbert, *Dead Certainty: The Death Penalty and the Problem of Judgment* (Stanford, CA: Stanford University Press, 2007); Lee Epstein and Joseph F. Kobylka, *The Supreme Court and Legal Change: Abortion and the Death Penalty* (Chapel Hill: University of North Carolina Press, 1992); Stephen P. Garvey, ed., *Beyond Repair? America's Death Penalty* (Durham, NC: Duke University Press, 2002); Roger G. Hood, *Death Penalty: A Worldwide Perspective* (New York: Oxford University Press, 2002); Michael Meltsner, *Cruel and Unusual: The Supreme Court and Capital Punishment* (New York: Random House, 1973); David M. Oshinsky, *Capital Punishment on Trial:* Furman v. Georgia *and the Death Penalty in Modern America* (Lawrence: University Press of Kansas, 2010); Austin Sarat, *When the State Kills: Capital Punishment and the American Condition* (Princeton, NJ: Princeton University Press, 2001); Thomas G. Walker, *Eligible for Execution: The Story of the Daryl Atkins Case* (Washington, DC: CQ Press, 2009).

---

31. In *Smith v. Doe,* decided on the same day, the Court ruled, 6–3, that Alaska's Megan's law, which applied to sex offenders who had been convicted prior to the law's passage, did not violate the ex post facto clause of the Constitution. That clause prohibits punishments applied retroactively, but, according to the majority, Megan's laws are not punishments.

Books on other topics relating to attorneys, trials, and punishments include George Fisher, *Plea Bargaining's Triumph* (Stanford, CA: Stanford University Press, 2004); Brandon L. Garrett, *Convicting the Innocent: Where Criminal Prosecutions Go Wrong* (Cambridge, MA: Harvard University Press, 2011); Milton Heumann, *Plea Bargaining* (Chicago: University of Chicago Press, 1978); Anthony Lewis, *Gideon's Trumpet* (New York: Vintage Books, 1964); Michael Lynch, Simon A. Cole, Ruth McNally, and Kathleen Jordan. *Truth Machine: The Contentious History of DNA Fingerprinting* (Chicago: University of Chicago Press, 2008); Keally McBride, *Punishment and Political Order* (Ann Arbor: University of Michigan Press, 2007); Jay A. Sigler, *Double Jeopardy: The Development of Legal and Social Policy* (Ithaca, NY: Cornell University Press, 1969); William J. Stuntz, *The Collapse of American Criminal Justice* (Cambridge, MA: Belknap Press, 2011); George C. Thomas, *Double Jeopardy: The History, the Law* (New York: Oxford University Press, 1998); George C. Thomas, *The Supreme Court on Trial: How the American Justice System Sacrifices Innocent Defendants* (Ann Arbor: University of Michigan Press, 2008); Mary Vogel, *Coercion to Compromise: Plea Bargaining, the Courts, and the Making of Political Authority* (New York: Oxford University Press, 2007); Franklin E. Zimring, Gordon Hawkins, and Sam Kamin, *Punishment and Democracy: Three Strikes and You're Out in California* (New York: Oxford University Press, 2001).

PART IV

Civil Rights

Civil Rights and the Constitution

I N MARKED CONTRAST to the colonial period, when most citizens came from British roots, Americans today are from many different backgrounds. Immigration has diversified the population, and this trend is expected to continue. Americans are a people of wide-ranging religions, races, ethnic backgrounds, and levels of wealth. Given this diversity, the motto "E pluribus unum," or "One from many," sometimes appears to be more of a challenge than a statement of fact. In spite of the differences among Americans, however, the nation has pledged itself to fairness and equality. All Americans are to be free from unconstitutional discrimination, to have equal opportunity, and to have the right to participate fully in the political process.

Even so, at times people feel they have been mistreated by their government, not because of what they have done but because of who they are. They claim that discrimination has occurred because of race, creed, national origin, gender, economic status, sexual orientation, or some other characteristic that government should not use as a basis for policy. When disputes over such charges arise, the court system provides a venue for their resolution. In the chapters in Part IV, we discuss the civil rights of Americans and how the Supreme Court has interpreted them. By *civil rights* we mean those legal provisions emanating from the concept of equality. Unlike civil liberties issues, which focus on personal freedoms protected by the Bill of Rights, civil rights issues involve the status of persons

with shared characteristics who historically have been disadvantaged in some way. Civil rights laws attempt to guarantee full and equal citizenship for such persons and to protect them from arbitrary and capricious treatment. Chapter 13 examines discrimination, and Chapter 14 explores the rights of political participation. Before we confront those subjects, however, a review of some basic concepts of history and law might be useful.

Today, we are used to hearing not only about charges of discrimination but also about Supreme Court rulings on the proper meaning of the Constitution governing such issues. These phenomena are comparatively recent. Although "equality" in the United States was relatively advanced for the period, colonial Americans discriminated in a number of ways that we now consider abhorrent. The most significant breach of fundamental equality was the institution of slavery. In spite of the Declaration of Independence, which proclaimed that all men are created equal, the enslavement of Africans brought to North America against their will was politically accepted, although not universally supported. The Constitution recognized this form of inequality, stipulating in Article I that a slave would be counted as three-fifths of a person for representation purposes; it also gave slavery a degree of protection by prohibiting any federal restrictions on the importation of slaves until 1808. Other forms of discrimination also were common. Voting qualifications, for example, were quite restrictive: only men could vote, and in some states only men who owned property could vote.

Guarantees of equality did not officially become part of the Constitution until after the Civil War. When the Radical Republicans took control of the legislative branch, three constitutional amendments, generally referred to as the Civil War amendments, were proposed and ratified. They incorporated into the Constitution what had been won on the battlefield and dramatically changed the concept of civil rights in the United States. The Thirteenth Amendment, ratified in 1865, unambiguously ended the institution of slavery. Although there have been some disputes over the involuntary servitude prohibition (in relation, for example, to the military draft), the slavery issue, over which the nation had been divided since the Constitutional Convention, finally was put to rest. The other two amendments, the Fourteenth and Fifteenth, have generated a great deal of litigation and many Supreme Court cases, and we discuss them in turn.

THE FOURTEENTH AMENDMENT

The Fourteenth Amendment, ratified in 1868, is unlike the other two because of its length and complexity. The first section is the most significant: it states that U.S. citizenship is superior to state citizenship, constitutionally reinforcing the Civil War outcome of national superiority over states' rights. This idea was a dramatic change from the pre–Civil War concept that national citizenship was dependent on state citizenship. The first section also includes the due process clause and privileges or immunities clause we discussed in earlier chapters, as well as the equal protection clause. Because this last clause forms the basis of constitutional protections against discrimination, we describe it in some detail. The remaining parts of the Fourteenth Amendment require the former slaves to be fully counted for representational purposes, impose (with few exceptions) universal adult male suffrage, restrict the civil rights of certain participants in the rebellion, and guarantee the public debt resulting from the war.

The Supreme Court and Equal Protection of the Laws

An analysis of the wording of the equal protection clause helps us to understand what it covers and what its limitations are. It says, "[N]or shall any State . . . deny to any person within its jurisdiction the equal protection of the laws."

The first significant element of the clause is the word *state*. The members of Congress who drafted the Fourteenth Amendment were concerned primarily with the danger of the states (especially those in the South) imposing discriminatory laws. With the Radical Republicans—who were deeply committed to an abolition ideology—in control of Congress and the White House, the legislators had little fear that the federal government would impose discriminatory policies. Consequently, the prohibitions of the clause apply only to the states and their political subdivisions, such as counties and cities.

Second, the amendment protects *all* persons within a state's jurisdiction, not just former slaves. In an early dispute over the amendment, the Supreme Court acknowledged its broad applicability. *Yick Wo v. Hopkins* (1886) concerned the discriminatory enforcement of fire safety regulations in San Francisco. The Court held that the equal protection clause applies to persons other than black Americans, also protecting noncitizens who are targets of discrimination by the state.

Finally, the clause outlaws a denial of equal protection of the laws; in other words, it prohibits discrimination. Any person within a state's jurisdiction is constitutionally entitled to be treated equitably, to be free from arbitrary and unreasonable treatment at the hands of the state government.

The wording of the equal protection clause means that before an individual can legitimately assert a claim of its violation, two important elements must be demonstrated. First, the aggrieved party must prove some form of unequal treatment or discrimination. Second, there must be state action; that is, the discrimination must have been initiated or supported by the state or its local governments. These two requirements have undergone substantial interpretation by the justices of the Supreme Court, and we need to understand what is included in each requirement.

Discrimination. Discrimination simply means to distinguish between people or things. It occurs in many forms, not all of which are prohibited by the Constitution. For example, in administering an admissions program, a state university must discriminate among its applicants. It admits some, rejects others. Decisions usually are based on applicants' high school grades, standardized test scores, and letters of recommendation. The university admits those who, based on valid predictors of performance, have the best chance to succeed. Those who are rejected usually accept the decision because the university's admissions criteria appear reasonable. But the reaction would be quite different if an applicant received a letter from a state college that said, "In spite of your demonstrated potential for college studies, we cannot admit you because of our policy not to accept students of your religion." In this case, the rejected applicant would rightly feel victimized by unreasonable discrimination.

What rule of law distinguishes acceptable discrimination from that which violates the Constitution? The Supreme Court answered this question by declaring that the equal protection clause goes no further than prohibiting "invidious discrimination"[1]—that is, discrimination that is arbitrary and capricious, unequal treatment that has no rational basis. Reasonable discrimination, on the other hand, is not unconstitutional. When the state treats two individuals differently, we need to ask what criteria the state is using to distinguish them. If two surgeons perform heart operations on patients and one is thrown in jail and the other is not, we might feel that the imprisoned person has not been treated fairly. Our opinion would change, however, if we learned that the jailed person had never been to medical school and was not licensed. Here the state would be discriminating on the basis of legitimate, reasonable criteria. The equal protection clause demands that similarly situated persons be treated equally. The two surgeons, because of their vastly different qualifications, are not similarly situated, and consequently the Constitution does not require that they be treated the same.

Almost every government action involves some form of discrimination. Most are perfectly legitimate, although all those affected might not agree. For example, when a state government passes an income tax law that imposes a higher rate on the wealthy than it does on the poor, the rich may feel they are the targets of unconstitutional discrimination. When individuals believe they have been denied equal protection at the hands of the state, the courts must decide if the government's discrimination runs afoul of the Fourteenth Amendment. When it comes to taxes, the courts have ruled that progressive rate structures are not invidious, but reasonable.

To assist the judiciary in deciding such disputes, the Supreme Court has developed three basic tests of the equal protection clause. Which test is applied in any given case is determined by the alleged discrimination and the government interests at stake.

The traditional test used to decide discrimination cases is the *rational basis* test. When using this approach to the Constitution, the justices ask: Is the challenged discrimination rational? Or is it arbitrary and capricious? If a state passes a law that says a person must be at least eighteen years old to enter a legally binding contract, it is imposing an age-based discrimination. Individuals under eighteen are not granted the right to consummate legal agreements; those over eighteen are. If a dispute over the validity of this law were brought to court, the judge would have to decide whether the state had acted reasonably to achieve a legitimate government objective.[2] Using the rational basis test, the Court generally defers to the state and presumes the validity of the government's action. The burden of proof rests with the party challenging the law to establish that the statute is irrational. Unless the Court has determined otherwise, discrimination claims proceed according to the rules of the rational basis test.

The second test is called the *suspect class* or *strict scrutiny* test. This test is used when the state discriminates on the basis of a criterion that the Supreme Court has declared to be inherently suspect or when there is a claim that the discrimination adversely affects the exercise of a fundamental right. A suspect classification is based on characteristics assumed to be irrational. The Supreme Court has ruled, for example, that race is a suspect class. Laws that discriminate on racial grounds are given strict scrutiny by the courts. The reason for moving racial discrimination from the rational basis test to the suspect class test is that the Supreme Court has concluded that racial criteria are inherently arbitrary, that compelling state interests are rarely (if ever) served by treating people differently according to race. For a law to be valid under strict scrutiny, it must be found to advance a compelling state interest by the least restrictive means available. When the suspect class test is used, the Court presumes that the state action is unconstitutional, and the burden of proof is on the government to demonstrate that the law is constitutional.

---

1. See *Williamson v. Lee Optical* (1955).

2. See *McGowan v. Maryland* (1961).

Given the rules associated with these two tests, it should be obvious that it is much easier to establish that a violation of the Constitution has occurred if the suspect class test is used. Therefore, many cases before the Supreme Court have been filed by attorneys representing groups seeking that classification. The Court has ruled that suspect class status should be accorded only to those groups that constitute discrete and insular minorities that have experienced a history of unequal treatment and a lack of political power.[3] Applying such criteria is difficult and has given rise to sharp divisions of opinion among the justices.

Legal battles over what rules should apply to sex discrimination cases were particularly difficult for the Court to resolve.[4] A majority could not agree to elevate sex to suspect class status, but there was substantial opinion that the rational basis test was also inappropriate for dealing with sex discrimination. This conflict gave rise to a third test of the equal protection clause, the *intermediate* (or *heightened*) *scrutiny* test. This test holds that to be valid the unequal treatment must serve important government objectives and must be substantially related to the achievement of those objectives.[5] In recent years, the Court has added that under this test a state must provide an exceedingly persuasive justification for any discriminatory classifications. As such, this test falls squarely between the rational basis test and the suspect class test *(see Table IV-1)*.

This three-tiered approach can be confusing, and the Supreme Court has been neither clear nor consistent in applying the principles. Justice Thurgood Marshall in **Dunn v. Blumstein** (1972) acknowledged that the tests do not have the "precision of mathematical formulas." Justice Byron R. White hinted that in reality the Court may be using a spectrum of tests rather than three separate tests. Frustration over the status of the equal protection clause tests prompted Justice John Paul Stevens to claim in his concurring opinion in *Cleburne v. Cleburne Living Center* (1985) that a continuum of standards was being used. Not persuaded of the wisdom of the Court's approach, Stevens has argued that a single test should be adopted for all equal protection claims. In spite of these criticisms, the Court

has stuck to the three-tiered approach, which reflects the belief that the more historically disadvantaged and politically powerless a class of people has been, the greater justification government must provide for any state action that discriminates against the members of that class.

State Action. As noted, the equal protection clause specifically prohibits discrimination by any state. The Supreme Court has interpreted this concept to include a wide array of state actions—statutes, their enforcement and administration, and the actions of state officials. We have already mentioned *Yick Wo v. Hopkins,* in which the Court struck down a fire safety regulation that was racially neutral as written but enforced in a discriminatory manner against Chinese laundry operators. State action includes the policies of political subdivisions such as towns, cities, counties, and special-purpose agencies. The states are prohibited from engaging in invidious discrimination either directly or indirectly. A city, for instance, may not run its municipal swimming pools in a racially segregated manner, nor may it donate the pools to a private organization that will restrict pool use to a particular racial group. In whatever form, however, some element of state action supporting invidious discrimination must be shown before a violation of the equal protection clause occurs.

This requirement means that discrimination by purely private individuals or organizations is not prohibited by the equal protection clause. A white apartment house owner who refuses to rent to an African American family is not in violation of the Constitution; neither is a restaurant manager who will not serve Latinos, a private club that will not admit women, or an employer who will not hire applicants over forty years of age. In each of these cases there is ample evidence of irrational discrimination, but no state action. The discrimination is conducted by private individuals or organizations. These forms of discrimination may well be in violation of any number of state or federal statutes, but they do not offend the equal protection clause of the Fourteenth Amendment.

Moreover, because it is restricted to the states, the equal protection clause does not prohibit the federal government from engaging in discrimination. The Supreme Court, therefore, faced a difficult situation in 1954 in the school desegregation cases. The best-known of these is *Brown v. Board of Education*

---

3. See *United States v. Carolene Products* (1938); *San Antonio Independent School District v. Rodriguez* (1973).

4. See, for example, **Frontiero v. Richardson** (1973).

5. *Craig v. Boren* (1976).

TABLE IV-1   Equal Protection Tests

TEST	EXAMPLE OF APPLICABILITY	VALIDITY STANDARD
Rational basis test	Age discrimination	The law must be a *reasonable* measure designed to achieve a *legitimate* government purpose.
Intermediate (heightened) scrutiny test	Sex discrimination	The law must be *substantially related* to the achievement of an *important* government objective.
Suspect class (strict scrutiny) test	Race discrimination	The law must be the *least restrictive* means available to achieve a *compelling* state interest.

of Topeka, Kansas, but *Brown* was only one of several cases involving the same basic issue. In ***Bolling v. Sharpe*** the Court faced the thorny issue of racial segregation in the Washington, D.C., public schools. The District of Columbia is not a state, and in the 1950s Congress was the ultimate authority over Washington, as it is today. The equal protection clause was not applicable there. Given the political situation at the time, the Court had to find a way to declare all segregated schools unconstitutional.

The justices found a solution in the due process clause of the Fifth Amendment, which states, "No person shall . . . be deprived of life, liberty, or property, without due process of law." This guarantee of essential fairness applies to the federal government and was used by the justices in *Bolling* as a bar against racial discrimination. Chief Justice Earl Warren explained for a unanimous Court:

The Fifth Amendment, which is applicable in the District of Columbia, does not contain an equal protection clause as does the Fourteenth Amendment which applies only to the states. But the concepts of equal protection and due process, both stemming from our American ideal of fairness, are not mutually exclusive. The "equal protection of the laws" is a more explicit safeguard of prohibited unfairness than "due process of law," and, therefore, we do not imply that the two are always interchangeable phrases. But, as this Court has recognized, discrimination may be so unjustifiable as to be violative of due process.

Although Warren cautioned that the due process clause and the equal protection clause could not be used interchangeably, the Court consistently has ruled that both provisions stand for the same general principles. In most areas of discrimination law (but not all), the justices have applied the same standards to both state and federal governments by using these two constitutional provisions. As a rule, any discriminatory action by a state found to be in violation of the equal protection clause would also be a violation of the Fifth Amendment if engaged in by the federal government. We should, however, understand which provision of the Constitution is offended when invidious discrimination is practiced by either state governments or the federal government. If the U.S. National Park Service were to require racially segregated campgrounds at Yellowstone, it would violate the due process clause of the Fifth Amendment; if a state imposed the same restriction at a state park, it would violate the equal protection clause of the Fourteenth Amendment.

Congressional Enforcement of the Fourteenth Amendment

The civil rights of Americans are defined and protected by more than just the Constitution. Over the years Congress has passed laws designed to enforce and extend constitutional guarantees *(see Box IV-1)*. These laws expand prohibitions against discriminatory behavior, give the federal executive branch authority to enforce civil rights protections, and enlarge the opportunities for aggrieved parties to seek redress in the courts. The rules of evidence and procedure in some of these laws make it easier for litigants to prevail by proving a violation of a civil rights statute rather than a constitutional violation.

The authority for Congress to pass such laws can be found in several constitutional provisions. Each Civil War amendment contains a section granting Congress the power to enforce the amendment with appropriate legislation. Consequently, these amendments have had considerable impact not only because of their basic substantive content but also because they gave Congress new legislative power. Immediately following the Civil War, Congress used this authority to pass

BOX IV-1 A SAMPLE OF MAJOR CIVIL RIGHTS ACTS

Since the end of the Civil War, Congress has enacted scores of civil rights statutes. In what follows we describe a few of the more prominent acts.

CIVIL RIGHTS ACTS OF 1866, 1870, 1871, AND 1875

Congress passed these laws after the Civil War to provide African Americans with equal political and legal rights, but it later repealed many of them, and the Supreme Court struck down others. For example, in the *Civil Rights Cases* (1883), the Court invalidated the "public accommodation" provision of the 1875 act, which guaranteed "[t]hat citizens of every race and color," regardless of whether they had been slaves, "be entitled to the full and equal enjoyment of the accommodations, advantages, facilities, and privileges of inns, public conveyances on land or water, theaters, and other places of public amusement."

Today, a few major provisions remain from the acts of 1866 and 1871. One makes it a federal crime for any person acting under the authority of a state law to deprive another of any rights protected by the Constitution or by laws of the United States. Another authorizes suits for civil damages against state or local officials by persons whose rights are abridged. Others permit actions against persons who conspire to deprive people of their rights.

CIVIL RIGHTS ACTS OF 1957 AND 1960

These acts were the first major civil rights laws passed since the 1875 act, and they were largely (but not exclusively) designed to secure voting rights for African Americans. Many viewed them as weak and, ultimately, ineffective. The

1957 legislation did, however, create the Civil Rights Commission to investigate civil rights violations and make policy recommendations. The 1957 act also established the Civil Rights Division in the Department of Justice and empowered the U.S. attorney general to bring suit against any deprivation of voting rights.

EQUAL PAY ACT OF 1963

Passed as an amendment to the Fair Labor Standards Act, this law prohibits discrimination in wages based on sex. It mandates that men and women receive the same pay "for equal work on jobs, the performance of which requires equal skill, effort, and responsibility, and which are performed under similar working conditions." It excluded wages paid pursuant to seniority or merit systems, among other exceptions.

CIVIL RIGHTS ACTS OF 1964 AND 1968

Considered by some commentators to be among the most important civil rights laws ever enacted by Congress, the Civil Rights Act of 1964 was designed to eradicate discrimination in many areas of American social, economic, and political life. Major provisions include Title I (on voting rights), which outlaws discrimination in voter registration and outlines procedures for expedited review of voting rights litigation. Title II (on public accommodations) guarantees that "all persons shall be entitled to the full and equal enjoyment of the goods, services, facilities, and privileges, advantages, and accommodations of any place of public accommodation, including hotels, restaurants, and theaters." Titles III and IV cover desegregation of public facilities and education, and empower the attorney general to initiate

laws intended to give the new amendments teeth. For example, the Civil Rights Act of 1866, passed over the veto of President Andrew Johnson, guaranteed blacks the right to purchase, lease, and use real property. The Supreme Court upheld the law, ruling that the Thirteenth Amendment's enforcement section gave Congress the power not only to outlaw slavery but also to legislate against the "badges and incidents of slavery."[6] Much of the federal regulation on fair housing is based on this authority.

Congress learned by trial and error to ground legislation in the correct Civil War amendment. In 1883 the Supreme Court handed down its decisions in the ***Civil Rights Cases,*** which involved challenges to the Civil Rights Act of 1875, a statute based on the Fourteenth Amendment that made discrimination in public accommodations unlawful. Because the law covered privately owned businesses, the owners of hotels, entertainment facilities, and transportation companies claimed that Congress had exceeded the authority granted to it by the amendment. The Court, with only one justice dissenting, struck down the statute,

6. *Jones v. Alfred Mayer, Inc.* (1968).

desegregation suits. Title VI prohibits discrimination in projects funded by the federal government. Finally, Title VII guarantees equal opportunity in the employment context by making it illegal, for example, for employers with fifteen or more employees "to fail or refuse to hire or to discharge any individual, or otherwise to discriminate against any individual with respect to his compensation, terms, conditions, or privileges of employment, because of such individual's race, color, religion, sex, or national origin."

As comprehensive as it was, the Civil Rights Act of 1964 did not cover discrimination in housing. Four years later, Congress enacted the Civil Rights Act of 1968, which prohibits discrimination in the sale, rental, advertising, and financing of housing based on race, religion, national origin, (and as later amended) sex, handicapped status, or presence of children in a household. Under the law, it is unlawful to refuse to sell a house to a buyer on any of these grounds (race, religion, and so on).

VOTING RIGHTS ACT OF 1965

Another major law, the Voting Rights Act of 1965 (and subsequent renewals) sought to eradicate racial discrimination in voting. For more on this law, see *South Carolina v. Katzenbach (excerpted in Chapter 14, pages 732-735)*, a 1966 case in which the Supreme Court upheld its constitutionality.

AGE DISCRIMINATION IN EMPLOYMENT ACT OF 1967

This act bans employment discrimination based on age. It covers individuals who are forty and older and applies to employers with twenty or more employees.

TITLE IX OF THE EDUCATION AMENDMENTS OF 1972

This provision bars sex discrimination in federally funded education programs. It covers a range of programs, but it is probably best known for prohibiting sex discrimination in college sports.

AMERICANS WITH DISABILITIES ACT OF 1990

Signed into law by President George H. W. Bush, this law (often called the ADA) sought to eliminate discrimination against the disabled in the spheres of employment and public services and accommodations. It defines *disability* as "a physical or mental impairment that substantially limits one or more of the major life activities."

CIVIL RIGHTS ACT OF 1991

Congress enacted this law primarily to override several decisions issued by the Supreme Court during its 1988 term, all of which made it more difficult for litigants to challenge discriminatory employment practices in the employment context. Legislators thought the Court's decisions had "weakened the scope and effectiveness of Federal civil rights protections" and set out to strengthen them.

SOURCES: Jody Feder, *Federal Civil Rights Statutes: A Primer*, CRS Report for Congress, September 9, 2005; William N. Eskridge Jr., Philip P. Frickey, and Elizabeth Garrett, *Cases and Materials on Legislation* (St. Paul, MN: West, 2001).

---

holding that any legislation based on the Fourteenth Amendment could regulate only discrimination promoted by state action. Discrimination by private individuals was not covered by the amendment, and, therefore, Congress could not prohibit it through an enforcement statute.

Congress eventually was able to pierce the private discrimination veil by finding a different constitutional grant of power upon which to base the Civil Rights Act of 1964. The most comprehensive civil rights statute ever, the law regulated discrimination in employment, education, and public accommodations. It placed restrictions on federal appropriations and programs to ensure that nondiscrimination principles were followed in any activity supported by the U.S. government. The act outlawed discrimination based not only on race but on other factors as well, such as sex, national origin, and religion. Much of what was regulated by the statute was private behavior, including prohibitions of discrimination by restaurants, hotels, and other privately run public accommodations. Rather than the Fourteenth Amendment, Congress used the commerce clause of Article I. That clause gives the national legislature the power to regulate interstate commerce, and the provisions of the 1964 Civil

Rights Act apply to all activities in interstate commerce. The Supreme Court upheld the constitutionality of the law and gave it increased effectiveness by broadly defining what is considered to be within interstate commerce.[7]

Since then, Congress has expanded the scope of federal regulation over civil rights by passing amendments to the 1964 act and by enacting additional legislation (see Box IV-1). For example, the Civil Rights Act of 1968 attempted to remove discrimination in the sale, rental, or financing of housing, and the Americans with Disabilities Act of 1990 extended federal protections to the disabled in employment, public services, and access to public places. As a result of such legislative actions, a large portion of federal civil rights law is based on congressional statutes rather than on constitutional provisions.

Federal civil rights laws provide great opportunities for those who wish to challenge discriminatory behavior. Not only do these statutes regulate private-sector discrimination, but they also frequently impose thresholds of proof that are easier to satisfy than those the Supreme Court requires for constitutional challenges. For example, under the civil rights laws a worker claiming employment discrimination based on race may not have to establish discriminatory intent (a requirement for a violation of the Constitution) but may instead submit statistical evidence that, regardless of intent, an employer's policies have a racially disparate impact. Because of the growth of civil rights laws, the federal courts today hear many more cases involving alleged violations of civil rights statutes than cases claiming a violation of the Constitution.

THE FIFTEENTH AMENDMENT

The Fifteenth Amendment removed race as a condition by which the right to vote could be denied. Unlike the Thirteenth Amendment, which was almost self-executing, the policy expressed so clearly in the Fifteenth Amendment in 1870 did not become a reality until almost a century later. Stubborn resistance by the southern states denied black citizens full participatory rights. It was not until the 1960s, when the nation renewed its commitment to civil rights, that equality in voting rights was substantially achieved.

---

7. In *Heart of Atlanta Motel v. United States* (1964) the Supreme Court upheld the public accommodations provisions of the law, thereby giving constitutional approval for Congress to expand civil rights protections by using the commerce power.

The long delay in implementing the principles of the Fifteenth Amendment has several explanations. Although the nation's leaders seemed unshakably committed to equality right after the Civil War, they soon turned their attention to other matters. Issues ranging from political corruption to the nation's industrialization moved to the top of the political agenda. At the same time, the white power structure of the prewar South began to reassert itself. Although forced to accept the Civil War amendments as a condition of rejoining the Union, the southern states survived Reconstruction and, once freed from the direct supervision of their victors, began to reinstitute discriminatory laws. Slavery was never again seriously considered, but, in its place, racial segregation became the official policy. For years the federal legislative and executive branches showed little interest in pursuing civil rights issues. And, even though the Supreme Court issued several important rulings, the nation did not turn its attention to freedom from discrimination and full participatory rights for all until the civil rights movement gained momentum in the 1960s.

The Fifteenth Amendment extended significant powers to the federal government to preserve fairness and equality in the political process. So too did the Nineteenth, Twenty-fourth, and Twenty-sixth Amendments, which, respectively, expanded the electorate by limiting state discrimination based on sex or on the ability to pay a tax and by lowering the voting age. From the enforcement provisions of these four voting rights amendments, Congress has passed a number of statutes ensuring the integrity of the election process. The most important of these is the Voting Rights Act of 1965, which has been strengthened by amendment over the years. This statute provided the machinery for federal enforcement and prosecution of voting rights violations. Its provisions have been the catalyst for significant growth in voter registration rates among segments of the population where political participation historically has been depressed.

Because this volume deals with constitutional law, our discussion of the various forms of discrimination focuses on the civil rights guarantees provided in the three Civil War amendments. As you read the cases and narrative to follow, however, keep in mind that in many areas Congress has passed statutes that extend those constitutional provisions to create various legal rights that go well beyond protections included in the Constitution itself.

13 Discrimination

I N A 1987 ADDRESS, delivered amid the planning for the bicentennial celebration of the Constitution, Justice Thurgood Marshall said the document was "defective from the start," that its first words—"We the People"—left out the majority of Americans because the phrase did not include women and blacks. He further alleged:

These omissions were intentional. . . . The record of the Framers' debates on the slave question is especially clear: The Southern states acceded to the demands of the New England states for giving Congress broad power to regulate commerce in exchange for the right to continue the slave trade. The economic interests of the regions coalesced.

One does not have to agree with Marshall to believe that discrimination has been a difficult and persistent problem for the United States since its beginnings. Although the founders were considered the vanguard of enlightened politics, different treatment based on race, economic status, religious affiliation, and sex was the rule in the colonies. And since those early years of nationhood, issues of discrimination have persisted on the country's political agenda. During the nineteenth century, slavery eroded national unity. Although officially settled by the Civil War and the constitutional amendments that followed, racial inequity did not disappear. Rather, it continued through the Jim Crow era and the organized civil rights struggle, and it persists today.

Recent years have seen the national spotlight turned on claims of unfair treatment based on sex, sexual orientation, national origin, economic status, age, and physical ability. Attempts to force government to address these claims have engendered counterclaims by those who fear that a government overly sensitive to the needs of minorities will deprive the majority of its rights. With each new argument, the issues become more complex. This chapter explores the kinds of discrimination that have occurred (and continue to occur) in American society and how the Supreme Court has responded. We also consider contemporary remedies that have been offered to blunt the effects of past discrimination.

RACIAL DISCRIMINATION

The institution of slavery is a blight on the record of a nation that otherwise has led the way in protecting individual rights. From 1619, when the first slaves were brought to Jamestown, to the ratification of the Civil War amendments 250 years later, people of African ancestry were considered an inferior race; they could be bought, sold, and used as personal property. Although some states extended various civil and political rights to emancipated slaves and their descendants, the national Constitution did not recognize African Americans as full citizens. In *Scott v. Sandford* (1857), Chief Justice Roger Brooke Taney, delivering the opinion of the Court, described the prevailing view of blacks when the Constitution was written:

They had for more than a century before been regarded as beings of an inferior order, and altogether unfit to associate with the white race, either in social or political relations; and so far inferior, that they had no rights which the white man was bound to respect; and that the negro might justly and lawfully be reduced to slavery for his benefit. He was bought and sold, and treated as an ordinary article of merchandise and traffic, whenever a profit could be made by it. This opinion was at that time fixed and universal in the civilized portion of the white race.

The Court's decision in *Scott* interpreted the Constitution in a way consistent with this view and helped set the stage for the Civil War. The ruling, which held that a black slave could not become a full member of the political community and be entitled to the constitutional privileges of citizens, undermined the legitimacy of the Court and damaged Taney's reputation forever. Union victories on the battlefield reunited the country, and the Thirteenth, Fourteenth, and Fifteenth Amendments ended slavery, guaranteed equal protection of the laws, and conferred full national citizenship on African Americans.

Congress moved with dispatch to give force to the new amendments, but the Supreme Court did not act with the same level of zeal. Although the justices supported the claims of the newly emancipated blacks in some cases, they did not construe the new amendments broadly, nor did they enthusiastically support new legislation designed to enforce them. In the **Slaughterhouse Cases** (1873), for example, the Court interpreted the Fourteenth Amendment's privileges or immunities clause quite narrowly. A broader view might have provided opportunities for women and blacks to bring cases based on this clause to the Court. In *United States v. Harris* and the **Civil Rights Cases**, both decided in 1883, the justices nullified major provisions of the Ku Klux Klan Act of 1871 and the Civil Rights Act of 1875 for attempting to prevent discriminatory actions by private institutions. It was clear that the battle for legal equality of the races was far from over.

"Separate but Equal"

By the end of the nineteenth century, the Supreme Court still had not answered what was perhaps the most important question arising from the Fourteenth Amendment: What is equal protection? As the vitality of the Reconstruction Acts and federal efforts to enforce them gradually waned, the political forces of the old order began to reassert control in the South. From the 1880s to the 1950s, a period known as the Jim Crow era, what progress had been made toward achieving racial equality not only came to a halt but also began to be reversed. The South, where 90 percent of the black minority population lived, began to enact laws that reimposed an inferior legal status on African Americans and required a strict separation of the races. Northern liberals were of little help. With the battle against slavery won, they turned their attention to other issues.

Although the Constitution made it clear that slavery was dead and the right to vote could not be denied on the basis of race, the validity of many other racially based state actions remained unresolved. With more conservative political forces gaining power in Congress, it was left to the Court, still smarting from the *Scott* debacle, to give meaning to the phrase *equal protection of the laws.*

The most important case of this period was *Plessy v. Ferguson* (1896), which forced the justices to confront directly the meaning of equality under the Constitution. At odds were the equal protection clause of the Fourteenth Amendment and a host of segregation statutes by then in force in the southern and border states. While reading *Plessy,* note that the Court uses the reasonableness standard (rational basis test) to interpret the equal protection clause. Ironically, Justice Henry B. Brown, a Lincoln Republican and New Englander who supported the abolitionist movement, wrote the majority opinion upholding the separation standards of the South. Justice John Marshall Harlan (I), an aristocratic Kentuckian whose family had owned slaves, wrote the lone dissent. Harlan's opinion is considered a classic and one of the most prophetic dissents ever registered.

Plessy v. Ferguson

163 U.S. 537 (1896)
http://laws.findlaw.com/US/163/537.html
Vote: 7 (Brown, Field, Fuller, Gray, Peckham, Shiras, White)
    1 (Harlan)

OPINION OF THE COURT: *Brown*
DISSENTING OPINION: *Harlan*
NOT PARTICIPATING: *Brewer*

FACTS:

Following the lead of Florida, Mississippi, and Texas, Louisiana passed a statute in 1890 ordering the separation of the races on all railroads. In response, a group of New Orleans residents of black and mixed-race heritage formed the Citizens Committee to Test the Constitutionality of the Separate Car Law.[1] The railroads, which found compliance with the segregation law costly, supported the group's efforts. Attempts to have the judiciary invalidate the statute were partially successful when the Louisiana Supreme Court struck down the law as it applied to passengers crossing state lines because it placed an unconstitutional burden on interstate commerce. This decision, however, left unanswered the question of segregated travel wholly within the state's borders.

The committee hired Albion Tourgée, a former Union army officer, to lead the legal attack on the railroad segregation statute. Tourgée, who had served as a journalist, lawyer, and judge in North Carolina and New York, was one of the nation's most prominent civil rights advocates. Part of his strategy was to select an individual of mixed-race background to violate the segregation statute as it applied to intrastate travel. Homer Adolph Plessy, who had been active in civil rights efforts in New Orleans for some time, was selected. Plessy described himself as being "of seven-eighths Caucasian and one-eighth African blood."

On June 7, 1892, Plessy bought a first-class rail ticket from New Orleans to Covington, Louisiana. He took a seat in a car reserved for white passengers. Tourgée and the committee had enlisted the cooperation of the railroad to have Plessy arrested for violating the statute. He was taken off the train and held in a New Orleans jail to await trial.

Tourgée moved to block the trial on the ground that the segregation law was in violation of the U.S. Constitution's Thirteenth and Fourteenth Amendments. Judge John Ferguson denied the motion, and appeal was taken to the Louisiana Supreme Court. The state high court, under the leadership of Chief Justice Francis Tillou Nicholls, who, as governor two years earlier, had signed the segregation statute into law, denied Plessy's petition, and the case moved to the U.S. Supreme Court.

Attorney and equal rights activist Albion Tourgée, who argued Homer Plessy's case and lost in the Supreme Court. Justice Harlan's lone dissent said that the Constitution must be color-blind, a phrase suggested by Tourgée's brief.

For the plaintiff-in-error, Homer Adolph Plessy:

- The statute is manifestly directed at the black race. It imposes a badge of servitude.
- The statute does not define the races. The law inappropriately gives railroad conductors the discretion to determine what constitutes "white" and "colored" people and to assign individuals to a racial group.
- The law violates the privileges or immunities of U.S. citizenship because it restricts the right of free travel, and it deprives an ejected paying passenger liberty and property without due process of law.
- The law violates basic human rights by separating husband from wife and mother from child in the case of interracial families.

For the defendant-in-error, J. H. Ferguson:

- The regulation of intrastate commerce lies exclusively within the state's police powers.
- A separation of passengers solely on the basis of race is a reasonable regulation, provided that accommodations are equal in quality and convenience and the same price is charged.

---

1. For a more complete description of the facts in this case, see Ellen Holmes Pearson, "Homer Plessy: Validation of Jim Crow," in *100 Americans Making Constitutional History,* ed. Melvin I. Urofsky (Washington, DC: CQ Press, 2004), 159–161.

- There is no discrimination based on race. Individuals of both races equally are required to ride in cars assigned them. The cars were equal in quality of accommodations.
- The law imposes no form of servitude or badge of slavery.

MR. JUSTICE BROWN DELIVERED THE OPINION OF THE COURT.

This case turns upon the constitutionality of an act of the General Assembly of the State of Louisiana, passed in 1890, providing for separate railway carriages for the white and colored races. . . .

By the Fourteenth Amendment, all persons born or naturalized in the United States, and subject to the jurisdiction thereof, are made citizens of the United States and of the State wherein they reside; and the States are forbidden from making or enforcing any law which shall abridge the privileges or immunities of citizens of the United States, or shall deprive any person of life, liberty or property without due process of law, or deny to any person within their jurisdiction the equal protection of the laws. . . .

The object of the amendment was undoubtedly to enforce the absolute equality of the two races before the law, but in the nature of things it could not have been intended to abolish distinctions based upon color, or to enforce social, as distinguished from political equality, or a commingling of the two races upon terms unsatisfactory to either. Laws permitting, and even requiring, their separation in places where they are liable to be brought into contact do not necessarily imply the inferiority of either race to the other, and have been generally, if not universally, recognized as within the competency of the state legislatures in the exercise of their police power. The most common instance of this is connected with the establishment of separate schools for white and colored children, which has been held to be a valid exercise of the legislative power even by courts of States where the political rights of the colored race have been longest and most earnestly enforced.

One of the earliest of these cases is that of *Roberts v. City of Boston* [1849], in which the Supreme Judicial Court of Massachusetts held that the general school committee of Boston had power to make provision for the instruction of colored children in separate schools established exclusively for them, and to prohibit their attendance upon the other schools. . . .

Laws forbidding the intermarriage of the two races may be said in a technical sense to interfere with the freedom of contract, and yet have been universally recognized as within the police power of the State.

The distinction between laws interfering with the political equality of the negro and those requiring the separation of the two races in schools, theatres and railway carriages has been frequently drawn by this court. Thus in *Strauder v. West Virginia* [1880] it was held that a law of West Virginia limiting to white male persons, 21 years of age and citizens of the State, the right to sit upon juries, was a discrimination which implied a legal inferiority in civil society, which lessened the security of the right of the colored race, and was a step toward reducing them to a condition of servility. Indeed, the right of a colored man that, in the selection of jurors to pass upon his life, liberty, and property, there shall be no exclusion of his race, and no discrimination against them because of color, has been asserted in a number of cases. . . .

So far, then, as a conflict with the Fourteenth Amendment is concerned, the case reduces itself to the question whether the statute of Louisiana is a reasonable regulation, and with respect to this there must necessarily be a large discretion on the part of the legislature. In determining the question of reasonableness it is at liberty to act with reference to the established usages, customs and traditions of the people, and with a view to the promotion of their comfort, and the preservation of the public peace and good order. Gauged by this standard, we cannot say that a law which authorizes or even requires the separation of the two races in public conveyances is unreasonable, or more obnoxious to the Fourteenth Amendment than the acts of Congress requiring separate schools for colored children in the District of Columbia, the constitutionality of which does not seem to have been questioned, or the corresponding acts of state legislatures.

We consider the underlying fallacy of the plaintiff's argument to consist in the assumption that the enforced separation of the two races stamps the colored race with a badge of inferiority. If this be so, it is not by reason of anything found in the act, but solely because the colored race chooses to put that construction upon it. The argument necessarily assumes that if, as has been more than once the case, and is not unlikely to be so again, the colored race should become the dominant power in the state legislature, and should enact a law in precisely similar terms, it would thereby relegate the white race to an inferior position. We imagine that the white race, at least, would not acquiesce in this assumption. The argument also assumes that social prejudices may be overcome by legislation, and that equal rights cannot be secured to the negro except by an enforced commingling of the two races. We cannot accept this proposition. If the two races are to meet upon terms of social equality, it must be the result of natural affinities, a mutual appreciation of each other's merits and a voluntary consent of individuals. . . . Legislation is powerless to eradicate racial instincts or to abolish distinctions based upon physical differences, and the attempt to do so can only result in accentuating the difficulties of the present situation. If the civil and political rights of both races be equal one cannot be inferior to the other civilly or politically. If one race be inferior to the other socially, the Constitution of the United States cannot put them upon the same plane. . . .

The judgment of the court below is, therefore,

Affirmed.

MR. JUSTICE HARLAN dissenting.

In respect of civil rights, common to all citizens, the Constitution of the United States does not, I think, permit any public authority to know the race of those entitled to be protected in the enjoyment of such rights. Every true man has pride of race, and under appropriate circumstances when the rights of others, his equals before the law, are not to be affected, it is his privilege to express such pride and to take such action based upon it as to him seems proper. But I deny that any legislative body or judicial tribunal may have regard to the race of citizens when the civil rights of those citizens are involved. Indeed, such legislation, as that here in question, is inconsistent not only with that equality of rights which pertains to citizenship, National and State, but with the personal liberty enjoyed by every one within the United States.

The Thirteenth Amendment does not permit the withholding or the deprivation of any right necessarily inhering in freedom. It not only struck down the institution of slavery as previously existing in the United States, but it prevents the imposition of any burdens or disabilities that constitute badges of slavery or servitude. It decreed universal civil freedom in this country. This court has so adjudged. But that amendment having been found inadequate to the protection of the rights of those who had been in slavery, it was followed

by the Fourteenth Amendment, which added greatly to the dignity and glory of American citizenship, and to the security of personal liberty. . . . These two amendments, if enforced according to their true intent and meaning, will protect all the civil rights that pertain to freedom and citizenship. Finally, and to the end that no citizen should be denied, on account of his race, the privilege of participating in the political control of his country, it was declared by the Fifteenth Amendment that "the right of citizens of the United States to vote shall not be denied or abridged by the United States or by any State on account of race, color or previous condition of servitude."

These notable additions to the fundamental law were welcomed by the friends of liberty throughout the world. They removed the race line from our governmental systems. They had, as this court has said, a common purpose, namely, to secure "to a race recently emancipated, a race that through many generations have been held in slavery, all the civil rights that the superior race enjoy." . . .

If a State can prescribe, as a rule of civil conduct, that whites and blacks shall not travel as passengers in the same railroad coach, why may it not so regulate the use of the streets of its cities and towns as to compel white citizens to keep on one side of a street and black citizens to keep on the other? Why may it not, upon like grounds, punish whites and blacks who ride together in street cars or in open vehicles on a public road or street? Why may it not require sheriffs to assign whites to one side of a courtroom and blacks to the other? And why may it not also prohibit the commingling of the two races in the galleries of legislative halls or in public assemblages convened for the consideration of the political questions of the day? Further, if this statute of Louisiana is consistent with the personal liberty of citizens, why may not the State require the separation in railroad coaches of native and naturalized citizens of the United States, or of Protestants and Roman Catholics? . . .

The white race deems itself to be the dominant race in this country. And so it is, in prestige, in achievements, in education, in wealth and in power. So, I doubt not, it will continue to be for all time, if it remains true to its great heritage and holds fast to the principles of constitutional liberty. But in view of the Constitution, in the eye of the law, there is in this country no superior, dominant, ruling class of citizens. There is no caste here. Our Constitution is color-blind, and neither knows nor tolerates classes among citizens. In respect of civil rights, all citizens are equal before the law. The humblest is the peer of the most powerful. The law regards man as man, and takes no account of his surroundings or of his color when his civil rights as guaranteed by the supreme law of the land are involved. It is, therefore, to be regretted that this high tribunal, the final expositor of the fundamental law of the land, has reached the conclusion that it is competent for a State to regulate the enjoyment by citizens of their civil rights solely upon the basis of race.

In my opinion, the judgment this day rendered will, in time, prove to be quite as pernicious as the decision made by this tribunal in the *Dred Scott Case*. . . .

I am of opinion that the statute of Louisiana is inconsistent with the personal liberty of citizens, white and black, in that State, and hostile to both the spirit and letter of the Constitution of the United States. If laws of like character should be enacted in the several States of the Union, the effect would be in the highest degree mischievous. Slavery, as an institution tolerated by law, would, it is true, have disappeared from our country, but there would remain a power in the States, by sinister legislation, to interfere with the full enjoyment of the blessings of freedom; to regulate civil rights, common to all citizens, upon the basis of race; and to place in a condition of legal inferiority a large body of American citizens, now constituting a part of the political community called the People of the United States, for whom, and by whom through representatives, our government is administered. Such a system is inconsistent with the guarantee given by the Constitution to each State of a republican form of government, and may be stricken down by Congressional action, or by the courts in the discharge of their solemn duty to maintain the supreme law of the land, anything in the constitution or laws of any State to the contrary notwithstanding.

For the reason stated, I am constrained to withhold my assent from the opinion and judgment of the majority.

The *Plessy* decision's "separate but equal" doctrine ushered in full-scale segregation in the southern and border states. According to the Court, separation did not constitute inequality under the Fourteenth Amendment; if the facilities and opportunities were somewhat similar, the equal protection clause permitted the separation of the races. Encouraged by the ruling, the legislatures of the South passed a wide variety of statutes to keep blacks segregated from the white population. The segregation laws affected transportation, schools, hospitals, parks, public restrooms and water fountains, libraries, cemeteries, recreational facilities, hotels, restaurants, and almost every other public and commercial facility.

These laws, coupled with segregated private lives, inevitably resulted in two separate societies.

Early Battles for Equality

During the first half of the twentieth century, the separate but equal doctrine dominated race relations law. The southern states continued to pass and enforce segregationist laws, largely insulated from legal attack. Over the years, however, it became clear that the "equality" part of the separate but equal doctrine was being ignored.

As the inequality of segregated public facilities grew worse, the disadvantages of the black population increased. The disparities extended to almost every area of life, but they were felt most keenly in education. Whites and blacks were given access to public schools, but the black schools, at all levels, received support and funding far inferior to that of the white institutions.

These conditions spurred the growth of civil rights groups dedicated to eradicating segregation. None was more prominent than the National Association for the Advancement of Colored People (NAACP) and its affiliate, the Legal Defense and Educational Fund (commonly referred to as the Legal Defense Fund, or LDF). Thurgood Marshall, who had been associated with the NAACP since he graduated first in his class at Howard University Law School, became the head of the LDF in 1940 and initiated a twenty-year campaign in the courts to win equal rights for black Americans.

Not surprisingly, one of the NAACP's earliest legal victories, ***Missouri ex rel. Gaines v. Canada*** (1938), concerned public education. Lloyd Gaines, a Missouri resident, had graduated from the all-black Lincoln University and applied for admission to the University of Missouri's law school. He was denied admission because of his race. Missouri did not have a law school for its African American citizens, so the state offered to send qualified black students to law school in a neighboring state that did not have segregationist policies. The Supreme Court concluded, 7–2, that the Missouri plan to pay out-of-state tuition did not meet the obligations imposed by the equal protection clause. The state then moved to establish a law school for blacks at Lincoln. Although *Gaines* imposed little substantive change, it served notice that segregation policies were about to undergo close evaluation. At the time, this idea had little popular support. Polls showed that two-thirds of Americans believed that blacks and whites should attend separate schools. By the late 1940s, however, change was in the air. Some of the impetus grew out of the

Under the rule of law established in **Plessy v. Ferguson (1896)**, *states could require racial separation if facilities for blacks and whites were of equal quality. In public education, black schools were not always equal to those reserved for whites.*

nation's experiences during World War II. With the support and approval of Presidents Franklin D. Roosevelt and Harry S. Truman, strict separation in the armed forces was reduced, and black and white soldiers fought together on the battlefields. At home, workers of both races joined to produce the arms and equipment necessary to support the war effort.

When the war was over, black soldiers returned to the United States intent on pursuing better lives for themselves and their families. Once they had experienced something different, there was little likelihood that blacks would be satisfied with a segregated society. Many whites, having had their first substantial contacts with blacks during the war, began questioning the wisdom of segregation.

It was in this new political climate that the LDF achieved some of its most impressive victories. One of those came in *Sweatt v. Painter* (1950), in which Marshall and his staff launched a frontal attack on the separate but equal doctrine in public school education.[2]

2. Another came in *Shelley v. Kraemer* (1948), involving restrictive covenants, which prevented private property owners from selling their homes to nonwhites. We consider that case in the section on state action in race discrimination.

They hoped the Court would overturn *Plessy,* but at a minimum they demanded that the justices ensure that facilities and opportunities were truly equal. Although the Court's decision was not everything civil rights advocates hoped for, it marked another significant step in the development of race relations law. As you read Chief Justice Frederick M. Vinson's opinion for the Court, note the emphasis he places on the importance of equal facilities for black and white students.

Sweatt v. Painter

339 U.S. 629 (1950)
http://laws.findlaw.com/US/339/629.html
Vote: 9 (Black, Burton, Clark, Douglas, Frankfurter,
Jackson, Minton, Reed, Vinson)
    0

OPINION OF THE COURT: *Vinson*

FACTS:

In 1946, H. M. Sweatt, a Texas postal worker, applied for admission to the racially segregated University of Texas Law School. His application was rejected on the exclusive ground that he was black. Because there was no Texas law school that admitted African Americans, Sweatt filed suit demanding that the University of

Texas admit him. Given the *Gaines* precedent, the trial court judge was aware that Sweatt had a strong case. Rather than grant Sweatt's motion, however, he continued the case for six months to allow the state time to address the problem. The state hastily established an interim law school for blacks in Austin that was to open in February 1947. A permanent black law school, part of the Texas State University for Negroes, was later to open in Houston.

When the six-month period ended in December 1946, the judge dismissed Sweatt's complaint on the ground that the state was meeting its obligations under the equal protection clause. Sweatt served notice of appeal, refusing to attend the new school. Supported by the NAACP and the LDF, Sweatt challenged the school as substantially inferior to the University of Texas Law School. The Texas courts concluded that the two schools were "substantially equivalent," and appeal was taken to the U.S. Supreme Court, where Sweatt asked the justices to reconsider *Plessy*'s separate but equal principle. Sweatt's appeal was supported by amicus curiae briefs submitted by the U.S. government as well as by a number of organizations such as the American Federation of Teachers and the American Jewish Committee. Eleven southern and border states filed briefs supporting Texas.

ARGUMENTS:

For the petitioner, Heman Marion Sweatt:

- There is no rational basis for the assumption underlying the Texas law that the races have different intellectual potentialities and therefore should be educated in separate schools.
- *Plessy v. Ferguson* does not apply because the separate facilities here are not equal in terms of physical plant, budget, faculty, library, reputation, etc.
- If the Court decides that *Plessy* is applicable, it should reconsider that precedent and overrule it.

For the respondent, Theophilus Shickel Painter, President of the University of Texas:

- *Plessy v. Ferguson* and subsequent decisions pertaining to higher education hold that a state may provide equal education to all its citizens while separating them on the basis of race.
- The history of the Fourteenth Amendment does not indicate it was intended to prevent the state from providing separate and equal facilities for white and Negro students.

- There is ample evidence that the admissions requirements, curriculum, classrooms, faculty, etc. of the Texas State University for Negroes Law School and the University of Texas Law School are equal.

 MR. CHIEF JUSTICE VINSON DELIVERED THE OPINION OF THE COURT.

This case and *McLaurin v. Oklahoma State Regents* [1950] present different aspects of this general question: To what extent does the Equal Protection Clause of the Fourteenth Amendment limit the power of a state to distinguish between students of different races in professional and graduate education in a state university? . . .

The University of Texas Law School, from which petitioner was excluded, was staffed by a faculty of sixteen full-time and three part-time professors, some of whom are nationally recognized authorities in their field. Its student body numbered 850. The library contained over 65,000 volumes. Among the other facilities available to the students were a law review, moot court facilities, scholarship funds, and Order of the Coif affiliation. The school's alumni occupy the most distinguished positions in the private practice of the law and in the public life of the State. It may properly be considered one of the nation's ranking law schools.

The law school for Negroes which was to have opened in February, 1947, would have had no independent faculty or library. The teaching was to be carried on by four members of the University of Texas Law School faculty, who were to maintain their offices at the University of Texas while teaching at both institutions. Few of the 10,000 volumes ordered for the library had arrived; nor was there any full-time librarian. The school lacked accreditation.

Since the trial of this case, respondents report the opening of a law school at the Texas State University for Negroes. It is apparently on the road to full accreditation. It has a faculty of five full-time professors; a student body of 23; a library of some 16,500 volumes serviced by a full-time staff; a practice court and legal aid association; and one alumnus who has become a member of the Texas Bar.

Whether the University of Texas Law School is compared with the original or the new law school for Negroes, we cannot find substantial equality in the educational opportunities offered white and Negro law students by the State. In terms of number of the faculty, variety of courses and opportunity for specialization, size of student body, scope of the library, availability of law review and similar activities, the University of Texas

Law School is superior. What is more important, the University of Texas Law School possesses to a far greater degree those qualities which are incapable of objective measurement but which make for greatness in a law school. Such qualities, to name but a few, include reputation of the faculty, experience of the administration, position and influence of the alumni, standing in the community, traditions and prestige. It is difficult to believe that one who had a free choice between these law schools would consider the question close.

Moreover, although the law is a highly learned profession, we are well aware that it is an intensely practical one. The law school, the proving ground for legal learning and practice, cannot be effective in isolation from the individuals and institutions with which the law interacts. Few students and no one who has practiced law would choose to study in an academic vacuum, removed from the interplay of ideas and the exchange of views with which the law is concerned. The law school to which Texas is willing to admit petitioner excludes from its student body members of the racial groups which number 85% of the population of the State and include most of the lawyers, witnesses, jurors, judges and other officials with whom petitioner will inevitably be dealing when he becomes a member of the Texas Bar. With such a substantial and significant segment of society excluded, we cannot conclude that the education offered petitioner is substantially equal to that which he would receive if admitted to the University of Texas Law School.

It may be argued that excluding petitioner from that school is no different from excluding white students from the new law school. This contention overlooks realities. It is unlikely that a member of a group so decisively in the majority, attending a school with rich traditions and prestige which only a history of consistently maintained excellence could command, would claim that the opportunities afforded him for legal education were unequal to those held open to petitioner. That such a claim, if made, would be dishonored by the State, is no answer. "Equal protection of the laws is not achieved through indiscriminate imposition of inequalities." *Shelley v. Kraemer* (1948).

It is fundamental that these cases concern rights which are personal and present. This Court has stated unanimously that "The State must provide [legal education] for [petitioner] in conformity with the equal protection clause of the Fourteenth Amendment and provide it as soon as it does for applicants of any other group." . . . In *Missouri ex rel. Gaines v. Canada* (1938), the Court, speaking through Chief Justice Hughes, declared that "petitioner's right was

a personal one. It was as an individual that he was entitled to the equal protection of the laws, and the State was bound to furnish him within its borders facilities for legal education substantially equal to those which the State there afforded for persons of the white race, whether or not other negroes sought the same opportunity." These are the only cases in this Court which present the issue of the constitutional validity of race distinctions in state-supported graduate and professional education.

In accordance with these cases, petitioner may claim his full constitutional right: legal education equivalent to that offered by the State to students of other races. Such education is not available to him in a separate law school as offered by the State. We cannot, therefore, agree with respondents that the doctrine of *Plessy v. Ferguson* (1896) requires affirmance of the judgment below. Nor need we reach petitioner's contention that *Plessy v. Ferguson* should be reexamined in the light of contemporary knowledge respecting the purposes of the Fourteenth Amendment and the effects of racial segregation.

We hold that the Equal Protection Clause of the Fourteenth Amendment requires that petitioner be admitted to the University of Texas Law School. The judgment is reversed and the cause is remanded for proceedings not inconsistent with this opinion.

Reversed.

The same day the Court decided *Sweatt,* it also handed the LDF a victory in **McLaurin v. Oklahoma State Regents** (1950), which took another step toward racial equality in higher education. *McLaurin* highlights an interesting aspect of the desegregation battle—the fear held by many segregationists that blacks and whites in school together would lead to interracial dating and marriage.[3] To comply with judicial decisions, the University of Oklahoma admitted black graduate students when these students could not obtain the desired degrees at minority schools. However, to protect against the possibilities of interracial marriage, the university restricted blacks to segregated areas of classrooms, libraries, and dining halls. Fraternization between the races was almost impossible.

To neutralize this fear of interracial marriage, the LDF chose George W. McLaurin to challenge the university's segregationist policies. McLaurin was a black graduate

---

3. For a discussion of this issue, see Richard Kluger, *Simple Justice,* rev. ed. (New York: Knopf, 2004), especially chap. 12.

student, already holding a master's degree, who was pursuing a doctorate in education. What made him perfect to challenge the separatist regulations was that McLaurin was sixty-eight years old and unlikely to marry a fellow student. Although McLaurin's suit was unsuccessful in the lower courts, the Supreme Court unanimously found Oklahoma's system in violation of the equal protection clause.

Race Discrimination and the Warren Court: The Demise of *Plessy*

At the beginning of the 1950s, conditions were ripe for a final assault on the half-century-old separate but equal doctrine. Civil rights groups continued to marshal legal arguments and political support to eliminate segregation. Legal challenges to a wide array of discriminatory laws were filed throughout the country, and the Justice Department under President Truman supported these efforts. The Supreme Court, through its unanimous rulings in favor of racial equality in higher education, appeared on the verge of seriously considering an end to *Plessy.* In addition, a significant leadership change took place on the Court. Chief Justice Vinson died on September 8, 1953, and was replaced by California governor Earl Warren, who, in contrast to his predecessor, was comfortable with activist judicial policies.

All of these factors combined to produce *Brown v. Board of Education of Topeka, Kansas* (1954), which many consider to be the Supreme Court's most significant decision of the twentieth century. Unlike earlier civil rights cases that involved relatively small professional and graduate education programs, the *Brown* case challenged official racial segregation in the nation's primary and secondary public schools. The decision affected thousands of school districts concentrated primarily in the southern and border states. Moreover, it was apparent to all that the precedent to be set for public education would be extended to other areas as well.

As you read Warren's opinion for a unanimous Court, note how the concept of equality has changed. No longer does the Court examine only physical facilities and tangible items such as buildings, libraries, teacher qualifications, and funding levels; instead, it emphasizes the intangible negative impact of racial segregation on children. Warren's opinion includes a footnote listing social science references as authorities for his arguments. The opinion was criticized for citing sociological and psychological studies to support the Court's conclusions rather than confining the analysis exclusively to legal arguments. Are these criticisms valid? Should the Court take social science evidence into account in arriving at constitutional decisions? Note how similar Warren's opinion is to Justice Harlan's lone dissent in *Plessy.*

Brown v. Board of Education (I)

347 U.S. 483 (1954)
http://laws.findlaw.com/US/347/483.html
Vote: 9 (Black, Burton, Clark, Douglas, Frankfurter,
*   Jackson, Minton, Reed, Warren)*
*   0*

OPINION OF THE COURT: *Warren*

FACTS:

The Court consolidated five cases involving similar issues for consideration at the same time; *Brown v. Board of Education* was one of these cases. Part of the

Linda Brown at age nine. Her father joined the suit that led to the desegregation of the nation's public schools. Oliver Brown was upset that Linda had to travel two and a half miles to school even though the family lived close to Sumner, a white school. Despite their victory, Linda never went to Sumner School; by the time the decision was rendered, she was old enough for the junior high, a school that had been integrated since 1879.

total desegregation litigation strategy orchestrated by Marshall and funded by the NAACP, these cases challenged the segregated public schools of Delaware, Kansas, South Carolina, Virginia, and the District of Columbia. The most prominent lawyers in the civil rights movement, Spottswood Robinson III, Louis Redding, Jack Greenberg, Constance Baker Motley, Robert Carter, and James Nabrit Jr., prepared them. As Marshall had expected, the suits were unsuccessful at the trial level, with the lower courts relying on *Plessy* as precedent. The leading lawyer for the states was John W. Davis, a prominent constitutional attorney who had been a Democratic candidate for president in 1924. (Davis had reportedly once been offered a nomination to the Court by President Warren G. Harding.)

Linda Carol Brown was an eight-year-old black girl whose father, Oliver Brown, was an assistant pastor of a Topeka church. The Browns lived in a predominantly white neighborhood only a short distance from an elementary school. Under Kansas law, cities with populations of more than fifteen thousand were permitted to administer racially segregated schools, and the Topeka Board of Education required its elementary schools to be racially divided. The Browns did not want their daughter to be sent to the school reserved for black students. It was far from home, and they considered the trip dangerous. In addition, their neighborhood school was a good one, and the Browns wanted their daughter to receive an integrated education. They filed suit challenging the segregated school system as violating their daughter's rights under the equal protection clause of the Fourteenth Amendment.

The Brown appeal was joined by those from the other four suits, and the cases were argued in December 1952. The following June, the Court asked the cases to be reargued in December 1953, with special emphasis to be placed on a series of questions dealing with the history and meaning of the Fourteenth Amendment. This delay also allowed the newly appointed Earl Warren to participate fully in the decision. Six months later, on May 17, 1954, the Court issued its ruling.

ARGUMENTS:

For the appellants, Oliver Brown, et al.:

- When distinctions are imposed by the state based on race and color alone, the actions are patently arbitrary and capricious and in violation of the Fourteenth Amendment [*Yick Wo v. Hopkins* (1886), *Smith v. Allwright* (1944), *Sweatt v. Painter* (1950), etc.].

- The evolution of the Supreme Court's racial discrimination jurisprudence has rendered *Plessy v. Ferguson* no longer applicable.

- Social science evidence clearly establishes that official racial separation is detrimental to the segregated group no matter how equal the facilities. Among other adverse effects, segregation instills a sense of inferiority.

For the appellees, Board of Education of Topeka, Kansas, et al.:

- By any measure of the quality of physical facilities, curriculum, teacher training, and school transportation, the segregated schools in Topeka are equal.

- *Plessy v. Ferguson* remains good law and should control this case.

- There have been no findings that the specific children involved in this litigation have suffered any damages from attending segregated schools.

> **MR. CHIEF JUSTICE WARREN DELIVERED THE OPINION OF THE COURT.**

In each of the cases, minors of the Negro race, through their legal representatives, seek the aid of the courts in obtaining admission to the public schools of their community on a nonsegregated basis. In each instance, they had been denied admission to schools attended by white children under laws requiring or permitting segregation according to race. This segregation was alleged to deprive the plaintiffs of the equal protection of the laws under the Fourteenth Amendment. . . .

The plaintiffs contend that segregated public schools are not "equal" and cannot be made "equal," and that hence they are deprived of the equal protection of the laws. Because of the obvious importance of the question presented, the Court took jurisdiction. Argument was heard in the 1952 Term, and reargument was heard this Term on certain questions propounded by the Court.

Reargument was largely devoted to the circumstances surrounding the adoption of the Fourteenth Amendment in 1868. It covered exhaustively consideration of the Amendment in Congress, ratification by the states, then existing practices in racial segregation, and the views of proponents and opponents of the Amendment. This discussion and our own investigation convince us that, although these sources cast some light, it is not enough to resolve the problem with which we are faced. At best, they are inconclusive. . . .

An additional reason for the inconclusive nature of the Amendment's history, with respect to segregated schools, is the status of public education at that time. In the South, the movement toward free common schools, supported by general taxation, had not yet taken hold. Education of white children was largely in the hands of private groups. Education of Negroes was almost nonexistent, and practically all of the race were illiterate. In fact, any education of Negroes was forbidden by law in some states. Today, in contrast, many Negroes have achieved outstanding success in the arts and sciences as well as in the business and professional world. It is true that public school education at the time of the Amendment had advanced further in the North, but the effect of the Amendment on Northern States was generally ignored in the congressional debates. Even in the North, the conditions of public education did not approximate those existing today. The curriculum was usually rudimentary; ungraded schools were common in rural areas; the school term was but three months a year in many states; and compulsory school attendance was virtually unknown. As a consequence, it is not surprising that there should be so little in the history of the Fourteenth Amendment relating to its intended effect on public education.

In the first cases in this Court construing the Fourteenth Amendment, decided shortly after its adoption, the Court interpreted it as proscribing all state-imposed discriminations against the Negro race. The doctrine of "separate but equal" did not make its appearance in this Court until 1896 in the case of *Plessy v. Ferguson,* involving not education but transportation. American courts have since labored with the doctrine for over half a century. . . .

Here, unlike *Sweatt v. Painter,* there are findings below that the Negro and white schools involved have been equalized, or are being equalized, with respect to buildings, curricula, qualifications and salaries of teachers, and other "tangible" factors. Our decision, therefore, cannot turn on merely a comparison of these tangible factors in the Negro and white schools involved in each of the cases. We must look instead to the effect of segregation itself on public education.

In approaching this problem, we cannot turn the clock back to 1868 when the Amendment was adopted, or even to 1896 when *Plessy v. Ferguson* was written. We must consider public education in the light of its full development and its present place in American life throughout the Nation. Only in this way can it be determined if segregation in public schools deprives these plaintiffs of the equal protection of the laws.

Today, education is perhaps the most important function of state and local governments. Compulsory school attendance laws and the great expenditures for education both demonstrate our recognition of the importance of education to our democratic society. It is required in the performance of our most basic public responsibilities, even service in the armed forces. It is the very foundation of good citizenship. Today it is a principal instrument in awakening the child to cultural values, in preparing him for later professional training, and in helping him to adjust normally to his environment. In these days, it is doubtful that any child may reasonably be expected to succeed in life if he is denied the opportunity of an education. Such an opportunity, where the state has undertaken to provide it, is a right which must be made available to all on equal terms.

We come then to the question presented: Does segregation of children in public schools solely on the basis of race, even though the physical facilities and other "tangible" factors may be equal, deprive the children of the minority group of equal educational opportunities? We believe that it does.

In *Sweatt v. Painter,* in finding that a segregated law school of Negroes could not provide them equal educational opportunities, this Court relied in large part on "those qualities which are incapable of objective measurement but which make for greatness in a law school." In *McLaurin v. Oklahoma State Regents,* the Court, in requiring that a Negro admitted to a white graduate school be treated like all other students, again resorted to intangible considerations: " . . . his ability to study, to engage in discussions and exchange views with other students, and, in general, to learn his profession." Such considerations apply with added force to children in grade and high schools. To separate them from others of similar age and qualifications solely because of their race generates a feeling of inferiority as to their status in the community that may affect their hearts and minds in a way unlikely ever to be undone. The effect of this separation on their educational opportunities was well stated by a finding in the Kansas case by a court which nevertheless felt compelled to rule against the Negro plaintiffs:

Segregation of white and colored children in public schools has a detrimental effect upon the colored children. The impact is greater when it has the sanction of

Pictured on the steps of the U.S. Supreme Court are the NAACP Legal Defense Fund lawyers who argued the school segregation cases that resulted in the Brown v. Board of Education *precedent. Left to right: Howard Jenkins, James M. Nabrit Jr., Spottswood W. Robinson III, Frank Reeves, Jack Greenberg, Special Counsel Thurgood Marshall, Louis Redding, U. Simpson Tate, and George E. C. Hayes. Missing is Robert L. Carter, who argued the Topeka case.*

the law; for the policy of separating the races is usually interpreted as denoting the inferiority of the negro group. A sense of inferiority affects the motivation of a child to learn. Segregation with the sanction of law, therefore, has a tendency to [retard] the educational and mental development of negro children and to deprive them of some of the benefits they would receive in a racial[ly] integrated school system.

Whatever may have been the extent of psychological knowledge at the time of *Plessy v. Ferguson,* this finding is amply supported by modern authority.* Any

*K. B. Clark, *Effect of Prejudice and Discrimination On Personality Development* (Midcentury White House Conference on Children and Youth, 1950); Witmer and Kotinsky, *Personality in the Making* (1952), C. Vi; Deutscher and Chein, *The Psychological Effects of Enforced Segregation: A Survey of Social Science Opinion,* 26 J. Psychol. 259 (1948); Chein, *What are the Psychological Effects of Segregation Under Conditions Of Equal Facilities?* 3 Int. J. Opinion and Attitude Res. 229 (1949); Brameld, *Educational Costs, In Discrimination and National Welfare* (Maciver, Ed., 1949), 44–48; Frazier, The Negro in the United States (1949), 674–681. And see generally Myrdal, *An American Dilemma* (1944).

language in *Plessy v. Ferguson* contrary to this finding is rejected.

We conclude that in the field of public education the doctrine of "separate but equal" has no place. Separate educational facilities are inherently unequal. Therefore, we hold that the plaintiffs and others similarly situated for whom the actions have been brought are, by reason of the segregation complained of, deprived of the equal protection of the laws guaranteed by the Fourteenth Amendment. . . .

Because these are class actions, because of the wide applicability of this decision, and because of the great variety of local conditions, the formulation of decrees in these cases presents problems of considerable complexity. On reargument, the consideration of appropriate relief was necessarily subordinated to the primary question—the constitutionality of segregation in public education. We have now announced that such segregation is a denial of the equal protection of the laws. In order that we may have the full assistance of the parties in formulating decrees, the cases will be restored to the docket, and the parties are requested to present further argument on Questions 4 and 5 previously propounded by the Court for the reargument this Term.* The Attorney General of the United States is again invited to participate. The Attorneys General of the states requiring or permitting segregation in public education will also be permitted to appear as amici curiae upon request to do so by September 15, 1954, and submission of briefs by October 1, 1954.

It is so ordered.

Note the final paragraph of the Court's unanimous decision in *Brown,* asking the attorneys to return the next year and argue the issue of remedies. The justices recognized that agreeing that racial separation in the public schools was unconstitutional was not the same as deciding how to end the practice and what would replace it.

The result of the Court's request, commonly referred to as *Brown II* (1955), set the stage for public school desegregation battles that were to dominate the national agenda for the next decade and still linger today in some districts. As you read *Brown II,* consider how the justices dealt with two basic questions: Who was to be responsible for implementing school desegregation, and on what kind of schedule?

Brown v. Board of Education (II)

349 U.S. 294 (1955)
http://laws.findlaw.com/US/349/294.html
Vote: 9 (Black, Burton, Clark, Douglas, Frankfurter,
    Harlan, Minton, Reed, Warren)
    0

OPINION OF THE COURT: Warren

---

*4. Assuming it is decided that segregation in public schools violates the Fourteenth Amendment

(a)   would a decree necessarily follow providing that, within the limits set by normal geographic school districting, Negro children should forthwith be admitted to schools of their choice, or

(b)   may this Court, in the exercise of its equity powers, permit an effective gradual adjustment to be brought about from existing segregated systems to a system not based on color distinctions?

5. On the assumption on which questions 4(a) and (b) are based, and assuming further that this Court will exercise its equity powers to the end described in question 4(b), should this Court formulate detailed decrees in these cases;

(a)   if so, what specific issues should the decrees reach;

(b)   should this Court appoint a special master to hear evidence with a view to recommending specific terms for such decrees;

(c)   should this Court remand to the courts of first instance with directions to frame decrees in these cases and, if so, what general directions should the decrees of this Court include and what procedures should the courts of first instance follow in arriving at the specific terms of more detailed decrees?

FACTS:

In *Brown I* the Court restored the cases to the docket and requested further arguments on the question of remedies. The justices invited the U.S. attorney general and the attorneys general of all states that maintained segregated schools, in addition to the parties, to present their views.

The NAACP asked the Court to order an immediate end to racial separation. Representatives of the federal government recommended a specific timetable for local governments to develop their desegregation plans. Attorneys for the southern states cited substantial difficulties standing in the way of compliance with *Brown I* and requested its gradual implementation. In *Brown II,* therefore, the Court had to struggle with these competing claims over the schedule for desegregation, as well as the question of who would be responsible for implementing the plan.

ARGUMENTS:

For the appellants, Oliver Brown, et al.:

- Within the limits of normal geographic school districting, Negro children should be admitted to the school of their choice immediately.

- Only an order to desegregate as quickly as administrative and mechanical procedures can be completed will vindicate the constitutional rights that have been violated. Desegregation should occur no later than the next academic year.

- There is no evidence that gradual desegregation will be better, smoother, or more effective.

- If the Court allows "effective gradual adjustment," it should remand these cases to the trial court with specific directions to begin the process immediately and to set an outer time limit. Safeguards must be imposed to protect against "gradual" becoming "interminable."

For the appellees, Board of Education of Topeka, Kansas, et al.:

- The transition to a desegregated system should take place gradually and in an orderly manner. School districts face differing conditions that determine the speed at which desegregation can effectively occur.

- Immediate desegregation would be done too hurriedly, without adequate investigation of the facts or careful thought and reflection. This would lead to confusion and an interruption of the educational process detrimental to all children.

- Should the Court allow "effective gradual adjustment" to a desegregated system, the school boards should be permitted to manage the transition subject to the trial court retaining equity jurisdiction over the process.

MR. CHIEF JUSTICE WARREN DELIVERED THE OPINION OF THE COURT.

These cases were decided on May 17, 1954. The opinions of that date, declaring the fundamental principle that racial discrimination in public education is unconstitutional, are incorporated herein by reference. All provisions of federal, state, or local law requiring or permitting such discrimination must yield to this principle. There remains for consideration the manner in which relief is to be accorded. . . .

Full implementation of these constitutional principles may require solution of varied local school problems. School authorities have the primary responsibility for elucidating, assessing, and solving these problems; courts will have to consider whether the action of school authorities constitutes good faith implementation of the governing constitutional principles. Because of their proximity to local conditions and the possible need for further hearings, the courts which originally heard these cases can best perform this judicial appraisal. Accordingly, we believe it appropriate to remand the cases to those courts.

In fashioning and effectuating the decrees, the courts will be guided by equitable principles. Traditionally, equity has been characterized by a practical flexibility in shaping its remedies and by a facility for adjusting and reconciling public and private needs. These cases call for the exercise of these traditional attributes of equity power. At stake is the personal interest of the plaintiffs in admission to public schools as soon as practicable on a nondiscriminatory basis. To effectuate this interest may call for elimination of a variety of obstacles in making the transition to school systems operated in accordance with the constitutional principles set forth in our May 17, 1954, decision. Courts of equity may properly take into account the public interest in the elimination of such obstacles in a systematic and effective manner. But it should go without saying that the vitality of these constitutional principles cannot be allowed to yield simply because of disagreement with them.

While giving weight to these public and private considerations, the courts will require that the defendants make a prompt and reasonable start toward full compliance with our May 17, 1954, ruling. Once such a start has been made, the courts may find that additional time is necessary to carry out the ruling in an effective manner. The burden rests upon the defendants to establish that such time is necessary in the public interest and is consistent with good faith compliance at the earliest practicable date. To that end, the courts may consider problems related to administration, arising from the physical condition of the school plant, the school transportation system, personnel, revision of school districts and attendance areas into compact units to achieve a system of determining admission to the public schools on a nonracial basis, and revision of local laws and regulations which may be necessary in solving the foregoing problems. They will also consider the adequacy of any plans the defendants may propose to meet these problems and to effectuate a transition to a racially nondiscriminatory school system. During this period of transition, the courts will retain jurisdiction of these cases.

The judgments below . . . are accordingly reversed, and the cases are remanded to the District Courts to take such proceedings and enter such orders and decrees consistent with this opinion as are necessary and proper to admit to public schools on a racially nondiscriminatory basis with all deliberate speed the parties to these cases. . . .

It is so ordered.

Brown I and *Brown II* are extraordinary Court opinions, true landmarks in American legal history. In *Brown I,* Chief Justice Warren, while not explicitly overturning *Plessy,* effectively gutted it. At least "in the field of education," Warren wrote, "the doctrine of 'separate but equal' has no place. Separate educational facilities are inherently unequal." In *Brown II* he laid out a plan for the implementation of that constitutional principle. On the question of who should be responsible for implementation, the justices held that the primary duty for ending segregation rested with local school boards. These political bodies carried out the general administration of the schools, and they should be responsible for implementing desegregation. The Court, however, was aware that many school boards would resist the change. In most states, board members were elected by the people, and desegregation was not popular with the electorate. To ensure that the school boards acted properly, the Court gave oversight responsibilities to the federal district courts, the trial courts of general jurisdiction for the federal system. Because they are the federal

BOX 13-1   ONE CHILD'S SIMPLE JUSTICE

Linda Brown Buckner, now a Head Start teacher in Topeka, Kansas, was eight years old in 1951 when her father, Oliver, included her in a lawsuit to desegregate public schools that led to the Supreme Court's landmark *Brown v. Board of Education* decision in 1954.

"I was just starting school when the local NAACP was recruiting people to join its case. Topeka had eighteen elementary schools for whites and four for African Americans. The closest school to my family was four blocks away, the Sumner School. But I went to Monroe Elementary School, which was two and a half miles across town. Often, I came home crying because it was so cold waiting for the bus.

"My father hadn't been involved with the NAACP, but he was upset with the distance I had to go. One of his childhood friends was Charles Scott, one of the attorneys for the case, and Dad agreed to try to enroll me at the Sumner School. Dad's name wasn't first alphabetically, and my sister Cheryl always suspected there was sexism involved in his name coming first in the court records: among the twelve other plaintiffs, he was the only man.

"The day the decision was handed down, my mother was home and heard it on the radio. The news was shared with the family, and there was a rally that evening at the Monroe School. But I never did go to the Sumner School. That fall I went to the junior-high school, which had been integrated in Topeka since 1879."

SOURCE: Copyright © 1993 *U.S. News and World Report*, L.P. Reprinted with permission.

courts closest to the people, their judges understand local conditions. In addition, district court judges enjoy life tenure; they are appointed, not elected. If school boards failed to live up to the expectation of *Brown I,* district judges were instructed to use their equity jurisdiction to fashion whatever remedies were necessary to achieve desegregation. This grant of authority allowed the judges to impose plans especially tailored to meet the specific conditions of the district's schools.

The Court sidestepped the question of the desegregation schedule. Rather than set a timetable, the Court ordered that desegregation take place "with all deliberate speed." This standard acknowledged that the situation in each district would determine how rapidly desegregation could progress. It also may have been a necessary compromise among the justices to achieve a unanimous ruling.[4]

Realizing that the decisions would be controversial and generate resistance, especially in the South, and that the Court had no way to enforce them, Warren went to great pains to unite the Court. He believed that unanimous opinions, written by him, would encourage voluntary compliance. He was wrong, as was Marshall, who predicted that segregated schools would be eliminated within five years of the *Brown* decision.[5] The unanimous decisions did not impress southern politicians, who did little to implement them. In fact, during the 1950s they adopted the strategy that "as long as we can legislate, we can segregate" and enacted hundreds of laws designed to thwart integration. "Impeach Earl Warren" posters and billboards became a common sight on southern roads. The U.S. Congress and the president did little to counter this trend. As one scholar characterized Dwight D. Eisenhower's position, "Thurgood Marshall got his decision, now let him enforce it."[6] Some members of Congress were so outraged by *Brown* and other liberal decisions that they introduced more than fifty Court-curbing bills during the period.

What was the upshot of the lack of federal support and defiance in the South? One result was that through the 1950s, *Brown* had little impact on public education in the United States. As Table 13-1 shows, in 1954, 0.001 percent of all southern black schoolchildren attended schools with whites; by 1960 that figure was only 0.16 percent. Segregated education remained a fact of life in the American South well into the 1960s.

---

4. Bernard Schwartz, *Super Chief* (New York: New York University Press, 1983).

5. We adopt the material in this paragraph and the next from Gerald N. Rosenberg, *The Hollow Hope* (Chicago: University of Chicago Press, 1991), chap. 3.

6. Jack Peltason, *Fifty-eight Lonely Men* (Urbana: University of Illinois Press, 1971), 54.

This is not to say that *Brown* was an insignificant decision. To the contrary, many point to *Brown*'s substantial long-term effects. By placing civil rights on the political agenda, the case may have spurred the civil rights movement of the 1960s, which in turn generated significant federal action. Congress finally passed civil rights legislation with some teeth *(see Box IV-1, pages 608–609)*, and, under the administration of President Lyndon Johnson, the Justice Department became an active participant in school desegregation litigation. As a result, as Table 13-1 depicts, by 1972 the percentage of black schoolchildren in southern and border states attending schools with whites increased to more than 90 percent.

School Desegregation in the Post-*Brown* Era

In the public education cases that followed *Brown II*, the Warren Court justices held steadfast in their desegregation goals. One example is ***Cooper v. Aaron*** (1958), in which the Court responded firmly to popular resistance in Arkansas by declaring that violence or threats of violence would not be allowed to slow the progress toward full desegregation. ***Griffin v. Prince Edward County School Board*** (1964) is another. There, the Court stopped a Virginia plan to close down public schools rather than integrate them. Also, in ***Green v. School Board of New Kent County*** (1968) the justices

struck down a "freedom of choice" plan as failing to bring about a nondiscriminatory school system. By the mid-1960s the justices had begun to lose patience. Justice Hugo Black remarked in his opinion for the Court in *Griffin* that "there has been entirely too much deliberation and not enough speed" in enforcing *Brown*'s desegregation mandate.

In short, the Warren Court tried to make it clear that dilatory tactics would not be tolerated.[7] But the resistance continued. The freedom given to district judges to approve desegregation plans led to a wide variety of schemes, some of which school officials criticized for going too far and some of which civil rights advocates disparaged for not going far enough. The specific methods of integration commonly were attacked for exceeding the powers of the district courts.

Clearing up the confusion was left to the Burger Court. In 1971 it accepted an appeal that it saw as a vehicle for the declaration of authoritative rules to govern the desegregation process. The case, *Swann v. Charlotte-Mecklenburg Board of Education,* involved challenges to a desegregation plan imposed by a district judge on North Carolina's largest city. As you read Chief Justice Warren Burger's opinion for a unanimous Court, note the wide range of powers the Court approves for imposing remedies once a violation of the Constitution has been demonstrated. Would Chief Justice Warren and the members of his Court have approved?

TABLE 13-1	Percentage of Black Students Attending School with Whites, Southern States, 1954–1972		
YEAR	PERCENTAGE	YEAR	PERCENTAGE
1954	0.001	1962	0.45
1955	0.12	1963	1.2
1956	0.14	1964	2.3
1957	0.15	1965	6.1
1958	0.13	1966	16.9
1959	0.16	1968	32.0
1960	0.16	1970	85.9
1961	0.24	1972	91.3

SOURCE: Lee Epstein, Jeffrey A. Segal, Harold J. Spaeth, and Thomas G. Walker, *The Supreme Court Compendium: Data, Decisions, and Developments,* 5th ed. (Washington, DC: CQ Press, 2012), Table 9-3.

Swann v. Charlotte-Mecklenburg Board of Education

402 U.S. 1 (1971)
http://laws.findlaw.com/US/402/1.html
Oral arguments are available at http://www.oyez.org.
Vote: 9 (Black, Blackmun, Brennan, Burger, Douglas, Harlan, Marshall, Stewart, White)
    0

OPINION OF THE COURT: Burger

FACTS:

This case resulted from a long-standing legal dispute over the desegregation of schools in Charlotte, North Carolina. As part of the efforts to bring the district into compliance, the Charlotte schools were consolidated with the surrounding Mecklenburg County schools. The combined district covered 550 square miles, with 107 schools and an enrollment of 84,000

---

7. See *Alexander v. Holmes Board of Education* (1969).

children; 71 percent of the students were white, and 29 percent were black.

As a result of a plan imposed by the courts in 1965, desegregation began in earnest, but the results were not satisfactory. Two-thirds of the 21,000 black students in Charlotte attended schools that were at least 98 percent black. All parties agreed that the plan was not working, but there was considerable controversy over what to do. When the school board failed to submit a suitable plan, the district court appointed John Finger, an educational consultant, to devise one. The minority members of the school board and the U.S. Department of Health, Education, and Welfare also offered plans. After considerable legal maneuvering, the district court imposed the Finger plan, part of which was later approved by the court of appeals. Both the plaintiffs and the school board appealed to the Supreme Court.

ARGUMENTS:

For the petitioners, James Swann, et al.:

- The Charlotte-Mecklenburg schools are unconstitutionally segregated. *Green v. New Kent County School Board* (1968) requires the dismantling of such dual-race school systems.
- The district court did not impose racial balancing quotas, but used a set of flexible desegregation goals.
- Busing has long been an accepted and effective way to carry out desegregation plans.
- Desegregation plans are judged by their effectiveness, and the plan approved by the district court will achieve a unitary school system.

For the respondent, Charlotte-Mecklenburg Board of Education:

- The Constitution does not require a racial balancing plan that results in each school within the district reflecting the black/white ratio of the entire district.
- The lower courts erred by ordering racial balancing with compulsory busing as a means to achieve it.
- Desegregation plans should be evaluated by a "rule of reason," not a "rule of absolutes."
- Nondiscriminatory geographic attendance zones, including those that promote neighborhood schools, supported by a majority to minority transfer program, are sufficient to establish a unitary school system where no student is excluded from any school because of race.

MR. CHIEF JUSTICE BURGER DELIVERED THE OPINION OF THE COURT.

Nearly 17 years ago this Court held, in explicit terms, that state-imposed segregation by race in public schools denies equal protection of the laws. At no time has the Court deviated in the slightest degree from that holding or its constitutional underpinnings. . . .

Over the 16 years since *Brown II*, many difficulties were encountered in implementation of the basic constitutional requirement that the State not discriminate between public school children on the basis of their race. Nothing in our national experience prior to 1955 prepared anyone for dealing with changes and adjustments of the magnitude and complexity encountered since then. Deliberate resistance of some to the Court's mandates has impeded the good-faith efforts of others to bring school systems into compliance. The detail and nature of these dilatory tactics have been noted frequently by this Court and other courts. . . .

The problems encountered by the district courts and courts of appeals make plain that we should now try to amplify guidelines, however incomplete and imperfect, for the assistance of school authorities and courts. The failure of local authorities to meet their constitutional obligations aggravated the massive problem of converting from the state-enforced discrimination of racially separate school systems. This process has been rendered more difficult by changes since 1954 in the structure and patterns of communities, the growth of student population, movement of families, and other changes, some of which had marked impact on school planning, sometimes neutralizing or negating remedial action before it was fully implemented. Rural areas accustomed for half a century to the consolidated school systems implemented by bus transportation could make adjustments more readily than metropolitan areas with dense and shifting population, numerous schools, congested and complex traffic patterns.

The objective today remains to eliminate from the public schools all vestiges of state-imposed segregation. Segregation was the evil struck down by *Brown I* as contrary to the equal protection guarantees of the Constitution. That was the violation sought to be corrected by the remedial measures of *Brown II*. That was the basis for the holding in *Green* [*v. School Board of New Kent County*, 1968] that school authorities are "clearly charged with the affirmative duty to take whatever steps might be necessary to convert to a unitary system in which racial discrimination would be eliminated root and branch."

If school authorities fail in their affirmative obligations under these holdings, judicial authority may be invoked. Once a right and a violation have been shown, the scope of a district court's equitable powers to remedy past wrongs is broad, for breadth and flexibility are inherent in equitable remedies. . . .

This allocation of responsibility once made, the Court attempted from time to time to provide some guidelines for the exercise of the district judge's discretion and for the reviewing function of the courts of appeals. However, a school desegregation case does not differ fundamentally from other cases involving the framing of equitable remedies to repair the denial of a constitutional right. The task is to correct, by a balancing of the individual and collective interests, the condition that offends the Constitution.

In seeking to define even in broad and general terms how far this remedial power extends it is important to remember that judicial powers may be exercised only on the basis of a constitutional violation. Remedial judicial authority does not put judges automatically in the shoes of school authorities whose powers are plenary. Judicial authority enters only when local authority defaults.

School authorities are traditionally charged with broad power to formulate and implement educational policy and might well conclude, for example, that in order to prepare students to live in a pluralistic society each school should have a prescribed ratio of Negro to white students reflecting the proportion for the district as a whole. To do this as an educational policy is within the broad discretionary powers of school authorities; absent a finding of a constitutional violation, however, that would not be within the authority of a federal court. As with any equity case, the nature of the violation determines the scope of the remedy. In default by the school authorities of their obligation to proffer acceptable remedies, a district court has broad power to fashion a remedy that will assure a unitary school system. . . .

We turn now to the problem of defining with more particularity the responsibilities of school authorities in desegregating a state-enforced dual school system in light of the Equal Protection Clause. Although the several related cases before us are primarily concerned with problems of student assignment, it may be helpful to begin with a brief discussion of other aspects of the process.

In *Green,* we pointed out that existing policy and practice with regard to faculty, staff, transportation, extracurricular activities, and facilities were among the most important indicia of a segregated system. Independent of student assignment, where it is possible to identify a "white school" or a "Negro school" simply by reference to the racial composition of teachers and staff, the quality of school buildings and equipment, or the organization of sports activities, a prima facie case of violation of substantive constitutional rights under the Equal Protection Clause is shown.

When a system has been dual in these respects, the first remedial responsibility of school authorities is to eliminate invidious racial distinctions. . . .

The construction of new schools and the closing of old ones are two of the most important functions of local school authorities and also two of the most complex. . . .

In ascertaining the existence of legally imposed school segregation, the existence of a pattern of school construction and abandonment is thus a factor of great weight. In devising remedies where legally imposed segregation has been established, it is the responsibility of local authorities and district courts to see to it that future school construction and abandonment are not used and do not serve to perpetuate or reestablish the dual system. When necessary, district courts should retain jurisdiction to assure that these responsibilities are carried out.

The central issue in this case is that of student assignment, and there are essentially four problem areas:

(1) to what extent racial balance or racial quotas may be used as an implement in a remedial order to correct a previously segregated system;

(2) whether every all-Negro and all-white school must be eliminated as an indispensable part of a remedial process of desegregation;

(3) what the limits are, if any, on the rearrangement of school districts and attendance zones, as a remedial measure; and

(4) what the limits are, if any, on the use of transportation facilities to correct state-enforced racial school segregation.

(1) Racial Balances or Racial Quotas

The constant theme and thrust of every holding from *Brown I* to date is that state-enforced separation of races in public schools is discrimination that violates the

Equal Protection Clause. The remedy commanded was to dismantle dual school systems. . . .

Our objective in dealing with the issues presented by these cases is to see that school authorities exclude no pupil of a racial minority from any school, directly or indirectly, on account of race; it does not and cannot embrace all the problems of racial prejudice, even when those problems contribute to disproportionate racial concentrations in some schools.

In this case it is urged that the District Court has imposed a racial balance requirement of 71%–29% on individual schools. . . .

As the voluminous record in this case shows, the predicate for the District Court's use of the 71%–29% ratio was twofold: first, its express finding, approved by the Court of Appeals and not challenged here, that a dual school system had been maintained by the school authorities at least until 1969; second, its finding, also approved by the Court of Appeals, that the school board had totally defaulted in its acknowledged duty to come forward with an acceptable plan of its own, notwithstanding the patient efforts of the District Judge who, on at least three occasions, urged the board to submit plans. As the statement of facts shows, these findings are abundantly supported by the record. . . .

We see therefore that the use made of mathematical ratios was no more than a starting point in the process of shaping a remedy, rather than an inflexible requirement. From that starting point the District Court proceeded to frame a decree that was within its discretionary powers, as an equitable remedy for the particular circumstances. As we said in *Green,* a school authority's remedial plan or a district court's remedial decree is to be judged by its effectiveness. Awareness of the racial composition of the whole school system is likely to be a useful starting point in shaping a remedy to correct past constitutional violations. In sum, the very limited use made of mathematical ratios was within the equitable remedial discretion of the District Court.

(2) One-race Schools

The record in this case reveals the familiar phenomenon that in metropolitan areas minority groups are often found concentrated in one part of the city. In some circumstances certain schools may remain all or largely of one race until new schools can be provided or neighborhood patterns change. Schools all or predominantly of one race in a district of mixed population will require close scrutiny to determine that school assignments are not part of state enforced segregation.

In light of the above, it should be clear that the existence of some small number of one-race, or virtually one-race, schools within a district is not in and of itself the mark of a system that still practices segregation by law. The district judge or school authorities should make every effort to achieve the greatest possible degree of actual desegregation and will thus necessarily be concerned with the elimination of one-race schools. No per se rule can adequately embrace all the difficulties of reconciling the competing interests involved; but in a system with a history of segregation the need for remedial criteria of sufficient specificity to assure a school authority's compliance with its constitutional duty warrants a presumption against schools that are substantially disproportionate in their racial composition. Where the school authority's proposed plan for conversion from a dual to a unitary system contemplates the continued existence of some schools that are all or predominately of one race, they have the burden of showing that such school assignments are genuinely nondiscriminatory. The court should scrutinize such schools, and the burden upon the school authorities will be to satisfy the court that their racial composition is not the result of present or past discriminatory action on their part. . . .

(3) Remedial Altering of Attendance Zones

The maps submitted in these cases graphically demonstrate that one of the principal tools employed by school planners and by courts to break up the dual school system has been a frank—and sometimes drastic—gerrymandering of school districts and attendance zones. An additional step was pairing, "clustering," or "grouping" of schools with attendance assignments made deliberately to accomplish the transfer of Negro students out of formerly segregated Negro schools and transfer of white students to formerly all-Negro schools. More often than not, these zones are neither compact nor contiguous; indeed they may be on opposite ends of the city. As an interim corrective measure, this cannot be said to be beyond the broad remedial powers of a court.

Absent a constitutional violation there would be no basis for judicially ordering assignment of students on a racial basis. All things being equal, with no history of discrimination, it might well be desirable to assign pupils to schools nearest their homes. But all things are not equal in a system that has been deliberately constructed and maintained to enforce racial segregation. The remedy for such segregation may be administratively awkward, inconvenient, and even bizarre in some situations and may impose burdens on some; but all awkwardness and inconvenience cannot be avoided in the interim period when remedial adjustments are being made to eliminate the dual school systems. . . .

We hold that the pairing and grouping of noncontiguous school zones is a permissible tool and such action is to be considered in light of the objectives sought. . . . Conditions in different localities will vary so widely that no rigid rules can be laid down to govern all situations.

(4) Transportation of Students

The scope of permissible transportation of students as an implement of a remedial decree has never been defined by this Court and by the very nature of the problem it cannot be defined with precision. No rigid guidelines as to student transportation can be given for application to the infinite variety of problems presented in thousands of situations. Bus transportation has been an integral part of the public education system for years, and was perhaps the single most important factor in the transition from the one-room schoolhouse to the consolidated school. Eighteen million of the Nation's public school children, approximately 39%, were transported to their schools by bus in 1969–1970 in all parts of the country.

The importance of bus transportation as a normal and accepted tool of educational policy is readily discernible in this . . . case. . . . The Charlotte school authorities did not purport to assign students on the basis of geographically drawn attendance zones until 1965 and then they allowed almost unlimited transfer privileges. The District Court's conclusion that assignment of children to the school nearest their home serving their grade would not produce an effective dismantling of the dual system is supported by the record.

Thus the remedial techniques used in the District Court's order were within that court's power to provide equitable relief; implementation of the decree is well within the capacity of the school authority.

The decree provided that the buses used to implement the plan would operate on direct routes. Students would be picked up at schools near their homes and transported to the schools they were to attend. The trips for elementary school pupils average about seven miles and the District Court found that they would take "not over 35 minutes at the most." This system compares favorably with the transportation plan previously operated in Charlotte under which each day 23,600 students on all grade levels were transported an average of 15 miles one way for an average trip requiring over an hour. In these circumstances, we find no basis for holding that the local school authorities may not be required to employ bus transportation as one tool of school desegregation. Desegregation plans cannot be limited to the walk-in school.

An objection to transportation of students may have validity when the time or distance of travel is so great as to either risk the health of the children or significantly impinge on the educational process. District courts must weigh the soundness of any transportation plan in light of what is said in subdivisions (1), (2), and (3) above. It hardly needs stating that the limits on time of travel will vary with many factors, but probably with none more than the age of the students. The reconciliation of competing values in a desegregation case is, of course, a difficult task with many sensitive facets but fundamentally no more so than remedial measures courts of equity have traditionally employed.

The Court of Appeals, searching for a term to define the equitable remedial power of the district courts, used the term "reasonableness." . . . On the facts of this case, we are unable to conclude that the order of the District Court is not reasonable, feasible and workable. However, in seeking to define the scope of remedial power or the limits on remedial power of courts in an area as sensitive as we deal with here, words are poor instruments to convey the sense of basic fairness inherent in equity. Substance, not semantics, must govern, and we have sought to suggest the nature of limitations without frustrating the appropriate scope of equity. . . .

. . . The order of the District Court . . . is . . . affirmed.

It is so ordered.

The Court's decision in *Swann* reaffirmed the broad powers of district courts in implementing desegregation. Plans imposed by the courts can affect teacher placement, school construction and maintenance, staff assignment, and funding equalization among schools within the district. Judges may use the overall racial composition of the district's students to set goals for racial balance in individual schools. Courts are empowered to use a wide arsenal of student placement strategies, including rearrangement of attendance zones and the politically unpopular imposition of forced busing.

In spite of the generally sweeping powers given to the district judges, a careful reading of Burger's opinion reveals certain limits. First, this judicial authority can be used only when the courts have determined that a particular district has violated the Constitution—that is to say, when black schools are the result of past or continuing de jure (by law) discrimination. In these instances, district courts should presume that government actors intended to create the segregation, and the courts' powers to address the situation are remedial. Questions of school administration are to be left to local school officials unless unconstitutional discrimination has occurred and the districts have not made the necessary corrections. Second, the remedy imposed must be tailored to compensate for the violation. In Burger's terms, "The nature of the violation determines the scope of the remedy."

These limits have at times been obstacles to achieving effective integration, especially in large metropolitan areas in the North where many independent school districts may be in operation and some may be made up of one race. True integration can take place only if multiple districts are brought into a single plan. But before a desegregation plan can be imposed, unconstitutional discrimination must be found to have occurred within that particular district. Violations are difficult to prove in northern cities where segregation laws never were in effect and segregated neighborhoods grew up without obvious government involvement. In these cases the segregation may exist de facto (in fact) but may not be the result of past or continuing de jure discrimination.[8]

Many school districts came under court supervision shortly after *Brown*. Judges monitored all significant actions taken by these districts to ensure that desegregation efforts continued and that resegregation was not encouraged. For the first three decades following the *Brown* ruling, judicial supervision of districts with histories of official segregation tended to be quite exacting. In the early 1990s, however, the Supreme Court began to ease the obligation of federal district judges to monitor the integration efforts of local school boards. In **Board of Education of Oklahoma City Public Schools v. Dowell** (1991), for example, the Court confronted the issue of resegregation caused by residential patterns. It held that judicial supervision

of the district could end as long as state-sanctioned discrimination had ceased and resegregation was the result of the private residential choices of parents. Similarly, **Freeman v. Pitts** (1992) permitted district judges to release school districts from supervision incrementally as the schools met desegregation goals for various parts of their programs. Civil rights groups criticized these decisions, claiming that the Court was retreating from the principles set in *Brown*.[9]

Although the Supreme Court's involvement in school desegregation cases has declined in recent years, it has not disappeared. In more contemporary controversies, the justices have faced integration plans attacked for placing excessive emphasis on race. Good examples are *Parents Involved in Community Schools v. Seattle School District No. 1* (2007) and *Meredith v. Jefferson County Board of Education* (2007).

Parents Involved in Community Schools v. Seattle School District No. 1

Meredith v. Jefferson County Board of Education

551 U.S. 701 (2007)
http://laws.findlaw.com/US/000/05-908.html
Oral arguments are available at http//www.oyez.org.
Vote: 5 (Alito, Kennedy, Roberts, Scalia, Thomas)
      4 (Breyer, Ginsburg, Souter, Stevens)

OPINION OF THE COURT: Roberts
CONCURRING OPINIONS: Kennedy, Thomas
DISSENTING OPINIONS: Breyer, Stevens

FACTS:

The Supreme Court consolidated these two cases in order to consider their central issue: the use of race as a criterion in the assignment of individual students to public schools.

The Seattle School District voluntarily adopted a plan for assigning students to its ten public high schools that included a combination of student preference rankings and tie-breaker procedures. Incoming ninth graders submitted a rank ordering of their preferred school options. When those preferences

---

8. See, for example, the Court's response to the Detroit metropolitan area desegregation plans in **Milliken v. Bradley** (1974).

9. The justices, however, made it clear that when effects of state-sponsored segregation persisted, the Court would order that actions be taken to bring the schools into compliance with the Constitution. An example is **United States v. Fordice** (1992), in which the justices found the desegregation efforts of Mississippi's higher education system to be unacceptably ineffective.

Kathleen Brose, left, and her attorney, Harry Korrell, speak to reporters on June 28, 2007, following the Supreme Court's decision in their favor in Parents Involved in Community Schools v. Seattle School District No. 1. *Brose became a plaintiff when her daughter was denied admission to highly rated Ballard High School based on the Seattle school system's racial distribution policies.*

resulted in a school being oversubscribed, preference was given first to students who had a sibling in that school. The second tie-breaker was race. The city system's total student population was approximately 41 percent white and 59 percent students from other racial backgrounds. If an oversubscribed school was not within 10 percentage points of this balance, it was classified as "integration positive," and students whose race would bring the school closer to racial balance were given priority. The third tie-breaker was the proximity of the student's residence to the school. The Seattle School District never operated unconstitutionally segregated schools and was never placed under court-ordered desegregation. Parents Involved in Community Schools, a nonprofit organization of parents whose children had been or might be denied access to their preferred schools because of race, filed suit challenging the constitutionality of the assignment procedure. The Ninth Circuit Court of Appeals upheld the assignment policy.

The Jefferson County Board of Education operates the public school system of metropolitan Louisville, Kentucky. In 1973, the federal courts found that the district maintained a racially segregated school system and placed it under court supervision. In 2000, the district was found to be in compliance with the law, and court supervision ended. In 2001, the Board of Education adopted a pupil assignment policy for its nonmagnet schools. The racial breakdown for students in the system was 34 percent black and 66 percent white. The plan required all nonmagnet schools

to maintain a black enrollment of no lower than 15 percent and no higher than 50 percent. The system grouped its schools into geographical clusters and students were assigned to a cluster on the basis of residence. The parents of incoming students ranked their two top choices from among the schools in their cluster. Students of parents who did not submit rankings were assigned by the district. Assignment decisions were based on available space and the district's racial guidelines. Once a school reached the extremes of the racial policy, no student was assigned to that school who would contribute to the school's racial imbalance. Once a student was assigned to a school, the student's parents could request a transfer, but racial balance was taken into account in granting such requests.

Crystal Meredith, whose son Joshua had been denied a requested transfer to the school of his choice because he is white, filed suit claiming the assignment policy violated the Fourteenth Amendment. The Sixth Circuit Court of Appeals upheld the policy.

ARGUMENTS:

For the petitioners, Parents Involved in Community Schools and Crystal Meredith:

- By using racial distributions of the district to establish quantitative diversity requirements for individual schools, the school boards are engaged in racial balancing.
- Racial balancing is not permitted here because neither district is engaged in unconstitutional segregation.

- Unlike the affirmative action plan approved in *Grutter v. Bollinger,* race is the only diversity factor considered in these plans and is the sole factor for determining the school assignments of some children.
- The racial criteria used in these plans constitute a racial quota.

For the respondents, Seattle School District No. 1 and Jefferson County Board of Education:

- The challenged policies pursue the compelling interests of (1) achieving the educational benefits of a diverse student body, (2) reducing the negative effects of racial isolation, and (3) preventing segregated housing patterns from denying all students equal access to schools of their choice.
- The districts have no interest in racial balancing.
- Completely race-neutral policies would not achieve the desired goals.
- The plans are narrowly tailored to achieve the desired objectives. The use of race is limited and flexible. The plans are not intended to be permanent.

> **CHIEF JUSTICE ROBERTS ANNOUNCED THE JUDGMENT OF THE COURT, AND DELIVERED THE OPINION OF THE COURT WITH RESPECT TO PARTS I, II, III–A, AND III–C, AND AN OPINION WITH RESPECT TO PARTS III–B AND IV, IN WHICH JUSTICES SCALIA, THOMAS, AND ALITO JOIN.**

I

Both cases present the same underlying legal question—whether a public school that had not operated legally segregated schools or has been found to be unitary may choose to classify students by race and rely upon that classification in making school assignments. . . .

II

[Jurisdictional issues. Omitted.]

III

A

It is well established that when the government distributes burdens or benefits on the basis of individual racial classifications, that action is reviewed under strict scrutiny. *Johnson v. California* (2005); *Grutter v. Bollinger* (2003); *Adarand [Constructors v. Peña* (1995)]. . . . In order to satisfy this searching standard of review, the school districts must demonstrate that the use of individual racial classifications in the assignment plans here under review is "narrowly tailored" to achieve a "compelling" government interest.

. . . [O]ur prior cases, in evaluating the use of racial classifications in the school context, have recognized two interests that qualify as compelling. The first is the compelling interest of remedying the effects of past intentional discrimination. See *Freeman v. Pitts* (1992). Yet the Seattle public schools have not shown that they were ever segregated by law, and were not subject to court-ordered desegregation decrees. The Jefferson County public schools were previously segregated by law and were subject to a desegregation decree entered in 1975. In 2000, the District Court that entered that decree dissolved it, finding that Jefferson County had "eliminated the vestiges associated with the former policy of segregation and its pernicious effects," and thus had achieved "unitary" status.

. . . We have emphasized that the harm being remedied by mandatory desegregation plans is the harm that is traceable to segregation, and that "the Constitution is not violated by racial imbalance in the schools, without more." *Milliken v. Bradley* (1977). Once Jefferson County achieved unitary status, it had remedied the constitutional wrong that allowed race-based assignments. Any continued use of race must be justified on some other basis.

The second government interest we have recognized as compelling for purposes of strict scrutiny is the interest in diversity in higher education upheld in *Grutter.* . . .

The entire gist of the analysis in *Grutter* was that the admissions program at issue there focused on each applicant as an individual, and not simply as a member of a particular racial group. The classification of applicants by race upheld in *Grutter* was only as part of a "highly individualized, holistic review." As the Court explained, "[t]he importance of this individualized consideration in the context of a race-conscious admissions program is paramount." The point of the narrow tailoring analysis in which the *Grutter* Court engaged was to ensure that the use of racial classifications was indeed part of a broader assessment of diversity, and not simply an effort to achieve racial balance, which the Court explained would be "patently unconstitutional."

In the present cases, by contrast, race is not considered as part of a broader effort to achieve "exposure to widely diverse people, cultures, ideas, and viewpoints;" race, for some students, is determinative standing alone. . . .

In upholding the admissions plan in *Grutter,* though, this Court relied upon considerations unique to institutions of higher education, noting that in light of "the expansive freedoms of speech and thought associated with the university environment, universities occupy a special niche in our constitutional tradition. . . .

B

. . . In briefing and argument before this Court, Seattle contends that its use of race helps to reduce racial concentration in schools and to ensure that racially concentrated housing patterns do not prevent nonwhite students from having access to the most desirable schools. Jefferson County has articulated a similar goal, phrasing its interest in terms of educating its students "in a racially integrated environment." Each school district argues that educational and broader socialization benefits flow from a racially diverse learning environment, and each contends that because the diversity they seek is racial diversity—not the broader diversity at issue in *Grutter*—it makes sense to promote that interest directly by relying on race alone. . . .

. . . [I]t is clear that the racial classifications employed by the districts are not narrowly tailored to the goal of achieving the educational and social benefits asserted to flow from racial diversity. In design and operation, the plans are directed only to racial balance, pure and simple, an objective this Court has repeatedly condemned as illegitimate. . . .

. . . [T]he racial demographics in each district—whatever they happen to be—drive the required "diversity" numbers. The plans here are not tailored to achieving a degree of diversity necessary to realize the asserted educational benefits; instead the plans are tailored . . . to "the goal established by the school board of attaining a level of diversity within the schools that approximates the district's overall demographics." . . .

In fact, in each case the extreme measure of relying on race in assignments is unnecessary to achieve the stated goals, even as defined by the districts. For example, at Franklin High School in Seattle, the racial tiebreaker was applied because nonwhite enrollment exceeded 69 percent, and resulted in an incoming ninth-grade class in 2000–2001 that was 30.3 percent Asian-American, 21.9 percent African-American, 6.8 percent Latino, 0.5 percent Native-American, and 40.5 percent Caucasian. Without the racial tiebreaker, the class would have been 39.6 percent Asian-American, 30.2 percent African-American, 8.3 percent Latino, 1.1 percent

Native-American, and 20.8 percent Caucasian. When the actual racial breakdown is considered, enrolling students without regard to their race yields a substantially diverse student body under any definition of diversity.

. . . Here the racial balance the districts seek is a defined range set solely by reference to the demographics of the respective school districts.

This working backward to achieve a particular type of racial balance, rather than working forward from some demonstration of the level of diversity that provides the purported benefits, is a fatal flaw under our existing precedent. We have many times over reaffirmed that "[r]acial balance is not to be achieved for its own sake." *Freeman.* See also *Richmond v. J. A. Croson Co. Grutter* itself reiterated that "outright racial balancing" is "patently unconstitutional."

Accepting racial balancing as a compelling state interest would justify the imposition of racial proportionality throughout American society, contrary to our repeated recognition that "[a]t the heart of the Constitution's guarantee of equal protection lies the simple command that the Government must treat citizens as individuals, not as simply components of a racial, religious, sexual or national class." *Miller v. Johnson* (1995). . . .

The principle that racial balancing is not permitted is one of substance, not semantics. Racial balancing is not transformed from "patently unconstitutional" to a compelling state interest simply by relabeling it "racial diversity." While the school districts use various verbal formulations to describe the interest they seek to promote—racial diversity, avoidance of racial isolation, racial integration—they offer no definition of the interest that suggests it differs from racial balance. . . .

C

The districts assert, as they must, that the way in which they have employed individual racial classifications is necessary to achieve their stated ends. The minimal effect these classifications have on student assignments, however, suggests that other means would be effective. Seattle's racial tiebreaker results, in the end, only in shifting a small number of students between schools. . . .

Similarly, Jefferson County's use of racial classifications has only a minimal effect on the assignment of students. Elementary school students are assigned to their first- or second-choice school 95 percent of the time. . . .

While we do not suggest that *greater* use of race would be preferable, the minimal impact of the districts' racial classifications on school enrollment casts doubt on the necessity of using racial classifications. . . .

The districts have also failed to show that they considered methods other than explicit racial classifications to achieve their stated goals. Narrow tailoring requires "serious, good faith consideration of workable race-neutral alternatives," *Grutter,* and yet in Seattle several alternative assignment plans—many of which would not have used express racial classifications—were rejected with little or no consideration. Jefferson County has failed to present any evidence that it considered alternatives, even though the district already claims that its goals are achieved primarily through means other than the racial classifications. . . .

IV

. . . In *Brown v. Board of Education* (1954) (*Brown I*), we held that segregation deprived black children of equal educational opportunities regardless of whether school facilities and other tangible factors were equal, because government classification and separation on grounds of race themselves denoted inferiority. It was not the inequality of the facilities but the fact of legally separating children on the basis of race on which the Court relied to find a constitutional violation in 1954. The next Term, we accordingly stated that "full compliance" with *Brown I* required school districts "to achieve a system of determining admission to the public schools *on a nonracial basis.*" *Brown II* (emphasis added).

The parties and their *amici* debate which side is more faithful to the heritage of *Brown,* but the position of the plaintiffs in *Brown* was spelled out in their brief and could not have been clearer: "[T]he Fourteenth Amendment prevents states from according differential treatment to American children on the basis of their color or race." . . .

Before *Brown,* schoolchildren were told where they could and could not go to school based on the color of their skin. The school districts in these cases have not carried the heavy burden of demonstrating that we should allow this once again—even for very different reasons. For schools that never segregated on the basis of race, such as Seattle, or that have removed the vestiges of past segregation, such as Jefferson County, the way "to achieve a system of determining admission to the public schools on a nonracial basis" is to stop assigning students on a racial basis. The way to stop discrimination on the basis of race is to stop discriminating on the basis of race.

The judgments of the Courts of Appeals for the Sixth and Ninth Circuits are reversed, and the cases are remanded for further proceedings.

It is so ordered.

JUSTICE THOMAS, concurring.

Today, the Court holds that state entities may not experiment with race-based means to achieve ends they deem socially desirable. I wholly concur in The Chief Justice's opinion . . .

Because this Court has authorized and required race-based remedial measures to address *de jure* segregation, it is important to define segregation clearly and to distinguish it from racial imbalance. In the context of public schooling, segregation is the deliberate operation of a school system to "carry out a governmental policy to separate pupils in schools solely on the basis of race." *Swann v. Charlotte-Mecklenburg Bd. of Ed.* (1971). In *Brown,* this Court declared that segregation was unconstitutional under the Equal Protection Clause of the Fourteenth Amendment.

Racial imbalance is the failure of a school district's individual schools to match or approximate the demographic makeup of the student population at large. Racial imbalance is not segregation. Although presently observed racial imbalance might result from past *de jure* segregation, racial imbalance can also result from any number of innocent private decisions, including voluntary housing choices. Because racial imbalance is not inevitably linked to unconstitutional segregation, it is not unconstitutional in and of itself.

Although there is arguably a danger of racial imbalance in schools in Seattle and Louisville, there is no danger of resegregation. No one contends that Seattle has established or that Louisville has reestablished a dual school system that separates students on the basis of race. . . . [R]acial imbalance without intentional state action to separate the races does not amount to segregation. To raise the specter of resegregation to defend these programs is to ignore the meaning of the word and the nature of the cases before us. . . .

What was wrong in 1954 cannot be right today. . . . None of the considerations trumpeted by the dissent is relevant to the constitutionality of the school boards' race-based plans because no contextual detail—or collection of contextual details—can "provide refuge from the principle that under our Constitution, the government may not make distinctions on the basis of race."

In place of the color-blind Constitution, the dissent would permit measures to keep the races together and proscribe measures to keep the races apart. Although no such distinction is apparent in the Fourteenth Amendment, the dissent would constitutionalize today's faddish social theories that embrace that distinction. The Constitution is not that malleable. Even if current social theories favor classroom racial engineering as necessary to "solve the problems at hand," the Constitution enshrines principles independent of social theories. Indeed, if our history has taught us anything, it has taught us to beware of elites bearing racial theories. See, e.g., *Dred Scott v. Sandford* (1857). Can we really be sure that the racial theories that motivated *Dred Scott* and *Plessy* are a relic of the past or that future theories will be nothing but beneficent and progressive? That is a gamble I am unwilling to take, and it is one the Constitution does not allow.

The plans before us base school assignment decisions on students' race. Because "[o]ur Constitution is color-blind, and neither knows nor tolerates classes among citizens," such race-based decisionmaking is unconstitutional. I concur in the Chief Justice's opinion so holding.

JUSTICE KENNEDY, concurring in part and concurring in the judgment.

I . . . join Parts I and II [III-A and III-C] of the Court's opinion. . . .

. . . The plurality opinion is too dismissive of the legitimate interest government has in ensuring all people have equal opportunity regardless of their race. The plurality's postulate that "[t]he way to stop discrimination on the basis of race is to stop discriminating on the basis of race" is not sufficient to decide these cases. Fifty years of experience since *Brown v. Board of Education* (1954) should teach us that the problem before us defies so easy a solution. School districts can seek to reach *Brown*'s objective of equal educational opportunity. The plurality opinion is at least open to the interpretation that the Constitution requires school districts to ignore the problem of *de facto* resegregation in schooling. I cannot endorse that conclusion. To the extent the plurality opinion suggests the Constitution mandates that state and local school authorities must accept the status quo of racial isolation in schools, it is, in my view, profoundly mistaken. . . .

This Nation has a moral and ethical obligation to fulfill its historic commitment to creating an integrated society that ensures equal opportunity for all of its children. . . . What the government is not permitted to do, absent a showing of necessity not made here, is to classify every student on the basis of race and to assign each of them to schools based on that classification. Crude measures of this sort threaten to reduce children to racial chits valued and traded according to one school's supply and another's demand. . . .

With this explanation I concur in the judgment of the Court.

JUSTICE STEVENS, dissenting.

There is a cruel irony in The Chief Justice's reliance on our decision in *Brown v. Board of Education* (1955). The first sentence in the concluding paragraph of his opinion states: "Before *Brown,* schoolchildren were told where they could and could not go to school based on the color of their skin." This sentence reminds me of Anatole France's observation: "[T]he majestic equality of the la[w], forbid[s] rich and poor alike to sleep under bridges, to beg in the streets, and to steal their bread." The Chief Justice fails to note that it was only black schoolchildren who were so ordered; indeed, the history books do not tell stories of white children struggling to attend black schools. In this and other ways, The Chief Justice rewrites the history of one of this Court's most important decisions.

The Chief Justice rejects the conclusion that the racial classifications at issue here should be viewed differently than others, because they do not impose burdens on one race alone and do not stigmatize or exclude. . . .

. . . It is my firm conviction that no Member of the Court that I joined in 1975 would have agreed with today's decision.

JUSTICE BREYER, with whom JUSTICE STEVENS, JUSTICE SOUTER, and JUSTICE GINSBURG join, dissenting.

These cases consider the longstanding efforts of two local school boards to integrate their public schools. . . .

This context is *not* a context that involves the use of race to decide who will receive goods or services that are normally distributed on the basis of merit and which are in short supply. It is not one in which race-conscious limits stigmatize or exclude; the limits at issue do not pit the races against each other or otherwise significantly exacerbate racial tensions. They do not impose burdens unfairly upon members of one race alone but instead seek benefits for members of all races alike. The context here is one of racial limits that seek, not to keep the races apart, but to bring them together. . . .

. . . The plans before us satisfy the requirements of the Equal Protection Clause. . . .

Four basic considerations have led me to this view. First, the histories of Louisville and Seattle reveal complex circumstances and a long tradition of conscientious efforts by local school boards to resist racial segregation in public schools. . . .

Second, since this Court's decision in *Brown,* the law has consistently and unequivocally approved of both voluntary and compulsory race-conscious measures to combat segregated schools. The Equal Protection Clause, ratified following the Civil War, has always distinguished in practice between state action that excludes and thereby subordinates racial minorities and state action that seeks to bring together people of all races. From *Swann* to *Grutter,* this Court's decisions have emphasized this distinction, recognizing that the fate of race relations in this country depends upon unity among our children, "for unless our children begin to learn together, there is little hope that our people will ever learn to live together." (Marshall, J.).

Third, the plans before us, subjected to rigorous judicial review, are supported by compelling state interests and are narrowly tailored to accomplish those goals. . . .

Fourth, the plurality's approach risks serious harm to the law and for the Nation. Its view of the law rests either upon a denial of the distinction between exclusionary and inclusive use of race-conscious criteria in the context of the Equal Protection Clause, or upon such a rigid application of its "test" that the distinction loses practical significance. Consequently, the Court's decision today slows down and sets back the work of local school boards to bring about racially diverse schools. . . .

. . . [W]hat of the hope and promise of Brown? For much of this Nation's history, the races remained divided. It was not long ago that people of different races drank from separate fountains, rode on separate buses, and studied in separate schools. In this Court's finest hour, *Brown v. Board of Education* challenged this history and helped to change it. For *Brown* held out a promise. It was a promise embodied in three Amendments designed to make citizens of slaves. It was the promise of true racial equality—not as a matter of fine words on paper, but as a matter of everyday life in the Nation's cities and schools. It was about the nature of a democracy that must work for all Americans. It sought one law, one Nation, one people, not simply as a matter of legal principle but in terms of how we actually live. . . .

. . . The last half-century has witnessed great strides toward racial equality, but we have not yet realized the promise of *Brown*. To invalidate the plans under review is to threaten the promise of Brown. The plurality's position, I fear, would break that promise. This is a decision that the Court and the Nation will come to regret.

I must dissent.

In these cases the school systems classified students on the basis of race as part of their policies intended to improve the level of school integration. The Court's majority held that such policies, even if pursued for benign reasons, can violate the Constitution—especially if the districts are already in compliance with the Constitution and their policies have racial balancing characteristics. The four dissenters, of course, saw the actions of the school boards much differently, finding that race can be taken into account as part of a narrowly tailored attempt to improve educational diversity and racial inclusiveness. The Court's ruling had a major impact in the area of school desegregation law, and, as we shall see later in this chapter, it also had an influence on the Court's affirmative action policies.

Expanding the Application of *Brown*

The death of the separate but equal doctrine brought about by *Brown* had widespread ramifications for American society. Parties soon began to file lawsuits requesting that the courts apply *Brown*'s principles to racially discriminatory state and local policies beyond the public education sphere. In these post-*Brown* disputes the justices faithfully applied the 1954 precedent. The Court presumed that racial classifications used to discriminate against African Americans violated the equal protection clause, and states attempting to justify such actions faced a heavy burden of proof. As members of a suspect class, black litigants enjoyed the advantages of the strict scrutiny test. These factors made it difficult for the states to withstand the attacks made against discriminatory policies and practices. One by one, the legal barriers between the races fell.

An illustration of the Warren Court's approach to racial equality is the ruling in *Loving v. Virginia* (1967), which concerned the part of life segregationist forces least wanted to see integrated—marriage. When *Loving* came to the Court, sixteen states, all of them southern or border, had miscegenation statutes that made interracial marriages unlawful. Other states, including Arizona, California, Colorado, Indiana, and Oregon, had only recently repealed similar laws. The *Loving* case presents an interesting twist on the equality issue: Are blacks and whites treated equally if both are prohibited from marrying outside their respective races?

Loving v. Virginia

388 U.S. 1 (1967)
http://laws.findlaw.com/US/388/1.html
Oral arguments are available at http://www.oyez.org.
Vote: 9 (Black, Brennan, Clark, Douglas, Fortas,
     Harlan, Stewart, Warren, White)
     0

OPINION OF THE COURT: *Warren*
CONCURRING OPINION: *Stewart*

FACTS:

In June 1958, two Virginia residents, Mildred Jeter, a black woman, and Richard Loving, a white man, were married in Washington, D.C. *(see Box 13-2).* They returned to Virginia to live, but later that year they were charged with evading the state's antimiscegenation law by leaving the state to be married with the intent to return. The crime called for a sentence of up to five years in the state penitentiary. They pleaded guilty to the charge and were each sentenced to one year in jail. The judge suspended the sentences on condition that the Lovings leave Virginia and not return for twenty-five years. In handing down the sentence, the judge said, "Almighty God created the races white, black, yellow, malay and red, and he placed them on separate continents. And but for the interference with his arrangement there would be no cause for such marriages. The fact that he separated the races shows that he did not intend for the races to mix."

The Lovings moved to Washington. In 1963, with the help of an American Civil Liberties Union attorney, they initiated a suit to have the sentence set aside on the ground that it violated their rights under the equal protection clause of the Fourteenth Amendment. The Virginia Supreme Court upheld the constitutionality of the law and affirmed the original convictions.

ARGUMENTS:

For the appellants, Richard Perry Loving and Mildred Jeter Loving:
- The law is a relic of slavery and an expression of modern-day racism.

- The law perpetuates a caste system based on race and the inferiority of black persons who are deemed unworthy to marry whites.
- *Brown v. Board of Education* (1954) should control this case. It violates the Fourteenth Amendment's equal protection clause to criminalize an otherwise lawful act solely on the basis of race.
- The law also violates the Fourteenth Amendment's due process clause by denying a basic human right to be free to choose one's own marriage partner.

For the appellee, Commonwealth of Virginia:
- The debates over proposing and ratifying the Fourteenth Amendment show conclusively that the framers did not intend to ban antimiscegenation laws; a majority of states that supported the amendment continued to have and enforce laws against interracial marriage after ratification.
- Both whites and blacks are equally punished for marrying outside their race. There is no unequal treatment of the races.
- The wisdom of a particular law is to be determined by the legislative branch.
- Marriage regulation is best left to the states' police powers.

 MR. CHIEF JUSTICE WARREN DELIVERED THE OPINION OF THE COURT.

This case presents a constitutional question never addressed by this Court: whether a statutory scheme adopted by the State of Virginia to prevent marriages between persons solely on the basis of racial classifications violates the Equal Protection and Due Process Clauses of the Fourteenth Amendment. For reasons which seem to us to reflect the central meaning of those constitutional commands, we conclude that these statutes cannot stand consistently with the Fourteenth Amendment. . . .

While the state court is no doubt correct in asserting that marriage is a social relation subject to the State's police power, the State does not contend in its argument before this Court that its powers to regulate marriage are unlimited notwithstanding the commands of the Fourteenth Amendment. Instead, the State argues that the meaning of the Equal Protection Clause, as illuminated by the statements of the Framers, is only that state penal laws containing an interracial element as part of the definition of the offense must apply equally to whites and Negroes in the sense that members of each

BOX 13-2   INTERMARRIAGE BROKEN UP BY DEATH

Mildred Jeter Loving is part of history, but she doesn't like a lot of fuss about it. She is alone now. Her husband, Richard, died in 1975. Their three children are grown. Her life is quiet, slowed by rheumatoid arthritis. Of publicity, she says politely, "It's not my style."

Mildred, who is black, and Richard, who was white, married in 1958. She was seventeen and he was twenty-four. She did not even know the marriage was illegal. Maybe her husband did; she isn't sure. She thought they took their vows in the District because there was less red tape to go through there than in Virginia.

They were caught, convicted, exiled, then allowed to return home a few years later while their case rose to the Supreme Court, which in 1967 ruled in *Loving v. Virginia* that the state's antimiscegenation law was unconstitutional and the Lovings could no longer be hounded by authorities. Fifteen other southern states had such laws and they too were dealt a death blow that day.

Her church in Central Point, Virginia, presented her with a plaque earlier this year to commemorate what the Lovings had done. "The preacher at my church classified me with Rosa Parks," she said, referring to the woman credited with starting the Montgomery, Alabama, bus boycott. "I don't feel like that. Not at all. What happened, we really didn't intend for it to happen. What we wanted, we wanted to come home."

The nine-year court battle began at 2 a.m. one day in July 1958, when a Caroline County, Virginia, sheriff roused the Lovings from sleep and took them to the Bowling Green jail house.

"Somebody had to tell, but I have no idea who it could have been," Loving says, laughing softly. "I guess we had one enemy."

They were sentenced several months later to a year in jail each, which Judge Leon M. Bazile said would be suspended if they agreed to stay out of Virginia for twenty-five years.

They moved to the District, where they lived with one of Mildred's cousins on Neal Street, N.E. Richard worked as an auto mechanic. All three of their children were born here. They missed Virginia all the while.

Mildred Loving, now fifty-two, wrote for help to then-U.S. Attorney General Robert F. Kennedy. Bernard S.

Richard and Mildred Loving at a press conference after the Supreme Court ruled in their favor, overturning the state's antimiscegenation law.

Cohen, an attorney with the American Civil Liberties Union, wound up with the case.

Cohen was eager to take it, viewing it as a clear shot at the last legal vestiges of *de jure* racism: the antimiscegenation laws, once prevalent in more than half the states, remained while other official forms of racism had fallen. Justice Harry L. Carrico of the state supreme court wrote the 1966 opinion upholding the law, saying there were no "sound judicial reasons" to overturn it. A year later, the U.S. Supreme Court disagreed.

Reflecting on the case, Cohen said it was filled with ironies. "It was ironical that her husband was killed in an auto accident just a few years after they finally got peace. And the irony that the justice of the Virginia Supreme Court who wrote the decision upholding the constitutionality of the law is now the chief justice" of the high court. "And another irony is that I am now a member of that legislature."

race are punished to the same degree. Thus, the State contends that, because its miscegenation statutes punish equally both the white and the Negro participants in an interracial marriage, these statutes, despite their reliance on racial classifications, do not constitute an invidious discrimination based upon race. The second argument advanced by the State assumes the validity of its equal application theory. The argument is that, if the Equal Protection Clause does not outlaw miscegenation statutes because of their reliance on racial classifications, the question of constitutionality would thus become whether there was any rational basis for a State to treat interracial marriages differently from other marriages. On this question, the State argues, the scientific evidence is substantially in doubt and, consequently, this Court should defer to the wisdom of the state legislature in adopting its policy of discouraging interracial marriages.

Because we reject the notion that the mere "equal application" of a statute containing racial classifications is enough to remove the classifications from the Fourteenth Amendment's proscription of all invidious racial discriminations, we do not accept the State's contention that these statutes should be upheld if there is any possible basis for concluding that they serve a rational purpose. . . . In the case at bar, we deal with statutes containing racial classifications, and the fact of equal application does not immunize the statute from the very heavy burden of justification which the Fourteenth Amendment has traditionally required of state statutes drawn according to race. . . .

The State finds support for its "equal application" theory in the decision of the Court in *Pace v. Alabama* (1883). In that case, the Court upheld a conviction under an Alabama statute forbidding adultery or fornication between a white person and a Negro which imposed a greater penalty than that of a statute proscribing similar conduct by members of the same race. The Court reasoned that the statute could not be said to discriminate against Negroes because the punishment for each participant in the offense was the same. However, as recently as the 1964 Term, in rejecting the reasoning of that case, we stated "*Pace* represents a limited view of the Equal Protection Clause which has not withstood analysis in the subsequent decisions of this Court." As we there demonstrated, the Equal Protection Clause requires the consideration of whether the classifications drawn by any statute constitute an arbitrary and invidious discrimination. The

clear and central purpose of the Fourteenth Amendment was to eliminate all official state sources of invidious racial discrimination in the States.

There can be no question but that Virginia's miscegenation statutes rest solely upon distinctions drawn according to race. The statutes proscribe generally accepted conduct if engaged in by members of different races. Over the years, this Court has consistently repudiated "[d]istinctions between citizens solely because of their ancestry" as being "odious to a free people whose institutions are founded upon the doctrine of equality." *Hirabayashi v. United States* (1943). At the very least, the Equal Protection Clause demands that racial classifications, especially suspect in criminal statutes, be subjected to the "most rigid scrutiny," *Korematsu v. United States* (1944), and, if they are ever to be upheld, they must be shown to be necessary to the accomplishment of some permissible state objective, independent of the racial discrimination which it was the object of the Fourteenth Amendment to eliminate. . . .

There is patently no legitimate overriding purpose independent of invidious racial discrimination which justifies this classification. The fact that Virginia prohibits only interracial marriages involving white persons demonstrates that the racial classifications must stand on their own justification, as measures designed to maintain White Supremacy. We have consistently denied the constitutionality of measures which restrict the rights of citizens on account of race. There can be no doubt that restricting the freedom to marry solely because of racial classifications violates the central meaning of the Equal Protection Clause.

These statutes also deprive the Lovings of liberty without due process of law in violation of the Due Process Clause of the Fourteenth Amendment. The freedom to marry has long been recognized as one of the vital personal rights essential to the orderly pursuit of happiness by free men.

Marriage is one of the "basic civil rights of man," fundamental to our very existence and survival. To deny this fundamental freedom on so unsupportable a basis as the racial classifications embodied in these statutes, classifications so directly subversive of the principle of equality at the heart of the Fourteenth Amendment, is surely to deprive all the State's citizens of liberty without due process of law. The Fourteenth Amendment requires that the freedom of choice to marry not be restricted by invidious racial discriminations. Under our Constitution, the freedom to marry or not marry a person of another race resides with the individual and cannot be infringed by the State.

These convictions must be reversed.

It is so ordered.

The *Loving* decision illustrates the Warren Court's rejection of discriminatory racial classifications. Government policies that allocated benefits or imposed penalties exclusively on the basis of race rarely survived Supreme Court scrutiny, especially when such laws or programs placed minorities at a disadvantage or were based on racial stereotypes. The Court has continued the Warren Court's constitutional condemnation of blatant racial discrimination. ***Palmore v. Sidoti*** (1984) provides a good example.

A Florida couple, Linda and Anthony J. Sidoti, both Caucasian, divorced in May 1980. The court awarded custody of the couple's three-year-old daughter, Melanie, to her mother, Linda Sidoti. In September 1981, Anthony Sidoti filed a petition requesting a change in the custody arrangement because of new conditions. He objected to his former wife cohabiting with a black man, Clarence Palmore Jr., whom she married two months after the court action was initiated. Sidoti also made several allegations of improper child care. A court counselor investigated the child-care situation, and although there was no evidence of serious neglect, the counselor recommended a change in custody on the ground that the child would be forced to suffer significant environmental pressures stemming from the mother's choice of a lifestyle "unacceptable to the father and to society." The judge agreed, concluding that the best interests of the child would be served by awarding custody to the father. He gave the following reason for his decision:

The father's evident resentment of the mother's choice of a black partner is not sufficient to wrest custody from the mother. It is of some significance, however, that the mother did see fit to bring a man into her home and carry on a sexual relationship with him without being married to him. Such action tended to place gratification of her own desires ahead of her concern for the child's future welfare. This Court feels that despite the strides that have been made in bettering relations between the races in this country, it is inevitable that Melanie will, if allowed to remain in her present situation and attains school age and [is] thus more vulnerable to peer pressures, suffer from the social stigmatization that is sure to come.

A Florida appellate court upheld the judge's custody ruling, but the Supreme Court reversed. Chief Justice Burger's opinion for the Court was short, direct, and endorsed unanimously by the other justices:

The court [below] correctly stated that the child's welfare was the controlling factor. But that court was entirely candid and made no effort to place its holding on any ground other than race. Taking the court's findings and rationale at face value, it is clear that the outcome would have been different had petitioner married a Caucasian male of similar respectability. A core purpose of the Fourteenth Amendment was to do away with all governmentally imposed discrimination based on race. Classifying persons according to their race is more likely to reflect racial prejudice than legitimate public concerns; the race, not the person, dictates the category. Such classifications are subject to the most exacting scrutiny; to pass constitutional muster, they must be justified by a compelling governmental interest and must be "necessary . . . to the accomplishment" of their legitimate purpose. See *Loving v. Virginia* (1967).

The State, of course, has a duty of the highest order to protect the interests of minor children, particularly those of tender years. . . . It would ignore reality to suggest that racial and ethnic prejudices do not exist or that all manifestations of those prejudices have been eliminated. There is a risk that a child living with a stepparent of a different race may be subject to a variety of pressures and stresses not present if the child were living with parents of the same racial or ethnic origin.

The question, however, is whether the reality of private biases and the possible injury they might inflict are permissible considerations for removal of an infant child from the custody of its natural mother. We have little difficulty concluding that they are not. The Constitution cannot control such prejudices but neither can it tolerate them. Private biases may be outside the reach of the law, but the law cannot, directly or indirectly, give them effect.

Brown, Loving, and *Palmore* involve challenges to laws or regulations that show racial bias in their wording or in their application. In dealing with this kind of case, contemporary Courts have had little trouble finding violations of the Constitution and striking down the discriminatory policies. The intent to discriminate, however, is not always so evident. Some laws are written in language that is racially neutral, but their impacts disproportionately disadvantage a particular racial group. What about a law that is passed to accomplish a legitimate government purpose, with no racially discriminatory intent? Are such laws unconstitutional if they have a racially disproportionate impact?

Washington v. Davis (1976) presented this question to the Court. At issue was a standard verbal ability, reading, and vocabulary examination that all applicants to the police force in Washington, D.C., were required to take. Unsuccessful black applicants challenged the exam, pointing out that the test had a disproportionately negative effect on black candidates; in fact, four times as many blacks as whites failed. A federal appeals court agreed. It held that the racially disproportionate impact of the examination, standing alone and without regard to proof of discriminatory intent, was sufficient to invalidate it on constitutional grounds. But, in a 7–2 decision, the Supreme Court reversed.

Writing for the Court, Justice Byron R. White emphasized that a successful constitutional challenge requires proof of discriminatory intent. Although disproportionate impact may be relevant to determining discriminatory intent, it is insufficient on its own to establish the presence of a discriminatory purpose. The Court's decision in *Washington v. Davis* was a blow to civil rights groups, making it more difficult than before for such groups to prevail in litigation.[10]

State Action Requirement

As *Washington v. Davis* shows, a party to a suit must prove more than just unequal treatment to establish a constitutional violation. An equally important question is, who is doing the discriminating? The equal protection clause of the Fourteenth Amendment and the due process clause of the Fifth prohibit only discriminatory policies that are initiated, enforced, or supported by the government. As the Court emphasized in the **Civil Rights Cases** (1883), the Constitution does not prohibit discrimination that takes place exclusively in the private sector. To be successful, therefore, constitutional challenges must fulfill the "state action" requirement; in other words, they must prove

some form of state or federal involvement in the discrimination. Some of the Supreme Court's most difficult tasks have involved reaching decisions on what constitutes state action.

One of the earliest and most important state action controversies focused on restrictive housing covenants, a common form of racial discrimination during the first half of the twentieth century. These covenants were private contractual arrangements, covering whole neighborhoods or subdivisions, that prohibited individual home owners from selling their property to nonwhites. The agreements were binding on all subsequent owners of the property. Racially restrictive covenants were a response to black migration into northern cities and to a 1917 Supreme Court decision, *Buchanan v. Warley,* striking down state laws that mandated racial segregation in housing. Whites opposed to residential integration viewed restrictive covenants as a way to keep blacks from moving into their neighborhoods.

The covenants were so effective that civil rights groups, especially the NAACP's LDF, considered their elimination—along with school segregation—a top priority. But they posed a vexing problem for such organizations because the state was not responsible for passing or maintaining them; in other words, the state action necessary to create a violation of the Fourteenth Amendment's equal protection clause did not *seem* to be present.

The state action requirement posed no obstacle for civil rights litigants seeking to challenge public school segregation because that policy was clearly the result of action by the government or its officials. The state action requirement was, however, a serious problem for legal challenges to private discrimination. African Americans often were denied access to public accommodations such as restaurants and hotels. Restrictive covenants and other "gentlemen's agreements" kept them from buying or renting the property of their choice. In all these cases, private enterprises and the individuals who owned properties simply refused to do business with blacks. Such discrimination, without any government involvement, appeared beyond the reach of the Constitution.

Even so, LDF attorneys pushed forward, developing imaginative arguments to convince judges that state action was present in these seemingly private cases. *Shelley v. Kraemer* (1948) was among their first attempts to do so before the Supreme Court. In this

---

10. In his *Washington v. Davis* opinion, Justice White pointed out that under some federal civil rights statutes disproportionate impact is enough to trigger a violation of the law. Therefore, it may be easier for civil rights advocates to win suits under congressional statutes than to claim a violation of the Constitution.

case, the Court found the presence of state action in an essentially private matter, the purchase of a house. Some have criticized the *Shelley* case for adopting an inappropriately broad definition of what constitutes state action. Those who drafted and ratified the equal protection clause, it is argued, had no intention of prohibiting such indirect government involvement. Were the justices wrong in their interpretation of the concept of state action? Or did the Court appropriately condemn a form of discrimination that could not have existed without state support?

Shelley v. Kraemer

334 U.S. 1 (1948)
http://laws.findlaw.com/US/334/1.html
Vote: 6 (Black, Burton, Douglas, Frankfurter, Murphy, Vinson)
   0

OPINION OF THE COURT: *Vinson*

NOT PARTICIPATING: *Jackson, Reed, Rutledge*

FACTS:

J. D. and Ethel Lee Shelley, an African American couple, moved from Mississippi to Missouri just before World War II. When their family grew to six children, the Shelleys decided to move from their poor, predominantly black neighborhood to a more desirable location. On August 11, 1945, the Shelleys bought a house in the Grand Prairie neighborhood of St. Louis, a white residential area with only a few houses occupied by blacks.[11]

Two months later, on October 9, Louis and Fern Kraemer, along with other property owners in the neighborhood, filed suit asking the court to divest the Shelleys of their property. They based their suit on a violation of a restrictive covenant signed in 1911. This covenant was a legal contract signed by thirty neighborhood property owners who agreed that for fifty years they would not allow their respective properties to be occupied by any person not of the Caucasian race. This restriction was binding upon subsequent owners of the properties as well as the original parties. The Shelley house was covered by the agreement, and the white property owners demanded that it be enforced.

The Missouri Supreme Court ruled that the covenant should be enforced. The Shelleys, represented by Thurgood Marshall and the LDF staff, appealed to the U.S. Supreme Court, and the case was combined with a similar one from Michigan. The Justice Department

---

11. For more on this case, see Clement E. Vose, *Caucasians Only* (Berkeley: University of California Press, 1959).

and a host of civil rights organizations submitted briefs supporting Marshall's position.

ARGUMENTS:

For the petitioners, J. D. Shelley and Ethel Lee Shelley:

- A contract that on the basis of race denies the right to acquire, occupy, and use property is void for being contrary to public policy and therefore unenforceable.
- In *Buchanan v. Warley* (1917) the Court declared that state interference with property rights on the basis of race is not a legitimate exercise of state police power.
- The restrictive covenants in question deprive the petitioners of their right to acquire property solely on the basis of race, and when the state enforces those private agreements it becomes a party to the discrimination.
- The state action can occur by actions of the judicial branch as well as the legislative and executive branches.

For the respondents, Louis Kraemer and Fern Kraemer:

- Contrary to the petitioner's claim, the contract in question does not violate any state or federal law and therefore cannot be declared contrary to public policy.
- The contract in question is a private agreement between individual private parties over the sale or transfer of private property. It involves no state action and therefore the Fourteenth Amendment does not apply.
- The Fourteenth Amendment is prohibitive of state action only when the state acts in its own right, not when a state court is called upon to decide private rights.
- The petitioners would have the Court rule that the Missouri judiciary cannot enforce private contracts like the one in question. Such a ruling would deprive the respondents of their rights to property and contracts and deny them access to the courts for adjudication of their rights.

● MR. CHIEF JUSTICE VINSON DELIVERED THE OPINION OF THE COURT.

Whether the equal protection clause of the Fourteenth Amendment inhibits judicial enforcement by state courts of restrictive covenants based on race or color is a question which this Court has not heretofore been

In 1948 the Supreme Court held that the state of Missouri had engaged in unconstitutional discrimination when it enforced a restrictive covenant that prevented J. D. and Ethel Lee Shelley and their six children from retaining ownership of their newly purchased home in St. Louis.

called upon to consider. . . . Here the particular patterns of discrimination and the areas in which the restrictions are to operate, are determined, in the first instance, by the terms of agreements among private individuals. Participation of the State consists in the enforcement of the restrictions so defined. The crucial issue with which we are here confronted is whether this distinction removes these cases from the operation of the prohibitory provisions of the Fourteenth Amendment.

Since the decision of this Court in the *Civil Rights Cases* (1883), the principle has become firmly embedded in our constitutional law that the action inhibited by the first section of the Fourteenth Amendment is only such action as may fairly be said to be that of the States. That Amendment erects no shield against merely private conduct, however discriminatory or wrongful.

We conclude, therefore, that the restrictive agreements standing alone cannot be regarded as violative of any rights guaranteed to petitioners by the Fourteenth Amendment. So long as the purposes of those agreements are effectuated by voluntary adherence to their terms, it would appear clear that there has been no action by the State and the provisions of the Amendment have not been violated.

But here there was more. These are cases in which the purposes of the agreements were secured only by judicial enforcement by state courts of the restrictive terms of the agreements. The respondents urge that judicial enforcement of private agreements does not amount to state action; or, in any event, the participation of the State is so attenuated in character as not to amount to state action within the meaning of the Fourteenth Amendment. . . .

That the action of state courts and judicial officers in their official capacities is to be regarded as action of the State within the meaning of the Fourteenth Amendment, is a proposition which has long been established by decisions of this Court. That principle was given expression in the earliest cases involving the construction of the terms of the Fourteenth Amendment. . . .

The short of the matter is that from the time of the adoption of the Fourteenth Amendment until the present, it has been the consistent ruling of this Court that the action of the States to which the Amendment has reference includes action of state courts and state judicial officials. Although, in construing the terms of the Fourteenth Amendment, differences have from time to time been expressed as to whether particular types of state action may be said to offend the Amendment's prohibitory provisions, it has never been suggested that state court action is immunized from the operation of those provisions simply because the act is that of the judicial branch of the state government.

Against this background of judicial construction, extending over a period of some three-quarters of a century, we are called upon to consider whether enforcement by state courts of the restrictive agreements in these cases may be deemed to be the acts of those States; and, if so, whether that action has denied these petitioners the equal protection of the laws which the Amendment was intended to insure.

We have no doubt that there has been state action in these cases in the full and complete sense of the phrase. The undisputed facts disclose that petitioners were willing purchasers of properties upon which they desired to establish homes. The owners of the properties were willing sellers; and contracts of sale were accordingly consummated. It is clear that but for the active intervention of the state courts, supported by the full panoply of state power, petitioners would have been free to occupy the properties in question without restraint.

These are not cases, as has been suggested, in which the States have merely abstained from action, leaving private individuals free to impose such discriminations as they see fit. Rather, these are cases in which the States have made available to such individuals the full coercive power of government to deny to petitioners, on the grounds of race or color, the enjoyment of property rights in premises which petitioners are willing and financially able to acquire and which the grantors are willing to sell. The difference between judicial enforcement and nonenforcement of the restrictive covenants is the difference to petitioners between being denied rights of property available to other members of the community and being accorded full enjoyment of those rights on an equal footing. . . .

State action, as that phrase is understood for the purposes of the Fourteenth Amendment, refers to exertions of state power in all forms. And when the effect of that action is to deny rights subject to the protection of the Fourteenth Amendment, it is the obligation of this Court to enforce the constitutional commands.

We hold that in granting judicial enforcement of the restrictive agreements in these cases, the States have denied petitioners the equal protection of the laws and that, therefore, the action of the state courts cannot stand. We have noted that freedom from discrimination by the States in the enjoyment of property rights was among the basic objectives sought to be effectuated by the framers of the Fourteenth Amendment. That such discrimination has occurred in these cases is clear. Because of the race or color of these petitioners they have been denied rights of ownership or occupancy enjoyed as a matter of course by other citizens of different race or color. . . .

The problem of defining the scope of the restrictions which the Federal Constitution imposes upon exertions of power by the States has given rise to many of the most persistent and fundamental issues which this Court has been called upon to consider. That problem was foremost in the minds of the framers of the Constitution, and, since that early day, has arisen in a multitude of forms. The task of determining whether the action of a State offends constitutional provisions is one which may not be undertaken lightly. Where, however, it is clear that the action of the State violates the terms of the fundamental charter, it is the obligation of this Court so to declare.

The historical context in which the Fourteenth Amendment became a part of the Constitution should not be forgotten. Whatever else the framers sought to achieve, it is clear that the matter of primary concern was the establishment of equality in the enjoyment of basic civil and political rights and the preservation of those rights from discriminatory action on the part of the States based on considerations of race or color. Seventy-five years ago this Court announced that the provisions of the Amendment are to be construed with this fundamental purpose in mind. Upon full consideration, we have concluded that in these cases the States have acted to deny petitioners the equal protection of the laws guaranteed by the Fourteenth Amendment.

Reversed.

In *Shelley* the Vinson Court adopted the LDF's broad approach to the state action requirement of the Fourteenth Amendment—at least in the area of restrictive covenants. In *Burton v. Wilmington Parking Authority* (1961), the Warren Court revisited *Shelley v. Kraemer* and, more generally, the state action requirement of the Fourteenth Amendment. In this case a black man was discriminated against by a privately owned and operated business, and, therefore, the equal protection clause did not seem to apply. But the attorneys representing William Burton argued that the state was indeed a participant in the discrimination. Was the Court's ruling a natural application of *Shelley*? Or was the involvement of the state government too remote to warrant an application of the Fourteenth Amendment?

Burton v. Wilmington Parking Authority

365 U.S. 715 (1961)
http://laws.findlaw.com/US/365/715.html
Vote: 6 (Black, Brennan, Clark, Douglas, Stewart, Warren)
     3 (Frankfurter, Harlan, Whittaker)

OPINION OF THE COURT: *Clark*
CONCURRING OPINION: *Stewart*
DISSENTING OPINIONS: *Frankfurter, Harlan*

FACTS:

In August 1958, William Burton parked his car in a downtown parking garage in Wilmington, Delaware, and went to the Eagle Coffee Shoppe, a restaurant located within the parking structure. Burton was denied service in the restaurant because he was black.

The parking garage was built, owned, and operated by the Wilmington Parking Authority, a city agency. Before the structure was completed, it had become clear that parking revenues alone would be insufficient to repay the loans and bonds that had financed the construction. To increase revenues, the parking authority leased space in the building to private businesses, including the Eagle Coffee Shoppe, which had a thirty-year lease to operate a restaurant in the garage. The Eagle Corporation invested some $220,000 of its own money to convert the space for restaurant use. The parking authority, under the terms of the lease, provided certain materials and services for the operation, and the city collected more than $28,000 in annual rent from Eagle. In addition, state law permitted restaurant operators to deny service to any person who would be offensive to a majority of customers or would injure the business.

Burton filed suit, claiming that his rights under the equal protection clause had been violated. The parking authority disagreed, arguing that the discrimination was purely private, with the state having no substantive involvement. The trial court ruled in favor of Burton, finding that the lease arrangement did not insulate the parking authority from the discrimination of its tenant. The Delaware Supreme Court, however, reversed, holding that Eagle was operating in a purely private capacity.

ARGUMENTS:

For the appellant, William H. Burton:

- The parking authority cannot exempt itself from the Constitution by leasing space to a private party.
- Racial discrimination cannot constitutionally occur in a place maintained by public funds.

- Because it operates in a public building, the Eagle Coffee Shoppe is not acting in a completely private capacity.
- The state participates in the discrimination by allowing the proprietor of a restaurant to deny service to anyone the proprietor thinks will be offensive to other customers or be detrimental to the business.

For the appellees, Wilmington Parking Authority and the Eagle Coffee Shoppe:

- The discriminatory actions of the Eagle Coffee Shoppe are completely private, and consequently the Fourteenth Amendment does not apply.
- The parking authority has no control over the Eagle Coffee Shoppe, either by statute or by terms of the lease.
- A private entity does not become part of state government just because it leases space from the government.

◥ **MR. JUSTICE CLARK DELIVERED THE OPINION OF THE COURT.**

It is clear, as it always has been since the *Civil Rights Cases* [1883], that "Individual invasion of individual rights is not the subject-matter of the [Fourteenth] amendment," and that private conduct abridging individual rights does no violence to the Equal Protection Clause unless to some significant extent the State in any of its manifestations has been found to have become involved in it. Because the virtue of the right to equal protection of the laws could lie only in the breadth of its application, its constitutional assurance was reserved in terms whose imprecision was necessary if the right were to be enjoyed in the variety of individual-state relationships which the Amendment was designed to embrace. For the same reason, to fashion and apply a precise formula for recognition of state responsibility under the Equal Protection Clause is an "impossible task" which "This Court has never attempted." . . .

The trial court's disposal of the issues on summary judgment has resulted in a rather incomplete record, but the opinion of the Supreme Court as well as that of the Chancellor presents the facts in sufficient detail for us to determine the degree of state participation in Eagle's refusal to serve petitioner. In this connection the Delaware Supreme Court seems to have placed controlling emphasis on its conclusion, as to the accuracy of which there is doubt, that only some 15% of the total cost of the facility was "advanced" from public funds; that the cost of the entire facility was allocated three-fifths to the space for commercial leasing and two-fifths to parking space; that anticipated revenue from parking was only some 30.5% of the total income, the balance of which was expected to be earned by the leasing; that the Authority had no original intent to place a restaurant in the building, it being only a happenstance resulting from the bidding; that Eagle expended considerable moneys on furnishings; that the restaurant's main and marked public entrance is on Ninth Street without any public entrance direct from the parking area; and that "the only connection Eagle has with the public facility . . . is the furnishing of the sum of $28,700 annually in the form of rent which is used by the Authority to defray a portion of the operating expense of an otherwise unprofitable enterprise." While these factual considerations are indeed validly accountable aspects of the enterprise upon which the State has embarked, we cannot say that they lead inescapably to the conclusion that state action is not present. Their persuasiveness is diminished when evaluated in the context of other factors which must be acknowledged.

The land and building were publicly owned. As an entity, the building was dedicated to "public uses" in performance of the Authority's "essential governmental functions." The costs of land acquisition, construction, and maintenance are defrayed entirely from donations by the City of Wilmington, from loans and revenue bonds and from the proceeds of rentals and parking services out of which the loans and bonds were payable. Assuming that the distinction would be significant, the commercially leased areas were not surplus state property, but constituted a physically and financially integral and, indeed, indispensable part of the State's plan to operate its project as a self-sustaining unit. Upkeep and maintenance of the building, including necessary repairs, were responsibilities of the Authority and were payable out of public funds. It cannot be doubted that the peculiar relationship of the restaurant to the parking facility in which it is located confers on each an incidental variety of mutual benefits. Guests of the restaurant are afforded a convenient place to park their automobiles, even if they cannot enter the restaurant directly from the parking area. Similarly, its convenience for diners may well provide additional demand for the Authority's parking facilities. Should any improvements effected in the leasehold by Eagle become part of the realty, there is no possibility of increased taxes being passed on to it since the fee is held by a tax-exempt government agency. Neither can it be ignored, especially in view of Eagle's affirmative allegation that for it to serve Negroes would injure its business, that profits earned by discrimination not only contribute to, but also are indispensable elements in, the financial success of a governmental agency.

Addition of all these activities, obligations and responsibilities of the Authority, the benefits mutually conferred, together with the obvious fact that the restaurant is operated as an integral part of a public building devoted to a public parking service, indicates that degree of state participation and involvement in discriminatory action which it was the design of the Fourteenth Amendment to condemn. It is irony amounting to grave injustice that in one part of a single building, erected and maintained with public funds by an agency of the State to serve a public purpose, all persons have equal rights, while in another portion, also serving the public, a Negro is a second-class citizen, offensive because of his race, without rights and unentitled to service, but at the same time fully enjoys equal access to nearby restaurants in wholly privately owned buildings. As the Chancellor pointed out, in its lease with Eagle the Authority could have affirmatively required Eagle to discharge the responsibilities under the Fourteenth Amendment imposed upon the private enterprise as a consequence of state participation. But no State may effectively abdicate its responsibilities by either ignoring them or by merely failing to discharge them whatever the motive may be. It is of no consolation to an individual denied the equal protection of the laws that it was done in good faith. . . . By its inaction, the Authority, and through it the State, has not only made itself a party to the refusal of service, but has elected to place its power, property and prestige behind the admitted discrimination. The State has so far insinuated itself into a position of interdependence with Eagle that it must be recognized as a joint participant in the challenged activity, which, on that account, cannot be considered to have been so "purely private" as to fall without the scope of the Fourteenth Amendment.

Because readily applicable formulae may not be fashioned, the conclusions drawn from the facts and circumstances of this record are by no means declared as universal truths on the basis of which every state leasing agreement is to be tested. Owing to the very "largeness" of government, a multitude of relationships might appear to some to fall within the Amendment's embrace, but that, it must be remembered, can be determined only in the framework of the peculiar facts or circumstances present. Therefore respondents' prophecy of nigh universal application of a constitutional precept so peculiarly dependent for its invocation upon appropriate facts fails to take into account "Differences in circumstances which beget appropriate differences in law." Specifically defining the limits of our inquiry, what we hold today is that when a State leases public property in the manner and for the purpose shown to have been the case here, the proscriptions of the Fourteenth Amendment must be complied with by the lessee as certainly as though they were binding covenants written into the agreement itself. . . .

Reversed and remanded.

Burton demonstrates the Warren Court's willingness to impose an expansive view of state action, even in the face of lingering hostility toward its *Brown* decision. But, as we shall soon discover, *Burton* did not eliminate the public/private distinction.

Along those lines is the Burger Court's decision in *Moose Lodge 107 v. Irvis* (1972), which suggests that the definition of state action has its limits. Note how Justice William Rehnquist distinguishes the state's involvement here from Delaware's relationship with the Eagle Coffee Shoppe. Is his argument that the *Burton* precedent is inapplicable convincing? Would finding state action in this case blur any meaningful state/private distinction? Or is Justice William J. Brennan more persuasive when he argues that the state was involved in racial discrimination? If the Court had taken the dissenters' position, what implications would this have had for other private organizations, such as country clubs and fraternal organizations?

Moose Lodge No. 107 v. Irvis

407 U.S. 163 (1972)
http://laws.findlaw.com/US/407/163.html
Oral arguments are available at http://www.oyez.org.
Vote: 6 (Blackmun, Burger, Powell, Rehnquist, Stewart, White)
     3 (Brennan, Douglas, Marshall)

OPINION OF THE COURT: *Rehnquist*
DISSENTING OPINIONS: *Brennan, Douglas*

FACTS:

A white member in good standing of the Harrisburg, Pennsylvania, Moose Lodge, accompanied by a guest, entered the lodge's dining room and bar and requested service. The lodge employees refused to serve him because his guest, K. Leroy Irvis, was black. Irvis was also a member of the Pennsylvania state legislature. Lodge 107, part of the national Moose organization, was subject to the rules of its Supreme Lodge, which limited membership to Caucasians and permitted members to entertain only Caucasian guests on the premises. Irvis sued the lodge, claiming that he had been denied his rights under the equal protection clause of the Fourteenth Amendment. His suit was based on the theory that by granting the Moose Lodge a liquor license, the state of Pennsylvania was approving the organization's racially discriminatory policies. A federal court ruled in favor of Irvis, declaring that the lodge's liquor license would be invalid until such time as the discriminatory practices ceased. The lodge appealed.

ARGUMENTS:

For the appellant, Moose Lodge No. 107:

- The right to choose one's social intimates and to form a club that expresses one's likes and dislikes is protected against government interference by the constitutional rights of privacy and association.
- Moose Lodge is a private, not-for-profit, noncommercial organization that exists for its members only and does not seek public patronage. It is not a public accommodation.
- Granting a liquor license to a private club does not convert it into a state actor any more than granting a driver's license, a building permit, or a marriage license transforms the recipients of those licenses into state actors.

For the appellee, K. Leroy Irvis:

- The state cannot command, support, or encourage racial discrimination by a private party. By granting a liquor license to the lodge, the state has approved its operations.
- There are only a limited number of liquor licenses available in the state. Granting one to the lodge is a state endorsement.
- With a state liquor license the lodge gains preferred pricing when purchasing alcohol from state stores, the right to resell the alcohol, and exemption from certain state restrictions (e.g., Sunday liquor sales). The state, therefore, has become significantly involved with the lodge and also becomes party to the racial discrimination that the lodge practices.

MR. JUSTICE REHNQUIST DELIVERED THE OPINION OF THE COURT.

Moose Lodge is a private club in the ordinary meaning of that term. It is a local chapter of a national fraternal organization having well-defined requirements for membership. It conducts all of its activities in a building that is owned by it. It is not publicly funded. Only members and guests are permitted in any lodge of the order; one may become a guest only by invitation of a member or upon invitation of the house committee.

Appellee, while conceding the right of private clubs to choose members upon a discriminatory basis, asserts that the licensing of Moose Lodge to serve liquor by the Pennsylvania Liquor Control Board amounts to such state involvement with the club's activities as to make its discriminatory practices forbidden by the Equal Protection Clause of the Fourteenth Amendment. . . . We conclude that Moose Lodge's refusal to serve food and beverages to a guest by reason of the fact that he was a Negro does not, under the circumstances here presented, violate the Fourteenth Amendment.

In 1883, this Court in *The Civil Rights Cases* set forth the essential dichotomy between discriminatory action by the State, which is prohibited by the Equal Protection Clause, and private conduct, "however discriminatory or wrongful," against which that clause "erects no shield." That dichotomy has been subsequently reaffirmed in *Shelley v. Kraemer* and in *Burton v. Wilmington Parking Authority.*

While the principle is easily stated, the question of whether particular discriminatory conduct is private, on the one hand, or amounts to "state action," on the other hand, frequently admits of no easy answer. "Only by sifting facts and weighing circumstances can the non-obvious involvement of the State in private conduct be attributed its true significance."

Our cases make clear that the impetus for the forbidden discrimination need not originate with the State if it is state action that enforces privately originated discrimination. *Shelley v. Kraemer.* The Court held in *Burton v. Wilmington Parking Authority* that a private restaurant owner who refused service because of a customer's race violated the Fourteenth Amendment, where the restaurant was located in a building owned by a state-created parking authority and leased from the authority. The Court, after a comprehensive review of the relationship between the lessee and the parking authority concluded that the latter had "so far

insinuated itself into a position of interdependence with Eagle [the restaurant owner] that it must be recognized as a joint participant in the challenged activity, which, on that account, cannot be considered to have been so 'purely private' as to fall without the scope of the Fourteenth Amendment."

The Court has never held, of course, that discrimination by an otherwise private entity would be violative of the Equal Protection Clause if the private entity receives any sort of benefit or service at all from the State, or if it is subject to state regulation in any degree whatever. Since state-furnished services include such necessities of life as electricity, water, and police and fire protection, such a holding would utterly emasculate the distinction between private as distinguished from state conduct set forth in *The Civil Rights Cases* and adhered to in subsequent decisions. Our holdings indicate that where the impetus for the discrimination is private, the State must have "significantly involved itself with invidious discriminations" in order for the discriminatory action to fall within the ambit of the constitutional prohibition. . . .

Here there is nothing approaching the symbiotic relationship between lessor and lessee that was present in *Burton,* where the private lessee obtained the benefit of locating in a building owned by the state-created parking authority, and the parking authority was enabled to carry out its primary public purpose of furnishing parking space by advantageously leasing portions of the building constructed for that purpose to commercial lessees such as the owner of the Eagle Restaurant. Unlike *Burton,* the Moose Lodge building is located on land owned by it, not by any public authority. Far from apparently holding itself out as a place of public accommodation, Moose Lodge quite ostentatiously proclaims the fact that it is not open to the public at large. Nor is it located and operated in such surroundings that although private in name, it discharges a function or performs a service that would otherwise in all likelihood be performed by the State. In short, while Eagle was a public restaurant in a public building, Moose Lodge is a private social club in a private building.

With the exception hereafter noted, the Pennsylvania Liquor Control Board plays absolutely no part in establishing or enforcing the membership or guest policies of the club that it licenses to serve liquor. There is no suggestion in this record that Pennsylvania law, either as written or as applied, discriminates against minority groups either in their right to apply for club licenses themselves or in their right to purchase and be served liquor in places of public accommodation. The only effect that the state licensing of Moose Lodge to serve liquor can be said to have on the right of any other Pennsylvanian to buy or be served liquor on premises other than those of Moose Lodge is that for some purposes club licenses are counted in the maximum number of licenses that may be issued in a given municipality. . . .

The District Court was at pains to point out in its opinion what it considered to be the "pervasive" nature of the regulation of private clubs by the Pennsylvania Liquor Control Board. As that court noted, an applicant for a club license must make such physical alterations in its premises as the board may require, must file a list of the names and addresses of its members and employees, and must keep extensive financial records. The board is granted the right to inspect the licensed premises at any time when patrons, guests, or members are present.

However detailed this type of regulation may be in some particulars, it cannot be said to in any way foster or encourage racial discrimination. Nor can it be said to make the State in any realistic sense a partner or even a joint venturer in the club's enterprise. The limited effect of the prohibition against obtaining additional club licenses when the maximum number of retail licenses allotted to a municipality has been issued, when considered together with the availability of liquor from hotel, restaurant, and retail licensees, falls far short of conferring upon club licensees a monopoly in the dispensing of liquor in any given municipality or in the State as a whole. We therefore hold that . . . the operation of the regulatory scheme enforced by the Pennsylvania Liquor Control Board does not sufficiently implicate the State in the discriminatory guest policies of Moose Lodge to make the latter "state action" within the ambit of the Equal Protection Clause of the Fourteenth Amendment.

Reversed and remanded.

MR. JUSTICE BRENNAN . . . *dissenting.*

When Moose Lodge obtained its liquor license, the State of Pennsylvania became an active participant in the operation of the Lodge bar. Liquor licensing laws are only incidentally revenue measures; they are primarily pervasive regulatory schemes under which the State dictates and continually supervises virtually every detail of the operation of the licensee's business. Very few, if any, other licensed businesses experience such complete state involvement. Yet the Court holds that such involvement does not constitute "state action" making the Lodge's refusal to serve a guest liquor solely because of his race a violation of the Fourteenth Amendment. The vital flaw in the Court's reasoning is its complete disregard of the fundamental value underlying the "state action" concept. . . .

Plainly, the State of Pennsylvania's liquor regulations intertwine the State with the operation of the Lodge bar in a "significant way [and] lend [the State's] authority to the sordid business of racial discrimination." . . .

This is thus a case requiring application of the principle that until today has governed our determinations of the existence of "state action": "Our prior decisions leave no doubt that the mere existence of efforts by the State, through legislation or otherwise, to authorize, encourage, or otherwise support racial discrimination in a particular facet of life constitutes illegal state involvement in those pertinent private acts of discrimination that subsequently occur."

I therefore dissent and would affirm the final decree entered by the District Court.

Did the Burger Court retreat from *Shelley* and *Burton,* or did it merely draw a sensible distinction between private and public discrimination for purposes of the Fourteenth Amendment? We leave these questions to you to address, but note that the three dissenters in *Moose Lodge No. 107*—Brennan, Marshall, and Douglas—had been members of the Warren Court's liberal majority responsible for expanding the rights of racial minorities.

Remember that victims of invidious discrimination may find recourse in federal or state statutes that outlaw private forms of discrimination when state action is not present or is difficult to prove. Governments enjoy a number of powers, especially those over commercial activities, that permit regulating certain forms of private discriminatory behavior. Although the Supreme Court ruled in *Moose Lodge No. 107* that state action had not contributed to the discrimination, several states have used the power to regulate alcoholic beverages as a means of combating racial bias. For example, in 1973 the Supreme Court upheld a Maine regulation that made the granting of a liquor license contingent on nondiscriminatory service policies.[12]

---

12. *B.P.O.E. Lodge No. 2043 v. Ingraham* (1973).

SEX DISCRIMINATION

Before *Brown v. Board of Education,* groups and individuals challenging practices as racially discriminatory had a major obstacle to overcome: *Plessy v. Ferguson.* Lawsuits based on claims of sex discrimination were also handicapped and for even longer periods of time. Indeed, before the 1970s, the few sex discrimination cases that reached the Supreme Court often ended in decisions that reinforced traditional views of sex roles. In **Bradwell v. Illinois** (1873), for example, the Court heard a challenge to an action by the Illinois Supreme Court denying Myra Bradwell a license to practice law solely because of her sex. The Court, with only Chief Justice Salmon P. Chase dissenting, upheld the state action. Justice Joseph P. Bradley's concurring opinion, which Justices Noah H. Swayne and Stephen J. Field joined, illustrates the attitude of the legal community toward women. Bradley said that he gave his "heartiest concurrence" to contemporary society's "multiplication of avenues for women's advancement." But he added, "The natural and proper timidity and delicacy which belongs to the female sex evidently unfits it for many of the occupations of civil life." This condition, according to Bradley, was the product of divine ordinance. Two years later, in *Minor v. Happersett* (1875), the Court upheld Missouri's denial of voting rights to women, a precedent in effect until ratification of the Nineteenth Amendment in 1920.

Similar decisions came early in the twentieth century. The majority opinion in the 1908 case of *Muller v. Oregon,* in which the Court upheld a maximum-work-hours law that covered only women, echoed Justice Bradley's view of women.[13] Writing for the Court, Justice David J. Brewer noted:

That woman's physical structure and the performance of maternal functions place her at a disadvantage in the struggle for subsistence is obvious. This is especially true when the burdens of motherhood are upon her. Even when they are not, by abundant testimony of the medical fraternity continuance for a long time on her feet at work, repeating this from day to day, tends to injurious effects upon her body, and, as healthy mothers are essential to vigorous offspring, the physical well-being of women becomes an object of public interest and care in order to preserve the strength and vigor of the race.

---

13. At the time of their implementation, statutes such as the one at issue in *Muller* were seen as a progressive step to protect women in the workforce. Today, this kind of law, based as it is on an assumption of the inferiority of women, is considered paternalistic.

Myra Bradwell studied law with her husband, a judge, and edited and published the Chicago Legal News, *the most important legal publication in the Midwest. Although she passed the bar exam, the Illinois Supreme Court refused to admit her to the state bar because of her sex. She appealed to the U.S. Supreme Court, but lost.*

As late as 1948, the Court upheld the right of the state to ban women from certain occupations. In *Goesaert v. Cleary,* decided that year, the justices declared valid a Michigan law that barred a woman from becoming a bartender unless she was a member of the bar owner's immediate family. In explaining the ruling, Justice Felix Frankfurter wrote, "The fact that women may now have achieved the virtues that men have long claimed as their prerogatives and now indulge in vices that men have long practiced, does not preclude the States from drawing a sharp line between the sexes, certainly in such matters as the regulation of the liquor traffic." In a comparatively modern case, *Hoyt v. Florida* (1961), the justices upheld a Florida law that automatically exempted women from jury duty unless they asked to serve.

While the Court continued to articulate a traditional view of women, the growing strength of the women's movement in the 1960s prompted legislatures

BOX 13-3   MAJOR CONGRESSIONAL ACTION ON WOMEN'S RIGHTS

1960s

• Title VII of the Civil Rights Act of 1964 makes it unlawful for an employer "to refuse to hire . . . any individual . . . because of such individual's race, color, religion, sex, or national origin" except where "religion, sex, or national origin" is a bona fide occupational qualification necessary to the normal operation of that particular business.

• Equal Pay Act of 1963 requires employers to pay men and women performing equal work equal salaries.

1970s

• Equal rights amendment (ERA) sent to the states for ratification in 1972. This amendment would have declared, "Equality of rights under the law shall not be denied or abridged by the United States or by any State on account of sex."

• Expansion of Title VII's ban on employment discrimination to cover employees of state and local governments.

• Title IX of the education amendments (passed in 1972) states, "No person in the United States shall, on the basis of sex, be excluded from participation in, be denied benefits of, or be subjected to discrimination under any educational program or activity receiving Federal financial assistance."

• Pregnancy Discrimination Act of 1978 forbids employment discrimination on grounds of pregnancy.

• Application in 1974 of the Civil Rights Act of 1968 to sex discrimination. The act prohibits discrimination in the advertising, financing, sale, or rental of housing.

1980s

• Civil Rights Restoration Act of 1988 extends Title IX coverage to all operations of state or local units and to private organizations if federal aid is given to the enterprises as a whole or if the enterprises are "principally engaged" in providing education, housing, health care, parks, or social services.

• An attempt in Congress to repropose the ERA falls short of the two-thirds requirement.

1990s

• Civil Rights Act of 1991 reaffirms and expands protections against discrimination in employment.

• The Family and Medical Leave Act of 1993 allows individuals who work for employers with fifty or more employees to take up to twelve weeks of unpaid leave to stay home with a new baby or sick parent, child, or spouse or to recover from an illness.

• Violence Against Women Act, initially passed in 1994 and subsequently modified, provides law enforcement assistance and authorizes federal support for social programs designed to combat domestic violence.

SOURCES: Leslie Friedman Goldstein, *The Constitutional Rights of Women* (Madison: University of Wisconsin Press, 1988); Susan Gluck Mezey, *In Pursuit of Equality* (New York: St. Martin's Press, 1992); and National Organization for Women, Legislative Updates, http://www.now.org/issues/legislat/index.html.

to act. Congress passed a number of federal statutes extending equal rights to women, among them the Equal Pay Act of 1963, which requires equal pay for equal work, and the 1964 Civil Rights Act, which forbids discrimination based on sex in the area of employment *(see Box 13-3)*. Many states passed similar laws to eliminate discriminatory conditions in the marketplace and in state legal codes. In addition to these legislative actions, in 1972 Congress proposed an amendment to the Constitution. Known as the equal rights amendment (ERA), it declared, "Equality of rights under the law shall not be denied or abridged by the United States or by any State on account of sex." Although the amendment ultimately failed to attain

support of the required number of states, the very fact that Congress proposed it (and later extended the deadline for ratification) indicated changing views toward women.

Standard of Scrutiny

While continuing to press for the ERA, women's rights organizations also turned to the courts for redress of their grievances. Like the advocates for black Americans, many in the women's movement believed that the due process and equal protection clauses held the potential for ensuring women's rights, and they began organizing to assert their claims in court.

One of the first such cases to reach the Supreme Court was *Reed v. Reed* (1971). In this case, the justices considered the validity of an Idaho inheritance statute that used sex classifications, which ACLU attorneys, including Ruth Bader Ginsburg, challenged as a violation of the equal protection clause of the Fourteenth Amendment.

It was clear from the outset that the same requirements that had developed in race relations cases would apply here: the statute's challenger would have to demonstrate both invidious discrimination and state action before a violation could be found. What was not so clear was the standard of scrutiny the justices would use. In the racial discrimination cases, the Court had declared strict scrutiny the appropriate standard. Racial minorities were considered a suspect class, and, therefore, classifications based on race were presumed to be unconstitutional. The state had a heavy burden of proof if it wished to show that a law based on race was the least restrictive means to achieve a compelling state interest. Much of the success enjoyed by civil rights groups was due to this favorable legal status. Ginsburg and other advocates of equal rights for women hoped the Court would adopt the same standard for sex discrimination claims. Did the justices go along?

Sally Reed, pictured with Boise attorney Allen Derr, who represented her in oral arguments before the Supreme Court, challenged an Idaho law that gave preference to males over females in designating administrators of estates. **Reed v. Reed** *ushered in the modern era of sex discrimination litigation.*

Reed v. Reed

404 U.S. 71 (1971)
http://laws.findlaw.com/US/404/71.html
Oral arguments are available at http://www.oyez.org.
Vote: 7 (Blackmun, Brennan, Burger, Douglas, Marshall, Stewart, White)
   0
OPINION OF THE COURT: *Burger*

FACTS:

Richard Reed was Sally and Cecil Reed's adopted son. He died in 1967 at the age of sixteen in Ada County, Idaho, leaving no will. The Reeds, who had divorced several years before Richard's death, became involved in a legal dispute over who should administer his estate. The child's property was negligible, consisting of a few personal items and a small savings account. The total value was less than $1,000. The probate court judge appointed Cecil Reed administrator of the estate, in accordance with Idaho law. Section 15-312 of the Idaho Code stipulated that when a person died intestate (without a will) an administrator would be appointed according to a list of priority relationships.

First priority went to a surviving spouse, second priority to children, third to parents, and so forth. Section 15-314 of the statute stated that in the case of competing petitions from otherwise qualified individuals of the same priority relationship, "males must be preferred to females."

Sally Reed challenged the law as a violation of the equal protection clause of the Fourteenth Amendment. The state district court agreed with her argument, but the Idaho Supreme Court reversed. With assistance of Ginsburg and other ACLU lawyers, Sally Reed and her attorney Allen Derr took the case to the U.S. Supreme Court. There she asked the justices to adopt a strict scrutiny approach to sex discrimination cases, but they also suggested that the law was unconstitutional even under a less rigorous standard.

ARGUMENTS:

For the appellant, Sally M. Reed:
- The Idaho statute subordinating women to men without regard to individual capacity creates a suspect classification requiring close judicial scrutiny.

- The suspect class designation is appropriate because women, like African Americans, have suffered long-standing discrimination, because sex is an easily identifiable and immutable characteristic, and because women are sparsely represented in political offices.
- Biological differences have nothing to do with the ability to be an effective administrator of an estate.
- The law is based on administrative convenience only. There is no substantial relationship between the law and any permissible government interest.

For the appellee, Cecil R. Reed:

- The statute was enacted to reduce the time, trouble, and expense of probating small estates as well as to eliminate costly contests over who should administer such estates. This case demonstrates the need for administrative efficiency. Richard's estate has an estimated value of only $745.
- The argument that the discrimination against women is comparable to the enslavement of African Americans is not valid.
- The legislators who enacted this statute recognized that on average men had higher education levels and more experience in financial affairs than women, making it rational to prefer men over women in settling small estates.

MR. CHIEF JUSTICE BURGER DELIVERED THE OPINION OF THE COURT.

Having examined the record and considered the briefs and oral arguments of the parties, we have concluded that the arbitrary preference established in favor of males by §15-314 of the Idaho Code cannot stand in the face of the Fourteenth Amendment's command that no State deny the equal protection of the laws to any person within its jurisdiction.

Idaho does not, of course, deny letters of administration to women altogether. Indeed, under §15-312, a woman whose spouse dies intestate has a preference over a son, father, brother, or any other male relative of the decedent. Moreover, we can judicially notice that in this country, presumably due to the greater longevity of women, a large proportion of estates, both intestate and under wills of decedents, are administered by surviving widows.

Section 15-314 is restricted in its operation to those situations where competing applications for letters of administration have been filed by both male and female members of the same entitlement class established by §15-312. In such situations, §15-314 provides that different treatment be accorded to the applicants on the basis of their sex; it thus establishes a classification subject to scrutiny under the Equal Protection Clause.

In applying that clause, this Court has consistently recognized that the Fourteenth Amendment does not deny to States the power to treat different classes of persons in different ways. The Equal Protection Clause of that amendment does, however, deny to States the power to legislate that different treatment be accorded to persons placed by a statute into different classes on the basis of criteria wholly unrelated to the objective of that statute. A classification "must be reasonable, not arbitrary, and must rest upon some ground of difference having a fair and substantial relation to the object of the legislation, so that all persons similarly circumstanced shall be treated alike." The question presented by this case, then, is whether a difference in the sex of competing applicants for letters of administration bears a rational relationship to a state objective that is sought to be advanced by the operation of §§15-312 and 15-314.

In upholding the latter section, the Idaho Supreme Court concluded that its objective was to eliminate one area of controversy when two or more persons, equally entitled under §15-312, seek letters of administration and thereby present the probate court "with the issue of which one should be named." The court also concluded that where such persons are not of the same sex, the elimination of females from consideration "is neither an illogical nor arbitrary method devised by the legislature to resolve an issue that would otherwise require a hearing as to the relative merits . . . of the two or more petitioning relatives. . . ."

Clearly the objective of reducing the workload on probate courts by eliminating one class of contests is not without some legitimacy. The crucial question, however, is whether §15-314 advances that objective in a manner consistent with the command of the Equal Protection Clause. We hold that it does not. To give a mandatory preference to members of either sex over members of the other, merely to accomplish the elimination of hearings on the merits, is to make the very kind of arbitrary legislative choice forbidden by the Equal Protection Clause of the Fourteenth Amendment; and whatever may be said as to the positive values of avoiding intrafamily controversy, the choice in this context may not lawfully be mandated solely on the basis of sex.

We note finally that if §15-314 is viewed merely as a modifying appendage to §15-312 and aimed at the same objective, its constitutionality is not thereby saved. The objective of §15-312 clearly is to establish degrees of entitlement of various classes of persons in accordance with their varying degrees and kinds of relationship to the intestate. Regardless of their sex, persons within any one of the enumerated classes of that section are similarly situated with respect to that objective. By providing dissimilar treatment for men and women who are thus similarly situated, the challenged section violates the Equal Protection Clause. The judgment of the Idaho Supreme Court is reversed and the case remanded for further proceedings not inconsistent with this opinion.

Reversed and remanded.

The Court's unanimous decision in *Reed* applied two important principles to sex discrimination. First, the Court refused to accept Idaho's defense of its statute. The state had contended that it was inefficient to hold full court hearings on the relative merits of competing candidates to administer estates, especially small estates. Imposing arbitrary criteria saved court time and avoided intrafamily squabbles. The

Supreme Court held that administrative convenience is no justification for violating the Constitution. Second, defenders of the Idaho law argued that the arbitrary favoring of males over females made sense because, in most cases, the male will have had more education and experience in financial matters than the competing female. In rejecting this argument, the justices said that laws containing overbroad, sex-based assumptions violate the equal protection clause.

The *Reed* case also signaled that the justices were receptive to sex discrimination claims and would not hesitate to strike down state laws that imposed arbitrary sex classifications. This turn of events was certainly good news for women's rights advocates, but the standard used in the case was not. Chief Justice Burger invoked the rational basis test (rather than strict scrutiny), holding that laws based on gender classifications must be reasonable and have a rational relationship to a state objective. The Idaho law was sufficiently arbitrary to fail the rational basis test, but other laws and policies might well survive it.

Two years later the controversy over the appropriate standard of scrutiny for sex discrimination cases once again reached the justices. In *Frontiero v. Richardson*

Sharron and Joseph Frontiero. She challenged U.S. military regulations that treated male and female officers differently in determining eligibility for dependent benefits. Frontiero v. Richardson *sparked a major battle over the appropriate standard to use in deciding sex discrimination claims.*

(1973) an Air Force lieutenant claimed that the military's benefits policy discriminated on the basis of sex in violation of the Fifth Amendment's due process clause. Her argument rested on the fact that husbands of female officers were not eligible for benefits without proof that the husband was financially dependent upon his wife. However, male officers did not face the same obstacle. Their wives were presumed to be financially dependent and were automatically entitled to benefits. The Air Force argued that its policy was rational because the husbands of female officers usually had careers of their own and did not rely on their wives' income, whereas most spouses of male officers did receive a majority of their financial support from their husbands.

With only justice William Rehnquist dissenting, the Court struck down the benefits eligibility rules. Following *Reed v. Reed,* the justices concluded that the military regulations were impermissibly based on overbroad gender-based assumptions and could not be justified on the basis of administrative convenience.

Although there was overwhelming agreement on the case outcome, the justices remained far apart on the question of the appropriate level of scrutiny to apply. Four justices argued that sex should be elevated to a suspect class, and four remained wedded to the rational basis test. Justice Potter Stewart held the deciding vote, but he failed to make his preferences known. In one line, Stewart indicated that he found the Air Force regulation unconstitutional without saying what standard he applied.

Absent a Court majority in *Frontiero* voting to change the prevailing test, sex discrimination remained governed by the rational basis approach. Three years later, however, the Court finally resolved the standards issue. In *Craig v. Boren* (1976) the justices adopted an entirely new standard of scrutiny for sex discrimination cases. This test, known as intermediate or heightened scrutiny, requires that laws that classify on the basis of sex be substantially related to an important government objective. It appealed especially to justices in the center of the Court who were not happy with either the conservative rational basis test or the liberal suspect class test. Observe how Brennan, writing for the Court, justifies the new test as being consistent with *Reed* and how he treats the use of social science evidence. Also read carefully Rehnquist's dissenting opinion rejecting the new test, especially as beneficially applied to men.

Craig v. Boren

429 U.S. 190 (1976)
http://laws.findlaw.com/US/429/190.html
Oral arguments are available at http://www.oyez.org.
Vote: 7 (Blackmun, Brennan, Marshall, Powell, Stevens, Stewart, White)
    2 (Burger, Rehnquist)

OPINION OF THE COURT: *Brennan*
CONCURRING OPINIONS: *Powell, Stevens*
OPINION CONCURRING IN JUDGMENT: *Stewart*
OPINION CONCURRING IN PART: *Blackmun*
DISSENTING OPINIONS: *Burger, Rehnquist*

FACTS:

In 1972 Oklahoma enacted a statute setting the age of legal majority for both males and females at eighteen. Before then, females reached legal age at eighteen and males at twenty-one.[14] The equalization statute, however, contained one exception. Males could not purchase beer, even with the low 3.2 percent alcohol level, until they reached twenty-one; females could buy beer at eighteen. The state differentiated between the sexes in response to statistical evidence indicating a greater tendency for males ages eighteen to twenty-one to be involved in alcohol-related traffic accidents, including fatalities.

Viewing the Oklahoma law as a form of sex discrimination, Mark Walker, a twenty-year-old Oklahoma State University student who wanted to buy beer, and Carolyn Whitener, the owner of the Honk-N-Holler convenience store, who wanted to sell it, brought suit in federal trial court challenging the law on equal protection grounds. While the case slowly progressed, Walker turned twenty-one and was no longer subject to the state restrictions on purchasing alcohol. To protect against the case being declared moot, eighteen-year-old Curtis Craig replaced his friend Walker as the lead party.

Craig and Whitener argued that the Oklahoma law should be evaluated on the basis of strict scrutiny. The state disagreed. It urged the trial court to apply the rational basis test. Under that test, the law was clearly constitutional, the state claimed, because statistics demonstrated that compared to women, men in the eighteen-to-twenty age category "drive more, drink more, and commit more alcohol-related offenses."

While acknowledging that the U.S. Supreme Court decisions were murky, a three-judge district court ruled that the rational basis test was the appropriate standard to apply. In doing so the judges concluded

---

14. For more on this case, see Lee Epstein and Jack Knight, *The Choices Justices Make* (Washington, DC: CQ Press, 1998).

that the statistical evidence supporting the differences in male and female drinking and driving behavior was sufficient to justify the state's sex-based alcohol policy. Craig and Whitener appealed to the U.S. Supreme Court.

The state continued to advocate for the continued use of the rational basis test, and Craig and Whitener for strict scrutiny. Craig and Whitener also opened the door to a compromise. Their brief cited a passage written by Justice Harry Blackmun in *Stanton v. Stanton* (1975), another dispute over sex differences and legal maturation. In deciding that case (and also avoiding the level of scrutiny issue) Blackmun wrote for the majority, "We therefore conclude that under any test—compelling state interest, or rational basis, or *something in between*—[the statute] does not survive an equal protection attack" (emphasis added). This suggested that the justices might be open to a compromise, some level of scrutiny between rational basis and strict scrutiny. An amicus curiae brief, written on behalf of the ACLU by Ruth Bader Ginsburg, also emphasized the possibility of an "in between" solution to the level of scrutiny standoff.

ARGUMENTS:

For the appellants, Curtis Craig and Carolyn Whitener:

- Based on recent decisions such as *Reed v. Reed* (1971), *Frontiero v. Richardson* (1973), and *Stanton v. Stanton* (1975), the Oklahoma statute unconstitutionally discriminates on the basis of sex.
- It is time to elevate sex discrimination to suspect class status.
- The statistics provided by the state regarding alcohol-related offenses committed in the eighteen-to-twenty-one-year-old age group are flawed and invalid.
- The law is irrational in that it only prohibits sales to minor males by licensed vendors of 3.2 percent beer. It does not bar minor males from securing the beverage from an older male relative or even a younger female friend.

For the appellees, David Boren, Governor of Oklahoma, et al.:

- The lower court correctly used the rational basis test in deciding this case.
- The Twenty-first Amendment gives the states wide latitude in regulating alcohol.
- The statistics clearly show that males under twenty-one years are responsible for a disproportionately large share of alcohol-related offenses.
- The state's interest in preventing slaughter and property damage on the highways is sufficient to justify the statute.

Mark Walker, left, an Oklahoma State University student, joined with beer vender Carolyn Whitener, middle, to challenge the state's drinking age law that treated males and females differently. When Walker turned twenty-one and was no longer adversely affected by the law, he persuaded freshman fraternity brother Curtis Craig, right, to join the lawsuit.

Analysis may appropriately begin with the reminder that *Reed* [*v. Reed*, 1971] emphasized that statutory classifications that distinguish between males and females are "subject to scrutiny under the Equal Protection Clause." To withstand constitutional challenge, previous cases establish that classifications by gender must serve important governmental objectives and must be substantially related to achievement of those objectives. Thus, in *Reed,* the objectives of "reducing the workload on probate courts" and "avoiding intrafamily controversy" were deemed of insufficient importance to sustain use of an overt gender criterion in the appointment of administrators of intestate decedents' estates. Decisions following *Reed* similarly have rejected administrative ease and convenience as sufficiently important objectives to justify gender-based classifications. . . .

Reed v. Reed has also provided the underpinning for decisions that have invalidated statutes employing gender as an inaccurate proxy for other, more germane bases of classification. Hence, "archaic and overbroad" generalizations could not justify use of a gender line in determining eligibility for certain governmental entitlements. Similarly, increasingly outdated misconceptions concerning the role of females in the home rather than in the "marketplace and world of ideas" were rejected as loose-fitting characterizations incapable of supporting state statutory schemes that were premised upon their accuracy. In light of the weak congruence between gender and the characteristic or trait that gender purported to represent, it was necessary that the legislatures choose either to realign their substantive laws in a gender-neutral fashion, or to adopt procedures for identifying those instances where the sex-centered generalization actually comported with fact.

In this case, too, "*Reed,* we feel, is controlling. . . ." We turn then to the question whether, under *Reed,* the difference between males and females with respect to the purchase of 3.2% beer warrants the differential in age drawn by the Oklahoma statute. We conclude that it does not.

The District Court recognized that *Reed v. Reed* was controlling. In applying the teachings of that case, the court found the requisite important governmental objective in the traffic-safety goal proffered by the Oklahoma Attorney General. It then concluded that the statistics introduced by the appellees established that the gender-based distinction was substantially related to achievement of that goal.

. . . Clearly, the protection of public health and safety represents an important function of state and local governments. However, appellees' statistics in our view cannot support the conclusion that the gender-based distinction closely serves to achieve that objective and therefore the distinction cannot under *Reed* withstand equal protection challenge.

The appellees introduced a variety of statistical surveys. First, an analysis of arrest statistics for 1973 demonstrated that 18–20-year-old male arrests for "driving under the influence" and "drunkenness" substantially exceeded female arrests for that same age period. Similarly, youths aged 17–21 were found to be overrepresented among those killed or injured in traffic accidents, with males again numerically exceeding females in this regard. Third, a random roadside survey in Oklahoma City revealed that young males were more inclined to drive and drink beer than were their female counterparts. Fourth, Federal Bureau of Investigation nationwide statistics exhibited a notable increase in arrests for "driving under the influence." Finally, statistical evidence gathered in other jurisdictions, particularly Minnesota and Michigan, was offered to corroborate Oklahoma's experience by indicating the pervasiveness of youthful participation in motor vehicle accidents following the imbibing of alcohol. . . .

Even were this statistical evidence accepted as accurate, it nevertheless offers only a weak answer to the equal protection question presented here. The most focused and relevant of the statistical surveys, arrests of 18–20-year-olds for alcohol-related driving offenses, exemplifies the ultimate unpersuasiveness of this evidentiary record. Viewed in terms of the correlation between sex and the actual activity that Oklahoma seeks to regulate—driving while under the influence of alcohol—the statistics broadly establish that .18% of females and 2% of males in that age group were arrested for that offense. While such a disparity is not trivial in a statistical sense, it hardly can form the basis for employment of a gender line as a classifying device. Certainly if maleness is to serve as a proxy for drinking and driving, a correlation of 2% must be considered an unduly tenuous "fit." Indeed, prior cases have consistently rejected the use of sex as a decisionmaking factor even though the statutes in question certainly rested on far more predictive empirical relationships than this.

Moreover, the statistics exhibit a variety of other shortcomings that seriously impugn their value to equal protection analysis. Setting aside the obvious methodological problems, the surveys do not adequately justify the salient features of Oklahoma's gender-based traffic-safety law. None purports to measure the use and dangerousness of 3.2% beer as opposed to alcohol generally, a detail that is of particular importance since, in light of its low alcohol level, Oklahoma apparently considers the 3.2% beverage to be "nonintoxicating." Moreover, many of the studies, while graphically documenting the unfortunate increase in driving while under the influence of alcohol, make no effort to relate their findings to age-sex differentials as involved here. Indeed, the only survey that explicitly centered its attention upon young drivers and their use of beer—albeit apparently not of the diluted 3.2% variety—reached results that hardly can be viewed as impressive in justifying either a gender or age classification.

There is no reason to belabor this line of analysis. It is unrealistic to expect either members of the judiciary or state officials to be well versed in the rigors of experimental or statistical technique. But this merely illustrates that proving broad sociological propositions by statistics is a dubious business, and one that inevitably is in tension with the normative philosophy that underlies the Equal Protection Clause. Suffice to say that the showing offered by the appellees does not satisfy us that sex represents a legitimate, accurate proxy for the regulation of drinking and driving. In fact, when it is further recognized that Oklahoma's statute prohibits only the selling of 3.2% beer to young males and not their drinking the beverage once acquired (even after purchase by their 18–20-year-old female companions), the relationship between gender and traffic safety becomes far too tenuous to satisfy *Reed*'s requirement that the gender-based difference be substantially related to achievement of the statutory objective.

We hold, therefore, that under *Reed*, Oklahoma's 3.2% beer statute invidiously discriminates against males 18–20 years of age.

Reversed.

MR. JUSTICE REHNQUIST, dissenting.

The Court's disposition of this case is objectionable on two grounds. First is its conclusion that men challenging a gender-based statute which treats them less favorably than women may invoke a more stringent standard of judicial review than pertains to most other types of classifications. Second is the Court's enunciation of this standard, without citation to any source, as being that "classification by gender must serve *important* governmental objectives and must be *substantially* related to achievement of those objectives." (Emphasis added.) The only redeeming feature of the Court's opinion, to my mind, is that it apparently signals a retreat by those who joined the plurality opinion in *Frontiero v. Richardson* (1973) from their view that sex is a "suspect" classification for purposes of equal protection analysis. I think the Oklahoma statute challenged here need pass only the "rational basis" equal protection analysis expounded in cases such as *McGowan v. Maryland* (1961) and *Williamson v. Lee Optical Co.* (1955), and I believe that it is constitutional under that analysis.

In *Frontiero v. Richardson,* the opinion for the plurality sets forth the reasons of four Justices for concluding that sex should be regarded as a suspect classification for purposes of equal protection analysis. These reasons center on our Nation's "long and unfortunate history of sex discrimination," which has been reflected in a whole range of restrictions on the legal rights of women, not the least of which have concerned the ownership of property and participation in the electoral process. Noting that the pervasive and persistent nature of the discrimination experienced by women is in part the result of their ready identifiability, the plurality rested its invocation of strict scrutiny largely upon the fact that "statutory distinctions between the sexes often have the effect of invidiously relegating the entire class of females to inferior legal status without regard to the actual capabilities of its individual members."

Subsequent to *Frontiero,* the Court has declined to hold that sex is a suspect class, and no such holding is imported by the Court's resolution of this case. However, the Court's application here of an elevated or "intermediate" level scrutiny, like that invoked in cases dealing with discrimination against females, raises the question of why the statute here should be treated any differently from countless legislative classifications unrelated to sex which have been upheld under a minimum rationality standard.

Most obviously unavailable to support any kind of special scrutiny in this case, is a history or pattern of past discrimination, such as was relied on by the plurality in *Frontiero* to support its invocation of strict scrutiny. There is no suggestion in the Court's opinion that males in this age group are in any way peculiarly disadvantaged, subject to systematic discriminatory treatment, or otherwise in need of special solicitude from the courts.

The Court does not discuss the nature of the right involved, and there is no reason to believe that it sees the purchase of 3.2% beer as implicating any important interest, let alone one that is "fundamental" in the constitutional sense of invoking strict scrutiny. Indeed, the Court's accurate observation that the statute affects the selling but not the drinking of 3.2% beer further emphasizes the limited effect that it has on even those persons in the age group involved. There is, in sum, nothing about the statutory classification involved here to suggest that it affects an interest, or works against a group, which can claim under the Equal Protection Clause that it is entitled to special judicial protection.

It is true that a number of our opinions contain broadly phrased dicta implying that the same test should be applied to all classifications based on sex, whether affecting females or males. However, before today, no decision of this Court has applied an elevated level of scrutiny to invalidate a statutory discrimination harmful to males, except where the statute impaired an important personal interest protected by the Constitution. There being no such interest here, and there being no plausible argument that this is a discrimination against females, the Court's reliance on our previous sex-discrimination cases is ill-founded. It treats gender classification as a talisman which—without regard to the rights involved or the persons affected—calls into effect a heavier burden of judicial review.

The Court's conclusion that a law which treats males less favorably than females "must serve important governmental objectives and must be substantially related to achievement of those objectives" apparently comes out of thin air. The Equal Protection Clause contains no such language, and none of our previous cases adopt that standard. I would think we have had enough difficulty with the two standards of review which our cases have recognized—the norm of "rational basis," and the "compelling state interest" required where a "suspect classification" is involved—so as to counsel weightily against the insertion of still another "standard" between those two. How is this Court to divine what objectives are important? How is it to determine whether a particular law is "substantially" related to the achievement of such objective, rather than related in some other way to its achievement? Both of the phrases used are so diaphanous and elastic as to invite subjective judicial preferences or prejudices relating to particular types of legislation, masquerading as judgments whether such legislation is directed at "important" objectives or, whether the relationship to those objectives is "substantial" enough.

I would have thought that if this Court were to leave anything to decision by the popularly elected branches of the Government, where no constitutional claim other than that of equal protection is invoked, it would be the decision as to what governmental objectives to be achieved by law are "important," and which are not. As for the second part of the Court's new test, the Judicial Branch is probably in no worse position than the Legislative or Executive Branches to determine if there is any rational relationship between a classification and the purpose which it might be thought to serve. But the introduction of the adverb "substantially" requires courts to make subjective judgments as to operational effects, for which neither their expertise nor their access to data fits them. And even if we manage to avoid both confusion and the mirroring of our own preferences in the development of this new doctrine, the thousands of judges in other courts who must interpret the Equal Protection Clause may not be so fortunate.

The Court's ruling in *Craig v. Boren* had little impact on the parties to the case *(see Box 13-4)*, but the decision fundamentally changed sex discrimination law. The intermediate scrutiny test—requiring that laws that classify on the basis of sex be substantially related to an important government objective—was adopted by a narrow margin. Nevertheless, *Craig v. Boren* established the elevated level of scrutiny standard that has been used in sex discrimination cases ever since. The battle between strict scrutiny advocates and rational basis proponents ended with neither side able to claim a total victory.

The Court's Application of Intermediate Scrutiny

Unlike the rational basis test and the suspect class standard, intermediate scrutiny presumes neither the constitutional validity nor the constitutional invalidity of a challenged statute. It should not be surprising, therefore, that when applying this standard the Court sometimes voids sex-based classifications and occasionally upholds them. In the following pages, we consider cases that show these different results. Are there common features of laws that the justices have voided or upheld? Or has the Court applied the midlevel standard in haphazard fashion?

BOX 13-4 AFTERMATH . . . *CRAIG V. BOREN*

On January 12, 1976, the Supreme Court announced that it had accepted the case of *Craig v. Boren* for full consideration later that year. The news naturally excited Mark Walker, the former Oklahoma State University student who first initiated the legal action after becoming upset that a twenty-year-old male could be drafted and sent to war but could not buy a beer in Oklahoma. He eagerly awaited the oral arguments scheduled for October.

Tragically, however, Walker did not live to see the arguments or experience victory when the Supreme Court issued a ruling in his favor. On May 8, 1976, Mark Walker died in an auto accident. He was driving outside Stillwater when in the opposite lane one car was struck by another, causing the first vehicle to cross the median and crash head-on into the car driven by Walker.

Carolyn Whitener, the beer vendor who joined Walker's lawsuit challenging the constitutionality of the Oklahoma law, was owner of the Honk-N-Holler convenience store on Sixth and Knoblock Streets in Stillwater. At one time, together with her husband, she owned eleven such stores. Later the Whiteners sold the stores and went into the computer equipment business. Because

of her role in the *Craig* case, she was inducted into the Oklahoma Women's Hall of Fame in 2009 for her contributions to sexual equality.

Curtis Craig, Mark Walker's college friend who became the lead litigant when Walker turned twenty-one and was no longer affected by the challenged law, graduated with a B.S. degree from Oklahoma State University. He later received his law degree from the University of Tulsa. Craig subsequently had a long career as vice president and general counsel for the Tulsa-based Explorer Pipeline Company.

David Boren, who defended the state law against the constitutional challenge, was governor of Oklahoma from 1975 to 1979. In 1978 he won election to the U.S. Senate; he was reelected in 1984 and again in 1990, when he captured 83 percent of the vote. He stepped down from his Senate seat in 1994 to assume the presidency of the University of Oklahoma, a position he continues to hold.

SOURCES: R. Darcy and Jenny Sanbrano, "Oklahoma in the Development of Equal Rights: The ERA, 3.2% Beer, Juvenile Justice, and *Craig v. Boren*," *Oklahoma City University Law Review* 22 (1997): 1009–1049; Martindale. com, http://martindale.com; *Okie Women*, March 22, 2009; *Tulsa World*, March 25, 2009; University of Oklahoma, Office of the President, http://www.ou.edu/president/biography.html.

Gender-Based Classifications the Court Has Voided. The sex discrimination cases we have examined so far—*Reed, Frontiero,* and *Craig*—are what some legal scholars refer to as "easy" cases.[15] The practices under review were based on old-fashioned, stereotypical generalizations about sex differences that often included assumptions of female inferiority. The law at issue in *Reed,* for example, was based on the outdated assumption that men are better than women in business matters. Such laws cannot withstand even a minimal level of review, much less the stricter standard articulated in *Craig.* In other words, the Court has made it clear that governments cannot base sex distinctions on outdated presumptions about the "proper" role of women in American society.

Decisions in the area of sex-segregated education illustrate the point nicely. The Court's first full-fledged ruling on the subject came in **Mississippi University**

for Women v. Hogan (1982). This suit, filed by a male who was denied admission to a nursing program, challenged state-operated single-sex schools. Although the state had expanded the choices and opportunities for females by creating a women's college, critics charged that the program was based on an outmoded notion that women need an environment protected from men to succeed academically.

The admissions policies of the Mississippi University for Women (MUW) provided an opportunity for Justice Sandra Day O'Connor, the first woman appointed to the Supreme Court, to express her legal views on laws that classify according to sex. She started her majority opinion by reiterating the Court's approach to sex discrimination:

We begin our analysis aided by several firmly established principles. Because the challenged policy expressly discriminates among applicants on the basis of gender, it is subject to scrutiny under the Equal Protection Clause of the Fourteenth Amendment. *Reed v. Reed* (1971). That this statutory policy

---

15. We adapt this discussion from Susan Gluck Mezey, *In Pursuit of Equality* (New York: St. Martin's Press, 1992), 20–27.

discriminates against males rather than against females does not exempt it from scrutiny or reduce the standard of review. Our decisions also establish that the party seeking to uphold a statute that classifies individuals on the basis of their gender must carry the burden of showing an "exceedingly persuasive justification" for the classification. The burden is met only by showing at least that the classification serves "important governmental objectives and that the discriminatory means employed" are "substantially related to the achievement of those objectives."

Although the test for determining the validity of a gender-based classification is straightforward, it must be applied free of fixed notions concerning the roles and abilities of males and females. Care must be taken in ascertaining whether the statutory objective itself reflects archaic and stereotypic notions. Thus, if the statutory objective is to exclude or "protect" members of one gender because they are presumed to suffer from an inherent handicap or to be innately inferior, the objective itself is illegitimate.

O'Connor then firmly asserted that the Mississippi program was repugnant to the Fourteenth Amendment because of its presumptions of the inferiority of women:

Rather than compensate for discriminatory barriers faced by women, MUW's policy of excluding males from admission to the School of Nursing tends to perpetuate the stereotyped view of nursing as an exclusively woman's job. By assuring that Mississippi allots more openings in its state-supported nursing schools to women than it does to men, MUW's admissions policy lends credibility to the old view that women, not men, should become nurses, and makes the assumption that nursing is a field for women a self-fulfilling prophecy. Thus, we conclude that, although the State recited a "benign, compensatory purpose," it failed to establish that the alleged objective is the actual purpose underlying the discriminatory classification.

The dissenting justices, through an opinion by Justice Powell, took issue with O'Connor's analysis. They suggested that the majority imposed an unwise uniformity and deprived women of educational choices and alternatives:

The Court's opinion bows deeply to conformity. Left without honor—indeed, held unconstitutional—is an element of diversity that has characterized much of American education and enriched much of American life. The Court in effect holds today that no State now may provide even a single institution of higher learning open only to women students. It gives no heed to the efforts of the State of Mississippi to provide abundant opportunities for young men and young women to attend coeducational institutions, and none to the preferences of the more than 40,000 young women who over the years have evidenced their approval of an all-women's college by choosing Mississippi University for Women (MUW) over seven coeducational universities within the State. The Court decides today that the Equal Protection Clause makes it unlawful for the State to provide women with a traditionally popular and respected choice of educational environment. It does so in a case instituted by one man, who represents no class, and whose primary concern is personal convenience.

Despite these words, the *Mississippi University for Women* decision *seemed* to settle the matter of government-operated single-sex schools—they violate the Constitution. By the time of the decision, most single-sex public colleges, including the U.S. military academies, had initiated coeducational admissions policies. However, state schools in Virginia (Virginia Military Institute, or VMI) and South Carolina (The Citadel) resolutely resisted compliance with the decision. Both VMI and The Citadel had long traditions of offering a military-style education to all-male student bodies. When female applicants sued the schools claiming a violation of the Constitution and federal law, the institutions responded with a spirited legal defense of their traditions. They asserted that their military nature distinguished them from other colleges and universities and that introducing coeducational instruction would require changes that would alter the nature of the schools. When the case involving VMI reached the Supreme Court, the Clinton Justice Department asked the Court to abandon the use of intermediate scrutiny and adopt the suspect class test as the appropriate standard for use in sex discrimination cases.

United States v. Virginia

518 U.S. 515 (1996)
http://laws.findlaw.com/US/518/515.html
Oral arguments are available at http://www.oyez.org.
Vote: 7 (Breyer, Ginsburg, Kennedy, O'Connor, Rehnquist, Souter, Stevens)
       1 (Scalia)

OPINION OF THE COURT: *Ginsburg*
CONCURRING OPINION: *Rehnquist*
DISSENTING OPINION: *Scalia*
NOT PARTICIPATING: *Thomas*

Virginia Military Institute, founded in 1839, was the only one among Virginia's fifteen state-supported institutions of higher learning with a single-sex admissions policy. VMI's distinctive mission was to produce "citizen-soldiers," men prepared to take leadership positions in military and civilian life. VMI trained its 1,300 cadets through an "adversative" model of education that emphasized physical rigor, mental stress, absolute equality of treatment, absence of privacy, minute regulation of behavior, and indoctrination in desirable values. The cadets lived in spartan barracks where surveillance was constant and privacy nonexistent. They were required to wear military uniforms, eat together in the mess hall, and participate in military drills. The school imposed a hierarchical class system, with freshmen, known as "rats," accorded the lowest status.

In 1990, in response to a letter of complaint from a female high school student, the United States sued the Commonwealth of Virginia and VMI, alleging that VMI's men-only admissions policy violated the equal protection clause of the Fourteenth Amendment. The district court ruled in favor of the state, concluding that single-sex education yielded substantial benefits and that having a single-sex institution added diversity of opportunity to the range of educational options offered by Virginia. The court of appeals reversed, holding that the state could not justify offering a unique educational opportunity to men but not to women.

In response, the state created the Virginia Women's Institute for Leadership (VWIL) to operate as a parallel program for women. The VWIL was located on the campus of Mary Baldwin College, a private women's college a short distance from the VMI campus. This new state-supported program was designed to provide an education that would train female "citizen-soldiers" to take leadership positions in American society, but many acknowledged that the funding, facilities, and academic programs at VWIL were inferior to the resources at VMI.

Once the VWIL was established, Virginia returned to the district court for judicial approval of the continuation of the all-male VMI admissions policy. The district court supported the state's position, and the court of appeals generally affirmed by a divided vote. The United States and Virginia asked the U.S. Supreme Court to review various aspects of the case. The United States argued that the VWIL was an insufficient remedy to compensate for VMI's violation of the equal

protection clause. The state countered that removing the single-sex nature of the VMI would destroy the institution. Justice Clarence Thomas, whose son, Jamal, was attending VMI when the Court heard this appeal, did not participate in the decision.

For the petitioner, United States:
- *Mississippi University for Women v. Hogan* (1982) held that a state violates the equal protection clause of the Fourteenth Amendment when it denies admission to an institution of higher education on the basis of sex unless it has an "exceedingly persuasive justification" for doing so.
- Sex discrimination should be evaluated by a strict scrutiny standard.
- Establishing the women-only leadership program at Mary Baldwin College is an unsatisfactory and unconstitutional response. Eliminating the males-only admissions policy is the only adequate remedy.
- The state has failed to prove that admitting women to VMI would destroy the educational mission of the institution.

For the respondent, Commonwealth of Virginia:
- A primarily coeducational state higher education system with single-sex alternatives for both men and women does not violate the equal protection clause. Single-sex educational settings provide benefits to some students that cannot be attained in a coeducational environment.
- Coeducation at VMI would destroy important elements of its adversative system, thereby eliminating diversity while offering no educational opportunity to women that is not already available elsewhere.
- The VWIL program fully remedies any constitutional violation that may have existed as a result of VMI's single-sex admissions policy. Differences between VWIL and VMI are pedagogically justified and not based on archaic stereotypes.
- Intermediate scrutiny is now an established standard for use in sex discrimination cases and should not be abandoned.

JUSTICE GINSBURG DELIVERED THE OPINION OF THE COURT.

Virginia's public institutions of higher learning include an incomparable military college, Virginia Military Institute (VMI). The United States maintains that the Constitution's equal protection guarantee precludes Virginia from reserving exclusively to men the unique educational opportunities VMI affords. We agree. . . .

The heightened review standard our precedent establishes does not make sex a proscribed classification. Supposed "inherent differences" are no longer accepted as a ground for race or national origin classifications. See *Loving v. Virginia* (1967). Physical differences between men and women, however, are enduring: "[T]he two sexes are not fungible; a community made up exclusively of one [sex] is different from a community composed of both." *Ballard v. United States* (1946).

"Inherent differences" between men and women, we have come to appreciate, remain cause for celebration, but not for denigration of the members of either sex or for artificial constraints on an individual's opportunity. . . . [S]uch classifications may not be used, as they once were, to create or perpetuate the legal, social, and economic inferiority of women.

Measuring the record in this case against the review standard just described, we conclude that Virginia has shown no "exceedingly persuasive justification" for excluding all women from the citizen-soldier training afforded by VMI. We therefore affirm the Fourth Circuit's initial judgment, which held that Virginia had violated the Fourteenth Amendment's Equal Protection Clause. Because the remedy proffered by Virginia—the Mary Baldwin VWIL program—does not cure the constitutional violation, *i.e.,* it does not provide equal opportunity, we reverse the Fourth Circuit's final judgment in this case.

The Fourth Circuit initially held that Virginia had advanced no state policy by which it could justify, under equal protection principles, its determination "to afford VMI's unique type of program to men and not to women." Virginia challenges that "liability" ruling and asserts two justifications in defense of VMI's exclusion of women. First, the Commonwealth contends, "single-sex education provides important educational benefits" and the option of single-sex education contributes to "diversity in educational approaches." Second, the Commonwealth argues, "the unique VMI method of character development and leadership training," the school's adversative approach, would have to be modified were VMI to admit women. We consider these two justifications in turn.

Single-sex education affords pedagogical benefits to at least some students, Virginia emphasizes, and that reality is uncontested in this litigation. Similarly, it is not disputed that diversity among public educational institutions can serve the public good. But Virginia has not shown that VMI was established, or has been maintained, with a view to diversifying, by its categorical exclusion of women, educational opportunities within the State. In cases of this genre, our precedent instructs that "benign" justifications proffered in defense of categorical exclusions will not be accepted automatically; a tenable justification must describe actual state purposes, not rationalizations for actions in fact differently grounded.

Mississippi Univ. for Women [v. Hogan (1982)] is immediately in point. There the State asserted, in justification of its exclusion of men from a nursing school, that it was engaging in "educational affirmative action" by "compensat[ing] for discrimination against women." Undertaking a "searching analysis," the Court found no close resemblance between "the alleged objective" and "the actual purpose underlying the discriminatory classification." Pursuing a similar inquiry here, we reach the same conclusion. . . .

[W]e find no persuasive evidence in this record that VMI's male-only admission policy "is in furtherance of a state policy of 'diversity.'" No such policy, the Fourth Circuit observed, can be discerned from the movement of all other public colleges and universities in Virginia away from single-sex education. That court also questioned "how one institution with autonomy, but with no authority over any other state institution, can give effect to a state policy of diversity among institutions." A purpose genuinely to advance an array of educational options, as the Court of Appeals recognized, is not served by VMI's historic and constant plan—a plan to "affor[d] a unique educational benefit only to males." However "liberally" this plan serves the State's sons, it makes no provision whatever for her daughters. That is not *equal* protection.

Virginia next argues that VMI's adversative method of training provides educational benefits that cannot be made available, unmodified, to women. Alterations to accommodate women would necessarily be "radical," so "drastic," Virginia asserts, as to transform, indeed "destroy," VMI's program. Neither sex would be favored by the transformation, Virginia maintains: Men would be deprived of the unique opportunity currently available to them; women would not gain that opportunity because their participation would "eliminat[e] the very aspects of [the] program that distinguish [VMI] from . . . other institutions of higher education in Virginia."

The District Court forecast from expert witness testimony, and the Court of Appeals accepted, that coeducation would materially affect "at least these three aspects of VMI's program—physical training, the absence of privacy, and the adversative approach." And it is uncontested that women's admission would require accommodations, primarily in arranging housing assignments and physical training programs for female cadets. It is also undisputed, however, that "the VMI methodology could be used to educate women." The District Court even allowed that some women may prefer it to the methodology a women's college might pursue. "[S]ome women, at least, would want to attend [VMI] if they had the opportunity," the District Court recognized, and "some women," the expert testimony established, "are capable of all of the individual activities required of VMI cadets." The parties, furthermore, agree that *"some women can meet the physical standards [VMI] now impose[s] on men."* In sum, as the Court of Appeals stated, "neither the goal of producing citizen soldiers," VMI's *raison d'être,* "nor VMI's implementing methodology is inherently unsuitable to women." . . .

The United States does not challenge any expert witness estimation on average capacities or preferences of men and women. Instead, the United States emphasizes that time and again since this Court's turning point decision in *Reed v. Reed* (1971), we have cautioned reviewing courts to take a "hard look" at generalizations or "tendencies" of the kind pressed by Virginia, and relied upon by the District Court. State actors controlling gates to opportunity, we have instructed, may not exclude qualified individuals based on "fixed notions concerning the roles and abilities of males and females." *Mississippi Univ. for Women; J.E.B. [v. Alabama ex rel. T.B.* (1994)]. . . .

Women's successful entry into the federal military academies, and their participation in the Nation's military forces, indicate that Virginia's fears for the future of VMI may not be solidly grounded. The State's justification for excluding all women from "citizen-soldier" training for which some are qualified, in any event, cannot rank as "exceedingly persuasive," as we have explained and applied that standard. . . .

In the second phase of the litigation, Virginia presented its remedial plan—maintain VMI as a male-only college and create VWIL as a separate program for women. . . .

A remedial decree, this Court has said, must closely fit the constitutional violation; it must be shaped to place persons unconstitutionally denied an opportunity or advantage in "the position they would have occupied in the absence of [discrimination]." See *Milliken v. Bradley* (1977). The constitutional violation in this case is the categorical exclusion of women from an extraordinary educational opportunity afforded men. A proper remedy for an unconstitutional exclusion, we have explained, aims to "eliminate [so far as possible] the discriminatory effects of the past" and to "bar like discrimination in the future." *Louisiana v. United States* (1965).

Virginia chose not to eliminate, but to leave untouched, VMI's exclusionary policy. For women only, however, Virginia proposed a separate program, different in kind from VMI and unequal in tangible and intangible facilities. Having violated the Constitution's equal protection requirement, Virginia was obliged to show that its remedial proposal "directly address[ed] and relate[d] to" the violation, *i.e.,* the equal protection denied to women ready, willing, and able to benefit from educational opportunities of the kind VMI offers. Virginia described VWIL as a "parallel program," and asserted that VWIL shares VMI's mission of producing "citizen-soldiers" and VMI's goals of providing "education, military training, mental and physical discipline, character . . . and leadership development." If the VWIL program could not "eliminate the discriminatory effects of the past," could it at least "bar like discrimination in the future"? A comparison of the programs said to be "parallel" informs our answer. . . .

VWIL affords women no opportunity to experience the rigorous military training for which VMI is famed. . . .

VWIL students participate in ROTC and a "largely ceremonial" Virginia Corps of Cadets, but Virginia deliberately did not make VWIL a military institute. The VWIL House is not a military-style residence and VWIL students need not live together throughout the 4-year program, eat meals together, or wear uniforms during the school day. VWIL students thus do not experience the "barracks" life "crucial to the VMI experience," the spartan living arrangements designed to foster an "egalitarian ethic." "[T]he most important aspects of the VMI educational experience occur in the barracks," the District Court found, yet Virginia deemed that core experience nonessential, indeed inappropriate, for training its female citizen-soldiers.

VWIL students receive their "leadership training" in seminars, externships, and speaker series, episodes and encounters lacking the "[p]hysical rigor, mental stress, . . .

minute regulation of behavior, and indoctrination in desirable values" made hallmarks of VMI's citizen-soldier training. . . .

In myriad respects other than military training, VWIL does not qualify as VMI's equal. VWIL's student body, faculty, course offerings, and facilities hardly match VMI's. Nor can the VWIL graduate anticipate the benefits associated with VMI's 157-year history, the school's prestige, and its influential alumni network.

Mary Baldwin College, whose degree VWIL students will gain, enrolls first-year women with an average combined SAT score about 100 points lower than the average score for VMI freshmen. The Mary Baldwin faculty holds "significantly fewer Ph.D.'s," and receives substantially lower salaries than the faculty at VMI.

Mary Baldwin does not offer a VWIL student the range of curricular choices available to a VMI cadet. . . .

Although Virginia has represented that it will provide equal financial support for in-state VWIL students and VMI cadets, and the VMI Foundation has agreed to endow VWIL with $5.4625 million, the difference between the two schools' financial reserves is pronounced. Mary Baldwin's endowment, currently about $19 million, will gain an additional $35 million based on future commitments; VMI's current endowment, $131 million—the largest per-student endowment in the Nation—will gain $220 million.

The VWIL student does not graduate with the advantage of a VMI degree. Her diploma does not unite her with the legions of VMI "graduates [who] have distinguished themselves" in military and civilian life. . . .

Virginia, in sum, while maintaining VMI for men only, has failed to provide any "comparable single-gender women's institution." Instead, the Commonwealth has created a VWIL program fairly appraised as a "pale shadow" of VMI in terms of the range of curricular choices and faculty stature, funding, prestige, alumni support and influence. . . .

. . . [W]e rule here that Virginia has not shown substantial equality in the separate educational opportunities the State supports at VWIL and VMI. . . .

. . . Women seeking and fit for a VMI-quality education cannot be offered anything less, under the State's obligation to afford them genuinely equal protection. . . .

For the reasons stated, the initial judgment of the Court of Appeals is affirmed, the final judgment of the Court of Appeals is reversed, and the case is remanded for further proceedings consistent with this opinion.

It is so ordered.

Reversed and remanded.

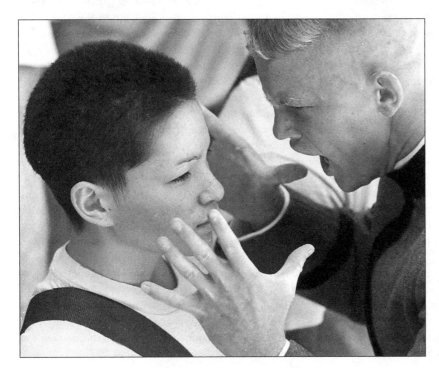

A member of the Virginia Military Institute cadre, right, yells at a female "rat" in 1998. Women were not allowed to attend VMI, with its "adversative" model of education, until the Supreme Court's 1996 decision in United States v. Virginia.

CHIEF JUSTICE REHNQUIST, concurring in judgment.

Two decades ago in *Craig v. Boren* (1976), we announced that "[t]o withstand constitutional challenge, . . . classifications by gender must serve important governmental objectives and must be substantially related to achievement of those objectives." We have adhered to that standard of scrutiny ever since. While the majority adheres to this test today, it also says that the State must demonstrate an "'exceedingly persuasive justification'" to support a gender-based classification. It is unfortunate that the Court thereby introduces an element of uncertainty respecting the appropriate test.

While terms like "important governmental objective" and "substantially related" are hardly models of precision, they have more content and specificity than does the phrase "exceedingly persuasive justification." That phrase is best confined, as it was first used, as an observation on the difficulty of meeting the applicable test, not as a formulation of the test itself. To avoid introducing potential confusion, I would have adhered more closely to our traditional, "firmly established" standard that a gender-based classification "must bear a close and substantial relationship to important governmental objectives."

JUSTICE SCALIA, dissenting.

Today the Court shuts down an institution that has served the people of the Commonwealth of Virginia with pride and distinction for over a century and a half. To achieve that desired result, it rejects (contrary to our established practice) the factual findings of two courts below, sweeps aside the precedents of this Court, and ignores the history of our people. As to facts: it explicitly rejects the finding that there exist "gender-based developmental differences" supporting Virginia's restriction of the "adversative" method to only a men's institution, and the finding that the all-male composition of the Virginia Military Institute (VMI) is essential to that institution's character. As to precedent: it drastically revises our established standards for reviewing sex-based classifications. And as to history: it counts for nothing the long tradition, enduring down to the present, of men's military colleges supported by both States and the Federal Government.

Much of the Court's opinion is devoted to deprecating the closed-mindedness of our forebears with regard to women's education, and even with regard to the treatment of women in areas that have nothing to do with education. Closed-minded they were—as every age is, including our own, with regard to matters it cannot

guess, because it simply does not consider them debatable. The virtue of a democratic system with a First Amendment is that it readily enables the people, over time, to be persuaded that what they took for granted is not so, and to change their laws accordingly. That system is destroyed if the smug assurances of each age are removed from the democratic process and written into the Constitution. So to counterbalance the Court's criticism of our ancestors, let me say a word in their praise: they left us free to change. The same cannot be said of this most illiberal Court, which has embarked on a course of inscribing one after another of the current preferences of the society (and in some cases only the countermajoritarian preferences of the society's law-trained elite) into our Basic Law. Today it enshrines the notion that no substantial educational value is to be served by an all-men's military academy—so that the decision by the people of Virginia to maintain such an institution denies equal protection to women who cannot attend that institution but can attend others. Since it is entirely clear that the Constitution of the United States—the old one—takes no sides in this educational debate, I dissent. . . .

To reject the Court's disposition today, however, it is not necessary to accept my view that the Court's made-up tests cannot displace long-standing national traditions as the primary determinant of what the Constitution means. It is only necessary to apply honestly the test the Court has been applying to sex-based classifications for the past two decades. It is well settled, as JUSTICE O'CONNOR stated some time ago for a unanimous Court, that we evaluate a statutory classification based on sex under a standard that lies "[b]etween th[e] extremes of rational basis review and strict scrutiny." *Clark v. Jeter* (1988). We have denominated this standard "intermediate scrutiny" and under it have inquired whether the statutory classification is "substantially related to an important governmental objective." . . .

Although the Court in two places recites the test as stated in [*Mississippi University for Women v.*] *Hogan* [1982], which asks whether the State has demonstrated "that the classification serves important governmental objectives and that the discriminatory means employed are substantially related to the achievement of those objectives," the Court never answers the question presented in anything resembling that form. When it engages in analysis, the Court instead prefers the phrase "exceedingly persuasive justification" from *Hogan.* The Court's nine invocations of that phrase and even its fanciful description of that imponderable as "the core instruction" of the Court's decisions in *J.E.B. v. Alabama ex rel. T.B.* (1994) and *Hogan* would be unobjectionable if the Court acknowledged that *whether* a "justification" is "exceedingly persuasive" must be assessed by asking "[whether] the classification serves important governmental objectives and [whether] the discriminatory means employed are substantially related to the achievement of those objectives." Instead, however, the Court proceeds to interpret "exceedingly persuasive justification" in a fashion that contradicts the reasoning of *Hogan* and our other precedents. . . .

Justice Brandeis said it is "one of the happy incidents of the federal system that a single courageous State may, if its citizens choose, serve as a laboratory; and try novel social and economic experiments without risk to the rest of the country." *New State Ice Co. v. Liebmann* (1932) (dissenting opinion). But it is one of the unhappy incidents of the federal system that a self-righteous Supreme Court, acting on its Members' personal view of what would make a "more perfect Union," (a criterion only slightly more restrictive than a "more perfect world"), can impose its own favored social and economic dispositions nationwide. As today's disposition, and others this single Term, show, this places it beyond the power of a "single courageous State," not only to introduce novel dispositions that the Court frowns upon, but to reintroduce, or indeed even adhere to, disfavored dispositions that are centuries old. See, *e.g., BMW of North America, Inc. v. Gore* (1996); *Romer v. Evans* (1996). The sphere of self-government reserved to the people of the Republic is progressively narrowed.

Although the Court struck down VMI's single-sex admissions policy, the justices still did not adopt the strict scrutiny standard for sex discrimination cases. Officially, they remained wedded to the intermediate scrutiny standard. Both the concurring and dissenting opinions criticized the majority for injecting the "exceedingly persuasive justification" element into the intermediate scrutiny test, even though the requirement was not new. Justice Stewart had used it in *Personnel Administrator of Massachusetts v. Feeney* (1979), as had Justice Marshall in *Kirchberg v. Feenstra* (1981) and Justice O'Connor in *Mississippi University for Women v. Hogan.* In the VMI case, however, this element appears to be more firmly fixed in the Court's sex discrimination jurisprudence.

United States v. Virginia also serves as an example of the obstacles those who must implement Supreme Court rulings may face. The case was a bitter defeat for VMI and The Citadel, which had spent millions of dollars defending their all-male policies and now had to spend additional funds to accommodate women. Nor did the first women cadets have an easy time. Of the four women who initially enrolled in The Citadel, two dropped out after alleging that they were assaulted, hazed, and sexually harassed. Several male cadets accused of the hazing resigned, and others were disciplined.

Both schools acted to remedy the problems of assimilating women into their environments. Some progress has been made, yet today less than 10 percent of these institutions' matriculated students are women. The events surrounding the transition of these previously all-male colleges to coeducational institutions clearly show the limitations of formal Court decisions. Simply because the justices render a decision does not mean that barriers between the sexes—just like those between the races—will fall overnight.

Gender-Based Classifications the Court Has Upheld. The cases in the previous section suggest that the Court, in applying the heightened scrutiny standard, has been unwilling to tolerate government actions that are based on outmoded stereotypes of women. On the whole, that is true. Data show that in the years since *Reed,* the justices have ruled in favor of the sex discrimination claim in more than half their cases.

There is at least one category of litigation, however, in which the Court has been less willing to strike down sex-based laws: cases involving physical differences between men and women.[16] In contrast to the "easy" cases you just read, these are "difficult" because they are based on actual differences rather than on outmoded stereotypes. The difficult cases raise a fundamental problem for the Court, which is that in all discrimination cases (regardless of what standard of scrutiny courts impose) claims of unequal treatment must be based only on comparisons of persons "similarly situated." For some purposes men and women are not similarly situated because of the real and immutable physical differences between them. The most obvious of these differences lies in the role each sex plays in human reproduction. Only women can become

---

16. Mezey, *In Pursuit of Equality,* 25–27.

pregnant, and the Constitution does not require that such an essential difference be ignored in the law.

To illustrate, consider **Michael M. v. Superior Court of Sonoma County** (1981). This case had its origins in June 1978, when Michael M., a seventeen-year-old boy, and two friends approached Sharon, who was sixteen, and her sister at a bus stop. It was around midnight and both Michael and Sharon had been drinking. During the course of their encounter, Michael and Sharon split off from the others. First they went into some bushes, where they hugged and kissed. Later, after Sharon's sister had left, Sharon and Michael walked to a nearby park, laid down on a bench, and continued kissing. Michael tried to convince Sharon to remove her clothes and have sexual relations. When Sharon refused, Michael hit her in the face. Then, in Sharon's words, "I let him do what he wanted to do."

Michael M. was charged with a violation of Section 261.5 of the California penal code, which prohibits "an act of sexual intercourse accomplished with a female not the wife of the perpetrator, where the female is under the age of 18 years." This statutory rape law makes males alone criminally liable for the act of sexual intercourse. Michael M. moved to have the criminal prosecution dropped on the grounds that Section 261.5 invidiously discriminates on the basis of sex and therefore violates the equal protection clause.

The Supreme Court upheld the law. Writing for the plurality, Justice Rehnquist explained why penalizing men but not women was constitutionally permissible. The sexes are not always similarly situated, he wrote, and the Constitution does not require things that are different in fact to be treated as if they were the same. The state can recognize in its policies that only women can become pregnant. Furthermore, the state has a strong interest in preventing illegitimate pregnancies among teenage girls. The state's law is substantially related to this interest. A state, therefore, may attack the problem of teenage pregnancy directly by prohibiting a male from having sexual intercourse with a minor female.

In some cases the justices have also permitted nonreproductive physical differences to be taken into account. A good example is the military draft case **Rostker v. Goldberg** (1981). Because historically wars have centered on physical combat, males have had the primary responsibility and opportunity to serve in the armed forces. Physical differences between men and women led to this custom, which has been reinforced by the way society views sex roles.

The federal legislation challenged in this case continued the policy of distinguishing men and women with respect to military service. The case also involved Congress's constitutional power to raise and regulate the armed forces. Traditionally, when the legislature has acted under this authority, the Court has accorded it great deference.

Rostker involved an attack on the federal Selective Service Act. The law authorizes the president of the United States to require every male citizen and resident alien between the ages of eighteen and twenty-six to register for the draft. In 1971 a lawsuit was filed challenging the constitutionality of the law. The suit became dormant, however, when the draft registration requirement was suspended in 1975. Circumstances changed in 1980 with the Soviet invasion of Afghanistan. To ensure military preparedness, President Jimmy Carter reactivated the registration program. At the same time, he asked Congress to amend the law to require females as well as males to register. Congress refused and appropriated only enough money to administer the registration of males.

The long-dormant suit was reactivated. On July 18, 1980, just three days before registration was to begin, a federal district court declared the law unconstitutional because its single-sex provisions violated the due process clause of the Fifth Amendment. Bernard Rostker, the director of the Selective Service, appealed the decision to the Supreme Court.

The justices upheld the registration law. Writing for a six-justice majority, William Rehnquist explained that the exclusion of women from the draft was not a product of traditional female stereotypes. Rather, the question was studied and debated extensively in Congress. In the end, the legislature concluded that the purpose of the draft was to raise combat troops. Since women were not eligible for direct combat duty, there was little reason to include them in the draft process. The Court deferred to the judgment of Congress. If women were not to be used in combat, they were not similarly circumstanced with men with respect to raising combat troops. The male-only registration program therefore was substantially related to the important government interest in raising soldiers for combat duty. Intermediate scrutiny requirements were satisfied.

Much has changed with respect to the role of women in the military since the *Rostker* decision was handed down. Women now represent 15–20 percent of all U.S. military forces, a far cry from the years before 1967, when the number of women was capped at 2 percent of the total. The percentage of women serving in reserve and National Guard units is even higher. Women now fly combat missions, serve as military police, and drive convoy protection vehicles. They qualify for 95 percent of all positions in the armed services. The exceptions are those tasks that require special physical characteristics (Special Operations) and direct ground combat, and even these restrictions have been under serious review. Women have constituted about 12 percent of the troops serving in the recent conflicts in Afghanistan and Iraq and have accounted for approximately 2 percent of the war-related fatalities. Given these changes, do you think the ruling in *Rostker* would be the same if the case were heard today?

DISCRIMINATION BASED ON SEXUAL ORIENTATION

Discrimination against gays and lesbians differs in at least two important ways from race and sex discrimination. First, although federal laws prohibit various forms of discrimination based on race and sex, national laws do not explicitly protect homosexuals. In fact, the U.S. government maintains policies that discriminate on the basis of sexual orientation. For example, in 1996 Congress passed the Defense of Marriage Act, which denies federal recognition of same-sex marriages and permits the states to refuse to recognize same-sex marriages performed in other states. Also in 1996, Congress refused to extend the remedies of the 1964 Civil Rights Act to sexual orientation, a move that would have prohibited job discrimination based on sexual orientation.

Second, although Americans' views about blacks and women have changed significantly and in a positive direction since the 1960s, the general public has been somewhat slower to alter its views of gays and lesbians. However, movement in public opinion has been consistently in the direction of increased support for gay rights.[17] Gallup Polls in 2011, for example, found

17. Public opinion data described in this paragraph are based on results of polling by the Gallup Organization in 2011 (http://www.gallup.com/poll/1651/gay-lesbian-rights.aspx) as well a review of multiple polls reported by PollingReport.com (http://www.pollingreport.com/civil.htm).

that 57 percent of the American public thought that homosexuality should be considered an acceptable alternative lifestyle (up from 34 percent in 1982). Polls by multiple public opinion organizations that same year found that the nation was roughly evenly divided over the legalization of same-sex marriage, whereas fifteen years earlier only about a quarter of Americans favored the right of gays to marry.

The Supreme Court's record in the area of discrimination based on sexual orientation is decidedly mixed. For years the Court avoided the issue in spite of efforts by gay rights groups to promote the expansion of legal protections for homosexuals. In Chapter 10 we discussed *Bowers v. Hardwick* (1986) and *Lawrence v. Texas* (2003), in which the Court first upheld anti-sodomy laws and then reversed itself seventeen years later. In *Lawrence* the Court based its ruling on the Constitution's privacy guarantees to protect private, consensual sexual behavior from criminal prosecution. That decision therefore has no direct relevance to the Court's interpretation of the equal protection clause as it applies to general discrimination against gays and lesbians. To date the Court's most important ruling on discriminatory behavior based on sexual orientation is *Romer v. Evans* (1996). Given the justices' general reluctance to accept such disputes, Court observers were interested in how the justices would decide this case, but, perhaps more important, they were also concerned about the standard of scrutiny the justices would use.

Romer v. Evans
517 U.S. 620 (1996)
http://laws.findlaw.com/US/517/620.html
Oral arguments are available at http://www.oyez.org.
Vote: 6 (Breyer, Ginsburg, Kennedy, O'Connor, Souter, Stevens)
3 (Rehnquist, Scalia, Thomas)
OPINION OF THE COURT: Kennedy
DISSENTING OPINION: Scalia

FACTS:

This case involved a challenge to an amendment to the Colorado state constitution, which had been adopted by statewide initiative. The initiative arose in response to local laws passed by communities such as Boulder, Aspen, and Denver making sexual orientation an impermissible ground upon which to discriminate. In effect, the local laws gave sexual orientation the same status as race, sex, and other protected categories. To reverse this trend and remove the possibility of future legislation, a sufficient number of citizens signed a petition to place a proposed constitutional amendment on the ballot for the November 1992 elections. Known as Amendment 2, it passed with the support of 53.4 percent of those voting. The amendment stated:

Neither the State of Colorado, through any of its branches or departments, nor any of its agencies, political subdivisions, municipalities or school districts, shall enact, adopt or enforce any statute, regulation, ordinance or policy whereby homosexual, lesbian or bisexual orientation, conduct, practices or relationships shall constitute or otherwise be the basis of or entitle any person or class of persons to have or claim any minority status, quota preferences, protected status or claim of discrimination. This Section of the Constitution shall be in all respects self-executing.

Almost immediately Richard G. Evans, a gay employee in the office of the mayor of Denver, other citizens, and several Colorado local governments sued Governor Roy Romer and the state of Colorado, claiming that the new amendment was in violation of the Fourteenth Amendment's equal protection clause. The amendment, they contended, prohibited gays from using the political process to secure legal protections against discrimination. The Colorado Supreme Court struck down the amendment, 6–1, and the state appealed to the U.S. Supreme Court.

ARGUMENTS:

For the petitioners, Roy Romer, Governor, and the State of Colorado:

- Federal courts have uniformly rejected the claim that sexual orientation is a suspect or semi-suspect classification. Therefore, rational basis is the appropriate test to use. Thus, Amendment 2 carries a strong presumption of constitutionality.
- Amendment 2 does not infringe on the right to vote or on any other right of political participation. Opponents of Amendment 2 are free to use the same political mechanisms for its repeal (the constitutional amendment process) that amendment supporters used to secure its adoption.

Attorney Jean Dubofsky hugs Priscilla Inkpen, one of the plaintiffs who challenged Colorado's anti-gay rights initiative, after the Supreme Court ruled the measure unconstitutional. Richard Evans, the first named plaintiff in the case, is at left.

- Amendment 2 advances legitimate state interests (e.g., uniformity of state civil rights laws, promotion of religious liberty, promotion of associational freedoms).
- A state may provide more protections than are required by the U.S. Constitution, but may also rescind those extra protections without violating the Constitution.

For the respondents, Richard G. Evans, et al.:

- A state law that singles out gay people and intentionally denies them all effective opportunity to seek relief from discrimination through the political process requires heightened scrutiny.
- Amendment 2 prohibits gay people from seeking any relief from any level of government for any claim of discrimination against them.
- The right to equal political access belongs to all the people, not just to members of groups that courts have declared to be a suspect class.
- Amendment 2 advances no legitimate purpose, but can only be explained by antipathy toward a particular group.

JUSTICE KENNEDY DELIVERED THE OPINION OF THE COURT.

One century ago, the first Justice Harlan admonished this Court that the Constitution "neither knows nor tolerates classes among citizens." *Plessy v. Ferguson* (1896) (dissenting opinion). Unheeded then, those words now are understood to state a commitment to the law's neutrality where the rights of persons are at stake. The Equal Protection Clause enforces this principle and today requires us to hold invalid a provision of Colorado's Constitution. . . .

Soon after Amendment 2 was adopted, this litigation to declare its invalidity and enjoin its enforcement was commenced in the District Court for the City and County of Denver. . . .

The trial court granted a preliminary injunction to stay enforcement of Amendment 2, and an appeal was taken to the Supreme Court of Colorado. Sustaining the interim injunction and remanding the case for further proceedings, the State Supreme Court held that Amendment 2 was subject to strict scrutiny under the Fourteenth Amendment because it infringed the fundamental right of gays and lesbians to participate in the political process. . . . On remand, the State advanced various

arguments in an effort to show that Amendment 2 was narrowly tailored to serve compelling interests, but the trial court found none sufficient. It enjoined enforcement of Amendment 2, and the Supreme Court of Colorado, in a second opinion, affirmed the ruling. We granted certiorari and now affirm the judgment, but on a rationale different from that adopted by the State Supreme Court.

The State's principal argument in defense of Amendment 2 is that it puts gays and lesbians in the same position as all other persons. So, the State says, the measure does no more than deny homosexuals special rights. This reading of the amendment's language is implausible. We rely not upon our own interpretation of the amendment but upon the authoritative construction of Colorado's Supreme Court. The state court, deeming it unnecessary to determine the full extent of the amendment's reach, found it invalid even on a modest reading of its implications. The critical discussion of the amendment, set out . . . [by the Colorado Supreme Court], is as follows:

The immediate objective of Amendment 2 is, at a minimum, to repeal existing statutes, regulations, ordinances, and policies of state and local entities that barred discrimination based on sexual orientation. . . .

The "ultimate effect" of Amendment 2 is to prohibit any governmental entity from adopting similar, or more protective statutes, regulations, ordinances, or policies in the future unless the state constitution is first amended to permit such measures.

Sweeping and comprehensive is the change in legal status effected by this law. So much is evident from the ordinances that the Colorado Supreme Court declared would be void by operation of Amendment 2. Homosexuals, by state decree, are put in a solitary class with respect to transactions and relations in both the private and governmental spheres. The amendment withdraws from homosexuals, but no others, specific legal protection from the injuries caused by discrimination, and it forbids reinstatement of these laws and policies.

The change that Amendment 2 works in the legal status of gays and lesbians in the private sphere is far-reaching, both on its own terms and when considered in light of the structure and operation of modern anti-discrimination laws. That structure is well illustrated by contemporary statutes and ordinances prohibiting discrimination by providers of public accommodations. . . .

Amendment 2 bars homosexuals from securing protection against the injuries that these public-accommodations laws address. That in itself is a severe consequence, but there is more. Amendment 2, in addition, nullifies specific legal protections for this targeted class in all transactions in housing, sale of real estate, insurance, health and welfare services, private education, and employment.

Not confined to the private sphere, Amendment 2 also operates to repeal and forbid all laws or policies providing specific protection for gays or lesbians from discrimination by every level of Colorado government. . . . The repeal of these measures and the prohibition against their future reenactment demonstrates that Amendment 2 has the same force and effect in Colorado's governmental sector as it does elsewhere and that it applies to policies as well as ordinary legislation.

Amendment 2's reach may not be limited to specific laws passed for the benefit of gays and lesbians. It is a fair, if not necessary, inference from the broad language of the amendment that it deprives gays and lesbians even of the protection of general laws and policies that prohibit arbitrary discrimination in governmental and private settings. . . .

. . . [W]e cannot accept the view that Amendment 2's prohibition on specific legal protections does no more than deprive homosexuals of special rights. To the contrary, the amendment imposes a special disability upon those persons alone. Homosexuals are forbidden the safeguards that others enjoy or may seek without constraint. They can obtain specific protection against discrimination only by enlisting the citizenry of Colorado to amend the state constitution or perhaps, on the State's view, by trying to pass helpful laws of general applicability. This is so no matter how local or discrete the harm, no matter how public and widespread the injury. We find nothing special in the protections Amendment 2 withholds. These are protections taken for granted by most people either because they already have them or do not need them; these are protections against exclusion from an almost limitless number of transactions and endeavors that constitute ordinary civic life in a free society.

The Fourteenth Amendment's promise that no person shall be denied the equal protection of the laws must coexist with the practical necessity that most legislation classifies for one purpose or another, with resulting disadvantage to various groups or persons. We have attempted to reconcile the principle with the reality by stating that, if a law neither burdens a fundamental right nor targets a suspect class, we will uphold the legislative classification so long as it bears a rational relation to some legitimate end. See, *e.g., Heller v. Doe* (1993).

Amendment 2 fails, indeed defies, even this conventional inquiry. First, the amendment has the peculiar property of imposing a broad and undifferentiated disability on a single named group, an exceptional and, as we shall explain, invalid form of legislation. Second, its sheer breadth is so discontinuous with the reasons offered for it that the amendment seems inexplicable by anything but animus toward the class that it affects; it lacks a rational relationship to legitimate state interests.

Taking the first point, even in the ordinary equal protection case calling for the most deferential of standards, we insist on knowing the relation between the classification adopted and the object to be attained. The search for the link between classification and objective gives substance to the Equal Protection Clause; it provides guidance and discipline for the legislature, which is entitled to know what sorts of laws it can pass; and it marks the limits of our own authority. In the ordinary case, a law will be sustained if it can be said to advance a legitimate government interest, even if the law seems unwise or works to the disadvantage of a particular group, or if the rationale for it seems tenuous. . . . By requiring that the classification bear a rational relationship to an independent and legitimate legislative end, we ensure that classifications are not drawn for the purpose of disadvantaging the group burdened by the law.

Amendment 2 confounds this normal process of judicial review. It is at once too narrow and too broad. It identifies persons by a single trait and then denies them protection across the board. The resulting disqualification of a class of persons from the right to seek specific protection from the law is unprecedented in our jurisprudence. . . .

It is not within our constitutional tradition to enact laws of this sort. Central both to the idea of the rule of law and to our own Constitution's guarantee of equal protection is the principle that government and each of its parts remain open on impartial terms to all who seek its assistance. . . . Respect for this principle explains why laws singling out a certain class of citizens for disfavored legal status or general hardships are rare. A law declaring that in general it shall be more difficult for one group of citizens than for all others to seek aid from the government is itself a denial of equal protection of the laws in the most literal sense. . . .

. . . [L]aws of the kind now before us raise the inevitable inference that the disadvantage imposed is born of animosity toward the class of persons affected. . . . Even laws enacted for broad and ambitious purposes often can be explained by reference to legitimate public policies which justify the incidental disadvantages they impose on certain persons. Amendment 2, however, in making a general announcement that gays and lesbians shall not have any particular protections from the law, inflicts on them immediate, continuing, and real injuries that outrun and belie any legitimate justifications that may be claimed for it. We conclude that, in addition to the far-reaching deficiencies of Amendment 2 that we have noted, the principles it offends, in another sense, are conventional and venerable; a law must bear a rational relationship to a legitimate governmental purpose, and Amendment 2 does not.

The primary rationale the State offers for Amendment 2 is respect for other citizens' freedom of association, and in particular the liberties of landlords or employers who have personal or religious objections to homosexuality. Colorado also cites its interest in conserving resources to fight discrimination against other groups. The breadth of the Amendment is so far removed from these particular justifications that we find it impossible to credit them. We cannot say that Amendment 2 is directed to any identifiable legitimate purpose or discrete objective. It is a status-based enactment divorced from any factual context from which we could discern a relationship to legitimate state interests; it is a classification of persons undertaken for its own sake, something the Equal Protection Clause does not permit.

We must conclude that Amendment 2 classifies homosexuals not to further a proper legislative end but to make them unequal to everyone else. This Colorado cannot do. A State cannot so deem a class of persons a stranger to its laws. Amendment 2 violates the Equal Protection Clause, and the judgment of the Supreme Court of Colorado is affirmed.

It is so ordered.

JUSTICE SCALIA, with whom THE CHIEF JUSTICE and JUSTICE THOMAS join, dissenting.

The Court has mistaken a Kulturkampf [a cultural conflict between religious and civil authorities] for a fit of spite. The constitutional amendment before us here is not the manifestation of a "'bare . . . desire to harm'" homosexuals, but is rather a modest attempt by seemingly tolerant Coloradans to preserve traditional sexual mores against the efforts of a politically powerful minority to revise those mores through use of the laws. That objective, and the means chosen to achieve it, are not only unimpeachable under any constitutional doctrine hitherto pronounced (hence the opinion's heavy reliance

upon principles of righteousness rather than judicial holdings); they have been specifically approved by the Congress of the United States and by this Court.

In holding that homosexuality cannot be singled out for disfavorable treatment, the Court contradicts a decision, unchallenged here, pronounced only 10 years ago, see *Bowers v. Hardwick,* and places the prestige of this institution behind the proposition that opposition to homosexuality is as reprehensible as racial or religious bias. Whether it is or not is *precisely* the cultural debate that gave rise to the Colorado constitutional amendment (and to the preferential laws against which the amendment was directed). Since the Constitution of the United States says nothing about this subject, it is left to be resolved by normal democratic means, including the democratic adoption of provisions in state constitutions. This Court has no business imposing upon all Americans the resolution favored by the elite class from which the Members of this institution are selected, pronouncing that "animosity" toward homosexuality is evil. I vigorously dissent. . . .

. . . [T]he principle underlying the Court's opinion is that one who is accorded equal treatment under the laws, but cannot as readily as others obtain *preferential* treatment under the laws, has been denied equal protection of the laws. If merely stating this alleged "equal protection" violation does not suffice to refute it, our constitutional jurisprudence has achieved terminal silliness. . . .

. . . The Court's opinion contains grim, disapproving hints that Coloradans have been guilty of "animus" or "animosity" toward homosexuality, as though that has been established as Unamerican. Of course it is our moral heritage that one should not hate any human being or class of human beings. But I had thought that one could consider certain conduct reprehensible—murder, for example, or polygamy, or cruelty to animals—and could exhibit even "animus" toward such conduct. Surely that is the only sort of "animus" at issue here: moral disapproval of homosexual conduct. . . .

But though Coloradans are, as I say, *entitled* to be hostile toward homosexual conduct, the fact is that the degree of hostility reflected by Amendment 2 is the smallest conceivable. The Court's portrayal of Coloradans as a society fallen victim to pointless, hate-filled "gay-bashing" is so false as to be comical. Colorado not only is one of the 25 States that have repealed their anti-sodomy laws, but was among the first to do so. But the society that eliminates criminal punishment for homosexual acts does not necessarily abandon the view that homosexuality is morally wrong and socially harmful;

often, abolition simply reflects the view that enforcement of such criminal laws involves unseemly intrusion into the intimate lives of citizens. . . .

When the Court takes sides in the culture wars, it tends to be with the knights rather than the villeins—and more specifically with the Templars, reflecting the views and values of the lawyer class from which the Court's Members are drawn. How that class feels about homosexuality will be evident to anyone who wishes to interview job applicants at virtually any of the Nation's law schools. The interviewer may refuse to offer a job because the applicant is a Republican; because he is an adulterer; because he went to the wrong prep school or belongs to the wrong country club; because he eats snails; because he is a womanizer; because she wears real-animal fur; or even because he hates the Chicago Cubs. But if the interviewer should wish not to be an associate or partner of an applicant because he disapproves of the applicant's homosexuality, *then* he will have violated the pledge which the Association of American Law Schools requires all its member-schools to exact from job interviewers: "assurance of the employer's willingness" to hire homosexuals. This law-school view of what "prejudices" must be stamped out may be contrasted with the more plebeian attitudes that apparently still prevail in the United States Congress, which has been unresponsive to repeated attempts to extend to homosexuals the protections of federal civil rights laws, and which took the pains to exclude them specifically from the Americans With Disabilities Act of 1990.

Today's opinion has no foundation in American constitutional law, and barely pretends to. The people of Colorado have adopted an entirely reasonable provision which does not even disfavor homosexuals in any substantive sense, but merely denies them preferential treatment. Amendment 2 is designed to prevent piece-meal deterioration of the sexual morality favored by a majority of Coloradans, and is not only an appropriate means to that legitimate end, but a means that Americans have employed before. Striking it down is an act, not of judicial judgment, but of political will. I dissent.

The majority's opinion is a strong statement against laws that single out homosexuals for discriminatory treatment, but the ruling is also important for other reasons. The justices explicitly distanced themselves from the "strict scrutiny" approach of the Colorado Supreme Court and did not even engage in a full discussion of the relative merits of the three equal protection tests as applied to gay rights. Instead, the Court concluded

that Amendment 2 offends even the lowest level of scrutiny (rational basis), leaving little necessity to engage in additional argument regarding an appropriate test. The Court struck down Amendment 2, but it created no new rights or protections for homosexuals.

So, despite *Romer*'s importance, it will not be the Court's last word on the rights of gays and lesbians. *Romer,* along with *Lawrence v. Texas,* undoubtedly will encourage additional constitutional challenges of laws having a discriminatory impact on homosexuals.

One issue that is already a matter of political and legal controversy is same-sex marriage. A large majority of states have followed Congress's lead, passing legislation that bans such unions, while others are moving in the opposite direction. The controversy has been fought in courts, in legislative chambers, and at the ballot box. The issue became especially prominent in 2003 when the Massachusetts Supreme Judicial Court held, 4–3, in *Goodridge v. Department of Public Health* that state laws allowing only heterosexual couples to marry discriminated against gay persons in violation of the state constitution. Shortly thereafter the court clarified that allowing gay couples to enter into civil unions, but not legal marriages, was not an acceptable substitute for full equality. As a consequence, in 2004 Massachusetts became the first state to allow gay couples to marry. By 2012 six other states and the District of Columbia, by legislative action or judicial decree, had taken similar actions. Other states have recognized domestic partnerships or otherwise have extended many of the advantages of traditional marriage to gay couples. On the other side of the controversy, twenty-eight states have placed the issue on the ballot, and in all of these states the voters have endorsed the traditional view of marriage as a union between one man and one woman. In a handful of states the issue remains hotly contested, with final determinations resting on future legislative actions or court decisions.

Thus far, legal battles over state bans on same-sex marriages largely have been fought in state courts and on state constitutional grounds. One reason for this strategy has been the reluctance of gay rights supporters to take their disputes to a U.S. Supreme Court composed of justices who are not seen as being particularly sympathetic to their cause or eager to take on the issue. Recently, however, a number of legal actions have been filed in federal courts, including challenges to the constitutionality of the federal Defense of Marriage Act. It is inevitable that the Supreme Court will soon face the question of whether state and federal prohibitions against same-sex marriages violate the due process and equal protection provisions of the U.S. Constitution, as well as raising privacy concerns *(see Chapter 10)*.

Other questions regarding the treatment of homosexuals loom as well. Sooner or later, the justices must determine the appropriate standard of scrutiny to be used in cases alleging discrimination based on sexual orientation. As Box 13-5 illustrates, several other nations have already confronted such issues.

BOX 13-5   GAY RIGHTS LAW IN GLOBAL PERSPECTIVE

In many areas, law scholars agree, the United States differs from other democracies in its legal treatment of gays and lesbians. For example, with the exception of several former republics of the Soviet Union, no country in Europe prohibits private consensual homosexual relations. The European Court of Human Rights has held that laws prohibiting sodomy violate the "right to privacy" under the European Convention for the Protection of Human Rights. In addition, in 1994 the United Nations Human Rights Committee ruled that the antisodomy law passed by the Australian state of Tasmania violated the privacy and nondiscrimination provisions of the International Covenant on Civil and Political Rights (ICCPR). These rulings stood in marked contrast to the U.S. Supreme Court's approach to sodomy prior to 2003, when the justices handed down *Lawrence v. Texas (see Chapter 10)*.

Moreover, at a time when U.S. (federal) law denies recognition of same-sex marriages, some countries are reconsidering their bans or at least contemplating legislation that would recognize gay and lesbian partnerships. In response to court rulings voiding his country's definition of marriage as a union between a man and woman, the Canadian prime minister introduced legislation to allow same-sex marriages. That legislation passed in 2005, making Canada the fourth country to recognize same-sex marriages (the others are the Netherlands, Belgium, and Spain). Since then, six others have legalized them (Argentina, Iceland, Portugal, South Africa, Norway, and Sweden). Other nations, such as Denmark, have moved or are moving in the direction of providing benefits to same-sex couples traditionally enjoyed by those legally married, as have some U.S. states, including Massachusetts, which recognizes gay marriages.

Many countries provide various protections against discrimination based on sexual orientation. Some of these protections are laws, such as Costa Rica's, which reads: "Whoever practices any form of discrimination, based on race, nationality, gender, age, political opinion, sexual orientation, social position, economic situation, marriage status, or diseases will be sanctioned by the law with twenty to sixty days in jail." Other protections have come in the form of constitutional provisions or court interpretations of those provisions. South Africa was the first country to prohibit discrimination based on sexual orientation explicitly in its constitution (which bans discrimination on the basis of "race, gender, sex, pregnancy, marital status, ethnic or social origin, colour, sexual orientation, age, disability, religion, conscience, belief, culture, language and birth"). Others, including Ecuador and Fiji, have followed suit. Courts in some nations have read their constitutional documents to accomplish similar ends. So, for example, the Canadian Supreme Court read the relevant clause in its country's charter—"Every individual is equal before and under the law and has the right to the equal protection and equal benefit of the law without discrimination and, in particular, without discrimination based on race, national or ethnic origin, colour, religion, sex, age, or mental or physical disability"—to cover sexual orientation.

Despite these steps, gays and lesbians still remain the targets of discrimination throughout the world. In 2011, Hungary passed an amendment to its constitution prohibiting same-sex marriages. Although Fiji's constitution prohibits discrimination on the basis of sexual orientation, its laws prohibit government recognition of same-sex marriages. Poland explicitly rejected national and international attempts to include sexual orientation as a ground for nondiscrimination in its new constitution, though it is now considering legislation to allow same-sex partnerships. More generally, however, according to a 2011 United Nations report, seventy-six countries have laws that "are used to criminalize people on the basis of sexual orientation or gender identity." In at least five, the country can punish consensual adult homosexual conduct by death. The report also notes that violence against gays and lesbians continues throughout the world, as it does in the United States.

SOURCES: James D. Wilets, "Using International Law to Vindicate the Civil Rights of Gays and Lesbians in United States Courts," *Columbia Human Rights Law Review* 27 (1995): 33–56; Edward H. Sadtler, "A Right to Same-Sex Marriage under International Law: Can It Be Vindicated in the United States?," *Virginia Journal of International Law* 40 (1999): 405–447; Martha Bailey, "How Will Canada Respond to Foreign Same-Sex Marriages?," *Creighton Law Review* 32 (1998): 105–119; and United Nations Human Rights Web site, http://www.ohchr.org/EN/Pages/WelcomePage.aspx.

DISCRIMINATION BASED ON ECONOMIC STATUS

As with matters of race and gender, society's views on economic status have changed. In the early days of our nation, wealth was considered a reflection of individual worth. The poor were thought to be less deserving. The free enterprise philosophy that emphasized personal economic responsibility discouraged public policies designed to help the less fortunate. The fact that people could be imprisoned for failure to pay debts—a contrast with today's more lenient treatment under the bankruptcy laws—reflects that period's hard-line approach to economic failure. Even a sitting Supreme Court justice, James Wilson, was imprisoned in 1796 because of a failure to satisfy his creditors. In *City of New York v. Miln* (1837) the Court supported the power of the state to take "precautionary measures against the moral pestilence of paupers."

As American society has evolved, the plight of the poor has become a major public policy concern. Although opinions differ widely on the proper role of government in addressing poverty, housing, and health care, the U.S. political system has developed social programs that would have been inconceivable to leaders during the nation's formative years. Moreover, economic disadvantage, at least according to the Supreme Court, is no longer a justification for denying a person full political and social rights. We have already seen, for example, that the Court has extended certain rights, such as government-provided attorneys, to indigent criminal defendants. It has also ruled on government policies discriminating against the poor, including welfare programs that require individuals to live in a particular state for a specified amount of time before receiving benefits.

When the Court examines such policies, what standard of review does it use? The level of scrutiny varies depending on the nature of the right in question. If the classification burdens a "fundamental" right, the justices apply strict scrutiny; if not, they invoke the rational basis standard.

Shapiro v. Thompson (1969) nicely illustrates the point. This case involved the kind of law we just mentioned—that is, to obtain welfare benefits some states required applicants to live in the state for one year. The states argued that the residency requirement was necessary for fiscal reasons. They claimed that those who require welfare assistance when they first move to a state are likely to become continuing burdens. If a state can deter such people from moving there in the first place by denying them welfare benefits during the first year, the state can continue to provide aid to longtime residents.

Writing for the Court, Justice Brennan disagreed. He concluded that the "states do not use and have no need to use the one-year requirement for the governmental purposes suggested. Thus, even under traditional equal protection tests a classification of welfare applicants according to whether they have lived in the State for one year would seem irrational and unconstitutional." But he went on to say:

The traditional criteria do not apply in these cases. Since the classification here touches on the fundamental right of interstate movement, its constitutionality must be judged by the stricter standard of whether it promotes a compelling state interest. Under this standard, the waiting-period requirement clearly violates the Equal Protection Clause.

In other words, a rational basis standard normally would be appropriate in cases involving classifications based on wealth, but when a fundamental right also is involved—here, the right to interstate travel—the standard is elevated. In **Saenz v. Roe** (1999) the Court reaffirmed *Shapiro v. Thompson* by striking down a California law that imposed similar economic disadvantages on new residents who moved into the state. The Court invoked the same logic in **Harper v. Virginia State Board of Elections** (1966), in which it struck down poll taxes as infringing on the fundamental right to vote.

When a fundamental right is not involved, however, the justices have tended to stick with the rational basis standard. An example is *San Antonio Independent School District v. Rodriguez* (1973), a case of enormous importance. First, it involved the right of children to receive a public education, the surest way for the disadvantaged to improve their prospects for economic and social advancement. Second, it questioned the constitutionality of the way Texas funded public schools. Education is the most expensive of all state programs, and any change in the method of distributing these funds can have a tremendous impact. Third, the Texas system challenged here was similar to schemes used by most states in determining the allocation of education dollars. Whatever the Court decided, this case was going to be significant economically and socially.

At its heart was the contention that the Texas system for funding schools discriminated against the poor. It was undeniable that children who lived in wealthy school districts had access to a higher-quality education than children in poor districts. But does this difference violate the Constitution? In large measure, the answer depends on which equal protection standard is used. Under strict scrutiny the Texas funding system almost certainly would fall. But before strict scrutiny can be applied, as we now know, one of two requirements has to be met. Either the poor, like black Americans in the racial discrimination cases, would have to be declared a suspect class, or the right to an education would have to be declared a fundamental right. If the Court failed to support one of these positions, the rational basis test would control, and the state plan likely would stand. As you read Justice Powell's decision, think about his reasoning and conclusions on these two points.

Demetrio Rodriguez and other Mexican American parents challenged the Texas public school financing system as discriminatory on the basis of economic status, but in 1973 the Supreme Court ruled against them.

San Antonio Independent School District v. Rodriguez

411 U.S. 1 (1973)
http://laws.findlaw.com/US/411/1.html
Oral arguments are available at http://www.oyez.org.
Vote: 5 (Blackmun, Burger, Powell, Rehnquist, Stewart)
   4 (Brennan, Douglas, Marshall, White)

OPINION OF THE COURT: Powell

CONCURRING OPINION: Stewart

DISSENTING OPINIONS: Brennan, Marshall, White

FACTS:

Demetrio Rodriguez and other Mexican American parents whose children attended the public schools of the Edgewood Independent School District in San Antonio, Texas, were concerned about the quality of the local schools. The Edgewood district was about 90 percent Mexican American and quite poor. Efforts to improve the children's schools were unsuccessful due to insufficient funding. Because the state formula for distributing education funds resulted in low levels of financial support for economically depressed districts,

the parents filed suit to declare the state funding system in violation of the equal protection clause. The funding program guaranteed each child in the state a minimum basic education by appropriating funds to local school districts through a complex formula designed to take into account economic variations across school districts. Local districts levied property taxes to meet their assigned contributions to the state program, but they also could use the property taxing power to obtain additional funds for the schools within their own districts.

The Edgewood district had an assessed property value per pupil of $5,960, the lowest in the San Antonio area. It taxed its residents at a rate of $1.05 per $100 in assessed valuation, the area's highest rate. This local tax yielded $26 per pupil above the contributions that had to be made to the state for the 1967–1968 school year. Funds from the state added $222 per pupil, and federal programs contributed $108. These sources combined for a total of $356 per pupil for the year. In the nearby

Alamo Heights district, property values amounted to $49,000 per pupil, which was taxed at a rate of $0.85 per $100 of assessed valuation. These property taxes yielded $333 additional available revenues per pupil. Combined with $225 from state funds and $36 from federal sources, Alamo Heights enjoyed a total funding level of $594 per pupil.

The suit filed by Rodriguez and the other parents was based on these disparities. Although the residents of Edgewood taxed themselves at a much higher rate, the yield from local taxes in Alamo Heights was almost thirteen times greater. To achieve equal property tax dollars with Alamo Heights, Edgewood would have had to raise its tax rate to $13 per $100 in assessed valuation, but state law placed a $1.50 ceiling on such taxes. There was no way for the Edgewood parents to achieve funding equality.

A three-judge federal court agreed with the Rodriguez suit, finding that the Texas funding program invidiously discriminated against children on the basis of economic status. According to the federal court, the poor were a suspect class, and education was a fundamental right. The state appealed to the Supreme Court. Twenty-five states filed amicus curiae briefs supporting the Texas funding system. Groups such as the NAACP, the ACLU, and the American Education Association filed briefs backing Rodriguez.

ARGUMENTS:

For the appellant, San Antonio
Independent School District:

- The respondents' argument is based on an invalid assumption that the amount of expenditures per pupil is an accurate measure of educational quality.
- Rights are fundamental if they are rooted in some provision of the Constitution or have been declared so by the Supreme Court. Education does not fall into either category.
- The Supreme Court has never declared economic status a suspect classification.
- The state's financing system is rational. It provides for a basic education for all children, and it allows local districts to use their own funds to supplement educational budgets as they see fit.

For the appellees, Demitrio Rodriguez, et al.:

- The state has made education a function of the wealth of the school district in which the child lives. The state itself drew the district boundary lines.
- Education is a prerequisite for fully participating in the nation's political, social, and cultural life. It is the most effective path to socioeconomic advancement. Education, therefore, is a fundamental right.
- The Texas system discriminates against those living in poor districts, primarily minorities and the economically disadvantaged. These individuals cannot escape the educational system by moving to a wealthy district or sending their children to private schools. The poor should be considered a suspect class.
- The Texas financing system should be evaluated using strict scrutiny.

 MR. JUSTICE POWELL DELIVERED THE OPINION OF THE COURT.

Texas virtually concedes that its historically rooted dual system of financing education could not withstand the strict judicial scrutiny that this Court has found appropriate in reviewing legislative judgments that interfere with fundamental constitutional rights or that involve suspect classifications. If, as previous decisions have indicated, strict scrutiny means that the State's system is not entitled to the usual presumption of validity, that the State rather than the complainants must carry a "heavy burden of justification," that the State must demonstrate that its educational system has been structured with "precision," and is "tailored" narrowly to serve legitimate objectives and that it has selected the "less drastic means" for effectuating its objectives, the Texas financing system and its counterpart in virtually every other State will not pass muster. The State candidly admits that "[n]o one familiar with the Texas system would contend that it has yet achieved perfection." Apart from its concession that educational financing in Texas has "defects" and "imperfections," the State defends the system's rationality with vigor and disputes the District Court's finding that it lacks a "reasonable basis."

This, then, establishes the framework for our analysis. We must decide, first, whether the Texas system of financing public education operates to the disadvantage of some suspect class or impinges upon a fundamental right explicitly or implicitly protected by the Constitution, thereby requiring strict judicial scrutiny. If so, the judgment of the District Court should be affirmed. If not, the Texas scheme must still be examined to determine whether it rationally furthers some legitimate, articulated state purpose and therefore does not constitute an invidious discrimination in violation of the Equal Protection Clause of the Fourteenth Amendment. . . .

. . . [F]or the several reasons that follow, we find neither the suspect-classification nor the fundamental-interest analysis persuasive.

The wealth discrimination discovered by the District Court in this case, and by several other courts that have recently struck down school-financing laws in other States, is quite unlike any of the forms of wealth discrimination heretofore reviewed by this Court. Rather than focusing on the unique features of the alleged discrimination, the courts in these cases have virtually assumed their findings of a suspect classification through a simplistic process of analysis: since, under the traditional systems of financing public schools, some poorer people receive less expensive educations than other more affluent people, these systems discriminate on the basis of wealth. This approach largely ignores the hard threshold questions, including whether it makes a difference for purposes of consideration under the Constitution that the class of disadvantaged "poor" cannot be identified or defined in customary equal protection terms, and whether the relative—rather than absolute—nature of the asserted deprivation is of significant consequence. Before a State's laws and the justification for the classifications they create are subjected to strict judicial scrutiny, we think these threshold considerations must be analyzed more closely than they were in the court below. . . .

. . . First, in support of their charge that the system discriminates against the "poor," appellees have made no effort to demonstrate that it operates to the peculiar disadvantage of any class fairly definable as indigent, or as composed of persons whose incomes are beneath any designated poverty level. Indeed, there is reason to believe that the poorest families are not necessarily clustered in the poorest property districts. A recent and exhaustive study of school districts in Connecticut concluded that . . . the poor were clustered around commercial and industrial areas—those same areas that provide the most attractive sources of property tax income for school districts. Whether a similar pattern would be discovered in Texas is not known, but there is no basis on the record in this case for assuming that the poorest people—defined by reference to any level of absolute impecunity—are concentrated in the poorest districts.

Second, neither appellees nor the District Court addressed the fact that, unlike each of the foregoing cases, lack of personal resources has not occasioned an absolute deprivation of the desired benefit. The argument here is not that the children in districts having relatively low assessable property values are receiving no public education; rather, it is that they are receiving a poorer quality education than that available to children in districts having more assessable wealth. Apart from the unsettled and disputed question whether the quality of education may be determined by the amount of money expended for it, a sufficient answer to appellees' argument is that, at least where wealth is involved, the Equal Protection Clause does not require absolute equality or precisely equal advantages. . . .

For these two reasons—the absence of any evidence that the financing system discriminates against any definable category of "poor" people or that it results in the absolute deprivation of education—the disadvantaged class is not susceptible of identification in traditional terms. . . .

However described, it is clear that appellees' suit asks this Court to extend its most exacting scrutiny to review a system that allegedly discriminates against a large, diverse, and amorphous class, unified only by the common factor of residence in districts that happen to have less taxable wealth than other districts. The system of alleged discrimination and the class it defines have none of the traditional indicia of suspectness: the class is not saddled with such disabilities, or subjected to such a history of purposeful unequal treatment, or relegated to such a position of political powerlessness as to command extraordinary protection from the majoritarian political process.

We thus conclude that the Texas system does not operate to the peculiar disadvantage of any suspect class. But in recognition of the fact that this Court has never heretofore held that wealth discrimination alone provides an adequate basis for invoking strict scrutiny, appellees have not relied solely on this contention. They also assert that the State's system impermissibly interferes with the exercise of a "fundamental" right and that accordingly the prior decisions of this Court require the application of the strict standard of judicial review. It is this question—whether education is a fundamental right, in the sense that it is among the rights and liberties protected by the Constitution—which has so consumed the attention of courts and commentators in recent years. . . .

Nothing this Court holds today in any way detracts from our historic dedication to public education. We are in complete agreement with the conclusion of the three-judge panel below that "the grave significance of education both to the individual and to our society" cannot be doubted. But the importance of a service performed by the State does not determine whether it must be regarded as fundamental for purposes of examination under the Equal Protection Clause. . . .

. . . It is not the province of this Court to create substantive constitutional rights in the name of guaranteeing equal protection of the laws. Thus, the key to discovering whether education is "fundamental" is not to be found in comparisons of . . . relative societal significance. . . . Rather, the answer lies in assessing whether there is a right to education explicitly or implicitly guaranteed by the Constitution.

Education, of course, is not among the rights afforded explicit protection under our Federal Constitution. Nor do we find any basis for saying it is implicitly so protected. As we have said, the undisputed importance of education will not alone cause this Court to depart from the usual standard for reviewing a State's social and economic legislation. It is appellees' contention, however, that education is distinguishable from other services and benefits provided by the State because it bears a peculiarly close relationship to other rights and liberties accorded protection under the Constitution. Specifically, they insist that education is itself a fundamental personal right because it is essential to the effective exercise of First Amendment freedoms and to intelligent utilization of the right to vote. In asserting a nexus between speech and education, appellees urge that the right to speak is meaningless unless the speaker is capable of articulating his thoughts intelligently and persuasively. The "marketplace of ideas" is an empty forum for those lacking basic communicative tools. Likewise, they argue that the corollary right to receive information becomes little more than a hollow privilege when the recipient has not been taught to read, assimilate, and utilize available knowledge. . . .

We need not dispute any of these propositions. The Court has long afforded zealous protection against unjustifiable governmental interference with the individual's rights to speak and to vote. Yet we have never presumed to possess either the ability or the authority to guarantee to the citizenry the most *effective* speech or the most *informed* electoral choice. That these may be desirable goals of a system of freedom of expression and of a representative form of government is not to be doubted. These are indeed goals to be pursued by a people whose thoughts and beliefs are freed from governmental interference. But they are not values to be implemented by judicial intrusion into otherwise legitimate state activities.

Even if it were conceded that some identifiable quantum of education is a constitutionally protected prerequisite to the meaningful exercise of either right, we have no indication that the present levels of educational expenditures in Texas provide an education that falls short. . . .

We have carefully considered each of the arguments supportive of the District Court's finding that education is a fundamental right or liberty and have found those arguments unpersuasive. . . .

In its reliance on state as well as local resources, the Texas system is comparable to the systems employed in virtually every other State. The power to tax local property for educational purposes has been recognized in Texas at least since 1883. When the growth of commercial and industrial centers and accompanying shifts in population began to create disparities in local resources, Texas undertook a program calling for a considerable investment of state funds. . . .

. . . While assuring a basic education for every child in the State, it permits and encourages a large measure of participation in and control of each district's schools at the local level. . . .

The persistence of attachment to government at the lowest level where education is concerned reflects the depth of commitment of its supporters. In part, local control means . . . the freedom to devote more money to the education of one's children. Equally important, however, is the opportunity it offers for participation in the decisionmaking process that determines how those local tax dollars will be spent. Each locality is free to tailor local programs to local needs. Pluralism also affords some opportunity for experimentation, innovation, and a healthy competition for educational excellence. An analogy to the Nation-State relationship in our federal system seems uniquely appropriate. Mr. Justice Brandeis identified as one of the peculiar strengths of our form of government each State's freedom to "serve as a laboratory; and try novel social and economic experiments." No area of social concern stands to profit more from a multiplicity of viewpoints and from a diversity of approaches than does public education.

Appellees do not question the propriety of Texas' dedication to local control of education. To the contrary, they attack the school-financing system precisely because, in their view, it does not provide the same level of local control and fiscal flexibility in all districts. Appellees suggest that local control could be preserved and promoted under other financing systems that resulted in more equality in educational expenditures. While it is no doubt true that reliance on local property taxation for school revenues provides less freedom of choice with respect to expenditures for some districts than for others, the existence of "some inequality" in the manner in which the State's rationale is achieved is not alone a sufficient basis for striking down the entire system. . . .

In sum, to the extent that the Texas system of school financing results in unequal expenditures between children who happen to reside in different districts, we cannot say that such disparities are the product of a system that is so irrational as to be invidiously discriminatory. Texas has acknowledged its shortcomings and has persistently endeavored—not without some success—to ameliorate the differences in levels of expenditures without sacrificing the benefits of local participation. The Texas plan is not the result of hurried, ill-conceived legislation. It certainly is not the product of purposeful discrimination against any group or class. On the contrary, it is rooted in decades of experience in Texas and elsewhere, and in major part is the product of responsible studies by qualified people. . . .

These practical considerations, of course, play no role in the adjudication of the constitutional issues presented here. But they serve to highlight the wisdom of the traditional limitations on this Court's function. The consideration and initiation of fundamental reforms with respect to state taxation and education are matters reserved for the legislative processes of the various States, and we do no violence to the values of federalism and separation of powers by staying our hand. We hardly need add that this Court's action today is not to be viewed as placing its judicial imprimatur on the status quo. The need is apparent for reform in tax systems which may well have relied too long and too heavily on the local property tax. And certainly innovative thinking as to public education, its methods, and its funding is necessary to assure both a higher level of quality and greater uniformity of opportunity. These matters merit the continued attention of the scholars who already have contributed much by their challenges. But the ultimate solutions must come from the lawmakers and from the democratic pressures of those who elect them.

Reversed.

MR. JUSTICE MARSHALL . . . *dissenting.*

The Court today decides, in effect, that a State may constitutionally vary the quality of education which it offers its children in accordance with the amount of taxable wealth located in the school districts within which they reside. The majority's decision represents an abrupt departure from the mainstream of recent state and federal court decisions concerning the unconstitutionality of state educational financing schemes dependent upon taxable local wealth. More unfortunately, though, the majority's holding can only be seen as a retreat from our historic commitment to equality of educational opportunity and as unsupportable acquiescence in a system which deprives children in their earliest years of the chance to reach their full potential as citizens. The Court does this despite the absence of any substantial justification for a scheme which arbitrarily channels educational resources in accordance with the fortuity of the amount of taxable wealth within each district.

In my judgment, the right of every American to an equal start in life, so far as the provision of a state service as important as education is concerned, is far too vital to permit state discrimination on grounds as tenuous as those presented by this record. Nor can I accept the notion that it is sufficient to remit these appellees to the vagaries of the political process which, contrary to the majority's suggestion, has proved singularly unsuited to the task of providing a remedy for this discrimination. I, for one, am unsatisfied with the hope of an ultimate "political" solution sometime in the indefinite future while, in the meantime, countless children unjustifiably receive inferior educations that "may affect their hearts and minds in a way unlikely ever to be undone." I must therefore respectfully dissent. . . .

. . . I must . . . voice my disagreement with the Court's rigidified approach to equal protection analysis. The Court apparently seeks to establish today that equal protection cases fall into one of two neat categories which dictate the appropriate standard of review—strict scrutiny or mere rationality. But this Court's decisions in the field of equal protection defy such easy categorization. A principled reading of what this Court has done reveals that it has applied a spectrum of standards in reviewing discrimination allegedly violative of the Equal Protection Clause. This spectrum clearly comprehends variations in the degree of care with which the Court will scrutinize particular classifications, depending, I believe, on the constitutional and societal importance of the interest adversely affected and the recognized invidiousness of the basis upon which the particular classification is drawn. I find in fact that many of the Court's recent decisions embody the very sort of reasoned approach to equal protection analysis for which I previously argued— that is, an approach in which "concentration [is] placed upon the character of the classification in question, the relative importance to individuals in the class discriminated against of the governmental benefits that they do not receive, and the asserted state interests in support of the classification."

I therefore cannot accept the majority's labored efforts to demonstrate that fundamental interests, which call for strict scrutiny of the challenged classification, encompass only established rights which we are somehow bound to recognize from the text of the Constitution itself. To be sure, some interests which the Court has deemed to be fundamental for purposes of equal protection analysis are themselves constitutionally protected rights. . . . But it will not do to suggest that the "answer" to whether an interest is fundamental for purposes of equal protection analysis is always determined by whether that interest "is a right . . . explicitly or implicitly guaranteed by the Constitution."

I would like to know where the Constitution guarantees the right to procreate, *Skinner v. Oklahoma* (1942), or the right to vote in state elections, *e.g., Reynolds v. Sims* (1964), or the right to an appeal from a criminal conviction, *e.g., Griffin v. Illinois* (1956). These are instances in which, due to the importance of the interests at stake, the Court has displayed a strong concern with the existence of discriminatory state treatment. But the Court has never said or indicated that these are interests which independently enjoy full-blown constitutional protection. . . .

. . . [I]f the discrimination inherent in the Texas scheme is scrutinized with the care demanded by the interest and classification present in this case, the unconstitutionality of that scheme is unmistakable.

The decision in *Rodriguez* was a blow to civil rights advocates. It had a substantial impact on education by validating financing systems that perpetuated inequity. Many states, however, reacted by adjusting their financing schemes to reduce funding disparities, and some state supreme courts even found unequal funding systems to be in violation of state constitutional provisions.

In terms of constitutional development, the ruling introduced problems for future litigation. The Court

expressly held that the poor were not a suspect class. Unlike other groups that were granted such status, such as black Americans and aliens, the poor were neither an easily identified group nor politically powerless; as a group they did not have a significant history of overt discrimination. The decision not to elevate the poor to suspect class status meant that a rational basis test would be used in economic discrimination cases in which a fundamental right was not at issue. This test provides the government with an advantage in demonstrating that challenged laws are valid.

In addition, the Court in *Rodriguez* held that education, unlike the right to interstate travel, was not a fundamental right under the Constitution. This holding also created potential problems for future cases. Advocates of the poor have concentrated their efforts on education because of its crucial role in human development. By not according it fundamental right status, the Court decreased the chances of successful legal action on behalf of the disadvantaged.

DISCRIMINATION AGAINST ALIENS

The Supreme Court generally has sympathized with the rights of noncitizens, a position consistent with the country's relatively generous immigration and naturalization policies. Although aliens legally in the United States do not enjoy the full range of rights and liberties granted to American citizens, they are entitled to certain protections under the Constitution. The Court has a history of striking down state laws that unnecessarily discriminate against aliens. As early as *Yick Wo v. Hopkins* (1886) the justices held that a resident alien was entitled to equal protection guarantees. Since then, the Court has nullified laws that prohibit resident aliens from obtaining civil service employment, receiving financial aid for college, becoming members of the bar, or even getting fishing licenses.[18] In fact, in *Graham v. Richardson* (1971), a challenge to the denial of public assistance to an alien, the Court accorded suspect class status to noncitizens, explaining:

[C]lassifications based on alienage, like those based on nationality or race, are inherently suspect and subject to close judicial scrutiny. Aliens as a class are a prime example of a

---

18. Respectively, *Sugarman v. Dougall* (1973), *Nyquist v. Mauclet* (1977), *In re Griffiths* (1973), and *Takahashi v. Fish and Game Commission* (1948).

"discrete and insular" minority . . . for whom such heightened judicial solicitude is appropriate.

This position is based on the recognition that aliens who lawfully reside in the United States are politically powerless because they can neither vote nor hold office. Yet they pay taxes, support the economy, serve in the military, and contribute to society in other ways, and, if they otherwise qualify for government benefits or opportunities, they should not be denied them on the basis of noncitizenship alone.

Has the Court been faithful to *Graham*? The answer is mixed, or, as Justice Powell once put it, "The decisions of this Court regarding the permissibility of statutory classifications involving aliens have not formed an unwavering line."[19] In some instances, such as *Nyquist v. Mauclet* (1977)—involving a New York policy that barred certain resident aliens from receiving state financial assistance for higher education—the justices reiterated the lesson of *Graham* and held that state classifications based on alienage are "inherently suspect and subject to close judicial scrutiny." At the opposite end of the spectrum is *Foley v. Connelie* (1978), in which a divided Court concluded that the Constitution is not violated when a state denies an alien a job in law enforcement. The justices held that it is not necessary to apply strict scrutiny when a government can demonstrate that citizenship bears a rational relationship to the job.

Cases such as *Graham*, *Nyquist*, and *Foley* have a common characteristic: all deal with disputes brought by aliens who legally resided in the United States. Illegal or undocumented aliens present an entirely different issue. Should illegal aliens be entitled to the same benefits and social services enjoyed by citizens and resident aliens? To what extent does the Constitution protect undocumented aliens from discriminatory treatment? In *Plyler v. Doe* (1982) the justices confronted these controversial questions.

Plyler v. Doe

457 U.S. 202 (1982)
http://laws.findlaw.com/US/457/202.html
Oral arguments are available at http://www.oyez.org.
Vote: 5 (Blackmun, Brennan, Marshall, Powell, Stevens)
    4 (Burger, O'Connor, Rehnquist, White)
OPINION OF THE COURT: *Brennan*
CONCURRING OPINIONS: *Blackmun, Marshall, Powell*
DISSENTING OPINION: *Burger*

---

19. *Ambach v. Norwick* (1979).

FACTS:

In May 1975, the Texas legislature revised its laws to withhold from local school districts any state funds for the education of children who were not legal U.S. residents. The law also allowed local school districts to deny enrollment to any student who was an undocumented alien under Section 21.031 of the Texas Education Code. In September 1977, a suit was filed against James Plyler, superintendent of the Tyler Texas Independent School District, on behalf of school-age children of Mexican origin who lived in Smith County, Texas. Because they could not prove their legal status, these children had been denied admission to school.

The state argued that the increase in undocumented aliens and the children's educational deficiencies had placed a tremendous burden on public schools in Texas. Providing free education for these children depleted the schools' resources and detracted from the quality of education available to citizens and legal residents. The trial court, however, was not convinced by these arguments, concluding instead that the state law violated the equal protection clause of the Fourteenth Amendment. The judgment was affirmed by the appeals court, and the state asked the Supreme Court to reverse.

ARGUMENTS:

For the appellants, James Plyler, Superintendent of the Tyler Independent School District, and the State of Texas:

- Education is not a fundamental right (*San Antonio Independent School District v. Rodriguez*). The Court should proceed using the rational basis test.
- The statute prevents the state's resources from being used to educate undocumented populations from Mexico and other countries. These children often require expensive special services.
- The statute also advances the state interest in discouraging illegal immigration.

For the appellees, J. and R. Doe, et al.:

- The plain meaning of the equal protection clause and its history compel the conclusion that the Fourteenth Amendment applies to undocumented children.
- Unlike *San Antonio v. Rodriguez,* where children were denied an equal education, the children here, all minorities and poor, are denied any public education at all. This justifies using a strict scrutiny standard.

- The state is punishing innocent children for the illegal acts of their parents.
- The statute cannot be justified as a means of discouraging illegal immigration.

JUSTICE BRENNAN DELIVERED THE OPINION OF THE COURT.

The Equal Protection Clause directs that "all persons similarly circumstanced shall be treated alike." . . . But so too, "[t]he Constitution does not require things which are different in fact or opinion to be treated in law as though they were the same." . . . The initial discretion to determine what is "different" and what is "the same" resides in the legislatures of the States. A legislature must have substantial latitude to establish classifications that roughly approximate the nature of the problem perceived, that accommodate competing concerns both public and private, and that account for limitations on the practical ability of the State to remedy every ill. In applying the Equal Protection Clause to most forms of state action, we thus seek only the assurance that the classification at issue bears some fair relationship to a legitimate public purpose.

But we would not be faithful to our obligations under the Fourteenth Amendment if we applied so deferential a standard to every classification. The Equal Protection Clause was intended as a restriction on state legislative action inconsistent with elemental constitutional premises. Thus we have treated as presumptively invidious those classifications that disadvantage a "suspect class," or that impinge upon the exercise of a "fundamental right." With respect to such classifications, it is appropriate to enforce the mandate of equal protection by requiring the State to demonstrate that its classification has been precisely tailored to serve a compelling governmental interest. In addition, we have recognized that certain forms of legislative classification, while not facially invidious, nonetheless give rise to recurring constitutional difficulties; in these limited circumstances we have sought the assurance that the classification reflects a reasoned judgment consistent with the ideal of equal protection by inquiring whether it may fairly be viewed as furthering a substantial interest of the State. . . .

Sheer incapability or lax enforcement of the laws barring entry into this country, coupled with the failure to establish an effective bar to the employment of undocumented aliens, has resulted in the creation of a substantial "shadow population" of illegal migrants—numbering in the millions—within our borders. This situation raises the specter of a permanent caste of undocumented resident aliens, encouraged by some to remain here as a source of cheap labor, but nevertheless denied the benefits that our society makes available to citizens and lawful residents. The existence of such an underclass presents most difficult problems for a Nation that prides itself on adherence to principles of equality under law.

The children who are plaintiffs in these cases are special members of this underclass. Persuasive arguments support the view that a State may withhold its beneficence from those whose very presence within the United States is the product of their own unlawful conduct. These arguments do not apply with the same force to classifications imposing disabilities on the minor children of such illegal entrants. At the least, those who elect to enter our territory by stealth and in violation of our law should be prepared to bear the consequences, including, but not limited to, deportation. But the children of those illegal entrants are not comparably situated. Their "parents have the ability to conform their conduct to societal norms," and presumably the ability to remove themselves from the State's jurisdiction; but the children who are plaintiffs in these cases "can affect neither their parents' conduct nor their own status." . . . Even if the State found it expedient to control the conduct of adults by acting against their children, legislation directing the onus of a parent's misconduct against his children does not comport with fundamental conceptions of justice. . . .

Of course, undocumented status is not irrelevant to any proper legislative goal. Nor is undocumented status an absolutely immutable characteristic since it is the product of conscious, indeed unlawful, action. But [section] 21.031 is directed against children, and imposes its discriminatory burden on the basis of a legal characteristic over which children can have little control. It is thus difficult to conceive of a rational justification for penalizing these children for their presence within the United States. Yet that appears to be precisely the effect of section 21.031.

Public education is not a "right" granted to individuals by the Constitution. *San Antonio Independent School Dist. v. Rodriguez* (1973). But neither is it merely some governmental "benefit" indistinguishable from other forms of social welfare legislation. Both the importance of education in maintaining our basic institutions, and the lasting impact of its deprivation on the life of the child, mark the distinction. The "American people have always regarded education and [the] acquisition of knowledge as matters of supreme importance." . . .

In addition to the pivotal role of education in sustaining our political and cultural heritage, denial of education to some isolated group of children poses an affront to one of the goals of the Equal Protection Clause: the abolition of governmental barriers presenting unreasonable obstacles to advancement on the basis of individual merit. Paradoxically, by depriving the children of any disfavored group of an education, we foreclose the means by which that group might raise the level of esteem in which it is held by the majority. But more directly, "education prepares individuals to be self-reliant and self-sufficient participants in society." . . .

These well-settled principles allow us to determine the proper level of deference to be afforded 21.031. Undocumented aliens cannot be treated as a suspect class because their presence in this country in violation of federal law is not a "constitutional irrelevancy." Nor is education a fundamental right; a State need not justify by compelling necessity every variation in the manner in which education is provided to its population. . . . But more is involved in these cases than the abstract question whether 21.031 discriminates against a suspect class, or whether education is a fundamental right. Section 21.031 imposes a lifetime hardship on a discrete class of children not accountable for their disabling status. The stigma of illiteracy will mark them for the rest of their lives. By denying these children a basic education, we deny them the ability to live within the structure of our civic institutions, and foreclose any realistic possibility that they will contribute in even the smallest way to the progress of our Nation. In determining the rationality of 21.031, we may appropriately take into account its costs to the Nation and to the innocent children who are its victims. In light of these countervailing costs, the discrimination contained in 21.031 can hardly be considered rational unless it furthers some substantial goal of the State.

It is the State's principal argument, and apparently the view of the dissenting Justices, that the undocumented status of these children vel non [or not] establishes a sufficient rational basis for denying them benefits that a State might choose to afford other residents. . . . Indeed, in the State's view, Congress' apparent disapproval of the presence of these children within the United States, and the evasion of the federal regulatory program that is the mark of undocumented status, provides authority for its decision to impose upon them special disabilities. Faced with an equal protection challenge respecting the treatment of aliens, we agree that the courts must be attentive to congressional policy; the exercise of congressional power might well affect the State's prerogatives to afford differential treatment to a particular class of aliens. But we are unable to find in the congressional immigration scheme any statement of policy that might weigh significantly in arriving at an equal protection balance concerning the State's authority to deprive these children of an education. . . .

To be sure, like all persons who have entered the United States unlawfully, these children are subject to deportation. . . . But there is no assurance that a child subject to deportation will ever be deported. An illegal entrant might be granted federal permission to continue to reside in this country, or even to become a citizen. . . . In light of the discretionary federal power to grant relief from deportation, a State cannot realistically determine that any particular undocumented child will in fact be deported until after deportation proceedings have been completed. It would of course be most difficult for the State to justify a denial of education to a child enjoying an inchoate federal permission to remain. . . .

. . . Apart from the asserted state prerogative to act against undocumented children solely on the basis of their undocumented status—an asserted prerogative that carries only minimal force in the circumstances of these cases—we discern three colorable state interests that might support 21.031.

First, appellants appear to suggest that the State may seek to protect itself from an influx of illegal immigrants. While a State might have an interest in mitigating the potentially harsh economic effects of sudden shifts in population, 21.031 hardly offers an effective method of dealing with an urgent demographic or economic problem. There is no evidence in the record suggesting that illegal entrants impose any significant burden on the State's economy. To the contrary, the available evidence suggests that illegal aliens underutilize public services, while contributing their labor to the local economy and tax money to the state fisc. . . . The dominant incentive for illegal entry into the State of Texas is the availability of employment; few if any illegal immigrants come to this country, or presumably to the State of Texas, in order to avail themselves of a free education. Thus, even making the doubtful assumption that the net impact of illegal aliens on the economy of the State is negative, we think it clear that "[c]harging tuition to undocumented children constitutes a ludicrously ineffectual attempt to stem the tide of illegal immigration," at least when compared with the alternative of prohibiting the employment of illegal aliens. . . .

Second, while it is apparent that a State may "not . . . reduce expenditures for education by barring [some arbitrarily chosen class of] children from its schools," . . . appellants suggest that undocumented children are appropriately singled out for exclusion because of the special burdens they impose on the State's ability to provide high-quality public education. But the record in no way supports the claim that exclusion of undocumented children is likely to improve the overall quality of education in the State. . . . And, after reviewing the State's school financing mechanism, the District Court . . . concluded that barring undocumented children from local schools would not necessarily improve the quality of education provided in those schools. . . . Of course, even if improvement in the quality of education were a likely result of barring some number of children from the schools of the State, the State must support its selection of this group as the appropriate target for exclusion. In terms of education cost and need, however, undocumented children are "basically indistinguishable" from legally resident alien children. . . .

Finally, appellants suggest that undocumented children are appropriately singled out because their unlawful presence within the United States renders them less likely than other children to remain within the boundaries of the State, and to put their education to productive social or political use within the State. Even assuming that such an interest is legitimate, it is an interest that is most difficult to quantify. The State has no assurance that any child, citizen or not, will employ the education provided by the State within the confines of the State's borders. In any event, the record is clear that many of the undocumented children disabled by this classification will remain in this country indefinitely, and that some will become lawful residents or citizens of the United States. It is difficult to understand precisely what the State hopes to achieve by promoting the creation and perpetuation of a subclass of illiterates within our boundaries, surely adding to the problems and costs of unemployment, welfare, and crime. It is thus clear that whatever savings might be achieved by denying these children an education, they are wholly insubstantial in light of the costs involved to these children, the State, and the Nation.

If the State is to deny a discrete group of innocent children the free public education that it offers to other children residing within its borders, that denial must be justified by a showing that it furthers some substantial state interest. No such showing was made here. Accordingly, the judgment of the Court of Appeals in each of these cases is affirmed.

JUSTICE MARSHALL, concurring.

While I join the Court opinion, I do so without in any way retreating from my opinion in *San Antonio Independent School District v. Rodriguez* (1973) (dissenting opinion). I continue to believe that an individual's interest in education is fundamental, and that this view is amply supported "by the unique status accorded public education by our society, and by the close relationship between education and some of our most basic constitutional values."

CHIEF JUSTICE BURGER, with whom JUSTICE WHITE, JUSTICE REHNQUIST, and JUSTICE O'CONNOR join, dissenting.

Were it our business to set the Nation's social policy, I would agree without hesitation that it is senseless for an enlightened society to deprive any children—including illegal aliens—of an elementary education. I fully agree that it would be folly—and wrong—to tolerate creation of a segment of society made up of illiterate persons, many having a limited or no command of our language. However, the Constitution does not constitute us as "Platonic Guardians" nor does it vest in this Court the authority to strike down laws because they do not meet our standards of desirable social policy, "wisdom," or "common sense." . . . We trespass on the assigned function of the political branches under our structure of limited and separated powers when we assume a policy-making role as the Court does today. . . .

The Constitution does not provide a cure for every social ill, nor does it vest judges with a mandate to try to remedy every social problem. . . . Moreover, when this Court rushes in to remedy what it perceives to be the failings of the political processes, it deprives those processes of an opportunity to function. When the political institutions are not forced to exercise constitutionally allocated powers and responsibilities, those powers, like muscles not used, tend to atrophy. Today's cases, I regret to say, present yet another example of unwarranted judicial action which in the long run tends to contribute to the weakening of our political processes.

Congress, "vested by the Constitution with the responsibility of protecting our borders and legislating with respect to aliens," . . . bears primary responsibility for addressing the problems occasioned by the millions of illegal aliens flooding across our southern border. Similarly, it is for Congress, and not this Court, to assess the "social costs borne by our Nation when select groups are denied the means to absorb the values and skills upon which our social order rests." . . . While the "specter of a permanent caste" of illegal Mexican residents of the United States is indeed a disturbing one, . . . it is but one segment of a larger problem, which is for the political branches to solve. I find it difficult to believe that Congress would long tolerate such a self-destructive result—that it would fail to deport these illegal alien families or to provide for the education of their children. Yet instead of allowing the political processes to run their course—albeit with some delay—the Court seeks to do Congress' job for it, compensating for congressional inaction. It is not unreasonable to think that this encourages the political branches to pass their problems to the Judiciary.

The solution to this seemingly intractable problem is to defer to the political processes, unpalatable as that may be to some.

How the Court will treat future claims of discrimination against aliens remains to be seen. What is beyond dispute is the inevitable growth of lawsuits claiming unfair treatment based on alien status. The nation's political leaders have yet to agree on a satisfactory immigration policy. Moreover, the government has been unable to control the flow of undocumented aliens into the United States, a condition that results in additional burdens placed on the states for education, health care, housing, and other government services. The expenses associated with providing such programs have prompted calls to curb state benefits for individuals unlawfully residing in the United States. Several states, led by Arizona and Alabama, have reacted by passing legislation aimed at discouraging illegal immigration and imposing punitive policies on undocumented aliens. These laws have already spawned significant lawsuits challenging their constitutionality. Furthermore, rising negative sentiment toward aliens from nations associated with terrorism has produced conditions that are likely to result in additional discrimination disputes.

REMEDYING THE EFFECTS OF DISCRIMINATION: AFFIRMATIVE ACTION

Creating appropriate standards for interpreting the equal protection principles of the Constitution and determining when governments have engaged in impermissible discrimination are, as we now know, exceedingly difficult tasks. And even when they have been accomplished, the Court's business is not finished. In addition to condemning unconstitutional discrimination, the Court confronts the problem of remedies, which entails consideration of acceptable ways to eliminate the discrimination, to implement nondiscriminatory policies, and to compensate the victims of discrimination.

For some discrimination issues remedial action is minimal: striking down a statute is often sufficient. For example, nullifying Idaho's discriminatory inheritance statute in *Reed v. Reed* required no significant remedial action. The state simply had to decide future estate administration issues without regard to sex. Declaring Virginia's miscegenation law a violation of the equal protection clause in the *Loving* decision also needed no follow-up action. Virginia was plainly barred from any future prosecutions of such cases.

For other discrimination issues, however, the enforcement of the Court's orders can be a lengthy, complex process. Timetables for change, compliance standards, and methods of implementation pose troublesome choices, and conditions are exacerbated when the affected populations resist the change. The integration of the public schools is an obvious and painful example.

The Supreme Court not only has created rules for implementing its own equal protection decisions but also has heard cases challenging the antidiscrimination policies imposed by Congress and the state legislatures. Beginning in the late 1960s, many political bodies asserted that the Fifth and Fourteenth Amendments demanded more than the elimination of overt discrimination; they also required positive actions taken by government to ensure that equality is achieved and the effects of past discrimination are eliminated. This philosophy gave rise to the controversy over affirmative action.

Programs in affirmative action generally take one of two approaches to reducing the effects of past discrimination. The first provides preferences for historically disadvantaged groups (women and racial minorities) in hiring, promotion, and admission to education and training programs. The second, often referred to as minority set-aside programs, requires that a certain proportion of government business be awarded to companies operated by minority owners. These programs, proponents argue, offer viable ways for women and minorities to become full participants in the nation's economy. Opponents, however, see these policies as nothing more than unconstitutional reverse discrimination.

Affirmative Action Origins

Affirmative action programs have their roots in presidential orders, issued as early as the 1940s, that expanded government employment opportunities for black Americans. These programs received their most significant boost in 1965, when President Lyndon Johnson issued Executive Order 11246, which instructed the Labor Department to ensure that businesses contracting with the federal government were nondiscriminatory. To meet the requirements, government contractors altered their employment policies and recruited minority workers.

Over the years, these requirements were strengthened and expanded. Failure to comply with the government's principles of nondiscriminatory employment was grounds for stripping a business or institution of its federal contract or appropriated funds. Moreover, some state and local governments adopted similar programs, many aggressively establishing numerical standards for minority participation. Private businesses also began to adopt programs to increase the numbers of women and minorities in their workforces, especially in positions where their numbers historically had been low. Are these programs desirable? Constitutional? Such questions have generated debates in political and legal circles.

Those supporting affirmative action marshal a number of arguments. First, taking issue with Justice Harlan's assertion in his *Plessy v. Ferguson* dissent that the Constitution is "color-blind," supporters hold that characteristics associated with disadvantaged status must be considered and taken into account. Special programs and incentives for people from disadvantaged groups are warranted to eradicate and compensate for the effects of past discrimination.

Second, advocates suggest that affirmative action plans do not benefit just one or two groups in society; rather, they benefit the entire community. These programs strengthen the country by taking advantage of the talents of all its citizens participating in a diverse political and economic system. Without these plans, many members of society would remain shut out of certain careers, returning the country to the days of white male domination.

Opponents of special programs, however, see things very differently. Many valued goods and opportunities in society—jobs, promotions, and admission to education and training programs—are scarce at times. When, instead of merit alone, factors such as race and sex are used to determine who obtains these opportunities, the losers may feel themselves victimized and claim reverse discrimination. The principles of equal protection, affirmative action opponents assert, should prohibit discrimination against whites and men just as they prohibit discrimination against blacks and women. Those who have been negatively affected by it view affirmative action as inconsistent with the nation's commitment to equal opportunity.

In addition, opponents note two legal obstacles to affirmative action programs: the Constitution and the Civil Rights Act of 1964. Opponents claim that the equal protection clause of the Fourteenth Amendment and the due process clause of the Fifth prohibit the government from giving special consideration to individuals because of their race, sex, or national origin. As Justice Stewart once wrote: "The Fourteenth Amendment was adopted to ensure that every person must be treated equally by each State regardless of the color of his skin. The Amendment promised to carry to its necessary conclusion a fundamental principle upon which this Nation had been founded—that the law would honor no preference based on lineage."[20] The Civil Rights Act of 1964, specifically Title VII, states, with respect to private employment, that race, color, religion, sex, and national origin cannot be used to discriminate against any employee. It further holds:

It shall be an unlawful employment practice for an employer ... to limit, segregate, or classify his employees or applicants for employment in any way which would deprive or tend to deprive any individual of employment opportunities or otherwise adversely affect his status as an employee, because of such individual's race, color, religion, sex, or national origin.

20. Dissent in *Fullilove v. Klutznick* (1980).

Title VI of the same statute contains similar provisions for state and local government programs that receive federal funding. These provisions were originally intended to prohibit discrimination against members of groups that historically have been the victims of prejudice. Whether giving preference to such individuals, at the possible expense of others, also violates these constitutional or statutory provisions was for the Supreme Court to determine.

The Court Enters the Fray

Which side of this debate would the Court favor? This question was very much on the minds of civil rights groups, scholars, and the public when the justices agreed to hear *Regents of the University of California v. Bakke* (1978), an equal protection clause challenge to a public university's policy to admit a specific number of minority applicants.

The stakes were high. For civil rights groups, the case represented a threat to the best way yet devised to eliminate the effects of past discrimination and bring minority students into professional programs. For opponents of affirmative action, it was an opportunity to overturn the growing burden of paying for the sins of the past and return to a system based on merit. Fifty-seven friend of the court briefs were filed by various organizations and interested parties.

The justices were deeply divided over this case. Four gave strong support to affirmative action programs, four others had serious reservations about them, and Justice Powell found himself in the middle. Portions of his opinion announcing the judgment of the Court were supported by one set of four justices, and other parts were joined by an entirely different group of four. As the "swing" vote in this case, Powell was effectively able to determine what the Constitution means with respect to affirmative action programs. What did he conclude?

Regents of the University of California v. Bakke

438 U.S. 265 (1978)
http://laws.findlaw.com/US/438/265.html
Oral arguments are available at http://www.oyez.org.
Vote: 5 (Burger, Powell, Rehnquist, Stevens, Stewart)
    4 (Blackmun, Brennan, Marshall, White)

OPINION ANNOUNCING THE JUDGMENT OF THE COURT: *Powell*
OPINION CONCURRING IN PART AND DISSENTING IN PART:
  Blackmun, Brennan, Marshall, White (jointly authored)
SEPARATE OPINION: *White*
SEPARATE OPINION: *Marshall*
SEPARATE OPINION: *Blackmun*
OPINION CONCURRING IN PART AND DISSENTING IN PART:
  Stevens

FACTS:

The medical school of the University of California at Davis began operations in 1968. In its first two years, it admitted only three minority students, all Asians. To improve minority participation, the school developed two admissions programs to fill the one hundred seats in its entry class—a regular admissions program and a special admissions program. The regular admissions program worked in the customary way: applicants were evaluated on the basis of undergraduate grades, standardized test scores, letters of recommendation, extracurricular activities, and an interview. The special admissions program was for applicants who indicated that they were economically or educationally disadvantaged or were black, Chicano, Asian, or Native American. Such applicants could choose to go through the regular admissions process or to be referred to a special admissions committee. Special admissions applicants were judged on the same characteristics as the regular applicants, but they competed only against each other. The school reserved sixteen seats to be filled from the special admissions pool. Many white applicants, claiming poverty, indicated a desire to be considered by the special admissions committee, but none was admitted. All specially admitted students were members of the designated minority groups.

Allan Bakke, a white male, graduated with honors in engineering from the University of Minnesota and was a Vietnam War veteran. He worked for the National Aeronautics and Space Administration and received his master's degree in engineering from Stanford. Developing an interest in a medical career, Bakke took extra science courses and did volunteer work in a local hospital. At age thirty-three, he applied for admission to the 1973 entry class of the medical school at Davis. He was rejected. He applied in 1974 and was again rejected. Because applicants admitted under the special admissions program were, at least statistically, less qualified than he (*see Table 13-2*), Bakke sued for admission, claiming that the university's dual admissions program violated the equal protection clause of the Fourteenth Amendment.

The state trial court struck down the special program, declaring that race could not be constitutionally taken into account in deciding who would be admitted, but the court refused to order Bakke's admission.

Both Bakke and the university appealed. The California Supreme Court found the special admissions program unconstitutional, holding that "no applicant may be rejected because of his race, in favor of another who is less qualified, as measured by standards applied without regard to race." The state supreme court's order to admit Bakke was stayed pending the university's appeal to the U.S. Supreme Court.

ARGUMENTS:

For the petitioner, Regents of the University of California:

- The legacy of racial discrimination continues to burden the advancement of discrete and insular minorities. One result has been a scarcity of physicians having minority racial and ethnic backgrounds.
- Standard forms of nondiscriminatory admissions policies have proven inadequate to remedy this problem. More aggressive, race-sensitive, remedial programs, like the one challenged here, are necessary.
- Strict scrutiny should not be applied to benign, race-based programs designed to assist historically disadvantaged groups.
- No matter what standard of scrutiny is used, the university's admissions program is constitutionally valid.

For the respondent, Allan Bakke:

- The special admissions program reserved sixteen of the one hundred entry class places for members of favored racial and ethnic groups. Because of his racial and ethnic background, Bakke was unable to compete for these positions. This constitutes a quota.
- Fourteenth Amendment rights are personal in nature. The university's quota system instead imposes a system of group rights.
- There is a well-recognized distinction between affirmative action, which takes positive steps to integrate the races and provide equal opportunity, and rigid quotas.
- The California Supreme Court correctly ruled that racial classifications such as this one must be evaluated according to strict scrutiny.

 MR. JUSTICE POWELL ANNOUNCED THE JUDGMENT OF THE COURT.

Petitioner does not deny that decisions based on race or ethnic origin by faculties and administrations of state universities are reviewable under the Fourteenth Amendment. For his part, respondent does not argue that all racial or ethnic classifications are *per se* invalid. The parties do disagree as to the level of judicial scrutiny to be

TABLE 13-2 Admissions Data for the Entering Class of the Medical School of the University of California at Davis, 1973 and 1974

	SGPAA	OGPAB	MCAT (PERCENTILES)			
			VERBAL	QUANTITATIVE	SCIENCE	GEN. INFOR.
Class Entering in 1973						
Bakke	3.44	3.46	96	94	97	72
Average of regular admittees	3.51	3.49	81	76	83	69
Average of special admittees	2.62	2.88	46	24	35	33
Class Entering in 1974						
Bakke	3.44	3.46	96	94	97	72
Average of regular admittees	3.36	3.29	69	67	82	72
Average of special admittees	2.42	2.62	34	30	37	18

SOURCE: *Regents of the University of California v. Bakke* (1978).

a. Science grade point average.

b. Overall grade point average.

applied to the special admissions program. Petitioner argues that the court below erred in applying strict scrutiny, as this inexact term has been applied in our cases. That level of review, petitioner asserts, should be reserved for classifications that disadvantage "discrete and insular minorities." Respondent, on the other hand, contends that the California court correctly rejected the notion that the degree of judicial scrutiny accorded a particular racial or ethnic classification hinges upon membership in a discrete and insular minority and duly recognized that the "rights established [by the Fourteenth Amendment] are personal rights."

En route to this crucial battle over the scope of judicial review, the parties fight a sharp preliminary action over the proper characterization of the special admissions program. Petitioner prefers to view it as establishing a "goal" of minority representation in the Medical School. Respondent, echoing the courts below, labels it a racial quota.

This semantic distinction is beside the point: The special admissions program is undeniably a classification based on race and ethnic background. To the extent that there existed a pool of at least minimally qualified minority applicants to fill the 16 special admissions seats, white applicants could compete only for 84 seats in the entering class, rather than the 100 open to minority applicants. Whether this limitation is described as a quota or a goal, it is a line drawn on the basis of race and ethnic status.

The guarantees of the Fourteenth Amendment extend to all persons. Its language is explicit: "No State shall . . . deny to any person within its jurisdiction the equal protection of the laws." It is settled beyond question that the "rights created by the first section of the Fourteenth Amendment are, by its terms, guaranteed to the individual. The rights established are personal rights." The guarantee of equal protection cannot mean one thing when applied to one individual and something else when applied to a person of another color. If both are not accorded the same protection, then it is not equal. . . .

Racial and ethnic distinctions of any sort are inherently suspect and thus call for the most exacting judicial examination. . . .

Although many of the Framers of the Fourteenth Amendment conceived of its primary function as bridging the vast distance between members of the Negro race and the white "majority," the Amendment itself was framed in universal terms, without reference to color, ethnic origin, or condition of prior servitude. . . .

Petitioner urges us to adopt for the first time a more restrictive view of the Equal Protection Clause and hold that discrimination against members of the white "majority" cannot be suspect if its purpose can be characterized as "benign." The clock of our liberties, however, cannot be turned back to 1868. It is far too late to argue that the guarantee of equal protection to *all* persons permits the recognition of special wards entitled to a degree of protection greater than that accorded others. "The Fourteenth Amendment is not directed solely against discrimination due to a 'two-class theory'—that is, based upon differences between 'white' and Negro." . . .

If it is the individual who is entitled to judicial protection against classifications based upon his racial or ethnic background because such distinctions impinge upon personal rights, rather than the individual only because of his membership in a particular group, then constitutional standards may be applied consistently. Political judgments regarding the necessity for the particular classification may be weighed in the constitutional balance, but the standard of justification will remain constant. This is as it should be, since those political judgments are the product of rough compromise struck by contending groups within the democratic process. When they touch upon an individual's race or ethnic background, he is entitled to a judicial determination that the burden he is asked to bear on that basis is precisely tailored to serve a compelling governmental interest. The Constitution guarantees that right to every person regardless of his background. . . .

We have held that in "order to justify the use of a suspect classification, a State must show that its purpose or interest is both constitutionally permissible and substantial, and that its use of the classification is 'necessary . . . to the accomplishment' of its purpose or the safeguarding of its interest." The special admissions program purports to serve the purposes of: (i) "reducing the historic deficit of traditionally disfavored minorities in medical schools and in the medical profession"; (ii) countering the effects of societal discrimination; (iii) increasing the number of physicians who will practice in communities currently underserved; and (iv) obtaining the educational benefits that flow from an ethnically diverse student body. It is necessary to decide which, if any, of these purposes is substantial enough to support the use of a suspect classification.

If petitioner's purpose is to assure within its student body some specified percentage of a particular group merely because of its race or ethnic origin, such a preferential purpose must be rejected not as insubstantial but as facially invalid. Preferring members of any one group for no reason other than race or ethnic origin is discrimination for its own sake. This the Constitution forbids.

The State certainly has a legitimate and substantial interest in ameliorating, or eliminating where feasible, the disabling effects of identified discrimination. The line of school desegregation cases, commencing with *Brown*, attests to the importance of this state goal and the commitment of the judiciary to affirm all lawful means toward its attainment. In the school cases, the States were required by court order to redress the wrongs worked by specific instances of racial discrimination. That goal was far more focused than the remedying of the effects of "societal discrimination," an amorphous concept of inquiry that may be ageless in its reach into the past.

We have never approved a classification that aids persons perceived as members of relatively victimized groups at the expense of other innocent individuals in the absence of judicial, legislative, or administrative findings of constitutional or statutory violations. After such findings have been made, the governmental interest in preferring members of the injured groups at the expense of others is substantial, since the legal rights of the victims must be vindicated. In such a case, the extent of the injury and the consequent remedy will have been judicially, legislatively, or administratively defined. Also, the remedial action usually remains subject to continuing oversight to assure that it will work the least harm possible to other innocent persons competing for the benefit. Without such findings of constitutional or statutory violations, it cannot be said that the government has any greater interest in helping one individual than in refraining from harming another. Thus, the government has no compelling justification for inflicting such harm.

Petitioner does not purport to have made, and is in no position to make, such findings. Its broad mission is education, not the formulation of any legislative policy or the adjudication of particular claims of illegality. . . . Before relying upon these sorts of findings in establishing a racial classification, a governmental body must have the authority and capability to establish, in the record, that the classification is responsive to identified discrimination. Lacking this capability, petitioner has not carried its burden of justification on this issue.

Hence, the purpose of helping certain groups whom the faculty of the Davis Medical School perceived as victims of "societal discrimination" does not justify a classification that imposes disadvantages upon persons like respondent, who bear no responsibility for whatever harm the beneficiaries of the special admissions program are thought to have suffered. To hold otherwise would be to convert a remedy heretofore reserved for violations of legal rights into a privilege that all institutions throughout the Nation could grant at their pleasure to whatever groups are perceived as victims of societal discrimination. That is a step we have never approved.

Petitioner identifies, as another purpose of its program, improving the delivery of health-care services to communities currently underserved. It may be assumed that in some situations a State's interest in facilitating the health care of its citizens is sufficiently compelling to support the use of a suspect classification. But there is virtually no evidence in the record indicating that petitioner's special admissions program is either needed or geared to promote that goal. . . .

Petitioner simply has not carried its burden of demonstrating that it must prefer members of particular ethnic groups over all other individuals in order to promote better health-care delivery to deprived citizens. Indeed, petitioner has not shown that its preferential classification is likely to have any significant effect on the problem.

The fourth goal asserted by petitioner is the attainment of a diverse student body. This clearly is a constitutionally permissible goal for an institution of higher education. Academic freedom, though not a specifically enumerated constitutional right, long has been viewed as a special concern of the First Amendment. The freedom of a university to make its own judgments as to education includes the selection of its student body. . . .

The atmosphere of "speculation, experiment and creation"—so essential to the quality of higher education—is widely believed to be promoted by a diverse student body. As the Court noted in *Keyishian* [v. *Board of Regents of the University of the State of New York*, 1967] it is not too much to say that the "nation's future depends upon leaders trained through wide exposure" to the ideas and mores of students as diverse as this Nation of many peoples.

Thus, in arguing that its universities must be accorded the right to select those students who will contribute the most to the "robust exchange of ideas," petitioner invokes a countervailing constitutional interest, that of the First Amendment. In this light, petitioner must be viewed as seeking to achieve a goal that is of paramount importance in the fulfillment of its mission.

It may be argued that there is greater force to these views at the undergraduate level than in a medical school where the training is centered primarily on professional competency. But even at the graduate level, our tradition and experience lend support to the view that the contribution of diversity is substantial. . . . Physicians serve a heterogeneous population. An otherwise qualified medical student with a particular background—whether it be ethnic, geographic, culturally advantaged or disadvantaged—may bring to a professional school of medicine experiences, outlooks, and ideas that enrich the training of its student body and better equip its graduates to render with understanding their vital service to humanity.

Ethnic diversity, however, is only one element in a range of factors a university properly may consider in attaining the goal of a heterogeneous student body. Although a university must have wide discretion in making the sensitive judgments as to who should be admitted, constitutional limitations protecting individual rights may not be disregarded. Respondent urges—and the courts below have held—that petitioner's dual admissions program is a racial classification that impermissibly infringes his rights under the Fourteenth Amendment. As the interest of diversity is compelling in the context of a university's admissions program, the question remains whether the program's racial classification is necessary to promote this interest.

It may be assumed that the reservation of a specified number of seats in each class for individuals from the preferred ethnic groups would contribute to the attainment of considerable ethnic diversity in the student body. But petitioner's argument that this is the only effective means of serving the interest of diversity is seriously flawed. In a most fundamental sense the argument misconceives the nature of the state interest that would justify consideration of race or ethnic background. It is not an interest in simple ethnic diversity, in which a specified percentage of the student body is in effect guaranteed to be members of selected ethnic groups, with the remaining percentage an undifferentiated aggregation of students. The diversity that furthers a compelling state interest encompasses a far broader array of qualifications and characteristics of which racial or ethnic origin is but a single though important element. Petitioner's special admissions program, focused solely on ethnic diversity, would hinder rather than further attainment of genuine diversity.

Nor would the state interest in genuine diversity be served by expanding petitioner's two-track system into a multitrack program with a prescribed number of seats set aside for each identifiable category of applicants. Indeed, it is inconceivable that a university would thus pursue the logic of petitioner's two-track program to the illogical end of insulating each category of applicants with certain desired qualifications from competition with all other applicants.

The experience of other university admissions programs, which take race into account in achieving the educational diversity valued by the First Amendment, demonstrates that the assignment of a fixed number of places to a minority group is not a necessary means toward that end. An illuminating example is found in the Harvard College program. . . .

In such an admissions program, race or ethnic background may be deemed a "plus" in a particular applicant's file, yet it does not insulate the individual from comparison with all other candidates for the available seats. The file of a particular black applicant may be examined for his potential contribution to diversity without the factor of race being decisive when compared, for example, with that of an applicant identified as an Italian American if the latter is thought to exhibit qualities more likely to promote beneficial educational pluralism. Such qualities could include exceptional personal talents, unique work or service experience, leadership potential, maturity, demonstrated compassion, a history of overcoming disadvantage, ability to communicate with the poor, or other qualifications deemed important. In short, an admissions program operated in this way is flexible enough to consider all pertinent elements of diversity in light of the particular qualifications of each applicant, and to place them on the same footing for consideration, although not necessarily according them the same weight. Indeed, the weight attributed to a particular quality may vary from year to year depending upon the "mix" both of the student body and the applicants for the incoming class.

This kind of program treats each applicant as an individual in the admissions process. The applicant who loses out on the last available seat to another candidate receiving a "plus" on the basis of ethnic background will not have been foreclosed from all consideration for that seat simply because he was not the right color or had the wrong surname. It would mean only that his combined qualifications, which may have included similar nonobjective factors, did not outweigh those of the other applicant. His qualifications would have been weighed fairly and competitively, and he would have no basis to complain of unequal treatment under the Fourteenth Amendment.

It has been suggested that an admissions program which considers race only as one factor is simply a subtle and more sophisticated—but no less effective—means of according racial preference than the Davis program. A facial intent to discriminate, however, is evident in petitioner's preference program and not denied in this case. No such facial infirmity exists in an admissions program where race or ethnic background is simply one element—to be weighed fairly against other elements—in the selection process. . . . And a court would not assume that a university, professing to employ a facially nondiscriminatory admissions policy, would operate it as a cover for the functional equivalent of a quota system. In short, good faith would be presumed in the absence of a showing to the contrary in the manner permitted by our cases.

In summary, it is evident that the Davis special admissions program involves the use of an explicit racial classification never before countenanced by this Court. It tells applicants who are not Negro, Asian, or Chicano that they are totally excluded from a specific percentage of the seats in an entering class. No matter how strong their qualifications, quantitative and extracurricular, including their own potential for contribution to educational diversity, they are never afforded the chance to compete with applicants from the preferred groups for the special admissions seats. At the same time, the preferred applicants have the opportunity to compete for every seat in the class.

The fatal flaw in petitioner's preferential program is its disregard of individual rights as guaranteed by the Fourteenth Amendment. Such rights are not absolute. But when a State's distribution of benefits or imposition of burdens hinges on ancestry or the color of a person's skin, that individual is entitled to a demonstration that the challenged classification is necessary to promote a substantial state interest. Petitioner has failed to carry this burden. For this reason, that portion of the California court's judgment holding petitioner's special admissions program invalid under the Fourteenth Amendment must be affirmed.

In enjoining petitioner from ever considering the race of any applicant, however, the courts below failed to recognize that the State has a substantial interest that legitimately may be served by a properly devised admissions program involving the competitive consideration of race and ethnic origin. For this reason, so much of the California court's judgment as enjoins petitioner from any consideration of the race of any applicant must be reversed.

With respect to respondent's entitlement to an injunction directing his admission to the Medical School, petitioner has conceded that it could not carry its burden of proving that, but for the existence of its unlawful special admissions program, respondent still would not have been admitted. Hence, respondent is entitled to the injunction, and that portion of the judgment must be affirmed.

Affirmed in part and reversed in part.

Opinion of MR. JUSTICE BRENNAN, MR. JUSTICE WHITE, MR. JUSTICE MARSHALL, and MR. JUSTICE BLACKMUN, *concurring in the judgment in part and dissenting in part.*
Unquestionably we have held that a government practice or statute which restricts "fundamental rights" or which contains "suspect classifications" is to be subjected to "strict scrutiny," and can be justified only if it furthers a compelling government purpose and, even then, only if no less restrictive alternative is available. But no fundamental right is involved here. Nor do whites, as a class, have any of the "traditional indicia of suspectness: the class is not saddled with such disabilities, or subjected to such a history of purposeful unequal treatment, or relegated to such a position of political powerlessness as to command extraordinary protection from the majoritarian political process."

Moreover, if the University's representations are credited, this is not a case where racial classifications are "irrelevant, and therefore prohibited." Nor has anyone suggested that the University's purposes contravene the cardinal principle that racial classifications that stigmatize—because they are drawn on the presumption that one race is inferior to another or because they put the weight of government behind racial hatred and separatism—are invalid without more.

On the other hand, the fact that this case does not fit neatly into our prior analytic framework for race cases does not mean that it should be analyzed by applying the very loose rational-basis standard of review that is the very least that is always applied in equal protection cases. . . . Instead, a number of considerations—developed in gender-discrimination cases but which carry even more force when applied to racial classifications—lead us to conclude that racial classifications designed to further remedial purposes "'must serve important

Twice rejected for admission to the medical school of the University of California at Davis, Allan Bakke, center, filed suit challenging school policy that admitted minority students with grades and test scores lower than his. Bakke's suit led to the Supreme Court's first major statement on the constitutionality of affirmative action programs.

governmental objectives, and must be substantially related to achievement of those objectives.'"

First, race, like, "gender-based classifications, too often [has] been inexcusably utilized to stereotype and stigmatize politically powerless segments of society." While a carefully tailored statute designed to remedy past discrimination could avoid these vices, we nonetheless have recognized that the line between honest and thoughtful appraisal of the effects of past discrimination and paternalistic stereotyping is not so clear, and that a statute based on the latter is patently capable of stigmatizing all women with a badge of inferiority. State programs designed ostensibly to ameliorate the effects of past racial discrimination obviously create the same hazard of stigma, since they may promote racial separatism and reinforce the views of those who believe that members of racial minorities are inherently incapable of succeeding on their own.

Second, race, like gender and illegitimacy, is an immutable characteristic which its possessors are powerless to escape or set aside. While a classification is not per se invalid because it divides classes on the basis of an immutable characteristic, it is nevertheless true that such divisions are contrary to our deep belief that "legal burdens should bear some relationship to individual responsibility or wrongdoing" and that advancement sanctioned, sponsored, or approved by the State should ideally be based on individual merit or achievement, or at the least on factors within the control of an individual.

Because this principle is so deeply rooted it might be supposed that it would be considered in the legislative process and weighed against the benefits of programs preferring individuals because of their race. But this is not necessarily so: The natural consequence of our governing processes [may well be] that the most "discrete and insular" of whites . . . will be called upon to bear the immediate, direct costs of benign discrimination. Moreover, it is clear from our cases that there are limits beyond which majorities may not go when they classify on the basis of immutable characteristics. Thus, even if the concern for individualism is weighed by the political process, that weighing cannot waive the personal rights of individuals under the Fourteenth Amendment.

In sum, because of the significant risk that racial classifications established for ostensibly benign purposes can be misused, causing effects not unlike those created by invidious classifications, it is inappropriate to inquire only whether there is any conceivable basis that might sustain such a classification. Instead, to justify such a classification, an important and articulated purpose for its use must be shown. In addition, any statute must be stricken that stigmatizes any group or that singles out those least well represented in the political process to bear the brunt of a benign program. . . .

Davis' articulated purpose of remedying the effects of past societal discrimination is, under our cases, sufficiently important to justify the use of race-conscious admissions programs where there is a sound basis for concluding that minority underrepresentation is substantial and chronic, and that the handicap of past discrimination is impeding access of minorities to the Medical School.

Justice Powell's opinion was a victory for Allan Bakke, who won admission to the medical school at Davis after a long legal battle *(see Box 13-6)*. The justices, however, were sharply divided not only in their views of affirmative action programs but also over the legal grounds on which to rest the Court's ruling.

Four justices—Burger, Stewart, Rehnquist, and Stevens—preferred not to address the constitutional issues in *Bakke*. Instead, they concluded that the university had violated Bakke's rights under Title VI of the Civil Rights Act of 1964, which states: "No person in the United States shall, on the ground of race, color, or national origin, be excluded from participation in, be denied the benefits of, or be subjected to discrimination under any program or activity receiving Federal financial assistance." By deciding for Bakke on statutory grounds, they argued, they avoided the controversy over

the constitutionality of the affirmative action program.

Four justices, led by Brennan, argued that intermediate scrutiny was the appropriate standard to use in "benign" discrimination cases, and that the University of California's program was constitutional under that analysis. Four other justices preferred to invalidate the university's admissions policy on statutory grounds. This split left Justice Powell holding the balance of power. His opinion argued that strict scrutiny was the appropriate standard, and that although a diverse student body was a compelling state interest, the use of quotas was an impermissible means of achieving that interest. Because Powell's opinion failed to gather majority support, its precedential value was diminished, but over time the conclusions Powell reached became the primary guiding principles in the affirmative action controversy.

The *Bakke* decision struck down the use of racial quotas and found fault with programs reserved exclusively for minority individuals, but the decision permitted less extreme forms of affirmative action. This aspect of the decision encouraged government agencies as well as private organizations and corporations to develop

---

BOX 13-6 AFTERMATH . . . ALLAN BAKKE

After securing his right to attend medical school, Allan Bakke asked the University of California to pay his legal expenses. When the university refused that request, Bakke sued. The California Superior Court ordered the university to compensate Bakke $183,089 to cover the fees of lead attorney Reynold Colvin and his associates. This was only a portion of the $437,295 Bakke had requested.

While the battle over legal fees was being fought, Bakke, at age thirty-eight and more than five years after his initial application for admission, entered the medical school at the University of California at Davis. When he arrived on campus in September 1978, more than one hundred demonstrators were protesting the Supreme Court's ruling, chanting, "Smash the *Bakke* decision now!" Bakke quietly entered the medical school building unrecognized by the protesters.

Bakke's medical school years were generally uneventful. His fellow students paid little attention to the manner in which he had gained acceptance to the school. The fact that Bakke was married and had three children distanced

him somewhat from his classmates and many of their activities outside the classroom.

At age forty-two, four years after his admission, Allan Bakke graduated with his doctor of medicine degree. On March 18, 1982, the school held a ceremony during which the postgraduate assignments of the members of the graduating class were announced. One observer described Bakke as receiving the loudest applause of all when it was announced that he had been selected for a prestigious internship at the Mayo Clinic in his native state of Minnesota.

After completing his internship, Bakke continued at the Mayo Clinic for a four-year residency in anesthesiology. He then went into private practice as an anesthesiologist for the Olmsted Medical Group in Rochester, Minnesota. By nature a very quiet and private person, Bakke never discussed his famous lawsuit publicly.

SOURCES: Howard Ball, *The Bakke Case: Race, Education, and Affirmative Action* (Lawrence: University Press of Kansas, 2000); *New York Times,* December 6, 1981, March 19 and June 4, 1982, November 2, 1986; *San Francisco Chronicle,* November 3, 1986; *Washington Post,* January 15, 1980.

programs to benefit individuals from historically disadvantaged groups. Such programs gave rise to challenges that they violated the 1964 Civil Rights Act or the Constitution's equal protection guarantees. In the years immediately following *Bakke,* the Supreme Court was generally sympathetic to such programs, especially when the affirmative action policies were adopted to address the effects of long-standing discriminatory practices. The programs were also on strong footing if they were temporary, flexible, and narrowly tailored to correct the effects of unlawful discrimination and did not overly burden innocent parties.

For example, in *United Steelworkers of America v. Weber* (1979) the justices rejected a Civil Rights Act challenge to a training program established by the Kaiser Aluminum Company and the steelworkers union. The program was a response to a situation in which only 1.83 percent of the skilled labor positions at a Kaiser plant in Gramercy, Louisiana, were held by black workers, although 39 percent of the workforce was black. The training program ignored the traditional union seniority system and admitted equal numbers of black and white applicants. As a result some white applicants were rejected, even though they had more seniority than black members who were admitted. The justices found that the program was voluntary, temporary, and narrowly tailored to break down old patterns of segregation. Furthermore, no white workers were discharged, demoted, or absolutely barred from being admitted.

During the post-*Bakke* period, the justices often judged the validity of the affirmative action program by the extent of the racial discrimination that previously had occurred. The more extreme the revealed racial bias, the more aggressive the Court allowed the affirmative action efforts to be. An example is *United States v. Paradise* (1987), a challenge to a court-ordered affirmative action program for the Alabama Department of Public Safety. In 1972 a federal district judge found that in the thirty-seven year history of the department, not one black state trooper had been hired. Over the next twelve years the federal courts repeatedly found the department to be in violation of the law and imposed various hiring and promotion goals for minority employees. The state consistently failed to meet these goals, at which point the district court ordered a 50 percent minority promotion quota. Because of the extreme nature of the racial discrimination that had occurred in the past and the failure of the state to correct the department's racially biased hiring and promotion practices, the Supreme Court upheld the use of racial quotas against claims that the plan violated the equal protection clause.

In addition to affirmative action programs designed to assist racial minorities, the justices gave support to plans that favored women, especially when the plans were applied to employment situations where females had been historically denied opportunity.[21] These plans tended to receive Supreme Court approval if they were temporary, flexible, and narrowly tailored and did not place undue burdens on opportunities available to males.

Minority Set-Asides

Minority set-aside programs are closely related to other affirmative action plans and share underlying philosophies and goals. Minority set-asides attempt to enhance the prospects of disadvantaged groups by granting them special considerations in the awarding of government contracts and benefits. The justification for such programs is the long history of discrimination against minority-owned businesses in general commercial activity and in their providing goods and services for the government. Set-asides are based on the idea that just eliminating discrimination in the granting of government contracts will not result in more business for minority-owned firms. Because of past discrimination, many minority businesses lack capital, management experience, and bonding eligibility. They cannot compete successfully with more solid, better-financed firms owned by whites. Consequently, minority set-aside programs propose, for a time, to reserve a percentage of government business and contracts for minority-owned enterprises.

Set-aside programs received their first significant review by the Court in 1980 in *Fullilove v. Klutznick,* a case testing the Public Works Employment Act of 1977. A provision of that law directed that in federally financed state public works projects, 10 percent of the goods and services had to be procured from minority-owned businesses. A minority-owned business was defined as a company at least 50 percent owned by citizens of the United States who were African American, Spanish-speaking, Asian, Native American, Eskimo, or Aleut. A group of contractors

---

21. See, for example, *Johnson v. Transportation Agency of Santa Clara County, California* (1987).

attacked the constitutionality of the statute, claiming economic injury due to its enforcement.

The Supreme Court, 6–3, upheld the validity of the law as a remedial action to correct a history of discrimination in government contracting. Despite the vote, the divisions among the justices were many and deep. They wrote five different opinions, and no opinion garnered the support of more than three. Burger, Powell, and White held that the law was constitutional as a necessary means of advancing a compelling government interest. In their view, the law was a narrow and carefully tailored measure to eliminate a particular type of discrimination. Blackmun, Brennan, and Marshall also supported the law's validity. They adhered to their views expressed in *Bakke,* giving strong support for the use of quotas as a means to alleviate discrimination. Rehnquist, Stewart, and Stevens dissented. Stewart argued that the Constitution should be hostile to all racial classifications.

The decision in *Fullilove* encouraged federal agencies as well as state and local governments that wanted to use the same kind of remedial approach to set up their own programs. Often these new programs contained more aggressive provisions than before, and they provoked the increasingly conservative Supreme Court to apply more rigorous scrutiny.

The first sign that the Court was becoming less sympathetic to affirmative action and minority set-aside programs was ***City of Richmond v. J. A. Croson Co.*** (1989). In 1983, Richmond's city council, which consisted of five black and four white members, adopted the Minority Utilization Plan. The ordinance required businesses contracting with the city to award 30 percent of the dollar amount of the contract to minority-owned subcontractors. Minority businesses were defined as enterprises at least 51 percent owned by persons who were African American, Spanish-speaking, Asian, Native American, Eskimo, or Aleut. The minority businesses did not have to be located in Richmond.

The purpose of the plan was to correct the effects of past racial discrimination. Richmond's population was 50 percent black, but between 1978 and 1983 less than 1 percent of the city's construction business had been awarded to minority contractors.

J. A. Croson Company had been awarded a contract to install plumbing fixtures at the city jail, but it had difficulty finding a minority-owned company to supply the materials at a cost that would allow Croson to complete the job for the amount specified in the

contract. When Richmond refused Croson's request either to rebid the contract or waive the minority participation rule, the company challenged the Minority Utilization Plan as a violation of the equal protection clause.

The Supreme Court held that the Richmond minority set-aside program violated the Constitution. In her opinion for the Court, Justice O'Connor found multiple defects in the Richmond plan. The record included little hard evidence of city discrimination against African American contractors in Richmond. Rather, the low rates of minority participation stemmed from a lack of minority-owned businesses in the area. In addition, the record showed no proof of any discrimination against companies owned by persons who were Spanish-speaking, Asian, Native American, Eskimo, or Aleut. The city failed to provide a compelling rationale for the 30 percent requirement; rather, it appeared to be an arbitrarily set threshold. If the plan was intended to combat racial discrimination against Richmond minority contractors, why did the plan allow qualifying contracts to go to out-of-state minority-owned businesses? If the city found black-owned businesses to have been discriminated against, why did the plan include firms owned by Eskimos and Aleuts, groups that were virtually nonexistent in Richmond?

In judging the constitutional validity of the Richmond set-aside program, the majority applied the strict scrutiny standard. Strict scrutiny requires government programs to be narrowly tailored to achieve a compelling state interest. Because the challenged program failed to meet that standard, it violated the equal protection clause.

The Court's condemnation of Richmond's minority set-aside program was a clear signal to other state and local governments that any plan to increase business for minority-owned enterprises was going to be difficult to justify. The decision clearly stated that the strict scrutiny test was the appropriate standard to be employed in such cases. This encouraged majority-owned businesses that wanted to challenge such plans.

The very next year, in ***Metro Broadcasting v. Federal Communications Commission*** (1990), however, the Court approved the FCC's use of minority preferences. The purpose of the FCC plan was to encourage minority ownership of radio and television stations. Unlike most forms of commercial activity, the number of radio and television stations that can operate in a particular market is limited. Because of this constraint and because broadcasters use the public airwaves, the federal government—through the FCC—decides who is to be granted a license to broadcast. The process of obtaining a license can be highly competitive.

Writing for the five-person majority, Justice Brennan held the federal government to more lenient standards than the states: "We hold that the FCC minority ownership policies pass muster under the test we announce today. First, we find that they serve the important governmental objective of broadcast diversity. Second, we conclude that they are substantially related to the achievement of that objective." In effect the Court was holding that federal set-aside and affirmative action programs would be evaluated according to an intermediate scrutiny standard, a significantly lower benchmark than the strict scrutiny analysis the justices earlier had applied to state and local programs. To this, Justice O'Connor, who wrote the majority opinion in *City of Richmond,* registered a strong dissent:

At the heart of the Constitution's guarantee of equal protection lies the simple command that the Government must treat citizens "as individuals, not 'as simply components of a racial, religious, sexual or national class.'" Social scientists may debate how people's thoughts and behavior reflect their background, but the Constitution provides that the Government may not allocate benefits and burdens among individuals based on the assumption that race or ethnicity determines how they act or think. To uphold the challenged programs, the Court departs from these fundamental principles and from our traditional requirement that racial classifications are permissible only if necessary and narrowly tailored to achieve a compelling interest. This departure marks a renewed toleration of racial classifications and a repudiation of our recent affirmation that the Constitution's equal protection guarantees extend equally to all citizens. The Court's application of a lessened equal protection standard to congressional actions finds no support in our cases or in the Constitution.

The gap between *City of Richmond* and *Metro Broadcasting* added more confusion to this area of the law. The Court had applied strict scrutiny to state and local programs but intermediate scrutiny to federal plans. Would the Court continue to hold the federal government and the states to different standards? This question became all the more important because, by the time the justices heard a 1995 minority set-aside case, *Adarand Constructors, Inc. v. Peña,* the Court's membership had changed. Justice Brennan's majority opinion in *Metro*

Broadcasting was his last after an illustrious career of thirty-four years on the Court. During that time, he had been a steadfast defender of liberal principles in constitutional interpretation. Brennan's 1990 retirement was followed the next year by Thurgood Marshall's. Like Brennan, Marshall had consistently supported vigorous affirmative action efforts.

President George H. W. Bush appointed David Souter to Brennan's seat and Clarence Thomas to Marshall's. Given the close vote on most affirmative action appeals and the nearly even division between liberal and conservative justices on an appropriate rule of law to govern these issues, the Brennan and Marshall retirements were a blow to affirmative action supporters. Then President Bill Clinton appointed Ruth Bader Ginsburg and Stephen Breyer to replace White and Blackmun, which put two new Democrats on the bench. Would they provide the Court with enough votes to uphold affirmative action programs, or would the worst fears of supporters of preferential treatment be realized in *Adarand*?

Adarand Constructors, Inc. v. Peña

515 U.S. 200 (1995)
http://laws.findlaw.com/US/515/200.html
Oral arguments are available at http://www.oyez.org.
Vote: 5 (Kennedy, O'Connor, Rehnquist, Scalia, Thomas)
    4 (Breyer, Ginsburg, Souter, Stevens)

OPINION OF THE COURT: O'Connor
CONCURRING OPINIONS: Scalia, Thomas
DISSENTING OPINIONS: Ginsburg, Souter, Stevens

FACTS:

This case involved the validity of minority preferences in federal construction projects. Challenged was a clause in Federal Highway Division contracts issued under the Federal Construction Procurement Program. These contracts were authorized by two statutes: the Small Business Act of 1954, as amended (SBA), and the Surface Transportation and Uniform Relocation Assistance Act of 1987 (STURAA). The preference policy called for the prime contractor to be paid a bonus if at least 10 percent of the overall contract amount was subcontracted to "disadvantaged business enterprises" (DBEs), small businesses that are minority owned and operated.

In 1989 the Federal Highway Division awarded a prime contract for highway work in Colorado to Mountain Gravel and Construction Company.

Adarand Constructors, owned and operated by a white male, submitted the lowest subcontract bid to do guardrail work on the project, but the guardrail contract went to Gonzales Construction, a minority-owned firm. Because Mountain Gravel awarded the subcontract to a DBE, it received a $10,000 bonus.

Adarand filed suit against Secretary of Transportation Federico Peña, claiming that the preference policy violated the due process clause of the Fifth Amendment. The federal program was upheld at the trial level. The Tenth Circuit Court of Appeals affirmed, holding that Supreme Court precedent allowed more latitude to the federal government in implementing race-conscious programs (*Metro Broadcasting*) than was permitted the states (*Croson*). Adarand requested Supreme Court review.

ARGUMENTS:

For the petitioner, Adarand Constructors, Inc.

- The federal procurement program challenged here makes race a determining factor in many federal construction subcontract decisions.
- Strict scrutiny should be the standard of review for race-conscious procurement programs. *Metro Broadcasting v. FCC* (1990) allowed for a lower standard of scrutiny for federal race-based programs, but that case involved First Amendment interests not present here. *City of Richmond v. Croson* (1989) should control.
- Because there is no evidence of any pattern of racial discrimination in federal procurement programs, there is no compelling interest to initiate this race-based procurement policy.
- Because this program is not limited in extent or duration, it is not narrowly tailored.

For the respondents, Federico Peña, Secretary of the Department of Transportation, et al.:

- The Act encourages, but does not require, hiring disadvantaged business enterprises (DBEs) as subcontractors.
- The program is designed to aid socially and economically disadvantaged companies. Minority-owned businesses are presumed to be disadvantaged, but that presumption can be rebutted.
- There is no quota or specified set-aside.
- *Metro Broadcasting v. FCC* (1990) held that intermediate scrutiny should be used to evaluate federal affirmative action programs. *Fullilove v. Klutznick* (1980) should control.

Randy Pech, owner of a guardrail installation company in Colorado Springs, challenged a federal minority set-aside program in Adarand Constructors, Inc. v. Peña.

> JUSTICE O'CONNOR ANNOUNCED THE JUDGMENT OF THE COURT AND DELIVERED AN OPINION . . . WHICH IS FOR THE COURT EXCEPT INSOFAR AS IT MIGHT BE INCONSISTENT WITH THE VIEWS EXPRESSED IN JUSTICE SCALIA'S CONCURRENCE. . . .

Adarand's claim arises under the Fifth Amendment to the Constitution, which provides that "No person shall . . . be deprived of life, liberty, or property, without due process of law." Although this Court has always understood that Clause to provide some measure of protection against arbitrary treatment by the Federal Government, it is not as explicit a guarantee of equal treatment as the Fourteenth Amendment, which provides that "No State shall . . . deny to any person within its jurisdiction the equal protection of the laws." Our cases have accorded varying degrees of significance to the difference in the language of those two Clauses. We think it necessary to revisit the issue here. . . .

In *Bolling v. Sharpe* (1954), the Court for the first time explicitly questioned the existence of any difference between the obligations of the Federal Government and the States to avoid racial classifications. . . . *Bolling*'s facts concerned school desegregation, but its reasoning was not so limited. The Court's observations that "[d]istinctions between citizens solely because of their ancestry are by their very nature odious," *Hirabayashi* [*v. United States,* 1943], and that "all legal restrictions which curtail the civil rights of a single racial group are immediately suspect," *Korematsu* [*v. United States,* 1944], carry no less force in the context of federal action than in the context of action by the States—indeed, they first appeared in cases concerning action by the Federal Government. . . .

Later cases in contexts other than school desegregation did not distinguish between the duties of the States and the Federal Government to avoid racial classifications. Consider, for example, the following passage from *McLaughlin v. Florida,* a 1964 case that struck down a race-based state law:

[W]e deal here with a classification based upon the race of the participants, which must be viewed in light of the historical fact that the central purpose of the Fourteenth Amendment was to eliminate racial discrimination emanating from official sources in the States. This strong policy renders racial classifications 'constitutionally suspect,' *Bolling v. Sharpe;* and subject to the 'most rigid scrutiny,' *Korematsu v. United States;* and 'in most circumstances irrelevant' to any constitutionally acceptable legislative purpose, *Hirabayashi v. United States.*

McLaughlin's reliance on cases involving federal action for the standards applicable to a case involving state legislation suggests that the Court understood the standards for federal and state racial classifications to be the same.

Cases decided after *McLaughlin* continued to treat the equal protection obligations imposed by the Fifth and the Fourteenth Amendments as indistinguishable. . . . *Loving v. Virginia* [1967], which struck down a race-based state law, cited *Korematsu* for the proposition that "the Equal Protection Clause demands that racial classifications . . . be subjected to the 'most rigid scrutiny.'" The various opinions in *Frontiero v. Richardson* (1973), which concerned sex discrimination by the Federal Government, took their equal protection standard of review from *Reed v. Reed* (1971), a case that invalidated sex discrimination by a State, without mentioning any possibility of a difference between the standards applicable to state and federal action. Thus, in 1975, the Court stated explicitly that "[t]his Court's approach to Fifth Amendment equal protection claims has always been precisely the same as to equal protection claims under

the Fourteenth Amendment." *Weinberger v. Wiesenfeld;* see also *Buckley v. Valeo* (1976); *United States v. Paradise* (1987). . . .

Most of the cases discussed above involved classifications burdening groups that have suffered discrimination in our society. In 1978, the Court confronted the question whether race-based governmental action designed to benefit such groups should also be subject to "the most rigid scrutiny." *Regents of Univ. of California v. Bakke* involved an equal protection challenge to a state-run medical school's practice of reserving a number of spaces in its entering class for minority students. The petitioners argued that "strict scrutiny" should apply only to "classifications that disadvantage 'discrete and insular minorities.'" *Bakke* did not produce an opinion for the Court, but Justice Powell's opinion announcing the Court's judgment rejected the argument. . . .

Two years after *Bakke,* the Court faced another challenge to remedial race-based action, this time involving action undertaken by the Federal Government. In *Fullilove v. Klutznick* (1980), the Court upheld Congress' inclusion of a 10% set-aside for minority-owned businesses in the Public Works Employment Act of 1977. As in *Bakke,* there was no opinion for the Court. Chief Justice Burger, in an opinion joined by Justices White and Powell, observed that "[a]ny preference based on racial or ethnic criteria must necessarily receive a most searching examination to make sure that it does not conflict with constitutional guarantees." . . .

In *Wygant v. Jackson Board of Ed.* (1986), the Court considered a Fourteenth Amendment challenge to another form of remedial racial classification. The issue in *Wygant* was whether a school board could adopt race-based preferences in determining which teachers to lay off. Justice Powell's plurality opinion observed that "the level of scrutiny does not change merely because the challenged classification operates against a group that historically has not been subject to governmental discrimination." . . . In other words, "racial classifications of any sort must be subjected to 'strict scrutiny.'" (O'CONNOR, J, concurring in part and concurring in judgment). . . .

The Court's failure to produce a majority opinion in *Bakke, Fullilove,* and *Wygant* left unresolved the proper analysis for remedial race-based governmental action. . . .

The Court resolved the issue, at least in part, in 1989. *Richmond v. J. A. Croson Co.* concerned a city's determination that 30% of its contracting work should go to minority-owned businesses. A majority of the Court in *Croson* held that "the standard of review under the

Equal Protection Clause is not dependent on the race of those burdened or benefited by a particular classification," and that the single standard of review for racial classifications should be "strict scrutiny." . . .

With *Croson,* the Court finally agreed that the Fourteenth Amendment requires strict scrutiny of all race-based action by state and local governments. But *Croson* of course had no occasion to declare what standard of review the Fifth Amendment requires for such action taken by the Federal Government. . . .

Despite lingering uncertainty in the details, however, the Court's cases through *Croson* had established three general propositions with respect to governmental racial classifications. First, skepticism: "'[a]ny preference based on racial or ethnic criteria must necessarily receive a most searching examination,'" *Wygant, Fullilove, McLaughlin, Hirabayashi.* . . . Second, consistency: "the standard of review under the Equal Protection Clause is not dependent on the race of those burdened or benefited by a particular classification," *Croson, Bakke.* . . . And third, congruence: "[e]qual protection analysis in the Fifth Amendment area is the same as that under the Fourteenth Amendment," *Buckley v. Valeo, Weinberger v. Wiesenfeld, Bolling v. Sharpe.* Taken together, these three propositions lead to the conclusion that any person, of whatever race, has the right to demand that any governmental actor subject to the Constitution justify any racial classification subjecting that person to unequal treatment under the strictest judicial scrutiny. . . .

A year later, however, the Court took a surprising turn. *Metro Broadcasting, Inc. v. FCC* (1990) involved a Fifth Amendment challenge to two race-based policies of the Federal Communications Commission. In *Metro Broadcasting,* the Court repudiated the long-held notion that "it would be unthinkable that the same Constitution would impose a lesser duty on the Federal Government" than it does on a State to afford equal protection of the laws, *Bolling.* It did so by holding that "benign" federal racial classifications need only satisfy intermediate scrutiny, even though *Croson* had recently concluded that such classifications enacted by a State must satisfy strict scrutiny. . . .

By adopting intermediate scrutiny as the standard of review for congressionally mandated "benign" racial classifications, *Metro Broadcasting* departed from prior cases in two significant respects. First, it turned its back on *Croson*'s explanation of why strict scrutiny of all governmental racial classifications is essential. . . .

Second, *Metro Broadcasting* squarely rejected one of the three propositions established by the Court's earlier equal protection cases, namely, congruence between the standards applicable to federal and state racial classifications, and in so doing also undermined the other two—skepticism of all racial classifications, and consistency of treatment irrespective of the race of the burdened or benefited group. Under *Metro Broadcasting,* certain racial classifications ("benign" ones enacted by the Federal Government) should be treated less skeptically than others; and the race of the benefited group is critical to the determination of which standard of review to apply. *Metro Broadcasting* was thus a significant departure from much of what had come before it.

The three propositions undermined by *Metro Broadcasting* all derive from the basic principle that the Fifth and Fourteenth Amendments to the Constitution protect persons, not groups. It follows from that principle that all governmental action based on race—a group classification long recognized as "in most circumstances irrelevant and therefore prohibited," *Hirabayashi*—should be subjected to detailed judicial inquiry to ensure that the personal right to equal protection of the laws has not been infringed. These ideas have long been central to this Court's understanding of equal protection, and holding "benign" state and federal racial classifications to different standards does not square with them. "[A] free people whose institutions are founded upon the doctrine of equality," *ibid.,* should tolerate no retreat from the principle that government may treat people differently because of their race only for the most compelling reasons. Accordingly, we hold today that all racial classifications, imposed by whatever federal, state, or local governmental actor, must be analyzed by a reviewing court under strict scrutiny. In other words, such classifications are constitutional only if they are narrowly tailored measures that further compelling governmental interests. To the extent that *Metro Broadcasting* is inconsistent with that holding, it is overruled. . . .

Because our decision today alters the playing field in some important respects, we think it best to remand the case to the lower courts for further consideration in light of the principles we have announced. . . .

It is so ordered.

JUSTICE SCALIA, concurring in part and concurring in the judgment.

I join the opinion of the Court . . . except insofar as it may be inconsistent with the following: In my view, government can never have a "compelling interest" in discriminating on the basis of race in order to "make up" for past racial discrimination in the opposite direction. Individuals who have been wronged by unlawful racial discrimination should be made whole; but under our Constitution there can be no such thing as either a creditor or a debtor race. That concept is alien to the Constitution's focus upon the individual. . . . To pursue the concept of racial entitlement—even for the most admirable and benign of purposes—is to reinforce and preserve for future mischief the way of thinking that produced race slavery, race privilege and race hatred. In the eyes of government, we are just one race here. It is American.

It is unlikely, if not impossible, that the challenged program would survive under this understanding of strict scrutiny, but I am content to leave that to be decided on remand.

JUSTICE THOMAS, concurring in part and concurring in the judgment.

That these programs may have been motivated, in part, by good intentions cannot provide refuge from the principle that under our Constitution, the government may not make distinctions on the basis of race. As far as the Constitution is concerned, it is irrelevant whether a government's racial classifications are drawn by those who wish to oppress a race or by those who have a sincere desire to help those thought to be disadvantaged. There can be no doubt that the paternalism that appears to lie at the heart of this program is at war with the principle of inherent equality that underlies and infuses our Constitution. . . .

These programs not only raise grave constitutional questions, they also undermine the moral basis of the equal protection principle. Purchased at the price of immeasurable human suffering, the equal protection principle reflects our Nation's understanding that such classifications ultimately have a destructive impact on the individual and our society. Unquestionably, "[i]nvidious [racial] discrimination is an engine of oppression." It is also true that "[r]emedial" racial preferences may reflect "a desire to foster equality in society." But there can be no doubt that racial paternalism and its unintended consequences can be as poisonous and pernicious as any other form of discrimination. So-called "benign" discrimination teaches many that because of chronic and apparently immutable handicaps, minorities cannot compete with them without their patronizing indulgence. Inevitably, such programs engender attitudes of superiority or, alternatively, provoke resentment among those who believe that they have been wronged by the government's use of race. These programs stamp minorities with a badge of inferiority and may cause them to develop dependencies or to adopt an attitude that they are "entitled" to preferences. . . .

In my mind, government-sponsored racial discrimination based on benign prejudice is just as noxious as discrimination inspired by malicious prejudice. In each instance, it is racial discrimination, plain and simple.

JUSTICE STEVENS, with whom JUSTICE GINSBURG joins, dissenting.

The Court's concept of "consistency" assumes that there is no significant difference between a decision by the majority to impose a special burden on the members of a minority race and a decision by the majority to provide a benefit to certain members of that minority notwithstanding its incidental burden on some members of the majority. In my opinion that assumption is untenable. There is no moral or constitutional equivalence between a policy that is designed to perpetuate a caste system and one that seeks to eradicate racial subordination. Invidious discrimination is an engine of oppression, subjugating a disfavored group to enhance or maintain the power of the majority. Remedial race-based preferences reflect the opposite impulse: a desire to foster equality in society. No sensible conception of the Government's constitutional obligation to "govern impartially," *Hampton v. Mow Sun Wong* (1976), should ignore this distinction. . . .

The Court's concept of "congruence" assumes that there is no significant difference between a decision by the Congress of the United States to adopt an affirmative-action program and such a decision by a State or a municipality. In my opinion that assumption is untenable. It ignores important practical and legal differences between federal and state or local decisionmakers. . . .

The Court's holding in *Fullilove* surely governs the result in this case. . . . In no meaningful respect is the current scheme more objectionable than the 1977 Act. Thus, if the 1977 Act was constitutional, then so must be the SBA and STURAA. . . .

My skeptical scrutiny of the Court's opinion leaves me in dissent. The majority's concept of "consistency" ignores a difference, fundamental to the idea of equal protection, between oppression and assistance. The majority's concept of "congruence" ignores a difference, fundamental to our constitutional system, between the Federal Government and the States. And the majority's concept of stare decisis ignores the force of binding precedent. I would affirm the judgment of the Court of Appeals.

JUSTICE SOUTER, with whom JUSTICE
GINSBURG and JUSTICE BREYER join, dissenting.

. . . I agree with JUSTICE STEVENS' conclusion that stare decisis compels the application of *Fullilove*. Although *Fullilove* did not reflect doctrinal consistency, its several opinions produced a result on shared grounds that petitioner does not attack: that discrimination in the construction industry had been subject to government acquiescence, with effects that remain and that may be addressed by some preferential treatment falling within the congressional power under section 5 of the Fourteenth Amendment. Once *Fullilove* is applied, as Justice Stevens points out, it follows that the statutes in question here (which are substantially better tailored to the harm being remedied than the statute endorsed in *Fullilove*) pass muster under Fifth Amendment due process and Fourteenth Amendment equal protection. . . .

JUSTICE GINSBURG, with whom
JUSTICE BREYER joins, dissenting.

The divisions in this difficult case should not obscure the Court's recognition of the persistence of racial inequality and a majority's acknowledgment of Congress' authority to act affirmatively, not only to end discrimination, but also to counteract discrimination's lingering effects. Those effects, reflective of a system of racial caste only recently ended, are evident in our workplaces, markets, and neighborhoods. . . . Bias both conscious and unconscious, reflecting traditional and unexamined habits of thought, keeps up barriers that must come down if equal opportunity and nondiscrimination are ever genuinely to become this country's law and practice.

Given this history and its practical consequences, Congress surely can conclude that a carefully designed affirmative action program may help to realize, finally, the "equal protection of the laws" the Fourteenth Amendment has promised since 1868.

The Court's decision to apply the same strict standards to the federal government as to state and local governments was important. Although the ruling does not strike down all affirmative action programs, it holds them to very exacting standards.

The Court Reconsiders Its Affirmative Action Policies

Decisions such as *Croson* and *Adarand* cast considerable doubt on the constitutional viability of affirmative action programs. This uncertainty was reinforced when the Court began rejecting plans that took race into account in constructing legislative districts *(see Chapter 14)*. Court observers began to speculate that the justices had turned away from the principles set in Justice Powell's opinion in *Bakke* and had become less open to minority preference programs of all kinds.

Encouraged by these events, opponents of affirmative action programs orchestrated political and legal efforts to eliminate them. In several instances they were successful. For example, California, Florida, and Washington enacted measures by popular initiative or legislative action that banned the use of racial preferences. In *Hopwood v. Texas* (1996) the Fifth Circuit Court of Appeals ruled that preferential college admissions policies violated the Constitution, a decision binding on the three states under its jurisdiction (Texas, Mississippi, and Louisiana). Several district courts around the country came to similar conclusions.

Where they were prohibited by law or judicial order, the elimination of affirmative action programs had a demonstrable impact. In California's university system, for example, the proportion of African American and Hispanic students dropped substantially. The population of white students remained relatively constant or declined slightly at some schools. The largest beneficiaries of race-blind admissions were Asian students, whose numbers increased significantly.[22] The University of Texas at Austin experienced similar enrollment patterns, with declines in the number of African American and Hispanic students and increases in Asians. The university's student body became less reflective of the state's population. In 2002 black enrollment was only 3 percent of the entry class, but blacks constituted 11 percent of the Texas population; Hispanics represented 14 percent of the freshman class, but 32 percent of the state population. On the other hand, Asians made up only 3 percent of the state population, but 18 percent of the entry class.[23] Faced with such statistics, those colleges and universities that had been forced to abandon preference programs worked to develop race-neutral methods of improving diversity.

With the nation's states and judicial districts taking different positions on the question, it was inevitable that the U.S. Supreme Court would attempt to clarify

---

22. Jacques Steinberg, "The New Calculus of Diversity on Campus," *New York Times,* February 2, 2003.

23. Ibid.

the constitutionality of affirmative action. The show-down occurred in 2003 when the justices took up two appeals challenging affirmative action at the University of Michigan. One suit, *Gratz v. Bollinger,* attacked the university's undergraduate admissions policies, and the the other, *Grutter v. Bollinger,* challenged admissions to the university's law school. In both cases the admissions policies had been adopted voluntarily rather than in response to a court order to compensate for past constitutional violations.

Speculation on the outcome of the Court's deliberations generally conceded that the votes of seven of the nine justices were all but certain. Justices Stevens, Souter, Ginsburg, and Breyer had records of consistent support for the limited use of racial preferences. On the other side, Chief Justice Rehnquist and Justices Scalia and Thomas had consistently and vigorously opposed affirmative action. Most observers believed that Justices O'Connor and Kennedy held the key to the outcome. For affirmative action to receive constitutional approval, at least one of these two moderate conservatives would have to vote with the Court's liberal bloc.

Would the Court reaffirm Justice Powell's *Bakke* decision, or would the more recent pattern of rejecting race-based policies prevail? Would the justices remain committed to the strict scrutiny test for deciding racial preference cases? If so, would the creation of a diverse student body qualify as a sufficiently compelling state interest to justify taking race into account?

In what follows, we discuss both cases and provide an excerpt of the Court's decision in *Grutter v. Bollinger.*

Grutter v. Bollinger

539 U.S. 306 (2003)
http://laws.findlaw.com/US/539/306.html
Oral arguments are available at http://www.oyez.org.
Vote: 5 (Breyer, Ginsburg, O'Connor, Souter, Stevens)
    4 (Kennedy, Rehnquist, Scalia, Thomas)
OPINION OF THE COURT: *O'Connor*
CONCURRING OPINION: *Ginsburg*
DISSENTING OPINIONS: *Rehnquist, Kennedy*
**OPINION CONCURRING IN PART AND DISSENTING
   IN PART:** *Thomas*

FACTS:

Gratz v. Bollinger (2003) involved the University of Michigan's undergraduate admissions policies. Jennifer Gratz and Patrick Hamacher, both white Michigan residents, applied for admission, Gratz in 1995 and Hamacher in 1997. Based on their academic credentials, Gratz fell into the university's "well-qualified" category and Hamacher was judged to be "qualified." The university denied them admission. Gratz and Hamacher sued the university, in the name of president Lee Bollinger, claiming that their rejections were due to the university's racial preference policies.

Barbara Grutter, shown in her Plymouth, Michigan, home in 2003, challenged the constitutionality of the University of Michigan Law School's admissions policies. In Grutter v. Bollinger, *the Supreme Court found that the school's affirmative action admissions program did not violate the equal protection clause.*

Committed to having a diverse student body, the university employed various methods of enhancing the admissions opportunities for applicants from underrepresented groups, specifically African Americans, Hispanics, and Native Americans. When Gratz applied, the policy of the university was to add 0.5 to the grade point averages of applicants from the designated minority groups, to use different grade point average/test score grids for minority and nonminority students, and to protect a number of slots for certain kinds of students, including minority applicants. The university later changed its policies, eliminating the protected slots and instead assigning points to applicants based on academic and nonacademic factors. One hundred points were needed to be admitted. To promote a diverse student body, the university gave 20 points automatically to every applicant from the designated underrepresented groups. The case focused on this revised system.

In *Grutter v. Bollinger,* a forty-three-year-old white Michigan resident, Barbara Grutter, applied for admission to the University of Michigan Law School in 1996, presenting a 3.8 undergraduate grade point average from Michigan State University and a 161 law school admissions test score. She was first placed on the school's waiting list but was ultimately denied admission. She sued the university, claiming that her rejection was due to an admissions policy that awarded racial preferences in violation of the equal protection clause.

The law school, one of the nation's finest, annually received about 3,500 applications for the 350 seats in its first-year class. The school sought the most capable class of students possible, but it also wanted to admit students with varying backgrounds and experiences. To achieve a diverse student body, the school looked beyond grade point averages and test scores. It did not confine diversity to racial and ethnic categories, nor did it limit the number of factors that might be considered in assembling a diverse student body. It did, however, make a commitment to African American, Hispanic, and Native American applicants who, without a special consideration, might be underrepresented. The law school wanted a "critical mass" of minority students so they would not be isolated or feel like spokespersons for their races. The law school argued that such a critical mass was necessary to attain the educational benefits of a diverse student body.

At trial, law school admissions officers testified that the "critical mass" goal did not imply any particular proportion of the entry class. No predetermined number of points was given to minority applicants; rather, each application was individually considered on its own merits. During the admissions process, school officials kept daily watch over the number of minority students who had been admitted. Expert testimony indicated that in 2000, 35 percent of underrepresented minority candidates were admitted, but if race had not been considered only 10 percent of minority applications would have been successful.

Gratz and *Grutter* attracted significant amicus curiae participation. A collection of conservative groups with long histories of opposing racial preferences supported the rejected students' position, but the most important amicus brief was that of Solicitor General Theodore Olson, who expressed the Bush administration's opposition to the admissions policies. Supporting the university was an even larger group of interests. Among them, as expected, were an array of traditional civil rights groups, but, surprisingly, briefs were also submitted by individuals associated with the military and business interests.

In *Gratz* the Court, by a 6–3 vote, found that the university's admissions policies violated the equal protection clause. The justices ruled that the automatic distribution of 20 points, or one-fifth of those necessary for admission, to every underrepresented minority applicant, solely because of race, was not narrowly tailored to achieve the goal of educational diversity. The system lacked the necessary individualized consideration that Justice Powell had emphasized in *Bakke,* and it elevated race to the point that it became a decisive factor for virtually every minimally qualified minority applicant. Both O'Connor and Kennedy, the two swing justices, voted against the university and joined the majority opinion.

Gratz was a victory for affirmative action opponents, but *Grutter* was a very different matter. Here the Court considered whether the goal of a diverse law school student body was a compelling government interest and whether an individualized preference policy passed constitutional muster.

ARGUMENTS:

For the petitioner, Barbara Grutter:
- Justice Powell's opinion in *Bakke* announced the judgment of the Court, not an opinion of the Court.
- The law school's policy of admitting "meaningful numbers" or a "critical mass" of specified minority

students amounts to the functional equivalent of a race-balancing quota.

- The enormous size of the preference given to minority applicants creates a "two-track" or "dual" admissions program.
- The law school's admissions program is not narrowly tailored because, among other factors, it has no durational limit and there is no rationale for selecting those minority groups included in the program and those minorities groups excluded.

For the respondents, Lee Bollinger, President, and the Board of Regents of the University of Michigan:

- In *Regents of the University of California v. Bakke* (1978) the Court recognized that a diverse student body is a compelling interest. *Bakke* should not be disturbed.
- There are no race-neutral alternatives capable of producing a diverse student body without abandoning academic selectivity.
- The program does not use quotas or set-asides. Rather, the program is individualized, competitive, and modest in scope and does not unduly burden nonminority applicants.
- It is rational to tailor the program to attract meaningful numbers of African American, Hispanic, and Native American students.

JUSTICE O'CONNOR DELIVERED THE OPINION OF THE COURT.

We last addressed the use of race in public higher education over 25 years ago. In the landmark [*Regents of the University of California v.*] *Bakke* [1978] case, we reviewed a racial set-aside program that reserved 16 out of 100 seats in a medical school class for members of certain minority groups. The decision produced six separate opinions, none of which commanded a majority of the Court. Four Justices would have upheld the program against all attack on the ground that the government can use race to "remedy disadvantages cast on minorities by past racial prejudice." Four other Justices avoided the constitutional question altogether and struck down the program on statutory grounds. Justice Powell provided a fifth vote not only for invalidating the set-aside program, but also for reversing the state court's injunction against any use of race whatsoever. The only holding for the Court in *Bakke* was that a "State has a substantial interest that legitimately may be served by a properly devised admissions

program involving the competitive consideration of race and ethnic origin." Thus, we reversed that part of the lower court's judgment that enjoined the university "from any consideration of the race of any applicant."

Since this Court's splintered decision in *Bakke,* Justice Powell's opinion announcing the judgment of the Court has served as the touchstone for constitutional analysis of race-conscious admissions policies. Public and private universities across the Nation have modeled their own admissions programs on Justice Powell's views on permissible race-conscious policies. . . .

Justice Powell began by stating that "[t]he guarantee of equal protection cannot mean one thing when applied to one individual and something else when applied to a person of another color. If both are not accorded the same protection, then it is not equal." In Justice Powell's view, when governmental decisions "touch upon an individual's race or ethnic background, he is entitled to a judicial determination that the burden he is asked to bear on that basis is precisely tailored to serve a compelling governmental interest." Under this exacting standard, only one of the interests asserted by the university survived Justice Powell's scrutiny.

First, Justice Powell rejected an interest in "'reducing the historic deficit of traditionally disfavored minorities in medical schools and in the medical profession'" as an unlawful interest in racial balancing. Second, Justice Powell rejected an interest in remedying societal discrimination because such measures would risk placing unnecessary burdens on innocent third parties "who bear no responsibility for whatever harm the beneficiaries of the special admissions program are thought to have suffered." Third, Justice Powell rejected an interest in "increasing the number of physicians who will practice in communities currently underserved," concluding that even if such an interest could be compelling in some circumstances the program under review was not "geared to promote that goal."

Justice Powell approved the university's use of race to further only one interest: "the attainment of a diverse student body." With the important proviso that "constitutional limitations protecting individual rights may not be disregarded," Justice Powell grounded his analysis in the academic freedom that "long has been viewed as a special concern of the First Amendment." Justice Powell emphasized that nothing less than the "'nation's future depends upon leaders trained through wide exposure' to the ideas and mores of students as diverse as this Nation of many peoples." In seeking the "right to select those students who will contribute the most to the 'robust exchange of ideas,'" a university seeks "to achieve a goal that is of paramount importance in the fulfillment of its mission." Both "tradition and experience lend support to the view that the contribution of diversity is substantial."

Justice Powell was, however, careful to emphasize that in his view race "is only one element in a range of factors a university properly may consider in attaining the goal of a heterogeneous student body." . . .

. . . [T]oday we endorse Justice Powell's view that student body diversity is a compelling state interest that can justify the use of race in university admissions.

The Equal Protection Clause provides that no State shall "deny to any person within its jurisdiction the equal protection of the laws." Because the Fourteenth Amendment "protect[s] *persons,* not *groups,*" all "governmental action based on race—a *group* classification long recognized as in most circumstances irrelevant and therefore prohibited—should be subjected to detailed judicial inquiry to ensure that the *personal* right to equal protection of the laws has not been infringed." *Adarand Constructors, Inc. v. Peña* (1995). . . . It follows from this principle that "government may treat people differently because of their race only for the most compelling reasons." . . .

The Law School's educational judgment that such diversity is essential to its educational mission is one to which we defer. The Law School's assessment that diversity will, in fact, yield educational benefits is substantiated by respondents and their *amici.* Our scrutiny of the interest asserted by the Law School is no less strict for taking into account complex educational judgments in an area that lies primarily within the expertise of the university. Our holding today is in keeping with our tradition of giving a degree of deference to a university's academic decisions, within constitutionally prescribed limits. . . .

As part of its goal of "assembling a class that is both exceptionally academically qualified and broadly diverse," the Law School seeks to "enroll a 'critical mass' of minority students." The Law School's interest is not simply "to assure within its student body some specified percentage of a particular group merely because of its race or ethnic origin." That would amount to outright racial balancing, which is patently unconstitutional. Rather, the Law School's concept of critical mass is defined by reference to the educational benefits that diversity is designed to produce.

These benefits are substantial. As the District Court emphasized, the Law School's admissions policy promotes "cross-racial understanding," helps to break down racial stereotypes, and "enables [students] to better understand persons of different races." These benefits are "important and laudable," because "classroom discussion is livelier, more spirited, and simply more enlightening and interesting" when the students have "the greatest possible variety of backgrounds."

The Law School's claim of a compelling interest is further bolstered by its *amici,* who point to the educational benefits that flow from student body diversity. In addition to the expert studies and reports entered into evidence at trial, numerous studies show that student body diversity promotes learning outcomes, and "better prepares students for an increasingly diverse workforce and society, and better prepares them as professionals."

These benefits are not theoretical but real, as major American businesses have made clear that the skills needed in today's increasingly global marketplace can only be developed through exposure to widely diverse people, cultures, ideas, and viewpoints. What is more, high-ranking retired officers and civilian leaders of the United States military assert that, "[b]ased on [their] decades of experience," a "highly qualified, racially diverse officer corps . . . is essential to the military's ability to fulfill its principle mission to provide national security." . . .

Moreover, universities, and in particular, law schools, represent the training ground for a large number of our Nation's leaders. . . .

In order to cultivate a set of leaders with legitimacy in the eyes of the citizenry, it is necessary that the path to leadership be visibly open to talented and qualified individuals of every race and ethnicity. . . .

Even in the limited circumstance when drawing racial distinctions is permissible to further a compelling state interest, government is still "constrained in how it may pursue that end: [T]he means chosen to accomplish the [government's] asserted purpose must be specifically and narrowly framed to accomplish that purpose." *Shaw v. Hunt* (1996). . . .

To be narrowly tailored, a race-conscious admissions program cannot use a quota system—it cannot "insulat[e] each category of applicants with certain desired qualifications from competition with all other applicants." *Bakke.* Instead, a university may consider race or ethnicity only as a "'plus' in a particular applicant's file," without "insulat[ing] the individual from comparison with all other candidates for the available seats." In other words, an admissions program must be "flexible enough to consider all pertinent elements of diversity in light of the particular qualifications of each applicant, and to place them on the same footing for consideration, although not necessarily according them the same weight." . . .

We are satisfied that the Law School's admissions program, like the Harvard plan described by Justice Powell, does not operate as a quota. Properly understood, a "quota" is a program in which a certain fixed number or proportion of opportunities are "reserved exclusively for certain minority groups." Quotas "impose a fixed number or percentage which must be attained, or which cannot be exceeded," and "insulate the individual from comparison with all other candidates for the available seats." In contrast, "a permissible goal . . . require[s] only a good-faith effort . . . to come within a range demarcated by the goal itself," and permits consideration of race as a "plus" factor in any given case while still ensuring that each candidate "compete[s] with all other qualified applicants." . . .

Here, the Law School engages in a highly individualized, holistic review of each applicant's file, giving serious consideration to all the ways an applicant might contribute to a diverse educational environment. The Law School affords this individualized consideration to applicants of all races. There is no policy, either *de jure* or *de facto,* of automatic acceptance or rejection based on any single "soft" variable. . . .

What is more, the Law School actually gives substantial weight to diversity factors besides race. The Law School frequently accepts nonminority applicants with grades and test scores lower than underrepresented minority applicants (and other nonminority applicants) who are rejected. This shows that the Law School seriously weighs many other diversity factors besides race that can make a real and dispositive difference for nonminority applicants as well. By this flexible approach, the Law School sufficiently takes into account, in practice as well as in theory, a wide variety of characteristics besides race and ethnicity that contribute to a diverse student body. . . .

Petitioner and the United States argue that the Law School's plan is not narrowly tailored because race-neutral means exist to obtain the educational benefits of student body diversity that the Law School seeks. We disagree. Narrow tailoring does not require exhaustion of every conceivable race-neutral alternative. Nor does it

require a university to choose between maintaining a reputation for excellence or fulfilling a commitment to provide educational opportunities to members of all racial groups. Narrow tailoring does, however, require serious, good faith consideration of workable race-neutral alternatives that will achieve the diversity the university seeks.

We agree with the Court of Appeals that the Law School sufficiently considered workable race-neutral alternatives. . . .

We acknowledge that "there are serious problems of justice connected with the idea of preference itself." *Bakke*. Narrow tailoring, therefore, requires that a race-conscious admissions program not unduly harm members of any racial group. . . . To be narrowly tailored, a race-conscious admissions program must not "unduly burden individuals who are not members of the favored racial and ethnic groups."

We are satisfied that the Law School's admissions program does not. Because the Law School considers "all pertinent elements of diversity," it can (and does) select nonminority applicants who have greater potential to enhance student body diversity over underrepresented minority applicants. As Justice Powell recognized in *Bakke,* so long as a race-conscious admissions program uses race as a "plus" factor in the context of individualized consideration, a rejected applicant "will not have been foreclosed from all consideration for that seat simply because he was not the right color or had the wrong surname. . . . His qualifications would have been weighed fairly and competitively, and he would have no basis to complain of unequal treatment under the Fourteenth Amendment."

We agree that, in the context of its individualized inquiry into the possible diversity contributions of all applicants, the Law School's race-conscious admissions program does not unduly harm nonminority applicants.

We are mindful, however, that "[a] core purpose of the Fourteenth Amendment was to do away with all governmentally imposed discrimination based on race." *Palmore v. Sidoti* (1984). Accordingly, race-conscious admissions policies must be limited in time. . . . We see no reason to exempt race-conscious admissions programs from the requirement that all governmental use of race must have a logical end point. . . .

In the context of higher education, the durational requirement can be met by sunset provisions in race-conscious admissions policies and periodic reviews to determine whether racial preferences are still necessary to achieve student body diversity. Universities in California,

Florida, and Washington State, where racial preferences in admissions are prohibited by state law, are currently engaged in experimenting with a wide variety of alternative approaches. Universities in other States can and should draw on the most promising aspects of these race-neutral alternatives as they develop. . . .

. . . It has been 25 years since Justice Powell first approved the use of race to further an interest in student body diversity in the context of public higher education. Since that time, the number of minority applicants with high grades and test scores has indeed increased. We expect that 25 years from now, the use of racial preferences will no longer be necessary to further the interest approved today.

In summary, the Equal Protection Clause does not prohibit the Law School's narrowly tailored use of race in admissions decisions to further a compelling interest in obtaining the educational benefits that flow from a diverse student body. . . . The judgment of the Court of Appeals for the Sixth Circuit, accordingly, is affirmed.

It is so ordered.

CHIEF JUSTICE REHNQUIST, with whom JUSTICE SCALIA, JUSTICE KENNEDY, and JUSTICE THOMAS join, dissenting.
I agree with the Court that, "in the limited circumstance when drawing racial distinctions is permissible," the government must ensure that its means are narrowly tailored to achieve a compelling state interest. I do not believe, however, that the University of Michigan Law School's (Law School) means are narrowly tailored to the interest it asserts. The Law School claims it must take the steps it does to achieve a "critical mass" of underrepresented minority students. But its actual program bears no relation to this asserted goal. Stripped of its "critical mass" veil, the Law School's program is revealed as a naked effort to achieve racial balancing. . . .

. . . Respondents explain that the Law School seeks to accumulate a "critical mass" of *each* underrepresented minority group. But the record demonstrates that the Law School's admissions practices with respect to these groups differ dramatically and cannot be defended under any consistent use of the term "critical mass."

From 1995 through 2000, the Law School admitted between 1,130 and 1,310 students. Of those, between 13 and 19 were Native American, between 91 and 108 were African-Americans, and between 47 and 56 were Hispanic.

If the Law School is admitting between 91 and 108 African-Americans in order to achieve "critical mass," thereby preventing African-American students from feeling "isolated or like spokespersons for their race," one would think that a number of the same order of magnitude would be necessary to accomplish the same purpose for Hispanics and Native Americans. Similarly, even if all of the Native American applicants admitted in a given year matriculate, which the record demonstrates is not at all the case, how can this possibly constitute a "critical mass" of Native Americans in a class of over 350 students? In order for this pattern of admission to be consistent with the Law School's explanation of "critical mass," one would have to believe that the objectives of "critical mass" offered by respondents are achieved with only half the number of Hispanics and one-sixth the number of Native Americans as compared to African-Americans. But respondents offer no race-specific reasons for such disparities. Instead, they simply emphasize the importance of achieving "critical mass," without any explanation of why that concept is applied differently among the three underrepresented minority groups.

These different numbers, moreover, come only as a result of substantially different treatment among the three underrepresented minority groups, as is apparent in an example offered by the Law School and highlighted by the Court. . . . The Law School states that "[s]ixty-nine minority applicants were rejected between 1995 and 2000 with at least a 3.5 [grade point average] and a [score of] 159 or higher on the [law school admissions test]" while a number of Caucasian and Asian-American applicants with similar or lower scores were admitted.

Review of the record reveals only 67 such individuals. Of these 67 individuals, 56 were Hispanic, while only 6 were African-American, and only 5 were Native American. This discrepancy reflects a consistent practice. For example, in 2000, 12 Hispanics who scored between a 159–160 on the LSAT and earned a GPA of 3.00 or higher applied for admission and only 2 were admitted. Meanwhile, 12 African-Americans in the same range of qualifications applied for admission and all 12 were admitted. Likewise, that same year, 16 Hispanics who scored between a 151–153 on the LSAT and earned a 3.00 or higher applied for admission and only 1 of those applicants was admitted. Twenty-three similarly qualified African-Americans applied for admission and 14 were admitted.

These statistics have a significant bearing on petitioner's case. Respondents have *never* offered any race-specific arguments explaining why significantly more individuals from one underrepresented minority group are needed in order to achieve "critical mass" or further student body diversity. They certainly have not explained why Hispanics, who they have said are among "the groups most isolated by racial barriers in our country," should have their admission capped out in this manner. True, petitioner is neither Hispanic nor Native American. But the Law School's disparate admissions practices with respect to these minority groups demonstrate that its alleged goal of "critical mass" is simply a sham. . . .

I do not believe that the Constitution gives the Law School such free rein in the use of race. . . . [T]his is precisely the type of racial balancing that the Court itself calls "patently unconstitutional."

JUSTICE KENNEDY, dissenting.

The Law School has the burden of proving, in conformance with the standard of strict scrutiny, that it did not utilize race in an unconstitutional way. *Adarand Constructors.* . . . At the very least, the constancy of admitted minority students and the close correlation between the racial breakdown of admitted minorities and the composition of the applicant pool . . . require the Law School either to produce a convincing explanation or to show it has taken adequate steps to ensure individual assessment. The Law School does neither.

The obvious tension between the pursuit of critical mass and the requirement of individual review increased by the end of the admissions season. Most of the decisions where race may decide the outcome are made during this period. The admissions officers consulted the daily reports which indicated the composition of the incoming class along racial lines. . . .

The consultation of daily reports during the last stages in the admissions process suggests there was no further attempt at individual review save for race itself. The admissions officers could use the reports to recalibrate the plus factor given to race depending on how close they were to achieving the Law School's goal of critical mass. The bonus factor of race would then become divorced from individual review; it would be premised instead on the numerical objective set by the Law School.

The Law School made no effort to guard against this danger. It provided no guidelines to its admissions personnel on how to reconcile individual assessment with the directive to admit a critical mass of minority students. . . .

To be constitutional, a university's compelling interest in a diverse student body must be achieved by a system where individual assessment is safeguarded through the entire process. . . . The Law School failed to comply with this requirement, and by no means has it carried its burden to show otherwise by the test of strict scrutiny.

JUSTICE SCALIA, with whom JUSTICE THOMAS joins, concurring in part and dissenting in part.

Unlike a clear constitutional holding that racial preferences in state educational institutions are impermissible, or even a clear anticonstitutional holding that racial preferences in state educational institutions are OK, today's [decision] seems perversely designed to prolong the controversy and the litigation. Some future lawsuits will presumably focus on whether the discriminatory scheme in question contains enough evaluation of the applicant "as an individual," and sufficiently avoids "separate admissions tracks." . . . Some will focus on whether a university has gone beyond the bounds of a "good faith effort" and has so zealously pursued its "critical mass" as to make it an unconstitutional *de facto* quota system, rather than merely "a permissible goal." Other lawsuits may focus on whether, in the particular setting at issue, any educational benefits flow from racial diversity. Still other suits may challenge the bona fides of the institution's expressed commitment to the educational benefits of diversity that immunize the discriminatory scheme in *Grutter.* (Tempting targets, one would suppose, will be those universities that talk the talk of multiculturalism and racial diversity in the courts but walk the walk of tribalism and racial segregation on their campuses—through minority-only student organizations, separate minority housing opportunities, separate minority student centers, even separate minority-only graduation ceremonies.) And still other suits may claim that the institution's racial preferences have gone below or above the mystical *Grutter* approved "critical mass." Finally, litigation can be expected on behalf of minority groups intentionally short changed in the institution's composition of its generic minority "critical mass." I do not look forward to any of these cases. The Constitution proscribes government discrimination on the basis of race, and state-provided education is no exception.

**JUSTICE THOMAS, with whom JUSTICE SCALIA joins . . . ,
concurring in part and dissenting in part.**

Frederick Douglass, speaking to a group of abolitionists almost 140 years ago, delivered a message lost on today's majority:

"[I]n regard to the colored people, there is always more that is benevolent, I perceive, than just, manifested towards us. What I ask for the negro is not benevolence, not pity, not sympathy, but simply *justice*. The American people have always been anxious to know what they shall do with us. . . . I have had but one answer from the beginning. Do nothing with us! Your doing with us has already played the mischief with us. Do nothing with us! If the apples will not remain on the tree of their own strength, if they are worm-eaten at the core, if they are early ripe and disposed to fall, let them fall! . . . And if the negro cannot stand on his own legs, let him fall also. All I ask is, give him a chance to stand on his own legs! Let him alone! . . . [Y]our interference is doing him positive injury." What the Black Man Wants: An Address Delivered in Boston, Massachusetts, on 26 January 1865.

Like Douglass, I believe blacks can achieve in every avenue of American life without the meddling of university administrators. Because I wish to see all students succeed whatever their color, I share, in some respect, the sympathies of those who sponsor the type of discrimination advanced by the University of Michigan Law School (Law School). The Constitution does not, however, tolerate institutional devotion to the status quo in admissions policies when such devotion ripens into racial discrimination. Nor does the Constitution countenance the unprecedented deference the Court gives to the Law School, an approach inconsistent with the very concept of "strict scrutiny."

No one would argue that a university could set up a lower general admission standard and then impose heightened requirements only on black applicants. Similarly, a university may not maintain a high admission standard and grant exemptions to favored races. . . .

The majority upholds the Law School's racial discrimination not by interpreting the people's Constitution, but by responding to a faddish slogan of the

cognoscenti. . . . I agree with the Court's holding that racial discrimination in higher education admissions will be illegal in 25 years. I respectfully dissent from the remainder of the Court's opinion and the judgment, however, because I believe that the Law School's current use of race violates the Equal Protection Clause and that the Constitution means the same thing today as it will in 300 months. . . .

The strict scrutiny standard that the Court purports to apply in this case was first enunciated in *Korematsu v. United States* (1944). There the Court held that "[p]ressing public necessity may sometimes justify the existence of [racial discrimination]; racial antagonism never can." This standard of "pressing public necessity" has more frequently been termed "compelling governmental interest." . . .

Where the Court has accepted only national security . . . as a justification for racial discrimination, I conclude that only those measures the State must take to provide a bulwark against anarchy, or to prevent violence, will constitute a "pressing public necessity." . . .

The Constitution abhors classifications based on race, not only because those classifications can harm favored races or are based on illegitimate motives, but also because every time the government places citizens on racial registers and makes race relevant to the provision of burdens or benefits, it demeans us all. . . .

. . . Today, the Court insists on radically expanding the range of permissible uses of race to something as trivial (by comparison) as the assembling of a law school class. I can only presume that the majority's failure to justify its decision by reference to any principle arises from the absence of any such principle. . . .

The Court bases its unprecedented deference to the Law School—a deference antithetical to strict scrutiny—on an idea of "educational autonomy" grounded in the First Amendment. In my view, there is no basis for a right of public universities to do what would otherwise violate the Equal Protection Clause. . . .

Moreover one would think, in light of the Court's decision in *United States v. Virginia* (1996), that before being given license to use racial discrimination, the Law School would be required to radically reshape its admissions process, even to the point of sacrificing some elements of its character. In *Virginia,* a majority of the Court, without a word about academic freedom, accepted the all-male Virginia Military Institute's (VMI) representation that some changes in its "adversative" method of education would be required with the admission of women, but did not defer to VMI's judgment that these changes would be too great. Instead, the Court concluded that they were "manageable." That case involved sex discrimination, which is subjected to intermediate, not strict, scrutiny. So in *Virginia,* where the standard of review dictated that greater flexibility be granted to VMI's educational policies than the Law School deserves here, this Court gave no deference. Apparently where the status quo being defended is that of the elite establishment—here the Law School—rather than a less fashionable Southern military institution, the Court will defer without serious inquiry and without regard to the applicable legal standard.

Virginia is also notable for the fact that the Court relied on the "experience" of formerly single-sex institutions, such as the service academies, to conclude that admission of women to VMI would be "manageable." Today, however, the majority ignores the "experience" of those institutions that have been forced to abandon explicit racial discrimination in admissions.

The sky has not fallen at Boalt Hall at the University of California, Berkeley, for example. Prior to Proposition 209's adoption of Cal. Const., Art. 1, §31(a), which bars the State from "grant[ing] preferential treatment . . . on the basis of race . . . in the operation of . . . public education," Boalt Hall enrolled 20 blacks and 28 Hispanics in its first-year class for 1996. In 2002, without deploying express racial discrimination in admissions, Boalt's entering class enrolled 14 blacks and 36 Hispanics. Total underrepresented minority student enrollment at Boalt Hall now exceeds 1996 levels. Apparently the Law School cannot be counted on to be as resourceful. The Court is willfully blind to the very real experience in California and elsewhere, which raises the inference that institutions with "reputation[s] for excellence" rivaling the Law School's have satisfied their sense of mission without resorting to prohibited racial discrimination. . . .

. . . [N]o modern law school can claim ignorance of the poor performance of blacks, relatively speaking, on the Law School Admissions Test (LSAT). Nevertheless, law schools continue to use the test and then attempt to "correct" for black underperformance by using racial discrimination in admissions so as to obtain their aesthetic student body. The Law School's continued adherence to measures it knows produce racially skewed results is not entitled to deference by this Court. . . .

Having decided to use the LSAT, the Law School must accept the constitutional burdens that come with this decision. The Law School may freely continue to employ the LSAT and other allegedly merit-based standards in whatever fashion it likes. What the Equal Protection Clause forbids, but the Court today allows, is the use of these standards hand-in-hand with racial discrimination. An infinite variety of admissions methods are available to the Law School. Considering all of the radical thinking that has historically occurred at this country's universities, the Law School's intractable approach toward admissions is striking.

The Court will not even deign to make the Law School try other methods, however, preferring instead to grant a 25-year license to violate the Constitution. And the same Court that had the courage to order the desegregation of all public schools in the South now fears, on the basis of platitudes rather than principle, to force the Law School to abandon a decidedly imperfect admissions regime that provides the basis for racial discrimination.

. . . I believe what lies beneath the Court's decision today are the benighted notions that one can tell when racial discrimination benefits (rather than hurts) minority groups, and that racial discrimination is necessary to remedy general societal ills. This Court's precedents supposedly settled both issues, but clearly the majority still cannot commit to the principle that racial classifications are *per se* harmful and that almost no amount of benefit in the eye of the beholder can justify such classifications. . . .

The silence in this case is deafening to those of us who view higher education's purpose as imparting knowledge and skills to students, rather than a communal, rubber-stamp, credentialing process. The Law School is not looking for those students who, despite a lower LSAT score or undergraduate grade point average, will succeed in the study of law. The Law School seeks only a facade—it is sufficient that the class looks right, even if it does not perform right.

The Law School tantalizes unprepared students with the promise of a University of Michigan degree and all of the opportunities that it offers. These overmatched students take the bait, only to find that they cannot succeed in the cauldron of competition. . . . While these students may graduate with law degrees, there is no evidence that they have received a qualitatively better legal education (or become better lawyers) than if they had gone to a less "elite" law school for which they were better prepared. And the aestheticists will never address the real problems facing "underrepresented minorities," instead continuing their social experiments on other people's children.

. . . "These programs stamp minorities with a badge of inferiority and may cause them to develop dependencies or to adopt an attitude that they are 'entitled' to preferences" [*Adarand,* THOMAS, J., concurring in part and concurring in judgment].

It is uncontested that each year, the Law School admits a handful of blacks who would be admitted in the absence of racial discrimination. Who can differentiate between those who belong and those who do not? The majority of blacks are admitted to the Law School because of discrimination, and because of this policy all are tarred as undeserving. This problem of stigma does not depend on determinacy as to whether those stigmatized are actually the "beneficiaries" of racial discrimination. When blacks take positions in the highest places of government, industry, or academia, it is an open question today whether their skin color played a part in their advancement. The question itself is the stigma— because either racial discrimination did play a role, in which case the person may be deemed "otherwise unqualified," or it did not, in which case asking the question itself unfairly marks those blacks who would succeed without discrimination. . . .

For the immediate future . . . the majority has placed its *imprimatur* on a practice that can only weaken the principle of equality embodied in the Declaration of Independence and the Equal Protection Clause. "Our Constitution is color-blind, and neither knows nor tolerates classes among citizens." *Plessy v. Ferguson* (1896) (HARLAN, J., dissenting). It has been nearly 140 years since Frederick Douglass asked the intellectual ancestors of the Law School to "[d]o nothing with us!" and the Nation adopted the Fourteenth Amendment. Now we must wait another 25 years to see this principle of equality vindicated. I therefore respectfully dissent from the remainder of the Court's opinion and the judgment.

Grutter was an important victory for the supporters of affirmative action, especially in the area of higher education. The Court held that educational diversity constitutes a compelling state interest and that affirmative action programs, if properly tailored, are a constitutionally acceptable means of achieving the state's goals. Contrary to its findings in *Gratz,* the majority

concluded that the law school's admissions process was based on a flexible, individualized consideration of applications in which race was only one of several diversity factors taken into account. Consistent with Justice Powell's opinion in *Bakke,* race was a "plus" in the application process. Race did not automatically determine acceptance or rejection. As such, it met the majority's approval. The Court's ruling provides constitutionally valid guidelines for affirmative action programs that other colleges and universities can use, but only where state laws do not otherwise prohibit the use of racial and ethnic preferences.

Court observers have speculated that amicus curiae participation may have exerted significant influence on the outcome in *Grutter.* Seen as especially important were the positions taken by the military and major corporations such as General Motors and 3M. These interests, not usually advocates of liberal policies, spoke with powerful voices on the value of affirmative action programs, and O'Connor repeatedly quoted their positions in her opinion for the Court. Also important was the law school community, which expressed overwhelming support for the importance of diverse student bodies in the training of the nation's lawyers.

In spite of the Court's decision, a number of questions remain unanswered: Did the Court adequately distinguish between a valid "critical mass" and an unconstitutional "quota"? Is the Court's *Grutter* rationale applicable only to the university setting, or can it be extended to minority set-aside programs as well? Is there danger that a flexible, individualized consideration of applications might unconstitutionally place excessive emphasis on race, and, if so, how would we know if it occurred? Is Justice O'Connor's comment concerning a twenty-five-year constitutional limit on affirmative action programs an important part of this ruling or just tangential speculation? These and other questions undoubtedly mean that the legal battle over affirmative action is far from over and the appropriate legal standards are not yet permanently fixed *(see Box 13-7).*

Court observers inevitably began to speculate whether the justices would remain true to the principles laid out in *Grutter.* After all, the vote in *Grutter* was very fragile, with the outcome resting largely on Justice O'Connor's decision to side with her more liberal colleagues, a somewhat surprising vote given the hard lines she had taken against other affirmative

BOX 13-7 AFFIRMATIVE ACTION/MINORITY SET-ASIDE PRINCIPLES

Critics have faulted the Supreme Court's affirmative action and minority set-aside decisions for failing to develop a consistent and coherent set of legal principles. The unstable majorities that have controlled these cases surely have contributed to this result. Although the Court seems to have settled on strict scrutiny as the appropriate test to decide such cases, various aspects of a challenged affirmative action plan may have an important bearing on its validity. No absolutes exist, but certain characteristics make minority enhancement plans more acceptable.

An affirmative action or minority set-aside program is more likely to be found constitutional if it

1. is narrowly tailored to achieve a compelling government interest;

2. is enacted in response to clear and demonstrable acts of unconstitutional or illegal discrimination, or is intended to eliminate the continuing effects of that illegal discrimination;

3. is designed to assist only those groups who have been the victims of illegal discrimination;

4. is not based on racial, ethnic, or gender stereotypes, or presumes the inferiority of such groups;

5. avoids the use of quotas and does not absolutely bar any group from competing or participating;

6. is temporary, with clear indicators of plan termination when certain thresholds are met;

7. seeks to eliminate racial imbalance, not maintain racial balance;

8. is based on data from relevant labor pools or other appropriate statistical comparisons;

9. does not trammel the rights of the majority;

10. provides new benefits to minorities rather than taking already earned benefits away from the majority;

11. is imposed by a federal court as a remedy for demonstrated constitutional violations; and

12. is imposed where the government's interest cannot reasonably be attained through the use of alternative plans that are neutral with respect to race, sex, or ethnicity.

---

action programs in *Croson, Metro Broadcasting,* and *Adarand Constructors.*

The Court's future affirmative action policy became even less clear three years later when Justice O'Connor retired from the Court and was replaced by the more conservative Samuel Alito. To what extent would this change affect the Court's position on affirmative action programs?

Two subsequent decisions have signaled that the Court may be moving away from its liberal *Grutter* decision. The first came with the Court's decision in *Parents Involved in Community Schools v. Seattle School District No. 1* (2007) and its companion case *Meredith v. Jefferson County Board of Education* (2007). As you will recall from our discussion earlier in this chapter, in these cases a five-justice majority struck down the policies of two public school systems that took race into account in assigning individual students to specific public schools. The Court rejected the argument that the school boards were pursuing academic diversity, finding instead that the programs promoted racial balancing.

Perhaps more telling was the Court's decision in ***Ricci v. DeStefano*** (2009). This dispute began when the personnel department of the city of New Haven,

Connecticut, contracted with an outside company to develop a written and oral examination to be used to identify the most qualified candidates for promotion in the city fire department. In 2003 the department sought to fill by promotion several captain and lieutenant vacancies. Under the city's employment rules, the promotions had to be made from among the top three performers on the examination. Seventy-seven candidates took the examination for promotion to lieutenant (forty-three whites, nineteen blacks, and fifteen Hispanics). Based on the test results and the "top three" rule, ten firefighters qualified for immediate promotion consideration—all of them white. Forty-one firefighters competed for promotion to captain (twenty-five white, eight black, and eight Hispanic). Seven whites and two Hispanics performed sufficiently well to be considered for the available captain rank vacancies. Faced with this racially disproportionate outcome and fearing a potential Civil Rights Act lawsuit, the city, after considerable deliberation, decided not to certify the results. No firefighter was promoted.

One Hispanic and seventeen white firefighters who had passed the examination but were denied a chance

Frank Ricci, right, and his attorney, Karen Torre, stand outside the New Haven courthouse on June 29, 2009, following the U.S. Supreme Court's ruling that Ricci and other firefighters were unlawfully denied promotions when the city discarded results of employment examinations that would have led to racially disproportionate promotion outcomes.

at promotion filed suit alleging that by failing to certify the test results the city violated their rights under the Civil Rights Act and the equal protection clause of the Fourteenth Amendment. They charged that the city's decision was racially discriminatory. After the plaintiffs had prepared in good faith for the test and scored well on it, their examination scores were not accepted only because the city did not like the prospect of promoting so many non-minorities. The district court and the court of appeals upheld the city's actions, finding that the decision to cancel the test results was based on a desire to avoid litigation and a commitment to diversity. Because no promotions were made, the lower courts concluded, applicants of all races were treated equally.

On review the Supreme Court found that the plaintiff firefighters had suffered discrimination contrary to the commands of Title VII of the Civil Rights Act. The city's action was motivated by the fact that certifying the test results would have resulted in too many white firefighters and not enough minorities being promoted. Canceling the test results violated the Civil Rights Act as "disparate treatment" based on race. The city's defense (that certifying the results would have a racially disproportionate impact and invite a lawsuit from minority candidates) was insufficient to justify its action.

Having ruled in favor of the complaining firefighters on the Civil Rights Act question, the justices found no reason to address the constitutional issue of a possible equal protection clause violation. This prompted Justice Scalia to comment that the Court was only "postpon[ing] the evil day" on which the Court will have to confront the question of inconsistencies between the Civil Rights Act and the Fourteenth Amendment.

Ricci was decided by a 5–4 vote. The majority consisted of the three remaining dissenters in *Grutter* (Kennedy, Scalia, and Thomas) along with the recently appointed Chief Justice Roberts and Justice Alito. All four dissenters (Breyer, Ginsburg, Souter, Stevens) had formed the majority in *Grutter* (along with the departed Justice O'Connor). Although *Ricci* did not address constitutional issues, the decision suggests that a majority of the justices may no longer fully subscribe to the *Grutter* ruling. Opponents of affirmative action have recognized this change in the ideological balance of the Court and the opportunities it may present them. Consequently, a number of legal challenges to affirmative action practices have been filed. The Court has already agreed to hear one case involving an attack on the affirmative action policies of the University of Texas. Other such appeals are likely to follow. What this means for future affirmative action disputes remains to be seen. For now we can conclude that the situation is highly fluid.

CONTEMPORARY DEVELOPMENTS IN DISCRIMINATION LAW

The continuing debate over affirmative action supports this point: discrimination issues continue to evolve, as they have since the Fourteenth Amendment was ratified in 1868. Many discrimination disputes involve new variations on old themes. The battle continues over which of the competing equal protection standards should be used to decide claims of gender and sexual orientation discrimination. Questions continue to arise regarding equitable treatment of the poor with respect to education and other government services. And we are a long way from resolving all of the questions surrounding illegal immigration.

Other issues are new, brought to the courts by groups that have only recently reached a critical stage in their numbers and organizational strength. Some groups, once silent, are now poised to make their demands. The disabled are increasingly politicized and have pushed for reforms from both the legislative and judicial branches. As members of the post–World War II baby boom generation enter their senior years, age discrimination complaints are likely to explode. Claims of discrimination based on physical disability, mental handicap, and diseases such as cancer, AIDS, alcoholism, and drug addiction have become common and promise to escalate in number.

In addition, new conditions give rise to new issues. Following the September 2001 terrorist attacks, many called for restrictions to be placed on those entering the United States from Islamic nations. Even American citizens with Middle Eastern origins were considered suspect. Large segments of the citizenry supported applying racial profiling to Muslims in the United States as an antiterrorism measure: old issues of discrimination based on race and national origin had become relevant to a new segment of the population.

In other words, issue evolution characterizes the history of discrimination law. Americans frequently rethink concepts of equality and fair treatment, sometimes concluding that previously acceptable practices have discriminatory effects. Fluctuations in economic and political power alter the methods used to pursue equality demands. As such changes occur, the nature of the discrimination issues brought to the courts also changes. We see no evidence that this process will stop. Rather, it is inevitable that the Supreme Court's docket will include appeals asking the justices to consider new questions that arise from the changing sociopolitical environment.

The evolution of discrimination law is further affected by the ideological positions of the men and women who occupy the federal judiciary. During a single term, a president can use the judicial appointment power to change significantly the ideological makeup of the lower federal courts. A president who serves two terms almost always has the opportunity to appoint more than half of the sitting federal judges. As the White House moves from the control of one political party to another, the federal judiciary may shift from being liberal to conservative, or vice versa, on discrimination and other controversial issues. At the Supreme Court level, votes on important discrimination cases are often very close. In the area of affirmative action, for example, the most important decisions (*Bakke, Adarand, Grutter,* and *Ricci*) were decided by a single vote. The pattern of retirements and appointments to the Court therefore takes on special significance. In this ideologically charged environment, it is inevitable that a nomination to the nation's highest court will become the centerpiece for an intense partisan battle.

ANNOTATED READINGS

A rich and interesting literature focuses on unconstitutional discrimination and the history of civil rights in the United States. Some of these works trace the history of the struggle for equal rights, such as Terry H. Anderson, *The Pursuit of Fairness: A History of Affirmative Action* (New York: Oxford University Press, 2004); Deborah Hellman, *When Is Discrimination Wrong?* (Cambridge, MA: Harvard University Press, 2008); Michael J. Klarman, *From Jim Crow to Civil Rights: The Supreme Court and the Struggle for Racial Equality* (New York: Oxford University Press, 2004); Richard Kluger, *Simple Justice,* rev. ed. (New York: Knopf, 2004); and Alexander Tsesis, *We Shall Overcome: A History of Civil Rights and the Law* (New Haven, CT: Yale University Press, 2008).

Other studies examine particular areas of civil rights law, including Susan Gluck Mezey, *Elusive Equality: Women's Rights, Public Policy, and the Law* (Boulder, CO: Lynne Rienner, 2003); Susan Gluck Mezey, *Gay Families and the Courts* (Lanham, MD: Rowman

& Littlefield, 2009); John S. Park, *Elusive Citizenship: Immigration, Asian Americans, and the Paradox of Civil Rights* (New York: New York University Press, 2004); Daniel R. Pinello, *Gay Rights and American Law* (New York: Cambridge University Press, 2003); Girardeau A. Spann, *Race against the Court: The Supreme Court and Minorities in Contemporary America* (New York: New York University Press, 1993); Mark Strasser, *Same-Sex Unions across the United States* (Durham, NC: Carolina Academic Press, 2011); and John H. Vinzant, *The Supreme Court's Role in American Indian Policy* (El Paso, TX: LFB Scholarly Publishing, 2009).

A large number of other works provide in-depth studies of landmark Supreme Court decisions. Among them are Howard Ball, *The Bakke Case: Race, Education, and Affirmative Action* (Lawrence: University Press of Kansas, 2000); Richard C. Cortner, *Civil Rights and Public Accommodations: The Heart of Atlanta and McClung Cases* (Lawrence: University Press of Kansas, 2001); Bernard Schwartz, *Swann's Way: The School Busing Case and the Supreme Court* (New York: Oxford University Press, 1986); Paul A. Sracic, *San Antonio v. Rodriguez and the Pursuit of Equal Education: The Debate over Discrimination and School Funding* (Lawrence: University Press of Kansas, 2006); and Philippa Strum, *Women in the Barracks: The VMI Case and Equal Rights* (Lawrence: University Press of Kansas, 2002).

14 Voting and Representation

F OR ANY GOVERNMENT built on a foundation of popular sovereignty, voting and representation are of critical importance. Through these mechanisms, the people express their political will and ultimately control the institutions of government. Representative democracy can function properly only when the citizenry has full rights to regular and meaningful elections and when the system is structured so that public officials act on behalf of their constituents. If any segment of society is denied the right to vote or is deprived of legitimate representation, the ideals of a republican form of government are not completely realized. Because elections and representation are the primary links between the people and their government, it is not surprising that the history of the United States is replete with struggles over rights of political participation. At both the state and federal levels, political battles have been fought over legislative initiatives and proposed constitutional amendments that affect voting rights. Some of these disputes ultimately came to the Supreme Court for decisions on the exercise of the franchise and the allocation of representation.

ELECTIONS AND THE COURT

Political questions are generally considered outside the judiciary's sphere of authority. In the area of elections and voting rights, however, the political and the legal often overlap, making the boundaries of judicial authority difficult to discern. Undoubtedly, the judiciary is capable of resolving disputes over voting rights deprivations or claims that constitutional or statutory election procedures were not properly followed. Questions concerning which candidate is best suited for public office or which candidate won a particular election, however, are not within the jurisdiction of the courts; instead, such questions are to be settled by the political process. The Constitution recognizes this fact. Article I, Section 5, for example, stipulates that "Each House [of Congress] shall be the Judge of the Elections, Returns, and Qualifications of its own Members." But on occasion the courts are asked to resolve voting rights claims that may determine the outcomes of particular elections. Under such circumstances, the issue of proper judicial behavior is often raised. Should the courts become involved in this kind of dispute, or should they defer to the political branches?

The propriety of the Supreme Court entering the electoral process was never more vigorously debated than during the presidential election of 2000, when the justices decided to accept a challenge to vote-counting procedures in Florida. With the votes in every other state tabulated, the election was deadlocked between Vice President Al Gore of Tennessee and Governor George W. Bush of Texas. The candidate who received Florida's contested electoral votes would be the winner of the presidency. The Supreme Court's decision in *Bush v. Gore* (2000) had a dramatic effect on the election outcome.

Bush v. Gore

531 U.S. 98 (2000)
http://laws.findlaw.com/US/531/98.html
Oral arguments are available at http://www.oyez.org.
Vote: 5 (Kennedy, O'Connor, Rehnquist, Scalia, Thomas)
4 (Breyer, Ginsburg, Souter, Stevens)

OPINION OF THE COURT: Per curiam
CONCURRING OPINION: Rehnquist
DISSENTING OPINIONS: Breyer, Ginsburg, Souter, Stevens

FACTS:

The presidential election of November 7, 2000, was one of the closest races in American history. On election night it became clear that the battle between Republican Governor Bush and Democratic Vice President Gore for the 270 electoral votes necessary for victory would be decided by the outcome in Florida.

The first vote counts in Florida gave Governor Bush a lead of some 1,780 votes out of 6 million cast. This narrow margin triggered an automatic machine recount held on November 10. The results gave Bush a victory, but the margin had slipped to a scant 250 votes, with absentee overseas ballots still to be counted. By this time, charges and countercharges of voting irregularities had led to lawsuits and political protests. As the various issues sorted themselves out over the ensuing days, the outcome of the election appeared to hinge on one major issue: large numbers of undercounted ballots in a select number of traditionally Democratic counties. Undercounted ballots were those for which vote-counting machines did not register a presidential preference. In many cases such undercounting was the result of a failure by the voter to perforate the computer-read punch card ballot. In other cases, machine malfunction may have been the cause. Gore supporters demanded a hand recount of the undercounted ballots.

Three statutory deadlines imposed obstacles for the labor-intensive and time-consuming manual recounts. First, Florida law directed the secretary of state to certify the election results by November 18. Second, federal law provided that if all controversies and contests over a state's electors were resolved by December 12, the state's slate would be considered conclusive and beyond challenge (the so-called safe-harbor provision). And third, federal law set December 18 as the date the electors would cast their ballots.

As the manual recounts proceeded, it became clear that the process would not be completed prior to the November 18 deadline for certification. Florida's Republican secretary of state, Katherine Harris, announced her intention to certify the vote on November 18 regardless of the ongoing recounts. Gore forces went to court to block Harris from doing so. A unanimous Florida Supreme Court, emphasizing that every cast vote should be counted, ruled that the recounts should continue and extended the certification date to November 26. Believing the Florida court had exceeded its authority, Bush's lawyers appealed this decision to the U.S. Supreme Court. On December 4 the justices set aside the Florida court's certification extension and asked the court to explain the reasoning behind its decision (*Bush v. Palm Beach Canvassing Board,* 2000). In the meantime, on November 26 Secretary Harris certified that George W. Bush had won the state by 537 votes.

Four days after the U.S. Supreme Court's decision, the Florida high court, in response to an appeal by Vice President Gore, ordered a new statewide manual recount of all undervotes to begin immediately. The recounts were to be conducted by local officials guided only by the instruction to determine voter intent on each ballot. Governor Bush appealed this decision to the U.S. Supreme Court. On December 9 the justices scheduled the case for oral argument and ordered the recounts to stop pending a final decision.

A primary question facing the Court was this: Did the Florida Supreme Court violate the equal protection clause of the Fourteenth Amendment when it ordered a recount to take place without setting a single uniform standard for determining voter intent? Also of concern was whether the Florida Supreme Court's order violated federal law by altering previously established vote count procedures.

A badly divided Supreme Court issued its ruling on December 12. The per curiam opinion for the majority focuses on the equal protection claim. The concurring and dissenting opinions include a wide range of views on the issues presented and debate what remedies should be imposed for any constitutional or statutory violations found.

ARGUMENTS:

For the petitioners, George W. Bush and Richard Cheney:

- The procedures used by the Florida Supreme Court conflict with state legislation on resolution of election disputes. Therefore, the court's orders violate the U.S. Constitution (Article II, Section 2), which gives state legislatures exclusive authority over the selection of presidential electors.

Theresa LePore, Palm Beach County election supervisor, examines a ballot during the manual recount following the disputed 2000 presidential election in Florida.

- The procedures used by the court also conflict with a federal "safe harbor" provision (3 U.S.C. sec. 5) requiring that election disputes be settled according to procedures established prior to the election.
- A lack of uniform standards for recounting ballots means that identical ballots cast in different counties will be counted differently. This violates voters' Fourteenth Amendment equal protection rights.
- The standardless recounting of ballots violates the Fourteenth Amendment's due process clause, which requires clear, consistent, and prospective rules.

For the respondents, Albert Gore Jr., et al.:

- The decision of the state supreme court does not violate Article II, Section 2, of the Constitution because it is presumed that any law passed by a state legislature is subject to judicial interpretation and review.
- The state court's recount orders do not change state law and therefore are not in conflict with the "safe

harbor" provision. Even so, although compliance has certain benefits, states are not required to adhere to all the components of the "safe harbor" provision.

- The state supreme court's order to use an "intent of the voter" standard for the recount is consistent with state law and sufficiently clear and uniform to meet equal protection and due process requirements.

PER CURIAM.

The closeness of this election, and the multitude of legal challenges which have followed in its wake, have brought into sharp focus a common, if heretofore unnoticed, phenomenon. Nationwide statistics reveal that an estimated 2% of ballots cast do not register a vote for President for whatever reason, including deliberately choosing no candidate at all or some voter error, such as voting for two candidates or insufficiently marking a ballot. In certifying election results, the votes eligible for inclusion in the certification are the votes meeting the properly established legal requirements.

This case has shown that punch card balloting machines can produce an unfortunate number of ballots which are not punched in a clean, complete way by the voter. After the current counting, it is likely legislative bodies nationwide will examine ways to improve the mechanisms and machinery for voting.

The individual citizen has no federal constitutional right to vote for electors for the President of the United States unless and until the state legislature chooses a statewide election as the means to implement its power to appoint members of the Electoral College. U.S. Const., Art. II, §1. This is the source for the statement in *McPherson v. Blacker* (1892) that the State legislature's power to select the manner for appointing electors is plenary; it may, if it so chooses, select the electors itself, which indeed was the manner used by State legislatures in several States for many years after the Framing of our Constitution. History has now favored the voter, and in each of the several States the citizens themselves vote for Presidential electors. When the state legislature vests the right to vote for President in its people, the right to vote as the legislature has prescribed is fundamental; and one source of its fundamental nature lies in the equal weight accorded to each vote and the equal dignity owed to each voter. The State, of course, after granting the franchise in the special context of Article II, can take back the power to appoint electors.

The right to vote is protected in more than the initial allocation of the franchise. Equal protection applies as well to the manner of its exercise. Having once granted the right to vote on equal terms, the State may not, by later arbitrary and disparate treatment, value one person's vote over that of another. . . .

There is no difference between the two sides of the present controversy on these basic propositions. Respondents say that the very purpose of vindicating the right to vote justifies the recount procedures now at issue. The question before us, however, is whether the recount procedures the Florida Supreme Court has adopted are consistent with its obligation to avoid arbitrary and disparate treatment of the members of its electorate.

Much of the controversy seems to revolve around ballot cards designed to be perforated by a stylus but which, either through error or deliberate omission, have not been perforated with sufficient precision for a machine to count them. In some cases a piece of the card—a chad—is hanging, say by two corners. In other cases there is no separation at all, just an indentation.

The Florida Supreme Court has ordered that the intent of the voter be discerned from such ballots. For purposes of resolving the equal protection challenge, it is not necessary to decide whether the Florida Supreme Court had the authority under the legislative scheme for resolving election disputes to define what a legal vote is and to mandate a manual recount implementing that definition. The recount mechanisms implemented in response to the decisions of the Florida Supreme Court do not satisfy the minimum requirement for non-arbitrary treatment of voters necessary to secure the fundamental right. Florida's basic command for the count of legally cast votes is to consider the "intent of the voter." This is unobjectionable as an abstract proposition and a starting principle. The problem inheres in the absence of specific standards to ensure its equal application. The formulation of uniform rules to determine intent based on these recurring circumstances is practicable and, we conclude, necessary.

The law does not refrain from searching for the intent of the actor in a multitude of circumstances; and in some cases the general command to ascertain intent is not susceptible to much further refinement. In this instance, however, the question is . . . how to interpret the marks or holes or scratches on an inanimate object, a piece of cardboard or paper which, it is said, might not have registered as a vote during the machine count. The fact-finder confronts a thing, not a person. The search for intent can be confined by specific rules designed to ensure uniform treatment.

The want of those rules here has led to unequal evaluation of ballots in various respects. As seems to have been acknowledged at oral argument, the standards for accepting or rejecting contested ballots might vary not only from county to county but indeed within a single county from one recount team to another.

The record provides some examples. A monitor in Miami-Dade County testified at trial that he observed that three members of the county canvassing board applied different standards in defining a legal vote. And testimony at trial also revealed that at least one county changed its evaluative standards during the counting process. Palm Beach County, for example, began the process with a 1990 guideline which precluded counting completely attached chads, switched to a rule that considered a vote to be legal if any light could be seen through a chad, changed back to the 1990 rule, and then abandoned any pretense of a *per se* rule, only to have a court order that the county consider dimpled chads legal. This is not a process with sufficient guarantees of equal treatment. . . .

The State Supreme Court ratified this uneven treatment. It mandated that the recount totals from two counties, Miami-Dade and Palm Beach, be included in the certified total. The court also appeared to hold *sub silentio* that the recount totals from Broward County, which were not completed until after the original November 14 certification by the Secretary of State, were to be considered part of the new certified vote totals even though the county certification was not contested by Vice President Gore. Yet each of the counties used varying standards to determine what was a legal vote. Broward County used a more forgiving standard than Palm Beach County, and uncovered almost three times as many new votes, a result markedly disproportionate to the difference in population between the counties.

In addition, the recounts in these three counties were not limited to so-called undervotes but extended to all of the ballots. The distinction has real consequences. A manual recount of all ballots identifies not only those ballots which show no vote but also those which contain more than one, the so-called overvotes. Neither category will be counted by the machine. This is not a trivial concern. At oral argument, respondents estimated there are as many as 110,000 overvotes statewide. As a result, the citizen whose ballot was not read by a machine because he failed to vote for a candidate in a way readable by a machine may still have his vote counted in a manual recount; on the other hand, the citizen who marks two candidates in a way discernable by the machine will not have the same opportunity to have his vote count, even if a manual examination of the ballot would reveal the requisite indicia of intent. Furthermore, the citizen who marks two candidates, only one of which is discernable by the machine, will have his vote counted even though it should have been read as an invalid ballot. The State Supreme Court's inclusion of vote counts based on these variant standards exemplifies concerns with the remedial processes that were under way.

That brings the analysis to yet a further equal protection problem. The votes certified by the court included a partial total from one county, Miami-Dade. The Florida Supreme Court's decision thus gives no assurance that the recounts included in a final certification must be complete. Indeed, it is respondent's submission that it would be consistent with the rules of the recount procedures to include whatever partial counts are done by the time of final certification, and we interpret the Florida Supreme Court's decision to permit this. This accommodation no doubt results from the truncated contest period established by the Florida Supreme Court in *Bush I,* at respondents' own urging. The press of time does not diminish the constitutional concern. A desire for speed is not a general excuse for ignoring equal protection guarantees.

In addition to these difficulties the actual process by which the votes were to be counted under the Florida Supreme Court's decision raises further concerns. That order did not specify who would recount the ballots. The county canvassing boards were forced to pull together ad hoc teams comprised of judges from various Circuits who had no previous training in handling and interpreting ballots. Furthermore, while others were permitted to observe, they were prohibited from objecting during the recount.

The recount process, in its features here described, is inconsistent with the minimum procedures necessary to protect the fundamental right of each voter in the special instance of a statewide recount under the authority of a single state judicial officer. Our consideration is limited to the present circumstances, for the problem of equal protection in election processes generally presents many complexities.

The question before the Court is not whether local entities, in the exercise of their expertise, may develop different systems for implementing elections. Instead, we are presented with a situation where a state court with the power to assure uniformity has ordered a statewide recount with minimal procedural safeguards. When

a court orders a statewide remedy, there must be at least some assurance that the rudimentary requirements of equal treatment and fundamental fairness are satisfied.

Given the Court's assessment that the recount process underway was probably being conducted in an unconstitutional manner, the Court stayed the order directing the recount so it could hear this case and render an expedited decision. The contest provision, as it was mandated by the State Supreme Court, is not well calculated to sustain the confidence that all citizens must have in the outcome of elections. The State has not shown that its procedures include the necessary safeguards. The problem, for instance, of the estimated 110,000 overvotes has not been addressed. . . .

Upon due consideration of the difficulties identified to this point, it is obvious that the recount cannot be conducted in compliance with the requirements of equal protection and due process without substantial additional work. It would require not only the adoption (after opportunity for argument) of adequate statewide standards for determining what is a legal vote, and practicable procedures to implement them, but also orderly judicial review of any disputed matters that might arise. In addition, the Secretary of State has advised that the recount of only a portion of the ballots requires that the vote tabulation equipment be used to screen out undervotes, a function for which the machines were not designed. If a recount of overvotes were also required, perhaps even a second screening would be necessary. Use of the equipment for this purpose, and any new software developed for it, would have to be evaluated for accuracy by the Secretary of State, as required by [Florida law].

The Supreme Court of Florida has said that the legislature intended the State's electors to "participat[e] fully in the federal electoral process," as provided in 3 U.S.C. §5. That statute, in turn, requires that any controversy or contest that is designed to lead to a conclusive selection of electors be completed by December 12. That date is upon us, and there is no recount procedure in place under the State Supreme Court's order that comports with minimal constitutional standards. Because it is evident that any recount seeking to meet the December 12 date will be unconstitutional for the reasons we have discussed, we reverse the judgment of the Supreme Court of Florida ordering a recount to proceed.

Seven Justices of the Court agree that there are constitutional problems with the recount ordered by the Florida Supreme Court that demand a remedy. The only disagreement is as to the remedy. Because the Florida Supreme

Court has said that the Florida Legislature intended to obtain the safe-harbor benefits of 3 U.S.C. §5, JUSTICE BREYER's proposed remedy—remanding to the Florida Supreme Court for its ordering of a constitutionally proper contest until December 18—contemplates action in violation of the Florida election code, and hence could not be part of an "appropriate" order authorized by [Florida law].

None are more conscious of the vital limits on judicial authority than are the members of this Court, and none stand more in admiration of the Constitution's design to leave the selection of the President to the people, through their legislatures, and to the political sphere. When contending parties invoke the process of the courts, however, it becomes our unsought responsibility to resolve the federal and constitutional issues the judicial system has been forced to confront.

The judgment of the Supreme Court of Florida is reversed, and the case is remanded for further proceedings not inconsistent with this opinion. . . .

CHIEF JUSTICE REHNQUIST, with whom JUSTICE SCALIA and JUSTICE THOMAS join, concurring.

We join the *per curiam* opinion. . . .

We deal here not with an ordinary election, but with an election for the President of the United States. . . .

In most cases, comity and respect for federalism compel us to defer to the decisions of state courts on issues of state law. . . . But there are a few exceptional cases in which the Constitution imposes a duty or confers a power on a particular branch of a State's government. This is one of them. Article II, §1, cl. 2, provides that "[e]ach State shall appoint, in such Manner as the *Legislature* thereof may direct," electors for President and Vice President. (Emphasis added.) Thus, the text of the election law itself, and not just its interpretation by the courts of the States, takes on independent significance. . . .

In Florida, the legislature has chosen to hold statewide elections to appoint the State's 25 electors. Importantly, the legislature has delegated the authority to run the elections and to oversee election disputes to the Secretary of State (Secretary) and to state circuit courts. Isolated sections of the code may well admit of more than one interpretation, but the general coherence of the legislative scheme may not be altered by judicial interpretation so as to wholly change the statutorily provided apportionment of responsibility among these various bodies. In any election but a Presidential election, the Florida Supreme Court can give as little or as much deference to Florida's executives as it chooses, so far as Article II is concerned, and this Court will have no cause

to question the court's actions. But, with respect to a Presidential election, the court must be both mindful of the legislature's role under Article II in choosing the manner of appointing electors and deferential to those bodies expressly empowered by the legislature to carry out its constitutional mandate. . . .

This inquiry does not imply a disrespect for state *courts* but rather a respect for the constitutionally prescribed role of state *legislatures.* To attach definitive weight to the pronouncement of a state court, when the very question at issue is whether the court has actually departed from the statutory meaning, would be to abdicate our responsibility to enforce the explicit requirements of Article II.

JUSTICE STEVENS, with whom JUSTICE GINSBURG and JUSTICE BREYER join, dissenting.

In the interest of finality . . . the majority effectively orders the disenfranchisement of an unknown number of voters whose ballots reveal their intent—and are therefore legal votes under state law—but were for some reason rejected by ballot-counting machines. It does so on the basis of the deadlines set forth in Title 3 of the United States Code. But . . . those provisions merely provide rules of decision for Congress to follow when selecting among conflicting slates of electors. They do not prohibit a State from counting what the majority concedes to be legal votes until a bona fide winner is determined. . . . Thus, nothing prevents the majority, even if it properly found an equal protection violation, from ordering relief appropriate to remedy that violation without depriving Florida voters of their right to have their votes counted. As the majority notes, "[a] desire for speed is not a general excuse for ignoring equal protection guarantees." . . .

What must underlie petitioners' entire federal assault on the Florida election procedures is an unstated lack of confidence in the impartiality and capacity of the state judges who would make the critical decisions if the vote count were to proceed. Otherwise, their position is wholly without merit. The endorsement of that position by the majority of this Court can only lend credence to the most cynical appraisal of the work of judges throughout the land. It is confidence in the men and women who administer the judicial system that is the true backbone of the rule of law. Time will one day heal the wound to that confidence that will be inflicted by today's decision. One thing, however, is certain. Although we may never know with complete certainty the identity of the winner of this year's Presidential election, the identity of the loser is perfectly clear. It is the Nation's confidence in the judge as an impartial guardian of the rule of law.

I respectfully dissent.

JUSTICE SOUTER, with whom JUSTICE BREYER joins and with whom JUSTICE STEVENS and JUSTICE GINSBURG join with regard to all but [the paragraphs dealing with the equal protection issue], dissenting.

The Court should not have reviewed either *Bush v. Palm Beach County Canvassing Bd.* or this case, and should not have stopped Florida's attempt to recount all under-vote ballots by issuing a stay of the Florida Supreme Court's orders during the period of this review. If this Court had allowed the State to follow the course indicated by the opinions of its own Supreme Court, it is entirely possible that there would ultimately have been no issue requiring our review, and political tension could have worked itself out in the Congress. . . . The case being before us, however, its resolution by the majority is another erroneous decision. . . .

[Only the issue of whether the manner of interpreting markings on disputed ballots violates equal protection presents] a meritorious argument for relief, as this Court's *Per Curiam* opinion recognizes. It is an issue that might well have been dealt with adequately by the Florida courts if the state proceedings had not been interrupted, and if not disposed of at the state level it could have been considered by the Congress in any electoral vote dispute. But because the course of state proceedings has been interrupted, time is short, and the issue is before us, I think it sensible for the Court to address it.

Petitioners have raised an equal protection claim, in the charge that unjustifiably disparate standards are applied in different electoral jurisdictions to otherwise identical facts. It is true that the Equal Protection Clause does not forbid the use of a variety of voting mechanisms within a jurisdiction, even though different mechanisms will have different levels of effectiveness in recording voters' intentions; local variety can be justified by concerns about cost, the potential value of innovation, and so on. But evidence in the record here suggests that a different order of disparity obtains under rules for determining a voter's intent that have been applied (and could continue to be applied) to identical types of ballots used in identical brands of machines and exhibiting identical physical characteristics (such as "hanging" or "dimpled" chads). I can conceive of no legitimate state interest served by these differing treatments of the expressions of voters' fundamental rights. The differences appear wholly arbitrary.

In deciding what to do about this, we should take account of the fact that electoral votes are due to be cast in six days. I would therefore remand the case to the courts of Florida with instructions to establish uniform standards for evaluating the several types of ballots that have prompted differing treatments, to be applied within and among counties when passing on such identical ballots in any further recounting (or successive recounting) that the courts might order.

Unlike the majority, I see no warrant for this Court to assume that Florida could not possibly comply with this requirement before the date set for the meeting of electors, December 18. . . . To recount these [disputed votes] manually would be a tall order, but before this Court stayed the effort to do that the courts of Florida were ready to do their best to get that job done. There is no justification for denying the State the opportunity to try to count all disputed ballots now.

I respectfully dissent.

JUSTICE GINSBURG, with whom JUSTICE STEVENS joins, and with whom JUSTICE SOUTER and JUSTICE BREYER join [except as to the portion of the opinion dealing with the equal protection claim], dissenting.

I agree with JUSTICE STEVENS that petitioners have not presented a substantial equal protection claim. Ideally, perfection would be the appropriate standard for judging the recount. But we live in an imperfect world, one in which thousands of votes have not been counted. I cannot agree that the recount adopted by the Florida court, flawed as it may be, would yield a result any less fair or precise than the certification that preceded that recount.

Even if there were an equal protection violation, I would agree with JUSTICE STEVENS, JUSTICE SOUTER, and JUSTICE BREYER that the Court's concern about "the December 12 deadline," is misplaced. . . .

The Court assumes that time will not permit "orderly judicial review of any disputed matters that might arise." But no one has doubted the good faith and diligence with which Florida election officials, attorneys for all sides of this controversy, and the courts of law have performed their duties. Notably, the Florida Supreme Court has produced two substantial opinions within 29 hours of oral argument. In sum, the Court's conclusion that a constitutionally adequate recount is impractical is a prophecy the Court's own judgment will not allow to be tested. Such an untested prophecy should not decide the Presidency of the United States.

I dissent.

JUSTICE BREYER, with whom JUSTICE STEVENS and JUSTICE GINSBURG join . . . and with whom JUSTICE SOUTER joins . . . dissenting.

The Court was wrong to take this case. It was wrong to grant a stay. It should now vacate that stay and permit the Florida Supreme Court to decide whether the recount should resume.

The political implications of this case for the country are momentous. But the federal legal questions presented, with one exception, are insubstantial. . . .

. . . [T]here is no justification for the majority's remedy, which is simply to reverse the lower court and halt the recount entirely. An appropriate remedy would be, instead, to remand this case with instructions that, even at this late date, would permit the Florida Supreme Court to require recounting *all* undercounted votes in Florida, including those from Broward, Volusia, Palm Beach, and Miami-Dade Counties, whether or not previously recounted prior to the end of the protest period, and to do so in accordance with a single-uniform standard. . . .

I respectfully dissent.

The Court's decision in *Bush v. Gore* was the final chapter in the presidential election controversy of 2000 *(see Box 14-1)*. By stopping the Florida recount, the Court removed Vice President Gore's last hope of capturing the state's twenty-five electoral votes

BOX 14-1   AFTERMATH . . . *BUSH V. GORE*

The announcement of the Supreme Court's decision in *Bush v. Gore* (2000) effectively ended the 2000 presidential election campaign. On December 13, 2000, the day after the justices ruled, Vice President Al Gore announced that he was ending his campaign: "I accept the finality of this outcome. . . . And tonight, for the sake of our unity as a people and the strength of our democracy, I offer my concession." Florida officials quickly certified the state's twenty-five electoral votes for Texas governor George W. Bush.

Florida's electoral votes gave Bush a total of 271, just one more than needed to become the forty-third president of the United States. Although Bush had won the Electoral College, he became only the fourth president in U.S. history to win office while losing the popular vote to his chief opponent. Vice President Gore captured 48.39 percent of the popular vote, as opposed to Governor Bush's 47.88 percent. Before Bush only John Quincy Adams in 1824, Rutherford B. Hayes in 1876, and Benjamin Harrison in 1888 had been elected president without leading in the popular vote count.

Because of the voting controversies in Florida, many states revised their election laws and upgraded voting equipment to avoid similar problems in future elections. The two Florida officials at the center of the controversy, Governor Jeb Bush, the president-elect's brother, and Secretary of State Katherine Harris, continued their political careers. Jeb Bush was reelected governor of Florida in 2002, and Harris won a congressional seat that same year. Theodore Olson, the lawyer who successfully argued George Bush's case before the Supreme Court, was appointed solicitor general of the United States by the new president.

Gore seriously considered undertaking a rematch against President Bush in the 2004 election, but in late 2002 he announced that he would not be a candidate for his party's nomination. He instead focused his efforts on environmental policy. *An Inconvenient Truth*, a film about global warming that Gore wrote and narrated, won the 2006 Academy Award for Best Documentary. In 2007 Gore received the Nobel Peace Prize for his efforts to combat global climate change. George Bush was reelected to the presidency in 2004.

Public opinion polls taken after the Court's ruling showed that a large majority of Americans accepted Bush as the legitimate president, and, contrary to many predictions, the polls failed to find any appreciable decline in public support for the Supreme Court as the result of its incursion into the 2000 presidential election. For example, a Harris Poll taken in 2000 before the election found that 34 percent of the American people had "great confidence" in the Supreme Court. Harris repeated the poll in January 2001, shortly after *Bush v. Gore*, and discovered virtually no change: 35 percent of the respondents expressed "great confidence" in the Court. Two years later the figure again was 34 percent.[1]

---

[1] A summary of polling data on the public's confidence in the Supreme Court can be found in Lee Epstein, Jeffrey A. Segal, Harold J. Spaeth, and Thomas G. Walker, *The Supreme Court Compendium: Data, Decisions, and Developments*, 5th ed. (Washington, DC: CQ Press, 2012), Table 8-29.

and guaranteed that Governor Bush would become the next president. Although much of the nation was happy to see the election finally resolved, the Court's action caused intense debate in political and academic circles. Not only was there a question of whether the Supreme Court should have heard the case in the first place, but also many believed that the justices' votes were excessively influenced by their own political preferences. The five-justice majority ruling in favor of Bush (Rehnquist, Kennedy, O'Connor, Scalia, and Thomas) was composed only of Republicans, and the Court's sole Democrats (Ginsburg and Breyer) favored Gore's position.

VOTING RIGHTS

When the framers met in Philadelphia in 1787, the thirteen states already had election systems, with their own voter qualification requirements and procedures for selecting state and local officials. By European standards of that time, the states were quite liberal in extending the right to vote.[1] Suffrage was far from universal, however. Ballot access generally was granted only to free adult males, and in several states only to those men who owned sufficient property. Women, slaves, Indians, minors, and the poor could not vote. Some states prohibited Jews and Catholics from voting.

With state systems in place, the framers saw no reason to create a separate set of qualifications for participating in federal elections. Because there was little uniformity from state to state and qualifications often changed, the addition of a new body of federal voting requirements could cause conflict. Moreover, under the Constitution, only one agency of the new national government, the House of Representatives, was to be elected directly by the people, another reason the federal government need not develop its own voter rolls. The Constitution therefore left voting qualifications to the states. Specifically, in Article I, Section 2, the Constitution says with respect to House elections that "the Electors in each State shall have the Qualifications requisite for Electors of the most numerous Branch of the State Legislature." If citizens were qualified to cast ballots in their states' legislative elections, they were also qualified to vote in

congressional elections. The authority of the states to set voting rights policy began to change after the Civil War, when the power to regulate elections began steadily shifting toward the federal government.

Ratification of four constitutional amendments substantially limited the states' authority to restrict the right to vote. The first was the Fifteenth Amendment in 1870. Part of the Reconstruction legislation initiated by the Radical Republicans after the Civil War, the Fifteenth Amendment removed from the states the power to deny voting rights on the basis of race, color, or previous condition of servitude. It prohibits such discrimination by either the federal government or the states, but the obvious target was the southern states. Most members of the Reconstruction Congress reasoned that unless some action was taken to protect the political rights of the newly freed slaves, the majority white southerners would reinstitute measures to deny black citizens full participation.

Fifty years later the Constitution was again amended to expand the electorate. The Nineteenth Amendment, ratified in 1920, stipulated that the right to vote could not be denied on account of sex. Its acceptance represented decades of effort by supporters of female suffrage. Although some states had already modified their laws to allow women to vote, a change in the Constitution was necessary to extend the right uniformly across the nation.

The third voter qualification amendment went into effect in 1964. The Twenty-fourth Amendment denied the federal government and the states the power to impose a poll tax as a voter qualification for federal elections. The levying of a tax on the right to vote was a common practice in the South and was identified by Congress as one of many tactics used to keep African Americans from voting, and thereby circumventing the clear intent of the Fifteenth Amendment.

In 1971 the last of the voting rights amendments, the Twenty-sixth, was ratified. It set eighteen years as the minimum voting age for all state and federal elections. Before 1971 individual states determined the minimum voting age, which ranged from eighteen to twenty-one. Earlier, Congress had attempted to impose the eighteen-year minimum through legislation, but in *Oregon v. Mitchell* (1970) the justices by a 5–4 vote held that Congress had the power under Article I to set a minimum age for voting in federal elections but could not impose an age standard on state and local elections. Rather than face the possible confusion of

---

1. Melvin I. Urofsky and Paul Finkelman, *A March of Liberty: A Constitutional History of the United States,* 2nd ed., vol. 1 (New York: Oxford University Press, 2002), 296.

conflicting sets of qualifications, Congress abrogated the impact of the *Mitchell* ruling by proposing the Twenty-sixth Amendment.

Each of these four constitutional changes altered the balance of authority over the establishment of voter qualifications. The states retained the basic right to set such qualifications, but with restrictions. States may no longer abridge voting rights by denying access to the ballot to otherwise qualified voters on the basis of race, sex, age, or ability to pay a tax. Moreover, any state actions affecting voting rights also are constrained by the Fourteenth Amendment's guarantee of the equal protection of the laws. In addition to limiting state power, the voting rights amendments increased congressional authority. The Fourteenth, Fifteenth, Nineteenth, Twenty-fourth, and Twenty-sixth Amendments declare: "The Congress shall have the power to enforce this article by appropriate legislation." These enforcement clauses grant Congress authority over an area that originally had been left entirely to the states.

Congress has not been reluctant to use its enforcement authority. Shortly after ratification of the Fourteenth and Fifteenth Amendments, it demonstrated the federal government's interest in extending the franchise to blacks by passing the Enforcement Act of 1870. This statute made it unlawful for state election officials to discriminate against African Americans in the application of state voting regulations. It also made acts of electoral corruption, including bribery, violence, and intimidation, federal crimes. The following year Congress passed the Enforcement Act of 1871, which allowed for federal supervision of congressional elections. The federal government also intervened to stem the growing incidence of private intimidation of black voters with the Ku Klux Klan Act of 1871, giving the president broad powers to combat conspiracies against voting rights.

The Supreme Court's response to these post–Civil War enforcement statutes was mixed. In some of their decisions the justices questioned the breadth of the congressional actions that regulated state elections beyond the specific racial purposes of the Fifteenth Amendment. For example, in *United States v. Reese* (1876) the justices declined to uphold the indictment of a Kentucky election official who refused to register a qualified black voter for a state election. The Court justified its conclusion on the ground that the Enforcement Act of 1870 was too broadly drawn. On the same day as *Reese,* and for the same reason, the Court in

United States v. Cruikshank dismissed the federal indictments of ninety-six Louisiana whites who were charged with intimidating potential black voters by shooting them.

The Court was also reluctant to approve sanctions under the Ku Klux Klan Act when the prosecution centered on purely private behavior (*United States v. Harris,* 1883). However, in *Ex parte Yarbrough* (1884) the justices gave strong support to federal enforcement actions against even private behavior when the right to vote in national elections was abridged. Similarly, in *Ex parte Clark* (1880), *Ex parte Siebold* (1880), and *United States v. Gale* (1883) the Court approved criminal charges against state officials who compromised the integrity of federal elections.

Although these enforcement measures had an impact on the South, their influence was short-lived. By the 1890s the zeal behind the Reconstruction efforts had waned. White southerners had regained control of their home states and had begun passing measures to restrict black participation in state and federal elections. The Jim Crow era had begun. The Civil War amendments officially had reduced the power of the states to discriminate and given regulatory authority to the federal government, but full voting rights were not a reality until after the civil rights movement of the mid-twentieth century.

State Restrictions on Voting

In 1869, during the congressional debate over the Fifteenth Amendment, Senator Waitman T. Willey, a Republican from West Virginia, proclaimed from the Senate floor:

This amendment, when adopted, will settle the question for all time of negro suffrage in the insurgent States, where it has lately been extended under the pressure of congressional legislation, and will preclude the possibility of any future denial of this privilege by any change in the constitutions of those States.

In retrospect, it would be hard to imagine a more overly optimistic prediction of the impact of the Fifteenth Amendment. Although ratification meant that the states were constitutionally prohibited from engaging in racial discrimination in extending the right to vote, the southern states, once out from under the policies of Reconstruction, acted to keep blacks from voting.

Actions by the southern states to limit black participation in voting took many forms, including white-only voting in Democratic Party primary elections, poll taxes, difficult registration requirements, literacy and understanding tests, and outright intimidation. These strategies were very effective. Black participation at the ballot box in the South was negligible well into the middle of the twentieth century.

Beginning in the 1960s the federal government took measures to reduce racial discrimination in voting. All three branches were involved: Congress passed legislation to enforce voting rights and remove legal barriers to the ballot box; the executive branch brought suits against state governments and election officials who deprived blacks of their rights; and the judiciary heard legal disputes over claims of voting discrimination. For example, in *Louisiana v. United States* (1965) the Supreme Court struck down Louisiana's "understanding test," which permitted local voting registrars to determine whether individuals attempting to register had a sufficient understanding of state and federal constitutions to be qualified to vote. The decisions of these local voting officials often were based exclusively on race. In striking down this practice, the Court gave a stern warning that it would no longer tolerate state schemes designed to deny individuals, particularly minorities, access to the ballot.

Racially discriminatory state practices were not the only barriers to voting that the Court struck down in the 1960s and 1970s. In *Harper v. Virginia State Board of Elections* (1966) the justices found that poll taxes imposed as a requirement to vote in *state* elections violated the Fourteenth Amendment. This decision, coupled with the Twenty-fourth Amendment's prohibition against poll taxes in *federal* elections, effectively eliminated willingness or ability to pay a tax as a voting rights requirement. In *Kramer v. Union Free School District* (1969), the Court removed ownership or rental of real property as a requirement some states had imposed for voting on certain property tax issues. Similarly, in *Dunn v. Blumstein* (1972) the Court struck down state laws that established residency requirements of up to a year as a voting prerequisite. The justices held that a thirty-day requirement would be sufficient for the state to ensure that only bona fide residents voted.

The Voting Rights Act of 1965

Although Supreme Court decisions did much to define the right to vote and limit state actions that restricted the franchise, judicial rulings alone were insufficient to bring about major changes—particularly with respect

President Lyndon B. Johnson signs into law the Voting Rights Act on August 6, 1965.

to voting participation among minorities. Too many alternative measures, many of them informal, were available to block or delay the effective exercise of the right to vote. Registration numbers in the southern states highlight the fact that victories in court do not necessarily translate into social change. According to Justice Department statistics, between 1958 and 1964 black voter registration in Alabama rose to 19.4 percent from 14.2 percent. From 1956 to 1965 Louisiana black registration increased only to 31.8 percent from 31.7 percent. And in Mississippi between 1954 and 1964 black registration rates rose to only 6.4 percent from 4.4 percent. In each of these states the white registration rates were fifty or more percentage points higher than black rates. These figures convinced Congress that its strategy of passing legislation to expand opportunities for taking civil rights claims to court had been ineffective and that a more aggressive policy was required. President Lyndon Johnson is reported to have instructed Attorney General Nicholas Katzenbach to "write the god-damnedest, toughest voting rights act that you can devise."[2] The result was the Voting Rights Act of 1965, the most comprehensive statute ever enacted by Congress to enforce the guarantees of the Fifteenth Amendment.

The provisions of the Voting Rights Act did not apply equally to all sections of the country. Instead, the act targeted certain areas. The coverage formula stipulated that the most stringent provisions of the statute would govern all states or counties that met these two criteria: a discriminatory test or device was in operation in November 1964, and less than 50 percent of the voting-age population was registered to vote or voted in the 1964 presidential general election.

In 1965 the states covered were Alabama, Alaska, Georgia, Louisiana, Mississippi, South Carolina, and Virginia, as well as portions of Arizona, Hawaii, Idaho, and North Carolina. A "bail-out" provision allowed a state or political subdivision to get itself removed from coverage by convincing the U.S. District Court for the District of Columbia that it had not practiced any discrimination for five years. The act's most significant provision authorized the U.S. attorney general to appoint federal examiners to supervise registration and voting procedures when the Justice Department

determined that low black participation rates were likely due to racial discrimination. The law prohibited literacy tests and stipulated that any changes in state election laws had to be approved by the U.S. attorney general or the U.S. District Court for the District of Columbia before they could take effect. The 1965 Voting Rights Act was Congress's most comprehensive intervention ever into the states' traditional powers over voter qualifications, and it was not surprising that a southern state, South Carolina, almost immediately challenged it as exceeding constitutional limits on federal power.

South Carolina v. Katzenbach

383 U.S. 301 (1966)
http://laws.findlaw.com/US/383/301.html
Oral arguments are available at http://www.oyez.org.
Vote: 8 (Brennan, Clark, Douglas, Fortas, Harlan, Stewart, Warren, White)
  1 (Black)

OPINION OF THE COURT: *Warren*

OPINION CONCURRING IN PART AND DISSENTING IN PART: *Black*

FACTS:

To gain a review of the Voting Rights Act, South Carolina instituted legal action against Attorney General Katzenbach, asking that he be enjoined from enforcing the act's provisions. Because the dispute involved a state suing a citizen of another state, and because of the importance of the issues involved, the Supreme Court accepted the case under its original jurisdiction. The hearing before the Court involved not only South Carolina and the federal government but also other states the Court invited to participate. Five states (all southern) appeared in support of South Carolina, and twenty-one states submitted legal arguments urging the Court to approve the act.

ARGUMENTS:

For the plaintiff, State of South Carolina:

- The act is not an "appropriate" law to enforce the Fifteenth Amendment. It unconstitutionally curtails the state's right to determine voter qualifications in violation of Article I, Sections 2 and 4, and the Seventeenth Amendment.
- The act violates the fundamental constitutional principle of equality of statehood.
- The act imposes an arbitrary and irrebuttable presumption of racial discrimination because of low voter turnout rates, yet voter turnout is primarily affected by political and economic factors.

---

2. Quoted in Howard Ball, "The Voting Rights Act of 1965," in *The Oxford Companion to the Supreme Court of the United States*, ed. Kermit L. Hall (New York: Oxford University Press, 1992), 903.

- Literacy tests promote the intelligent and informed use of the ballot. Allowing illiterates to vote would put the state's interests in the hands of unqualified voters.

For the defendant, Nicholas de B. Katzenbach, Attorney General of the United States:

- Section 2 of the Fifteenth Amendment gives Congress comprehensive authority to protect and enforce a citizen's right to vote free of racial discrimination. The provisions of the act, including federal review of new voting procedures and the use of federal examiners, represent a proper exercise of congressional power to enforce the amendment.
- The act's "triggering mechanism" provides a fair and reasonable formula for determining what states and political subdivisions fall under the law's coverage.
- Literacy tests and other devices may operate as engines of racial discrimination.
- When tests are used to establish voter qualifications and less than half of the voting population participates, it is reasonable to suspect discrimination. The act gives a state the opportunity to prove that no illegal discrimination has taken place.

MR. CHIEF JUSTICE WARREN DELIVERED THE OPINION OF THE COURT.

The Voting Rights Act was designed by Congress to banish the blight of racial discrimination in voting, which has infected the electoral process in parts of our country for nearly a century. The Act creates stringent new remedies for voting discrimination where it persists on a pervasive scale, and in addition the statute strengthens existing remedies for pockets of voting discrimination elsewhere in the country. Congress assumed the power to prescribe these remedies from §2 of the Fifteenth Amendment, which authorizes the National Legislature to effectuate by "appropriate" measures the constitutional prohibition against racial discrimination in voting. We hold that the sections of the Act which are properly before us are an appropriate means for carrying out Congress' constitutional responsibilities and are consonant with all other provisions of the Constitution. We therefore deny South Carolina's request that enforcement of these sections of the Act be enjoined.

The constitutional propriety of the Voting Rights Act of 1965 must be judged with reference to the historical experience which it reflects. Before enacting the measure, Congress explored with great care the problem of racial discrimination in voting. The House and Senate Committees on the Judiciary each held hearings for nine days and received testimony from a total of 67 witnesses. More than three full days were consumed discussing the bill on the floor of the House, while the debate in the Senate covered 26 days in all. At the close of these deliberations, the verdict of both chambers was overwhelming. The House approved the bill by a vote of 328–74, and the measure passed the Senate by a margin of 79–18.

Two points emerge vividly from the voluminous legislative history of the Act contained in the committee hearings and floor debates. First: Congress felt itself confronted by an insidious and pervasive evil which had been perpetuated in certain parts of our country through unremitting and ingenious defiance of the Constitution. Second: Congress concluded that the unsuccessful remedies which it had prescribed in the past would have to be replaced by sterner and more elaborate measures in order to satisfy the clear commands of the Fifteenth Amendment. . . .

The Voting Rights Act of 1965 reflects Congress' firm intention to rid the country of racial discrimination in voting. The heart of the Act is a complex scheme of stringent remedies aimed at areas where voting discrimination has been most flagrant. Section 4(a)–(d) lays down a formula defining the States and political subdivisions to which these new remedies apply. The first of the remedies, contained in §4(a), is the suspension of literacy tests and similar voting qualifications for a period of five years from the last occurrence of substantial voting discrimination. Section 5 prescribes a second remedy, the suspension of all new voting regulations pending review by federal authorities to determine whether their use would perpetuate voting discrimination. The third remedy, covered in §§6(b), 7, 9, and 13(a), is the assignment of federal examiners on certification by the Attorney General to list qualified applicants who are thereafter entitled to vote in all elections.

Other provisions of the Act prescribe subsidiary cures for persistent voting discrimination. Section 8 authorizes the appointment of federal poll-watchers in places to which federal examiners have already been assigned. Section 10(d) excuses those made eligible to vote in sections of the country covered by §4(b) of the Act from paying accumulated past poll taxes for state and local elections. Section 12(e) provides for balloting by persons denied access to the polls in areas where federal examiners have been appointed.

The remaining remedial portions of the Act are aimed at voting discrimination in any area of the country where it may occur. Section 2 broadly prohibits the use of voting rules to abridge exercise of the franchise on racial grounds. Sections 3, 6(a), and 13(b) strengthen existing procedures for attacking voting discrimination by means of litigation. Section 4(e) excuses citizens educated in American schools conducted in a foreign language from passing English-language literacy tests. Section 10(a)–(c) facilitates constitutional litigation challenging the imposition of all poll taxes for state and local elections. Sections 11 and 12(a)–(d) authorize civil and criminal sanctions against interference with the exercise of rights guaranteed by the Act. . . .

These provisions of the Voting Rights Act of 1965 are challenged on the fundamental ground that they exceed the powers of Congress and encroach on an area reserved to the States by the Constitution. . . .

The ground rules for resolving this question are clear. The language and purpose of the Fifteenth Amendment, the prior decisions construing its several provisions, and the general doctrines of constitutional interpretation, all point to one fundamental principle. As against the reserved powers of the States, Congress may use any rational means to effectuate the constitutional prohibition of racial discrimination in voting. . . .

Section 1 of the Fifteenth Amendment declares that "[t]he right of citizens of the United States to vote shall not be denied or abridged by the United States or by any State on account of race, color, or previous condition of servitude." This declaration has always been treated as self-executing and has repeatedly been construed, without further legislative specification, to invalidate state voting qualifications or procedures which are discriminatory on their face or in practice. . . . [T]he Fifteenth Amendment expressly declares that "Congress shall have power to enforce this article by appropriate legislation." . . . Accordingly, in addition to the courts, Congress has full remedial powers to effectuate the constitutional prohibition against racial discrimination in voting.

Congress has repeatedly exercised these powers in the past, and its enactments have repeatedly been upheld. . . . On the rare occasions when the Court has found an unconstitutional exercise of these powers, in its opinion Congress had attacked evils not comprehended by the Fifteenth Amendment.

The basic test to be applied in a case involving §2 of the Fifteenth Amendment is the same as in all cases concerning the express powers of Congress with relation to the reserved powers of the States. Chief Justice Marshall laid down the classic formulation, 50 years before the Fifteenth Amendment was ratified:

Let the end be legitimate, let it be within the scope of the constitution, and all means which are appropriate, which are plainly adapted to that end, which are not prohibited, but consist with the letter and spirit of the constitution, are constitutional. *McCulloch v. Maryland.*

The Court has subsequently echoed his language in describing each of the Civil War Amendments:

Whatever legislation is appropriate, that is, adapted to carry out the objects the amendments have in view, whatever tends to enforce submission to the prohibitions they contain, and to secure to all persons the enjoyment of perfect equality of civil rights and the equal protection of the laws against State denial or invasion, if not prohibited, is brought within the domain of congressional power. *Ex parte Virginia.*

. . . We therefore reject South Carolina's argument that Congress may appropriately do no more than to forbid violations of the Fifteenth Amendment in general terms—that the task of fashioning specific remedies or of applying them to particular localities must necessarily be left entirely to the courts. Congress is not circumscribed by any such artificial rules under §2 of the Fifteenth Amendment. . . .

Congress exercised its authority under the Fifteenth Amendment in an inventive manner when it enacted the Voting Rights Act of 1965. First: The measure prescribes remedies for voting discrimination which go into effect without any need for prior adjudication. This was clearly a legitimate response to the problem, for which there is ample precedent under other constitutional provisions. . . .

Second: The Act intentionally confines these remedies to a small number of States and political subdivisions which in most instances were familiar to Congress by name. This, too, was a permissible method of dealing with the problem. Congress had learned that substantial voting discrimination presently occurs in certain sections of the country, and it knew no way of accurately forecasting whether the evil might spread elsewhere in the future. In acceptable legislative fashion, Congress chose to limit its attention to the geographic areas where immediate action seemed necessary. . . .

After enduring nearly a century of widespread resistance to the Fifteenth Amendment, Congress has marshalled an array of potent weapons against the evil, with authority in the Attorney General to employ them effectively. Many of the areas directly affected by this development have indicated their willingness to abide by any restraints legitimately imposed upon them. We here hold that the portions of the Voting Rights Act properly before us are a valid means for carrying out the commands of the Fifteenth Amendment. Hopefully, millions of nonwhite Americans will now be able to participate for the first time on an equal basis in the government under which they live. We may finally look forward to the day when truly "[t]he right of citizens of the United States to vote shall not be denied or abridged by the United States or by any State on account of race, color, or previous condition of servitude."

The bill of complaint is

Dismissed.

MR. JUSTICE BLACK, concurring and dissenting.

Though . . . I agree with most of the Court's conclusions, I dissent from its holding that every part of §5 of the Act is constitutional. . . . I think this section is unconstitutional on at least two grounds.

(a) The Constitution gives federal courts jurisdiction over cases and controversies only. If it can be said that any case or controversy arises under this section which gives the District Court for the District of Columbia jurisdiction to approve or reject state laws or constitutional amendments, then the case or controversy must be between a State and the United States Government. But it is hard for me to believe that a justiciable controversy can arise in the constitutional sense from a desire by the United States Government or some of its officials to determine in advance what legislative provisions a State may enact or what constitutional amendments it may adopt. If this dispute between the Federal Government and the States amounts to a case or controversy it is a far cry from the traditional constitutional notion of a case or controversy as a dispute over the meaning of enforceable laws or the manner in which they are applied. . . .

(b) My second and more basic objection to §5 is that Congress has here exercised its power under §2 of the Fifteenth Amendment through the adoption of means that conflict with the most basic principles of the Constitution. . . . Section 5, by providing that some of the States cannot pass state laws or adopt state constitutional amendments without first being compelled to beg federal authorities to approve their policies, so distorts our constitutional structure of government as to render any distinction drawn in the Constitution between state and federal power almost meaningless. One of the most basic premises upon which our structure of government was founded was that the Federal Government was to have certain specific and limited powers and no others, and all other power was to be reserved either "to the States respectively, or to the people." Certainly if all the provisions of our Constitution which limit the power of the Federal Government and reserve other power to the States are to mean anything, they mean at least that the States have power to pass laws and amend their constitutions without first sending their officials hundreds of miles away to beg federal authorities to approve them. Moreover, it seems to me that §5, which gives federal officials power to veto state laws they do not like is in direct conflict with the clear command of our Constitution that "The United States shall guarantee to every State in this Union a Republican Form of Government." I cannot help but believe that the inevitable effect of any such law which forces any one of the States to entreat federal authorities in far-away places for approval of local laws before they can become effective is to create the impression that the State or States treated in this way are little more than conquered provinces. . . .

. . . I would hold §5 invalid for the reasons stated above with full confidence that the Attorney General has ample power to give vigorous, expeditious and effective protection to the voting rights of all citizens.

With the Court's approval of the Voting Rights Act, the federal government was free to launch a vigorous campaign to make the goals of the Fifteenth Amendment a reality. The executive branch actively enforced the law, and Congress periodically strengthened and extended its provisions. These efforts, coupled with large-scale voter registration drives conducted by civil rights organizations, resulted in southern blacks being registered to vote at rates only slightly below those of whites.

The history of voting rights in the United States shows the steady expansion of the electorate. The barriers of race, sex, economic status, and residency that once blocked millions of Americans from participating in the electoral process have been torn down. Few legitimate reasons currently exist for the government to deny someone the right to vote. Voter education projects and registration drives have encouraged people to participate in the political process. Reformed registration laws make it easier than ever to qualify to vote. Early voting opportunities and vote-by-mail options now allow participation by citizens who otherwise might not be able to get to the polls on the official election day. In spite of these legal and constitutional reforms, American elections are characterized by relatively low voter turnout. As Box 14-2 illustrates, the electoral participation rates of Americans do not compare favorably to those of many other nations.

Although the Voting Rights Act contributed significantly to the expansion of political participation among minority groups, states that came under the coverage of the act lost a degree of sovereignty. Unlike other states, which were able to change their electoral and representational laws at will, covered states were required by Section 5 of the act to obtain federal approval before implementing any legislation affecting voting rights or procedures. The imposition of such federal authority over the states was considered constitutionally acceptable only as long as the patterns and practices of racial discrimination

continued. Section 5 was considered to be a temporary measure, originally lasting only five years, but Congress repeatedly saw reason to extend its life.

As the nation entered the twenty-first century, southern states began to argue that it was time they were released from the restrictions imposed by the Voting Rights Act. The old ways of racial discrimination in voting had long since been abolished, they claimed. In 1964, for example, there were fewer than three hundred black local officials nationwide, but by 2009 the figure had risen to more than ten thousand. Additionally, the nation had elected its first African American president. Civil rights advocates, of course, argued that the Voting Rights Act had been a major factor in the progress that had been made and feared that a repeal of the act would provide an opportunity for discrimination to return. In 2006, when Congress extended the Voting Rights Act for another twenty-five years, a legal battle became inevitable.

The unlikely challenger of the act was the Northwest Austin Municipal Utility District, a small provider of

---

BOX 14-2   VOTING IN GLOBAL PERSPECTIVE

Although Americans have fought hard to remove legal barriers to the vote—property requirements, literacy tests, and laws prohibiting women and minorities from voting—many do not exercise their voting rights. Turnout for the 2008 presidential election was only about 58 percent of the voting-age population. Overall voter turnout in the United States tends to lag behind that in many other countries, as the presidential (or equivalent) election data in this table illustrate.

COUNTRY	YEAR	PERCENTAGE TURNOUT OF VOTING-AGE POPULATION	COUNTRY	YEAR	PERCENTAGE TURNOUT OF VOTING-AGE POPULATION
Argentina	2007	72.2	Peru	2011	86.2
Austria	2010	49.1	Philippines	2004	75.1
Brazil	2010	77.3	Poland	2010	54.5
Chile	2010	59.1	Portugal	2011	51.9
Costa Rica	2010	62.3	Russian Federation	2008	65.4
Finland	2006	77.6	Taiwan	2008	74.7
France	2007	76.8	Uganda	2011	55.3
Iceland	2004	63.7	Ukraine	2010	68.0
Kenya	2007	54.5	United States	2008	57.5
Mexico	2006	63.3	Venezuela	2006	76.3
Panama	2009	69.0			

SOURCE: Institute for Democracy and Electoral Assistance, http://www.idea.int/vt/view_data.cfm#cq_presidential.

utility services to a portion of Travis County, Texas. The district is run by a board consisting of five elected directors who serve staggered four-year terms. The district does not register voters—the county handles that task— but it does administer elections. The district had never been charged in any racial discrimination complaint. However, as a political subdivision of Texas, it is subject to the Voting Rights Act.[3] Consequently, when the district decided to move its primary polling place from a private residence to a more convenient public school building, it was required to seek federal approval.

Instead, the district filed suit in federal court challenging Section 5. First, the district sought to take advantage of the law's "bail-out" provision, which would allow it to be removed from Voting Rights Act coverage if it could prove that, among other things, it had not engaged in racial discrimination for the past five years. Second, if the federal court would not grant bail-out relief, the district requested that the court find Section 5 unconstitutional. In extending the act for another twenty-five years, the district argued, Congress had failed to take into account the changes that had taken place in voting participation that made Section 5 unnecessary.

The trial court denied the district's petition to be removed from Voting Rights Act coverage. Interpreting the statute narrowly, the court ruled that the bail-out procedure applied only to political subdivisions that registered voters. The court also rejected the district's claim that Section 5 was unconstitutional. The district appealed to the U.S. Supreme Court.

Civil rights advocates expressed considerable concern that the Court might hold Section 5 unconstitutional. When the justices announced their decision in *Northwest Austin Municipal Utility District No. 1 v. Holder* (2009), however, the Voting Rights Act had survived. Chief Justice Roberts's opinion for the Court included a number of critical comments about the constitutionality of the law, but the justices, in restrained fashion, opted not to decide the dispute on constitutional grounds. Rather, they concluded that the district court had misinterpreted the bail-out provision. That option, according to the Court, was open to political subdivisions such as the Northwest Austin Municipal Utility District even if they had no voter

---

3. In addition to Texas, the states of Alabama, Alaska, Arizona, Georgia, Louisiana, Mississippi, South Carolina, and Virginia were subject to Section 5's preclearance requirements in 2012. Portions of California, Florida, Michigan, New Hampshire, New York, North Carolina, and South Dakota also fell under Voting Rights Act coverage.

registration responsibilities. The decision allowed the district to pursue an exemption from the law and the justices to avoid making a controversial constitutional ruling. Eight justices agreed with this outcome. Only Clarence Thomas expressed a preference to tackle the constitutional issue and to strike down Section 5.

The Court's decision to avoid confronting the issue of Section 5's constitutionality likely only delayed the inevitable. Following the announcement of that decision, the attorneys general of several states affected by the Voting Rights Act began to develop litigation strategies for new constitutional attacks on the legislation. They argue that the racial discrimination in voting rights that Section 5 was designed to combat is a thing of the past. As a consequence, the law's requirement that the covered states must obtain federal approval before they can put any election-related laws into effect diminishes the states' sovereignty without a constitutionally justified reason for doing so. If successful, these lawsuits would eliminate the toughest and most effective section of the Voting Rights Act. Should such a result occur, states would still be prohibited from discriminating on the basis of race in extending the right to vote, but no longer would a covered state have to subject election-related legislative acts to the burdensome preclearance process.

Contemporary Restrictions on the Right to Vote

The drama over the 2000 presidential election in Florida was followed by a number of similarly close elections in other states. These electoral experiences underscored two important realities. First, every vote is important. As a consequence, any rules or policies that restrict voting opportunities must be taken seriously. And second, the procedures used to administer elections and count votes needed significant attention. Evidence mounted that bureaucratic errors and mechanical malfunctions frequently resulted in failure to count the votes of many citizens. Inevitably, charges of voter fraud and lawsuits challenging electoral outcomes became increasingly common.

Congress and the states responded by searching for ways to ensure the integrity of the electoral process. This included efforts to make voting procedures more uniform and vote-counting mechanisms more accurate, as well as initiatives to protect the system against voter fraud. Electoral reforms, however, always have the potential of affecting partisan interests. As a consequence, any proposal for change faced a number of common questions: Would the advocated reform improve the honesty of the electoral process? Would the suggested change have a negative impact on the voting rights of any segment of the population? Would the proposed change advantage one political party over another?

One of the more controversial suggested reforms was a requirement that voters present government-issued photographic identification at the polls. The goal was to prohibit individuals from illegally casting ballots in the name of registered voters who might have died or moved to other states. While such a requirement might seem reasonable on its face, opponents claimed that it would impose an undue burden on the poor and the elderly, who are less likely to have such identification. Republicans tended to support this reform, while Democrats, who feared an adverse impact on groups of voters who traditionally support the party, opposed it. When the state of Indiana passed a voter ID law in 2005, the stage was set for a constitutional battle over the statute's validity. The Supreme Court tackled the question in *Crawford v. Marion County Election Board* in 2008.

Crawford v. Marion County Election Board

553 U.S. 181 (2008)
http://laws.findlaw.com/US/000/07-21.html
Oral arguments are available at http://www.oyez.org.
Vote: 6 (Alito, Kennedy, Roberts, Scalia, Stevens, Thomas)
    3 (Breyer, Ginsburg, Souter)

OPINION ANNOUNCING THE JUDGMENT OF THE COURT: *Stevens*
OPINION CONCURRING IN THE JUDGMENT: *Scalia*
DISSENTING OPINIONS: *Breyer, Souter*

FACTS:

With the stated goals of discouraging and preventing voter fraud, the Republican-dominated Indiana legislature in 2005 enacted the "Voter ID Law" (SEA 483) requiring citizens to present government-issued photo identification at the polls in order to vote in any primary or general election. The requirement did not apply to absentee votes submitted by mail, and exceptions were made for residents of state-licensed facilities such as nursing homes. A voter who had the required ID but failed to bring it to the polls could cast a provisional vote that would be counted if the voter brought proper identification to the circuit court clerk within ten days. Similar provisional ballot procedures were available for those who had religious objections to

On May 6, 2008, polling inspector Julie McGuire, a Roman Catholic nun, was forced to turn away about a dozen of her fellow nuns from a nearby South Bend convent for not having proper identification. McGuire had frequently informed the sisters, most of them elderly, that under Indiana's new voter registration law they would need to show an identification card from the state Bureau of Motor Vehicles before they would be able to cast a ballot.

being photographed. The state Bureau of Motor Vehicles offered free photo identification cards to those who did not already possess a driver's license or other acceptable identification. A photo ID was not required to register to vote or to vote absentee.

Shortly after the law's enactment, a coalition of individuals and groups representing the interests of minorities and the poor challenged the law. In addition, the Indiana and Marion County Democratic Party organizations filed suit to have the law declared unconstitutional. These parties claimed that the law violated the Fourteenth Amendment by substantially burdening the right to vote and arbitrarily disenfranchising voters who could not obtain the identification cards easily.

After consolidating these challenges into a single case, the district court ruled for the state and a divided court of appeals affirmed, concluding that the benefit of reducing the risk of fraud offset the burden on voters.

For the petitioners, William Crawford, et al.:

- Voting is a fundamental right, and the law imposes a significant burden on thousands of prospective Indiana voters. Most affected are the poor and the elderly.
- Indiana's provisional voting process, rather than easing the burden, actually imposes an additional barrier for those who are unable to produce acceptable identification at the polls.
- Indicative of the ID law's lack of narrow tailoring is that it applies to voting at polling places (where no evidence of voter fraud has been presented) but does not apply to absentee balloting (where there have been proven instances of voter fraud).
- The law was motivated primarily by partisan advantage.

For the respondent, State of Indiana:

- The petitioners have failed to produce a single voter who has been unable to vote because of the voter identification law. A study has shown that 99 percent of Indiana voters already possess the required identification.
- The voter identification law is a reasonable, nondiscriminatory method of deterring voter fraud and is part of a larger effort to modernize voting procedures.
- The law accommodates those who do not have identification through its provisional voting procedures and other waivers (e.g., the elderly are automatically eligible to vote by mail, where photo identification is not required).
- The law not only deters polling place voter fraud but also helps preserve public confidence in electoral integrity.

JUSTICE STEVENS ANNOUNCED THE JUDGMENT OF THE COURT AND DELIVERED AN OPINION IN WHICH THE CHIEF JUSTICE AND JUSTICE KENNEDY JOIN.

In *Harper v. Virginia Bd. of Elections* (1966), the Court held that Virginia could not condition the right to vote in a state election on the payment of a poll tax of $1.50. We rejected the dissenters' argument that the interest in promoting civic responsibility by weeding out those voters who did not care enough about public affairs to pay a small sum for the privilege of voting provided a rational basis for the tax. Applying a stricter standard, we concluded that a State "violates the Equal Protection Clause of the Fourteenth Amendment whenever it makes the affluence of the voter or payment of any fee an electoral standard." We used the term "invidiously discriminate" to describe conduct prohibited under that standard. . . . Although the State's justification for the tax was rational, it was invidious because it was irrelevant to the voter's qualifications.

Thus, under the standard applied in *Harper,* even rational restrictions on the right to vote are invidious if they are unrelated to voter qualifications. In *Anderson v. Celebrezze* (1983), however, we confirmed the general rule that "evenhanded restrictions that protect the integrity and reliability of the electoral process itself" are not invidious and satisfy the standard set forth in *Harper.* Rather than applying any "litmus test" that would neatly separate valid from invalid restrictions, we concluded that a court must identify and evaluate the interests put forward by the State as justifications for the burden imposed by its rule, and then make the "hard judgment" that our adversary system demands. . . .

. . . The State has a valid interest in participating in a nationwide effort to improve and modernize election procedures that have been criticized as antiquated and inefficient. The State also argues that it has a particular interest in preventing voter fraud in response to a problem that is in part the product of its own maladministration—namely, that Indiana's voter registration rolls include a large number of names of persons who are either deceased or no longer live in Indiana. Finally, the State relies on its interest in safeguarding voter confidence. Each of these interests merits separate comment.

Election Modernization

Two recently enacted federal statutes have made it necessary for States to reexamine their election procedures. Both contain provisions consistent with a State's choice to use government-issued photo identification as a relevant source of information concerning a citizen's eligibility to vote. . . .

Of course, neither [statute] required Indiana to enact SEA 483, but they do indicate that Congress believes that photo identification is one effective method of establishing a voter's qualification to vote and that the integrity of elections is enhanced through improved technology. That conclusion is also supported by a report issued shortly after the enactment of SEA 483 by the Commission on Federal Election Reform chaired by former President Jimmy Carter and former Secretary of State James A. Baker III. . . .

Voter Fraud

The only kind of voter fraud that SEA 483 addresses is in-person voter impersonation at polling places. The record contains no evidence of any such fraud actually occurring in Indiana at any time in its history. Moreover, petitioners argue that provisions of the Indiana Criminal Code punishing such conduct as a felony provide adequate protection against the risk that such conduct will occur in the future. It remains true, however, that flagrant examples of such fraud in other parts of the country have been documented throughout this Nation's history by respected historians and journalists, that occasional examples have surfaced in recent years, and that Indiana's own experience with fraudulent voting in the 2003 Democratic primary for East Chicago Mayor—though perpetrated using absentee ballots and not in-person fraud—demonstrate that not only is the risk of voter fraud real but that it could affect the outcome of a close election.

There is no question about the legitimacy or importance of the State's interest in counting only the votes of eligible voters. Moreover, the interest in orderly administration and accurate recordkeeping provides a sufficient justification for carefully identifying all voters participating in the election process. While the most effective method of preventing election fraud may well be debatable, the propriety of doing so is perfectly clear.

In its brief, the State argues that the inflation of its voter rolls provides further support for its enactment of SEA 483. . . . Indiana's lists of registered voters included the names of thousands of persons who had either moved, died, or were not eligible to vote because they had been convicted of felonies. . . . Even though Indiana's own negligence may have contributed to the serious inflation of its registration lists when SEA 483 was enacted, the fact of inflated voter rolls does provide a neutral and nondiscriminatory reason supporting the State's decision to require photo identification.

Safeguarding Voter Confidence

Finally, the State contends that it has an interest in protecting public confidence "in the integrity and legitimacy of representative government." While that interest is closely related to the State's interest in preventing voter fraud, public confidence in the integrity of the electoral process has independent significance, because it encourages citizen participation in the democratic process. . . .

States employ different methods of identifying eligible voters at the polls. Some merely check off the names of registered voters who identify themselves; others require voters to present registration cards or other documentation before they can vote; some require voters to sign their names so their signatures can be compared with those on file; and in recent years an increasing number of States have relied primarily on photo identification. A photo identification requirement imposes some burdens on voters that other methods of identification do not share. . . .

The burdens that are relevant to the issue before us are those imposed on persons who are eligible to vote but do not possess a current photo identification that complies with the requirements of SEA 483. The fact that most voters already possess a valid driver's license, or some other form of acceptable identification, would not save the statute under our reasoning in *Harper,* if the State required voters to pay a tax or a fee to obtain a new photo identification. But just as other States provide free voter registration cards, the photo identification cards issued by Indiana's BMV are also free. For most voters who need them, the inconvenience of making a trip to the BMV, gathering the required documents, and posing for a photograph surely does not qualify as a substantial burden on the right to vote, or even represent a significant increase over the usual burdens of voting.

Both evidence in the record and facts of which we may take judicial notice, however, indicate that a somewhat heavier burden may be placed on a limited number of persons. They include elderly persons born out-of-state, who may have difficulty obtaining a birth certificate; persons who because of economic or other personal limitations may find it difficult either to secure a copy of their birth certificate or to assemble the other required documentation to obtain a state-issued identification; homeless persons; and persons with a religious objection to being photographed. . . .

The severity of that burden is, of course, mitigated by the fact that, if eligible, voters without photo identification may cast provisional ballots that will ultimately be counted. To do so, however, they must travel to the circuit court clerk's office within 10 days to execute the required affidavit. It is unlikely that such a requirement would pose a constitutional problem unless it is wholly unjustified. And even assuming that the burden may not be justified as to a few voters, that conclusion is by no means sufficient to establish petitioners' right to the relief they seek in this litigation.

Given the fact that petitioners have advanced a broad attack on the constitutionality of SEA 483, seeking relief that would invalidate the statute in all its applications, they bear a heavy burden of persuasion. . . .

Petitioners ask this Court, in effect, to perform a unique balancing analysis that looks specifically at a small number of voters who may experience a special burden under the statute and weighs their burdens against the State's broad interests in protecting election integrity. Petitioners urge us to ask whether the State's interests justify the burden imposed on voters who cannot afford or obtain a birth certificate and who must make a second trip to the circuit court clerk's office after voting. But on the basis of the evidence in the record it is not possible to quantify either the magnitude of the burden on this narrow class of voters or the portion of the burden imposed on them that is fully justified.

First, the evidence in the record does not provide us with the number of registered voters without photo identification. . . .

Further, the deposition evidence presented in the District Court does not provide any concrete evidence of the burden imposed on voters who currently lack photo identification. . . .

The record says virtually nothing about the difficulties faced by either indigent voters or voters with religious objections to being photographed. . . . The record does contain the affidavit of one homeless woman who has a copy of her birth certificate, but was denied a photo identification card because she did not have an address. But that single affidavit gives no indication of how common the problem is.

In sum, on the basis of the record that has been made in this litigation, we cannot conclude that the statute imposes "excessively burdensome requirements" on any class of voters. . . . When we consider only the statute's broad application to all Indiana voters we conclude that it "imposes only a limited burden on voters' rights." The "'precise interests'" advanced by the State are therefore sufficient to defeat petitioners' facial challenge to SEA 483. . . .

In their briefs, petitioners stress the fact that all of the Republicans in the General Assembly voted in favor of SEA 483 and the Democrats were unanimous in opposing it. . . . It is fair to infer that partisan considerations may have played a significant role in the decision to enact SEA 483. If such considerations had provided the only justification for a photo identification requirement, we may also assume that SEA 483 would suffer the same fate as the poll tax at issue in *Harper*.

But if a nondiscriminatory law is supported by valid neutral justifications, those justifications should not be disregarded simply because partisan interests may have provided one motivation for the votes of individual legislators. The state interests identified as justifications for SEA 483 are both neutral and sufficiently strong to require us to reject petitioners' facial attack on the statute. The application of the statute to the vast majority of Indiana voters is amply justified by the valid interest in protecting "the integrity and reliability of the electoral process."

The judgment of the Court of Appeals is affirmed.

JUSTICE SCALIA, with whom JUSTICE THOMAS and JUSTICE ALITO join, concurring in the judgment.

The universally applicable requirements of Indiana's voter-identification law are eminently reasonable. The burden of acquiring, possessing, and showing a free photo identification is simply not severe, because it does not "even represent a significant increase over the usual burdens of voting." And the State's interests are sufficient to sustain that minimal burden. That should end the matter. That the State accommodates some voters by permitting (not requiring) the casting of absentee or provisional ballots is an indulgence—not a constitutional imperative that falls short of what is required.

JUSTICE SOUTER, with whom JUSTICE GINSBURG joins, dissenting.

Indiana's "Voter ID Law" threatens to impose nontrivial burdens on the voting right of tens of thousands of the State's citizens and a significant percentage of those individuals are likely to be deterred from voting. The statute is unconstitutional under the balancing standard of *Burdick v. Takushi* (1992): a State may not burden the right to vote merely by invoking abstract interests, be they legitimate, or even compelling, but must make a particular, factual showing that threats to its interests outweigh the particular impediments it has imposed. The State has made no such justification here, and as to some aspects of its law, it has hardly even tried. I therefore respectfully dissent from the Court's judgment sustaining the statute. . . .

Without a shred of evidence that in-person voter impersonation is a problem in the State, much less a crisis, Indiana has adopted one of the most restrictive photo identification requirements in the country. The State recognizes that tens of thousands of qualified voters lack the necessary federally issued or state-issued identification, but it insists on implementing the requirement immediately, without allowing a transition period for targeted efforts to distribute the required identification to individuals who need it. The State hardly even tries to explain its decision to force indigents or religious objectors to travel all the way to their county seats every time they wish to vote. . . . It is impossible to say, on this record, that the State's interest in adopting its signally inhibiting photo identification requirement has been shown to outweigh the serious burdens it imposes on the right to vote. . . .

The Indiana Voter ID Law is thus unconstitutional: the state interests fail to justify the practical limitations placed on the right to vote, and the law imposes an unreasonable and irrelevant burden on voters who are poor and old.

JUSTICE BREYER, dissenting.

Indiana's statute requires registered voters to present photo identification at the polls. It imposes a burden upon some voters, but it does so in order to prevent fraud, to build confidence in the voting system, and thereby to maintain the integrity of the voting process. In determining whether this statute violates the Federal Constitution, I would balance the voting-related interests that the statute affects, asking "whether the statute burdens any one such interest in a manner out of proportion to the statute's salutary effects upon the others (perhaps, but not necessarily, because of the existence of a clearly superior, less restrictive alternative)." Applying this standard, I believe the statute is unconstitutional because it imposes a disproportionate burden upon those eligible voters who lack a driver's license or other statutorily valid form of photo ID.

REGULATION OF ELECTION CAMPAIGNS

Following the 1968 presidential election and associated Watergate controversy, the integrity of federal election campaigns became a national issue. In 1974 Congress moved to reform presidential elections, especially with respect to the role of campaign contributions and expenditures, by amending the Federal Election Campaign Act of 1971 (FECA). The law restricted how much individuals and groups could contribute to candidates, parties, and political action committees (PACs) for use in federal elections. It also imposed record-keeping requirements and provided for federal funding of presidential election campaigns. In *Buckley v. Valeo* (1976) the Supreme Court upheld these provisions but struck down others that limited independent campaign expenditures and candidate expenditures of personal funds. The Court's decision rested on an assumption that placing a ceiling on campaign expenditures was equivalent to restricting political speech. In addition, the justices balanced the need to secure the integrity of federal elections against the right to political expression. The Court concluded that reducing electoral corruption was a sufficient interest to limit campaign contributions, but not to restrict campaign expenditures.

In the years following the implementation of FECA, political strategists developed creative ways to circumvent the law. First, campaign contributors were able to exploit a loophole that distinguished money given to a candidate's political campaign from contributions made to political party organizations for "party-building" activities or "get-out-the-vote" drives. FECA clearly regulated and limited the amount of money that could be given to a campaign organization in support of a candidate ("hard money"), but did not regulate general funds given to political parties ("soft money"). Funded by soft money, political parties designed advertising campaigns that supported their candidates without explicit entreaties to voters to cast their ballots for them. The result, as illustrated in Table 14-1, was an exponential growth of soft money in campaigns and a weakening of FECA.

Second, interest groups and other entities launched "issue campaigns" that promoted certain public policies. These campaigns were unregulated because, at least on their face, they did not advocate voting for any particular candidate. In fact, as long as the advertisements avoided certain "trigger words," such as "Vote for John Smith" or "Defeat Nancy Johnson," they were considered issue ads outside the reach of FECA regulation. Often the ads promoted or attacked policies or positions clearly associated with specific candidates and even praised or criticized the candidates themselves, and they appeared during the heat of a political campaign. Again, these activities tended to undermine the policy goals of FECA.

TABLE 14-1 Growth of Soft Money (millions of dollars)

	1991–1992	1993–1994	1995–1996	1997–1998	1999–2000
Democrats					
Hard money	$155.5	$121.1	$210.0	$153.4	$269.9
Soft money	36.3	49.1	122.3	91.5	243.1
Republicans					
Hard money	266.3	223.7	407.5	273.6	447.4
Soft money	49.8	52.5	141.2	131.0	244.4
TOTAL	$507.9	$446.4	$881.0	$649.5	$1,204.8

SOURCES: Federal Election Commission; "Debating McCain-Feingold," *CQ Weekly*, March 10, 2001, 526.

Dissatisfaction with the inability of FECA to control the growing problems related to soft-money contributions and issue advertising prompted Congress to pass the Bipartisan Campaign Reform Act of 2002 (BCRA), which placed new restrictions on political contributions and expenditures. The law was immediately challenged as conflicting with *Buckley*. In addition, many believed it was an unconstitutional restraint on political speech.

First, Title I of BCRA dealt with soft money. It prohibited the national political parties from raising or spending soft money, barred officeholders and candidates for federal office from soliciting or receiving soft money, and prevented state and local party organizations from spending soft money to promote or attack candidates for federal office. Essentially, all money donated to candidates, national political parties, and some other political organizations became hard money regulated by the federal election laws.

Second, Title II prohibited labor unions and corporations, including incorporated interest groups, from using their general funds to engage in "electioneering communication," defined as advertising (primarily televised) clearly referring to a candidate for federal office that appears within sixty days of a general election or thirty days of a primary election and targets the relevant constituency. The law also required comprehensive disclosure and record keeping related to such advertising. Exempt from these restrictions were media corporations and nonprofit organizations that took no contributions from for-profit corporations.

Third, to compensate political organizations for the loss of soft-money contributions, the law increased the ceiling on hard-money contributions and allowed some of the limitations to be adjusted periodically for inflation. Based on the adjusted limits in effect for the 2012 federal elections, individuals were permitted to give up to $2,500 per election to a candidate, $30,800 annually to a national political party, $10,000 annually to a state or local party, and $5,000 annually to a political action committee. In aggregate, such contributions could not exceed $117,000 per two-year election cycle (with limits of $46,200 to all candidates and $70,800 to groups such as national political parties and PACs).

Given these new restrictions, it was predictable that the law would be challenged. The provisions that restricted the freedom of corporations and labor unions to make independent campaign expenditures seemed particularly vulnerable given the ruling in *Buckley v. Valeo,* which tended to equate spending with speech. Supporters of the law were, however, encouraged by the Supreme Court's decision in *Austin v. Michigan Chamber of Commerce* (1990), in which the justices upheld a state law that prohibited corporations from making independent campaign contributions from their general treasuries in support of or opposition to candidates for state office.

A number of individuals and organizations challenged BCRA as soon as it became effective. The challengers included groups that rarely found themselves on the same side of public policy issues: the National Rifle Association, the National Right to Life Committee, the American Civil Liberties Union, the California Democratic Party, the Republican National Committee, the Chamber of Commerce of the United States, and the AFL/CIO. All believed that the new law violated the First Amendment. Most vigorously attacked were the soft-money and issue advocacy provisions. The attacks on the new law were consolidated into a single dispute, with the lawsuit filed by Senator Mitch McConnell, R-Ky., designated as the lead case. This dispute presented the Court with a conflict between two important values: the freedom of speech and the need to protect the real and perceived integrity of the electoral process.

In *McConnell v. Federal Election Commission* (2003) the Court upheld BCRA against arguments that Congress had exceeded its authority and that the law violated the First Amendment, but the Court was badly fractured. A five-justice majority, representing the more liberal justices, reasoned that Congress had the authority to protect the integrity of the electoral process by imposing the restrictions included in BCRA. The four dissenters, all from the Court's more conservative wing, expressed strong disagreement with the decision, calling it a sad day for the First Amendment. Crucial to the decision was Justice Sandra Day O'Connor, generally regarded as a swing vote. She decided in favor of the law's validity.

The unstable nature of the Court's position on campaign finance reform became even more so when Justice O'Connor retired and was replaced by Justice Samuel Alito in 2006. Just five months after Alito took his seat, the Court in *Randall v. Sorrell* (2006) struck down a Vermont law that placed stringent ceilings on campaign contributions. Among its other provisions, the law limited individual donations to candidates for statewide office to $400 per two-year election cycle, with lower limits of $200 for some local offices. The law also put strict ceilings on the amount of money candidates could spend. The Court invalidated the law, saying that the Constitution is violated when contribution and spending limitations, like those imposed by the Vermont law, become so severe as to damage freedom of speech interests.

Two years later, in *Davis v. Federal Election Commission* (2008), the justices declared unconstitutional the so-called millionaire's amendment to BCRA. This provision dealt with wealthy candidates who in large part finance their own campaigns with personal funds. Under the law, once those personal funds exceeded a particular threshold as determined by a complex statistical formula, supporters of the self-financing candidate's opponent were allowed to donate up to three times the regular contribution limits permitted under BCRA. Supporters of the self-financing candidate, however, were required to abide by the normal contribution ceilings. The law was designed to reduce the advantage of wealthy candidates, but the justices found that it placed an impermissible burden on candidates' First Amendment rights to use their own money for campaign speech.

The *Randall* and *Davis* decisions gave way to speculation that the *McConnell* ruling no longer had the support of the Court's majority. In both decisions Justice Alito voted with the conservative bloc to strike down the campaign finance restrictions. It appeared that the Court now had a five-justice majority opposed on First Amendment grounds to strong limitations on campaign finance. That speculation was tested in the watershed case of *Citizens United v. Federal Election Commission*.

Citizens United v. Federal Election Commission

558 U.S. ___ (2010)

http://laws.findlaw.com/us/000/08-205.html
Oral arguments are available at http://www.oyez.org.
Vote: 5 (Alito, Kennedy, Roberts, Scalia, Thomas)
    4 (Breyer, Ginsburg, Sotomayor, Stevens)

OPINION OF THE COURT: Kennedy

CONCURRING OPINIONS: Roberts, Scalia

OPINIONS CONCURRING IN PART AND DISSENTING IN PART:
    Stevens, Thomas

FACTS:

In January 2008, Citizens United, a nonprofit corporation that receives some funding from for-profit organizations, released *Hillary: The Movie,* a documentary film critical of then-senator Hillary Clinton, a candidate for the Democratic presidential nomination. The film depicted Clinton as unfit for the presidency. Anticipating that it would make the film available on cable television through video-on-demand programming, Citizens United produced television advertisements promoting the documentary to run on broadcast and cable television. Concerned about possible civil and criminal penalties for violating campaign finance laws, Citizens United initiated legal action against the Federal Election Commission (FEC), arguing that (1) section 203 of the Bipartisan Campaign Reform Act (BCRA), which prohibits corporations and labor unions from using general treasury funds to finance independent electioneering communications, is unconstitutional as applied to *Hillary*; and (2) BCRA's disclaimer, disclosure, and reporting requirements (sections 201 and 311) are unconstitutional as applied to *Hillary*

Citizens United president David Bossie stands outside the Supreme Court on January 21, 2010, after hearing the Court's ruling in Citizens United v. FCC.

and the advertisements. A three-judge district court ruled in favor of the FEC, and Citizens United appealed.

The full opinion in this case runs almost two hundred pages. The excerpt provided here focuses on the issue of the right of corporations to engage in political speech.

ARGUMENTS:

For the appellant, Citizens United:

- The government may not suppress political speech except when necessary to prevent corruption or the appearance of corruption.
- *Hillary* is not express advocacy. No compelling interest supports the government's effort to prohibit video-on-demand distribution of Citizens United's feature-length documentary film.
- *Austin v. Michigan State Chamber of Commerce* (1990) should be overruled. It was wrongly decided and is flatly at odds with the well-established principle that First Amendment protections do not depend on the identity of the speaker.

For the appellee, Federal Election Commission:

- The Supreme Court has approved the power of Congress to restrict corporations from using their treasury funds to finance express advocacy or its functional equivalent.

- *Hillary* is the functional equivalent of express advocacy because it focuses on Senator Clinton's candidacy and character.
- There is no exception under the law for feature-length films or video-on-demand distribution.

JUSTICE KENNEDY DELIVERED THE OPINION OF THE COURT.

In this case we are asked to reconsider *Austin* [*v. Michigan Chamber of Commerce* (1990)] and, in effect, *McConnell* [*v. Federal Election Commission* (2003)]. It has been noted that "*Austin* was a significant departure from ancient First Amendment principles," *Federal Election Comm'n v. Wisconsin Right to Life, Inc.* (2007) [*WRTL*]. We agree with that conclusion and hold that stare decisis does not compel the continued acceptance of *Austin*. The Government may regulate corporate political speech through disclaimer and disclosure requirements, but it may not suppress that speech altogether. We turn to the case now before us. . . .

The law before us is an outright ban, backed by criminal sanctions. Section 441b [of the U.S. code] makes it a felony for all corporations—including non-profit advocacy corporations—either to expressly advocate the election or defeat of candidates or to broadcast electioneering communications within 30 days of a primary election and 60 days of a general election. . . .

Section 441b's prohibition on corporate independent expenditures is thus a ban on speech. As a "restriction on the amount of money a person or group can spend on political communication during a campaign," that statute "necessarily reduces the quantity of expression by restricting the number of issues discussed, the depth of their exploration, and the size of the audience reached." *Buckley v. Valeo* (1976). Were the Court to uphold these restrictions, the Government could repress speech by silencing certain voices at any of the various points in the speech process. If §441b applied to individuals, no one would believe that it is merely a time, place, or manner restriction on speech. Its purpose and effect are to silence entities whose voices the Government deems to be suspect.

Speech is an essential mechanism of democracy, for it is the means to hold officials accountable to the people. The right of citizens to inquire, to hear, to speak, and to use information to reach consensus is a precondition to enlightened self-government and a necessary means to protect it. The First Amendment "'has its fullest and most urgent application' to speech uttered during a campaign for political office." *Eu v. San Francisco County Democratic Central Comm* (1989).

For these reasons, political speech must prevail against laws that would suppress it, whether by design or inadvertence. Laws that burden political speech are "subject to strict scrutiny," which requires the Government to prove that the restriction "furthers a compelling interest and is narrowly tailored to achieve that interest." [WRTL] While it might be maintained that political speech simply cannot be banned or restricted as a categorical matter, the quoted language from *WRTL* provides a sufficient framework for protecting the relevant First Amendment interests in this case. We shall employ it here.

Premised on mistrust of governmental power, the First Amendment stands against attempts to disfavor certain subjects or viewpoints. Prohibited, too, are restrictions distinguishing among different speakers, allowing speech by some but not others. As instruments to censor, these categories are interrelated: Speech restrictions based on the identity of the speaker are all too often simply a means to control content.

Quite apart from the purpose or effect of regulating content, moreover, the Government may commit a constitutional wrong when by law it identifies certain preferred speakers. By taking the right to speak from some and giving it to others, the Government deprives the disadvantaged person or class of the right to use speech to strive to establish worth, standing, and respect for the speaker's voice. The Government may not by these means deprive the public of the right and privilege to determine for itself what speech and speakers are worthy of consideration. The First Amendment protects speech and speaker, and the ideas that flow from each.

The Court has upheld a narrow class of speech restrictions that operate to the disadvantage of certain persons, but these rulings were based on an interest in allowing governmental entities to perform their functions. The corporate independent expenditures at issue in this case, however, would not interfere with governmental functions, so these cases are inapposite. These precedents stand only for the proposition that there are certain governmental functions that cannot operate without some restrictions on particular kinds of speech. By contrast, it is inherent in the nature of the political process that voters must be free to obtain information from diverse sources in order to determine how to cast their votes. At least before *Austin,* the Court had not allowed the exclusion of a class of speakers from the general public dialogue.

We find no basis for the proposition that, in the context of political speech, the Government may impose restrictions on certain disfavored speakers. Both history and logic lead us to this conclusion.

The Court has recognized that First Amendment protection extends to corporations. [E.g., *First National Bank of Boston v. Bellotti* (1978); *Doran v. Salem Inn, Inc.* (1975); *Southeastern Promotions, Ltd. v. Conrad* (1975); *Cox Broadcasting Corp. v. Cohn* (1975); *Miami Herald Publishing Co. v. Tornillo* (1974); *New York Times Co. v. United States* (1971); *Time, Inc. v. Hill* (1967); *New York Times Co. v. Sullivan* (1964); *Turner Broadcasting System, Inc. v. FCC* (1997); *Young v. American Mini Theatres, Inc.* (1976); *Gertz v. Robert Welch, Inc.* (1974).]

This protection has been extended by explicit holdings to the context of political speech. Under the rationale of these precedents, political speech does not lose First Amendment protection "simply because its source is a corporation." *Bellotti.* The Court has thus rejected the argument that political speech of corporations or other associations should be treated differently under the First Amendment simply because such associations are not "natural persons." . . .

"We thus find no support in the First . . . Amendment, or in the decisions of this Court, for the proposition that speech that otherwise would be within the protection of the First Amendment loses that protection simply because its source is a corporation that cannot prove, to the satisfaction of a court, a material effect on its business or property. . . . [That proposition] amounts to an impermissible legislative prohibition of speech based on the identity of the interests that spokesmen may represent in public debate over controversial issues and a requirement that the speaker have a sufficiently great interest in the subject to justify communication. [*Bellotti*]

"In the realm of protected speech, the legislature is constitutionally disqualified from dictating the subjects about which persons may speak and the speakers who may address a public issue." [*Bellotti*]

It is important to note that the reasoning and holding of *Bellotti* did not rest on the existence of a viewpoint-discriminatory statute. It rested on the principle that the Government lacks the power to ban corporations from speaking.

Bellotti did not address the constitutionality of the State's ban on corporate independent expenditures to support candidates. In our view, however, that restriction would have been unconstitutional under *Bellotti*'s central principle: that the First Amendment does not allow political speech restrictions based on a speaker's corporate identity.

Thus the law stood until *Austin. Austin* "uph[eld] a direct restriction on the independent expenditure of funds for political speech for the first time in [this Court's] history." There, the Michigan Chamber of Commerce sought to use general treasury funds to run a newspaper ad supporting a specific candidate. Michigan law, however, prohibited corporate independent expenditures that supported or opposed any candidate for state office. A violation of the law was punishable as a felony. The Court sustained the speech prohibition.

To bypass *Buckley* and *Bellotti,* the *Austin* Court identified a new governmental interest in limiting political speech: an antidistortion interest. *Austin* found a compelling governmental interest in preventing "the corrosive and distorting effects of immense aggregations of wealth that are accumulated with the help of the corporate form and that have little or no correlation to the public's support for the corporation's political ideas."

The Court is thus confronted with conflicting lines of precedent: a pre-*Austin* line that forbids restrictions on political speech based on the speaker's corporate identity and a post-*Austin* line that permits them. No case before *Austin* had held that Congress could prohibit independent expenditures for political speech based on the speaker's corporate identity. Before *Austin* Congress had enacted legislation for this purpose, and the

Government urged the same proposition before this Court. [See *Federal Election Comm'n v. Massachusetts Citizens for Life, Inc.* (1986) and *California Medical Assn. v. Federal Election Comm'n* (1981).] In neither of these cases did the Court adopt the proposition.

In its defense of the corporate-speech restrictions in §441b, the Government notes the antidistortion rationale on which *Austin* and its progeny rest in part, yet it all but abandons reliance upon it. . . .[T]he Government does little to defend it. And with good reason, for the rationale cannot support §441b.

If the First Amendment has any force, it prohibits Congress from fining or jailing citizens, or associations of citizens, for simply engaging in political speech. If the antidistortion rationale were to be accepted, however, it would permit Government to ban political speech simply because the speaker is an association that has taken on the corporate form. The Government contends that *Austin* permits it to ban corporate expenditures for almost all forms of communication stemming from a corporation. If *Austin* were correct, the Government could prohibit a corporation from expressing political views in media beyond those presented here, such as by printing books. . . . This troubling assertion of brooding governmental power cannot be reconciled with the confidence and stability in civic discourse that the First Amendment must secure. . . .

It is irrelevant for purposes of the First Amendment that corporate funds may "have little or no correlation to the public's support for the corporation's political ideas." All speakers, including individuals and the media, use money amassed from the economic marketplace to fund their speech. The First Amendment protects the resulting speech, even if it was enabled by economic transactions with persons or entities who disagree with the speaker's ideas.

Austin's antidistortion rationale would produce the dangerous, and unacceptable, consequence that Congress could ban political speech of media corporations. Media corporations are now exempt from §441b's ban on corporate expenditures. Yet media corporations accumulate wealth with the help of the corporate form, the largest media corporations have "immense aggregations of wealth," and the views expressed by media corporations often "have little or no correlation to the public's support" for those views. *Austin*. Thus, under the Government's reasoning, wealthy media corporations could have their voices diminished to put them on par with other media entities. There is no precedent for permitting this under the First Amendment. . . .

Austin interferes with the "open marketplace" of ideas protected by the First Amendment. It permits the Government to ban the political speech of millions of associations of citizens. Most of these are small corporations without large amounts of wealth. This fact belies the Government's argument that the statute is justified on the ground that it prevents the "distorting effects of immense aggregations of wealth." *Austin.* It is not even aimed at amassed wealth. . . .

The purpose and effect of this law is to prevent corporations, including small and nonprofit corporations, from presenting both facts and opinions to the public. . . .

Even if §441b's expenditure ban were constitutional, wealthy corporations could still lobby elected officials, although smaller corporations may not have the resources to do so. And wealthy individuals and unincorporated associations can spend unlimited amounts on independent expenditures. Yet certain disfavored associations of citizens—those that have taken on the corporate form—are penalized for engaging in the same political speech.

When Government seeks to use its full power, including the criminal law, to command where a person may get his or her information or what distrusted source he or she may not hear, it uses censorship to control thought. This is unlawful. The First Amendment confirms the freedom to think for ourselves. . . .

Our precedent is to be respected unless the most convincing of reasons demonstrates that adherence to it puts us on a course that is sure error. "Beyond workability, the relevant factors in deciding whether to adhere to the principle of stare decisis include the antiquity of the precedent, the reliance interests at stake, and of course whether the decision was well reasoned." *Montejo v. Louisiana* (2009).

These considerations counsel in favor of rejecting *Austin,* which itself contravened this Court's earlier precedents in *Buckley* and *Bellotti.*

For the reasons above, it must be concluded that *Austin* was not well reasoned. The Government defends *Austin,* relying almost entirely on "the quid pro quo interest, the corruption interest or the shareholder interest," and not *Austin*'s expressed antidistortion rationale. When neither party defends the reasoning of a precedent, the principle of adhering to that precedent through stare decisis is diminished. . . .

Due consideration leads to this conclusion: *Austin* should be and now is overruled. We return to the principle established in *Buckley* and *Bellotti* that the Government may not suppress political speech on the basis of the speaker's corporate identity. No sufficient governmental interest justifies limits on the political speech of nonprofit or for-profit corporations.

Given our conclusion we are further required to overrule the part of *McConnell* that upheld BCRA §203's extension of §441b's restrictions on corporate independent expenditures. The *McConnell* Court relied on the antidistortion interest recognized in *Austin* to uphold a greater restriction on speech than the restriction upheld in *Austin,* and we have found this interest unconvincing and insufficient. This part of *McConnell* is now overruled. . . .

[*Affirmed in part, reversed in part.*]

JUSTICE SCALIA, with whom JUSTICE ALITO joins, and with whom JUSTICE THOMAS joins in part, concurring.

The [First] Amendment is written in terms of "speech," not speakers. Its text offers no foothold for excluding any category of speaker, from single individuals to partnerships of individuals, to unincorporated associations of individuals, to incorporated associations of individuals—and the dissent offers no evidence about the original meaning of the text to support any such exclusion. We are therefore simply left with the question whether the speech at issue in this case is "speech" covered by the First Amendment. No one says otherwise. A documentary film critical of a potential Presidential candidate is core political speech, and its nature as such does not change simply because it was funded by a corporation. Nor does the character of that funding produce any reduction whatever in the "inherent worth of the speech" and "its capacity for informing the public[.]" *Bellotti.* Indeed, to exclude or impede corporate speech is to muzzle the principal agents of the modern free economy. We should celebrate rather than condemn the addition of this speech to the public debate.

JUSTICE STEVENS, with whom JUSTICE GINSBURG, JUSTICE BREYER, and JUSTICE SOTOMAYOR join, concurring in part and dissenting in part.

The real issue in this case concerns how, not if, the appellant may finance its electioneering. Citizens United is a wealthy nonprofit corporation that runs a political action committee (PAC) with millions of dollars in assets. Under the Bipartisan Campaign Reform Act of 2002 (BCRA), it could have used those assets to televise and promote *Hillary: The Movie* wherever and whenever it wanted to. It also could have spent unrestricted sums to broadcast *Hillary* at any time other than the 30 days before the last primary election. Neither Citizens United's nor any other corporation's speech has been "banned." All that the parties dispute is whether Citizens United had a right to use the funds in its general treasury to pay for broadcasts during the 30-day period. The notion that the First Amendment dictates an affirmative answer to that question is, in my judgment, profoundly misguided. Even more misguided is the notion that the Court must rewrite the law relating to campaign expenditures by for-profit corporations and unions to decide this case.

The basic premise underlying the Court's ruling is its iteration, and constant reiteration, of the proposition that the First Amendment bars regulatory distinctions based on a speaker's identity, including its "identity" as a corporation. While that glittering generality has rhetorical appeal, it is not a correct statement of the law. Nor does it tell us when a corporation may engage in electioneering that some of its shareholders oppose. It does not even resolve the specific question whether Citizens United may be required to finance some of its messages with the money in its PAC. The conceit that corporations must be treated identically to natural persons in the political sphere is not only inaccurate but also inadequate to justify the Court's disposition of this case.

In the context of election to public office, the distinction between corporate and human speakers is significant. Although they make enormous contributions to our society, corporations are not actually members of it. They cannot vote or run for office. Because they may be managed and controlled by nonresidents, their interests may conflict in fundamental respects with the interests of eligible voters. The financial resources, legal structure, and instrumental orientation of corporations raise legitimate concerns about their role in the electoral process. Our lawmakers have a compelling constitutional basis, if not also a democratic duty, to take measures designed to guard against the potentially deleterious effects of corporate spending in local and national races. . . .

I am not an absolutist when it comes to stare decisis, in the campaign finance area or in any other. No one is. But if this principle is to do any meaningful work in supporting the rule of law, it must at least demand a significant justification, beyond the preferences of five Justices, for overturning settled doctrine. "[A] decision to overrule should rest on some special reason over and above the belief that a prior case was wrongly decided." *Planned Parenthood of Southeastern Pa. v. Casey* (1992). No such justification exists in this case, and to the

contrary there are powerful prudential reasons to keep faith with our precedents.

In the end, the Court's rejection of *Austin* and *McConnell* comes down to nothing more than its disagreement with their results. Virtually every one of its arguments was made and rejected in those cases, and the majority opinion is essentially an amalgamation of resuscitated dissents. The only relevant thing that has changed since *Austin* and *McConnell* is the composition of this Court. Today's ruling thus strikes at the vitals of stare decisis, "the means by which we ensure that the law will not merely change erratically, but will develop in a principled and intelligible fashion" that "permits society to presume that bedrock principles are founded in the law rather than in the proclivities of individuals." *Vasquez v. Hillery* (1986). . . .

Today's decision is backwards in many senses. It elevates the majority's agenda over the litigants' submissions, facial attacks over as-applied claims, broad constitutional theories over narrow statutory grounds, individual dissenting opinions over precedential holdings, assertion over tradition, absolutism over empiricism, rhetoric over reality. Our colleagues have arrived at the conclusion that *Austin* must be overruled and that §203 is facially unconstitutional only after mischaracterizing both the reach and rationale of those authorities, and after bypassing or ignoring rules of judicial restraint used to cabin the Court's lawmaking power. Their conclusion that the societal interest in avoiding corruption and the appearance of corruption does not provide an adequate justification for regulating corporate expenditures on candidate elections relies on an incorrect description of that interest, along with a failure to acknowledge the relevance of established facts and the considered judgments of state and federal legislatures over many decades.

In a democratic society, the longstanding consensus on the need to limit corporate campaign spending should outweigh the wooden application of judge-made rules. The majority's rejection of this principle "elevate[s] corporations to a level of deference which has not been seen at least since the days when substantive due process was regularly used to invalidate regulatory legislation thought to unfairly impinge upon established economic interests." *Bellotti.* At bottom, the Court's opinion is thus a rejection of the common sense of the American people, who have recognized a need to prevent corporations from undermining self-government since the founding, and who have fought against the distinctive corrupting potential of corporate electioneering since the days of Theodore Roosevelt. It is a strange time to repudiate that common sense. While American democracy is imperfect, few outside the majority of this Court would have thought its flaws included a dearth of corporate money in politics.

JUSTICE THOMAS, concurring in part and dissenting in part.

. . . Political speech is entitled to robust protection under the First Amendment. Section 203 of the Bipartisan Campaign Reform Act of 2002 (BCRA) has never been reconcilable with that protection. By striking down §203, the Court takes an important first step toward restoring full constitutional protection to speech that is "indispensable to the effective and intelligent use of the processes of popular government." *McConnell.* I dissent from [a part] of the Court's opinion, however, because the Court's constitutional analysis

does not go far enough. The disclosure, disclaimer, and reporting requirements in BCRA §§201 and 311 are also unconstitutional. . . .

Citizens United was a major defeat for those who supported restrictions on corporate participation in election campaigns. Although the decision did not upset a long-standing ban on corporate donations directly to political candidates, it provided constitutional protection for the right of unions and corporations to use their funds to support their own independent political advertising. The decision was quite controversial. With several of the justices in attendance, President Obama even condemned the ruling during his nationally televised 2010 State of the Union address. In addition, the decision had profound effects on the conduct of election campaigns *(see Box 14-3).*

BOX 14-3   AFTERMATH . . . *CITIZENS UNITED* AND THE RISE OF THE SUPER PAC

Political Action Committees (PACs) have long been a fixture of American politics. These organizations raise funds for political purposes, make financial contributions to political candidates, and engage in political communications of their own. Most traditional PACs are created by unions, corporations, trade associations, or other organized interests with the goal of raising funds and using them to support candidates and causes that further their sponsors' political and policy goals. The amount of money an individual can contribute to a PAC is limited under federal law, and so is the amount of money a PAC can contribute to a political candidate.

The Supreme Court's decision in *Citizens United v. FEC* (2010) held that labor unions and corporations have a First Amendment right to spend their own money in whatever amounts they wish for direct political advertising. This decision was followed by an important 2010 court of appeals ruling, *SpeechNow.Org v. Federal Election Commission,* which had the effect of removing federal contribution and spending limitations on organizations that use their funds only for political expenditures independent of candidates or political parties.

These two decisions gave rise to a new variety of political action committee—the "independent expenditure-only committee," better known as the Super PAC. Like traditional PACs, Super PACs must register with the Federal Election Commission and must generally disclose the contributions they receive. But unlike traditional PACS, Super

PACs do not contribute to candidates or parties. Rather, a Super PAC carries out a single function—the independent expenditure of campaign funds. As long as the organization remains independent of any candidate and does not coordinate its efforts with any candidate's campaign, it may receive and spend unlimited amounts of money for the election or defeat of anyone running for public office. As a consequence, the Super PAC has become a way in which corporations, unions, and wealthy individuals may contribute large sums of money for political purposes.

Super PACs began playing a significant role in American politics during the 2012 presidential campaign. Each major candidate in the primary and general elections enjoyed the support of a Super PAC dedicated to advancing the candidate's electoral prospects. These Super PACs often were created and run by friends and former associates of the candidates. They attracted and spent millions of dollars on political advertising favoring their candidates—all outside the campaign finance limitations imposed by federal law on candidates and political parties. Although these Super PACs remained officially independent of the candidates they supported, there is little doubt that the leaders of these organizations understood the political strategies and advertising messages that would be most beneficial to their candidates' causes.

The rise of the Super PAC gave truth to the statement made by Justices Stevens and O'Connor in their opinion for the Court in *McConnell v. FEC*: "Money, like water, will always find an outlet."

POLITICAL REPRESENTATION

Having the right to vote and the promise of honest elections does not guarantee that everyone shares equally in political influence. The United States is not a direct democracy; consequently, few public policy decisions are made in the voting booth. In a republican form of government, most political decisions are made by officials elected by the people from defined geographical districts. The duty of these officials is to represent the interests of their constituencies in the policy-making process.

How well and how equitably this representational process works depends in part on how the boundary lines of political units are drawn. Because district lines determine political representation, the authority to draw those boundaries carries with it a great deal of political power. Skillful construction of political subdivisions can be used to great advantage, and politicians have never been reluctant to use this power to advance their own interests. Since 1812 the art of structuring legislative districts to ensure political success has been known as *gerrymandering*. The term refers to the political maneuverings of Massachusetts governor Elbridge Gerry, who convinced the state legislature to draw district lines so that his partisan supporters would have a high probability of reelection. Gerrymandered districts frequently are characterized by the rather strange geographical configurations necessary to achieve the desired political ends.

Historically, the establishment or modification of district lines has been a political matter. Battles over drawing the boundaries of political subdivisions usually are fought within the halls of state legislatures. When officials use inappropriate criteria for drawing boundaries or when the process results in the discriminatory treatment of certain groups of voters, however, serious legal or even constitutional questions may arise. In such cases the courts may be called upon to intervene in what is otherwise a legislative duty.

The Reapportionment Controversy

In drafting Article I of the Constitution, the framers clearly intended that representation in the lower house of Congress would be based on population. Each state was allotted at least one representative, with additional seats based on the number of persons residing within state boundaries.

In 1812 Elkanah Tinsdale lampooned the political maneuverings of Governor Elbridge Gerry of Massachusetts, who deftly engineered the construction of constituency boundaries to aid in the election of a member of his own party. Because the district resembled a salamander in the cartoonist's illustration, the term gerrymander has come to mean the drawing of political district lines for partisan advantage.

The Constitutional Convention wisely anticipated that the population would grow and that people would move from one state to another. The framers determined that the number of congressional seats allocated to each state would be reformulated every ten years following the national census. States that grew in population would gain more congressional representation, and those that lost population would have less representation. This process remains relatively unchanged today. The number of seats in the House of Representatives is fixed by federal law, currently at 435. Every ten years, when the U.S. Bureau of the Census completes its work, the allocation of those 435 seats among the states must be recalculated to reflect changes since the previous population count. Following the 2010 census, for example, Texas gained four House seats, Florida increased by two, and the states of Arizona, Georgia, Nevada, South Carolina, Utah, and Washington each added one more congressional representative. By contrast, Ohio and New York each lost two seats, and the states of Illinois, Iowa, Louisiana, Massachusetts, Michigan, Missouri, New Jersey, and Pennsylvania all lost one.

Following the census, each state is told the number of representatives it will have for the next decade. The state legislature then geographically divides the state into separate congressional districts, each of which elects a member of Congress. This scheme is known as the single-member constituency system of representation.[4] Political representation is equitable only if the state legislature constructs its congressional districts so that each contains approximately the same number of residents.

The process of devising legislative districts is called *apportionment.* When the legislature creates equally populated districts, the system is properly apportioned. When the districts are not in proper balance—that is, when some districts have substantially larger populations than others—they are said to be malapportioned. A state can be malapportioned if the legislature does not draw the district lines properly or fails to adjust boundaries to keep pace with population shifts.

Representational districts are used for other government units as well as for congressional seats. The state legislatures, for example, generally are based on the single-member constituency system, as are many county commissions and city councils. Even special-purpose commissions, such as boards of education and public utility districts, often follow the same scheme. In each case, a legislative body must create districts from which representatives will be selected. The same apportionment concepts apply to these bodies as to congressional districts.

Constitutional issues related to apportionment began to arise in the 1940s. Spurred by industrialization, two major wars, and an economic depression, many Americans had moved from rural areas and small towns into urban centers during the first half of the twentieth century. The cities grew rapidly while agricultural areas declined, but state legislatures failed to respond adequately to these migration patterns by reapportioning their congressional and state legislative districts. The more rural interests dominated state legislatures, the less incumbent legislators wished to consider redistricting. If the districts were apportioned properly, that would mean fewer legislative seats for the rural areas, and that meant abolishing some seats

---

4. During the first half century of the nation's history, it was common for the states to select their delegates to the House of Representatives on an at-large basis rather than using the single-member constituency plan.

held by incumbents. At the midpoint of the twentieth century, many states had not reapportioned since the 1900 census.

The first major apportionment case to come before the Supreme Court was ***Colegrove v. Green*** (1946), a challenge to the congressional districts in Illinois, where the largest district had almost nine times as many residents as the smallest. This imbalance was attacked on the ground that it resulted in a system that violated the Constitution's guarantee of a republican form of government. The Supreme Court, however, refused to rule on the case, holding, 4–3, that reapportionment was a political issue that should be resolved at the ballot box and not in court.

The Court's admonishment presented an insurmountable problem for urban residents living in disproportionately large districts. Many states were so badly malapportioned, and the dominant rural interests so opposed to change, that electing enough state legislators sympathetic to reapportionment was almost impossible. But the Court maintained its position that reapportionment questions were outside the purview of judicial scrutiny. Meanwhile, the census figures for 1950 and 1960 indicated that the malapportionment problem was growing.

In the early 1960s the Supreme Court's position began to soften. This change was prompted not only by a greater awareness of the problems associated with malapportionment but also by significant personnel changes on the Court. Of the four justices who had voted against Kenneth Colegrove's demand for reapportionment in 1948, only Felix Frankfurter remained on the bench, and the Court, now under the leadership of Earl Warren, expressed its willingness to accept rights violations claims.

In 1962 the Court decided ***Baker v. Carr,*** in which a group of urban residents from Tennessee challenged the way their state legislative districts were drawn. Although this case involved representation in the state assembly rather than in Congress, the factual parallels between *Baker* and *Colegrove* were notable. The central question in *Baker* was whether the federal courts have jurisdiction over apportionment cases. Rather than basing their jurisdictional claim on the Constitution's republican form of government guarantee, as *Colegrove* had done, the plaintiffs in *Baker* argued that the malapportioned Tennessee legislature violated the Fourteenth Amendment's equal protection clause.

If the Court did not alter its position that apportionment was a political question over which the federal courts had no say, urban residents would continue to find their representational voice diluted by legislatures dominated by rural interests. But a decision that granted federal court jurisdiction undoubtedly would set off an avalanche of litigation throughout the nation.

The justices considered the *Baker* case with extreme care.[5] The Court heard six hours of oral argument on two separate occasions. The justices deliberated at length in conference. The opinions took up 163 pages in *U.S. Reports* and covered a wide range of subjects, such as the political question doctrine, the guarantee and equal protection clauses, standing, and justiciability.

With only Frankfurter and John Marshall Harlan (II) in dissent, the Court held that the federal judiciary has authority to hear challenges to state districting systems and that equal protection arguments present justiciable issues not barred by the political question doctrine. Although the Court confined itself to these jurisdictional issues, the ruling in *Baker* opened the Supreme Court's doors to reapportionment cases, and most observers believed that the justices were prepared to initiate significant changes in the nation's system of political representation.

The next major reapportionment case was **Wesberry v. Sanders** (1964), which involved a challenge to the way Georgia apportioned its congressional districts. Although this case involved only Georgia, the malapportionment there was typical of most states following the 1960 census.

James P. Wesberry and other qualified voters of Georgia's Fifth Congressional District filed suit against the governor, Carl Sanders, and other state officials. The plaintiffs claimed that the state's congressional districting system violated the federal Constitution. The Fifth (metropolitan Atlanta) was the largest of Georgia's ten congressional districts, with a population of 823,680. By comparison, the Ninth District had only 272,154 residents, and the population of the average district was 394,312. This inequality meant that the Fifth District's legislator represented two to three times as many people as the other members of Congress from Georgia. The districting scheme dated

from 1931, and no effort to bring the districts into balance had occurred since then.

The justices held that this condition of significant malapportionment violated Article I, Section 2, of the Constitution, which says, "The House of Representatives shall be composed of Members chosen every second Year by the People of the several States." To satisfy that constitutional provision, the Court ruled, the congressional districts within a state must be as equal in population as practicably possible. The decision required the state legislature to redraw its congressional districts to meet this standard.

Wesberry, however, did not resolve the reapportionment controversy. A more difficult and politically charged issue centered on malapportionment within the state legislatures. It was one thing to command the state legislators to alter the boundaries of congressional districts, but still another to require them to reapportion their own legislative districts. Many legislators would regard such an action as an infringement on their state's sovereignty. In addition, the wholesale alteration of state legislative districts would mean that many state representatives would lose their districts or become politically vulnerable, and legislative power would shift from rural to urban interests. That the state legislatures were less than enthusiastic about such prospects is hardly surprising.

It did not take the Supreme Court long to address the dilemma of the state legislatures. Only four months after the *Wesberry* ruling, the Court announced its decision in *Reynolds v. Sims.* Although *Reynolds* shares with *Wesberry* questions of representational equality, the legal bases for the two cases are different. Article I, Section 2, of the Constitution, upon which the *Wesberry* outcome rested, concerns only the U.S. House of Representatives. Consequently, a challenge to state representational schemes had to be based on other grounds. In addition, all state legislatures except Nebraska's are bicameral, leaving open for dispute whether both houses of the state assembly must be population based. Note in Chief Justice Warren's majority opinion in *Reynolds* how the Court reaches a conclusion consistent with *Wesberry* while using entirely different constitutional grounds. Is the Court's holding on bicameralism reasonable? Or should the states be allowed to base representation in one house of the legislature on interests other than population alone? How compelling is Justice Harlan's dissent?

---

5. See J. W. Peltason, "*Baker v. Carr,*" in *The Oxford Companion,* 56–59.

Reynolds v. Sims

377 U.S. 533 (1964)
http://laws.findlaw.com/US/377/533.html
Oral arguments are available at http://www.oyez.org.
Vote: 8 (Black, Brennan, Clark, Douglas, Goldberg, Stewart, Warren, White)
  1 (Harlan)

OPINION OF THE COURT: *Warren*
CONCURRING OPINIONS: *Clark, Stewart*
DISSENTING OPINION: *Harlan*

FACTS:

Alabama's 1901 constitution authorized a state legislature of 106 House members and 35 senators. These legislators were to represent districts created generally on the basis of population equality. Although obliged to reapportion following each national census, the legislature had never altered the districts that were originally drawn following the 1900 census. Because of population shifts and a state constitutional requirement that each county, regardless of size, have at least one representative, Alabama had become severely malapportioned. In the state House of Representatives, the most populous legislative district had sixteen times as many people as the least populous. Conditions in the state Senate were even more inequitable. The largest senatorial district had a population forty-one times that of the smallest. As was the case in other states, rural areas enjoyed representation levels far higher than their populations warranted. For example, rural Lowndes County had one senator for its 15,417 citizens, while urban Jefferson County's single senator represented more than 600,000 residents.

O. M. Sims and other voters from urban counties filed suit against a group of state officials to have the Alabama system declared unconstitutional as a violation of the equal protection clause of the Fourteenth Amendment. Pressured by the threat of legal action in light of the Supreme Court's decision in *Baker v. Carr,* the state legislature offered two reapportionment plans to improve the situation. A three-judge district court declared the existing system unconstitutional and the proposed reforms inadequate. The judges imposed a temporary reapportionment plan, and the state appealed to the Supreme Court. The *Reynolds* case was one of six state legislative reapportionment disputes the Supreme Court heard at the same time. The others came from Colorado, Delaware, Maryland, New York, and Virginia. The justices used the opinion in *Reynolds* as the primary vehicle for articulating the Court's position on the state redistricting issue.

ARGUMENTS:

For the appellants, B. A. Reynolds and other State of Alabama officials:

- The Supreme Court should reconsider its decision in *Baker v. Carr* and return authority over legislative apportionment to the states.
- Under the Alabama constitution each county is entitled to at least one representative in the state House with additional representatives distributed on the basis of population. This is similar to the way states are represented in Congress.
- The state legislature developed a reapportionment plan that was declared unconstitutional by the district court even before it was voted on by the people. That plan would have followed the federal Senate model by allowing each county to have one senator and to base House districts on population.
- Population disparities are not invidious if they are designed rationally to protect rural interests from being dominated by big cities.

For the appellee, O. M. Sims, et al.:

- *Baker v. Carr* should be reaffirmed, and the federal courts should retain jurisdiction over this dispute.
- The existing apportionment of the Alabama legislature and the modifications proposed by the legislature all leave the state's representational scheme malapportioned and out of compliance with the equal protection clause of the Fourteenth Amendment.
- The district court should be authorized to continue to impose relief on behalf of the millions of Alabamans who have been denied their representational rights.

 MR. CHIEF JUSTICE WARREN DELIVERED THE OPINION OF THE COURT.

Legislators represent people, not trees or acres. Legislators are elected by voters, not farms or cities or economic interests. As long as ours is a representative form of government, and our legislatures are those instruments of government elected directly by and directly representative of the people, the right to elect legislators in a free and unimpaired fashion is a bedrock of our political system. It could hardly be gainsaid that a constitutional claim had been asserted by an allegation that certain otherwise qualified voters had been entirely prohibited from voting for members of their state legislature. And, if a State should provide that the votes of citizens in one part of the State should be given two times, or five times, or 10 times the weight of votes of citizens in another part of the State, it could hardly be contended that the right to vote of those residing in the disfavored areas had not been effectively diluted. It would appear extraordinary to suggest that a State could be constitutionally permitted to enact a law providing that certain of the State's voters could vote two, five, or 10 times for their legislative representatives, while voters living elsewhere could vote only once. And it is inconceivable that a state law to the effect that, in counting votes for legislators, the votes of citizens in one part of the State would be multiplied by two, five, or 10 while the votes of persons in another area would be counted only at face value, could be constitutionally sustainable. Of course, the effect of state legislative districting schemes which give the same number of representatives to unequal numbers of constituents is identical. Overweighting and overvaluation of the votes of those living here has the certain effect of dilution and undervaluation of the votes of those living there. The resulting discrimination against those individual voters living in disfavored areas is easily demonstrable mathematically. Their right to vote is simply not the same right to vote as that of those living in a favored part of the State. Two, five, or 10 of them must vote before the effect of their voting is equivalent to that of their favored neighbor. Weighting the votes of citizens differently, by any method or means, merely because of where they happen to reside, hardly seems justifiable. One must be ever aware that the Constitution forbids "sophisticated as well as simple-minded modes of discrimination." . . .

Logically, in a society ostensibly grounded on representative government, it would seem reasonable that a majority of the people of a State could elect a majority of that State's legislators. To conclude differently, and to sanction minority control of state legislative bodies, would appear to deny majority rights in a way that far surpasses any possible denial of minority rights that might otherwise be thought to result. Since legislatures are responsible for enacting laws by which all citizens are to be governed, they should be bodies which are collectively responsive to the popular will. And the concept of equal protection has been traditionally viewed as requiring the uniform treatment of persons standing in the same relation to the governmental action questioned or challenged. With respect to the allocation of legislative representation, all voters, as citizens of a State, stand in the same relation regardless of where

they live. Any suggested criteria for the differentiation of citizens are insufficient to justify any discrimination, as to the weight of their votes, unless relevant to the permissible purposes of legislative apportionment. Since the achieving of fair and effective representation for all citizens is concededly the basic aim of legislative apportionment, we conclude that the Equal Protection Clause guarantees the opportunity for equal participation by all voters in the election of state legislators. Diluting the weight of votes because of place of residence impairs basic constitutional rights under the Fourteenth Amendment just as much as invidious discriminations based upon factors such as race or economic status. . . .

We are told that the matter of apportioning representation in a state legislature is a complex and many-faceted one. We are advised that States can rationally consider factors other than population in apportioning legislative representation. We are admonished not to restrict the power of the States to impose differing views as to political philosophy on their citizens. We are cautioned about the dangers of entering into political thickets and mathematical quagmires. Our answer is this: a denial of constitutionally protected rights demands judicial protection; our oath and our office require no less of us. . . . To the extent that a citizen's right to vote is debased, he is that much less a citizen. The fact that an individual lives here or there is not a legitimate reason for overweighting or diluting the efficacy of his vote. The complexions of societies and civilizations change, often with amazing rapidity. A nation once primarily rural in character becomes predominantly urban. Representation schemes once fair and equitable become archaic and outdated. But the basic principle of representative government remains, and must remain, unchanged—the weight of a citizen's vote cannot be made to depend on where he lives. Population is, of necessity, the starting point for consideration and the controlling criterion for judgment in legislative apportionment controversies. A citizen, a qualified voter, is no more nor no less so because he lives in the city or on the farm. This is the clear and strong command of our Constitution's Equal Protection Clause. This is an essential part of the concept of a government of laws and not men. This is at the heart of Lincoln's vision of "government of the people, by the people, [and] for the people." The Equal Protection Clause demands no less than substantially equal state legislative representation for all citizens, of all places as well as of all races.

We hold that, as a basic constitutional standard, the Equal Protection Clause requires that the seats in both houses of a bicameral state legislature must be apportioned on a population basis. Simply stated, an individual's right to vote for state legislators is unconstitutionally impaired when its weight is in a substantial fashion diluted when compared with votes of citizens living in other parts of the State. . . .

Legislative apportionment in Alabama is signally illustrative and symptomatic of the seriousness of this problem in a number of the States. At the time this litigation was commenced, there had been no reapportionment of seats in the Alabama Legislature for over 60 years. Legislative inaction, coupled with the unavailability of any political or judicial remedy, had resulted, with the passage of years, in the perpetuated scheme becoming little more than an irrational anachronism. Consistent failure by the Alabama Legislature to comply with state constitutional requirements as to the frequency of reapportionment and the bases of legislative representation resulted in a minority stranglehold on the State Legislature. Inequality of representation in one house added to the inequality in the other. . . . Since neither of the houses of the Alabama Legislature, under any of the three plans considered by the District Court, was apportioned on a population basis, we would be justified in proceeding no further. However, one of the proposed plans, that contained in the so-called 67-Senator Amendment, at least superficially resembles the scheme of legislative representation followed in the Federal Congress. Under this plan, each of Alabama's 67 counties is allotted one senator, and no counties are given more than one Senate seat. Arguably, this is analogous to the allocation of two Senate seats, in the Federal Congress, to each of the 50 States, regardless of population. Seats in the Alabama House, under the proposed constitutional amendment, are distributed by giving each of the 67 counties at least one, with the remaining 39 seats being allotted among the more populous counties on a population basis. This scheme, at least at first glance, appears to resemble that prescribed for the Federal House of Representatives, where the 435 seats are distributed among the States on a population basis, although each State, regardless of its population, is given at least one Congressman. Thus, although there are substantial differences in underlying rationale and results, the 67-Senator Amendment, as proposed by the Alabama Legislature, at least arguably presents for

consideration a scheme analogous to that used for apportioning seats in Congress. . . .

We agree with the District Court, and find the federal analogy inapposite and irrelevant to state legislative districting schemes. Attempted reliance on the federal analogy appears often to be little more than an after-the-fact rationalization offered in defense of maladjusted state apportionment arrangements. The original constitutions of 36 of our States provided that representation in both houses of the state legislatures would be based completely, or predominantly, on population. And the Founding Fathers clearly had no intention of establishing a pattern or model for the apportionment of seats in state legislatures when the system of representation in the Federal Congress was adopted. . . .

The system of representation in the two Houses of the Federal Congress is one ingrained in our Constitution, as part of the law of the land. It is one conceived out of compromise and concession indispensable to the establishment of our federal republic. Arising from unique historical circumstances, it is based on the consideration that in establishing our type of federalism a group of formerly independent States bound themselves together under one national government. . . .

Political subdivisions of States—counties, cities, or whatever—never were and never have been considered as sovereign entities. Rather, they have been traditionally regarded as subordinate governmental instrumentalities created by the State to assist in the carrying out of state governmental functions. . . . The relationship of the States to the Federal Government could hardly be less analogous.

Thus, we conclude that the plan contained in the 67-Senator Amendment for apportioning seats in the Alabama Legislature cannot be sustained by recourse to the so-called federal analogy. Nor can any other inequitable state legislative apportionment scheme be justified. . . .

By holding that as a federal constitutional requisite both houses of a state legislature must be apportioned on a population basis, we mean that the Equal Protection Clause requires that a State make an honest and good faith effort to construct districts, in both houses of its legislature, as nearly of equal population as is practicable. We realize that it is a practical impossibility to arrange legislative districts so that each one has an identical number of residents, or citizens, or voters. Mathematical exactness or precision is hardly a workable constitutional requirement. . . .

A State may legitimately desire to maintain the integrity of various political subdivisions, insofar as possible, and provide for compact districts of contiguous territory in designing a legislative apportionment scheme. Valid considerations may underlie such aims. Indiscriminate districting, without any regard for political subdivision or natural or historical boundary lines, may be little more than an open invitation to partisan gerrymandering. Single-member districts may be the rule in one State, while another State might desire to achieve some flexibility by creating multimember or floterial districts. Whatever the means of accomplishment, the overriding objective must be substantial equality of population among the various districts, so that the vote of any citizen is approximately equal in weight to that of any other citizen in the State.

History indicates, however, that many States have deviated, to a greater or lesser degree, from the equal-population principle in the apportionment of seats in at least one house of their legislatures. So long as the divergences from a strict population standard are based on legitimate considerations incident to the effectuation of a rational state policy, some deviations from the equal-population principle are constitutionally permissible with respect to the apportionment of seats in either or both of the two houses of a bicameral state legislature. But neither history alone, nor economic or other sorts of group interests, are permissible factors in attempting to justify disparities from population-based representation. Citizens, not history or economic interests, cast votes. Considerations of area alone provide an insufficient justification for deviations from the equal population principle. . . .

We find, therefore, that the action taken by the District Court in this case, in ordering into effect a reapportionment of both houses of the Alabama Legislature for purposes of the 1962 primary and general elections, by using the best parts of the two proposed plans which it had found, as a whole, to be invalid, was an appropriate and well-considered exercise of judicial power. Admittedly, the lower court's ordered plan was intended only as a temporary and provisional measure and the District Court correctly indicated that the plan was invalid as a permanent apportionment. In retaining jurisdiction while deferring a hearing on the issuance of a final injunction in order to give the provisionally reapportioned legislature an opportunity to act effectively, the court below proceeded in a proper fashion.

It is so ordered.

MR. JUSTICE HARLAN, *dissenting.*

In these cases the Court holds that seats in the legislatures of six States are apportioned in ways that violate the Federal Constitution. Under the Court's ruling it is bound to follow that the legislature in all but a few of the other 44 States will meet the same fate. These decisions, with *Wesberry v. Sanders,* involving congressional districting by the States, and *Gray v. Sanders,* relating to elections for statewide office, have the effect of placing basic aspects of state political systems under the pervasive overlordship of the federal judiciary. Once again, I must register my protest.

Today's holding is that the Equal Protection Clause of the Fourteenth Amendment requires every State to structure its legislature so that all the members of each house represent substantially the same number of people; other factors may be given play only to the extent that they do not significantly encroach on this basic "population" principle. Whatever may be thought of this holding as a piece of political ideology—and even on that score the political history and practices of this country from its earliest beginnings leave wide room for debate . . . — I think it demonstrable that the Fourteenth Amendment does not impose this political tenet on the States or authorize this Court to do so.

The Court's constitutional discussion, found in its opinion in the Alabama cases, is remarkable . . . for its failure to address itself at all to the Fourteenth Amendment as a whole or to the legislative history of the Amendment pertinent to the matter at hand. Stripped of aphorisms, the Court's argument boils down to the assertion that appellees' right to vote has been invidiously "debased" or "diluted" by systems of apportionment which entitle them to vote for fewer legislators than other voters, an assertion which is tied to the Equal Protection Clause only by the constitutionally frail tautology that "equal" means "equal."

Had the Court paused to probe more deeply into the matter, it would have found that the Equal Protection Clause was never intended to inhibit the States in choosing any democratic method they pleased for the apportionment of their legislatures. This is shown by the language of the Fourteenth Amendment taken as a whole, by the understanding of those who proposed and ratified it, and by the political practices of the States at the time the Amendment was adopted. It is confirmed by numerous state and congressional actions since the adoption of the Fourteenth Amendment, and by the common understanding of the Amendment as evidenced by subsequent constitutional amendments and decisions of this Court before *Baker v. Carr* made an abrupt break with the past in 1962. . . .

So far as the Federal Constitution is concerned, the complaints in these cases should all have been dismissed below for failure to state a cause of action because what has been alleged or proved shows no violation of any constitutional right.

Justice Harlan's dissent in *Reynolds* predicting that the legislatures of all the states would be affected by the Court's one person, one vote principle proved to be accurate. At first, some states resisted complying with the Court's ruling. Opponents of the decision began a campaign to amend the Constitution to provide states the authority to have at least one house of their legislatures based on factors other than population, but the proposal failed to garner sufficient support. As the states began the Court-imposed reapportionment process, opposition started to wane. Today, reapportionment of congressional and state legislative districts routinely occurs each decade following the national census.

Upon his retirement, Chief Justice Warren said that, in his opinion, the reapportionment decisions were the most significant rulings rendered during his sixteen-year tenure. That statement was remarkable, considering that under his leadership the Court handed down landmark decisions on race relations, criminal justice, obscenity, libel, and school prayer.

Representational Equality: Applicability and Measurement

Although *Wesberry* and *Reynolds* made it clear that the Constitution demanded population-based representational units for the U.S. House of Representatives and both houses of state legislatures, the question of applying the one person, one vote principle to other governing bodies remained open. As early as 1963, when it struck down Georgia's county unit system of electing governors in *Gray v. Sanders,* the Supreme Court indicated a willingness to apply principles of population equality to political entities other than legislatures. It appeared quite possible that the justices would impose equal protection standards on the thousands of local government commissions, councils, and boards to which Americans regularly elect representatives. Most of these bodies were loosely based on population, but they could not meet the exacting standards of the reap-

An editorial cartoon depicting the disparity in political power held by rural interests before such decisions as Reynolds v. Sims.

portionment rulings. Did the Constitution demand that these governing bodies be properly apportioned in the same manner as state legislatures? Supporters of representational equality sponsored numerous lawsuits asking the judiciary to extend the one person, one vote rule to these local government units.

In ***Avery v. Midland County*** (1968) the Court ruled on a challenge to the representational system used to elect a county government. The seat of Midland County, Texas, contained more than 95 percent of the county's population but was only given 20 percent of the representatives on the governing commission. The Court struck down this scheme, holding that the equal protection principles that govern representation in the state legislature also control representation on elected local government bodies. In ***Hadley v. Junior College District*** (1970) the justices extended the same principles to elected special-purpose boards that exercise legislative functions. In *Board of Estimate of New York v. Morris* (1989) the Supreme Court unanimously struck down the system used for selecting members of New

York City's Board of Estimate, which gave equal representation to each of the five New York boroughs even though they had substantially unequal populations. The Court's position has been relatively clear: the equal protection clause demands that the principle of one person, one vote applies to local governing bodies that are elected and exercise legislative or general governing powers. The basic rule was articulated well in *Hadley*:

[W]henever a state or local government decides to select persons by popular election to perform governmental functions, the Equal Protection Clause of the Fourteenth Amendment requires that each qualified voter must be given an equal opportunity to participate in that election, and when members of an elected body are chosen from separate districts, each district must be established on a basis that will insure, as far as is practicable, that equal numbers of voters can vote for proportionally equal numbers of officials.

In its early apportionment decisions, the Supreme Court emphasized the need for population-based representational schemes. The justices used phrases such as "one person, one vote," "substantial equality," and "as equal as practicably possible" to refer to this standard. But the Court did not define what is meant by such equality. Although the justices regularly acknowledged that mathematical precision could not be expected, they failed to say what variation among districts would be constitutionally tolerated. Redistricting is a complex process, and, even with the assistance of sophisticated computer technology, drawing boundaries that create districts of nearly perfect equality is difficult. Adding to the burden are the demands of partisan, racial, ethnic, and economic interests for political power.

For the state legislatures involved in this process, it would be helpful for the Supreme Court to designate a minimum level of deviation that is constitutionally permissible. Such a de minimis standard would give legislators a guide as to what population equality means in practice. But in the Missouri congressional reapportionment case of *Kirkpatrick v. Preisler* (1969) the Court explicitly refused to provide any specified mathematical standard of equality. For the majority, Justice William J. Brennan explained:

We reject Missouri's argument that there is a fixed numerical or percentage population variance small enough to be considered *de minimis* and to satisfy without question the "as nearly as practicable" standard. The whole thrust of the "as nearly as practicable" approach is inconsistent with adoption of fixed numerical standards which excuse population variances without regard to the circumstances of each particular case.

In this decision, the Court declared Missouri's reapportionment plan to be unconstitutional in spite of the relatively small 1.6 percent average deviation from the ideal. The state had failed to convince the Court's majority that it had made a good-faith attempt to achieve equality.

The Court's policy of imposing exacting standards for congressional districts continued in **Karcher v. Daggett** (1983). This case involved the New Jersey legislature's redistricting scheme when the state lost one congressional seat following the 1980 census. After fierce political battles, the legislature passed a reapportionment plan in which the difference between the largest and smallest districts was 3,674, or a disparity of 0.6984 percent. Before passing this plan, the legislature considered several alternatives that would have created an even smaller difference. The reapportionment law was challenged in court. Justice Brennan, for a five-justice majority, struck down the plan, finding that the legislature had not demonstrated a good-faith attempt to achieve population equality. The state failed to show that there were convincing reasons why plans allowing greater equality were not adopted. Four justices in the minority, led by Byron White, attacked the majority for "unreasonable insistence on an unattainable perfection in the equalizing of congressional districts." Furthermore, the minority argued that, absent extraordinary circumstances, plans with deviations of less than 5 percent from absolute equality ought to be considered close enough to meet constitutional standards.

It is important to keep in mind that in *Karcher v. Daggett* the Supreme Court interpreted Article I, Section 2, of the Constitution, which deals with the election of members to the U.S. House of Representatives. The majority's rather strict approach to equality standards for congressional districts is not necessarily applicable to the apportionment of state and local governments, which is governed by the equal protection clause of the Fourteenth Amendment. In fact, the Supreme Court has allowed the states greater latitude in devising reapportionment plans and has tolerated larger deviation from absolute equality than it has with the creation of congressional constituencies.

For example, in **Mahan v. Howell** (1973) the justices examined a reapportionment plan for the Virginia House of Delegates that had an average deviation from perfect equality of 3.89 percent and a 16.4 percent variance between the largest and smallest districts. These deviations were due, in part, to the state's preference for drawing legislative district lines that followed existing city and county political boundaries. In upholding the plan, the Court emphasized the ruling in *Reynolds v. Sims* that "so long as the divergences from a strict population standard are based on legitimate considerations incident to the effectuation of a rational state policy, some deviations from the equal-population principle are constitutionally permissible with respect to the apportionment of seats in either or both of the two houses of a bicameral state legislature." Respecting the integrity of political subdivision boundaries in constructing a reapportionment plan, the justices ruled, advances a rational state policy.

In a number of decisions, the Court has continued to follow the guidelines set in *Mahan*. For example, in *Gaffney v. Cummings* (1973) the justices upheld a Connecticut state legislative redistricting plan with a maximum 7.83 percent deviation from ideal equality, in part because the state provided evidence that the particular plan preserved political fairness. In *White v. Regester* (1973) a Texas state reapportionment scheme with a 9.9 percent maximum variation from the ideal was upheld, with the Court concluding that the threshold for a prima facie case of invidious discrimination had not been passed. On the same day, almost as if to emphasize the differences, in *White v. Weiser* (1973) the Court struck down a Texas congressional redistricting plan that contained substantially less deviation from perfect equality than did the state scheme the justices had upheld.

In developing state apportionment rules under the equal protection clause, the Supreme Court has even accepted the de minimis position that it explicitly rejected in a number of congressional redistricting cases. In *Brown v. Thomson* (1983) Justice Lewis F. Powell, speaking for the Court, stated: "Our decisions have established, as a general matter, that an apportionment plan with a maximum population deviation under 10% falls within this category of minor deviations. . . . A plan with larger disparities in population, however, creates a prima facie case of discrimination and therefore must be justified by the State." The *Brown* case centered on a Wyoming redistricting plan that included a maximum deviation of 89 percent from perfect equality. This large variation was caused by the representation given to one isolated and sparsely populated county. The Court upheld the law, concluding that

the state had provided convincing, nondiscriminatory reasons for allowing this exception to the one person, one vote rule. Ironically, *Brown* was handed down the same day that the Court, in *Karcher v. Daggett,* struck down New Jersey's congressional reapportionment with its maximum deviation of less than 1 percent and rejected a de minimis rationale for use in such cases.

Although the Court has been divided in its application of reapportionment rules developed since *Baker v. Carr,* it has not abandoned the basic principle underlying these cases: representational units must be based on the one person, one vote principle.

Political Representation and Minority Rights

As long as the one person, one vote principle is observed, the Supreme Court generally has allowed the states freedom in constructing representational districts. That latitude, however, is not without limit. The Court always has been aware that representational schemes that satisfy standards of numerical equality may still offend basic constitutional principles. Plans that discriminate on the basis of race or ethnicity have been of particular concern. The justices have served notice that boundary lines cannot be drawn in a way that dilutes the political power of minorities.

An early example of how lines can be drawn to change the influence of minorities is shown in **Gomillion v. Lightfoot** (1960). Prior to 1957 the city limits of Tuskegee, Alabama, formed a square that covered the entire urban area. With the growing civil rights activism of the time and the increasing tendency of black citizens to vote, the white establishment in Tuskegee feared a loss of political control. Consequently, members of the Alabama legislature sympathetic to the city's white leaders successfully sponsored a bill that changed the boundary lines. No longer a square, the altered city limits formed, in Justice Frankfurter's words, "an uncouth twenty-eight-sided figure."

The effect of the redistricting was phenomenal. The law removed from the city all but four or five of its four hundred black voters, but no white voters. The black plaintiffs, now former residents of Tuskegee, claimed that their removal from the city denied them the right to vote on the basis of race and, therefore, violated their Fifteenth Amendment rights. The city did not deny that race was at issue but claimed that the state of Alabama had an unrestricted right to draw city boundaries as it saw fit and that the courts could not intervene to limit that authority. A unanimous Supreme Court ruled to the contrary, holding that when an otherwise lawful exercise of state power is used to circumvent a federally protected right, the courts may indeed intervene. A legislative act that removes citizens from the municipal voting rolls in a racially discriminatory fashion violates the Fifteenth Amendment.

Beginning in the 1970s, the issue of race and representation took on a new twist when legislatures started to enact districting plans designed to ensure the election of minority officials. They created "majority-minority" districts, representational units in which a majority of the residents were members of a particular minority group. These districts virtually ensured the election of minority officeholders. In *United Jewish Organizations of Williamsburgh v. Carey* (1977) the Supreme Court upheld such legislative actions. For the Court, Justice White declared:

[T]he Constitution does not prevent a State subject to the Voting Rights Act from deliberately creating or preserving black majorities in particular districts.... [N]either the Fourteenth nor the Fifteenth Amendment mandates any per se rule against using racial factors in districting and apportionment.... The permissible use of racial criteria is not confined to eliminating the effects of past discriminatory districting or apportionment.

The decisions in *United Jewish Organizations* and subsequent cases encouraged state legislatures to engage in such racially aware districting practices. Civil rights groups and other liberal organizations had been advocating this practice as the only meaningful way to guarantee African Americans, Hispanics, and other minorities a fair share of legislative seats.

In promoting this cause, advocates of increasing the political power of minorities received significant support from the Justice Department under Presidents Ronald Reagan and George H. W. Bush. Why would two Republican administrations back efforts to increase the number of black representatives, especially since these legislators probably would be Democrats? The answer is simple. When lines are drawn to create districts with high concentrations of black voters, the other districts become more white and more Republican. In other words, by creating a few districts dominated by minorities, the state legislatures also create other districts that are more likely to elect Republicans.

In many states the reapportionment battles that followed the 1990 census were not over one person, one vote issues; rather, they focused on drawing district boundary lines in a manner that would increase the number of minority officeholders. The successful creation of districts with heavy concentrations of racial and ethnic minorities had its intended effect. In the 1992 congressional elections, sixteen new black representatives were elected, bringing the total membership of the Congressional Black Caucus to thirty-nine. Eight newly elected Hispanic representatives also took their seats after the 1992 elections.

To draw these new majority-minority districts, state legislatures often had to engage in quite creative districting methods. Critics contended that legislators went too far, frequently establishing district boundaries that were highly irregular in shape and sprawled across large areas. It was one thing, they argued, to create districts that did not purposefully dilute minority voting strength, but a much different thing to base representational boundaries exclusively on race. As a consequence, lawsuits filed in Florida, Georgia, Louisiana, North Carolina, and Texas challenged the constitutionality of many new districts.

The first appeal to reach the Supreme Court was *Shaw v. Reno* (1993), a challenge to two majority-minority congressional districts in North Carolina. The decision in that case shocked the civil rights community; the Court ruled that congressional districts created to maximize minority representation may be unconstitutional under some circumstances. At constitutional risk were district lines that created bizarrely shaped configurations explainable in racial terms only. After establishing this new standard, the justices sent the case back down to the lower courts for additional proceedings.

The Court made no final determination in *Shaw* regarding the constitutionality of the challenged district, and the 5–4 vote left the districting waters muddy. It did not take long, however, for the Court to accept another case, a challenge to a majority-minority district in Georgia. As you read *Miller v. Johnson* (1995), pay close attention to the different views expressed.

Miller v. Johnson

515 U.S. 900 (1995)
http://laws.findlaw.com/US/515/900.html
Oral arguments are available at http://www.oyez.org.
Vote: 5 (Kennedy, O'Connor, Rehnquist, Scalia, Thomas)
  4 (Breyer, Ginsburg, Souter, Stevens)
OPINION OF THE COURT: *Kennedy*
CONCURRING OPINION: *O'Connor*
DISSENTING OPINIONS: *Ginsburg, Stevens*

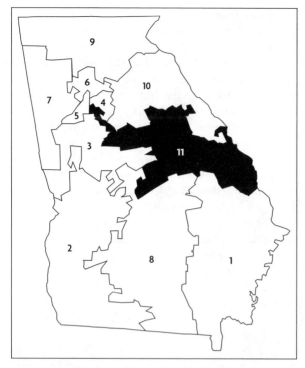

Georgia's Eleventh Congressional District was challenged in Miller v. Johnson *(1995). Although its shape is not generally irregular, note the district's fingerlike extensions to the northwest, northeast, and west. These were designed to incorporate high concentrations of black voters in Savannah, Augusta, and Atlanta.*

FACTS:

Following the 1990 census, Georgia, like many other states, was obliged to redraw the lines of its eleven congressional districts. The state legislature passed a plan in 1991 that included two districts with a majority of black voters. Because Georgia is subject to the provisions of the Voting Rights Act, the plan went to the Justice Department for approval (preclearance). The Justice Department rejected the plan, holding that it did not give sufficient attention to black voting strength. The state revised its apportionment plan, but the new version still had only two majority-black districts and also failed to receive approval. In 1992 the state passed a new districting plan that met with Justice Department approval. This legislation created three majority-black districts: the Second (southwest Georgia), the Fifth (Atlanta), and the Eleventh, the district challenged in this case.

The Eleventh District ran diagonally across the state from the edge of Atlanta to the Atlantic Ocean. It included portions of urban Atlanta, Savannah,

and Augusta, as well as sparsely populated, but overwhelmingly black, rural areas in the central part of the district. The Eleventh covered 6,784 square miles, splitting eight counties and five cities along the way. Numerous narrow land bridges were used to link areas with significant black populations. The district was 60 percent black. In the 1992 and 1994 congressional elections, district voters sent Cynthia McKinney, a black Democrat, to the House of Representatives. The other two majority-minority districts in Georgia also elected black representatives.

In 1994 five white voters from the Eleventh District, including Davida Johnson, filed suit. They claimed that the legislature violated the equal protection clause of the Fourteenth Amendment by adopting a redistricting plan driven primarily by considerations of race. A three-judge federal court, applying principles articulated in *Shaw v. Reno,* struck down the district. The Constitution was violated, the judges ruled, because race was the overriding, predominant factor employed to determine the lines of the district. Democratic governor Zell Miller appealed to the Supreme Court on behalf of the state.

ARGUMENTS:

For the appellants, Zell Miller, Governor of Georgia, et al.:

- The lower court and the appellees support a motivational standard (e.g., "was race a substantial or motivating consideration" in the construction of the districts) for evaluating the constitutionality of a districting plan. This ignores the conclusion in *Shaw v. Reno* that only district lines drawn in a bizarre and highly irregular fashion are constitutionally suspect.
- The lines of the Eleventh District challenged here were drawn with the goal of creating a district comprising mainly minority voters, but the shape of the district was made as regular as possible.
- The standard for regularity should be whether the state used traditional political building blocks to construct the district. Here the district's boundaries follow county lines as well as geographical and political markers of local significance that are independent of race.

For the appellees, Davida Johnson, et al.:

- Unconstitutional racial gerrymandering occurs when the state draws district lines in a way that artificially manipulates noncompact dispersed minority populations into a majority-black district without regard for the state's traditional districting principles.

- Under the Fourteenth Amendment, racial classifications are presumptively invalid unless they meet strict scrutiny standards.

- To establish a violation of the equal protection clause it is enough to show that the district lines are unexplainable on grounds other than race.

- The creation of a district such as this one is not required by the Voting Rights Act or the Constitution.

JUSTICE KENNEDY DELIVERED THE OPINION OF THE COURT.

The Equal Protection Clause of the Fourteenth Amendment provides that no State shall "deny to any person within its jurisdiction the equal protection of the laws." Its central mandate is racial neutrality in governmental decisionmaking. Though application of this imperative raises difficult questions, the basic principle is straightforward: "Racial and ethnic distinctions of any sort are inherently suspect and thus call for the most exacting judicial examination. . . . This perception of racial and ethnic distinctions is rooted in our Nation's constitutional and demographic history." *Regents of Univ. of California v. Bakke* (1978) (opinion of Powell, J.). This rule obtains with equal force regardless of "the race of those burdened or benefited by a particular classification." *Richmond v. J. A. Croson Co.* (1989) (plurality opinion). Laws classifying citizens on the basis of race cannot be upheld unless they are narrowly tailored to achieving a compelling state interest.

In *Shaw v. Reno* [1993] we recognized that these equal protection principles govern a State's drawing of congressional districts, though, as our cautious approach there discloses, application of these principles to electoral districting is a most delicate task. Our analysis began from the premise that "[l]aws that explicitly distinguish between individuals on racial grounds fall within the core of [the Equal Protection Clause's] prohibition." This prohibition extends not just to explicit racial classifications, but also to laws neutral on their face but "'unexplainable on grounds other than race.'" Applying this basic Equal Protection analysis in the voting rights context, we held that "redistricting legislation that is so bizarre on its face that it is 'unexplainable on grounds other than race,' . . . demands the same close scrutiny that we give other state laws that classify citizens by race."

This case requires us to apply the principles articulated in *Shaw* to the most recent congressional redistricting plan enacted by the State of Georgia. . . .

. . . Just as the State may not, absent extraordinary justification, segregate citizens on the basis of race in its public parks, buses, golf courses, beaches, and schools, so did we recognize in *Shaw* that it may not separate its citizens into different voting districts on the basis of race. The idea is a simple one: "At the heart of the Constitution's guarantee of equal protection lies the simple command that the Government must treat citizens 'as individuals, not "as simply components of a racial, religious, sexual or national class."'" *Metro Broadcasting, Inc. v. FCC* (1990) (O'Connor, J., dissenting). When the State assigns voters on the basis of race, it engages in the offensive and demeaning assumption that voters of a particular race, because of their race, "think alike, share the same political interests, and will prefer the same candidates at the polls." Race-based assignments "embody stereotypes that treat individuals as the product of their race, evaluating their thoughts and efforts—their very worth as citizens—according to a criterion barred to the Government by history and the Constitution." They also cause society serious harm. As we concluded in *Shaw*:

Racial classifications with respect to voting carry particular dangers. Racial gerrymandering, even for remedial purposes, may balkanize us into competing racial factions; it threatens to carry us further from the goal of a political system in which race no longer matters—a goal that the Fourteenth and Fifteenth Amendments embody, and to which the Nation continues to aspire. It is for these reasons that race-based districting by our state legislatures demands close judicial scrutiny.

Our observation in *Shaw* of the consequences of racial stereotyping was not meant to suggest that a district must be bizarre on its face before there is a constitutional violation. Nor was our conclusion in *Shaw* that in certain instances a district's appearance (or, to be more precise, its appearance in combination with certain demographic evidence) can give rise to an equal protection claim, a holding that bizarreness was a threshold showing, as appellants believe it to be. Our circumspect approach and narrow holding in *Shaw* did not erect an artificial rule barring accepted equal protection analysis in other redistricting cases. Shape is relevant not because bizarreness is a necessary element of the constitutional wrong or a threshold requirement of proof, but because it may be persuasive circumstantial evidence that race for its own sake, and not other districting principles, was the legislature's dominant and controlling rationale in drawing its district lines. The logical implication, as courts applying *Shaw* have recognized, is that parties may rely on evidence other than bizarreness to establish race-based districting.

Our reasoning in *Shaw* compels this conclusion. We recognized in *Shaw* that, outside the districting context, statutes are subject to strict scrutiny under the Equal Protection Clause not just when they contain express racial classifications, but also when, though race neutral on their face, they are motivated by a racial purpose or object. . . .

Shaw applied these same principles to redistricting. "In some exceptional cases, a reapportionment plan may be so highly irregular that, on its face, it rationally cannot be understood as anything other than an effort to 'segregat[e] . . . voters' on the basis of race." In other cases, where the district is not so bizarre on its face that it discloses a racial design, the proof will be more "difficul[t]." Although it was not necessary in *Shaw* to consider further the proof required in these more difficult cases, the logical import of our reasoning is that evidence other than a district's bizarre shape can be used to support the claim. . . .

In sum, we make clear that parties alleging that a State has assigned voters on the basis of race are neither confined in their proof to evidence regarding the district's geometry and makeup nor required to make a threshold showing of bizarreness. Today's case requires us further to consider the requirements of the proof necessary to sustain this equal protection challenge.

. . . Electoral districting is a most difficult subject for legislatures, and so the States must have discretion to exercise the political judgment necessary to balance competing interests. Although race-based decision-making is inherently suspect, until a claimant makes a showing sufficient to support that allegation the good faith of a state legislature must be presumed. The courts, in assessing the sufficiency of a challenge to a districting plan, must be sensitive to the complex interplay of forces that enter a legislature's redistricting calculus. Redistricting legislatures will, for example, almost always be aware of racial demographics; but it does not follow that race predominates in the redistricting process. The distinction between being aware of racial considerations and being motivated by them may be difficult to make. This evidentiary difficulty, together with the sensitive nature of redistricting and the presumption of good faith that must be accorded legislative enactments, requires courts to exercise extraordinary caution in adjudicating claims that a state has drawn district lines on the basis of race. The plaintiff's burden is to show, either through circumstantial evidence of a district's shape and demographics or more direct evidence going to legislative purpose, that race was the predominant factor motivating the legislature's decision to place a significant number of voters within or without a particular district. To make this showing, a plaintiff must prove that the legislature subordinated traditional race-neutral districting principles, including but not limited to compactness, contiguity, respect for political subdivisions or communities defined by actual shared interests, to racial considerations. Where these or other race-neutral considerations are the basis for redistricting legislation, and are not subordinated to race, a state can "defeat a claim that a district has been gerrymandered on racial lines." *Shaw*. These principles inform the plaintiff's burden of proof at trial. . . .

In our view, the District Court applied the correct analysis, and its finding that race was the predominant factor motivating the drawing of the Eleventh District was not clearly erroneous. The court found it was "exceedingly obvious" from the shape of the Eleventh District, together with the relevant racial demographics, that the drawing of narrow land bridges to incorporate within the District outlying appendages containing nearly 80% of the district's total black population was a deliberate attempt to bring black populations into the district. Although by comparison with other districts the geometric shape of the Eleventh District may not seem bizarre on its face, when its shape is considered in conjunction with its racial and population densities, the story of racial gerrymandering seen by the District Court becomes much clearer. Although this evidence is quite compelling, we need not determine whether it was, standing alone, sufficient to establish a *Shaw* claim that the Eleventh District is unexplainable other than by race. The District Court had before it considerable additional evidence showing that the General Assembly was motivated by a predominant, overriding desire to assign black populations to the Eleventh

District and thereby permit the creation of a third majority-black district. . . .

The court found that "it became obvious," both from the Justice Department's objection letters and the three preclearance rounds in general, "that [the Justice Department] would accept nothing less than abject surrender to its maximization agenda." It further found that the General Assembly acquiesced and as a consequence was driven by its overriding desire to comply with the Department's maximization demands. . . .

In light of its well-supported finding, the District Court was justified in rejecting the various alternative explanations offered for the District. Although a legislature's compliance with "traditional districting principles such as compactness, contiguity, and respect for political subdivisions" may well suffice to refute a claim of racial gerrymandering, *Shaw,* appellants cannot make such a refutation where, as here, those factors were subordinated to racial objectives. Georgia's Attorney General objected to the Justice Department's demand for three majority-black districts on the ground that to do so the State would have to "violate all reasonable standards of compactness and contiguity." This statement from a state official is powerful evidence that the legislature subordinated traditional districting principles to race when it ultimately enacted a plan creating three majority-black districts, and justified the District Court's finding that "every [objective districting] factor that could realistically be subordinated to racial tinkering in fact suffered that fate."

Nor can the State's districting legislation be rescued by mere recitation of purported communities of interest. The evidence was compelling "that there are no tangible 'communities of interest' spanning the hundreds of miles of the Eleventh District." A comprehensive report demonstrated the fractured political, social, and economic interests within the Eleventh District's black population. It is apparent that it was not alleged shared interests but rather the object of maximizing the District's black population and obtaining Justice Department approval that in fact explained the General Assembly's actions. A State is free to recognize communities that have a particular racial makeup, provided its action is directed toward some common thread of relevant interests. . . . But where the State assumes from a group of voters' race that they "think alike, share the same political interests, and will prefer the same candidates at the polls," it

engages in racial stereotyping at odds with equal protection mandates.

Race was, as the District Court found, the predominant, overriding factor explaining the General Assembly's decision to attach to the Eleventh District various appendages containing dense majority-black populations. As a result, Georgia's congressional redistricting plan cannot be upheld unless it satisfies strict scrutiny, our most rigorous and exacting standard of constitutional review.

To satisfy strict scrutiny, the State must demonstrate that its districting legislation is narrowly tailored to achieve a compelling interest. There is a "significant state interest in eradicating the effects of past racial discrimination." *Shaw.* The State does not argue, however, that it created the Eleventh District to remedy past discrimination, and with good reason: there is little doubt that the State's true interest in designing the Eleventh District was creating a third majority-black district to satisfy the Justice Department's preclearance demands. . . . Whether or not in some cases compliance with the Voting Rights Act, standing alone, can provide a compelling interest independent of any interest in remedying past discrimination, it cannot do so here. As we suggested in *Shaw,* compliance with federal antidiscrimination laws cannot justify race-based districting where the challenged district was not reasonably necessary under a constitutional reading and application of those laws. The congressional plan challenged here was not required by the Voting Rights Act under a correct reading of the statute. . . .

We do not accept the contention that the State has a compelling interest in complying with whatever preclearance mandates the Justice Department issues. When a state governmental entity seeks to justify race-based remedies to cure the effects of past discrimination, we do not accept the government's mere assertion that the remedial action is required. Rather, we insist on a strong basis in evidence of the harm being remedied. "The history of racial classifications in this country suggests that blind judicial deference to legislative or executive pronouncements of necessity has no place in equal protection analysis." *Croson.* Our presumptive skepticism of all racial classifications prohibits us as well from accepting on its face the Justice Department's conclusion that racial districting is necessary under the Voting Rights Act. Where a State relies on the Department's determination that race-based districting is necessary to comply with the Voting Rights Act, the judiciary retains an independent obligation in adjudicating consequent equal protection challenges to ensure that the State's actions are narrowly tailored to achieve a compelling interest. See *Shaw*. Were we to accept the Justice Department's objection itself as a compelling interest adequate to insulate racial districting from constitutional review, we would be surrendering to the Executive Branch our role in enforcing the constitutional limits on race-based official action. We may not do so. . . .

The Voting Rights Act, and its grant of authority to the federal courts to uncover official efforts to abridge minorities' right to vote, has been of vital importance in eradicating invidious discrimination from the electoral process and enhancing the legitimacy of our political institutions. Only if our political system and our society cleanse themselves of that discrimination will all members of the polity share an equal opportunity to gain public office regardless of race. As a Nation we share both the obligation and the aspiration of working toward this end. The end is neither assured nor well served, however, by carving electorates into racial blocs. "If our society is to continue to progress as a multiracial democracy, it must recognize that the automatic invocation of race stereotypes retards that progress and causes continued hurt and injury." It takes a shortsighted and unauthorized view of the Voting Rights Act to invoke that statute, which has played a decisive role in redressing some of our worst forms of discrimination, to demand the very racial stereotyping the Fourteenth Amendment forbids.

The judgment of the District Court is affirmed, and the case is remanded for further proceedings consistent with this decision.

It is so ordered.

JUSTICE GINSBURG, with whom JUSTICES STEVENS, BREYER, . . . and . . . SOUTER join . . . , dissenting.

Before *Shaw v. Reno* (1993), this Court invoked the Equal Protection Clause to justify intervention in the quintessentially political task of legislative districting in two circumstances: to enforce the one-person-one-vote requirement, see *Reynolds v. Sims* (1964); and to prevent dilution of a minority group's voting strength.

In *Shaw,* the Court recognized a third basis for an equal protection challenge to a State's apportionment plan. The Court wrote cautiously, emphasizing that judicial intervention is exceptional: "[S]trict [judicial] scrutiny" is in order, the Court declared, if a district is "so extremely irregular on its face that it rationally can be viewed only as an effort to segregate the races for purposes of voting." . . .

The problem in *Shaw* was not the plan architects' consideration of race as relevant in redistricting. Rather, in the Court's estimation, it was the virtual exclusion of other factors from the calculus. Traditional districting practices were cast aside, the Court concluded, with race alone steering placement of district lines.

The record before us does not show that race similarly overwhelmed traditional districting practices in Georgia. Although the Georgia General Assembly prominently considered race in shaping the Eleventh District, race did not crowd out all other factors, as the Court found it did in North Carolina's delineation of the *Shaw* district.

In contrast to the snake-like North Carolina district inspected in *Shaw,* Georgia's Eleventh District is hardly "bizarre," "extremely irregular," or "irrational on its face." Instead, the Eleventh District's design reflects significant consideration of "traditional districting factors (such as keeping political subdivisions intact) and the usual political process of compromise and trades for a variety of nonracial reasons." . . .

Nor does the Eleventh District disrespect the boundaries of political subdivisions. Of the 22 counties in the District, 14 are intact and 8 are divided. That puts the Eleventh District at about the state average in divided counties. . . .

Evidence at trial similarly shows that considerations other than race went into determining the Eleventh District's boundaries. . . .

Georgia's Eleventh District, in sum, is not an outlier district shaped without reference to familiar districting techniques. . . .

The Court suggests that it was not Georgia's legislature, but the U.S. Department of Justice, that effectively drew the lines, and that Department officers did so with nothing but race in mind. . . .

And although the Attorney General refused preclearance to the first two plans approved by Georgia's legislature, the State was not thereby disarmed; Georgia could have demanded relief from the Department's objections by instituting a civil action in the United States District Court for the District of Columbia, with ultimate review in this Court. Instead of pursuing that avenue, the State chose to adopt the plan here in controversy—a plan the State forcefully defends before us. We should respect Georgia's choice by taking its position on brief as genuine.

Along with attention to size, shape, and political subdivisions, the Court recognizes as an appropriate districting principle, "respect for . . . communities defined by actual shared interests." The Court finds no community here, however, because a report in the record showed "fractured political, social, and economic interests within the Eleventh District's black population." But ethnicity itself can tie people together, as volumes of social science literature have documented—even people with divergent economic interests. For this reason, ethnicity is a significant force in political life. . . .

To accommodate the reality of ethnic bonds, legislatures have long drawn voting districts along ethnic lines. Our Nation's cities are full of districts identified by their ethnic character—Chinese, Irish, Italian, Jewish, Polish, Russian, for example. . . .

To separate permissible and impermissible use of race in legislative apportionment, the Court orders strict scrutiny for districting plans "predominantly motivated" by race. No longer can a State avoid judicial oversight by giving—as in this case—genuine and measurable consideration to traditional districting practices. Instead, a federal case can be mounted whenever plaintiffs plausibly allege that other factors carried less weight than race. This invitation to litigate against the State seems to me neither necessary nor proper.

The Court derives its test from diverse opinions on the relevance of race in contexts distinctly unlike apportionment. The controlling idea, the Court says, is "'the simple command [at the heart of the Constitution's guarantee of equal protection] that the Government must treat citizens as individuals, not as simply components of a racial, religious, sexual or national class.'"

In adopting districting plans, however, States do not treat people as individuals. Apportionment schemes, by their very nature, assemble people in groups. States do not assign voters to districts based on merit or achievement, standards States might use in hiring employees or engaging contractors. Rather, legislators classify voters in groups—by economic, geographical, political, or social characteristics—and then "reconcile the competing claims of [these] groups." *Davis v. Bandemer* (1986) (O'CONNOR, J., concurring in judgment).

That ethnicity defines some of these groups is a political reality. Until now, no constitutional infirmity has been seen in districting Irish or Italian voters together, for example, so long as the delineation does not abandon familiar apportionment practices. If Chinese-Americans and Russian-Americans may seek and secure group recognition in the delineation of voting districts, then African-Americans should not be dissimilarly treated. Otherwise, in the name of equal protection, we would shut out "the very minority group whose history in the United States gave birth to the Equal Protection Clause." See *Shaw* (STEVENS, J., dissenting). . . .

Only after litigation—under either the Voting Rights Act, the Court's new *Miller* standard, or both—will States now be assured that plans conscious of race are safe. Federal judges in large numbers may be drawn into the fray. This enlargement of the judicial role is unwarranted. The reapportionment plan that resulted from Georgia's political process merited this Court's approbation, not its condemnation.

Accordingly, I dissent.

With *Miller v. Johnson* the Court continued on its path of applying strict scrutiny standards to legislative redistricting designed to create majority-minority districts. Once again, the decision was the result of a 5–4 voting split. Conservative justices Kennedy, O'Connor, Rehnquist, Scalia, and Thomas formed a solid bloc against districts with boundaries that were "unexplainable on grounds other than race" and legislatures that had "subordinated traditional race-neutral districting principles . . . to racial considerations." This same five-justice coalition had constituted the majority in *Shaw v. Reno* two years earlier. Liberal justices Breyer, Ginsburg, Souter, and Stevens expressed their solidarity with legislative and executive branch efforts to enhance the representation of historically disadvantaged minorities. As the data in Box 14-4 show, these efforts have met with a degree of success.

In spite of the consistency in the direction of the Court's rulings, the law pertaining to majority-minority districts lacks clarity. How much attention can the legislature give to racial considerations without violating the Fourteenth Amendment? At what point

BOX 14-4   AFTERMATH . . . *MILLER V. JOHNSON*

The immediate impact of *Miller v. Johnson*, which struck down Georgia's redistricting plan, was to send the map back to the state legislature for revision. Despite numerous attempts, the lawmakers were unable to develop an acceptable plan, and the task of redesigning the congressional districts fell to the federal district court. After considering several plans, the court approved a scheme that included only one majority-black district. This judicially imposed redistricting plan was challenged by civil rights advocates. The Supreme Court upheld the plan in *Abrams v. Johnson* (1997), with the justices divided into the same 5–4 voting blocs that occurred in *Shaw v. Reno* and *Miller v. Johnson.*

Despite this legal setback, Georgia's African American representatives held their positions in Congress. Congresswoman Cynthia McKinney, whose district was the primary target of the *Miller v. Johnson* litigation, found herself representing a district that was 58.4 percent white. She captured 58 percent of the vote in 1996 and 61 percent in 1998. Congressman Sanford Bishop's Second District became 59.5 percent white under the revised apportionment plan; he was reelected with 54 percent of the vote in 1996 and 57 percent in 1998. John Lewis, the lone representative of a majority-black district, ran unopposed in 1996 and received 79 percent of the vote in 1998.

Following the 2000 census, Georgia gained an additional congressional seat, prompting the legislature to redraw the state's congressional districts. The new apportionment plan included two majority-black districts. In the 2002 through 2010 elections, four of Georgia's thirteen congressional districts sent African American representatives to Congress. In *Georgia v. Ashcroft* (2003) the

YEAR	HISPANIC REPRESENTATIVES	BLACK REPRESENTATIVES
1985	11	20
1987	11	22
1989	10	23
1991	11	26
1993	17	39
1995	17	39
1997	17	37
1999	19	37
2001	19	37
2003	22	37
2005	22	40
2007	22	42
2009	27	41
2011	30	44

SOURCES: Norman J. Ornstein, Thomas E. Mann, and Michael J. Malbin, *Vital Statistics on Congress, 1999–2000* (Washington, DC: AEI Press, 2000); Michael Barone and Grant Ujifusa, with Richard E. Cohen and Charles E. Cook Jr., *The Almanac of American Politics 2000* (Washington, DC: National Journal, 1999); Associated Press, January 7, 2003; and Ethnic Majority, http://www.ethnicmajority.com/congress.htm.

justices rejected a Voting Rights Act claim that the new plan excessively retrograded black voting strength. After the 2010 census, Georgia gained a fourteenth congressional seat that again required the state legislature to reapportion. In response, the state legislature passed a redistricting plan that included four majority-minority districts. The plan received the approval of the Justice Department.

Data for the entire House of Representatives show that between 1985 and 2011 the number of African American representatives more than doubled, and that of Hispanic representatives nearly tripled.

---

do traditional race-neutral factors take a subordinate position to racial factors? Perhaps these questions will be answered as the Court responds to the next round of challenges to state reapportionment efforts.

ANNOTATED READINGS

A great deal of scholarly attention has been devoted to the subject of voting rights, much of it dealing with various forms of discrimination. A representative sample of these works includes Charles V. Hamilton, *The Bench and Ballot: Southern Federal Judges and Black Voters* (New York: Oxford University Press, 1973); Richard L. Hasen, *The Supreme Court and Election Law: Judging Equality from* Baker v. Carr *to* Bush v. Gore (New York: New York University Press, 2003); David Michael Hudson, *Along Racial Lines: Consequences of the 1965 Voting Rights Act* (New York: Peter Lang, 1998); Alexander Keyssar, *The Right to Vote: The Contested*

History of Democracy in the United States (New York: Basic Books, 2000); Daniel McCool, Susan M. Olson, and Jennifer L. Robinson, *Native Vote: American Indians, the Voting Rights Act, and the Right to Vote* (New York: Cambridge University Press, 2007); Robert J. Norell, *Reaping the Whirlwind: The Civil Rights Movement in Tuskegee* (Chapel Hill: University of North Carolina Press, 1998); Anthony A. Peacock, *Deconstructing the Republic: Voting Rights, the Supreme Court, and the Founders' Republicanism Reconsidered* (Washington, DC: AEI Press, 2008); Donald Greer Stephenson Jr., *The Right to Vote: Rights and Liberties under the Law* (Santa Barbara, CA: ABC-CLIO, 2004); Richard M. Valelly, *Two Reconstructions: The Struggle for Black Enfranchisement* (Chicago: University of Chicago Press, 2004); and Charles L. Zelden, *The Battle for the Black Ballot:* Smith v. Allwright *and the Defeat of the Texas All-White Primary* (Lawrence: University Press of Kansas, 2004).

Other authors have focused on representation and apportionment issues. Their efforts have spanned a wide variety of topics, including historical development, limitations on judicial power, practical reapportionment problems, and the effects of malapportionment. Among these efforts are Dean Alfange Jr., "Gerrymandering and the Constitution: Into the Thorns of the Thicket at Last," *Supreme Court Review* (1986): 175–257; Dewey M. Clayton, *African Americans and the Politics of Congressional Redistricting* (New York: Garland, 2000); Richard C. Cortner, *The Apportionment Cases* (Knoxville: University of Tennessee Press, 1970); Bernard Grofman, *Political Gerrymandering and the Courts* (New York: Agathon Press, 1990); Anthony Peacock, ed., *Affirmative Action and Representation:* Shaw v. Reno *and the Future of Voting Rights* (Durham, NC: Carolina Academic Press, 1997); Richard K. Scher, Jon L. Mills, and John J. Hotaling, *Voting Rights and Democracy: The Law and Politics of Districting* (Chicago: Nelson-Hall, 1997); Bernard Taper, Gomillion v. Lightfoot: *Apartheid in Alabama* (New York: McGraw-Hill, 1967); Dianne T. Thompson, *Congressional Districting in North Carolina: Reconsidering Traditional Criteria* (New York: FB Scholarly Publishing, 2002); and Tinsley E. Yarbrough, *Race and Redistricting: The* Shaw-Cromartie *Cases* (Lawrence: University Press of Kansas, 2002).

The Supreme Court's role in the presidential election of 2000 has received a great deal of criticism and analysis. Some of the better examples include Alan M. Dershowitz, *Supreme Injustice: How the High Court Hijacked Election 2000* (New York: Oxford University Press, 2001); Howard Gillman, *The Votes That Counted: How the Court Decided the 2000 Presidential Election* (Chicago: University of Chicago Press, 2001); Abner Greene, *An Understanding the 2000 Election: A Guide to the Legal Battles That Decided the Presidency* (New York: New York University Press, 2001); and Richard A. Posner, *Breaking the Deadlock: The 2000 Election, the Constitution, and the Courts* (Princeton, NJ: Princeton University Press, 2001).

Reference Material

Appendixes

APPENDIX 1

Constitution of the United States

WE THE PEOPLE of the United States, in Order to form a more perfect Union, establish Justice, insure domestic Tranquility, provide for the common defence, promote the general Welfare, and secure the Blessings of Liberty to ourselves and our Posterity, do ordain and establish this Constitution for the United States of America.

ARTICLE I

Section 1. All legislative Powers herein granted shall be vested in a Congress of the United States, which shall consist of a Senate and House of Representatives.

Section 2. The House of Representatives shall be composed of Members chosen every second Year by the People of the several States, and the Electors in each State shall have the Qualifications requisite for Electors of the most numerous Branch of the State Legislature.

No Person shall be a Representative who shall not have attained to the age of twenty five Years, and been seven Years a Citizen of the United States, and who shall not, when elected, be an Inhabitant of that State in which he shall be chosen.

[Representatives and direct Taxes shall be apportioned among the several States which may be included within this Union, according to their respective Numbers, which shall be determined by adding to the whole Number of free Persons, including those bound to Service for a Term of Years, and excluding Indians not taxed, three fifths of all other Persons.][1] The actual Enumeration shall be made within three Years after the first Meeting of the Congress of the United States, and within every subsequent Term of ten Years, in such Manner as they shall by Law direct. The Number of Representatives shall not exceed one for every thirty Thousand, but each State shall have at Least one Representative; and until such enumeration shall be made, the State of New Hampshire shall be entitled to chuse three, Massachusetts eight, Rhode-Island and Providence Plantations one, Connecticut five, New-York six, New Jersey four, Pennsylvania eight, Delaware one, Maryland six, Virginia ten, North Carolina five, South Carolina five, and Georgia three.

When vacancies happen in the Representation from any State, the Executive Authority thereof shall issue Writs of Election to fill such Vacancies.

The House of Representatives shall chuse their Speaker and other Officers; and shall have the sole Power of Impeachment.

Section 3. The Senate of the United States shall be composed of two Senators from each State, [chosen by the Legislature thereof,][2] for six Years; and each Senator shall have one Vote.

---

1. The part in brackets was changed by Section 2 of the Fourteenth Amendment.

2. The part in brackets was changed by the first paragraph of the Seventeenth Amendment.

Immediately after they shall be assembled in Consequence of the first Election, they shall be divided as equally as may be into three Classes. The Seats of the Senators of the first Class shall be vacated at the Expiration of the second Year, of the second Class at the Expiration of the fourth Year, and of the third Class at the Expiration of the sixth Year, so that one third may be chosen every second Year; [and if Vacancies happen by Resignation, or otherwise, during the Recess of the Legislature of any State, the Executive thereof may make temporary Appointments until the next Meeting of the Legislature, which shall then fill such Vacancies.][3]

No Person shall be a Senator who shall not have attained to the Age of thirty Years, and been nine Years a Citizen of the United States, and who shall not, when elected, be an Inhabitant of that State for which he shall be chosen.

The Vice President of the United States shall be President of the Senate, but shall have no Vote, unless they be equally divided.

The Senate shall chuse their other Officers, and also a President pro tempore, in the Absence of the Vice President, or when he shall exercise the Office of President of the United States.

The Senate shall have the sole Power to try all Impeachments. When sitting for that Purpose, they shall be on Oath or Affirmation. When the President of the United States is tried, the Chief Justice shall preside: And no Person shall be convicted without the Concurrence of two thirds of the Members present.

Judgment in Cases of Impeachment shall not extend further than to removal from Office, and disqualification to hold and enjoy any Office of honor, Trust or Profit under the United States: but the Party convicted shall nevertheless be liable and subject to Indictment, Trial, Judgment and Punishment, according to Law.

Section 4. The Times, Places and Manner of holding Elections for Senators and Representatives, shall be prescribed in each State by the Legislature thereof; but the Congress may at any time by Law make or alter such Regulations, except as to the Places of chusing Senators.

The Congress shall assemble at least once in every Year, and such Meeting shall [be on the first Monday in December],[4] unless they shall by Law appoint a different Day.

Section 5. Each House shall be the Judge of the Elections, Returns and Qualifications of its own Members, and a Majority of each shall constitute a Quorum to do Business; but a smaller Number may adjourn from day to day, and may be authorized to compel the Attendance of absent Members, in such Manner, and under such Penalties as each House may provide.

Each House may determine the Rules of its Proceedings, punish its Members for disorderly Behaviour, and, with the Concurrence of two thirds, expel a Member.

Each House shall keep a Journal of its Proceedings, and from time to time publish the same, excepting such Parts as may in their Judgment require Secrecy; and the Yeas and Nays of the Members of either House on any question shall, at the Desire of one fifth of those Present, be entered on the Journal.

Neither House, during the Session of Congress, shall, without the Consent of the other, adjourn for more than three days, nor to any other Place than that in which the two Houses shall be sitting.

Section 6. The Senators and Representatives shall receive a Compensation for their Services, to be ascertained by Law, and paid out of the Treasury of the United States. They shall in all Cases, except Treason, Felony and Breach of the Peace, be privileged from Arrest during their Attendance at the Session of their respective Houses, and in going to and returning from the same; and for any Speech or Debate in either House, they shall not be questioned in any other Place.

No Senator or Representative shall, during the Time for which he was elected, be appointed to any civil Office under the Authority of the United States, which shall have been created, or the Emoluments whereof shall have been encreased during such time; and no Person holding any Office under the United States, shall be a Member of either House during his Continuance in Office.

Section 7. All Bills for raising Revenue shall originate in the House of Representatives; but the Senate may propose or concur with Amendments as on other Bills.

Every Bill which shall have passed the House of Representatives and the Senate, shall, before it become a Law, be presented to the President of the United

---

3. The part in brackets was changed by the second paragraph of the Seventeenth Amendment.

4. The part in brackets was changed by Section 2 of the Twentieth Amendment.

States; If he approve he shall sign it, but if not he shall return it, with his Objections to that House in which it shall have originated, who shall enter the Objections at large on their Journal, and proceed to reconsider it. If after such Reconsideration two thirds of that House shall agree to pass the Bill, it shall be sent, together with the Objections, to the other House, by which it shall likewise be reconsidered, and if approved by two thirds of that House, it shall become a Law. But in all such Cases the Votes of both Houses shall be determined by Yeas and Nays, and the Names of the Persons voting for and against the Bill shall be entered on the Journal of each House respectively. If any Bill shall not be returned by the President within ten Days (Sundays excepted) after it shall have been presented to him, the Same shall be a Law, in like Manner as if he had signed it, unless the Congress by their Adjournment prevent its Return, in which Case it shall not be a Law.

Every Order, Resolution, or Vote to which the Concurrence of the Senate and House of Representatives may be necessary (except on a question of Adjournment) shall be presented to the President of the United States; and before the Same shall take Effect, shall be approved by him, or being disapproved by him, shall be repassed by two thirds of the Senate and House of Representatives, according to the Rules and Limitations prescribed in the Case of a Bill.

Section 8. The Congress shall have Power To lay and collect Taxes, Duties, Imposts and Excises, to pay the Debts and provide for the common Defence and general Welfare of the United States; but all Duties, Imposts and Excises shall be uniform throughout the United States;

To borrow Money on the credit of the United States;

To regulate Commerce with foreign Nations, and among the several States, and with the Indian Tribes;

To establish an uniform Rule of Naturalization, and uniform Laws on the subject of Bankruptcies throughout the United States;

To coin Money, regulate the Value thereof, and of foreign Coin, and fix the Standard of Weights and Measures;

To provide for the Punishment of counterfeiting the Securities and current Coin of the United States;

To establish Post Offices and post Roads;

To promote the Progress of Science and useful Arts, by securing for limited Times to Authors and Inventors the exclusive Right to their respective Writings and Discoveries;

To constitute Tribunals inferior to the supreme Court;

To define and punish Piracies and Felonies committed on the high Seas, and Offences against the Law of Nations;

To declare War, grant Letters of Marque and Reprisal, and make Rules concerning Captures on Land and Water;

To raise and support Armies, but no Appropriation of Money to that Use shall be for a longer Term than two Years;

To provide and maintain a Navy;

To make Rules for the Government and Regulation of the land and naval Forces;

To provide for calling forth the Militia to execute the Laws of the Union, suppress Insurrections and repel Invasions;

To provide for organizing, arming, and disciplining, the Militia, and for governing such Part of them as may be employed in the Service of the United States, reserving to the States respectively, the Appointment of the Officers, and the Authority of training the Militia according to the discipline prescribed by Congress;

To exercise exclusive Legislation in all Cases whatsoever, over such District (not exceeding ten Miles square) as may, by Cession of particular States, and the Acceptance of Congress, become the Seat of the Government of the United States, and to exercise like Authority over all Places purchased by the Consent of the Legislature of the State in which the Same shall be, for the Erection of Forts, Magazines, Arsenals, dock-Yards, and other needful Buildings;—And

To make all Laws which shall be necessary and proper for carrying into Execution the foregoing Powers, and all other Powers vested by this Constitution in the Government of the United States, or in any Department or Officer thereof.

Section 9. The Migration or Importation of such Persons as any of the States now existing shall think proper to admit, shall not be prohibited by the Congress prior to the Year one thousand eight hundred and eight, but a Tax or duty may be imposed on such Importation, not exceeding ten dollars for each Person.

The Privilege of the Writ of Habeas Corpus shall not be suspended, unless when in Cases of Rebellion or Invasion the public Safety may require it.

No Bill of Attainder or ex post facto Law shall be passed.

No Capitation, or other direct, Tax shall be laid, unless in Proportion to the Census or Enumeration herein before directed to be taken.[5]

No Tax or Duty shall be laid on Articles exported from any State.

No Preference shall be given by any Regulation of Commerce or Revenue to the Ports of one State over those of another; nor shall Vessels bound to, or from, one State, be obliged to enter, clear, or pay Duties in another.

No Money shall be drawn from the Treasury, but in Consequence of Appropriations made by Law; and a regular Statement and Account of the Receipts and Expenditures of all public Money shall be published from time to time.

No Title of Nobility shall be granted by the United States: And no Person holding any Office of Profit or Trust under them, shall, without the Consent of the Congress, accept of any present, Emolument, Office, or Title, of any kind whatever, from any King, Prince, or foreign State.

Section 10. No State shall enter into any Treaty, Alliance, or Confederation; grant Letters of Marque and Reprisal; coin Money; emit Bills of Credit; make any Thing but gold and silver Coin a Tender in Payment of Debts; pass any Bill of Attainder, ex post facto Law, or Law impairing the Obligation of Contracts, or grant any Title of Nobility.

No State shall, without the Consent of the Congress, lay any Imposts or Duties on Imports or Exports, except what may be absolutely necessary for executing it's inspection Laws: and the net Produce of all Duties and Imposts, laid by any State on Imports or Exports, shall be for the Use of the Treasury of the United States; and all such Laws shall be subject to the Revision and Controul of the Congress.

No State shall, without the Consent of Congress, lay any Duty of Tonnage, keep Troops, or Ships of War in time of Peace, enter into any Agreement or Compact with another State, or with a foreign Power, or engage in War, unless actually invaded, or in such imminent Danger as will not admit of delay.

ARTICLE II

Section 1. The executive Power shall be vested in a President of the United States of America. He shall hold his Office during the Term of four Years, and, together with the Vice President, chosen for the same Term, be elected, as follows

Each State shall appoint, in such Manner as the Legislature thereof may direct, a Number of Electors, equal to the whole Number of Senators and Representatives to which the State may be entitled in the Congress: but no Senator or Representative, or Person holding an Office of Trust or Profit under the United States, shall be appointed an Elector.

[The Electors shall meet in their respective States, and vote by Ballot for two Persons, of whom one at least shall not be an Inhabitant of the same State with themselves. And they shall make a List of all the Persons voted for, and of the Number of Votes for each; which List they shall sign and certify, and transmit sealed to the Seat of the Government of the United States, directed to the President of the Senate. The President of the Senate shall, in the Presence of the Senate and House of Representatives, open all the Certificates, and the Votes shall then be counted. The Person having the greatest Number of Votes shall be the President, if such Number be a Majority of the whole Number of Electors appointed; and if there be more than one who have such Majority, and have an equal Number of Votes, then the House of Representatives shall immediately chuse by Ballot one of them for President; and if no Person have a Majority, then from the five highest on the list the said House shall in like Manner chuse the President. But in chusing the President, the Votes shall be taken by States, the Representation from each State having one Vote; A quorum for this Purpose shall consist of a Member or Members from two thirds of the States, and a Majority of all the States shall be necessary to a Choice. In every Case, after the Choice of the President, the Person having the greatest Number of Votes of the Electors shall be the Vice President. But if there should remain two or more who have equal Votes, the Senate shall chuse from them by Ballot the Vice President.][6]

The Congress may determine the Time of chusing the Electors, and the Day on which they shall give their Votes; which Day shall be the same throughout the United States.

No Person except a natural born Citizen, or a Citizen of the United States, at the time of the Adoption

---

5. The Sixteenth Amendment gave Congress the power to tax incomes.

6. The material in brackets has been superseded by the Twelfth Amendment.

of this Constitution, shall be eligible to the Office of President; neither shall any Person be eligible to that Office who shall not have attained to the Age of thirty five Years, and been fourteen Years a Resident within the United States.

In Case of the Removal of the President from Office, or of his Death, Resignation, or Inability to discharge the Powers and Duties of the said Office,[7] the Same shall devolve on the Vice President, and the Congress may by Law provide for the Case of Removal, Death, Resignation or Inability, both of the President and Vice President, declaring what Officer shall then act as President, and such Officer shall act accordingly, until the Disability be removed, or a President shall be elected.

The President shall, at stated Times, receive for his Services, a Compensation, which shall neither be encreased nor diminished during the Period for which he shall have been elected, and he shall not receive within that Period any other Emolument from the United States, or any of them.

Before he enter on the Execution of his Office, he shall take the following Oath or Affirmation:—"I do solemnly swear (or affirm) that I will faithfully execute the Office of President of the United States, and will to the best of my Ability, preserve, protect and defend the Constitution of the United States."

Section 2. The President shall be Commander in Chief of the Army and Navy of the United States, and of the Militia of the several States, when called into the actual Service of the United States; he may require the Opinion, in writing, of the principal Officer in each of the executive Departments, upon any Subject relating to the Duties of their respective Offices, and he shall have Power to grant Reprieves and Pardons for Offences against the United States, except in Cases of Impeachment.

He shall have Power, by and with the Advice and Consent of the Senate, to make Treaties, provided two thirds of the Senators present concur; and he shall nominate, and by and with the Advice and Consent of the Senate, shall appoint Ambassadors, other public Ministers and Consuls, Judges of the supreme Court, and all other Officers of the United States, whose Appointments are not herein otherwise provided for, and which shall be established by Law: but the Congress may by Law vest the Appointment of such inferior Officers, as they think proper, in the President alone, in the Courts of Law, or in the Heads of Departments.

The President shall have Power to fill up all Vacancies that may happen during the Recess of the Senate, by granting Commissions which shall expire at the End of their next Session.

Section 3. He shall from time to time give to the Congress Information of the State of the Union, and recommend to their Consideration such Measures as he shall judge necessary and expedient; he may, on extraordinary Occasions, convene both Houses, or either of them, and in Case of Disagreement between them, with Respect to the Time of Adjournment, he may adjourn them to such Time as he shall think proper; he shall receive Ambassadors and other public Ministers; he shall take Care that the Laws be faithfully executed, and shall Commission all the Officers of the United States.

Section 4. The President, Vice President and all civil Officers of the United States, shall be removed from Office on Impeachment for, and Conviction of, Treason, Bribery, or other high Crimes and Misdemeanors.

ARTICLE III

Section 1. The judicial Power of the United States, shall be vested in one supreme Court, and in such inferior Courts as the Congress may from time to time ordain and establish. The Judges, both of the supreme and inferior Courts, shall hold their Offices during good Behaviour, and shall, at stated Times, receive for their Services, a Compensation, which shall not be diminished during their Continuance in Office.

Section 2. The judicial Power shall extend to all Cases, in Law and Equity, arising under this Constitution, the Laws of the United States, and Treaties made, or which shall be made, under their Authority;—to all Cases affecting Ambassadors, other public Ministers and Consuls;—to all Cases of admiralty and maritime Jurisdiction;—to Controversies to which the United States shall be a Party;—to Controversies between two or more States;—between a State and Citizens of another State;[8]—between Citizens of different States;—between Citizens of the same State claiming Lands under Grants of different States, and between a State, or the Citizens thereof, and foreign States, Citizens or Subjects.[8]

In all Cases affecting Ambassadors, other public Ministers and Consuls, and those in which a State

---

7. This provision has been affected by the Twenty-fifth Amendment.

8. These clauses were affected by the Eleventh Amendment.

shall be Party, the supreme Court shall have original Jurisdiction. In all the other Cases before mentioned, the supreme Court shall have appellate Jurisdiction, both as to Law and Fact, with such Exceptions, and under such Regulations as the Congress shall make.

The Trial of all Crimes, except in Cases of Impeachment, shall be by Jury; and such Trial shall be held in the State where the said Crimes shall have been committed; but when not committed within any State, the Trial shall be at such Place or Places as the Congress may by Law have directed.

Section 3. Treason against the United States, shall consist only in levying War against them, or in adhering to their Enemies, giving them Aid and Comfort. No Person shall be convicted of Treason unless on the Testimony of two Witnesses to the same overt Act, or on Confession in open Court.

The Congress shall have Power to declare the Punishment of Treason, but no Attainder of Treason shall work Corruption of Blood, or Forfeiture except during the Life of the Person attainted.

ARTICLE IV

Section 1. Full Faith and Credit shall be given in each State to the public Acts, Records, and judicial Proceedings of every other State. And the Congress may by general Laws prescribe the Manner in which such Acts, Records and Proceedings shall be proved, and the Effect thereof.

Section 2. The Citizens of each State shall be entitled to all Privileges and Immunities of Citizens in the several States.

A Person charged in any State with Treason, Felony, or other Crime, who shall flee from Justice, and be found in another State, shall on Demand of the executive Authority of the State from which he fled, be delivered up, to be removed to the State having Jurisdiction of the Crime.

[No Person held to Service or Labour in one State, under the Laws thereof, escaping into another, shall, in Consequence of any Law or Regulation therein, be discharged from such Service or Labour, but shall be delivered up on Claim of the Party to whom such Service or Labour may be due.]9

Section 3. New States may be admitted by the Congress into this Union; but no new State shall be

formed or erected within the Jurisdiction of any other State; nor any State be formed by the Junction of two or more States, or Parts of States, without the Consent of the Legislatures of the States concerned as well as of the Congress.

The Congress shall have Power to dispose of and make all needful Rules and Regulations respecting the Territory or other Property belonging to the United States; and nothing in this Constitution shall be so construed as to Prejudice any Claims of the United States, or of any particular State.

Section 4. The United States shall guarantee to every State in this Union a Republican Form of Government, and shall protect each of them against Invasion; and on Application of the Legislature, or of the Executive (when the Legislature cannot be convened) against domestic Violence.

ARTICLE V

The Congress, whenever two thirds of both Houses shall deem it necessary, shall propose Amendments to this Constitution, or, on the Application of the Legislatures of two thirds of the several States, shall call a Convention for proposing Amendments, which, in either Case, shall be valid to all Intents and Purposes, as Part of this Constitution, when ratified by the Legislatures of three fourths of the several States, or by Conventions in three fourths thereof, as the one or the other Mode of Ratification may be proposed by the Congress; Provided [that no Amendment which may be made prior to the Year One thousand eight hundred and eight shall in any Manner affect the first and fourth Clauses in the Ninth Section of the first Article; and]10 that no State, without its Consent, shall be deprived of its equal Suffrage in the Senate.

ARTICLE VI

All Debts contracted and Engagements entered into, before the Adoption of this Constitution, shall be as valid against the United States under this Constitution, as under the Confederation.

This Constitution, and the Laws of the United States which shall be made in Pursuance thereof; and all Treaties made, or which shall be made, under the Authority of the United States, shall be the supreme

---

9. This paragraph has been superseded by the Thirteenth Amendment.

10. Obsolete.

Law of the Land; and the Judges in every State shall be bound thereby, any Thing in the Constitution or Laws of any State to the Contrary notwithstanding.

The Senators and Representatives before mentioned, and the Members of the several State Legislatures, and all executive and judicial Officers, both of the United States and of the several States, shall be bound by Oath or Affirmation, to support this Constitution; but no religious Test shall ever be required as a Qualification to any Office or public Trust under the United States.

ARTICLE VII

The Ratification of the Conventions of nine States, shall be sufficient for the Establishment of this Constitution between the States so ratifying the Same. Done in Convention by the Unanimous Consent of the States present the Seventeenth Day of September in the Year of our Lord one thousand seven hundred and Eighty seven and of the Independence of the United States of America the Twelfth. IN WITNESS whereof We have hereunto subscribed our Names,

George Washington,
President and deputy from Virginia.

New Hampshire:	John Langdon, Nicholas Gilman.
Massachusetts:	Nathaniel Gorham, Rufus King.
Connecticut:	William Samuel Johnson, Roger Sherman.
New York:	Alexander Hamilton.
New Jersey:	William Livingston, David Brearley, William Paterson, Jonathan Dayton.
Pennsylvania:	Benjamin Franklin, Thomas Mifflin, Robert Morris, George Clymer, Thomas FitzSimons, Jared Ingersoll, James Wilson, Gouverneur Morris.
Delaware:	George Read, Gunning Bedford Jr., John Dickinson, Richard Bassett, Jacob Broom.
Maryland:	James McHenry, Daniel of St. Thomas Jenifer, Daniel Carroll.
Virginia:	John Blair, James Madison Jr.
North Carolina:	William Blount, Richard Dobbs Spaight, Hugh Williamson.
South Carolina:	John Rutledge, Charles Cotesworth Pinckney, Charles Pinckney, Pierce Butler.
Georgia:	William Few, Abraham Baldwin.

[The language of the original Constitution, not including the Amendments, was adopted by a convention of the states on September 17, 1787, and was subsequently ratified by the states on the following dates: Delaware, December 7, 1787; Pennsylvania, December 12, 1787; New Jersey, December 18, 1787; Georgia, January 2, 1788; Connecticut, January 9, 1788; Massachusetts, February 6, 1788; Maryland, April 28, 1788; South Carolina, May 23, 1788; New Hampshire, June 21, 1788.

Ratification was completed on June 21, 1788.

The Constitution subsequently was ratified by Virginia, June 25, 1788; New York, July 26, 1788; North Carolina, November 21, 1789; Rhode Island, May 29, 1790; and Vermont, January 10, 1791.]

AMENDMENTS

Amendment I

(First ten amendments ratified December 15, 1791.)

Congress shall make no law respecting an establishment of religion, or prohibiting the free exercise thereof; or abridging the freedom of speech, or of the press; or the right of the people peaceably to assemble, and to petition the Government for a redress of grievances.

Amendment II

A well regulated Militia, being necessary to the security of a free State, the right of the people to keep and bear Arms, shall not be infringed.

Amendment III

No Soldier shall, in time of peace be quartered in any house, without the consent of the Owner, nor in time of war, but in a manner to be prescribed by law.

Amendment IV

The right of the people to be secure in their persons, houses, papers, and effects, against unreasonable searches and seizures, shall not be violated, and no Warrants shall issue, but upon probable cause, supported by Oath or affirmation, and particularly describing the place to be searched, and the persons or things to be seized.

Amendment V

No person shall be held to answer for a capital, or otherwise infamous crime, unless on a presentment or indictment of a Grand Jury, except in cases arising in the land or naval forces, or in the Militia, when in actual service in time of War or public danger; nor shall any person be subject for the same offence to be twice put in jeopardy of life or limb; nor shall be compelled in any criminal case to be a witness against himself, nor be deprived of life, liberty, or property, without due process of law; nor shall private property be taken for public use, without just compensation.

Amendment VI

In all criminal prosecutions, the accused shall enjoy the right to a speedy and public trial, by an impartial jury of the State and district wherein the crime shall have been committed, which district shall have been previously ascertained by law, and to be informed of the nature and cause of the accusation; to be confronted with the witnesses against him; to have compulsory process for obtaining witnesses in his favor, and to have the Assistance of Counsel for his defence.

Amendment VII

In Suits at common law, where the value in controversy shall exceed twenty dollars, the right of trial by jury shall be preserved, and no fact tried by a jury, shall be otherwise re-examined in any Court of the United States, than according to the rules of the common law.

Amendment VIII

Excessive bail shall not be required, nor excessive fines imposed, nor cruel and unusual punishments inflicted.

Amendment IX

The enumeration in the Constitution, of certain rights, shall not be construed to deny or disparage others retained by the people.

Amendment X

The powers not delegated to the United States by the Constitution, nor prohibited by it to the States, are reserved to the States respectively, or to the people.

Amendment XI

(Ratified February 7, 1795)

The Judicial power of the United States shall not be construed to extend to any suit in law or equity, commenced or prosecuted against one of the United States by Citizens of another State, or by Citizens or Subjects of any Foreign State.

Amendment XII

(Ratified June 15, 1804)

The Electors shall meet in their respective states and vote by ballot for President and Vice-President, one of whom, at least, shall not be an inhabitant of the same state with themselves; they shall name in their ballots the person voted for as President, and in distinct ballots the person voted for as Vice-President, and they shall make distinct lists of all persons voted for as President, and of all persons voted for as Vice-President, and of the number of votes for each, which lists they shall sign and certify, and transmit sealed to the seat of the government of the United States, directed to the President of the Senate;—The President of the Senate shall, in the presence of the Senate and House of Representatives, open all the certificates and the votes shall then be counted;—The person having the greatest number of votes for President, shall be the President, if such number be a majority of the whole number of Electors appointed; and if no person have such majority, then from the persons having the highest numbers not exceeding three on the list of those voted for as President, the House of Representatives shall choose immediately, by ballot, the President. But in choosing the President, the votes shall be taken by states, the representation from each state having one vote; a quorum for this purpose shall consist of a member or members from two-thirds of the states, and a majority of all the states shall be necessary to a choice. [And if the House of Representatives shall not choose a President whenever the right of choice shall devolve upon them, before the fourth day of March next following, then the Vice-President shall act as President, as in the case of the death or other constitutional disability of the

President.][11] The person having the greatest number of votes as Vice-President, shall be the Vice-President, if such number be a majority of the whole number of Electors appointed, and if no person have a majority, then from the two highest numbers on the list, the Senate shall choose the Vice-President; a quorum for the purpose shall consist of two-thirds of the whole number of Senators, and a majority of the whole number shall be necessary to a choice. But no person constitutionally ineligible to the office of President shall be eligible to that of Vice-President of the United States.

Amendment XIII

(Ratified December 6, 1865)

Section 1. Neither slavery nor involuntary servitude, except as a punishment for crime whereof the party shall have been duly convicted, shall exist within the United States, or any place subject to their jurisdiction.

Section 2. Congress shall have power to enforce this article by appropriate legislation.

Amendment XIV

(Ratified July 9, 1868)

Section 1. All persons born or naturalized in the United States, and subject to the jurisdiction thereof, are citizens of the United States and of the State wherein they reside. No State shall make or enforce any law which shall abridge the privileges or immunities of citizens of the United States; nor shall any State deprive any person of life, liberty, or property, without due process of law; nor deny to any person within its jurisdiction the equal protection of the laws.

Section 2. Representatives shall be apportioned among the several States according to their respective numbers, counting the whole number of persons in each State, excluding Indians not taxed. But when the right to vote at any election for the choice of electors for President and Vice President of the United States, Representatives in Congress, the Executive and Judicial officers of a State, or the members of the Legislature thereof, is denied to any of the male inhabitants of such State, being twenty-one years of age,[12] and citizens of the United States, or in any way abridged, except for participation in rebellion, or other crime, the basis of representation therein shall be reduced in the proportion

which the number of such male citizens shall bear to the whole number of male citizens twenty-one years of age in such State.

Section 3. No person shall be a Senator or Representative in Congress, or elector of President and Vice President, or hold any office, civil or military, under the United States, or under any State, who, having previously taken an oath, as a member of Congress, or as an officer of the United States, or as a member of any State legislature, or as an executive or judicial officer of any State, to support the Constitution of the United States, shall have engaged in insurrection or rebellion against the same, or given aid or comfort to the enemies thereof. But Congress may by a vote of two-thirds of each House, remove such disability.

Section 4. The validity of the public debt of the United States, authorized by law, including debts incurred for payment of pensions and bounties for services in suppressing insurrection or rebellion, shall not be questioned. But neither the United States nor any State shall assume or pay any debt or obligation incurred in aid of insurrection or rebellion against the United States, or any claim for the loss or emancipation of any slave; but all such debts, obligations and claims shall be held illegal and void.

Section 5. The Congress shall have power to enforce, by appropriate legislation, the provisions of this article.

Amendment XV

(Ratified February 3, 1870)

Section 1. The right of citizens of the United States to vote shall not be denied or abridged by the United States or by any State on account of race, color, or previous condition of servitude.

Section 2. The Congress shall have power to enforce this article by appropriate legislation.

Amendment XVI

(Ratified February 3, 1913)

The Congress shall have power to lay and collect taxes on incomes, from whatever source derived, without apportionment among the several States, and without regard to any census or enumeration.

Amendment XVII

(Ratified April 8, 1913)

The Senate of the United States shall be composed of two Senators from each State, elected by the people

---

11. The part in brackets has been superseded by Section 3 of the Twentieth Amendment.

12. See the Nineteenth and Twenty-sixth Amendments.

thereof, for six years; and each Senator shall have one vote. The electors in each State shall have the qualifications requisite for electors of the most numerous branch of the State legislatures.

When vacancies happen in the representation of any State in the Senate, the executive authority of such State shall issue writs of election to fill such vacancies: *Provided,* That the legislature of any State may empower the executive thereof to make temporary appointments until the people fill the vacancies by election as the legislature may direct.

This amendment shall not be so construed as to affect the election or term of any Senator chosen before it becomes valid as part of the Constitution.

Amendment XVIII

(Ratified January 16, 1919)

Section 1. After one year from the ratification of this article the manufacture, sale, or transportation of intoxicating liquors within, the importation thereof into, or the exportation thereof from the United States and all territory subject to the jurisdiction thereof for beverage purposes is hereby prohibited.

Section 2. The Congress and the several States shall have concurrent power to enforce this article by appropriate legislation.

Section 3. This article shall be inoperative unless it shall have been ratified as an amendment to the Constitution by the legislatures of the several States, as provided in the Constitution, within seven years from the date of the submission hereof to the States by the Congress.][13]

Amendment XIX

(Ratified August 18, 1920)

The right of citizens of the United States to vote shall not be denied or abridged by the United States or by any State on account of sex.

Congress shall have power to enforce this article by appropriate legislation.

Amendment XX

(Ratified January 23, 1933)

Section 1. The terms of the President and Vice President shall end at noon on the 20th day of January, and the terms of Senators and Representatives at noon on the 3d day of January, of the years in which such terms would have ended if this article had not been ratified; and the terms of their successors shall then begin.

Section 2. The Congress shall assemble at least once in every year, and such meeting shall begin at noon on the 3d day of January, unless they shall by law appoint a different day.

Section 3.[14] If, at the time fixed for the beginning of the term of the President, the President elect shall have died, the Vice President elect shall become President. If a President shall not have been chosen before the time fixed for the beginning of his term, or if the President elect shall have failed to qualify, then the Vice President elect shall act as President until a President shall have qualified; and the Congress may by law provide for the case wherein neither a President elect nor a Vice President elect shall have qualified, declaring who shall then act as President, or the manner in which one who is to act shall be selected, and such person shall act accordingly until a President or Vice President shall have qualified.

Section 4. The Congress may by law provide for the case of the death of any of the persons from whom the House of Representatives may choose a President whenever the right of choice shall have devolved upon them, and for the case of the death of any of the persons from whom the Senate may choose a Vice President whenever the right of choice shall have devolved upon them.

Section 5. Sections 1 and 2 shall take effect on the 15th day of October following the ratification of this article.

Section 6. This article shall be inoperative unless it shall have been ratified as an amendment to the Constitution by the legislatures of three-fourths of the several States within seven years from the date of its submission.

Amendment XXI

(Ratified December 5, 1933)

Section 1. The eighteenth article of amendment to the Constitution of the United States is hereby repealed.

Section 2. The transportation or importation into any State, Territory, or possession of the United States for delivery or use therein of intoxicating liquors, in violation of the laws thereof, is hereby prohibited.

Section 3. This article shall be inoperative unless it shall have been ratified as an amendment to the Constitution by conventions in the several States, as

---

13. This Amendment was repealed by Section 1 of the Twenty-first Amendment.

14. See the Twenty-fifth Amendment.

provided in the Constitution, within seven years from the date of the submission hereof to the States by the Congress.

Amendment XXII

(Ratified February 27, 1951)

Section 1. No person shall be elected to the office of the President more than twice, and no person who has held the office of President, or acted as President, for more than two years of a term to which some other person was elected President shall be elected to the office of the President more than once. But this Article shall not apply to any person holding the office of President when this Article was proposed by the Congress, and shall not prevent any person who may be holding the office of President, or acting as President, during the term within which this Article become operative from holding the office of President or acting as President during the remainder of such term.

Section 2. This article shall be inoperative unless it shall have been ratified as an amendment to the Constitution by the legislatures of three-fourths of the several States within seven years from the date of its submission to the States by the Congress.

Amendment XXIII

(Ratified March 29, 1961)

Section 1. The District constituting the seat of Government of the United States shall appoint in such manner as the Congress may direct:

A number of electors of President and Vice President equal to the whole number of Senators and Representatives in Congress to which the District would be entitled if it were a State, but in no event more than the least populous State; they shall be in addition to those appointed by the States, but they shall be considered, for the purposes of the election of President and Vice President, to be electors appointed by a State; and they shall meet in the District and perform such duties as provided by the twelfth article of amendment.

Section 2. The Congress shall have power to enforce this article by appropriate legislation.

Amendment XXIV

(Ratified January 23, 1964)

Section 1. The right of citizens of the United States to vote in any primary or other election for President or Vice President, for electors for President or Vice President, or for Senator or Representative in Congress, shall not be denied or abridged by the United States or any State by reason of failure to pay any poll tax or other tax.

Section 2. The Congress shall have power to enforce this article by appropriate legislation.

Amendment XXV

(Ratified February 10, 1967)

Section 1. In case of the removal of the President from office or of his death or resignation, the Vice President shall become President.

Section 2. Whenever there is a vacancy in the office of the Vice President, the President shall nominate a Vice President who shall take office upon confirmation by a majority vote of both Houses of Congress.

Section 3. Whenever the President transmits to the President pro tempore of the Senate and the Speaker of the House of Representatives his written declaration that he is unable to discharge the powers and duties of his office, and until he transmits to them a written declaration to the contrary, such powers and duties shall be discharged by the Vice President as Acting President.

Section 4. Whenever the Vice President and a majority of either the principal officers of the executive departments or of such other body as Congress may by law provide, transmit to the President pro tempore of the Senate and the Speaker of the House of Representatives their written declaration that the President is unable to discharge the powers and duties of his office, the Vice President shall immediately assume the powers and duties of the office as Acting President.

Thereafter, when the President transmits to the President pro tempore of the Senate and the Speaker of the House of Representatives his written declaration that no inability exists, he shall resume the powers and duties of his office unless the Vice President and a majority of either the principal officers of the executive department or of such other body as Congress may by law provide, transmit within four days to the President pro tempore of the Senate and the Speaker of the House of Representatives their written declaration that the President is unable to discharge the powers and duties of his office. Thereupon Congress shall decide the issue, assembling within forty-eight hours for that purpose if not in session. If the Congress, within twenty-one days after receipt of the latter written declaration, or, if Congress is not in session, within twenty-one days after Congress is required to assemble, determines by two-thirds vote of both Houses that the President is unable to discharge the powers and duties of his office, the Vice President shall continue to discharge the same as Acting President; otherwise, the President shall resume the powers and duties of his office.

Amendment XXVI

(Ratified July 1, 1971)

Section 1. The right of citizens of the United States, who are eighteen years of age or older, to vote shall not be denied or abridged by the United States or by any State on account of age.

Section 2. The Congress shall have power to enforce this article by appropriate legislation.

Amendment XXVII

(Ratified May 7, 1992)

No law varying the compensation for the services of the Senators and Representatives shall take effect, until an election of Representatives shall have intervened.

SOURCE: *United States Government Manual, 1993–94* (Washington, DC: Government Printing Office, 1993), 5–20.

APPENDIX 2

The Justices

T HE JUSTICES OF THE Supreme Court are listed below in alphabetical order, each with birth and death years, state from which he or she was appointed, political party affiliation at time of appointment, educational institutions attended, appointing president, confirmation date and vote, date of service termination, and major preappointment offices and activities.

Alito, Samuel A., Jr. (1950–). New Jersey. Republican. Princeton, Yale. Nominated associate justice by George W. Bush; confirmed 2006 by 58–42 vote. Federal appeals court judge.

Baldwin, Henry (1780–1844). Pennsylvania. Democrat. Yale. Nominated associate justice by Andrew Jackson; confirmed 1830 by 41–2 vote; died in office 1844. U.S. representative.

Barbour, Philip Pendleton (1783–1841). Virginia. Democrat. College of William and Mary. Nominated associate justice by Andrew Jackson; confirmed 1836 by 30–11 vote; died in office 1841. Virginia state legislator, U.S. representative, U.S. Speaker of the House, state court judge, federal district court judge.

Black, Hugo Lafayette (1886–1971). Alabama. Democrat. Birmingham Medical College, University of Alabama. Nominated associate justice by Franklin Roosevelt; confirmed 1937 by 63–16 vote; retired 1971. Alabama police court judge, county solicitor, U.S. senator.

Blackmun, Harry Andrew (1908–1999). Minnesota. Republican. Harvard. Nominated associate justice by Richard Nixon; confirmed 1970 by 94–0 vote; retired 1994. Federal appeals court judge.

Blair, John, Jr. (1732–1800). Virginia. Federalist. College of William and Mary; Middle Temple (England). Nominated associate justice by George Washington; confirmed 1789 by voice vote; resigned 1796. Virginia legislator, state court judge, delegate to Constitutional Convention.

Blatchford, Samuel (1820–1893). New York. Republican. Columbia. Nominated associate justice by Chester A. Arthur; confirmed 1882 by voice vote; died in office 1893. Federal district court judge, federal circuit court judge.

Bradley, Joseph P. (1813–1892). New Jersey. Republican. Rutgers. Nominated associate justice by Ulysses S. Grant; confirmed 1870 by 46–9 vote; died in office 1892. Private practice.

Brandeis, Louis Dembitz (1856–1941). Massachusetts. Republican. Harvard. Nominated associate justice by Woodrow Wilson; confirmed 1916 by 47–22 vote; retired 1939. Private practice.

Brennan, William Joseph, Jr. (1906–1997). New Jersey. Democrat. University of Pennsylvania, Harvard. Received recess appointment from Dwight Eisenhower to be associate justice 1956; confirmed 1957 by voice vote; retired 1990. New Jersey Supreme Court.

Brewer, David Josiah (1837–1910). Kansas. Republican. Wesleyan, Yale, Albany Law School. Nominated associate justice by Benjamin Harrison; confirmed 1889 by 53–11 vote; died in office 1910. Kansas state court judge, federal circuit court judge.

Breyer, Stephen G. (1938–). Massachusetts. Democrat. Stanford, Oxford, Harvard. Nominated associate justice by Bill Clinton; confirmed 1994 by 87–9 vote. Law professor; chief counsel, Senate Judiciary Committee; federal appeals court judge.

Brown, Henry B. (1836–1913). Michigan. Republican. Yale, Harvard. Nominated associate justice by Benjamin Harrison; confirmed 1890 by voice vote; retired 1906. Michigan state court judge, federal district court judge.

Burger, Warren Earl (1907–1995). Virginia. Republican. University of Minnesota, St. Paul College of Law. Nominated chief justice by Richard Nixon; confirmed 1969 by 74–3 vote; retired 1986. Assistant U.S. attorney general, federal appeals court judge.

Burton, Harold Hitz (1888–1964). Ohio. Republican. Bowdoin College, Harvard. Nominated associate justice by Harry Truman; confirmed 1945 by voice vote; retired 1958. Ohio state legislator, mayor of Cleveland, U.S. senator.

Butler, Pierce (1866–1939). Minnesota. Republican. Carleton College. Nominated associate justice by Warren G. Harding; confirmed 1922 by 61–8 vote; died in office 1939. Minnesota county attorney, private practice.

Byrnes, James Francis (1879–1972). South Carolina. Democrat. Privately educated. Nominated associate justice by Franklin Roosevelt; confirmed 1941 by voice vote; resigned 1942. South Carolina local solicitor, U.S. representative, U.S. senator.

Campbell, John Archibald (1811–1889). Alabama. Democrat. Franklin College (University of Georgia), U.S. Military Academy. Nominated associate justice by Franklin Pierce; confirmed 1853 by voice vote; resigned 1861. Alabama state legislator.

Cardozo, Benjamin Nathan (1870–1938). New York. Democrat. Columbia. Nominated associate justice by Herbert Hoover; confirmed 1932 by voice vote; died in office 1938. State court judge.

Catron, John (1786–1865). Tennessee. Democrat. Self-educated. Nominated associate justice by Andrew Jackson; confirmed 1837 by 28–15 vote; died in office 1865. Tennessee state court judge, state chief justice.

Chase, Salmon Portland (1808–1873). Ohio. Republican. Dartmouth. Nominated chief justice by Abraham Lincoln; confirmed 1864 by voice vote; died in office 1873. U.S. senator, Ohio governor, U.S. secretary of the Treasury.

Chase, Samuel (1741–1811). Maryland. Federalist. Privately educated. Nominated associate justice by George Washington; confirmed 1796 by voice vote; died in office 1811. Maryland state legislator, delegate to Continental Congress, state court judge.

Clark, Tom Campbell (1899–1977). Texas. Democrat. University of Texas. Nominated associate justice by Harry Truman; confirmed 1949 by 73–8 vote; retired 1967. Texas local district attorney, U.S. attorney general.

Clarke, John Hessin (1857–1945). Ohio. Democrat. Western Reserve University. Nominated associate justice by Woodrow Wilson; confirmed 1916 by voice vote; resigned 1922. Federal district judge.

Clifford, Nathan (1803–1881). Maine. Democrat. Privately educated. Nominated associate justice by James Buchanan; confirmed 1858 by 26–23 vote; died in office 1881. Maine state legislator, state attorney general, U.S. representative, U.S. attorney general, minister to Mexico.

Curtis, Benjamin Robbins (1809–1874). Massachusetts. Whig. Harvard. Nominated associate justice by Millard Fillmore; confirmed 1851 by voice vote; resigned 1857. Massachusetts state legislator.

Cushing, William (1732–1810). Massachusetts. Federalist. Harvard. Nominated associate justice by George Washington; confirmed 1789 by voice vote; died in office 1810. Massachusetts state court judge, Electoral College delegate.

Daniel, Peter Vivian (1784–1860). Virginia. Democrat. Princeton. Nominated associate justice by Martin Van Buren; confirmed 1841 by 22–5 vote; died in office 1860. Virginia state legislator, state Privy Council member, federal district court judge.

Davis, David (1815–1886). Illinois. Republican. Kenyon College, Yale. Nominated associate justice by Abraham Lincoln; confirmed 1862 by voice vote; resigned 1877. Illinois state legislator, state court judge.

Day, William Rufus (1849–1923). Ohio. Republican. University of Michigan. Nominated associate justice by Theodore Roosevelt; confirmed 1903 by voice vote; resigned 1922. Ohio state court judge, U.S. secretary of state, federal court of appeals judge.

Douglas, William Orville (1898–1980). Connecticut. Democrat. Whitman College, Columbia. Nominated associate justice by Franklin Roosevelt; confirmed 1939 by 62–4 vote; retired 1975. Law professor, member of the Securities and Exchange Commission.

Duvall, Gabriel (1752–1844). Maryland. Democratic-Republican. Privately educated. Nominated associate justice by James Madison; confirmed 1811 by voice vote; resigned 1835. Maryland state legislator, U.S. representative, state court judge, presidential elector, comptroller of the U.S. Treasury.

Ellsworth, Oliver (1745–1807). Connecticut. Federalist. Princeton. Nominated chief justice by George Washington; confirmed 1796 by 21–1 vote; resigned 1800. Connecticut state legislator, delegate to Continental Congress and Constitutional Convention, state court judge, U.S. senator.

Field, Stephen J. (1816–1899). California. Democrat. Williams College. Nominated associate justice by Abraham Lincoln; confirmed 1863 by voice vote; retired 1897. California state legislator, California Supreme Court.

Fortas, Abe (1910–1982). Tennessee. Democrat. Southwestern College, Yale. Nominated associate justice by Lyndon Johnson; confirmed 1965 by voice vote; resigned 1969. Counsel for numerous federal agencies, private practice.

Frankfurter, Felix (1882–1965). Massachusetts. Independent. College of the City of New York, Harvard. Nominated associate justice by Franklin Roosevelt; confirmed 1939 by voice vote; retired 1962. Law professor, War Department law officer, assistant to secretary of war, assistant to secretary of labor, War Labor Policies Board chairman.

Fuller, Melville Weston (1833–1910). Illinois. Democrat. Bowdoin College, Harvard. Nominated chief justice by Grover Cleveland; confirmed 1888 by 41–20 vote; died in office 1910. Illinois state legislator.

Ginsburg, Ruth Bader (1933–). New York. Democrat. Columbia. Nominated associate justice by Bill Clinton; confirmed 1993 by 96–3 vote. Law professor, federal court of appeals judge.

Goldberg, Arthur J. (1908–1990). Illinois. Democrat. Northwestern. Nominated associate justice by John Kennedy; confirmed 1962 by voice vote; resigned 1965. Secretary of labor.

Gray, Horace (1828–1902). Massachusetts. Republican. Harvard. Nominated associate justice by Chester A. Arthur; confirmed 1881 by 51–5 vote; died in office 1902. Massachusetts Supreme Court justice.

Grier, Robert Cooper (1794–1870). Pennsylvania. Democrat. Dickinson College. Nominated associate justice by James Polk; confirmed 1846 by voice vote; retired 1870. Pennsylvania state court judge.

Harlan, John Marshall (1833–1911). Kentucky. Republican. Centre College, Transylvania University. Nominated associate justice by Rutherford B. Hayes; confirmed 1877 by voice vote; died in office 1911. Kentucky attorney general.

Harlan, John Marshall (1899–1971). New York. Republican. Princeton, Oxford, New York Law School. Nominated associate justice by Dwight Eisenhower; confirmed 1955 by 71–11 vote; retired 1971. Chief counsel for New York State Crime Commission, federal court of appeals.

Holmes, Oliver Wendell, Jr. (1841–1935). Massachusetts. Republican. Harvard. Nominated associate justice by Theodore Roosevelt; confirmed 1902 by voice vote; retired 1932. Law professor; justice, Supreme Judicial Court of Massachusetts.

Hughes, Charles Evans (1862–1948). New York. Republican. Colgate, Brown, Columbia. Nominated associate justice by William Howard Taft; confirmed 1910 by voice vote; resigned 1916; nominated chief justice by Herbert Hoover; confirmed 1930 by 52–26 vote; retired 1941. New York governor, U.S. secretary of state, Court of International Justice judge.

Hunt, Ward (1810–1886). New York. Republican. Union College. Nominated associate justice by Ulysses S. Grant; confirmed 1872 by voice vote; retired 1882. New York state legislator, mayor of Utica, state court judge.

Iredell, James (1751–1799). North Carolina. Federalist. English schools. Nominated associate justice by George Washington; confirmed 1790 by voice vote; died in office 1799. Customs official, state court judge, state attorney general.

Jackson, Howell Edmunds (1832–1895). Tennessee. Democrat. West Tennessee College, University of Virginia, Cumberland University. Nominated associate justice by Benjamin Harrison; confirmed 1893 by voice vote; died in office 1895. Tennessee state legislator, U.S. senator, federal circuit court judge, federal court of appeals judge.

Jackson, Robert Houghwout (1892–1954). New York. Democrat. Albany Law School. Nominated associate justice by Franklin Roosevelt; confirmed 1941 by voice vote; died in office 1954. Counsel for Internal Revenue Bureau and Securities and Exchange Commission, U.S. solicitor general, U.S. attorney general.

Jay, John (1745–1829). New York. Federalist. King's College (Columbia University). Nominated chief justice by George Washington; confirmed 1789 by voice vote; resigned 1795. Delegate to Continental Congress, chief justice of New York, minister to Spain and Great Britain, secretary of foreign affairs.

Johnson, Thomas (1732–1819). Maryland. Federalist. Privately educated. Nominated associate justice by George Washington; confirmed 1791 by voice vote; resigned 1793. Delegate to Annapolis Convention and Continental Congress, Maryland governor, state legislator, state court judge.

Johnson, William (1771–1834). South Carolina. Democratic-Republican. Princeton. Nominated associate justice by Thomas Jefferson; confirmed 1804 by voice vote; died in office 1834. South Carolina state legislator, state court judge.

Kagan, Elena (1960–). Massachusetts. Democrat. Princeton, Oxford, Harvard. Nominated associate justice by Barack Obama; confirmed 2010 by 63–37 vote. Law professor and dean, solicitor general of the United States.

Kennedy, Anthony McLeod (1936–). California. Republican. Stanford, London School of Economics, Harvard. Nominated associate justice by Ronald Reagan; confirmed 1988 by 97–0 vote. Federal appeals court judge.

Lamar, Joseph Rucker (1857–1916). Georgia. Democrat. University of Georgia, Bethany College, Washington and Lee. Nominated associate justice by William Howard Taft; confirmed 1910 by voice vote; died in office 1916. Georgia state legislator, Georgia Supreme Court.

Lamar, Lucius Quintus Cincinnatus (1825–1893). Mississippi. Democrat. Emory College. Nominated associate justice by Grover Cleveland; confirmed 1888 by 32–28 vote; died in office 1893. Georgia state legislator, U.S. representative, U.S. senator, U.S. secretary of the interior.

Livingston, Henry Brockholst (1757–1823). New York. Democratic-Republican. Princeton. Nominated associate justice by Thomas Jefferson; confirmed 1806 by voice vote; died in office 1823. New York state legislator, state court judge.

Lurton, Horace Harmon (1844–1914). Tennessee. Democrat. University of Chicago, Cumberland. Nominated associate justice by William Howard Taft; confirmed 1909 by voice vote; died in office 1914. Tennessee Supreme Court, federal court of appeals judge.

Marshall, John (1755–1835). Virginia. Federalist. Privately educated, College of William and Mary. Nominated chief justice by John Adams; confirmed

1801 by voice vote; died in office 1835. Virginia state legislator, minister to France, U.S. representative, U.S. secretary of state.

Marshall, Thurgood (1908–1993). New York. Democrat. Lincoln University, Howard University. Nominated associate justice by Lyndon Johnson; confirmed 1967 by 69–11 vote; retired 1991. Chief counsel for the NAACP Legal Defense Fund, federal court of appeals judge, U.S. solicitor general.

Matthews, Stanley (1824–1889). Ohio. Republican. Kenyon College. Nominated associate justice by Rutherford B. Hayes; no Senate action on nomination; renominated associate justice by James A. Garfield; confirmed 1881 by 24–23 vote; died in office 1889. Ohio state legislator, state court judge, U.S. attorney for southern Ohio, U.S. senator.

McKenna, Joseph (1843–1926). California. Republican. Benicia Collegiate Institute. Nominated associate justice by William McKinley; confirmed 1898 by voice vote; retired 1925. California state legislator, U.S. representative, federal court of appeals judge, U.S. attorney general.

McKinley, John (1780–1852). Alabama. Democrat. Self-educated. Nominated associate justice by Martin Van Buren; confirmed 1837 by voice vote; died in office 1852. Alabama state legislator, U.S. senator, U.S. representative.

McLean, John (1785–1861). Ohio. Democrat. Privately educated. Nominated associate justice by Andrew Jackson; confirmed 1829 by voice vote; died in office 1861. U.S. representative, Ohio Supreme Court justice, commissioner of U.S. General Land Office, U.S. postmaster general.

McReynolds, James Clark (1862–1946). Tennessee. Democrat. Vanderbilt, University of Virginia. Nominated associate justice by Woodrow Wilson; confirmed 1914 by 44–6 vote; retired 1941. U.S. attorney general.

Miller, Samuel Freeman (1816–1890). Iowa. Republican. Transylvania University. Nominated associate justice by Abraham Lincoln; confirmed 1862 by voice vote; died in office 1890. Medical doctor, private law practice, justice of the peace.

Minton, Sherman (1890–1965). Indiana. Democrat. Indiana University, Yale. Nominated associate justice by Harry Truman; confirmed 1949 by 48–16 vote; retired 1956. U.S. senator, federal court of appeals judge.

Moody, William Henry (1853–1917). Massachusetts. Republican. Harvard. Nominated associate justice by Theodore Roosevelt; confirmed 1906 by voice vote;

retired 1910. Massachusetts local district attorney, U.S. representative, secretary of the navy, U.S. attorney general.

Moore, Alfred (1755–1810). North Carolina. Federalist. Privately educated. Nominated associate justice by John Adams; confirmed 1799 by voice vote; resigned 1804. North Carolina legislator, state attorney general, state court judge.

Murphy, William Francis (Frank) (1880–1949). Michigan. Democrat. University of Michigan, London's Inn (England), Trinity College (Ireland). Nominated associate justice by Franklin Roosevelt; confirmed 1940 by voice vote; died in office 1949. Michigan state court judge, mayor of Detroit, governor of the Philippines, governor of Michigan, U.S. attorney general.

Nelson, Samuel (1792–1873). New York. Democrat. Middlebury College. Nominated associate justice by John Tyler; confirmed 1845 by voice vote; retired 1872. Presidential elector, state court judge, New York Supreme Court chief justice.

O'Connor, Sandra Day (1930–). Arizona. Republican. Stanford. Nominated associate justice by Ronald Reagan; confirmed 1981 by 99–0 vote; retired 2006. Arizona state legislator, state court judge.

Paterson, William (1745–1806). New Jersey. Federalist. Princeton. Nominated associate justice by George Washington; confirmed 1793 by voice vote; died in office 1806. New Jersey attorney general, delegate to Constitutional Convention, U.S. senator, New Jersey governor.

Peckham, Rufus Wheeler (1838–1909). New York. Democrat. Albany Boys' Academy. Nominated associate justice by Grover Cleveland; confirmed 1895 by voice vote; died in office 1909. New York local district attorney, city attorney, state court judge.

Pitney, Mahlon (1858–1924). New Jersey. Republican. Princeton. Nominated associate justice by William Howard Taft; confirmed 1912 by 50–26 vote; retired 1922. U.S. representative, New Jersey state legislator, New Jersey Supreme Court, chancellor of New Jersey.

Powell, Lewis Franklin, Jr. (1907–1998). Virginia. Democrat. Washington and Lee, Harvard. Nominated associate justice by Richard Nixon; confirmed 1971 by 89–1 vote; retired 1987. Private practice, Virginia State Board of Education president, American Bar Association president, American College of Trial Lawyers president.

Reed, Stanley Forman (1884–1980). Kentucky. Democrat. Kentucky Wesleyan, Yale, Virginia, Columbia,

University of Paris. Nominated associate justice by Franklin Roosevelt; confirmed 1938 by voice vote; retired 1957. Federal Farm Board general counsel, Reconstruction Finance Corporation general counsel, U.S. solicitor general.

Rehnquist, William Hubbs (1924–2005). Arizona. Republican. Stanford, Harvard. Nominated associate justice by Richard Nixon; confirmed 1971 by 68–26 vote; nominated chief justice by Ronald Reagan; confirmed 1986 by 65–33 vote; died in office 2005. Private practice, assistant U.S. attorney general.

Roberts, John G., Jr. (1955–). Maryland. Republican. Harvard. Nominated associate justice by George W. Bush 2005; nomination withdrawn; nominated chief justice by George W. Bush; confirmed 2005 by 78–22 vote. Federal appeals court judge.

Roberts, Owen Josephus (1875–1955). Pennsylvania. Republican. University of Pennsylvania. Nominated associate justice by Herbert Hoover; confirmed 1930 by voice vote; resigned 1945. Private practice, Pennsylvania local prosecutor, special U.S. attorney.

Rutledge, John (1739–1800). South Carolina. Federalist. Middle Temple (England). Nominated associate justice by George Washington; confirmed 1789 by voice vote; resigned 1791. Nominated chief justice by George Washington August 1795 and served as recess appointment; confirmation denied and service terminated December 1795. South Carolina legislator, state attorney general, governor, chief justice of South Carolina, delegate to Continental Congress and Constitutional Convention.

Rutledge, Wiley Blount (1894–1949). Iowa. Democrat. Maryville College, University of Wisconsin, University of Colorado. Nominated associate justice by Franklin Roosevelt; confirmed 1943 by voice vote; died in office 1949. Law professor, federal court of appeals judge.

Sanford, Edward Terry (1865–1930). Tennessee. Republican. University of Tennessee, Harvard. Nominated associate justice by Warren G. Harding; confirmed 1923 by voice vote; died in office 1930. Assistant U.S. attorney general, federal district court judge.

Scalia, Antonin (1936–). Virginia. Republican. Georgetown, Harvard. Nominated associate justice by Ronald Reagan; confirmed 1986 by 98–0 vote. Assistant U.S. attorney general, law professor, federal court of appeals judge.

Shiras, George, Jr. (1832–1924). Pennsylvania. Republican. Ohio University, Yale. Nominated associate justice by Benjamin Harrison; confirmed 1892 by voice vote; retired 1903. Private practice.

Sotomayor, Sonia (1954–). New York. Democrat. Princeton, Yale. Nominated associate justice by Barack Obama; confirmed 2009 by 68–31 vote. New York state assistant district attorney, federal district court judge, federal appeals court judge.

Souter, David Hackett (1939–). New Hampshire. Republican. Harvard, Oxford. Nominated associate justice by George Bush; confirmed 1990 by 90–9 vote; retired 2009. New Hampshire attorney general, state court judge, federal appeals court judge.

Stevens, John Paul (1920–). Illinois. Republican. Chicago, Northwestern. Nominated associate justice by Gerald Ford; confirmed 1975 by 98–0 vote; retired 2010. Federal court of appeals judge.

Stewart, Potter (1915–1985). Ohio. Republican. Yale, Cambridge. Received recess appointment from Dwight Eisenhower to be associate justice in 1958; confirmed 1959 by 70–17 vote; retired 1981. Cincinnati city council, federal court of appeals judge.

Stone, Harlan Fiske (1872–1946). New York. Republican. Amherst College, Columbia. Nominated associate justice by Calvin Coolidge; confirmed 1925 by 71–6 vote; nominated chief justice by Franklin Roosevelt; confirmed 1941 by voice vote; died in office 1946. Law professor, U.S. attorney general.

Story, Joseph (1779–1845). Massachusetts. Democratic-Republican. Harvard. Nominated associate justice by James Madison; confirmed 1811 by voice vote; died in office 1845. Massachusetts state legislator, U.S. representative.

Strong, William (1808–1895). Pennsylvania. Republican. Yale. Nominated associate justice by Ulysses S. Grant; confirmed 1870 by voice vote; retired 1880. U.S. representative, Pennsylvania Supreme Court justice.

Sutherland, George (1862–1942). Utah. Republican. Brigham Young, University of Michigan. Nominated associate justice by Warren G. Harding; confirmed 1922 by voice vote; retired 1938. Utah state legislator, U.S. representative, U.S. senator.

Swayne, Noah Haynes (1804–1884). Ohio. Republican. Privately educated. Nominated associate justice by Abraham Lincoln; confirmed 1862 by 38–1 vote; retired 1881. Ohio state legislator, local prosecutor, U.S. attorney for Ohio, Columbus city councilman.

Taft, William Howard (1857–1930). Connecticut. Republican. Yale, Cincinnati. Nominated chief justice by Warren G. Harding; confirmed 1921 by voice vote; retired 1930. Ohio local prosecutor, state court judge, U.S. solicitor general, federal court of appeals judge, governor of the Philippines, secretary of war, U.S. president.

Taney, Roger Brooke (1777–1864). Maryland. Democrat. Dickinson College. Nominated associate justice by Andrew Jackson; nomination not confirmed 1835; nominated chief justice by Andrew Jackson; confirmed 1836 by 29–15 vote; died in office 1864. Maryland state legislator, state attorney general, acting secretary of war, secretary of the Treasury (nomination later rejected by Senate).

Thomas, Clarence (1948–). Georgia. Republican. Holy Cross, Yale. Nominated associate justice by George H. W. Bush; confirmed 1991 by 52–48 vote. U.S. Department of Education assistant secretary for civil rights, Equal Employment Opportunity Commission chairman, federal appeals court judge.

Thompson, Smith (1768–1843). New York. Democratic-Republican. Princeton. Nominated associate justice by James Monroe; confirmed 1823 by voice vote; died in office 1843. New York state legislator, state court judge, secretary of the navy.

Todd, Thomas (1765–1826). Kentucky. Democratic-Republican. Liberty Hall (Washington and Lee). Nominated associate justice by Thomas Jefferson; confirmed 1807 by voice vote; died in office 1826. Kentucky state court judge, state chief justice.

Trimble, Robert (1776–1828). Kentucky. Democratic-Republican. Kentucky Academy. Nominated associate justice by John Quincy Adams; confirmed 1826 by 27–5 vote; died in office 1828. Kentucky state legislator, state court judge, U.S. attorney, federal district court judge.

Van Devanter, Willis (1859–1941). Wyoming. Republican. Indiana Asbury University, University of Cincinnati. Nominated associate justice by William Howard Taft; confirmed 1910 by voice vote; retired 1937. Cheyenne city attorney, Wyoming Territorial legislature, Wyoming Supreme Court, assistant U.S. attorney general, federal court of appeals judge.

Vinson, Frederick Moore (1890–1953). Kentucky. Democrat. Centre College. Nominated chief justice by Harry Truman; confirmed 1946 by voice vote; died in office 1953. U.S. representative, federal appeals court judge, director of Office of Economic Stabilization, secretary of the Treasury.

Waite, Morrison Remick (1816–1888). Ohio. Republican. Yale. Nominated chief justice by Ulysses S. Grant; confirmed 1874 by 63–0 vote; died in office 1888. Private practice, Ohio state legislator.

Warren, Earl (1891–1974). California. Republican. University of California. Recess appointment as chief justice by Dwight Eisenhower 1953; confirmed 1954 by voice vote; retired 1969. California local district attorney, state attorney general, governor.

Washington, Bushrod (1762–1829). Virginia. Federalist. College of William and Mary. Nominated associate justice by John Adams; confirmed 1798 by voice vote; died in office 1829. Virginia state legislator.

Wayne, James Moore (1790–1867). Georgia. Democrat. Princeton. Nominated associate justice by Andrew Jackson; confirmed 1835 by voice vote; died in office 1867. Georgia state legislator, mayor of Savannah, state court judge, U.S. representative.

White, Byron Raymond (1917–2002). Colorado. Democrat. University of Colorado, Oxford, Yale. Nominated associate justice by John Kennedy; confirmed 1962 by voice vote; retired 1993. Deputy U.S. attorney general.

White, Edward Douglass (1845–1921). Louisiana. Democrat. Mount St. Mary's College, Georgetown. Nominated associate justice by Grover Cleveland; confirmed 1894 by voice vote; nominated chief justice by William Howard Taft; confirmed 1910 by voice vote; died in office 1921. Louisiana state legislator, Louisiana Supreme Court justice, U.S. senator.

Whittaker, Charles Evans (1901–1973). Missouri. Republican. University of Kansas City. Nominated associate justice by Dwight Eisenhower; confirmed 1957 by voice vote; retired 1962. Federal district court judge, federal appeals court judge.

Wilson, James (1742–1798). Pennsylvania. Federalist. University of St. Andrews (Scotland). Nominated associate justice by George Washington; confirmed 1789 by voice vote; died in office 1798. Delegate to Continental Congress and Constitutional Convention.

Woodbury, Levi (1789–1851). New Hampshire. Democrat. Dartmouth, Tapping Reeve Law School. Nominated associate justice by James Polk; confirmed 1846 by voice vote; died in office 1851. New Hampshire state legislator, state court judge, governor, U.S. senator, secretary of the navy, secretary of the Treasury.

Woods, William B. (1824–1887). Georgia. Republican. Western Reserve College, Yale. Nominated associate justice by Rutherford B. Hayes; confirmed 1880 by 39–8 vote; died in office 1887. Ohio state legislator, Alabama chancellor, federal circuit court judge.

APPENDIX 3

Glossary

Abstention: A doctrine or policy of the federal courts to refrain from deciding a case so that the issues involved may first be definitively resolved by state courts.

Acquittal: A decision by a court that a person charged with a crime is not guilty.

Advisory opinion: An opinion issued by a court indicating how it would rule on a question of law should such a question come before it in an actual case. U.S. federal courts do not hand down advisory opinions, but some state courts do.

Affidavit: A written statement of facts voluntarily made under oath or affirmation.

Affirm: To uphold a decision of a lower court.

A fortiori: With greater force or reason.

Aggravating circumstances: Conditions that increase the seriousness of a crime but are not a part of its legal definition.

Amicus curiae: "Friend of the court." A person (or group), not a party to a case, who submits views (usually in the form of written briefs) on how the case should be decided.

Ante: Prior to.

Appeal: The procedure by which a case is taken to a superior court for a review of the lower court's decision.

Appellant: The party dissatisfied with a lower court ruling who appeals the case to a superior court for review.

Appellate jurisdiction: The legal authority of a superior court to review and render judgment on a decision by a lower court.

Appellee: The party usually satisfied with a lower court ruling against whom an appeal is taken.

Arbitrary: Unreasonable; capricious; not done in accordance with established principles.

Arguendo: In the course of argument.

Arraignment: A formal stage of the criminal process in which the defendants are brought before a judge and are confronted with the charges against them, and they enter a plea to those charges.

Arrest: The act of physically taking into custody or otherwise depriving of freedom a person suspected of violating the law.

Attainder, Bill of: A legislative act declaring a person or easily identified group of people guilty of a crime and imposing punishments without the benefit of a trial. Such legislative acts are prohibited by the U.S. Constitution.

Attest: To swear to; to be a witness.

Bail: A security deposit, usually in the form of cash or bond, that allows a person accused of a crime to be released from jail and guarantees the accused's appearance at trial.

Balancing test: A process of judicial decision making in which the court weighs the relative merits of the rights of the individual against the interests of the government.

Bench trial: A trial, without a jury, conducted before a judge.

Bicameral: Having two houses within a given legislative body, as does the U.S. Congress.

Bona fide: Good faith.

Brandeis brief: A legal argument that stresses economic and sociological evidence along with traditional legal authorities. Named for Louis Brandeis, who pioneered the use of such briefs.

Brief: A written argument of law and fact submitted to the court by an attorney representing a party having an interest in a lawsuit.

Case: A legal dispute or controversy brought to a court for resolution.

Case-in-chief: The primary evidence offered by a party in a court case.

Case law: Law that has evolved from past court decisions, as opposed to law created by legislative acts.

Case or controversy rule: The constitutional requirement that courts may hear only real disputes brought by adverse parties.

Certification: A procedure whereby a lower court requests that a superior court rule on specified legal questions so that the lower court may correctly apply the law.

Certiorari, Writ of: An order of an appellate court to an inferior court to send up the records of a case that the appellate court has elected to review. The primary method by which the U.S. Supreme Court exercises its discretionary jurisdiction to accept appeals for a full hearing.

Civil law: Law that deals with the private rights of individuals (e.g., property, contracts, negligence), as contrasted with criminal law.

Class action: A lawsuit brought by one or more persons who represent themselves and all others similarly situated.

Collateral estoppel: A rule of law that prohibits an already settled issue from being relitigated in another form.

Comity: The principle by which the courts of one jurisdiction give respect and deference to the laws and legal decisions of another jurisdiction.

Common law: Law that has evolved from usage and custom as reflected in the decisions of courts.

Compensatory damages: A monetary award, equivalent to the loss sustained, to be paid to an injured party by the party at fault.

Concurrent powers: Authority that may be exercised by both the state and federal governments.

Concurring opinion: A separate opinion written by a judge who agrees with the opinion of the court but expresses additional views (called a *regular concurrence*), or a separate opinion written by a judge who agrees with the court's disposition of a case but disagrees with the rationale used by the majority to reach that disposition (called a *special concurrence*).

Confrontation: The right of a criminal defendant to see the testimony of prosecution witnesses and subject such witnesses to cross-examination.

Consent decree: A court-ratified agreement voluntarily reached by parties to settle a lawsuit.

Constitutional court: A court created under authority of Article III of the Constitution. Judges serve for terms of good behavior and are protected against having their salaries reduced by the legislature.

Contempt: A purposeful failure to carry out an order of a court (civil contempt) or a willful display of disrespect for the court (criminal contempt).

Contraband: Articles that are illegal to possess.

Courts of appeals (federal): The intermediate-level appellate courts in the federal system, each of which has jurisdiction over a particular region known as a circuit.

Criminal law: Law governing the relationship between individuals and society. Deals with the enforcement of laws and the punishment of those who, by breaking laws, commit crimes.

Curtilage: The land and outbuildings immediately adjacent to a home and regularly used by its occupants.

Declaratory judgment: A court ruling determining a legal right or interpretation of the law, but not imposing any relief or remedy.

De facto: In fact, actual.

Defendant: A party at the trial level being sued in a civil case or charged with a crime in a criminal case.

De jure: As a result of law or official government action.

De minimis: Small or unimportant. A de minimis issue is considered one too trivial for a court to consider.

Demurrer: A motion to dismiss a lawsuit in which the defendant admits to the facts alleged by the plaintiff but contends that those facts are insufficient to justify a legal cause of action.

De novo: New, from the beginning.

Deposition: Sworn testimony taken out of court.

Dicta (or Obiter dicta): Those portions of a judge's opinion that are not essential to deciding the case.

Directed verdict: An action by a judge ordering a jury to return a specified verdict.

Discovery: A pretrial procedure whereby one party to a lawsuit gains access to information or evidence held by the opposing party.

Dissenting opinion: A formal written expression by a judge who disagrees with the result reached by the majority.

Distinguish: A court's explanation of why a particular precedent is inapplicable to the case under consideration.

District courts: The trial courts of general jurisdiction in the federal system.

Diversity jurisdiction: The authority of federal courts to hear cases in which a party from one state is suing a party from another state.

Docket: The schedule of cases to be heard by a court.

Double jeopardy: The trying of a defendant a second time for the same offense. Prohibited by the Fifth Amendment to the Constitution.

Due process: Government procedures that follow principles of essential fairness.

Eminent domain: The authority of the government to take private property for public purpose.

En banc: An appellate court hearing with all the judges of the court participating.

Enjoin: An order from a court requiring a party to do or refrain from doing certain acts.

Entrapment: Situation in which law enforcement officials induce an otherwise innocent person into the commission of a criminal act.

Equity: Law based on principles of fairness rather than strictly applied statutes.

Error, Writ of: An order issued by an appeals court commanding a lower court to send up the full record of a case for review.

Exclusionary rule: A principle of law that illegally gathered evidence may not be admitted in court.

Exclusive powers: Powers reserved for either the federal government or the state governments, but not exercised by both.

Ex parte: A hearing in which only one party to a dispute is present.

Ex post facto law: A criminal law passed by the legislature and made applicable to acts committed prior to passage of the law. Prohibited by the U.S. Constitution.

Ex rel: Upon information from. Used to designate a court case instituted by the government but instigated by a private party.

Ex vi termini: From the force or very meaning of the term or expression.

Federal question: A legal issue based on the U.S. Constitution, laws, or treaties.

Felony: A serious criminal offense, usually punishable by incarceration of one year or more.

Gerrymander: To construct political boundaries for the purpose of giving advantage to a particular political party or interest.

Grand jury: A panel of twelve to twenty-three citizens who review prosecutorial evidence to determine if there are sufficient grounds to issue an indictment binding an individual over for trial on criminal charges.

Guilty verdict: A determination that a person accused of a criminal offense is legally responsible as charged.

Habeas corpus: "You have the body." A writ issued to determine if a person held in custody is being unlawfully detained or imprisoned.

Harmless error: An error occurring in a court proceeding that is insufficient in magnitude to justify the overturning of the court's final determination.

Hearsay: Testimony not based on the personal knowledge of the witness, but a repetition of what the witness has heard others say.

Immunity: An exemption from prosecution granted in exchange for testimony.

In camera: A legal hearing held in the judge's chambers or otherwise in private.

Incorporation: The process whereby provisions of the Bill of Rights are declared to be included in the due process guarantee of the Fourteenth Amendment and made applicable to state and local governments.

Indictment: A document issued by a grand jury officially charging an individual with criminal violations and binding the accused over for trial.

In forma pauperis: "In the form of a pauper." A special status granted to indigents that allows them to proceed without payment of court fees and to be exempt from certain procedural requirements.

Information: A document serving the same purpose as an indictment but issued directly by the prosecutor.

Infra: Below.

Injunction: A writ prohibiting the person to whom it is directed from committing certain specified acts.

In pari materia: On the same subject.

In re: "In the matter of." The designation used in a judicial proceeding in which there are no formal adversaries.

In rem An act directed against a thing and not against a person.

Inter alia: Among other things.

Interlocutory decree: A provisional action that temporarily settles a legal question pending the final determination of a dispute.

Judgment of the court: The final ruling of a court, independent of the legal reasoning supporting it.

Judicial activism: A philosophy that courts should not be reluctant to review and if necessary strike down legislative and executive actions.

Judicial notice: The recognition by a court of the truth of certain facts without requiring one of the parties to put them into evidence.

Judicial restraint: A philosophy that courts should defer to the legislative and executive branches whenever possible.

Judicial review: The authority of a court to determine the constitutionality of acts committed by the legislative and executive branches and to strike down acts judged to be in violation of the Constitution.

Jurisdiction: The authority of a court to hear and decide legal disputes and to enforce its rulings.

Justiciable: Capable of being heard and decided by a court.

Legislative court: A court created by Congress under authority of Article I of the Constitution to assist in carrying out the powers of the legislature.

Litigant: A party to a lawsuit.

Magistrate: A low-level judge with limited authority.

Mandamus: "We command." A writ issued by a court commanding a public official to carry out a particular act or duty.

Mandatory jurisdiction: A case that a court is required to hear.

Marque and reprisal: An order from the government of one country requesting and legitimating the seizure of persons and property of another country. Prohibited by the U.S. Constitution.

Merits: The central issues of a case.

Misdemeanor: A less serious criminal act, usually punishable by less than one year of incarceration.

Mistrial: A trial that is prematurely ended by a judge because of procedural irregularities.

Mitigating circumstances: Conditions that lower the moral blame of a person who commits a criminal act, but do not justify or excuse the act.

Moot: A question presented in a lawsuit that cannot be answered by a court either because the issue has resolved itself or conditions have so changed that the court is unable to grant the requested relief.

Motion: A request made to a court for a certain ruling or action.

Natural law: Law considered applicable to all persons in all nations because it is thought to be basic to human nature.

Nolle prosequi: The decision of a prosecutor to drop criminal charges against an accused.

Nolo contendere: No contest. A plea entered by a criminal defendant in which the accused does not admit guilt but submits to sentencing and punishment as if guilty.

Opinion of the court: An opinion announcing the judgment and reasoning of a court endorsed by a majority of the judges participating.

Order: A written command issued by a judge.

Original jurisdiction: The authority of a court to try a case and to decide it, as opposed to appellate jurisdiction.

Per curiam: An unsigned or collectively written opinion issued by a court.

Peremptory challenge: An attorney's excusing a prospective juror without explaining the reasons for doing so.

Per se: In and of itself.

Petitioner: A party seeking relief in court.

Petit jury: A trial court jury to decide criminal or civil cases.

Plaintiff: The party who brings a legal action to court for resolution or remedy.

Plea bargain: An arrangement in a criminal case in which the defendant agrees to plead guilty in return for the prosecutor reducing the criminal charges or recommending a lenient sentence.

Plurality opinion: An opinion announcing the judgment of a court with supporting reasoning that is not endorsed by a majority of the justices participating.

Police powers: The power of the state to regulate for the health, safety, morals, and general welfare of its citizens.

Political question: An issue more appropriate for determination by the legislative or executive branch than by the judiciary.

Precedent: A previously decided case that serves as a guide for deciding a current case.

Preemption: A doctrine under which an area of authority previously left to the states is, by act of

Congress, brought into the exclusive jurisdiction of the federal government.

Prima facie: "At first sight." A case that is sufficient to prevail unless effectively countered by the opposing side.

Pro bono publico: "For the public good." Usually refers to legal representation done without fee for some charitable or public purpose.

Pro se: A person who appears in court without an attorney.

Punitive damages: A monetary award (separate from compensatory damages) imposed by a court for punishment purposes to be paid by the party at fault to the injured party.

Quash: To annul, vacate, or totally do away with.

Ratio decidendi: A court's primary reasoning for deciding a case the way it did.

Recuse: The action taken by a judge not to participate in a case because of conflict of interest or other disqualifying condition.

Remand: To send a case back to an inferior court for additional action.

Res judicata: A legal issue that has been finally settled by a court judgment.

Respondent: The party against whom a legal action is filed.

Reverse: An action by an appellate court setting aside or changing a decision of a lower court.

Ripeness: A condition in which a legal dispute has evolved to the point where the issues it presents can be effectively resolved by a court.

Selective incorporation: The policy of the Supreme Court to decide incorporation issues on a case-by-case, right-by-right basis.

Show cause: A judicial order commanding a party to appear in court and explain why the court should not take a proposed action.

Solicitor general: Justice Department official whose office represents the federal government in all litigation before the U.S. Supreme Court.

Standing; standing to sue: The right of parties to bring legal actions because they are directly affected by the legal issues raised.

Stare decisis: "Let the decision stand." The doctrine that once a legal issue has been settled it should be followed as precedent in future cases presenting the same question.

State action: An action taken by an agency or official of a state or local government.

Stay: To stop or suspend.

Strict construction: Narrow interpretation of the provisions of laws.

Subpoena ad testificandum: An order compelling a person to testify before a court, legislative hearing, or grand jury.

Subpoena duces tecum: An order compelling a person to produce a document or other piece of physical evidence that is relevant to issues pending before a court, legislative hearing, or grand jury.

Sub silentio: "Under silence." A court action taken without explicit notice or indication.

Summary judgment: A decision by a court made without a full hearing or without receiving briefs or oral arguments.

Supra: Above.

Temporary restraining order: A judicial order prohibiting certain challenged actions from being taken prior to a full hearing on the question.

Test: A criterion or set of criteria used by courts to determine if certain legal thresholds have been met or constitutional provisions violated.

Three-judge court: A special federal court, made up of appellate and trial court judges, created to expedite the processing of certain issues made eligible for such priority treatment by congressional statute.

Ultra vires: Actions taken that exceed the legal authority of the person or agency performing them.

Usus loquendi: The common usage of ordinary language.

Vacate: To void or rescind.

Vel non: "Or not."

Venireman: A juror.

Venue: The geographical jurisdiction in which a case is heard.

Voir dire: "To speak the truth." The stage of a trial in which potential jurors are questioned to determine their competence to sit in judgment of a case.

Warrant: A judicial order authorizing an arrest or search and seizure.

Writ: A written order of a court commanding the recipient to perform or not to perform certain specified acts.

APPENDIX 4

Online Case Archive Index

S PACE LIMITATIONS PREVENT us from including in this volume excerpts of every important Supreme Court decision dealing with constitutional rights and liberties. To make a larger number of cases available to instructors and students, we have created an online archive, which currently contains more than two hundred decisions *(see list below)*. In the text, boldface case names indicate that they can be found in the archive. As the Court hands down new rulings of significance, we will add them to the archive to ensure that the materials available to our readers will always be current. Access the archive at http://clca.cqpress.com.

Adamson v. California (1947)
Adderley v. Florida (1966)
Aguilar v. Felton (1985)
Agurs; United States v. (1976)
Akron v. Akron Center for Reproductive Health (1983)
Alabama v. Shelton (2002)
American Booksellers Association v. Hudnut (1986)
American Communications Association v. Douds (1950)
Apodaca v. Oregon (1972)
Argersinger v. Hamlin (1972)
Arizona v. Hicks (1987)
Ashcroft v. ACLU (2002)
Ashcroft v. ACLU II (2004)

Ashcroft v. Free Speech Coalition (2002)
Ashe v. Swenson (1970)
Associated Press v. Walker (1967)
Avery v. Midland County (1968)
Baker v. Carr (1962)
Ballard; United States v. (1944)
Barker v. Wingo (1972)
Barnes v. Glen Theatre (1991)
Baze v. Rees (2008)
Berkemer v. McCarty (1984)
Betts v. Brady (1942)
Bigelow v. Virginia (1975)
Blakely v. Washington (2004)
Board of Education of Kiryas Joel Village School District v. Grumet (1994)
Board of Education of Oklahoma City Public Schools v. Dowell (1991)
Board of Education v. Allen (1968)
Board of Regents of the University of Wisconsin System v. Southworth (2000)
Bob Jones University v. United States (1983)
Bolling v. Sharpe (1954)
Booker; United States v. (2005)
Bowers v. Hardwick (1986)
Bradfield v. Roberts (1899)
Bradwell v. Illinois (1873)
Brady v. Maryland (1963)
Braunfeld v. Brown (1961)
Brewer v. Williams (1977)

Case Index

See also Appendix 4 for Online Case Archive Index. Bold type indicates a case for which an excerpted opinion appears in the book.

Subject Index

IMAGE CREDITS

ABOUT THE AUTHORS

Lee Epstein is Provost Professor of Law & Political Science and Rader Family Trustee Chair in Law at the University of Southern California.. She is also a fellow of the American Academy of Arts and Sciences and the American Academy of Political and Social Science. She is author, coauthor, or editor of fifteen books, including *The Supreme Court Compendium: Data, Decisions, and Developments,* 5th edition, with Jeffrey A. Segal, Harold J. Spaeth, and Thomas G. Walker; *Courts, Judges, and Politics,* 6th edition, with Walter F. Murphy, C. Herman Pritchett, and Jack Knight; and *Advice and Consent: The Politics of Judicial Appointments,* with Jeffrey A. Segal. Her most recent book is *The Behavior of Federal Judges: A Theoretical and Empirical Study of Rational Choice* (2012), with William M. Landes and Richard A. Posner.

Thomas G. Walker is Goodrich C. White Professor of Political Science at Emory University, where he has won several teaching awards for his courses on constitutional law and the judicial process. He received his Ph.D. from the University of Kentucky. His book, *A Court Divided,* written with Deborah J. Barrow, won the prestigious V. O. Key Award for the best book on southern politics. He is coauthor of *The Supreme Court Compendium: Data, Decisions, and Developments,* 5th edition (2012), with Lee Epstein, Jeffrey A. Segal, and Harold J. Spaeth, and author of *Eligible for Execution* (2009).

⑤SAGE research**methods**

The essential online tool for researchers from the world's leading methods publisher

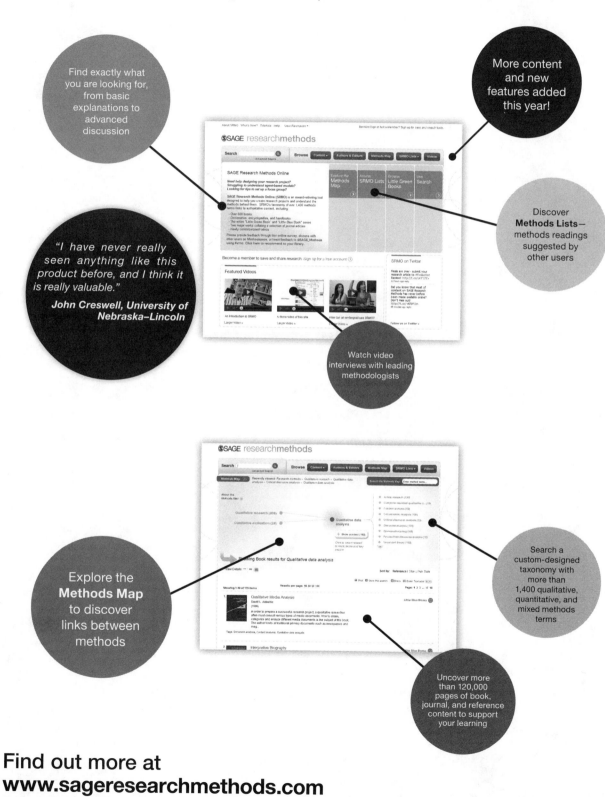

Find exactly what you are looking for, from basic explanations to advanced discussion

More content and new features added this year!

"I have never really seen anything like this product before, and I think it is really valuable."

John Creswell, University of Nebraska–Lincoln

Discover **Methods Lists**— methods readings suggested by other users

Watch video interviews with leading methodologists

Explore the **Methods Map** to discover links between methods

Search a custom-designed taxonomy with more than 1,400 qualitative, quantitative, and mixed methods terms

Uncover more than 120,000 pages of book, journal, and reference content to support your learning

Find out more at
www.sageresearchmethods.com